Organizational Behavior Case for Discussion assists
...dents in the transition from textbook learning to real-world
...lication.

e "Bodacious" Success of Oprah (Ch. 1)
e Sky's the Limit at Lockheed Martin (Ch. 2)
.S Delivers Diversity to Diverse World (Ch. 3)
...uing Employees at the World's Largest Firm (Ch. 4)
...en Employees are Owners (Ch. 5)
...warding Employees (Ch. 6)
...ployee Participation at Chaparral Steel (Ch. 7)
...warding the Hourly Worker (Ch. 8)
...er the Edge (Ch. 9)
...ale of Two Companies (Ch. 10)
...ng Groups to Get Things Done (Ch. 11)
...ne of Us Is as Smart as All of Us (Ch. 12)
...w Do You Manage Magic? (Ch. 13)
...Corporate Marriage Made in Heaven (Not!) (Ch. 14)
e Most Stressful Conditions (Ch. 15)
...Company Divided Against Itself Cannot Stand (Ch. 16)
...structuring at Cisco (Ch. 17)
...crosoft: Cult or Culture? (Ch. 18)
...ange of Direction at Schwab (Ch. 19)

 Experiencing Organizational Behavior exercises
continue students' transition to real-world application
by asking them to work together to apply concepts to
their own surroundings.

...lating OB and Popular Culture (Ch. 1)
...naging in Today's Organization (Ch. 2)
...derstanding Your Own Stereotypes and Attitudes Toward
...Others (Ch. 3)
...tching Personalities and Jobs (Ch. 4)
...lating Your Needs to the Theories of Motivation (Ch. 5)
...derstanding the Dynamics of Expectancy Theory (Ch. 6)
...arning About Job Design (Ch. 7)
...ing Compensation to Motivate Workers (Ch. 8)
...arning How Stress Affects You (Ch. 9)
e Importance of Feedback in Oral Communication (Ch. 10)
...arning the Benefits of a Group (Ch. 11)
...ing Teams (Ch. 12)
...derstanding Successful and Unsuccessful Leadership (Ch. 13)
...arning About Ethics and Power (Ch. 14)
...ogrammed and Nonprogrammed Decisions (Ch. 15)
...derstanding Organization Structure (Ch. 16)
...dying a Real Organization (Ch. 17)
...lture of the Classroom (Ch. 18)
...nning a Change at the University (Ch. 19)

 Self-Assessment Exercises give students the opportunity to apply concepts to brief self-assessment or diagnostic activities.

Assessing Your Own Theory X and Theory Y Tendencies (Ch. 1)
Assessing Your Own Management Skills (Ch. 2)
Cross-Cultural Awareness (Ch. 3)
Assessing Your Locus of Control (Ch. 4)
Assessing Your Own Needs (Ch. 5)
Assessing Your Equity Sensitivity (Ch. 6)
The Job Characteristics Inventory (Ch. 7)
Diagnosing Poor Performance and Enhancing Motivation (Ch. 8)
Are You Type A or Type B? (Ch. 9)
Diagnosing Your Listening Skills (Ch. 10)
Group Cohesiveness (Ch. 11)
Understanding the Benefits of Teams (Ch. 12)
Applying Vroom's Decision Tree Approach (Ch. 13)
Are You a Charismatic Leader? (Ch. 14)
Rational Versus Practical Approaches to Decision Making (Ch. 15)
Making Delegation Work (Ch. 16)
Diagnosing Organization Structure (Ch. 17)
An Empowering Culture: What It Is and What It Is Not (Ch. 18)
Support for Change (Ch. 19)

 Building Managerial Skills exercises require students to
consider a situation and make decisions as a manager in
order to change the course of events in the workplace.

OB Online exercises direct students to go to the web site
of a company or organization or to search the Web for
information about some topic illustrating how organizations are approaching issues discussed in the chapter.

The **Integrative Running Case** at the end of each part provides
an opportunity for students to discuss an actual ongoing management situation with significant organizational behavior facets.

The Downfall of Enron (Part 1)
The Downfall of Enron—The People (Part 2)
The Downfall of Enron—The Leadership (Part 3)
The Downfall of Enron—The Organization (Part 4)

WITHDRAWN

SEVENTH EDITION

Organizational Behavior

Managing People and Organizations

▼ ▼ ▼

Gregory Moorhead

Arizona State University

▼ ▼ ▼

Ricky W. Griffin

Texas A&M University

Houghton Mifflin Company   Boston   New York

For my family: Linda, Alex, and Lindsay. —G.M.

For my daughter Ashley: Still a sweet and shining star moving boldly forward through life's big adventure. —R.W.G.

Editor-in-Chief: *George T. Hoffman*
Development Editor: *Jessica Carlisle*
Editorial Assistant: *Eve Nicolaou*
Senior Project Editor: *Rachel D'Angelo Wimberly*
Editorial Assistant: *May Jawdat*
Senior Production/Design Coordinator: *Sarah L. Ambrose*
Senior Manufacturing Coordinator: *Priscilla Bailey*
Marketing Manager: *Steven W. Mikels*
Marketing Associate: *Lisa E. Boden*

Cover Design: Illustration by Todd Davidson

Photo Credits   p. 4, ©Harry Borden/IPG/Cpi; p. 9, Courtesy of AT&T Archives; p. 14, Richard Vogel/AP/Wide World; p. 29, © James Leynse/Corbis SABA; p. 34, © Katherine Lambert; p. 38, Jeff Kowalsky/Bloomberg News/Landov; p. 41, © Russ Quackenbush; p. 55, © Juliana Sohn/M.S. Logan Ltd.; p. 63, © Greg Girard/Contact Press Images; p. 67, Gene Puskar/AP/Wide World; p. 89, Peter Cosgrove/AP/Wide World; p. 94, Courtesy of Lockheed Martin; p. 103, © France Ruffenach; p. 115, Dave Caulkin/AP/Wide World; p. 123, © Allessandra Sanguenetti; p. 129, freediver AFP Photo/Jacques Munch; p. 142, © Steve Labadassa; p. 144, Saureb Das/AP/Wide World; p. 154, ©Jeff Mermelstein; p. 168, © Peter M. Fisher/Corbis; p. 175, © Taro Yamasaki/People Weekly/Time, Inc.; p. 181, © Christina Caturano/Boston Globe; p. 192, © Dorothy Low/People Weekly/Time, Inc.; p. 200, photo by Monica Lopossay Riesser, The Baltimore Sun; p. 202, Beck Group © Bryce Duffy/Corbis; p. 207, © Mike DeHoog/Tom DiPace Photography, Inc.; p. 225, © Mark Wilson/Getty Images; p. 232, Justin Lane/The New York Times; p. 236, © Todd Buchanan; p. 253, Fritz Hoffmann/Document China; p. 255, © Robert Burroughs; p. 260, Robert Brenner/PhotoEdit; p. 266, © Katie Murray; p. 284, John Russell/AP/Wide World; p. 290, © Timothy Fadek/Gamma; p. 293, © Barbel Schmidt; p. 300, © Erica Berger/Corbis Outline; p. 316, © John R. Boehm; p. 321, Kathy Willens/AP/Wide World; p. 324, © Thomas Broening; p. 326, © Pablo Bartholomew/MediaWeb India; p. 340, Amy Sancetta/AP/Wide World; p. 348, © Jose Azel/Aurora & Quanta Productions; p. 353, © Michele Asselin; p. 355, © Margaret Salmon and Dean Wiand; p. 367, © 2002 Peter Serling. All Rights Reserved.; p. 369, Dan Bayer/AP/Wide World; p. 371, © Axel Koester; p. 383, © Brooks Kraft/Gamma; p. 403, © David McLain/Aurora & Quanta Productions; p. 409, Laura Pedrick/The New York Times; p. 419, Chicago Tribune photo by John Lee; p. 432, Guy Stubbs Photographer Copyright; p. 435, © Robert Semeniuk; p. 446, © Gerry Gropp; p. 463, Michael Newman/PhotoEdit; p. 478, Mark Richards/People Weekly/Time, Inc.; p. 483, © Axel Koester; p. 497, © Michael L. Abramson; p. 502, © Ethan Hill; p. 509, © Greg Miller; p. 512, © Bruce Zake; p. 526, Mark Ralston/SCMP; p. 535, Everett Collection; p. 538, United Way © Daniel Levin.

Printed in the U.S.A.

Library of Congress Control Number: 2002109651

ISBN: 0-618-30587-4

2 3 4 5 6 7 8 9—DOW—07 06 05 04 03

Brief Contents

Part I   Introduction to Organizational Behavior

1 An Overview of Organizational Behavior   1
2 Managing People and Organizations   27
3 Managing Global and Workforce Diversity   52

Part II   Individual Processes in Organizations

4 Foundations of Individual Behavior   85
5 Need-Based Perspectives on Motivation   113
6 Process-Based Perspectives on Motivation   137
7 Job Design, Employee Participation, and Alternative Work Arrangements   163
8 Goal Setting, Performance Management, and Rewards   189
9 Managing Stress and the Work-Life Balance   219

Part III   Interpersonal Processes in Organizations

10 Communication in Organizations   248
11 Group Dynamics   280
12 Using Teams in Organizations   312
13 Leadership Models and Concepts   338
14 Leadership and Influence Processes   365
15 Decision Making and Negotiation   393

Part IV   Organizational Processes and Characteristics

16 Dimensions of Organization Structure   429
17 Organization Design   458
18 Organization Culture   491
19 Organization Change and Development   521

Appendix A   Research Methods in Organizational Behavior   554

Appendix B   Career Dynamics   562

Endnotes 579
Glossary 601
Name Index 614
Organization Index 620
Subject Index 622

Contents

Part I   Introduction to Organizational Behavior

I An Overview of Organizational Behavior   1

What is Organizational Behavior?   3
The Meaning of Organizational Behavior 3   The Importance of Organizational Behavior 5

The Historical Roots of Organizational Behavior   5
The Scientific Management Era 6   Classical Organization Theory 7

The Emergence of Organizational Behavior   7
Precursors of Organizational Behavior 8   The Hawthorne Studies 8   ■ *Working with Diversity 10*   The Human Relations Movement 10   Toward Organizational Behavior: The Value of People 12

Contemporary Organizational Behavior   12
■ *Business of Ethics 13*   Characteristics of the Field 13
Basic Concepts of the Field 15   ■ *Mastering Change 17*

Contextual Perspectives on Organizational Behavior   17
Systems and Contingency Perspectives 17   Contemporary Applied Perspectives 21

Organizational Behavior Case for Discussion: *The "Bodacious" Success of Oprah*   **22**
Experiencing Organizational Behavior: *Relating OB and Popular Culture*   **24**
Self-Assessment Exercise: *Assessing Your Own Theory X and Theory Y Tendencies*   **24**
OB Online   25
Building Managerial Skills   25

2 Managing People and Organizations   27

Managerial Perspectives on Organizational Behavior   29

Basic Management Functions, Roles, and Skills   30
Fundamental Managerial Functions 30   ■ *World View 31*   Basic Managerial Roles 32
Critical Managerial Skills 34

Organizational Challenges   36
Workforce Expansion and Reduction 36   The New Workplace 37   ■ *Mastering Change 39*   Organization Change 39   Information Technology 40   New Ways of Organizing 40

Environmental Challenges   40
Competitive Strategy 40   Globalization 41   Ethics and Social Responsibility 42
■ *Business of Ethics 43*   Quality and Productivity 44   Manufacturing and Service Technology 44

Managing for Effectiveness   45

Individual-Level Outcomes 45   Group- and Team-Level Outcomes 46
Organization-Level Outcomes 46

Organizational Behavior Case for Discussion: *The Sky's the Limit at Lockheed Martin* **48**

Experiencing Organizational Behavior: *Managing in Today's Organization* **49**

Self-Assessment Exercise: *Assessing Your Own Management Skills* **50**

OB Online   51

Building Managerial Skills   51

3   **Managing Global and Workforce Diversity   52**

The Nature of Diversity in Organizations   54

What Is Workforce Diversity? 54   Who Will Be the Workforce of the Future? 56
Global Workforce Diversity 57   The Value of Diversity 58

The Emergence of International Management   61

The Growth of International Business 61   Trends in International Business 62
Cross-Cultural Differences and Similarities 63

Dimensions of Diversity   66

Primary Dimensions of Diversity 66   ■ *World View 69*   Secondary Dimensions of
Diversity 71

Managing the Multicultural Organization   71

Managerial Behavior Across Cultures 71   ■ *Business of Ethics 72*   Multicultural
Organization as Competitive Advantage 73   Creating the Multicultural Organization 74

Organizational Behavior Case for Discussion: *UPS Delivers Diversity to Diverse World* **77**

Experiencing Organizational Behavior: *Understanding Your Own Stereotypes and Attitudes Toward Others* **79**

Self-Assessment Exercise: *Cross-Cultural Awareness* **80**

OB Online   81

Building Managerial Skills   81

Part I Integrative Running Case: *The Downfall of Enron* **82**

Part II   Individual Processes in Organizations

4   **Foundations of Individual Behavior   85**

People in Organizations   87
Psychological Contracts 87   ■ The Person-Job Fit 89   ■ *Talking Technology 90*
Individual Differences 91

Personality and Organizations   91
The "Big Five" Personality Traits 91   The Myers-Briggs Framework 93
Other Personality Traits at Work 93

Attitudes in Organizations   95
How Attitudes are Formed 95   ■ *Business of Ethics 96*   ■ *Mastering Change 98*
Key Work-Related Attitudes 99   Affect and Mood in Organizations 100

Perception in Organizations   100

Basic Perceptual Processes 101   Perception and Attribution 102

Creativity in Organizations   102

The Creative Individual 103   The Creative Process 104   Enhancing Creativity in Organizations 105

Types of Workplace Behavior   106

Performance Behaviors 106   Dysfunctional Behaviors 106
Organizational Citizenship 107

Organizational Behavior Case for Discussion: *Valuing Employees at the World's Largest Firm*   **109**

Experiencing Organizational Behavior: *Matching Personalities and Jobs*   **110**

Self-Assessment Exercise: *Assessing Your Locus of Control*   **111**

OB Online   112

Building Managerial Skills   112

5 Need-Based Perspectives on Motivation   113

The Nature of Motivation   115

The Importance of Motivation 115   ■ *Business of Ethics 116*   The Motivational Framework 117   Needs and Motives in Organizations 118   ■ *Mastering Change 119*

Historical Perspectives on Motivation   120

Early Views of Motivation 120   The Scientific Management Approach 120
The Human Relations Approach 121

Need Theories of Motivation   121

The Hierarchy of Needs 121   ■ *World View 124*   ERG Theory 125

The Dual-Structure Theory   126

Development of the Theory 126   Evaluation of the Theory 127

Other Important Needs   128

The Need for Achievement 128   The Need for Affiliation 130
The Need for Power 130

Integrating the Need-Based Perspectives   131

Organizational Behavior Case for Discussion: *When Employees Are Owners*   **133**

Experiencing Organizational Behavior: *Relating Your Needs to the Theories of Motivation*   **134**

Self-Assessment Exercise: *Assessing Your Own Needs*   **135**

OB Online   136

Building Managerial Skills   136

6 Process-Based Perspectives on Motivation   137

The Equity Theory of Motivation   139

Forming Equity Perceptions 139   ■ *Working with Diversity 140*   Responses to Equity and Inequity 140   Evaluation and Implications 141

The Expectancy Theory of Motivation   143

The Basic Expectancy Model 143   The Porter-Lawler Model 145   Evaluation and Implications 146   ■ *Talking Technology 147*

Learning and Motivation   148

How Learning Occurs 148   Reinforcement Theory and Learning 149   Related Aspects of Learning 153

Organizational Behavior Modification   155

Behavior Modification in Organizations 155   The Effectiveness of OB Mod 157   The Ethics of OB Mod 157

Attribution and Motivation   158

Organizational Behavior Case for Discussion   159

Experiencing Organizational Behavior: *Understanding the Dynamics of Expectancy Theory*   160

Self-Assessment Exercise: *Assessing Your Equity Sensitivity*   161

OB Online   162

Building Managerial Skills   162

7   Job Design, Employee Participation, and Alternative Work Arrangements   163

Motivation and Employee Performance   165

The Evolution of Job Design   166

■ *Mastering Change 167*   Job Specialization 168   ■ *Talking Technology 169*
Early Alternatives to Job Specialization 170   Job Enrichment 171

The Job Characteristics Approach   172

The Job Characteristics Theory 173   Social Information and Job Design 175

Participation, Empowerment, and Motivation   176

Early Perspectives on Participation and Empowerment 176   Areas of Participation 177   Techniques and Issues in Empowerment 177

Alternative Work Arrangements   178

Variable Work Schedules 178   Flexible Work Schedules 179   Job Sharing 180   Telecommuting 181   ■ *Business of Ethics 182*

Organizational Behavior Case for Discussion: *Employee Participation at Chaparral Steel*   183

Experiencing Organizational Behavior: *Learning About Job Design*   185

Self-Assessment Exercise: *The Job Characteristics Inventory*   186

OB Online   188

Building Managerial Skills   188

8   Goal Setting, Performance Management, and Rewards   189

Goal Setting and Motivation   191

Goal-Setting Theory 191   Broader Perspectives on Goal Setting 193
Evaluation and Implications 194

Performance Management in Organizations 195

The Nature of Performance Management 195   Purposes of Performance Measurement
196   Performance Measurement Basics 196   ■ *Talking Technology 198*

Performance Measurement and Total Quality Management 199

Continuous Improvement 199   The Learning Organization 201

Individual Rewards in Organizations 202

■ *Working with Diversity 203*   Roles, Purposes, and Meanings of Rewards 203
Types of Rewards 204   ■ *Business of Ethics 206*

Managing Reward Systems 209

Linking Performance and Rewards 210   Flexible Reward Systems 210   Participative
Pay Systems 211   Pay Secrecy 211   Expatriate Compensation 211

Organizational Behavior Case for Discussion: *Rewarding the Hourly Worker* 214

Experiencing Organizational Behavior: *Using Compensation to Motivate Workers* 215

Self-Assessment Exercise: *Diagnosing Poor Performance and Enhancing Motivation* 217

OB Online 218

Building Managerial Skills 218

9 **Managing Stress and the Work-Life Balance** 219

The Nature of Stress 221

Stress Defined 221   The Stress Process 221

Individual Differences and Stress 222

Type A and B Personality Profiles 222   ■ *Mastering Change 223*
Hardiness and Optimism 225

Common Causes of Stress 226

Organizational Stressors 226   ■ *Talking Technology 229*   Life Stressors 230

Consequences of Stress 233

Individual Consequences 233   Organizational Consequences 233   Burnout 234

Managing Stress in the Workplace 234

Individual Coping Strategies 235   Organizational Coping Strategies 237

Work-Life Linkages 238

Fundamental Work-Life Relationships 238   ■ *Working With Diversity 239*
Balancing Work-Life Linkages 239

Organizational Behavior Case for Discussion: *Over the Edge* 241

Experiencing Organizational Behavior: *Learning How Stress Affects You* 242

Self-Assessment Exercise: *Are You Type A or Type B?* 243

OB Online 244

Building Managerial Skills 244

Part II Integrative Running Case: *The Downfall of Enron—The People* 245

Part III Interpersonal Processes in Organizations

10 Communication in Organizations 248

The Nature of Communication in Organizations 250

The Purposes of Communication in Organizations 250   Communication Across Cultures 250   ■ *Mastering Change 252*

Methods of Communication 253

Written Communication 253   Oral Communication 254
Nonverbal Communication 255

The Communication Process 256

Source 256   Encoding 257   Transmission 257   Decoding 257
■ *Talking Technology 258*   Receiver 259   Feedback 259   Noise 259

Electronic Information Processing and Telecommunications 260

■ *Business of Ethics 262*

Communication Networks 263

Small-Group Networks 263   Organizational Communication Networks 265

Managing Communication 268

Improving the Communication Process 268   Improving Organizational Factors in Communication 271

Organizational Behavior Case for Discussion: *A Tale of Two Companies* **275**
Experiencing Organizational Behavior: *The Importance of Feedback in Oral Communication* **276**
Self-Assessment Exercise: *Diagnosing Your Listening Skills* **277**
OB Online 278
Building Managerial Skills 278

11 Group Dynamics 280

Overview of Groups and Group Dynamics 282

"Group" Defined 282   The Importance of Studying Groups 283   Group Formation 284
■ *Mastering Change 285*

Types of Groups 286

Formal Groups 286   Informal Groups 287

Stages of Group Development 288

Mutual Acceptance 288   Communication and Decision Making 289
Motivation and Productivity 289   Control and Organization 290

Group Performance Factors 291

Composition 292   Size 293   Norms 294   Cohesiveness 295

Intergroup Dynamics 297

Conflict in Groups and Organizations 298

■ *Working With Diversity 299*   The Nature of Conflict 300   Reactions to Conflict 301
Managing Conflict 303

Managing Group and Intergroup Dynamics in Organizations 304

Organizational Behavior Case for Discussion: *Using Groups to Get Things Done* **307**

Experiencing Organizational Behavior: *Learning the Benefits of a Group* **308**

Self-Assessment Exercise: *Group Cohesiveness* **309**

OB Online 310

Building Managerial Skills 310

12 **Using Teams in Organizations 312**

Differentiating Teams from Groups 313

■ *Working With Diversity 315*   Job Categories 316   Authority 317   Reward Systems 317

Benefits and Costs of Teams in Organizations 318

Enhanced Performance 318   Employee Benefits 319   Reduced Costs 319
■ *Talking Technology 320*   Organizational Enhancements 320   Costs of Teams 321

Types of Teams 322

Quality Circles 322   Work Teams 323   Problem-Solving Teams 323
Management Teams 323   Product Development Teams 324   Virtual Teams 325

Implementing Teams in Organizations 325

Planning the Change 325   Phases of Implementation 328

Essential Team Issues 331

Team Performance 331   ■ *Business of Ethics 332*   Start at the Top 333

Organizational Behavior Case for Discussion: *None of Us Is as Smart as All of Us* **334**

Experiencing Organizational Behavior: *Using Teams* **336**

Self-Assessment Exercise: *Understanding the Benefits of Teams* **336**

OB Online 337

Building Managerial Skills 337

13 **Leadership Models and Concepts 338**

The Nature of Leadership 340

The Meaning of Leadership 340   Leadership Versus Management 340

Early Approaches to Leadership 342

Trait Approaches to Leadership 342   ■ *Mastering Change 343*
Behavioral Approaches to Leadership 344   ■ *World View 345*

The LPC Theory of Leadership 348

Task Versus Relationship Motivation 348   Situational Favorableness 349
Evaluation and Implications 351

The Path-Goal Theory of Leadership 351

Basic Premises 351   ■ *Working With Diversity 352*   Evaluation and Implications 354

Vroom's Decision Tree Approach to Leadership   354

Basic Premises *354*   Evaluation and Implications *358*

Other Contemporary Approaches to Leadership   358

The Leader-Member Exchange Model *358*   The Hersey and Blanchard Model *359*

Organizational Behavior Case for Discussion: *How Do You Manage Magic?*   **361**

Experiencing Organizational Behavior: *Understanding Successful and Unsuccessful Leadership*   **362**

Self-Assessment Exercise: Applying Vroom's Decision Tree Approach   363

OB Online   363

Building Managerial Skills   363

14   Leadership and Influence Processes   365

Leadership as Influence   366

Influence-Based Approaches to Leadership   367

Transformational Leadership *367*   Charismatic Leadership *368*   ■ *Mastering Change 370*

Leadership Substitutes: Can Leadership Be Irrelevant?   370

The Nature of Leadership Substitutes *370*   Workplace Substitutes *371*   Superleadership *372*

Power in Organizations   372

The Nature of Power *372*   Types of Power *373*   The Uses of Power in Organizations *375*

Politics and Political Behavior   380

The Pervasiveness of Political Behavior *380*   ■ *Business of Ethics 381*   Managing Political Behavior *382*

Impression Management in Organizations   386

Organizational Behavior Case for Discussion: *A Corporate Marriage Made in Heaven (Not!)*   **388**

Experiencing Organizational Behavior: *Learning About Ethics and Power*   **390**

Self-Assessment Exercise: *Are You a Charismatic Leader?*   **390**

OB Online   392

Building Managerial Skills   392

15   Decision Making and Negotiation   393

The Nature of Decision Making   395

Types of Decisions *395*   Information Required for Decision Making *396*

The Decision-Making Process   398

The Rational Approach *399*   ■ *Mastering Change 400*   The Behavioral Approach *403*   The Practical Approach *404*   The Personal Approach *405*

Related Behavioral Aspects of Decision Making   408

Ethics and Decision Making *408*   Escalation of Commitment *409*   ■ *Business of Ethics 410*

Group Decision Making   411

Group Polarization 411   Groupthink 412   Participation 414
Group Problem Solving 415

Negotiation   417

Approaches to Negotiation 417   ■ *World View 418*   Win-Win Negotiation 419

Organizational Behavior Case for Discussion: *The Most Stressful Conditions*   **421**

Experiencing Organizational Behavior: *Programmed and Nonprogrammed Decisions*   **423**

Self-Assessment Exercise: *Rational Versus Practical Approaches to Decision Making*   **424**

OB Online   **424**

Building Managerial Skills   **424**

Part III Integrative Running Case: *The Downfall of Enron—The Leadership*   **426**

Part IV   Organizational Processes and Characteristics

16 Dimensions of Organization Structure   429

The Nature of Organization Structure   431

Organization Defined 431   Organization Structure 431   ■ *Mastering Change 433*

Structural Configuration   433

Division of Labor 434   Coordinating the Divided Tasks 436   ■ *World View 439*

Structure and Operations   443

Centralization 443   Formalization 444

Responsibility and Authority   445

Responsibility 445   Authority 446   ■ *Business of Ethics 447*   An Alternative View of
Authority 448

Classic Views of Structure   448

Ideal Bureaucracy 449   The Classic Principles of Organizing 449
Human Organization 451

Organizational Behavior Case for Discussion: *A Company Divided Against Itself Cannot
Stand*   **454**

Experiencing Organizational Behavior: *Understanding Organization Structure*   **455**

Self-Assessment Exercise: *Making Delegation Work*   **456**

OB Online   **457**

Building Managerial Skills   **457**

17 Organization Design   458

Contingency Approaches to Organization Design   460

Strategy, Structural Imperatives, and Strategic Choice   461

Strategy 461   Structural Imperatives 461   ■ *Talking Technology 467*
Strategic Choice 470   ■ *World View 471*   ■ *Business of Ethics 472*

Organizational Designs   473

Mechanistic and Organic Designs 473   Sociotechnical Systems Designs 473
Mintzberg's Designs 475   Matrix Organization Design 479   Virtual Organizations 481

Contemporary Organization Design 481

Reengineering the Organization 482   Rethinking the Organization 482
Global Organization Structure and Design Issues 483   Dominant Themes of
Contemporary Designs 484

Organizational Behavior Case for Discussion: *Restructuring at Cisco* **486**

Experiencing Organizational Behavior: *Studying a Real Organization* **487**

Self-Assessment Exercise: *Diagnosing Organization Structure* **488**

OB Online 489

Building Managerial Skills 490

18 **Organization Culture 491**

The Nature of Organization Culture 492

What Is Organization Culture? 493   ■ *World View 495*   Historical Foundations 496
■ *Working with Diversity 499*   Culture Versus Climate 500

Creating the Organization Culture 500

Establish Values 500   Create Vision 501   Initiate Implementation Strategies 501
Reinforce Cultural Behaviors 502

Approaches to Describing Organization Culture 502

The Ouchi Framework 503   The Peters and Waterman Approach 505

Emerging Issues in Organization Culture 507

Innovation 507   Empowerment 509   ■ *Mastering Change 510*   Procedural Justice 511

Managing Organization Culture 511

Taking Advantage of the Existing Culture 511   Teaching the Organization Culture:
Socialization 512   Changing the Organization Culture 513

Organizational Behavior Case for Discussion: *Microsoft: Cult or Culture?* **516**

Experiencing Organizational Behavior: *Culture of the Classroom* **518**

Self-Assessment Exercise: *An Empowering Culture: What It Is and What It Is Not* **518**

OB Online 519

Building Managerial Skills 519

19 **Organization Change and Development 521**

Forces for Change 523

People 523   Technology 524   ■ *Working with Diversity 525*   Information Processing
and Communication 525   Competition 526   ■ *Talking Technology 527*

Processes for Planned Organization Change 527

Lewin's Process Model 528   The Continuous Change Process Model 528

Organization Development 530

Organization Development Defined 531   Systemwide Organization Development 531
Task and Technological Change 533   Group and Individual Change 534

Resistance to Change 538

Organizational Sources of Resistance 539   ■ *Mastering Change 540*   Individual Sources
of Resistance 541

Managing Successful Organization Change and Development 542
Consider International Issues 543   Take a Holistic View 543   Start Small 543
Secure Top Management Support 544   Encourage Participation 544
Foster Open Communication 544   Reward Contributors 544

Organizational Behavior Case for Discussion: *Change of Direction at Schwab* **546**
Experiencing Organizational Behavior: *Planning a Change at the University* **548**
Self-Assessment Exercise: *Support for Change* **549**
OB Online 549
Building Managerial Skills 550
Part IV Integrative Running Case: *The Downfall of Enron—The Organization* **551**

Appendix A **Research Methods in Organizational Behavior 554**
The Role of Theory and Research 554
Purposes of Research 555
The Scientific Research Process 555
Types of Research Designs 556
Case Study 556   Field Survey 557   Laboratory Experiment 558   Field Experiment 558
Methods of Gathering Data 559
Questionnaires 559   Interviews 559   Observation 559   Nonreactive Measures 559
Related Issues in Research 560
Causality 560   Reliability and Validity 560   Ethical Concerns 561

Appendix B **Career Dynamics 562**
Individual and Organizational Perspectives on Careers 563
Career Choices 564
Choice of Occupation 566   Choice of Organization 568   Changes in Midcareer 568
Career Stages 569
Entry 569   Trial 569   Establishment 571   Mastery 571   Exit 572   Mentoring 573
Organizational Career Planning 574
Purposes of Career Planning 574   Types of Career Programs 575
Career Management 577   Results of Career Planning 578

Endnotes 579
Glossary 601
Name Index 614
Organization Index 620
Subject Index 622

Preface

New Challenges for the New Century

WOW!! How things are changing in the new century! As we wrote the previous edition (the sixth), everyone was excited about the opportunities of the new century. Optimism was everywhere: for the new e-business, the Internet, an ever-expanding stock market, and a truly global marketplace. Now, three years later, the United States is in a recession, layoffs are commonplace, and while the Internet is still expanding, e-business is now in retrenchment. The stock market has plummeted and may take years to recover. Terrorism has invaded our peaceful world, threatening more people in scarier ways. The threat and existence of military conflicts in various parts of the world makes the business world less than stable. And all of those ubiquitous Top Ten Lists of the previous century are now forgotten as organizations struggle to figure out the new world order for their businesses, and then how to survive in it.

Focusing on how to survive and thrive in this ever-changing world is as important as ever. Computers are having the impact that was predicted twenty to thirty years ago. With computers and the advances in communications technology, we are certainly in the Internet age. The Internet age is so much more than just a faster way to communicate, however. Everything that people do is now done faster. In organizations, managers do not have the luxury of making significant changes and then sitting back to watch as the system adjusts and restabilizes, and these changes have an impact on operations. Previously, managers had the time to take measurements on the impact of the change and make more adjustments. Managers now must make a change and then prepare for the next change before the first one has fully taken effect. All of these changes that organizations are making—downsizing, merging, valuing diversity, acquiring, reengineering, and going global—are made at warp speed. Managers are creating new business, e.g., creating on-line stores that cannibalize their existing sales and distribution systems, before they know if Internet shopping will even work for their business. All of these changes require people to make the decisions and carry them out.

"Most managers now seem to understand that they will find competitive advantage by tapping employees' most essential humanity, their ability to create, judge, imagine, and build relationships. The champion managers of the Infotech Age will be those who do it fastest and best."—Geoffrey Colvin, "Managing in the Info Era," Fortune, March 6, 2000, pp. F-6–F-9, quote on p. F-9.

As we prepared this edition of *Organizational Behavior: Managing People and Organizations*, we considered what we had learned in the past and what new managers will need over the next few years, given the grave uncertainties that managers are facing. We realize that we cannot prepare them for every possibility and dilemma they will face in their management careers—their careers, after all, may last 40 years or longer! The world is already changing too fast for that.

We realize that we need to equip today's students with a perspective on managing people that allows them to create, judge, imagine, and build relationships, rather than provide every answer to every dilemma. That perspective needs to provide a firm grasp of the fundamentals of human behavior in organizations—the basic foundations of behavior so that they can develop new answers to the new problems they encounter. That perspective must also provide the background of the theories and approaches, not simply so they can answer questions on an exam, but so they can go back to the basics, the fundamentals, when things perplex them. A famous golf coach tells his students that if they go into a slump in hitting the golf ball, then they should always go back to the basics, and check the fundamentals in order to get back on track. The same works in managing people in organizations. As new challenges are thrust on us from around the world by global competition, new technologies, newer and faster information processes, new world-wide uncertainties and customers who demand the best in quality and service, the next generation of managers will need to go back to basics—the fundamentals—then combine those basics with valid new experiences in a complex world, and then develop creative new solutions, processes, products, or services to succeed and even gain a competitive advantage.

The Text That Meets the Challenge

This edition of *Organizational Behavior: Managing People and Organizations* takes on that charge by providing the basics in each area, bolstered by the latest research in the field, and infused with examples of what companies are doing in each area. We have made some changes in how the material is presented. We open each chapter with a textual introduction that weaves in a new opening incident and provides an immediate example of how the topic of the chapter is relevant in organizations. The chapter outlines and chapter objectives are available on the student web site as well as in the *Instructor's Resource Manual* for use in planning the discussion of the chapter material. We have further expanded the learning materials at the end of each chapter in order to provide more opportunities to work with the chapter content. In addition to the end of chapter case, experiencing exercise, and self-assessment exercise, we have revised the former Internet exercise to be a more practical OB Online, plus added an opportunity for students to build their own managerial skills, with the Building Management Skills exercise. We have kept the more in-depth case that is presented at the end of each part of the book. This edition's running case follows the blockbuster developments of the Enron case that rocked the business world in the recent past.

The text is presented in a dynamic and contemporary fashion, using more and bolder colors, more pictures, different print styles, and quotations by real managers about real organizational situations. We present the material in a fashion that is like popular business periodicals, and the book reads like a contemporary business magazine while still covering the basic foundation material of the field. Our students have remarked how easy it is to read this book and really get into the material. (They say they never count the pages they have left to read in each chapter in this book the way they do in other texts!)

In this edition we have kept the popular call-out quotes to emphasize bold statements made by contemporary organizational leaders talking about real managerial issues. We have resisted the recently popular trend of authors and publishers to cut the heart of the book in an effort to make books thinner. Several editions ago we cut out some material and rewrote other parts in a briefer form in an effort to reduce the mass of the book. Whereas those changes were favorably received, we have not gone any further in this downsizing in order to maintain the integrity of the book as truly representative of the field. We have left the meat. The basic theoretical approaches and developments that are the heart of this field are discussed in enough detail that students will understand them, yet not in so exhaustive fashion that they are overwhelmed.

Organizational Behavior: Managing People and Organizations, Seventh Edition, prepares and energizes managers of the future for the complex and challenging tasks of the new century while it preserves the past contributions of the classics. It is comprehensive in its presentation of practical perspectives, backed up by the research and learning of the experts. We expect each reader to be inspired by the most exciting task of the new century: managing people in organizations.

Content and Organization

The seventh edition of *Organizational Behavior: Managing People and Organizations* has essentially the same overall organization and topical presentation as did the previous edition. That is one of the benefits of a book in its seventh edition: we no longer have to experiment with different ways of combining the topics into chapters and parts. Based on feedback from reviewers, the current organization fits the way that many instructors prefer to approach the topics in their courses. We have, however, updated much of the research and added topics that needed attention throughout the text. Part I discusses the managerial context of organizational behavior. In Chapter 1 we describe Yellow Corporation and the role people have played in its transformation. This opening case provides an effective vehicle to introduce basic concepts of the field, to discuss the importance of the study of organizational behavior, and to give a brief history of the field, and sets the stage for study of the field. In Chapter 2 we develop a managerial perspective on the field by describing how Continental Airlines effectively integrated basic and sound management techniques with respect and consideration for the employees and led a remarkable turnaround that helped the firm navigate a post-9/11 world. This chapter develops a managerial perspective on organizational behavior and describes the manager's job in terms of its functions, roles, and skills. New material on workforce expansion and information technology has been added as part of the discussion of managerial challenges. Chapter 3 has been a real hit with users of the sixth edition. It combined former chapters on diversity and international issues to form a cohesive treatment of global issues and workforce diversity. In addition to the discussion of diversity programs in operation at Procter & Gamble we have updated the data on the changing workforce and added special features on the special problems of working women in Asia, how some managers are bringing spirituality into the workplace, and how UPS is diversifying its workforce to meet the challenges of an increasingly diverse world. The first three chapters, therefore, constitute an in-depth look at the context within which organizational behavior takes place.

Part II includes six chapters that focus on key aspects of individual processes in organizations: individual differences and perception, motivation, employee performance, and stress. Chapter 4 presents the foundations for understanding individual behavior in organizations by discussing the psychological nature of people, elements of personality, individual attitudes, perceptual processes, and creativity. We use numerous examples to illustrate some of the difficulties of dealing with the individuality of employees. Chapters 5 and 6 focus on the two primary categories of motivation theories: need-based approaches and process-based approaches. Although some may view this material as rather dull recitations of old theories, these two chapters are spiked with great real-world examples of how the basic approaches are meaningfully used in organizations today. Motivation techniques used by big companies such as Lucent Technologies, Ford Motor Company, and Commerce Bancorp are used throughout these chapters. Chapters 7 and 8 focus on specific methods, techniques, and strategies managers use to affect individual performance in organizations. Chapter 7 makes the transition from the theories to actual organizational practice by discussing job design, employee participation, and alternative work arrangements, including an expanded section on job sharing. To round out our study of individual/organizational motivation and performance, Chapter 8 provides the next practical step in motivation by focusing on goal setting, performance measurement, and rewards. The chapter includes special features on actual techniques, such as accelerated reviews, and pay and benefit practices at General Motors and Honda. Part II closes with the very important topics of work stress and work-life balance in Chapter 9. It presents the latest research on stress at work and shows how companies are paying more attention to the individual work-life balance and the needs of their employees. Included in this chapter is also a new discussion of the role of information technology in work stress.

In Part III we move from the individual aspects of organizational behavior to the more interpersonal aspects of the field, including communication, groups and teams, leadership and influence processes, and decision making. Chapter 10 describes the behavioral aspects of communication in organizations. Since most college and university business programs typically include one or two courses in communication, it is not our intent here to replicate that material. We do, however, provide an overview of the communication process, discuss important aspects of international communication, describe communication networks in organizations, and examine the impacts of computerized information processing and telecommunications in a variety of organizational settings. Chapters 11 and 12 are a two-chapter sequence on groups and teams in organizations. We believe there is too much important material to just have one chapter on these topics. Therefore, we present the basics of understanding the dynamics of small group behavior in Chapter 11 and discuss the more applied material on teams in Chapter 12. In this manner readers get to understand the more basic processes first before attacking the more complex issues in developing teams in organizations. New material on affinity groups has been added to Chapter 11, as well as examples from business— Lockheed Martin—and the business of sports—New York Yankees (the most successful sports franchise in history). Chapter 12 uses diverse examples, such as glass blowing and the Mayo Clinic, to illustrate the differences between groups and teams, the benefits and costs of teams, and the steps for implementing a team-based organization. We present leadership in a two-chapter sequence, examining models and concepts in Chapter 13 and influence processes in Chapter 14. These chapters present several new examples of non-traditional leaders such as Andy Pearson, CEO of Tricon, James Mullen, CEO of Biogen, and Susan Lyne, president of ABC Entertainment, in its coverage of the historical views of leadership; the basic trait, behavioral, and situational views; and contemporary views. This chapter includes a discussion of the role of gender in leadership and the newest version of the Vroom decision tree model of leadership. Closely related to leadership is the more complex topic of influence processes, discussed in Chapter 14.

The chapter moves from influence-based leadership approaches—transformational and charismatic leadership—to a discussion of substitutes for leadership, and then describes power and political behavior in organizations—both highly influence related phenomena. Finally, the last chapter in Part III on Interpersonal Processes in Organizations is Chapter 15, Decision Making and Negotiation. As we did in the sixth edition, we include group decision making in this chapter in order to present a cohesive discussion of individual and group decision making. Special features in this chapter include a discussion of decisions made at MTV by Bill Roedy and firms affected by the 9/11 terrorists attacks.

In Part IV we address more macro and system-wide aspects of organizational behavior. Chapter 16, the first of a two-chapter sequence on organization structure and design, describes the basic building blocks of organizations—division of labor, specialization, centralization, formalization, responsibility, and authority—and then presents the classical view of organizations of Weber, Fayol, and Likert. Special features describe the organization structure problems of AOL, Daimler-Chrysler, Deutsche Bank, General Electric, and Sapient. Chapter 17 describes more about the factors and the process through which the structure of an organization is matched to fit the demands of change, new technology, and expanding competition, including global issues and describes the restructuring problems at AT&T, Wal-Mart, Dell Computers, and Cisco. A special focus on ethics is highlighted in the organizational problems faced by ImClone Systems. Chapter 18 moves on to the more elusive concept of organizational culture. We differentiate culture from climate and describe the classic views of culture, as described by Peters and Waterman, Deal and Kennedy, and Ouchi. We strengthened the discussion of the process of creating the organizational culture and present special features on the unusual problems faced by Southwest Airlines as they try to maintain their culture following the retirement of Herb Kelleher, the eclectic culture of ING Corporation, the problems of women working at WalMart, and difficulties inherent in meshing the cultures of HP and Compaq. The final chapter, Chapter 19, could really be the cornerstone of every chapter, because it presents the classical and contemporary views of organizational change. Due to the demands on organizations today, as stated earlier and by every management writer alive, change is the order of the day, the year, the decade, and the new century. The only constant in organizations today is constant change. Changes at Vivendi, Avon, Context Integration, and Electronic Data Systems Corporation provide powerful illustrations of the necessity and complexity of change.

Features of the Book

This edition of *Organizational Behavior: Managing People and Organizations* is guided by our continuing devotion to the preparation of the next generation of managers. This is reflected in four key elements of the book which we believe stem from this guiding principle: a strong student orientation; contemporary content; a real world, applied approach; and effective pedagogy.

Student Orientation

We believe that students, instructors, and other readers will agree with our students' reactions to the book as being easy and even enjoyable to read with its direct and active style. We have tried to retain the comprehensive nature of the book while writing in a style that is active and lively and geared to the student reader. We want your students to enjoy reading the book while they learn from it. As an example, here is an unsolicited quote from a professor whose students used this book this past semester.

"My students liked your textbook a lot (so did I)! They said the theories are described in ways that are clear and to-the-point. Interestingly, the engineers (about half of my students) said your book was extremely helpful because the theories were new to them."—Lynne McClure, Ph.D., Arizona State University

The cartoons and their content-rich captions tie the humorous intent of the cartoons to the concepts in the text. All of the figures include meaningful captions, again to tie the figure directly to the concepts. The end-of-chapter features retain the popular experiential exercises and the diagnostic questionnaire, or self-assessments, and the real-world cases that show how the chapter material relates to actual practice.

We have changed the running case at the end of each of the four parts of the book to provide a more current, deeper, and more integrative real-world example. These end-of-part cases describe the interesting management problems in the Enron situation that dominated the front pages of the world's newspapers, as well as the business section. We did not have to look very far to find this classic story. We hope you and your students enjoy considering the issues of this disaster.

Contemporary Content Coverage

This edition continues our tradition of presenting the most modern management approaches as expressed in the popular press and the academic research. The basic structure of the book remains the same, but you will find new items that represent the most recent research in many areas of the book.

Real World, Applied Approach

The organizations cited in the opening incidents, examples, cases, and boxed features throughout this edition represent a blend of large, well-known and smaller, less well-known organizations so that students will see the applicability of the material in a variety of organizational settings. Each chapter opens and closes with concrete examples of relevant topics from the chapter. The running end-of-part case on the Enron disaster provides a more in-depth case for class discussion. Each chapter also contains two or three boxes, selected from the five types of boxed features included in this edition. Each box has a unique, identifying icon that distinguishes it and makes it easier for students to identify.

 Each *Talking Technology* box describes how a company uses advances in computer and information technology to improve its business.

 Each *Mastering Change* box shows an organization rethinking its methods of operation to respond to changes in the business climate.

Each *Business of Ethics* box explores an organization dealing with ethical issues.

 Each *Working with Diversity* box describes an organization meeting the needs of its increasingly diverse work force.

 Each *World View* box examines an issue an organization and the people in it face as the organization expands its global operations.

Effective Pedagogy

Our guiding intent continues to be to put together a package that enhances student learning. The package includes several features of the book, many of which have already been mentioned.

- Each chapter begins with a Management Preview and ends with a Synopsis.
- *Discussion Questions* at the end of each chapter stimulate interaction among students and provide a guide to complete studying of the chapter concepts.
- An *Experiencing Organizational Behavior* exercise at the end of each chapter helps students make the transition from textbook learning to real world applications. The end-of-chapter case, "Organizational Behavior Case for Discussion" also assists in this transition.
- A *Self-Assessment* activity at the end of each chapter gives students the opportunity to apply a concept from the chapter to a brief self-assessment or diagnostic activity.
- The *OB Online* feature encourages students to reach beyond the text to find organizations or other resources on the Web that illustrate the issues discussed in the chapter.
- The brand new *Building Managerial Skills* activity provides an opportunity for students to "get their hands dirty" and really use something discussed in the chapter.
- The Integrative Running Case at the end of each part on the Enron collapse provides an opportunity for students to discuss an actual ongoing management situation with significant organizational behavior facets.
- Figures, tables, photographs, and cartoons offer visual and humorous support for the text content. Explanatory captions to figures, photographs, and cartoons enhance their pedagogical value.
- A running marginal glossary and a complete glossary at the end of the book provide additional support for identifying and learning key concepts.

A new design reflects this edition's content, style, and pedagogical program. The colors remain bold to reflect the dynamic nature of the behavioral and managerial challenges facing managers today, and all interior photographs are new to this edition and have been specially selected to highlight the dynamic world of organizational behavior. Call-out quotes like you might find in many popular business magazines are found throughout every chapter to call special attention to what real managers are saying about managing people in organizations.

We would like to hear from you about your experiences in using the book. We want to know what you like and what you do not like about it. Please write to us via email to tell us about your learning experiences with the book. You may contact us at:

<table>
<tr><td>Greg Moorhead</td><td>Ricky Griffin</td></tr>
<tr><td>greg.moorhead@asu.edu</td><td>RGriffin@tamu.edu</td></tr>
</table>

A Complete Teaching and Learning Package

A complete package of teaching and learning support materials accompanies the seventh edition.

For Students

The *Student Web Site* provides additional information, study aids, activities, and resources that help reinforce the concepts presented in the text. The site includes: learning objectives; brief chapter outlines; chapter summaries; the OB Online exercises from the text with relevant links and any necessary updates; ACE self-tests; a glossary of key terms; flash cards for reviewing the key terms; additional cases; convenient chapter links to the organizations highlighted in the text; and a resource center with links to various sites of general organizational behavior interest.

OB in Action, Seventh Edition, by Steven Wolff provides additional cases and hands-on experiential exercises to help students bridge the gap between theory and practice. Working individually or with teams, students tackle problems and find solutions, using organizational theories as their foundation. The author brings his extensive experience in both university classroom and executive training and development settings to his work in creating this new edition.

For Instructors

The *Instructor's Resource Manual,* revised by Bruce Barringer, *University of Central Florida,* includes for each chapter a synopsis, learning objectives, detailed lecture outline, suggested answers to the text questions and activities, and a supplemental mini-lecture. Also included are a section on learning and teaching ideologies, suggested course outlines, suggestions on how to use the mini-lectures, and a transition guide to help current users of the sixth edition move easily to this new edition.

The *Test Bank,* prepared by David Glew, *The University of Tulsa,* has been thoroughly revised to match changes in the new edition and contains multiple-choice, true/false, completion, matching, and essay questions for every chapter. A text page reference and learning-level indicator accompanies each question. A *call-in test service* is also available.

The new *HM ClassPrep with HM Testing* is offered on CD-ROM and is designed to assist the instructor with in-class lectures and text preparation. The *ClassPrep* component includes key pieces of the *Instructor's Resource Manual* in electronic format as well as a complete PowerPoint package that includes key figures from the text. Also included on the CD is *HM Testing*. This computerized version of the *Test Bank* allows instructors to select, edit, and add questions, or generate randomly selected questions to produce a test master for easy duplication. Online Testing and Gradebook functions allow instructors to administer tests via their local area network or the World Wide Web, set up classes, record grades from tests or assignments, analyze grades, and product class and individual statistics. This program can be used on both PCs and Macintosh computers.

The completely new password-protected *Instructor Web Site* provides several tools to help prepare and deliver lectures: downloadable files of the *Instructor's Resource Manual*; downloadable PowerPoint® slides; suggested answers to the activities on the Student Web Site, and the Video Guide with video summaries, suggested uses, and questions for discussion.

A detailed set of ***PowerPoint Slides***, available on both the ***Instructor Web Site*** and the ***HM ClassPrep CD***, combines clear, concise text and art to create a complete lecture package with more than 20 slides per chapter. Instructors can use the slides as-is or edit them. Slides also can be printed for lecture notes and class distribution.

A set of full-color ***transparencies*** includes 100 images that highlight key figures and definitions from the text as well as additional images that can be used to enhance lecture presentation.

A special set of ***videos*** is provided to enhance the teaching package. Focusing on key topics of organizational behavior, the videos present additional material to help bring the concepts to life. Teaching notes and suggestions are also provided.

The ***Instructor's Resource Manual*** for *OB in Action* provides requirements, objectives, background, suggested outlines and timing for each exercise, and it flags some issues that may be raised. It also includes curve balls for instructors to use when groups come to facile or premature decisions.

Acknowledgments

Although this book bears our two names, numerous people have contributed to it. Through the years we have had the good fortune to work with many fine professionals who helped us to sharpen our thinking about this complex field and to develop new and more effective ways of discussing it. Their contributions were essential to the development of this edition. Any and all errors of omission, interpretation, and emphasis remain the responsibility of the authors.

Several reviewers made essential contributions to the development of this and previous editions. We would like to express a special thanks to them for taking the time to provide us with their valuable assistance:

Abdul Aziz, *College of Charleston*
Steve Ball, *Cleary College*
Brendan Bannister, *Northeastern University*
Greg Baxter, *Southeastern Oklahoma State University*
Jon W. Beard, *Texas A&M University*
Mary-Beth Beres, *Mercer University Atlanta*
Ronald A. Bigoness, *Stephen F. Austin State University*
Allen Bluedorn, *University of Missouri Columbia*
Murray Brunton, *Central Ohio Technical College*
John Bunch, *Kansas State University*
Mark Butler, *San Diego State University*
Richard R. Camp, *Eastern Michigan University*
Anthony Chelte, *Western New England College*
Dan R. Dalton, *Indiana University Bloomington*
Carla L. Dando, *Idaho State University*
T. K. Das, *Baruch College*
George deLodzia, *University of Rhode Island*
Ronald A. DiBattista, *Bryant College*
Thomas W. Dougherty, *University of Missouri Columbia*
Cathy Dubois, *Kent State University*
Earlinda Elder-Albritton, *Detroit College of Business*
Stanley W. Elsea, *Kansas State University*
Maureen J. Fleming, *The University of Montana—Missoula*
Joseph Forest, *Georgia State University*
Eliezer Geisler, *Northeastern Illinois University*
Robert Giacalone, *University of Richmond*
Lynn Harland, *University of Nebraska at Omaha*
Stan Harris, *Lawrence Tech University*
Nell Hartley, *Robert Morris College*
Peter Heine, *Stetson University*
William Hendrix, *Clemson University*
John Jermier, *University of South Florida*
Avis L. Johnson, *University of Akron*
Bruce Johnson, *Gustavus Adolphus College*
Gwen Jones, *Bowling Green State University*
Robert T. Keller, *University of Houston*

Michael Klausner, *University of Pittsburgh at Bradford*
Stephen Kleisath, *University of Wisconsin*
Barbara E. Kovatch, *Rutgers University*
David R. Lee, *University of Dayton*
Richard Leifer, *Rensselaer Polytechnic Institute*
Robert Leonard, *Lebanon Valley College*
Peter Lorenzi, *University of Central Arkansas*
Joseph B. Lovell, *California State University, San Bernardino*
Patricia Manninen, *North Shore Community College*
Edward K. Marlow, *Eastern Illinois University*
Edward Miles, *Georgia State University*
C. W. Millard, *University of Puget Sound*
Alan N. Miller, *University of Nevada Las Vegas*
Herff L. Moore, *University of Central Arkansas*
Robert Moorman, *West Virginia University*
Stephan J. Motowidlo, *Pennsylvania State University*
Richard T. Mowday, *University of Oregon*
Margaret A. Neale, *Northwestern University*
Christopher P. Neck, *Virginia Tech*
Linda L. Neider, *University of Miami*
Mary Lippitt Nichols, *University of Minnesota Minneapolis*
Ranjna Patel, *Bethune-Cookman College*
Robert J. Paul, *Kansas State University*
Pamela Pommerenke, *Michigan State University*
James C. Quick, *University of Texas at Arlington*
Richard Raspen, *Wilkes University*
Elizabeth Rawlin, *University of South Carolina*
Joan B. Rivera, *West Texas A&M University*
Bill Robinson, *Indiana University of Pennsylvania*
Hannah Rothstein, *CUNY—Baruch College*
Carol S. Saunders, *Florida Atlantic University*
Constance Savage, *Ashland University*
Mary Jane Saxton, *University of Colorado at Denver*
Ralph L. Schmitt, *Macomb Community College*
Randall S. Schuler, *New York University*
Amit Shah, *Frostburg State University*
Gary Shields, *Wayne State University*
Randall G. Sleeth, *Virginia Commonwealth University*
William R. Stevens, *Missouri Southern State College*
Steve Taylor, *Boston College*
Donald Tompkins, *Slippery Rock University*
Ahmad Tootoonchi, *Frostburg State University*
Matthew Valle, *Troy State University at Dothan*
Linn Van Dyne, *Michigan State University*
David D. Van Fleet, *Arizona State University West*
Bobby C. Vaught, *Southwest Missouri State University*
Sean Valentine, *University of Wyoming*
Jack W. Waldrip, *American Graduate School of International Management*
John P. Wanous, *The Ohio State University*
Judith Y. Weisinger, *Northeastern University*
Albert D. Widman, *Berkeley College*

The seventh edition could never have been completed without the support of Arizona State University and Texas A&M University. Bill Glick, chair of the Management Department; Larry Penley, dean of the W. P. Carey School of Business at Arizona State University; and Jerry Strawser, dean of the Mays Business School at Texas A&M University, facilitated our work by providing environments that encourage scholarly activities and contributions to the field. Several secretaries and graduate and undergraduate assistants were also involved in the development of the seventh edition. We extend our appreciation to Phyllis Washburn, Linda Perry, and Emily Emmer.

We would also like to acknowledge the outstanding team of professionals at Houghton Mifflin Company who helped us prepare this book. Jessica Carlisle and Rachel D'Angelo Wimberly have done yeoman's work in pulling all of the parts of this book together and shepherding it through the process. George Hoffman, Susan Kahn, and Steve Mikels were also key players in planning the book and supplements package from start to finish. Others who made significant contributions to this edition's team are Lisa Boden, Sarah Ambrose, Priscilla Bailey, Katie Huha, and May Jawdat.

Finally, we would like to acknowledge the daily reminders that we get from our families of the importance of our work. As we wrote each revision, our families grew and changed, just as we did. Neither of our wives is doing the same things that they were when we wrote the first edition, and the children are out of college and even graduates in some cases. Often one of them will tell us that one of their friends is in our class or is using our book. Such comments make us feel really old, but they also provide us with some of the best reasons for doing what we do. We get long distance phone calls asking how the book is going and are often chastised for not meeting a deadline. With all of the changes in our lives, we devoted the time and energy to prepare this revision. Without the love and support of our families our lives would be far less enriched and meaningful. It is with all of our love that we dedicate this book to them.

G.M.

R.W.G.

1 An Overview of Organizational Behavior

Management Preview

▶ Effectively managing an organization's resources is one of the most critical activities in any complex society. Human behaviors, decisions, and actions, in turn, play vital and pervasive roles throughout every aspect of both management processes and organizations. Thus, understanding human behavior in organizational settings is a fundamental necessity for all managers, including both current practitioners and those who aspire to hold management positions in the future. In this opening chapter, we introduce you to the meaning of organizational behavior and then trace its development from its earliest simple concepts through modern times as it has evolved into a complex and multidisciplinary field capable of explaining many different forms of complex organizational phenomena. We conclude the chapter by presenting useful contextual perspectives that effectively link the field's theoretical concepts with the practical elements of organizational realities. First, though, we begin by illustrating how one manager, Bill Zollars, has effectively capitalized on the people at Yellow Freight to revitalize the firm and transform it into a model of twenty-first-century excellence.

▼ ▼ ▼

Since its founding in 1923, Yellow Corporation has led the transportation industry by using its trucks to haul large, heavy items between major shipping centers in the United States, Canada, and Mexico. For decades the firm focused on ways to increase its efficiency, such as ensuring that all trucks were full before they left the warehouse and using an inflexible delivery schedule to reduce last-minute changes. But Yellow was the victim of its own success—as operational efficiency increased, customer service was given less attention, allowing newer and more responsive companies to lure away many of the firm's customers. Even worse, the customers most likely to seek a different, more service-oriented transportation provider were also the very ones who were willing to pay premium prices for the extra service.

Bill Zollars was intrigued by the opportunity to revitalize the carrier, accepting the role of chief executive officer (CEO) of Yellow Freight in 1996. James Welch, president and chief operating officer, recollects, "We were a defensive company—a follower, not a leader. We were yearning for leadership. This company was ready for change." Zollars understood that successful organizational transformation would need to be profound, altering the attitudes, behaviors, and performance of each of the firm's 30,000 employees.

Communication was one key to Zollars's management revolution at Yellow. The CEO spent eighteen months traveling to the company's several hundred locations in order to talk face to face with customers and employees at all levels. He repeatedly put forth his message of the need for enhanced customer service, but the meetings consisted of more than just empty promises and motivational speeches. Zollars was the first Yellow manager to accurately report the true defect rate—the percentage of shipments that were late, wrong, or damaged. Yellow employees were stunned to learn that their defect rate was a whopping 40 percent, but that knowledge was necessary to provide motivation and a benchmark for improvement. Zollars also instituted the company's first ongoing program for surveying customer satisfaction and then reporting the results openly throughout the company.

"If people doing the work don't believe what's coming from the leadership, it doesn't get implemented. Period."—Bill Zollars, CEO of Yellow Freight

Zollars's leadership created a sense of motivation and pride among employees, which in turn led to continuing high levels of productivity and performance. He made a real effort to listen to his employees, entertain their suggestions, and give them additional authority to make decisions. He earned an enviable reputation for honesty and commitment, attempting to "walk the walk" as well as "talk the talk." Zollars asserts, "If people doing the work don't believe what's coming from the leadership, it doesn't get implemented. Period."

Technology also played an important role in Yellow's success. The firm implemented a variety of automated systems to improve customer service and satisfaction. The systems provide up-to-the-minute information about a shipment's progress via the Internet, maintain a customer database that enables faster scheduling, and develop the truck loading procedures and routes that will ensure on-time delivery. However, the real technology success story at Yellow isn't merely the innovative and efficient use of technology but rather the savvy application of those systems to support employees and customers.

Perhaps the most challenging and yet the most important change at Yellow was the re-envisioning of the company's mission from delivery of freight to customer service. When the firm's employees saw their primary goal as the efficient movement of cargo, the firm focused on one set of processes. Today, thanks to the efforts of Zollars and other managers, employees realize that supporting customers by meeting their delivery needs is their paramount task. This shift in perspective enables the firm to provide better service to its customers, to develop innovative new products and services, to improve its performance, and ultimately, to compete successfully in an increasingly tough industry. As Bill Zollars says in the firm's 2000 Annual Report, "Our business really isn't about moving freight. It's about earning the trust of the consumers of our services."

References: Matthew Boyle, "America's Most Admired Companies: The Right Stuff," *Fortune*, March 4, 2002. www.fortune.com on March 6, 2002; Chuck Salter, "Fresh Start 2002: On the Road Again," *Fast Company*, January 2002, pp. 50–58 (quotation on p. 57). See www.fastcompany.com; "Yellow Corporation 2000 Annual Report," March 2001. www.yellowcorp.com on March 6, 2002.

B ill Zollars's success at Yellow Freight has been based on a number of different factors, including his skills as a manager and his understanding of the importance of other people. He clearly recognizes the value of control and operational systems in a successful organization. But perhaps even more importantly, he sees the value of people as a key determinant of success. Indeed, no manager can succeed without the assistance of others. Thus, any manager—whether responsible for an industrial giant like General Electric, Honda, IBM, or British Airways; the Boston Celtics basketball team; the Mayo Clinic; or a local Pizza Hut restaurant—must strive to understand the people who work in the organization. This book is about those people. It is also about the organization itself and the managers who operate it. The study of organizations and of the people who work in them together constitutes the field of organizational behavior. Our starting point in exploring this field begins with a more detailed discussion of its meaning and its importance to managers.

What Is Organizational Behavior?

Organizational behavior (OB) is the study of human behavior in organizational settings, the interface between human behavior and the organization, and the organization itself.

W hat exactly is meant by the term "organizational behavior"? And why should it be studied? Answers to these two fundamental questions will both help establish our foundation for discussion and analysis and help you better appreciate how and why understanding the field can be of value to you in the future.

The Meaning of Organizational Behavior

figure 1.1

The Nature of Organizational Behavior

The field of organizational behavior attempts to understand human behavior in organizational settings, the organization itself, and the individual-organization interface. As illustrated here, these areas are highly interrelated. Thus, although it is possible to focus on only one of these areas at a time, a complete understanding of organizational behavior requires knowledge of all three areas.

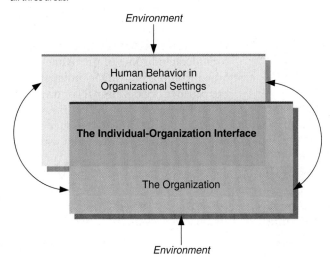

Organizational behavior (OB) is the study of human behavior in organizational settings, of the interface between human behavior and the organization, and of the organization itself.[1] Although we can focus on any one of these three areas, we must remember that all three are ultimately necessary for a comprehensive understanding of organizational behavior. For example, we can study individual behavior (such as the behavior of Bill Zollars or of one of his Yellow Freight employees) without explicitly considering the organization. But because the organization influences and is influenced by the individual, we cannot fully understand the individual's behavior without learning something about the organization. Similarly, we can study organizations (such as Yellow Freight itself) without focusing explicitly on the people within them. But again, we are looking at only a portion of the puzzle. Eventually we must consider the other pieces as well as the whole.

Figure 1.1 illustrates this view of organizational behavior. It shows the linkages among human behavior in organizational settings, the individual-organization interface, the organization, and the environment surrounding the

When people hear the name of a business their first thought is usually of a building, a product, a logo or slogan. But in reality it is people who are the essence of any organization. From the top managers who establish corporate strategy to the rank-and-file workers who perform basic tasks to the custodial crew cleaning up at the end of the day, it is the people of a business who ultimately determine its success or failure. And more and more enlightened companies today are recognizing the critical importance of attracting and retaining the very best workers possible. Take Pret A Manger, for instance. Pret A Manger is a London-based fast-food company that is revolutionizing the industry. On the heels of its success in the United Kingdom, the company is now beginning an ambitious expansion into the United States. And it plans to rely heavily on the skills and abilities of workers like these to fuel its success. The company strives to attract bright and energetic workers by offering managers schedules that exclude nights and weekends, and hosting weekly "pub nights" for all employees. Pret hopes that policies and perks like this will attract and retain enthusiastic and satisfied workers who will in turn pass on that enthusiasm and satisfaction to customers.

organization. Each individual brings to an organization a unique set of personal background and characteristics as well as experiences from other organizations. In considering the people who work in organizations, therefore, a manager must look at the unique perspective each individual brings to the work setting. For example, suppose The Home Depot hires a consultant to investigate employee turnover. As a starting point, the consultant might analyze the types of people the company usually hires. The goal would be to learn as much as possible about the nature of the company's workforce as individuals—their expectations, their personal goals, and so forth.

But individuals do not work in isolation. They come in contact with other people and with the organization in a variety of ways. Points of contact include managers, coworkers, the formal policies and procedures of the organization, and various changes implemented by the organization. Over time, the individual changes, too, as a function both of personal experiences and maturity and of work experiences and the organization. The organization, in turn, is affected by the presence and eventual absence of the individual. Clearly, then, managers must also consider how the individual and the organization interact. Thus, the consultant studying turnover at The Home Depot might next look at the orientation procedures for newcomers to the organization. The goal of this phase of the study would be to understand some of the dynamics of how incoming individuals interact with the broader organizational context.

An organization, of course, exists before a particular person joins it and continues to exist after he or she leaves. Thus, the organization itself represents a crucial third perspective from which to view organizational behavior. For instance, the consultant studying turnover would also need to study the structure and culture of The Home Depot. An understanding of factors such as the performance evaluation and reward systems, the decision-making and communication patterns, and the design of the firm itself can provide added insight into why some people choose to leave a company and others elect to stay.

Thus, the field of organizational behavior is both exciting and complex. Myriad variables and concepts accompany the interactions just described, and together these factors greatly complicate the manager's ability to understand, appreciate, and manage others in the organization. They also provide unique and important opportunities to enhance personal and organizational effectiveness.

The Importance of Organizational Behavior

The importance of organizational behavior may now be clear, but we should take a few moments to make it even more explicit. Most people are born and educated in organizations, acquire most of their material possessions from organizations, and die as members of organizations. Many of our activities are regulated by the various organizations that make up our governments. And most adults spend the better part of their lives working in organizations. Because organizations influence our lives so powerfully, we have every reason to be concerned about how and why those organizations function.

In our relationships with organizations, we may adopt any one of several roles or identities. For example, we can be consumers, employees, or investors. Since most readers of this book are either present or future managers, we will adopt a managerial perspective throughout our discussion. The study of organizational behavior can greatly clarify the factors that affect how managers manage. Hence, the field attempts to describe the complex human context of organizations and to define the opportunities, problems, challenges, and issues associated with that realm. The value of organizational behavior is that it isolates important aspects of the manager's job and offers specific perspectives on the human side of management: people as organizations, people as resources, and people as people.

Clearly, then, an understanding of organizational behavior can play a vital role in managerial work. To use the knowledge provided by this field most effectively, however, managers must thoroughly understand its various concepts, assumptions, and premises. To provide the groundwork for this understanding, we start by looking at the field's historical roots.

The Historical Roots of Organizational Behavior

Many disciplines, such as physics and chemistry, are literally thousands of years old. Management has also been around in one form or another for centuries. For example, the writings of Aristotle and Plato abound with references to and examples of management concepts and practices. But because serious interest in the study of management did not emerge until around the turn of the twentieth century, the study of organizational behavior is only a few decades old.[2]

"Business history lets us look at what we did right and, more important, it can help us be right the next time."—Alfred D. Chandler Jr., noted business historian[3]

One reason for the relatively late development of management as a scientific field is that few large business organizations existed before the nineteenth century. Although management is just as important to a small organization as to a large one, large firms were needed to provide both a stimulus and a laboratory for management research. A second reason is that many of the first people who took an interest in studying organizations were economists who initially assumed that management practices at the organizational level are by nature efficient and effective; therefore, they concentrated on higher levels of analysis such as national economic policy and industrial structures.

Interestingly, many contemporary managers have come to appreciate the value of history. For example, managers can glean useful organizational insights from such diverse works as Homer's *Iliad*, Machiavelli's *The Prince*, Sun Tsu's *The Art of War*, Musashi's *The Book of Five Rings*, and Chaucer's *The Canterbury Tales*. And some organizations, such as Polaroid and Wells Fargo, have corporate historians to help preserve their past. Others, such as Shell Oil and Coca-Cola, openly proclaim their heritage as part of their employee orientation programs and often stress their rich histories as part of their advertising and public relations activities.[4]

The Scientific Management Era

Scientific management, one of the first approaches to management, focused on the efficiency of individual workers.

One of the first approaches to the study of management, popularized during the early 1900s, was **scientific management.** Scientific management was developed primarily in the United States. It focused primarily on the efficiency of individual workers. Several individuals helped develop and promote scientific management, including Frank and Lillian Gilbreth (whose lives were portrayed in a book and a subsequent movie, *Cheaper by the Dozen*), Henry Gantt, and Harrington Emerson. But Frederick W. Taylor is most closely identified with this approach.[5] Early in his life, Taylor developed an interest in efficiency and productivity. While working as a foreman at Midvale Steel Company in Philadelphia from 1878 to 1890, he became aware of a phenomenon he called "soldiering"—employees working at a pace much slower than their capabilities. Because most managers had never systematically studied jobs in the plant—and, in fact, had little idea how to gauge worker productivity—they were completely unaware of this practice.

To counteract the effects of soldiering, Taylor developed several innovative techniques. For example, he scientifically studied all the jobs in the Midvale plant and developed a standardized method for performing each one. He also installed a piece-rate pay system in which each worker was paid for the amount of work that individual completed during the workday rather than for the time spent on the job. (Taylor believed that money was the only important motivational factor in the workplace.) These innovations boosted productivity markedly and are the foundation of scientific management.

After leaving Midvale, Taylor spent several years working as a management consultant for industrial firms. At Bethlehem Steel Company, he developed several efficient techniques for loading and unloading rail cars. At Simonds Rolling Machine Company, he redesigned jobs, introduced rest breaks to combat fatigue, and implemented a piece-rate pay system. In every case, Taylor claimed his ideas and methods greatly improved worker output. His book *Principles of Scientific Management*, published in 1911, was greeted with enthusiasm by practicing managers and quickly became a standard reference.

"It's [Frederick Taylor's] ideas that determine how many burgers McDonald's expects its flippers to flip or how many callers the phone company expects its operators to assist."—Robert Kanigel, Taylor's biographer[6]

Scientific management quickly became a mainstay of business practice. Among other things, it facilitated job specialization and mass production, profoundly influencing the U.S. business system.[7] It also demonstrated to managers the importance of enhancing performance and productivity and confirmed their influence on these matters. For example, firms such as UPS and McDonald's today still use some of the basic concepts introduced during the scientific management era in their efforts to become ever more efficient.

Taylor had his critics, however. Labor opposed scientific management because its explicit goal was to get more output from workers. Congress investigated Taylor's methods and ideas because some argued that his incentive system would dehumanize the workplace and reduce workers to little more than drones. Later theorists recognized that Taylor's views of employee motivation were inadequate and narrow. And recently there have been allegations that Taylor falsified some of his research findings and paid someone to do his writing for him. Nevertheless, scientific management represents a key milestone in the development of management thought.[8]

Classical Organization Theory

Classical organization theory, another early approach to management, focused on how organizations can be structured most effectively to meet their goals.

During the same era, another perspective on management theory and practice was also emerging. Generally referred to as **classical organization theory,** this perspective was concerned with structuring organizations effectively. Whereas scientific management studied how individual workers could be made more efficient, classical organization theory focused on how a large number of workers and managers could be organized most effectively into an overall structure. Interestingly, whereas scientific management was generally an American phenomenon, classical organization theory has a much more international heritage.

Henri Fayol (a French executive and engineer), Lyndall Urwick (a British executive), and Max Weber (a German sociologist) were major contributors to classical organization theory. Weber, the most prominent of the three, proposed a "bureaucratic" form of structure that he believed would work for all organizations.[9] Although today the term "bureaucracy" conjures up images of paperwork, red tape, and inflexibility, in Weber's model bureaucracy embraced logic, rationality, and efficiency. Weber assumed that the bureaucratic structure would always be the most efficient approach. (Such a blanket prescription represents what is now called a universal approach.) Table 1.1 summarizes the elements of Weber's ideal bureaucracy.

In contrast to Weber's views, contemporary organization theorists recognize that different organization structures may be appropriate in different situations. However, like scientific management, classical organization theory played a key role in the development of management thought, and Weber's ideas and the concepts associated with his bureaucratic structure are still interesting and relevant today. (Chapters 16 and 17 discuss contemporary organization theory.)

The Emergence of Organizational Behavior

Rationality, efficiency, and standardization were the central themes of both scientific management and classical organization theory. The roles of individuals and groups in organizations were either ignored altogether or given only minimal attention. A few early writers and managers, however, recognized the importance of individual and social processes in organizations.

table 1.1

Elements of Weber's Ideal Bureaucracy

Elements	Comments
1. **Rules and Procedures**	A consistent set of abstract rules and procedures should exist to ensure uniform performance.
2. **Distinct Division of Labor**	Each position should be filled by an expert.
3. **Hierarchy of Authority**	The chain of command should be clearly established.
4. **Technical Competence**	Employment and advancement should be based on merit.
5. **Segregation of Ownership**	Professional managers rather than owners should run the organization.
6. **Rights and Properties of the Position**	These should be associated with the organization, not with the person who holds the office.
7. **Documentation**	A record of actions should be kept regarding administrative decisions, rules, and procedures.

Precursors of Organizational Behavior

In the early nineteenth century, Robert Owen, a British industrialist, attempted to better the condition of industrial workers. He improved working conditions, raised minimum ages for hiring children, introduced meals for employees, and shortened working hours. In the early twentieth century, the noted German psychologist Hugo Münsterberg argued that the field of psychology could provide important insights into areas such as motivation and the hiring of new employees. Another writer in the early 1900s, Mary Parker Follett, believed that management should become more democratic in its dealings with employees. An expert in vocational guidance, Follett argued that organizations should strive harder to accommodate their employees' human needs.[10] Indeed, as the "Working with Diversity" box clearly indicates, Follett's work, neglected in the years following her death, foreshadowed many of today's most popular and widely used management innovations.

Like Follett's perspective, the views of Owen and Münsterberg were not widely shared by practicing managers. Not until the 1930s did management's perception of the relationship between the individual and the workplace change significantly. At that time, a series of now-classic research studies led to the emergence of organizational behavior as a field of study.

The Hawthorne Studies

The **Hawthorne studies** were conducted between 1927 and 1932 at Western Electric's Hawthorne plant near Chicago. (General Electric initially sponsored the research but withdrew its support after the first study was finished.) Several researchers were involved, the best known being William Dickson, chief of Hawthorne's Employee Relations Research Department, who initiated the research, and Elton Mayo and Fritz Roethlisberger, Harvard faculty members and consultants, who were called in after some of the more interesting findings began to surface.[11]

The first major experiment at Hawthorne investigated the effects of different levels of lighting on productivity. The researchers systematically manipulated the lighting of the area in which a group of women worked. The group's productivity

The Hawthorne studies, conducted between 1927 and 1932, led to some of the first discoveries of the importance of human behavior in organizations.

The Hawthorne studies were a series of early experiments that focused new attention on the role of human behavior in the workplace. In one experiment involving this group of workers, for example, researchers monitored how productivity changed as a result of changes in working conditions. To the surprise of the researchers, behavioral processes apparently played a major role in the productivity gains that were achieved. These findings, in turn, served as a catalyst for other major research projects designed to learn more about the role of human behavior at work. The Hawthorne studies and subsequent research thus led directly to the emergence of organizational behavior as an important field of study in the business world.

was measured and compared with that of another group (the control group), whose lighting was left unchanged. As lighting was increased for the experimental group, productivity went up—but, surprisingly, so did the productivity of the control group. Even when lighting was subsequently reduced, the productivity of both groups continued to increase. Not until the lighting had become almost as dim as moonlight did productivity start to decline. This result led the researchers to conclude that lighting had no relationship to productivity—and it was at this point that General Electric withdrew its sponsorship of the project!

In another major experiment, a piecework incentive system was established for a nine-person group that assembled terminal banks for telephone exchanges. Scientific management would have predicted that each individual would work as hard as he or she could to maximize personal income. But the Hawthorne researchers instead found that the group as a whole established an acceptable level of output for its members. Individuals who failed to meet this level were dubbed "chiselers," and those who exceeded it by too much were branded "rate busters." A worker who wanted to be accepted by the group could not produce at too high or too low a level. Thus, as a worker approached the accepted level each day, he or she slowed down to avoid overproducing.

After a follow-up interview program with several thousand workers, the Hawthorne researchers concluded that the human element in the workplace was considerably more important than previously believed. The lighting experiment, for example, suggested that productivity might increase simply because workers were singled out for special treatment and thus perhaps felt more valued. In the incentive system experiment, being accepted as a part of the group evidently meant more to the workers than earning extra money. Several other studies supported the overall conclusion that individual and social processes are too important to ignore.

WORKING WITH DIVERSITY

▶ The Mother of Them All?

The business section of virtually any bookstore today carries literally dozens of books extolling the virtues of empowerment and cross-functional work teams and dozens of other books stressing the importance of knowledge-based leadership and organizational flexibility. Interestingly, however, many of these same "cutting-edge" ideas were also set forth around eighty years ago by a management pioneer named Mary Parker Follett.

Follett was born in Quincy, Massachusetts, in 1868. After graduating from Radcliffe College, she taught political science for several years. During this period of her life, her social circle came to include a number of influential and wealthy philanthropists and business leaders. One of these leaders became enthralled with her views regarding wages and work structures and began providing her with a monthly stipend so that she could devote more time to pursuing her ideas and interests.

With her new freedom to explore her theories, she began a long and serious study of organizations and how they functioned. One of her first messages involved worker participation. She warned, for example, that the bureaucratic model of organization just then coming into vogue might tend to bury the knowledge and ability of workers at lower levels in the hierarchy while simultaneously eliminating an important motivational factor, self-control.

Follett was also among the first to recognize the potential value of cross-functional work teams. She believed, for example, that authority in an organization should be distributed laterally across departments rather than vertically up and down the hierarchy. This approach, she argued,

"People often puzzle about who is the father of management. I don't know who the father was, but I have no doubt about who was the mother."—Sir Peter Parker, London School of Economics chairman

would result in collaboration based on expertise rather than on power or position. And indeed, power itself needed rethinking, at least in Follett's view. Most managers and management experts of her day thought that managers should strive to precisely define and allocate power on the basis of hierarchical position. Follett, meanwhile, suggested that power should instead be based on knowledge and expertise—again, notions currently popular in most modern organizations.

As her ideas began to take shape, so too did her influence. She became a widely respected authority in the field and a popular speaker to business groups. And some managers no doubt tried to implement her ideas in their own organizations. Ultimately, however, Follett's views fell from favor after her death in 1933. Most experts at that time were advocating different notions and methods, and without Follett on the scene to personally champion her ideas, they soon fell from favor, and her work fell into obscurity. But today her writings have found new favor among managers and management theorists, and Follett is winning the status and recognition as an important management pioneer that she so richly deserves.

References: Dana Wechsler Linden, "The Mother of Them All," *Forbes,* January 16, 1995, pp. 75–76 (quote on p. 76); Daniel Wren, *The Evolution of Management Theory,* 4th ed. (New York: Wiley, 1994).

Like the work of Taylor, unfortunately, the Hawthorne studies recently have been called into question. Critics cite deficiencies in research methods and alternative explanations of the findings. Again, however, these studies played a major role in the advancement of the field and are still among its most frequently cited works.[12]

The Human Relations Movement

The Hawthorne studies created quite a stir among managers, providing the foundation for an entirely new approach to management known as the human relations

As the field of organizational behavior began to emerge, managers came to better appreciate the importance of human behavior at work and the social environment of the organization. This view is not to say, of course, that the social environment is the only thing that matters. If a manager were to take the approach reflected here, for example, the firm would probably not survive for very long. Enlightened managers should remember that a variety of things, including technology, profitability, and the social environment, are all important. Successful organizations are usually those that optimize these and other imperatives in an effective manner.

The human relations movement, the beginning of organizational behavior, was based on the assumption that employee satisfaction is a key determinant of performance.

Theory X, described by Douglas McGregor, indicates an approach to management that takes a negative and pessimistic view of workers.

Theory Y, also described by McGregor, reflects an approach to management that offers a more positive and optimistic perspective on workers.

"*You know what I think, folks? Improving technology isn't important. Increased profits aren't important. What's important is to be warm, decent human beings.*"

movement. The basic premises underlying the **human relations movement** were that people respond primarily to their social environment, that motivation depends more on social needs than on economic needs, and that satisfied employees work harder than unsatisfied employees. This perspective represented a fundamental shift away from the philosophy and values of scientific management and classical organization theory. The cartoon above provides a humorous take on this view when carried to the extreme.

The works of Douglas McGregor and Abraham Maslow perhaps best exemplified the early values of the human relations approach to management.[13] McGregor is best known for his classic book, *The Human Side of Enterprise*, in which he identified two opposing perspectives that he believed typified managerial views of employees. Some managers, McGregor said, subscribed to what he labeled Theory X, whose characteristics are summarized in Table 1.2. **Theory X** takes a pessimistic view of human nature and employee behavior. In many ways, it is consistent with the premises of scientific management. A much more optimistic and positive view of employees is found in Theory Y, also summarized in Table 1.2. **Theory Y**, which is generally representative of the human relations perspective, was the approach McGregor himself advocated.

In 1943, Abraham Maslow published a pioneering theory of employee motivation that became well known and widely accepted among managers. Maslow's theory, which we describe in detail in Chapter 5, assumes that motivation arises from a hierarchical series of needs. As the needs at each level are satisfied, the individual progresses to the next higher level.

The Hawthorne studies and the human relations movement played major roles in developing the foundations for the field of organizational behavior. Some of the early theorists' basic premises and assumptions were incorrect, however. For example, most human relationists believed that employee attitudes such as job satisfaction are the major causes of employee behaviors such as job performance. As

table 1.2

Theory X and Theory Y

Theory X Assumptions	Theory Y Assumptions
1. People do not like work and try to avoid it.	1. People do not naturally dislike work; work is a natural part of their lives.
2. People do not like work, so managers have to control, direct, coerce, and threaten employees to get them to work toward organizational goals.	2. People are internally motivated to reach objectives to which they are committed.
3. People prefer to be directed, to avoid responsibility, to want security; they have little ambition.	3. People are committed to goals to the degree that they receive personal rewards when they reach their objectives.
	4. People will seek and accept responsibility under favorable conditions.
	5. People have the capacity to be innovative in solving organizational problems.
	6. People are bright, but under most organizational conditions, their potentials are underutilized.

Reference: Douglas McGregor, *The Human Side of Enterprise* (New York: McGraw-Hill, 1960), pp. 33–34, 47–48.

we explain in Chapter 6, however, this usually is not the case at all. Also, many of the human relationists' views were unnecessarily limited and situation specific. Thus, there was still plenty of room for refinement and development in the emerging field of human behavior in organizations.

Toward Organizational Behavior: The Value of People

Organizational behavior began to emerge as a mature field of study in the late 1950s and early 1960s.[14] That period witnessed the field's evolution from the simple assumptions and behavioral models of the human relationists to the concepts and methodologies of a true scientific discipline. Since that time, organizational behavior as a scientific field of inquiry has made considerable strides, although there have been occasional steps backward as well. Overall, however, managers increasingly recognize the value of human resources and strive to better understand people and their roles in complex organizations and competitive business situations.[15] Of course, as illustrated in the "Business of Ethics" box, there is still considerable controversy about how corporations attach a price tag to the value and contributions of various individuals in an organization. Many of the ideas discussed in this book have emerged over the past two decades. We turn now to contemporary organizational behavior.

Contemporary Organizational Behavior

Two fundamental characteristics of contemporary organizational behavior warrant special discussion. Furthermore, a particular set of concepts is generally accepted as defining the field's domain.

BUSINESS OF ETHICS

Putting a Price on Talent Can Be a Slippery Slope

American corporations paid their top managers more money in 2001 than ever before in U.S. history and more than any other nation. In part, the high level of compensation can be explained by the nature of the job itself—executives deserve large salaries because their jobs are difficult and require specialized skills. Another explanation is the economic principle of supply and demand. Few possess the experience and training necessary to head a major corporation, so high demand for executive talent leads to high compensation.

For companies with financial difficulties or impending bankruptcies, however, there is a third explanation: the need for retention. Top managers are likely to look for employment elsewhere when bankruptcy threatens, but companies in dire circumstances often hope to retain their most experienced managers to help them through the difficult period. Thus, troubled firms often rely on bonuses as additional compensation designed to discourage top managers from "jumping ship."

But what seems like a sound business policy can have severe negative consequences for other interested parties. For example, Enron reportedly paid over $55 million in bonuses to about five hundred key personnel after beginning bankruptcy proceedings. That money could have instead been used to pay employees, retirees, investors, and suppliers of the failed firm. Investors and employees have reacted to this practice by often seeking to overthrow retention bonus plans in bankruptcy court before the compensation can be paid. This has happened in cases involving steel maker LTV, Polaroid, and Burlington Industries, the clothing manufacturer.

Groups opposed to the bonus plans claim that such bonuses reward the managers who are most directly responsible for the company's current problems. They also assert that such payments are unfair to lower-level employees, who are least able to find another job and who have the fewest personal resources to sustain them through a period of unemployment. Personal finance advisors counsel employees of companies facing bankruptcy to seek other employment, demand a retention bonus, and even hire a lawyer." By definition, bankruptcy is a world inhabited by companies that have trouble keeping promises. It's a world where promises aren't kept and there isn't enough to go around," says Stephen Bubo, a bankruptcy attorney with the Chicago law firm D'Ancono and Pflaum. Workers and investors of failed companies, who have been stripped of their jobs and billions of investment dollars, would surely agree.

"By definition, bankruptcy is a world inhabited by companies that have trouble keeping promises."—Stephen Bobo, bankruptcy attorney with the Chicago law firm D'Ancona & Pflaum

References: Stephanie Armour, "Use of Retention Bonuses Draws Fire: Select Few Get Cash While Others Face Financial Ruin," *USA Today,* February 14, 2002. See www.usatoday.com/money; Victoria Zunitch, "What If Your Company Fails?: Five Ways to Protect Your Finances and Career When Your Employer Goes Bankrupt," *CNN/Money* online magazine, January 23, 2002 (quotation). money.cnn.com on February 25, 2002; Stephanie Armour, "Polaroid Retirees Lose Benefits," *USA Today,* January 14, 2002. www.usatoday.com/money on February 25, 2002.

Characteristics of the Field

Researchers and managers who use concepts and ideas from organizational behavior must recognize that it has an interdisciplinary focus and a descriptive nature; that is, it draws from a variety of other fields and it attempts to describe behavior (rather than to predict how behavior can be changed in consistent and predictable ways).

An Interdisciplinary Focus   In many ways, organizational behavior synthesizes several other fields of study. Perhaps the greatest contribution is from psychology, especially organizational psychology. Psychologists study human behavior whereas organizational psychologists deal specifically with the behavior of people in organizational settings. Many of the concepts that interest psychologists, such as individual differences and motivation, are also central to students of organizational behavior. These concepts are covered in Chapters 4–9.

Sociology, too, has had a major impact on the field of organizational behavior. Sociologists study social systems such as families, occupational classes, and organizations. Because a major concern of organizational behavior is the study of organization structures, the field clearly overlaps with areas of sociology that focus on the organization as a social system. Chapters 16–19 reflect the influence of sociology on the field of organizational behavior.

Anthropology is concerned with the interactions between people and their environments, especially their cultural environment. Culture is a major influence on the structure of organizations and on the behavior of people in organizations. Culture is discussed in Chapters 3 and 18.

Political science also interests organizational behaviorists. We usually think of political science as the study of political systems such as governments. But themes of interest to political scientists include how and why people acquire power and such topics as political behavior, decision making, conflict, the behavior of interest groups, and coalition formation. These are also major areas of interest in organizational behavior, as is reflected in Chapters 13–15.

Economists study the production, distribution, and consumption of goods and services. Students of organizational behavior share the economist's interest in areas such as labor market dynamics, productivity, human resource planning and forecasting, and cost-benefit analysis. Chapters 2, 7, and 8 most strongly illustrate these issues.

Engineering has also influenced the field of organizational behavior. Industrial engineering in particular has long been concerned with work measurement, productivity measurement, work-flow analysis and design, job design, and labor relations. Obviously, these areas are also relevant to organizational behavior and are discussed in Chapters 2, 7, and 12.

Contemporary organizational behavior reinforces the need for a strong interdisciplinary focus. For example, consider these Vietnamese employees working in a Nike contract factory in their homeland. Managers cannot simply take their understanding of U.S. workers and blindly apply it in a setting such as this. Instead, managers need to have an understanding of how psychological, sociological, anthropological, political, and economic forces vary across cultures in general and how they apply to Vietnam in particular if they are to work effectively in that country.

Most recently, medicine has come into play in connection with the study of human behavior at work, specifically in the area of stress. Increasingly, research is showing that controlling the causes and consequences of stress in and out of organizational settings is important for the well-being of both the individual and the organization. Chapter 9 is devoted to stress.

A Descriptive Nature   A primary goal of studying organizational behavior is to describe relationships among two or more behavioral variables. The theories and concepts of the field, for example, cannot predict with certainty that changing a specific set of workplace variables will improve an individual employee's performance by a certain amount. At best, the field can suggest that certain general concepts or variables tend to be related to one another in particular settings. For instance, research might indicate that in one organization, employee satisfaction and individual perceptions of working conditions are positively related. However, we may not know if better working conditions lead to more satisfaction, if more-satisfied people see their jobs differently than dissatisfied people, or if both satisfaction and perceptions of working conditions are actually related through other variables. Also, the relationship between satisfaction and perceptions of working conditions observed in one setting may be considerably stronger, weaker, or nonexistent in other settings.

Organizational behavior is descriptive for several reasons: the immaturity of the field, the complexities inherent in studying human behavior, and the lack of valid, reliable, and accepted definitions and measures. However, whether the field will ever be able to make definitive predictions and prescriptions is still an open question. But even if researchers never succeed in such endeavors, the value of studying organizational behavior is firmly established. Because behavioral processes pervade most managerial functions and roles, and because the work of organizations is done primarily by people, the knowledge and understanding gained from the field can help managers significantly in many ways.[16]

Basic Concepts of the Field

The central concepts of organizational behavior can be grouped into three basic categories: (1) individual processes, (2) interpersonal processes, and (3) organizational processes and characteristics. As Figure 1.2 shows, these categories provide the basic framework for this book.

Chapter 2 develops a managerial perspective on organizational behavior and links the core concepts of organizational behavior with actual management for organizational effectiveness. Chapter 3 discusses two increasingly important areas of organizational behavior, global and workforce diversity. Together, the three chapters in Part I provide a fundamental introduction to organizational behavior.

The six chapters of Part II cover individual processes in organizations. Chapter 4 explores key individual differences in such characteristics as personality and attitude. As a preview, the "Mastering Change" box discusses individual attitudes toward change. Chapters 5 and 6 provide in-depth coverage of an especially important topic, employee motivation in organizations. Chapters 7 and 8 are devoted to various methods and strategies that managers can use to enhance employee motivation and performance. Finally, Chapter 9 covers the causes and consequences of stress in the workplace.

figure 1.2

The Framework for Understanding Organizational Behavior

Organizational behavior is an exciting and complex field of study. The specific concepts and topics that constitute the field can be grouped into three categories: individual, interpersonal, and organizational processes and characteristics. Here these concepts and classifications are used to provide an overall framework for the organization of this book.

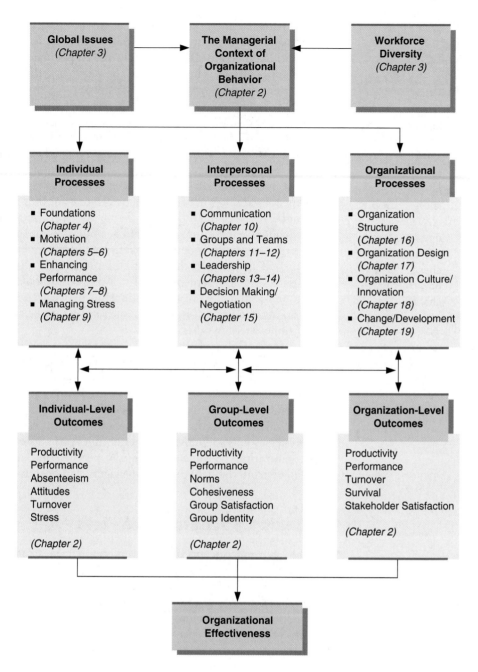

Part III is devoted to interpersonal processes in organizations. Chapter 10 covers interpersonal communication, and Chapter 11 is devoted to group dynamics. Chapter 12 describes how managers are using teams in organizations today. Chapters 13 and 14 discuss leadership models and concepts. Chapter 15 covers decision making and negotiation.

Part IV is devoted to organizational processes and characteristics. Chapter 16 describes organization structure; Chapter 17 is an in-depth treatment of organization design. Organization culture and innovation are discussed in Chapter 18.

MASTERING CHANGE

▶ *Positive Attitudes Toward Change*

The prevailing wisdom today is that most people tend to resist change. Supposedly, it makes them uncomfortable, it creates uncertainty, and it makes both work and life increasingly ambiguous. Yet the results of one recent survey were just the opposite—most of the people included in the study actually felt very comfortable with change!

The study in question surveyed one thousand randomly selected adults and focused only on one specific area of change—changes in technology. Interviewers asked respondents how comfortable they were with the rate of technological change in the world today. Perhaps surprisingly, 20 percent indicated they were very comfortable, and another 27 percent said they were somewhat comfortable. A whopping 41 percent replied that they were simply comfortable. At the other extreme, only 11 percent said they

were not at all comfortable. The final 1 percent either indicated they were unsure or refused to participate. The researchers noted that these findings had a margin of error of about 3 percent in either direction.

"While change may sometimes have its downside, people seem surprisingly comfortable today with changes in technology."—representative of The Tarrance Group

Although different studies might yield different results, this survey clearly indicates that most people are indeed comfortable with technological change. This may come as welcome news to those who have expressed concerns or fears that technological change may be happening too quickly.

Reference: "Most Comfortable with Changes," *USA Today*, March 11, 2002, p. 1A.

Organization change and development are covered in Chapter 19. Finally, research methods in organizational behavior and career dynamics are covered in Appendices 1 and 2.

Contextual Perspectives on Organizational Behavior

Several contextual perspectives have also influenced organizational behavior: the systems and contingency perspectives, the interactional view, and contemporary applied perspectives. Many of the concepts and theories discussed in the chapters that follow reflect these perspectives; they represent basic points of view that influence much of our contemporary thinking about behavior in organizations.

Systems and Contingency Perspectives

The systems and contingency perspectives share related viewpoints on organizations and how they function. Each is concerned with interrelationships among organizational elements and between organizational and environmental elements.

A system is a set of interrelated elements functioning as a whole.

The Systems Perspective   The systems perspective, or the theory of systems, was first developed in the physical sciences, but it has been extended to other areas such as management.[17] A **system** is an interrelated set of elements that function

figure 1.3

The Systems Approach to Organizations

The systems approach to organizations provides a useful framework for understanding how the elements of an organization interact among themselves and with their environment. Various inputs are transformed into different outputs, with important feedback from the environment. If managers do not understand these interrelations, they may tend to ignore their environment or to overlook important interrelationships within their organization.

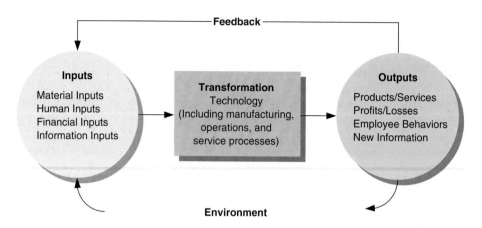

as a whole. Figure 1.3 shows a general framework for viewing organizations as systems.

According to this perspective, an organizational system receives four kinds of inputs from its environment: material, human, financial, and informational. The organization then combines and transforms the inputs and returns them to the environment in the form of products or services, profits or losses, employee behaviors, and new information. Then the system receives feedback from the environment regarding these outputs.

As an example, we can apply systems theory to Shell Oil Company. Material inputs include pipelines, crude oil, and the machinery used to refine petroleum. Human inputs are oil field workers, refinery workers, office staff, and other people employed by the company. Financial inputs take the form of money received from oil and gas sales, stockholder investment, and so forth. Finally, the company receives information inputs from forecasts about future oil supplies, geological surveys on potential drilling sites, sales projections, and similar analyses.

Through complex refining and other processes, these inputs are combined and transformed to create products such as gasoline and motor oil. As outputs, these products are sold to the consuming public. Profits from operations are fed back into the environment through taxes, investments, and dividends; losses, when they occur, affect the environment by reducing stockholders' incomes. In addition to having on-the-job contacts with customers and suppliers, employees live in the community and participate in a variety of activities away from the workplace, and their behavior is influenced in part by their experiences as Shell workers. Finally, information about the company and its operations is also released into the environment. The environment, in turn, responds to these outputs and influences future inputs. For example, consumers may buy more or less gasoline depending on the quality and price of Shell's product, and banks may be more or less willing to lend Shell money based on financial information released about the company.

The systems perspective is valuable to managers for a variety of reasons. First, it underscores the importance of an organization's environment. Failing to acquire the appropriate resources and to heed feedback from the environment, for instance, can be disastrous. The systems perspective also helps managers conceptualize the flow and interaction of various elements of the organization as they enter the system, are transformed by it, and then reenter the environment. Many of the

figure 1.4

**Universal versus
Contingency Approach**

*Managers once believed that
they could identify the "one
best way" of solving problems
or reacting to situations. Here
we illustrate a more realistic view,
the contingency approach. The
contingency approach suggests
that approaches to problems and
situations are contingent on
elements of the situation.*

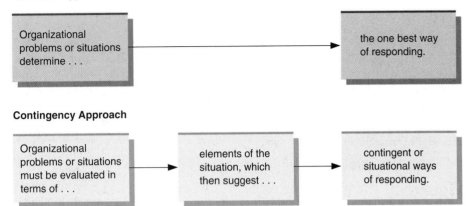

The contingency perspective
suggests that in most
organizations, situations and
outcomes are contingent
on, or influenced by, other
variables.

basic management concepts introduced in Chapter 2 rely heavily on the systems
perspective.

The Contingency Perspective   Another useful viewpoint for understanding behavior
in organizations comes from the **contingency perspective.** In the earlier days of
management studies, managers searched for universal answers to organizational
questions. They sought prescriptions, the "one best way" that could be used in any
organization under any conditions, searching, for example, for forms of leadership
behavior that would always lead employees to be more satisfied and to work
harder. Eventually, however, researchers realized that the complexities of human
behavior and organizational settings make universal conclusions virtually impossible. They discovered that in organizations, most situations and outcomes are contingent; that is, the relationship between any two variables is likely to be contingent on, or to depend on, other variables.[18]

Figure 1.4 distinguishes the universal and contingency perspectives. The universal model, shown at the top of the figure, presumes a direct cause-and-effect
linkage between variables. For example, it suggests that whenever a manager encounters a certain problem or situation (such as motivating employees to work
harder), a universal approach exists (such as raising pay or increasing autonomy)
that will lead to the desired outcome. The contingency perspective, on the other
hand, acknowledges that several other variables alter the direct relationship. In
other words, the appropriate managerial action or behavior in any given situation
depends on the elements of that situation.

The field of organizational behavior gradually has shifted from a universal
approach in the 1950s and early 1960s to a contingency perspective. The contingency perspective is especially strong in the areas of motivation (Chapters 5
and 6), job design (Chapter 7), leadership (Chapters 13 and 14), and organization design (Chapter 17), but it is becoming increasingly important throughout
the field.

When Rod Canion founded Compaq Computer Corporation in 1982, he focused on building expensive, complicated, high-quality computers for the business market. That formula led to enormous success for Compaq, which five years
later became the fastest firm ever to enter the *Fortune* 500 list of the largest 500

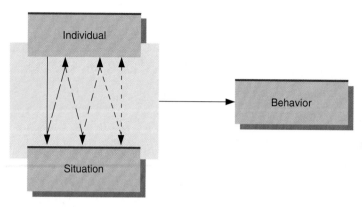

figure 1.5

The Interactionist Perspective on Behavior in Organizations

When people enter an organization, their own behaviors and actions shape that organization in various ways. Similarly, the organization itself shapes the behaviors and actions of each individual who becomes a part of it. This interactionist perspective can be useful in explaining organizational behavior.

corporations in the United States. When the environment of the computer industry shifted to a more marketing-oriented business stressing affordability and user-friendliness in 1991, however, Canion was unable to shift his own thinking and management style. That is, he did not recognize that circumstances had so radically changed that a new approach to managing the firm was needed. Compaq's board of directors eventually replaced him with Eckhard Pfeiffer, a German marketing specialist. Pfeiffer quickly altered the firm's strategy and soon had it back on a fast-growth trajectory. And for the next several years Compaq again grew rapidly and was the envy of the industry. But by 1999, the environment had again changed and, like his predecessor, Pfeiffer failed to realize that different strategies were needed. Thus, Compaq's board replaced him with Michael Capellas, hoping that under new leadership the firm could again get back on track. Capellas did indeed help Compaq right itself once again, but then decided that the firm would be most effective if it merged with Hewlett-Packard in 2002. Both Canion and Pfeiffer achieved dramatic success when each was running Compaq; nevertheless, each also fell from grace when the business environment shifted and the firm's leadership failed to adjust in concert. Capellas, however, did eventually respond to the changing environment by deciding that the firm actually needed to merge with HP in order to maintain its success. In each case, then, appropriate managerial action depended on the environment of the computer industry and Compaq's strategies relative to that environment.

Interactionalism: People and Situations   Interactionalism is another useful perspective from which to better understand behavior in organizational settings. First presented in terms of interactional psychology, this view assumes that individual behavior results from a continuous and multidirectional interaction between the characteristics of the person and the characteristics of the situation. More specifically, **interactionalism** attempts to explain how people select, interpret, and change various situations.[19] Figure 1.5 illustrates this perspective. Note that the individual and the situation are presumed to interact continuously. This interaction is what determines the individual's behavior.

Interactionalism suggests that individuals and situations interact continuously to determine individuals' behavior.

The interactional view implies that simple cause-and-effect descriptions of organizational phenomena are not enough. For example, one set of research studies may suggest that job changes lead to improved employee attitudes. Another set of studies may propose that attitudes influence how people perceive their jobs in the first place. Both positions are probably incomplete: Employee attitudes may influence job perceptions, but these perceptions may in turn influence future attitudes. Because interactionalism is a fairly recent contribution to the field, it is less prominent in the chapters that follow than the systems and contingency theories. Nonetheless, the interactional view appears to offer many promising ideas for future development.

Contemporary Applied Perspectives

In recent years, books written for the so-called popular press have also had a major impact on both the field of organizational behavior and the practice of management.[20] This trend first became noticeable in the 1980s with the success of books such as William Ouchi's *Theory Z*, Thomas Peters and Robert Waterman's *In Search of Excellence*, and Terrence Deal and Allan Kennedy's *Corporate Cultures*. Each of these books spent time on the *New York Times* bestseller list and was virtually required reading for any manager who wanted to appear informed. Biographies of executives such as Bill Gates and Jack Welch have also received widespread attention.

"You are what you read."—Martha Finney, business writer[21]

More recently, other applied authors have had a similar impact. Among the most popular applied authors today are Peter Senge, Stephen Covey, Tom Peters, John Kotter, Michael Porter, and Gary Hamel. Their books highlight the management practices—many of them directly linked to concepts from organizational behavior—of successful firms such as Kodak, IBM, and Shell. In addition, a new body of writing focusing specifically on feminist issues in management has also begun to emerge.[22]

Scott Adams, creator of the popular comic strip *Dilbert*, also remains popular today. Adams himself is a former communications industry worker who developed his strip to illustrate some of the absurdities of contemporary organizational life. The daily strip is routinely posted outside office doors, above copy machines, and beside water coolers in hundreds of offices. (And indeed, you may find a few of them posted in this book!) Adams's books now routinely top bestseller lists, and many people regularly visit the Dilbert web site. Adams's work is satirical, but it seems to reflect the actual perceptions of many people who work in organizations today.

Synopsis

Organizational behavior is the study of human behavior in organizational settings, the interface between human behavior and the organization, and the organization itself. The study of organizational behavior is important because organizations have a powerful influence over our lives.

Serious interest in the study of management first developed around the beginning of this century. Two of the earliest approaches were scientific management (best represented by the work of Taylor) and classical organization theory (exemplified by the work of Weber).

Organizational behavior began to emerge as a scientific discipline as a result of the Hawthorne studies. McGregor and Maslow led the human relations movement that grew out of those studies.

Contemporary organizational behavior attempts to describe, rather than prescribe, behavioral forces in organizations. Ties to psychology, sociology, anthropology, political science, economics, engineering, and medicine make organizational behavior an interdisciplinary field.

The basic concepts of the field are divided into three categories: individual processes, interpersonal processes, and organizational processes and characteristics. Those categories form the framework for the organization of this book.

Important contextual perspectives on the field of organizational behavior are the systems and contingency perspectives, interactionism, and contemporary applied perspectives.

Discussion Questions

1. Some people have suggested that understanding human behavior at work is the single most important requirement for managerial success. Do you agree or disagree with this statement? Why?

2. In what ways is organizational behavior comparable to functional areas such as finance, marketing, and production? In what ways is it different from these areas? Is it similar to statistics in any way?

3. Identify some managerial jobs that are highly affected by human behavior and others that are less so. Which would you prefer? Why?

4. Besides those cited in the text, what reasons can you think of for the importance of organizational behavior?

5. Suppose you have to hire a new manager. One candidate has outstanding technical skills but poor interpersonal skills. The other has exactly the opposite mix of skills. Which would you hire? Why?

6. Some people believe that individuals working in an organization have a basic human right to satisfaction with their work and to the opportunity to grow and develop. How would you defend this position? How would you argue against it?

7. Many universities offer a course in industrial or organizational psychology. The content of those courses is quite similar to the content of this one. Do you think that behavioral material is best taught in a business or in a psychology program, or is it best to teach it in both?

8. Do you believe the field of organizational behavior has the potential to become prescriptive as opposed to descriptive? Why or why not?

9. Are the notions of systems, contingency, and interactionalism mutually exclusive? If not, describe ways in which they are related.

10. Get a recent issue of a popular business magazine such as *Business Week* or *Fortune* and scan its major articles. Do any of them reflect concepts from organizational behavior? Describe.

11. Do you read *Dilbert*? Do you think it accurately describes organization life? Are there other comic strips that also reflect life and work in contemporary organizations?

Organizational Behavior Case for Discussion

The "Bodacious" Success of Oprah

Oprah Winfrey uses the word "bodacious" to describe herself, saying, "I feel more bodacious in stepping out and telling people what my message is." "Bodacious" is a Southern regional term, probably formed as a blend of "bold" and "audacious," which seems to be an apt description of Winfrey herself. Although Winfrey is CEO of privately owned Harpo, Inc., valued at $575 million, ranks third on *Fortune's* list of the most powerful women in business, and teaches management at Northwestern University's Kellogg School of Business, she is unable to read a financial statement.

Winfrey claims she is driven by creativity, not by money or acclaim. Her employees note that she is generous with praise but pays little attention to external recognition. Despite her apparent lack of interest in fame and fortune, Harpo ("Oprah" spelled backwards) is very profitable, most notably because of the Oprah television show, the number one talk show for the last sixteen years and the number three show overall, with revenues of $300 million annually. Other Winfrey holdings, together totaling just under $1 billion, include *The Oprah Magazine*; Harpo Films, which produces television movies; an 8 percent stake in the women's cable company Oxygen Media; $52 million of Viacom stock options; and a conservative portfolio of investments and real estate.

Winfrey is an unlikely candidate for business leadership—female, ethnic, and possessing a background of abuse and rural poverty. Her personality, too, is unconventional. She is disarmingly honest about her own shortcomings. She cultivates a "just-one-of-the-girls" persona, talking about her struggles with weight and the thrill of kissing Tom Cruise. Winfrey prefers not to see herself as a businesswoman: "[My business decisions are] leaps of faith. If I called a strategic-planning meeting, there would be dead silence, then people would fall out of their chairs laughing." She ignores conventional business wisdom when making her business decisions, often hiring friends, refusing to sell shares in her company, and limiting licensing of the Oprah brand to products that she controls personally. But Winfrey understands people, and that is the foundation of her success as a manager.

Winfrey use the details of her personal life to establish a rapport with her many fans. Public knowledge of her humble origins and childhood abuse seems to enable others, even those who may feel ignored by other segments of society, to identify with her success in the face of adversity. Her somewhat "preachy" style appeals to the twenty-five-to-forty-five-year-old women who are her primary customers. Her intimate relationship with her customers has led her into numerous and varied aspects of women's lives, including their interest in celebrities, pop psychology, home decorating, parenting, women's health, and even spirituality. Winfrey establishes the same types of close relationships with her employees and is known for showing, and requiring, great loyalty.

As a manager, Winfrey's very personal approach works at times. "It's all about character with Oprah. We investment bankers do the same sort of thing—try to figure out what people are made of—but with Oprah, it's like someone is looking into your soul," says Nancy Peretsman, an investment banker at Allen & Co. At other times, she can be narcissistic, according to one former employee. She has also been criticized for her need to control and her notorious ability to change her mind, characterized by some as indecisiveness. A frank assessment of Winfrey's skills as a manager will probably not be available because Winfrey requires everyone she hires to sign a highly unusual lifetime confidentiality agreement, defending this move by asserting, "You wouldn't say it's harsh if you were in the tabloids all the time."

One of Winfrey's biggest challenges seems to be maintaining the balance between Oprah the person and Oprah the brand. Like Martha Stewart, who has marketed her name, image, and values for public consumption, Winfrey is balancing the public and the private. And that means finding a way to control the use of her very personal brand. When Winfrey addresses the question of licensing her name for products created by others, she explains, "If I lost control of the business, I'd lose myself—or at least the ability to be myself. Owning myself is a way to be myself." Winfrey has decided to discontinue her monthly reading club recommendations, and she recently announced that she would retire after 2005. Yet those plans are still not certain. Winfrey sees herself as being on the verge of even greater accomplishments, saying, "I believe I'm just getting started. The TV show is just the foundation. . . . If you're open to the possibilities, your life gets grander, bigger, bolder!"

"[My business decisions are] leaps of faith."—Oprah Winfrey, CEO of Harpo, Inc.

References: The Oprah.com web site. www.oprah.com on April 8, 2002; www.galegroup.com/free-resources/bhm/bio/winfrey_o.htm on April 8, 2002; Patricia Sellers, "The Business of Being Oprah," *Fortune*, April 1, 2002, pp. 50–64 (quotation p. 58). See www.fortune.com; "The Top 25 Managers of the Year," *Business Week*, January 14, 2002, pp. 52–53 (quotation p. 63). See www.businessweek.com; Janet Guyon, "The Power 50," *Fortune*, October 15, 2001. www.fortune.com on April 8, 2002; *The American Heritage Dictionary of the English Language*, 4th ed. Boston: Houghton Mifflin Company, 2000. www.dictionary.com on April 8, 2002; *The Afro-American Almanac*, 7th ed. (Gale Group, 1997).

Case Questions

1. In what ways does Oprah Winfrey differ from managers in most other large organizations? Consider her personal characteristics and her behavior.
2. In your opinion, will the differences you noted in your answer to question 1 be an advantage for Winfrey's organization? In what ways? In what ways will the differences be a disadvantage?
3. Which of the individual, group, and organizational processes are being handled effectively by Winfrey? Which of the processes seem to be receiving less of her attention? What are the likely outcomes, based on Winfrey's pattern of strengths and weaknesses?

Experiencing Organizational Behavior

Relating OB and Popular Culture

Purpose: This exercise will help you appreciate the importance and pervasiveness of organizational behavior concepts and processes in both contemporary organizational settings and popular culture.

Format: Your instructor will divide the class into groups of three to five members. Each group will be assigned a specific television program to watch before the next class meeting.

Procedure: Arrange to watch the program as a group. Each person should have a pad of paper and a pencil handy. As you watch the show, jot down examples of individual behavior, interpersonal dynamics, organizational characteristics, and other concepts and processes relevant to organizational behavior. After the show, spend a few minutes comparing notes. Compile one list for the entire group. (It is advisable to turn off the television set during this discussion!)

During the next class meeting, have someone in the group summarize the plot of the show and list the concepts it illustrated. The following television shows

are especially good for illustrating behavioral concepts in organizational settings:

Network Shows	*Syndicated Shows*
Survivor	*Seinfeld*
The West Wing	*Cheers*
N.Y.P.D. Blue	*Star Trek*
The Drew Carey Show	*Home Improvement*
24	*L.A. Law*
C.S.I.	*Gilligan's Island*

Follow-up Questions

1. What does this exercise illustrate about the pervasiveness of organizations in our contemporary society?
2. What recent or classic movies might provide similar kinds of examples?
3. Do you think television programs from countries other than the United States would provide more or fewer examples of shows set in organizations?

 # Self-Assessment Exercise

Assessing Your Own Theory X and Theory Y Tendencies

The questions below are intended to provide insights into your tendencies toward Theory X or Theory Y management styles. Answer each of the following questions on the scale by circling the number that best reflects your feelings. For example, circle a "5" for a statement if you strongly agree with it, or a "2" if you disagree with it.

1. Most employees today are lazy and have to be forced to work hard.

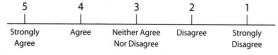

2. People in organizations are only motivated by extrinsic rewards such as pay and bonuses.

3. Most people do not like to work.

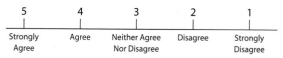

4. Most people today generally avoid responsibility.

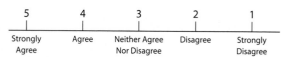

5. Many employees in big companies today do not accept the company's goals but instead work only for their own welfare.

6. Most people are not innovative and are not interested in helping their employer solve problems.

5	4	3	2	1
Strongly Agree	Agree	Neither Agree Nor Disagree	Disagree	Strongly Disagree

7. Most people need someone else to tell them how to do their job.

5	4	3	2	1
Strongly Agree	Agree	Neither Agree Nor Disagree	Disagree	Strongly Disagree

8. Many people today have little ambition, preferring to stay where they are and not work hard for advancement.

5	4	3	2	1
Strongly Agree	Agree	Neither Agree Nor Disagree	Disagree	Strongly Disagree

9. Work is not a natural activity for most people and instead is something they feel they have to do.

5	4	3	2	1
Strongly Agree	Agree	Neither Agree Nor Disagree	Disagree	Strongly Disagree

10. Most employees today are not interested in utilizing their full potential and capabilities.

5	4	3	2	1
Strongly Agree	Agree	Neither Agree Nor Disagree	Disagree	Strongly Disagree

Instructions: Add up the responses you have for each question. If you scored 40 or above, you have clear tendencies toward the Theory X view of management. If you scored 20 or below, you have clear tendencies toward the Theory Y view of management. If you scored between 20 and 40, your tendencies fall in between the extreme Theory X and Y viewpoints, and you have a more balanced approach. [*Note:* This brief instrument has not been scientifically validated and is to be used for classroom discussion purposes only.]

 # OB Online

1. Find a company web site that stresses the firm's history. What role, if any, does that history seem to play in the way that the firm is currently managed?
2. Do a web search using the key word "bureaucracy." Based on a representative sample of sites identified by your search, what is the prevailing meaning that most people seem to attach to this term?
3. Do a web search for the key term "Hawthorne studies." What additional information beyond that provided in this text do these sites contain?
4. Visit Amazon.com or another Internet book retailer and identify the top ten best-selling business books today. What, if anything, do they seem to have in common?

 # Building Managerial Skills

Exercise Overview: Conceptual skills refer to a manager's ability to think in the abstract while diagnostic skills focus on responses to situations. These skills must frequently be used together to better understand the behavior of others in the organization, as illustrated by this exercise.

Exercise Background: Human behavior is a complex phenomenon in any setting but is especially so in organizations. Understanding how and why people choose particular behaviors can be difficult and frustrating but also quite important. Consider, for example, the following scenario.

Sandra Buckley has worked in your department for several years. Until recently, she was a model employee. She always arrived on time, or early, for work and stayed late whenever necessary to get her assignments done. She was upbeat and cheerful and worked very hard. She frequently said that the company was the best place she had ever worked and that you were the perfect boss.

About six months ago, however, you began to notice changes in Sandra's behavior. She began to come in late occasionally, and you cannot remember the last time she agreed to work past 5:00 P.M. She also complains a lot. Other workers have started to avoid her because she is so negative all the time. You also suspect that she may be looking for a new job.

Exercise Task: Using the scenario previously described as background, do the following:

1. Assume that you have done some background work to find out what has happened. Write a brief case with more information that explains why Sandra's behavior has changed (i.e., your case might include the fact that you recently promoted someone else when Sandra might have expected to get the job). Make the case as descriptive as possible.

2. Relate elements of your case to the various behavioral concepts discussed in this chapter.

3. Decide whether or not you might be about to resolve things with Sandra in order to overcome whatever issues have arisen.

4. Which behavioral process or concept discussed in this chapter is easiest to change? Which is the most difficult to change?

2 Managing People and Organizations

Management Preview

▶ Effective management is the key to organizational success. Of course, figuring out how to manage effectively is sometimes akin to searching for the proverbial alchemist's stone. One reason for this is that effective management requires a level of understanding of human behavior that is both complex and elusive, again reinforcing the need for current and future managers to be familiar with the basic concepts and processes of behavior in organizations. This chapter relates the general field of management to the more specific field of organizational behavior. We start by developing a managerial perspective on organizational behavior. Then we characterize the manager's job in terms of its functions, roles, and requisite skills. Next, we identify and discuss a variety of organizational and environmental challenges in a context of organizational behavior. We conclude by discussing how an understanding of organizational behavior can enhance the manager's ability to achieve effectiveness. First, however, we examine how one manager, Bonnie Reitz, has helped Continental Airlines weather the effects of September 11 on the airline industry by successfully integrating basic and sound management techniques with respect and consideration for the employees who work there.

▼ ▼ ▼

The terrorist attacks of September 11, 2001, had wide-ranging consequences for organizations and individuals in the United States and around the world. One industry that was particularly hard hit was the U.S. airline industry. The crisis was especially challenging for Continental Airlines, which had just spent the last few years rebuilding its reputation after bankruptcies in 1983 and 1990 and a near-bankruptcy in 1994.

Through the late 1990s, slowly, gradually, both employees and travelers began to regain trust in the company. During this time Continental Airlines Senior Vice President for Sales and Marketing Bonnie Reitz worked tirelessly to reestablish relationships with customers, especially the business frequent flyers who are the most profitable segment of air travelers. A turning point was reached when Continental CEO Gordon Bethune invited one hundred of the airlines' top customers to a party at his home, during which he apologized for Continental's past negligence and promised increased responsiveness in the future. This event strongly underscored his message to the company's employees: "We're going to do what customers want us to do."

Today, Reitz is faced with the difficult tasks of reassuring customers that air travel remains safe and efficient while at the same time supporting Continental employees through the layoffs that inevitably followed the terrorist attacks. She has continued to rely on the management principle of honest communication, telling Continental workers that "they were great" and emphasizing that it wasn't their fault." Although the downsizing came as a shock to employees who felt they had job security, for the most part their confidence in the firm remains high. One laid-off employee gave his collection of souvenir travel pins to his boss, asking his superior to keep it safe and repeating his convictions that Continental would recover and that he would be rehired. (About half of the 12,000 employees who were laid off have been rehired.)

"[September 11] takes us back to all of the things we laid the groundwork for."
—*Bonnie Reitz, senior vice president for sales and distribution, Continental Airlines*

In order to keep the company in business during this troubled time for the airline industry, Reitz is continuing her campaign to win travelers through increased personal contact with key customers. She has doubled the size of the sales staff that handles corporate accounts and has changed the focus of Continental's advertising to providing information and safety updates. Reitz firmly believes that emphasizing relationships and communication is the best way to restore profitability. She explains, "[September 11] takes us back to all of the things we laid the groundwork for."

What does the future hold for Continental and other U.S. airlines? With the start of the economic downturn in 2001, the industry was expected to incur a $3 billion loss. After the events of September 11, however, the losses for 2001 exceeded $7 billion, even when offset by government aid. Traffic fell more than 40 percent immediately following the attacks and by mid-2002 was still more than 10 percent below 2000 levels. Other factors plaguing the industry include intense price competition, aging fleets of planes, high levels of debt, and rising fuel, labor, and security costs. Based on its improved relationships with customers and employees as well as on increased efficiency, Continental is well poised to take advantage of its growth as the market for air travel recovers. If the airline can use its focus on people to engineer one recovery, perhaps it can do so a second time—or, as the firm states on the cover of its 2001 annual report, "Times have changed. Our commitment hasn't."

References: Air Transport Association of America, Inc., "State of the Industry: Recent Trends for U.S. Air Carriers," March 6, 2002. www.airlines.org on March 8, 2002; "Continental Airlines 2001 Annual Report," January 2002. www.continental.com/corporate on March 8, 2002; Keith H. Hammonds, "Business Fights Back: Continental's Turnaround Pilot," *Fast Company*, December 2001, pp. 96–101 (quotation p. 98). See www.fastcompany.com.

Both Bonnie Reitz and Gordon Bethune clearly recognize that if an organization is to succeed, its managers cannot rely solely on either operations or people. Instead, they must appropriately meld both operations and people effectively to ensure organizational success. Since today's competitive environment is driven by such forces as globalization, technology, and downsizing, it is more important than ever for managers to hone their craft to a fine art. Whether taking courses in local business programs, going through in-house training programs, or visiting other successful firms, managers are constantly seeking new ways to perform their tasks more effectively. The nature of managerial work varies from company to company and continues to evolve, but one common thread is evident in most managerial activity: interacting with other people. Indeed, the typical day for most managers is devoted almost entirely to interacting with others. Thus, the management process and the behavior of people in organizations are undeniably intertwined.

Managerial Perspectives on Organizational Behavior

Virtually all organizations have managers with titles such as chief financial officer, marketing manager, director of public relations, vice president for human resources, and plant manager. But probably no organization has a position called "organizational behavior manager." The reason for this is simple: Organizational behavior is not a designated function or area. Rather, an understanding of organizational behavior is a perspective or set of tools that all managers can use to carry out their jobs more effectively.[1]

An appreciation and understanding of organizational behavior helps managers better recognize why others in the organization behave as they do.[2] For example, most managers in an organization are directly responsible for the work-related behaviors of a set of other people—their immediate subordinates. Typical managerial activities in this realm include motivating employees to work harder, ensuring that employees' jobs are properly designed, resolving conflicts, evaluating performance,

Concepts and processes from the field of organizational behavior permeate virtually every aspect of management. Consider, for example, the success enjoyed by Pfizer, an international leader in the pharmaceutical industry. Among its other benefits, Pfizer provides its employees with fitness centers, yoga classes, prenatal and nutritional counseling, on-site doctors who provide diabetes screening and flu shots, and subsidized cafeterias (including a $1.75 omelet bar and take-home dinners for families). Pfizer employees, in turn, recognize how much the firm values their contributions and are steadfastly loyal and dedicated to the firm's success.

and helping workers set goals to achieve rewards. The field of organizational behavior abounds with models and research relevant to each of these functions.[3]

Unless they happen to be chief executive officers (CEOs), managers also report to others in the organization (and even the CEO reports to the board of directors). In dealing with these individuals, an understanding of basic issues associated with leadership, power and political behavior, decision making, organization structure and design, and organization culture can be extremely beneficial. Again, the field of organizational behavior provides numerous valuable insights into these processes.

Managers can also use their knowledge of organizational behavior to better understand their own needs, motives, behaviors, and feelings, which will help them improve their decision-making capabilities, control stress, communicate better, and comprehend how career dynamics unfold. The study of organizational behavior provides insights into all of these concepts and processes.

Managers interact with a variety of colleagues, peers, and coworkers inside the organization. An understanding of attitudinal processes, individual differences, group dynamics, intergroup dynamics, organization culture, and power and political behavior can help managers handle such interactions more effectively. Organizational behavior provides a variety of practical insights into these processes. Virtually all of the behavioral processes already mentioned are also valuable in interactions with people outside the organization—suppliers, customers, competitors, government officials, representatives of citizens' groups, union officials, and potential joint venture partners. In addition, a special understanding of the environment, technology, and global issues is valuable. Again, organizational behavior offers managers many different insights into how and why things happen as they do.

"We spend all our time on people. The day we screw up the people thing, this company is over."—Jack Welch, retired CEO of General Electric[4]

Finally, these patterns of interactions hold true regardless of the type of organization. Whether a business is large or small, domestic or international, growing or stagnating, its managers perform their work within a social context. And the same can be said of managers in health care, education, government, and student organizations such as fraternities, sororities, and professional clubs.

We see, then, that it is essentially impossible to understand and practice management without considering the numerous areas of organizational behavior. And as the "World View" box illustrates, as more and more organizations hire managers from other countries, the processes of understanding human behavior in organizations will almost certainly become increasingly more complicated. We now turn to discussing the nature of the manager's job in more detail.

Basic Management Functions, Roles, and Skills

There are many different ways to conceptualize the job of a contemporary manager.[5] The most widely accepted approaches, however, are from the perspectives of basic managerial functions, common managerial roles, and fundamental managerial skills.[6]

Fundamental Managerial Functions

Managers in all organizations engage in four basic functions. These functions are generally referred to as planning, organizing, leading, and controlling. All organi-

WORLD VIEW

U.S. Firms Turn to Foreign-Born CEOs

Given the significant impact that globalization and diversity are having on U.S. firms, it comes as no surprise that American companies are increasingly hiring foreign-born managers, even at the highest levels. Managers who have lived overseas and experienced other cultures firsthand have a unique contribution to make to multinational firms. They are able to bring a deep understanding of the social and business forces at work in other regions.

> *"Change is easier in the U.S.A.; companies and employees are more adaptable."—Lars Nyberg, CEO of NCR*

The list of foreign-born CEOs of U.S. companies represents an impressive variety of industries and countries. Rakesh Ganwal, a native of India, serves as CEO of US Airways. The CEO of Computer Associates, Sanjay Kumar, is a native of Sri Lanka. Others include Pharmacia CEO Fred Hassan, a Pakistani; Goodyear CEO Samir Gibara, an Egyptian of Lebanese descent; Aramark CEO Joseph Neubauer, an Israeli; and United Airlines President Ronojoy Dutta, an Indian. In addition, Avon Products is headed by Andrea Jung, a Canadian-born woman of Chinese ancestry; NCR Corporation is led by Lars Nyberg, a native of Sweden; and Ford Motors, the fourth-largest firm in the world, was directed by Jacques Nasser, an Australian of Lebanese descent, until 2001.

Why do foreign-born CEOs head so many American firms? One answer is the U.S. companies' flexibility and willingness to take risks. Nyberg, responding to a question about the possibility of a European firm hiring an American-born CEO, says, "The European networks are tighter. It would

be a challenge. Change is easier in the U.S.A.; companies and employees are more adaptable." Many of the foreign-born CEOs first came to the United States as college students, drawn by the superior educational opportunities and quality of life. Jay Sidhu, CEO of Massachusetts-based Sovereign Bank, asserts, "The people you see over here [in the United States] are among the best from elsewhere." Many of the CEOs also cite the better entrepreneurial business spirit in America as compared with that in many other nations.

A foreign-born CEO experiences many challenges when leading an American organization, from communication and management style to social norms and work practices. For example, Nyberg claims that European and Asian management styles are more consensus based while American CEOs are given more individual decision-making authority. His number one tip for foreign-born CEOs of American firms: "Adjust to the U.S. culture. Don't expect American employees to adjust to your culture."

References: "The 25 Most Influential Global Executives," *Time*, December 2, 2001. www.time.com on March 31, 2002; Del Jones, "USA Plucks CEOs from All Across the World," *USA Today*, October 21, 2001, p. B1. See www.usatoday.com; Del Jones, "Ideas Can Get Lost in the Translation," *USA Today*, October 2, 2001 (quotation). www.usatoday.com on March 31, 2002.

zations also use four kinds of resources: human, financial, physical, and information. As illustrated in Figure 2.1, managers combine these resources through the four basic functions, with the ultimate purpose of efficiently and effectively attaining the goals of the organization. That is, the figure shows how managers apply the basic functions across resources to advance the organization toward its goals.

Planning is the process of determining an organization's desired future position and the best means of getting there.

Planning   **Planning,** the first managerial function, is the process of determining the organization's desired future position and deciding how best to get there. The planning process at Sears, for example, includes studying and analyzing the environment, deciding on appropriate goals, outlining strategies for achieving those goals, and developing tactics to help execute the strategies. Behavioral processes and characteristics pervade each of these activities. Perception, for instance, plays a major role in environmental scanning, and creativity and motivation influence how managers establish goals, strategies, and tactics for their organization. Larger corporations such

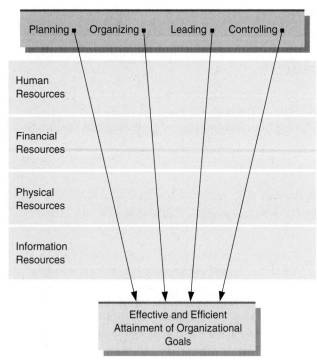

figure 2.1

Basic Managerial Functions

Managers engage in the four basic functions of planning, organizing, leading, and controlling. These functions are applied to human, financial, physical, and information resources, with the ultimate purpose of attaining organizational goals efficiently and effectively.

Organizing is the process of designing jobs, grouping jobs into units, and establishing patterns of authority between jobs and units.

Leading is the process of getting the organization's members to work together toward achieving the organization's goals.

Controlling is the process of monitoring and correcting the actions of the organization and its members to keep them directed toward their goals.

Key interpersonal roles are the figurehead, the leader, and the liaison.

as General Electric and IBM usually rely on their top management teams to handle most planning activities. In smaller firms, the owner usually takes care of planning.

Organizing   The second managerial function is **organizing**—the process of designing jobs, grouping jobs into manageable units, and establishing patterns of authority among jobs and groups of jobs. This process produces the basic structure, or framework, of the organization. For large organizations such as Sears, that structure can be extensive and complicated. Smaller firms can often function with a relatively simple and straightforward form of organization. As noted earlier, the processes and characteristics of the organization itself are a major theme of organizational behavior.

Leading   **Leading,** the third managerial function, is the process of motivating members of the organization to work together toward achieving the organization's goals. A Sears manager, for example, must hire people, train them, and motivate them. Major components of leading include motivating employees, managing group dynamics, and the actual process of leadership. These are all closely related to major areas of organizational behavior. All managers, whether they work in a huge multinational corporation or a small neighborhood business, must understand the importance of leading.

Controlling   The fourth managerial function, **controlling,** is the process of monitoring and correcting the actions of the organization and its people to keep them headed toward their goals. A Sears manager has to control costs, inventory, and so on. Again, behavioral processes and characteristics are a key part of this function. Performance evaluation, reward systems, and motivation, for example, all apply to control. Control is of vital importance to all businesses, but it may be especially critical to smaller ones. General Motors, for example, can easily withstand a loss of several thousand dollars due to poor control, but an equivalent loss may be devastating to a small firm.

Basic Managerial Roles

In an organization, as in a play or a movie, a role is the part a person plays in a given situation. Managers often play a number of different roles. Much of our knowledge about managerial roles comes from the work of Henry Mintzberg.[7] Mintzberg identified ten basic managerial roles clustered into three general categories; they are listed in Table 2.1.

Interpersonal Roles   The **interpersonal roles** are primarily social in nature; that is, they are roles in which the manager's main task is to relate to other people in

table 2.1

Important Managerial Roles

Category	Role	Example
Interpersonal	Figurehead	Attend employee retirement ceremony
	Leader	Encourage workers to increase productivity
	Liaison	Coordinate activities of two committees
Informational	Monitor	Scan *Business Week* for information about competition
	Disseminator	Send out memos outlining new policies
	Spokesperson	Hold press conference to announce new plant
Decision-making	Entrepreneur	Develop idea for new product and convince others of its merits
	Disturbance handler	Resolve dispute
	Resource allocator	Allocate budget requests
	Negotiator	Settle new labor contract

certain ways. The manager sometimes may serve as a *figurehead* for the organization. Taking visitors to dinner and attending ribbon-cutting ceremonies are part of the figurehead role. In the role of *leader*, the manager works to hire, train, and motivate employees. Finally, the *liaison* role consists of relating to others outside the group or organization. For example, a manager at Intel might be responsible for handling all price negotiations with a key supplier of electronic circuit boards. Obviously, each of these interpersonal roles involves behavioral processes.

Key informational roles are the monitor, the disseminator, and the spokesperson.

Informational Roles   The three **informational roles** involve some aspect of information processing. The *monitor* actively seeks information that might be of value to the organization in general or to specific managers. The manager who transmits this information to others is carrying out the role of *disseminator*. The *spokesperson* speaks for the organization to outsiders. A manager chosen by Dell Computer to appear at a press conference announcing a new product launch or other major deal, such as a recent decision to undertake a joint venture with Microsoft, would be serving in this role. Again, behavioral processes are part of each of these roles because information is almost always exchanged between people.

Important decision-making roles are the entrepreneur, the disturbance handler, the resource allocator, and the negotiator.

Decision-Making Roles   Finally, there are also four **decision-making roles.** The *entrepreneur* voluntarily initiates change, such as innovations or new strategies, in the organization. The *disturbance handler* helps settle disputes between various parties, such as other managers and their subordinates. The *resource allocator* decides who will get what—how resources in the organization will be distributed among various individuals and groups. The *negotiator* represents the organization in reaching agreements with other organizations, such as when settling contracts between

Management involves four basic functions, ten roles, and four fundamental skills. The work of Claire Fraser, President of the Institute for Genomic Research, clearly illustrates several of these. Her current challenges include supervising research leading to new scientific breakthroughs, managing the Institute's most talented employees, keeping abreast of all current developments in her field, and managing several on-going applied and basic research programs.

management and labor unions. Again, behavioral processes clearly are crucial in each of these decisional roles.

Critical Managerial Skills

Another important element of managerial work is possessing the skills necessary to carry out basic functions and fill fundamental roles. In general, most successful managers have a strong combination of technical, interpersonal, conceptual, and diagnostic skills.[8]

Technical Skills   **Technical skills** are abilities necessary to accomplish specific tasks within the organization. Designing a new modem for Dell Computer, developing a new formula for a frozen-food additive for Conagra, and writing a press release for Exxon require all technical skills. Hence, these skills are generally associated with the operations employed by the organization in its production processes. For example, Bill Hewlett and David Packard, founders of Hewlett-Packard, began their careers as engineers. They still work hard today to keep abreast of new technology—their technical skills are an important part of

Technical skills are the skills necessary to accomplish specific tasks within the organization.

their success. Other examples of managers with strong technical skills include H. Lee Scott (president and CEO of Wal-Mart, who started his career as a store manager) and Gordon Bethune (CEO of Continental, a former pilot).

The manager uses interpersonal skills to communicate with, understand, and motivate individuals and groups.

Interpersonal Skills   The manager uses **interpersonal skills** to communicate with, understand, and motivate individuals and groups. As we noted, managers spend a large portion of their time interacting with others, so it is clearly important that they get along with other people. Gordon Bethune, CEO of Continental Airlines, is one of the most admired business leaders in America. Part of his success is attributable to how he deals with people in the firm; he treats them with dignity and respect and is always open and direct when he talks to them. For example, he refers to everyone in the firm, from baggage handlers to pilots to executives, as his coworkers, and he is candid when he has to relay bad news.

The manager uses conceptual skills to think in the abstract.

Conceptual Skills   **Conceptual skills** involve the manager's ability to think in the abstract. A manager with strong conceptual skills is able to see the "big picture." That is, she or he can see opportunity where others perceive roadblocks or problems. For example, after Steve Wozniak and Steve Jobs built a small computer of their own design in a garage, Wozniak saw just a new toy that could be tinkered with. Jobs, however, saw far more and convinced his partner that they should start a company to make and sell the computers. Thus was born Apple Computer.

Successful managers need to have several basic skills, including diagnostic skills. This "manager," for example, has just realized that the earlier he gets started in the morning, the more worms he is likely to get! In real businesses, parallels might include understanding the relationship between how rewards are distributed and worker satisfaction, the quality of products and services and customer satisfaction, and managerial honesty and employee trust.

Diagnostic Skills   Most successful managers also bring diagnostic skills to the organization. **Diagnostic skills** allow managers to better understand cause-and-effect relationships and to recognize the optimal solutions to problems. For example, when Gordon Bethune took over Continental, he immediately began searching for ways to turn the failing company around. It was his diagnostic skills that enabled him to first recognize the enormous costs being incurred because of late departures and arrivals, then to identify the reasons for this problem, and, finally, to determine how to most effectively change things in order to solve the problem. The cartoon provides another illustration of diagnostic skills.

The manager uses diagnostic skills to understand cause-and-effect relationships and to recognize the optimal solutions to problems.

Of course, not every manager has an equal measure of these four basic types of skills, nor are equal measures critical. As shown in Figure 2.2, for example, the optimal skills mix tends to vary with the manager's level in the organization. First-line managers generally need to depend more on their technical and

figure 2.2

Managerial Skills at Different Organizational Levels

Most managers need technical, interpersonal, conceptual, and diagnostic skills, but the importance of these skills varies by level in the organization. As illustrated here, conceptual and diagnostic skills are usually more important for top managers in organizations whereas technical and interpersonal skills may be more important for first-line managers.

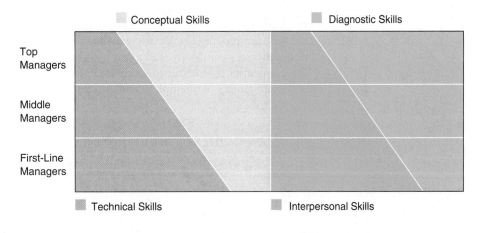

interpersonal skills and less on their conceptual and diagnostic skills. Top managers tend to exhibit the reverse combination—more emphasis on conceptual and diagnostic skills and less dependence on technical and interpersonal skills. Middle managers require a more even distribution of skills. Similarly, the mix of skills needed can vary, depending on economic prosperity. One recent survey suggested that during very tough economic times, the most important skills for a CEO are that he or she be an effective communicator and motivator, be decisive, and be a visionary.[9]

Organizational Challenges

Organizational behavior has several implications for various organizational and environmental challenges. From the organizational perspective, particularly important challenges are workforce expansions and reductions, the new workplace, organization change, information technology, and new ways of organizing.

Workforce Expansion and Reduction

One important organizational challenge involves workforce expansion and reduction. During the last ten years alone, for instance, many organizations have had to first reduce their workforces during the economic slowdown in the early 1990s, then expand by hiring new employees during the boom period of the late 1990s, and then reduce them once again as a result of another economic downturn that began in 2001.

Downsizing is the process of purposely becoming smaller by reducing the size of the workforce or shedding divisions or businesses.

Downsizing   **Downsizing** is purposely becoming smaller by reducing the size of the workforce or by shedding entire divisions or businesses. Downsizing became common in the mid-1980s. For example, General Motors, IBM, and AT&T each underwent major downsizing efforts involving thousands of employees. More recently, because of declining sales of Western-style boots, Justin Industries closed two of its factories, putting 260 people out of work. And growing international competition recently compelled Kellogg Company to recently shut down much of its oldest factory, cutting 550 jobs. In addition, most major airlines eliminated thousands of jobs in the wake of September 11.

Organizations undergoing such downsizing must be concerned about managing the effects of these cutbacks, not only for those employees who are let go but also for those who continue—albeit with reduced security. We should note, of course, that downsizing sometimes has surprisingly positive results. The firm that cuts staff presumably lowers its costs. But the people who leave may find that they are happier as well. Many start their own businesses, and some find employment with companies that better meet their needs and goals. Unfortunately, others suffer the indignities of unemployment and financial insecurity.

"I think they could try a little bit harder to bring more jobs in here. The community is going to suffer tremendously, as are we."—Debra Robinson, Kellogg employee whose job was eliminated[10]

Expansion   During boom periods like the late 1990s, downsizing and reductions give way in many sectors of the economy to growth and expansion. Indeed, in some sectors, especially those involving high-technology and intensive knowledge work, such severe labor shortages sometimes exist that firms may have to pay hefty signing bonuses and provide an array of benefits and perks. A clear understanding of organizational behavior can help managers in this situation in a variety of ways. These include attracting new workers in sufficient numbers and with necessary skills and abilities, retaining both newer and older workers in the face of alternative work options, and blending newer and older workers into a harmonious and effective workforce.

Simultaneously, even during the best of times, managers should be somewhat cautious to avoid overexpanding too quickly. That is, if an organization hires more workers than it can sustain, as soon as economic growth slows or the firm's fortunes stall, managers may once again find themselves in the position of having to reduce their workforce all over again. To help buffer against this possibility, many firms, especially larger ones, rely on temporary workers to add to their workforce to meet expansion needs without incurring too great a commitment to providing those workers with long-term job security. Organizational behavior concepts again help managers here deal with issues arising from blending permanent and temporary workers together in a single job setting.

The New Workplace

As previously implied, workplaces are also changing. These changes relate in part to both workforce reductions and expansion. But even more central to the idea of workplace change are such elements as workforce diversity and the characteristics of new workers themselves.

Workforce Diversity   The management of diversity is another important organizational challenge today. The term "diversity" refers to differences among people. Diversity may be reflected along numerous dimensions, but most managers tend to focus on age, gender, ethnicity, and physical abilities and disabilities.[11] For example, the average age of workers in the United States is gradually increasing. This is partly because of declining birthrates and partly because people are living and working longer. Many organizations are finding retirees to be excellent part-time and temporary employees. McDonald's has hired hundreds of elderly workers in recent years. Apple Computer has used many retired workers for temporary assignments and projects. By hiring retirees, the organization gets the expertise of skilled workers, and the individuals get extra income and an opportunity to continue to use their skills.

An increasing number of women have also entered the American workforce. In 1950, only about one-third of American women worked outside their homes; today almost two-thirds work part-time or full-time outside the home. Many occupations traditionally dominated by women—nursing, teaching, being a secretary—continue to be popular with females. But women have also increasingly moved into occupations previously dominated by males, becoming lawyers, physicians, and executives. Further, many blue-collar jobs are being sought more often by women, and they are more frequently occupying both positions of business ownership as entrepreneurs and slots as senior executives in major corporations. Likewise, more and more men are also entering occupations previously dominated

Managing today takes a keen understanding of the attitudes, goals, and needs of the members of the organization. Consider, for example, the case of Tom Ridge, tapped by President Bush to lead the Homeland Security Department. As currently proposed, the new agency would be created by merging 22 existing agencies and employing a total of 170,000 people. Ridge must figure out how to integrate disparate missions and structures while simultaneously focusing employees on both their current tasks and their new ones. And he can only be successful if he truly understands and appreciates the dynamics of human behavior in organizations.

by women. For example, there are more male office assistants and nurses today than ever before.

The ethnic composition of the workplace is also changing. One obvious change has been the increasing number of Hispanics and black Americans entering the workplace.[12] Further, many of these individuals now hold executive positions. In addition, there has been a dramatic influx of immigrant workers during the last few years. Immigrants and refugees from Central America and Asia have entered the American workforce in record numbers.

The passage of the Americans with Disabilities Act also brought to the forefront the importance of providing equal employment opportunities for people with various disabilities. As a result, organizations are attracting qualified employees from groups that they may perhaps once have ignored. Clearly, then, along just about any dimension imaginable, the workforce is becoming more diverse. Workforce diversity enhances the effectiveness of most organizations, but it also provides special challenges for managers. We return to these issues in Chapter 3.

Characteristics of The New Workforce   Aside from its new demographic composition, the workforce today is changing in other ways. During the 1980s, many people entering the workforce were what came to be called "yuppies," slang for "young urban professionals." These individuals were highly motivated by career prospects, sought employment with big corporations, and were often willing to make work their highest priority. Thus, they put in long hours and could be expected to remain loyal to the company, regardless of what happened.

But younger people entering the workforce in the 1990s, however, were frequently quite different from their predecessors. Sometimes called "Generation X," these workers were less devoted to long-term career prospects and less willing to adapt to a corporate mindset that stressed conformity and uniformity. Instead, they often sought work in smaller, more entrepreneurial firms that allowed flexibility and individuality. They also put a premium on lifestyle considerations, often putting location high on their list of priorities when selecting an employer. And, of course, new workers entering the workforce in the first years of this century are likely to be different still from their counterparts both in the 1980s and in the 1990s.

Thus, managers are increasingly faced with challenges. First they must create an environment that will be attractive to today's worker. Second, they must address the challenge of providing new and different incentives to keep people motivated

MASTERING CHANGE

▶ *Change Alone Is Unchanging*

"Change alone is unchanging," according to Greek philosopher Heraclitus, writing about 500 B.C. This idea certainly applies to business leaders, who constantly face myriad changes in their firms and their environments, ranging from workforce changes to globalization to technological innovations. Yet even in the rapidly changing world of business, 2001 stands out as a year in which numerous, extreme, and unpredictable changes were the norm. The year began under the cloud of a worldwide economic recession followed by the terrorist attacks of September 11. Then came the declaration of war on terrorism and the Enron scandal.

The best managers, therefore, are those who can support their organizations through such times of change. For example, Louis V. Gerstner Jr., CEO of IBM, has spent the last nine years pushing the giant firm into new areas. Today IBM is more flexible and diverse, generating 60 percent of its sales from overseas and reporting profits of $7.7 billion in 2001, a year when the technology industry suffered serious declines. At Verizon, co-CEOs Charles Lee and Ivan Seidenberg have been working for two years to integrate GTE and Bell Atlantic into one smoothly functioning firm. Lee says, "Anybody who says it can't be done: Wrong. Anybody who says it's easy: Also wrong."

Even changes that seem to be overwhelmingly negative can have some positive outcomes. Lehman Brothers,

an investment banking firm, suffered severe damage to its Wall Street headquarters building on September 11, but CEO Richard S. Fuld Jr. found his employees more motivated after the attacks. He notes, "It was that horrible, unfortunate event that got my people to come together in such a strong way."

Some managers are struggling to find a means to cope with negative changes. With the downturn in the electronics industry, Motorola and its CEO, Christopher

> *"Anybody who says it can't be done: Wrong. Anybody who says it's easy: Also wrong."—Charles Lee, co-CEO of Verizon Communications*

Galvin, are facing their first-ever operating loss in 71 years. Hilton hotels, headed by Stephen Bollenbach, are suffering from the decline in travel after September 11. One thing seems certain—those firms that respond effectively to changes will prosper while those that keep on with "business as usual" will be left behind in the competitive race.

References: IBM corporate web site, page describing Louis V. Gerstner Jr., CEO. www.ibm.com/lvg on April 4, 2002; "The Top 25 Managers of the Year," *Business-Week*, January 14, 2002, pp. 52–53 (quotation p. 63). See www.businessweek.com; Robert Andrews, Mary Biggs, Michael Seidel et al. [eds.], *The Columbia World of Quotations*, New York: Columbia University Press, 1996. www.bartleby.com/100 on April 4, 2002.

and interested in their work. Finally, managers must build enough flexibility into the organization to accommodate an ever-changing set of lifestyles and preferences.

Organization Change

Managers must be prepared to address organization change.[13] This has always been a concern, but the rapid, constant environmental change faced by businesses today has made change management even more critical. Simply put, an organization that fails to monitor its environment and to change to keep pace with that environment is doomed to failure. But more and more managers are seeing change as an opportunity, not a cause for alarm. Indeed, some managers think that if things get too calm in an organization and people start to become complacent, managers should shake things up to get everyone energized. Change is explored more fully in the "Mastering Change" box; we also discuss the management of organizational change in more detail in Chapter 19.

Information Technology

New technology, especially as it relates to information, also poses an increasingly important challenge for managers. Specific forms of hardware such as cellular phones and fax machines have made it easier than ever for managers to communicate with each other. At the same time, these innovations have increased the work pace for managers, cut into their time for thoughtful contemplation of decisions, and increased the amount of information they must process.

"Over the past couple of decades, I've watched industries be transformed by the use of information systems and incredible visual displays."—Dr. Laura Esserman, surgeon[14]

The Internet and World Wide Web, intranets, local area networks, and the increased use of email and voicemail have also changed the manager's job.[15] On the one hand, these tools make it easier to acquire, process, and disseminate information. But they also increase the risk that the manager will get distracted by superfluous information or become so wrapped up in communication as to give too little time to other important management functions. A related issue is the increased capabilities this technology provides for people to work at places other than their offices.[16] Chapter 10 examines some of these issues in more depth.

New Ways of Organizing

A final organizational challenge today is dealing with the complex array of new ways of organizing that managers can consider.[17] Recall from Chapter 1 that early organization theorists such as Max Weber advocated "one best way" of organizing. These organizational prototypes generally resembled pyramids—tall structures with power controlled at the top and rigid policies and procedures governing most activities. Now, however, many organizations seek greater flexibility and the ability to respond more quickly to their environment by adopting flat structures. These structures are characterized by few levels of management; broad, wide spans of management; and fewer rules and regulations. The increased use of work teams also goes hand in hand with this new approach to organizing. We will examine these new ways of organizing in Chapters 12 and 17.

Environmental Challenges

Managers also face numerous environmental challenges. The environmental issues most relevant to the domain of organizational behavior are competitive strategy, globalization, ethics and social responsibility, quality and productivity, and manufacturing and service technology.

Competitive Strategy

A competitive strategy is an outline of how a business intends to compete with other firms in the same industry.

A firm's **competitive strategy** explains how it intends to compete with other firms in the same industry. In general, most firms adopt one of three business strategies.[18] A firm using a *differentiation strategy* attempts to make its products or services at least appear to be different from others in the marketplace. For example, Rolex has created the image that its watches are of higher quality and prestige than

Today's competitive environment and the relentless move toward globalization combine to make management and organizational behavior increasingly complex for today's managers. For example, Harley-Davidson has faced increasingly stiff competition in recent years from German bikes made by BMW and Japanese bikes made by Honda and Kawasaki. While Harley has an almost cult-like following among its current owners, potential new customers have been deterred by long waits for new products and the image of Harley as appealing to middle-aged riders longing to look rebellious. To help overcome these obstacles, Harley has initiated a new program called Rider's Edge, a two and a half-day training program to introduce potential customers to motorcycle ownership. This first-time Harley rider, for example, is learning from Rider's Edge instructor Paul Lessard.

those offered by its competitors so that it can charge a higher price. Other firms that have successfully used this model are BMW, Calvin Klein, and Nikon.

A firm that adopts a *cost leadership strategy*, on the other hand, works aggressively to push its costs as low as possible. This allows the firm to charge a lower price for its products or services and thus gain more market share. Bic, the French firm, uses cost leadership to sell its inexpensive disposable ballpoint pens. Timex and Texas Instruments also use this strategy to sell watches and calculators, respectively.

Finally, a *focus strategy* involves targeting products or services to meet the unique needs of a specific customer group. Fiesta Mart, a Houston-based supermarket, has prospered by targeting that city's large Hispanic population. Customers at a Fiesta store can buy Mexican soft drinks, corn husks for wrapping tamales, and other ethnic products not readily available at other supermarkets.

A firm's managers must know its business strategy when hiring employees. For example, if the business strategy calls for differentiation, the firm will need employees who can produce higher-quality products or services and project a differentiated image. On the other hand, a cost leadership strategy dictates the need for people who can keep focused on cost cutting and who respond well to tight cost controls. Finally, a focus strategy requires people who clearly understand the target population being courted by the firm.[19]

Globalization

It is no secret that the world economy is becoming increasingly global in character.[20] But often people do not realize the true magnitude of this globalization trend or the complexities it creates for managers. Consider, for example, the impact of international businesses on our daily lives. We wake to the sound of Panasonic alarm clocks made in Japan. For breakfast we drink milk from Carnation—a subsidiary of Nestlé, a Swiss firm—and coffee ground from Colombian beans. We dress in clothes sewn in Taiwan and drive a Japanese automobile. Along the way, we stop and buy gas imported from the Middle East by Shell, a Dutch company. Of course, U.S. citizens are not alone in experiencing the effects of globalization. Indeed, people in other countries eat at McDonald's restaurants and snack on Mars candy bars and Coca-Cola soft drinks. They drive Fords, use IBM computers, and wear Levi jeans. They use Kodak film and fly on Boeing airplanes.

The globalization trend started right after World War II. The U.S. economy emerged strong and intact. U.S. businesses were the dominant worldwide suppliers in virtually all major industries. But war-torn Europe and the Far East rebuilt. Businesses there were forced to build new plants and other facilities, and their citizens turned to their work as a source of economic security. As a result, these economies grew in strength, and each developed competitive advantages. Today those advantages are being exploited to their fullest.

The situation is further confounded by the rapid change that has characterized the international arena. When the 1980s began, the Eastern bloc countries (including what was then East Germany) were going nowhere economically, the Japanese and German economies (then just West Germany) were dominant, many observers were writing off the United States, and countries such as South Korea and Taiwan played only minor roles. As the 1990s began, however, much of the Eastern bloc had embraced capitalism and opened their markets, Japan was slowing down, the United States was coming back, Germany had unified, and South Korea and Taiwan had become powerhouses. And in the early years of the twenty-first century, Pacific Asia continues to struggle with a major financial crisis, Hong Kong has become a part of China, and both China and India are emerging as strong economic powers. Vietnam is again an important market, and the European Union and NAFTA have defined major new trading blocs.

Managing in a global economy poses many different challenges and opportunities. For example, at a macro level, property ownership arrangements vary widely. So does the availability of natural resources and components of the infrastructure as well as the role of government in business. For our purposes, a very important consideration is how behavioral processes vary widely across cultural and national boundaries. Values, symbols, and beliefs differ sharply among cultures. Different work norms and the role work plays in a person's life influence patterns of both work-related behavior and attitudes toward work. They also affect the nature of supervisory relationships, decision-making styles and processes, and organizational configurations. Group and intergroup processes, responses to stress, and the nature of political behaviors also differ from culture to culture.

Ethics and Social Responsibility

Another environmental challenge that has taken on renewed importance concerns ethics and social responsibility. An individual's **ethics** are his or her beliefs about what is right and wrong or good and bad. **Social responsibility,** meanwhile, is the organization's obligation to protect and contribute to the social environment in which it functions. Thus, the two concepts are related, but they are also distinct from each other.

Both ethics and social responsibility have taken on new significance in recent years. Scandals in organizations ranging from Royal Caribbean Cruise Lines (improper dumping of waste) to Tyco (improper use of company assets for the benefit of senior managers) to various Olympics committees (bribery of government officials)

Individual ethics are personal beliefs about what is right and wrong or good and bad.

An organization's social responsibility is its obligation to protect or contribute to the social environment in which it functions.

▶ BUSINESS OF ETHICS

▶ The Ethics of Employee Stock Ownership

The recent bankruptcy at Enron and the public disclosure of the unethical and dishonest behaviors that contributed to the failure have sent a chill through managers and employees around the world. Trust between workers and their leaders seems to be at an all-time low. One laid-off manager at Global Crossing, which declared bankruptcy in January 2002, asserts, "Whatever company I work for in the future, I'll never again trust at face value what top executives say." Others view the lack of trust as a symptom of a larger failure in American society. Richard Tetlow, Harvard professor, believes, "Enron is more than an accounting failure. It represents a mentality [of greed] that we've all been part of."

"Whatever company I work for in the future, I'll never again trust at face value what top executives say."—A laid-off manager at Global Crossing

Worker compensation in the form of stock or stock options is an area beset with ethical concerns for both the firms and the employees. Organizations want their employees to own company stock because ownership more closely aligns the interests of the employee with the interests of the firm. In other words, workers are more likely to act in a way that benefits the firm when they are also stockholders. Offering employees stock and stock options is also a good choice for new or struggling companies because this form of compensation doesn't require the use of cash.

But stock ownership by employees also has a dark side. Employers control the investment of the 401(k) funds, and many companies are choosing to invest heavily in their own company, thereby increasing workers' investment risk. Employees are thus doubly vulnerable— if the company experiences financial difficulties, they may lose their jobs while simultaneously losing much of the value of their retirement funds. (Nationwide, the average is 19 percent investment in the employing firm.)

Also, some critics note that employees are more likely to overlook ethical violations if they believe the company stands to profit from the dishonest practices. In addition, corporate tax policy gives companies favorable tax deductions when they contribute stock options to employees' 401(k) retirement funds. This policy allows companies to compensate workers without showing the full expense, a practice which tends to inflate earnings. Finally, issuance of options does not create new shares of stock outstanding; therefore, the firm's earnings per share remain high, a situation which makes the stock more attractive to potential investors.

There are numerous other ethical issues surfacing in companies facing financial troubles, including bonuses paid to executives, reduction in promised retirement benefits, and the deliberately misleading use of accounting information. With more bankruptcies looming in today's uncertain economy, there will surely be new ethical dilemmas appearing soon.

References: Carol Hymowitz, "In the Lead: Managers Must Respond to Employee Concerns about Honest Business," *Wall Street Journal*, February 19, 2002. See www.wsj.com; Jeffrey L. Seglin, "The Right Thing: Do Stock Options Buy Silence?" *New York Times*, February 17, 2002, p. BU-4. See www.nytimes.com; Jeffrey H. Birnbaum, "The Enron Effect," *Fortune*, January 22, 2002. www.fortune.com on February 25, 2002.

have made headlines around the world. And of course, the fallout from the Enron scandal will no doubt continue for years. From the social responsibility angle, increasing attention has been focused on pollution and the obligation of businesses to help clean up our environment, business contributions to social causes, and similar issues.

Leadership, organization culture, and group norms—all important organizational behavior concepts—are relevant in managing these processes.[21] For example, part of Enron's collapse has been attributed to a work culture that promoted overly aggressive competition among its own employees, group norms that made it acceptable to take risks that others would deem unacceptable, and top management leadership that continued to encourage questionable business practices. The "Business of Ethics" box explores several issues additionally related to the firm's failure.

Quality and Productivity

Quality is the total set of features and characteristics of a product or service that determine its ability to satisfy stated or implied needs.

Another competitive challenge that has attracted much attention is quality and productivity. **Quality** is the total set of features and characteristics of a product or service that define its ability to satisfy a stated or implied need of customers or consumers.[22] Quality is an important issue for several reasons. First, more and more organizations are using quality as a basis for competition. For example, Continental Airlines' advertising campaigns routinely stress the firm's high rankings in the J. D. Powers survey of customer satisfaction.

Second, improving quality tends to increase productivity because making higher-quality products generally results in less waste and rework. Third, enhancing quality lowers costs. Whistler Corporation once found that it was using 100 of its 250 employees to repair defective radar detectors that were built incorrectly the first time.

Productivity is an indicator of how much an organization is creating relative to its inputs.

Quality is also important because of its relationship to productivity. In a general sense, **productivity** is an indicator of how much an organization is creating relative to its inputs. For example, if Honda can produce a car for $15,000 while General Motors needs $17,000 to produce a comparable car, Honda is clearly more productive. Experts suggest numerous techniques and strategies for improving productivity. Many of these center around increased cooperation and participation on the part of workers. Ultimately, then, managers and workers will need to work in greater harmony and with unity of purpose. The implications for organizational behavior are obvious: The more closely people work together, the more important it is to understand behavioral processes and concepts.

Indeed, many of the things organizations can do to enhance the quality of their products and services depend on the people who work for them. Motivating employees to get involved in quality improvement efforts, increasing the level of participation throughout the organization, and rewarding people on the basis of contributions to quality are common suggestions—and all rely on human behavior.

Manufacturing and Service Technology

Technology is the mechanical and intellectual processes used to transform inputs into products and services.

A final environmental challenge confronting managers today is the set of issues involving technology. **Technology** is the set of processes the organization uses to transform resources into goods and services. Traditionally, most businesses were manufacturers—they used tangible resources like raw materials and machinery to create tangible products such as automobiles and steel.

Managing this form of technology requires managers to keep abreast of new types of technology and to make appropriate investments to acquire new manufacturing equipment. In addition, training employees for this type of work and then evaluating their performance was once a relatively straightforward undertaking.

In recent years, however, the service sector of the economy has become much more important. Indeed, services now account for well over half of the gross domestic product in the United States and play a similarly important role in many other industrialized nations as well. Service technology involves the use of both tangible resources (such as machinery) and intangible resources (such as intellectual property) to create intangible services (such as a haircut, insurance protection, or transportation between two cities). Because of the intangible properties associated with services, training and performance evaluation are obviously more complex. Many other managerial activities must also be approached in fundamentally different ways in service-based organizations.

Managing for Effectiveness

E arlier in this chapter we noted that managers work toward various goals. We are now in a position to elaborate on the nature of these goals in detail. In particular, as shown in Figure 2.3, goals—or outcomes—exist at three specific levels in an organization: individual-level outcomes, group-level outcomes, and organizational-level outcomes. Of course, it may sometimes be necessary to make tradeoffs among these different kinds of outcomes, but, in general, each is seen as a critical component of organizational effectiveness. The sections that follow elaborate on these different levels in more detail.

Individual-Level Outcomes

Several different outcomes at the individual level are important to managers. Given the focus of the field of organizational behavior, it should not be surprising that most of these outcomes are directly or indirectly addressed by various theories and models.

Individual Behaviors   First, several individual behaviors result from a person's participation in an organization. One important behavior is productivity. A person's productivity is an indicator of his or her efficiency and is measured in terms of the products or services created per unit of input. For example, if Bill makes 100 units of a product in a day, and Sara makes only 90 units in a day, then assuming that the units are of the same quality and that Bill and Sara earn the same wages, Bill is more productive than Sara.

Performance, another important individual-level outcome variable, is a somewhat broader concept. It is made up of all work-related behaviors. For example, even though Bill is highly productive, it may also be that he refuses to work overtime, expresses negative opinions about the organization at every opportunity, and will do nothing unless it falls precisely within the boundaries of his job. Sara, on the other hand, may always be willing to work overtime, is a positive representative of

figure 2.3

Managing for Effectiveness

Managers work to optimize a variety of individual-level, group-level, and organization-level outcomes. It is sometimes necessary to make tradeoffs among the different types and levels of outcomes, but each is an important determinant of organizational effectiveness.

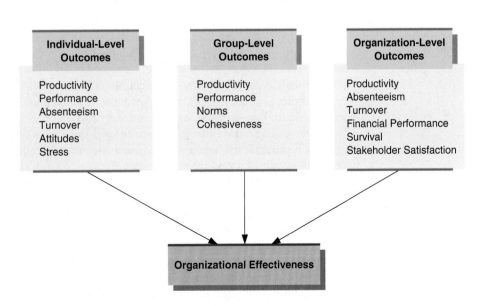

the organization, and goes out of her way to make as many contributions to the organization as possible. Based on the full array of behaviors, then, we might conclude that Sara actually is the better performer.

Two other important individual-level behaviors are absenteeism and turnover. Absenteeism is a measure of attendance. Although virtually everyone misses work occasionally, some people miss far more than others. Some look for excuses to miss work and call in sick regularly just for some time off; others miss work only when absolutely necessary. Turnover occurs when a person leaves the organization. If the individual who leaves is a good performer or if the organization has invested heavily in training the person, turnover can be costly.

Individual Attitudes   Another set of individual-level outcomes influenced by managers consists of individual attitudes. (We discuss attitudes more fully in Chapter 4.) Levels of job satisfaction or dissatisfaction, organizational commitment, and organizational involvement all play an important role in organizational behavior.

Stress   Stress, discussed more fully in Chapter 9, is another important individual-level outcome variable. Given its costs, both personal and organizational, it should not be surprising that stress is becoming an increasingly more important topic for both researchers in organizational behavior and practicing managers.

Group- and Team-Level Outcomes

Another set of outcomes exists at the group and team level. Some of these outcomes parallel the individual-level outcomes just discussed. For example, if an organization makes extensive use of work teams, team productivity and performance are important outcome variables. On the other hand, even if all the people in a group or team have the same or similar attitudes toward their jobs, the attitudes themselves are individual-level phenomena. Individuals, not groups, have attitudes.

But groups or teams can also have unique outcomes that individuals do not share. For example, as we will discuss in Chapter 11, groups develop norms that govern the behavior of individual group members. Groups also develop different levels of cohesiveness. Thus, managers need to assess both common and unique outcomes when considering the individual and group levels.

Organization-Level Outcomes

Finally, a set of outcome variables exists at the organization level. As before, some of these outcomes parallel those at the individual and group levels, but others are unique. For example, we can measure and compare organizational productivity. We can also develop organization-level indicators of absenteeism and turnover. But profitability is generally assessed only at the organizational level.

Organizations are also commonly assessed in terms of financial performance: stock price, return on investment, growth rates, and so on. They are also evaluated in terms of their ability to survive and of the extent to which they satisfy important stakeholders such as investors, government regulators, employees, and unions.

Clearly, then, the manager must balance different outcomes across all three levels of analysis. In many cases, these outcomes appear to contradict one another. For example, paying workers high salaries can enhance satisfaction and reduce turnover, but it also may detract from bottom-line performance. Similarly, exerting strong pressure to increase individual performance may boost short-term profitability but increase turnover and job stress. Thus, the manager must look at the full array of outcomes and attempt to balance them in an optimal fashion. The manager's ability to do this is a major determinant of the organization's success.

Synopsis

By its very nature, management requires an understanding of human behavior to help managers better comprehend those at different levels in the organization, those at the same level, those in other organizations, and themselves.

The manager's job can be characterized in terms of four functions, three sets of roles, and four skills. The basic managerial functions are planning, organizing, leading, and controlling. The roles consist of three interpersonal roles, three informational roles, and four decision-making roles. The four basic skills necessary for effective management are technical, interpersonal, conceptual, and diagnostic skills.

Several organizational challenges confront managers. One major organizational challenge is workforce expansion and reduction. Another is the new workplace itself. Organization change also poses significant organizational challenges for managers. Information technology and new ways of organizing are two other important organizational challenges.

There are also several important environmental challenges to consider. Determining the most effective competitive strategy and matching people to that strategy is one important challenge. Today, global competition is one of the most critical environmental challenges. Ethics and social responsibility are significant as well. The manager must also emphasize product and service quality and manage technology successfully.

Managing for effectiveness involves balancing a variety of individual-level, group- and team-level, and organization-level outcome variables.

Discussion Questions

1. Is it possible for managers to worry too much about the behavior of their subordinates? Why or why not?

2. The text identifies four basic managerial functions. Based on your own experiences or observations, provide examples of each function.

3. Which managerial skills do you think are among your strengths? Which are among your weaknesses? How might you improve the latter?

4. The text argues that we cannot understand organizations without understanding the behavior of the people within them. Do you agree or disagree with this assertion? Why?

5. Interview a local manager or business owner to find out his or her views on the importance of individual behavior to the success of the organization. Then report your findings to the class.

6. What advice would you give managers to help them prepare better to cope with changes in workforce diversity?

7. How has information technology changed your role as a student? Have the changes been positive or negative?

8. Identify firms that use each of the three competitive strategies noted in the text.

9. Of the five environmental challenges noted in the text, which do you think is most important? Which is least important? Give reasons for your answers.

10. Are there any businesses that have not been affected by globalization? Explain.

11. What individual-, group-, or organization-level outcome variables of consequence can you identify beyond those noted in the text?

Organizational Behavior Case for Discussion

The Sky's the Limit at Lockheed Martin

October 26, 2001, was a triumphant day for Lockheed Martin and for Tom Burbage, aeronautics engineer, executive vice president, and head of the firm's Joint Strike Fighter program. The aeronautics contractor had just been chosen by the Department of Defense to develop and manufacture its new Joint Strike Fighter (JSF) jet, beating rivals Boeing and McDonnell Douglas. Lockheed received $19 billion to begin the design, and the 6,000-aircraft, 40-year contract is expected to ultimately be worth as much as $200 billion. The win established Lockheed as the leading maker of fighter jets and as the supplier for the U.S. Air Force, Navy, and Marines as well as for the U.K. Royal Air Force and Royal Navy. Other aeronautics firms would be left hoping for a spot as a subcontractor on the gigantic project. In the aeronautics industry, Lockheed has often been considered an also-ran and far from competitive with industry leader Boeing. So how did the firm come to win this highly lucrative defense contract?

It might have had something to do with the attitude expressed by Darleen Druyun, acquisition chief for the Air Force. At the time, she noted, "This competition is not about an airplane. It's about a management team." It was clear that all three of the bidders for the contract had excellent technical skills and could produce an acceptable product. What the Pentagon was looking for was the management experience and ability that would enable the winner to coordinate the costly and complex project.

Perhaps the key decision made at Lockheed was naming Burbage to head the program. Burbage credits his time as a Navy test pilot with teaching him leadership and management skills. In one early military experience, he commanded a team on board an aircraft carrier. He used extravagant rewards, such as flying top-performing sailors into Naples for a weekend jaunt, and as a result, his crew had the best performance record ever attained. He explained, "[Y]ou can build a high-performing team in some pretty austere environments. But first, you've got to take care of your people. And second, you've got to understand the difference between the carrot and the stick—and in my view, the former is a lot more useful than the latter. In the end, I stopped trying to motivate people. I learned that if you recognize and reward them, people will motivate themselves."

One problem Burbage encountered was an internal rift within the firm—two divisions of Lockheed were competing for control of the project. "Lockheed wasn't known for pulling teams together," says Martin Taylor, BAE's program manager on the JSF project. Another manager at Lockheed, Harry Blot, saw that Lockheed lacked some of the skills needed to complete the project and recommended that the firm partner with rivals BAE and Northrup Grumman. At first, the competitors were concerned. "Lockheed and Northrup have battled each other for sixty years. At the time, I couldn't believe it: We're supposed to *partner* with these guys?" questioned Martin McLaughlin, a Northrup manager. Representatives from the three firms met, and, according to Taylor, they "expected the discussions to revolve around how to divide the work. But as it turned out, Lockheed was more interested in how [they would] build a relationship." Lockheed made the unheard-of decision to grant Northrup and BAE a 30 percent financial and strategic share in the program—effectively treating them as equals rather than as subcontractors.

Lockheed maintained an intense focus on the needs of its customers, the U.S. and U.K. military forces, as well as the allied forces around the world who are also expected to adopt the JSF jet. The U.S. Navy would be purchasing more planes than any other group, but the Marines were more assertive and had the greatest political and military influence. When the Marines demanded that the jet be able to make vertical landings on smaller ships, Lockheed made that criterion one of their core requirements. Designing a system for vertical lift for such a large jet had never been done. When the process hit a snag, engineers worked around the clock for three weeks to solve the problem together.

Burbage's team anticipated problems and planned strategies for addressing them in advance of need. Managers from the three partner firms worked together to create an extensive list of lessons learned based on their combined experience of modern aircraft development programs. In a technique that Burbage has dubbed the "premortem," they compared that list to their ten-year schedule, identifying high-risk points. Solutions for these high-risk points are already being worked out years before they will be implemented. This preplanning allows the team to have confidence in its deadlines, which are critical to the survival of the JSF program.

Burbage claims, "If you can't control your schedule, the implication is that you can't control costs. And if you can't control costs, you won't keep the [military] services interested in funding your program."

Lockheed is on track to reach its goal of having a flying prototype by 2005. This accomplishment, while great, is even more extraordinary in light of the challenges that had to be overcome to reach this point. Loren Thompson, a defense analyst at the Lexington Institute, explains it best: "The Lockheed guys were like the patient who undergoes heart surgery while running for his life. They had to fix themselves in the midst of the biggest battle they'd ever been in."

"I stopped trying to motivate people. . . . [I]f you recognize and reward them, people will motivate themselves."—Tom Burbage, Lockheed Martin executive vice president

References: Bill Breen, "High Stakes, Big Bets," *Fast Company*, April 2002, pp. 66–78. See www.fastcompany.com; Bill Breen, "Leadership Voyage," *Fast Company*, April 2002 (quotation). www.fastcompany.com on April 4, 2002; Massachusetts Institute of Technology Engineering Systems Division, "Special Seminar: Lockheed Martin Aeronautics Company." www.mit.edu/headline/seminar0306.htm on April 4, 2002; Michael A. Dornheim, "Boeing: Lift Fan Put LockMart Over the Top in JSF Competition," *Aviation Week & Space Technology*, March 12, 2002. www.aviationnow.com/content/publication on April 4, 2002.

Case Questions

1. How do the actions of Burbage and other Lockheed managers exemplify the four fundamental functions of management? Give specific examples of actions which fall into each of the four categories.
2. Which of the managerial skills does Burbage display?
3. What types of organizational and environmental challenges do you expect Lockheed JSF managers to encounter as they complete the project?

 # Experiencing Organizational Behavior

Managing in Today's Organization

Purpose: This exercise is intended to help you develop a deeper and more complete appreciation of the complexities and nuances of managing individual behavior in organizational settings.

Format: You will first develop a scenario regarding a behavior problem of your own choosing, along with a recommended course of action. You will then exchange scenarios with a classmate and compare recommendations.

Procedure: Select one of the organizational challenges (downsizing, workforce diversity, the new workforce, change, information technology, or new ways of organizing) or environmental challenges (competitive strategy, global competition, ethics and social responsibility, quality and productivity, or technology) discussed in this chapter. Working alone (perhaps as an outside-of-class assignment, if requested by your instructor), write a brief scenario (one page or less) describing a hypothetical organization facing that challenge. Your scenarios should provide a bit of background about the firm, the specific challenge it is facing, and some detail about why that particular challenge is relevant.

On a separate page, recommend a course of action that a manager might take to address that challenge. For example, if your challenge is to cope with a new form of technology or a need to enhance quality, your recommendation might be to form employee advisory groups to help implement the technology or to establish a new employee reward system to improve quality. Try hard to clearly and logically link the scenario to the recommendation and provide enough detail so that the appropriateness of your plan is readily apparent.

Next, exchange scenarios with one of your classmates. Without discussing it, read the classmate's scenario and develop your own recommendations to address it. After you have finished, verbally summarize your recommendations for your colleague and listen to his or her summary of recommendations for your scenario. Then exchange the written recommendations you prepared for your own scenarios and read them. Discuss similarities and differences between the two sets of recommendations. Explain the logic behind the recommendations you originally proposed and listen carefully to the logic your colleague used to develop his or her own recommendations.

Follow-up Questions

1. Were the two sets of recommendations basically the same or basically different? Did the discussion alter your view of what should be done?

2. The contingency view, discussed in Chapter 1, would suggest that different courses of action might be equally effective. How likely is it that each of the two sets of recommendations you and your colleague developed might work?

 # Self-Assessment Exercise

Assessing Your Own Management Skills

The questions below are intended to provide insights into your confidence about your capabilities regarding the management skills discussed in this chapter. Answer each question by circling the scale value that best reflects your feelings.

1. I generally do well in quantitative courses like math, statistics, accounting, and finance.

2. I get along well with most people.

3. It is usually easy for me to see how material in one of my classes relates to material in other classes.

4. I can usually figure out why a problem occurred.

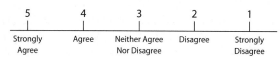

5. When I am asked to perform a task or to do some work, I usually know how to do it or else can figure it out pretty quickly.

6. I can usually understand why people behave as they do.

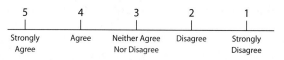

7. I enjoy classes that deal with theories and concepts.

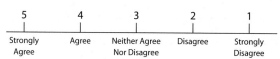

8. I usually understand why things happen as they do.

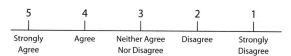

9. I like classes that require me to "do things"—write papers, solve problems, research new areas, and so forth.

10. Whenever I work in a group, I can usually get others to accept my opinions and ideas.

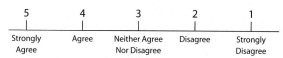

11. I am much more interested in understanding the "big picture" than in dealing with narrow, focused issues.

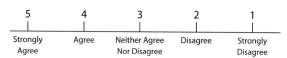

12. When I know what I am supposed to do, I can usually figure out how to do it.

Instructions: Add up your point values for questions 1, 5, and 9; this total reflects your assessment of your technical skills. The point total for questions 2, 6, and 10 reflects interpersonal skills; the point total for questions 3, 7, and 11 reflects conceptual skills; the point total for questions 4, 8, and 12 reflects diagnos-tic skills. Higher scores indicate stronger confidence in that realm of management. [*Note:* This brief instrument has not been scientifically validated and is to be used for classroom discussion only.]

OB Online

1. Use the Internet to research Continental's current performance.
2. Find news stories on the Internet that illustrate managers actually engaging in the basic functions of planning, organizing, leading, and controlling. For instance, an article telling of a manager setting new goals or outlining a new strategy for his or her business would illustrate planning.
3. Research the Internet to identify at least two companies that have recently announced workforce reductions.
4. Find a story on the Internet that involves ethics and social responsibility.

Building Managerial Skills

Exercise Overview: Conceptual skills involve the manager's ability to think in the abstract. This exercise will help you extend your conceptual skills by identifying potential generalizations of management functions, roles, and skills across a variety of organizations.

Exercise Background: This introductory chapter discusses four basic management functions, ten common managerial roles, and four vital management skills. It is frequently asserted that management is applicable to a wide variety of organizations.

Identify one large business, one small business, one educational organization, one health-care organization, and one government organization. These might be organizations about which you have some personal knowledge or simply organizations that you recognize. Next, imagine yourself in the position of a top manager in each organization.

Write the names of the five organizations across the top of a sheet of paper. List the four functions, ten roles, and four skills down the left side of the paper. Then think of a situation, problem, or opportunity relevant to the intersection of each row and column on the paper. For example, how might a manager in a government organization engage in planning and need diagnostic skills? Similarly, how might a manager in a small business carry out the organizing function and play the role of negotiator?

Exercise Task

1. What meaningful similarities can you identify across the five columns?

2. What meaningful differences can you identify across the five columns?

3. Based on your assessment of the similarities and differences previously identified, how easy or difficult do you think it might be for a manager to move from one type of organization to another?

3 Managing Global and Workforce Diversity

Management Preview

▶ Business and the workforce in organizations are becoming increasingly global and diverse. These developments affect our lives as workers and managers and pose numerous challenges. In some organizations the transformation is due to changing demographics among the general population of society whereas in other situations the increasing diversity is caused by the globalization of an organization's products, services, suppliers, customers, and employees. Regardless of the cause of the diversity in an organization, the result is that management must deal with the diversity and develop ways to manage it. In this chapter we explore how to manage these cross-cultural issues. We first examine the different types and sources of diversity affecting organizations today. We then trace the emergence of international management issues and describe the dimensions and the complexities of this organizational diversity. Next, we discuss the primary and secondary dimensions of diversity. We also examine cross-cultural factors that affect individual, interpersonal, and organizational issues. We conclude with some comments on managing multicultural and multinational organizations. First, though, we begin by describing the diversity programs in operation at Procter & Gamble.

▼ ▼ ▼

Procter & Gamble (P&G) produces a wide variety of items, including such popular U.S. brand names as Tide, Crest, Always, Pampers, Cover Girl, Olay, Secret, Scope, Charmin, Ivory, Folgers, and Pringles. The company, with more than 250 brands, is the largest producer of products for the home, products that are primarily purchased by women. A 1999 survey by P&G found that women control 80 percent of family purchasing decisions. Therefore, it makes sense that P&G would be a leader in the hiring and promotion of women in order to match the diversity represented by their customers. This was not the case until recently, but P&G, known for its effective marketing campaigns, has now focused its abilities on the goal of attracting and retaining more women.

The problem was clear—too many women were leaving P&G, with few remaining to be promoted to top management ranks. The probelm even became evident in meetings when thirty people, not one of them female, might be discussing a diaper or makeup brand. The solution was clear, too—find out why women were leaving the company and respond. Some of the new initiatives at P&G include local task forces for each facility, diversity specialists in the human resources departments, flexible work arrangements, generous family leave, and sabbaticals. A companywide survey identified areas of concern, and another survey gathered insights from those who had recently quit. The "Careers" page of the company web site lists "We show respect for all individuals" as the firm's number one principle, supported by the statements "We believe that all individuals can and want to contribute" and "We value differences."

One-third of the P&G vice presidents today are women, up from 5 percent in 1992, and two members of its board of directors are female (up from zero in 1992). Women head some of P&G's most important brands, including Tide, the firm's best seller. P&G was recognized by *Business Ethics* as one of the one hundred best corporate citizens, gaining the number five spot, in part for its diversity programs. P&G's web site states, "Of the approximately 700 firms [being evaluated for this distinction], P&G is the only company that has ranked within the top 5 for all years of this ranking."

"Our ability to develop new consumer insights . . . is the best possible testimony to the power of diversity that any organization could ever have."—John E. Pepper, *Procter & Gamble chairman*

However, progress can be slow. In 1998, an article in the *Cincinnati Post* named four P&G female vice presidents who were likely to gain further recognition. By 2001, two of them had been promoted to global group vice presidents; the other two had left the firm. One reason for the slow pace of change is P&G's strict policy of internal promotion. P&G's strong culture is another barrier to change. "It's such a strong culture; they really want sameness," says former P&G manager Juelene Beck.

Business Ethics found that companies on its "100 Best" list had significantly higher financial performance than did comparable firms not on the list. P&G management also equates diversity with success. "Our success as a global company is a direct result of our diverse and talented workforce. Our ability to develop new consumer insights and ideas and to execute in a superior way across the world is the best possible testimony to the power of diversity that any organization could ever have," says John E. Pepper, P&G Chairman.

References: "Careers," "Diversity," "Purpose, Values, Principles," Procter and Gamble web site. www.pg.com and www.pgcareers.com on May 4, 2002; "2001 Annual 10-K Report," Procter and Gamble, p. 38; Mary Miller, "The 100 Best Corporate Citizens for 2002," *Business Ethics*, March/April 2001. www.business-ethics.com on May 4, 2002; Tara Parker-Pope, "P&G retools to keep more female employees," *The Cincinnati Post*, September 14, 1998, p. 7B; Lindsey Arent, "How Women Buy, and Why," *Wired*, November 17, 1999. www.wired.com on May 4, 2002.

More and more organizations are developing and expanding their internal and external programs in the areas of diversity, and most are finding that doing so makes good business sense. Organizations such as Procter & Gamble, AT&T, Denny's (Advantica), Ernst and Young, the Anderson School at UCLA, Pitney Bowes, and Pfizer are using innovative ways to utilize an increasingly diverse workforce through various diversity initiatives, diversity roundtables, diversity seminars, and diversity marketing to reach new employees, suppliers, and customers that make a difference on the bottom line. It is essential that managers be aware of the different aspects of diversity, the wide range of diversity programs in use, and the impact of diversity on corporate performance. We start this chapter with a more detailed discussion of the meaning and nature of diversity in organizations.

The Nature of Diversity in Organizations

You have no doubt heard the term "diversity" many times, but what does it mean in the workplace today? Usually when we speak of diversity, we think only of the gender, racial, and ethnic differences in the workforce. More broadly, the term refers to a mixture of items, objects, or people that are characterized by differences and similarities.[1] The similarities can be as important as the differences. After all, none of us are exactly alike. We may be similar but never the same. Thus, it is important to note that although two employees may have the same gender, ethnicity, and even university education, they are different employees who may act differently and react differently to various management styles. In the workplace, we refer to this variation with such terms as "cultural diversity," "workforce diversity," and "cultural variety." Managers have to deal simultaneously with similarities and differences among people in organizations.[2] They must deal with diversity within their own organizations and in the organizations they encounter all over the world. The opportunities and difficulties inherent in managing multicultural organizations will be a key management challenge in the twenty-first century.

The increasing diversity of the workforce is due to four trends. First, as the job market evolves and changes from good to bad, it becomes very important to find the best workers and then utilize them to best serve the organization. Layoffs are costly, as are recruiting and hiring new employees. During economic downturns, companies such as Silicon Graphics struggle to make sure that no one group of employees is disproportionately affected by layoffs, for example.[3] Second, more companies are focusing their marketing efforts on the increasing buying power in the minority markets. A diverse, or segmented, marketing effort requires a marketing team that represents the markets being targeted. As an example, McDonalds, number three on *Fortune's* list of the fifty best companies for minorities, is diversifying what it buys as well as what it sells by buying $3 billion a year from minority-owned firms.[4] Third, more companies are seeking to expand their markets around the world. It takes more diverse thinking to effectively reach global markets. Finally, companies that have sought to reach globally via expansion, acquisitions, and mergers inevitably go through a period of consolidation to reduce duplication of efforts around the world and to capitalize on the synergies of cross-border operations. Typically, consolidation means that employees from around the world are thrust together in newly streamlined units, resulting in more diverse groups. These four trends, then, are the drivers behind the increasing diversity in the workforce.[5]

What Is Workforce Diversity?

Workforce diversity is the similarities and differences in such characteristics as age, gender, ethnic heritage, physical abilities and disabilities, race, and sexual orientation among the employees of organizations.

Workforce diversity is the similarities and differences in such characteristics as age, gender, ethnic heritage, physical abilities and disabilities, race, and sexual orientation among the employees of organizations. 3M defines its goals regarding workforce diversity as "valuing uniqueness, while respecting differences, maximizing individual potentials, and synergizing collective talents and experiences for the growth and success of 3M."[6] In a diverse workforce, managers are compelled to recognize and handle the similarities and differences that exist among the people in the organization.

Coca-Cola CEO Douglas Daft (second from left) is shown with some of the employees who represent the company's drive to diversify its workforce. At Coke, forty percent of new hires are minorities. This comes after a racial discrimination suit in 2000 that cost the company $192 million. And they are not only at the lower levels of the organization: minorities now makeup thirty percent of the executive committee of the Board of Directors.

Employees' conceptions of work, expectations of rewards from the organization, and practices in relating to others are all influenced by diversity.[7] Managers of diverse work groups need to understand how the social environment affects employees' beliefs about work, and they must have the communication skills to develop confidence and self-esteem in members of diverse work groups. Many people tend to stereotype others in organizations. As described in Chapter 4, a **stereotype** is a generalization about a person or a group of persons based on certain characteristics or traits. Many managers fall into the trap of stereotyping workers as being like themselves and sharing a manager's orientation toward work, rewards, and relating to coworkers. However, if workers do not share those views, values, and beliefs, problems can arise. A second situation involving stereotyping occurs when managers stereotype workers according to some particular group such as age, gender, race, ethnic origin, or other characteristic. It is often easier for managers to group people based on easily identifiable characteristics and to treat these groups as "different." Managers who stereotype workers based on assumptions about the characteristics of their group tend to ignore individual differences, which leads to making rigid judgments about others that do not take into account the specific person and the current situation.[8]

Stereotypes tend to become rigid judgments about others that ignore the specific person and the current situation. Acceptance of stereotypes can lead to the dangerous process of prejudice toward others.

Stereotypes can lead to the even more dangerous process of prejudice toward others. **Prejudices** are judgments about others that reinforce beliefs about superiority and inferiority. They can lead to an exaggerated assessment of the worth of one group and a diminished assessment of the worth of others.[9] When people prejudge others, they make assumptions about the nature of the others that may or may not be true, and they manage accordingly. In other words, people build job descriptions, reward systems, performance appraisal systems, and management systems and policies that fit their stereotypes.

Prejudices are judgments about others that reinforce beliefs about superiority and inferiority.

Management systems built on stereotypes and prejudices do not meet the needs of a diverse workforce. An incentive system may offer rewards that people do not value, job descriptions that do not fit the jobs and the people who do them, and performance evaluation systems that measure the wrong things. In addition, those who engage in prejudice and stereotyping fail to recognize employees' distinctive individual talents, a situation which often leads these employees to lose self-esteem and possibly have lower levels of job satisfaction and performance. Stereotypes can also become self-fulfilling prophecies.[10] If we assume someone is incompetent and treat the person as though he or she is, over time the employee may begin to share the same belief. This can lead to reduced productivity, lower creativity, and lower morale.

Of course, managers caught in this counterproductive cycle can change. As a first step, they must recognize that diversity exists in organizations. Only then can they begin to manage it appropriately. Managers who do not recognize diversity may face an unhappy, disillusioned, and underutilized workforce.

Who Will Be the Workforce of the Future?

Employment statistics can help us understand just how different the workforce of the future will be. Figure 3.1 compares the workforce composition of 1990 to projections for 2010. All workforce segments will increase as a percentage of the total workforce except the white male segment, which declines from 47.4 percent to 43.2 percent. This may not seem too dramatic, but it follows decades in which the

figure 3.1

Workforce Composition: 1990–2010

In the period between 1990 and 2010, all workforce segments are expected to increase as a percentage of the total workforce except the white male segment, which declines from 47.4 percent to 43.2 percent.

Reference: Bureau of Labor Statistics, *Monthly Labor Review*, November 2001.

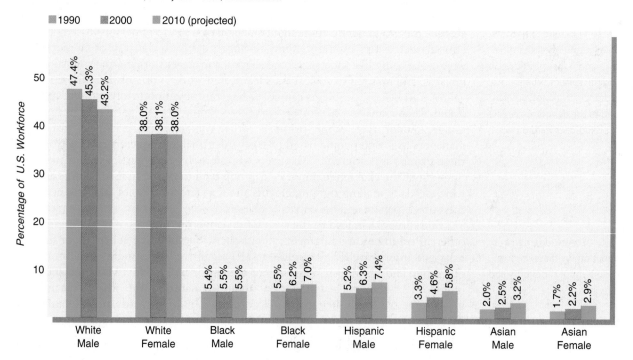

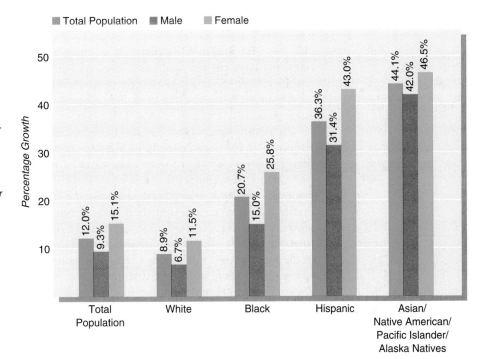

figure 3.2

Expected Percentage of Growth in Workforce: 2000–2010

There is no question that the composition of the workforce is changing in the United States. For the period from 2000 to 2010, the growth rate in all segments is higher for women than for men and higher for nonwhites than for whites.

Reference: Bureau of Labor Statistics, *Monthly Labor Review*, November 2001.

white males have dominated the workforce, making up well over 50 percent of it. When one considers that the total U.S. workforce is expected to be over 150 million people in 2010, a 4 percent drop represents a significant decline.[11]

We can also examine the nature of the growth in the workforce over the ten-year period from 2000 to 2010. Figure 3.2 shows the percentage of the growth attributable to each segment. Although the overall workforce growth is expected to be 12 percent, the growth rate for white males is expected to be only 6.7 percent. Females are expected to increase their percentage in the workforce by 15.1 percent, so that more than 62 percent of the women in the United States are expected to be working in 2010.

"In 2000, 48.2 percent of the labor force was age 40 or older; by 2010, more than one half of the labor force will be in this age category." —Howard Fullerton, Jr. and Mitra Toossi, Bureau of Labor Statistics[12]

Examining the age ranges of the workforce gives us another view of the changes. In contrast to its standing in earlier decades, the sixteen-to-twenty-four age group will grow more rapidly than the overall population—an increase of 3.4 million (14.8 percent) between 2000 and 2010. The number of workers in the twenty-five-to-fifty-four age group is expected to increase by 5 million (5.0 percent), and the number of workers in the fifty-five and older group is expected to increase by 8.5 million (46.6 percent).[13]

Global Workforce Diversity

Similar statistics on workforce diversity are found in other countries. In Canada, for instance, minorities are the fastest-growing segment of the population and the workforce. In addition, women make up two-thirds of the growth in the Canadian workforce, increasing from 35 percent in the 1970s to 45 percent in 1991.[14] These changes have initiated a workforce revolution in offices and factories throughout Canada. Managers and employees are learning to adapt to changing demographics. One study found that 81 percent of the organizations surveyed by the Conference Board of Canada include diversity management programs for their employees.[15]

Increasing diversity in the workplace is even more dramatic in Europe, where employees have been crossing borders for many years. In fact, as of 1991, more than 2 million Europeans were working in another European country. When the European Union opened borders in 1992, this number increased significantly. It was expected that opening borders among the European community members primarily would mean relaxing trade restrictions so that goods and services could move among the member countries. In addition, however, workers were also free to move, and they have taken advantage of the opportunity. It is clear that diversity in the workforce is more than a U.S. phenomenon. Many German factories now have a very diverse workforce that includes many workers from Turkey. Several of the newly emerging economies in Central Europe are encountering increasing diversity in their workforce. Poland, Hungary, and the Czech Republic are experiencing an influx of workers from the Ukraine, Afghanistan, Sri Lanka, China, and Somalia.[16]

Companies throughout Europe are learning to adjust to the changing workforce. Amadeus Global Travel Distribution serves the travel industry, primarily in Europe, but its staff of 650 is composed of individuals from thirty-two different countries. Amadeus developed a series of workshops to teach managers how to lead multicultural teams. Such seminars also teach them how to interact better with peers, subordinates, and superiors who come from a variety of countries.[17] Other companies experiencing much the same phenomenon in Europe and doing something about it include Mars, Digital Equipment, Hewlett-Packard Spain, Fujitsu in Spain, and British Petroleum. Companies in Asia are also encountering increasing diversity. In Thailand, where there is a shortage of skilled and unskilled workers because of rapid industrialization and slow population growth, there is a growing demand for foreign workers to fill the gap, which creates problems integrating local and foreign workers.[18] Thus, the issues of workforce diversity are not prevalent only in the United States. The emergence of international management is discussed in the next major section of this chapter. But first, we describe why it is important to value diversity rather than just tolerate it.

The Value of Diversity

In the traditional view, the United States was seen as a "melting pot" of people from many different countries, cultures, and backgrounds. For centuries, it was assumed that people who were different or new to something should assimilate themselves into the existing situation. Although equal employment opportunity and accompanying affirmative action legislation have had significant effects on diversifying workplaces, they sometimes focused on bringing into the workplace people from culturally different groups and fully assimilating them into the existing organization. In organizations, however, integration proved to be difficult. People were slow to change and usually resistant to the change. Substantive career advancement opportunities rarely materialized for those who were "different."

The issue of workforce diversity has become increasingly more important in the last few years as employees, managers, consultants, and the government finally realized that the composition of the workforce affects organizational productivity. Today, instead of a melting pot, the workplace in the United States is regarded as more of a tossed salad made up of a delightful mosaic of different flavors, colors, and textures. Rather than trying to assimilate those who are different into a single organizational culture, the current view holds that organizations need to celebrate the differences and utilize the variety of talents, perspectives, and backgrounds of all employees.

Valuing diversity means putting an end to the assumption that everyone who is not a member of the dominant group must assimilate.

Benefits of Valuing Diversity   **Valuing diversity** means putting an end to the assumption that everyone who is not a member of the dominant group must assimilate. This is not easily accomplished in most organizations. Truly valuing diversity is not merely giving lip service to an ideal, putting up with a necessary evil, promoting a level of tolerance for those who are different, or tapping into the latest fad. It is an opportunity to develop and utilize all of the human resources available to the organization for the benefit of the workers as well as the organization. Later in this chapter we discuss the benefits of creating a multicultural organization.

"Diversifying our staff is not some side project. It is a core part of our business strategy."—Jay Harris, publisher, San Jose Mercury News[19]

Valuing diversity is not just the right thing to do for workers; it is the right thing to do for the organization, financially and economically. One of the most important benefits of diversity is the richness of ideas and perspectives that it makes available to the organization. Rather than relying on one homogeneous dominant group for new ideas and alternative solutions to increasingly complex problems, companies that value diversity have access to more perspectives of a problem. These fresh perspectives may lead to development of new products, opening of new markets, or improving service to existing customers.

Overall, the organization wins when it truly values diversity. A worker whom the organization values is more creative and productive. Valued workers in diverse organizations experience less interpersonal conflict because the employees understand each other. When employees of different cultural groups, backgrounds, and values understand each other, they have a greater sense of teamwork, stronger identification with the team, and deeper commitment to the organization and its goals.

Assimilation is the process through which members of a minority group are forced to learn the ways of the dominant group. In organizations, this means that when people of different types and backgrounds are hired, the organization attempts to mold them to fit the existing organizational culture.

Assimilation   **Assimilation** is the process through which members of a minority group are forced to learn the ways of the majority group. In organizations this entails hiring people from diverse backgrounds and attempting to mold them to fit into the existing organizational culture. One way that companies attempt to make people fit in is by requiring that employees speak only one language. In Chicago, Carlos Solero was fired three days after he refused to sign a work agreement that included a policy of English-only at a suburban manufacturing plant. Management said the intent of the English-only policy was to improve communication among workers at the plant. In response, Solero and seven other Spanish speakers filed lawsuits against the plant. [20] Attempts to assimilate diverse workers by imposing English-only rules can lead to a variety of organizational problems. Most organizations develop systems such as performance evaluation and incentive programs that reinforce the values of the dominant

"Wilkens, the next time we catch you coming to work in a suit and tie,
I'm afraid we're going to have to let you go."

Fitting into the corporate model is not exactly what it used to be with all of the Internet start-ups these days. In this situation, the "boss" expects the older gentleman in the suit and tie to conform to the more informal "dress code." But fitting in is not necessarily the best in every situation. Doing the right job in the right way is more important than wearing the right clothes and fitting in. The lessons of valuing diversity should have shown us that by now.

Reference: *Fast Company*, February–March 1999, p. 66. Richard Cline

group. (Chapter 18 discusses organizational culture as a means of reinforcing the organizational values and affecting the behavior of workers.) By universally applying the values of the majority group throughout the organization, assimilation tends to perpetuate false stereotypes and prejudices. Workers who are different are expected to meet the standards for dominant group members.[21] Sometimes those standards can pertain to dress, as shown in the cartoon on the left.

Dominant groups tend to be self-perpetuating. Majority group members may avoid people who are "different" simply because they find communication difficult. Moreover, informal discussions over coffee and lunch and during after-hours socializing tend to be limited to people in the dominant group. What happens? Those who are not in the dominant group miss out on the informal communication opportunities in which office politics, company policy, and other issues are often discussed in great detail. Subsequently, employees not in the dominant group often do not understand the more formal communication and may not be included in necessary action taken in response. The dominant group likewise remains unaware of opinions from the "outside."

Similarly, since the dominant group makes decisions based on their values and beliefs, the minority group has little say in decisions regarding compensation, facility location, benefit plans, performance standards, and other work issues that pertain directly to all workers. Workers who differ from the majority very quickly get the idea that to succeed in such a system, one must be like the dominant group in terms of values and beliefs, dress, and most other characteristics. Since success depends on assimilation, differences are driven underground.

Most organizations have a fairly predictable dominant group. Table 3.1 shows the results of interviews with members of several organizations who were asked to list the attributes reinforced by their organization's culture. Typically, white men in organizations view themselves as quite diverse. Others in the organizations view them as quite homogeneous, however, having attributes similar to those listed. Also typically, those who work in these dominant groups tend to be less aware of the problems that homogeneity can cause. Generally, those not in the dominant group feel the effects more keenly.

Not paying attention to cultural diversity can be very costly to the organization. In addition to blocking minority involvement in communication and decision making, it can result in tensions among workers, lower productivity, increased costs due to increasing absenteeism, increased employee turnover, increased equal employment opportunity and harassment suits, and lower morale among the workers.[22]

table 3.1

Attributes Reinforced by the Culture in Typical Organizations

- Rational, linear thinker
- Impersonal management style
- Married with children
- Quantitative
- Adversarial
- Careerist
- Individualistic
- Experience in competitive team sports
- In control
- Military veteran

- Age 35–49
- Competitive
- Protestant or Jewish
- College graduate
- Tall
- Heterosexual
- Predictable
- Excellent physical condition
- Willing to relocate

Reference: Marilyn Loden and Judy B. Rosener, *Workforce America! Managing Employee Diversity as a Vital Resource* (Homewood, Ill.: Business One Irwin, 1991), p. 43. Copyright © 1991 by Business One Irwin. Used with permission.

The Emergence of International Management

A primary source of diversity in organizations is the increasing globalization of organizations and management. However, in many ways, international management is nothing new. Centuries ago, the Roman army was forced to develop a management system to deal with its widespread empire.[23] Likewise, the Olympic games, the Red Cross, and many similar organizations have international roots. From a business standpoint, however, international management is relatively new, at least in the United States.

The Growth of International Business

In 1990, the volume of international trade in current dollars was almost thirty times greater than the amount in 1960, and the figures are projected to continue escalating. What has led to this dramatic increase? As Figure 3.3 shows, four major factors account for much of the momentum.

First, communication and transportation have advanced dramatically over the past few decades. Telephone service has improved, communication networks span the globe and can interact via satellite, and once-remote areas have become accessible. Telephone service in some developing countries is now almost entirely by cellular phone technology rather than land-based wired telephone service. Fax machines and electronic mail allow managers to send documents around the world in seconds as opposed to the days it took just a few years ago. In short, it is simply easier to conduct international business today.

figure 3.3

Forces That Have Increased International Business

Movement along the continuum from domestic to international business is due to four forces. Businesses subject to these forces are becoming more international.

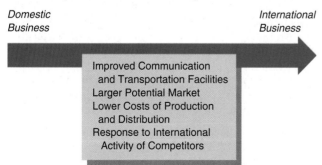

Domestic Business → International Business

Improved Communication and Transportation Facilities
Larger Potential Market
Lower Costs of Production and Distribution
Response to International Activity of Competitors

Second, businesses have expanded internationally to increase their markets. Companies in smaller countries, such as Nestlé in Switzerland, recognized long ago that their domestic markets were too small to sustain much growth and therefore moved into international activities. Many U.S. firms, on the other hand, had all the business they could handle until recently; hence, they are just beginning to consider international opportunities. As U.S. companies grow internationally, they have to confront many differences in the ways various countries conduct business. Differences in laws, local customs, tariffs, and exchange rates are only a few of these. In spite of the Foreign Corrupt Practices Act in the United States, some companies are having difficulty finding legal ways to do business, and individuals are still getting into trouble. For example, in 1999 Saybolt, Inc. pled guilty to paying a $50,000 bribe to Panamanian government officials within the Panamanian Ministry of Commerce and Industries to obtain a lease from the government for a laboratory site adjacent to the Panama Canal. David H. Mean, who was then president of Saybolt, was convicted of conspiracy, violation of the Foreign Corrupt Practices Act, and interstate travel to promote bribery.[24] Companies in the tobacco industry have significantly increased their global efforts and are currently embroiled in a global controversy over whether it is ethical to advertise tobacco products heavily around the world.

Third, more and more firms are moving into the international realm to control costs, especially to reduce labor costs. Plans to cut costs in this way do not always work out as planned, but many firms are successfully using inexpensive labor in Asia and Mexico.[25] In searching for lower labor costs, some companies have discovered well-trained workers and built more efficient plants that are closer to international markets.[26]

Finally, many organizations have become international in response to competition. If an organization starts gaining strength in international markets, its competitors often must follow suit to avoid falling too far behind in sales and profitability. Exxon Mobil Corporation and Texaco realized they had to increase their international market share to keep pace with foreign competitors such as BP Amoco p.l.c. and Royal Dutch/Shell.

Trends in International Business

The most striking trend in international business is obvious: growth. More and more businesses are entering the international marketplace, including many smaller firms. We read a great deal about the threat of foreign companies. For example, for many years successful Japanese automobile firms such as Toyota and Nissan produced higher-quality cars for lower prices than did U.S. firms. What we often overlook, however, is the success of U.S. firms abroad. Ford, for example, has long had a successful business in Europe and today employs less than half its total workforce on U.S. soil. And U.S. firms make dozens of products better than anyone else in the world.[27] General Motors Europe has had strong sales in Europe since 1985, rising to a 12.6 percent market share, the second best in Europe, behind Volkswagen.[28] In addition, many foreign firms (BMW and Mercedes) are now producing their products in the United States because of the lower wage rates, better tax rates, and improved quality.

Business transactions are also becoming increasingly blurred across national boundaries. Ford owns 25 percent of Mazda, General Motors and Toyota have a joint venture in California, Ford and Volkswagen have one in Argentina, and Honda and British Sterling have one worldwide. Indeed, some experts have started predict-

These four workers in Alcatel's switch-making plant in Shanghai, China, exemplify the rapid changes in manufacturing in that country. Once known for cheap and low-skilled labor that made cheap trinkets, toys, textiles, and knock-offs of higher quality goods, China has become a haven for high-tech manufacturing. Sophisticated electronic equipment, photonics, ceramic casings, liquid crystal display screens, digital switching systems and much more are now among the goods being produced there. China's emergence is creating rapid shifts in investment around the world, as manufacturers move to take advantage of the cheaper labor, high quality workmanship, sophisticated engineering expertise, and proximity to the huge Chinese marketplace. Investment that used to go to Japan and other countries in Southeast Asia is now going to China. In fact, Japanese, European, and United States producers of high tech equipment, such as OMRON, Nokia, and Alcatel, are now investing billions in new manufacturing plants in China.

ing that some multinational firms will soon start to lose their national identity altogether and become truly global corporations. Car makers are now becoming global, with mergers taking place all over the globe. Ford owns Jaguar, Daimler-Benz merged with Chrysler, BMW controls Rover, and everyone is looking at the Korean automakers.

International involvement has also increased across not-for-profit organizations. Universities offer study programs abroad, health-care and research programs span national boundaries, international postal systems are working more closely together, and athletic programs are increasingly being transplanted to different cultures.

Events in other parts of the world are having major effects on business. The unification of Germany and the movement of the formerly communist-controlled countries in Central Europe toward free-market economies are providing many new opportunities and challenges to business. In many ways, then, we are becoming a truly global economy. No longer will a firm be able to insulate itself from foreign competitors or opportunities. Thus, it is imperative that every manager develop and maintain at least a rudimentary understanding of the dynamics of international management.[29]

Cross-Cultural Differences and Similarities

Since the primary concern of this discussion is human behavior in organizational settings, we focus on differences and similarities in behavior across cultures. Unfortunately, research in this area is still relatively new. Thus, many of the research findings we can draw on are preliminary at best.

General Observations   In this section we describe a few general observations about similarities and differences across cultures. First, cultures and national boundaries do not necessarily coincide. Some areas of Switzerland are very much like Italy, other parts like France, and still other parts like Germany. Similarly, within the United States there are profound cultural differences among southern California, Texas, and the East Coast.[30]

Given this basic assumption, one review of the literature on international management reached five basic conclusions.[31] First, behavior in organizational settings indeed varies across cultures. Thus, employees in companies based in Japan, the United States, and Germany are likely to have different attitudes and patterns of behavior. The behavior patterns are likely to be widespread and pervasive within an organization.

Second, culture itself is one major cause of this variation. Culture is the set of shared values, often taken for granted, that help people in a group, organization, or society understand which actions are considered acceptable and which are deemed unacceptable (we use this same definition in our discussion of organizational culture in Chapter 18). Thus, although the behavioral differences just noted may be caused in part by different standards of living, different geographical conditions, and so forth, culture itself is a major factor apart from other considerations.

Third, although behavior within organizational settings (e.g., motivation and attitudes) remains quite diverse across cultures, organizations and the way they are structured appear to be increasingly similar. Hence, managerial practices at a general level may be more and more alike, but the people who work within organizations still differ markedly.

Fourth, the same manager behaves differently in different cultural settings. A manager may adopt one set of behaviors when working in one culture but change those behaviors when moved to a different culture. For example, Japanese executives who come to work in the United States slowly begin to act more like U.S. managers and less like Japanese managers. This is often a source of concern for them when they are transferred back to Japan.[32]

Finally, cultural diversity can be an important source of synergy in enhancing organizational effectiveness. More and more organizations are coming to appreciate the virtues of cultural diversity, but they still know surprisingly little about how to manage it.[33] Organizations that adopt a multinational strategy can—with effort—become more than a sum of their parts. Operations in each culture can benefit from operations in other cultures through an enhanced understanding of how the world works.[34]

Specific Cultural Issues   Geert Hofstede, a Dutch researcher, studied workers and managers in sixty countries and found that attitudes and behaviors differed significantly because of the values and beliefs in the various countries.[35] Table 3.2 shows how Hofstede's categories help us summarize differences for several countries.

The two primary dimensions that Hofstede found are the individualism/collectivism continuum and power distance. **Individualism** exists to the extent that people in a culture define themselves by referring to themselves as singular persons rather than as part of one or more groups or organizations. At work, people from more individualistic cultures tend to be more concerned about themselves than about their work group, individual tasks are more important than relationships, and hiring and promotion are based on skills and rules. **Collectivism,** on the other hand, is characterized by tight social frameworks in which people tend to base their identities on the group or organization to which they belong. At work, this means that employee-employer links are more like family relationships, relationships are more important than individuals or tasks, and hiring and promotion are based on group membership. In the United States, a very individualistic culture, it is important to perform better than others and to stand out from the crowd. In Japan, a more collectivist culture, an individual tries to fit in with the group, strives for harmony, and prefers stability.

Power distance, which can also be called **orientation to authority,** is the extent to which less powerful people accept the unequal distribution of power. In

Individualism is the extent to which people place primary value on themselves.

Collectivism is the extent to which people emphasize the good of the group or society.

Power distance (orientation to authority) is the extent to which less powerful persons accept the unequal distribution of power.

Country	Individualism/ Collectivism	Power Distance	Uncertainty Avoidance	Masculinity	Long-Term Orientation
Canada	H	M	M	M	L
Germany	M	M	M	M	M
Israel	M	L	M	M	(no data)
Italy	H	M	M	H	(no data)
Japan	M	M	H	H	H
Mexico	H	H	H	M	(no data)
Pakistan	L	M	M	M	L
Sweden	H	M	L	L	M
United States	H	M	M	M	L
Venezuela	L	H	M	H	(no data)

Note: H=high; M=moderate; L=low. These are only ten of the more than sixty countries that Hofstede and others have studied.

References: Adapted from Geert Hofstede and Michael Harris Bond, "The Confucius Connection: From Cultural Roots to Economic Growth," *Organizational Dynamics,* Spring 1988, pp. 5–21. Geert Hofstede, "Motivation, Leadership, and Organization: Do American Theories Apply Abroad?" *Organizational Dynamics,* Summer 1980, pp. 42–63.

table 3.2

Work-Related Differences in Ten Countries

countries such as Mexico and Venezuela, for example, people prefer to be in a situation in which the authority is clearly understood and lines of authority are never bypassed. On the other hand, in countries such as Israel and Denmark, authority is not as highly respected and employees are quite comfortable circumventing lines of authority to accomplish something. People in the United States tend to be mixed, accepting authority in some situations but not in others.

Uncertainty avoidance, which can also be called **preference for stability,** is the extent to which people feel threatened by unknown situations and prefer to be in clear and unambiguous situations. People in Japan and Mexico prefer stability to uncertainty, whereas uncertainty is normal and accepted in Sweden, Hong Kong, and the United Kingdom. **Masculinity,** which can also be called **assertiveness** or **materialism,** is the extent to which the dominant values in a society emphasize aggressiveness and the acquisition of money and things as opposed to concern for people, relationships among people, and the overall quality of life. People in the United States are moderate on both the uncertainty avoidance and masculinity scales. Japan and Italy score high on the masculinity scale while Sweden scores low.

Hofstede's framework was later expanded to include **long-term** versus **short-term orientation.** Long-term values include focusing on the future, working on projects that have a distant payoff, persistence, and thrift. Short-term values are more oriented toward the past and the present and include respect for traditions and social obligations. Japan, Hong Kong, and China are highly long-term oriented. The Netherlands and Germany are moderately long-term oriented. The United States, Indonesia, West Africa, and Russia are more short-term oriented. Certain aspects of the culture of a specific country can change over time.

Hofstede's research presents only one of several ways of categorizing differences across many different countries and cultures. His system is, however, widely

Uncertainty avoidance (preference for stability) is the extent to which people prefer to be in clear and unambiguous situations.

Masculinity (assertiveness or materialism) is the extent to which the dominant values in a society emphasize aggressiveness and the acquisition of money and material goods rather than concern for people, relationships among people, and the overall quality of life.

People with a short-term orientation focus on the past or present; people with a long-term orientation focus on the future.

accepted and used by many companies. The important issue is that people from diverse cultures value things differently from each other and that all employees need to take these differences into account as they work.

Dimensions of Diversity

People do not have to be from different countries to have different values. Within a single country—be it the United States, Italy, or the Former Yugoslav Republic of Macedonia—there are significant differences in values, beliefs, and the normally accepted ways of doing things. In the United States, race and gender were considered the primary dimensions of diversity during the past two decades. The earliest civil rights laws were aimed at correcting racial segregation. Other laws have dealt with discrimination on the basis of gender, age, and disability. However, diversity entails broader issues than these. In the largest sense, the diversity of the workforce refers to all of the ways that employees are similar and different. The importance of renewed interest in diversity is that it helps organizations reap the benefits of all the similarities and differences among workers. For the purposes of discussion, we have divided the many aspects of diversity into primary and secondary dimensions.

Primary Dimensions of Diversity

The **primary dimensions of
diversity** are factors that are
either inborn or exert extraordinary influence on early
socialization: age, ethnicity,
gender, physical abilities, race,
and sexual orientation.

The **primary dimensions of diversity** are those factors that are either inborn or exert extraordinary influence on early socialization. These include age, race and ethnicity, gender, physical and mental abilities, and sexual orientation.[36] These factors make up the essence of who we are as human beings. They define us to others, and because of how others react to them, these factors also define us to ourselves. These characteristics are enduring aspects of our human personality, and they sometimes present extremely complex problems to managers. In this section, we highlight a few issues surrounding the primary dimensions.

Age   The age issue is multifaceted and very individualistic. As people age, they become more diverse in more ways. As the United States and the world's economy and labor productivity continue to grow, the demand for labor is expected to grow at 2 percent annually. At the same time, fewer people are entering the workforce, and the workforce is growing older overall as the baby boomers move into the over-fifty age range. The median age of the workforce increased from 36.6 years in 1990 to 39.3 years in 2000 and is expected to be 40.6 years by 2010.[37] In addition, the labor force participation rate for workers over sixty-five is expected to increase from 12.8 to 14.8 percent from 2000 to 2010.[38] This trend subsumes another— workforce participation rates for women over age fifty are increasing faster than for men over fifty; thus, women constitute more of the increase in older workers.

"The 55-to-64 age group will increase by 11 million persons over the 2000–2010 period—more than any other group."—Howard Fullerton Jr. and Mitra Toossi, Bureau of Labor Statistics [39]

Several aspects of these data require managerial attention. First, benefit packages may need to be changed to appeal to older workers. For example, for workers

Ariko Iso became the National Football League's first female trainer in 2002. Although 47.9% of the members of the National Athletic Trainers' Association are women, prior to her taking the job with the Pittsburgh Steelers, none had broken into the male-dominated, professional level of the sport. Iso has a Master's degree in the field and worked her way up in the industry. She has served at the University level, where she was involved with several sports, including football, and as a part-time summer intern with the Steelers. The Steelers maintain that she was not hired because of her gender, but because of her expertise as an athletic trainer. The players seem to like her work and claim she is a very good trainer.

with no children at home, family benefit packages may not be as attractive. Second, as the population ages, more people are living well into their eighties. A man who reaches age sixty-five is expected to live fourteen more years. A woman who reaches age sixty-five is expected to live another eighteen-and-a-half years. The over-eighty-five age group is the fastest-growing segment of the population.[40] Therefore, this age group's children, who may be over fifty and still active in the workforce, may need to become primary caregivers for their elderly parents. Primary caregivers for the elderly face increased stress, take more unscheduled days off, have more late arrivals and early departures, have above-average telephone use, and are absent more often.

Older workers may need additional and different training in new technologies and equipment to accommodate their special needs. For example, consider the functioning of the eye. As people get older, the amount of light that reaches the retina of the eye falls by about 50 percent because of the gradual yellowing of the lens. This changes perceptions of blue, green, and gray. The average sixty-year-old needs two-and-a-half times as much light to read comfortably as the average twenty-year-old.[41] Differences also exist in manual dexterity, hearing, perception, cognition, strength, and agility. Managers will need to adjust physical facilities, equipment, and training methods to expect maximum productivity from the entire workforce. In the past, little allowance was made for a worker who could not conform to the standard equipment and expectations of the workplace. In the future, the workplace will need to adjust to older workers.

Race and Ethnicity   Racial and ethnic cultural differences may be more important than most managers initially realize because critical differences exist across cultures in attitudes toward, beliefs about, and values surrounding work. The data show that people of different racial and ethnic backgrounds are increasing in number and in percentage of the workforce. Although much has been accomplished in recent years, racial and ethnic minorities still believe that a significant barrier exists that keeps them from the top executive positions in U.S. companies. One of the primary reasons for turnover or attrition among women and minorities is the "glass ceiling" barrier that exists in U.S. companies. The diversity director in one high-tech company estimates that the cost of recruiting and training one new worker to replace one who voluntarily leaves exceeds $112,000.[42] Another cost is lower morale and productivity among those who do not leave. Companies today simply cannot afford to ignore the impact of racial and ethnic differences in the workforce. The glass ceiling is still in place for minorities and women in spite of the years of progress and the new emphasis on valuing diversity.

Gender   Women were one of the first groups to be emphasized in the early attempts at providing equal employment opportunity and affirmative action. Many organizations have always included at least some women, of course; the issue now is that women hold positions other than secretary, nurse, teacher, and receptionist. Many companies have discovered that women hold many other types of jobs and are moving into more all the time. Apple found that over 40 percent of the sales force were women, who were generating more than $1.5 billion in sales.[43] Xerox noted that its workforce has changed significantly. For example, during the 1980s, the number of women increased from 29 to 32 percent of its workforce, the number of female managers doubled from 10 to 20 percent, the number of female professionals increased from 18 to 29 percent, and the number of females in the sales force almost doubled from 22 to 41 percent.[44] After recognizing this trend, Xerox increased its efforts to move more women into sales, professional, and managerial jobs, and developed programs to help all employees work together in its newly diverse workforce.

Until recently, most managers assumed that women should be treated the same way as men and that they had the same reactions to issues. This is not always the case, however. Following a sales meeting, for example, men often go to the hotel bar for relaxation and an inevitable continuation of discussions. Women, however, often feel uncomfortable having social drinks with the men in the bar and therefore are often excluded from the continued discussions. Similar feelings arise when men leave a meeting to go to golf clubs, some of which prohibit women. Situations such as these may exclude women from valuable socialization processes necessary for groups to coordinate activities and accomplish goals and may have the unintended but systematic effect of excluding women from top management positions. Companies have found simple solutions to some of these situations by having sales meetings in conference centers and bringing refreshments into the meeting rooms after the meetings so all can participate in the follow-up sessions. Hosting dinners in the conference center can also help keep everyone involved after the formal meeting. The increasing number of women in the workforce means that employees with different attitudes, backgrounds, and capabilities need to be utilized, possibly in different ways than were previously the norm in many organizations.

During the 1970s and early 1980s, the women's movement enabled women to make great strides toward true equality in society in general and in the workplace specifically. Such strides are also being made in Asia, as discussed in the "World View" box. Despite these advances, women's wages are still lower than men's, and most U.S. organizations have a glass ceiling that excludes many women from upper-

WORLD VIEW

Equality for Asian Women in the Workforce

Diversity consists of the similarities and differences that exist in a workforce regarding age, gender, ethnicity, and other personal characteristics. Diversity, then, is always defined with regard to a specific group of workers and will concern different issues in different populations. Equality for women in the U.S. workforce has tended to focus on issues such as childcare, equal pay for equal work, and the "glass ceiling" effect. Female workers in Asia face the same issues, but with significant differences.

During the Cultural Revolution of the 1960s and 70s, Chinese women were officially accorded equal social and political status with men. "Women can hold up half the sky," in the words of former Chairman Mao Zedong. From that time forward, Chinese women experienced less hiring discrimination than did Western women, although they also suffered from the glass ceiling effect. Bonnie Furst, a PricewaterhouseCoopers human resources manager, says, "Many of my Chinese colleagues prefer to work in China where gender is less of an issue, all things considered.... When I came to China ten years ago, my being a woman was less of an issue in everyday work life than it was in the [United States] and Japan, right up to the top levels."

However, in many Asian societies, women still struggle for respect and equality. Consider the case of female business managers in Japan. In the last ten years, the percentage of women managers has grown from a mere 0.04 percent to reach 8.9 percent. However, compare these numbers with the percentage of women managers in Hong Kong, up from 16 percent to 22 percent. In addition, Japanese women are often guided into fields such as human resources or services, in which pay and job security are typically lower than for manufacturing or technical positions.

Wiwam Tharahirunchote, a female finance company director in Thailand, claims, "Discrimination is gone." But

> *"Many of my Chinese colleagues prefer to work in China where gender is less of an issue, all things considered."*
> —Bonnie Furst, PricewaterhouseCoopers human resources manager

she also believes that women aren't suited to jobs in construction or engineering, explaining, "Women just don't have the physical strength to do that kind of thing" says, Doris Lau, HSBC bank vice president, "The male executive I believe could work longer hours than the female" she also maintains, "Women shouldn't enter into contract negotiations." Rochana Kosiyanon worked for DuPont in America for nine years before returning to Thailand to become managing director of a consulting firm. She asserts that gender discrimination was more of a problem in the United States than in her homeland. However, she also acknowledges, "[If a wife is successful in business], she may not be a wife for much longer. Asian male egos are fragile."

References: "Breaking Glass: Chinese Women on the Rise," *Business Beijing*, November 2001, pp. 26–31; Carol Hymowitz, "The Glass Ceiling's Jagged Edge—In a Slowing Economy, Women Who Achieved Now Face Sharper Scrutiny," *Asian Wall Street Journal*, March 16, 2001, p. W3; Samantha Marshall, "Women Stereotyping Women—Compounding Glass Ceiling, Some Women May Construct Their Own Workplace Barriers," *Asian Wall Street Journal*, May 21, 1999, p. 3.

level positions. Moreover, in the late 1980s and 1990s, there seems to have been a type of backlash on the part of some men against the progress made by women. This backlash can take many forms. It may become apparent when men are asked about their views of the women's movement. When men are "passed over" for promotions, for admission to some graduate schools, and for other forms of advancement or opportunity, they often blame the women's movement as a force behind reverse discrimination. Some people blame all sorts of social ills on the women's movement, including increases in crime, divorce, and stress levels at work.[45]

In reality, extreme positions for or against the women's movement may not be constructive, and efforts to solve gender-based problems and inequities may be hindered by various groups calling names and pointing fingers. For managers, it is important to recognize that strong feelings exist on both sides, and that addressing tensions in the workplace over equality for all types of workers is paramount if managers and workers are to get their work done and reach organizational goals.

Different Abilities   An often misunderstood group, one that is more diverse than any other, is people whose abilities are in some way limited when compared with those of the general population. Disabilities may be of many different types. Some persons have missing or nonfunctioning limbs, some have sensory impairments, others have problems related to diseases such as multiple sclerosis, and still others have mental limitations of various kinds. The rights of these people are protected under the Americans with Disabilities Act and the Rehabilitation Act. Employers cannot discriminate in any way regarding employment of people with disabilities, and employers must make reasonable accommodations in the workplace to assist employees on the job. These workers are best referred to as "differently abled" or "physically or mentally challenged" to indicate respect for the abilities that make them unique and capable of making valuable contributions to the organization.[46]

Physically or mentally challenged people are just like everyone else except for their one disability. They have to live, eat, sleep, and support themselves by working. They are often excellent employees in jobs appropriate for their skill types and levels. Reasonable accommodations to allow people to work may include such matters as equipment purchase or modification, restructuring of jobs, reassignment to other jobs, making facilities accessible, modifying work schedules, and modifying examination and training materials.[47] Each case needs to be considered individually, and accommodations should be made for that specific case. One accommodation that is often important is the reaction of coworkers to the hiring of a physically or mentally challenged person. It may take some training and personal accommodation for the other members of the work group to adjust.

Many companies have attempted to appropriately accommodate differently challenged workers. Lotus Development has a hiring program that works in conjunction with Greater Boston Rehabilitation Services to hire differently abled workers in its assembly, packing, and shipping departments. Lotus provides a shuttle bus to the plant from the local train station and provides job coaches, special equipment, and new training programs to ensure the success of each worker. In addition, other Lotus employees participate in awareness programs to ease the entry of the new workers into the company. Eastman Kodak's warehouse in Oak Brook, Illinois, includes five employees who are both deaf and mute. The order-filling accuracy of these employees exceeds that of other employees and is more than 99 percent. Eastman Kodak accommodated these employees by placing them in an area that had no forklifts or other heavy equipment and by adding special telephones that use a keyboard and screen for communication.[48]

Sexual Orientation   Another dimension of diversity that may make some people uncomfortable but which is receiving increasing attention in organizations is sexual orientation. As in the population in general, it is estimated that 10 percent of the workforce is homosexual. Homosexuals work in all types of industries, including finance, insurance, science, engineering, and computers.[49] Although some homosexuals no longer try to hide their sexual preference, many still feel that they must keep it a secret. A California judge ordered a Shell Oil subsidiary to pay $5.3 million in damages to a worker who was fired because of his homosexuality.[50] On the other hand, companies such as Levi Strauss, Apple Computer, Digital Equipment Corporation, Boeing, DuPont, and Xerox have lesbian and gay groups that operate openly, holding meetings, orientation sessions, and special gay pride weeks. As open as some companies have become, however, many critics still complain that a glass ceiling exists for homosexual managers ready to advance to executive positions. Companies must also decide whether to extend dependent health coverage to gay and lesbian partners, as Kodak and IBM did in 1996.[51]

Secondary Dimensions of Diversity

Secondary dimensions of diversity include factors that are important to us as individuals and that to some extent define us to others but are less permanent and can be adapted or changed: educational background, geographical location, income, marital status, military experience, parental status, religious beliefs, and work experience.

Secondary dimensions of diversity include factors that matter to us as individuals and that to some extent define us to others but which are less permanent than primary dimensions and can be adapted or changed. These include educational background, geographical location, income, marital status, military experience, parental status, religious beliefs, and work experience. These factors may influence our lives as much as the primary dimensions. Many veterans of the Persian Gulf War and the war in Afghanistan, for example, were profoundly affected by their experience of serving in the military. The influence of religion and spirituality, two secondary dimensions, is becoming more commonplace at work, as discussed in the "Business of Ethics" box.

The impact of secondary dimensions may differ at various times in our lives. For example, moving to another part of the country or world may be traumatic for a parent with several children; a person with no close ties or dependents, on the other hand, may find it exciting. Family experiences may also influence a manager's degree of sympathy for the disruptions of work life that sometimes occur because of personal responsibilities.

Employees enter the workforce with unique experiences and backgrounds that affect their perspective of work rules, work expectations, and personal concerns. Although employees may have essentially the same work hours, job description, tenure with the company, and compensation, their reactions to the work situation may differ significantly because of differences in these primary and secondary dimensions of diversity.

Managing the Multicultural Organization

The multicultural organization has six characteristics: pluralism, full structural integration, full integration of informal networks, an absence of prejudice and discrimination, equal identification among employees with organizational goals for majority and minority groups, and low levels of intergroup conflict.

Taking advantage of diversity in organizations poses difficult challenges, but it also presents new opportunities. Simply announcing that the organization values diversity is not enough. It requires that management develop a **multicultural organization** in which employees of mixed backgrounds, experiences, and cultures can contribute and achieve their fullest potential to benefit both themselves and the organization. Management must plan to manage diversity throughout the organization and work hard to implement the plan.

Managerial Behavior Across Cultures

Some individual variations in people from different cultures shape the behavior of both managers and employees. Other differences are much more likely to influence managerial behavior.[52] In general, these differences relate to managerial beliefs about the role of authority and power in the organization. For example, managers in Indonesia, Italy, and Japan tend to believe that the purpose of an organization structure is to let everyone know who his or her boss is (medium to high power distance). Managers in the United States, Germany, and Great Britain,

BUSINESS OF ETHICS

▶ *Spiritual Faith in the Workplace*

After decades of a declining interest in religion, Americans are turning again to church and faith. According to a 1999 survey, 55 percent of U.S. citizens attend church at least once per month, compared to 40 percent in Canada, 25 percent in England and Germany, and 17 percent in France. The change may be due to the impact of the aging baby boomers, who are focusing more attention on spiritual matters as they enter middle age. The events of September 11 may also be responsible for a more intense focus on spirituality.

> *"Spirituality is in convergence with all the cutting-edge thinking in management and organizational behavior."*
> —Hamilton Beazley, professor, George Washington University

A few companies have always encouraged spirituality in the workplace. ServiceMaster, which owns Merry Maids, Terminix, and other service businesses, states its first objective as "To honor God in all we do." ServiceMaster CEO Carlos Cantu says, "I just cannot envision my success . . . without the foundation of my faith in God." Tom Monaghan, founder of Domino's Pizza, took a thirty-month leave of absence to build missions in Central America. Monaghan also founded Legatus, an association for Catholic CEOs that has 450 members.

Today, employees in many organizations are using their religious values to help them become better workers and managers. Dallas attorney Thomas Crisman takes one month each year to practice Buddhist meditation in India in order to restore his compassion for others and reduce the impact of destructive emotions. Julius Walls Jr., CEO of Greyston Bakery, always hires the first job applicant he interviews in order to give everyone a chance at a job. After Catholic bishops issued a report critical of capitalism, a group of Chicago businesspeople founded BEEJ, Business Leaders for Excellence, Ethics, and Justice. Hamilton Beazley, a former business manager and currently a professor, says, "Spirituality is in convergence with all the cutting-

edge thinking in management and organizational behavior. It creates a higher-performing organization."

Others, however, are concerned that the use of religious faith as a management tool blunts the spiritual message. "This [integration] is about who you are, your being, your character," says David Miller, an expert on the integration of work and faith. But some feel that religious expression is inappropriate at work and may create division among workers. Others point out that religion and profit-making are often at odds. Dick Green, president of Blistex, believes that his religious convictions have sometimes led him to make decisions that were not optimal for the firm, but he says, "I don't think I can make a business decision and ignore who I am."

The complexity of spiritual faith makes it difficult to apply in work settings. Is it more charitable to retain highly paid Americans or to transfer production overseas, a move that benefits the poor of other nations? For workers looking for more meaning in their lives, specific answers to these types of questions are not as important as the opportunity to express their spirituality wherever they are, even at work.

References: Marc Gunther, "God & Business," *Fortune*, July 9, 2001, pp. 59–80 (quote, p. 80); Ronald Inglehart and Wayne E. Baker, "Modernization, Secularization, Globalization and the Persistence of Tradition," *Millennial Symposium of the American Sociological Review*, February 1999; Dan Culloton, "Leadership Fostered on Faith," *Daily Herald* (Arlington Heights, IL), June 26, 1997; Laurel Campbell, "Discipline, Faith Made Winner," *Commercial Appeal* (Memphis, TN), April 20, 1997, p. C1; Rachel Konrad, "Founder Doesn't Want Domino's Product Line to Stray from Pizza," *Detroit Free Press*, November 13, 1996.

in contrast, believe that organization structure is intended to coordinate group behavior and effort (low power distance). On another dimension, Italian and German managers believe it is acceptable to bypass one's boss to get things done, but among Swedish and British managers, bypassing one's superior is strongly prohibited.

Figure 3.4 illustrates findings on another interesting point. Managers in Japan strongly believe that a manager should be able to answer any question he or she is asked. Thus, they place a premium on expertise and experience. At the other ex-

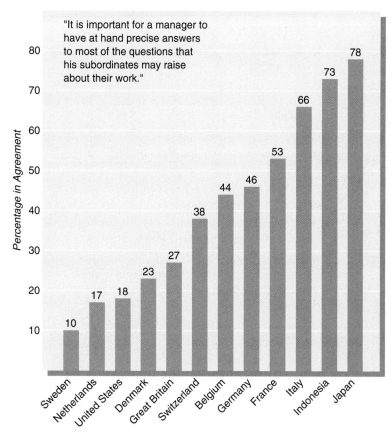

figure 3.4

Differences Across Cultures in Managers' Beliefs About Answering Questions from Subordinates

Subordinates in various cultures have different beliefs regarding managers' ability to provide definite, precise answers to questions. Japan has the strongest expectations; Sweden has the weakest.

Reference: Reprinted from *International Studies of Management and Organization*, vol. XIII, no. 1–2, Spring–Summer 1983, by permission of M. E. Sharpe, Inc., Armonk, N.Y. 10504.

treme are Swedish managers, who have the least concern about knowing all the answers. They view themselves as problem solvers and facilitators who make no claim to omnipotence.

Some recent evidence suggests that managerial behavior is rapidly changing, at least among European managers. In general, these managers are becoming more career oriented, better educated, more willing to work cooperatively with labor, more willing to delegate, and more cosmopolitan.[53]

Multicultural Organization as Competitive Advantage

Movement toward better management of a diverse workforce usually begins for one or more of three reasons. Some companies, such as Xerox, were obliged to develop better management of a workforce made more diverse by affirmative action. Other companies, such as Digital Equipment and Hewlett-Packard, grew very quickly to remain competitive and then realized that they had to work with multicultural constituencies. A third group of companies, which includes Avon Products, needed to have a diverse workforce to match the diversity in the marketplace.[54] Companies of all three types need to manage their multicultural workforce better to gain a competitive advantage in the marketplace. Business leaders, consultants, and academic scholars contend that having a multicultural organization can create competitive advantage in the six ways shown in Table 3.3: cost, resource acquisition, marketing, creativity, problem solving, and system flexibility. Thus, a diverse workforce should be highly valued and managed well for reasons beyond the fact that doing so is socially responsible.[55]

Since the workforce is becoming more diverse, the companies that value and integrate diverse employees the fastest and the best will reap the most benefits. Lower personnel costs and improved quality of personnel are two obvious benefits for such companies. In addition, access to diverse perspectives in problem solving, decision making, creativity, and product development and marketing activities is essential to creating a competitive advantage in the increasingly dynamic global marketplace.

table 3.3

Six Ways That Managing Diversity Can Create Competitive Advantage

Advantage	Contribution
Cost	Managing diversity well can trim the costs of integrating diverse workers.
Resource Acquisition	Companies that have the best reputation for managing diverse employees will have the best chance of hiring the best available diverse personnel.
Marketing	Increased insight and cultural sensitivity will improve the development and marketing of products and services for diverse segments of the population.
Creativity	Diversity of perspectives will improve levels of creativity throughout the organization.
Problem Solving	Problem solving and decision making will improve through groups with more diverse perspectives.
System Flexibility	Tolerance and valuing of diverse perspectives throughout the organization will make the organization more fluid, more flexible, and more responsive to environmental changes.

Reference: Adapted from Taylor H. Cox and Stacy Blake, "Managing Cultural Diversity: Implications for Organizational Competitiveness," *Academy of Management Executive*, August 1991, p. 47. Copyright 1991 by ACADEMY OF MANAGEMENT. Reproduced with permission of ACADEMY OF MANAGEMENT via Copyright Clearance Center.

Creating the Multicultural Organization

A multicultural organization has six characteristics: pluralism, full structural integration, full integration of informal networks, an absence of prejudice and discrimination, equal identification with organizational goals for all groups, and low levels of intergroup conflict.[56] Developing the multicultural organization requires commitment from top management and a clear vision of the benefits of multiculturalism for the future of the organization. To achieve each of these characteristics requires specific activities, as shown in Table 3.4.

A pluralistic organization has diverse membership and takes steps to fully involve all people who differ from the dominant group.

A **pluralistic organization** is one that has mixed membership and takes steps to fully involve all people who differ from the dominant group. Creating pluralism requires training and orientation programs that increase awareness of cultural differences and build skills for working together. Programs that describe how people of different ages and genders differ in some respects but are similar in others can be included in programs for new and existing employees. Language and culture training can help employees in the majority group better understand those from different cultures. Companies such as Motorola and Pace Foods offer language training on company time and at company expense.

Organizations have several ways to ensure that minority groups have input. First, minorities should be included in regular meetings at all levels. For example, *USA Today*'s daily news meetings include members of varied racial, ethnic, education, and geographic groups.[57] Second, the organization must foster the development of minority advisory groups that meet regularly to discuss organizational issues and encourage top management to consult regularly with the groups. Organizations can also foster pluralism throughout the organization by explicitly stating in their mission statements and strategic policies that it is an integral part of the organization.

table 3.4

Creating the Multicultural Organization: Above All— Top Management Support Throughout!

Characteristic	Tools
Pluralism	Training and orientation programs, ensuring minority group input, putting diversity into mission statements
Full Structural Integration	Education, training, affirmative action, performance appraisal and reward systems, benefits, work schedules
Integration of Informal Networks	Mentoring, social events, support groups
Absence of Prejudice	EEO seminars, focus groups, bias-reduction training programs, task forces
Equal Identification with Goals	Input of minority group into mission, goals, and strategies
Minimal Intergroup Conflict	Survey feedback, conflict reduction training

Reference: Adapted from Taylor H. Cox Jr., "The Multicultural Organization," *Academy of Management Executive*, August 1991, p. 41. Copyright 1991 by ACADEMY OF MANAGEMENT. Reproduced with permission of ACADEMY OF MANAGEMENT via Copyright Clearance Center.

When an organization has minority-group members serving at all levels, performing all functions, and participating in all work groups, we say it has achieved full structural integration. This requires distributing education specialties and skill differences equally throughout the organization. Therefore, organizations must develop and support educational programs and skill building at all levels. They also must hire and promote minority-group members into positions at all levels and jobs that perform all organizational functions.

Performance measurement and reward systems, which are discussed in Chapter 8, also need to be changed to promote pluralism. Organizations need to determine how much managers incorporate multiculturalism into their work groups and whether they hire and promote with proper sensitivity to multicultural concerns. Desired changes need to be rewarded through formal incentives. Benefit plans and work schedules also need to be altered to accommodate differences in employee family situations, needs, and values.

Mentoring programs, special social events, and support groups for minorities can foster integration in informal networks. One might think such special groups and events would create more differences, but in practice they have the opposite effect. They give minority groups outlets to express their cultural identity and share part of themselves with dominant groups. Dominant group members can then better understand the cultural heritage and traditions of minority members.

Several means can be used to create a bias-free organization. Equal-opportunity seminars have been used to increase awareness among employees for quite a while. In addition, organizations can conduct in-house focus groups to examine attitudes and beliefs about cultural differences and organizational practices. They can also sponsor bias-reduction training programs, one- or two-day workshops designed to help employees identify and begin to modify negative attitudes toward people who are different. These programs usually include exercises and role-plays that expose stereotypes about minority group members and help build the skills to eliminate these stereotypes. Another way to move toward a bias-free organization is to create task forces to monitor organizational policies and practices for evidence of unfairness. Such task forces need to be composed of employees from every level and those who perform the full range of organizational functions to ensure that top management is committed. All minorities should be represented to ensure that the full spectrum of views is considered.

Employees develop a sense of identity with the organization's mission, goals, and strategies as a result of utilizing all of the tools and techniques already discussed. When members of different groups participate fully in determining the organization's direction and deciding how to meet its goals, they better understand the organization and their place within it. Through training programs, mentoring programs, support groups, social events, and bias-free organization practices, employees who are different from the dominant group can become an integral part of the organization.

Intergroup conflict can be minimized in several ways. As discussed in Chapter 9, some forms of conflict can be healthy if they stimulate creativity in problem solving and decision making. However, conflict based on cultural differences that divides employees along cultural lines is usually considered unhealthy and detrimental to the multicultural organization. Survey feedback processes can be used to expose beliefs and attitudes toward others and to measure the success of the multicultural effort. Providing feedback to all relevant groups is important to ensure openness throughout the organization. Special training in conflict resolution has also been shown to help managers learn the skills of mediation and listening that are so important for managing conflict.

An integrated program involving activities of the sort described here can help an organization become truly multicultural. The transition is not easy or quick, but once multiculturalism has been achieved, it can give to the organization advantages in the struggle to compete successfully.

Synopsis

Workforce diversity is a function of the similarities and differences among employees in such characteristics as age, gender, ethnic heritage, physical or mental ability or disability, race, and sexual orientation. Managers of diverse work groups need to understand how their members' social conditioning affects their beliefs about work and must have the communication skills to develop confidence and self-esteem in their employees.

Stereotypes can lead to prejudice toward others; prejudice consists of judgments concerning the superiority or inferiority of others that can lead to exaggerating the worth of one group while disparaging the worth of others. Management systems built on stereotypes and prejudices are inappropriate for a diverse workforce.

Employment statistics show that the future workforce will be radically different from the workforce of today. The goal of valuing diversity is to utilize all of the differences among workers for the benefit of the workers and the organization.

International business has rapidly become an important part of almost every manager's life and is likely to become even more important in the future. Managers need to recognize that employees from different backgrounds are similar in some respects and different in others.

Diversity can be categorized as having primary and secondary dimensions. The primary dimensions of diversity are those that are either inborn or exert extraordinary influence on early socialization; dimensions of this type are age, ethnicity, gender, physical or mental abilities, race, and sexual orientation. Secondary dimensions of diversity include factors that are important to us as individuals and that to some extent define us to others but which are less permanent and can be adapted or changed: educational background, geographical location, income, marital status, military experience, parental status, religious beliefs, and work experience.

A multicultural organization is one in which employees of different backgrounds, experiences, and cultures can contribute and achieve their fullest potential for the benefit of both themselves and the organization. Developing a multicultural organization is a significant step in managing a diverse workforce and may be crucial to sustaining a competitive advantage in the marketplace. A multicultural organization has six characteristics: pluralism, full structural integration, full integration of informal networks, an absence of prejudice and discrimination, equal identification with organizational goals among employees from both majority and minority groups, and low levels of intergroup conflict.

Discussion Questions

1. Why do organizations need to be interested in managing diversity? Is it a legal or moral obligation, or does it have some other purpose?

2. Summarize in your own words what the statistics tell us about the workforce of the future.

3. What are the two major differences between the primary and secondary dimensions of diversity? Which particular dimension seems to you to be the most difficult to deal with in organizations?

4. Identify ways in which the internationalization of business affects businesses in your community.

5. All things considered, do you think people from diverse cultures are more alike or more different? Explain the reasons for your answer.

6. What stereotypes exist about the motivational patterns of workers from other cultures?

7. What is the difference between assimilation of minority groups and valuing diversity in organizations?

8. Why does multiculturalism contribute to competitive advantage for an organization?

9. What are the characteristics of a multicultural organization?

10. Discuss three techniques that can contribute to the development of a multicultural organization.

Organizational Behavior Case for Discussion

UPS Delivers Diversity to Diverse World

United Parcel Service (UPS) is a highly diverse organization and winner of the 2001 Ron Brown Award for Corporate Citizenship, the only presidential award for corporate leadership. The package delivery firm has appeared on *Fortune's* "Best Companies for Minorities" list for three consecutive years. UPS's awards—slots on numerous "best" lists, dozens of diversity awards—are well deserved. Overall, one-third of UPS employees are ethnic or racial minority members and 20 percent are female. UPS Human Resources Director Terri Champion explains, "We try to have our workforce reflect the community in which we work."

The company's commitment to diversity goes beyond merely hiring minorities and women to promoting these groups into managerial positions. UPS has 49,000 managers in the United States; 25 percent of these are members of racial minorities and 25 percent are female. "At UPS, it's not where you're from or what you look like; it's how much you care and how good you are at your job," according to Hugo Parades. Parades, a Hispanic American who was originally hired as a package unloader, is now a UPS district manager who oversees 3,800 workers and millions of dollars in sales. The company hires women and minorities into traditionally white, male-dominated fields. Of its 4,000 information technology workers, 1,000 are minorities and 1,100 are women. UPS also looks beyond the diversity elements of race and gender, hiring persons with disabilities, non-English speakers, and seniors. Its Welfare to Work programs have moved more than 35,000 former welfare recipients into full-time jobs with benefits. In addition to its focus on workforce diversity, the delivery firm seeks to increase diversity among its suppliers and customers. UPS is partnered with more than 25,000 small minority- and women-owned businesses in the United States, with a combined contract value of almost $600 million annually.

A true commitment to diversity requires that the firm take action and expend funds to support its values. UPS enrolls its senior managers in a community internship program in which managers spend one month working full-time with diverse and disadvantaged populations such as residents of nursing homes, the mentally handicapped, and the homeless. These experiences give managers a better appreciation of the needs and talents of often-overlooked groups. A program that provides education and internship opportunities for minority youth, developed in partnership with the NAACP, has helped hundreds of disadvantaged young people find jobs at UPS. The company has also given designated purchasing staff in each local office the responsibility of identifying and encouraging applications from minority-owned suppliers.

Today, firms recognize that diversity in the workforce and supplier network is necessary to cope with increasing customer diversity. Virginia Clarke, cohead of the diversity practice at executive-search firm Spencer Stuart, says, "There is a strong business case [for diversity] now. If you have any doubts about it, just look at the 2000 census figures. A third of all Americans belong to a minority group. . . . [A] diverse workplace isn't a luxury—it's a necessity." UPS also sees its commitment to diversity as helping to attract and retain talented personnel, increase creativity, and give the firm a competitive advantage. On its web site, the firm states, "We consider diversity a mindset of inclusiveness, respect and cooperation—a visible core value that helps drive the way we do business with our customers and suppliers—and strengthens our bonds with a multi-cultural community of friends and neighbors." The largest package delivery business in the world, UPS moves 13.6 million packages daily, with a net worth of 6 percent of the U.S. gross domestic product. Its service requires the efforts of more than 370,000 employees who operate in more than 200 countries around the world. With this level of operational complexity, diversity is a must.

Diversity remains a challenging issue for many firms. Nationwide, the number of minorities in senior positions is higher than ever, but 45 percent of minority executives have been the target of racial slurs or jokes, and this statistic only includes deliberate acts, not unintentional slights. In spite of the diversity programs at UPS, problem areas still exist. For example, Bill Lewis, a UPS driver, confronted his boss about years of harassment only to have his boss reply, "I will never apologize to a black boy." Frustrated by senior managers' inaction, Lewis and others have filed class action lawsuits and made complaints to the Equal Employment Opportunity Commission. UPS executives point to the firm's excellent record on diversity while also acknowledging that some individuals within the company may be prejudiced and engage in discrimination. Lea Soupata, senior vice president for Human Resources at UPS, says, "We're going to have [racial discrimination] cases, because . . . we have 300-and-something thousand people. We're not perfect. But to categorize the entire company as racist, . . . it's painful." The challenge for the firm lies in ensuring that its values of inclusion are communicated and implemented throughout the organization.

"[I]t's not where you're from or what you look like; it's how much you care and how good you are at your job."—Hugo Parades, UPS district manager

References: Jennifer Merritt, "Wanted: A Campus That Looks Like America," *Business Week*, March 11, 2002. www.businessweek.com on March 28, 2002; "The Ron Brown Award for Corporate Leadership," The Conference Board. www.ron-brown-award.org/winners on February 26, 2002; "Helping People Succeed" and "Supplier Diversity," UPS company web site (quotation). www.community.ups.com on February 23, 2002; "UPS Seeks Diverse Pros to Fuel Its Needs," *Diversity/Careers*, August–September, 2001. www.diversitycareers.com on February 23, 2002; Jeremy Kahn, "Best Companies for Minorities: Diversity Trumps the Downturn," *Fortune*, July 9, 2001. www.fortune.com on March 28, 2002; Stephanie N. Mehta, "Best Companies for Minorities: What Minority Employees Really Want," *Fortune*, July 10, 2000. www.fortune.com on March 28, 2002; John Koenig, "UPS Trains Its Managers by Putting Them in Shoes of Less Fortunate," *Orlando Sentinel*, July 6, 1998, p. 5; Cynthia Mitchell, "Charges Daunting to Delivery Giant," *Atlanta Journal Constitution*, June 15, 1997, p. D5.

Case Questions

1. According to the case, which dimensions of diversity are present at UPS?
2. What steps has UPS taken to create a multicultural organization?
3. What actions could UPS take in the future to better manage its diverse workforce?

Experiencing Organizational Behavior

Understanding Your Own Stereotypes and Attitudes Toward Others

Purpose: This exercise will help you better understand your own stereotypes and attitudes toward others.

Format: You will be asked to evaluate a situation and the assumptions you make in doing so. Then you will compare your results with those of the rest of the class.

Procedure

1. Read the following description of the situation to yourself, and decide who it is that is standing at your door and why you believe it to be that person. Make some notes that explain your rationale for eliminating the other possibilities and selecting the one that you did. Then answer the follow-up questions.
2. Working in small groups or with the class as a whole, discuss who might be standing at your door and why you believe it to be that person. Using the grid at the end of this exercise, record the responses of class members.
3. In class discussion, reflect on the stereotypes used to reach a decision and consider the following:
   a. How hard was it to let go of your original belief once you had formed it?
   b. What implications do first impressions of people have concerning how you treat them, what you expect of them, and your assessment of whether the acquaintance is likely to go beyond the initial stage?
   c. What are the implications of your responses to these questions concerning how you, as a manager, might treat a new employee? What will the impact be on that employee?
   d. What are the implications of your answers for yourself in terms of job hunting?

Situation: You have just checked into a hospital room for some minor surgery the next day. When you get to your room, you are told that the following people will be coming to speak with you within the next several hours.

1. The surgeon who will do the operation
2. A nurse
3. The secretary for the department of surgery
4. A representative of the company that supplies televisions to the hospital rooms
5. A technician who does laboratory tests
6. A hospital business manager
7. The dietitian

You have never met any of these people before and do not know what to expect.

About half an hour after your arrival, a woman who seems to be of Asian ancestry appears at your door dressed in a straight red wool skirt, a pink-and-white-striped polyester blouse with a bow at the neck, and red medium-high-heeled shoes that match the skirt. She is wearing gold earrings, a gold chain necklace, a gold wedding band, and a white hospital laboratory coat. She is carrying a clipboard.

Follow-up Questions

1. Of the seven people listed, which of them is standing at your door? How did you reach this conclusion?
2. If the woman had not been wearing a white hospital laboratory coat, how might your perceptions of her have differed? Why?
3. If you find out that she is the surgeon who will be operating on you in the morning, and you thought initially that she was someone else, how confident do you now feel in her ability as a surgeon? Why?

Reasons		Number Who Made This Selection
Surgeon		
Nurse		
Secretary		
Television Representative		
Laboratory Technician		
Business Manager		
Dietitian		

Reference: Adapted from Janet W. Wohlberg and Scott Weighart, *OB in Action: Cases and Exercises.* Copyright © 1992 by Houghton Mifflin Company. Used by permission.

Self-Assessment Exercise

Cross-Cultural Awareness

The following questions are intended to provide insights into your awareness of other cultures. Please indicate the best answers to the questions listed below. There is no passing or failing answer. Use the following scale, recording it in the space before each question.

1 = definitely no   2 = not likely   3 = not sure
4 = likely   5 = definitely yes

_____ 1. I can effectively conduct business in a language other than my native language.

_____ 2. I can read and write a language other than my native language with great ease.

_____ 3. I understand the proper protocol for conducting a business card exchange in at least two countries other than my own.

_____ 4. I understand the role of the *keiretsu* in Japan or the *chaebol* in Korea.

_____ 5. I understand the differences in manager-subordinate relationships in two countries other than my own.

_____ 6. I understand the differences in negotiation styles in at least two countries other than my own.

_____ 7. I understand the proper protocols for gift giving in at least three countries.

_____ 8. I understand how a country's characteristic preference for individualism versus collectivism can influence business practices.

_____ 9. I understand the nature and importance of demographic diversity in at least three countries.

_____ 10. I understand my own country's laws regarding giving gifts or favors while on international assignments.

_____ 11. I understand how cultural factors influence the sales, marketing, and distribution systems of different countries.

_____ 12. I understand how differences in male-female relationships influence business practices in at least three countries.

_____ 13. I have studied and understand the history of a country other than my native country.

_____ 14. I can identify the countries of the European Union without looking them up.

_____ 15. I know which gestures to avoid using overseas because of their obscene meanings.

_____ 16. I understand how the communication style practiced in specific countries can influence business practices.

_____ 17. I know in which countries I can use my first name with recent business acquaintances.

_____ 18. I understand the culture and business trends in major countries in which my organization conducts business.

_____ 19. I regularly receive and review news and information from and about overseas locations.

_____ 20. I have access to and utilize a cultural informant before conducting business at an overseas location.

_____ = Total Score

When you have finished, add up your score and compare it with those of others in your group. Discuss the areas of strengths and weaknesses of the group members. [Note: This brief instrument has not been scientifically validated and is to be used for classroom discussion purposes only.]

Reference: Neal R. Goodman, "Cross-Cultural Training for the Global Executive," in Richard W. Brislin and Tomoko Yoshida (eds.), _Improving Intercultural Interactions_, pp. 35–36, copyright © 1994 by Sage Publications, Inc. Reprinted by permission of Sage Publications, Inc.

OB Online

1. Use the Internet to research Denny's/Advantica to find out what Denny's has done to overcome charges of discrimination.
2. Find articles and news stories that describe what Denny's has done and how the actions have changed the company.
3. Several of the executives of Denny's have left the company to go to other companies. See if you can find news stories that describe who has left and determine why executives are leaving.

Building Managerial Skills

Exercise Overview: Conceptual skills refer to a manager's ability to think in the abstract while diagnostic skills focus on responses to situations. These skills must frequently be used together to better understand the behavior of others in an organization, as illustrated by the following exercise.

Exercise Background: We can read about creating an organization in which diverse workers are welcomed and included in everyday work activities. However, working with a diverse workforce everyday can be more difficult. Consider, for example, the following situation.

You are the office manager for a large call center in an urban area. You interview applicants, explain the type of work, and give them a quick, job-oriented test. At the call center employees sit at a desk in front of a computer screen and answer calls and inquiries about the products of several different companies. Employees must answer each call, determine the product, access the appropriate screen that contains all of the information about the product, and, if possible, complete the sale of the product and hopefully extend the purchase to related products. Employees must be able to use a computer and speak well. One day you interview and hire a new employee, Sarah Jane. She completes the simple test that involves sitting at the desk, using the computer, and answering mock calls. Consequently, you hire Sarah Jane, who reports to work the next Monday.

About two weeks after her first day, Sarah Jane shows up with her seeing-eye dog. Because the call stations are built to fit a normal-size person in a desk chair in front of a computer, there is no room for her rather large seeing-eye dog. Sarah Jane requests a special accommodation for her dog. Other employees are concerned about having a large dog sitting underneath the workstations and complain to you about the situation.

Exercise Task: Using the scenario previously described as background, do the following:

1. You have to decide what to do and have to write a report to your boss as well as to Sarah Jane and the other employees. What do you decide? Do you fire Sarah Jane because she is legally blind? Do you fire Sarah Jane because her dog is bothering the other employees just by sleeping underneath the workstations? Do you keep her and find her a separate workstation that is larger and would allow her dog to sleep under it without bothering the other employees?

2. Let's say that you fire her and two weeks later you get a call from her attorney, who is threatening to sue you for violation of the Americans with Disabilities Act (ADA). What resources could you contact to help you determine your alternatives? (In many states there are offices to assist employers in complying with the ADA.) What are your responsibilities regarding the creation of accommodations for differently abled employees?

Part I   Integrative Running Case

The Downfall of Enron

No business episode of 2001 has been the subject of so much debate and despair as the swift descent of once-admired energy trader Enron. The saga of this firm, which rose to prominence as rapidly as it subsequently fell, serves as a kind of morality tale for corporations, regulators, and investors. The tragic effects of Enron's overreaching arrogance provide a textbook example of both the best and the worst of American business culture and practice. Although the catastrophe's complete impact cannot be determined yet, it seems likely that more than one major firm will cease to exist, several industries will experience radically changed environments, regulators and investors will modify their behavior, and all firms will be subjected to increased scrutiny and regulatory oversight. So how did one of the brightest stars of American business, the company that had been called "a proven winner" and "a New Economy wonder," come to epitomize one of capitalism's most serious weaknesses—unbridled and unprincipled greed?

Enron began innocently enough with the 1953 formation of the Houston Natural Gas Production Company, which owned a few gas wells near Corpus Christi, Texas. From that time into the 1980s, the company grew by merger and acquisition, and in 1985, it merged with InterNorth, Inc., changing its name to Enron. Kenneth Lay, CEO of Houston Natural Gas, was named chief executive. An important part of Lay's strategy for the firm was to diversify beyond the regulated and therefore relatively low-profit gas pipeline industry into unregulated markets. Jeffrey Skilling joined the firm in 1989, the same year that Enron began to offer financing to oil and gas producers through a subsidiary. Enron continued to expand into other utility businesses, especially electrical power generation and trading, and also increased its international presence with offices in Europe, India, and South America.

In 1999, the company first ventured into a radically new industry—broadband services. This unit traded excess Internet capacity, serving as an intermediary between buyers and sellers, in much the same way that it traded electrical power or natural gas. The company's new strategy was to become a trader for "every commodity on earth," and at the time seemed to be on its way to accomplishing that feat. By 2000, Enron was the sixth-largest energy company in the world based on market capitalization (the total value of the firm's outstanding shares of stock). *Forbes* recognized Enron as the thirty-sixth-largest firm in the United States overall and the seventh-largest in sales.

Meanwhile, profits abounded. Lay donated generously to the city of Houston, where Enron is headquartered, and in return was given naming privileges for its new sports venue, Enron Field. Lay also raised $100,000 for George W. Bush's election campaign and was rewarded with a personal invitation to the Washington inauguration, which included seating at a private White House luncheon with the president. Enron's annual stockholder meeting in January 2001 was a study in corporate egotism. Executives met at a San Antonio, Texas, hill country resort, and champagne and cigars were free for the taking. At this meeting, Lay boldly asserted that he expected Enron to become "the world's greatest company." On February 5, special bonus checks worth tens of millions of dollars were prepared for Enron executives. However, in what might have been the first outward sign of the trouble to come, Lay resigned as CEO in February 2001, keeping his position as chairman of the board, while Skilling was tapped to be his replacement.

On the surface, Enron had the appearance of assured success, but underneath, a tangled web of deceit was slowly emerging. *Fortune* writer Bethany McLean, who has covered Enron extensively, prepared an article titled "Is Enron Overpriced?" in March 2001, when the stock was valued at $80 per share, near its $90 per share high. The article, in part, noted, "The company remains largely impenetrable to outsiders, as even some of its admirers are quick to admit. Start with a pretty straightforward question: How exactly does Enron make its money? Details are hard to come by because Enron keeps many of the specifics confidential for what it terms 'competitive reasons.' And the numbers that Enron does present are often extremely complicated. Even quantitatively minded Wall Streeters who scrutinize the company for a living think so." Insiders saw problems, too. One of Enron's tax lawyers, Jordan Mintz, began work in the CFO's office in October 2000 and immediately had questions about some of the files he had read. Deals looked questionable, and many had not been signed by COO Skilling, as required by law. Mintz's boss, Chief Accounting Officer Richard A.

Causey, advised him to forget about it, telling him, "I wouldn't stick my neck out." When Mintz ignored the warning and emailed Skilling in spring of 2001 to ask him to sign the documents, his message went unanswered. In August 2001, accountant Sherron S. Watkins also noticed bookkeeping irregularities and wrote to Lay, who was now chairman. In response to the allegations contained in Watkins's message, the firm's attorneys, Vinson & Elkins, conducted interviews, but no further action was taken.

Ironically, accounting, an area often stereotyped as dull, lies at the heart of this complex and riveting story. Accounting problems first began to show up in small ways and to raise nagging questions; one problem area was a group of partnerships that Enron had spun off from its mainline operations. This is a common type of corporate risk management which allows a company to divest risky investments to separate partnerships that are then sold to outside investors who are willing to assume the increased risk. Accounting rules insist that the deals be done at "arm's length," meaning that the partnerships must be truly independent of their parent. In Enron's case, however, Chief Financial Officer Andrew S. Fastow and members of his staff owned the partnerships, a fact unknown to most Enron employees, auditors, and lawyers.

The lack of arm's-length, independent-party transactions led to some strange results. For example, when terms of the partnerships needed to be renegotiated, Fastow served as the representative for the partnerships while other financial managers, his subordinates, negotiated on behalf of Enron. Enron's board of directors approved Fastow's role in these negotiations, then asked Skilling to provide oversight. Enron profited tremendously from these deals since it recorded a profit on the initial sale while moving any associated expenses or losses off its books. The conflict of interest ran even deeper because more than a dozen Enron executives obtained securities brokers' licenses, and the firm owned an investment bank as a subsidiary. Skilling initiated this change, which allowed Enron to serve as the broker as well as the buyer and seller in some of its partnerships transactions. And Enron managers collected hefty fees for negotiating some of the firm's most costly and doomed investments.

Another example of creative accounting involved the partnerships that were financed with Enron stock. According to some of the legal requirements of the original deal, if Enron's stock price fell below a certain trigger, the partnership's assets and debts would revert to Enron. The triggers were intentionally set low, some as low as $28, at a time when Enron was trading at around $90. But when the scandal broke, the stock price fell rapidly, ending up below even the lowest trigger in a matter of weeks. Enron was then forced to account for the partnerships' losses on its financial reports, which ran in the hundreds of millions of dollars, negating Enron's annual profits several times over.

A third accounting problem was the extensive use of "off-the-books" transactions. Most corporations engage in some types of complex financial deals, and many do not report the results on their audited financial statements because current accounting rules do not require reporting when the parent company owns less than half of the voting stock of the partnership. A firm's involvement in these off-the-books deals means that investors and even stock analysts, who are paid to oversee and report on corporate finances, do not have access to all the information they need. Most companies claim that these transactions are so small the results would have only a negligible impact on earnings, but that was not the case at Enron, whose losses were at least $500 million. "Four or five [off-the-books partnerships] would be a lot," says lawyer Allen Tucci. But Enron was involved in over nine hundred of the complex deals, many of them located in countries which offer tax havens, further reducing Enron's expenses and artificially raising profits.

As Enron's troubles began to mount, a few analysts and industry observers questioned the firm's apparent profitability, but others determinedly defended the company. Amid these questions and the energy crisis in California, which had a negative impact on Enron's electricity trading unit, the stock price continued to fall. Skilling abruptly resigned from the firm in August 2001, and Lay returned to fill the CEO slot. By late September, the price had fallen below trigger levels, causing auditors at Arthur Andersen to unwind the deals, placing the full loss on Enron's books.

At about this time, Andersen employees realized that they had made a terrible mistake—in the previous year, they had overstated Enron's earnings by $1 billion. Although Andersen's accountants blamed the complexity of the deals for the errors, Enron was required to restate earnings to reflect much lower levels of profitability.

Enron's downward spiral accelerated, and the U.S. Securities and Exchange Commission (SEC), which regulates financial markets, began an investigation which widened in November 2001 to include Arthur Andersen. Fastow was put on administrative leave. Lay

had talks with several high-ranking government officials, including Federal Reserve Board Chairman Alan Greenspan, Treasury Secretary Paul H. O'Neill, and Commerce Secretary Donald L. Evans, to request government assistance, but all help was denied. Dynegy, another Houston-based energy company, had talks about a possible merger with Enron, but the increasing public disclosure of the firm's problems caused the merger to fall through. Finally, unable to meet its obligations, Enron filed for bankruptcy protection on December 2, 2001.

These are the bare facts. Understanding the causal factors behind the facts—the fundamental origins of the problems—is the diagnostic task that will be undertaken in Parts II, III, and IV of this Integrative Running Case.

"I wouldn't stick my neck out"— Richard A. Causey, Enron chief accounting officer, advising one of his subordinates, Enron lawyer Jordan Mintz

References: "History," Enron Oil & Gas Resources, Inc., web site. www.eogresources.com on June 25, 2002; Kurt Eichenwald, "A Handicapper's Guide to the Trial of Andersen," *New York Times*, May 5, 2002, p. BU4. See www.nytimes.com; Peter Elkind and Bethany McLean, "Is There Anything Enron Didn't Do?" *Fortune*, April 16, 2002. www.fortune.com on June 12, 2002; David Barboza, "Enron Cases Await. Let the Swaggering Begin." *New York Times*, March 23, 2002, pp. C1, 3. See www.nytimes.com; Kurt Eichenwald, "Through the Enron Looking Glass," *New York Times*, March 23, 2002, p. BU7. See www.nytimes.com; Daniel Altman, "Contracts So Complex They Imperil the System," *New York Times*, February 24, 2002, pp. BU1, 14. See www.nytimes.com; Jeremy Kahn, "Off Balance Sheet—And Out of Control," *Fortune*, February 18, 2002. www.fortune.com on June 27, 2002; Kurt Eichenwald, "Enron Buffed Image to a Shine Even as It Rotted From Within," *New York Times*, February 10, 2002, pp. 1, 28, 29 (quotation p. 29). See www.nytimes.com; "Enron Timeline," *Houston Chronicle*, January 17, 2002. www.chron.com on June 25, 2002; Bethany McLean, "Is Enron Overpriced?" *Fortune*, March 5, 2001. www.fortune.com on June 14, 2002; "2001 *Forbes* 500," *Forbes*, March 2001. www.forbes.com on June 25, 2002.

Integrative Case Questions

1. Based on information in the case about leaders Ken Lay and Jeffrey Skilling, describe the management functions, roles, and skills represented.

2. What were some of the organizational and environmental challenges faced by Enron throughout its history?

3. Enron was not an effective organization, that is, it did not accomplish what it set out to do. What do you think are the causes of its lack of effectiveness? Identify as many contributing factors as you can.

4 Foundations of Individual Behavior

Management Preview

▶ Think about human behavior as a jigsaw puzzle. Puzzles consist of various pieces that fit together in precise ways. And, of course, no two puzzles are exactly alike. They have different numbers of pieces, the pieces are of different sizes and shapes, and they fit together in different ways. The same can be said of human behavior and its determinants. Each of us is a whole picture, like a fully assembled jigsaw puzzle, but the puzzle pieces that define us and the way those pieces fit together are unique. Thus, every person in an organization is fundamentally different from everyone else. To be successful, managers must recognize that these differences exist and attempt to understand them. In this chapter we explore some of the key characteristics that differentiate people from one another in organizations. We first investigate the psychological nature of individuals in organizations. We then look at elements of people's personalities that can influence behavior and consider individual attitudes and their role in organizations. In subsequent sections we examine perception and creativity. We close this chapter with an examination of various kinds of workplace behaviors that affect organizational performance. We begin, however, by looking at the ways in which some companies are starting to change how they treat their employees.

▼ ▼ ▼

With the ever-increasing pressure to reduce costs and to function in a shrinking economy, many firms are searching for the next area to which they can apply cost-saving measures. Throughout the 1990s, companies used technological advances such as robotics and the Internet to reduce costs in areas as diverse as advertising, production, and purchasing. However, for most companies, costs in those areas have now been driven as low as possible. Consequently, some firms are presently turning to human resources for the next round of cuts.

Many corporations have reduced hiring or have begun laying off workers. Organizations realize that workers today have fewer options for employment, so they are not as worried that employees will leave to seek jobs elsewhere. "This may sound bad, but there are not a lot of good choices around," says Tom Newman, a vice president at Teradyne, Inc. Another of the first areas hit was employee perquisites, or "perks." Among the lost amenities were the closing of the employee bowling alley at an Austin-based high-tech firm, no more free massages at the desks of Wall Street bankers, and Xerox's firing of the "plant caretaker" (employees now must water their own office plants). Don't be fooled into thinking these issues are trivial, though. "There is a huge dent in morale when you take anything away from employees, no matter how miniscule it may look," according to workplace consultant Sharon Jordan-Evans.

Next in line for cuts are employee benefits—many firms have reduced their contributions to plans or have eliminated them altogether. Ford Motors and Lucent Technologies are just two of the many organizations contributing less for employee health insurance or retirement plans. Bonuses, sick leave, and vacation time are also being squeezed. As a last resort, some firms are even asking workers to accept pay cuts. Agilent Technology workers' pay declined 10 percent while Disney lowered some pay rates as much as 30 percent. "This was a cost structure that had gotten out of hand," claims Thomas Schumacher head of Walt Disney animation, referring to the $1 million salaries paid to the studio's star animators.

> *"People are lying low, but when the economy improves[,] they'll be out of here."*
> *— Anonymous company executive, after pay cuts at his firm*

However, the hazards of cutting incentives too much can include low morale, reduced productivity, or worse. When the Indiana Social Services Administration left job vacancies unfilled in 1990, the state led the country in the number of welfare fraud cases. And the effects of such measures can be long-lasting. One executive whose company instituted pay cuts says, "People are lying low, but when the economy improves[,] they'll be out of here." Workers complain that they should not bear a disproportionate share of the cost-cutting, and studies verify that median CEO compensation rose 7 percent in 2001 while worker pay rose just 3 percent and company profits fell 35 percent.

The good news for struggling firms is that there are cost-reducing incentives that are effective. The most powerful, and least expensive, perk can be time off from work. Up to 20 percent of workers would work fewer hours for lower pay. Siemens, a German electronics firm, is offering workers a year-long "time-out" with reduced pay and a guaranteed job when they return. "It's a possibility for us not to lose good workers despite bad times," says Siemens' spokesman Axel Heim. Companies are also finding that technology workers and professionals, who need to stay on the leading edge, want more training and increased job responsibilities. Patti Wilson, founder of a high-tech career-management firm, asserts, "[People] will jump jobs to learn more or stay if they feel that they're being challenged."

References: David Leonhardt, "Did Pay Incentives Cut Both Ways?" *New York Times*, April 7, 2002, pp. BU1–3. See www.nytimes.com; John Strauss, "Agency Workers Mull Pay Cut for Time Off," *Indianapolis Star*, March 11, 2002. www.indystar.com on April 10, 2002; Dean Foust and Michelle Conlin, "A Smarter Squeeze?" *Business Week*, December 31, 2001, pp. 42–44. See www.businessweek.com; Rick Perera, "Siemens Offers Workers 'Time-Outs' to Save Cash," *The Industry Standard*, August 31, 2001. www.thestandard.com on April 10, 2002; Tischelle George, "Bye-Bye, Employee Perks," *Information Week*, October 15, 2001. www.informationweek.com on April 10, 2002.

Relationships between businesses and their employees are clearly changing. Like parties in any contractual transaction, each side wants more for itself but wants to give less to the other side. One byproduct of this trend is that today many employees feel less loyalty to their employer than workers did in earlier days. At the same time, though, many managers seem willing to trade employee loyalty for lower costs and great flexibility. The key to knowing how business-employee relationships might work or backfire is an understanding of people in organizations and the various elements and characteristics that contribute to determining how and in what form they are willing to engage in behaviors that will benefit the organization.

People in Organizations

As a starting point for understanding the behavior of people in organizations, in turn, we examine the basic nature of the individual-organization relationship. Understanding this relationship helps us appreciate the nature of individual differences. That is, these differences play a critical role in determining various important workplace behaviors of special relevance to managers.

Psychological Contracts

A psychological contract is a person's set of expectations regarding what he or she will contribute to the organization and what the organization, in return, will provide to the individual.

An individual's contributions to an organization include such things as effort, skills, ability, time, and loyalty.

Organizations provide inducements to individuals in the form of tangible and intangible rewards.

Whenever we buy a car or sell a house, both buyer and seller sign a contract that specifies the terms of the agreement—who pays what to whom, when it is paid, and so forth. A psychological contract resembles a standard legal contract in some ways but is less formal and well defined. Specifically, a **psychological contract** is a person's overall set of expectations regarding what he or she will contribute to the organization and what the organization will provide in return.[1] Thus, unlike a business contract, a psychological contract is not written on paper, nor are all of its terms explicitly negotiated.

Figure 4.1 illustrates the essential nature of a psychological contract. The individual makes a variety of **contributions** to the organization—such things as effort, skills, ability, time, and loyalty. Jill Henderson, a branch manager for Merrill Lynch, uses her knowledge of financial markets and investment opportunities to help her clients make profitable investments. Her M.B.A. in finance, coupled with hard work and motivation, have led her to become one of the firm's most promising young managers. The firm believed she had these attributes when it hired her, of course, and expected that she would do well.

In return for these contributions, the organization provides **inducements** to the individual. Some inducements, such as pay and career opportunities, are tangible rewards. Others, such as job security and status, are more intangible. Jill Henderson started at Merrill Lynch at a very competitive salary and has received an attractive salary increase each of the six years she has been with the firm. She has also been promoted twice and expects another promotion—perhaps to a larger office—in the near future.

In this instance, both Jill Henderson and Merrill Lynch apparently perceive that the psychological contract is

figure 4.1

The Psychological Contract

Psychological contracts govern the basic relationship between people and organizations. Individuals contribute such things as effort and loyalty. Organizations, in turn, offer such inducements as pay and job security.

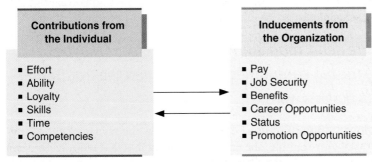

Contributions from the Individual	Inducements from the Organization
■ Effort	■ Pay
■ Ability	■ Job Security
■ Loyalty	■ Benefits
■ Skills	■ Career Opportunities
■ Time	■ Status
■ Competencies	■ Promotion Opportunities

Psychological contracts play an important role in the relationship between an organization and its employees. As long as both parties agree that the contributions provided by an employee and the inducements provided by the organization are balanced, both parties are satisfied and will likely maintain their relationship. But if a serious imbalance occurs, one or both parties may attempt to change the relationship. As illustrated here, for example, an employee who feels sufficiently dissatisfied may even resort to using company assets for his or her own personal gain.

Reference: DILBERT reprinted by permission of United Feature Syndicate, Inc.

fair and equitable. Both will be satisfied with the relationship and will do what they can to continue it. Henderson is likely to continue to work hard and effectively, and Merrill Lynch is likely to continue to increase her salary and give her promotions. In other situations, however, things might not work out as well. If either party sees an inequity in the contract, that party may initiate a change. The employee might ask for a pay raise or promotion, put forth less effort, or look for a better job elsewhere. The organization can also initiate change by training the worker to improve his or her skills, transferring the employee to another job, or by firing the person.

All organizations face the basic challenge of managing psychological contracts. They want value from their employees, and they need to give employees the right inducements. For instance, underpaid employees may perform poorly or leave for better jobs elsewhere. Similarly, as illustrated in the cartoon, an employee may even occasionally start to steal organizational resources as a way to balance the psychological contract. Overpaying employees who contribute little to the organization, though, incurs unnecessary costs.

Recent trends in downsizing and cutbacks have complicated the process of managing psychological contracts. For example, many organizations used to offer at least reasonable assurances of job permanence as a fundamental inducement to employees. Now, however, job permanence is less likely, so alternative inducements may be needed.[2] Among the new forms of inducements some companies are providing are such things as additional training opportunities and increased flexibility in working schedules.

"Loyalty. Gratitude. Fortitude. They're dead, man. And who's the culprit? Maybe corporate America. After all, it was the big companies that . . . ended the traditional employment contract."—Nina Munk, business writer[3]

Increased globalization of business also complicates the management of psychological contracts. For example, the array of inducements that employees deem to be of value varies across cultures. U.S. workers tend to value individual rewards and recognition, but Japanese workers are more likely to value group-based rewards and recognition. Workers in Mexico and Germany highly value leisure time and may thus prefer more time off from work whereas workers in China place a lower premium on time off. Several years ago the Lionel Train Company, maker of toy electric trains, moved its operations to Mexico to capitalize on cheaper labor. The firm encountered problems, however, when it could not hire enough motivated employees to maintain quality standards and ended up making a costly move back to the United States.

A related problem faced by international businesses is the management of psychological contracts for expatriate managers. In some ways, this process is more like a formal contract than are other employment relationships. Managers selected for a foreign assignment, for instance, are usually given some estimate of the duration of the assignment and receive various adjustments in their compensation package—cost-of-living adjustments, education subsidies for children, personal travel expenses, and so forth. When the assignment is over, the manager must then be integrated back into the domestic organization. During the duration of the assignment, however, the organization itself may have changed in many ways—new managers, new coworkers, new procedures, new business practices, and so forth. Thus, returning managers may very well come back to an organization that is quite different from the one they left and to a job quite different from what they expected.[4]

The Person-Job Fit

One specific aspect of managing psychological contracts is managing the person-job fit. A good **person-job fit** is one in which the employee's contributions match the inducements the organization offers. In theory, each employee has a specific

Person-job fit is the extent to which the contributions made by the individual match the inducements offered by the organization.

Understanding and managing person-job fit is an important element in effective psychological contracts. For example, consider the case of the crew members for the *Atlantis* space shuttle. Each had demonstrated both the technical skills necessary to perform in space as well as the emotional strength necessary to withstand the rigors of space travel. Further, they have also demonstrated the ability to work together as a team both in training and actual space missions. Clearly, then, each crew member has an advanced level of person-job fit.

TALKING TECHNOLOGY

▶ *The Ethics of Psychological Testing*

Technological innovation has provided new techniques for improved cost cutting and effectiveness; however, such innovations often have a downside. One of the most controversial innovations is the use of personality or psychological testing as a human resources tool.

No one is sure how many companies use standardized psychological testing, but estimates range from 15 percent to 40 percent. Whatever estimate you accept, the number of applicants tested is in the thousands, and firms report that their use of such tests is increasing. Corporations claim that the evaluations help them to select applicants as well as provide current employees with the best person-job fit.

What the tests are truly measuring is one concern. When applicants answer questions such as "Do you enjoy taking charge of new projects?" the temptation to be dishonest is great. Other questions—such as "Do you ever indulge in unusual sex practices?" or "Do you feel sure that there is only one true religion?"—are criticized as overly personal. Rent-A-Center and Target have both been hit with recent lawsuits for tests that allegedly violated workers' privacy. With other questions, the meaning of a particular response may be unclear. To measure risk taking, one test uses the statement "To me, crossing the ocean in a sailboat would be a wonderful adventure." But it's not clear whether a firm considers risk-taking employees desirable or undesirable.

Another area of concern is how employers will use the data. In one survey, as many as 70 percent of firms using psychological testing shared confidential information with other institutions such as government agencies or banks. Paradoxically, up to 75 percent barred employees from

> *"New technologies have improved [the tests'] accuracy and efficiency, [but] the types of things assessed have changed very little."*—Charles Wonderlic, president of Wonderlic Testing

seeing their own data! Some observers are concerned that a company that relies only on a single employment test may hire employees who are "clones," reducing opportunities for diversity and creativity. Others worry that the tests imply workers cannot overcome their tendencies.

The use of personal computers and the Internet has driven the explosion in personality testing, but thus far, high technology has had little impact on the fundamental nature of psychological testing. Charles Wonderlic, president of Wonderlic Testing, maintains, "New technologies have improved [the tests'] accuracy and efficiency, [but] the types of things assessed have changed very little."

References: Steve Bates, "Personality Counts," *HRMagazine*, February 2002, pp. 28–34 (quotation p. 34). See www.shrm.org/hrmagazine; Pamela Mendels, "Do You Have the Personality for Success?" *Business Week*, October 13, 2000. www.businessweek.com on April 12, 2002; Rodger Doyle, "By the Numbers: Privacy in the Workplace," *Scientific American*, January 1999. www.sciam.com on April 12, 2002.

set of needs that he or she wants fulfilled and a set of job-related behaviors and abilities to contribute. If the organization can take perfect advantage of those behaviors and abilities and exactly fulfill the worker's needs, it will have achieved a perfect person-job fit.

Of course, such a precise person-job fit is seldom achieved. For one thing, hiring procedures are imperfect. Managers can estimate employee skill levels when making hiring decisions and can improve them through training, but even simple performance dimensions are hard to measure objectively and validly. The "Talking Technology" box discusses how some firms are using psychological testing to improve their hiring procedures and thus enhance the person-job fit.

Another consideration is that both people and organizations change. An employee who initially finds a new job stimulating and exciting may consider the same job boring and monotonous a few years later. An organization that adopts new technology needs new skills from its employees. Finally, each person is unique. Measuring skills and performance is difficult enough; assessing attitudes and personality is far more complex. Each individual difference makes matching workers with jobs a difficult and complex process.[5]

Individual Differences

Individual differences are personal attributes that vary from one person to another.

As already noted, every individual is unique. **Individual differences** are personal attributes that vary from one person to another. Individual differences may be physical, psychological, or emotional. The individual differences that characterize a specific person make that person unique. As we see in the sections that follow, the basic categories of individual differences include personality, attitudes, perception, and creativity. First, however, we need to note the importance of the situation in assessing the individual's behavior.

Are the specific differences that characterize a given person good or bad? Do they contribute to or detract from performance? The answer, of course, is that it depends on the circumstances. One person may be dissatisfied, withdrawn, and negative in one job setting but satisfied, outgoing, and positive in another. Working conditions, coworkers, and leadership are just a few of the factors that affect how a person performs and feels about a job. Thus, whenever managers attempt to assess or account for individual differences among their employees, they must also be sure to consider the situation in which behavior occurs.

Since managers need to establish effective psychological contracts with their employees and achieve optimal fits between people and jobs, they face a major challenge in attempting to understand both individual differences and contributions in relation to inducements and contexts. A good starting point in developing this understanding is to appreciate the role of personality in organizations.

Personality and Organizations

The personality is the relatively stable set of psychological attributes that distinguish one person from another.

Personality is the relatively stable set of psychological attributes that distinguish one person from another. A longstanding debate among psychologists—often expressed as "nature versus nurture"—is the extent to which personality attributes are inherited from our parents (the "nature" argument) or shaped by our environment (the "nurture" argument). In reality, both biological and environmental factors play important roles in determining our personalities. Although the details of this debate are beyond the scope of our discussion here, managers should strive to understand basic personality attributes and how they can affect people's behavior in organizational situations, not to mention employees' perceptions of and attitudes toward the organization.

The "Big Five" Personality Traits

The "big five" personality traits are a set of fundamental traits that are especially relevant to organizations.

Psychologists have identified literally thousands of personality traits and dimensions that differentiate one person from another. But in recent years, researchers have identified five fundamental traits that are especially relevant to organizations. Because these five traits are so important and because they are currently receiving so much attention, they are now commonly called **the "big five" personality traits.** Figure 4.2 illustrates these traits.

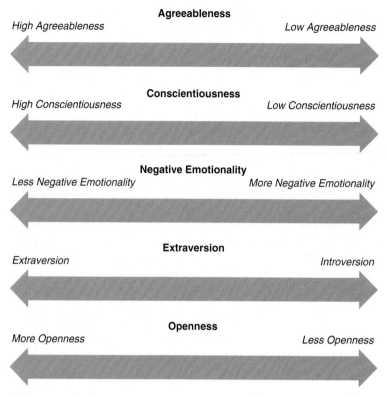

figure 4.2

The "Big Five" Personality Framework

The "big five" personality framework is currently very popular among researchers and managers. These five dimensions represent fundamental personality traits presumed to be important in determining the behaviors of individuals in organizations. In general, experts agree that personality traits closer to the left end of each dimension are more positive in organizational settings whereas traits closer to the right are less positive.

Agreeableness is the ability to get along with others.

Conscientiousness refers to the number of goals on which a person focuses.

Negative emotionality is characterized by moodiness and insecurity; those who have little negative emotionality are better able to withstand stress.

Extraversion is the quality of being comfortable with relationships; the opposite extreme, introversion, is characterized by more social discomfort.

Agreeableness refers to a person's ability to get along with others. Agreeableness causes some people to be gentle, cooperative, forgiving, understanding, and good-natured in their dealings with others. But it results in others being irritable, short-tempered, uncooperative, and generally antagonistic toward other people. Researchers have not yet fully investigated the effects of agreeableness, but it seems likely that highly agreeable people are better at developing good working relationships with coworkers, subordinates, and higher-level managers whereas less agreeable people are not likely to have particularly good working relationships. The same pattern might extend to relationships with customers, suppliers, and other key organizational constituents.

Conscientiousness refers to the number of goals on which a person focuses. People who focus on relatively few goals at one time are likely to be organized, systematic, careful, thorough, responsible, and self-disciplined; they tend to focus on a small number of goals at one time. Others, however, may pursue a wider array of goals, and, as a result, tend to be more disorganized, careless, and irresponsible as well as less thorough and self-disciplined. Research has found that more conscientious people tend to be higher performers than less conscientious people in a variety of different jobs. This pattern seems logical, of course, since conscientious people take their jobs seriously and approach their jobs in a highly responsible fashion.

The third of the "big five" personality dimensions is **negative emotionality.** People with less negative emotionality are relatively poised, calm, resilient, and secure; people with more negative emotionality are more excitable, insecure, reactive, and subject to extreme mood swings. People with less negative emotionality might be expected to better handle job stress, pressure, and tension. Their stability might also lead them to be considered more reliable than their less-stable counterparts.

Extraversion reflects a person's comfort level with relationships. Extroverts are sociable, talkative, assertive, and open to establishing new relationships. Introverts are much less sociable, talkative, and assertive, and are more reluctant to begin new relationships. Research suggests that extroverts tend to be higher overall job performers than introverts and that they are more likely to be attracted to jobs based on personal relationships, such as sales and marketing positions.

Openness is the capacity to entertain new ideas and to change as a result of learning new information.

Finally, **openness** reflects a person's rigidity of beliefs and range of interests. People with high levels of openness are willing to listen to new ideas and to change their own ideas, beliefs, and attitudes in response to new information. They also tend to have broad interests and to be curious, imaginative, and creative. On the other hand, people with low levels of openness tend to be less receptive to new ideas and less willing to change their minds. Further, they tend to have fewer and narrower interests and to be less curious and creative. People with more openness might be expected to be better performers because of their flexibility and the likelihood that they would be better accepted by others in the organization. Openness may also involve a person's willingness to accept change; people with high levels of openness may be more receptive to change whereas those with little openness may resist change.

The "big five" framework continues to attract the attention of both researchers and managers. The potential value of this framework is that it encompasses an integrated set of traits that appear to be valid predictors of certain behaviors in certain situations. Thus, managers who can both understand the framework and assess these traits in their employees are in a good position to understand how and why employees behave as they do. On the other hand, managers must be careful not to overestimate their ability to assess the "big five" traits in others. Even assessment using the most rigorous and valid measures is likely to be somewhat imprecise. Another limitation of the "big five" framework is that it is primarily based on research conducted in the United States. Thus, its generalizability to other cultures presents unanswered questions. Even within the United States, a variety of other factors and traits are also likely to affect behavior in organizations.

The Myers-Briggs Framework

Another interesting approach to understanding personalities in organizations is the Myers-Briggs framework. This system, based on the classical work of Carl Jung, differentiates people in terms of four general dimensions: sensing, intuiting, judging, and perceiving. Higher and lower positions in each of the dimensions are used to classify people into one of sixteen different personality categories.

The Myers-Briggs Type Indicator (MBTI) is a popular questionnaire some organizations use to assess personality types. Indeed, it is among the most popular selection instruments used today, with as many as 2 million people taking it each year. Research suggests that the MBTI is a useful method for determining communication styles and interaction preferences. In terms of personality attributes, however, questions exist about both the validity and the stability of the MBTI.

Other Personality Traits at Work

Besides the "big five" traits and the characteristics assessed by the Myers-Briggs framework, several other personality traits influence behavior in organizations. Among the most important are locus of control, self-efficacy, authoritarianism, Machiavellianism, self-esteem, and risk propensity.

Locus of control is the extent to which people believe their circumstances are a function of either their own actions or external factors beyond their control.

Locus of control is the extent to which people believe that their behavior has a real effect on what happens to them.[6] Some people, for example, believe that if they work hard, they will succeed. They may also believe that people who fail do so because they lack ability or motivation. People who believe that individuals are in control of their lives are said to have an internal locus of control. Other people think that fate, chance, luck, or other people's behavior determines what happens to them. For example, an employee who fails to get a promotion may attribute that

Risk propensity is the degree to which a person is willing to take chances and make risky decisions. Top managers at Lockheed Martin demonstrated strong risk propensity in their recent quest to earn a $200 billion contract to build the new Joint Strike Fighter shown here. No less than three times did they essentially risk the future of the company in order to remain the leader in the bidding. Had they ultimately failed Lockheed Martin would have suffered the consequences for years.

failure to a politically motivated boss or just bad luck rather than to her or his own lack of skills or poor performance record. People who think that forces beyond their control dictate what happens to them are said to have an external locus of control.

Self-efficacy is a related but subtly different personality characteristic. A person's self-efficacy is that person's belief about his or her capabilities to perform a task. People with high self-efficacy believe that they can perform well on a specific task, but people with low self-efficacy tend to doubt their ability to perform a specific task. Self-assessments of ability contribute to self-efficacy, but so does the individual's personality. Some people simply have more self-confidence than others. This belief in their ability to perform a task effectively results in their being more self-assured and better able to focus their attention on performance.

Another important personality characteristic is **authoritarianism,** the extent to which a person believes that power and status differences are appropriate within hierarchical social systems such as organizations.[7] For example, people who are highly authoritarian may accept directives or orders from someone with more authority purely because the other

A person's self-efficacy is that person's beliefs about his or her capabilities to perform a task.

Authoritarianism is the belief that power and status differences are appropriate within hierarchical social systems such as organizations.

People who possess the personality trait of Machiavellianism behave to gain power and control the behavior of others.

person is "the boss." On the other hand, people who are not highly authoritarian, although they may still carry out reasonable directives from the boss, are more likely to question things, express disagreement with the boss, and even refuse to carry out orders if they are for some reason objectionable. A highly authoritarian manager may be relatively autocratic and demanding, and highly authoritarian subordinates will be more likely to accept this behavior from their leader. On the other hand, a less authoritarian manager may allow subordinates a bigger role in making decisions, and less authoritarian subordinates will respond positively to this behavior. (This trait is also quite similar to the concept of power orientation discussed in Chapter 3.)

Machiavellianism is another important personality trait. This concept is named after Niccolo Machiavelli, a sixteenth-century author. In his book *The Prince*, Machiavelli explained how the nobility could more easily gain and use power. The term "Machiavellianism" is now used to describe behavior directed at gaining power and controlling the behavior of others. Research suggests that the degree of Machiavellianism varies from person to person. More Machiavellian individuals tend to be rational and nonemotional, may be willing to lie to attain their personal goals, put little emphasis on loyalty and friendship, and enjoy manipulating others' behavior. Less Machiavellian individuals are more emotional, less willing to lie to succeed, value loyalty and friendship highly, and get little personal pleasure from manipulating others.

Self-esteem is the extent to which a person believes that he or she is a worthwhile and deserving individual.

Self-esteem is the extent to which a person believes that he or she is a worthwhile and deserving individual. People with high self-esteem are more likely to seek higher-status jobs, be more confident in their ability to achieve higher levels of performance, and derive greater intrinsic satisfaction from their accomplishments. In contrast, people with less self-esteem may be more content to remain in lower-level jobs, be less confident of their ability, and focus more on extrinsic rewards. Among the major personality dimensions, self-esteem is the one that has been most widely studied in other countries. Although more research is clearly needed, the published evidence suggests that self-esteem as a personality trait does indeed exist in a variety of countries and that its role in organizations is reasonably important across different cultures.

A person's risk propensity is the degree to which he or she is willing to take chances and make risky decisions.

Risk propensity is the degree to which a person is willing to take chances and make risky decisions. Managers with high risk propensity, for example, might experiment with new ideas and gamble on new products. They might also lead the organization in new and different directions. Such managers might be a catalyst for innovation, or on the other hand, might jeopardize the continued well-being of the organization if the risky decisions prove to be bad ones. Managers with low risk propensity might lead an organization to stagnation and excessive conservatism, or they might help the organization successfully weather turbulent and unpredictable times by maintaining stability and calm. Thus, the potential consequences of a manager's risk propensity depend heavily on the organization's environment. The "Business of Ethics" box explores risk propensity from another perspective—that of whistleblowing employees.

Attitudes in Organizations

Attitudes are a person's complexes of beliefs and feelings about specific ideas, situations, or other people.

People's attitudes also affect their behavior in organizations. **Attitudes** are complexes of beliefs and feelings that people have about specific ideas, situations, or other people. Attitudes are important because they are the mechanisms through which most people express their feelings. An employee's statement that he thinks he is underpaid by the organization reflects his feelings about his pay. Similarly, when a manager says that she likes the new advertising campaign, she is expressing her feelings about the organization's marketing efforts.

How Attitudes Are Formed

Attitudes are formed by a variety of forces, including our personal values, our experiences, and our personalities. For example, if we value honesty and integrity, we may form especially favorable attitudes toward a manager whom we believe to be very honest and moral. Similarly, if we have had negative and unpleasant experiences with a particular coworker, we may form an unfavorable attitude toward her. Any of the "big five" or individual personality traits may also influence our attitudes. Understanding the basic structure of an attitude helps us see how attitudes are formed and can be changed.

Attitude Structure   Attitudes are usually viewed as stable dispositions to behave toward objects in a certain way. For any number of reasons, a person might decide that he or she does not like a particular political figure or a certain restaurant (a

BUSINESS OF ETHICS

▶ Whistleblowers Face Risks

Whistleblowers often risk their reputations and careers to stop corporate wrongdoing. Surely such action illustrates a commitment to their companies. So whistleblowers should be rewarded by the organizations they are struggling to improve, right? Wrong!

In August 2001, on the day Kenneth L. Lay was appointed CEO of Enron, he received a letter from Vice President Sherron S. Watkins detailing her concerns about Enron's accounting practices. In her note, she says, "I am incredibly nervous that we will implode in a wave of accounting scandals. . . . I realize that a lot of smart people, . . . including A A & Co. [Enron auditor, Arthur Anderson] have blessed the accounting treatment. None of that will protect Enron if these transactions are ever disclosed in the bright light of day." Watkins's fears eventually proved to be exactly on target, but Lay and others had ignored her warnings.

Enron fell apart in December 2001, partly due to the problems disclosed by Watkins, so she did not sacrifice her job for her whistleblowing activities. But many others have experienced such a fate. Among them are Allison K. Schieffelin, a top performer at Wall Street firm Morgan Stanley, who had been earning an annual salary of more than $1 million. Although Schieffelin loved her job, calling herself "the most reluctant plaintiff on the planet," she filed suit with the Equal Employment Opportunity Commission in 1998, citing unwelcome sexual advances and a glass ceiling against promotion of women to higher levels. In alleged retaliation for her lawsuit, she was abruptly fired and not even allowed to clean out her desk before being escorted from the building.

Companies use a "nuts and sluts" approach to discredit whistleblowers and ruin their reputations, accord-

> *"Companies use a 'nuts and sluts' approach to discredit whistleblowers."*—Roberta Ann Johnson, author of Whistleblowing: Power and Policy from the Inside Out

ing to Roberta Ann Johnson, author of *Whistleblowing: Power and Policy from the Inside Out.* C. Fred Alford, in his book *Whistleblowers: Broken Lives and Organizational Power*, notes that it's not uncommon for whistleblowers to lose their jobs, even though such action is illegal. Some also lose their families, their friends, and their homes.

In spite of the risks, whistleblowers persist, motivated by their consciences to speak out. On the positive side, public sentiment about whistleblowing appears to be changing. Far from being outcast by corporate society, Enron's Watkins has been publicly lauded as "an icon of workplace integrity" and "a fearless upholder of business ethics."

References: Patrick McGeehan, "Wall Street Highflier to Outcast: A Woman's Story," *New York Times*, February 10, 2002, pp. BU1–BU12. See www.nytimes.com; Marci Alboher Nusbaum, "Blowing the Whistle: Not for the Fainthearted," *New York Times*, February 10, 2002, p. BU10. See www.nytimes.com; Joann S. Lublin, "Saving Your Career After Earning a Name as a Whistle-Blower," *Wall Street Journal*, February 5, 2002. See www.wsj.com; Wendy Zellner, "A Hero—And a Smoking-Gun Letter," *Business Week*, January 28, 2002, pp. 34–35. See www.businessweek.com.

disposition). We would expect that person to express consistently negative opinions of the candidate or restaurant and to maintain the consistent, predictable intention of not voting for the political candidate or eating at the restaurant. In this view, attitudes contain three components: affect, cognition, and intention.

Affect is a person's feelings toward something.

A person's **affect** is his or her feelings toward something. In many ways, affect is similar to emotion—it is something over which we have little or no conscious control. For example, most people react to words such as "love," "hate," "sex," and "war" in a manner that reflects their feelings about what those words convey. Similarly, you may like one of your classes, dislike another, and be indifferent toward a third. If the class you dislike is an elective, you may not be particularly concerned.

But if it is the first course in your chosen major, your affective reaction may cause you considerable anxiety.

A person's cognitions constitute the knowledge that person presumes to have about something.

Cognition is the knowledge a person presumes to have about something. You may believe you like a class because the textbook is excellent, the class meets at your favorite time, the instructor is outstanding, and the workload is light. This "knowledge" may be true, partially true, or totally false. For example, you may intend to vote for a particular candidate because you think you know where the candidate stands on several issues. In reality, depending on the candidate's honesty and your understanding of his or her statements, the candidate's thinking on the issues may be exactly the same as yours, partly the same, or totally different. Cognitions are based on perceptions of truth and reality, and, as we note later, perceptions agree with reality to varying degrees.

An intention is a component of an attitude that guides a person's behavior.

Intention guides a person's behavior. If you like your instructor, you may intend to take another class from him or her next semester. Intentions are not always translated into actual behavior, however. If the instructor's course next semester is scheduled for 8:00 A.M., you may decide that another instructor is just as good. Some attitudes, and their corresponding intentions, are much more central and significant to an individual than others. You may intend to do one thing (take a particular class) but later alter your intentions because of a more significant and central attitude (fondness for sleeping late).

Cognitive Dissonance   When two sets of cognitions or perceptions are contradictory or incongruent, a person experiences a level of conflict and anxiety called **cognitive dissonance.** Cognitive dissonance also occurs when people behave in a fashion that is inconsistent with their attitudes.[8] For example, a person may realize that smoking and overeating are dangerous yet continue to do both. Because the attitudes and behaviors are inconsistent with each other, the person probably will experience a certain amount of tension and discomfort and may try to reduce these feelings by changing the attitude, altering the behavior, or perceptually distorting the circumstances. For example, the dissonance associated with overeating might be resolved by the person's continually deciding to go on a diet "next week."

Cognitive dissonance is the anxiety that a person experiences when she or he simultaneously possesses two sets of knowledge or perceptions that are contradictory or incongruent.

Cognitive dissonance affects people in a variety of ways. We frequently encounter situations in which our attitudes conflict with each other or with our behaviors. Dissonance reduction is the way we deal with these feelings of discomfort and tension. In organizational settings, people thinking about leaving the organization may wonder why they continue to stay and work hard. As a result of this dissonance, they may conclude that the company is not so bad after all, that they have no immediate options elsewhere, or that they will leave "soon."

Attitude Change   Attitudes are not as stable as personality attributes. For example, learning new information about a person may change attitudes. A manager may have a negative attitude about a new colleague because of his lack of job-related experience. After working with the new person for a while, however, the manager may come to realize that the person is actually very talented and subsequently develop a more positive attitude. Likewise, if object of an attitude changes, a person's attitude toward that object may also change. Suppose, for example, that employees feel underpaid and, as a result, have negative attitudes toward the company's reward system. A big salary increase may cause these attitudes to become more positive. In fact, companies themselves have adopted new attitudes toward employees' ability to adapt and create. The "Mastering Change" box

MASTERING CHANGE

▶ *Changing the Way Companies Change*

After many years of improving organizational technology and work processes, some managers are now concentrating on changing the way people think. For instance, many corporate leaders are coming to realize that internal mental processes such as attitudes, perception, and creativity are the fundamental sources of individual behavior. And the most thoughtful plans, the most remarkable innovations, and the most appealing products are not worth very much without the support that comes from the sum of thousands of individual actions. "[W]hat I [previously] failed to recognize was that the way people think is far more important than the tools they use," says Dennis Pawley, a former Chrysler executive, now head of Lean Learning, a change consulting firm.

"Learning" has become the new corporate rallying cry. Corporations and consulting firms are developing training programs to teach workers how to learn. But many are finding that teaching people how to learn is much harder than teaching them specific skills. Peter Senge, a noted management guru, claims that organizations need to develop an increased sensitivity to human relationships at work. He explains, "[To change companies], we keep bringing in mechanics—when what we need are gardeners. We keep trying to drive change—when what we need to do is cultivate change." Senge agrees with a concept also articulated by Pawley: "The people who do the work should be the ones to improve the work." Senge asserts that in his extensive experience as a management consultant, he has "never seen a suc-

cessful organizational-learning program rolled out from the top [of the organization]. Not a single one."

So if change requires learning, and learning requires that organizations become more humane and experimen-

> *"We keep trying to drive change—when what we need to do is cultivate change."—Peter Senge, management expert*

tal, how exactly can training programs get workers to learn better? Most effective programs begin by selecting a motivated team, usually at the middle-management level. Then, training is provided to them through a variety of media, including case studies, role playing, teaching, reading, and lectures. Next, students are asked to take their "book knowledge" and apply it in simulated environments. Lean Learning, for example, assigns students the task of reworking a toy-airplane assembly line to make it more efficient. To reinforce the lessons learned mentally and physically, workers are asked to use journals and dialogues to express their feelings and reflections. Finally, students who have been transformed are themselves now ready to transform by spreading their learning throughout their organizations.

References: Lean Learning Center web site, "How You Will Learn." www.leanlearningcenter.com on April 11, 2002; Fara Warner, "Think Lean," *Fast Company*, February 2002, pp. 40–42. See www.fastcompany.com; Alan M. Webber, "Will Companies Ever Learn?" *Fast Company*, October 2000. www.fastcompany.com on April 11, 2002; Alan M. Webber, "Learning for a Change," *Fast Company*, May 1999, (quotation). www.fastcompany.com on April 11, 2002.

describes some company efforts to train workers to learn better and be more receptive to change.

Attitudes can also change when the object of the attitude becomes less important or less relevant to the person. For example, suppose an employee has a negative attitude about his company's health insurance. When his spouse gets a new job with an organization that has outstanding family insurance benefits, his attitude toward his own insurance may become more moderate simply because he no longer has to worry about it. Finally, as noted earlier, individuals may change their attitudes as a way to reduce cognitive dissonance.

Deeply rooted attitudes that have a long history are, of course, resistant to change. For example, over a period of years a former airline executive named Frank Lorenzo developed a reputation in the industry of being antiunion and for cutting wages and benefits. As a result, employees throughout the industry came to dislike and distrust him. When he took over Eastern Airlines, its employees had such a strong attitude of distrust toward him that they could never agree to cooperate with any of his programs or ideas. Some of them actually cheered months later when Eastern went bankrupt, even though the action cost them their own jobs!

Key Work-Related Attitudes

People in an organization form attitudes about many different things. Employees are likely to have attitudes about their salary, their promotion possibilities, their boss, employee benefits, the food in the company cafeteria, and the color of the company softball team uniforms. Of course, some of these attitudes are more important than others. Especially important attitudes are job satisfaction and organizational commitment.

Job Satisfaction   **Job satisfaction** reflects the extent to which people find gratification or fulfillment in their work. Extensive research on job satisfaction shows that personal factors such as an individual's needs and aspirations determine this attitude, along with group and organizational factors such as relationships with coworkers and supervisors and working conditions, work policies, and compensation.[9]

Job satisfaction is the extent to which a person is gratified or fulfilled by his or her work.

A satisfied employee tends to be absent less often, to make positive contributions, and to stay with the organization.[10] In contrast, a dissatisfied employee may be absent more often, may experience stress that disrupts coworkers, and may be continually looking for another job. Contrary to what a lot of managers believe, however, high levels of job satisfaction do not necessarily lead to higher levels of productivity.[11] One survey indicated that, also contrary to popular opinion, Japanese workers are less satisfied with their jobs than their counterparts in the United States are.[12]

Organizational Commitment   **Organizational commitment,** sometimes called "job commitment," reflects an individual's identification with and attachment to the organization. A highly committed person will probably see herself as a true member of the firm (for example, referring to the organization in personal terms such as "we make high-quality products"), overlook minor sources of dissatisfaction, and see herself remaining a member of the organization. In contrast, a less committed person is more likely to see himself as an outsider (for example, referring to the organization in less personal terms like "they don't pay their employees very well"), to express more dissatisfaction about things, and to not see himself as a long-term member of the organization.[13]

Organizational commitment is a person's identification with and attachment to an organization.

Organizations can do few definitive things to promote satisfaction and commitment, but some specific guidelines are available. For one thing, if the organization treats its employees fairly and provides reasonable rewards and job security, its employees are more likely to be satisfied and committed. Allowing employees to have a say in how things are done can also promote these attitudes. Designing jobs so that they are stimulating can enhance both satisfaction and commitment. Research suggests that Japanese workers may be more committed to their organizations than are U.S. workers.[14] Other research suggests that some of the factors that may lead to commitment—including extrinsic rewards, role clarity, and participative management— are the same across different cultures.[15]

Affect and Mood in Organizations

People who possess *positive affectivity* are upbeat and optimistic, have an overall sense of well-being, and see things in a positive light.

People characterized by *negative affectivity* are generally downbeat and pessimistic, see things in a negative way, and seem to be in a bad mood.

Researchers have recently started to renew their interest in the affective component of attitudes. Recall from our previous discussion that the affect component of an attitude reflects our emotions. Managers once believed that emotion and feelings varied among people from day to day, but research now suggests that although some short-term fluctuation does indeed occur, there are also underlying stable predispositions toward fairly constant and predictable moods and emotional states.[16]

Some people, for example, tend to have a higher degree of **positive affectivity.** This means that they are relatively upbeat and optimistic, that they have an overall sense of well-being, and that they usually see things in a positive light. Thus, they always seem to be in a good mood. People with more **negative affectivity** are just the opposite. They are generally downbeat and pessimistic, and they usually see things in a negative way. They seem to be in a bad mood most of the time.

[Mary Kay] "is a company that understands that positive emotions can be good for the soul."—Gloria Mayfield Banks, senior sales director, Mary Kay, Inc.[17]

Of course, as noted previously, short-term variations can occur among even the most extreme types. People with a lot of positive affectivity, for example, may still be in a bad mood if they have just been passed over for a promotion, gotten extremely negative performance feedback, or been laid off or fired, for instance. Similarly, those with negative affectivity may be in a good mood—at least for a short time—if they have just been promoted, received very positive performance feedback, or had other good things befall them. After the initial impact of such an event wears off, however, those with positive affectivity generally return to their normal positive mood whereas those with negative affectivity gravitate back to their normal bad mood.

Perception in Organizations

Perception is the set of processes by which an individual becomes aware of and interprets information about the environment.

Perception—the set of processes by which an individual becomes aware of and interprets information about the environment—is another important element of workplace behavior. If everyone perceived everything in the same way, things would be a lot simpler (and a lot less exciting!). Of course, just the opposite is true: People perceive the same things in very different ways.[18] Moreover, people often assume that reality is objective, that we all perceive the same things in the same way. To test this idea, we could ask students at the University of Florida and Florida State University to describe the most recent football game between their schools. We probably would hear two conflicting stories. These differences would arise primarily because of perception. The two sets of fans "saw" the same game but interpreted it in sharply contrasting ways.

Since perception plays a role in a variety of workplace behaviors, managers should understand basic perceptual processes. As implied in our definition, perception actually consists of several distinct processes. Moreover, in perceiving we receive information in many guises, from spoken words to visual images of movements and forms. Through perceptual processes, the receiver assimilates the varied types of incoming information for the purpose of interpreting it.[19]

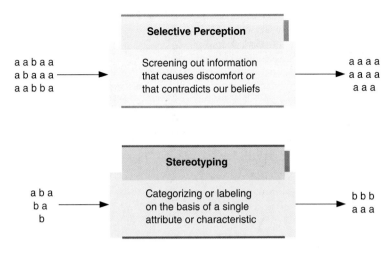

figure 4.3

Basic Perceptual Processes

Perception determines how we become aware of information from our environment and how we interpret it. Selective perception and stereotyping are particularly important perceptual processes that affect behavior in organizations.

Selective perception is the process of screening out information that we are uncomfortable with or that contradicts our beliefs.

Stereotyping is the process of categorizing or labeling people on the basis of a single attribute.

Basic Perceptual Processes

Figure 4.3 shows two basic perceptual processes that are particularly relevant to managers—selective perception and stereotyping.

Selective Perception **Selective perception** is the process of screening out information that makes us uncomfortable or that contradicts our beliefs. For example, suppose a manager is exceptionally fond of a particular worker. The manager has a very positive attitude about the worker and thinks he is a top performer. One day the manager notices that the worker seems to be goofing off. Selective perception may cause the manager to quickly forget what he has observed. Similarly, suppose a manager has formed a very negative image of a particular worker. She thinks this worker is a poor performer who never does a good job. When she happens to observe an example of high performance from the worker, she may quickly forget it. In one sense, selective perception is beneficial because it allows us to disregard minor bits of information. Of course, the benefit occurs only if our basic perception is accurate. If selective perception causes us to ignore important information, however, it can become quite detrimental.

Stereotyping **Stereotyping** is categorizing or labeling people on the basis of a single attribute. Certain forms of stereotyping can be useful and efficient. Suppose, for example, that a manager believes that communication skills are important for a particular job and that speech communication majors tend to have exceptionally good communication skills. As a result, whenever he interviews candidates for jobs, he pays especially close attention to speech communication majors. To the extent that communication skills truly predict job performance and that majoring in speech communication does indeed provide those skills, this form of stereotyping can be beneficial. However, common attributes from which people often stereotype are race and sex. Of course, stereotypes along these lines are inaccurate and can be harmful. For example, suppose a human resource manager forms the stereotype that women can only perform certain tasks and that men are best suited for other tasks. To the extent that these beliefs affect the manager's hiring practices, he or she is (1) costing the organization valuable talent for both sets of jobs, (2) violating federal law, and (3) behaving unethically.

"Based on repeated sightings by large numbers of people exchanging and confirming their impressions over time, stereotypes are no more than a mass exercise in inductive reasoning."—Dan Seligman, business writer[20]

figure 4.4

The Attribution Process

The attribution process involves observing behavior and then attributing causes to it. Observed behaviors are interpreted in terms of their consensus, their consistency, and their distinctiveness. The interpretations result in behavior being attributed to either internal or external causes.

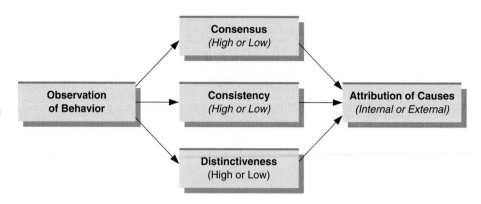

Perception and Attribution

Attribution theory suggests that we attribute causes to behavior based on our observations of certain characteristics of that behavior.

Attribution theory has extended our understanding of how perception affects behavior in organizations.[21] **Attribution theory** suggests that we observe behavior and then attribute causes to it. That is, we attempt to explain why people behave as they do. The process of attribution is based on perceptions of reality, and these perceptions may vary widely among individuals.

Figure 4.4 illustrates the basic attribution theory framework. To start the process, we observe behavior, either our own or someone else's. We then evaluate that behavior in terms of its degrees of consensus, consistency, and distinctiveness. Consensus is the extent to which other people in the same situation behave in the same way. Consistency is the degree to which the same person behaves in the same way at different times. Distinctiveness is the extent to which the same person behaves in the same way in different situations. We form impressions or attributions as to the causes of behavior based on various combinations of consensus, consistency, and distinctiveness. We may believe the behavior is caused internally (by forces within the person) or externally (by forces in the person's environment).

For example, suppose you observe one of your subordinates being rowdy, disrupting others' work and generally making a nuisance of himself. If you can understand the causes of this behavior, you may be able to change it. If the employee is the only one engaging in the disruptive behavior (low consensus), if he behaves like this several times each week (high consistency), and if you have seen him behave like this in other settings (low distinctiveness), a logical conclusion would be that internal factors are causing his behavior.

Suppose, however, that you observe a different pattern: Everyone in the person's work group is rowdy (high consensus), and although the particular employee often is rowdy at work (high consistency), you have never seen him behave this way in other settings (high distinctiveness). This pattern indicates that something in the situation is causing the behavior—that is, that the causes of the behavior are external.

Creativity in Organizations

Creativity is a person's ability to generate new ideas or to conceive of new perspectives on existing ideas.

Creativity is yet another important component of individual behavior in organizations. **Creativity** is the ability to generate new ideas or to conceive of new perspectives on existing ideas. What makes a person creative? How do people become creative? How does the creative process work? Although psychologists have not yet completely answered these questions, examining a few general patterns helps us understand the sources of individual creativity within organizations.[22]

The Creative Individual

Numerous researchers have attempted to describe the common attributes of creative individuals. These attributes generally fall into three categories: background experiences, personal traits, and cognitive abilities.

Background Experiences and Creativity   Researchers have observed that many creative individuals were raised in environments that nurtured creativity. Mozart was raised in a family of musicians and began composing and performing music at age six. Pierre and Marie Curie, great scientists in their own right, raised a daughter, Irene, who won the Nobel Prize in chemistry. Thomas Edison's creativity was nurtured by his mother. However, people with very different background experiences have also been creative. The African-American abolitionist and writer Frederick Douglass was born into slavery in Tuckahoe, Maryland, and had very limited opportunities for education. Nonetheless, his powerful oratory and creative thinking helped lead to the Emancipation Proclamation, which outlawed slavery in the United States.

Creativity is the ability to generate new ideas or to conceive of new perspectives on existing ideas. For example, one of the most significant innovations in the food industry in the last few years has been "salad in a bag." And we owe that innovation to Drew and Myra Goodman. The Goodmans were barely surviving farming a small plot of land; to save time they pre-bagged salads for themselves every Sunday night. One day they decided to see if a San Francisco natural foods market was interested in selling them. The rest, as they say, is history—today the Goodmans own Earthbound Farms and sell over $200 million in packaged salads a year.

Personal Traits and Creativity   Certain personal traits have also been linked to creativity in individuals. The traits shared by most creative people are openness; an attraction to complexity; high levels of energy, independence, and autonomy; strong self-confidence; and a strong belief that one is, in fact, creative. Individuals who possess these traits are more likely to be creative than are those who do not.

Cognitive Abilities and Creativity   Cognitive abilities are an individual's power to think intelligently and to analyze situations and data effectively. Intelligence may be a precondition for individual creativity—although most creative people are highly intelligent, not all intelligent people are necessarily creative. Creativity is also linked with the ability to think divergently and convergently. Divergent thinking allows people to see differences among situations, phenomena, or events. Convergent thinking allows people to

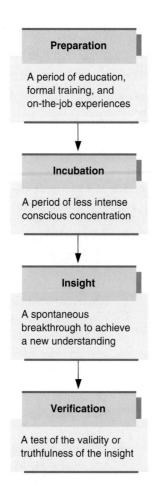

figure 4.5

The Creative Process

The creative process generally follows the four steps illustrated here. Of course, there are exceptions, and the process is occasionally different. In most cases, however, these steps capture the essence of the creative process.

Preparation usually the first stage in the creative process, includes education and formal training.

incubation is the stage of less intense conscious concentration during which a creative person lets the knowledge and ideas acquired during preparation mature and develop.

see similarities among situations, phenomena, or events. Creative people are generally very skilled at both divergent and convergent thinking.

Interestingly, Japanese managers have recently questioned their own creative ability. The concern is that their emphasis on group harmony has perhaps stifled individual initiative and hampered the development of individual creativity. As a result, many Japanese firms, including Omron Corporation, Fuji Photo, and Shimizu Corporation, have launched employee training programs intended to boost the creativity of their employees.[23]

The Creative Process

Although creative people often report that ideas seem to come to them "in a flash," individual creative activity actually tends to progress through a series of stages. Figure 4.5 summarizes the major stages of the creative process. Not all creative activity follows these four stages, but much of it does.

Preparation   The creative process normally begins with a period of **preparation.** Formal education and training are usually the most efficient ways to acquire a strong foundation of knowledge. To make a creative contribution to business management or business services, people must usually receive formal training and education in business. This is one reason for the strong demand for undergraduate and master's-level business education. Formal business education can help a person get "up to speed" and begin making creative contributions quickly. Managers' experiences on the job after completing formal training can also contribute to the creative process. In an important sense, the education and training of creative people never really ends. It continues as long as they remain interested in the world and curious about how things work.

Incubation   The second phase of the creative process is **incubation**—a period of less intense conscious concentration during which the knowledge and ideas acquired during preparation mature and develop. A curious aspect of incubation is that it is often helped along by pauses in concentrated rational thought. Some creative people rely on physical activity such as jogging or swimming to provide a break from thinking. Others read or listen to music. Sometimes sleep may even supply the needed pause. While out rowing one day, David Morse, a research scientist at Corning, hit on the answer to a difficult product improvement. Morse had a special interest in a new line of cookware called Visions. These glass pots and pans had many advantages over traditional cookware, but no one at Corning had succeeded in putting a nonstick surface on the glass. Looking for a solution to this problem, Morse put in many long days in the laboratory, but it was during his hours of rowing that the ideas and concepts that would enable him to devise a nonstick coating began to come together and mature. Morse may never have been able to solve this technical problem if he had not taken the time to let his ideas incubate.

Insight is the stage in the creative process when all the scattered thoughts and ideas that were maturing during incubation come together to produce a breakthrough.

Insight   Usually occurring after preparation and incubation, **insight** is a breakthrough in which the creative person achieves a new understanding of some problem or situation. Insight represents a coming together of all the scattered thoughts and ideas that were maturing during incubation. It may occur suddenly or develop slowly over time. Insight can be triggered by some external event, such as a new experience or an encounter with new data that forces the individual to think about old issues and problems in new ways, or it can be a completely internal event in which patterns of thought finally coalesce in ways that generate new understanding.

One manager's key insight led to a complete restructuring of Citibank's back room operations. The term "back room operations" refers to the enormous avalanche of paperwork that a bank must process to serve its customers—listing checks and deposits, updating accounts, and preparing bank statements. Historically, back room operations at Citibank had been managed as if they were part of the regular banking operation. When John Reed, then vice president, arrived on the scene, he realized that these operations had more to do with manufacturing than with banking and could be managed as a paper-manufacturing process. On the basis of this insight, he hired former manufacturing managers from Ford and other automobile companies. By reconceptualizing the nature of back room operations, Reed substantially reduced costs for Citibank.

In verification, the final stage of the creative process, the validity or truthfulness of the insight is determined.

Verification   Once an insight has occurred, **verification** determines the validity or truthfulness of the insight. For many creative ideas, verification includes scientific experiments to determine whether the insight actually leads to the results expected. In David Morse's case, the insight concerning how to apply a nonstick coating on glass pots was verified in several important experiments and practical trials. Without these experiments and trials, Morse's idea would have remained an interesting concept with little practical application. Verification may also include the development of a product or service prototype. A prototype is one product (or very few) built to see if the ideas behind them actually work. Product prototypes are rarely sold to the public but are very valuable in verifying the insights developed in the creative process. Once the new product or service has been developed, verification in the marketplace is the ultimate test of the creative idea behind it.

Enhancing Creativity in Organizations

Managers who wish to enhance and promote creativity in their organizations can do so in a variety of ways. One important method is to make it a part of the organization's culture, often through explicit goals. Firms that truly want to stress creativity, such as 3M and Rubbermaid, for example, state as goals that some percentage of future revenues are to be gained from new products. This clearly communicates that creativity and innovation are valued.

Another important part of enhancing creativity is to reward creative successes while also being careful not to punish creative failures. Many ideas that seem worthwhile on paper fail to pan out in reality. If the first person to come up with an idea that fails is fired or otherwise punished, others in the organization will become more cautious in their own work, and fewer creative ideas will emerge.

"They say that genius is 99 percent perspiration and 1 percent inspiration. Most companies have that 99 percent. It's the 1 percent that's really hard, and that's why our clients are asking us to work with their people and not just their products."
—Dennis Boyle, partner at Ideo, a respected creativity consulting firm[24]

Types of Workplace Behavior

Workplace behavior is a pattern of action by the members of an organization that directly or indirectly influences organizational effectiveness.

Now that we have looked closely at how individual differences can influence behavior in organizations, let's turn our attention to what we mean by workplace behavior. **Workplace behavior** is a pattern of action by the members of an organization that directly or indirectly influences the organization's effectiveness. One way to talk about workplace behavior is to describe its impact on performance and productivity, absenteeism and turnover, and organizational citizenship. Unfortunately, employees can exhibit dysfunctional behaviors as well.

Performance Behaviors

Performance behaviors are the total set of work-related behaviors that the organization expects the individual to display.

Performance behaviors are the total set of work-related behaviors that the organization expects the individual to display. You might think of these as the "terms" of the psychological contract. For some jobs, performance behaviors can be narrowly defined and easily measured. For example, an assembly-line worker who sits by a moving conveyor and attaches parts to a product as it passes by has relatively few performance behaviors. He or she is expected to remain at the workstation and correctly attach the parts. Performance can often be assessed quantitatively by counting the percentage of parts correctly attached.

For many other jobs, however, performance behaviors are more diverse and much more difficult to assess. For example, consider the case of a research-and-development scientist at Merck. The scientist works in a lab trying to find new scientific breakthroughs that have commercial potential. The scientist must apply knowledge learned in graduate school and experience gained from previous research. Intuition and creativity are also important. And the desired breakthrough may take months or even years to accomplish. Organizations rely on a number of different methods to evaluate performance. The key, of course, is to match the evaluation mechanism with the job being performed.

Dysfunctional Behaviors

Dysfunctional behaviors are work-related behaviors that detract from organizational performance.

Some work-related behaviors are dysfunctional in nature. That is, **dysfunctional behaviors** are those that detract from, rather than contribute to, organizational performance. Two of the more common ones are absenteeism and turnover.

Absenteeism occurs when an individual does not show up for work.

Absenteeism occurs when an employee does not show up for work. Some absenteeism has a legitimate cause, such as illness, jury duty, or a death or illness in the family. At other times, the employee may report a feigned legitimate cause that is actually just an excuse to stay home. When an employee is absent, legitimately or not, her or his work either does not get done at all or a substitute must be hired to do it. In either case, the quantity or quality of actual output is likely to suffer. Obviously, some absenteeism is expected, but organizations strive to minimize feigned absenteeism and reduce legitimate absences as much as possible.

Turnover occurs when people quit their jobs.

Turnover occurs when people quit their jobs. An organization usually incurs costs in replacing workers who have quit, and if turnover involves especially productive people, it is even more costly. Turnover seems to result from a number of factors, including aspects of the job, the organization, the individual, the labor market, and family influences. In general, a poor person-job fit is also a likely cause of turnover. People may also be prone to leave an organization if its inflexibility makes it difficult to manage family and other personal matters, and they may be more likely to stay if an organization provides sufficient flexibility to make it easier to balance work and nonwork considerations. One Chick-fil-A operator in Texas has cut the turnover rate in his stores by offering flexible work schedules, college scholarships, and such perks as free bowling trips.[25]

Other forms of dysfunctional behavior may be even more costly for an organization. Theft and sabotage, for example, result in direct financial costs for an organization. Sexual and racial harassment also cost an organization, both indirectly (by lowering morale, producing fear, and driving off valuable employees) and directly (through financial liability if the organization responds inappropriately). Workplace violence is also a growing concern in many organizations. Violence by disgruntled workers or former workers results in dozens of deaths and injuries each year.[26]

Organizational Citizenship

A person's degree of organizational citizenship is the extent to which that individual's behavior makes a positive overall contribution to the organization.

Managers strive to minimize dysfunctional behaviors while trying to promote organizational citizenship. **Organizational citizenship** refers to the behavior of individuals who make a positive overall contribution to the organization.[27] Consider, for example, an employee who does work that is acceptable in terms of both quantity and quality. However, she refuses to work overtime, won't help newcomers learn the ropes, and is generally unwilling to make any contribution beyond the strict performance of her job. This person may be seen as a good performer, but she is not likely to be seen as a good organizational citizen.

Another employee may exhibit a comparable level of performance. In addition, however, he always works late when the boss asks him to, he takes time to help newcomers learn their way around, and he is perceived as being helpful and committed to the organization's success. He is likely to be seen as a better organizational citizen.

A complex mosaic of individual, social, and organizational variables determine organizational citizenship behaviors. For example, the personality, attitudes, and needs (discussed in Chapter 5) of the individual must be consistent with citizenship behaviors. Similarly, the social context, or work group, in which the individual works must facilitate and promote such behaviors (we discuss group dynamics in Chapter 11). And the organization itself, especially its culture, must be capable of promoting, recognizing, and rewarding these types of behaviors if they are to be maintained. The study of organizational citizenship is still in its infancy, but preliminary research suggests that it may play a powerful role in organizational effectiveness.

Synopsis

Understanding individuals in organizations is important for all managers. A basic framework for facilitating this understanding is the psychological contract—people's expectations regarding what they will contribute to the organization and what they will get in return. Organizations strive to achieve an optimal person-job fit, but this process is complicated by the existence of individual differences.

Personalities are the relatively stable sets of psychological and behavioral attributes that distinguish one person from another. The "big five" personality traits are agreeableness, conscientiousness, negative emotionality, extraversion, and openness. Other important personality traits include locus of control, self-efficacy, authoritarianism, Machiavellianism, self-esteem, and risk propensity.

Attitudes are based on emotion, knowledge, and intended behavior. Cognitive dissonance results from contradictory or incongruent attitudes, behaviors, or both. Job satisfaction or dissatisfaction and organizational commitment are important work-related attitudes. Employees' moods, assessed in terms of positive or negative affectivity, also impact attitudes in organizations.

Perception is the set of processes by which a person becomes aware of and interprets information about the environment. Basic perceptual processes include selective perception and stereotyping. Perception and attribution are also closely related.

Creativity is a person's ability to generate new ideas or to conceive of new perspectives on existing ideas. Background experiences, personal traits, and cognitive abilities affect an individual's creativity. The creative process usually involves four steps: preparation, incubation, insight, and verification.

Workplace behavior is a pattern of action by the members of an organization that directly or indirectly influences organizational effectiveness. Performance behaviors are the set of work-related behaviors the organization expects the individual to display to fulfill the psychological contract. Dysfunctional behaviors include absenteeism and turnover as well as theft, sabotage, and violence. Organizational citizenship entails behaviors that make a positive overall contribution to the organization.

Discussion Questions

1. What is a psychological contract? Why is it important? What psychological contracts do you currently have?

2. Sometimes people describe an individual as having "no personality." What is wrong with this statement? What does this statement actually mean?

3. Describe how the "big five" personality attributes might affect a manager's own behavior in dealing with subordinates.

4. What are the components of an individual's attitude?

5. Think of a person whom you know who seems to have positive affectivity. Think of another who has more negative affectivity. How constant are they in their expressions of mood and attitude?

6. How does perception affect behavior?

7. What stereotypes have you formed about people? Are they good or bad?

8. Describe a situation in which you came up with a new idea by following the basic steps of the creative process described in the text.

9. Identify and describe several important workplace behaviors.

10. As a manager, how would you go about trying to make someone a better organizational citizen?

Organizational Behavior Case for Discussion

Valuing Employees at the World's Largest Firm

In April of 2002, according to *Fortune* magazine, Wal-Mart became the largest company in the world, based on sales. The discounter is the first service company ever to top that list. *Fortune* began publishing its list in 1955, before Wal-Mart was founded, and the largest firm that first year was General Motors. GM and Exxon have remained in the number one and number two spots until Wal-Mart's coup. The retailer's growth has been phenomenal since its 1962 founding. In 1979, Wal-Mart had annual sales of $1 billion; in 1993, $1 billion was just one week's sales; in 2001, just one day's. However, today Wal-Mart, like other American companies, is facing the challenge of maintaining profitability in a tough economy.

Wal-Mart CEO Lee Scott says, "We have not seen any marked increase in the level of consumer spending [in 2002]." In response, the retailer is aggressively adding new, larger stores that are open longer hours—1400 of them are open twenty-four hours. This means that the firm's need for workers continues to grow rapidly. Also, through the 1990s, Wal-Mart sustained an 8 to 9 percent increase in sales annually and a 23 to 25 percent increase in profits. However, Wal-Mart stores last year had sales growth of less than 6 percent, and profits grew just 9 percent. Although still much greater than competitors' growth, Wal-Mart's reduced growth is not rising to meet management expectations. Consequently, its expenses must continually be reduced to maintain target profit margins.

The good news is that Wal-Mart has usually enjoyed a very harmonious relationship with its employees. The firm pays its hourly workers less than many of its competitors, but its corporate culture provides workers with a sense that the company cares about them and their families. Wal-Mart's psychological contract is a product of founder Sam Walton's values. In his autobiography, Walton says, "If you're good to people, and fair with them, . . . they will eventually decide that you're on their side." During Walton's tenure as CEO, Wal-Mart employees had benefits and family-friendly policies such as time-and-a-half pay for working on Sunday, starting pay that was always above minimum wage, an internal promotion policy (70 percent of store managers were once hourly associates), and the opportunity for even low-wage workers to own stock and receive retirement benefits. Walton himself was a charismatic figure, someone who truly listened to what workers had to say.

Unfortunately for workers, the constant pressure to reduce expenses, large store sizes, and twenty-four-hour store hours make it hard for Wal-Mart managers to maintain the personal touch that Walton employed so well. More and more Wal-Mart managers have come to believe that their contract with workers isn't being honored or just isn't working. Stan Fortune, former Wal-Mart manager, asserts, "My job was brainwashing. My job was to take you from your job across town and make you want to work for me, regardless of the pay. I'm almost embarrassed to say it, but that's what I did."

Of course, workers aren't living up to their end of the bargain, either. With little personal contact with their managers, some workers miss work frequently or quit unexpectedly. "We had five call in and quit one day," says Stephanie Haynes, manager at the Madisonville, Texas, store. And Walton himself noted, as stores were being built in more urban areas, "We have more trouble coming up with educated people who want to work in our industry, or with people of the right moral character and integrity." Workers in a Las Vegas store are considering unionizing, and if they choose to do so, they will be the first Wal-Mart employees ever to be represented by a union. And that could change the entire character of Wal-Mart's business.

There are some signs that the retailing giant may be returning to more profitable times. Rival Kmart recently declared bankruptcy while Wal-Mart's stock price increased 41 percent since September 2001, compared with a 33 percent improvement for all retail stores. But the discounter still faces complex challenges, especially in managing its growing labor force. Wal-Mart's growth over the next five years will rely on international markets. Stock analyst Jeff Klinefelter says, "I have no doubt they can [become the dominant retailer] globally. But it's going to change the profile of the company." Unhappy employees are less optimistic. Once, every Wal-Mart employee wore a blue apron that read, "Our people make the difference." Today, that apron slogan has been changed to "How may I help you?" For Wal-Mart workers, that change signals a shift in focus away from the worker and toward the customer. To ensure its success, Wal-Mart must find a way to provide what employees need, motivating them to continue to provide quality customer service.

"My job was brainwashing." —Stan Fortune, former Wal-Mart manager, now a union organizer in Las Vegas

References: "Fourteen Top CEOs (and One President) Gauge the Year Ahead," *Fortune*, April 15, 2002. www.fortune.com on April 15, 2002; Brian O'Keefe, "The High Price of Being No. 1," *Fortune*, April 15, 2002. www.fortune.com on April 15, 2002; Cait Murphy, "Now That Wal-Mart Is America's Largest Corporation, the Service Economy Wears the Crown," *Fortune*, April 15, 2002. www.fortune.com on April 15, 2002; Mark Gimein, "Sam Walton Made Us a Promise," *Fortune*, March 18, 2002, pp. 120–130 (quotation p. 124).

Case Questions

1. According to the psychological contract that was previously observed in use at Wal-Mart, what were the employee contributions and the organizational inducements? In your opinion, was the contract fair and equitable? Why or why not?
2. According to the psychological contract that is currently in use at Wal-Mart, what are the employee contributions and the organizational inducements? Is the contract fair and equitable, in your opinion? Why or why not?
3. What do you suggest that Wal-Mart managers do to better manage their firm's organization culture as the company continues to grow?

 # Experiencing Organizational Behavior

Matching Personalities and Jobs

Purpose: This exercise will give you insights into the importance of personality in the workplace and into some of the difficulties associated with assessing personality traits.

Format: You will first try to determine which personality traits are most relevant to different jobs. You will then write a series of questions to help assess or measure those traits in prospective employees.

Procedure: First, read each of the job descriptions below.

Sales Representative

This position involves calling on existing customers to ensure that they continue to be happy with your firm's products. The sales representative also works to get customers to buy more of your products and to attract new customers. A sales representative must be aggressive but not pushy.

Office Manager

The office manager oversees the work of a staff of twenty secretaries, receptionists, and clerks. The manager hires them, trains them, evaluates their performance, and sets their pay. The manager also schedules working hours and, when necessary, disciplines or fires workers.

Warehouse Worker

Warehouse workers unload trucks and carry shipments to shelves for storage. They also pull orders for customers from shelves and take products for packing. The job requires that workers follow orders precisely; there is little room for autonomy or interaction with others during work.

Working alone, think of a single personality trait that you think is especially important for a person to be able to perform each of these three jobs effectively. Next, write five questions that will help you assess how an applicant scores on that particular trait. These questions should be of the type that can be answered on a five-point scale (i.e., strongly agree, agree, neither agree nor disagree, disagree, strongly disagree).

After completing your questions, exchange them with one of your classmates. Pretend you are a job applicant. Provide honest and truthful answers to your partner's questions. After you have both finished, discuss the traits each of you identified for each position and how well you think your classmate's questions actually measure those traits.

Follow-up Questions

1. How easy is it to measure personality?
2. How important do you believe it is for organizations to consider personality in hiring decisions?
3. Do perceptions and attitudes affect how people answer personality questions?

Self-Assessment Exercise

Assessing Your Locus of Control

Read each pair of statements below and indicate whether you agree more with statement A or with statement B. There are no right or wrong answers. In some cases, you may agree somewhat with both statements; choose the one with which you agree more.

——— 1. A. Making a lot of money is largely a matter of getting the right breaks.
      B. Promotions are earned through hard work and persistence.

——— 2. A. There is usually a direct correlation between how hard I study and the grades I get.
      B. Many times the reactions of teachers seem haphazard to me.

——— 3. A. The number of divorces suggests that more and more people are not trying to make their marriages work.
      B. Marriage is primarily a gamble.

——— 4. A. It is silly to think you can really change another person's basic attitudes.
      B. When I am right, I can generally convince others.

——— 5. A. Getting promoted is really a matter of being a little luckier than the next person.
      B. In our society, a person's future earning power is dependent upon her or his ability.

——— 6. A. If one knows how to deal with people, they are really quite easily led.
      B. I have little influence over the way other people behave.

——— 7. A. The grades I make are the result of my own efforts; luck has little or nothing to do with it.

      B. Sometimes I feel that I have little to do with the grades I get.

——— 8. A. People like me can change the course of world affairs if we make ourselves heard.
      B. It is only wishful thinking to believe that one can readily influence what happens in our society at large.

——— 9. A. A great deal that happens to me probably is a matter of chance.
      B. I am the master of my life.

———10. A. Getting along with people is a skill that must be practiced.
      B. It is almost impossible to figure out how to please some people.

Give yourself 1 point each if you chose the following answers: 1B, 2A, 3A, 4B, 5B, 6A, 7A, 8A, 9B, 10A.

Sum your scores and interpret them as follows:

8–10 = high internal locus of control
6–7   = moderate internal locus of control
5   = mixed internal/external locus of control
3–4   = moderate external locus of control
1–2   = high external locus of control

(Note: This is an abbreviated version of a longer instrument. The scores obtained here are only an approximation of what your score might be on the complete instrument.)

Reference: Adapted from J. B. Rotter, "External Control and Internal Control," *Psychology Today*, June 1971, p. 42. Reprinted with permission from *Psychology Today Magazine*. Copyright © 1971 Sussex Publishers, Inc.

OB Online

1. Find an organization that seems to openly address the issue of person-job fit on its recruiting web site. Look for such things as a discussion of what the organization expects from its employees and what it in turn offers to them.

2. Pick six companies with which you are familiar and visit their web sites. What examples illustrating perception can you identify?

3. Find a consulting firm on the Internet that offers services such as conducting attitude surveys. As a manager, how willing would you be to buy such services?

4. Search the Internet and find two or three recent high-profile examples of dysfunctional behavior, such as theft or violence, in an organization.

Building Managerial Skills

Exercise Overview: Conceptual skills are the manager's ability to think in the abstract. This exercise will help you apply conceptual skills in a way designed to better understand the concepts of attitude formation and cognitive dissonance.

Exercise Task: Begin by considering the following situation. Assume that a new restaurant has just opened near your house, apartment, or dorm. You decide to give it a try and have one of the worse nights of your life. You wait thirty minutes to get seated, and then another thirty minutes before your waitperson stops by. The menu you are handed is dirty, and your water glass has a dead fly floating in it. Your food is served cold (unintentionally), the waitperson spills food on you when clearing the table, the food is way overpriced, and when you return to your car you find that it has been towed! All in all, not a pleasant experience. As a result, you vow to never set foot back in that restaurant again.

Now suppose that there is someone that you have been trying for months to date. While he or she seems to have an interest in dating you as well, circumstances have always kept the two of you apart. This person has just called you, however, and indicated a strong interest in going out with you next week, but only if the two of you can have dinner at the restaurant you hate.

Using the situation above as background, answer the following questions:

1. Explain how your attitude about the restaurant was formed.

2. Explain how your attitude toward the other person was formed.

3. Explain what you would do when confronted with this choice.

4. Explain the role of cognitive dissonance in this situation.

5 Need-Based Perspectives on Motivation

Management Preview

▶ Given the complex array of individual differences discussed in Chapter 4, it should be obvious that people work for a wide variety of different reasons. Some people want money, some want challenge, and some want power. What each unique person in an organization wants from work plays an instrumental role in determining that person's motivation to work. As we see in this chapter, motivation is vital to all organizations. Indeed, the difference between highly effective organizations and less effective ones often lies in the motivations of their members. Thus, managers need to understand the nature of individual motivation, especially as it applies to work situations. This is the first of two chapters dealing with employee motivation. Here we examine need-based perspectives on motivation. (Some researchers call these "content perspectives.") In Chapter 6, we explore process-based perspectives on motivation. First, however, we discuss how some managers are beginning to recognize that employee needs for friendship and other kinds of interpersonal relationships are more important than they had previously believed.

▼ ▼ ▼

Theories of employee motivation abound. The "need theories" describe motivation as arising from unsatisfied human desires or needs. Thus, for example, workers are motivated by pay because they can then use their earnings to buy things that they desire or need, such as food, shelter, or entertainment. This logical relationship between pay and motivation has been recognized and used by managers for more than one hundred years. Many motivation theories or frameworks also include various other widely recognized needs such as the needs for recognition, for achievement, for job security, and for various status symbols like big offices.

Some managers are also beginning to recognize that the needs for human friendship, belonging, and connectedness are perhaps more important than they had previously imagined. Given the growing use of teams in the workplace, it follows that these needs can interact with teamwork settings in very powerful ways. According to Peter Grazier, consultant for Team Building, Inc., "[Successful teams] are well balanced in both technical and human skills. The people on these teams genuinely like each other and work hard to develop and maintain their relationships. Although they are probably not aware that research supports this behavior, they just seem to understand that it's a lot easier to support your team member when you have a good relationship." The surge in interest in interpersonal relationships is partly due to the downsizing, reorganizations, and mergers which characterize today's competitive economy. As firms reallocate human resources to meet their changing needs, workers are often separated from their long-time associates. The events of September 11 also focused attention on the value of close personal relationships at work and a supportive work group. Kent Bailey, psychology professor emeritus at Virginia Commonwealth University, asserts that because people today spend more time at work than at home, coworkers often become "psychological kin."

"[I]t's almost embarrassing to admit that things like sharing and compassion and trust are important."—Tim Sanders, Yahoo! chief solutions officer and author of Love Is the Killer App: How to Win Business and Influence Friends

The effects of losing work friends are subtle, but they can be devastating. One consequence is experiencing feelings of sadness, alienation, and even depression. "You lose people who know who you are when you let your hair down, when you're not putting on a business face," claims one manager who was reassigned. Another outcome is the loss of productivity that occurs when a team gains new members. It takes time for a team to develop productive and efficient working relationships. Grazier claims that teams that lack close friendships will suffer from a lack of support, openness, praise, and communication.

Some organizations are beginning to recognize and encourage the positive power of friendships. One Wall Street investment firm gives employees time off to lunch with work friends—and even pays the check. The company benefits by receiving information, referrals, or opportunities and gains an inexpensive form of business research. Tim Sanders, Yahoo!'s chief solutions officer who wrote *Love Is the Killer App: How to Win Business and Influence Friends,* clearly was inspired by Dale Carnegie's 1937 book *How to Win Friends and Influence People.* Sanders says," [B]ecause there is so much cynicism in our culture, it's almost embarrassing to admit that things like sharing and compassion and trust are important, essential both to business success and to finding happiness in one's work." He emphasizes unselfishness, saying, "Behave this way not because you expect something in return, but because it's the right way to behave. The less you expect in return for acts of professional generosity, the more you'll receive."

References: Peter Grazier, "Team Motivation," Team Building, Inc., web site (quotation). www.teambuildinginc.com on April 29, 2002; Anne Fisher, "Networking for Fun and Profit," *Fortune,* April 1, 2002. www.fortune.com on April 28, 2002; Sue Shellenbarger, "Along with Benefits and Pay, Employees Seek Friends on the Job," *Wall Street Journal,* February 20, 2002; Anne Fisher, "Be a 'Lovecat' at Work?" *Fortune,* February 11, 2002. www.fortune.com on April 28, 2002; Tim Sanders, *Love Is the Killer App: How to Win Business and Influence Friends* (Crown Publishing, 2002).

Many people would readily acknowledge that they value their friends and acquaintances. But understanding how the importance of such relationships translates into behavior in organizational settings is a complex challenge. For example, it might seem obvious that an organization can enhance the motivation of its employees by creating conditions that foster and promote friendships and other close personal relationships. But the same company may face motivational problems at a later time if it must transfer employees to different work settings or layoff members of its workforce to reduce costs.

Complicating matters even further is the fact that the strength or importance of social relationships to motivation will vary from person to person from very strong and meaningful to relatively weak and inconsequential. And, of course, people are likely to have a complex array of needs that include things other than friendships—things such as pay, security, and so forth. Thus, managers need to understand the different needs that motivate people to behave in various ways in order to capitalize most effectively on that motivation and provide truly meaningful rewards and recognition for their employees.

The Nature of Motivation

Motivation is the set of forces that leads people to behave in particular ways.

Motivation is the set of forces that causes people to engage in one behavior rather than some alternative behavior.[1] Students who stay up all night to ensure that their term papers are the best they can be, salespeople who work on Saturdays to get ahead, and doctors who make follow-up phone calls to patients to check on their conditions are all motivated people. Of course, students who avoid the term paper by spending the day at the beach, salespeople who go home early to escape a tedious sales call, and doctors who skip follow-up calls to have more time for golf are also motivated, but their goals are different. From the manager's viewpoint, the objective is to motivate people to behave in ways that are in the organization's best interest.[2]

The Importance of Motivation

Managers strive to motivate people in the organization to perform at high levels. This means getting them to work hard, to come to work regularly, and to make positive contributions to the organization's mission. But job performance depends on ability and environment as well as motivation. This relationship can be stated as follows:

$$P = M + A + E$$

Motivation is the set of forces that cause people to engage in one behavior rather than some alternative behavior. Consider, for example, tennis star Serena Williams. She and her sister Venus are the current stars of the professional tennis circuit, often facing each other in major championship finals and routinely generating higher television ratings than their male counterparts. But far from a game, professional tennis is a grueling profession that requires sacrifice and hard work. Motivation clearly plays a pivotal role in Williams' quest to remain at the upper echelon of this profession.

BUSINESS OF ETHICS

▶ *What's the Price of Motivation?*

Would you feel motivated if your boss gave you a pizza? What if she gave you a trip to the Super Bowl? Can the matter of motivation be reduced to a mere commercial transaction? As George Bernard Shaw asks, "Now that we have established what you are, madam, it is simply a matter of deciding on the price?"

There's no doubt that companies benefit from increased worker motivation. Studies show that workers who report high motivation are more productive and innovative, have lower absenteeism and turnover, and provide better customer service. What's never been demonstrated is a sure method for achieving motivation and avoiding the sticky ethical issues that can arise.

Ethical concerns about giving rewards for performance include the following:

■ Workers may feel that rewards trivialize their significant contributions. Some employees compare rewards to bribes; others to implicit threats.

■ It's hard to determine who deserves rewards. "The positive sometimes is negative because it seems unfair," according to motivational consultant Alex Heim.

■ Workers may become used to receiving rewards and expect them frequently, becoming unsatisfied and demanding if rewards don't arrive. "Downstream, the grand scheme doesn't always work. The fallout is disenchantment," says Joe Magliochetti, CEO of Dana, a supplier to the auto industry.

■ Rewards, which can cost hundreds of thousands of dollars, have no demonstrated relationship to a company's bottom line and may take funds away from other, more worthy programs.

"Downstream, the grand scheme doesn't always work. The fallout is disenchantment."—Joe Magliochetti, CEO of Dana Corporation

Combine these concerns with the observation that increases in productivity due to rewards are fleeting, if they exist at all, and you will see why many companies are disillusioned. Nevertheless, motivation remains a critical issue—a recent poll found that one-fifth of workers are so negative that they poison others and that their employers would be better off without them.

This fact is not lost on such high-performing organizations as Microsoft, Sun Microsystems, and GE, who no longer try to motivate everyone. Former GE CEO Jack Welch claims, "A company that bets its future on its people must remove that lower 10 percent, and keep removing it every year." Welch's tough-love philosophy may be the most motivating message, in effect telling workers, "My way or the highway."

References: Michelle Conlin, "The Big Squeeze on Workers," *Business Week*, May 13, 2002. www.businessweek.com on May 17, 2002; Nancy K. Austin, "Get Happy! Please," *Fortune*, May 1, 2002. www.fortune.com on May 17, 2002; Del Jones, "Firms Spend Billions to Fire Up Workers—With Little Luck," *USA Today*, May 10, 2001, p. 1A (quotation). See www.usatoday.com.

with P = performance, M = motivation, A = ability, and E = environment. To reach high levels of performance, an employee must want to do the job well (motivation), must be able to do the job effectively (ability), and must have the materials, resources, equipment, and information to do the job (environment). A deficiency in any one of these areas hurts performance. A manager should thus strive to ensure that all three conditions are met.[3]

In most settings motivation is the most difficult of these factors to manage. If an employee lacks the ability to perform, she or he can be sent to training programs to learn new job skills. If the person cannot learn those skills, she or he can be transferred to a simpler job and replaced with a more skilled worker. If an employee lacks materials, resources, equipment, and/or information, the manager can take steps to provide them. For example, if a worker cannot complete a project without sales forecast data from marketing, the manager can contact marketing and request that information. But if motivation is deficient, the manager faces the more complex situation of determining what will motivate the employee to work harder. This point is explored further in the "Business of Ethics" box.

The Motivational Framework

We can start to understand motivation by looking at need deficiencies and goal-directed behaviors. Figure 5.1 shows the basic motivational framework we use to organize our discussion. A **need**—something an individual requires or wants—is the starting point.[4] Motivated behavior usually begins when a person has one or more important needs. Although a need that is already satisfied may also motivate behavior (for example, the need to maintain a standard of living one has already achieved), unmet needs usually result in more intense feelings and behavioral changes. For example, if a person has yet to attain the standard of living she desires, this unmet need may stimulate her to action.

A need deficiency usually triggers a search for ways to satisfy it. Consider a person who feels her salary and position are deficient because she wants more income and because they do not reflect the importance to the organization of the work she does. She may feel she has three options: to simply ask for a raise and a promotion, to work harder in the hope of earning a raise and a promotion, or to look for a new job with a higher salary and a more prestigious title.

Next comes a choice of goal-directed behaviors. Although a person might pursue more than one option at a time (such as working harder while also looking for another job), most effort is likely to be directed at one option. In the next phase, the person actually carries out the behavior chosen to satisfy the need. She will probably begin putting in longer hours, working harder, and so forth. She will next experience either rewards or punishment as a result of this choice. She may perceive her situation to be punishing if she ends up earning no additional recognition and not getting a promotion or pay raise. Alternatively, she may actually be rewarded by getting the raise and promotion because of her higher performance.

Finally, the person assesses the extent to which the outcome achieved fully addresses the original need deficiency. Suppose the person wanted a 10 percent raise and a promotion to vice president. If she got both, she should be satisfied. On the other hand, if she got only a 7 percent raise and a promotion to associate vice president, she will have to decide whether to keep trying, to accept what she got, or to choose one of the other options considered earlier. (Sometimes, of course, a need may go unsatisfied altogether despite the person's best efforts.) The cartoon on page 118 illustrates a clear case of a person not achieving need fulfillment as he might have expected!

> A **need** is anything an individual requires or wants.

figure 5.1

The Motivational Framework

This framework provides a useful way to see how motivational processes occur. When people experience a need deficiency, they seek ways to satisfy it, which results in a choice of goal-directed behaviors. After performing the behavior, the individual experiences rewards or punishments that affect the original need deficiency.

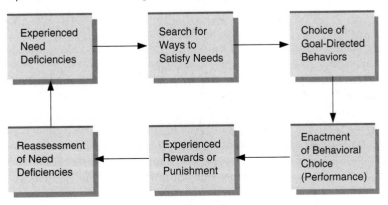

Money, of course, plays an important role in a person's decisions about where to work and how much effort to actually devote to the job. If people do choose to work hard and subsequently feel rewarded for their efforts, they are likely to be even more motivated to work hard in the future. But if, as in Dagwood Bumstead's case, people make meaningful contributions to the organization but still don't share in the benefits, they may be less motivated to do so in the future.

Reference: Reprinted with Special Permission of King Features Syndicate.

Needs and Motives in Organizations

Primary needs are the basic physical requirements necessary to sustain life.

Secondary needs are requirements learned from the environment and culture in which the person lives.

As just noted, a need is simply something a person requires or wants. Not surprisingly, people have many different needs. These needs can be grouped into two categories: primary and secondary needs. **Primary needs** are things that people require to live and to sustain themselves, such as food, water, and shelter from the environment. Needs of this type are instinctive and physiologically based. **Secondary needs,** on the other hand, are perceived requirements based more on mental processes and are learned from the environment and culture in which the person lives. Examples include the needs for achievement, autonomy, power, status, order, affiliation, and understanding.

Secondary needs often arise in organizational settings, so it is especially important to consider them when examining motivated behavior. For example, if people are to be satisfied with their psychological contracts with their organization, the inducements offered by the organization must be consistent with their own unique needs. A nice office and job security may not be sufficient if the employee is primarily seeking income and promotion opportunities.

People's needs also change with time. When you graduate and accept a new job, you may be very satisfied with your compensation. But if you do not receive a raise for several years, you will eventually become quite dissatisfied. Thus, efforts designed to motivate employees to behave in a certain way may lose their effectiveness as employees satisfy one set of needs and begin to identify another set. Some firms use flexible reward systems in an attempt to satisfy an array of different needs for different individuals.

A Motive is a factor that determines a person's choice of one course of behavior from among several possibilities.

A **motive** is a person's reason for choosing one behavior from among several choices. Motives are derived from needs in that most behaviors are undertaken to satisfy one or more needs. For example, a person may decide to have lunch to satisfy a need for food. He might choose to go to McDonald's because it's right across the street and service is fast and convenient, the Taco Bell three blocks away because he's in the mood for Mexican food, or another spot simply because it's on the way to an afternoon business appointment. The reasons for each choice, then, reflect a motive.

Needs, motives, and behavior are interrelated in a fairly simple and straightforward manner. A need serves as a stimulus for action. Motives are the channels through which the individual thinks the need can best be satisfied and thus reflect the person's behavioral choices. Finally, the manifestation of motives is actual behavior. For example, suppose an employee wants to advance her career to gain income and prestige (needs). She decides to work harder and do higher-quality work to impress her boss (motives). Therefore, she works later each evening, comes into the office on Saturday, and pays more attention to detail as she strives for perfection (behaviors).

Motives can vary considerably in the extent to which they require detailed and conscious deliberation and complexity. A simple decision about where to have a routine lunch, for example, can usually be made quickly and without much thought whereas a decision about where to take an important client to lunch might require more consideration. Similarly, a major decision that affects a person's career or family may take much longer and involve many other factors. The "Mastering Change" feature discusses how some people are making different decisions about how to fulfill various needs today.

MASTERING CHANGE

▶ Tradeoffs in the Hierarchy of Needs

Everyone agrees that the world is changing, but one area that seems virtually immune to change is human nature. Therefore, need theories of motivation, which are based upon human yearnings from our lowest instincts to our highest dreams, should be an unchanging constant. However, even within this seemingly inflexible framework, the emphasis that employees place on various types of needs is changing.

Employee job satisfaction is an area of critical concern for both workers and their employers. One recent study claims that 20 percent of American workers are so negative and unproductive that they actually reduce the performance of their unit. And all workers, even those who are currently satisfied, have vivid memories of a job that made them miserable.

Some people really love their work but are unhappy about side effects. Consider the veterinarian who is allergic to dogs. She would never consider quitting because other than having to endure constant sneezing and rashes, she finds that the job is a perfect fit. Writers develop repetitive-motion wrist injuries; chefs cut their fingers. Stories of seasick sailors are many. Nevertheless, one explains, "[Sailing] is the only way I can really see the world." Other workers may have loved their jobs in the beginning, but the nature of the jobs may have changed over time. An engineer who loves to tinker was promoted to a management position and now spends all his time on

paperwork and meetings. Sometimes, the person-job fit isn't right, as when one guitarist briefly took a sales position. He recalls, "I was completely and agonizingly miserable every minute of every day I was there."

What these workers have in common is a job that doesn't perfectly fill their needs. The veterinarian, writers,

"I was completely and agonizingly miserable every minute of every day."—A former salesman, now a rock guitarist

chefs, and sailors have accepted less fulfillment of their need for health in order to fulfill higher needs. The engineer chooses to stay in the management position for higher pay—another needs tradeoff. The guitarist was fortunate in recognizing that music would be a more rewarding career for him and gave up a steady income to pursue the work he loves.

The current trend is for young workers, the hardest hit by unemployment in today's economy, to return to school. This is a convenient solution to a difficult problem, but perhaps those young people are simply choosing to fulfill their esteem and achievement needs.

References: Lisa Belkin, "When the Job You Love Makes You Ill," *New York Times*, April 14, 2002, p. WC1. See www.nytimes.com; Melanie Payne, "Looking for Your Labor of Love," *The Eagle* (Bryan-College Station, Texas), December 2, 2001 (quotation). See www.theeagle.com; "Climbing Out of the Job Pool," *Business Week*, February 25, 2002. www.businessweek.com on May 18, 2002.

Historical Perspectives on Motivation

Historical views on motivation, although not always accurate, are of interest for several reasons. For one thing, they provide a foundation for contemporary thinking about motivation. For another, because they generally were based on common sense and intuition, an appreciation of their strengths and weaknesses can help managers gain useful insights into employee motivation in the workplace.

Early Views of Motivation

We introduced the personality trait of Machiavellianism in Chapter 4. Recall that this trait centers on the need for power. To the extent that individuals actually want power, this need provides motivation and could therefore be considered one of the first approaches to understanding motivated behavior. But hedonism was a more far-reaching concept that shaped early thinking about motivation.

The concept of *hedonism*—the idea that people seek pleasure and comfort and try to avoid pain and discomfort—dominated early thinking on human motivation.[5] Although this notion seems reasonable as far as it goes, there are many kinds of behavior that it cannot explain. For example, why do recreational athletes exert themselves willingly and regularly whereas a hedonist would prefer to relax? Why did so many people risk their lives for others on September 11, 2001? Why do volunteers work tirelessly to collect money for charitable causes? And why do some employees work extra hard while a hedonist would prefer to loaf? As experts recognized that hedonism is an extremely limited—and often incorrect—view of human behavior, other perspectives emerged.

The Scientific Management Approach

The scientific management approach assumes that employees are motivated by money.

As we noted in Chapter 1, Frederick W. Taylor, the chief advocate of **scientific management,** assumed that employees are economically motivated and work to earn as much money as they can.[6] Taylor once used the case of a Bethlehem Steelworker named Schmidt to illustrate the importance of money in motivation. Schmidt's job was to move heavy pieces of iron from one pile to another. He appeared to be doing an adequate job and regularly met the standard quota of 12.5 tons per day. Taylor, however, believed that Schmidt was strong enough to do much more. To test his ideas, Taylor designed a piece-rate pay system that would award Schmidt a certain sum of money for each ton of iron he loaded. Then he had the following conversation with Schmidt and observed his work:

Taylor: "Schmidt, are you a high-priced man?"

Schmidt: "Well, I don't know what you mean." [Several minutes of conversation ensue.]

Taylor: "Well, if you are a high-priced man, you will do exactly as this [supervisor] tells you tomorrow, from morning until night. When he tells you to pick up [a piece of iron] and walk, you pick it up and walk, and when he tells you to sit down and rest, you sit down and rest. You do that right straight through the day. And what's more, no back talk. Do you understand that?"

The next day Schmidt started to work and all day long, and at regular intervals, was told by the supervisor who stood over him with a watch, "Now pick up a pig and walk. Now sit down and rest. Now walk, now rest. . . ." He worked when he was told to work and rested when he was told to rest, and at half-past five in the afternoon, he had loaded 47.5 tons on the car. According to Taylor, Schmidt practically never failed to work at this pace and do the task that was given him during the three years Taylor was at Bethlehem.[7]

Historical evidence suggests that Taylor may have fabricated the conversation just related and that Schmidt himself may have been an invention.[8] Even if this is true, however, Taylor's willingness to lie shows just how strongly he believed in his economic view of human motivation and in the need to spread the doctrine. But researchers also soon recognized that scientific management's assumptions about motivation could not always explain complex human behavior. The next perspective on motivation to emerge was the human relations approach.

The Human Relations Approach

The human relations approach to motivation suggests that favorable employee attitudes result in motivation to work hard.

The **human relations approach,** which we also discussed in Chapter 1, arose from the Hawthorne studies.[9] Douglas McGregor's popular Theory X and Theory Y, for example, exemplified this view of employee motivation. The human relations perspective suggested that people are motivated by things other than money; in particular, it maintains that employees are motivated by and respond to their social environment at work. Favorable employee attitudes such as job satisfaction were presumed to result in improved employee performance. In Chapter 6, we explore this relationship in more detail. At this point it is sufficient to say, as we did in Chapter 1, that the human relations approach left many questions about human behavior unanswered. However, one of the primary theorists associated with this movement, Abraham Maslow, helped develop an important need theory of motivation.

Need Theories of Motivation

Need theories of motivation assume that need deficiencies cause behavior.

Need theories represent the starting point for most contemporary thought on motivation, although these theories also attracted critics.[10] The basic premise of **need theories,** consistent with our motivation framework introduced earlier, is that humans are motivated primarily by deficiencies in one or more important needs or need categories. Need theorists have attempted to identify and categorize the needs that are most important to people. As indicated earlier, some observers call these "content theories" because they deal with the content, or substance, of what motivates behavior. The best-known need theories are the hierarchy of needs and the ERG theory.

The Hierarchy of Needs

Maslow's hierarchy of needs theory assumes that human needs are arranged in a hierarchy of importance.

The hierarchy of needs, developed by psychologist Abraham Maslow in the 1940s, is the best-known need theory.[11] Influenced by the human relations school, Maslow argued that human beings are "wanting" animals: They have innate desires to satisfy a given set of needs. Furthermore, Maslow believed that these needs are arranged in a hierarchy of importance, with the most basic needs at the foundation of the hierarchy.

Figure 5.2 shows Maslow's **hierarchy of needs.** The three sets of needs at the bottom of the hierarchy are called deficiency needs, because they must be satisfied

figure 5.2

The Hierarchy of Needs

Maslow's hierarchy of needs consists of five basic categories of needs. This figure illustrates both general and organizational examples of each type of need. Of course, each individual has a wide variety of specific needs within each category.

Reference: Adapted from Abraham H. Maslow, "A Theory of Human Motivation," *Psychological Review*, vol. 50, 1943, pp. 374–396.

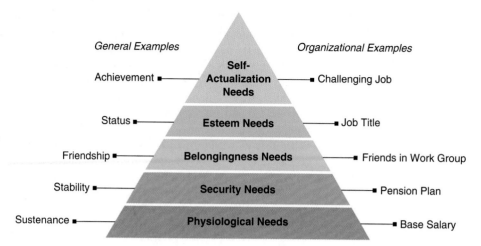

for the individual to be fundamentally comfortable. The top two sets of needs are termed growth needs because they focus on personal growth and development.

The most basic needs in the hierarchy are *physiological needs*. They include the needs for food, sex, and air. Next in the hierarchy are *security needs*: things that offer safety and security, such as adequate housing and clothing and freedom from worry and anxiety. *Belongingness needs*, the third level in the hierarchy, are primarily social. Examples include the need for love and affection and the need to be accepted by peers. The fourth level, *esteem needs*, actually encompasses two slightly different kinds of needs: the need for a positive self-image and self-respect and the need to be respected by others. At the top of the hierarchy are *self-actualization needs*. These involve a person's realizing her full potential and becoming all that she can be.

"Its nice to have a job that pays halfway decent, if you've got to do it."—Joe Sizemore, hourly wage earner at a factory in Blacksburg, Virginia[12]

Maslow believed that each need level must be satisfied before the level above it can become important. Thus, once physiological needs have been satisfied, their importance diminishes, and security needs emerge as the primary sources of motivation. This escalation up the hierarchy continues until the self-actualization needs become the primary motivators. Suppose, for example, that Jennifer Wallace earns all the money she needs and is very satisfied with her standard of living. Additional income may have little or no motivational impact on her behavior. Instead, Jennifer will strive to satisfy other needs, such as a desire for higher self-esteem.

However, if a previously satisfied lower-level set of needs becomes deficient again, the individual returns to that level. For example, suppose that Jennifer unexpectedly loses her job. At first, she may not be too worried because she has savings and confidence that she can find another good job. As her savings dwindle, however, she will become increasingly motivated to seek new income. Initially, she may seek a job that both pays well and that satisfies her esteem needs. But as her financial situation grows increasingly more grim, she may lower her expectations

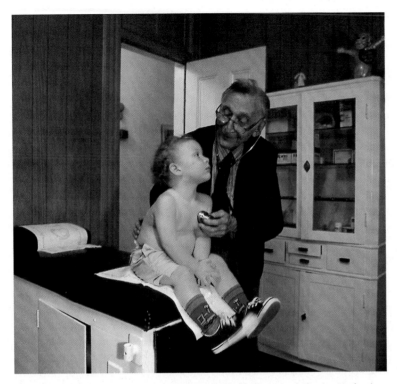

Need theories of motivation assume that need deficiencies cause behavior. Maslow's need hierarchy culminates with self-actualization needs, involving potential and fulfillment. Take Dr. Salvator Altchek, for example. Dr. Altchek practiced medicine in Brooklyn for 67 years. For over 60 of those years he continued to make house calls, and he only charged $5 per visit for his services. Dr. Altchek clearly had all of the material possessions he needed and so chose to devote his life to helping others. And the needs that motivated this behavior had nothing to do with material things.

regarding esteem and instead focus almost exclusively on simply finding a job with a reliable paycheck.

In most businesses, physiological needs are probably the easiest to evaluate and to meet. Adequate wages, toilet facilities, ventilation, and comfortable temperatures and working conditions are measures taken to satisfy this most basic level of needs. Security needs in organizations can be satisfied by such things as job continuity (no layoffs), a grievance system (to protect against arbitrary supervisory actions), and an adequate insurance and retirement system (to guard against financial loss from illness and to ensure retirement income).

Most employees' belongingness needs are satisfied by family ties and group relationships both inside and outside the organization. In the workplace, people usually develop friendships that provide a basis for social interaction and can play a major role in satisfying social needs. Managers can help satisfy these needs by fostering a sense of group identity and interaction among employees. At the same time, managers can be sensitive to the probable effects on employees (such as low performance and absenteeism) of family problems or lack of acceptance by coworkers. Esteem needs in the workplace are met at least partially by job titles, choice offices, merit pay increases, awards, and other forms of recognition. Of course, to be sources of long-term motivation, tangible rewards such as these must be distributed equitably and be based on performance.

Self-actualization needs are perhaps the hardest to understand and the most difficult to satisfy. For example, it is difficult to assess how many people completely meet their full potential. In most cases, people who are doing well on Maslow's hierarchy will have satisfied their esteem needs and will be moving toward self-actualization. Working toward self-actualization, rather than actually achieving it, may be the ultimate motivation for most people.

Research shows that the need hierarchy does not generalize very well to other countries. For example, in Greece and Japan, security needs may motivate employees more than self-actualization needs. Likewise, belongingness needs are especially important in Sweden, Norway, and Denmark. Research has also found differences in the relative importance of different needs in Mexico, India, Peru, Canada, Thailand, Turkey, and Puerto Rico.[13] The "World View" box discusses the problems Saudi Arabian businesses have encountered when trying to change the needs, values, and motives of their new workforce to suit their purposes.

WORLD VIEW

Different Culture, Different Needs

Changing the work-related needs, motives, and values of one person in an organization is a daunting challenge. Consider, then, the difficulties inherent in trying to change the needs, motives, and values of an entire population. This is exactly the task being confronted by businesses in Saudi Arabia. For decades Saudi Arabia relied heavily on so-called "guest workers" to perform most of its menial and service-oriented jobs. People from Pakistan, Egypt, and the Philippines, for example, found it easy to enter Saudi Arabia and find steady work performing jobs that locals found unattractive. Companies in Saudi Arabia routinely hired these guest workers for less attractive jobs and paid them relatively low wages. Most guest workers found jobs as restaurant workers, security guards, custodians and maintenance people, and package couriers.

Recently, however, the government of Saudi Arabia has had to change its liberal guest worker policy. For one thing, a huge baby boom of Saudis is now reaching employment age, and there aren't enough jobs to go around. For another, the government, a large employer itself, is in the midst of downsizing and has fewer jobs to offer citizens. As a result, officials are now taking a much harder stance on guest workers. Few new guest workers are being admitted. As current workers' visas expire, they are not being renewed, so those workers are being forced to leave the country. A new law bans foreign workers from owning cars. In some cities in Saudi Arabia, a retail store can be closed down automatically if someone other than a Saudi national is working behind the counter. And the government has ordered all companies to increase the native workforce 5 percent each year.

A problem, however, arises from the prevailing work ethic of Saudi workers. Because most have grown up in a privileged setting and have had autonomy over where and when they worked, they find it difficult to adjust to more regimented and routine work situations. For example, a typical Saudi trying to cope with a new job situation has difficulty understanding why he can't come to work at 9:00 A.M. instead of 8:00 and make up the time by simply

> *"If I'm supposed to be here at 8 and I come in at 9, why can't I stay until 3:30 instead of 2:30?"—Khalid Al Sharif, Saudi worker fired for repeatedly coming to work late*

working an hour longer in the evening. Progress is being made in some companies, but others still face major challenges. For example, McDonald's is having trouble attracting enough qualified Saudis to hold management positions in its restaurants. Most Saudis consider restaurant work demeaning, regardless of the actual position held.

And even though many workers are trying, they still have a difficult time adjusting to a traditional work environment. For example, when initiating higher-level business dealings in Saudi Arabia, it is typical to spend a considerable time exchanging information and asking questions about one another's families. The young Saudis now working in lower-level positions still adhere to this practice in some cases and may trade as many as a dozen or more pleasantries with one another before getting down to business. They are also prone to showing unfailing hospitality to visitors. This approach is desirable in some situations, but in others it can be quite dysfunctional. For example, some Saudi workers have been known to walk off their job at a busy airline counter to have tea with a friend who has strolled up. Saudis consider it rude not to be sociable with visitors, regardless of the circumstance!

References: "Certain Work Is Foreign to Saudis, But That's Changing," *Wall Street Journal,* September 12, 1996, pp. A1, A4 (quotation on p. A1). Ricky W. Griffin and Michael W. Pustay, *International Business: A Managerial Perspective,* 3rd ed., Chapter 14 (Upper Saddle River, N.J.: Prentice Hall, 2002).

Maslow's need hierarchy makes a certain amount of intuitive sense. And because it was the first motivation theory to become popular, it is also one of the best known among practicing managers. However, research has revealed a number of deficiencies in the theory. For example, five levels of needs are not always present, the actual hierarchy of needs does not always conform to Maslow's model, and need structures are more unstable and variable than the theory would lead us to believe.[14] And sometimes managers are overly clumsy or superficial in their attempts to use a theory such as this one. Thus, the theory's primary contribution seems to lie in providing a general framework for categorizing needs.

ERG Theory

The ERG theory describes existence, relatedness, and growth needs.

The ERG theory, developed by Yale psychologist Clayton Alderfer, is another historically important need theory of motivation.[15] In many respects, **ERG theory** extends and refines Maslow's needs hierarchy concept, although there are also several important differences between the two. The *E, R,* and *G* stand for three basic need categories: existence, relatedness, and growth. *Existence needs*—those necessary for basic human survival—roughly correspond to the physiological and security needs of Maslow's hierarchy. *Relatedness needs*, those involving the need to relate to others, are similar to Maslow's belongingness and esteem needs. Finally, *growth needs* are analogous to Maslow's needs for self-esteem and self-actualization.

In contrast to Maslow's approach, ERG theory suggests that more than one kind of need, for example, relatedness and growth needs, may motivate a person at the same time. A more important difference from Maslow's hierarchy is that ERG theory includes a satisfaction-progression component and a frustration-regression component (see Figure 5.3). The satisfaction-progression concept suggests that after satisfying one category of needs, a person progresses to the next level. On this point, the need hierarchy and ERG theory agree. The need hierarchy, however, assumes the individual remains at the next level until the needs at that level are satisfied. In contrast, the frustration-regression component of ERG theory suggests that a person who is frustrated by trying to satisfy a higher level of needs eventually will regress to the preceding level.[16]

Suppose, for instance, that Nick Hernandez has satisfied his basic needs at the relatedness level and now is trying to satisfy his growth needs. That is, he has many friends and social relationships and is now trying to learn new skills and advance in his career. For a variety of reasons, such as organizational constraints (i.e., few challenging jobs, a glass ceiling, etc.) and the lack of opportunities to advance, he is unable to satisfy those needs. No matter how hard he tries, he seems stuck in his current position. According to ERG theory, frustration of his growth needs will cause Nick's relatedness needs to once again become dominant as motivators. As a result, he will put renewed interest into making friends and developing social relationships.

figure 5.3

The ERG Theory

The ERG theory includes an important process missing from other needs hierarchies—the frustration-regression component, which suggests that if a person becomes frustrated attempting to satisfy one level of needs, he or she may regress to a need level that was previously satisfied. Only if a need level is satisfied does the person progress to a higher level.

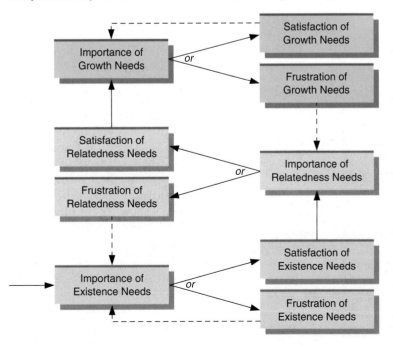

The Dual-Structure Theory

Another important foundational theory of motivation is the dual-structure theory, which is in many ways similar to the need theories just discussed. This theory was originally called the "two-factor theory," but the more contemporary name used here is more descriptive. This theory has played a major role in managerial thinking about motivation, and even though few researchers today accept the theory, it is nevertheless widely known and accepted among practicing managers.

The dual-structure theory identifies motivation factors, which affect satisfaction, and hygiene factors, which determine dissatisfaction.

Development of the Theory

Frederick Herzberg and his associates developed the **dual-structure theory** in the late 1950s and early 1960s.[17] Herzberg began by interviewing approximately two hundred accountants and engineers in Pittsburgh. He asked them to recall times when they felt especially satisfied and motivated by their jobs and times when they felt particularly dissatisfied and unmotivated. He then asked them to describe what caused the good and bad feelings. The responses to the questions were recorded by the interviewers and later subjected to content analysis. (In a content analysis, the words, phrases, and sentences used by respondents are analyzed and categorized according to their meanings.)

To his surprise, Herzberg found that entirely different sets of factors were associated with the two kinds of feelings about work. For example, a person who indicated "low pay" as a source of dissatisfaction would not necessarily identify "high pay" as a source of satisfaction and motivation. Instead, people associated entirely different causes, such as recognition or achievement, with satisfaction and motivation.

The findings led Herzberg to conclude that prevailing thinking about satisfaction and motivation was incorrect. As Figure 5.4 shows, at the time job satisfaction was being viewed as a single construct ranging from satisfaction to dissatisfaction. If this were the case, Herzberg reasoned, one set of factors should therefore influence movement back and forth along the continuum. But because his research had identified differential influences from two differ-

figure 5.4

The Dual-Structure Theory of Motivation

The traditional view of satisfaction suggested that satisfaction and dissatisfaction were opposite ends of a single dimension. Herzberg's dual-structure theory found evidence of a more complex view. In this theory, motivation factors affect one dimension, ranging from satisfaction to no satisfaction. Other workplace characteristics, called "hygiene factors," are assumed to affect another dimension, ranging from dissatisfaction to no dissatisfaction.

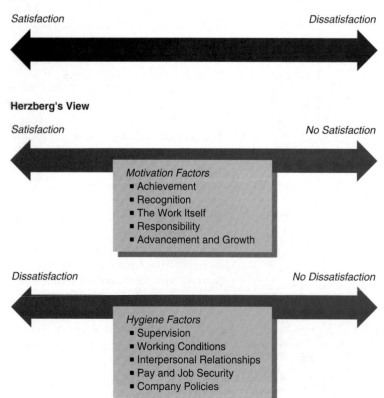

ent sets of factors, Herzberg argued that two different dimensions must be involved. Thus, he saw motivation as a dual-structured phenomenon.

Figure 5.4 also illustrates the dual-structure concept that there is one dimension ranging from satisfaction to no satisfaction and another ranging from dissatisfaction to no dissatisfaction. The two dimensions must presumably be associated with the two sets of factors identified in the initial interviews. Thus, this theory proposed, employees might be either satisfied or not satisfied and, at the same time, dissatisfied or not dissatisfied.[18]

In addition, Figure 5.4 lists the primary factors identified in Herzberg's interviews. **Motivation factors** such as achievement and recognition were often cited by people as primary causes of satisfaction and motivation. When present in a job, these factors apparently could cause satisfaction and motivation; when they were absent, the result was feelings of no satisfaction rather than dissatisfaction. The other set of factors, **hygiene factors,** came out in response to the question about dissatisfaction and lack of motivation. The respondents suggested that pay, job security, supervisors, and working conditions, if seen as inadequate, could lead to feelings of dissatisfaction. When these factors were considered acceptable, however, the person still was not necessarily satisfied; rather, he or she was simply not dissatisfied.[19]

Motivation factors are intrinsic to the work itself and include factors such as achievement and recognition.

Hygiene factors are extrinsic to the work itself and include factors such as pay and job security.

"Offering flexible work hours, generous stock options, and an anything-goes dress code isn't enough, it turns out, if the office is dingy, dull or developer-conceived rather than custom-made."—Kevin Helliker, Wall Street Journal *reporter*[20]

To use the dual-structure theory in the workplace, Herzberg recommended a two-stage process. First, the manager should try to eliminate situations that cause dissatisfaction, which Herzberg assumed to be the more basic of the two dimensions. For example, suppose that Susan Kowalski wants to use the dual-structure theory to enhance motivation in the group of seven technicians she supervises. Her first goal would be to achieve a state of no dissatisfaction by addressing hygiene factors. Imagine, for example, that she discovers that their pay is a bit below market rates and that a few of them are worried about job security. Her response would be to secure a pay raise for them and to allay their concerns about job security.

According to the theory, once a state of no dissatisfaction exists, trying to further improve motivation through hygiene factors is a waste of time. At that point, the motivation factors enter the picture. Thus, when Susan Kowalski is sure that she has adequately dealt with hygiene issues, she should try to increase opportunities for achievement, recognition, responsibility, advancement, and growth. As a result, she would be helping her subordinates feel satisfied and motivated.

Unlike many other theorists, Herzberg described explicitly how managers could apply his theory. In particular, he developed and described a technique called "job enrichment" for structuring employee tasks.[21] (We discuss job enrichment in Chapter 7.) Herzberg tailored this technique to his key motivation factors. This unusual attention to application may explain the widespread popularity of the dual-structure theory among practicing managers.

Evaluation of the Theory

Because it gained popularity so quickly, the dual-structure theory has been scientifically scrutinized more than almost any other organizational behavior theory.[22] The results have been contradictory, to say the least. The initial study by Herzberg and his associates supported the basic premises of the theory, as did a few follow-up studies.[23] In general, studies that use the same methodology as Herzberg did (content analysis of recalled incidents) tend to support the theory. However, this methodology has itself been criticized, and studies that use other methods to measure satisfaction and dissatisfaction frequently obtain results quite different from Herzberg's.[24] If the theory is "method bound," as it appears to be, its validity is therefore questionable.

Several other criticisms have been directed against the theory. Critics say the original sample of accountants and engineers may not represent the general working population. Furthermore, they maintain that the theory fails to account for individual differences. Also, subsequent research has found that a factor such as pay may affect satisfaction in one sample and dissatisfaction in another and that the effect of a given factor depends on the individual's age and organizational level. In addition, the theory does not define the relationship between satisfaction and motivation.

Research has also suggested that the dual-structure framework varies across cultures. Only limited studies have been conducted, but findings suggest that employees in New Zealand and Panama assess the impact of motivation and hygiene factors differently than U.S. workers.[25] It is not surprising, then, that the dual-structure theory is no longer held in high esteem by organizational behavior researchers. Indeed, the field has since adopted far more complex and valid conceptualizations of motivation, most of which we discuss in Chapter 6. But because of its initial popularity and its specific guidance for application, the dual-structure theory merits a special place in the history of motivation research.

Other Important Needs

Each theory discussed so far describes interrelated sets of important individual needs within specific frameworks. Several other key needs have been identified; these needs are not allied with any single integrated theoretical perspective. The three most frequently mentioned are the needs for achievement, affiliation, and power.

The Need for Achievement

The need for achievement is the desire to accomplish a task or goal more effectively than was done in the past.

The **need for achievement** is most frequently associated with the work of David McClelland.[26] This need arises from an individual's desire to accomplish a goal or task more effectively than in the past. Need for achievement has been studied at both the individual and societal levels. At the individual level, the primary aim of research has been to pinpoint the characteristics of those who have a high need for achievement, the outcomes associated with a high need for achievement, and the methods for increasing the need for achievement.

"There's a self-imposed pressure when you get into an environment like HP's [Hewlett-Packard] and you're surrounded by overachievers. You want to be successful and you want the company to be successful."—Craig Byquist, HP manufacturing engineering manager[27]

Characteristics of High-Need Achievers   Individuals who have a high need for achievement tend to set moderately difficult goals and to make moderately risky decisions. For example, when people playing ring toss are allowed to stand anywhere they want to, players with a low need for achievement tend to stand either so close to the target that there is no challenge or so far away that they have little chance of hitting the mark. High-need achievers, however, stand at a distance that offers challenge but also allows frequent success. Suppose, for example, that Mark Cohen, a regional manager for a national retailer, sets a sales increase goal for his stores of either 1 percent or 50 percent. The first goal is probably too easy, and the second is probably impossible to reach. But a mid-range goal of, say, 15 percent might present a reasonable challenge and be within reach. Accepting this goal might more accurately reflect a high need for achievement.

High-need achievers also want immediate, specific feedback on their performance. They want to know how well they did something as quickly after finishing it as possible. For this reason, high-need achievers frequently take jobs in sales, where they get almost immediate feedback from customers, and avoid jobs in areas such as research and development, where tangible progress is slower and feedback comes at longer intervals. If Mark Cohen only asks his managers for their sales performance on a periodic basis, he might not have a high need for achievement. But if he is constantly calling each store manager in his territory to ask about their sales increases, this activity indicates a high need for achievement on his part.

The need for achievement is the desire to accomplish a task or goal more effectively than in the past. Frenchman Guillaume Néry recently set a new world record for diving with no breathing apparatus. Armed only with a set of fins, Néry swam below 87 meters of water (about 285 feet) in 2 minutes and 40 seconds. Only a strong need for achievement could have motivated such a feat.

Preoccupation with work is another characteristic of high-need achievers. They think about it on their way to the workplace, during lunch, and at home. They find it difficult to put their work aside, and they become frustrated when they must stop working on a partly completed project. If Cohen seldom thinks about his business in the evening, he may not be a high-need achiever. However, if work is always on his mind, he might indeed be a high-need achiever.

Finally, high-need achievers tend to assume personal responsibility for getting things done. They often volunteer for extra duties and find it difficult to delegate part of a job to someone else. Accordingly, they derive a feeling of accomplishment when they have done more work than their peers without the assistance of others. Suppose Mark Cohen visits a store one day and finds that the merchandise is poorly displayed, that the floor is dirty, and that sales clerks don't seem motivated to help customers. If he has a low need for achievement, he might point the problems out to the store manager and then leave. But if his need for achievement is high, he may very well stay in the store for a while, personally supervising the changes that need to be made.

Consequences of Achievement   Although high-need achievers tend to be successful, they often do not achieve top management posts. The most common explanation is that although high need for achievement helps these people advance quickly through the ranks, the traits associated with the need often conflict with the requirements of high-level management positions. Because of the amount of work they are expected to do, top executives must be able to delegate tasks to others. In addition, they seldom receive immediate feedback, and they often must make decisions that are either more or less risky than those with which a high-need achiever would be comfortable.[28] High-need achievers tend to do well as individual entrepreneurs with little or no group reinforcement. Steve Jobs, the cofounder of both Apple Computer and NeXT Computer, and Bill Gates, founder and CEO of Microsoft, are both recognized as being high-need achievers.

Achievement and Economic Development   McClelland also conducted research on the need for achievement at the societal level. He believed that a nation's level of economic prosperity correlates with its citizens' need for achievement.[29] The higher the percentage of a country's population that has a high need for achievement, the stronger and more prosperous the nation's economy; conversely, the lower the percentage, the weaker the economy. The reason for this correlation is that high-need achievers tend toward entrepreneurial success. Hence, one would expect a country with many high-need achievers to have a high level of business activity and economic stimulation.

The Need for Affiliation

The need for affiliation is the need for human companionship.

Individuals also experience the **need for affiliation**—the need for human companionship.[30] This view, of course, is consistent with the chapter's opening vignette. Researchers recognize several ways that people with a high need for affiliation differ from those with a lower need. Individuals with a high need tend to want reassurance and approval from others and usually are genuinely concerned about others' feelings. They are likely to act and think as they believe others want them to, especially those with whom they strongly identify and desire friendship. As we might expect, people with a strong need for affiliation most often work in jobs with a lot of interpersonal contact, such as sales and teaching positions.

For example, suppose that Watanka Jackson is seeking a job as a geologist or petroleum field engineer, a job that will take her into remote areas for long periods of time with little interaction with coworkers. Aside from her academic training, one reason for the nature of her job search might be that she has a low need for affiliation. In contrast, a classmate of hers, William Pfeffer, may be seeking a job in the corporate headquarters of a petroleum company. His preferences might be dictated, at least in part, by a desire to be around other people in the workplace; he thus has a higher need for affiliation.

The Need for Power

The need for power is the desire to control the resources in one's environment.

A third major individual need is the **need for power**—the desire to control one's environment, including financial, material, informational, and human resources.[31] People vary greatly along this dimension. Some individuals spend much time and energy seeking power; others avoid power if at all possible. People with a high need for power can be successful managers if three conditions are met. First, they must seek power for the betterment of the organization rather than for their own interests. Second, they must have a fairly low need for affiliation because fulfilling a personal need for power may well alienate others in the workplace. Third, they need plenty of self-control to curb their desire for power when it threatens to interfere with effective organizational or interpersonal relationships.[32]

Integrating the Need-Based Perspectives

This chapter has examined several views of individual motives and needs. Despite their differences, the theories intersect at several points. Both the need hierarchy and the ERG theory, for instance, determined a hierarchy of needs whereas the dual-structure theory proposed two discrete continuums for two need categories. The individual needs identified by each of the three theories are actually strikingly similar. Figure 5.5 illustrates the major likenesses among them.

The hygiene factors described by the dual-structure theory correspond closely to the lower three levels of the need hierarchy. In particular, pay and working conditions correspond to physiological needs, job security and company

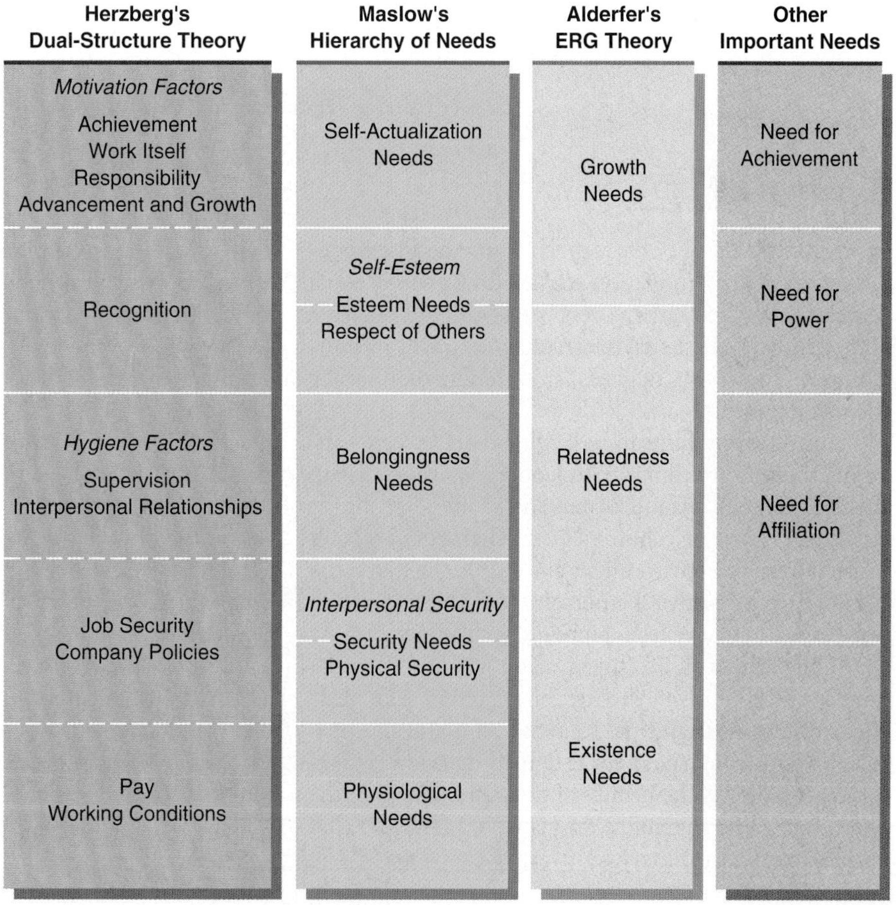

figure 5.5

Parallels Among the Need-Based Perspectives on Motivation

Each of the need theories of motivation reflects its own unique concepts and ideas, but there are also many commonalties and parallels among them. For example, as shown here, certain hygiene factors from the dual-structure theory, such as supervision and interpersonal relations, correspond closely with Maslow's belongingness needs, the ERG theory's relatedness needs, and the need for affiliation.

Herzberg's Dual-Structure Theory	Maslow's Hierarchy of Needs	Alderfer's ERG Theory	Other Important Needs
Motivation Factors Achievement Work Itself Responsibility Advancement and Growth	Self-Actualization Needs	Growth Needs	Need for Achievement
Recognition	*Self-Esteem* Esteem Needs Respect of Others		Need for Power
Hygiene Factors Supervision Interpersonal Relationships	Belongingness Needs	Relatedness Needs	Need for Affiliation
Job Security Company Policies	*Interpersonal Security* Security Needs Physical Security		
Pay Working Conditions	Physiological Needs	Existence Needs	

policies correspond to security needs, and supervision and interpersonal relations correspond to belongingness needs. Meanwhile, the dual-structure motivation factors parallel the top two levels of the need hierarchy. Recognition, for example, is comparable to esteem; achievement, the work itself, responsibility, and advancement and growth might all be categorized as part of the self-actualization process.

There are also clear similarities between Maslow's need hierarchy and the ERG theory. The existence needs in the ERG theory correspond to the physiological and physical security needs in the hierarchy perspective. The relatedness needs overlap with the interpersonal security needs, the belongingness needs, and the need for respect from others in the need hierarchy. Finally, the growth needs correspond to Maslow's self-esteem and self-actualization needs.

The independent individual needs we discussed can also be correlated with the need theories. The need for affiliation clearly is analogous to relatedness needs in the ERG theory, belongingness needs in the need hierarchy, and interpersonal relations in the dual-structure theory. The need for power overlaps with the ERG theory's relatedness and growth needs; the need for achievement parallels ERG's growth needs and the need hierarchy's self-actualization needs.

Unfortunately, despite the many conceptual similarities among the need theories that have emerged over the years, the theories share an inherent weakness—they do an adequate job of describing the factors that motivate behavior, but they tell us very little about the actual processes of motivation.[33] Even if two people are obviously motivated by interpersonal needs, they may pursue quite different paths to satisfy those needs. In Chapter 6, we describe other theories that try to solve that part of the motivation puzzle.

Synopsis

Motivation is the set of forces that cause people to behave as they do. Motivation starts with a need. People search for ways to satisfy their needs and then behave accordingly. Their behavior results in rewards or punishment. To varying degrees, an outcome may satisfy the original need.

A need is anything an individual requires or wants. Primary needs are things that people require to sustain themselves, such as food, water, and shelter. Secondary needs are more psychological in character and are learned from the environment and culture in which the person lives. A motive is a person's reason for choosing one certain behavior from among several choices.

The earliest view of motivation was based on the concept of hedonism, the idea that people seek pleasure and comfort and try to avoid pain and discomfort. Scientific management extended this view, asserting that money is the primary human motivator in the workplace. The human relations view suggested that social factors are primary motivators.

According to Abraham Maslow, human needs are arranged in a hierarchy of importance, from physiological to security to belongingness to esteem and, finally, to self-actualization. The ERG theory is a refinement of Maslow's original hierarchy that includes a frustration-regression component.

In Herzberg's dual-structure theory, satisfaction and dissatisfaction are two distinct dimensions instead of opposite ends of the same dimension. Motivation factors are presumed to affect satisfaction and hygiene factors to affect dissatisfaction. Herzberg's theory is well known among managers but has several deficiencies.

Other important individual needs include the needs for achievement, affiliation, and power. Each of these specific needs has been studied in isolation, and each seems to play a meaningful role in motivation for some people.

Discussion Questions

1. Is it possible for someone to be unmotivated, or is all behavior motivated?

2. In what meaningful ways might the motivational process vary in different cultures?

3. Is it useful to characterize motivation in terms of a deficiency? Why or why not? Is it possible to characterize motivation in terms of excess? If so, how?

4. When has your level of performance been directly affected by your motivation? By your ability? By the environment?

5. What similarities exist between the views of human motivation of scientific management theorists and those of human relations theorists? How do they differ?

6. Identify examples from your own experience that support, and others that refute, Maslow's hierarchy of needs theory.

7. Do you think the hierarchy of needs theory or the ERG model has the greatest value? Explain.

8. Do you agree or disagree with the basic assumptions of Herzberg's dual-structure theory? Why?

9. Which of the need theories discussed in the chapter has the most practical value for managers? Which one has the least practical value?

10. How do you evaluate yourself in terms of your needs for achievement, affiliation, and power?

11. Do you agree or disagree that the need for achievement can be learned? Do you think it might be easier to learn it as a young child or as an adult?

Organizational Behavior Case for Discussion

When Employees Are Owners

What do W. L. Gore, maker of Goretex; a San Diego-based engineering firm named SAIC; and an engine rebuilder called Springfield Remanufacturing that was created as a spin-off from International Harvester have in common? One fundamental similarity is that each firm is owned by its employees. Unlike corporations with many public stockholders or most private firms, which are owned by one or a few individuals, employee-owned firms are private firms in which employees are the primary owners.

Employee ownership is not a new concept in the United States, where cooperatives have owned businesses since Revolutionary War times. During the early part of the twentieth century, labor unions made such tremendous strides forward in improving working conditions and pay that there was little interest in employee ownership. In the 1970s, however, interest in employee ownership was revived at least in part because of the creation of employee stock ownership plans, which contribute company stock to retirement accounts. Twelve percent of the U.S. workforce—about 15 million individuals—have some company ownership while the proportion of ownership ranges from less than 1 percent to 100 percent. Most employee-owned firms were previously profitable divisions of larger corporations that were sold to employees during a divestiture.

Publix Super Markets is a success story—it's the largest employee-owned firm in the United States, with 120,000 employees, 700 store locations in the Southeast, and annual sales of $15.3 billion. The firm has appeared on *Fortune*'s "100 Best Companies to Work For" list for the last five years, is one of *Fortune*'s "Most Admired Companies," wins awards for supporting diversity and families, and in 2002, ranked first in customer satisfaction in its industry. The firm attributes this remarkable success to the fact that it is 100 percent owned by employees. When the United Food and Commercial Workers Union (UFCW) recently tried to organize Publix workers, fewer than 20 percent voted in favor. "On their own time and at their own expense, our [employees] have campaigned against the UFCW. . . . Their voices have now been heard," says Publix spokesperson Lee Brunson.

Employee ownership better aligns the interests of individual workers with the interests of the firm. Ownership also gives workers a sense of loyalty and commitment that is rare in today's uncertain corporate environments. According to Louise Brown, a Gore employee, "Nobody's afraid to jump in. Whenever you need to get the job done, people are always ready to do it." Other benefits of employee ownership include greater job security—Publix has never laid off an employee—and higher creativity. Worker loyalty translates into lower costs because productivity tends to be higher and turnover lower at employee-owned firms.

But there are some inherent risks in employee ownership as well. One potential problem is highlighted by the difficulties at United Airlines, which is 55 percent owned by employees. The company has had continuing struggles with labor unions, especially the powerful pilots' union. Recently, for example, the union's contract remained expired for over a year before an agreement could be reached. Distrust and resentment from both management and labor continue at United in spite of the employee ownership. United's experience contrasts sharply with that of Southwest Airlines, a firm known for its strong company loyalty and productivity and low turnover. The company is only 13 percent employee owned, but the organization culture motivates employees to feel a pride in ownership, which is greater than that felt by United's workers.

At Springfield Remanufacturing, managers found that it was important to educate workers about financial information. CEO Jack Stack organized weekly "huddles" in which all workers in the firm, from top managers to hourly wage earners, meet to discuss company data. "It's about truly understanding the business," says Stack. Workers learned to make use of costs data when making choices such as whether to repair or replace an engine part. Within three years, the firm's stock price soared from $0.10 to $13.60 per share, and 82 percent of that increase was owned by employees.

Virginia Vanderslice of Praxis Consulting claims that employee-owned firms can be high-performing organizations if the organization culture is participa-

tive and empowering. According to Vanderslice, neither participation nor ownership alone creates high performance—rather, the two must be used together. "At some point, employees in companies that have participation without ownership begin asking themselves: 'Why should I participate? What's in it for me?'" Corey Rosen, executive director of the National Center for Employee Ownership, says that it's critical to give workers a meaningful stake in the company, whether it is ownership of shares or the opportunity to participate in decision making. Rosen advises workers, "What's really important is to have an influence on the way you do your day-to-day job."

"What's really important is to have an influence on the way you do your day-to-day job."—Corey Rosen, executive director, National Center for Employee Ownership

References: "Awards," "Careers," "Facts and Figures," "News Room," Publix Super Markets web site. www.publix.com on April 30, 2002; "History," The Worker-Ownership Institute web site. www.workerownership.org on April 29, 2002; Virginia Vanderslice, "Creating Ownership When You Already Have Participation," National Center for Employee Ownership web site. www.nceo.org on April 29, 2002; Wendy Zellner, "What's Weighing Down the Big Carriers," *Business Week*, April 29, 2002. www.businessweek.com on April 30, 2002; Laird Harrison, "We're All the Boss," *Time*, April 8, 2002, Inside Business Bonus pages (quotation); Jacquelyn Yates and Marilyn Kelly, "The 100 Largest Majority Employee-Owned Companies (and What Makes Them Great)," "The Employee Ownership 100," *Business Ethics*, September-October 2000. www.business-ethics.com on April 30, 2002.

Case Questions

1. Using Maslow's hierarchy of needs, as described in Chapter 5 of your text, explain why having ownership of their company is motivating to workers.
2. Would employee ownership be considered a motivation factor or a hygiene factor according to Herzberg's dual-structure theory? Why?
3. What additional actions could managers take to improve employee motivation, other than giving ownership and allowing participation? Use need theories of motivation to answer this question.

 ## Experiencing Organizational Behavior

Relating Your Needs to the Theories of Motivation

Purpose: This exercise asks you to apply the theories discussed in the chapter to your own needs and motives.

Format: First, you will develop a list of things you want from life. Then you will categorize them according to one of the theories in the chapter. Next, you will discuss your results with a small group of classmates.

Procedure: Prepare a list of approximately fifteen things you want from life. These can be very specific (such as a new car) or very general (such as a feeling of accomplishment in school). Try to include some things you want right now and other things you want later in life. Next, choose the one motivational theory discussed in this chapter that best fits your set of needs. Classify each item from your "wish list" in terms of the need or needs it might satisfy.

Your instructor will then divide the class into groups of three. Spend a few minutes in the group discussing each person's list and its classification according to needs.

After the small-group discussions, your instructor will reconvene the entire class. Discussion should center on the extent to which each theory can serve as a useful framework for classifying individual needs. Students who found that their needs could be neatly categorized and those who found little correlation between their needs and the theories are especially encouraged to share their results.

Follow-up Questions

1. As a result of this exercise, do you now have more or less trust in need theories as viable management tools?
2. Could a manager use some form of this exercise in an organizational setting to enhance employee motivation?

 # Self-Assessment Exercise

Assessing Your Own Needs

Introduction: Needs are one factor that influences motivation. The following assessment surveys your judgments about your personal needs that might be partially shaping your motivation.

Introduction: Judge how descriptively accurate each of the following statements is about you. You may find making a decision difficult in some cases, but you should force a choice. Record your answers next to each statement according to the following scale:

Very Descriptive of Me   = 5
Fairly Descriptive of Me   = 4
Somewhat Descriptive of Me   = 3
Not Very Descriptive of Me   = 2
Not Descriptive of Me at All   = 1

_____ 1. I aspire to accomplish difficult tasks, maintain high standards, and am willing to work toward distant goals.

_____ 2. I enjoy being with friends and people in general and accept people readily.

_____ 3. I am easily annoyed and am sometimes willing to hurt people to get my way.

_____ 4. I try to break away from restraints or restrictions of any kind.

_____ 5. I want to be the center of attention and enjoy having an audience.

_____ 6. I speak freely and tend to act on the "spur of the moment."

_____ 7. I assist others whenever possible, giving sympathy and comfort to those in need.

_____ 8. I believe in the saying that "there is a place for everything and everything should be in its place." I dislike clutter.

_____ 9. I express my opinions forcefully, enjoy the role of leader, and try to control my environment as much as I can.

_____ 10. I want to understand many areas of knowledge and value synthesizing ideas and generalization.

Interpretation: This set of needs was developed by H. A. Murray, a psychologist, in 1938, and operationalized by another psychologist, J. W. Atkinson. These needs correspond one-to-one to the items on the assessment questionnaire. Known as Murray's Manifest Needs because they are visible through behavior, they are

1. Achievement
2. Affiliation
3. Aggression
4. Autonomy

5. Exhibition
6. Impulsivity
7. Nurturance
8. Order
9. Power
10. Understanding

Although little research has evaluated Murray's theory, the different needs have been researched. People seem

to have a different profile of needs underlying their motivations at different ages. The more any one or more are descriptive of you, the more you see yourself as having that particular need active in your motivational makeup. For more information, see H. A. Murray, *Explorations in Personality* (New York: Oxford University Press, 1938); and J. W. Atkinson, *An Introduction to Motivation* (Princeton, N.J.: Van Nostrand, 1964).

OB Online

1. Use a search engine to locate web sites that deal with such topics as human needs and motivation. Then discuss how the information you found relates to this chapter.
2. Find two web sites that discuss Frederick Taylor and his work. Then explain how they relate to the discussion in this chapter.

3. Find a web site that discusses Herzberg's theory. Determine whether the site presents a positive, negative, or balanced assessment.
4. Use a search engine to find more information about the need for achievement, affiliation, or power. Then discuss how the information you found relates to this chapter.

Building Managerial Skills

Exercise Overview: Conceptual skills are the manager's ability to think in the abstract. This exercise will help you apply conceptual skills to better understand the need for achievement.

Exercise Task: First, identify someone you consider to have a high need for achievement. This individual can be a friend, family member, classmate, business associate, or coworker. Next, interview this individual. Using questions in your own words, try to assess how this individual measures up on the following five characteristics of high need achievers:

- Sets moderately difficult goals
- Makes moderately risky decisions
- Wants specific and immediate feedback
- Is preoccupied with task
- Assumes personal responsibility

Finally, based on the answers to your questions, further assess (or reassess) the extent to which this individual truly has a high need for achievement.

6 Process-Based Perspectives on Motivation

Management Preview

The process-based perspectives on motivation focus on how people behave in their efforts to satisfy their needs.

▶ In Chapter 5 we introduced the concept of employee motivation in organizations and discussed several need-based perspectives. The general distinction between those basic approaches and the more advanced theories discussed in this chapter rests on the difference between *content* and *process*. The need-based theories reflect a content perspective in that they attempt to describe what factor or factors motivate behavior—they try to list specific things that motivate behavior. The more sophisticated **process-based perspectives** introduced in this chapter focus on how motivated behavior occurs—they explain how people go about satisfying their needs. Process-based perspectives also describe how people choose among behavioral alternatives. We begin this chapter by discussing the equity theory of motivation, and then we describe the expectancy theory. Next, we discuss learning and reinforcement, organizational behavior modification, and attribution theory. First, though, let's examine how motivation has played a key role in the success of Commerce Bancorp.

▼ ▼ ▼

I f you're like most people, it's been a while since you were inside your bank actually communicating face to face with an employee. Driven by cost concerns, many banks are actually discouraging customers from entering their building and instead are relying on drive-through windows, the Internet, or ATM machines for many routine transactions. And when you do need to visit the bank's building, you probably often encounter those inconvenient "banker's hours." One firm, though, New Jersey–based Commerce Bancorp, is virtually alone in encouraging use of branches and staying open longer hours, including nights, weekends, and holidays. "Everyone else has given up on branches, . . . but people will always choose to bank in person. The problem with most banks is that they abuse their customers every day. We want to wow ours," says CEO Vernon Hill. The heart of the firm's customer service strategy is having high-performing employees who can welcome customers, serve them efficiently, and build lasting personal relationships.

Hill, a former property locator for McDonald's, thinks of his business as retailing rather than banking. Says Dennis DiFlorio, chief retail officer, "The greatest insult you can give someone here is to say, 'You're thinking like a banker.'" To help employees shift their focus from money to providing customers with that "wow" service experience, new hires receive training at Commerce University. Hill tells the new managers, "We're asking you to forget the way you delivered your skills at other banks. In many ways, you have joined a service cult."

The "Kill a Stupid Rule" program pays $50 when workers identify a rule that interferes with great customer service. Even job applicants must have the right attitude. "This is not the job for someone who's interested in being cool or indifferent," says Wow Department Vice President John Manning. After being carefully selected and trained, Commerce employees regularly earn rewards, which can be $5,000 when a competing nearby branch bank closes, balloon bouquets, congratulatory notes, or pictures with Mr. C or Buzz, the company's mascots. Silliness and fun, two qualities that are rarely encouraged in the staid banking industry, prevail at Commerce. For example, the Wow Patrol routinely visits branches, rewarding high-performing staffers while singing songs, giving candy to customers, and leading group cheers.

"This is not the job for someone who's interested in being cool or indifferent."
—John Manning, Wow Department vice president, Commerce Bancorp

Commerce's organization culture emphasizes rewarding high performers. Maintaining the consistency of rewards and using desirable rewards are also priorities. Mystery shoppers report on every detail of their experience, so having just one associate who gives incorrect information or fails to smile can keep the entire branch from getting a "wow" rating. Managers are competitive for the scarce rewards, says Jennifer Perrone, an assistant manager. "I don't want to give it [the trophy] up. I'm obsessed with it. I leave notes for my tellers in the drive-through all the time to remind them to smile," she adds.

Having highly motivated employees seems to be paying off for Commerce. For example, Commerce holds market shares of up to 50 percent in some cities while paying below-average interest. Their high deposits give the company a larger and cheaper pool of money to lend. The high levels of customer satisfaction and profits have brought the attention of investors—Commerce stock value is increasing at a time when most bank stocks are declining. At Commerce bank, the motivation seems to be contagious.

References: "Branch Locations," Commerce Bancorp web site. bank.commerceonline.com on May 1, 2002; "Business Summary: Commerce Bancorp," "Analysts' Opinions," *Business Week* web site. research.businessweek.com on May 1, 2002; "Zacks Issues Recommendations on 4 Stocks: CHS, EMC, CBH, and PG," Hoover's Online web site. hoovnews.hoovers.com on May 1, 2002; Chuck Salter, "Customer Service: Commerce Bank," *Fast Company*, Fifth Annual Best of the Business issue, May 2002, pp. 80–91 (quotation p. 86). See www.fastcompany.com; Steve Watkins, "It's a Bank, It's a Retail Firm, It's . . . Both?" *Investor's Business Daily*, February 4, 2002. www.investors.com on May 1, 2002; Jeffrey R. Kosnett, "Ready for Long-Term Commitment?" *Kiplinger's*, November 2001. www.kiplinger.com on May 1, 2002; Jack Milligan, "He'll Take Manhattan," *U.S. Banker*, October 1, 2001. www.us-banker.com on May 1, 2002.

Commerce Bancorp is clearly working to create a business model that is unique in its industry. The firm wants to instill high levels of motivation in all its employees, for example, and anticipates that this motivation will translate into higher earnings for the company itself. But rather than relying simply on bigger rewards, Commerce is trying to make motivation a fundamental business principle. This approach, in turn, provides interesting insights into how motivational processes work in organizations. Specifically, various complex theories and frameworks that describe or address motivational processes can shed new light on how and why employees behave as they do and help managers structure rewards and other work-related outcomes so as to enhance employee motivation and performance.[1] We begin our discussion of these theories and frameworks with equity theory.

The Equity Theory of Motivation

Equity theory focuses on people's desire to be treated with what they perceive as equity and to avoid perceived inequity.

Equity is the belief that we are being treated fairly in relation to others; inequity is the belief that we are being treated unfairly in relation to others.

The **equity theory** of motivation is based on the relatively simple premise that people in organizations want to be treated fairly.[2] The theory defines **equity** as the belief that we are being treated fairly in relation to others and **inequity** as the belief that we are being treated unfairly compared with others. Equity theory is just one of several theoretical formulations derived from social comparison processes. Social comparisons involve evaluating our own situation in terms of others' situations. In this chapter, we focus mainly on equity theory because it is the most highly developed of the social comparison approaches and the one that applies most directly to the work motivation of people in organizations.

Forming Equity Perceptions

People in organizations form perceptions of the equity of their treatment through a four-step process. First, they evaluate how they are being treated by the firm. Second, they form a perception of how a "comparison-other" is being treated. The comparison-other might be a person in the same work group, someone in another part of the organization, or even a composite of several people scattered throughout the organization.[3] Third, they compare their own circumstances with those of the comparison-other and then use this comparison as the basis for forming an impression of either equity or inequity. Fourth, depending on the strength of this feeling, the person may choose to pursue one or more of the alternatives discussed in the next section.

Equity theory describes the equity comparison process in terms of an input-to-outcome ratio. Inputs are an individual's contributions to the organization—such factors as education, experience, effort, and loyalty. Outcomes are what the person receives in return—pay, recognition, social relationships, intrinsic rewards, and similar things. In effect, then, this part of the equity process is essentially a personal assessment of one's psychological contract. A person's assessments of inputs and outcomes for both self and others are based partly on objective data (for example, the person's own salary) and partly on perceptions (such as the comparison-other's level of recognition). The equity comparison thus takes the following form:

$$\frac{\text{Outcomes (self)}}{\text{Inputs (self)}} \quad \text{compared with} \quad \frac{\text{Outcomes (other)}}{\text{Inputs (other)}}$$

If the two sides of this psychological equation are comparable, the person experiences a feeling of equity; if the two sides do not balance, a feeling of inequity results. We should stress, however, that a perception of equity does not require that the perceived outcomes and inputs be equal, but only that their ratios be the same. A person may believe that his comparison-other deserves to make more

WORKING WITH DIVERSITY

Are Female CEOs Underpaid?

In general, compensation is based on two sets of factors: the labor market and the nature of the job itself. As a result, corporate CEOs are generally very highly paid because few people are qualified and because the position is both demanding and very difficult. And indeed, CEO compensation in the United States is quite high. But meaningful differences among CEO salaries nevertheless exist. Although it may be no surprise that female CEOs are paid less than their male counterparts, it may come as a shock that female CEOs are also paid less than women in lower-ranking positions.

Of the top twenty male earners, fourteen are CEOs while just one female CEO is among the top twenty women earners. Andrea Jung, the CEO of Avon Products, is the highest-paid American female CEO, and her salary lags behind those of thirteen other businesswomen. Her compensation in 2001 wasn't miserly at $7.7 million, including $2 million in salary and $5.7 million in long-term pay. However, it's nowhere near the total compensation of Yahoo! Senior Vice President Heather Killen, who earned $32.7 million, or Charles Schwab Chief Information Officer Dawn G. Lepore, who received $22.3 million. Also included in the list of top female earners are vice presidents, chief operating officers, and chief financial officers from firms such as 3Com, Wells Fargo Bank, Lucent, and Goldman Sachs and grocer Safeway. After Jung, the next female CEOs on the list are Marion Sandler of Golden West Financial (number twenty-four with $4 mil-lion) and Carly Fiorina of Hewlett-Packard (number twenty-six with $3.7 million).

Differences exist because some CEOs, such as Lillian Vernon, took voluntary pay cuts after their companies' poor financial results last year. Also, female top managers

> *"The more senior [the women managers] get, the more subtle the barriers become, and the more profoundly they operate."*—Debra Meyerson, visiting professor, Stanford University

are more common at traditional, older firms, which pay less than technology companies. According to Mary C. Mattis, research fellow at women's business think tank Catalyst, "Generally speaking, the new industries are not level playing fields for women." Debra Meyerson, a visiting professor at Stanford University, believes that gender barriers remain even at the top level: "The more senior [the women managers] get, the more subtle the barriers become, and the more profoundly they operate." Pay differentials violate the principles of equity theory, but the real story is that today there are more female top managers, and their compensation is growing. These trends can only be good for women—and for business.

References: Anne Fisher, "What Does It Take to Get a Man-Sized Salary?" *Fortune*, February 18, 2002. www.fortune.com on May 8, 2002; Louis Lavelle, "For Female CEOs, It's Stingy at the Top," *Business Week*, April 23, 2001, pp. 70–71 (quotation p. 71). See www.businessweek.com; Sue Zeidler, "Female CEOs Don't See Any Gender Bias on Internet," *Detroit News*, March 12, 2000. detnews.com on May 9, 2002.

money because she works harder, thus making her higher ratio of outcome to input acceptable. Only if the other person's outcomes seem disproportionate to her inputs does the comparison provoke a perception of inequity. The "Working with Diversity" box highlights some equity issues in the compensation of women executives in some firms.

Responses to Equity and Inequity

Figure 6.1 summarizes the results of an equity comparison. If a person feels equitably treated, she is generally motivated to maintain the status quo. For example, she will continue to provide the same level of input to the organization as long as her outcomes do not change and the inputs and outcomes of the comparison-other do not change. But a person who is experiencing inequity—real or imagined—is motivated to reduce it. Moreover, the greater the inequity, the stronger the level of motivation.

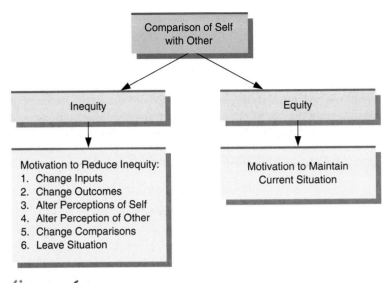

figure 6.1

Responses to Perceptions of Equity and Inequity

People form equity perceptions by comparing their situation with that of someone else. If they experience equity, they are motivated to maintain the current situation. If they experience inequity, they are motivated to use one or more of the strategies shown here to reduce the inequity.

People may use one of six common methods to reduce inequity.[4] First, we may change our own inputs. Thus, we may put more or less effort into the job, depending on which way the inequity lies, as a way to alter our ratio. If we believe we are being underpaid, for example, we may decide not to work as hard.

Second, we may change our own outcomes. We might, for example, demand a pay raise, seek additional avenues for growth and development, or even resort to stealing as a way to "get more" from the organization. Or we might alter our perceptions of the value of our current outcomes, perhaps by deciding that our present level of job security is greater and more valuable than we originally thought.

A third, more complex response is to alter our perceptions of ourselves and our behavior. After perceiving an inequity, for example, we may change our original self-assessment and decide that we are really contributing less but receiving more than we originally believed. For example, we might decide that we are not really working as many hours as we first thought—for example, that some of our time spent in the office is really just socializing and not really contributing to the organization.

Fourth, we may alter our perception of the other's inputs or outcomes. After all, much of our assessment of other people is based on perceptions, and perceptions can be changed. For example, if we feel underrewarded, we may decide that our comparison-other is working more hours than we originally believed—say by coming in on weekends and taking work home at night.

Fifth, we may change the object of comparison. We may conclude, for instance, that the current comparison-other is the boss's personal favorite, is unusually lucky, or has special skills and abilities. A different person would thus provide a more valid basis for comparison. Indeed, we might change comparison-others fairly often.

Finally, as a last resort, we may simply leave the situation. That is, we might decide that the only way to feel better about things is to be in a different situation altogether. Transferring to another department or seeking a new job may be the only way to reduce the inequity.

Evaluation and Implications

Most research on equity theory has been narrowly focused, dealing with only one ratio—between pay (hourly and piece-rate) and the quality or quantity of worker output given overpayment and underpayment.[5] Findings support the predictions of equity theory quite consistently, especially when the worker feels underpaid. When people being paid on a piece-rate basis experience inequity, they tend to reduce their inputs by decreasing quality and to increase their outcomes by producing more units of work. When a person paid by the hour experiences inequity, the theory predicts an increase in quality and quantity if the person feels overpaid and a decrease in quality and quantity if the person feels underpaid. Research provides stronger support for responses to underpayment than for responses to overpayment, but overall, most studies appear to uphold the basic premises of the theory. One interesting new twist on equity theory suggests that some people are more sensitive than others to perceptions of inequity. That is, some people pay a good deal of attention to their relative standing within the organization. Others focus more on their own situation without considering the situations of others.[6]

"It's really the high-performer we should be rewarding with time off, instead of seniority."—Bruce Tulgan, human resources consultant[7]

The equity theory of motivation suggests that people compare themselves with others in terms of their inputs to their organization relative to their outcomes. But in these days of high-stress jobs and overworked employees, equity perceptions may be about as stable as a house of cards. Take Sherri Stoddard, for example. Stoddard is a registered nurse. Efforts to lower health care costs have caused nurses to take on ever-growing patient loads. In addition, they often have mandatory overtime requirements and mountains of paperwork. While their compensation has grown slightly, many nurses like Stoddard are feeling that they are being asked to do too much for what they are paid.

Social comparisons clearly are a powerful factor in the workplace. For managers, the most important implication of equity theory concerns organizational rewards and reward systems. Because "formal" organizational rewards (pay, task assignments, and so forth) are more easily observable than "informal" rewards (intrinsic satisfaction, feelings of accomplishment, and so forth), they are often central to a person's perceptions of equity.

Equity theory offers managers three messages. First, everyone in the organization needs to understand the basis for rewards. If people are to be rewarded more for high-quality work rather than for quantity of work, for instance, that fact needs to be clearly communicated to everyone. Second, people tend to take a multifaceted view of their rewards; they perceive and experience a variety of rewards, some tangible and others intangible. Finally, people base their actions on their perceptions of reality. If two people make exactly the same salary, but each thinks the other makes more, each will base his or her experience of equity on the perception, not the reality. Hence, even if a manager believes two employees are being fairly rewarded, the employees themselves may not necessarily agree if their perceptions differ from the manager's.

The Expectancy Theory of Motivation

E xpectancy theory is a more encompassing model of motivation than equity theory. Over the years since its original formulation, the theory's scope and complexity have continued to grow.

The Basic Expectancy Model

The basic expectancy theory model emerged from the work of Edward Tolman and Kurt Lewin.[8] Victor Vroom, however, is generally credited with first applying the theory to motivation in the workplace.[9] The theory attempts to determine how individuals choose among alternative behaviors. The basic premise of **expectancy theory** is that motivation depends on how much we want something and how likely we think we are to get it.

A simple example further illustrates this premise. Suppose a recent college graduate is looking for her first managerial job. While scanning the want ads, she sees that Shell Oil is seeking a new executive vice president to oversee its foreign operations. The starting salary is $600,000. The student would love the job, but she does not bother to apply because she recognizes that she has no chance of getting it. Reading on, she sees a position that involves scraping bubble gum from underneath desks in college classrooms. The starting pay is $5.85 an hour, and no experience is necessary. Again, she is unlikely to apply—even though she assumes she could get the job, she does not want it.

Then she comes across an advertisement for a management training position with a large company known for being an excellent place to work. No experience is necessary, the primary requirement is a college degree, and the starting salary is $37,000. She will probably apply for this position because (1) she wants it, and (2) she thinks she has a reasonable chance of getting it. (Of course, this simple example understates the true complexity of most choices. Job-seeking students may have strong geographic preferences, have other job opportunities, and also be considering graduate school. Most decisions of this type, in fact, are quite complex.)

Figure 6.2 summarizes the basic expectancy model. The model's general components are effort (the result of motivated behavior), performance, and outcomes, consistent with our discussion in Chapter 5. Expectancy theory emphasizes the linkages among these elements, which are described in terms of expectancies and valences.

Effort-to-Performance Expectancy   **Effort-to-performance expectancy** is a person's perception of the probability that effort will lead to successful performance. If we believe our effort will lead to higher performance, this expectancy is very strong, perhaps approaching a probability of 1.0, where 1.0 equals absolute certainty that the outcome will occur. If we believe our performance will be the same no matter how much effort we make, our expectancy is very low—perhaps as low as 0, meaning that there is no probability that the outcome will occur. A person who thinks there is a moderate relationship between effort and subsequent performance—the normal circumstance—has an expectancy somewhere between 1.0 and 0. Mia Hamm, a star soccer player who believes that she has a great chance of scoring higher than any opponent when she puts forth maximum effort, clearly sees a link between her effort and performance.

Expectancy theory suggests that people are motivated by how much they want something and the likelihood they perceive of getting it.

Effort-to-performance expectancy is a person's perception of the probability that effort will lead to performance.

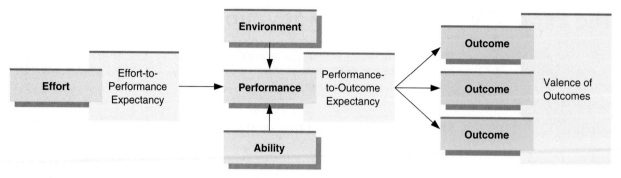

figure 6.2

The Expectancy Theory of Motivation

The expectancy theory is the most complex model of employee motivation in organizations. As shown here, the key components of expectancy theory are effort-to-performance expectancy, performance-to-outcome expectancy, and outcomes, each of which has an associated valence. These components interact with effort, the environment, and the ability to determine an individual's performance.

Performance-to-outcome expectancy is the individual's perception of the probability that performance will lead to certain outcomes.

Performance-to-Outcome Expectancy   **Performance-to-outcome expectancy** is a person's perception of the probability that performance will lead to certain other outcomes. If a person thinks a high performer is certain to get a pay raise, this expectancy is close to 1.0. At the other extreme, a person who believes raises are entirely independent of performance has an expectancy close to 0. Finally, if a person thinks performance has some bearing on the prospects for a pay raise, his or her expectancy is somewhere between 1.0 and 0. In a work setting, several performance-to-outcome expectancies are relevant because, as Figure 6.2 shows, several outcomes might logically result from performance. Each outcome, then, has its own expectancy. Green Bay's quarterback Brett Favre may believe that if he plays aggressively all the time (performance), he has a great chance of leading his team to the playoffs. Playing aggressively may win him individual honors like the Most Valuable Player award, but he may also experience more injuries and physical trauma. (All three anticipated results are outcomes.)

The expectancy theory of motivation suggests that people are motivated to pursue outcomes that they value and they believe they have a reasonable probability of attaining. Rock star Bono and treasury secretary Paul O'Neill recently toured impoverished areas of Africa together. The publicity generated by the anti-establishment rocker and the conservative government official odd couple has helped bring renewed attention to the problem. In a nutshell, the two individuals saw a problem, decided how they could help address it, and then worked together to accomplish their goal.

Outcomes and Valences   An **outcome** is anything that might potentially result from performance. High-level performance conceivably might produce such outcomes as a pay raise, a promotion, recognition from the boss, fatigue, stress, or less time to rest, among others. The **valence** of an outcome is the relative attractiveness or unattractiveness—the value—of that outcome to the person. Pay raises, promotions, and recognition might all have positive valences whereas fatigue, stress, and less time to rest might all have negative valences.

The strength of outcome valences varies from person to person. Work-related stress may be a significant negative factor for one person but only a slight annoyance to another. Similarly, a pay increase may have a strong positive valence for someone desperately in need of money, a slight positive valence for someone interested mostly in getting a promotion—or, for someone in an unfavorable tax position, even a negative valence!

The basic expectancy framework suggests that three conditions must be met before motivated behavior occurs. First, the effort-to-performance expectancy must be well above zero. That is, the worker must reasonably expect that exerting effort will produce high levels of performance. Second, the performance-to-outcome expectancies must be well above zero. Thus, the person must believe that performance will realistically result in valued outcomes. Third, the sum of all the valences for the potential outcomes relevant to the person must be positive. One or more valences may be negative as long as the positives outweigh the negatives. For example, stress and fatigue may have moderately negative valences, but if pay, promotion, and recognition have very high positive valences, the overall valence of the set of outcomes associated with performance will still be positive.

Conceptually, the valences of all relevant outcomes and the corresponding pattern of expectancies are assumed to interact in an almost mathematical fashion to determine a person's level of motivation. Most people do assess likelihoods of and preferences for various consequences of behavior, but they seldom approach them in such a calculating manner.

"Even if I were to get a better job offer somewhere else, I would have to think twice about giving up the kind of benefits that my company offers."—Katherine Lechler, graphics designer for CMP trade magazine[10]

The Porter-Lawler Model

The original presentation of expectancy theory placed it squarely in the mainstream of contemporary motivation theory. Since then, the model has been refined and extended many times. Most modifications have focused on identifying and measuring outcomes and expectancies. An exception is the variation of expectancy theory developed by Porter and Lawler. These researchers used expectancy theory to develop a novel view of the relationship between employee satisfaction and performance.[11] Although the conventional wisdom was that satisfaction leads to performance, Porter and Lawler argued the reverse: If rewards are adequate, high levels of performance may lead to satisfaction.

An outcome is anything that results from performing a particular behavior.

Valence is the degree of attractiveness or unattractiveness a particular outcome has for a person.

The Porter-Lawler model appears in Figure 6.3. Some of its features are quite different from the original version of expectancy theory. For example, the extended model includes abilities, traits, and role perceptions. At the beginning of the motivational cycle, effort is a function of the value of the potential reward for the employee (its valence) and the perceived effort-reward probability (an expectancy). Effort then combines with abilities, traits, and role perceptions to determine actual performance.

Performance results in two kinds of rewards. Intrinsic rewards are intangible—a feeling of accomplishment, a sense of achievement, and so forth. Extrinsic rewards are tangible outcomes such as pay and promotion. The individual judges the

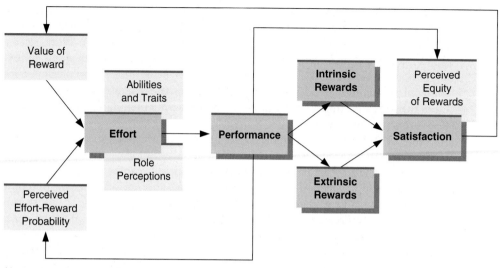

figure 6.3

The Porter-Lawler Model

The Porter and Lawler expectancy model provides interesting insights into the relationships between satisfaction and performance. As illustrated here, this model predicts that satisfaction is determined by the perceived equity of intrinsic and extrinsic rewards for performance. That is, rather than satisfaction causing performance, which many people might predict, this model argues that it is actually performance that eventually leads to satisfaction.

Reference: Figure from Porter, Lyman W., and Edward E. Lawler, *Managerial Attitudes and Performance.* Copyright © 1968. Reproduced by permission of the publisher, McGraw-Hill, Inc.

value of his or her performance to the organization and uses social comparison processes (as in equity theory) to form an impression of the equity of the rewards received. If the rewards are regarded as equitable, the employee feels satisfied. In subsequent cycles, satisfaction with rewards influences the value of the rewards anticipated, and actual performance following effort influences future perceived effort-reward probabilities. The "Talking Technology" box provides another perspective on performance and its relationship to motivation and satisfaction by examining older and younger workers' reactions to the addition of technology in the workplace.

Evaluation and Implications

Expectancy theory has been tested by many different researchers in a variety of settings and using a variety of methods.[12] As noted earlier, the complexity of the theory has been both a blessing and a curse.[13] Nowhere is this double-edged quality more apparent than in the research undertaken to evaluate the theory. Several studies have supported various parts of the theory. For example, both kinds of expectancy and valence have been found to be associated with effort and performance in the workplace.[14] Research has also confirmed expectancy theory's claims that people will not engage in motivated behavior unless they (1) value the expected rewards, (2) believe their efforts will lead to performance, and (3) believe their performance will result in the desired rewards.[15]

However, expectancy theory is so complicated that researchers have found it quite difficult to test. In particular, the measures of various parts of the model may

TALKING TECHNOLOGY

▶ *Technology as a Motivator?*

There was a time when blue-collar manufacturing jobs were the ideal career for those seeking refuge from the demands of technology. Through the 1970s, some production workers chose that line of work because they disliked school and didn't care to earn a college degree. One such worker, David Erb, a technician at Techneglas, Inc., recalls, "When I finished high school, I said: 'Enough.'" But those days are gone. Recent advances in high-tech manufacturing have made factory-floor occupations among the most technology intensive. Although some workers welcome the change, others are less enchanted by this brave new world.

The Columbus, Ohio, plant of Techneglas seems at first glance to be a throwback to earlier times—the firm makes the glass funnels for television-picture tubes. Right now, demand for TVs is robust, but flat-screen TVs that don't need picture tubes are beginning to find their way into homes. Within the plant, however, a technology revolution has taken place. New equipment includes electronic quality monitoring machines and computers on the factory floor.

All the plant workers are under constant pressure to learn new skills, but some older employees have taken early retirement rather than increase their computer or math skills. The plant has a learning center, but Heidi LoRash-Neuenschwander, who runs it, says, "Older workers often demand to know exactly what they're going to get out of learning new skills; while younger workers just want to learn." The younger workers often do have better technology skills; after all, most of them used personal computers in high school. But even when these workers' skills are weaker, everyone assumes that younger people understand technology better. David Erb sees another dif-

> *"Older workers often demand to know exactly what they're going to get out of learning new skills, while younger workers just want to learn."—Heidi LoRash-Neuenschwander, head of the learning lab at the Dayton, Ohio, Techneglas factory*

ference, too. According to him, younger employees often want the "latest and greatest" technology, even when the upgrade confers no real benefit.

One explanation for this generational technology divide is the difference in factors that motivate the two lands of workers. Older workers, nervous about retirement, tend to look for job stability and security. They say that younger workers look for any kind of labor-saving device because they are "lazy" and "just want to play." Younger workers, however, claim that learning about technology is "fun" and motivating in itself. Perhaps the difference can be explained by the Porter-Lawler extension to expectancy theory. Older workers want to be motivated first and then they will achieve high performance. For the younger employees, achievement may occur first, leading to higher motivation.

References: Aaron Bernstein, "Too Many Workers? Not for Long," *Business Week*, May 20, 2002. www.businessweek.com on May 19, 2002; Ed Michaels, Helen Handfield-Jones, and Beth Axelrod, *The War for Talent*, excerpt reprinted in *Business Week*, December 12, 2001. www.businessweek.com on May 19, 2002; Timothy Aeppel, "Young and Old See Technology Sparking Friction on Shop Floor," *Wall Street Journal*, April 7, 2000, pp. A1–A10 (quotation p. A10). See www.wsj.com.

lack validity, and the procedures for investigating relationships among the variables have often been less scientific than researchers would like. Moreover, people are seldom as rational and objective in choosing behaviors as expectancy theory implies. Still, the logic of the model, combined with the consistent, albeit modest, research support for it, suggests that the theory has much to offer.

Research has also suggested that expectancy theory is more likely to explain motivation in the United States than in other countries. People from the United States tend to be very goal-oriented and to think that they can influence their own success. Thus, under the right combinations of expectancies, valences, and outcomes, they will be highly motivated. But different patterns may exist in other countries. For example, many people from Moslem countries think that God determines the outcome of every behavior, so the concept of expectancy is not applicable.[16]

Because expectancy theory is so complex, it is difficult to apply directly in the workplace. A manager would need to figure out what rewards each employee wants and how valuable those rewards are to each person, measure the various expectancies, and finally adjust the relationships to create motivation. Nevertheless, expectancy theory offers several important guidelines for the practicing manager. The following are some of the more fundamental guidelines:

1. Determine the primary outcomes each employee wants.
2. Decide what levels and kinds of performance are needed to meet organizational goals.
3. Make sure the desired levels of performance are possible.
4. Link desired outcomes and desired performance.
5. Analyze the situation for conflicting expectancies.
6. Make sure the rewards are large enough.
7. Make sure the overall system is equitable for everyone.[17]

Learning and Motivation

Learning is a relatively permanent change in behavior or behavioral potential resulting from direct or indirect experience.

Learning is another key component in employee motivation. In any organization, employees quickly learn which behaviors are rewarded and which are ignored or punished. Thus, learning plays a critical role in maintaining motivated behavior. **Learning** is a relatively permanent change in behavior or behavioral potential that results from direct or indirect experience. For example, we can learn to use a new software application program by practicing and experimenting with its various functions and options.

How Learning Occurs

Classical conditioning is a simple form of learning that links a conditioned response with an unconditioned stimulus.

The Traditional View: Classical Conditioning   The most influential historical approach to learning is classical conditioning, developed by Ivan Pavlov in his famous experiments with dogs.[18] **Classical conditioning** is a simple form of learning in which a conditioned response is linked with an unconditioned stimulus. In organizations, however, only simple behaviors and responses can be learned in this manner. For example, suppose an employee receives very bad news one day from his boss. It's possible that the employee could come to associate, say, the color of the boss's suit that day with bad news. Thus, the next time the boss wears that same suit to the office, the employee may experience dread and foreboding.

But this form of learning is obviously simplistic and not directly relevant to motivation. Learning theorists soon recognized that although classical conditioning offered some interesting insights into the learning process, it was inadequate as an explanation of human learning. For one thing, classical conditioning relies on simple cause-and-effect relationships between one stimulus and one response; it cannot deal with the more complex forms of learned behavior that typify human beings. For another, classical conditioning ignores the concept of choice; it assumes that behavior is reflexive, or involuntary. Therefore, this perspective cannot explain situations in which people consciously and rationally choose one course of action from among many. Because of these shortcomings of classical conditioning, theorists eventually moved on to other approaches that seemed more useful in ex-

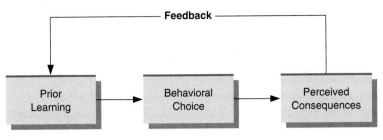

figure 6.4

Learning as a Cognitive Process

Contemporary thinking suggests that individual learning is a cognitive process. Specifically, the idea is that prior learning influences our behavioral choices. The perceived consequences of the choices we make regarding behavior become in turn a part of our learning and affect future behavioral choices.

plaining the processes associated with complex learning.

The Contemporary View: Learning as a Cognitive Process   Although it is not tied to a single theory or model, contemporary learning theory generally views learning as a cognitive process; that is, it assumes that people are conscious, active participants in how they learn. Figure 6.4 illustrates some underpinnings of the cognitive view of learning.[19]

First, the cognitive view suggests that people draw on their experiences and use past learning as a basis for their present behavior. These experiences represent knowledge, or cognitions. For example, an employee faced with a choice of job assignments will use previous experiences in deciding which one to accept. Second, people make choices about their behavior. The employee recognizes that she has two alternatives and chooses one. Third, people recognize the consequences of their choices. Thus, when the employee finds the job assignment rewarding and fulfilling, she will recognize that the choice was a good one and will understand why. Finally, people evaluate those consequences and add them to prior learning, which affects future choices. Faced with the same job choices next year, the employee will probably be motivated to choose the same one. As implied earlier, several perspectives on learning take a cognitive view. Perhaps foremost among them is reinforcement theory. Although reinforcement theory per se is not really new, it has only been applied to organizational settings in the last few years.

Reinforcement Theory and Learning

Reinforcement theory is based on the idea that behavior is a function of its consequences.

Reinforcement theory (also called "operant conditioning") is generally associated with the work of B. F. Skinner.[20] In its simplest form, **reinforcement theory** suggests that behavior is a function of its consequences.[21] Behavior that results in pleasant consequences is more likely to be repeated (the employee will be motivated to repeat the current behavior), and behavior that results in unpleasant consequences is less likely to be repeated (the employee will be motivated to engage in different behaviors). Reinforcement theory also suggests that in any given situation, people explore a variety of possible behaviors. Future behavioral choices are affected by the consequences of earlier behaviors. Cognitions, as already noted, also play an important role. Therefore, rather than assuming the mechanical stimulus-response linkage suggested by the traditional classical view of learning, contemporary theorists believe that people consciously explore different behaviors and systematically choose those that result in the most desirable outcomes.

Suppose a new employee at Monsanto in St. Louis wants to learn the best way to get along with his boss. At first, the employee is very friendly and informal, but the boss responds by acting aloof and, at times, annoyed. Because the boss does not react positively, the employee is unlikely to continue this behavior. In fact, the employee next starts acting more formal and professional and finds the boss much more receptive to this posture. The employee will probably continue this new set of behaviors because they have resulted in positive consequences.

Reinforcement is the consequences of behavior.

Positive reinforcement is a reward or other desirable consequence that a person receives after exhibiting behavior.

Avoidance, or negative reinforcement, is the opportunity to avoid or escape from an unpleasant circumstance after exhibiting behavior.

Types of Reinforcement in Organizations   The consequences of behavior are called **reinforcement.** Managers can use various kinds of reinforcement to affect employee behavior. The four basic forms of reinforcement—positive reinforcement, avoidance, extinction, and punishment—are summarized in Figure 6.5.

Positive reinforcement is a reward or other desirable consequence that follows behavior. Providing positive reinforcement after a particular behavior motivates employees to maintain or increase the frequency of that behavior. A compliment from the boss after an employee has completed a difficult job and a salary increase following a worker's period of high performance are examples of positive reinforcement. This type of reinforcement has been used at Corning's ceramics factory in Virginia, where workers receive bonuses for pulling blemished materials from assembly lines before they go into more expensive stages of production.[22] The cartoon illustrates another take on positive reinforcement!

Avoidance, also known as **negative reinforcement,** is another means of increasing the frequency of desirable behavior. Rather than receiving a reward fol-

figure 6.5

Kinds of Reinforcement

There are four basic kinds of reinforcement managers can use to motivate employee behavior. The first two, positive reinforcement and avoidance, can be used to motivate employees to continue to engage in desirable behaviors (such as working hard). The other two, extinction and punishment, might be used to motivate employees to change undesirable behaviors (such as goofing off).

Positive Reinforcement

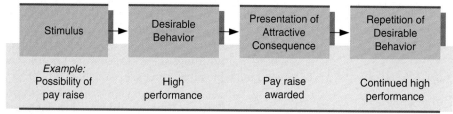

Avoidance

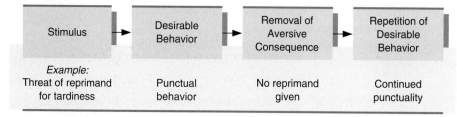

Extinction

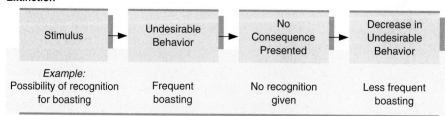

Punishment

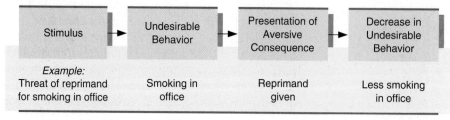

Positive reinforcement, of course, can be a powerful force in organizations and can help sustain motivated behaviors. But in order to really work, reinforcement should be of value to the individual and conform to one of the five schedules, as discussed in the text. However, if someone is truly desperate for a pat on the back, a simple device such as the one shown here might have some hidden market potential!

Reference: © Harley Schwadron

lowing a desirable behavior, the person is given the opportunity to avoid an unpleasant consequence. For example, suppose that a boss habitually criticizes employees who dress casually. To avoid criticism, an employee may routinely dress to suit the supervisor's tastes. The employee is thus motivated to engage in desirable behavior (at least from the supervisor's viewpoint) to avoid an unpleasant, or aversive, consequence.

Extinction decreases the frequency of behavior, especially behavior that was previously rewarded. If rewards are withdrawn for behaviors that were previously reinforced, the behaviors will probably become less frequent and eventually die out. For example, a manager with a small staff may encourage frequent visits from subordinates as a way of keeping in touch with what is going on. Positive reinforcement might include cordial conversation, attention to subordinates' concerns, and encouragement to come in again soon. As the staff grows, however, the manager may find that such unstructured conversations make it difficult to get her own job done. She then might begin to brush off casual conversation and reward only to-the-point "business" conversations. Withdrawing the rewards

Extinction decreases the frequency of behavior by eliminating a reward or desirable consequence that follows that behavior.

Punishment is an unpleasant, or aversive, consequence that results from behavior.

for casual chatting will probably extinguish that behavior. We should also note that if managers, inadvertently or otherwise, cease to reward valuable behaviors such as good performance and punctuality, those behaviors also may become extinct.

Punishment, like extinction, also tends to decrease the frequency of undesirable behaviors. **Punishment** is an unpleasant, or aversive, consequence of a behavior.[23] Examples of punishment are verbal or written reprimands, pay cuts, loss of privileges, layoffs, and termination. Many experts question the value of punishment and believe that managers use it too often and use it inappropriately. In some situations, however, punishment may be an appropriate tool for altering behavior. Many instances of life's unpleasantness teach us what to do by means of punishment. Falling off a bike, drinking too much, or going out in the rain without an umbrella all lead to punishing consequences (getting bruised, suffering a hangover, and getting wet), and we often learn to change our behavior as a result. Furthermore, certain types of undesirable behavior may have far-reaching negative effects if they go unpunished. For instance, an employee who sexually harasses a coworker, a clerk who steals money from the petty cash account, and an executive who engages in illegal stock transactions all deserve punishment.

Schedules of Reinforcement in Organizations   Should the manager try to reward every instance of desirable behavior and punish every instance of undesirable behavior? Or is it better to apply reinforcement according to some plan or schedule? As you

table 6.1

Schedules of
Reinforcement

Schedule of Reinforcement	Nature of Reinforcement
Continuous	Behavior is reinforced every time it occurs.
Fixed-Interval	Behavior is reinforced according to some predetermined, constant schedule based on time.
Variable-Interval	Behavior is reinforced after periods of time, but the time span varies from one time to the next.
Fixed-Ratio	Behavior is reinforced according to the number of behaviors exhibited, with the number of behaviors needed to gain reinforcement held constant.
Variable-Ratio	Behavior is reinforced according to the number of behaviors exhibited, but the number of behaviors needed to gain reinforcement varies from one time to the next.

table 6.1

Schedules of Reinforcement

Schedules of reinforcement indicate when or how often managers should reinforce certain behaviors.

With continuous reinforcement, behavior is rewarded every time it occurs.

Fixed-interval reinforcement provides reinforcement on a fixed time schedule.

Variable-interval reinforcement varies the amount of time between reinforcements.

Fixed-ratio reinforcement provides reinforcement after a fixed number of behaviors.

might expect, it depends on the situation. Table 6.1 summarizes five basic **schedules of reinforcement** that managers can use.

Continuous reinforcement rewards behavior every time it occurs. Continuous reinforcement is very effective in motivating desirable behaviors, especially in the early stages of learning. When reinforcement is withdrawn, however, extinction sets in very quickly. But continuous reinforcement poses serious difficulties because the manager must monitor every behavior of an employee and provide effective reinforcement. This approach, then, is of little practical value to managers. Offering partial reinforcement according to one of the other four schedules is much more typical.

Fixed-interval reinforcement is reinforcement provided on a predetermined, constant schedule. The Friday-afternoon paycheck is a good example of a fixed-interval reinforcement. Unfortunately, in many situations the fixed-interval schedule does not necessarily maintain high performance levels. If employees know the boss will drop by to check on them every day at 1:00 P.M., they may be motivated to work hard at that time, hoping to gain praise and recognition or to avoid the boss's wrath. At other times of the day, the employees probably will not work as hard because they have learned that reinforcement is unlikely except during the daily visit.

Variable-interval reinforcement also uses time as the basis for applying reinforcement, but it varies the interval between reinforcements. This schedule is inappropriate for paying wages, but it can work well for other types of positive reinforcement, such as praise and recognition, and for avoidance. Consider again the group of employees just described. Suppose that instead of coming by at exactly 1:00 P.M. every day, the boss visits at a different time each day: 9:30 A.M. on Monday, 2:00 P.M. on Tuesday, 11:00 A.M. on Wednesday, and so on. The following week, the times change. Because the employees do not know exactly when to expect the boss, they may be motivated to work hard for a longer period—until her visit. Afterward, though, they may drop back to lower levels because they have learned that she will not be back until the next day.

The fixed- and variable-ratio schedules gear reinforcement to the number of desirable or undesirable behaviors rather than to blocks of time. With **fixed-ratio reinforcement,** the number of behaviors needed to obtain reinforcement is constant. Assume, for instance, that a work group enters its cumulative performance totals into the firm's computer network every hour. The manager of the group uses the network to monitor its activities. He might adopt a practice of dropping by to praise the group every time it reaches a performance level of five hundred units. Thus, if the group does this three times on Monday, he stops by each time; if it reaches the mark only once on Tuesday, he stops by only once. The fixed-ratio schedule can be fairly effective in maintaining desirable behavior. Employees may acquire a sense of what it takes to be reinforced and may be motivated to maintain their performance.

With **variable-ratio reinforcement,** the number of behaviors required for reinforcement varies over time. An employee performing under a variable-ratio schedule is motivated to work hard because each successful behavior increases the probability that the next one will result in reinforcement. With this schedule, the exact number of behaviors needed to obtain reinforcement is not crucial; what is important is that the intervals between reinforcement not be so long that the worker gets discouraged and stops trying. The supervisor in the fixed-ratio example could reinforce his work group after it reaches performance levels of 325, 525, 450, 600, and so on. A variable-ratio schedule can be quite effective, but it is difficult and cumbersome to use when formal organizational rewards, such as pay increases and promotions, are the reinforcers. A fixed-interval system is the best way to administer these rewards.

Variable-ratio reinforcement varies the number of behaviors between reinforcements.

Related Aspects of Learning

Several additional aspects of learning also pertain to motivated behavior in organizations. Among them are reinforcement generalization, reinforcement discrimination, and social learning.

Reinforcement Generalization   **Reinforcement generalization** is the process through which a person extends recognition of similar or identical behavior-reinforcement relationships to different settings. People learn what behaviors are likely to produce reinforcement, and, when they encounter a similar behavior opportunity in different surroundings, they may expect the same response to elicit a similar consequence. For example, consider a plant manager for General Electric who has a history of effective troubleshooting. Over the years he has been assigned to several plants, each with a serious operating problem. After successfully dealing with the difficulties, he has always received an extended vacation, a bonus, and a boost in his base salary. He has learned the basic contingencies, or requirements, of reinforcement for his job: working hard and solving the plant's problems result in several positive reinforcers. When the manager gets his next assignment, he will probably generalize from his past experiences. Even though he will be in a different plant with different problems and employees, he will know what is expected of him and understand what it takes to be rewarded.

Reinforcement generalization is the process through which a person extends recognition of similar or identical behavior-reinforcement relationships to different settings.

Reinforcement Discrimination   **Reinforcement discrimination** is the ability to recognize differences in behavior-reinforcement relationships in different situations. It is the capacity to recognize that behaviors that were reinforced a certain way in one situation may be reinforced differently in a new situation. For example, a successful college coach taking a job coaching a professional team should understand that although the games may be similar, the players and their relationship with the team are very different. Indeed, a few years ago John Calipari left the job of head basketball coach at the University of Massachusetts for the same job with the NBA's New Jersey Nets. He was subsequently fired, in large part because he was unable to duplicate the successes at the professional level that he had enjoyed at the collegiate level. Had he recognized the differences from the beginning, he might very well have enjoyed greater success.

Reinforcement discrimination is the process of recognizing differences between behavior and reinforcement in different settings.

"People will say this isn't college basketball, but you reach back to past experiences when you're in a new position."—John Calipari, on his transition from college to NBA coach[24]

Similarly, suppose the troubleshooting plant manager is assigned to a plant that is running smoothly. His routine response to new situations has always been to identify and solve problems, but he now must discriminate between his new situation and his earlier ones. In this situation he may recognize that he needs a different set of behaviors, or responses, to meet performance expectations and receive positive reinforcement.

Social Learning in Organizations   In recent years, managers have begun to recognize the power of social learning. **Social learning** occurs when people observe the behaviors of others, recognize their consequences, and alter their own behavior as a result. A person can learn to do a new job by observing others or by watching videotapes. Or an employee may learn to avoid being late by seeing the boss chew out fellow workers. Social learning theory, then, suggests that individual behavior is determined by a person's cognitions and social environment. More specifically, people are presumed to learn behaviors and attitudes at least partly in response to what others expect of them.

Social learning occurs when people observe the behaviors of others, recognize their consequences, and alter their own behavior as a result.

Several conditions must be met to produce an appropriate environment for social learning. First, the behavior being observed and imitated must be relatively simple. Although we can learn by watching someone else how to push three or four buttons to set specifications on a machine or to turn on a computer, we probably cannot learn a complicated sequence of operations for the machine or how to run a complex software package without also practicing the various steps ourselves. Second, social learning usually involves observed and imitated behavior that is concrete, not intellectual. We can learn by watching others how to respond to the different behaviors of a particular manager or how to assemble a few component parts into a final assembled product. But we probably cannot learn through simple observation how to write computer software, how to write complicated text, how to conceptualize, or how to think abstractly. Finally, for social learning to occur, we must possess the physical ability to imitate the behavior observed. Most of us, even if we watch televised baseball games or tennis matches every weekend, cannot hit a fastball like Jason Giambi or execute a backhand like Venus Williams.

Reinforcement generalization is the process through which a person extends recognition of one situation to a similiar or identical situation. United Parcel Service has a program it calls Community Internship Program (CIP). UPS managers are encouraged to work on community service projects. This manager, for example, is fixing bicycles at a New York community center. One benefit of this program is that these managers can take what they learn about people in these settings and transfer that understanding back to the work place.

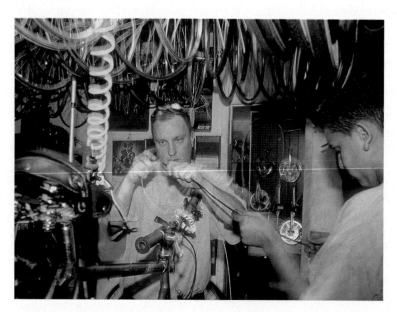

Social learning influences motivation in a variety of ways. Many of the behaviors we exhibit in our daily work lives are learned from others. Suppose a new employee joins an existing work group. She already has some basis for knowing how to behave from her education and previous experience. However, the group provides a set of very specific cues she can use to tailor her behavior to fit her new situation. The group may indicate how the organization expects its members to dress, how people are "supposed" to feel about the boss, and so forth. Hence, the employee learns how to behave in the new situation partly in response to what she already knows and partly in response to what others suggest and demonstrate.

Organizational Behavior Modification

Learning theory alone has important implications for managers, but organizational behavior modification has even more practical applications. Organizational behavior modification is an important application of reinforcement theory some managers use to enhance motivation and performance.

Behavior Modification in Organizations

Organizational behavior modification, or OB mod, is the application of reinforcement theory to people in organizational settings.

Organizational behavior modification, or **OB mod,** is the application of reinforcement theory to people in organizational settings.[25] Reinforcement theory says that we can increase the frequency of desirable behaviors by linking those behaviors with positive consequences and decrease undesirable behaviors by linking them with negative consequences. OB mod characteristically uses positive reinforcement to encourage desirable behaviors in employees. Figure 6.6 illustrates the basic steps in OB mod.

The first step is to identify performance-related behavioral events—that is, desirable and undesirable behaviors. A manager of an electronics store might decide that the most important behavior for salespeople working on commission is to greet customers warmly and show them the exact merchandise they came in to see. Note in Figure 6.6 that three kinds of organizational activity are associated with this behavior: the behavioral event itself, the performance that results, and the organizational consequences that befall the individual.

Next, the manager measures baseline performance—the existing level of performance for each individual. This usually is stated in terms of a percentage frequency across different time intervals. For example, the electronics store manager may observe that a particular salesperson presently is greeting around 40 percent of the customers each day as desired. Performance management techniques, described in Chapter 8, are used for this purpose.

The third step is to identify the existing behavioral contingencies, or consequences, of performance; that is, what happens now to employees who perform at various levels? If an employee works hard, does he or she get a reward or just get tired? The electronics store manager may observe that when customers are greeted warmly and assisted competently, they buy something 40 percent of the time whereas customers who are not properly greeted and assisted make a purchase only 20 percent of the time.

At this point, the manager develops and applies an appropriate intervention strategy. In other words, some element of the performance-reward linkage—structure, process, technology, groups, or task—is changed to make high-level performance more rewarding. Various kinds of positive reinforcement are used to guide employee behavior in desired directions. The electronics store manager might offer a sales commission plan whereby salespeople earn a percentage of the dollar amount taken in by each sale. The manager might also compliment salespeople who give appropriate greetings and ignore those who do not. This reinforcement helps shape the behavior of salespeople. In addition, an individual salesperson who does not get reinforced may imitate the behavior of more successful salespersons. In general, this step relies on the reward system in the organization, as discussed previously.

figure 6.6

Steps in Organizational Behavior Modification

Organizational behavior modification involves using reinforcement theory to motivate employee behavior. By employing the steps shown here, managers can often isolate behaviors they value and then link specific rewards to those behaviors. As a result, employees will be more likely to engage in those behaviors in the future.

Reference: "Steps in Organizational Behavior Modification," from *Personnel,* July–August 1974. Copyright © 1974 American Management Association. Reproduced with permission of American Management Association via Copyright Clearance Center.

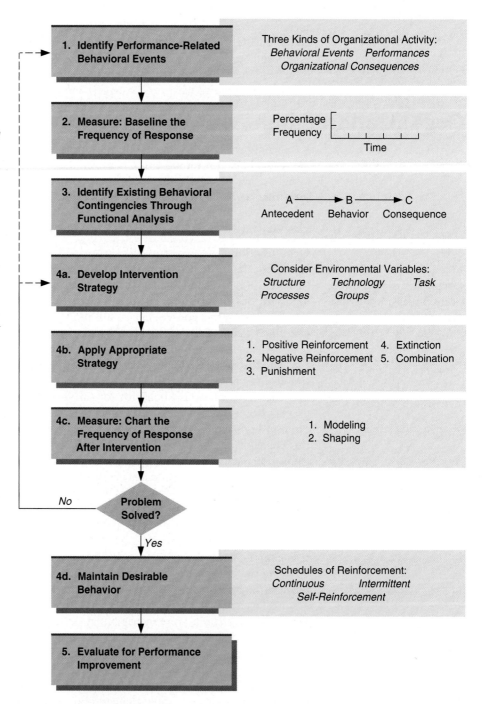

After the intervention step, the manager again measures performance to determine whether the desired effect has been achieved. If not, the manager must redesign the intervention strategy or repeat the entire process. For instance, if the salespeople in the electronics store are still not greeting customers properly, the manager may need to look for other forms of positive reinforcement—perhaps a higher commission.

If performance has increased, the manager must try to maintain the desirable behavior through some schedule of positive reinforcement. For example, higher commissions might be granted for every other sale, for sales over a certain dollar amount, and so forth. (As we saw earlier, a reinforcement schedule defines the interval at which reinforcement is given.)

Finally, the manager looks for improvements in individual employees' behavior. Here the emphasis is on offering significant longer-term rewards, such as promotions and salary adjustments, to sustain ongoing efforts to improve performance.

The Effectiveness of OB Mod

Since the OB mod approach is relatively simple, it has been used by many types of organizations, with varying levels of success.[26] A program at Emery Air Freight prompted much of the initial enthusiasm for OB mod, and other success stories have caught the attention of practicing managers.[27] B. F. Goodrich increased productivity over 300 percent and Weyerhaeuser increased productivity by at least 8 percent in three different work groups.[28] These results suggest that OB mod is a valuable method for improving employee motivation in many situations.

Turner Brothers Trucking, Inc., uses "behavioral observation of one another by workers, productivity bonuses that include a safety component, and measurement of learning from defensive driving courses by third-party road observations" as part of its OB mod program.—Garry M. Ritzky, human resources director for Turner Brothers Trucking, Inc.[29]

OB mod also has certain drawbacks. For one thing, not all applications have worked. A program at Standard Oil of Ohio was discontinued because it failed to meet its objectives; another program at Michigan Bell was only modestly successful. In addition, managers frequently have only limited means for providing meaningful reinforcement for their employees. Furthermore, much of the research testing OB mod has gone on in laboratories and thus is hard to generalize to the real world. And even if OB mod works for a while, the impact of the positive reinforcement may wane once the novelty has worn off, and employees may come to view it as a routine part of the compensation system.[30]

The Ethics of OB Mod

Although OB mod has considerable potential for enhancing motivated behavior in organizations, its critics raise ethical issues about its use. The primary ethical argument is that use of OB mod compromises individual freedom of choice. Managers may tend to select reinforcement contingencies that produce advantages for the organization with little or no regard for what is best for the individual employee. Thus, workers may be rewarded for working hard, producing high-quality products, and so forth. Behaviors that promote their own personal growth and development or that reduce their level of personal stress may go unrewarded.

An element of manipulation is also involved in OB mod. Indeed, its very purpose is to shape the behaviors of others. Thus, rather than giving employees an array of behaviors from which to choose, managers may continually funnel employee efforts through an increasingly narrow array of behavioral options so that they eventually have little choice but to select the limited set behaviors approved of by managers.

These ethical issues are, of course, real concerns that should not be ignored. At the same time, many other methods and approaches used by managers have the same goal of shaping behavior. Thus, OB mod is not really unique in its potential for misuse or misrepresentation. The keys are for managers to recognize and not abuse their ability to alter subordinate behavior and for employees to maintain control of their own work environment to the point that they are fully cognizant of the behavioral choices they are making.

Attribution and Motivation

Attribution theory suggests that employees observe their own behavior, determine whether it is a response to external or internal factors, and shape their future motivated behavior accordingly.

In Chapter 4, we discussed the role of attribution in perception. **Attribution theory** also has motivational implications. According to the attributional view of employee motivation, a person observes his or her behavior through the processes of self-perception. On the basis of these perceptions, the individual decides whether his or her behavior is a response primarily to external or to internal factors. A person who believes he is extrinsically motivated will seek extrinsic rewards, such as pay or status symbols, as future incentives. One who feels she is intrinsically motivated will look more for intrinsic incentives in the future.

Although little work has been done on attribution theory's applications to motivation, there have been some intriguing findings. For example, Deci reasoned that paying an intrinsically motivated person on an incentive basis (that is, providing extrinsic rewards) would make him or her more extrinsically motivated and less intrinsically motivated. Deci's research has indicated that if people are paid to do something they already like to do (that is, that they are intrinsically motivated to do), their level of "liking" diminishes. Furthermore, if the pay is later withheld, their level of effort also diminishes. Thus, attributional processes appear to play a meaningful role in employee motivation in the workplace.

Synopsis

The equity theory of motivation assumes that people want to be treated fairly. It hypothesizes that people compare their own input-to-outcome ratio in the organization with the ratio of a comparison-other. If they feel their treatment has been inequitable, they take steps to reduce the inequity.

Expectancy theory, a somewhat more complicated model, follows from the assumption that people are motivated to work toward a goal if they want it and think that they have a reasonable chance of achieving it. Effort-to-performance expectancy is the belief that effort will lead to performance. Performance-to-outcome expectancy is the belief that performance will lead to certain outcomes. Valence is the desirability to the individual of the various possible outcomes of performance. The Porter-Lawler version of expectancy theory provides useful insights into the relationship between satisfaction and performance. This model suggests that performance may lead to a variety of intrinsic and extrinsic rewards. When perceived as equitable, these rewards lead to satisfaction.

Learning also plays a role in employee motivation. Various kinds of reinforcement provided according to different schedules can increase or decrease motivated behavior. People can also generalize and discriminate among different behavior-reinforcement situations and are affected by social learning processes.

Organizational behavior modification is a strategy for using learning and reinforcement principles to enhance employee motivation and performance. This strategy relies heavily on the effective measurement of performance and the provision of rewards to employees after they perform at a high level.

Attribution processes also affect motivation. Attribution theory suggests that employees perceive their behavior as stemming from either external or internal causes and are motivated by rewards that correspond to the causes of their behavior.

Discussion Questions

1. Besides distinctions between need-based and process-based perspectives, are there any basic differences between the motivation theories discussed in Chapters 5 and 6?

2. Have you ever experienced inequity in a job or a class? How did it affect you?

3. Which is likely to be a more serious problem—perceptions of being underrewarded or perceptions of being overrewarded?

4. What are some managerial implications of equity theory beyond those discussed in the chapter?

5. Do you think expectancy theory is too complex for direct use in organizational settings? Why or why not?

6. Do the relationships between performance and satisfaction suggested by Porter and Lawler seem valid? Cite examples that both support and refute the model.

7. Have you ever experienced classical conditioning? If so, what were the circumstances?

8. Think of occasions on which you experienced each of the four types of reinforcement.

9. Identify the five types of reinforcement that you receive most often. On what schedule do you receive each of them?

10. What is your opinion about the ethics of OB mod?

11. Cite personal examples of attributional processes and motivation.

Organizational Behavior Case for Discussion

It's the classic "brilliant-plan-scribbled-on-a-cocktail-napkin" kind of story. In 1997, Frances Flood, president of the audio-conferencing company Gentner, mapped out the future of her firm on a restaurant place mat. The company was suffering from a host of problems: Flood and her boss, founder and CEO Russell Gentner, disagreed over the company's plans; the firm had a loss of $373,000; Research and Development wasted time on money-losing ideas; the product line was too diverse; the marketing team was too sluggish; investors and employees were discouraged. The situation seemed hopeless, but Flood knew that the audio-conferencing industry was ready to take off and that her company could participate in that growth.

Flood's plan to rescue the floundering firm was easy to scribble on that place mat but took several years to implement. Gentner had close ties to the company he had founded in 1981 to clean up audio signals such as phone calls for broadcast on radio or TV. When Gentner stepped down, Flood became CEO. She reorganized the company into just four product-related divisions, then took on engineering. The R & D group was innovative, but "[t]here was no laser-like focus. One day they'd be making a broadcast product. The next day it was something else," Flood says. She used manufacturing data to show engineers the cost-benefit tradeoff for each product. The result was a slimmed-down product lineup, with two-thirds of the products eliminated.

When employees balked at the changes, they were asked to resign, and ultimately about half of the workers left. "The old culture was very much about family," Flood claims. "In a professional organization everyone is accountable." To replace lost talent, the firm offered stock options to recruits, which will only become vested when Gentner reaches its profit targets.

Next, the CEO needed to get engineers focused on developing new products that would appeal to customers and be competitive in features and price. One quick strategy was to upgrade existing products. Flood motivated R & D workers by offering them a share of the profits if their developments went into production on time. After that incentive was offered, the product development cycle time shrank 30 percent.

Angelina Beitia, Gentner director of marketing, says, "The key to our continued success will be to combine our engineering excellence with world-class marketing." Each year Flood invents a marketing theme based on popular movies, with names such as "Mission: Possible" or "The Matrix." She engages in wacky stunts to pump up enthusiasm—such as leaving voicemail messages that begin, "Your mission, should you choose to accept it" or dressing in a black trench coat and sunglasses while screaming, "We won't conduct business as usual! We won't get sucked into the Matrix!" A wolf-related theme led to group howl-fests in the halls when a big contract was signed and to the distribution of Wolf Bucks, redeemable for cash and prizes when Gentner reaches profitability targets. According to Flood, employees love the rewards, even the little ones. "You'd think they'd won the lottery. Psychic income is huge," she maintains. Even the firm's web site conveys the message of "serious fun," saying, "At Gentner, we believe that it takes stamina, courage, and even a little lunacy to stay ahead of the pack."

There is also a more serious and down-to-earth side to Flood. In order to signal its new strategic direction, she changed the firm's name to ClearOne, based on a Massachusetts multimedia firm acquired in 2001. Another acquisition was Dublin-based Ivron Systems, a hardware manufacturer, that added video and web conferencing to the firm's audio expertise. Apparently, the changes are working. During Flood's tenure, Gentner's awards have included Ernst & Young's Entrepreneur of the Year Award, *Fortune*'s ranking of the firm as the number seven "Fastest-Growing Small Public Company," and placing number eighteen on Forbes's "200 Best Small Companies" list. The year 2002 brought an issuance of new stock that was well received by the market, as it should be: Earnings are growing an average of 75 percent annually, with fifteen consecutive quarters of profitability, a company first.

One of Flood's favorite group exercises asks managers on one side of the table to pretend that they are rowing a boat while the managers on the other side sit back, relaxing. After a few minutes, Flood asks, "What's happening to the boat? Well, the boat's going around in circles. We're on this little boat. We've got to get to the other side. Everyone's . . . got to do something. But don't just sit there because if you're just sitting there, . . . you're cargo. And there's no place for cargo on the boat." Flood sums up her view of the firm, saying, "It's definitely an unorthodox company without a doubt, but I think that's the magic. I do."

"Don't just sit there because if you [do], you're cargo. And there's no place for cargo on the boat." —Frances Flood, CEO, ClearOne Communications

References: "Gentner Communications: Philosophy/Vision," Monster.com web site. company.monster.com/gentner on May 19, 2002; Susan Sawatzki, "CEO Series: Frances Flood—President, CEO of SLC-Based Gentner Communications Corp." *AdNews Online*, November 29, 2001 (quotation). www.adnewsonline.com on May 19, 2002; "Gentner Shareholders Approve Name Change to ClearOne Communications," Gentner press release, November 15, 2001. www.clearone.com on May 19, 2002; Lea Goldman, "Over the Top," *Forbes*, October 29, 2001, pp. 146–147. See www.forbes.com; "Gentner Responds to Need for New Ways to Do Business; Unveils New Brand Identity Campaign," Gentner press release, October 23, 2001. www.clearone.com on May 19, 2002; "The FSB 100 List: America's Fastest-Growing Small Companies," *Fortune Small Business*, July 2, 2001. www.fortune.com on May 19, 2002; Walter Banks, "Gentner—Known by Its Dealers for High-End, Best-In-Breed Audio," CEOCFOInterviews.com, January 2001. www.ceocfointerviews.com on May 19, 2002.

Case Questions

Note: Gentner changed its name to ClearOne Communications in November 2001.

1. Using expectancy theory, explain the process by which Fran Flood motivates the workers at ClearOne.
2. Flood is providing positive reinforcement to her employees. What schedule of reinforcement is she using? What evidence in the case did you use in preparing your answer?
3. If you worked for Flood, would you be motivated by her? Why or why not?

Experiencing Organizational Behavior

Understanding the Dynamics of Expectancy Theory

Purpose: This exercise will help you recognize both the potential value and the complexity of expectancy theory.

Format: Working alone, you will be asked to identify the various aspects of expectancy theory that are pertinent to your class. You will then share your thoughts and results with some of your classmates.

Procedure: Considering your class as a workplace and your effort in the class as a surrogate for a job, do the following:

1. Identify six or seven things that might happen as a result of good performance in your class (for example, getting a good grade or a recommendation from your instructor). Your list must include at least one undesirable outcome (for example, a loss of free time).

2. Using a value of 10 for "extremely desirable," −10 for "extremely undesirable," and 0 for "complete neutrality," assign a valence to each outcome. In other words, the valence you assign to

each outcome should be somewhere between 10 and −10, inclusive.

3. Assume you are a high performer. On that basis, estimate the probability of each potential outcome. Express this probability as a percentage.

4. Multiply each valence by its associated probability and add the results. This total is your overall valence for high performance.

5. Assess the probability that if you exert effort, you will be a high performer. Express that probability as a percentage.

6. Multiply this probability by the overall valence for high performance calculated in step 4. This

score reflects your motivational force—that is, your motivation to exert strong effort.

Now form groups of three or four. Compare your scores on motivational force. Discuss why some scores differ widely. Also, note whether any group members had similar force scores but different combinations of factors leading to those scores.

Follow-up Questions

1. What does this exercise tell you about the strengths and limitations of expectancy theory?
2. Would this exercise be useful for a manager to run with a group of subordinates? Why or why not?

 # Self-Assessment Exercise

Assessing Your Equity Sensitivity

The questions that follow are intended to help you better understand your equity sensitivity. Answer each question on the scales by circling the number that best reflects your personal feelings.

1. I think it is important for everyone to be treated fairly.

2. I pay a lot of attention to how I am treated in comparison to how others are treated.

3. I get really angry if I think I'm being treated unfairly.

4. It makes me uncomfortable if I think someone else is not being treated fairly.

5. If I thought I were being treated unfairly, I would be very motivated to change things.

6. It doesn't really bother me if someone else gets a better deal than I do.

7. It is impossible for everyone to be treated fairly all the time.

8. When I'm a manager, I'll make sure that all of my employees are treated fairly.

9. I would quit my job if I thought I was being treated unfairly.

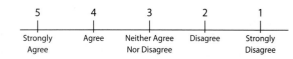

10. Short-term inequities are okay because things all even out in the long run.

5	4	3	2	1
Strongly Agree	Agree	Neither Agree Nor Disagree	Disagree	Strongly Disagree

Instructions: Add up your total points (note that some items have a "reversed" numbering arrangement). If you scored 35 or higher, you are highly sensitive to equity and fairness; 15 or lower, you have very little sensitivity to equity and fairness; between 35 and 15, you have moderate equity sensitivity.

 ## OB Online

1. Use the Internet to identify salary information for a group of individuals such as the members of a professional sports team or a college faculty. See if you can point out any potential equity problems or issues.
2. What role, if any, do you think the Internet plays today in how individuals form perceptions of equity?

3. Find a company web site that explicitly discusses the ways in which the firm links employee performance and rewards. How consistent is its message with expectancy theory?
4. Locate web sites that illustrate both reinforcement generalization and discrimination.

 ## Building Managerial Skills

Exercise Overview: Interpersonal skills—the ability to understand and motivate individuals and groups—are especially critical when managers attempt to deal with issues associated with equity and justice in the workplace. This exercise will provide you with insights into how these skills may be used.

Exercise Background: You are the manager of a group of professional employees in the electronics industry. One of your employees, David Brown, has asked to meet with you. You think you know what David wants to discuss, and you are unsure about how to proceed.

You hired David about ten years ago. During his time in your group, he has been a solid, but not an outstanding, employee. His performance, for example, has been satisfactory in every respect, but seldom outstanding. As a result, he has consistently received average performance evaluations, pay increases, and so forth. Indeed, he actually makes a somewhat lower salary today than do a few people in the group with less tenure but with stronger performance records.

The company has just announced an opening for a team leader position in your group, and you know that David wants the job. He feels that he has earned the opportunity to have the job on the basis of his consistent efforts. Unfortunately, you see things a bit differently. You really want to appoint another individual, Becky Thomas, to the job. Becky has worked for the firm for only six years, but she is your top performer. You want to reward her performance and think that she will do an excellent job. On the other hand, you do not want to lose David because he is a solid member of the group.

Exercise Task: Using the previous information, answer the following questions:

1. Using equity theory as a framework, how do you think David and Becky are likely to see the situation?
2. Outline a conversation with David in which you will convey your decision to him. What will you say?
3. What advice might you offer Becky in her new job? About interacting with David?
4. What other rewards might you offer David to keep him motivated?

7 Job Design, Employee Participation, and Alternative Work Arrangements

Management Preview

▶ Managers determine what jobs will be performed in their organizations and how those jobs will be performed. But managers must also determine how to motivate people and how to optimize their performance. The long-term key to success in business is to create jobs that optimize the organization's requirements for productivity and efficiency while simultaneously motivating and satisfying the employees who perform those jobs. As people and organizations change, and as we continue to learn more about management, it is important to look back occasionally at those jobs and make whatever changes are necessary to improve them. This chapter is the first of two that address the strategies managers use to optimize the performance of their employees. We begin with a discussion of job design, starting with a look at historical approaches to job design. Then we discuss an important contemporary perspective on jobs, the job characteristics theory. Next, we describe how social information affects job design and then review the importance of employee participation and empowerment. Finally, we discuss alternative work arrangements that can be used to enhance motivation and performance. First, though, we look at some contemporary approaches to changing jobs in order to improve organizational flexibility.

▼ ▼ ▼

Firms in today's economy are facing changes—mergers and acquisitions, lay-offs, plant closures, and globalization. Manufacturing firms have been especially hard hit by the changes, losing 1.7 million jobs in the United States between 1999 to 2002. In this volatile environment, companies must reduce expenses, but they also recognize that repeated cycles of hiring and firing drive workers out of the industry, costing firms more in the long run. "It's important to have a skill base and good loyal people who already know the company," says Richard Dillard, director of public affairs at Milliken & Company. To cope with hiring uncertainty, many firms are adapting by increasing job flexibility.

Each firm develops a customized approach to implementing job flexibility. For example, the South Carolina Nestlé's plant keeps a roster of part-time workers who can be called on a daily basis. Lincoln Electric, a Cleveland-based maker of welding equipment, moves workers between manufacturing positions and even into clerical jobs, paying different rates for each assignment. Lincoln's sales were down in 2001, so production supervisors moved into desk jobs. John Stropki, Lincoln's president of North American operations, says, "We pay [workers] for the job they are doing, not the job they used to do." Crown Mold and Machine transfers workers between day and night shifts at its Ohio fiberglass-mold factory. A & R Welding of Atlanta sends young, unmarried welders to out-of-state projects when local demand is slack. The Ohio plant of Blackhawk Automotive Plastics cross-trains employees to operate any of its plastic-forming machinery. "We're continually refining the process and reallocating people," explains Clifford Croley, a Blackhawk owner. When Milliken & Company closed a textile factory, laying off 190 employees in South Carolina, it rehired about 70 for nearby locations.

"It's important to have a skill base and good loyal people who already know the company."—Richard Dillard, director of public affairs, Milliken & Company

Employers appreciate the benefits of flexible job arrangements, including lower costs, less need for rehiring and retraining after a downsizing, and greater ease in scheduling staff. For workers, however, the reality is not always positive. Employees appreciate having more time to spend with family and benefits continuity but fear loss of seniority or pay. Rick Willard, a thirty-year Lincoln veteran, made $20 an hour until his plant was sold. Today, Lincoln is training him for a new job, and he is working longer while earning 40 percent less. Willard says, "Some people resent being moved. I was just worried [about] what type of job I would have. [Retraining is] good for the company. Sometimes it's good for the employees." It remains unclear whether internal flexibility works for all firms, but it seems to work best in manufacturing organizations. Economists Peter Cappelli and David Neumark, working with the National Bureau of Economic Research in 1999, found that only in manufacturing firms did the use of job flexibility reduce turnover.

Companies will no doubt continue to look for ways to increase their adaptability to change, and that could be a good thing for workers. E. Jeffrey Hill, research associate for Brigham Young University's Family Studies Department, takes a positive approach when he says, "As companies offer flexibility, . . . and more individuals use that flexibility, the work-family imbalance that was problematic for employees in the twilight of the twentieth century can become the balance so many seek in the twenty-first century."

References: E. Jeffrey Hill, "Flexible Schedules Help Employees Work More Without Complaint," Brigham Young University, May 19, 2001. www.newswise.com on May 5, 2002; Clare Ansberry, "In the New Workplace, Jobs Morph to Suit Rapid Pace of Change," *Wall Street Journal*, March 22, 2002, pp. A1–A7. See www.wsj.com; Peter Cappelli and David Neumark, "External Job Churning and Internal Job Flexibility," National Bureau of Economic Research, Working Paper No. w8111, February 2001. papers.nber.org on May 2, 2002.

Not all jobs are suitable for cross-training and frequent rotations in assignments, and certainly many workers have mixed feelings about such arrangements. But the very fact that some businesses are using this strategy underscores the growing need for flexibility in the workplace. In the discussion that follows, we will explore many of these problems and issues in more detail. First, however, we will introduce a general framework that can guide managers as they attempt to put into practice the various need- and process-based theories of motivation.

Motivation and Employee Performance

C hapters 5 and 6 described a variety of need- and process-based perspectives on motivation. We noted in those discussions, however, that no single theory or model completely explains motivation—each covers only some of the factors that actually result in motivated behavior. Moreover, even if one theory were applicable in a particular situation, a manager might still need to translate that theory into operational terms. Thus, while using the actual theories as tools, managers need to understand various operational procedures, systems, and methods for enhancing motivation and performance.

Figure 7.1 illustrates a basic framework for relating various theories of motivation to potential and actual motivation and to operational methods for translating this potential and actual motivation into performance. The left side of the figure illustrates that motivated behavior can be induced by need-based or process-based circumstances. That is, people may be motivated to satisfy various specific needs (as described by the various need-based theories in Chapter 5) or through various processes such as perceptions of inequity, expectancy relationships, and reinforcement contingencies (as described by the various process-based theories in Chapter 6).

These need- and process-based concepts result in the situation illustrated in the center of the figure—a certain potential exists for motivated behavior directed

figure 7.1

Enhancing Performance in Organizations

Managers can use a variety of methods to enhance performance in organizations. The need- and process-based perspectives on motivation explain some of the factors involved in increasing the potential for motivated behavior directed at enhanced performance. Managers can then use such means as goal setting, job design, alternative work arrangements, performance management, rewards, and organizational behavior modification to help translate this potential into actual enhanced performance.

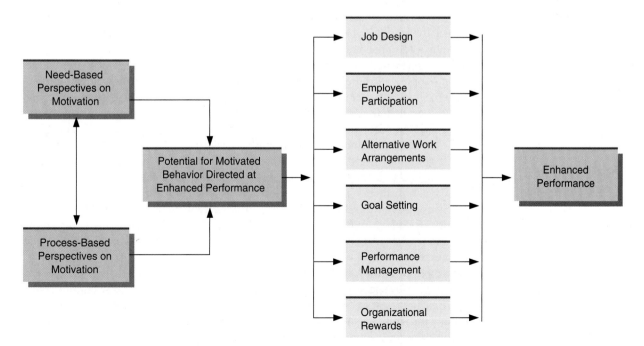

at enhanced performance. For example, suppose that an employee wants more social relationships—that is, he wants to satisfy belongingness, relatedness, or affiliation needs. This means that there is potential for the employee to want to perform at a higher level if he thinks that higher performance will satisfy those social needs. Likewise, if an employee's high performance in the past was followed by strong positive reinforcement, there is again a potential for motivation directed at enhanced performance.

But managers may need to take certain steps to translate the potential for motivation directed at enhanced performance into real motivation and real enhanced performance. In some cases, these steps may be tied to the specific need or process that has created the existing potential. For example, providing more opportunities for social interaction contingent on improved performance might capitalize on an employee's social needs. More typically, however, a manager needs to go further to help translate potential into real performance.

The right side of Figure 7.1 names some of the more common methods used to enhance performance. This chapter covers the first three—job design, employee participation and empowerment, and alternative work arrangements. The other three—goal setting, performance management, and organizational rewards—are discussed in Chapter 8.

The Evolution of Job Design

Job design is how organizations define and structure jobs.

Job design is an important method managers can use to enhance employee performance.[1] As the "Mastering Change" box suggests, one way that managers address job design is by being creative with techniques as straightforward as altering job titles.[2] **Job design** is how organizations define and structure jobs. As we will see, properly designed jobs can have a positive impact on the motivation, performance, and job satisfaction of those who perform them. On the other hand, poorly designed jobs can impair motivation, performance, and job satisfaction.

Until the nineteenth century, many families grew the things that they needed, especially food. General craft jobs became prevalent as people ceased or reduced their own food production, used their labor to produce other goods such as clothing and furniture, and traded these goods for food and other necessities. Over time, people's work became increasingly specialized as they followed this general pattern. For example, the general craft of clothing production splintered into specialized craft jobs such as weaving, tailoring, and sewing. This evolution toward specialization accelerated as the Industrial Revolution swept Europe in the 1700s and 1800s and the United States in the later 1800s.

The trend toward specialization eventually became a subject of formal study. The two most influential students of specialization were Adam Smith and Charles Babbage. Smith, an eighteenth-century Scottish economist, originated the phrase "division of labor" in his classic book *An Inquiry into the Nature and Causes of the Wealth of Nations*, published in 1776.[3] The book tells the story of a group of pin makers who specialized their jobs to produce many more pins per person in a day than each could have made by working alone.

In Smith's time, pin-making, like most other production work, was still an individual job. One person would perform all of the tasks required: drawing out a strip of wire, clipping it to the proper length, sharpening one end, attaching a head to the other end, and polishing the finished pin. With specialization, one person did nothing but draw out wire, another did the clipping, and so on. Smith attributed the

MASTERING CHANGE

▶ *What's In a Job Title?*

One often-overlooked aspect of job design is the creation of job titles. Businesses tend to rely on the same lackluster titles over and over: Production Supervisor, Administrative Clerk, Sales Associate, Vice President of Accounting. Although these titles may seem to be purely functional, they often are not. For example, what title should be given to the only employee who can speak Arabic with the firm's Middle Eastern customers? Is it fair to call the woman who controls access to the firm's CEO a secretary or, even worse, an assistant?

Boxer founder Nicholas Graham goes by the title of Chief Underpants Officer.

Other offbeat job titles include Manager of Mischief, Chief Privacy Officer, Idea Ambassador, Chief Detonator (the person who provides public relations for startups),

> *"The title is a combination of what I do in my personal life and what I do in my professional life."—Jill Darby Ellison, chief super mom, ActivityOne.com*

A recent business trend is to allow employees to develop their own creative, or even silly, job titles. These titles serve a variety of purposes: to express a worker's true contribution to the organization, to allow workers some autonomy and creative input, and to increase fun.

For example, Chief Super Mom Jill Darby Ellison uses her network of parents and knowledge of family events to contribute web content to ActivityOne.com, a firm that provides information about community events. When asked how she obtained the title, Ellison replies, "Well, it wasn't from a radioactive spider bite. The title is a combination of what I do in my personal life and what I do in my professional life." Seth Zuckerman was hired by Ecotrust to travel the West Coast communicating with grass-roots environmental efforts. He named his position "Circuit Rider," after the ministers who traveled from church to church in 1800s frontier America. International Paper's division heads have job titles such as Prince of Pine, Baron of Boards, Monarch of Mulch, and Marquis of Machinery. Joe

the Truth (the guy who always says the things that people don't want to hear), and Web Archaeologist. Would you prefer to be addressed as "Queen for the Day," "Top Dog," or "Minister of Comedy"? Or perhaps as "Slave Boy"? Tim Cleaver of Amazing Online Marketing explains, "Will Slave Boy be on my resumé? Sure. If a company doesn't want to hire me because I used to have a goofy title, I probably don't want to work there anyway."

References: Erika Germer, "Chief Privacy Officer," *Fast Company*, July 2001, p. 50. See www.fastcompany.com; Alison Overholt, "Slave Boy," *Fast Company*, June 2001, p. 56. See www.fastcompany.com; Nancy Einhart, "Idea Ambassador," *Fast Company*, April 2001, p. 66. See www.fastcompany.com; Annie F. Pyatak, "The Truth," *Fast Company*, April 2001, p. 74. See www.fastcompany.com; Jen Grasso, "Chief Super Mom," *Fast Company*, November 2000, p. 92 (quotations). See www.fastcompany.com; Christine Canabou, "Chief Detonator," *Fast Company*, July 2000, p. 64. See www.fastcompany.com; Lauren Heist, "Prince of Pine," *Fast Company*, June 2000, p. 72. See www.fastcompany.com; Erika Dykstra, "Manager of Mischief," *Fast Company*, December 1999, p. 66. See www.fastcompany.com; Erika Germer, "Circuit Rider," *Fast Company*, October 1999, p. 96. See www.fastcompany.com; Curtis Sittenfeld, "Web Archaeologist," *Fast Company*, December 1998, p. 52. See www.fastcompany.com; Curtis Sittenfeld, "Chief Underpants Officer," *Fast Company*, August 1998, p. 54. See www.fastcompany.com.

dramatic increases in output to factors such as increased dexterity owing to practice, decreased time changing from one production operation to another, and the development of specialized equipment and machinery. The basic principles described in *The Wealth of Nations* provided the foundation for the assembly line.

Charles Babbage wrote *On the Economy of Machinery and Manufactures* in 1832.[4] Extending Smith's work, Babbage cited several additional advantages of job specialization: relatively little time was needed to learn specialized jobs, waste decreased, workers needed to make fewer tool and equipment changes, and workers' skills improved through the frequent repetition of tasks.

As the Industrial Revolution spread to the United States from Europe, job specialization proliferated throughout industry. It began in the mid-1880s and reached its peak with the development of scientific management in the early 1900s.

Job Specialization

Job specialization, as advocated by scientific management, can help improve efficiency, but it can also promote monotony and boredom.

Frederick W. Taylor, the chief proponent of **job specialization,** argued that jobs should be scientifically studied, broken down into small component tasks, and then standardized across all workers doing the jobs.[5] (Recall our discussion of scientific management in Chapter 1.) Taylor's view was consistent with the premises of division of labor as discussed by Smith and Babbage. In practice, job specialization generally brought most, if not all, of the advantages its advocates claimed. Specialization paved the way for large-scale assembly lines and was at least partly responsible for the dramatic gains in output U.S. industry achieved for several decades after the turn of the century.

On the surface, job specialization appears to be a rational and efficient way to structure jobs. The jobs in many factories, for instance, are highly specialized and are often designed to maximize productivity. In practice, however, performing those jobs can cause problems, foremost among them the extreme monotony of highly specialized tasks. Consider the job of assembling toasters. A person who does the entire assembly may find the job complex and challenging, albeit inefficient. If the job is specialized so that the worker simply inserts a heating coil into the toaster as it passes along on an assembly line, the process may be efficient, but it is unlikely to interest or challenge the worker. A worker numbed by boredom and monotony may be less motivated to work hard and more inclined to do poor-quality work or to complain about the job. Moreover, related work pressure, as discussed in more detail in the "Talking Technology" box, can also result in more accidents. For these reasons, managers began to search for job design alternatives to specialization.

"Automation . . . has created work that is faster than ever before, subject to Orwellian control and electronic surveillance, and reduced to limited tasks that are numbingly repetitive, potentially crippling, and stripped of any meaningful skills or the chance to develop them."—Tony Horwitz, Wall Street Journal *reporter*[6]

Job specialization is still a cornerstone of work design in many sectors of the economy. While traditionally found in assembly line production settings such as automobile plants, the service sector has also found uses for job specialization. Most call centers such as this one, for instance, rely heavily on specialization. When calling an airline for reservations, for example, most consumers first select from an automated menu of services such as domestic flights, international flights, frequent flyer reward travel, and so forth. The caller is then routed to a specialist in that area.

TALKING TECHNOLOGY

▶ *Using Technology to Promote Worker Safety*

Forest-products businesses are not known for their safe, pleasant, and comfortable work environments. Paper and lumber factories are noisy and contain huge razor-toothed blades, chutes loaded with tons of lumber, and vats of boiling water and caustic chemicals. The products they make are heavy, awkward in size, and often full of splinters, and the machinery requires frequent maintenance and close worker contact with sharp edges and dangerous moving parts.

Georgia-Pacific Corporation, one of the world's largest forest-products businesses, has long had an unenviable safety record, even for this hazardous industry. For example, between 1986 and 1990, the firm averaged nine serious injuries per year per one hundred employees, and twenty-six workers lost their lives on the job. One factor that contributed to this situation was the emphasis top management continually gave to the importance of keeping production lines moving at all costs. As a result, workers attempted routine maintenance or repairs without shutting down the line. And if they didn't have a pair of safety gloves handy, they would carry heavy, sharp saw blades around with their bare hands rather than "waste" an extra few minutes to take appropriate safety precautions.

But all this started to change in the 1990s with a new top-management team who were appalled and embarrassed at the firm's poor safety record. Their starting point was altering the firm's culture to reinforce safe rather than risky behaviors. GP implemented an array of new rules and regulations that promote safe work and punish those who commit dangerous actions. The firm also initiated a behavior-based safety training program in which workers report on their own and others' safety actions online. Jim

Kelly, safety manager of a paper mill using the new system, says, "We want employees to . . . recognize when they are putting themselves at risk and [to] automatically modify their behavior before it results in an accident." Machine operator Darren Bailey agrees: "[The program] made this a safer mill because everyone is [now] more aware and

> *We want employees to . . . recognize when they are putting themselves at risk and [to] automatically modify their behavior before it results in an accident."—Jim Kelly, safety manager, Georgia-Pacific's Plattsburgh, N.Y., tissue mill*

everyone is watching out for each other." Personnel from the Occupational Safety and Health Administration (OSHA) conduct safety reviews of current plant designs over a collaborative Internet system and can even simulate worker behavior in a proposed factory design, thereby improving safety before a plant is even built.

The results have been impressive. In lumber processing, GP's current safety incident rate is one-fifth the industry average. At a previously hazardous plant, injuries now run about 0.7 per 100 workers annually—about one-third the rate for banks! Caution and adherence to safety procedures have also boosted productivity because stopping the production line to correct a problem takes only a few minutes whereas stopping it for an accident might cost hours—or even days.

References: Faith Keenan and Spencer E. Ante, "The New Teamwork," *Business Week*, February 18, 2002. www.businessweek.com on May 30, 2002; "OSHA VPP Requires a Team Approach," "Plattsburgh Mill Promotes Safety Through Observation," "Safety Measures," Georgia-Pacific web site. www.gp.com on May 30, 2002; "New Ways to Get Work Done," *Business Week*, February 18, 2002. www.businessweek.com on May 30, 2002.

One of the primary catalysts for this search was a famous 1952 study of jobs in the automobile industry. The purpose of this study was to assess how satisfied automobile workers were with various aspects of their jobs.[7] The workers indicated that they were reasonably satisfied with their pay, working conditions, and the quality of their supervision. However, they expressed extreme dissatisfaction with the actual work they did. The plants were very noisy, and the moving assembly line dictated a rigid, grueling pace. Jobs were highly specialized and standardized.

The workers complained about six facets of their jobs: mechanical pacing by an assembly line, repetitiveness, low skill requirements, involvement with only a portion of the total production cycle, limited social interaction with others in the workplace, and lack of control over the tools and techniques used in the job. These sources of dissatisfaction were a consequence of the job design prescriptions of scientific management. Thus, managers began to recognize that although job specialization might lead to efficiency, if carried too far, it would have a number of negative consequences.[8]

Early Alternatives to Job Specialization

In response to the automobile plant study, other reported problems with job specialization, and a general desire to explore ways to create less monotonous jobs, managers began to seek alternative ways to design jobs. Managers initially formulated two alternative approaches: job rotation and job enlargement.

Job rotation is systematically moving workers from one job to another in an attempt to minimize monotony and boredom.

Job Rotation   **Job rotation** involves systematically shifting workers from one job to another to sustain their motivation and interest. Figure 7.2 contrasts job rotation and job specialization. Under specialization, each task is broken down into small parts. For example, assembling fine writing pens such as those made by Mont Blanc

figure 7.2

Job Specialization, Rotation, and Enlargement

Job specialization involves breaking down a job into small component tasks. As illustrated here, each worker then performs one of these tasks. In job rotation, the tasks remain the same, but workers rotate among them. Job enlargement combines small tasks into somewhat larger ones; an individual worker is assigned to each of the new enlarged jobs.

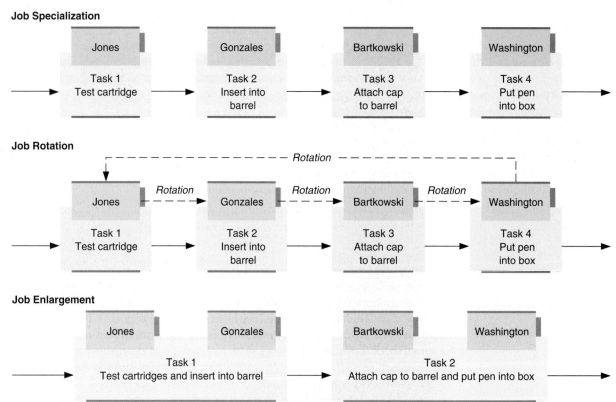

or Cross might involve four discrete steps: testing the ink cartridge, inserting the cartridge into the barrel of the pen, screwing the cap onto the barrel, and inserting the assembled pen into a box. One worker performs each of these four tasks.

When job rotation is introduced, the tasks themselves stay the same. However, as Figure 7.2 shows, the workers who perform them are systematically rotated across the various tasks. Jones, for example, starts out with task 1 (testing ink cartridges). On a regular basis—perhaps weekly or monthly—she is systematically rotated to task 2, to task 3, to task 4, and back to task 1. Gonzalez, who starts out on task 2 (inserting cartridges into barrels), rotates ahead of Jones to tasks 3, 4, 1, and back to 2.

Numerous firms have used job rotation, including American Cyanamid, Baker International, Ford, and Prudential Insurance. Job rotation did not entirely live up to its expectations, however.[9] The problem again was narrowly defined, routine jobs. If a rotation cycle takes workers through the same old jobs, the workers simply experience several routine and boring jobs instead of just one. Although a worker may begin each job shift with a bit of renewed interest, the effect usually is short-lived.

Rotation may also decrease efficiency. For example, it clearly sacrifices the proficiency and expertise that grow from specialization. At the same time, job rotation is an effective training technique because a worker rotated through a variety of related jobs acquires a larger set of job skills. Thus, there is increased flexibility in transferring workers to new jobs. Many U.S. firms now use job rotation for training or other purposes, but few rely on it to motivate workers. Pilgrim's Pride, one of the largest chicken-processing firms in the United States, uses job rotation, for instance, but not for motivation. Because workers in a chicken-processing plant are subject to cumulative trauma injuries such as carpel tunnel syndrome, managers at Pilgrim's believe that rotating workers across different jobs can reduce these injuries.[10]

Job Enlargement   **Job enlargement,** or horizontal job loading, is expanding a worker's job to include tasks previously performed by other workers. This process is also illustrated in Figure 7.2. Before enlargement, workers perform a single, specialized task; afterward, they have a "larger" job to do. Thus, after enlargement Jones and the other workers each performs a "bigger" job than he or she did previously. Thus, assembling the pens has been redefined as two tasks rather than four. Jones and Gonzalez do the first task while Bartkowski and Washington do the other. The logic behind this change is that the increased number of tasks in each job reduces monotony and boredom.

Maytag was one of the first companies to use job enlargement.[11] In the assembly of washing machine water pumps, for example, jobs done sequentially by six workers at a conveyor belt were modified so that each worker completed an entire pump alone. Other organizations that implemented job enlargement included AT & T, the U.S. Civil Service, and Colonial Life Insurance Company.

Unfortunately, job enlargement also failed to have the desired effects. Generally, if the entire production sequence consisted of simple, easy-to-master tasks, merely doing more of them did not significantly change the worker's job. If the task of putting two bolts on a piece of machinery was "enlarged" to putting on three bolts and connecting two wires, for example, the monotony of the original job essentially remained.

Job enlargement involves giving workers more tasks to perform.

Job Enrichment

Job rotation and job enlargement seemed promising but eventually disappointed managers seeking to counter the ill effects of extreme specialization. They failed partly because they were intuitive, narrow approaches rather than fully developed,

Job enrichment entails giving workers more tasks to perform and more control over how to perform them.

theory-driven methods. Consequently, a new, more complex approach to task design—job enrichment—was developed. **Job enrichment** is based on the dual-structure theory of motivation, which is discussed in Chapter 5. That theory contends that employees can be motivated by positive job-related experiences such as feelings of achievement, responsibility, and recognition. To achieve these, job enrichment relies on vertical job loading—not only adding more tasks to a job, as in horizontal loading, but also giving the employee more control over those tasks.[12]

AT&T, Texas Instruments, IBM, and General Foods have all used job enrichment. For example, AT&T utilized job enrichment in a group of eight typists who were responsible for preparing service orders. Managers believed turnover in the group was too high and performance too low. Analysis revealed several deficiencies in the work. The typists worked in relative isolation, and any service representative could ask them to type work orders. As a result, they had little client contact or responsibility, and they received scant feedback on their job performance. The job enrichment program focused on creating a typing team. Each member of the team was paired with a service representative, and the tasks were restructured: Ten discrete steps were replaced with three more complex ones. In addition, the typists began to get specific feedback on performance, and their job titles were changed to reflect their greater responsibility and status. As a result of these changes, the number of orders delivered on time increased from 27 to 90 percent, accuracy improved, and turnover decreased significantly.[13]

One of the first published reports on job enrichment told how Texas Instruments had used this technique to improve janitorial jobs. The company had given janitors more control over their schedules and let them sequence their own cleaning jobs and purchase their own supplies. As a direct result, turnover dropped, cleanliness improved, and the company reported estimated cost savings of approximately $103,000.[14]

At the same time, we should note that many job enrichment programs have failed. Some companies have found job enrichment to be cost ineffective, and others believe that it simply did not produce the expected results.[15] Several programs at Prudential Insurance, for example, were abandoned because managers believed they were benefiting neither employees nor the firm. Some of the criticism is associated with the dual-structure theory of motivation, on which job enrichment is based. In Chapter 5, we reviewed the major objections: The theory confuses employee satisfaction with motivation, is fraught with methodological flaws, ignores situational factors, and is not convincingly supported by research.

Because of these and other problems, job enrichment recently has fallen into disfavor among managers. Yet some valuable aspects of the concept can be salvaged. The efforts of managers and academic theorists ultimately have led to more complex and sophisticated viewpoints. Many of these advances are evident in the job characteristics approach, which we consider next.

The Job Characteristics Approach

The job characteristics approach focuses on the motivational attributes of jobs.

The **job characteristics approach** focuses on the specific motivational properties of jobs. The most current view is the job characteristics theory. The theory also suggests that social information affects job design properties.

The Job Characteristics Theory

The job characteristics theory identifies three critical psychological states: experienced meaningfulness of the work, experienced responsibility for work outcomes, and knowledge of results.

The **job characteristics theory,** diagrammed in Figure 7.3, was developed by Hackman and Oldham.[16] At the core of the theory is the idea of critical psychological states. These states are presumed to determine the extent to which characteristics of the job enhance employee responses to the task. The three critical psychological states are

1. *Experienced meaningfulness of the work*—the degree to which the individual experiences the job as generally meaningful, valuable, and worthwhile
2. *Experienced responsibility for work outcomes*—the degree to which individuals feel personally accountable and responsible for the results of their work
3. *Knowledge of results*—the degree to which individuals continuously understand how effectively they are performing the job

If employees experience these states at a sufficiently high level, they are likely to feel good about themselves and to respond favorably to their jobs. Hackman and Oldham suggest that the three critical psychological states are triggered by the following five characteristics of the job, or core job dimensions:

1. *Skill variety*—the degree to which the job requires a variety of activities that involve different skills and talents
2. *Task identity*—the degree to which the job requires completion of a "whole" and an identifiable piece of work; that is, the extent to which a job has a beginning and an end with a tangible outcome
3. *Task significance*—the degree to which the job affects the lives or work of other people, both in the immediate organization and in the external environment
4. *Autonomy*—the degree to which the job allows the individual substantial freedom, independence, and discretion to schedule the work and determine the procedures for carrying it out

figure 7.3

The Job Characteristics Theory

The job characteristics theory is an important contemporary model of how to design jobs. By using five core job characteristics, managers can enhance three critical psychological states. These states, in turn, can improve a variety of personal and work outcomes. Individual differences also affect how the job characteristics affect people.

Reference: From J. R. Hackman and G. R. Oldham, "Motivation Through the Design of Work: Test of a Theory," in *Organizational Behavior and Human Performance,* Volume 16, 250–279. Copyright 1976, Elsevier Science (USA), reproduced by permission of the publisher.

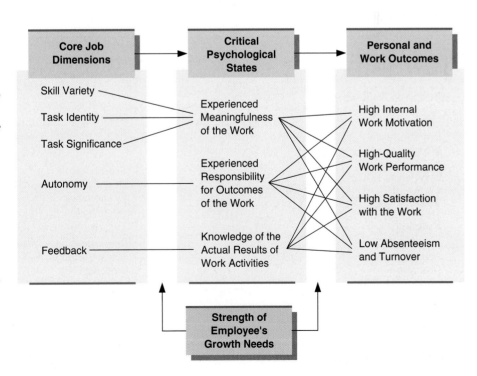

5. *Feedback*—the degree to which the job activities give the individual direct and clear information about the effectiveness of his or her performance

Figure 7.3 shows that these five job characteristics, operating through the critical psychological states, affect a variety of personal and work outcomes: high internal work motivation (that is, intrinsic motivation), high-quality work performance, high satisfaction with the work, and low absenteeism and turnover. The figure also suggests that individual differences play a role in job design. People with strong needs for personal growth and development will be especially motivated by the five core job characteristics. On the other hand, people with weaker needs for personal growth and development are less likely to be motivated by the core job characteristics.

Figure 7.4 expands the basic job characteristics theory by incorporating general guidelines to help managers implement it.[17] Managers can use such means as forming natural work units (that is, grouping similar tasks together), combining existing tasks into more complex ones, establishing direct relationships between workers and clients, increasing worker autonomy through vertical job loading, and opening feedback channels. Theoretically, such actions should enhance the motivational properties of each task. Using these guidelines, sometimes in adapted form, several firms, including 3M, Volvo, AT & T, Xerox, Texas Instruments, and Motorola, have successfully implemented job design changes.[18]

figure 7.4

Implementing the Job Characteristics Theory

Managers should use a set of implementation guidelines if they want to apply the job characteristics theory in their organization. This figure shows some of these guidelines. For example, managers can combine tasks, form natural work units, establish client relationships, vertically load jobs, and open feedback channels.

Reference: J. R. Hackman, G. R. Oldham, R. Janson, and K. Purdy, "A New Stage for Job Enrichment." Copyright © 1975 by the Regents of the University of California. Reprinted from *California Management Review*, vol. 17, no. 4. By permission of The Regents.

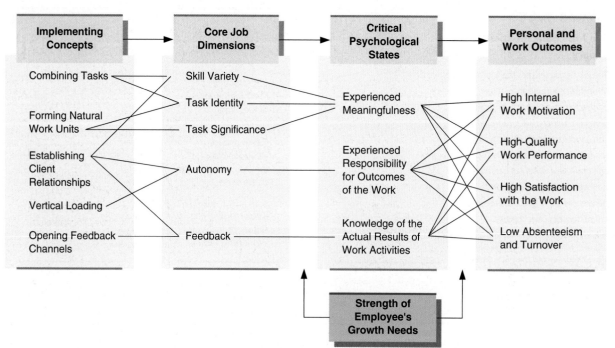

The experienced meaningfulness of the work, experienced responsibility for work outcomes, and knowledge of results are critical psychological states that impact how people respond to their jobs. Dr. Carolyn Stern was driven to become a doctor for just these reasons. Because she is deaf, it was very difficult for her to complete medical school. But today her disability enables her to effectively relate to her patients.

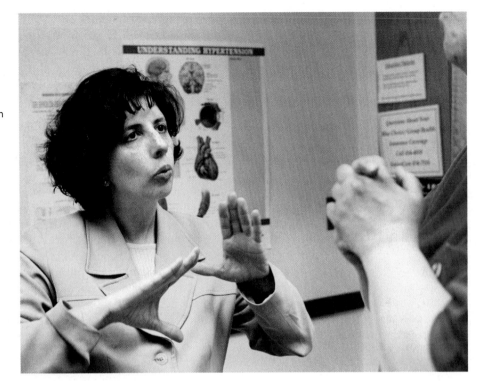

Much research has been devoted to this approach to job design.[19] This research has generally supported the theory, although performance has seldom been found to correlate with job characteristics.[20] Several apparent weaknesses in the theory have also come to light. First, the measures used to test the theory are not always as valid and reliable as they should be. Further, the role of individual differences frequently has not been supported by research. Finally, guidelines for implementation are not specific, so managers usually tailor them to their own particular circumstances. Still, the theory remains a popular perspective on studying and changing jobs.[21]

Social Information and Job Design

Recent research has also suggested that social information in the workplace may influence how individuals perceive and react to job characteristics.[22] For example, if a newcomer to the organization is told by a coworker, "You're really going to like it here because everybody gets along so well," that person may quickly decide that the job is best evaluated in terms of social interactions and that those interactions are satisfactory. But if the message is "You won't like it here because the boss is lousy and the pay is worse," the newcomer may become inclined to think that the job's most important elements are pay and interactions with the boss and that both are deficient.

This view has gotten mixed support from empirical research.[23] Indeed, research suggests that how people perceive their jobs is determined by a complex combination of both objective task characteristics and social information about those characteristics.[24] For example, positive social information and a well-designed job may produce more favorable results than either positive social information or a well-designed job would alone. Conversely, negative social information and a poorly designed job may produce more negative reactions than either negative social information or a poorly designed job would by itself. In situations where social information and job characteristics do not reinforce each other, they may cancel each other out. For example, negative social information may diminish the positive effects of a well-designed job whereas positive social information may at least partly offset the negative consequences of a poorly designed job.[25]

Participation, Empowerment, and Motivation

Participation entails giving employees a voice in making decisions about their own work.

Empowerment is the process of enabling workers to set their own work goals, make decisions, and solve problems within their sphere of responsibility and authority.

Participative management and empowerment are two more important methods managers can use to enhance employee motivation. In a sense, participation and empowerment are extensions of job design because each fundamentally alters how employees in an organization perform their jobs. **Participation** occurs when employees have a voice in decisions about their own work. (One important model that helps managers determine the optimal level of employee participation, the Vroom-Yetton-Jago model, is discussed in Chapter 13.) **Empowerment** is the process of enabling workers to set their own work goals, make decisions, and solve problems within their spheres of responsibility and authority. Thus, empowerment is a somewhat broader concept that promotes participation in a wide variety of areas, including but not limited to work itself, work context, and work environment.[26]

Early Perspectives on Participation and Empowerment

The human relations movement in vogue from the 1930s through the 1950s (see Chapter 1) assumed that employees who are happy and satisfied will work harder. This view stimulated management interest in having workers participate in a variety of organizational activities. Managers hoped that if employees had a chance to participate in decision making concerning their work environment, they would be satisfied, and this satisfaction would supposedly result in improved performance. However, managers tended to see employee participation merely as a way to increase satisfaction, not as a source of potentially valuable input. Eventually, managers began to recognize that employee input was useful in itself, apart from its presumed effect on satisfaction. In other words, they came to see employees as valued human resources who can contribute to organizational effectiveness.[27]

The role of participation and empowerment in motivation can be expressed in terms of both the need-based perspectives discussed in Chapter 5 and the expectancy theory discussed in Chapter 6. Employees who participate in decision making may be more committed to executing decisions properly. Furthermore, successfully making a decision, executing it, and then seeing the positive consequences can help satisfy one's need for achievement, provide recognition and responsibility, and enhance self-esteem. Simply being asked to participate in organizational decision making may also enhance an employee's self-esteem. In addition, participation should help clarify expectancies; that is, by participating in decision making, employees may better understand the linkage between their performance and the rewards they want most.

Areas of Participation

At one level, employees can participate in addressing questions and making decisions about their own jobs. Instead of just telling them how to do their jobs, for example, managers can ask employees to make their own decisions about how to do them. Based on their own expertise and experience with their tasks, workers might be able to improve their own productivity. In many situations, they might also be well qualified to make decisions about what materials to use, what tools to use, and so forth.

It might also help to let workers make decisions about administrative matters, such as work schedules. If jobs are relatively independent of one another, employees might decide when to change shifts, take breaks, go to lunch, and so forth. A work group or team might also be able to schedule vacations and days off for all of

"I give people license to be themselves and motivate others in that way. We give people the opportunity to be mavericks. You don't have to fit into a constraining mold at work."—Herb Kelleher, former CEO of Southwest Airlines[28]

its members. Furthermore, employees are getting increasing opportunities to participate in broader issues of product quality. Participation of this type has become a hallmark of successful Japanese and other international firms, and many U.S. companies have followed suit.[29]

Techniques and Issues in Empowerment

In recent years many organizations have actively sought ways to extend participation beyond the traditional areas. Simple techniques such as suggestion boxes and question-and-answer meetings allow a certain degree of participation, for example. The basic motive has been to better capitalize on the assets and capabilities inherent in all employees. Thus, many managers today prefer the term "empowerment" to "participation" because it implies a more comprehensive involvement.

One method some firms use to empower their workers is the use of work teams. This method grew out of early attempts to use what Japanese firms call "quality circles." A quality circle is a group of volunteer employees who voluntarily meet regularly to identify and propose solutions to problems related to quality. This use of quality circles quickly grew to encompass a wider array of work groups, now generally called "work teams." These teams are collections of employees empowered to plan, organize, direct, and control their own work. Their supervisor, rather than being a traditional "boss," plays more the role of a coach. We discuss work teams more fully in Chapter 12.

The other method some organizations use to facilitate empowerment is to change their overall method of organizing. The basic pattern is for an organization to eliminate layers from its hierarchy, thereby becoming much more decentralized. Power, responsibility, and authority are delegated as far down the organization as possible, so control of work is squarely in the hands of those who actually do it. Chapter 17 addresses these trends in more detail.

Regardless of the specific technique used, however, empowerment only enhances organizational effectiveness if certain conditions exist. First, the organization must be sincere in its efforts to spread power and autonomy to lower levels of the organization. Token efforts to promote participation in just a few areas are unlikely to succeed. This point is clearly illustrated in the cartoon. Second, the organization must be committed to maintaining participation and empowerment. Workers will be resentful if they are given more control only to later have it reduced or taken away altogether. Third, the organization must be systematic and patient in its efforts to empower workers. Turning over too much control too quickly can spell disaster. Finally, the organization must be prepared to increase its commitment to training. Employees being given more freedom concerning how they work are likely to need additional training to help them exercise that freedom most effectively.

Alternative Work Arrangements

Beyond the actual redesigning of jobs and the use of participation and empowerment, many organizations today are experimenting with a variety of alternative work arrangements. These arrangements are generally intended to enhance employee motivation and performance by giving workers more flexibility about how and when they work. Among the more popular alternative work arrangements are variable work schedules, flexible work schedules, job sharing, and telecommuting.[30]

Participation and empowerment can play powerful roles in motivating employees. But in order for these benefits to have any hope of fruition, managers must ensure that their efforts to involve employees in decision making are sincere and genuine. For example, if employees sense that their manager is asking for their opinion only for symbolic purposes and has already made a decision, things can backfire in unfortunate ways. In the instance shown here, the manager is asking for opinions through the suggestion box but is obviously not going to pay attention to what anyone has to say.

Reference: ©Harley Schwadron

"DON'T FORGET TO EMPTY THE SUGGESTION BOX."

Variable Work Schedules

There are many exceptions, of course, but the traditional work schedule in the United States has long been days that start at 8:00 or 9:00 in the morning and end at 5:00 in the evening, five days a week (and, of course, managers often work many additional hours outside of these times). Although the exact starting and ending times vary, most companies in other countries have also used a well-defined work schedule. But such a schedule makes it difficult for workers to attend to routine personal business—going to the bank, seeing a doctor or dentist for a checkup, having a parent-teacher conference, getting an automobile serviced, and so forth. Employees locked into this work schedule may find it necessary to take a sick or vacation day to handle these activities. On a more psychological level, some people may feel so powerless and constrained by their job schedules that they grow resentful and frustrated.

In a compressed work week, employees work a full forty-hour week in fewer than the traditional five days.

To help counter these problems, one alternative some businesses use is a compressed work schedule.[31] An employee following a **compressed work week** schedule works a full forty-hour week in fewer than the traditional five days. Most typically, this schedule involves working ten hours a day for four days, leaving an extra day off. Another alternative is for employees to work slightly less than ten hours a day but to complete the forty hours by lunchtime on Friday. And a few firms have tried having employees work twelve hours a day for three days, followed by four days off. Firms that have used these forms of compressed workweeks include John Hancock, Atlantic Richfield, and R. J. Reynolds. One problem with this schedule is that if everyone in the organization is off at the same time, the firm may have no one on duty to handle problems or deal with outsiders on the off day. On the other hand, if a company staggers days off across the workforce, people who don't get the more desirable days off (Monday and Friday, for most people) may be jealous or resentful. Another problem is that when employees put in too much time in a single day, they tend to get tired and perform at a lower level later in the day.

A popular schedule some organizations are beginning to use is called a "nine-eighty" schedule. Under this arrangement, an employee works a traditional schedule one week and a compressed schedule the next, getting every other Friday off. That is, they work eighty hours (the equivalent of two weeks of full-time work) in nine days. By alternating the regular and compressed schedules across half of its workforce, the organization is staffed at all times but still gives employees two additional full days off each month. Shell Oil and Amoco Chemicals are two businesses that currently use this schedule.

Flexible Work Schedules

Flexible work schedules, or flextime, give employees more personal control over the hours they work each day.

Another promising alternative work arrangement is **flexible work schedules,** sometimes called **flextime.** The compressed work schedules previously discussed give employees time off during "normal" working hours, but they must still follow a regular and defined schedule on the days when they do work. Flextime, however, usually gives employees less say about what days they work but more personal control over the times when they work on those days.[32]

Figure 7.5 illustrates how flextime works. The workday is broken down into two categories: flexible time and core time. All employees must be at their workstations during core time, but they can choose their own schedules during flexible time. Thus, one employee may choose to start work early in the morning and leave in mid-afternoon, another to start in the late morning and work until late afternoon, and a third to start early in the morning, take a long lunch break, and work until late afternoon.

The major advantage of this approach, as already noted, is that workers get to tailor their work day to fit their personal needs. A person who needs to visit the dentist in the late afternoon can just start work early. A person who stays out late one night can start work late the next day. And the person who needs to run some errands during lunch can take a longer midday break. On the other hand, flextime is more difficult to manage because others in the organization may not be sure when a person will be available for meetings other than during the core time. Expenses such as utilities will also be higher since the organization must remain open for a longer period each day.

figure 7.5

Flexible Work Schedules

Flexible work schedules are an important new work arrangement used in some organizations today. All employees must be at work during "core time." In the hypothetical example shown here, core time is from 9 to 11 A.M. and 1 to 3 P.M. The other time, then, is flexible—employees can come and go as they please during this time, as long as the total time spent at work meets organizational expectations.

In job sharing, two or more part-time employees share one full-time job.

6:00 A.M.	9:00 A.M. – 11:00 A.M.		1:00 P.M. – 3:00 P.M.	6:00 P.M.
Flexible Time	Core Time	Flexible Time	Core Time	Flexible Time

Some organizations have experimented with a plan in which workers set their own hours but then must follow that schedule each day. Others allow workers to modify their own schedule each day. Organizations that have used the flexible work schedule method for arranging work include Control Data Corporation, DuPont, Metropolitan Life, Texaco, and some offices in the U.S. government.

Job Sharing

Yet another potentially useful alternative work arrangement is job sharing. In **job sharing,** two part-time employees share one full-time job. Job sharing may be desirable for people who want to work only part-time or when job markets are tight. For its part, the organization can accommodate the preferences of a broader range of employees and may benefit from the talents of more people. Perhaps the simplest job-sharing arrangement to visualize is that of a receptionist. To share this job, one worker would staff the receptionist's desk from, say, 8:00 A.M. to noon each day, the office might close from noon to 1:00 P.M., and a second worker would staff the desk from 1:00 in the afternoon until 5:00. To the casual observer or visitor to the office, the fact that two people serve in one job is essentially irrelevant. The responsibilities of the job in the morning and the afternoon are not likely to be interdependent. Thus, the position can easily be broken down into two or perhaps even more components.

Organizations sometimes offer job sharing as a way to entice more workers to the organization. If a particular kind of job is difficult to fill, a job-sharing arrangement might make it more attractive to more people. There are also cost benefits for the organization. Since the employees may only be working part-time, the organization does not have to give them the same benefits that full-time employees receive. The organization can also tap into a wider array of skills when it provides job-sharing arrangements. The firm gets the advantage of the two sets of skills from one job.

Some workers like job sharing because it gives them flexibility and freedom. Certain workers, for example, may only want part-time work. Stepping into a shared job may also give them a chance to work in an organization that otherwise only wants to hire full-time employees. When the job sharer isn't working, she or he may attend school, take care of the family, or simply enjoy leisure time.

Job sharing does not work for every organization, and it isn't attractive to all workers, but it has produced enough success stories to suggest that it will be around for a long time. Among the organizations that are particularly committed to job-sharing programs are the Bank of Montreal, United Airlines, and the National School Board Association. Each of these organizations, and dozens more like them, reports that job sharing has become a critically important part of its human resource system. Although job sharing has not been scientifically evaluated, it appears to be a useful alternative to traditional work scheduling.

Job sharing is an alternative work arrangement in which two part-time employees share one full-time job. For example, Amy Frank (left) and Denise Brown share the job of vice president of fixed-income sales at Fleet-Boston. Frank works Monday, Tuesday, and Wednesday morning, while Brown works Wednesday afternoon, Thursday, and Friday. This arrangement allows each of them to pursue a career, earn a reasonable income, and spend time at home with their children.

Telecommuting

Telecommuting is a work arrangement in which employees spend part of their time working off-site.

A relatively new approach to alternative work arrangements is **telecommuting**— allowing employees to spend part of their time working off-site, usually at home. By using email, computer networks, and other technology, many employees can maintain close contact with their organization and do as much work at home as they could in their offices. The increased power and sophistication of modern communication technology is making telecommuting easier and easier.

"Working at home for me has been wonderful. I know my mom is O.K., and this allows me to focus on doing my job better."—Shelley Comes, quality consultant for Hewlett-Packard[33]

On the plus side, many employees like telecommuting because it gives them added flexibility. By spending one or two days a week at home, for instance, they have the same kind of flexibility to manage personal activities as is afforded by flextime or compressed schedules. Some employees also feel that they get more work done by staying at home because they are less likely to be interrupted. Organizations may benefit for several reasons as well: (1) They can reduce absenteeism and turnover since employees will need to take less "formal" time off, and (2) they can save on facilities such as parking spaces, because fewer people will be at work on any given day.

On the other hand, although many employees thrive under this arrangement, others do not. Some feel isolated and miss the social interaction of the workplace. Others simply lack the self-control and discipline to walk from the breakfast table to their desk and start working. The "Business of Ethics" box discusses another type of problem that concerns some organizations—the safety and health of their employees who are working at home. Managers may also encounter coordination difficulties in scheduling meetings and other activities that require face-to-face contact. Still, given the boom in communication technology and the pressures for flexibility, many more organizations will no doubt be using telecommuting in the years to come.[34]

BUSINESS OF ETHICS

Safety Starts at Home

It's an interesting convergence of legal and social trends. Under pressure from both workers and employers, the Occupational Safety and Health Administration (OSHA), recently changed the way it protects workers who work for their employers at home.

Prior to the new ruling, employers who asked workers to work from home—for example, by telecommuting or doing home manufacturing—were legally liable for ensuring that employees had a safe and hazard-free working environment at all times. That meant that employers had to inspect workers' homes to ensure that all safety requirements were being met. For example, the employer had to verify that there were two external exits, that no lead paint had been used on the walls, that the employee's chairs were ergonomically sound, and that the indoor air quality met OSHA standards. This stipulation led to somewhat absurd decisions, such as corporations allowing their employees to use home telephones but not home computers if the employees' monitors did not meet low-radiation requirements. The employer could also be held accountable for employees' unsafe behaviors, such as plugging too many electrical devices into one power outlet or standing on a chair rather than on a ladder to change a light bulb.

The OSHA ruling was very broad, requiring employers to take a proactive stance on home safety. "Even when the workplace is in a designated area in an employee's home, the employer retains some degree of control over the conditions of the 'work at home' agreement. Employers should exercise reasonable diligence to identify in advance the possible hazards associated with particular home work assignments. . . . [This] may necessitate an on-site examination of the working environment by the employer," according to a 1999 OSHA publication for employers. Employers found the requirements burdensome, especially as more workers began telecommuting. Employees, too, objected to the requirements as being too intrusive, invading the privacy of their homes.

"If you would be liable for your employees on-site, then you wouldn't be less liable just because you have someone working off-site."—Nicole Goluboff, attorney and specialist in the legal implications of telecommuting

Consequently, in 2000, OSHA backed down from its position on requirements, and the new policy became law in January 2001. However, it's still not clear how much responsibility a company has if a worker is injured at home. And there is now a new area of growing concern—cybercrime. Is a company liable if a client's confidential information is stolen because an employee's home computer didn't have hacker protection? What if the employee uses a home computer for business and also peddles online pornography? Nicole Goluboff, an attorney specializing in the legal implications of telecommuting, says, "If you would be liable for your employees on-site, then you wouldn't be less liable just because you have someone working off-site." Who knows where all this will lead? Only time—and the courts, no doubt—will tell.

References: Jeremy Quittner, "OSHA Won't Come Knockin' on the Home Office Door," *Business Week*, March 3, 2000. www.businessweek.com on May 30, 2002; "Occupational Injury and Illness Recording and Reporting Requirements," Occupational Health and Safety Administration web site, January 19, 2001. www.osha.gov on May 30, 2002; Chris Sandlund, "Telecommuting: A Legal Primer," *Business Week*, March 20, 2000 (quotation). www.businessweek.com on May 30, 2002.

Synopsis

Managers seek to enhance employee performance by capitalizing on the potential for motivated behavior intended to improve performance. Methods often used to translate motivation into performance involve job design, participation and empowerment, alternative work arrangements, performance management, goal setting, and rewards.

Job design is how organizations define and structure jobs. Historically, there was a general trend toward increasingly specialized jobs, but more recently the movement has consistently been away from extreme specialization. Two early alternatives to specialization were job rotation and job enlargement. Job enrichment approaches stimulated considerable interest in job design.

The job characteristics theory grew from early work on job enrichment. One basic premise of this theory is that jobs can be described in terms of a specific set of motivational characteristics. Another is that managers should work to enhance the presence of those motivational characteristics in jobs but should also take individual differences into account. Today the emerging opinion is that employees' job perceptions and attitudes are jointly determined by objective task properties and social information.

Participative management and empowerment can help improve employee motivation in many business settings. New management practices such as the use of various kinds of work teams and of flatter, more decentralized methods of organizing are intended to empower employees throughout the organization. Organizations that want to empower their employees need to understand a variety of issues as they go about promoting participation.

Alternative work arrangements are commonly used today to enhance motivated job performance. Among the more popular alternative arrangements are compressed workweeks, flexible work schedules, job sharing, and telecommuting.

Discussion Questions

1. What are the primary advantages and disadvantages of job specialization? Were they the same in the early days of mass production?

2. Under what circumstances might job enlargement be especially effective? Especially ineffective? How about job rotation?

3. Do any trends today suggest a return to job-specialization?

4. What are the strengths and weaknesses of job enrichment? When might it be useful?

5. Do you agree or disagree that individual differences affect how people respond to their jobs? Explain.

6. What are the primary similarities and differences between job enrichment and the approach proposed by job characteristics theory?

7. Can you recall any instances in which social information affected how you perceived or felt about something?

8. What are the motivational consequences of participative management from the frame of reference of expectancy and equity theories?

9. What motivational problems might result from an organization's attempt to set up work teams?

10. Which form of alternative work schedule might you prefer?

11. How do you think you would like telecommuting?

Organizational Behavior Case for Discussion

Employee Participation at Chaparral Steel

Although few people may have heard of Chaparral Steel, the company enjoys a stellar reputation as one of the most effective firms in the steel industry. Chaparral was founded in 1973 in a small town of Dallas and today enjoys annual sales of almost $500 million. In earlier times, most steel companies were large, bureaucratic operations like U.S. Steel (now USX) and Bethlehem Steel. However, increased competition from low-cost foreign steel firms—especially in Japan and Korea—has caused major problems for these manufacturers with their high overhead costs and inflexible modes of operation.

These competitive pressures, in turn, have also led to the formation of so-called minimills like Chaparral.

These minimills are consciously designed to be much smaller and more flexible than the traditional steel giants. Because of their size, technology, and flexibility, these firms are able to maintain much lower production costs and to respond more quickly to customer requests. Today, Chaparral is recognized as one of the best of this new breed of steel companies. For example, whereas most mills produce one ton of steel with an average of 3 to 5 hours of labor, Chaparral produces a ton with fewer than 1.2 hours of labor. Chaparral has also successfully avoided all efforts to unionize its employees.

Since its inception, Chaparral has been led by Gordon Forward. Forward knew that if Chaparral was going to succeed with what was then a new strategic orientation in the industry, it would also need to be managed in new and different ways. One of the first things he decided to do as a part of his new approach was to systematically avoid the traditional barriers that tend to be created between management and labor, especially in older industries like steel. For example, he mandated that there would be neither reserved parking spaces in the parking lot nor a separate dining area inside the plant for managers. Today everyone dresses casually at the work site, and people throughout the firm are on a first-name basis with one another. Workers take their lunch and coffee breaks whenever they choose, and coffee is provided free for everyone.

Forward also insisted that all employees be paid on a salary basis—no time clocks or time sheets for anyone, from the president down to the custodians. Workers are organized into teams, and each team selects its own "leader." The teams also interview and select new members as needed and are responsible for planning their own work, setting their own work schedules, and even allocating vacation days among themselves. And teams are also responsible for implementing any disciplinary actions that need to be taken toward a member. Finally, no one has a specific and narrowly defined job that must be routinely performed on a continuous and monotonous basis. That is, each team has an array of tasks and functions for which it is responsible; the teams themselves are encouraged to ensure that everyone on the team knows how to perform all of its assigned tasks and functions and to rotate people regularly across them.

Forward clearly believes in trusting everyone in the organization. For example, when the firm recently needed a new rolling mill lathe, it budgeted $1 million for its purchase, then put the purchase decision in the hands of an operating machinist. This machinist, in turn, investigated various options, visited other mills in Japan and Europe, and then recommended an alternative piece of machinery costing less than half of the budgeted amount. Forward also helped pioneer an innovative concept called "open-book management"—any employee at Chaparral can see any document, record, or other piece of information at any time and for any reason.

Chaparral also recognizes the importance of investing in and rewarding people. Continuous education is an integral part of the firm's culture, with a variety of classes being offered all the time. For example, one recent slate of classes included metallurgy, electronics, finance, and English. The classes are intended to be of value to both individual workers and to the organization as a whole. The classes are scheduled onsite and in the evening. Some include community college credit (there are tuition charges for these classes, although the company pays for half the costs) while others are noncredit only (there are no charges for these classes). Forward has a goal that at any given time at least 85 percent of Chaparral's employees will be enrolled in at least one class.

Everyone also participates in the good—and the bad—times at Chaparral. For example, all workers have a guaranteed base salary that is adequate but which, by itself, is below the standard market rate. However, in addition to their base pay, employees get pay-for-performance bonuses based on their individual achievements. Finally, there are also companywide bonuses paid to everyone on a quarterly basis. These bonuses are tied to overall company performance. The typical bonuses increase an employee's total compensation to a level well above the standard market rate. Thus, hard work and dedication on everyone's part means that everyone can benefit.

"Not only does Chaparral conduct a comprehensive screening of prospective applicants, but it [also] gives current employees an opportunity to talk with them."—U.S. Department of Labor, which selected Chaparral Steel as one of its "best practices" firms

References: "Chaparral Steel," Foundation for Enterprise Development web site (reporting the U.S. Department of Labor, Office of the American Workplace, "best practices" winners). www.fed.org on May 31, 2002; Ricky W.

Griffin and Ronald J. Ebert, *Business Essentials*, 2nd ed. (Englewood Cliffs, NJ.: Prentice Hall, 1998), p. 119; John Case, "HR Learns How to Open the Books," *HRMagazine*, May 1998, pp. 70–76; John Case, "Opening the Books," *Harvard Business Review*, March–April 1997, pp. 118–129; Brian Dumaine, "Chaparral Steel: Unleash Workers and Cut Costs," *Fortune*, May 18, 1992, p. 88.

Case Questions

1. Describe how managers at Chaparral Steel appear to be implementing various need- and process-based theories of motivation.

2. Discuss the apparent role and nature of job design at Chaparral.

3. Describe how Chaparral uses participation and empowerment to motivate its workers.

 # Experiencing Organizational Behavior

Learning About Job Design

Purpose: This exercise will help you assess the processes involved in designing jobs to make them more motivating.

Format: Working in small groups, you will diagnose the motivating potential of an existing job, compare its motivating potential to that of other jobs, suggest ways to redesign the job, and then assess the effects of your redesign suggestions on other aspects of the workplace.

Procedure: Your instructor will divide the class into groups of three or four people each. In assessing the characteristics of jobs, use a scale value of 1 ("very little") to 7 ("very high").

1. Using the scale values, assign scores on each core job dimension used in the job characteristics theory (see page 173) to the following jobs: secretary, professor, food server, auto mechanic, lawyer, short-order cook, department store clerk, construction worker, and newspaper reporter.

2. Researchers often assess the motivational properties of jobs by calculating their motivating potential score (MPS). The usual formula for MPS is

$$(\text{Variety} + \text{Identity} + \text{Significance})/3 \times \text{Autonomy} \times \text{Feedback}$$

Use this formula to calculate the MPS for each job in step 1.

3. Your instructor will now assign your group one of the jobs from the list. Discuss how you might reasonably go about enriching the job.

4. Calculate the new MPS score for the redesigned job, and check its new position in the rank ordering.

5. Discuss the feasibility of your redesign suggestions. In particular, look at how your recommended changes might necessitate changes in other jobs, in the reward system, and in the selection criteria used to hire people for the job.

6. Briefly discuss your observations with the rest of the class.

Follow-up Questions

1. How might the social-information-processing model explain some of your own perceptions in this exercise?

2. Are some jobs simply impossible to redesign?

Self-Assessment Exercise

The Job Characteristics Inventory

The questionnaire below was developed to measure the central concepts of the job characteristics theory. Answer the questions in relation to the job you currently hold or the job you most recently held.

Characteristics from Hackman and Oldham's Job Diagnostic Survey

Reference: *Work Redesign* by Hackman/Oldham, © Adapted by permission of Pearson Education, Inc., Upper Saddle River, NJ.

Skill Variety

1. How much *variety* is there in your job? That is, to what extent does the job require you to do many different things at work, using a variety of your skills and talents?

1	2	3	4	5	6	7
Very little; the job requires me to do the same routine things over and over again.			Moderate variety			Very much; the job requires me to do many different things, using a number of different skills and talents.

2. The job requires me to use a number of complex or high-level skills.

How accurate is the statement in describing your job?

1	2	3	4	5	6	7
Very inaccurate	Mostly inaccurate	Slightly inaccurate	Uncertain	Slightly accurate	Mostly accurate	Very accurate

3. The job is quite simple and repetitive.*

How accurate is the statement in describing your job?

1	2	3	4	5	6	7
Very inaccurate	Mostly inaccurate	Slightly inaccurate	Uncertain	Slightly accurate	Mostly accurate	Very accurate

Task Identity

1. To what extent does your job involve doing a *"whole" and identifiable piece of work*? That is, is the job a complete piece of work that has an obvious beginning and end? Or is it only a small *part* of the overall piece of work, which is finished by other people or by automatic machines?

1	2	3	4	5	6	7
My job is only a tiny part of the overall piece of work; the results of my activities cannot be seen in the final product or service.			My job is a moderate-sized "chunk" of the overall piece of work; my own contribution can be seen in the final outcome.			My job involves doing the whole piece of work, from start to finish; the results of my activities are easily seen in the final product or service.

2. The job provides me a chance to completely finish the pieces of work I begin.

How accurate is the statement in describing your job?

1	2	3	4	5	6	7
Very inaccurate	Mostly inaccurate	Slightly inaccurate	Uncertain	Slightly accurate	Mostly accurate	Very accurate

3. The job is arranged so that I do *not* have the chance to do an entire piece of work from beginning to end.*

How accurate is the statement in describing your job?

1	2	3	4	5	6	7
Very inaccurate	Mostly inaccurate	Slightly inaccurate	Uncertain	Slightly accurate	Mostly accurate	Very accurate

Task Significance

1. In general, how significant or important is your job? That is, are the results of your work likely to significantly affect the lives or well-being of other people?

1	2	3	4	5	6	7
Not very significant; the outcomes of my work are *not* likely to have important effects on other people.			Moderately significant			Highly significant; the outcomes of my work can affect other people in very important ways.

2. This job is one in which a lot of people can be affected by how well the work gets done.

How accurate is the statement in describing your job?

1	2	3	4	5	6	7
Very inaccurate	Mostly inaccurate	Slightly inaccurate	Uncertain	Slightly accurate	Mostly accurate	Very accurate

3. The job itself is *not* very significant or important in the broader scheme of things.*

How accurate is the statement in describing your job?

1	2	3	4	5	6	7
Very inaccurate	Mostly inaccurate	Slightly inaccurate	Uncertain	Slightly accurate	Mostly accurate	Very accurate

Autonomy

1. How much *autonomy* is there in your job? That is, to what extent does your job permit you to decide *on your own* how to go about doing your work?

1	2	3	4	5	6	7
Very little; the job gives me almost no personal "say" about how and when the work is done.			Moderate autonomy; many things are standardized and not under my control, but I can make some decisions about the work.			Very much; the job gives me almost complete responsibility for deciding how and when the work is done.

2. The job gives me considerable opportunity for independence and freedom in how I do the work.

How accurate is the statement in describing your job?

1	2	3	4	5	6	7
Very inaccurate	Mostly inaccurate	Slightly inaccurate	Uncertain	Slightly accurate	Mostly accurate	Very accurate

3. The job denies me any chance to use my personal initiative or judgment in carrying out the work.*

How accurate is the statement in describing your job?

1	2	3	4	5	6	7
Very inaccurate	Mostly inaccurate	Slightly inaccurate	Uncertain	Slightly accurate	Mostly accurate	Very accurate

Feedback

1. To what extent does *doing the job itself* provide you with information about your work performance? That is, does the actual *work itself* provide clues about how well you are doing—aside from any "feedback" coworkers or supervisors may provide?

1	2	3	4	5	6	7
Very little; the job itself is set up so I could work forever without finding out how well I am doing.			Moderately; sometimes doing the job provides "feedback" to me; sometimes it does not.			Very much; the job is set up so that I get almost constant "feedback" as I work about how well I am doing.

2. Just doing the work required by the job provides many chances for me to figure out how well I am doing.

How accurate is the statement in describing your job?

1	2	3	4	5	6	7
Very inaccurate	Mostly inaccurate	Slightly inaccurate	Uncertain	Slightly accurate	Mostly accurate	Very accurate

3. The job itself provides very few clues about whether or not I am performing well.*

How accurate is the statement in describing your job?

1	2	3	4	5	6	7
Very inaccurate	Mostly inaccurate	Slightly inaccurate	Uncertain	Slightly accurate	Mostly accurate	Very accurate

Scoring: Responses to the three items for each core characteristic are averaged to yield an overall score for that characteristic.

Items marked with an asterisk (*) should be scored as follows: 1 = 7; 2 = 6; 3 = 5; 6 = 2; 7 = 1

$$\text{Motivating potential score} \times \left(\frac{\text{Skill variety} \times \text{Task identity} \times \text{Task significance}}{3} \right) \times \text{Autonomy} \times \text{Feedback}$$

OB Online

1. Find the web site of a company that appears to promote job flexibility.
2. Visit the web sites of the companies listed in the text that have used alternative approaches to job design and see if you can find any evidence of what job design practices, if any, they seem to be promoting now.
3. Develop a framework that illustrates how the Internet might affect participation in the workplace. Use the Internet to find some evidence to support your framework.
4. Find the web sites of at least four companies that discuss alternative work arrangements as part of their human resources recruiting process.

Building Managerial Skills

Exercise Overview: Conceptual skills refer to a person's abilities to think in the abstract. This exercise will help you develop your conceptual skills as they relate to designing jobs.

Exercise Background: Begin by thinking of three different jobs, one that appears to have virtually no enrichment, one that seems to have moderate enrichment, and one that appears to have a great deal of enrichment. These jobs might be ones that you have personally held or ones that you have observed and about which you can make some educated or informed judgments.

Evaluate each job along the five dimensions described in the job characteristics theory. Next, see if you can identify ways to improve each of the five dimensions for each job. That is, see if you can determine how to enrich the jobs by using the job characteristics theory as a framework.

Finally, meet with a classmate and share results. See if you can improve your job enrichment strategy based on the critique offered by your classmate.

Exercise Task: Using the background information about the three jobs you examined as context, answer the following questions.

1. What job qualities make some jobs easier to enrich than others?

2. Can all jobs be enriched?

3. Even if a particular job can be enriched, does that always mean that it should be enriched?

4. Under what circumstances might an individual prefer to have a routine and unenriched job?

8 Goal Setting, Performance Management, and Rewards

Management Preview

▶ This chapter continues our discussion of how managers can use various strategies and techniques to enhance employee motivation and performance. Essentially, this chapter follows a logical progression of discrete activities that, taken together, provide an integrated, systematic approach to motivating employee performance. That sequence involves setting goals, evaluating performance, and providing rewards. We begin by examining the role and importance of goal setting in employee motivation. Next we introduce performance management and measurement. Then we discuss in more detail how a good performance management system contributes to total quality management. We subsequently turn to reward systems and their role in motivation. We conclude by identifying important types of rewards and exploring perspectives on managing reward systems. First, however, we describe how Honda is using access to training as a meaningful reward for employees.

▼ ▼ ▼

Employees often welcome the chance to obtain additional training, particularly if their employer is willing to foot the bill. Training is legitimately viewed as a means to increase the workers' skills; these new skills, in turn, can lead to enhanced opportunities for promotion and advancement. Training also provides some protection against job loss because skilled workers can more easily find new employment if their current jobs are eliminated. Employers also appreciate the benefit that training offers them: a more skilled and flexible workforce.

But have you ever heard of a company paying to train employees before they are hired? That's exactly what's happening at Honda's new minivan factory in Lincoln, Alabama. The automaker has built a $10 million pretraining facility, which includes replicas of Honda production equipment and multimedia classrooms. Andy Ritter, a Honda human resources manager, was chosen to lead the innovative project. He explains, "I knew I would need to find and train about 1,500 employees by April 2002. The clock was ticking." Ritter brought a staff of experienced Honda managers to the new facility. Jim Willman became part of Ritter's training team. Willman says, "Everything in Ohio [Honda's first U.S.

plant], I had inherited. The systems were in place; anyone could have done it. Andy [Ritter] gave me license to come down here and do it my way. He said, 'If it worked well in Ohio, we'll take it, but we don't have to use anything we're not comfortable with.'" Ken Pyo, who became the quality manager, maintains, "I saw an opportunity to live out a vision in quality that I had. It would have been very difficult for me to change things in Ohio because they're so instilled." Ritter's team effort resulted in the Alabama plant's opening six months earlier than scheduled.

"[Applicants] commit to . . . the program with no guarantees. If they survive until the end, it tells Honda something special about them."—Lee Hammett, training manager, Alabama Industrial Development Training

In the program, applicants for production work are screened for education, experience, and residency requirements. Those who pass the screening then participate in a six-week training course that meets in the evenings. Trainees learn many different types of information about working at Honda, including viewing a video of a Honda assembly line and discussing how to get along with Japanese coworkers. Hands-on training requires applicants to perform basic production tasks while a team of assessors grades their performance.

During the training, "[Honda explains everything] up front, so there's no surprise. About 15 percent drop out," according to Lee Hammett, training project manager for Alabama Industrial Development Training. Even after applicants successfully complete the training course, there's no job guarantee, just the chance to apply for open positions. Furthermore, applicants may even have to risk their current jobs to take the training—some local businesses have reportedly fired employees who sign up for the sessions. Hammett says that "99 percent of the people who participate in the training have full-time jobs. They commit to the time and effort of the program with no guarantees. If they survive until the end, it tells Honda something special about them." Thus far, 2,600 trainees have completed the course, with another 1,400 waiting. Feedback about the program has been positive. Wendy Curvin, now a quality administrator, explains, "They taught you how to do things over and over so you'd see what it was like, and I'm using things I learned in the classroom . . . every day."

References: Hiroyuki Yoshino, "Remarks: 2001 Year-End Press Conference," Honda web site. www.hondanews.com on May 5, 2002; Robert J. Grossman, "Made from Scratch," *HR Magazine*, April 2002, pp. 44–48 (quotation p. 48). See www.shrm.com; "The Top 25 Managers of the Year: Hiroyuki Yoshino of Honda Motor," *Business Week*, January 14, 2002. www.businessweek.com on May 5, 2002; "Online Extra: Q & A: Honda CEO Hiroyuki Yoshino," *Business Week Online*, June 11, 2001. www.businessweek.com on May 5, 2002.

For years management experts have advocated the importance of providing meaningful rewards for employees. But until recently, most firms focused primarily on pay as the basic reward offered to employees. As illustrated in the opening case, however, some forward-looking companies are realizing the benefit of offering new and innovative reward opportunities, including valuable job skills training. Of course, these companies and the employees they seek to reward each have important goals that they are hoping to achieve. Goals, then, play an important foundational role in motivating employee behavior. As you will see as we discuss goal setting, goals provide context and direction for assessing performance and allocating rewards.[1]

Goal Setting and Motivation

A goal is a desirable objective.

Goal setting is a very useful method of enhancing employee performance. From a motivational perspective, a **goal** is a desirable objective. Goals are used for two purposes in most organizations. First, they provide a useful framework for managing motivation. Managers and employees can set goals for themselves and then work toward them. Thus, if the organization's goal is to increase sales by 10 percent, a manager can use individual goals to help attain an overall goal. Second, goals are an effective control device; control is the monitoring by management of how well the organization is performing. Comparing people's short-term performances with their goals can be an effective way to monitor the organization's long-run performance.

Social learning theory perhaps best describes the role and importance of goal setting in organizations.[2] This perspective suggests that feelings of pride or shame about performance are a function of the extent to which people achieve their goals. A person who achieves a goal will be proud of having done so whereas a person who fails to achieve a goal will feel personal disappointment, and perhaps even shame. People's degree of pride or disappointment is affected by their **self-efficacy,** the extent to which they feel that they can still meet their goals even if they failed to do so in the past.

Our self-efficacy is the extent to which we believe we can accomplish our goals even if we failed to do so in the past.

Goal-Setting Theory

Social learning theory provides insights into why and how goals can motivate behavior. It also helps us understand how different people cope with failure to reach their goals. The research of Edwin Locke and his associates most clearly established the utility of goal-setting theory in a motivational context.[3]

Locke's goal-setting theory of motivation assumes that behavior is a result of conscious goals and intentions. Therefore, by setting goals for people in the organization, a manager should be able to influence their behavior. Given this premise, the challenge is to develop a thorough understanding of the processes by which people set goals and then work to reach them. In the original version of goal-setting theory, two specific goal characteristics—goal difficulty and goal specificity—were expected to shape performance.

Goal difficulty is the extent to which a goal is challenging and requires effort.

Goal Difficulty   **Goal difficulty** is the extent to which a goal is challenging and requires effort. If people work to achieve goals, it is reasonable to assume that they will work harder to achieve more difficult goals. But a goal must not be so difficult that it is unattainable. If a new manager asks her sales force to increase sales by 300 percent, the group may actually ignore her charge because they regard it as impossible to reach. A more realistic but still difficult goal—perhaps a 20 percent increase in sales—would probably be a better incentive. A substantial body of research supports the importance of goal difficulty.[4] In one study, managers at Weyerhauser set difficult goals for truck drivers hauling loads of timber from cutting sites to wood yards. Over a nine-month period, the drivers increased the quantity of wood they delivered by an amount that would have required $250,000 worth of new trucks at the previous per-truck average load.[5] Reinforcement also fosters motivation toward difficult goals. A person who is rewarded for achieving a difficult goal will be more inclined to strive toward the next difficult goal than will someone who received no reward for reaching the first goal.

Goals, or desirable objectives, play two important roles in organizations: they provide a framework for managing motivation and they are effective control devices. For example, Dr. Taryn Rose started her career as an orthopedic surgeon. But since one of her earliest interests was fashion, she was motivated to create fashionable women's footwear that was comfortable and less damaging to feet than traditional designer shoes. Motivated by her sense of style and her understanding of bone structures, she launched a line of designer shoes in 1997. Today the pricey shoes are sold in her two boutiques (in Beverly Hills and New York City) as well as in over 200 other retail outlets such as Neiman Marcus and Nordstrom. She still practices medicine, but spends most of her time running her growing shoe empire.

Goal specificity is the clarity and precision of a goal.

Goal Specificity

Goal specificity is the clarity and precision of the goal. A goal of "increasing productivity" is not very specific; a goal of "increasing productivity by 3 percent in the next six months" is quite specific. Some goals, such as those involving costs, output, profitability, and growth, can easily be stated in clear and precise terms. Other goals, such as improving employee job satisfaction and morale, company image and reputation, ethical behavior, and social responsibility, are much harder to state in specific terms.

Like difficulty, specificity has been shown to be consistently related to performance. The study of timber truck drivers previously mentioned also examined goal specificity. The initial loads the truck drivers were carrying were found to be 60 percent of the maximum weight each truck could haul. The managers set a new goal for drivers of 94 percent, which the drivers were soon able to reach. Thus, the goal was quite specific as well as difficult.

Locke's theory attracted much widespread interest and research support from both researchers and managers, so Locke, together with Gary Latham, eventually proposed an expanded model of the goal-setting process. The expanded model, shown in Figure 8.1, attempts to capture more fully the complexities of goal setting in organizations.

Goal acceptance is the extent to which a person accepts a goal as his or her own.

Goal commitment is the extent to which a person is personally interested in reaching a goal.

The expanded theory argues that goal-directed effort is a function of four goal attributes: difficulty and specificity, which we already discussed, and acceptance and commitment. **Goal acceptance** is the extent to which a person accepts a goal as his or her own. **Goal commitment** is the extent to which he or she is personally interested in reaching the goal. The manager who vows to take whatever steps are necessary to cut costs by 10 percent has made a commitment to achieving the goal.

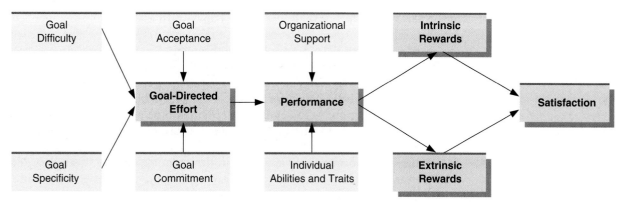

figure 8.1

The Goal-Setting Theory of Motivation

The goal-setting theory of motivation provides an important means of enhancing the motivation of employees. As illustrated here, appropriate goal difficulty, specificity, acceptance, and commitment contribute to goal-directed effort. This effort, in turn, has a direct impact on performance.

Reference: Goal-Setting Motivational Technique That Works by Gary P. Latham et al. Reprinted from *Organizational Dynamics*, Autumn, 1979, Latham et al: "The Goal-Setting Theory of Motivation" with permission from Elsevier Science.

Factors that can foster goal acceptance and commitment include participating in the goal-setting process, making goals challenging but realistic, and believing that goal achievement will lead to valued rewards.[6]

The interaction of goal-directed effort, organizational support, and individual abilities and traits determines actual performance. Organizational support is whatever the organization does to help or hinder performance. Positive support might mean providing whatever resources are needed to meet the goal; negative support might mean failing to provide such resources, perhaps due to cost considerations or staff reductions. Individual abilities and traits are the skills and other personal characteristics necessary to do a job. As a result of performance, a person receives various intrinsic and extrinsic rewards that, in turn, influence satisfaction. Note that the latter stages of this model are quite similar to those of the Porter and Lawler expectancy model discussed in Chapter 6.

Broader Perspectives on Goal Setting

Management by objectives **(MBO)** is a collaborative goal-setting process through which organizational goals cascade down throughout the organization.

Some organizations undertake goal setting from the somewhat broader perspective of **management by objectives**, or **MBO.** MBO is essentially a collaborative goal-setting process through which organizational goals systematically cascade down through the organization. Our discussion describes a generic approach, but many organizations adapt MBO to suit their own purposes.

A successful MBO program starts with top managers establishing overall goals for the organization. After these goals have been set, managers and employees throughout the organization collaborate to set subsidiary goals. First, the overall goals are communicated to everyone. Then each manager meets with each subordinate. During these meetings, the manager explains the unit goals to the subordinate, and the two together determine how the subordinate can contribute to the goals most effectively. The manager acts as a counselor and helps ensure that the subordinate develops goals that are verifiable. For example, a goal of "cutting costs by 5 percent" is verifiable whereas a goal of "doing my best" is not. Finally, manager and subordinate ensure that the subordinate has the resources needed to reach his or her goals. The entire process spirals downward as each subordinate meets with his or her own subordinates to develop their goals. Thus, as we noted earlier, the initial goals set at the top cascade down through the entire organization.

During the time frame set for goal attainment (usually one year), the manager periodically meets with each subordinate to check progress. It may be necessary to modify goals in light of new information, to provide additional resources, or to take some other action. At the end of the specified time period, managers hold a final evaluation meeting with each subordinate. At this meeting, manager and subordinate assess how well goals were met and discuss why. This meeting often serves as the annual performance review as well, determining salary adjustments and other rewards based on reaching goals. This meeting may also serve as the initial goal-setting meeting for the next year's cycle.

"Big, hairy, audacious goals . . . are a powerful way to stimulate progress—change, improvement, innovation, renewal—while simultaneously preserving your core values and purpose."—Jim Collins, management consultant[7]

Evaluation and Implications

Goal-setting theory has been widely tested in a variety of settings. Research has demonstrated fairly consistently that goal difficulty and specificity are closely associated with performance. Other elements of the theory, such as acceptance and commitment, have been studied less frequently. A few studies have shown the importance of acceptance and commitment, but little is currently known about how people accept and become committed to goals. Goal-setting theory may also focus too much attention on the short run at the expense of long-term considerations. Despite these questions, however, goal setting is clearly an important way for managers to convert motivation into actual improved performance.

From the broader perspective, MBO remains a very popular technique. Alcoa, Tenneco, Black & Decker, General Foods, and Du Pont, for example, have used versions of MBO with widespread success. The technique's popularity stems in part from its many strengths. For one thing, MBO clearly has the potential to motivate employees because it helps implement goal-setting theory on a systematic basis throughout the organization. It also clarifies the basis for rewards, and it can stimulate communication. Performance appraisals are easier and more clear-cut under MBO. Further, managers can use the system for control purposes.

However, using MBO also presents pitfalls, especially if a firm takes too many shortcuts or inadvertently undermines how the process is supposed to work. Sometimes, for instance, top managers do not really participate; that is, the goals really are established in the middle of the organization and may not reflect the real goals of top management. If employees believe this situation to be true, they may become cynical, interpreting the lack of participation by top management as a sign that the goals are not important and that their own involvement is therefore a waste of time. MBO also has a tendency to overemphasize quantitative goals to enhance verifiability. Another potential liability is that an MBO system requires a great deal of paperwork and record keeping since every goal must be documented. Finally, some managers do not really let subordinates participate in goal setting but, instead, merely assign goals and order subordinates to accept them.

On balance, MBO is often an effective and useful system for managing goal setting and enhancing performance in organizations. Research suggests that it can actually do many of the things its advocates claim but that it must also be handled carefully. In particular, most organizations need to tailor it to their own unique circumstances. Properly used, MBO can also be an effective approach to managing an organization's reward system. It requires, however, individual, one-on-one interactions between each supervisor and each employee, and these one-on-one interactions can often be difficult because of the time they take and the likelihood that at least some of them will involve critical assessments of unacceptable performance.

Performance Management in Organizations

As described earlier, most goals are oriented toward some element of performance. Managers can do a variety of things to enhance employee motivation and performance, including redesigning jobs, allowing greater participation, creating alternative work arrangements, and setting goals. They may also fail to do things that might have improved motivation and performance, and they may inadvertently even do things that reduce motivation and performance. Thus, it is clearly important that performance be approached as something that can and should be managed.

Performance measurement, or performance appraisal, is the process by which someone (1) evaluates an employee's work behaviors by measurement and comparison with previously established standards, (2) documents the results, and (3) communicates the results to the employee.

The Nature of Performance Management

The core of performance management is the actual measurement of the performance of an individual or group. **Performance measurement,** or **performance appraisal,** is the process by which someone (1) evaluates an employee's work behaviors by measurement and comparison with previously established standards, (2) documents the results, and (3) communicates the results to the employee.[8] A performance management system (PMS) comprises the processes and activities involved in performance appraisals, as shown in Figure 8.2.

figure 8.2

The Performance Management System

An organization's performance management system plays an important role in determining its overall level of effectiveness. This is especially true when the organization is attempting to employ total quality management. Key elements of a performance management system, as shown here, include the timing and frequency of evaluations, the choice of who does the evaluation, the choice of measurement procedures, the storage and distribution of performance information, and the recording methods. These elements are used by managers and employees in most organizations.

Simple performance appraisal involves a manager and an employee whereas the PMS incorporates the total quality management context along with the organizational policies, procedures, and resources that support the activity being approved. The timing and frequency of evaluations, choice of who appraises whom, measurement procedures, methods of recording the evaluations, and storage and distribution of information are all aspects of the PMS.

Purposes of Performance Measurement

Performance measurement may serve many purposes. The ability to provide valuable feedback is one critical purpose. Feedback, in turn, tells the employee where she or he stands in the eyes of the organization. Appraisal results, of course, are also used to decide and justify reward allocations. Performance evaluations may be used as a starting point for discussions of training, development, and improvement. Finally, the data produced by the performance appraisal system can be used to forecast future human resource needs, to plan management succession, and to guide other human resource activities such as recruiting, training, and development programs.

Providing job performance feedback is the primary use of appraisal information. Performance appraisal information can indicate that an employee is ready for promotion or that he or she needs additional training to gain experience in another area of company operations. It may also show that a person does not have the skills for a certain job and that another person should be recruited to fill that particular role. Other purposes of performance appraisal can be grouped into two broad categories, judgment and development, as shown in Figure 8.3.

Performance appraisals with a judgmental orientation focus on past performance and are concerned mainly with measuring and comparing performance and with the uses of the information generated. Appraisals with a developmental orientation focus on the future and use information from evaluations to improve performance. If improved future performance is the intent of the appraisal process, the manager may focus on goals or targets for the employee, on eliminating obstacles or problems that hinder performance, and on future training needs.

figure 8.3

Purposes of Performance Measurement

Performance measurement plays a variety of roles in most organizations. This figure illustrates that these roles can help managers judge an employee's past performance and help managers and employees improve future performance.

Basic Purpose of Performance Measurement: Provide Information About Work Performance	
Judgment of Past Performance	*Development of Future Performance*
Provide a basis for reward allocation Provide a basis for promotions, transfers, layoffs, and so on Identify high-potential employees Validate selection procedures Evaluate previous training programs	Foster work improvement Identify training and development opportunities Develop ways to overcome obstacles and performance barriers Establish supervisor-employee agreement on expectations

Performance Measurement Basics

Employee appraisals are common in every type of organization, but how they are performed may vary. Many issues must be considered in determining how to conduct an appraisal. Two of the most important issues are who does the appraisals and how often they are done.

The Appraiser In most appraisal systems, the employee's primary evaluator is the supervisor. This stems from the obvious fact that the supervisor is presumably in the best position to be aware of the employee's day-to-day performance. Further, it is the supervisor who has traditionally provided performance feedback to employees and determined performance-based rewards and sanctions. Problems often arise, however, if the supervisor has incomplete or distorted information about the employee's performance. For example, the supervisor may have little firsthand knowledge of the performance of an employee who works alone outside the company premises, such as a salesperson who makes solo calls on clients or a maintenance person who handles equipment problems in the field. Similar problems may arise when the supervisor has a limited understanding of the technical knowledge involved in an employee's job.

"We were miles apart on his performance. I thought it was adequate at best[;] he thought it was outstanding."—James Sauter, CEO of a newspaper publishing company[9]

One solution to these problems is a multiple-rater system that incorporates the ratings of several people familiar with the employee's performance. One possible alternative, for example, is to use the employee as an evaluator. Although they may not actually do so, most employees are actually very capable of evaluating themselves in an unbiased manner.

360-degree feedback is a performance management system in which people receive performance feedback from those on all sides of them in the organization— their boss, their colleagues and peers, and their own subordinates.

One of the more interesting approaches being used in many companies today is something called **360-degree feedback**—a performance management system in which people receive performance feedback from those on all "sides" of them in the organization—their boss, their colleagues and peers, and their own subordinates. Thus, the feedback comes from all around them, or from 360 degrees. This form of performance evaluation can be very beneficial to managers because it typically gives them a much wider range of performance-related feedback than a traditional evaluation provides. That is, rather than focusing narrowly on objective performance, such as sales increases or productivity gains, 360 feedback often focuses on such things as interpersonal relations and style. For example, one person may learn that she stands too close to other people when she talks, another that he has a bad temper. These are the kinds of things a supervisor might not even be aware of, much less report as part of a performance appraisal. Subordinates or peers are much more willing to provide this sort of feedback.

Of course, to benefit from 360-degree feedback, a manager must have a thick skin. The manager is likely to hear some personal comments on sensitive topics, which may be threatening. Thus, a 360-feedback system must be carefully managed so that its focus remains on constructive rather than destructive criticism.[10] Because of its potential advantages and in spite of its potential shortcomings, many companies today are using this approach to performance feedback. AT&T, Nestlé, Pitney Bowes, and Chase Manhattan Bank are just a few of the major companies today using 360-degree feedback to help managers improve a wide variety of performance-related behaviors.[11]

Frequency of the Appraisal Another important issue is the frequency of appraisals. Regardless of the employee's level of performance, the type of task, or the employee's need for information on performance, the organization usually conducts performance appraisals on a regular basis, typically once a year. Annual performance appraisals are convenient for administrative purposes such as record keeping and predictability. Some organizations also conduct appraisals semiannually.[12]

TALKING TECHNOLOGY

High-Tech Performance Measurement: Workers' Friend or Foe?

Advances in technology have enabled companies to gather, analyze, report, and use information in ways that would have been impossible a decade ago. One area in great need of improved accuracy and objectivity is worker performance measurement. "[W]hat was once a smushy, subjective effort by finger-in-the-wind managers is hitting new levels of scientific precision," says *Business Week* writer Michelle Conlin. British Airways manager Steven Pruneau claims that the productivity of his airline's physical and financial capital can be measured precisely with indicators such as the hours planes spend in the air versus on the ground, but he explains, "[We don't have] a fraction of that kind of information about the productivity of our other assets—our human capital."

Consider the effects of the technology revolution on performance measurement at household goods retailer Pier 1 Imports. In the past, daily sales reports could be calculated only at the end of the day, so employees didn't know how well they were doing until it was too late to do anything about it. Now, Pier 1 Imports uses information technology to tabulate sales continuously. In cities where Pier 1 has multiple stores, the same technology pits one store against the others because employees see their store's results as well as those of other stores. Employees check the sales performance data regularly and set improvement goals that enable the firm to boost sales and employees to increase their bonuses.

At British Airways, software monitors employees' every action, ensuring that their time in the break room or on a personal phone call doesn't get charged to the company. Progress toward corporate goals such as increased ticket sales and complaint resolutions is also tracked. The workers have instant access to their performance scores and can see the impact of incentive compensation on their daily pay.

> *"[Worker performance measurement] was once a smushy, subjective effort by finger-in-the-wind managers, [but now it] is hitting new levels of scientific precision."—Michelle Conlin, writer for* Business Week

Some firms are employing even more intrusive technologies, such as recording entry card data to determine what time workers arrive and leave and using security cameras—sometimes without notifying employees of their presence—in cubicles, hallways, and even restrooms. Software now enables managers to receive reports of every web site that their workers have accessed and also records employees' keystrokes. Many workers see the benefits of accurate and objective performance measurement, but others claim that the systems used invade workers' privacy. As technology continues to evolve, this debate is sure to continue.

References: James C. Cooper and Kathleen Madigan, "The Surprise Economy," *Business Week*, March 18, 2002. www.businessweek.com on May 30, 2002; Michelle Conlin, "The Software Says You're Just Average," *Business Week*, February 25, 2002 (quotation). www.businessweek.com on May 30, 2002; Karen E. Klein, "Making Performance Reviews Pay Off," *Business Week*, February 6, 2002. www.businessweek.com on May 30, 2002; Eric Wahlgren, "Have Investors Missed the Boat on Pier 1?" *Business Week*, December 21, 2001. www.businessweek.com on May 30, 2002.

Several systems for monitoring employee performance on an "as-needed" basis have been proposed as an alternative to the traditional annual system.

Managers in international settings must ensure that they incorporate cultural phenomena in their performance appraisal strategies. For example, in highly individualistic cultures such as that of the United States, appraising performance at the individual level is both common and accepted. But in collectivistic cultures such as Japan, performance appraisals almost always need to be focused more on group performance and feedback. And in countries where people put a lot of faith in destiny, fate, or some form of divine control, employees may not be receptive to performance feedback at all, believing that their actions are irrelevant to the results that follow them.

Performance Measurement and Total Quality Management

Total quality management (TQM) is a form of management that focuses on the customer, an environment of trust and openness, working in teams, breaking down internal organizational barriers, team leadership and coaching, shared power, and continuous improvement. Use of this approach often involves fundamental changes in the organization's culture.

An area in which performance management is especially important to many organizations today is total quality management. **Total quality management (TQM)** is a form of management that focuses on the customer, an environment of trust and openness, working in teams, breaking down internal organizational barriers, team leadership and coaching, shared power, and continuous improvement. Adapting TQM usually means fundamentally changing the organization's culture. In general, experts agree that to practice TQM, performance management is imperative. Indeed, virtually all of the winners of the Malcolm Baldrige National Quality Award have incorporated elements of TQM into their performance management systems. One of the basic tenets of TQM is continuous improvement.

Continuous Improvement

Some managers have traditionally approached performance as something to be maintained. That is, they assume that motivation, environment, and ability result in a constant level of performance. A logical extension of this assumption would be that performance will only increase when motivation, the environment, or ability improves. In this view, performance increases in a stair-step fashion—plateaus of stable or flat performance punctuated by periodic incremental increases. The left part of Figure 8.4 illustrates this view.

Continuous improvement is a perspective suggesting that performance should constantly be enhanced.

The premise of **continuous improvement,** in contrast, is that under a TQM program performance can—and should—be increased constantly. The right part of Figure 8.4 illustrates this viewpoint. The founder of the TQM philosophy, W. Edwards Deming, called for the elimination of numerical productivity and work-standard-type goals because they focused management's attention on short-run

figure 8.4

Incremental Versus Continuous Improvement

Traditional approaches to improving performance, as illustrated on the left of this figure, focused on incremental improvement. That is, managers assumed that motivation, environment, and ability resulted in a constant level of performance. Only by changing one or more of these elements could performance be improved. The concept of continuous improvement, illustrated on the right part of the figure, assumes that performance can be elevated on a constant basis.

Incremental Performance Improvement

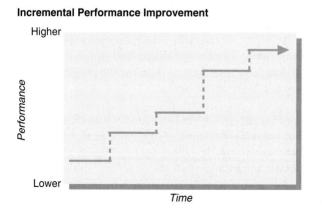

Continuous Improvement

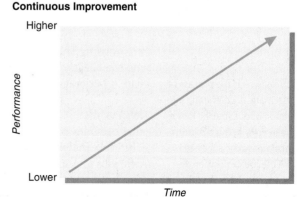

Performance management is a key component of any effective organization. Dr. Freeman Hrabowski relies heavily on performance management in his quest to simultaneously enhance the reputation of the University of Maryland Baltimore County and increase the number of African Americans who major in math and science and subsequently attend graduate school. To help advance these goals, Dr. Hrabowski aggressively recruits top students, sets high standards for them, nurtures their creativity, and keeps a close eye on how well his students perform. And in just a few years, UMBC has quickly established itself as a premier institution in a variety of technical fields.

targets and away from satisfying the customer. Instead, he proposed that the goals for employees, teams, and the organization as a whole be continuous improvement in quality and customer service, decreased cycle time, skill upgrading, reduced machine setup time, and increased machine run time. Although originally developed for traditional manufacturing settings, the concept of continuous improvement has been applied to a wide array of organizations.

The performance management systems that organizations use vary greatly in their methods and in their effectiveness. Some work, some don't, and some are constantly being changed in a search for improvements. Four factors are crucial in incorporating the principles of TQM into a performance management system and achieving continuous improvement: commitment to objectives, job analysis, a performance plan, and performance measurement.

Commitment to Objectives   A successful performance management system is based on a strong commitment from the entire organization, especially top management, to improve quality. This commitment is made manifest in the objectives of the system. Top managers must know what they want the PMS to accomplish and must communicate their objectives to those responsible for developing and managing the system. When objectives are clear and organizational commitment to quality improvement is strong, supervisors are confident that the time and effort they devote to performance management are worthwhile, which increases their interest in using the performance reviews to change behaviors and improve performance. Clearly stated objectives also allow managers to monitor the program, evaluate it periodically, and make any necessary adjustments.

Job analysis is the process of systematically gathering information about specific jobs to use in developing a performance measurement system, to write job or position descriptions, and to develop equitable pay systems.

Job Analysis   The second factor of an effective PMS is a sound job analysis system that provides comprehensive and accurate descriptions of all jobs in the organization. **Job analysis** is the process of systematically gathering information about specific jobs to use in developing a PMS, in writing job or position descriptions, and in developing equitable pay systems. To evaluate an employee's job performance fairly, the job must be precisely and clearly defined and well understood by managers.

A performance plan is an understanding between an employee and a manager concerning what and how a job is to be done such that both parties know what is expected and how success is defined and measured.

Performance Plan   Closely tied to the job analysis is the performance plan. A **performance plan** is an understanding between an employee and manager of what and how the job is to be done such that both parties know what is expected and how success is defined and measured. In TQM terms, a performance plan defines the areas of improvement that an employee is striving for. It also defines the goals and standards for improvement in quality or skills. A performance plan can help clarify mutual expectations, serve as the basis for periodic reviews, and reduce disagreements.

Measurement of Performance   The cornerstone of a good PMS is the method for measuring performance. Detailed descriptions of the many different methods for measuring performance are beyond the scope of this book; they are more appropriately covered in a course in human resource management or a specialized course in performance appraisal. However, we can present a few general comments about how to measure performance.

The measurement method provides the information managers use to make decisions about salary adjustment, promotion, transfer, training, and discipline. The courts and Equal Employment Opportunity guidelines have mandated that performance measurements be based on job-related criteria rather than on some other factor such as friendship, age, sex, religion, or national origin. In addition, to provide useful information for the decision maker, performance appraisals must be valid, reliable, and free of bias. They must not produce ratings that are consistently too lenient or too severe or that all cluster in the middle. They must also be free of perceptual and timing errors.

Some of the most popular methods for evaluating individual performance are graphic rating scales, checklists, essays or diaries, behaviorally anchored rating scales, and forced-choice systems. These systems are easy to use and familiar to most managers. However, two major problems are common to all individual methods: a tendency to rate most individuals at about the same level and the inability to discriminate among variable levels of performance.

Comparative methods evaluate two or more employees by comparing them with each other on various performance dimensions. The most popular comparative methods are ranking, forced distribution, paired comparisons, and the use of multiple raters in making comparisons. Comparative methods, however, are more difficult to use than the individual methods, are unfamiliar to many managers, and may require sophisticated development procedures and a computerized analytical system to extract usable information.

The Learning Organization

A learning organization is one that works to facilitate the lifelong learning and personal development of all of its employees while continually transforming itself to respond to changing demands and needs.

A recent refinement of the TQM approach is the so-called learning organization. Organizations that adopt this approach work to integrate continuous improvement with continuous employee learning and development. Specifically, a **learning organization** is one that works to facilitate the lifelong learning and personal development of all of its employees while continually transforming itself to respond to changing demands and needs.[13]

Managers might approach the concept of a learning organization from a variety of perspectives, but improved TQM, continuous improvement, and performance measurement are frequent goals. The idea is that the most consistent and logical strategy for achieving continuous improvement is to constantly upgrade employee talent, skill, and knowledge. For example, if each employee in an organization learns one new thing each day and can translate that knowledge into work-related

A learning organization is one that facilitates the lifelong earning and personal development of all of its employees while continuously transforming itself to respond to changing demands and needs. A good case-in-point is Beck Group. Its employees are empowered to do whatever is necessary to complete construction projects on time. And they receive constant training in how to better perform their jobs. These employees, for example, are learning how to use wireless communication devices to monitor construction and delivery schedules.

practice, continuous improvement logically follows. Indeed, organizations that wholeheartedly embrace this approach believe that only through constant employee learning can continuous improvement really occur.

In recent years many different organizations have implemented this approach. For example, the Shell Oil Company purchased an executive conference center north of its headquarters in Houston. The center features state-of-the-art classrooms and instructional technology, lodging facilities, a restaurant, and recreational amenities such as a golf course, swimming pool, and tennis courts. Line managers at the firm rotate through the Shell Learning Center, as the facility was renamed, and serve as teaching faculty. Such teaching assignments last any length from a few days to several months. At the same time, all Shell employees routinely attend training programs, seminars, and related activities to learn the latest information they need to contribute more effectively to the firm. Recent seminar topics included time management, implications of the Americans with Disabilities Act, balancing work and family demands, and international trade theory, among others.

Individual Rewards in Organizations

A s noted earlier, one of the primary purposes of performance management is to provide a basis for rewarding employees. We now turn our attention to rewards and their impact on employee motivation and performance. The

WORKING WITH DIVERSITY

How Firms Reward Minority Employees

African-American men earn just 75 cents on the dollar compared with the earnings of white males while Hispanic men earn just 62 cents. African-American and Hispanic women fare somewhat better, at 86 and 73 cents, respectively. Some of the earnings differential can be explained by differences in education, experience, or career choice, but even when these factors are considered, minorities' wages still lag behind. Some companies make an effort to reward all employees fairly. For example, at Applied Materials twelve of the top fifty earners are racial minorities.

Others have found different ways to reward minority employees in addition to or instead of through pay. One attractive feature at companies like BellSouth and Kodak is the presence of a Chief Diversity Officer, who is charged with managing diversity issues. Another rewarding factor is the presence of mentors and the guidance they provide. Dinah Moore, a senior vice president and African-American female, says, "[Mentoring is] one of the components that has kept me at Chase [Bank]." Her mentor, African-American female Pat Carmichael, senior vice president, feels that mentoring is an obligation: "When you go to meetings and don't see people who look like you, you start to wonder why that is. And how do I get involved so that when I leave, that isn't the case?"

Some firms put minorities on the company's board of directors, in the executive suite, and among the newly hired. For example, mortgage financier Fannie Mae hires minorities to fill 42 percent of its jobs; in addition, four of its eighteen board members are minorities. Advantica, owner of Denny's restaurants, used to be one of the worst firms for treatment of minorities and consequently faced numerous discrimination lawsuits. However, in 2001, *Fortune* named Advantica the best company in the United States for minorities, with minorities comprising 48 percent of its employees, 31 percent of its managers, and four of eleven board members.

> *"When you go to meetings and don't see people who look like you, you start to wonder why that is."—Pat Carmichael, senior vice president of Chase Bank and an African-American woman*

Providing rewards and fair treatment for minorities can create a strategic advantage for companies, especially in the retail and services sectors, areas in which employee satisfaction can have a direct impact on customers. Virginia Clarke, cohead of the diversity practice at Spencer Stuart, an executive search firm, maintains, "There is a strong business case [for diversity] now." With one-third of Americans presently belonging to a minority group, it seems clear that diversity is a necessity.

References: Noshua Watson, "Happy Companies Make Happy Investments," *Fortune*, May 27, 2002. www.fortune.com on May 29, 2002; "Report on the American Workforce," U.S. Department of Labor, Bureau of Labor Statistics web site, August 30, 2001. www.bls.gov on May 29, 2002; Fabiana Esposito, Sarah Garman, Jonathon Hickman, Noshua Watson, and Alynda Wheat, "America's 50 Best Companies for Minorities," *Fortune*, July 9, 2001, pp. 122–127. See www.fortune.com; Jeremy Kahn, "Diversity Trumps the Downturn," *Fortune*, July 9, 2001, pp. 114–116. See www.fortune.com; Stephanie N. Mehta, "Why Mentoring Works," *Fortune*, July 9, 2001, p. 117 (quotation). See www.fortune.com.

The reward system consists of all organizational components, including people, processes, rules and procedures, and decision-making activities, involved in allocating compensation and benefits to employees in exchange for their contributions to the organization.

reward system consists of all organizational components—including people, processes, rules and procedures, and decision-making activities—involved in allocating compensation and benefits to employees in exchange for their contributions to the organization.[14] As we examine organizational reward systems, it is important to keep in mind their role in psychological contracts (as discussed in Chapter 4) and employee motivation (as discussed in Chapters 5 and 6). Rewards constitute many of the inducements that organizations provide to employees as their part of the psychological contract, for example. Rewards also satisfy some of the needs employees attempt to meet through their choice of work-related behaviors.

Roles, Purposes, and Meanings of Rewards

The purpose of the reward system in most organizations is to attract, retain, and motivate qualified employees. The organization's compensation structure must be equitable and consistent to ensure equality of treatment and compliance with the law. Compensation should also be a fair reward for the individual's contributions to the organization, although in most cases these contributions are difficult, if not impossible, to measure objectively. Given this limitation, managers should be as fair and as equitable as possible. Finally, the system must be competitive in the external labor market for the organization to attract and retain competent workers in appropriate fields.[15]

Beyond these broad considerations, an organization must develop its philosophy of compensation based on its own conditions and needs, and this philosophy must be defined and built into the actual reward system. For example, Wal-Mart has a policy that none of its employees will be paid the minimum wage. Even though it may pay some people only slightly more than this minimum, the firm nevertheless wants to communicate to all workers that it places a higher value on their contributions than just having to pay them the lowest wage possible.

The organization needs to decide what types of behaviors or performance it wants to encourage with a reward system because what is rewarded tends to recur. Possible behaviors include performance, longevity, attendance, loyalty, contributions to the "bottom line," responsibility, and conformity. Performance measurement, as described earlier, assesses these behaviors, but the choice of which behaviors to reward is a function of the compensation system. A reward system must also take into account volatile economic issues such as inflation, market conditions, technology, labor union activities, and so forth.

> The surface value of a reward to an employee is its objective meaning or worth.

It is also important for the organization to recognize that organizational rewards have many meanings for employees. Intrinsic and extrinsic rewards carry both surface and symbolic value. The **surface value** of a reward to an employee is its objective meaning or worth. A salary increase of 5 percent, for example, means that an individual has 5 percent more spending power than before whereas a promotion, on the surface, means new duties and responsibilities. But managers must recognize that rewards also carry **symbolic value.** Consider what frequently happens when a professional sports team signs a top college prospect for a huge bonus and salary. The new player often feels enormous pressure to live up to the salary whereas veteran players may grumble that their pay should be increased to keep the salary structure in balance.

> The symbolic value of a reward to an employee is its subjective and personal meaning or worth.

Thus, rewards convey to people not only how much they are valued by the organization but also their importance relative to others. Consider again a 5 percent salary increase. If the recipient later finds out that everyone else got 3 percent or less, she will likely feel that she is very important to the organization, someone whose contributions are recognized and valued. On the other hand, if everyone else got at least 8 percent, the person will probably believe the organization places little value on her contributions. In short, then, managers need to tune in to the many meanings rewards can convey—not only to the surface messages but to the symbolic messages as well.

Types of Rewards

Most organizations use several different types of rewards. The most common are base pay (wages or salary), incentive systems, benefits, perquisites, and awards. These rewards are combined to create an individual's **compensation package.**

> An individual's compensation package is the total array of money (wages, salary, commission), incentives, benefits, perquisites, and awards provided by the organization.

Base Pay   For most people, the most important reward for work is the pay they receive. Obviously, money is important because of the things it can buy, but as we just noted, it can also symbolize an employee's worth. Pay is very important to an organization for a variety of reasons. For one thing, an effectively planned and managed pay system can improve motivation and performance. For another, employee compensation is a major cost of doing business—as much as 50 to 60 percent in many organizations—so a poorly designed system can be an expensive proposition. Finally, since pay is considered a major source of employee dissatisfaction, a poorly designed system can result in problems in other areas such as turnover and low morale.

Incentive systems are plans in which employees can earn additional compensation in return for certain types of performance.

Incentive Systems   **Incentive systems** are plans in which employees can earn additional compensation in return for certain types of performance. Examples of incentive programs include the following:

1. *Piecework programs*, which tie a worker's earnings to the number of units produced
2. *Gain-sharing programs*, which grant additional earnings to employees or work groups for cost-reduction ideas
3. *Bonus systems*, which provide managers with lump-sum payments from a special fund based on the financial performance of the organization or a unit
4. *Long-term compensation*, which gives managers additional income based on stock price performance, earnings per share, or return on equity
5. *Merit pay plans*, which base pay raises on the employee's performance
6. *Profit-sharing plans*, which distribute a portion of the firm's profits to all employees at a predetermined rate
7. *Employee stock option plans*, which set aside stock in the company for employees to purchase at a reduced rate

Plans oriented mainly toward individual employees may cause increased competition for the rewards and some possibly disruptive behaviors, such as sabotaging a coworker's performance, sacrificing quality for quantity, or fighting over customers. A group incentive plan, on the other hand, requires that employees trust one another and work together. Of course, incentive systems have advantages and disadvantages.

"Performance-based pay used to be limited to executives, managers, and sales forces. Now it's at the factory floor."—Marc Wallace, consultant[16]

Long-term compensation for executives is particularly controversial because of the large sums of money involved and the basis for the payments. The "Business of Ethics" box discusses this situation in more detail. Indeed, executive compensation is one of the more controversial subjects that U.S. businesses have had to face in recent years. News reports and the popular press seem to take great joy in telling stories about how this or that executive has just received a huge windfall from his or her organization. Clearly, successful top managers deserve significant rewards. The job of a senior executive, especially a CEO, is grueling and stressful and takes talent and decades of hard work to reach. Only a small handful of managers ever attain a top position in a major corporation. The question is whether some companies are overrewarding such managers for their contributions to the organization.[17]

When a firm is growing rapidly, and its profits are also growing rapidly, relatively few objections can be raised to paying the CEO well. However, objections arise when an organization is laying off workers, its financial performance is perhaps less than might be expected, and the CEO is still earning a huge amount of

BUSINESS OF ETHICS

CEOs Help Themselves to the Cookie Jar

On the surface it may seem that the compensation of Chief Executive Officers has started to decline in recent years. In 2001, for instance, annual CEO salaries and bonuses at the largest U.S. firms (those with revenues of $1 billion or more) fell 7.7 percent to an average of $1.32 million; median cash payments fell even more, plummeting 15 percent. This decline was apparently in response to a year in which the S & P 500 Index, a leading stock price indicator, declined 13 percent. But dig a little deeper, and a very different picture emerges. In reality, total compensation for CEOs, which includes stock awards, actually rose 24 percent in 2001, with the average CEO gaining $11.4 million from new stock options. "In bad years, CEOs should feel the same pain," says Drew Hambly, an analyst with the Investor Responsibility Research Center. "But year in and year out, these [people] continue to get compensation packages which aren't representative of stock performance."

CEOs have rare skills and abilities and can command high salaries, but do their contributions justify the high prices? In Germany and Japan, CEOs earn about twelve times more than the average worker; American CEOs, meanwhile, earn an average of 180 times more. The average European and Japanese compensation for CEOs is a "mere" $500,000. In addition, the compensation of other U.S. top managers is rising proportionally with that of the CEOs. Operations managers' total compensation averages $6 million; financial and legal managers, $3 million;

"Once CEOs have learned to help themselves to the cookie jar, they continue to do so."—Sarah Teslik, director, Council of Institutional Investors

and human resources and information managers, $2 million (again, at the largest firms). One of the most extreme cases is at Coca-Cola, where shares fell 23 percent during the same period that CEO Douglas Daft received a 17 percent salary increase and additional stock options and grants worth $93.6 million!

Overinflated CEO compensation hurts everyone. Shareholders want CEOs to share downside risk and are concerned about share value dilution as new shares are issued to cover options. In a year in which a record number of companies have sought pay cuts from employees, workers resent their bosses' high pay and the dilution of share value, which negatively impacts their retirement accounts. Customers, too, are not well served by compensation that leaves less money for innovation or quality improvements. And there's no sign that the trend will slow. According to Sarah Teslik, director of the Council of Institutional Investors, "Once CEOs have learned to help themselves to the cookie jar, they continue to do so. It's addictive."

References: Ken Belson, "Learning How to Talk about Salary in Japan," *New York Times*, April 7, 2002, p BU12. See www.nytimes.com; Claudia H. Deutsch, "Trailing the Chief in Pay, Too," *New York Times*, April 7, 2002, p. BU6. See www.nytimes.com; "Executive Pay: A Special Report," *New York Times*, April 7, 2002, pp. BU7–9. See www.nytimes.com; Gary Strauss, "CEOs Rarely Felt Shareholders' Financial Pain," *USA Today*, March 25, 2002, pp. 1B–3B. See www.usatoday.com.

money. It is these situations that dictate that a company's board of directors take a close look at the appropriateness of its actions.[18]

Benefits   Another major component of the compensation package is the employee benefits plan. **Benefits** are often called "indirect compensation." Typical benefits provided by businesses include the following:

Benefits are an important form of indirect compensation.

1. *Payment for time not worked*, both on and off the job. On-the-job free time includes lunch, rest, coffee breaks, and wash-up or get-ready time. Off-the-job time not worked includes vacation, sick leave, holidays, and personal days.
2. *Social Security contributions*. The employer contributes half the money paid into the system established under the Federal Insurance Contributions Act (FICA). The employee pays the other half.

Edgerrin James is a talented but often controversial running back for the Indianapolis Colts. He minces no words when it comes to what motivates him—money. He has a large contract, but a substantial portion of his income is tied to incentives. For instance, he earns additional money based on the number of times he carries the ball in a season, the number of yards he gains, and the number of touchdowns he scores. James has been criticized for not running out of bounds to stop the clock or for running too aggressively when the game's outcome was already determined. But he responds that to do any less reduces his income.

3. *Unemployment compensation.* People who have lost their jobs or are temporarily laid off get a percentage of their wages from an insurance-like program.
4. *Disability and workers' compensation benefits.* Employers contribute funds to help workers who cannot work due to occupational injury or ailment.
5. *Life and health insurance programs.* Most organizations offer insurance at a cost far below what individuals would pay to buy insurance on their own.
6. *Pension or retirement plans.* Most organizations offer plans to provide supplementary income to employees after they retire.

A company's Social Security, unemployment, and workers' compensation contributions are set by law. But how much to contribute for other kinds of benefits is up to each company. Some organizations contribute more to the cost of these benefits than others. Some companies pay the entire cost; others pay a percentage of the cost of certain benefits, such as health insurance, and bear the entire cost of other benefits. Offering benefits beyond wages became a standard component of compensation during World War II as a way to increase employee compensation when wage controls were in effect. Since then, competition for employees and employee demands (expressed, for instance, in union bargaining) have caused companies to increase these benefits. In many organizations today, benefits now account for 30 to 40 percent of the payroll.

The burden of providing employee benefits is growing heavier for firms in the United States than it is for organizations in other countries, especially among unionized firms. For example, consider the problem that General Motors faces. Workers at GM's brake factory in Dayton, Ohio, earn an average of $27 an hour in wages. They also earn another $16 an hour in benefits, including full health-care coverage with no deductibles, full pension benefits after thirty years of service, life and disability insurance, and legal services. Thus, GM's total labor costs per worker at the factory average $43 an hour. A German rival, Robert Bosch GmbH, meanwhile, has a nonunionized brake plant in South Carolina. It pays its workers an average of $18 an hour in wages, and its hourly benefit cost is around $5. Bosch's benefits include medical coverage with a $2,000 deductible, 401-K retirement plans with employee participation, and life and disability coverage. Bosch's total hourly labor costs per worker, therefore, are only $23. Toyota, Nissan, and Honda buy most of their brakes for their U.S. factories from Bosch whereas General Motors must use its own factory to supply brakes. Thus, foreign competitors realize considerable cost advantages over GM in the brakes they use, and this pattern runs across a variety of other component parts as well.[19]

Perquisites   Perquisites are special privileges awarded to selected members of an organization, usually top managers. For years, the top executives of many businesses were allowed privileges such as unlimited use of the company jet, motor home, vacation home, and executive dining room. In Japan, a popular perquisite is a paid membership in an exclusive golf club; a common perquisite in England is first-class travel. In the United States, the Internal Revenue Service has recently ruled that some "perks" constitute a form of income and thus can be taxed. This decision has substantially changed the nature of these benefits, but they have not entirely disappeared, nor are they likely to. Today, however, many perks tend to be more job-related. For example, popular perks currently include a car and driver (so that the executive can work while being transported to and from work) and cellular telephones (so that the executive can conduct business anywhere). More than anything else, though, perquisites seem to add to the status of their recipients and thus may increase job satisfaction and reduce turnover.[20]

Perquisites are special privileges awarded to selected members of an organization, usually top managers.

Awards   At many companies, employees receive awards for everything from seniority to perfect attendance, from zero defects (quality work) to cost reduction suggestions. Award programs can be costly in the time required to run them and in money if cash awards are given. But award systems can improve performance un-

Organizations often seek to recognize, reward, and motivate their best employees by giving them various awards. One long-standing tradition, for example, is to provide awards to long-term employees at key anniversary dates to reward their loyalty and dedication and to recognize the value of seniority. But in order for such programs to be effective, the awards and prizes themselves must have value to the employee being recognized. For example, as illustrated here, although some employees might regard extra time with their boss as a reward, others clearly see things in a different way!

DILBERT reprinted by permission of United Feature Syndicate, Inc.

der the right conditions. In one medium-size manufacturing company, careless work habits were pushing up the costs of scrap and rework (the cost of scrapping defective parts or reworking them to meet standards). Management instituted a zero-defects program to recognize employees who did perfect or near-perfect work. During the first month, two workers in shipping caused only one defect in over two thousand parts handled. Division management called a meeting in the lunchroom and recognized each worker with a plaque and a ribbon. The next month, the same two workers had two defects, so there was no award. The following month, the two workers had zero defects, and once again top management called a meeting to give out plaques and ribbons. Elsewhere in the plant, defects, scrap, and rework decreased dramatically as workers evidently sought recognition for quality work. What worked in this particular plant may or may not work in others. And, of course, as illustrated in the cartoon, managers and workers can sometimes have very different perceptions of the value of different awards!

Managing Reward Systems

Much of our discussion on reward systems has focused on general issues. As Table 8.1 shows, however, the organization must address other issues when developing organizational reward systems. The organization must consider its ability to pay employees at certain levels, economic and labor market conditions, and the impact of the pay system on organizational financial performance. In addition, the organization must consider the relationship between performance and

table 8.1

Issues to Consider in Developing Reward Systems

Issue	Important Examples
Pay Secrecy	• Open, closed, partial • Link with performance appraisal • Equity perceptions
Employee Participation	• By human resource department • By joint employee/management committee
Flexible System	• Cafeteria-style benefits • Annual lump sum or monthly bonus • Salary versus benefits
Ability to Pay	• Organization's financial performance • Expected future earnings
Economic and Labor Market Factors	• Inflation rate • Industry pay standards • Unemployment rate
Impact on Organizational Performance	• Increase in costs • Impact on performance
Expatriate Compensation	• Cost of living differentials • Managing related equity issues

rewards as well as the issues of reward system flexibility, employee participation in the reward system, pay secrecy, and expatriate compensation.

Linking Performance and Rewards

For managers to take full advantage of the symbolic value of pay, there must be a perception on the part of employees that their rewards are linked to their performance. For example, if everyone in an organization starts working for the same hourly rate and then receives a predetermined wage increase every six months or year, there is clearly no relationship between performance and rewards. Instead, the organization is indicating that all entry-level employees are worth the same amount, and pay increases are tied solely to the length of time an employee works in the organization. This holds true whether the employee is a top, average, or mediocre employee. The only requirement is that the employee work well enough to avoid being fired.

At the other extreme, an organization might attempt to tie all compensation to actual performance. Thus, each new employee might start at a different wage, as determined by his or her experience, education, skills, and other job-related factors. After joining the organization, the individual then receives rewards based on actual performance. One employee, for example, might start at $15 an hour because she has ten years of experience and a good performance record at her previous employer. Another might start the same job at a rate of $10.50 an hour because he has only four years' experience and an adequate but not outstanding performance record. Assuming the first employee performs up to expectations, she might also get several pay increases, bonuses, and awards throughout the year whereas the second employee might get only one or two small increases and no other rewards. Of course, organizations must ensure that pay differences are based strictly on performance (including seniority), not on factors that do not relate to performance (such as gender, ethnicity, or other discriminatory factors).

In reality, most organizations attempt to develop a reward strategy somewhere between these two extremes. Because it is really quite difficult to differentiate all the employees, most firms use some basic compensation level for everyone. For example, they might start everyone performing a specific job at the same rate, regardless of experience. They might also work to provide reasonable incentives and other inducements for high performers while making sure that they don't ignore the average employees. The key fact for managers to remember is simply that if they expect rewards to motivate performance, employees must see a clear, direct link between their own job-related behaviors and the attainment of those rewards.[21]

Flexible Reward Systems

A flexible reward system allows employees to choose the combination of benefits that best suits their needs.

Flexible, or cafeteria-style, reward systems are a recent and increasingly popular variation on the standard compensation system. A **flexible reward system** allows employees, within specified ranges, to choose the combination of benefits that best suits their needs. For example, a younger worker just starting out might prefer to have especially strong health-care coverage with few deductibles. A worker with a few years of experience might prefer to have more child-care benefits. A midcareer employee with more financial security might prefer more time off with pay. And older workers might prefer to have more rewards concentrated into their retirement plans.

Some organizations are starting to apply the flexible approach to pay. For example, employees sometimes have the option of taking an annual salary increase in one lump sum rather than in monthly increments. General Electric recently implemented such a system for some of its managers. UNUM Corporation, a large insurance firm, allows all of its employees the option of drawing a full third of their annual compensation in the month of January. This makes it easier for them to handle such major expenses as purchasing a new automobile, buying a home, or covering college education costs for children. Obviously, the administrative costs of providing this level of flexibility are greater, but many employees value this flexibility and may develop strong loyalty and attachment to an employer who offers this kind of compensation package.

Participative Pay Systems

In keeping with the current trend toward worker involvement in organizational decision making, employee participation in the pay process is also increasing. A participative pay system may involve the employee in the system's design, administration, or both. A pay system can be designed by staff members of the organization's human resources department, a committee of managers in the organization, an outside consultant, the employees, or a combination of these sources. Organizations that have used a joint management employee task force to design the compensation system have generally succeeded in designing and implementing a plan that managers could use and that employees believed in. Employee participation in administering the pay system is a natural extension of having employees participate in its design. Examples of companies that have involved employees in the administration of the pay system include Romac Industries, where employees vote on the pay of other employees; Graphic Controls, where each manager's pay is determined by a group of peers; and the Friedman-Jacobs Company, where employees set their own wages based on their perceptions of their performance.[22]

Pay Secrecy

When a company has a policy of open salary information, the exact salary amounts for employees are public knowledge. State governments, for instance, make public the salaries of everyone on their payrolls. A policy of complete secrecy means that no information is available to employees regarding other employees' salaries, average or percentage raises, or salary ranges. The National Labor Relations Board recently upheld an earlier ruling that an employer starting or enforcing a rule that forbids "employees to discuss their salaries" constitutes interference, restraint, and coercion of protected employee rights under the National Labor Relations Act. Although a few organizations have completely public or completely secret systems, most have systems somewhere in the middle.

Expatriate Compensation

Expatriate compensation is yet another important issue in managing reward systems.[23] Consider, for example, a manager living and working in Houston currently making $250,000 a year. That income allows the manager to live in a certain kind of home, drive a certain kind of car, have access to certain levels of medical care, and live a certain kind of lifestyle. Now suppose the manager is asked to accept a transfer to Tokyo, Geneva, or London, cities where the cost of living is considerably higher than in Houston. The same salary cannot begin to support a comparable lifestyle in those cities. Consequently, the employer is almost certain to redesign the manager's compensation package so that the employee's lifestyle in the new location will be comparable to that in the old.

Now consider a different scenario. Suppose the same manager is asked to accept a transfer to an underdeveloped nation. The cost of living in this nation might be quite low by U.S. standards. But there may also be relatively few choices in housing, poorer schools and medical care, a harsh climate, greater personal danger, or similar unattractive characteristics. The firm will probably have to pay the manager some level of additional compensation to offset the decrement in quality of lifestyle. Thus, developing rewards for expatriates is a complicated process.

Figure 8.5 illustrates the approach to expatriate compensation used by one major multinational corporation. The left side of the figure shows how a U.S. employee currently uses her or his salary—part of it goes for taxes, part is saved, and the rest is consumed. When a person is asked to move abroad, a human resource

figure 8.5

The Expatriate Compensation Balance Sheet

Organizations that ask employees to accept assignments in foreign locations must usually adjust their compensation levels to account for differences in cost of living and similar factors. Amoco uses the system shown here. The employee's domestic base salary is first broken down into the three categories shown on the left. Then adjustments are made by adding compensation to the categories on the right until an appropriate, equitable level of compensation is achieved.

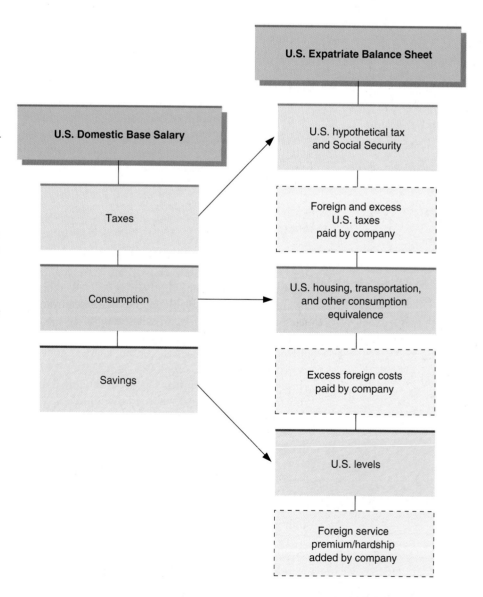

manager works with the employee to develop an equitable balance sheet for the new compensation package. As shown on the right side of the figure, the individual's compensation package will potentially consist of six components. First, the individual will receive income to cover what his or her taxes and Social Security payments in the United States will be. The individual may also have to pay foreign taxes and additional U.S. taxes as a result of the move, so the company covers these as well.

Next, the firm also pays an amount adequate to the employee's current consumption levels in the United States. If the cost of living is greater in the foreign location than at home, the firm pays the excess foreign costs. The employee also receives income for saving comparable to what he or she is currently saving. Finally, if the employee faces a hardship because of the assignment, an additional foreign service premium or hardship allowance is added by the firm. Not surprisingly, then, expatriate compensation packages can be very expensive for an organization and must be carefully developed and managed.[24]

Synopsis

A goal is a desirable objective. The goal-setting theory of motivation suggests that appropriate goal difficulty, specificity, acceptance, and commitment will result in higher levels of motivated performance. Management by objectives, or MBO, extends goal setting throughout an organization by cascading goals down from the top of the firm to the bottom.

Performance measurement is the process by which work behaviors are measured and compared with established standards and the results recorded and communicated. Its purposes are to evaluate employees' work performance and to provide information for organizational uses such as compensation, personnel planning, and employee training and development. Two primary issues in performance appraisal are who does the appraisals and how often they are done. Performance can be appraised through individual assessment methods (graphic rating scales, checklists, essays, behaviorally anchored rating scales, forced choice, and management by objectives); comparative techniques (ranking, forced distribution, and paired comparison); and new approaches that use multiple raters and comparative methods.

To practice total quality management, performance measurement is imperative. Continuous improvement, the foundation of total quality management, requires effective performance management. The essential elements for success of TQM are commitment to objectives, job analysis, performance plans, and measurement of performance. Learning organizations attempt to promote continuous improvement through a strategy of constant employee learning, training, and development.

The purpose of the reward system is to attract, retain, and motivate qualified employees and to maintain a pay structure that is internally equitable and externally competitive. Rewards have both surface and symbolic value. Rewards take the form of money, benefits, perquisites, awards, and incentives. Factors such as motivational impact, cost, and fit with the organizational system must be considered when designing or analyzing a reward system.

The effective management of a reward system requires that performance be linked with rewards. Managing rewards entails dealing with issues such as flexible reward systems, employee participation in the pay system, the secrecy of pay systems, and expatriate rewards.

Discussion Questions

1. Critique the goal-setting theory of motivation.

2. Develop a framework whereby an instructor could use goal setting in running a class such as this one.

3. Why are employees not simply left alone to do their jobs instead of having their performance measured and evaluated all the time?

4. In what ways is your performance as a student evaluated?

5. How can you apply total quality management to your job as an independent student?

6. Can performance on some jobs simply not be measured? Why or why not?

7. What conditions make it easier for an organization to achieve continuous improvement? What conditions make it more difficult?

8. As a student in this class, what "rewards" do you receive in exchange for your time and effort? What are the rewards for the professor who teaches this class? How do your contributions and rewards differ from those of some other student in the class?

9. Do you expect to obtain the rewards you discussed in question 8 on the basis of your intelligence, your hard work, the number of hours you spend in the library, your height, your good looks, your work experience, or some other personal factor?

10. What rewards are easiest for managers to control? What rewards are more difficult to control?

11. Often institutions in federal and state governments give the same percentage pay raise to all their employees. What do you think is the effect of this type of pay raise on employee motivation?

Organizational Behavior Case for Discussion

Rewarding the Hourly Worker

Hourly workers—people who are paid a set dollar amount for each hour they work—have long been the backbone of the U.S. economy. But times are changing, and with them so also is the lot of the hourly worker. As they can with most employment conditions, organizations are able to take a wider variety of approaches to managing compensation for hourly workers. And nowhere are these differences more apparent than in the contrasting conditions for hourly workers at General Motors and Wal-Mart.

General Motors is an old, traditional industrial company that until recently was the nation's largest employer. And for decades, its hourly workers have been protected by strong labor unions like the United Auto Workers (UAW). These unions, in turn, have forged contracts and established working conditions that almost seem archaic in today's economy. Consider, for example, the employment conditions of Tim Philbrick, a forty-two-year-old plant worker and union member at the firm's Fairfax plant near Kansas City who has worked for GM for twenty-three years.

Mr. Philbrick makes almost $20 an hour in base pay. With a little overtime, his annual earnings top $60,000. But even then, he is far from the highest-paid factory worker at GM. Skilled-trade workers like electricians and toolmakers make $2 to $2.50 an hour more, and with greater overtime opportunities often make $100,000 or more per year. Mr. Philbrick also gets a no-deductible health insurance policy that allows him to see any doctor he wants. He gets four weeks of vacation per year, plus two weeks off at Christmas and at least another week off in July. Mr. Philbrick gets two paid twenty-three-minute breaks and a paid thirty-minute lunch break per day. He also has the option of retiring after thirty years with full benefits.

GM estimates that, with benefits, its average worker makes more than $43 an hour. Perhaps not surprisingly, then, the firm is always looking for opportunities to reduce its workforce through attrition and cutbacks, with the goal of replacing production capacity with lower-cost labor abroad. The UAW, on the other hand, of course, is staunchly opposed to further workforce reductions and cutbacks. And long-standing work rules strictly dictate who gets overtime, who can be laid off and who can't, and myriad other employment conditions for Mr. Philbrick and his peers.

But the situation at GM is quite different—in a lot of ways—from conditions at Wal-Mart. Along many different dimensions Wal-Mart is slowly but surely supplanting General Motors as the quintessential U.S. corporation. For example, it is growing rapidly, is becoming more and more ingrained in the American lifestyle, and now employs more people than GM did in its heyday. But the hourly worker at Wal-Mart has a much different experience than the hourly worker at GM.

For example, consider Ms. Nancy Handley, a twenty-seven-year-old Wal-Mart employee who oversees the men's department at a big store in St. Louis. Jobs like Ms. Handley's pay between $9 and $11 an hour, or about $20,000 a year. About $100 a month is deducted from Ms. Handley's paycheck to help cover the costs of benefits. Her health insurance has a $250 deductible; she then pays 20 percent of her health-care costs as long as she uses a set of approved physicians. During her typical workday, Ms. Handley gets two fifteen-minute breaks and an hour for lunch, which are unpaid. Some feel that the conditions are inadequate. Barbara Ehrenreich, author of *Nickel and Dimed: On (Not) Getting By in America*, worked at a Wal-Mart while researching her book and now says, "Why would anybody put up with the wages we were paid?"

But Ms. Handley doesn't feel mistreated by Wal-Mart. Far from it, she says she is appropriately compensated for what she does. She has received three merit raises in the last seven years and has ample job security. Moreover, if she decides to try for advancement, Wal-Mart seems to offer considerable potential, promoting thousands of hourly workers a year to the ranks of management. And Ms. Handley is clearly not unique in her views—Wal-Mart employees routinely reject any and all overtures from labor unions.

In the twenty-first century, the gap between "Old Economy" and "New Economy" workers, between unionized manufacturing workers and nonunion or service workers, may be shrinking. Unions are losing their power in the auto industry, for example, as foreign-owned plants within the United States give makers such as Toyota and BMW, which are nonunion, a cost advantage over the Big Three U.S. automakers. U.S. firms are telling the UAW and other unions, "We're becoming noncompetitive, and unless you organize the [foreign-owned firms], we're going to have to modify the proposals we make to you." At the same time, Wal-Mart is facing lawsuits from employees who claim the retailer forced them to work unpaid overtime, among other charges. At a Las Vegas store, the firm faces its first union election. In a world where Wal-Mart now employs three times as many workers as GM, it may be inevitable that the retailer's labor will organize. On the other hand, will labor unions continue to lose their power to determine working conditions for America's workforce?

"Why would anybody put up with the wages we were paid?" —Barbara Ehrenreich, author of *Nickel and Dimed: On (Not) Getting By in America*

References: Joann Muller, "Can the UAW Stay in the Game?" *Business Week*, June 10, 2002. www.businessweek.com on June 3, 2002; Mark Gimein, "Sam Walton Made Us a Promise," *Fortune*, March 18, 2002. www.fortune.com on June 3, 2002; Barbara Ehrenreich, *Nickel and Dimed: On (Not) Getting By in America*, Metropolitan Books, May 2001 (quotation); "I'm Proud of What I've Made Myself Into—What I've Created," *Wall Street Journal*, August 28, 1997, pp. B1, B5; "That's Why I Like My Job . . . I Have an Impact on Quality," *Wall Street Journal*, August 28, 1997, pp. B1, B8.

Case Questions

1. Compare and contrast hourly working conditions at General Motors and Wal-Mart.
2. Describe the most likely role that the hourly compensation at these two companies plays in motivating employees.
3. Discuss how goal setting might be used for each of the two jobs profiled in this case.

Experiencing Organizational Behavior

Using Compensation to Motivate Workers

Purpose: The purpose of this exercise is to illustrate how compensation can be used to motivate employees.

Format: You will be asked to review eight managers and make salary adjustments for each.

Procedure: Listed below are your notes on the performance of eight managers who work for you. You (either individually or as a group, depending on your instructor's choice) have to recommend salary increases for eight managers who have just completed their first year with the company and are now to be considered for their first annual raise. Keep in mind that you may be setting precedents and that you need to keep salary costs down. However, there are no formal company restrictions on the kind of raises you can give. Indicate the sizes of the raise that you would like to give each manager by writing a percentage next to each name.

Variations: The instructor might alter the situation in one of several ways. One way is to assume that all of the eight managers entered the company at the same salary, say $30,000, which gives a total salary expense of $240,000. If upper management has allowed a salary raise pool of 10 percent of the current salary expenses, then you as the manager have $24,000 to give out as raises. In this variation, students can deal with actual dollar amounts rather than just percentages for the raises. Another interesting variation is to assume that all of the managers entered the company at different salaries, averaging $30,000. (The instructor can create many interesting possibilities for how these salaries might vary.) Then, the students can suggest salaries for the different managers.

_____ % Abraham McGowan. Abe is not, as far as you can tell, a good performer. You have checked your view with others, and they do not feel that he is effective either. However, you happen to know he has one of the toughest work groups to manage. His subordinates have low skill levels, and the work is dirty and hard. If you lose him, you are not sure whom you could find to replace him.

_____ % Benjy Berger. Benjy is single and seems to live the life of a carefree bachelor. In general, you feel that his job performance is not up to par, and some of his "goofs" are well known to his fellow employees.

_____ % Clyde Clod. You consider Clyde to be one of your best subordinates. However, it is obvious that other people do not consider him to be an effective manager. Clyde has married a rich wife, and as far as you know, he does not need additional money.

_____ %David Doodle. You happen to know from your personal relationship with "Doodles" that he badly needs more money because of certain personal problems he is having. As far as you are concerned, he also happens to be one of the best of your subordinates. For some reason, your enthusiasm is not shared by your other subordinates, and you have heard them make joking remarks about his performance.

_____ % Ellie Ellesberg. Ellie has been very successful so far in the tasks she has undertaken. You are particularly impressed by this since she has a hard job. She needs money more than many of the other people, and you are sure that they respect her because of her good performance.

_____ % Fred Foster. Fred has turned out to be a very pleasant surprise to you. He has done an excellent job and it is generally accepted among the others that he is one of the best people. This surprises you because he is generally frivolous and does not seem to care very much about money and promotion.

_____ % Greta Goslow. Your opinion is that Greta is just not cutting the mustard. Surprisingly enough, however, when you check to see how others feel about her, you discover that her work is very highly regarded. You also know that she badly needs a raise. She was just recently widowed and is finding it extremely difficult to support her household and her young family of four.

_____ % Harry Hummer. You know Harry personally, and he just seems to squander his money continually. He has a fairly easy job assignment, and your view is that he does not do it particularly well. You are, therefore, quite surprised to find that several of the other new managers think that he is the best of the new group.

After you have made the assignments for the eight people, you will have a chance to discuss them either in groups or in the larger class.

Follow-up Questions

1. Is there a clear difference between the highest and lowest performer? Why or why not?
2. Did you notice differences in the types of information that you had available to make the raise decisions? How did you use the different sources of information?
3. In what ways did your assignment of raises reflect different views of motivation?

Reference: Edward E. Lawler III, "Motivation Through Compensation," adapted by D. T. Hall, in *Instructor's Manual for Experiences in Management and Organizational Behavior* (New York: John Wiley & Sons, 1975). Reprinted by permission of the author.

Self-Assessment Exercise

Diagnosing Poor Performance and Enhancing Motivation

Introduction: Formal performance appraisal and feedback are part of assuring proper performance in an organization. The following assessment is designed to help you understand how to detect poor performance and overcome it.

Procedure: Please respond to the following statements by writing a number from the following rating scale in the left-hand column. Your answers should reflect your attitudes and behaviors as they are *now*.

Strongly agree   = 6
Agree   = 5
Slightly agree   = 4
Slightly disagree = 3
Disagree   = 2
Strongly disagree = 1

When another person needs to be motivated,

_____ 1. I always approach a performance problem by first establishing whether it is caused by a lack of motivation or ability.

_____ 2. I always establish a clear standard of expected performance.

_____ 3. I always offer to provide training and information, without offering to do the task myself.

_____ 4. I am honest and straightforward in providing feedback on performance and assessing advancement opportunities.

_____ 5. I use a variety of rewards to reinforce exceptional performance.

_____ 6. When discipline is required, I identify the problem, describe its consequences, and explain how it should be corrected.

_____ 7. I design task assignments to make them interesting and challenging.

_____ 8. I determine what rewards are valued by the person and strive to make those available.

_____ 9. I make sure that the person feels fairly and equitably treated.

_____ 10. I make sure that the person gets timely feedback from those affected by task performance.

_____ 11. I carefully diagnose the causes of poor performance before taking any remedial or disciplinary actions.

_____ 12. I always help the person establish performance goals that are challenging, specific, and time-bound.

_____ 13. Only as a last resort do I attempt to reassign or release a poorly performing individual.

_____ 14. Whenever possible, I make sure that valued rewards are linked to high performance.

_____ 15. I consistently discipline when effort is below expectations and capabilities.

_____ 16. I try to combine or rotate assignments so that the person can use a variety of skills.

_____ 17. I try to arrange for the person to work with others in a team, for the mutual support of all.

_____ 18. I make sure that the person is using realistic standards for measuring fairness.

_____ 19. I provide immediate compliments and other forms of recognition for meaningful accomplishments.

_____ 20. I always determine if the person has the necessary resources and support to succeed in the task.

OB Online

1. Locate the web site of a firm that indicates that it uses goal setting and/or MBO for its employees. How similar or different is the process described on the web site as compared with the models and approaches discussed in this chapter?

2. Find five company web sites that stress the importance of quality to the firm's mission and strategy. Identify the role of performance management in each firm's quality program.

3. Search for information on the Internet about 360-degree feedback. What kind of information is most widely available and accessible?

4. Find five company web sites that provide some information about the rewards that the firms make available to their employees. Relate each to the discussion in this chapter.

Building Managerial Skills

Exercise Overview: All managers must be able to communicate effectively with others in the organization. Communication is especially important in terms of dealing with employment-related issues.

Exercise Background: As noted in the chapter, many companies provide various benefits to their workers. These benefits may include such things as pay for time not worked, insurance coverage, pension plans, and so forth. These benefits are often very costly to the organization. Benefits often equal one-third or more of what employees are paid in wages and salaries. In some countries, such as Germany, the figures are even higher.

However, many employees often fail to appreciate the actual value of the benefits their employers provide to them. For example, they frequently underestimate the dollar value of their benefits. In addition, when comparing their income with that of others or when comparing alternative job offers, many people focus almost entirely on direct compensation—wages and salaries directly paid to the individual.

For example, consider a college graduate who has two offers. One job offer is for $40,000 a year, and the other is for $42,000. The individual is likely to see the second offer as being more desirable, even though the first offer may have sufficiently more attractive benefits that would make the total compensation packages equivalent to each other.

Exercise Task: With this information as context, respond to the following questions:

1. Why do you think most people focus on pay when assessing their compensation?

2. If you were the human resource manager for a firm, how would you go about communicating benefit values to your employees?

3. Suppose an employee comes to you and says that he is thinking about leaving for a "better job." You then learn that he is defining "better" only in terms of higher pay. How might you go about helping him compare the total compensation (including benefits) packages of his current job and of the "better job"?

4. Some firms today are cutting their benefits. How would you go about communicating a benefit cut to your employees?

9 Managing Stress and the Work-Life Balance

Management Preview

▶ Many people today work long hours, face constant deadlines, and are subject to pressure to produce more and more. Organizations and the people who run them are under constant pressure to increase income while keeping costs in check. To do things faster and better—but with fewer people—is the goal of many companies today. An unfortunate effect of this trend is to put too much pressure on people—operating employees, other managers, and oneself. The results can indeed be increased performance, higher profits, and faster growth. But stress, burnout, turnover, aggression, and other unpleasant side effects can also occur. In this chapter, we examine how and why stress occurs in organizations and how to better understand and control it. First, we explore the nature of stress. Then we look at such important individual differences as Type A and B personality profiles and their role in stress. Next, we discuss a number of causes of stress and consider the potential consequences of stress. We then highlight several things people and organizations can do to manage stress at work. We conclude by discussing an important factor related to stress—linkages between work and the nonwork parts of people's lives. But before we begin, let's examine how work is increasingly becoming a twenty-four-hour-a-day phenomenon.

▼ ▼ ▼

Business competition is undeniably becoming more intense. Increased free trade, the recession of 2000–2001, and the events of September 11 have led to difficult times in virtually every industry. And, unfortunately, workers' quality of life is one of the areas in which sacrifices are being made.

Many factories are scheduling continuous operations because it's too expensive to let an expensive facility remain idle. Plant closures and consolidations have contributed to the problem, and even automation is to blame—new plants are designed for continuous operation. "Once an operation goes 24/7, you don't want to mess with the schedule," says Tim Robertson, a spokesman for Exide Technologies. According to Bill Sirois, a consultant who specializes in helping companies implement a nonstop schedule, almost all companies begin twelve-hour work shifts when they move to continuous operations, and most also begin to rotate shifts in order to be fair to every employee. Workers, consequently, are working unusual hours, longer days, and longer weeks.

One negative outcome is fatigue. Mark Rosekind, president of Alertness Solutions, says, "Fatigue undermines every aspect of human capability—from decision-making abilities to alertness." Accidents are most likely to occur between 3 and 5 A.M., when workers are most tired. After twelve years of rotating shift work for Corning, Michael Tucker claims that fatigue and depression are related, explaining, "You're tired all the time, and it keeps you feeling down." Health problems run the gamut from lack of sleep to depression to increased blood pressure. To compound the difficulties, most workers are reluctant to report health or mental health concerns. Other workers complain about the disruption of their weekly routine. Without a fixed schedule, it's impossible for them to attend church regularly, coach children's sports, or take night school classes.

"Fatigue undermines every aspect of human capability—from decision-making abilities to alertness."—Mark Rosekind, president of Alertness Solutions, a Cupertino, California, consulting firm

In spite of their concerns, some workers appreciate the flexibility. Most employers offer some incentive—either increased pay to compensate for lost overtime, more weekends free, or help with child or elder care. In addition, unions, which generally oppose continuous operations, may be inclined to drop their objections if increased hiring occurs. When a Danville plant instituted a new plan, employees suddenly had one weekday free every week. "People with small children love it; they get more time with their children," says plant manager Darrell Finney.

Christopher J. Ruhm, an economist at the University of North Carolina at Greensboro who studies localized unemployment, takes this idea a step further. His studies demonstrate that being out of work, even involuntarily, leads to lower stress, less drinking and smoking, fewer accidents, and more exercise. Overall, a 1 percent increase in unemployment corresponds with a 0.5 percent decrease in the total death rate. According to Professor Ruhm, when employment is high, "people are so busy [that] they don't have time to invest in health. So they drink more, and eat unhealthily."

Whether the increase in working hours is perceived as primarily positive or negative, the situation is one that businesses will have to confront, and soon. With the increasing prevalence of both two-wage-earner families and single parents, the aging of America's population, and the recent upsurge in births to mothers in their forties and fifties, it seems that just about everyone will be needing more, not less, time off from work in the future.

References: Leslie Eaton, "So You Lost Your Job. Feel Better Now?" *New York Times*, April 7, 2002, p. WWC1. See www.nytimes.com; Michael Kinsman, "Paid-Time-Off Bank Benefits Boss, Workers," *San Diego Union-Tribune*, November 12, 2001. www.signonsandiego.com on April 10, 2002; Timothy Aeppel, "More Plants Go 24/7, and Workers Are Left at Sixes and Sevens," *Wall Street Journal*, July 24, 2001, pp. A1–A6 (quotation p. A6). See www.wsj.com.

Continuous work hours are becoming increasingly widespread. Although some people regard working at night and on the weekends as a way to help reduce stress during other periods of the week, others no doubt see night and weekend work itself as stressful. Moreover, when people work varying schedules, their relationships with their family and friends are also affected. To better understand how these processes affect different individuals, we first describe the nature of stress itself.

The Nature of Stress

M any people think of stress as a simple problem. In reality, however, stress is complex and often misunderstood.[1] To learn how job stress truly works, we must first define it and then describe the process through which it develops.

Stress Defined

Stress has been defined in many ways, but most definitions say that stress is caused by a stimulus, that the stimulus can be either physical or psychological, and that the individual responds to the stimulus in some way.[2] Therefore, we define **stress** as a person's adaptive response to a stimulus that places excessive psychological or physical demands on him or her.

Given the underlying complexities of this definition, we need to examine its components carefully. First is the notion of adaptation. As we will discuss presently, people may adapt to stressful circumstances in any of several ways. Second is the role of the stimulus. This stimulus, generally called a "stressor," is anything that induces stress. Third, stressors can be either psychological or physical. Finally, the demands the stressor places on the individual must be excessive for stress to actually result. Of course, what is excessive for one person may be perfectly tolerable for another. The point is simply that a person must perceive the demands as excessive or stress will not actually be present.

Stress is a person's adaptive response to a stimulus that places excessive psychological or physical demands on that person.

The Stress Process

Much of what we know about stress today can be traced to the pioneering work of Dr. Hans Selye.[3] Among Selye's most important contributions were his identification of the general adaptation syndrome and the concepts of eustress and distress.

The general adaptation syndrome (GAS) identifies three stages of response to a stressor: alarm, resistance, and exhaustion.

General Adaptation Syndrome Figure 9.1 graphically shows the **general adaptation syndrome (GAS).** According to this model, each of us has a normal level of resistance to stressful events. Some of us can tolerate a great deal of stress and others much less, but we all have a threshold at which stress starts to affect us.

The GAS begins when a person first encounters a stressor. The first stage is called "alarm." At this point, the person may feel some degree of panic and begin to wonder how to cope. The individual may also have to resolve a "fight-or-flight" question: Can I deal with this, or should I run away? For example, suppose a manager

figure 9.1

The General Adaptation Syndrome

The general adaptation syndrome, or GAS, perspective describes three stages of the stress process. The initial stage is called alarm. As illustrated here, a person's resistance often dips slightly below the normal level during this stage. Next comes actual resistance to the stressor, usually leading to an increase above the person's normal level of resistance. Finally, in stage 3, exhaustion may set in, and the person's resistance declines sharply below normal levels.

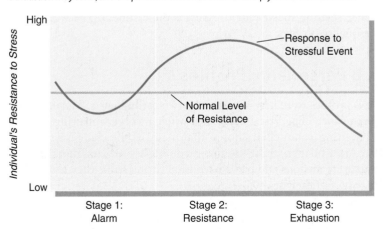

is assigned to write a lengthy report overnight. Her first reaction may be "How will I ever get this done by tomorrow?"

If the stressor is too extreme, the person may simply be unable to cope with it. In most cases, however, the individual gathers his or her strength (physical or emotional) and begins to resist the negative effects of the stressor. The manager with the long report to write may calm down, call home to tell her kids that she's working late, roll up her sleeves, order out for dinner, and get to work. Thus, at stage 2 of the GAS, the person is resisting the effects of the stressor.

Often, the resistance phase ends the GAS. If the manager completes the report earlier than she expected, she may drop it in her briefcase, smile to herself, and head home tired but happy. On the other hand, prolonged exposure to a stressor without resolution may bring on phase 3 of the GAS: exhaustion. At this stage, the person literally gives up and can no longer fight the stressor. For example, the manager may fall asleep at her desk at 3 A.M. and fail to finish the report.

Distress and Eustress   Selye also pointed out that the sources of stress need not be bad. For example, receiving a bonus and then having to decide what to do with the money can be stressful. So can getting a promotion, making a speech as part of winning a major award, getting married, and similar "good" things. Selye called this type of stress **eustress.** As we will see later, eustress can lead to a number of positive outcomes for the individual.

Of course, there is also negative stress. Called **distress,** this is what most people think of when they hear the word "stress." Excessive pressure, unreasonable demands on our time, and bad news all fall into this category. As the term suggests, this form of stress generally results in negative consequences for the individual.

For purposes of simplicity, we will continue to use the simple term "stress" throughout this chapter. But as you read and study the chapter, remember that stress can be either good or bad. It can motivate and stimulate us, or it can lead to any number of dangerous side effects. Recent research into this idea is also summarized in the "Mastering Change" box.

> Eustress is the pleasurable stress that accompanies positive events.
>
> Distress is the unpleasant stress that accompanies negative events.

Individual Differences and Stress

We have already alluded to the fact that stress can affect different people in different ways. Given our earlier discussion of individual differences back in Chapter 4, of course, this should come as no surprise.[4] The most fully developed individual difference relating specifically to stress is the distinction between Type A and Type B personality profiles.

Type A and B Personality Profiles

Type A and Type B profiles were first observed by two cardiologists, Meyer Friedman and Ray Rosenman.[5] They first got the idea when a worker repairing the upholstery on their waiting-room chairs noted that many of the chairs were worn only on the front. After further study, the two cardiologists realized that many of their heart patients were anxious and had a hard time sitting still—they were literally sitting on the edges of their seats!

Using this observation as a starting point, Friedman and Rosenman began to study the phenomenon more closely. They eventually concluded that their patients were exhibiting one of two very different types of behavior patterns. Their re-

MASTERING CHANGE

▶ *Stress: The Bad Side and the Good Side*

How many times have you said, "I'm so stressed out"? If you are like most workers, one-quarter to one-half of your workdays are stressful. Job stress is increasing, and, according to John Boudreau of Cornell University, its potential causes include lack of job security, too much red tape, confusion about career goals, and overemphasis on office politics. The National Institute of Occupational Safety and Health (NIOSH) notes that inappropriate task design, lack of participation in decision making, poor interpersonal relations, and dangerous work conditions also contribute to stress.

NIOSH defines job stress as "[T]he harmful physical and emotional responses that occur when the requirements of the job do not match the capabilities, resources, or needs of the worker." This bad stress, also called "hindrance" stress, has many negative consequences for both the worker and for the organization. Stress causes health problems such as fatigue, disturbed sleep, moodiness, high blood pressure, and stomach upset. Nineteen percent of sick days that workers take are actually "stress" days, and health care expenses for stressed workers are 50 percent above average. Stressed workers are also more violent and accident prone, and their productivity declines as stress increases.

However, experts are changing the way they think about stress, recognizing that some stress ("good" or "challenge" stress) may in fact be beneficial. NIOSH researchers maintain, "Challenge energizes us psychologically and phys-

ically, and it motivates us to learn new skills and master our jobs. When a challenge is met, we feel relaxed and satisfied. Thus, challenge is an important ingredient for healthy and productive work." Wendy Boswell, a Texas A & M professor,

"Challenge [good stress] is an important ingredient for healthy and productive work." — *National Institute of Occupational Safety and Health researchers*

agrees, noting that employees actively seek out challenge stress. Challenge stress has been associated with job satisfaction, productivity, and loyalty to the employer.

The good news is that bad stress can be managed. In one radical approach, individuals are advised to switch career paths if they find that their job doesn't meet their expectations. Other, less drastic steps that employees can employ include taking frequent breaks from work, exercising, or seeking counseling to learn to calm down quickly after an upset. Employers also can help by ensuring that workers have appropriate work loads, using care in assigning personnel to jobs, providing opportunities to communicate and learn about stress, and being sensitive to the other stressors in employees' lives, such as family responsibilities.

References: "Stress at Work," National Institute for Occupational Safety and Health web site (quotation). www.cdc.gov/niosh on May 10, 2002; Lisa Belkin, "When the Job You Love Makes You Ill," *New York Times*, April 14, 2002, p. WC1. See www.nytimes.com; Michael Kinsman, "Paid-Time-Off Bank Benefits Boss, Workers," *San Diego Union-Tribune*, November 12, 2001. www.signonsandiego.com on April 10, 2002; Sue Shellenbarger, "Learning How to Work with the Good Stress, Live Without the Bad," *Wall Street Journal*, July 25, 2001. See www.wsj.com.

Type A people are extremely competitive, are highly committed to work, and have a strong sense of time urgency.

Type B people are less competitive, are less committed to work, and have a weaker sense of time urgency.

search also led them to conclude that the differences were personality based. They labeled these two behavior patterns "Type A" and "Type B."

The extreme **Type A** individual is extremely competitive, very devoted to work, and has a strong sense of time urgency. Moreover, this person is likely to be aggressive, impatient, and highly work oriented. He or she has a lot of drive and motivation and wants to accomplish as much as possible in as short a time as possible. The manager highlighted in the cartoon is almost certainly a Type A individual!

The extreme **Type B** person, in contrast, is less competitive, is less devoted to work, and has a weaker sense of time urgency. This person feels less conflict with either people or time and has a more balanced, relaxed approach to life. She or he has more confidence and is able to work at a constant pace.

A common-sense expectation might be that Type A people are more successful than Type B people. In reality, however, this is not necessarily true—the Type B person is not necessarily any more or less successful than the Type A. There are

Among other things, Type A individuals are very devoted to work and have a lot of drive and motivation. This manager, for example, is clearly mixing business with pleasure! To the extent that he is choosing to keep in contact with his office while on vacation, he may see this activity as simply a part of his work. On the other hand, of course, people may suffer a variety of difficulties if they never disengage from work. Indeed, although Type A individuals may achieve rapid short-term career success, they may also be more susceptible to burnout later in life.

Reference: Roy Delgado & Associates.

" SURE, SURE ... I'M HAVING A GREAT VACATION .. "

several possible explanations for this. For example, Type A people may alienate others because of their drive and may miss out on important learning opportunities in their quest to get ahead. Type Bs, on the other hand, may have better interpersonal reputations and may learn a wider array of skills.

Friedman and Rosenman pointed out that most people are not purely Type A or Type B; instead, people tend toward one or the other type. For example, an individual might exhibit marked Type A characteristics much of the time but still be able to relax once in a while and even occasionally forget about time. Likewise, even the most "laid-back" Type B person may occasionally spend some time obsessing about work.

"I've literally lost my ability to relax." —George Bell, president of ExciteAtHome, an Internet firm[6]

Friedman and Rosenman's initial research on the Type A and Type B profile differences yielded some alarming findings. In particular, they suggested that Type As were much more likely to develop coronary heart disease than were Type Bs. In recent years, however, follow-up research by other scientists has suggested that the relationship between Type A behavior and the risk of coronary heart disease is not all that straightforward.

Although the reasons are unclear, recent findings suggest that Type As are much more complex than originally believed. For example, in addition to exhibiting the characteristics already noted, Type As are also more likely to be depressed and hostile. Any one of these characteristics or a combination of them can lead to heart problems. Moreover, different approaches to measuring Type A tendencies have yielded different results.

Finally, in one study that found Type As actually to be less susceptible to heart problems than Type Bs, the researchers offered an explanation consistent with earlier thinking: Because Type As are relatively compulsive, they may seek treatment earlier and are more likely to follow their doctors' orders![7]

Stress is how people respond to stimuli that result in excessive psychological or physical demands on them. Individuals who work in law enforcement and surveillance, for example, are subject to intense and constant pressure, even more so after the terrorist attacks of September 11, 2001. For instance, these officers must continuously monitor cameras focused on various Washington landmarks. If they respond too quickly to something suspicious they will be criticized for being overly zealous. But failing to respond to a real threat would be disastrous.

Hardiness and Optimism

Hardiness is a person's ability to cope with stress.

Two other important individual differences related to stress are hardiness and optimism. Research suggests that some people have what are termed hardier personalities than others.[8] **Hardiness** is a person's ability to cope with stress. People with hardy personalities have an internal locus of control, are strongly committed to the activities in their lives, and view change as an opportunity for advancement and growth. Such people are seen as relatively unlikely to suffer illness if they experience high levels of pressure and stress. On the other hand, people with low hardiness may have more difficulties in coping with pressure and stress.

Optimism is the extent to which a person sees life in relatively positive or negative terms.

Another potentially important individual difference is optimism. **Optimism** is the extent to which a person sees life in positive or negative terms. A popular expression used to convey this idea concerns the glass half filled with water. A person with a lot of optimism will tend to see it as half full whereas a person with less optimism (a pessimist) will often see it as half empty. Optimism is also related to positive and negative affectivity, as discussed earlier in Chapter 4. In general, optimistic people tend to handle stress better. They will be able to see the positive aspects of the situation and recognize that things may eventually improve. In contrast, less optimistic people may focus more on the negative aspects of the situation and expect things to get worse, not better.

Cultural differences also are important in determining how stress affects people. For example, research by Cary Cooper suggests that American executives may experience less stress than executives in many other countries, including Japan and Brazil. The major causes of stress also differ across countries. In Germany, for example, major causes of stress are time pressure and deadlines. In South Africa, long work hours more frequently lead to stress. And in Sweden, the major cause of stress is the encroachment of work on people's private lives.[9]

Other research suggests that women are perhaps more prone to experience the psychological effects of stress whereas men may report more physical effects.[10] Finally, some studies suggest that people who regard themselves as complex individuals are better able to handle stress than people who view themselves as relatively simple.[11] We should add, however, that the study of individual differences in stress is still in its infancy. It would therefore be premature to draw rigid conclusions about how different types of people handle stress.

Common Causes of Stress

Many things can cause stress. Figure 9.2 shows two broad categories: organizational stressors and life stressors. It also shows three categories of stress consequences: individual consequences, organizational consequences, and burnout.

figure 9.2

Causes and Consequences of Stress

The causes and consequences of stress are related in complex ways. As shown here, most common causes of stress can be classified as either organizational stressors or life stressors. Similarly, common consequences include individual and organizational consequences, as well as burnout.

Reference: Adapted from James C. Quick and Jonathan D. Quick, *Organizational Stress and Preventive Management* (McGraw-Hill, 1984) pp. 19, 44, and 76.

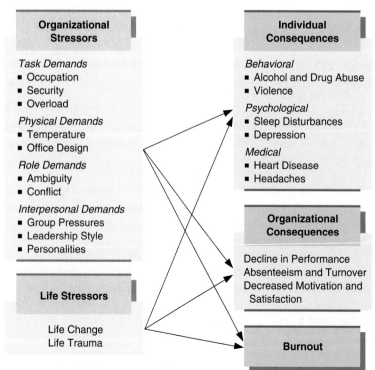

Organizational Stressors

Organizational stressors are various factors in the workplace that can cause stress. Four general sets of organizational stressors are task demands, physical demands, role demands, and interpersonal demands.

Task Demands Task demands are stressors associated with the specific job a person performs. Some occupations are by nature more stressful than others. The jobs of surgeons, air-traffic controllers, and professional football coaches are generally more stressful than those of general practitioners, airline ticket agents, and football team equipment managers. Table 9.1 lists a representative sample of stressful jobs from among a total set of 250 jobs studied. As you can see, the job of U.S. president was found to be the most stressful, followed by the jobs of firefighter and senior executive. Toward the middle of the distribution are jobs such as mechanical engineer, chiropractor, technical writer, and bank officer. The jobs of broadcast technician, bookkeeper, and actuary were among the least stressful jobs in this study.

Beyond specific task-related pressures, other aspects of a job may pose physical threats to a person's health. Unhealthy conditions exist in occupations such as coal mining and toxic waste handling. Security is another task demand that can cause stress. Someone in a relatively secure job is not likely to worry unduly about losing that position. Threats to job security can increase stress dramatically. For example, stress generally increases throughout an organization during a period of layoffs or immediately after a merger with another firm. This phenomenon has been observed at a number of organizations, including AT&T, Safeway, and Digital Equipment.

A final task demand stressor is overload. Overload occurs when a person simply has more work than he or she can handle. The overload can be either quantitative (the person has too many tasks to perform or too little time to perform them) or qualitative (the person may believe that he or she lacks the ability to do the job). We should note that the opposite of overload may also be undesirable. As Figure 9.3

Organizational stressors are factors in the workplace that can cause stress.

Task demands are stressors associated with the specific job a person performs.

table 9.1

The Most Stressful Jobs

How selected occupations ranked in an evaluation of 250 jobs*

Rank	Occupation	Stress Score	Rank	Occupation	Stress Score
1	U.S. president	176.6	103	Market-research analyst	42.1
2	Firefighter	110.9	104	Personnel recruiter	41.8
3	Senior executive	108.6	113	Hospital administrator	39.6
6	Surgeon	99.5	119	Economist	38.7
10	Air-traffic controller	83.1	122	Mechanical engineer	38.3
12	Public-relations executive	78.5	124	Chiropractor	37.9
16	Advertising account executive	74.6	132	Technical writer	36.5
17	Real-estate agent	73.1	144	Bank officer	35.4
20	Stockbroker	71.7	149	Retail salesperson	34.9
22	Pilot	68.7	150	Tax examiner/collector	34.8
25	Architect	66.9	154	Aerospace engineer	34.6
31	Lawyer	64.3	166	Industrial designer	32.1
33	Physician (general practitioner)	64.0	173	Accountant	31.1
35	Insurance agent	63.3	193	Purchasing agent	28.9
42	Advertising salesperson	59.9	194	Insurance underwriter	28.5
47	Auto salesperson	56.3	212	Computer programmer	26.5
50	College professor	54.2	216	Financial planner	26.3
60	School principal	51.7	229	Broadcast technician	24.2
67	Psychologist	50.0	241	Bookkeeper	21.5
81	Executive-search consultant	47.3	245	Actuary	20.2

*Among the criteria used in the rankings: overtime, quotas, deadlines, competitiveness, physical demands, environmental conditions, hazards encountered, initiative required, stamina required, win-lose situations, and working in the public eye.

Reference: The Most Stressful Jobs, February 26, 1996. Republished with permission of Dow Jones, from *Wall Street Journal*, February 26, 1996; permission conveyed through Copyright Clearance Center, Inc.

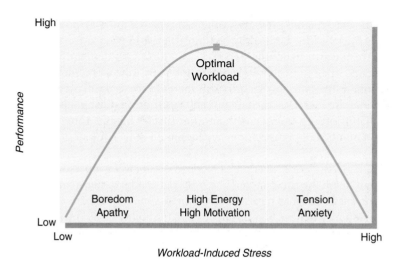

figure 9.3

Workload, Stress, and Performance

Too much stress is clearly undesirable, but too little stress can also lead to unexpected problems. For example, too little stress may result in boredom and apathy and be accompanied by low performance. And although too much stress can cause tension, anxiety, and low performance, for most people there is an optimal level of stress that results in high energy, motivation, and performance.

shows, low task demands can result in boredom and apathy just as overload can cause tension and anxiety. Thus, a moderate degree of workload-related stress is optimal because it leads to high levels of energy and motivation.

Physical Demands   The **physical demands** of a job are its physical requirements on the worker; these demands are a function of the physical characteristics of the setting and the physical tasks the job involves. One important element is temperature. Working outdoors in extreme temperatures can result in stress, as can working in an improperly heated or cooled office. Strenuous labor such as loading heavy cargo or lifting packages can lead to similar results. Office design also can be a problem. A poorly designed office can make it difficult for people to have privacy or can promote too much or too little social interaction. Too much interaction may distract a person from his or

Physical demands are stressors associated with the job's physical setting, such as the adequacy of temperature and lighting and the physical requirements the job makes on the employee.

her task whereas too little may lead to boredom or loneliness. Likewise, poor lighting, inadequate work surfaces, and similar deficiencies can create stress. In addition, shift work can cause disruptions for people because of the way it affects their sleep and leisure-time activities.

Role Demands   **Role demands** also can be stressful for people in organizations. A **role** is a set of expected behaviors associated with a particular position in a group or organization. As such, it has both formal (i.e., job-related and explicit) and in-

"It's hard to have a life when your hours are always changing."—unidentified shift worker[12]

Role demands are stressors associated with the role a person is expected to play.

A role is a set of expected behaviors associated with a particular position in a group or organization.

Role ambiguity arises when a role is unclear.

formal (i.e., social and implicit) requirements. People in an organization or work group expect a person in a particular role to act in certain ways. They transmit these expectations both formally and informally. Individuals perceive role expectations with varying degrees of accuracy and then attempt to enact those roles. However, "errors" can creep into this process, resulting in stress-inducing problems known as role ambiguity, role conflict, and role overload.

Role ambiguity arises when a role is unclear. If your instructor tells you to write a term paper but refuses to provide more information, you will probably experience ambiguity. You do not know what the topic is, how long the paper should be, what format to use, or when the paper is due. In work settings, role ambiguity can stem from poor job descriptions, vague instructions from a supervisor, or unclear cues from coworkers. The result is likely to be a subordinate who does not know what to do. Role ambiguity can thus be a significant source of stress.

TALKING TECHNOLOGY

Communication Technology Creates Stress

Once a rarity, cellular telephones are ubiquitous in society today. Walking through any large airport or business center, one notices dozens of people sitting in chairs, leaning against walls, or strolling around, conducting business on their cell phones. Other new communication technologies include personal digital assistants (PDAs) such as the Hewlett-Packard Jornada or the Palm Pilot as well as extra-small "sub-notebook" laptop computers. Some devices incorporate all three functions: phone access, computing ability, and Internet connectivity. Accessories (portable printers, folding keyboards) are also available. For those who don't want to learn an array of new technologies, Internet service providers make voicemail, email, and all other business information available over the World Wide Web through any conventional PC.

The advent of these new technologies has given many managers an opportunity to become considerably more productive. It's easier for them to supervise workers in remote locations, to stay in touch with clients and customers, and to share information with their home offices while traveling. At the same time, the devices create certain problems for many busy executives. Specifically, because these executives are always available for contact, they have less "down time" and fewer opportunities to disconnect from their work.

In the past, for example, managers had free time when they were traveling to and from work or when they were away from their offices at lunch. Now, many are readily accessible during these times. Consequently, what might have once been a nice one-hour break for lunch in the middle of the day may now be a continuation of work

"The cell phone is the entry point. The falling cost of technology makes it increasingly accessible to everyone."
— *Mohammed Yunus, banking executive*

as an individual makes and receives telephone calls while at the corner deli. Even vacations are falling victim to the technology—for example, parents vacationing at Disney World with their children can duck into the resort's Internet café to spend a few minutes online with their employees.

The astute manager who wants to regain some control over this aspect of his or her work life really has more control than might be expected. Simply put, all the manager has to do is turn the devices off. But with the increasing introduction of more ways to stay connected, it's getting harder and harder for stressed managers to have a few minutes of rest from the ongoing demands of the executive's life.

References: Chris Sandlund, "Stay Plugged In," *Fortune*, February 27, 2002. www.fortune.com on June 3, 2002; Eyal Ravinovitch, "Life in the Fast Lane," *Fortune*, February 1, 2002. www.fortune.com on June 3, 2002; "It Takes a Cell Phone," *Wall Street Journal*, June 25, 1999, pp. B1, B6 (quotation on p. B6). See www.wsj.com.

Role conflict occurs when the messages and cues constituting a role are clear but contradictory or mutually exclusive.

Role conflict occurs when the messages and cues from others about the role are clear but contradictory or mutually exclusive.[13] One common form is *interrole conflict*—conflict between roles. For example, if a person's boss says that to get ahead one must work overtime and on weekends, and the same person's spouse says that the person needs to spend more time at home with the family, conflict may result. *Intrarole conflict* may occur when the person gets conflicting demands from different sources within the context of the same role. A manager's boss may tell her that she needs to put more pressure on subordinates to follow new work rules. At the same time, her subordinates may indicate that they expect her to get the rules changed. Thus, the cues are in conflict, and the manager may be unsure about which course to follow.

Intrasender conflict occurs when a single source sends clear but contradictory messages. This might occur if the boss says one morning that there can be no more overtime for the next month but after lunch tells someone to work late that same evening. *Person-role conflict* results from a discrepancy between the role requirements and the individual's personal values, attitudes, and needs. If a person is told to do something unethical or illegal, or if the work is distasteful (for example, firing a close friend), person-role conflict is likely to result. Role conflict of all varieties is of particular concern to managers. Research has shown that conflict may occur in a variety of situations and may lead to a variety of adverse consequences, including stress, poor performance, and rapid turnover.

Role overload occurs when expectations for the role exceed the individual's capabilities.

A final consequence of a weak role structure is **role overload,** which occurs when expectations for the role exceed the individual's capabilities. When a manager gives an employee several major assignments at once while increasing the person's regular workload, the employee will probably experience role overload. Role overload may also result when an individual takes on too many roles at one time. For example, a person trying to work extra hard at his job, run for election to the school board, serve on a committee in church, coach Little League baseball, maintain an active exercise program, and be a contributing member to his family will probably encounter role overload.

Interpersonal demands are stressors associated with group pressures, leadership, and personality conflicts.

Interpersonal Demands   A final set of organizational stressors consists of three **interpersonal demands:** group pressures, leadership, and interpersonal conflict. Group pressures may include pressure to restrict output, pressure to conform to the group's norms, and so forth. For instance, as we have noted before, it is quite common for a work group to arrive at an informal agreement about how much each member will produce. Individuals who produce much more or much less than this level may be pressured by the group to get back in line. An individual who feels a strong need to vary from the group's expectations (perhaps to get a pay raise or promotion) will experience a great deal of stress, especially if acceptance by the group is also important to him or her.

Leadership style also may cause stress. Suppose an employee needs a great deal of social support from his leader. The leader, however, is quite brusque and shows no concern or compassion for him. This employee will probably feel stressed. Similarly, assume an employee feels a strong need to participate in decision making and to be active in all aspects of management. Her boss is very autocratic and refuses to consult subordinates about anything. Once again, stress is likely to result.

Finally, conflicting personalities and behaviors may cause stress. Conflict can occur when two or more people must work together even though their personalities, attitudes, and behaviors differ. For example, a person with an internal locus of control—that is, someone who always wants to control how things turn out, might become frustrated working with an external person who likes to wait and just let things happen. Likewise, a smoker and a nonsmoker who are assigned adjacent offices obviously will experience stress.[14]

Life Stressors

Stress in organizational settings also can be influenced by events that take place outside the organization. Life stressors can be categorized in terms of life change and life trauma.

A life change is any meaningful change in a person's personal or work situation; too many life changes can lead to health problems.

Life Change   Thomas Holmes and Richard Rahe first developed and popularized the notion of life change as a source of stress.[15] A **life change** is any meaningful change in a person's personal or work situation. Holmes and Rahe reasoned that major changes in a person's life can lead to stress and eventually to disease. Table 9.2 summarizes their findings on major life change events. Note that several of

Rank	Life Event	Mean Value	Rank	Life Event	Mean Value
1	Death of spouse	100	23	Son or daughter leaving home	29
2	Divorce	73	24	Trouble with in-laws	29
3	Marital separation	65	25	Outstanding personal achievement	28
4	Jail term	63	26	Spouse beginning or ending work	26
5	Death of close family member	63	27	Beginning or ending school	26
6	Personal injury or illness	53	28	Change in living conditions	25
7	Marriage	50	29	Revision of personal habits	24
8	Fired at work	47	30	Trouble with boss	23
9	Marital reconciliation	45	31	Change in work hours or conditions	20
10	Retirement	45	32	Change in residence	20
11	Change in health of family member	44	33	Change in schools	20
12	Pregnancy	40	34	Change in recreation	19
13	Sex difficulties	39	35	Change in church activities	19
14	Gain of new family member	39	36	Change in social activities	18
15	Business readjustment	39	37	Small mortgage or loan	17
16	Change in financial state	38	38	Change in sleeping habits	16
17	Death of close family friend	37	39	Change in the number of family get-togethers	15
18	Change to different line of work	36	40	Change in eating habits	15
19	Change in number of arguments with spouse	35	41	Vacation	13
20	Large mortgage*	31	42	Christmas or other major holiday	12
21	Foreclosure of mortgage or loan	30	43	Minor violations of the law	11
22	Change in responsibilities of work	29			

The amount of life stress that a person has experienced in a given period of time, say one year, is measured by the total number of life change units (LCUs). These units result from the addition of the values (shown in the right-hand column) associated with events that the person has experienced during the target time period.

Reference: Reprinted from *Journal of Psychosomatic Research,* vol. 11, Thomas H. Holmes and Richard H. Rahe, "The Social Adjustment Rating Scale," Copyright © 1967, with permission from Elsevier Science.

table 9.2

Life Changes and Life Change Units

these events relate directly (fired from work, retirement) or indirectly (change in residence) to work.

Each event's point value supposedly reflects the event's impact on the individual. At one extreme, a spouse's death, assumed to be the most traumatic event considered, is assigned a point value of 100. At the other extreme, minor violations of the law rank only 11 points. The points themselves represent life change units, or LCUs. Note also that the list includes negative events (divorce and trouble with the boss) as well as positive ones (marriage and vacations).

Life stressors can be addressed by different people in different ways. Take Brian Benavidez, for example. After being laid off from his job as an investment banker during the 2002 recession, Benavidez spent his days watching television. One day he watched a documentary about—of all things—hot dogs. But he also noticed that everyone engaged in the process of making, selling, and eating hot dogs seemed to be happy! So rather than trying to get back into the corporate rat race, he has decided to open his own hot dog stand.

Holmes and Rahe argued that a person can handle a certain threshold of LCUs, but beyond that level problems can set in. In particular, they suggest that people who encounter more than 150 LCUs in a given year will experience a decline in their health the following year. A score of between 150 and 300 LCUs supposedly carries a 50 percent chance of major illness whereas the chance of major illness is said to increase to 70 percent if the number of LCUs exceeds 300. These ideas offer some interesting insights into the potential cumulative impact of various stressors and underscore our limitations in coping with stressful events. However, research on Holmes and Rahe's proposals has provided only mixed support.

Life Trauma   Life trauma is similar to life change, but it has a narrower, more direct, and shorter-term focus. A **life trauma** is any upheaval in an individual's life that alters his or her attitudes, emotions, or behaviors. To illustrate, according to the life change view, a divorce adds to a person's potential for health problems in the following year. At the same time, the person will obviously also experience emotional turmoil during the actual divorce process itself. This turmoil is a form of life trauma and will clearly cause stress, much of which may spill over into the workplace.[16]

A life trauma is any upheaval in an individual's life that alters his or her attitudes, emotions, or behaviors.

Major life traumas that may cause stress include marital problems, family difficulties, and health problems initially unrelated to stress. For example, suppose a person learns she has developed arthritis that will limit her favorite activity, skiing. Her dismay over the news may translate into stress at work. Similarly, a worker coping with the traumatic aftermath of the death of his child will almost certainly go through difficult periods, some of which will affect his job performance. Millions of individuals experienced traumatic stress in the wake of the September 11 terrorist attacks.

Consequences of Stress

S tress can have a number of consequences. As we already noted, if the stress is positive, the result may be more energy, enthusiasm, and motivation. Of more concern, of course, are the negative consequences of stress. Referring back to Figure 9.2, we see that stress can produce individual consequences, organizational consequences, and burnout.

We should first note that many of the factors listed are obviously interrelated. For example, alcohol abuse is shown as an individual consequence, but it also affects the organization the person works for. An employee who drinks on the job may perform poorly and create a hazard for others. If the category for a consequence seems somewhat arbitrary, be aware that each consequence is categorized according to the area of its primary influence.

Individual Consequences

The individual consequences of stress, then, are the outcomes that mainly affect the individual. The organization also may suffer, either directly or indirectly, but it is the individual who pays the real price. Stress may produce behavioral, psychological, and medical consequences.

Behavioral Consequences   The behavioral consequences of stress may harm the person under stress or others. One such behavior is smoking. Research has clearly documented that people who smoke tend to smoke more when they experience stress. There is also evidence that alcohol and drug abuse are linked to stress, although this relationship is less well documented. Other possible behavioral consequences are accident proneness, violence, and appetite disorders.

Psychological Consequences   The psychological consequences of stress relate to a person's mental health and well-being. When people experience too much stress at work, they may become depressed or find themselves sleeping too much or not enough. Stress may also lead to family problems and sexual difficulties.

Medical Consequences   The medical consequences of stress affect a person's physical well-being. Heart disease and stroke, among other illnesses, have been linked to stress. Other common medical problems resulting from too much stress include headaches, backaches, ulcers and related stomach and intestinal disorders, and skin conditions such as acne and hives.

Organizational Consequences

Clearly, any of the individual consequences just discussed can also affect the organization. Other results of stress have even more direct consequences for organizations. These include decline in performance, withdrawal, and negative changes in attitudes.

"Today [companies] are looking at the economic cost of things like dual-career couples, single parents, and stress."—Bradley Googins, director of Boston College's Center for Corporate Community Relations[17]

Performance   One clear organizational consequence of too much stress is a decline in performance. For operating workers, such a decline can translate into poor-quality work or a drop in productivity. For managers, it can mean faulty decision-making or disruptions in working relationships as people become irritable and hard to get along with.

Withdrawal   Withdrawal behaviors also can result from stress. For the organization, the two most significant forms of withdrawal behavior are absenteeism and quitting. People who are having a hard time coping with stress in their jobs are more likely to call in sick or consider leaving the organization for good. Stress can also produce other, more subtle forms of withdrawal. A manager may start missing deadlines or taking longer lunch breaks. An employee may withdraw psychologically by ceasing to care about the organization and the job. As noted earlier, employee violence is a potential individual consequence of stress. This also has obvious organizational implications as well, especially if the violence is directed at another employee or at the organization in general.[18]

Attitudes   Another direct organizational consequence of employee stress relates to attitudes. As we just mentioned, job satisfaction, morale, and organizational commitment can all suffer, along with motivation to perform at high levels. As a result, people may be more prone to complain about unimportant things, do only enough work to get by, and so forth.

Burnout

Burnout, another consequence of stress, has clear implications for both people and organizations. **Burnout** is a general feeling of exhaustion that develops when a person simultaneously experiences too much pressure and has too few sources of satisfaction.[19]

Burnout generally develops in the following way. First, people with high aspirations and strong motivation to get things done are prime candidates for burnout under certain conditions. They are especially vulnerable when the organization suppresses or limits their initiative while constantly demanding that they serve the organization's own ends.

In such a situation, the individual is likely to put too much of himself or herself into the job. In other words, the person may well keep trying to meet his or her own agenda while simultaneously trying to fulfill the organization's expectations. The most likely effects of this situation are prolonged stress, fatigue, frustration, and helplessness under the burden of overwhelming demands. The person literally exhausts his or her aspirations and motivation, much as a candle burns itself out. Loss of self-confidence and psychological withdrawal follow. Ultimately, burnout results. At this point, the individual may start dreading going to work in the morning, may put in longer hours but accomplish less than before, and may generally display mental and physical exhaustion.[20]

> Burnout is a general feeling of exhaustion that develops when an individual simultaneously experiences too much pressure and has too few sources of satisfaction.

Managing Stress in the Workplace

Given that stress is widespread and so potentially disruptive in organizations, it follows that people and organizations should be concerned about how to manage it more effectively. And in fact they are. Many strategies have been developed to help manage stress in the workplace. Some are for individuals, and others are geared toward organizations.[21]

Individual Coping Strategies

Many strategies for helping individuals manage stress have been proposed. Figure 9.4 lists five of the more popular ones.

Exercise   Exercise is one method of managing stress. People who exercise regularly are less likely to have heart attacks than inactive people. More directly, research has suggested that people who exercise regularly feel less tension and stress, are more self-confident, and show greater optimism. People who do not exercise regularly feel more stress, are more likely to be depressed, and experience other negative consequences.

Relaxation   A related method of managing stress is relaxation. We noted at the beginning of the chapter that coping with stress requires adaptation. Proper relaxation is an effective way to adapt. Relaxation can take many forms. One way to relax is to take regular vacations. One study found that people's attitudes toward a variety of workplace characteristics improved significantly following a vacation.[22] People can also relax while on the job. For example, it has been recommended that people take regular rest breaks during their normal workday.[23] A popular way of resting is to sit quietly with closed eyes for ten minutes every afternoon. (Of course, it might be necessary to have an alarm clock handy!)

Time Management   Time management is often recommended for managing stress. The idea is that many daily pressures can be eased or eliminated if a person does a better job of managing time. One popular approach to time management is to make a list every morning of the things to be done that day. Then one groups the items on the list into three categories: critical activities that must be performed, important activities that should be performed, and optional or trivial things that

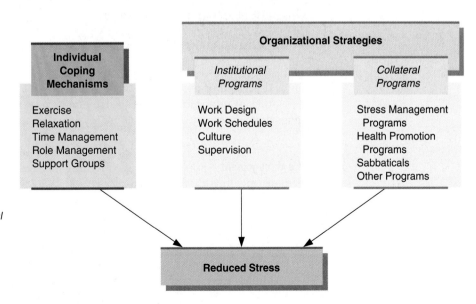

figure 9.4

Individual and Organizational Coping Strategies

Just as individual and organizational factors can cause stress, there are individual and organizational strategies for coping with stress. This figure shows the individual coping mechanisms most experts recommend and several institutional and collateral organizational programs.

Individuals and organizations can adopt a variety of coping strategies for enabling people to better deal with stress. At Baxter International, CEO Harry Kraemer sets a good example for his employees by making sure he has plenty of time for his family. Among its many benefits, Baxter offers its employees flexible work schedules. Kraemer argues that by allowing his employees to meet their personal and family needs first, the company then gets their full-time attention when they are at work. Following this policy allows the firm to retain its most valued employees and creates a true sense of camaraderie among its employees.

can be delegated or postponed. Then, of course, one does the things on the list in their order of importance. This strategy helps people get more of the important things done every day. It also encourages delegation of less important activities to others.

Role Management   Somewhat related to time management is the idea of role management, in which the individual actively works to avoid overload, ambiguity, and conflict. For example, if a person does not know what is expected of her, she should not sit and worry about it. Instead, she should ask for clarification from her boss. Another role management strategy is to learn to say "no." As simple as saying "no" might sound, many people create problems for themselves by always saying "yes." Besides working at their regular jobs, they agree to serve on committees, volunteer for extra duties, and accept extra assignments. Sometimes, of course, we have no choice but to accept an extra obligation (if our boss tells us to complete a new project, we will probably have to do it). In many cases, however, saying "no" is an option.[24]

Support Groups   A final method for managing stress is to develop and maintain support groups. A support group is simply a group of family members or friends with whom a person can spend time. Going out after work with a couple of coworkers to a basketball game, for example, can help relieve the stress that builds up during the day. Supportive family and friends can help people deal with normal stress on an ongoing basis. Support groups can be particularly useful during times of crisis. For example, suppose an employee has just learned that she did not get the promotion she has been working toward for months. It may help her tremendously if she has good friends to lean on, be it to talk to or to yell at.

Organizational Coping Strategies

Organizations are also increasingly realizing that they should be involved in managing their employees' stress. There are two different rationales for this view. One is that since the organization is at least partly responsible for creating the stress, it should help relieve it. The other is that workers experiencing lower levels of harmful stress will function more effectively. Two basic organizational strategies for helping employees manage stress are institutional programs and collateral programs.

"Employers are being held increasingly liable for job stress. From a financial perspective, employers are finding they have to do something."—*Paul Rosch, president of the American Institute of Stress*[25]

Institutional Programs   *Institutional programs* for managing stress are undertaken through established organizational mechanisms. For example, properly designed jobs (discussed in Chapter 7) and work schedules (also discussed in Chapter 7) can help ease stress. Shift work, in particular, can cause major problems for employees because they constantly have to adjust their sleep and relaxation patterns. Thus, the design of work and work schedules should be a focus of organizational efforts to reduce stress.

The organization's culture (covered in Chapter 18) also can be used to help manage stress. In some organizations, for example, there is a strong norm against taking time off or going on vacation. In the long run, such norms can cause major stress. Thus, the organization should strive to foster a culture that reinforces a healthy mix of work and nonwork activities.

Finally, supervision can play an important institutional role in managing stress. A supervisor can be a major source of overload. If made aware of their potential for assigning stressful amounts of work, supervisors can do a better job of keeping workloads reasonable.

Collateral Programs   In addition to institutional efforts aimed at reducing stress, many organizations are turning to collateral programs. A *collateral stress program* is an organizational program specifically created to help employees deal with stress. Organizations have adopted stress management programs, health promotion programs, and other kinds of programs for this purpose. More and more companies are developing their own programs or adopting existing programs of this type. For example, Lockheed Martin offers screening programs for its employees to detect signs of hypertension.

Many firms today also have employee fitness programs. These programs attack stress indirectly by encouraging employees to exercise, which is presumed to reduce stress. On the negative side, this kind of effort costs considerably more than stress management programs because the firm must invest in physical facilities. Still, more and more companies are exploring this option.[26] L. L. Bean, for example, has state-of-the-art fitness centers for its employees.

Finally, organizations try to help employees cope with stress through other kinds of programs. For example, existing career development programs, like the one at General Electric, are used for this purpose. Other companies use programs promoting everything from humor to massage to yoga as antidotes for stress.[27] Of course, little or no research supports some of the claims made by advocates of these programs. Thus, managers must take steps to ensure that any organizational effort to help employees cope with stress is at least reasonably effective.

Work-Life Linkages

At numerous points in this chapter we have alluded to relationships between a person's work and life. In this final brief section, we will make these relationships a bit more explicit. One important related issue, working women who sometimes must choose between career advancement and having children, is discussed in the "Working with Diversity" box.

Fundamental Work-Life Relationships

Work-life relationships can be characterized in any number of ways. Consider, for example, the basic dimensions of the part of a person's life tied specifically to work. Common dimensions would include such things as an individual's current job (including working hours, job satisfaction, and so forth), his or her career goals (the person's aspirations, career trajectory, and so forth), interpersonal relations at work (with the supervisor, subordinates, coworkers, and others), and job security.

Part of each person's life is also distinctly separate from work. These dimensions might include the person's spouse or life companion, dependents (such as children or elderly parents), personal life interests (hobbies, leisure time interests, religious affiliations, community involvement), and friendship networks.

"I'd like to participate more in school or camp stuff, but I can't manage my schedule in a way to allow that. I'm letting go of everything for myself, except for exercise on weekends. And I've given up any attempt to manage our finances."—Jeffrey Welch, staff worker in a large New York bank[28]

Work-life relationships are interrelationships between a person's work life and personal life.

Work-life relationships, then, include any relationships between dimensions of the person's work life and the person's personal life. For example, a person with numerous dependents (a nonworking spouse or domestic partner, dependent children, dependent parents, and so on) may prefer a job with a relatively high salary, fewer overtime demands, and less travel. On the other hand, a person with no de-

WORKING WITH DIVERSITY

The Not-Mommy Track

Women's advocates are applauding the progress that American firms have made in hiring and promoting women, especially the increase in female managers. About 75 percent of working-age women participate in the U.S. labor force, and women represent about 40 percent of all managers. On the downside, there is a growing realization that some women are making tremendous personal sacrifices to reach the top professional ranks. Whereas the "mommy track," the plight of working mothers, used to be a top diversity concern, a new issue is emerging.

Sylvia Ann Hewlett, author of the new book *Creating a Life: Professional Women and the Quest for Children*, claims, "One pair of figures from corporate America says it all: 49 percent of 40-year-old women executives earning $100,000 or more a year are childless while only 10 percent of 40-year-old male executives in an equivalent earnings bracket do not have children." According to a study conducted by Hewlett, most of the successful women she interviewed wanted to have children (only 14 percent did not) but found motherhood incompatible with the demands of a high-powered, high-stress career.

Hewlett's book has raised a firestorm of controversy. Some readers point out that work and child rearing are both demanding jobs and that "you can't have it all." Hewlett is quick to reply that work success apparently is not incompatible with fatherhood, only motherhood. Other readers rebut that argument, claiming that fatherhood is in fact made more difficult by a high-powered

career. One reader, James R. Maxeiner, says, "Success is not incompatible with being a biological father, but it may be incompatible with being a good father." Another group of critics claims that American working women are better off than working women elsewhere. In Japan for example, 73 percent of firms had women filling less than 10 percent

> *"[Forty-nine] percent of . . . women executives . . . are childless while only 10 percent of . . . male executives . . . do not have children."* —Sylvia Ann Hewlett, *author of* Creating a Life: Professional Women and the Quest for Children

of their management positions, and 13 percent had no women managers at all. Japanese firms may legally fire a woman who becomes pregnant, and most companies have strict policies against hiring mothers.

U.S. businesses have made great strides in hiring and promoting women, and have begun to consider work-life issues more seriously than ever before. However, clearly much remains to be done before American firms are truly "family friendly."

References: Sylvia Ann Hewlett, *Creating A Life: Professional Women and the Quest for Motherhood* (New York: Talk Miramax Books, 2002); "Workforce Diversity Program," Washington State Department of Personnel web site. hr.dop.wa.gov/wfd on May 5, 2002; Catherine Arnst, "The Loneliness of the High-Powered Woman," *Business Week,* April 29, 2002. www.businessweek.com on April 29, 2002; Robin Toner, "At the Table, but Not for Dinner," *New York Times,* April 28, 2002, p. WK3; Karen Alexander, "Making Room for Daddy, and a Job," *New York Times,* April 7, 2002, p. BU14; Lisa Belkin, "Motherhood, and Defining Success," *New York Times,* March 31, 2002, p. MB1; Lisa Belkin, "For Women, the Price of Success," *New York Times,* March 17, 2002, p. WC1.

pendents may be less interested in salary, more receptive to overtime, and more available for job-related travel.

Stress will occur when there is a basic inconsistency or incompatibility between a person's work and life dimensions. For example, if a person is the sole care provider for a dependent elderly parent and has a job that requires considerable travel and evening work, stress is likely to result.

Balancing Work-Life Linkages

Balancing work-life linkages is, of course, no easy thing to do. Demands from both sides can be extreme, and people may need to be prepared to make tradeoffs. The important thing is to recognize the potential tradeoffs in advance so that they can be carefully weighed, and a comfortable decision can be made. Some of the strategies for doing so were discussed earlier. For example, working for a company that offers flexible work schedules may be an attractive option.[29]

Individuals must also recognize the importance of long-term versus short-term perspectives in balancing their work and personal lives. For example, people may have to respond a bit more to work than to life demands in the early years of their careers. In midcareer, they may be able to achieve a more comfortable balance. And in later career stages, they may be able to put life dimensions first by refusing to relocate, by working shorter hours, and so forth.

People also have to decide for themselves what they value and what tradeoffs they are willing to make. For instance, consider the dilemma faced by a dual-career couple when one partner is being transferred to another city. One option is for one of the partners to subordinate her or his career for the other partner, at least temporarily. For example, the partner being transferred could turn the job down, risking a potential career setback or the loss of the job. Or the other partner could resign from his or her current position and seek another one in the new location. The couple might also decide to live apart, with one moving and the other staying. The partners might also come to realize that their respective careers are more important to them than their relationship and decide to go their separate ways.

Synopsis

Stress is a person's adaptive response to a stimulus that places excessive psychological or physical demands on that person. According to the general adaptation syndrome perspective, the three stages of response to stress are alarm, resistance, and exhaustion. Two important forms of stress are eustress and distress.

Type A personalities are more competitive and time driven than Type B personalities. Initial evidence suggested that Type As are more susceptible to coronary heart disease, but recent findings provide less support for this belief. Hardiness, optimism, cultural context, and gender may also affect stress.

Stress can be caused by many factors. Major organizational stressors are task demands, physical demands, role demands, and interpersonal demands. Life stressors include life change and life trauma.

Stress has many consequences. Individual consequences can include behavioral, psychological, and medical problems. On the organizational level, stress can affect performance and attitudes or cause withdrawal. Burnout is another possibility.

Primary individual mechanisms for managing stress are exercise, relaxation, time management, role management, and support groups. Organizations use both institutional and collateral programs to control stress.

People have numerous dimensions to their work and personal lives. When these dimensions are interrelated, individuals must decide for themselves which are more important and how to balance them.

Discussion Questions

1. Describe one or two recent times when stress had both good and bad consequences for you.

2. Describe a time when you successfully avoided stage 3 of the GAS and another time when you got to stage 3.

3. Do you consider yourself a Type A or a Type B person? Why?

4. Can a person who is a Type A change? If so, how?

5. What are the major stressors for a student?

6. Is an organizational stressor or a life stressor likely to be more powerful?

7. What consequences are students most likely to suffer as a result of too much stress?

8. Do you agree that a certain degree of stress is necessary to induce high energy and motivation?

9. What can be done to prevent burnout? If someone you know is suffering burnout, how would you advise that person to recover from it?

10. Do you practice any of the stress reduction methods discussed in the text? Which ones? Do you use others not mentioned in the text?

11. Has the work-life balance been an issue in your life?

Organizational Behavior Case for Discussion

Over the Edge

Almost everyone experiences stress in one form or another. The effects of stress may include such things as anxiety and high blood pressure. Occasionally, however, people are under so much stress that they are pushed over the edge. They reach a breaking point and take action that results in destruction and occasionally death. Consider the case of James Daniel Simpson, a quiet and reserved young man whom no one ever expected to cause trouble.

Throughout his high school years in El Paso, Simpson was quiet and reserved. He caused no problems but made few friends. Classmates and neighbors recall him as being polite and dependable. They also note that he didn't talk much and usually kept to himself. After graduating in 1985, he enrolled at the University of Texas at El Paso, but he did not graduate. Simpson subsequently worked in a variety of jobs until moving to Corpus Christi in 1992.

Soon after arriving there, Simpson went to work for the Walter Rossler Company. The firm performed consulting work for area refinery industries, specializing in ultrasonic inspections. Rossler paid $1,900 for Simpson to enroll in some training courses at a local college. Like other employees who took advantage of Rossler's training incentive, Simpson signed an agreement to repay the money if he left the company for any reason within three years of the date of the agreement. The agreement itself was dated November 3, 1993.

By all accounts, Simpson was an average worker—he was adequate but did not distinguish himself in any way. He occasionally came to work late, but his overall performance was satisfactory. The only major complaint that Simpson himself voiced was his objection to the company's policy requiring employees to come and go through the back door. He resented this policy because a few managers and secretaries were "exempt" and were allowed to use the front door.

In September 1994, he quit his job at Rossler and began to look for other work. After repeated attempts to recover the money it had spent for Simpson's training, the company filed a lawsuit against Simpson on November 1, 1994. The suit was eventually settled out of court, with Simpson agreeing to repay $700 of the total amount. Rossler also provided unsatisfactory references for Simpson as he continued to search for a new job.

Over the next six months, Simpson's savings dwindled, and his prospects for work disappeared. In February 1995, he bought two guns from a Corpus Christi gun dealer. One gun was a Ruger 9-mm semiautomatic pistol (an expensive handgun costing around $500); the other was an inexpensive .32-caliber handgun. Shortly thereafter, he ran out of money and pawned his television, one of his last assets.

On the afternoon of Monday, April 3, 1995, Simpson drove to a local park and fired several shots into the air. After leaving the park at around 4:30 P.M., he drove to the offices of Walter Rossler Company and parked in front of the building. His former coworkers at Rossler had often chided him for using an antitheft alarm in his old, beat-up Subaru. On this day, however, he did not bother to set the alarm.

He walked directly to the building and entered through the front door. Once inside, he systematically walked through the facility, shooting and killing five people. He appeared to be seeking out specific targets. The five individuals killed were Walter Charles Rossler (company president), Joann Rossler (corporate secretary), Patty Gilmore (secretary), Richard Lee Tomlinson (vice president for operations), and Derek Harrison (sales representative).

As he approached each one, Simpson first cursed the person and then shot him or her. Along the way, he bypassed at least two employees without so much as a second glance. He also spared Lisa Rossler, daughter of the owners, and her infant son. Simpson then walked out through the back door of the building and into a small shed. Once inside, he killed himself with a single shot to the head.

References: Joel H. Neuman and Robert A. Baron, "Workplace Violence and Workplace Aggression: Evidence Concerning Specific Forms, Potential Causes, and Preferred Targets," *Journal of Management*, 1998, vol. 24, no. 3, pp. 391–419; "Employers on Guard for Violence," *Wall Street Journal*, April 5, 1995, pp. 3A; "Dialing the Stress-Meter Down," *Newsweek*, March 6, 1995, p. 62.

Case Questions

1. Describe how stress may have played a role in this tragedy.
2. What individual and organizational sources of stress can be identified in this case?
3. Do you think that any of the individual or organizational strategies described in the chapter for dealing with stress could have kept this situation from occurring?

 # Experiencing Organizational Behavior

Learning How Stress Affects You

Purpose: This exercise is intended to help you develop a better understanding of how stress affects you.

Format: The following is a set of questions about your job. If you work, respond to the questions in terms of your job. If you do not work, respond to the questions in terms of your role as a student.

Procedure: This quiz will help you recognize your level of stress on the job. Take the test, figure your score, and then see if your stress level is normal, beginning to be a problem, or dangerous. Answer the following statements by putting a number in front of each:

1—seldom true
2—sometimes true
3—mostly true

_____ 1. Even over minor problems, I lose my temper and do embarrassing things, like yell or kick a garbage can.

_____ 2. I hear every piece of information or question as criticism of my work.

_____ 3. If someone criticizes my work, I take it as a personal attack.

_____ 4. My emotions seem flat whether I'm told good news or bad news about my performance.

_____ 5. Sunday nights are the worst time of the week.

_____ 6. To avoid going to work, I'd even call in sick when I'm feeling fine.

_____ 7. I feel powerless to lighten my work load or schedule, even though I've always got far too much to do.

_____ 8. I respond irritably to any request from coworkers.

_____ 9. On the job and off, I get highly emotional over minor accidents, such as typos or spilt coffee.

_____ 10. I tell people about sports or hobbies that I'd like to do but say I never have time because of the hours I spend at work.

_____ 11. I work overtime consistently yet never feel caught up.

_____ 12. My health is running down; I often have headaches, backaches, stomachaches.

_____ 13. If I even eat lunch, I do it at my desk while working.

_____ 14. I see time as my enemy.

_____ 15. I can't tell the difference between work and play; it all feels like one more thing to be done.

_____ 16. Everything I do feels like a drain on my energy.

_____ 17. I feel like I want to pull the covers over my head and hide.

_____ 18. I seem off center, distracted—I do things like walk into mirrored pillars in department stores and excuse myself.

_____19. I blame my family—because of them, I have to stay in this job and location.

_____20. I have ruined my relationship with coworkers whom I feel I compete against.

Scoring: Add up the points you wrote beside the questions. Interpret your score as follows:

20–29:   You have normal amounts of stress.

30–49:   Stress is becoming a problem. You should try to identify its source and manage it.

50–60:   Stress is at dangerous levels. Seek help, or it could result in worse symptoms such as alcoholism or illness.

Follow-up Questions

1. How valid do you think your score is?
2. Is it possible to anticipate stress ahead of time and plan ways to help manage it?

Reference: "Stress on the job? Ask yourself," *USA Today*, June 16, 1987. Copyright 1987, *USA Today*. Reprinted with permission.

 # Self-Assessment Exercise

Are You Type A or Type B?

This test will help you develop insights into your own tendencies toward Type A or Type B behavior patterns. Answer the questions honestly and accurately about either your job or your school, whichever requires the most time each week. Then calculate your score according to the instructions that follow the questions. Discuss your results with a classmate. Critique each other's answers and see if you can help each other develop a strategy for reducing Type A tendencies.

Choose from the following responses to answer the questions that follow:

a. Almost always true   c. Seldom true

b. Usually true   d. Never true

_____ 1. I do not like to wait for other people to complete their work before I can proceed with mine.

_____ 2. I hate to wait in most lines.

_____ 3. People tell me that I tend to get irritated too easily.

_____ 4. Whenever possible, I try to make activities competitive.

_____ 5. I have a tendency to rush into work that needs to be done before knowing the procedure I will use to complete the job.

_____ 6. Even when I go on vacation, I usually take some work along.

_____ 7. When I make a mistake, it is usually because I have rushed into the job before completely planning it through.

_____ 8. I feel guilty about taking time off from work.

_____ 9. People tell me I have a bad temper when it comes to competitive situations.

_____10. I tend to lose my temper when I am under a lot of pressure at work.

_____11. Whenever possible, I will attempt to complete two or more tasks at once.

_____12. I tend to race against the clock.

_____13. I have no patience with lateness.

_____14. I catch myself rushing when there is no need.

Score your responses according to the following key:

- *An intense sense of time urgency* is a tendency to race against the clock, even when there is little reason to. The person feels a need to hurry for hurry's sake alone, and this tendency has appropriately been called hurry sickness. Time urgency is measured by items 1, 2, 8, 12, 13, and 14. Every *a* or *b* answer to these six questions scores one point.

- *Inappropriate aggression and hostility* reveal themselves in a person who is excessively competitive and who cannot do anything for fun. This inappropriately aggressive behavior easily evolves into frequent displays of hostility, usually at the slightest provocation or frustration. Competitiveness and hostility are measured by items 3, 4, 9, and 10. Every *a* or *b* answer scores one point.

- *Polyphasic behavior* refers to the tendency to undertake two or more tasks simultaneously at inappropriate times. It usually results in wasted time because of an inability to complete the tasks. This behavior is measured by items 6 and 11. Every *a* or *b* answer scores one point.

- *Goal directedness without proper planning* refers to the tendency of an individual to rush into work without really knowing how to accomplish the desired result. This usually results in incomplete work or work with many errors, which in turn

leads to wasted time, energy, and money. Lack of planning is measured by items 5 and 7. Every *a* or *b* response scores one point.

TOTAL SCORE = _____

If your score is 5 or greater, you may possess some basic components of the Type A personality.

Reference: From Daniel A. Girdano, George S. Everly Jr., and Dorothy E. Dusek, *Controlling Stress and Tension: A Holistic Approach*. Copyright © 2001 by Allyn & Bacon. Reprinted by permission of Pearson Education, Inc.

OB Online

1. Use a search engine to find out how many web sites contain the word "stress." What conclusions can you draw from the sheer number of such sites?

2. Find a web site that features a corporate fitness center. Compare it with the web site for a nearby private fitness center. If you had a choice, which would you prefer to use? Why?

3. Locate five company web sites that directly discuss employee health and/or well-being and that at least appear to promote their concern as a benefit.

4. Locate a company web site that openly addresses issues associated with work and family relationships.

Building Managerial Skills

Exercise Overview: Time management skills help people prioritize work, work more efficiently, and delegate appropriately. Poor time management, in turn, may result in stress. This exercise will help you relate time management skills to stress reduction.

Exercise Background: Make a list of several of the major things that cause stress for you. Stressors might involve school (i.e., difficult classes, too many exams, and so on), work (i.e., financial pressures, demanding work schedule), and/or personal circumstances (i.e., friends, romance, family, and so on). Try to be as specific as possible. Also, try to identify at least ten different stressors.

Exercise Task: Using the list you have developed, do each of the following:

1. Evaluate the extent to which poor time management on your part plays a role in how each stressor affects you. For example, do exams cause stress because you delay studying for them?

2. Develop a strategy for using time more efficiently in relation to each stressor that relates to time.

3. Note interrelationships among different kinds of stressors and time. For example, financial pressures may cause you to work, but work may interfere with school. Can any of these interrelationships be more effectively managed in relation to available time?

4. How do you manage the stress in your life? Would it be possible for you to manage stress in a more time-effective manner?

Part II   Integrative Running Case

The Downfall of Enron—The People

Part I of the Integrative Running Case described an intricate scheme of questionable business practices that ultimately led to Enron's downfall. Individuals within the firm created and perpetuated the lies, but there were also individuals who refused to bend the rules. If Enron's sad story is primarily about a high-level fraud with Kenneth Lay, Jeffrey Skilling, and Andrew Fastow as the black-hatted villains, then the white hats are worn by the lower-level employees who spoke the truth in the face of indifference and outright hostility.

As with so much at Enron, appearances were deceiving. On the face of it, the company appeared to be doing everything right: recruiting top graduates, rewarding high performance, encouraging creativity, and adapting its strategy to a changing environment. The firm was glorified by management scholars and hyped by the media as a paragon firm of the New Economy. Lay and Skilling were lauded for their efforts in bringing what had formerly been a slowly growing, stodgy business into the twenty-first century. But the same behaviors that were applauded and rewarded also carried within them the seeds of Enron's destruction.

Enron preferred to hire ambitious recent college graduates. This practice kept the company's labor costs down (inexperienced workers earn less), increased innovation and creativity (new graduates have recently been exposed to cutting-edge techniques and are prone to take more risks), and most importantly, helped to socialize workers into Enron's culture and behavioral norms. The young employees were given a great deal of autonomy—new workers often were authorized to make trades of up to $5 million on their own. Advancement came quickly, with a 20 percent annual turnover due solely to promotion. Enron preferred to nurture a few star performers rather than build teamwork. Jon Katzenbach, one of Skilling's former McKinsey colleagues, says, "The lesson is you cannot rely solely on individual achievement to drive your performance over time. Companies with only that one path overemphasize it and run into trouble, switching over to vanity and greed." For the creative, driven individual, an Enron job was ideal, so the firm had no trouble recruiting talent even during the boom years of the 1990s.

However, some saw a downside to Enron's hiring practices. Jay Conger, a professor at London Business School, says, "One potential flaw in the model was that Enron managers tended to move relatively quickly. . . . If you move young people fast in[to] senior-level positions without industry experience and then allow them to make large trading decisions, that is a risky strategy." Lynda Clemmons is one employee who rapidly rose to power. Upon graduation, Clemmons joined Enron's oil and gas trading unit. She was promoted from an entry-level analyst position up through three successively higher organizational levels, ending up, at age 27, as a vice president in charge of her own business in just seven years. Her business, which was based on a concept she had developed, sold "weather derivatives," essentially a kind of insurance for electric-power buyers that protected them against price changes due to heat waves and cold snaps. Sales in Clemmons's unit were reportedly over $500 million per year, but it's clear that few profits ever developed from those sales. Of course, hiring inexperienced workers can be effective as long as adequate controls are in place. James O'Toole, a professor at the University of Southern California, explains, "In larger companies like IBM and GE, even though there is a movement toward youth, there are still enough older people around to mentor them. At Enron, you had a bunch of kids running loose without adult supervision." O'Toole's focus on mentoring is appropriate because so much of the behavior of individuals within organizations is influenced by training, culture, role models, mentoring, and other forms of learning.

For example, Enron publicly proclaimed its honesty—its 2000 Annual Report states, "We work with customers and prospects openly, honestly and sincerely. When we say we will do something, we do it; when we say we cannot or will not do something, then we won't do it." However, top executives were setting a bad example—in some cases, true honesty was impossible because employees were asked to approve deals made by their superiors. "If your boss was [fudging], and you [had] never worked anywhere else, you just assume[d] that everybody fudges earnings," says a former employee. "Once you [got] there and you realized how it was, [did] you stand up and lose your job? It was easy to get into, 'Well, everybody else is doing it, so maybe it isn't so bad.'" However, the questionable conduct wasn't confined to Enron; starting in October 2001, Andersen lead accountant David B. Duncan ordered his staff to shred documents and delete emails related to Enron just as the company's problems were coming to light.

Employees worked to increase Enron's stock price, the most important goal of top management and one that was repeated often and publicly. In March 2001, as he assumed the CEO position, Skilling was quizzed by reporters about Enron's stance on deregulation in the California energy industry. "We are doing the right thing. We are looking to create open, competitive, fair markets. . . . [so that] prices are lower and customers get better service," Skilling said. But when asked about his top priority as chief executive, he immediately replied, "To get the stock price up."

Skilling instituted a performance review system based on improvements in stock price that was widely disliked by employees. It asked every person who came in contact with an employee to participate in his or her review; in theory, this information could provide valuable feedback to workers and managers. Skilling apparently believed the system would reduce any bias in the reviews because of the participation of multiple raters. However, in practice, the performance reviews became a political mechanism because employees knew that the lowest 10 to 20 percent would be fired. Fastow, in particular, was known for using the system to get rid of workers who questioned his actions. One worker describes the situation after the initiation of the new performance review by saying, "This changed the entire atmosphere at Enron. It became a den of backstabbers and snitches. People felt like they had to make somebody else look bad so that they could advance. . . . People just wanted to get ahead, no matter what." With the performance review linked to pay—the top-ranking 5 percent got bonuses that were 66 percent higher than those given to the next 30 percent—the competitiveness increased rapidly.

In spite of the tremendous pressure to achieve financial results at any cost, some employees spoke out anonymously or through internal channels. Vice President and accountant Sherron S. Watkins became well known for her questioning of Enron executives. In August, when Lay returned to the chief executive position, he encouraged employees to address him directly about their concerns. Watkins responded with an email message that asked in part, "Has Enron become a risky place to work? [Can] those of us who

didn't get rich over the last few years . . . afford to stay?" After detailing many of the questionable transactions, the email continued with Watkins stating, "I am incredibly nervous that we will implode in a wave of accounting scandals." Lay asked the firm's lawyers, Vinson & Elkins, to investigate her claims. Attorneys interviewed CFO Fastow, Andersen lead accountant David B. Duncan, and others, concluding that there was no reason for concern. In hindsight, Watkins's fears seem wholly justified, though her attempt at whistleblowing went unheeded.

While Watkins was trying in vain to draw attention to problem areas, and thousands of other employees labored innocently, a few unscrupulous managers were apparently aware of the problems and determined to maximize their gains while they could. The deals fell somewhere in that ambiguous region between unethical and illegal, but one in particular evoked the wrath of employees: bonuses paid to top executives. Specifically, in the days just prior to the bankruptcy declaration, when thousands of employees were terminated, the company paid a total of $55 million in retention bonuses to a few hundred executives to ensure that they would not desert the company during the difficult period. Enron upset employees again when it chose to change administrators in its retirement program, thereby freezing all employee requests for changes from mid-October until the bankruptcy declaration on December 3, 2001. As more problems were publicly disclosed, employees had no chance to switch their retirement funds out of Enron stock and into other, safer investments. Perhaps unwisely, many had chosen to keep most or all of their funds in Enron stock, which fell from around $37 per share to just 11 cents while the accounts were frozen. Many employees then received a double blow—they lost both their jobs and their retirement accounts.

Employees were also unhappy about the way in which they were fired. Some received termination notices via voice mail; others found out by watching the evening news. One manager said that the firm would be in touch with employees through email and then shut down the company's email system. Many workers received assurances and then found themselves unemployed twenty-four hours later. Each was given just $4,500 in severance pay in spite of employment contract requirements. When employees complained, they were told to file a claim in bankruptcy court, but the law requires that all of a firm's other debts take precedence over employee claims. To add insult to injury, as employees removed their personal effects from the downtown high-rise offices, bus drivers refused to carry passengers with large boxes, and the Houston Police Department ticketed those who temporarily left their cars in the loading zone.

Hundreds of employees kept their jobs in acquired divisions that are still operating, but thousands are now out of work and bitter with blame for top managers. One says, "To me, the downfall of Enron can be summed up in one word: Greed! Upper management of Enron was filled with very young, mostly early 30s and 40s men and women who were promoted faster than they could move to their new office[s]. As their incomes grew, so did their heads and their selfishness. Once money, which meant Enron stock price, became the most important thing[,] ethics, morals and the financial safety of the company went out the window." Others claim, "I may find it very hard to commit to another company like I did with Enron. There may always be a part of me that will be guarded and never really feel secure on the job," and "I never thought the day would come that I was ashamed to say I worked at Enron."

"I never thought the day would come that I was ashamed to say I worked at Enron."—an anonymous former Enron employee.

References: Kurt Eichenwald, "Lawyer Balks at Discussing Enron Case," *New York Times*, March 23, 2002, p. C3. See www.nytimes.com; John A. Byrne, "At Enron, 'The Environment Was Ripe for Abuse,'" *Business Week*, February 25, 2002. www.businessweek.com on June 25, 2002; Tom Zeller, "The Tao of Enron: Well, It Sounded Good," *New York Times*, February 24, 2002, p. WK5. See www.nytimes.com; Kurt Eichenwald, "Enron Buffed Image to a Shine Even as It Rotted from Within," *New York Times*, February 10, 2002, pp. 1, 28, 29. See www.nytimes.com; "Enron Letters," *Houston Chronicle*, February 7 and 8, 2002 (quotation). www.chron.com on June 26, 2002; Bethany McLean, "Why Enron Went Bust," *Fortune*, December 24, 2001. www.fortune.com on June 27, 2002; "Our Values," Annual Report 2000, Enron web site. www.enron.com on June 28, 2002.

Integrative Case Questions

1. Describe the person-job fit for the typical Enron employee. In what ways did the fit help the company be more effective? In what ways did the fit make the company less effective?

2. What needs and processes motivated Enron workers? What actions did the company take to motivate its workers? Were the actions effective in producing motivation? Why or why not?

3. Describe Enron's performance management system. What are the potential advantages and disadvantages of this type of system? What could Enron have done differently to avoid or lessen the impact of the disadvantages?

10 Communication in Organizations

Management Preview

▶ Communication is something that most of us take for granted—we have been communicating for so long that we really pay little attention to the actual process. Even at work, we often focus more on doing our jobs and less on how we communicate about those jobs. However, since methods of communication change so rapidly, we need to pay more attention to the processes that effectively link what we do to others in the organization. In this chapter, we focus on the important processes of interpersonal communication and information processing. First, we discuss the importance of communication in organizations and some important aspects of international communication. Next, we describe the methods of organizational communication and examine the basic communication process. Then we examine the potential effects of computerized information technology and telecommunications. Next, we explore the development of communication networks in organizations. Finally, we discuss several common problems of organizational communication and methods of managing communication. First, though, we begin by describing how telecommunications are changing the way Reuters Group conducts its business.

▼ ▼ ▼

The past 150 years have brought extraordinary change to Reuters Group, the English news firm. The company was founded in the 1850s, with carrier pigeons as its fastest and most reliable means of communication. The company was one of the first to invest heavily in that "new" technology, the telegraph, during the 1860s and 1870s. In fact, the firm was the first to report to Europe the news of Abraham Lincoln's assassination and described the end of the Boer War to the English two days ahead of the official report. The firm also established a huge nonnews business that was based primarily on delivering financial quotes to customers through a proprietary network.

As new communication technologies—including satellites, cell phones, and the Internet—have been introduced, Reuters has struggled to keep up with the new demands placed on it by increasingly technology-savvy customers. Tom Glocer, who became CEO of Reuters in July 2001, has been faced with the task of transforming the company's communication strategy to fit today's communications environment. Glocer's vision of an Internet-based firm prevailed in the end. "What Tom did was to articulate the urgency of it," according to Devin Wenig, president of Reuters Information subsidiary. Glocer himself says modestly, "I was the dirt in the oyster."

He is finding that changing the way in which the firm communicates with customers affects everything that the firm does. The new technology requires more technical know-how and places less emphasis on Reuters' traditional strength in news reporting. The cost structure has changed, too—as the proprietary network is replaced by Internet-accessible information, subscription fees grow while hardware and labor costs shrink. Glocer fears that Internet sales will cannibalize the more profitable proprietary sales and that the firm will have to charge less for its Internet offerings. Even Glocer himself, a lawyer and self-described "computer geek," is a symbol of change within the firm because he is the first nonjournalist and the first American to head the company. One former Reuters executive says Glocer was "not part of the old boys' network," and Reuters' chairman calls Glocer's appointment, "a generational shift in leadership."

"I was the dirt in the oyster."—Tom Glocer, CEO of Reuters Group

Meanwhile, Reuters is reaping the benefits of adopting the newest technologies. Its customer base is expanding to include buyers who want only a small slice of the financial news, such as reports about currency trading in Brazilian reals or South African rand. Reuters' new system enables the firm to deliver customized portions of the news for a lower cost. While competitors such as Bloomberg continue to offer their traditional proprietary networks and to move into areas such as the financial cable network Bloomberg Television, Reuters is aggressively expanding into online services, including Instinet, an online financial trading subsidiary. Referring to Reuters' plan to invest in new technology, Derek Brown, an analyst with Robertson Stephens, says, "This is an example of a bricks-and-mortar media company adopting what I believe is a very sensible strategy." The giant firm is changing to keep up with the times, and it now remains to be seen whether Glocer and Reuters can make this "very sensible" strategy pay off.

References: "Famous Reuters' People" and "Reuters Media Statement," Reuters' corporate web site. www.reuters.com on April 25, 2002; Tom Lowry and Pallavi Gogoi, "Instinet: How Not to Run a Trading Company," *Business Week*, April 22, 2002. www.businessweek.com on April 25, 2002; Mark Gimein, "The Other Bloomberg: Bloomberg Television Trails CNBC," *Fortune*, April 1, 2002. www.fortune.com on April 25, 2002; Katrina Brooker, "London Calling," *Fortune*, April 2, 2001, pp. 131–136 (quotation p. 136); Amey Stone, "Now Comes the Real Test for Reuters' E-Strategy," *Business Week Online*, February 17, 2000. www.businessweek.com on April 25, 2002.

Advances in electronic communication technology have greatly changed how businesses and people communicate. Our lives, too, are now different simply because we are more mobile and can communicate so quickly in so many forms with anyone. In many cases, managers do not even have to go to the office anymore. Less than a generation ago not going to the office was most commonly a practice used by slackers and marginal performers, but now it may actually signal greater performance as managers move freely among work sites and interact with various stakeholders. Regardless of the technology involved, however, the basics of interpersonal communication remain important. Communication is important in all phases of organizational behavior, but it is especially crucial in decision making, performance appraisal, motivation, and ensuring that the organization functions effectively. We begin our discussion of the role communication plays in organizational behavior by presenting the most basic elements of communication.

The Nature of Communication in Organizations

Communication is the social
process in which two or more
parties exchange information
and share meaning.

Communication is the social process in which two or more parties exchange information and share meaning. Communication has been studied from many perspectives. In this section, we provide an overview of the complex and dynamic communication process and discuss some important issues relating to international communication in organizations.

The Purposes of Communication in Organizations

Communication among individuals and groups is vital in all organizations. Some of the purposes of organizational communication are shown in Figure 10.1. The primary purpose is to achieve coordinated action.[1] Just as the human nervous system responds to stimuli and coordinates responses by sending messages to the various parts of the body, communication coordinates the actions of the parts of an organization. Without communication, an organization would be merely a collection of individual workers doing separate tasks. Organizational action would lack coordination and would be oriented toward individual rather than organizational goals.

A second purpose of communication is information sharing. The most important information relates to organizational goals, which give members a sense of purpose and direction. Another information-sharing function of communication is to give specific task directions to individuals. Whereas information on organizational goals gives employees a sense of how their activities fit into the overall picture, task communication tells them what their job duties are and are not. Employees must also receive information on the results of their efforts, as in performance appraisals.

Communication is essential to the decision-making process as well, as we discuss in Chapter 15. Information and information sharing are needed to define problems, generate and evaluate alternatives, implement decisions, and control and evaluate results.

Finally, communication expresses feelings and emotions. Organizational communication is far from merely a collection of facts and figures. People in organizations, like people anywhere else, often need to communicate emotions such as happiness, anger, displeasure, confidence, and fear.

Communication Across Cultures

Communication is an element of interpersonal relations that obviously is

figure 10.1

Three Purposes of Organizational Communication

Achieving coordinated action is the prime purpose of communication in organizations. Sharing information properly and expressing emotions help achieve coordinated action.

table 10.1

Examples of International Communication Problems

Source of Problem	Examples
Language	One firm, trying to find a name for a new soap powder, tested the chosen name in fifty languages. In English, it meant "dainty." Translations into other languages meant "song" (Gaelic), "aloof" (Flemish), "horse" (African), "hazy" or "dimwitted" (Persian), and "crazy" (Korean). The name was obscene in several Slavic languages.
	The Chevy Nova was *no va* in Spanish, which means "doesn't go."
	Coca-Cola in Chinese meant "bite the head of a dead tadpole."
	Idioms cannot be translated literally: "to murder the King's English" becomes "to speak French like a Spanish cow" in French.
Nonverbal Signs	Shaking your head up and down in Greece means "no," and swinging it from side to side means "yes."
	In most European countries, it is considered impolite not to have both hands on the table.
	The American sign for "OK" is rude in Spain and vulgar in Brazil.

Colors	Green: Popular in Moslem countries
	  Suggests disease in jungle-covered countries
	  Suggests cosmetics in France, Sweden, and the Netherlands

	Red: Blasphemous in African countries Stands for wealth and masculinity in Great Britain
Product	Campbell Soup was unsuccessful in Britain until the firm added water to its condensed soup so the cans would be the same size as the cans of soup the British were used to purchasing.
	Long-life packaging, which is commonly used for milk in Europe, allows milk to be stored for months at room temperature if it is unopened. Americans are still wary of it.
	Coca-Cola had to alter the taste of its soft drink in China when the Chinese described it as "tasting like medicine."

References: Adapted from David A. Ricks, *Blunders in International Business* (Cambridge, Mass.: Blackwell Publishers, 1993); David A. Ricks, *Big Business Blunders: Mistakes in Multinational Marketing* (Homewood, Ill.: Dow Jones–Irwin, 1983); Nancy Bragganti and Elizabeth Devine, *The Traveler's Guide to European Customs and Manners* (St. Paul, Minn.: Meadowbrook Books, 1984); and several *Wall Street Journal* articles.

affected by the international environment, partly because of language issues and partly because of coordination issues.

Language   Differences in languages are compounded by the fact that the same word can mean different things in different cultures. For example, as Table 10.1 indicates, "Coca-Cola" means "bite the head of a dead tadpole" in the first Chinese characters that were used in its advertising. Finally, the company found other Chinese characters to use in advertising in China. The table lists other interesting examples of minor communication failures across cultures.

Note in the table that elements of nonverbal communication also vary across cultures. Colors and body language can convey quite a different message in one

MASTERING CHANGE

▶ Email's Effect on the English Language

With the widespread use of personal computers, the Internet, and email, it's clear that communication technology is rapidly changing. What might not be so obvious are the ways in which email technology is changing English language usage.

Email messages consist of written words and simple pictures, and therein lies the trouble. People want to use email to express complex ideas that involve emotions, subtlety, irony, and other elements that are difficult to express in writing. New uses of English are transforming "flat" written emails into three-dimensional, meaningful messages. These enhanced messages attempt to mimic human speech and face-to-face dialogues by using written words and symbols to convey nuances of meaning, body language, and even tone of voice.

Online acronyms express subtle aspects of messages and also save time in typing repetitious phrases. Common acronyms used today include BTW for "by the way," and FYI, which means "for your information." Other recently coined acronyms are IMHO for "in my humble opinion," LOL for "I laughed out loud," and TIA for "thanks in advance." B2B stands for "business to business," referring to communication between two firms, and *2* is also used to replace the word "too," as in the acronym U2 (you, too).

Email technology has also created new meanings for many older words. For example, "spam" is the name for unwanted, mass commercial solicitations whereas "bounce" refers to email messages that are returned to the sender. Email messages that are unreservedly hostile are referred to as "flames," and "flame" can also be used as a verb: "His

> *"The most difficult thing to convey in email is emotion."*
> —*Kaitlin Duck Sherwood, author of* Overcome Email Overload

joke wasn't funny, so he really got flamed!"

According to Kaitlin Duck Sherwood, author of *Overcome Email Overload,* "the most difficult thing to convey in email is emotion." Users can express emphasis or changes in tone of voice by using asterisks for emphasis: You *are* wrong. To convey hesitation or thoughtfulness, words can be typed with white space or repeated letters: Www..eeee..lllll. Body language is expressed simply with <L> for laughing and <Y> for yawning. An "emoticon" uses an icon or simple graphic to express emotions. Some typical emoticons include :-) for "happy", :-(for "sad", :-| for "skeptical", ;-) for "winking", :-O for "surprised", and :-P for "laughing". All that having been said, it's TTFN (ta-ta for now).

References: "High-Tech Dictionary," ComputerUser.com web site. www.computeruser.com/resources/dictionary/emoticons.html on April 30, 2002; Kaitlin Duck Sherwood, "A Beginner's Guide to Effective Email," World Wide Webfoot Press web site (quotation). www.webfoot.com on April 30, 2002; Virginia Shea, *Netiquette* (Albion Press, 1994). See www.netiquette.com.

culture than in another. For example, the American sign for "OK" (making a loop with thumb and first finger) is considered rude in Spain and vulgar in Brazil. Managers should be forewarned that they can take nothing for granted in dealing with people from other cultures. They must take the time to become as fully acquainted as possible with the verbal and nonverbal languages of a culture. And indeed, as the "Mastering Change" box illustrates, new forms of communication technology such as email are actually changing language itself.

Coordination   International communication is closely related to issues of coordination. For example, an American manager who wants to speak with his or her counterpart in Hong Kong, Singapore, Rome, or London must contend not only with language differences but also with a time difference of many hours. When the American manager needs to talk on the telephone, the Hong Kong executive may be home asleep. Consequently, organizations are employing increasingly innovative methods for coordinating their activities in scattered parts of the globe. Mer-

Communication across cultures is influenced by myriad factors, including language and technology. Consider, for instance, Anny Wong. Ms. Wong is a sales representative for Caterpillar, the U.S. equipment maker. She is shown here at a customer's work site in the People's Republic of China. She is using her cellular telephone to contact the client. The cultural context in which they are talking (a U.S. company, an Asian sales representative, and a Chinese client) will affect how effectively they communicate. And new technology makes the communication both faster and more complex.

rill Lynch, for example, has its own satellite-based telephone network to monitor and participate in the worldwide money and financial markets.[2]

Methods of Communication

The three primary methods of communicating in organizations are written, oral, and nonverbal. Often the methods are combined. Considerations that affect the choice of method include the audience (whether it is physically present), the nature of the message (its urgency or secrecy), and the costs of transmission. Figure 10.2 shows various forms each method can take.

Written Communication

Organizations typically produce a great deal of written communication of many kinds. A letter is a formal means of communicating with an individual, generally someone outside the organization. Probably the most common form of written communication in organizations is the office memorandum, or memo. Memos usually are addressed to a person or group inside the organization. They tend to deal with a single topic and are more impersonal (as they often are destined to reach more than one person) but less formal than letters. Most email is similar to the traditional memo, although it is even less formal.

"There's a tremendous over-reliance on email, which is leading to a lot of confusion, misunderstanding, anger, and frustration."—Quentin Schultz, communications expert[3]

Other common forms of written communication include reports, manuals, and forms. Reports generally summarize the progress or results of a project and often

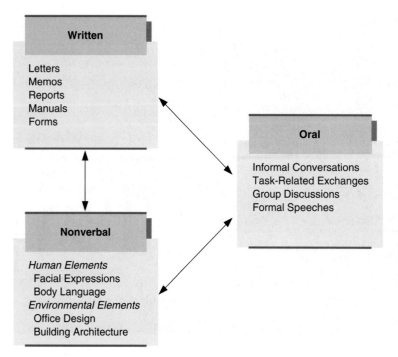

provide information to be used in decision making. Manuals have various functions in organizations. Instruction manuals tell employees how to operate machines; policy and procedures manuals inform them of organizational rules; operations manuals describe how to perform tasks and respond to work-related problems. Forms are standardized documents on which to report information. As such, they represent attempts to make communication more efficient and information more accessible. A performance appraisal form is an example. We should also note that although many of these forms of written communication have historically been used in a paper-based environment, they are increasingly being put on web sites and intranets in many larger companies today.

figure 10.2

Methods of Communication in Organizations

The three methods of communication in organizations are related to each other. Each one supplements the other, although each can also stand alone.

Oral Communication

The most prevalent form of organizational communication is oral. Oral communication takes place everywhere—in informal conversations, in the process of doing work, in meetings of groups and task forces, and in formal speeches and presentations. Recent studies identified oral communication skills as the number one criterion for hiring new college graduates.[4] Business school leaders have also been urged by industry to develop better communication skills in their graduates.[5] Even in Europe, employers have complained that the number one problem with current graduates is the lack of oral communication skills, citing cultural factors and changes in the educational process as primary causes.[6]

Oral forms of communication are particularly powerful because they include not only speakers' words but also their changes in tone, pitch, speed, and volume. As listeners, people use all of these cues to understand oral messages. Try this example with a friend or work colleague. Say this sentence several times, each time placing the emphasis on a different word: "The boss gave Joe a raise." See how the meaning changes depending on the emphasis! Moreover, receivers interpret oral messages in the context of previous communications and, perhaps, the reactions of other receivers. (Try saying another sentence before saying the phrase about the boss—such as "Joe is so lazy" or "Joe is such a good worker.") Quite often the top management of an organization sets the tone for oral communication throughout the organization.

The popular voicemail has all the characteristics of traditional verbal communication except that there is no feedback. The sender just leaves a message on the machine or network with no feedback or confirmation that the message was, or will be, received. With no confirmation, the sender does not know for sure whether the message will be received as he or she intended it. Therefore, it may be wise for the receiver of a voicemail to quickly leave a message on the sender's voicemail telling that the original message was received. But then the "great voicemail phone tag" is at its worst! Also, the receiver then has an excuse in the event that something goes wrong later and can always say that a return message was left on the sender's voicemail! The receiver could also pass the blame by saying that no such voice message was received. The lack of confirmation, or two-way communication, can lead to several problems, as will be discussed in later sections of this chapter.

Nonverbal Communication

Nonverbal communication includes all the elements associated with human communication that are not expressed orally or in writing. Sometimes nonverbal communication conveys more meaning than words do. Human elements of nonverbal communication include facial expressions and physical movements, both conscious and unconscious. Facial expressions have been categorized as (1) interest-excitement, (2) enjoyment-joy, (3) surprise-startle, (4) distress-anguish, (5) fear-terror, (6) shame-humiliation, (7) contempt-disgust, and (8) anger-rage.[7] The eyes are the most expressive component of the face.

Physical movements and "body language" are also highly expressive human elements. Body language includes both actual movement and body positions during communication. The handshake is a common form of body language. Other examples include making eye contact, which expresses a willingness to communicate; sitting on the edge of a chair, which may indicate nervousness or anxiety; and sitting back with arms folded, which may convey an unwillingness to continue the discussion. Table 10.1 lists examples of nonverbal sources of communication problems in other countries.

Environmental elements such as buildings, office space, and furniture can also convey messages. A spacious office, expensive draperies, plush carpeting, and elegant furniture can combine to remind employees or visitors that they are in the office of the president and CEO of the firm. On the other hand, the small metal desk set in the middle of the shop floor accurately communicates the organizational rank of a first-line supervisor. Thus, office arrangements convey status, power, and prestige and create

Nonverbal communication involves the use of facial expressions, physical movements, and environmental elements to convey meaning. These trainers use hand signals to guide dolphins to vocalize and jump. In much the same way, people use their eyes and faces, body language, and office arrangements to convey meaning to others as well. A facial expression of disinterest, sitting back in a chair with folded arms, and frequent glances at the clock will clearly convey to someone that you are not interested in what they may have to say.

an atmosphere for doing business. The physical setting can also be instrumental in the development of communication networks because a centrally located person can more easily control the flow of task-related information.

The Communication Process

Communication is a social process in which two or more parties exchange information and share meaning. The process is social because it involves two or more people. It is a two-way process and takes place over time rather than instantaneously. The communication process illustrated in Figure 10.3 shows a loop between the source and the receiver.[8] Note the importance of the feedback portion of the loop; upon receiving the message, the receiver responds with a message to the source to verify the communication. Each element of the basic communication process is important. If one part is faulty, the message may not be communicated as it was intended. A simple organizational example might be when a manager attempts to give direction to an employee regarding the order in which to perform two tasks. (We refer to this example again in later discussions.) The manager wants to send a message and have the employee understand precisely the meaning she intends. Each part of the communication process is described next.

Source

The source is the individual, group, or organization interested in communicating something to another party.

The **source** is the individual, group, or organization interested in communicating something to another party. In group or organizational communication, an individual may send the message on behalf of the organization. The source is responsible for preparing the message, encoding it, and entering it into the transmission medium. In some cases, the receiver chooses the source of information, as when a decision maker

figure 10.3
The Communication Process

The communication process is a loop that connects the sender and the receiver and operates in both directions. Communication is not complete until the original sender knows that the receiver understands the message.

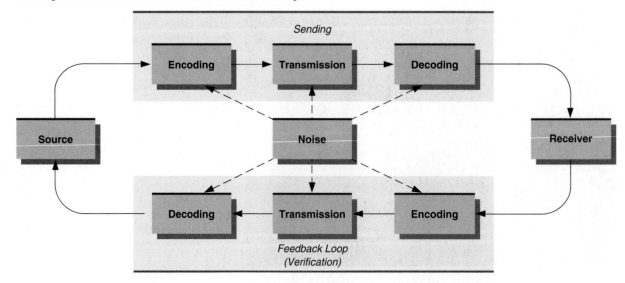

seeks information from trusted and knowledgeable individuals.[9] The source in organizational communication is often the manager giving directions to employees.

Encoding

Encoding is the process by which the message is translated from an idea or thought into transmittable symbols.

Encoding is the process by which the message is translated from an idea or thought into symbols that can be transmitted. The symbols may be words, numbers, pictures, sounds, or physical gestures and movements. In a simple example, the manager may use words in English as the symbols, usually spoken or written. The source must encode the message in symbols that the receiver can decode properly; that is, the source and the receiver must attach the same meaning to the symbols. When we use the symbols of a common language, we assume those symbols have the same meaning to everyone who uses them. However, the inherent ambiguity of symbol systems can lead to decoding errors. In verbal communication, for example, some words have different meanings for different people. Parents and children often use the same word, but the differences in their positions and ages may lead them to interpret words quite differently. If a manager only speaks Spanish and an employee only speaks German, the message is unlikely to be understood. The meanings of words used by the sender may differ depending on the nonverbal cues, such as facial expression, that the sender transmits along with them.

"From the point of view of the speakers, language is a symbolic system that they use to communicate."—Michael Agar, author of Language Shock—Understanding the Culture of Conversation[10]

Transmission

Transmission is the process through which the symbols that represent the message are sent to the receiver.

The medium is the channel, or path, through which the message is transmitted.

Transmission is the process through which the symbols that carry the message are sent to the receiver. The **medium** is the channel, or path, of transmission. The medium for face-to-face conversation is sound waves. The same conversation conducted over the telephone involves not only sound waves but also electrical impulses and the lines that connect the two phones. To tell the employee in what order to perform tasks, the manager could tell the employee face to face or use the telephone, a memo, email, or voicemail.

Communications media range from interpersonal media, such as talking or touching, to mass media, such as newspapers, magazines, or television broadcasts. The "Talking Technology" box describes an increasingly popular medium for communication, videoconferencing. Different media have different capacities for carrying information. For example, a face-to-face conversation generally has more carrying capacity than a letter because it allows the transmission of more than just words. In addition, the medium can help determine the effect the message has on the receiver. Calling a prospective client on the telephone to make a business proposal is a more personal approach than sending a letter and is likely to elicit a different response. It is important that a sender choose the medium that is most likely to correspond to the type of message that needs to be sent and understood.

Decoding

Decoding is the process by which the receiver of the message interprets its meaning.

Decoding is the process by which the receiver of the message interprets its meaning. The receiver uses knowledge and experience to interpret the symbols of the message; in some situations, he or she may consult an authority such as a dictionary

TALKING TECHNOLOGY

▶ *The Challenges of Videoconferencing*

Although the fundamental communications elements—sender, message, medium, receiver, feedback—have not changed, the varieties of available media have increased rapidly during the last century. One of the most recent advances is the use of videoconferencing, also called virtual conferencing or teleconferencing, in which participants at multiple locations simultaneously send and receive digital images and sound. Unlike other types of communication such as email, fax, or telephone, videoconferencing transmits both visual and audio signals. For the users, the experience is similar to attending a face-to-face meeting.

Videoconferencing provides some benefits that face-to-face meetings cannot. One benefit is the ability to have many participants at diverse locations come together without the expense or wasted time of international travel. Many corporations increased their use of videoconferencing due to the safety concerns, travel uncertainties, and travel restrictions imposed after the events of September 11.

The new technology has also facilitated some types of communication interactions that would have been very difficult or prohibitively expensive to conduct via older media. For example, medical specialists now use videoconferencing for diagnosis and supervision of surgery. Teachers instruct students at multiple sites, and students interact with the instructor and each other, as they would in a traditional classroom. Hundreds of universities worldwide now offer courses by videoconference, and some grant degrees to students who have been taught entirely by this method. At one school for the deaf, computing

technology translates voices into text, which appears on the screen with the speaker's image.

Videoconferencing is becoming a popular communication tool, but its primary difficulties are the same human factors that provide challenges in every communication situation. Body language, always tricky to interpret, is made even more problematic when the participants are from different cultures, and the relatively poor quality of

"Without meaningful personal interactions and doing 'real' work together, it's hard to build understanding and accountability." —Jon Katzenbach, author of The Discipline of Teams

digital images increases the ambiguity. Tone of voice provides an important clue to meaning, but it can be distorted when transmitted digitally. Even something as basic as time zones can create a problem. For example, if some participants are meeting at 2 A.M. local time, they may be tired and unfocused. Jon Katzenbach, author of *The Discipline of Teams,* recommends videoconferencing but also sees a continuing need for frequent face-to-face meetings. He maintains, "Without meaningful personal interactions and doing 'real' work together, it's hard to build understanding and accountability."

References: Paul Korzeniowski, "For Videoconferencing, New Desktop Systems Becoming Viable Option," *Investor's Business Daily,* February 21, 2002, p. A16; Gill Plimmer, "Tapping into Virtual Networks: Modern Technology Is Helping, Rather Than Hindering, the Future of the Conference," *Financial Times* (London, UK), February 15, 2002, p. 3; "The World's Fastest Growing Industry in 2002 Will Be Virtual Meetings," *Videoconferencing Insight Newsletter,* February 13, 2002 www.businesswire.com on February 14, 2002; Jon R. Katzenbach and Douglas R. Smith, *The Discipline of Teams* (New York: Wiley, 2001), quoted in Anne Fisher, "Virtual Teams and Long-Distance Meetings: More on Staying Grounded," *Fortune,* October 15, 2001. www.fortune.com on April 28, 2002.

or a code book. Up to this point, the receiver has been relatively inactive, but the receiver becomes more active in the decoding phase. The meaning the receiver attaches to the symbols may be the same as or different from the meaning intended by the source. If the meanings differ, of course, communication breaks down, and misunderstanding is likely. In our example, if the employee does not understand the language or a particular word, then the employee will not comprehend the same meaning as the sender (manager) and may do the tasks in the wrong order or not do them at all.

Receiver

The receiver is the individual, group, or organization that perceives the encoded symbols; the receiver may or may not decode them to try to understand the intended message.

The **receiver** of the message may be an individual, a group, an organization, or an individual acting as the representative of a group. The receiver decides whether to decode the message, whether to make an effort to understand it, and whether to respond. Moreover, the intended receiver may not get the message at all whereas an unintended receiver may, depending on the medium and the symbols used by the source and the attention level of potential receivers. An employee may share the same language (know the symbols) used by the manager but may not want to get the sender's meaning.

The key skill for proper reception of the message is good listening. The receiver may not concentrate on the sender, the message, or the medium such that the message is lost. Listening is an active process that requires as much concentration and effort from the receiver as sending the message does for the sender. The expression of emotions by the sender and receiver enters into the communication process at several points. First, the emotions may be part of the message, entering into the encoding process. For example, if the manager's directions are encoded with a sense of emotional urgency—for example, if they are given with a high-pitched or loud voice—the employee may move quickly to follow the directions. However, if the message is urgent, but the manager's tone of voice is low and does not send urgent signals, employees may not engage in quick action. Second, as the message is decoded, the receiver may let his or her emotions perceive a message different from what the sender intended. Third, emotion-filled feedback from the intended receiver can cause the sender to modify her or his subsequent message.

Feedback

Feedback is the process in which the receiver returns a message to the sender that indicates receipt of the message.

Feedback is the receiver's response to the message. Feedback verifies the message by telling the source whether the receiver received and understood the message. The feedback may be as simple as a phone call from the prospective client expressing interest in the business proposal or as complex as a written brief on a complicated point of law sent from an attorney to a judge. In our example, the employee can respond to the manager's directions by a verbal or written response indicating that he or she does or does not understand the message. Feedback could also be nonverbal, as when, in our example, the employee does not do either task. With typical voicemail, the feedback loop is missing, which can lead to many communication problems.

Noise

Noise is any disturbance in the communication process that interferes with or distorts communication.

Channel noise is a disturbance in communication that is primarily a function of the medium.

Noise is any disturbance in the communication process that interferes with or distorts communication. Noise can be introduced at virtually any point in the communication process. The principal type, called **channel noise,** is associated with the medium.[11] Radio static and "ghost" images on television are examples of channel noise. When noise interferes in the encoding and decoding processes, poor encoding and decoding can result. Emotions that interfere with an intended communication may also be considered a type of noise. An employee may not hear the directions given by the manager owing to noisy machinery on the shop floor or competing input from other people.

Noise is any disturbance in the communication process that interferes with or distorts communication. Take this busy scene in New York City, for example. Anyone attempting to have a quiet conversation or place a cellular telephone call would have difficulty in hearing and in being heard due to the traffic and large number of people around. While most work settings are likely to have fewer sources of noise than this, people in organizations must still contend with other people talking, equipment noises, and similar distractions.

Effective communication occurs when information or meaning has been shared by at least two people. Therefore, communication must include the response from the receiver back to the sender. The sender cannot know if the message has been conveyed as intended if there is no feedback from the receiver, as when we leave voicemail. Both parties are responsible for the effectiveness of the communication. The evolution of new technology in recent years presents novel problems in ensuring that communications work as sender and receiver expect them to.

Electronic Information Processing and Telecommunications

C hanges in the workplace are occurring at an astonishing rate. Many innovations are based on new technologies—computerized information processing systems, new types of telecommunication systems, the Internet, organizational intranets, and various combinations of these technologies. Experts have estimated that performance of new information technology (at the same cost) doubles every eighteen months.[12] Managers can now send and receive memos and other documents to and from one person or a group scattered around the world from their computers using the Internet, and they can do so in their cars or via their notebook computers and cellular phones on the commuter train. Soon they may be doing the same thing on their wristwatches. Employees are now telecommuting from home rather than going to the office every day. And whole new industries are developing around information storage, transmission, and retrieval that were not even dreamed of a few years ago.

"The number of email messages sent on an average day in the U.S. was 3.5 billion in 1999 and is expected to total 10 billion by 2004."—research by International Data Corporation[13]

The "office of the future" is here, but it just may not be in a typical office building. Every office now has a facsimile (fax) machine, a copier, and personal computers, many of them linked into a single integrated system and to numerous databases and electronic mail systems. Automobile companies advertise that their cars and trucks have equipment for your cellular telephone, computer, and fax machine. The electronic office links managers, clerical employees, professional workers, sales personnel, and often suppliers and customers as well in a worldwide communication network that uses a combination of computerized data storage, retrieval, and transmission systems.

In fact, the computer-integrated organization is becoming commonplace. Ingersol Milling Machine of Rockford, Illinois, boasts a totally computer-integrated operation in which all major functions—sales, marketing, finance, distribution, and manufacturing—exchange operating information quickly and continuously via computers. For example, product designers can send specifications directly to machines on the factory floor, and accounting personnel receive online information about sales, purchases, and prices instantaneously. The computer system parallels and greatly speeds up the entire process.

Computers are facilitating the increase in telecommuting across the United States and reducing the number of trips people make to the office to get work done. Almost ten years ago IBM provided many of its employees with notebook computers and told them not to come to the office but instead to use the computers to do the work out in the field and send it in electronically.[14] Other companies, such as Motorola and AT & T, have also encouraged such telecommuting by employees. Employees report increased productivity, less fatigue caused by commuting, reduced commuting expenses, and increased personal freedom. In addition, telecommuting may reduce air pollution and overcrowding. Some employees have reported, however, that they miss the social interaction of the office. Some managers have also expressed concerns about the quantity and quality of the work telecommuting employees do when away from the office. Another potential issue, the uses and abuses of email, a medium vital to telecommuters, is discussed in the "Business of Ethics" feature.

Research conducted among office workers using a new electronic office system indicated that attitudes toward the system were generally favorable. On the other hand, reduction of face-to-face meetings may depersonalize the office. Some observers are also concerned that companies are installing electronic systems with little consideration for the social structures of the office. As departments adopt computerized information systems, the activities of work groups throughout the organization are likely to become more interdependent, a situation which may alter power relationships among the groups. Most employees quickly learn the system of power, politics, authority, and responsibility in the office. A radical change in work and personal relationships caused by new office technology may disrupt normal ways of accomplishing tasks, thereby reducing productivity. Other potential problems include information overload, loss of records in a "paperless" office, and the dehumanizing consequences of using electronic equipment. In effect, new information processing and transmission technologies mean new media, symbols, message transmission methods, and networks for organizational communication.

The real increases in organizational productivity due to information technology may come from the ability to communicate in new and different ways rather than from simply speeding up existing communication patterns. For example, to remain competitive in a very challenging global marketplace, companies will need to be able to generate, disseminate, and implement new ideas more effectively. In effect, organizations will become "knowledge-based" learning organizations that are

BUSINESS OF ETHICS

Email—Friend or Foe?

Technological developments are creating ethical problems in many areas—consider cloning, satellite reconnaissance, and bioengineered foods. It seems that for every innovation that results in convenience or safety, a corresponding sacrifice is required. Use of the Internet and email, although undeniably convenient and efficient, presents business people with several vexing ethical issues.

In one set of age-old concerns, the Internet and email have merely substituted for more traditional forms of communication such as mail or telephone calls. Internet scams often mimic the form of classic swindles such as Ponzi or pyramid schemes with greater efficiency than before. Federal law enforcement personnel surf the Web looking for illegal or unethical practices, finding 1600 questionable sites in a typical "sting." Employers are using email to test employee loyalty, as in the case of the manager who sent false emails to his workers, pretending to be a recruiter from a competing firm. Any employees who responded to that email were passed over for promotion.

Other abuses arise from the capabilities of new, more sophisticated software. Email management software can legally be used by supervisors to monitor their employees' email. If the practice is undisclosed or used inappropriately, the employees' right to privacy can be infringed. Forty-six percent of employers monitor employee emails, most without the knowledge of their employees. "To help protect their businesses from potential liability or security threats, companies need a . . . monitoring system," explains William Caple, executive vice president of OTG Software, maker of email management systems.

Employees use email technology to post opinions about their employers to online message boards, and the results can be a wake-up call for managers. Agency.com CEO Kyle Shannon, whose company was slammed on Vault.com's public discussion boards, warns, "In this new information environment you've got to assume everyone

> *"In this new information environment you've got to assume everyone knows everything."* — *Kyle Shannon, Agency.com CEO*

knows everything. So being straight with employees is important. Don't spin anything. Don't try to hide anything." After viewing Vault.com, Shannon realized his employees felt ill prepared, stressed, and uninformed, so he recently hired a vice president of People Management to alleviate the workers' anxiety. Whether or not an employer responds to the message boards, just having an opportunity to "vent" can be a relief for upset employees. With the increasing number of innovations and the resulting spate of new ethical concerns, employees may need that opportunity more than ever.

References: "Press Release: Quantum Announces Network Attached Storage Solution Designed to Simplify E-Mail Management," OTG Software web site. www.otg.com on April 26, 2002; "OTG Software Introduces Transparent Email Surveillance for Policy Enforcement," *Business Wire*, December 5, 2001. www.businesswire.com on December 6, 2001; John Simons, "Stop Moaning about Gripe Sites and Log On," *Fortune*, April 2, 2001 (quotation). www.fortune.com on February 26, 2002; Michael Shrage, "E-Mail or E-Sting? Your Boss Knows, But He's Not Telling," *Fortune*, March 20, 2000, p. 240. See www.fortune.com; Daniel H. Pink, "America's Top Cybercop," *Fast Company*, October 2000. www.fastcompany.com on February 26, 2002.

continually generating new ideas to improve themselves. This can only occur when expert knowledge is communicated and available throughout the organization.

One of these new ways of communicating is idea sharing, or knowledge sharing, by sharing information on what practices work best. A computer-based system is necessary to store, organize, and then make available to others the best practices from throughout the company.[15] For example, Eli Lilly, a large pharmaceutical company, has developed a company-wide intranet for all of its sixteen thousand employees. This system makes available internal email, corporate policies, and directories and enables information sharing throughout the organization.[16] Electronic information technology is, therefore, speeding up existing communication and developing new types of organizational communication processes with potential new benefits and problems for managers.

Communication Networks

Communication links individuals and groups in a social system. Initially, task-related communication links develop in an organization so that employees can get the information they need to do their jobs and coordinate their work with that of others in the system. Over a long period, these communication relationships become a sophisticated social system composed of both small-group communication networks and a larger organizational network. These networks structure both the flow and the content of communication and support the organizational structure.[17] The pattern and content of communication also support the culture, beliefs, and value systems that enable the organization to operate.

Small-Group Networks

To examine interpersonal communication in a small group, we can observe the patterns that emerge as the work of the group proceeds, and information flows from some people in the group to others.[18] Four such patterns are shown in Figure 10.4. The lines identify the communication links most frequently used in the groups.

A **wheel network** is a pattern in which information flows between the person at the end of each spoke and the person in the middle. Those on the ends of the spokes do not directly communicate with each other. The wheel network is a feature of the typical work group, in which the primary communication occurs between the members and the group manager. In a **chain network,** each member communicates with the person above and below, except for the individuals on each end, who communicate with only one person. The chain network is typical of communication in a vertical hierarchy, in which most communication travels up and down the chain of command. Each person in a **circle network** communicates with the people on both sides but not with anyone else. The circle network often is found in task forces and committees. Finally, in an **all-channel network,** all members communicate with all the other members. The all-channel network often is found in informal groups that have no formal structure, leader, or task to accomplish.

Communication may be more easily distorted by noise when much is being communicated or when the communication must travel a great distance. Improvements in electronic communication technology, such as computerized mail systems and intranets, are reducing this effect. A relatively central position gives a person an opportunity to communicate with all of the other members, so a member in a relatively central position can control the information flow and may become a leader of the group. This leadership position is separate and distinct from the formal group structure, although a central person in a group may also emerge as a formal group leader over a long period.

Communication networks form spontaneously and naturally as interactions among workers continue. They are rarely permanent since they change as the tasks, interactions, and memberships change. The patterns and characteristics of small-group communication networks are determined by the factors summarized in Table 10.2 (on p. 265). The task is crucial in determining the pattern of the network. If the group's primary task is decision making, an all-channel network may develop to provide the information needed to evaluate all possible alternatives. If, however, the group's task mainly involves the sequential execution of individual

In a wheel network, information flows between the person at the end of each spoke and the person in the middle.

In a chain network, each member communicates with the person above and below, except for the individuals on each end, who communicate with only one person.

In a circle network, each member communicates with the people on both sides but with no one else.

In an all-channel network, all members communicate with all other members.

Communication networks form spontaneously and naturally as the interactions among workers continue over time.

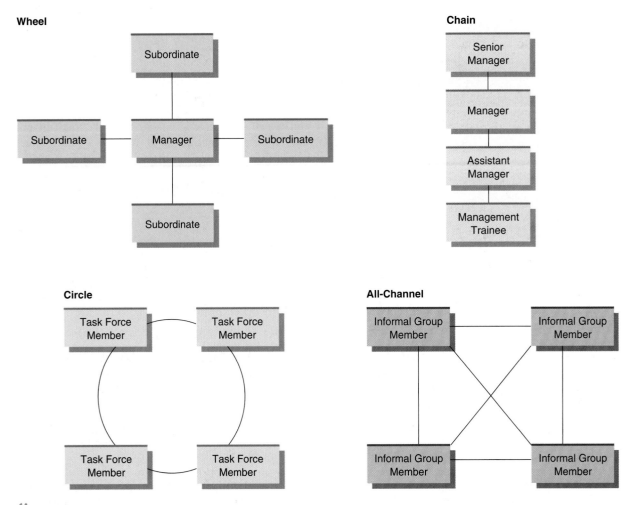

figure 10.4

Small-Group Communication Networks

These four types of communication networks are the most common in organizations. The lines represent the most frequently used communication links in small groups.

tasks, a chain or wheel network is more likely because communication among members may not be important to the completion of the tasks.

The environment (the type of room in which the group works or meets, the seating arrangement, the placement of chairs and tables, the geographical dispersion, and other aspects of the group's setting) can affect the frequency and types of interactions among members. For example, if most members work on the same floor of an office building, the members who work three floors down may be considered outsiders and develop weaker communication ties to the group. They may even form a separate communication network.

Personal factors also influence the development of the communication network. These include technical expertise, openness, speaking ability, and the degree to which members are acquainted with one another. For example, in a group concerned mainly with highly technical problems, the person with the most expertise may dominate the communication flow during a meeting.

table 10.2

Factors Influencing the
Development of Small-
Group Networks

Factor	Example
Task	Decision making
	Sequential production
Environment	Type of room, placement of chairs and tables, dispersion of members
Personal Characteristics	Expertise, openness, speaking ability, degree of familiarity among group members
Group Performance Factors	Composition, size, norms, cohesiveness

The group performance factors that influence the communication network include composition, size, norms, and cohesiveness. For example, group norms in one organization may encourage open communication across different levels and functional units whereas the norms in another organization may discourage such lateral and diagonal communication. These performance factors are discussed in Chapter 11.

Because the outcome of the group's efforts depends on the coordinated action of its members, the communication network strongly influences group effectiveness. Thus, to develop effective working relationships in the organization, managers need to make a special effort to manage the flow of information and the development of communication networks. Managers can, for example, arrange offices and work spaces to foster communication among certain employees. Managers may also attempt to involve members who typically contribute little during discussions by asking them direct questions such as "What do you think, Tom?" or "Maria, tell us how this problem is handled in your district." Methods such as the nominal group technique, discussed in Chapter 15, can also encourage participation.

One other factor that is becoming increasingly more important in the development of communication networks is the advent of electronic groups fostered by electronic distribution lists, chat rooms, discussion boards, and other computer networking systems. This form of communication results in a network of people who may have little or no face-to-face communication but still may be considered a group communication network. For example, your professor is probably a member of an electronic group of other professors who share an interest in the topic of this course. Through the electronic group, they keep up with new ideas in the field.

Organizational Communication Networks

An organization chart shows reporting relationships from the line worker up to the CEO of the firm. The lines of an organization chart may also represent channels of communication through which information flows, yet communication may also follow paths that cross traditional reporting lines. Information moves not only from the top down—from CEO to group members—but also upward from group members to the CEO. In fact, a good flow of information to the CEO is an important determinant of the organization's success.

Several companies have realized that the key to their continuing success was improved internal communication. General Motors was known for its extremely

Communication networks structure both the flow and the content of communication in organizations. Take Charlie Scharf, for example. He is the head of retail banking for Banc One and is shown here meeting with a group of branch employees in Ohio. The branch employees themselves form various small-group communication networks such as the wheel, the chain, and the circle. But when Mr. Scharf is involved the networks become more formalized. And he plays the role of gatekeeper by controlling the flow of information in and out of the branch employee networks.

formal, top-down communication system. In the mid-1980s, however, the formality of its system came under fire from virtually all of its stakeholders. GM's response was to embark on a massive communication improvement program that included sending employees to public-speaking workshops, improving the more than 350 publications that it sends out, providing videotapes of management meetings to employees, and using satellite links between headquarters and field operations to establish two-way conversations around the world.

Downward communication generally provides directions whereas upward communication provides feedback to top management. Communication that flows horizontally or crosses traditional reporting lines usually is related to task performance. For example, a design engineer, a manufacturing engineer, and a quality engineer may communicate about the details of a particular product design, thus making it easy to manufacture and inspect. Horizontal communication often travels faster than vertical communication because it need not follow organizational protocols and procedures.

Organizational communication networks may diverge from reporting relationships as employees seek better information with which to do their jobs. Employees often find that the easiest way to get their jobs done or to obtain the necessary information is to go directly to employees in other departments rather than through the formal channels shown on the organization chart. Figure 10.5 shows a simple organization chart and the organization's real communication network. The communication network links the individuals who most frequently communicate with one another; the firm's CEO, for example, communicates most often with employee 5. (This does not mean that individuals not linked in the communication network never communicate, but only means that their communications are relatively infrequent.) Perhaps the CEO and the employee interact frequently outside of work, in church, in service organizations such as Kiwanis, or at sporting events. Such interactions may lead to close friendships that carry over into business relationships. The figure also shows that the group managers do not have important roles in the communication network, contrary to commonsense expectations.

The gatekeeper has a strategic position in the network that allows him or her to control information moving in either direction through a channel.

The liaison serves as a bridge between groups, tying groups together and facilitating the communication flow needed to integrate group activities.

The cosmopolite links the organization to the external environment and may also be an opinion leader in the group.

The isolate and the isolated dyad tend to work alone and to interact and communicate little with others.

The roles that people play in organizational communication networks can be analyzed in terms of their contribution to the functioning of the network.[19] The most important roles are labeled in the bottom portion of Figure 10.5. A **gatekeeper** (employee 5) has a strategic position in the network that allows him or her to control information moving in either direction through a channel. A **liaison** (employee 15) serves as a bridge between groups, tying groups together and facilitating the communication flow needed to integrate group activities. Employee 13 performs the interesting function of **cosmopolite,** who links the organization to the external environment by, for instance, attending conventions and trade shows, keeping up with outside technological innovations, and having more frequent contact with sources outside the organization. This person may also be an opinion leader in the group. Finally, the **isolate** (employee 3) and the **isolated dyad** (employees 2 and 9) tend to work alone and to interact and communicate little with others.

Each of these roles and functions plays an important part in the overall functioning of the communication network and in the organization as a whole. Understanding these roles can help both managers and group members facilitate communication. For instance, the manager who wants to be sure that the CEO receives certain information is well advised to go through the gatekeeper. If the employee who has the technical knowledge necessary for a particular project is an isolate, the manager can take special steps to integrate the employee into the communication network for the duration of the project.

Recent research has indicated some possible negative impacts of communication networks. Employee turnover has been shown to occur in clusters related to employee communication networks.[20] That is, employees who communicate regularly in a network may share feelings about the organization and thus influence one another's intentions to stay or quit. Communication networks therefore may have both positive and negative consequences.

figure 10.5

Comparison of an Organization Chart and the Organization's Communication Network

A single organization chart compared with actual communication patterns are quite different from the reporting relationships shown in the organization chart.

Organization Chart

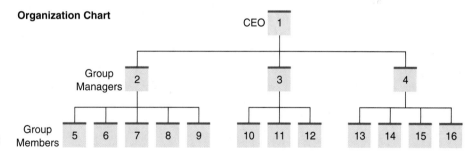

Communication Network of Most Frequent Communications for the Same Organization

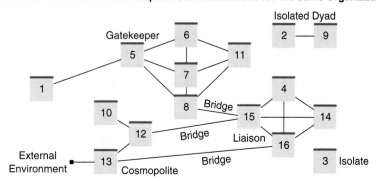

As we discuss in Chapters 16 and 17, a primary function of organizational structure is to coordinate the activities of many people doing specialized tasks. Communication networks in organizations provide this much-needed integration. In fact, in some ways, communication patterns influence organizational structure. Some companies are finding that the need for better communication forces them to create smaller divisions. The fewer managerial levels and improved team spirit of these divisions tend to enhance communication flows.

Managing Communication

Communication fidelity is the degree of correspondence between the message intended by the source and the message understood by the receiver.

As simple as the process of communication may seem, messages are not always understood. The degree of correspondence between the message intended by the source and the message understood by the receiver is called communication **fidelity.** Fidelity can be diminished anywhere in the communication process, from the source to the feedback. Moreover, organizations may have characteristics that impede the flow of information. Table 10.3 summarizes the most common types of breakdowns and barriers in organizational communication.

Improving the Communication Process

To improve organizational communication, one must understand potential problems. Using the basic communication process, we can identify several ways to overcome typical problems.

Source   The source may intentionally withhold or filter information on the assumption that the receiver does not need it to understand the communication. Withholding information, however, may render the message meaningless or cause an erroneous interpretation. For example, during a performance appraisal interview, a manager may not tell the employee all of the sources of information being used to make the evaluation, thinking that the employee does not need to know them. If the employee knew, however, he or she might be able to explain certain behaviors or otherwise alter the manager's perspective of the evaluation and thereby make it more accurate. Filtering may be more likely to occur in electronic communication such as email or voicemail since they carry an implied importance for brevity and conciseness. Selective filtering may cause a breakdown in communication that cannot be repaired, even with good follow-up communication.

To avoid filtering, the communicator needs to understand why it occurs. Filtering can result from a lack of understanding of the receiver's position, from

table 10.3

Communication Problems in Organizations

Root of the Problem	Type of Problem
Source	Filtering
Encoding and Decoding	Lack of common experience
	Semantics; jargon
	Medium problems
Receiver	Selective attention
	Value judgments
	Lack of source credibility
	Overload
Feedback	Omission
Organizational Factors	Noise
	Status differences
	Time pressures
	Overload
	Communication structure

the sender's need to protect his or her own power by limiting the receiver's access to information, or from doubts about what the receiver might do with the information. The sender's primary concern, however, should be the message. In essence, the sender must determine exactly what message he or she wants the receiver to understand, send the receiver enough information to understand the message but not enough to create an overload, and trust the receiver to use the information properly.

Encoding and Decoding   Encoding and decoding problems occur as the message is translated into or from the symbols used in transmission. Such problems can relate to the meaning of the symbols or to the transmission itself. As Table 10.3 shows, encoding and decoding problems include lack of common experience between source and receiver, problems related to semantics and the use of jargon, and difficulties with the medium. The cartoon illustrates another potential problem!

Clearly, the source and the receiver must share a common experience with the symbols that express the message if they are to encode and decode them in exactly the same way. People who speak different languages or come from different cultural backgrounds may experience problems of this sort. But even people who speak the same language can misunderstand each other.

Semantics is the study of language forms.

Semantics is the study of language forms, and semantic problems occur when people attribute different meanings to the same words or language forms. For example, J. Edgar Hoover, the legendary former director of the FBI, once jotted "watch the borders" on a memo he had received and sent it back to the senior agency manager who had written it. Only after dispatching several dozen agents to guard the border between the United States and Mexico did the agency manager learn what Hoover had actually meant—the margins on the memo were too narrow! Similarly, when discussing a problem employee, the division head may tell her assistant, "We need to get rid of this problem." The division head may have meant that the employee should be scheduled for more training or transferred to another division. However, the assistant may interpret the statement differently and fire the problem employee.

Jargon is the specialized or technical language of a trade, profession, or social group.

The specialized or technical language of a trade, field, profession, or social group is called jargon. **Jargon** may be a hybrid of standard language and the

One of the oldest barriers to effective communication in organizations is simply poor writing. If the sender jots down some instructions or other information, but the receiver cannot accurately read the intended message, any number of problems can arise. Of course, the simplest solution is for the receiver to simply ask the sender to "translate" what she or he has written. As shown here, though, some people are reluctant to take this step, and their reluctance can sometimes spell big trouble!

Reference: Reprinted with Special Permission of King Feature Syndicate.

specialized language of a group. For example, experts in the computer field use terms such as "gigs," "megs," "RAM," and "bandwidth" that have little or no meaning to those unfamiliar with computers. The use of jargon makes communication within a close group of colleagues more efficient and meaningful, but outside the group it has the opposite effect. Sometimes a source person comfortable with jargon uses it unknowingly in an attempt to communicate with receivers who do not understand it, thus causing a communication breakdown. In other cases, the source may use jargon intentionally to obscure meaning or to show outsiders that he or she belongs to the group that uses the language.

The use of jargon is acceptable if the receiver is familiar with it; otherwise, it should be avoided. Repeating a jargon-containing message in clearer terms should help the receiver understand it. In general, the source and the receiver should clarify the set of symbols to be used before they communicate. Also, the receiver can ask questions frequently and, if necessary, ask the source to repeat all or part of the message. The source must send the message through a medium appropriate to the message itself and to the intended receiver. For example, a commercial run on an AM radio station will not have its intended effect if the people in the desired market segment listen only to FM radio.

Largely influenced by the Enron debacle, many investors are increasingly beginning to scrutinize the financial reporting systems of larger companies. Coca-Cola, for instance, has recently seen its own accounting practices criticized in the media. These critics contend that the firm is using increasingly complex reporting methods to make its earnings seem higher than they would have been if simpler and more straightforward accounting practices had been used.[21]

Receiver   Several communication problems originate in the receiver, including problems with selective attention, value judgments, source credibility, and overload. Selective attention exists when the receiver attends only to selected parts of a message—a frequent occurrence with oral communication. For example, in a college class, some students may hear only part of the professor's lecture as their minds wander to other topics. To focus receivers' attention on the message, senders often engage in attention-getting behaviors such as varying the volume, repeating the message, and offering rewards.

Value judgments are influenced by the degree to which a message reinforces or challenges the receiver's basic personal beliefs. If a message reinforces the receiver's beliefs, he or she may pay close attention and believe it completely, without examination. On the other hand, if the message challenges those beliefs, the receiver may entirely discount it. Thus, if a firm's sales manager predicts that the demand for new baby-care products will increase substantially over the next two years, he may ignore reports that the birthrate is declining.

The receiver may also judge the credibility of the source of the message. If the source is perceived to be an expert in the field, the listener may pay close attention to the message and believe it. Conversely, if the receiver has little respect for the source, he or she may disregard the message. The receiver considers both the message and the source in making value judgments and determining credibility. An expert in nuclear physics may be viewed as a credible source if the issue is building a nuclear power plant, yet the same person's evaluation of the birthrate may be disregarded, perhaps correctly. This is one reason that trial lawyers ask expert witnesses about their education and experience at the beginning of their testimony: to establish credibility.

A receiver experiencing communication overload is receiving more information than she or he can process. In organizations, this can happen very easily; a receiver can be bombarded with computer-generated reports and messages from superiors, peers, and sources outside the organization. It is not unusual for middle managers or telecommuters to receive one hundred email messages per day. Unable to take in all the messages, decode them, understand them, and act on them, the receiver may use selective attention and value judgments to focus on the messages that seem most important. Although this type of selective attention is necessary for survival in an information-glutted environment, it may mean that vital information is lost or overlooked.[22]

Verification is the feedback portion of communication in which the receiver sends a message to the source indicating receipt of the message and the degree to which he or she understood the message.

Feedback   The purpose of feedback is **verification,** in which the receiver sends a message to the source indicating receipt of the message and the degree to which it was understood. Lack of feedback can cause at least two problems. First, the source may need to send another message that depends on the response to the first; if the source receives no feedback, the source may not send the second message or may be forced to send the original message again. Second, the receiver may act on the unverified message; if the receiver misunderstood the message, the resulting act may be inappropriate.

Because feedback is so important, the source must actively seek it, and the receiver must supply it. Often it is appropriate for the receiver to repeat the original message as an introduction to the response, although the medium or symbols used may be different. Nonverbal cues can provide instantaneous feedback. These include body language and facial expressions such as anger and disbelief.

The source needs to be concerned with the message, the symbols, the medium, and the feedback from the receiver. Of course, the receiver is concerned with these things, too, but from a different point of view. In general, the receiver needs to be source oriented just as the source needs to be receiver oriented. Table 10.4 gives specific suggestions for improving the communication process.

Improving Organizational Factors in Communication

Organizational factors that can create communication breakdowns or barriers include noise, status differences, time pressures, and overload. As previously stated, disturbances anywhere in the organization can distort or interrupt meaningful communication. Thus, the noise created by a rumored takeover can disrupt the orderly flow of task-related information. Kmart's stock dropped precipitously in early 2002 based on rumors that it would file bankruptcy. Although the retailer did indeed take this step several weeks later, rumor alone caused great damage to the company in the eyes of the investment community.[23]

Status differences between source and receiver can cause some of the communication problems just discussed. For example, a firm's chief executive officer may pay little attention to communications from employees far lower on the organization chart, and employees may pay little attention to communications from the CEO. Both are instances of selective attention prompted by the organization's status system. Time pressures and communication overloads are also detrimental to communication. When the receiver is not allowed enough time to understand incoming messages, or when there are too many messages, he or she may misunderstand or ignore some of them. Effective organizational communication

Focus	Source		Receiver	
	Question	Corrective Action	Question	Corrective Action
Message	What idea or thought are you trying to get across?	Give more information. Give less information. Give entire message.	What idea or thought does the sender want you to understand?	Listen carefully to the entire message, not just to part of it.
Symbols	Does the receiver use the same symbols, words, jargon?	Say it another way. Employ repetition. Use receiver's language or jargon. Before sending, clarify symbols to be used.	What symbols are being used—for example, foreign language, technical jargon?	Clarify symbols before communication begins. Ask questions. Ask sender to repeat message.
Medium	Is this a channel that the receiver monitors regularly? Sometimes? Never?	Use multiple media. Change medium. Increase volume (loudness).	What medium or media is the sender using?	Monitor several media.
Feedback	What is the receiver's reaction to your message?	Pay attention to the feedback, especially nonverbal cues. Ask questions.	Did you correctly interpret the message?	Repeat message.

table 10.4

Improving the Communication Process

provides the right information to the right person at the right time and in the right form.

The grapevine is an informal system of communication that coexists with the formal system.

Reduce Noise   Noise is a primary barrier to effective organizational communication. A common form of noise is the rumor **grapevine,** an informal system of communication that coexists with the formal system. The grapevine usually transmits information faster than official channels do. Because the accuracy of this information often is quite low, however, the grapevine can distort organizational communication. Management can reduce the effects of the distortion by using the grapevine as an additional channel for disseminating information and by constantly monitoring it for accuracy.

Foster Informal Communication   Thomas Peters and Robert Waterman once described communication in well-run companies as "a vast network of informal, open communications."[24] Informal communication fosters mutual trust, which minimizes the effects of status differences. Open communication can also contribute to better understanding between diverse groups in an organization. Monsanto Company created fifteen-member teams in its Agricultural Group, the primary objective being to increase communication and awareness among various diverse groups. Its Chemical Group set up diversity pairs of one supervisor and one worker to increase communication and awareness. In both cases, Monsanto found that increasing communication between people who were different paid handsome benefits for the organization.[25] Open communication also allows information to be communicated when it is needed rather than when the formal information system allows it to emerge. Peters and Waterman further describe communication in effective companies as chaotic and intense, supported by the reward structure and the physical arrangement of the facilities. This means that the performance appraisal and reward system, offices, meeting rooms, and work areas are designed to encourage frequent, unscheduled, and unstructured communication throughout the organization.

Develop a Balanced Information Network   Many large organizations have developed elaborate formal information networks to cope with the potential problems of information overload and time pressures. In many cases, however, the networks have created problems instead of solving them. Often they produce more information than managers and decision makers can comprehend and use in their jobs. The networks also often use only formal communication channels and ignore various informal lines of communication. Furthermore, they frequently provide whatever information the computer is set up to provide—information that may not apply to the most pressing problem at hand. The result of all these drawbacks is loss of communication effectiveness.

Organizations need to balance information load and information-processing capabilities. In other words, they must take care not to generate more information than people can handle. It is useless to produce sophisticated statistical reports that managers have no time to read. Furthermore, the new technologies that are making more information available to managers and decision makers must be unified to produce usable information. Information production, storage, and processing capabilities must be compatible with one another and, equally important, with the needs of the organization.

Some companies—for example, General Electric, McDonnell Douglas, Anheuser-Busch, and McDonald's—have formalized an upward communication system that uses a corporate "ombudsperson" position. A highly placed executive who is available outside the formal chain of command to hear employees' complaints usually holds this position. The system provides an opportunity for disgruntled employees to complain without fear of losing their jobs and may help some companies achieve a balanced communication system.

Synopsis

Communication is the process by which two parties exchange information and share meaning. It plays a role in every organizational activity. The purposes of communication in organizations are to achieve coordinated action, to share information, and to express feelings and emotions.

People in organizations communicate through written, oral, and nonverbal means. Written communications include letters, memos, email, reports, and the like. Oral communication is the type most commonly used. Personal elements, such as facial expressions and body language, and environmental elements, such as office design, are forms of nonverbal communication.

Communication among individuals, groups, or organizations is a process in which a source sends a message and a receiver responds. The source encodes a message into symbols and transmits it through a medium to the receiver, who decodes the symbols. The receiver then responds with feedback, an attempt to verify the meaning of the original message. Noise—anything that distorts or interrupts communication—may interfere in virtually any stage of the process.

The fully integrated communication-information office system—the electronic office—links personnel in a communication network through a combination of computers and electronic transmission systems. The full range of effects of such systems has yet to be fully realized.

Communication networks are systems of information exchange within organizations. Patterns of communication emerge as information flows from person to person in a group. Typical small-group communication networks include the wheel, chain, circle, and all-channel networks.

The organizational communication network, which constitutes the real communication links in an organization, usually differs from the arrangement on an organization chart. Roles in organizational communication networks include those of gatekeeper, liaison, cosmopolite, and isolate.

Managing communication in organizations involves understanding the numerous problems that can interfere with effective communication. Problems may arise from the communication process itself and from organizational factors such as status differences.

Discussion Questions

1. How is communication in organizations an individual process as well as an organizational process?

2. Discuss the three primary purposes of organizational communication.

3. Describe a situation in which you tried to carry on a conversation when no one was listening. Were any messages sent during the "conversation"?

4. A college classroom is a forum for a typical attempt at communication as the professor tries to communicate the subject to the students. Describe classroom communication in terms of the basic communication process outlined in the chapter.

5. Is there a communication network (other than professor-to-student) in the class in which you are using this book? If so, identify the specific roles that people play in the network. If not, why has no network developed? What would be the benefits of having a communication network in this class?

6. Why might educators typically focus most communication training on the written and oral methods and pay little attention to the nonverbal methods? Do you think that more training emphasis should be placed on nonverbal communication? Why or why not?

7. Is the typical classroom means of transferring information from professor to student an effective form of communication? Where does it break down? What are the communication problems in the college classroom?

8. Whose responsibility is it to solve classroom communication problems: the students', the professor's, or the administration's?

9. Have you ever worked in an organization in which communication was a problem? If so, what were some causes of the problem?

10. What methods were used, or should have been used, to improve communication in the situation you described in question 9?

11. Would the use of advanced computer information processing or telecommunications have helped solve the communications problem you described in question 9?

12. What types of communication problems will new telecommunications methods probably be able to solve? Why?

13. What types of communications would NOT be appropriate to send by email? Or by voicemail?

14. Which steps in the communication process are usually left out, or at least, poorly done when email and voicemail are used for communication?

Organizational Behavior Case for Discussion

A Tale of Two Companies

To quote Charles Dickens's *A Tale of Two Cities*, "It was the best of times[;] it was the worst of times." With apologies to Dickens, this description handily sums up the current state of affairs in the communications industry. Firms that are able to take advantage of technological developments prosper while firms that have remained in traditional markets are losing sales and profits. Agilent, an electronics component manufacturer, described the situation in its 2001 Annual Report: "The dramatic slowdown in the communications and semiconductor markets defined Agilent's second year as an independent company. After very strong growth in 1999 and 2000, the decline in demand in these markets was unprecedented in its speed and severity. . . . The downturn worsened as we moved through 2001."

EchoMail provides software that automatically processes, responds, stores and tracks email correspondence, reducing the time users spend on these chores. Founded by MIT scientists and headquartered in Cambridge, Massachusetts, home of Harvard and MIT, EchoMail has clients that include many large organizations such as AT & T, Compaq, Nike, and the U.S. Senate. EchoMail was used to create the controversial Calvin Klein advertisements that allowed consumers to email the "characters" in television or print ads and to receive customized, scripted emails in response. EchoMail is the oldest firm (at seven years) in the intelligent email response industry, which is predicted to grow to $340 million in sales by 2003. Thus, the firm is poised to take advantage of the expected flood of intelligent software users over the next decade, and it has recently hired sales and technical professionals.

Contrast EchoMail's situation with that of Agilent, which was created as a spinoff from Hewlett-Packard (HP) when that company refocused its businesses on computing and printing. The November 1999 initial public offering was the largest in Silicon Valley history, valued at $2.1 billion. With 43,000 employees in forty countries, Agilent is a leader in developing and manufacturing electrical components and testing equipment as well as in installation and maintenance services for its equipment. Agilent customers compete in a wide variety of industries, including agricultural chemicals, pharmaceuticals, petrochemicals, semiconductors, wireless communications, semiconductors, PCs, foods, appliances, and automotive, aerospace, and consumer products. Therefore, Agilent is vulnerable to economic downturns in which manufacturers reduce their purchases of equipment and services. Agilent has instituted pay cuts, and in 2001, the firm laid off 4,000 workers, with another 4,000 scheduled for layoffs in 2002.

But if Agilent seems to be facing a host of problems because of its dependence on a currently lackluster segment of the communications industry, there is also a bright side. Agilent considers itself the true heir of Hewlett-Packard founders Dave Packard and Bill Hewlett, who used participatory management, open-door policies and decision making by consensus to keep HP employees working together as a team. Agilent, which carefully built upon the foundation of HP's culture, also carefully worked to maintain its culture when things got tough. Initially, the company tried everything within its power to avoid layoffs—cost cutting, hiring freezes, and even pay cuts. Then, when layoffs became inevitable, CEO Ned Barnholt asked each manager to choose from among the employees known personally to them and insisted that workers be told face to face. Barnholt made the announcement himself, ensuring that employees heard the news from him and not from reporters. He described exactly how employees would be evaluated and how the layoffs would occur. In a rough, emotional tone of voice, he intoned, "This is the toughest decision of my career, but we've run out of alternatives."

As a result of his honest and sincere communication, most Agilent employees did not blame the firm or their supervisors. "I knew that this isn't the HP Way, and it's not what Bill and Dave [Hewlett and Packard] would have wanted, but if they were faced with the same situation, they would have had to do the exact same thing. I know Ned [CEO Barnholt] probably lost a lot [of sleep] having to get up there in front of everybody and make this announcement and have to let go people in his family," says Benjamin Steers, an Agilent employee.

EchoMail today is prospering as its new technology enables the firm to increase sales, profitability, and personnel. Agilent is facing declining markets for many of its traditional products. Its hope for the future is dependent upon its ability to innovate and develop new products. However, as Agilent is demonstrating, appropriate communication, especially of bad news, can be key to building a culture of responsibility, loyalty, and empathy.

"I know Ned [Barnholt, Agilent CEO] . . . probably lost a lot [of sleep] having to get up there in front of everybody and make this announcement"—Benjamin Steers, Agilent employee

References: "About Agilent," "History," "Industries," "2001 Annual Report," Agilent corporate web site. www.agilent.com on April 25, 2002; "About EchoMail," "Board of Directors," EchoMail corporate web site. www.interactive.com on April 25, 2002; Daniel Roth, "How to Cut Pay, Lay Off 8,000 People, and Still Have Workers Who Love You. It's Easy: Just Follow the Agilent Way," *Fortune*, February 4, 2002. www.fortune.com on April 25, 2002; Erin Allday, "Agilent Cuts 600 More Local Jobs," *Press Democrat* (Santa Rosa, CA), December 11, 2001, p. A1; John Evan Frook, "Technology Leads Prospects to Sales," *BtoB Magazine*, October 10, 2001. www.btobonline.com on April 26, 2002; Deborah Shapley, "Dr. E-Mail Will See You Now," *Technology Review*, January–February 2000, pp. 42–47; Roberta Fusaro, "E-Mail Adds Aura to Calvin Klein Campaign," *Computerworld*, November 30, 1998, p. 103.

Case Questions

1. How did Agilent's communication choices lead to an effective employee response to the recent downsizing?

2. Both Agilent and EchoMail are international firms, with production and sales locations in multiple countries. What are some of the potential problems or challenges presented by these firms' international involvement?

3. In Chapter 10, communication is described as reflecting the organization culture and as having the power to change the culture. How does the communication taking place in your Management classroom reflect your school's culture? Has communication at your school changed its culture, and if so, how?

Experiencing Organizational Behavior

The Importance of Feedback in Oral Communication

Purpose: This exercise demonstrates the importance of feedback in oral communication.

Format: You will be an observer or play the role of either a manager or an assistant manager trying to tell a coworker where a package of important materials is to be picked up. The observer's role is to make sure the other two participants follow the rules and to observe and record any interesting occurrences.

Procedure: The instructor will divide the class into groups of three. (Any extra members can be roving observers.) The three people in each group will take the roles of manager, assistant manager, and observer. In the second trial, the manager and the assistant manager will switch roles.

Trial 1: The manager and the assistant manager should turn their backs to each other so that neither can see the other. Here is the situation: The manager is in another city that he or she is not familiar with but that the assistant manager knows quite well. The

manager needs to find the office of a supplier to pick up drawings of a critical component of the company's main product. The supplier will be closing for the day in a few minutes; the drawings must be picked up before closing time. The manager has called the assistant manager to get directions to the office. However, the connection is faulty; the manager can hear the assistant manager, but the assistant manager can hear only enough to know the manager is on the line. The manager has redialed once, but there was no improvement in the connection. Now there is no time to lose. The manager has decided to get the directions from the assistant without asking questions.

Just before the exercise begins, the instructor will give the assistant manager a detailed map of the city that shows the locations of the supplier's office and the manager. The map will include a number of turns, stops, stoplights, intersections, and shopping centers between these locations. The assistant manager can study it for no longer than a minute or two. When the instructor gives the direction to start, the assistant manager describes to the manager how to get from his or her present location to the supplier's office. As the assistant manager gives the directions, the manager draws the map on a piece of paper.

The observer makes sure that no questions are asked, records the beginning and ending times, and notes how the assistant manager tries to communicate particularly difficult points (including points about which the manager obviously wants to ask questions) and any other noteworthy occurrences.

After all pairs have finished, each observer "grades" the quality of the manager's map by comparing it with the original and counting the number of obvious mistakes. The instructor will ask a few managers who believe they have drawn good maps to tell the rest of the class how to get to the supplier's office.

Trial 2: In trial 2, the manager and the assistant manager switch roles, and a second map is passed out to the new assistant managers. The situation is the same

as in the first trial except that the telephones are working properly and the manager can ask questions of the assistant manager. The observer's role is the same as in trial 1—recording the beginning and ending times, the methods of communication, and other noteworthy occurrences.

After all pairs have finished, the observers grade the maps, just as in the first trial. The instructor then selects a few managers to tell the rest of the class how to get to the supplier's office. The subsequent class discussion should center on the experiences of the class members and the follow-up questions.

Follow-up Questions

1. Which trial resulted in more accurate maps? Why?
2. Which trial took longer? Why?
3. How did you feel when a question needed to be asked but could not be asked in trial 1? Was your confidence in the final result affected differently in the two trials?

Self-Assessment Exercise

Diagnosing Your Listening Skills

Introduction: Good listening skills are essential for effective communication and are often overlooked when communication is analyzed. This self-assessment questionnaire examines your ability to listen effectively.

Instructions: Go through the following statements, checking "Yes" or "No" next to each one. Mark each question as truthfully as you can in light of your behavior in the last few meetings or gatherings you attended.

Yes   No

____ ____ 1. I frequently attempt to listen to several conversations at the same time.

____ ____ 2. I like people to give me only the facts and then let me make my own interpretation.

____ ____ 3. I sometimes pretend to pay attention to people.

____ ____ 4. I consider myself a good judge of non-verbal communications.

____ ____ 5. I usually know what another person is going to say before he or she says it.

____ ____ 6. I usually end conversations that don't interest me by diverting my attention from the speaker.

____ ____ 7. I frequently nod, frown, or in some other way let the speaker know how I feel about what he or she is saying.

____ ____ 8. I usually respond immediately when someone has finished talking.

____ ____ 9. I evaluate what is being said while it is being said.

____ ____ 10. I usually formulate a response while the other person is still talking.

____ ____ 11. The speaker's "delivery" style frequently keeps me from listening to content.

___ ___ 12. I usually ask people to clarify what they have said rather than guess at the meaning.

___ ___ 13. I make a concerted effort to understand other people's point of view.

___ ___ 14. I frequently hear what I expect to hear rather than what is said.

___ ___ 15. Most people feel that I have understood their point of view when we disagree.

Scoring

The correct answers according to communication theory are as follows:

No for statements 1, 2, 3, 5, 6, 7, 8, 9, 10, 11, 14.
Yes for statements 4, 12, 13, 15.

If you missed only one or two responses, you strongly approve of your own listening habits, and you are on the right track to becoming an effective listener in your role as manager. If you missed three or four responses, you have uncovered some doubts about your listening effectiveness, and your knowledge of how to listen has some gaps. If you missed five or more responses, you probably are not satisfied with the way you listen, and your friends and coworkers may not feel you are a good listener, either. Work on improving your active listening skills.

Reference: "Diagnosing Your Listening Skills," from Ethel C. Glenn and Elliott A. Pond, "Listening Self-Inventory," *Supervisory Management*, January 1989, pp. 12–15. Reprinted with permission of American Management Association via Copyright Clearance Center.

OB Online

1. Find the country-specific web sites of a single large company such as Coca-Cola, IBM, or Levi Strauss for at least three different countries. Then identify the similarities and differences among web sites.

2. Relate electronic communication to the three basic methods of communication. For example, can nonverbal messages be sent via email?

3. Identify how several different attributes of electronic communication can serve as noise. For example, cell phone static may make it difficult for the receiver to hear the sender.

4. Use the Internet to research the most frequently used methods of communicating in organizations.

Building Managerial Skills

Exercise Overview: Communication skills refer to a manager's ability both to convey ideas and information effectively to others and to receive ideas and information effectively from others. This exercise focuses on communication skills as they involve deciding how to best convey information.

Exercise Background: Assume that you are a middle manager for a large electronics firm. People in your organization generally use one of three means for communicating with one another. The most common way is oral communication, accomplished either face to face or by telephone. Electronic mail is also widely used. Finally, a surprisingly large amount of communication is still done on paper, such as through memos, reports, or letters.

During the course of a typical day, you receive and send a variety of messages and other communication. You generally use some combination of all of the communication methods previously noted during the course of any given day. The things that you need to communicate today include the following:

1. You need to schedule a meeting with five subordinates.

2. You need to congratulate a coworker who just had a baby.

3. You need to reprimand a staff assistant who has been coming to work late for the last several days.

4. You need to inform the warehouse staff that several customers have recently complained because their shipments were not properly packed.

5. You need to schedule a meeting with your boss.
6. You need to announce two promotions.
7. You need to fire someone who has been performing poorly for some time.
8. You need to inform several individuals about a set of new government regulations that will soon affect them.
9. You need to inform a supplier that your company will soon be cutting back on its purchases because a competing supplier has lowered its prices, and you plan to shift more of your business to that supplier.
10. You need to resolve a disagreement between two subordinates who both want to take their vacation at the same time.

Exercise Task: Using the information just presented, do the following:

1. Indicate which methods of communication would be appropriate for each situation.

2. Rank-order the methods for each communication situation from best to worst.

3. Compare your rankings with those of a classmate and discuss any differences.

11 Group Dynamics

Almost every person can identify several groups to which she or he belongs. Some groups are based in friendships and personal relationships whereas others are more formally established and may be part of a larger organization. All organizations have numerous groups that do some part of the organization's work. The performance and productivity of an organization is the total of the output and productivity of all of the individuals and groups that exist within it. Large companies around the world are restructuring their organizations around work groups and teams to increase productivity and innovation and improve customer service.

This chapter is the first of a two-chapter sequence on groups and teams in organizations—groups such as the traditional work groups to which most people belong in their work organizations, pit crews at stock-car races, the Zebra teams that reenergized the black-and-white photo-processing unit at Eastman Kodak, a football team, an engineering work group, or a group of nurses working the night shift at a local hospital. Here we cover the basics of group dynamics—the reasons for group formation, the types of groups in organizations, group performance factors, and the potential for conflict in groups. In Chapter 12, we consider how organizations are using teams today.

We begin this chapter by defining "group" and summarizing the importance of groups in organizations. We then describe different types of groups and discuss the stages in which they evolve from newly formed groups into mature, high-performing units. Next, we identify four key factors that affect group performance. We then move to a discussion of how groups interact with other groups in organizations and of conflict between groups in organizations. Finally, we summarize the important elements in managing groups in organizations. But first, we provide sketches that underscore the importance of groups to the successful performance of a variety of businesses today.

Many observers feared that recent advances in communications marked the end of face-to-face dialogues, human interaction, collaboration, and teamwork. Instead, companies today are finding that technology can enhance and extend the use of traditional team interactions. "There's an opportunity for a whole new level of business-performance improvements in the collaborative redesign of processes, using the Internet," according to James A. Champy, chairman of consulting at Perot Systems.

Lockheed Martin uses a system of ninety web software tools to coordinate a $200 billion project for building the next-generation stealth fighters. The manufacturer brings together 40,000 users, 80 subcontractors, and 187 locations around the world. Lockheed uses the Web to exchange documents and designs and to monitor project progress. "We're getting the best people, applying the best designs, from wherever we need them," says Mark Peden, Lockheed information systems vice president.

"Without meaningful personal interaction . . . , it's hard to build understanding and accountability."—*Jon Katzenbach, consultant, author of* The Discipline of Teams

At General Motors, web collaboration helps engineers and external parts suppliers work together on product design. Complex designs might involve fourteen worldwide sites in addition to the dozens of partner firms that create components and subsystems. By saving time, the engineers are able to complete three or four alternative designs instead of just one and still finish weeks sooner.

Prospective students at Yale University use an Internet-based system to investigate the school, complete an application, and apply for financial aid. Admissions staff around the country then share information about applicants, with online discussion and comments posted to documents. Nevertheless, the director of admissions, James Stevens, still notifies accepted applicants with a phone call. He explains, "[They will] hear from me personally. It is very important to us for people to understand how personal the experience is here."

General Electric holds virtual "company meetings," with speeches webcast to all of its locations simultaneously. Management shares financial results over the Internet with all employees. "There are no secrets. The whole organization has everything," says former CEO Jack Welch. He claims that the shared data facilitate building employees' trust and allow everyone to have the same information, thereby improving teamwork.

The Children's Hospital at Montefiore has integrated a patient-information system throughout the facility. Patients and family members use smart cards for customized access to information about illness and treatment, video games or movies on demand, and Internet access. "It's about the patient's ability to control [his or her] environment," says Jeb Weisman, software designer. David Rockwell, a lead designer of the system, says the intent is "to provide information, insight, and a sense of wonder and delight." Patients and their families thus become team members in their own treatment.

The technology is helpful, but it doesn't manage itself. Paul R. Gudonis, chairman and CEO of Genuity, Inc., says that although managers have made a good start in encouraging teams to use technology, "[t]hey've now found that it's going to take more effort offline to integrate offline and online processes to get the kind of changed behavior and benefits that they're looking for." And Jon

Katzenbach, consultant and author of *The Discipline of Teams*, claims, "Without meaningful personal interaction and doing 'real' work together, it's hard to build understanding and accountability"—reminding leaders of the continuing value of hands-on management and face-to-face meetings.

References: "Paul Gudonis, Chairman and CEO, Genuity, Inc." *Fast Company*. www.fastcompany.com on May 20, 2002; Polly LaBarre, "Strategic Innovation: The Children's Hospital at Montefiore," *Fast Company*, May 2002. www.fastcompany.com on May 20, 2002; Faith Keenan and Spencer E. Ante, "The New Teamwork," *Business Week*, February 18, 2002. www. businessweek.com on May 20, 2002; Anne Fisher, "Virtual Teams and Long-Distance Meetings: More on Staying Grounded," *Fortune*, October 15, 2001 (quotation). www.fortune.com on May 20, 200; Faith Keenan, "Giants Can Be Nimble," *Business Week Biz*, September 18, 2000. www.businessweek.com on May 20, 2002; Nadav Enbar, "Meet Yale's Admissions Director," *Business Week*, December 15, 1999. www.businessweek.com on May 20, 2002.

Understanding how and why people interact with one another is a complex process—whether the interaction occurs in a sports team, a work group, or a school committee. This is especially true when those individuals are members of the same group. Figure 11.1 presents a three-phase model of group dynamics. In the first phase, the reasons for forming the group determine what type of group it will be. A four-step process of group development occurs during the second stage; the precise nature of these steps depends on four primary group performance factors. In the final phase, a mature, productive, adaptive group has evolved. As the model shows, mature groups interact with other groups, meet goals, and sometimes have conflicts with other groups. This model serves as the framework for our discussion of groups in this chapter.

Overview of Groups and Group Dynamics

Work groups consist of people who are trying to make a living for themselves and their families. The work group is often the primary source of social identity for employees, and the nature of the group can affect their performance at work as well as their relationships outside the organization.[1] A group in an organization often takes on a life of its own that transcends the individual members.

"Group" Defined

A group is two or more people who interact with one another such that each person influences and is influenced by each other person.

Definitions of "group" are as abundant as studies of groups. Groups can be defined in terms of perceptions, motivation, organization, interdependencies, and interactions. We will define a **group** as two or more persons who interact with one another such that each person influences and is influenced by each other person.[2] The concept of interaction is essential to this definition. Two people who are physically near each other are not a group unless they interact and have some influence on each other. Coworkers may work side by side on related tasks, but if they do not interact, they are not a group. The presence of others may influence the performance of a group: An audience may stimulate the performance of actors, or an evaluator may inhibit the employee's behavior. However, neither the audience nor the evaluator can be considered part of a group unless interaction occurs.

Although groups often have goals, our definition does not state that group members must share a goal or motivation. This omission implies that members of a group may identify little or not at all with the group's goal. People can be a part of a group and enjoy the benefits of group membership without wanting to pursue any

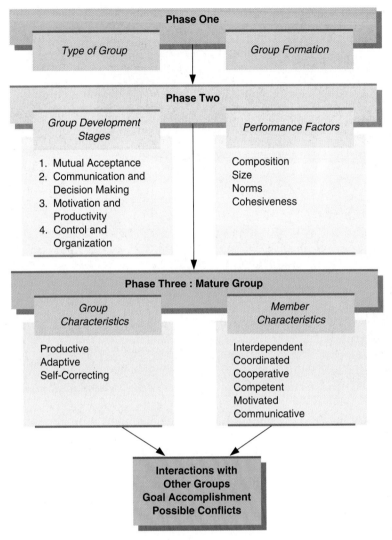

group goal. Members may satisfy needs just by being members, without pursuing anything. Of course, the quality of the interactions and the group's performance may be affected by members' lack of interest in the group goal.

Our definition of "group" also suggests a limit on group size. A collection of people so large that its members cannot interact with and influence one another does not meet this definition. And in reality, the dynamics of large assemblies of people usually differ significantly from those of small groups. Our focus in this chapter is on small groups in which the members interact with and influence one another.

The Importance of Studying Groups

We must study the behavior of people in group settings if we are to understand organizational behavior. Groups are everywhere in our society. Most people belong to several groups—family, bowling team, church group, fraternity or sorority, or work group at the office. Some groups are formally established in a work or social organization; others are more loosely knit associations of people.

To understand the behavior of people in organizations, we must understand the forces that affect individuals as well as how individuals affect the organization. The behavior of individuals both affects and is affected by the group. The accomplishments of groups are strongly influenced by the behavior of their individual members. For example, adding one key all-star player to a basketball team may make the difference between a bad season and a league championship. At the same time, groups have profound effects on the behaviors of their members. In 1999, the union for the umpires for Major League Baseball convinced its members that rather than strike, they should all resign, so most of them did in September 1999. Unfortunately, Major League Baseball called their bluff and accepted the resignations of twenty-two of them.[3] Thus, the behavior of many individuals was affected by factors within the group.

figure 11.1

A General Model of Group Dynamics

This model serves as the framework for this chapter. In phase one, the reasons for group formation determine what type of group it will be. In the second phase, groups evolve through four stages under the influence of four performance factors. Finally, a mature group emerges that interacts with other groups and can pursue organizational goals; conflicts with other groups sometimes occur.

Groups form as a way to meet individual and organizational needs. For example, each year the National Black MBA Association holds a meeting for its members. Individuals who attend make contacts, get acquainted with their peers, and form numerous groups. These groups are formed in response to similar goals, aspirations, interests, and experiences. Both the overall organization and the various groups that are formed help satisfy a variety of needs and offer networking and other support for their members.

From a managerial perspective, the work group is the primary means by which managers coordinate individuals' behavior to achieve organizational goals. Managers direct the activities of individuals, but they also direct and coordinate interactions within groups. For example, efforts to boost salespersons' performance have been shown to have both individual and group effects.[4] Therefore, the manager must pay attention to both the individual and the group when trying to improve employee performance. Managers must be aware of individual needs and interpersonal dynamics to manage groups effectively and efficiently because the behavior of individuals is key to the group's success or failure.[5] The "Mastering Change" box underscores this with its discussion of how creating Innovation Teams made up of employees from various divisions, levels, and geographical regions has helped boost innovation at Whirlpool.

Group Formation

Groups are formed to satisfy both organizational and individual needs. They form in organizations because managers expect people working together in groups to be better able to complete and coordinate organizational tasks. Organizations of all types are forming teams to improve some aspect of the work such as productivity or quality. Electromation created several worker-management teams to discuss absenteeism, pay scales, attendance bonuses, no-smoking policies, and communication.

Individuals join groups to satisfy a need. An employee may join a work group to get or keep a job. Individuals may form an informal group or join an existing one for many reasons: attraction to people in the group, to its activities (such as playing bridge, running marathons, or gardening), or to its goals. Some people join

MASTERING CHANGE

▶ *Ongoing Innovation at Whirlpool*

The appliance industry has been long considered one of the most predictable areas of business, with the same types of products—refrigerators, dishwashers, washers, and dryers—being sold to the same types of consumers. Competitors such as Whirlpool, General Electric, and Maytag have always competed by offering lower-cost and higher-quality products while reducing manufacturing and distribution costs. However, managers at Whirlpool found that using that proven strategy left the company stagnant, with little room to grow and change, so the company adopted a new strategy.

Today, Whirlpool is using its own employees as well as consumers to supply new, innovative ideas built around current lifestyles. Nancy Snyder, Whirlpool vice president, says, "We had this internal market of people we weren't tapping into. We wanted to get rid of the 'great man' theory that only one person . . . is responsible for innovation." In order to encourage creativity, the firm created a seventy-five-member Innovation Team made up of employees from every division, level, and geographical region to search the company for new ideas.

The change has been dramatic. One employee suggestion led to the creation of Whirlpool's new Inspired Chef division. The business uses home-based parties that feature chefs cooking gourmet meals for paying guests, with hopes of selling them the kitchenware needed to prepare the meals. A pilot program, with sixty chefs in six

"[T]his time, it feels like innovation has become a part of us . . ."—Nancy Snyder, Whirlpool vice president for Strategic Competency Creation

states, was a success, and a national rollout began in 2002. Listening to customers and workers has led to innovations such as a juicer that rotates more slowly to reduce frothing and an oven that cooks from the top and bottom simultaneously to enhance baking results. Other employee suggestions have resulted in the development of specialized washing machines for international customers, such as a washer that specializes in cleaning white clothes for the Indian market, in which whiteness is associated with good hygiene and purity.

Whirlpool's challenge is to sustain such creative efforts over the long term. J. D. Rapp, an Innovation Team leader, says, "With the constant pressure to innovate and change, creative ideas can end up being one-hit wonders." Nancy Snyder believes that the firm can extend its creative streak, saying, " [T]his time, it feels like innovation has become a part of us, that it's bigger than a specific project."

References: "Whirlpool's 2001 Annual Report: Chairman's Letter," "Whirlpool North America," Whirlpool web site. www.whirlpool.com on May 5, 2002; Fara Warner, "Recipe for Growth," *Fast Company*, October 2001, pp. 40–41 (quotation p. 41). See www.fastcompany.com; "Whirlpool Announces First Stage of Global Restructuring," *Appliance Manufacturer*, February 26, 2001. www.ammagazine.com on May 8, 2002.

groups just to have companionship or to be identified as members of the group. In any case, people join groups for personal need satisfaction. In other words, they expect that they will get something in return for their membership in the group.

Understanding why groups form is important in studying individual behavior in group situations. Suppose some people join a bridge group primarily for social contact. If a more competitive player substitutes for a regular player one evening, she or he joins the group (temporarily) with the goal of playing rigorous, competitive bridge. The substitute may be annoyed when the game slows down or stops altogether because the other players are absorbed in a discussion. The regular members, on the other hand, may be irritated when the substitute interrupts the discussion or criticizes his or her partner for faulty technique. To resolve the resulting conflict, one must understand the different reasons why each person joined the group. The inconsistencies in behavior arise because each member is trying to satisfy a different need. To settle the dispute, the regulars and the substitute may have to be more tolerant of each other's behavior, at least for the rest of the evening. Even if that occurs, however, the substitute player may not be invited back the next time a regular member cannot attend.

Thus, understanding why people join groups sheds light on apparent inconsistencies in behavior and the tensions likely to result from them. Managers are better equipped to manage certain kinds of conflict that arise in groups in organizations when they understand why groups form.

Types of Groups

Our first task in understanding group processes is to develop a typology of groups that provides insight into their dynamics. Groups may be loosely categorized according to their degrees of formalization (formal or informal) and permanence (relatively permanent or relatively temporary). Table 11.1 shows this classification scheme.

Formal Groups

A formal group is formed by an organization to do its work.

A command group is a relatively permanent, formal group with functional reporting relationships and is usually included in the organization chart.

A task group is a relatively temporary, formal group established to do a specific task.

Affinity groups are collections of employees from the same level in the organization who meet on a regular basis to share information, capture emerging opportunities, and solve problems.

Formal groups are established by the organization to do its work. Formal groups include command (or functional) groups, task groups, and affinity groups. A **command group** is relatively permanent and is characterized by functional reporting relationships such as having a group manager and those who report to the manager. Command groups are usually included in the organization chart. A **task group** is created to perform a specific task, such as solving a particular quality problem, and is relatively temporary. **Affinity groups** are relatively permanent collections of employees from the same level in the organization who meet on a regular basis to share information, capture emerging opportunities, and solve problems.[6]

In business organizations, most employees work in command groups, as typically specified on an official organization chart. The size, shape, and organization of a company's command groups can vary considerably. Typical command groups in organizations include the quality-assurance department, the industrial engineering department, the cost-accounting department, and the personnel department. Other types of command groups include work teams organized as in the Japanese style of management, in which subsections of manufacturing and assembly processes are each assigned to a team of workers. The team members decide among themselves who will perform each task.

Teams are becoming widespread in automobile manufacturing. For instance, General Motors has organized most of its highly automated assembly lines into work teams of between five and twenty workers. Although participative teams are becoming more popular, command groups, whether entire departments or sophisticated work teams, are the dominant type of work group in organizations. Federal Express organized its clerical workers into teams that manage themselves.

Task, or special-project, groups are usually temporary and are often established to solve a particular problem. The group usually dissolves once it solves the problem or makes recommendations. People typically remain members of their command groups, or functional departments, while simultaneously serving in a task group and continuing to carry out the normal duties of their jobs. The members' command group duties may be temporarily reduced if the task group requires a great deal of time and effort. Task groups exist in all types of organizations around the world. For example, the Pope once established a special task force of

table 11.1

Classification Scheme for Types of Groups

	Relatively Permanent	Relatively Temporary	
Formal	**Command Groups**	**Task Groups**	**Affinity Groups**
	Quality-assurance department Cost-accounting group	Search committee for a new school superintendent Task force on new-product quality	New product development group
Informal	**Friendship Groups**	**Interest Groups**	
	Friends who do many activities together (attend the theater, play games, travel)	Bowling group Women's network	

cardinals to study the financial condition of the Vatican and develop new ways to raise money.[7]

Affinity groups are a special type of formal group: They are set up by the organization, yet they are not really part of the formal organization structure. They are not really command groups because they are not part of the organizational hierarchy, yet they are not task groups because they stay in existence longer than any one task. Affinity groups are groups of employees who share roles, responsibilities, duties, and interests, and which represent horizontal slices of the normal organizational hierarchy. Because the members share important characteristics such as roles, duties, and levels, they are said to have an affinity for one another. The members of affinity groups usually have very similar job titles and similar duties but are in different divisions or departments within the organization.

"Through affinity groups, business leaders can tap into the latent knowledge, skills and abilities of the organization as it operates naturally."—Dominic J. Monetta, president of Resource Alternatives, Inc.[8]

Affinity groups meet regularly, and members have assigned roles such as recorder, reporter, facilitator, and meeting organizer. Members follow simple rules such as communicating openly and honestly, listening actively, respecting confidentiality, honoring time agreements, being prepared, staying focused, being individually accountable, and being supportive of each other and the group. The greatest benefits of affinity groups are that they cross existing boundaries of the organization and facilitate better communication among diverse departments and divisions across the organization.

Informal Groups

An informal group is established by its members.

Whereas formal groups are established by an organization, **informal groups** are formed by their members and consist of friendship groups, which are relatively

A friendship group is relatively permanent and informal and draws its benefits from the social relationships among its members.

An interest group is relatively temporary and informal and is organized around a common activity or interest of its members.

permanent, and interest groups, which may be shorter lived. **Friendship groups** arise out of the cordial relationships among members and the enjoyment they get from being together. **Interest groups** are organized around a common activity or interest, although friendships may develop among members.

Good examples of interest groups are the networks of working women that have developed. Many of these groups began as informal social gatherings of women who wanted to meet with other women working in male-dominated organizations, but they soon developed into interest groups whose benefits went far beyond their initial social purposes. The networks became information systems for counseling, job placement, and management training. Some networks were eventually established as formal, permanent associations; some remained informal groups based more on social relationships than on any specific interest; others were dissolved. These groups may be partly responsible for the dramatic increase in the percentage of women in managerial and administrative jobs.

Stages of Group Development

Groups are not static—they typically develop through a four-stage process: (1) mutual acceptance, (2) communication and decision making, (3) motivation and productivity, and (4) control and organization.[9] The stages and the activities that typify them are shown in Figure 11.2. We treat the stages as separate and distinct. It is difficult to pinpoint exactly when a group moves from one stage to another, however, because the activities in the phases tend to overlap.

Mutual Acceptance

The mutual acceptance stage of group development is characterized by members sharing information about themselves and getting to know each other.

In the **mutual acceptance** stage of group development, the group forms, and members get to know one another by sharing information about themselves. They often test one another's opinions by discussing subjects that have little to do with the group, such as the weather, sports, or recent events within the organization. Some aspects of the group's task, such as its formal objectives, may also be discussed at this stage. However, such discussion probably will not be very productive because the members are unfamiliar with one another and do not know how to evaluate one another's comments. If the members do happen to know one another already, this stage may be brief, but it is unlikely to be skipped altogether because this is a new group with a new purpose. Besides, there are likely to be a few members whom the others do not know well or at all.

"The first prerequisite of effective teamwork is trust."—John Mackey, CEO of Whole Foods[10]

As the members get to know one another, discussion may turn to more sensitive issues, such as the organization's politics or recent controversial decisions. At this stage, members may have little arguments and feud a bit as they explore one another's views on various issues and learn about each other's reactions, knowledge, and expertise. From the discussion, members come to understand how similar their beliefs and values are and the extent to which they can trust one another. Members may discuss their expectations about the group's activities in terms of their previous group and organizational experience.[11] Eventually, the conversation turns to the business of the group. When this discussion becomes serious, the group is moving to the next stage of development, communication and decision making.

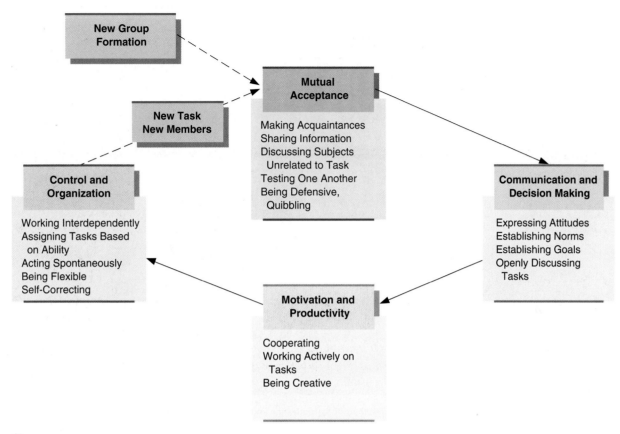

figure 11.2

Stages of Group Development

This figure shows the stages of evolution from a newly formed group to a mature group. Note that as new members are added or an existing group gets a new task, the group needs to go through the stages again.

Communication and Decision Making

In the communication and decision-making stage of group development, members discuss their feelings more openly and agree on group goals and individual roles in the group.

The group progresses to the **communication and decision-making** stage once group members have begun to accept one another. In this stage, members discuss their feelings and opinions more openly; they may show more tolerance for opposing viewpoints and explore different ideas to bring about a reasonable solution or decision. The membership usually begins to develop norms of behavior during this stage. Members discuss and eventually agree on the group's goals. Then they are assigned roles and tasks to accomplish the goals.

Motivation and Productivity

In the motivation and productivity stage of group development, members cooperate, help each other, and work toward accomplishing tasks.

In the next stage, **motivation and productivity,** the emphasis shifts away from personal concerns and viewpoints to activities that will benefit the group. Members perform their assigned tasks, cooperate with each other, and help others accomplish their goals. The members are highly motivated and may carry out their tasks creatively. In this stage, the group is accomplishing its work and moving toward the final stage of development.

As groups form they evolve through a series of stages. The third stage, motivation and productivity, centers on the group working to accomplish its task. The numerous groups—both formal and informal—that took part in rescue activities following the terrorist attacks of September 11, 2001, were clearly functioning at this stage of development. They worked together to both locate as many survivors as possible and to help identify those killed and/or missing.

Control and Organization

In the control and organization stage of group development, the group is mature; members work together and are flexible, adaptive, and self-correcting.

In the final stage, **control and organization,** the group works effectively toward accomplishing its goals. Tasks are assigned by mutual agreement and according to ability. In a mature group, the members' activities are relatively spontaneous and flexible rather than subject to rigid structural restraints. Mature groups evaluate their activities and potential outcomes and take corrective actions if necessary. The characteristics of flexibility, spontaneity, and self-correction are very important if the group is to remain productive over an extended period.

Not all groups go through all four stages. Some groups disband before reaching the final stage. Others fail to complete a stage before moving on to the next one. Rather than spend the time necessary to get to know one another and build trust, for example, a group may cut short the first stage of development because of pressure from its leader, from deadlines, or from an outside threat (such as the boss).[12] If members are forced into activities typical of a later stage while the work of an earlier stage remains incomplete, they are likely to become frustrated: The group may not develop completely and may be less productive than it could be.[13] Group productivity depends on successful development at each stage. A group that evolves fully through the four stages of development usually becomes a mature, effective group.[14] Its members are interdependent, coordinated, cooperative, competent at their jobs, motivated to do them, self-correcting, and in active communi-

Communication and decision-making are key stages of group development, but it looks like this team may have skipped an early stage like mutual acceptance. Groups need to openly discuss and agree on their goals, motivations, and individual roles before they can successfully accomplish tasks. It is essential that groups go through all four stages of development in order to become a mature, productive group.

Reference: © Randy Glasbergen

Copyright 2001 by Randy Glasbergen.
www.glasbergen.com

"My team is having trouble thinking outside the box. We can't agree on the size of the box, what materials the box should be constructed from, a reasonable budget for the box, or our first choice of box vendors."

cation with one another.[15] The process does not take a long time if the group makes a good, solid effort and pays attention to the processes. The cartoon presents an extreme view of the development process.

Finally, as working conditions and relationships change, either through a change in membership or when a task is completed and a new task is begun, groups may need to reexperience one or more of the stages of development to maintain the cohesiveness and productivity characteristic of a well-developed group. The San Francisco Forty-Niners, for example, returned from an NFL strike in 1987 to an uncomfortable and apprehension-filled period. Their coach, Bill Walsh, conducted rigorous practices but also allowed time for players to get together to air their feelings. Slowly, team unity returned, and players began joking and socializing again as they prepared for the rest of the 1987 season.[16] Their redevelopment as a mature group resulted in Super Bowl victories in 1989 and 1990.

Although these stages are not separate and distinct in all groups, many groups make fairly predictable transitions in activities at about the midpoint of the period available to complete a task.[17] A group may begin with its own distinctive approach to the problem and maintain it until about halfway through the allotted time. The midpoint transition is often accompanied by a burst of concentrated activity, reexamination of assumptions, dropping old patterns of activity, adopting new perspectives on the work, and making dramatic progress. Following these midpoint activities, the new patterns of activity may be maintained until close to the end of the period allotted for the activity. Another transition may occur just before the deadline. At this transition, groups often go into the completion stage, launching a final burst of activity to finish the job.

Group Performance Factors

The performance of any group is affected by several factors other than its reasons for forming and the stages of its development. In a high-performing group, a group synergy often develops in which the group's performance is more than the sum of the individual contributions of its members. Several additional factors may account for this accelerated performance.[18] The four basic **group performance factors** are composition, size, norms, and cohesiveness.

Composition

The composition of a group plays an important role in determining group productivity.[19] **Group composition** is most often described in terms of the homogeneity or heterogeneity of the members. A group is *homogeneous* if the members are similar in one or several ways that are critical to the work of the group, such as in age, work experience, education, technical specialty, or cultural background. In *heterogeneous* groups, the members differ in one or more ways that are critical to the work of the group. Homogeneous groups often are created in organizations when people are assigned to command groups based on a similar technical specialty. Although the people who work in such command groups may differ in some ways, such as in age or work experience, they are homogeneous in terms of a critical work performance variable: technical specialty.

Much research has explored the relationship between a group's composition and its productivity. The group's heterogeneity in terms of age and tenure with the group has been shown to be related to turnover: Groups with members of different ages and experiences with the group tend to experience frequent changes in membership.[20] Table 11.2 summarizes task variables that make a homogeneous or heterogeneous group more effective. A homogeneous group is likely to be more productive when the group task is simple, cooperation is necessary, the group tasks are sequential, or quick action is required. A heterogeneous group is more likely to be productive when the task is complex, requires a collective effort (that is, each member does a different task, and the sum of these efforts constitutes the group output), and demands creativity, and when speed is less important than thorough deliberations. For example, a group asked to generate ideas for marketing a new product probably needs to be heterogeneous to develop as many different ideas as possible.

The link between group composition and type of task is explained by the interactions typical of homogeneous and heterogeneous groups. A homogeneous group tends to have less conflict, fewer differences of opinion, smoother communication, and more interactions. When a task requires cooperation and speed, a homogeneous group is therefore more desirable. If, however, the task requires complex analysis of information and creativity to arrive at the best possible solution, a heterogeneous group may be more appropriate because it generates a wide range of viewpoints. More discussion and more conflict are likely, both of which can enhance the group's decision making.

Group composition becomes especially important as organizations become increasingly more diverse.[21] Cultures differ in the importance they place on group membership and in how they view authority, uncertainty, and other important factors. Increasing attention

Group performance factors—composition, size, norms, and cohesiveness—affect the success of the group in fulfilling its goals.

Group composition is the degree of similarity or difference among group members on factors important to the group's work.

table 11.2

Task Variables and Group Composition

A homogeneous group is more useful for:	A heterogeneous group is more useful for:
Simple tasks	Complex tasks
Sequential tasks	Collective tasks
Tasks that require cooperation	Tasks that require creativity
Tasks that must be done quickly	Tasks that need not be done quickly

Reference: Based on discussion in Bernard M. Bass and Edward C. Ryterband, *Organizational Psychology*, 2nd ed. (Allyn & Bacon, 1979). Reprinted by permission.

Group composition is an important factor in understanding group dynamics. These women recently attended a Women in Business seminar for women holding key executive positions in major corporations. The fact that they are all female gave them a shared frame-of-reference and common perspectives from which to identify key issues and to help shape the future of their respective businesses.

is being focused on how to deal with groups made up of people from different cultures.[22] In general, a manager in charge of a culturally diverse group can expect several things. First, members will probably distrust each other. Stereotyping also will present a problem, and communication problems will almost certainly arise. Thus, the manager needs to recognize that such groups will seldom function smoothly, at least at first. Managers may therefore need to spend more time helping a culturally diverse group through the rough spots as it matures, and they should allow a longer-than-normal time before expecting it to carry out its assigned task.

Many organizations are creating joint ventures and other types of alliances with organizations from other countries. Joint ventures have become common in the automobile and electronics industries, for example. However, managers from the United States tend to exhibit individualistic behaviors in a group setting whereas managers from more collectivistic countries, such as the People's Republic of China, tend to exhibit more group-oriented behaviors. Thus, when these two different types of managers work together in a joint venture, the managers must be trained to be cautious and understanding in their interactions and in the types of behaviors they exhibit. As we discussed in Chapter 3, all employees need training in how to work with people from different cultures.

Size

Group size is the number of members of the group; group size affects the number of resources available to perform the task.

A group can have as few as two members or as many members as can interact and influence one another. **Group size** can have an important effect on performance. A group with many members has more resources available and may be able to complete a large number of relatively independent tasks. In groups established to generate ideas, those with more members tend to produce more ideas, although the rate of increase in the number of ideas diminishes rapidly as the group grows.[23] Beyond a certain point, the greater complexity of interactions and communication may make it more difficult for a large group to achieve agreement.

Interactions and communication are much more likely to be formalized in larger groups. Large groups tend to set agendas for meetings and to follow a protocol or parliamentary procedure to control discussion. As a result, some time that otherwise might be available to work on tasks is taken up in administrative duties such as organizing and structuring the interactions and communications within the group. Also, the large size may inhibit participation of some people and increase absenteeism; some people may stop trying to make a meaningful contribution and may even stop coming to group meetings if their repeated attempts to contribute or participate are thwarted by the sheer number of similar efforts by other members. Furthermore, large groups present more opportunities for interpersonal attraction, leading to more social interactions and fewer task interactions. **Social loafing** is the tendency of some members of groups not to put forth as much effort in a group situation as they would working alone. Social loafing often results from the assumption by some members that if they do not work hard, other members will pick up the slack. How much of a problem this becomes depends on the nature of the task, the characteristics of the people involved, and the ability of the group leadership to be aware of the potential problem and do something about it.

The most effective size of a group, therefore, is determined by the group members' ability to interact and influence each other effectively. The need for interaction is affected by the maturity of the group, the tasks of the group, the maturity of individual members, and the ability of the group leader or manager to manage the communication, potential conflicts, and task activities. In some situations, the most effective group size is three or four; other groups can function effectively with fifteen or more members.

> Social loafing is the tendency of some members of groups to put forth less effort in a group than they would when working alone.

Norms

> A norm is a standard against which the appropriateness of a behavior is judged.

A **norm** is a standard against which the appropriateness of a behavior is judged. Thus, norms determine the behavior expected in a certain situation. Group norms usually are established during the second stage of group development (communication and decision making) and carried forward into the maturity stage. By providing a basis for predicting others' behaviors, norms enable people to behave in a manner consistent with and acceptable to the group. Without norms, the activities in a group would be chaotic.

"On great teams, players know their own roles and everyone else's role, too. The more you know about how a teammate plays his position, the better you'll play your own position."—Steve Bzomowski, former assistant basketball coach at Harvard University and president of Never Too Late Basketball Camps, Inc.[24]

Norms result from the combination of members' personality characteristics, the situation, the task, and the historical traditions of the group.[25] Lack of conformity to group norms may result in verbal abuse, physical threats, ostracism, or ejection from the group. Group norms are enforced, however, only for actions that are important to group members. For example, if the office norm is for employees to wear suits to convey a professional image to clients, a staff member who wears blue jeans and a sweatshirt violates the group norm and will hear about it quickly. But if the norm is that dress is unimportant because little contact with clients occurs in the office, the fact that someone wears blue jeans may not even be noticed.

Norms serve four purposes in organizations. First, they help the group survive. Groups tend to reject deviant behavior that does not help meet group goals or contribute to the survival of the group if it is threatened. Accordingly, a successful group that is not under threat may be more tolerant of deviant behavior. Second, they simplify and make more predictable the behaviors expected of group members. Because they are familiar with norms, members do not have to analyze each behavior and decide on a response. Members can anticipate the actions of others on the basis of group norms, usually resulting in increased productivity and goal attainment. Third, norms help the group avoid embarrassing situations. Group members often want to avoid damaging other members' self-images and are likely to avoid certain subjects that might hurt a member's feelings. And finally, norms express the central values of the group and identify the group to others. Certain clothes, mannerisms, or behaviors in particular situations may be a rallying point for members and may signify to others the nature of the group.[26]

Norms usually regulate the behavior of group members rather than their thoughts or feelings. Members thus may believe one thing but do another to maintain membership in a group. For example, during the so-called Iran-Contra Affair of 1985–1987, there were several meetings in which President Ronald Reagan and aides such as Lt. Col. Oliver North, National Security Advisor Robert McFarlane, and Central Intelligence Agency Director William Casey discussed the sale of arms to Iran in exchange for American hostages.[27] Secretary of State George P. Schultz and Secretary of Defense Caspar W. Weinberger were known to be against the sale of arms to Iran even indirectly, through Israel. The president and others strongly favored such arms sales and were eager to achieve the release of American hostages held in Iran. Thus, Schultz and Weinberger did not attend meetings in which further arms sales were authorized.[28] Although it is not clear whether the members excluded them or they excluded themselves by not attending, group norms clearly affected the meetings and outcomes. From the group's perspective, the norm was to go along with the group and approve the arms transfer. Anyone who continued to argue against the transfer would not be in the group. Thus, Schultz and Weinberger knew that they were in the minority and were making it uncomfortable for the president. If they wanted to maintain their valued membership in the president's cabinet as heads of two of the most powerful agencies of the executive branch, they knew they should not continue to cause trouble. Thus, group norms regarding how presidential advisors should act may have led them to decide not to attend.

Cohesiveness

Group cohesiveness is the extent to which a group is committed to staying together.

Group cohesiveness is the extent to which a group is committed to remaining together; it results from forces acting on the members to remain in the group. The forces that create cohesiveness are attraction to the group, resistance to leaving the group, and the motivation to remain a member of the group.[29] As shown in Figure 11.3, group cohesiveness is related to many aspects of group dynamics that we have already discussed—maturity, homogeneity, manageable size, and frequency of interactions.

The figure also shows that group cohesiveness can be increased by competition or by the presence of an external threat. Either factor can focus members' attention on a clearly defined goal and increase their willingness to work together. The threats by the Major League Baseball owners to use replacement umpires had the immediate effect of unifying the umpires against the owners. The umpires became

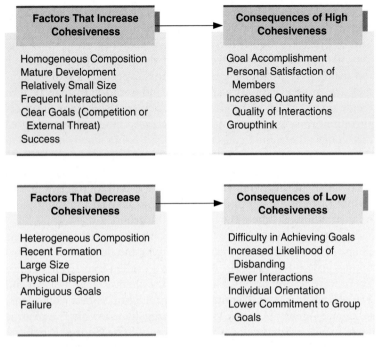

figure 11.3

Factors That Affect Group Cohesiveness and Consequences of Group Cohesiveness

The factors that increase and decrease cohesiveness and the consequences of high and low cohesiveness indicate that although it is often preferable to have a highly cohesive group, in some situations the effects of a highly cohesive group can be negative for the organization.

Groupthink occurs when a group's overriding concern is a unanimous decision rather than critical analysis of alternatives.

more cohesive and vowed more strongly than ever to stick together when they resigned. However, when the owners accepted the resignation of twenty-two umpires, the umpires tried to rescind their letters of resignation. The owners did not let them, and the courts upheld their right to do so. Similarly, in the Iran-Contra affair, the inner group (Casey, North, McFarlane, and Vice Admiral John M. Poindexter) became cohesive due to the need for secrecy and the threat of exposure by Congress and the media.

Finally, successfully reaching goals often increases the cohesiveness of a group because people are proud to be identified with a winner and to be thought of as competent and successful. This may be one reason behind the popular expression "Success breeds success." A group that is successful may become more cohesive and hence possibly even more successful. Of course, other factors can get in the way of continued success, such as personal differences, egos, and the lure of more individual success in other activities.

Research on group performance factors has focused on the relationship between cohesiveness and group productivity. Highly cohesive groups appear to be more effective at achieving their goals than groups that are low in cohesiveness, especially in research and development groups in U.S. companies.[30] However, highly cohesive groups will not necessarily be more productive in an organizational sense than groups with low cohesiveness. As Figure 11.4 illustrates, when a group's goals are compatible with the organizational goals, a cohesive group probably will be more productive than one that is not cohesive. In other words, if a highly cohesive group has the goal of contributing to the good of the organization, it is very likely to be productive in organizational terms. But if such a group decides on a goal that has little to do with the business of the organization, it will probably achieve its own goal even at the expense of any organizational goal. In a study of group characteristics and productivity, group cohesiveness was the only factor that was consistently related to high performance for research and development engineers and technicians.

Cohesiveness may also be a primary factor in the development of certain problems for some decision-making groups. An example is **groupthink,** which occurs when a group's overriding concern is a unanimous decision rather than critical analysis of alternatives.[31] (In Chapter 15 we go into more detail in describing groupthink.) These problems, together with the evidence regarding group cohesiveness and productivity, mean that a manager must carefully weigh the pros and cons of fostering highly cohesive groups.

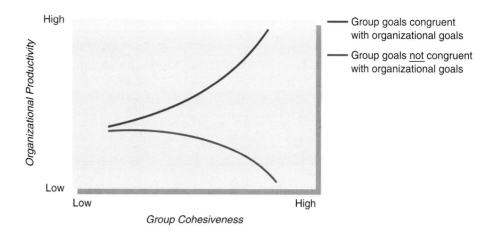

figure 11.4

Group Cohesiveness, Goals, and Productivity

This figure shows that the best combination is for the group to be cohesive and for the group's goals to be congruent with the organization's goals. The lowest potential group performance also occurs with highly cohesive groups when the group's goals are not consistent with the organization's goals.

Intergroup Dynamics

A group's contribution to an organization depends on its interactions with other groups as well as on its own productivity. Many organizations are expanding their use of cross-functional teams to address more complex and increasingly more important organizational issues. The result has been heightened emphasis on the teams' interactions with other groups. Groups that actively interact with other groups by asking questions, initiating joint programs, and sharing their team's achievements are usually the most productive.

Interactions are the key to understanding intergroup dynamics. The orientation of the groups toward their goals takes place under a highly complex set of conditions that determine the relationships among the groups. The most important of these factors are presented in the model of intergroup dynamics in Figure 11.5. The model emphasizes three primary factors that influence intergroup interactions: group characteristics, organizational setting, and task and situational bases of interaction.

First, we must understand the key characteristics of the interacting groups. Each group brings to the interaction its own unique features. As individuals become a part of a group, they tend to identify so strongly with the group that their views of other groups become biased, so harmonious relationships with other groups may be difficult to achieve.[32] Furthermore, the individuals in the group contribute to the group processes, and these contributions in turn influence the group's norms, size, composition, and cohesiveness; all of these factors affect the interactions with other groups. Thus, understanding the individuals in the group and the key characteristics of the group can help managers monitor intergroup interactions.

Second, the organizational setting in which the groups interact can have a powerful influence on intergroup interactions. The organization's structure, rules and procedures, decision-making processes, and goals and reward systems all affect interactions. For example, organizations in which frequent interactions occur and strong ties among groups exist usually are characterized as low-conflict organizations.[33] Third, the task and situational bases of interactions focus attention on the working relationships among the interacting groups and on the reasons for the interactions. As Figure 11.5 shows, five factors affect intergroup interactions: location, resources, time and goal interdependence, task uncertainty, and task interdependence. These factors both create the interactions and determine their characteristics,

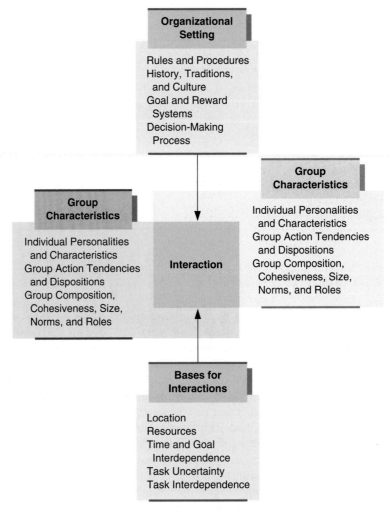

figure 11.5

Factors That Influence Intergroup Interactions

The nature of the interactions between groups depends on the characteristics of the groups involved, the organizational setting, and the task and situational setting for the interaction.

such as the frequency of interaction, the volume of information exchange among groups, and the type of coordination the groups need to interact and function. For example, if two groups depend heavily on each other to perform a task about which much uncertainty exists, they need a great deal of information from each other to define and perform the task.

Conflict in Groups and Organizations

Conflict is disagreement among parties. It has both positive and negative characteristics.

Conflict often occurs when groups interact in organizations. In its simplest form, **conflict** is disagreement among parties. When people, groups, or organizations disagree over significant issues, conflict is often the result. The "Working with Diversity" box describes how conflict can even arise among top-management

WORKING WITH DIVERSITY

CEOs Need Lesson in Teamwork

One of the most enduring management trends from the 1990s is the preference for using teams instead of traditional "command and control" structures. Teams are credited with increasing cooperation, decision making by consensus, and inclusion of diverse populations, and they have been widely studied, written about, and recommended (there are over 1,100 books on business teams listed for sale at amazon.com). Therefore, it is surprising to find that the one area of the firm that is least likely to be employing effective teamwork is the executive boardroom. Corporate insiders acknowledge that top-management teams are often one of the least inclusive, cooperative, and democratic units in an organization.

Top teams and CEOs preach the gospel of teamwork to their employees, so why don't they practice what they preach? One reason is the personalities of team members. Extremely competent members may not understand the benefits of teamwork, and their ambitions make it difficult to share decision-making power. Janet L. Spencer, team consultant, explains, "[Top-management team members] are super-accelerators, ambitious people, and there is only one seat higher than the one they now occupy: the top job." The experiences of successful managers in most companies point to the value of decisiveness, competition, and delegation. Some leaders worry that collaboration may be seen as weakness or incompetence. According to Spencer, "You would be amazed at the level of

threat some executives perceive from one another. You would think people this accomplished would feel secure, but they often don't."

Most top managers are understandably reluctant to use names in their stories, but when asked, they tell tales

> *"We can't expect managers reared along sharply competitive lines to become collaborative gurus overnight."*
> —Eric Simpson, associate of the Center for the Study of Work Teams, University of North Texas

of CEOs who make uninformed and hurried decisions, act unilaterally, insult employees, or even physically abuse them. Several high-profile CEOs, including Donald Trump, Larry Ellison of Oracle, and Martha Stewart, have been accused of less-than-exemplary behavior by former employees. Eric Simpson, an associate of the Center for the Study of Work Teams, says, "We can't expect managers reared along sharply competitive lines to become collaborative gurus overnight." Given the ways in which top-team members serve as important organizational role models, perhaps it's time they did.

References: "Special Report—The Crisis in Corporate Governance: Leadership," *Business Week*, May 6, 2002. www.businessweek.com on May 8, 2002; "Editorial—CEOs: Why They're So Unloved," *Business Week*, April 22, 2002. www.businessweek.com on May 8, 2002; Michael Finley, "All for One, but None for All?" *Across the Board*, January–February 2002, pp. 45–48 (quotation p. 47). See www.conference-board.org; Lisa DiCarlo, "Tale of the Tape," *Forbes*, September 27, 2001. www.forbes.com on May 8, 2002.

team members who advocate teamwork in their organizations. Often political behavior or battles over limited resources generate conflict between groups. In particular, it frequently occurs when a person or a group believes its attempts to achieve its goal are being blocked by another person or group. For example, conflict may arise over financial resources, the number of authorized positions in work groups, or the number of laptop computers to be purchased for departments. Conflict may also result from anticipating trouble. For example, a person may behave antagonistically toward another person whom he or she expects to pose obstacles to goal achievement.[34]

Although conflict often is considered harmful, and thus something to avoid, it can also have some benefits. A total absence of conflict can lead to apathy and lethargy. A moderate degree of focused conflict, on the other hand, can stimulate new ideas, promote healthy competition, and energize behavior. In some organizations, especially profit-oriented ones, many managers believe that conflict is

Conflict results from disagreement among parties (people and/or organizations). Dylan Lauren and her business partner, Jeff Rubin, have a unique way to resolve their conflicts. They each take a piece of gum, take three steps, and then blow a bubble. Whoever holds their bubble the longest wins and gets to decide how to do things. Ms. Lauren, for example, won the contest to determine the name of the candy store they opened on Manhattan's Upper East Side. The name? What else but Dylan's Candy Bar?

dysfunctional. On the other hand, many managers in not-for-profit organizations view conflict as beneficial and conducive to higher-quality decision making.[35]

The Nature of Conflict

Figure 11.6 illustrates the relationship between competition and conflict. Competition occurs when groups strive for the same goal, have little or no antagonism toward one another, and behave according to rules and procedures. In conflict, on the other hand, one group's goals jeopardize the other's, there is open antagonism among the groups, and few rules and procedures regulate behavior. When this happens, the goals become extremely important, the antagonism increases, rules and procedures are violated, and conflict occurs.[36] We have more to say about competition later in this section.

figure 11.6

Competition-Conflict Relationship

Although competition and conflict are similar, they also differ. Competition can lead to conflict when goals are threatened, open antagonism occurs, and rules are no longer observed.

Reactions to Conflict

The most common reactions to conflict are avoidance, accommodation, competition, collaboration, and compromise.[37] Whenever conflict occurs between groups or organizations, it is really the people who are in conflict. In many cases, however, people are acting as representatives of the groups to which they belong. In effect, they work together, representing their group as they strive to do their part in helping the group achieve its goals. Thus, whether the conflict is between people acting as individuals or people acting as representatives of groups, the five types of interactions can be analyzed in terms of relationships among the goals of the people or the groups they represent.

Reactions to conflict can be differentiated along two dimensions: how important each party's goals are to that party and how compatible the goals are, as shown in Figure 11.7. The importance of reaching a goal may range from very high to very low. The degree of **goal compatibility** is the extent to which the goals can be achieved simultaneously. In other words, the goals are compatible if one party can meet its goals without preventing the other from meeting its goals. The goals are incompatible if one party's meeting its goals prevents the other party from meeting its goals. The goals of different groups may be very compatible, completely incompatible, or somewhere in between.

Goal compatibility is the extent to which the goals of more than one person or group can be achieved at the same time.

Avoidance occurs when the interacting parties' goals are incompatible, and the interaction between groups is relatively unimportant to the attainment of the goals.

Avoidance   **Avoidance** occurs when an interaction is relatively unimportant to either party's goals, and the goals are incompatible, as in the bottom left corner of Figure 11.7. Because the parties to the conflict are not striving toward compatible goals, and the issues in question seem unimportant, the parties simply try to avoid interacting with one another. For example, one state agency may simply ignore another agency's requests for information. The requesting agency can then practice its own form of avoidance by not following up on the requests.

figure 11.7

Five Types of Reactions to Conflict

The five types of reactions to conflict stem from the relative importance of interaction to goal attainment and the degree of goal compatibility.

Reference: Adapted from Kenneth Thomas, "Conflict and Conflict Management," in Marvin Dunnette (ed.), *Handbook of Industrial and Organizational Psychology* (Chicago: Rand McNally, 1976), pp. 889–935. Reprinted by permission.

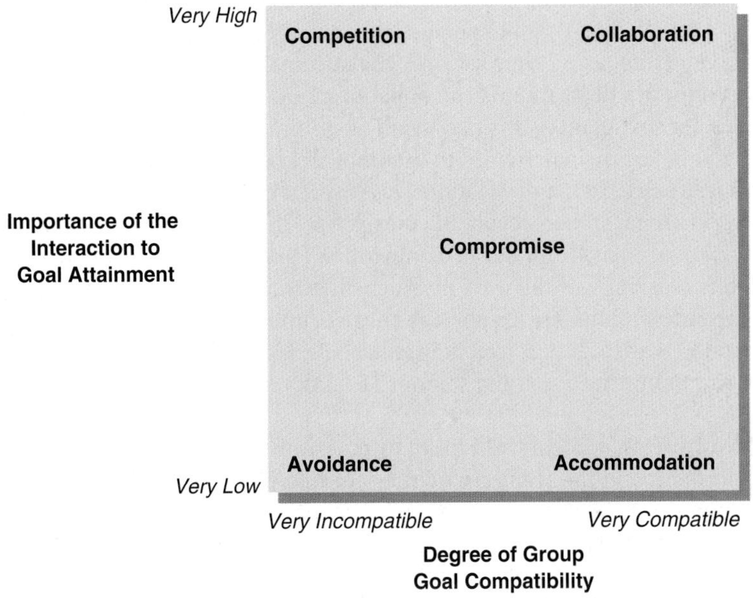

Accommodation   **Accommodation** occurs when the goals are compatible, but the interactions are not considered important to overall goal attainment, as in the bottom right corner of Figure 11.7. Interactions of this type may involve discussions of how the parties can accomplish their interdependent tasks with the least expenditure of time and effort. This type of interaction tends to be very friendly. For example, during a college's course scheduling period, potential conflict may exist between the marketing and management departments. Both departments offer morning

Accommodation occurs when the parties' goals are compatible, and the interaction between groups is relatively unimportant to the goals' attainment.

Competition occurs when the goals are incompatible, and the interactions between groups are important to meeting goals.

classes. Which department is allocated the 9:00 A.M. time slot and which one the 10:00 A.M. time slot is not that important to either group. Their overall goal is that the classes are scheduled so that students will be able to take courses.

Competition   **Competition** occurs when the goals are incompatible, and the interactions are important to each party's meeting its goals, as in the top left corner of Figure 11.7. If all parties are striving for a goal, but only one can reach the goal, the parties will be in competition. As we noted earlier, if a competitive situation gets out of control, as when overt antagonism occurs, and there are no rules or procedures to follow, then competition can result in conflict. Thus, competition may lead to conflict. Sometimes conflict can also change to competition if the parties agree to rules to guide the interaction, and conflicting parties agree not to be hostile toward each other.

In one freight warehouse and storage firm, the first, second, and third shifts each sought to win the weekly productivity prize by posting the highest productivity record. Workers on the winning shift received recognition in the company newspaper. Because the issue was important to each group, and the interests of the groups were incompatible, the result was competition.

The competition among the shifts encouraged each shift to produce more per week, which increased the company's output and eventually improved its overall welfare (and thus the welfare of each group). Both the company and the groups benefited from the competition because it fostered innovative and creative work methods, which further boosted productivity. After about three months, however, the competition got out of control. The competition among the groups led to poorer overall performance as the groups started to sabotage other shifts and inflate records. The competition became too important, open antagonism resulted, rules were ignored, and the competition changed to open conflict, resulting in actual decreases in work performance.[38]

Collaboration occurs when the interaction between groups is very important to goal attainment, and the goals are compatible.

Collaboration   **Collaboration** occurs when the interaction between groups is very important to goal attainment, and the goals are compatible, as in the top right corner of Figure 11.7. In the class scheduling situation mentioned earlier, conflict may arise over which courses to teach in the first semester and which ones in the second. Both departments would like to offer specific courses in the fall. However, by discussing the issue and refocusing their overall goals to match students' needs, the marketing and economics departments can collaborate on developing a proper sequence of courses. At first glance, this may seem to be simple interaction in which the parties participate jointly in activities to accomplish goals after agreeing on the goals and their importance. In many situations, however, it is no easy matter to agree on goals, their importance, and especially the means for achieving them. In a collaborative interaction, goals may differ but be compatible. Parties to a conflict may initially have difficulty working out the ways in which all can achieve their goals. However, because the interactions are important to goal attainment, the parties are willing to continue to work together to achieve the goals. Collaborative relationships can lead to new and innovative ideas and solutions to differences among the parties.

Compromise occurs when the interaction is moderately important to meeting goals, and the goals are neither completely compatible nor completely incompatible.

Compromise   **Compromise** occurs when the interactions are moderately important to goal attainment, and the goals are neither completely compatible nor completely incompatible. In a compromise situation, parties interact with others striving to achieve goals, but they may not aggressively pursue goal attainment in either a competitive or collaborative manner because the interactions are not that important to goal attainment. On the other hand, the parties may neither avoid one another nor be accommodating because the interactions are somewhat important. Often each party gives up something, but because the interactions are only moderately important, they do not regret what they have given up.

Contract negotiations between union and management are usually examples of compromise. Each side brings numerous issues of varying importance to the bargaining table. The two sides give and take on the issues through rounds of offers and counteroffers. The complexity of such negotiations is increasing as negotiations spread to multiple plants in different countries. Agreements between management and labor in a plant in the United States may be unacceptable to either or both parties in Canada. Weeks of negotiations ending in numerous compromises usually result in a contract agreement between the union and management.

In summary, when groups are in conflict, they may react in several different ways. If the goals of the parties are very compatible, the parties may engage in mutually supportive interactions—that is, collaboration or accommodation. If the goals are very incompatible, each may attempt to foster its own success at the expense of the other's, engaging in competition or avoidance.

Managing Conflict

One must know when to resolve conflict and when to stimulate it if one is to avoid its potentially disruptive effects.[39] When a potentially harmful conflict situation exists, a manager needs to engage in **conflict resolution.** As Figure 11.8 shows, conflict needs to be resolved when it causes major disruptions in the organization and absorbs time and effort that could be used more productively. Conflict should also be resolved when its focus is on the group's internal goals rather than on organizational goals.

Conflict resolution occurs when a manager resolves a conflict that has become harmful or serious.

"I've learned that confrontation doesn't have to be frightening or violent; you can confront people in a determined, respectful way. . . . Deal with it."—Joe Torre, manager, New York Yankees[40]

We describe the principal conflict-handling strategies later in this section. First, remember that sometimes a manager should be concerned about the absence of conflict. An absence of conflict may indicate that the organization is stagnant and that employees are content with the status quo. It may also suggest that work

figure 11.8

Conflict Management Alternatives

Conflict management may involve resolution or stimulation of conflict, depending on the situation.

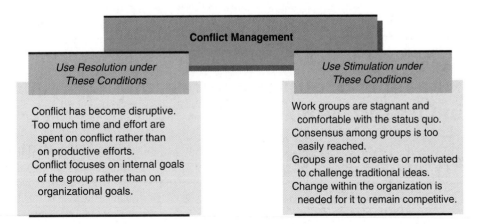

Conflict Management	
Use Resolution under These Conditions	*Use Stimulation under These Conditions*
Conflict has become disruptive. Too much time and effort are spent on conflict rather than on productive efforts. Conflict focuses on internal goals of the group rather than on organizational goals.	Work groups are stagnant and comfortable with the status quo. Consensus among groups is too easily reached. Groups are not creative or motivated to challenge traditional ideas. Change within the organization is needed for it to remain competitive.

Conflict stimulation is the creation and constructive use of conflict by a manager.

groups are not motivated to challenge traditional and well-accepted ideas. **Conflict stimulation** is the creation and constructive use of conflict by a manager. Its purpose is to bring about situations in which differences of opinion are exposed for examination by all. For example, if competing organizations are making significant changes in products, markets, or technologies, it may be time for a manager to stimulate innovation and creativity by challenging the status quo. Conflict may give employees the motivation and opportunity to reveal differences of opinion that they previously kept to themselves. When all parties to the conflict are interested enough in an issue to challenge other groups, they often expose their hidden doubts or opinions. These in turn, allow the parties to get to the heart of the matter and often to develop unique solutions to the problem. Indeed, the interactions may lead the groups to recognize that a problem in fact does exist. Conflict, then, can be a catalyst for creativity and change in an organization.

Several methods can be used to stimulate conflict under controlled conditions. These include altering the physical location of groups to stimulate more interactions, forcing more resource sharing, and implementing other changes in relationships among groups. In addition, training programs can be used to increase employee awareness of potential problems in group decision-making and group interactions. Adopting the role of "devil's advocate" in discussion sessions is another way to stimulate conflict among groups. In this role, a manager challenges the prevailing consensus to ensure that all alternatives have been critically appraised and analyzed. Although this role is often unpopular, employing it is a good way to stimulate constructive conflict.

Of course, too much conflict is also a concern. If conflict becomes excessive or destructive, the manager needs to adopt a strategy to reduce or resolve it. Managers should first attempt to determine the source of the conflict. If the source of destructive conflict is a particular person or two, it might be appropriate to alter the membership of one or both groups. If the conflict is due to differences in goals, perceptions of the difficulty of goal attainment, or the importance of the goals to the conflicting parties, then the manager can attempt to move the conflicting parties into one of the five types of reactions to conflict, depending on the nature of the conflicting parties.

A superordinate goal is an organizational goal that is more important to the well-being of the organization and its members than the more specific goals of interacting parties.

To foster collaboration, it might be appropriate to try to help people see that their goals are really not as different as they seem to be. The manager can help groups view their goals as part of a superordinate goal to which the goals of both conflicting parties can contribute. A **superordinate goal** is a goal of the overall organization and is more important to the well-being of the organization and its members than the more specific goals of the conflicting parties. If the goals are not really that important and are very incompatible, the manager may need to develop ways to help the conflicting parties avoid each other. Similarly, accommodation, competition, or compromise might be appropriate for the conflicting parties.

Managing Group and Intergroup Dynamics in Organizations

Managing groups in organizations is difficult. Managers must know what types of groups—command or task, formal or informal—exist in the organization. If a certain command group is very large, there will probably be several informal subgroups to be managed. A manager might want to take advantage of existing informal groups, "formalizing" some of them into command or task groups based on a subset of the tasks to be performed. Other informal groups may need to be broken up to make task assignment easier. In assigning tasks to people and subgroups, the manager must also consider individual motivations for joining groups and the composition of groups.

Quite often, a manager can help make sure a group develops into a productive unit by nurturing its activities in each stage of development. Helpful steps include encouraging open communication and trust among the members, stimulating discussion of important issues and providing task-relevant information at appropriate times, and helping analyze external factors such as competition and external threats and opportunities. Managers might also encourage the development of norms and roles within the group to help its development.

In managing a group, managers must consider both the goals of individual members and the goals of the group as a whole. Developing a reward structure that lets people reach their own goals by working toward those of the group can result in a very productive group. A manager may also be able to improve group cohesiveness, for example, by trying to stimulate competition, by provoking an external threat to the group, by establishing a goal-setting system, or by employing participative approaches.

Managers must carefully choose strategies for dealing with interactions among groups after thorough examination and analysis of the groups, their goals, their unique characteristics, and the organizational setting in which the interactions occur. Managers can use a variety of strategies to increase the efficiency of intergroup interactions. One common mechanism is to encourage groups to focus on a superordinate goal, as mentioned earlier. In other situations, management might want to use a **linking role,** a position for a person or group that coordinates the activities of two or more organizational groups.[41] This may add a layer of management, but in very important situations, it may be worthwhile. Finally, management may need to change reporting relationships, decision-making priorities, and rules and procedures to properly manage group interactions.

In summary, managers must be aware of the implications—organizational and social—of their attempts to manage people in groups. Groups affect how their members behave, and it is member behavior that adds up to total group performance. Groups are so prevalent in our society that managers must strive to understand them better.

> A linking role is a position for a person or group that serves to coordinate the activities of two or more organizational groups.

Synopsis

A group is two or more people who interact so as to influence one another. It is important to study groups because groups are everywhere in our society, because they can profoundly affect individual behavior, and because the behavior of individuals in a group is key to the group's success or failure. The work group is the primary means by which managers coordinate individual behavior to achieve organizational goals. Individuals form or join groups because they expect to satisfy personal needs.

Groups may be differentiated on the bases of relative permanence and degree of formality. The three types of formal groups are command, task, and affinity groups. Friendship and interest groups are the two types of informal groups. Command groups are relatively permanent work groups established by the organization and usually are specified on an organization chart. Task groups, although also established by the organization, are relatively temporary and exist only until the specific task is accomplished. Affinity groups are formed by the organization, are composed of employees at the same level and doing similar jobs, and come together regularly to share information and discuss organizational issues. In friendship groups, the affiliation among members arises from close social relationships and the enjoyment that comes from being together. The common bond in interest groups is the activity in which the members engage.

Groups develop in four stages: mutual acceptance, communication and decision making, motivation and productivity, and control and organization. Although the stages are sequential, they may overlap. A group that does not fully develop within each stage will not fully mature as a group, resulting in lower group performance.

Four additional factors affect group performance: composition, size, norms, and cohesiveness. The homogeneity of the people in the group affects the interactions that occur and the productivity of the group. The effect of increasing the size of the group depends on the nature of the group's tasks and the people in the group. Norms help people function and relate to one another in predictable and efficient ways. Norms serve four purposes: They facilitate group survival, simplify and make more predictable the behaviors of group members, help the group avoid embarrassing situations, and express the central values of the group and identify the group to others.

To comprehend intergroup dynamics, we must understand the key characteristics of groups: that each group is unique, that the specific organizational setting influences the group, and that the group's task and setting have an effect on group behavior. The five bases of intergroup interactions determine the characteristics of the interactions among groups, including their frequency, how much information is exchanged, and what type of interaction occurs.

Interactions among work groups involve some of the most complex relationships in organizations. They are based on five factors: location, resources, time and goal interdependence, task uncertainty, and task interdependence. Being physically near one another naturally increases groups' opportunities for interactions. If groups use the same or similar resources, or if one group can affect the availability of the resources needed by another group, the potential for frequent interactions increases. The nature of the tasks groups perform, including time and goal orientation, the uncertainties of group tasks, and group interdependencies, influences how groups interact.

Conflict is disagreement between parties; it is a common cause of stress in organizations. Five types of reactions to conflict are avoidance, accommodation, competition, collaboration, and compromise. The types of interactions are determined by the compatibility of goals and the importance of the interaction to group goal attainment. Managers should recognize that conflict can be beneficial as well as harmful.

Managers must be aware of the many factors that affect group performance and understand the individual as well as the group issues.

Discussion Questions

1. Why is it useful for a manager to understand group behavior? Why is it useful for an employee?

2. Our definition of a group is somewhat broad. Would you classify each of the following collections of people as a group? Explain why.

   a. Seventy thousand people at a football game

   b. Students taking this course

   c. People in an elevator

   d. People on an escalator

   e. Employees of IBM

   f. Employees of your local college bookstore

3. List four groups to which you belong. Identify each as formal or informal.

4. Explain why each group you listed in question 3 formed. Why did you join each group? Why might others have decided to join each group?

5. In which stage of development is each of the four groups listed in question 3? Did any group move too quickly through any of the stages? Explain.

6. Analyze the composition of two of the groups to which you belong. How are they similar in composition? How do they differ?

7. Are any of the groups to which you belong too large or too small to get their work done? If so, what can the leader or the members do to alleviate the problem?

8. List two norms each for two of the groups to which you belong. How are these norms enforced?

9. Discuss the following statement: "Group cohesiveness is the good, warm feeling we get from working in groups and is something that all group leaders should strive to develop in the groups they lead."

10. Consider one of the groups to which you belong and describe the interactions that group has with another group.

11. Do you agree or disagree with the assertion that conflict can be both good and bad? Cite examples of both cases.

Organizational Behavior Case for Discussion

Using Groups to Get Things Done

After years of difficulties and many attempts to change, a Myerstown, Pennsylvania, pharmaceutical plant, part of the Consumer Care Division of German-owned Bayer Corporation, instituted a teams-based change program. The facility had been sold several times in recent years and had operated under various organizations. The fifty-year-old factory was staffed at less than 50 percent when it was purchased by Bayer. There had been no plant manager for almost a year, and morale was at an all-time low. Worse yet, the factory was losing money, and the remaining employees feared a shutdown. The outlook was bleak, but in the absence of leadership from the top level, the Human Resources Department, under the guidance of director John Danchisko, decided that the employees themselves could turn the low-performing facility around.

First, ninety-three employees were selected at random to participate in seven focus groups. At the meetings, workers brainstormed the answers to open-ended questions such as "Why do people work here?" and "Why do people leave here?" Their answers were compiled and sent to every employee for comments and input. Employees were impressed; they liked the new proactive and collaborative management style. Rick Higley, a pharmaceutical operator, says, "The thing I really appreciated about the process was that the managers listened to what everyone had to say, treated us as equals, and really valued our opinions."

Next, an eighteen-member cross-functional team was formed to recommend and help implement improvements. The team approach was clearly popular because fifty people volunteered for those eighteen slots. The team focused on five key priorities:

1. *Define site goals and strategy and communicate them in interactive employee conferences.* Job security concerns and a need to see how shorter-term goals fit into the long-term strategy were important to employees.
2. *Develop a site communication process.* Employees felt that their best option for information was no better than a "rumor mill" while supervisors often weren't given critical information. Having consistency of information from the top to the bottom of the organization benefited everyone.
3. *Develop hourly employee and supervisory role definitions and competency profiles.* Changing ownership had led to too many abandoned programs, and training had been inconsistent. Decision-making authority, span of control, and management roles were just a few of the areas of confusion.
4. *Identify areas of perceived inconsistencies in site practices and policies and determine appropriate actions.* Employees wanted to ensure that any system used at the facility would be used consistently and that all workers would be treated the same.
5. *Develop a performance measurement process (a performance scorecard system).* Without some type of measurement system, workers and supervisors were unsure whether goals were being reached.

One of the biggest obstacles to change was the factory's past history of failed changes. An employee noted, "It would be nice if [managers] were really sincere in this, but we've all been through this before. I think this is going to be another flavor of the month." Employee skepticism began to change as the teams focused on what really mattered to the hourly workers.

Employees began by asking, "What's in it for me?" — but the teams proposed a pay-for-performance system, with employees earning up to an additional 8 percent on top of their base pay when profitability was above target.

In its first year, the facility reached four of its five financial goals and became profitable earlier than expected. Employee satisfaction is now up, and accidents are down. On-time completion of weekly production quotas has risen from 53 percent (about average for this industry) to 85 percent. In 2000, the plant received *Workforce* magazine's Optimas award for excellence in human resources. Management was so pleased with the results of the program that the teams have become permanent, with rotating membership. Danchisko says, "When we first started this, we didn't realize how big it would actually become for our site. Here we are, a few years down the road, and we're still heavily into this." The site's teams process has become a model for other Bayer facilities.

Werner Wenning, the new chairman of Bayer, has taken control of the firm at a difficult time. The stock price is declining, new products are slow to reach market, and the company is restructuring its divisional organization. Wenning admits that Bayer was too slow in its response to changing market conditions, noting, "In the future, we have to act more quickly." Perhaps the CEO ought to consider the team-based methods that were developed by his own employees at the Myerstown facility.

> **"The thing I really appreciated about the process was that the managers listened to what everyone had to say, treated us as equals, and really valued our opinions."— Rick Higley, a pharmaceutical operator for Bayer**

References: "About the Awards," *Workforce* web site. www.workforce.com on May 21, 2002; "2001 Bayer Annual Report," Bayer web site. www.bayer.com on May 21, 2002; Kerry Capell, "Bayer's Big Headache," *Business Week*, May 6, 2002. www.businessweek.com on May 21, 2002; John Danchisko, "Five Initiatives for Growth," *Workforce*, March 2000. www.workforce.com on April 30, 2002; Jennifer Koch Laabs, "Paving the Way to Profitability," *Workforce*, March 2000 (quotation). www.workforce.com on April 30, 2002; "Role Expectations for Supervisors at Bayer," *Workforce*, March 2000. www.workforce.com on May 21, 2002.

Case Questions

1. What type of group are the focus groups that were initially formed at Bayer's Myerstown facility? What type is the current eighteen-member, permanent group? What factors led you to make the choices you did?

2. Based on group performance factors, what do you predict will be the likely performance of the eighteen-member cross-functional team?

3. Initially, workers at the Myerstown plant were skeptical about the use of teams and resisted the change. What conflict resolution approach was used to address this problem? Is that the approach you would recommend for this situation? Why or why not?

Experiencing Organizational Behavior

Learning the Benefits of a Group

Purpose: This exercise demonstrates the benefits a group can bring to a task.

Format: You will be asked to do the same task both individually and as part of a group.

Procedure: You will need a pen or pencil and an 8 1/2" by 11" sheet of paper. Working alone, do the following:

Part 1

1. Write the letters of the alphabet in a vertical column down the left side of the paper: A–Z.
2. Your instructor will randomly select a sentence from any written document and read out loud the first twenty-six letters in that sentence. Write these letters in a vertical column immediately

to the right of the alphabet column. Everyone should have an identical set of twenty-six two-letter combinations.

3. Working alone, think of a famous person whose initials correspond to each pair of letters, and write the name next to the letters—for example, "MT Mark Twain." You will have ten minutes. Only one name per set is allowed. One point is awarded for each legitimate name, so the maximum score is twenty-six points.

4. After time expires, exchange your paper with another member of the class and score each other's work. Disputes about the legitimacy of names will be settled by the instructor. Keep your score for use later in the exercise.

Part 2

Your instructor will divide the class into groups of five to ten people. All groups should have approximately the same number of members. Each group now follows the procedure given in part 1. Again write the letters of the alphabet down the left side of the sheet of paper, this time in reverse order: Z–A. Your instructor will dictate a new set of letters for the second column. The time limit and scoring procedure are the same. The only difference is that the groups will generate the names.

Part 3

Each team identifies the group member who came up with the most names. The instructor places these "best" students into one group. Then all groups repeat part 2, but this time the letters from the reading will be in the first column and the alphabet letters will be in the second column.

Part 4

Each team calculates the average individual score of its members on part 1 and compares it with the team score from parts 2 and 3, kept separately. Your instructor will put the average individual score and team scores from each part of each group on the board.

Follow-up Questions

1. Are there differences in the average individual scores and the team scores? What are the reasons for the differences, if any?

2. Although the team scores in this exercise usually are higher than the average individual scores, under what conditions might individual averages exceed group scores?

Reference: Adapted from *The Handbook for Group Facilitators*, pp. 19–20. by John E. Jones and J. William Pfeiffer (eds.), Copyright © 1979 Pfeiffer. This material is used by permission of Pfeiffer/Jossey-Bass, Inc., a subsidiary of John Wiley & Sons, Inc.

 # Self-Assessment Exercise

Group Cohesiveness

Introduction: You are probably a member of many different groups: study groups for school, work groups, friendship groups within a social club such as a fraternity or sorority, and interest groups. You probably have some feel for how tightly knit or cohesive each of those groups is. This exercise will help you diagnose the cohesiveness of one of those groups.

Instructions: First, pick one of the small groups to which you belong for analysis. Be sure that it is a small group, say between three and eight people. Next, rate on the following scale of 1 (poorly) to 5 (very well) how well you feel the group works together.

1	2	3	4	5
Poorly	Not Very Well	About Average	Pretty Well	Very Well

How well does this group work together?

Now answer the following six questions about the group. Put a check in the blank next to the answer that best describes how you feel about each question.

1. How many of the people in your group are friendly toward each other?
   ____ (5) All of them
   ____ (4) Most of them
   ____ (3) Some of them
   ____ (2) A few of them
   ____ (1) None of them

2. How much trust is there among members of your group?
   ____ (1) Distrust
   ____ (2) Little trust

_____ (3) Average trust

_____ (4) Considerable trust

_____ (5) A great deal of trust

3. How much loyalty and sense of belonging is there among group members?

_____ (1) No group loyalty of sense of belonging

_____ (2) A little loyalty and sense of belonging

_____ (3) An average sense of belonging

_____ (4) An above-average sense of belonging

_____ (5) A strong sense of belonging

4. Do you feel that you are really a valuable part of your group?

_____ (5) I am really a part of my group.

_____ (4) I am included in most ways.

_____ (3) I am included in some ways but not others.

_____ (2) I am included in a few ways but not many.

_____ (1) I do not feel I really belong.

5. How friendly are your fellow group members toward each other?

_____ (1) Not friendly

_____ (2) Somewhat friendly

_____ (3) Friendly to an average degree

_____ (4) Friendlier than average

_____ (5) Very friendly

6. If you had a chance to work with a different group of people doing the same task, how would you feel about moving to another group?

_____ (1) I would want very much to move.

_____ (2) I would rather move than stay where I am.

_____ (3) It would make no difference to me.

_____ (4) I would rather stay where I am than move.

_____ (5) I would want very much to stay where I am.

Now add up the numbers you chose for all six questions and divide by 6. Total from all six questions = _____ / 6 = _____. This is the group cohesiveness score for your group.

Compare this number with the one you checked on the scale at the beginning of this exercise about how well you feel this group works together. Are they about the same, or are they quite different? If they are about the same, then you have a pretty good feel for the group and how it works. If they are quite different, then you probably need to analyze what aspects of the group functioning you misunderstood. (This is only part of a much longer instrument; it has not been scientifically validated in this form and is to be used for class discussion purposes only.)

Reference: The six questions were taken from the Groupthink Assessment Inventory by John R. Montanari and Gregory Moorhead, "Development of the Groupthink Assessment Inventory," *Educational and Psychological Measurement*, 1989, vol. 39, pp. 209–219. Reprinted by permission of Gregory Moorhead.

OB Online

1. Given the widespread adoption of the Internet, can a virtual group (i.e., one whose members interact electronically) be a group in the same way that a traditional face-to-face group can? Why or why not?

2. Use a search engine to find information about each of the types of groups identified in the chapter. Can you locate information about other types of groups?

3. In what ways might electronic interaction impact the stages of group development discussed in the chapter?

4. Describe the roles that the Internet and email might play in conflict. That is, in what ways might new forms of communication technologies both increase and decrease conflict in organizations?

Building Managerial Skills

Exercise Overview: A manager's interpersonal skills refer to her or his ability to understand how to motivate individuals and groups. Clearly, then, interpersonal skills play a major role in determining how well a manager can interact with others in a group setting. This exercise will allow you to practice your interpersonal skills in relation to just such a setting.

Exercise Background: You have just been transferred to a new position supervising a group of five employees. The business you work for is fairly small and has few rules and regulations. Unfortunately, the lack of rules and regulations is creating a problem that you must now address.

Specifically, two of the group members are nonsmokers. They are becoming increasingly more vocal about the fact that two other members of the group smoke at work. These two workers feel that the secondary smoke in the workplace is endangering their health and want to establish a no-smoking policy like those of many large businesses today.

The two smokers, however, argue that since the firm did not have such a policy when they started working there, it would be unfair to impose such a policy now. One of them, in particular, says that he turned down an attractive job with another company because he wanted to work in a place where he could smoke.

The fifth worker is also a nonsmoker but says that she doesn't care if others smoke. Her husband smokes at home anyway, she says, so she is used to being around smokers. You suspect that if the two vocal nonsmokers are not appeased, they may leave. At the same time, you also think that the two smokers will leave if you mandate a no-smoking policy. All five workers do good work, and you do not want any of them to leave.

Exercise Task: With this information as context, do the following:

1. Explain the nature of the conflict that exists in this work group.

2. Develop a course of action for dealing with the situation.

12 Using Teams in Organizations

Management Preview

Teams are an integral part of the management process in many organizations to-day. But the notion of using teams as a way of organizing work is not new. Neither is it an American or Japanese innovation. One of the earliest uses and analyses of teams was the work of the Tavistock Institute in the late 1940s in the United Kingdom (discussed in more detail in Chapter 17).[1] Major companies such as Hewlett-Packard, Xerox, Procter & Gamble, General Motors, and General Mills have been using teams as a primary means of accomplishing tasks for many years. The popular business press, such as *Fortune*, *Business Week*, *Forbes*, and the *Wall Street Journal*, regularly reports on the use of teams in businesses around the world. The use of teams is not a fad of the month or some new way to manipulate workers into producing more at their own expense to enrich owners. Managers and experts agree that using teams can be the way to organize and manage successfully in the twenty-first century.

This chapter presents a summary of many of the current issues involving teams in organizations. First, we define what "team" means and differentiate teams from normal work groups. We then discuss the rationale for using teams, including both the benefits and the costs. Next, we describe six types of teams in use in organizations today. Then we present the steps involved in implementing teams. Finally, we take a brief look at two essential issues that must be addressed. But first, we look at teams as they are used in one unconventional work setting.

For many of us, the creation of art is an individual achievement, one person's expression of his or her unique perspective. Imagine the painter alone behind the canvas with a personal vision. Or consider the solitary sculptor chipping away at a stone block. However, glass blowing, an ancient art in which the production methods, tools, and team organization have remained the same for 2,000 years, depends on the cooperation of a team of artists.

A glass-blowing team consists of a starter, a glass master, and assistants. The starter gathers molten glass from a 2,300-degree furnace into a glob on the tip of a hollow metal pipe and rotates the glob through molds to form the rough shape of the piece. The glass master then directs the starter and assistants as they blow, shape, cool, heat, cut, bend, color, and fuse blobs of white-hot liquid glass in order to create the finished item.

The process resembles a ballet, with each performer moving around the central piece. Correct timing and coordination are essential. In one situation a four-person team at Cloud Cap Glass in Montana has been working for an hour to create a stemmed goblet when something goes wrong. The worker gathering the small blob to "glue" the stem to the cup hesitates for a second, and as a result, the cup fuses to the metal tool gripping it. Silently, the team throws the ruined pieces into the waste can. Rich Langley, the glass master, says, "It's my fault. I've been practicing these goblets for two years. They're very complicated. But what it boils down to is that [this] was the first piece of the day. Later in the day, after we've worked on them for awhile, everybody's timing is in synch."

"This is a unique art form. It's not like painting, where it's just you and the canvas. It's a team effort."—Rich Langley, glass blower and owner, Cloud Cap Glass

Dale Chihuly of Seattle, the best-known American glass artist, runs his glass-blowing school based on techniques he learned from visits to international glass-works, especially the traditional schools on the island of Murano in Venice, Italy. While there, Chihuly witnessed the workings of hierarchical production teams in which each worker is given a specific role. His teachings have had a tremendous influence on American glass blowing—nearly every studio today uses the team techniques that he brought back to this country. Chihuly acts much like the director in a film production: He sets the stage, creates the concept, begins the action, and then allows each artist to fulfill his or her role with spontaneity. To inspire workers, he often plays music or hires a chef to prepare an elegant meal in the workspace. One of Chihuly's artists claims that his ideas become an integrated part of every worker. "When I work for Dale, I almost become him," says Flora Mace.

American teams tend to be more democratic than Italian teams, and Langley emphasizes the importance of every worker, saying, "This is a unique art form. It's not like painting, where it's just you and the canvas. It's a team effort." At first glance, glass blowing seems to be very different from business tasks, but corporate managers could learn much about creating cooperation and integration by observing the team approach used in this fascinating industry.

References: "The Art of Making Glass," Bendheim Glass Studios web site. www.bendheim.com on May 22, 2002; Karen Chambers, "With the Team," Dale Chihuly web site. www.chihuly.com on May 22, 2002; "Matthew's Biography," Thames Glass web site. www.thamesglass.com on May 22, 2002; Daryl Gadbow, "'Blow Hard': Teamwork and Timing Are Essentials at Florence Glass-Blowing Studio," *Missoulian* (Missoula, Montana), February 3, 2002 (quotation). See www.missoulian.com.

Glass blowing clearly requires an advanced level of teamwork. But so, too, do many organizations' tasks and responsibilities today. This chapter describes some of the techniques for making the best use of teams in organizations.

Differentiating Teams from Groups

Teams have been used, written about, and studied under many names and organizational programs: self-directed teams, self-managing teams, autonomous work groups, participative management, and many others. Groups and teams are not the same thing, although the two words are often used interchangeably in popular usage. A brief look at a dictionary shows that "group" usually refers to an assemblage of people or objects gathered together whereas "team" usually refers to people or animals organized to work together. Thus, a "team" places more emphasis on concerted action than a "group" does. In common, everyday usage, however, "committee," "group," "team," and "task force" are often used interchangeably.

In organizations, teams and groups are quite different. As we noted in Chapter 11, a group is two or more persons who interact with one another such that each person influences and is influenced by each other person. We specifically noted that individuals interacting and influencing each other need not have a common goal. The collection of people who happen to report to the same supervisor or manager in an organization can be called a "work group." Group members may be satisfying their own needs in the group and have little concern for a common objective. This is where a team and a group differ. In a team, all team members are committed to a common goal.

We could therefore say that a team is a group with a common goal. But teams differ from groups in other ways, too, and most experts are a bit more specific in defining teams. A more elaborate definition is this: "A **team** is a small number of people with complementary skills who are committed to a common purpose, performance goals, and approach for which they hold themselves mutually accountable."[2] Several facets of this definition need further explanation. A team includes few people, much like the small group described in Chapter 11, because the interaction and influence processes needed for the team to function can only occur when the number of members is small. When many people are involved, they have difficulty interacting and influencing each other, utilizing their complementary skills, meeting goals, and holding themselves accountable. Regardless of the name, by our definition, mature, fully developed teams are self-directing, self-managing, and autonomous. If they are not, then someone from outside the group must be giving directions, so the group cannot be considered a true team.[3]

A team is a small number of people with complementary skills who are committed to a common purpose, common performance goals, and an approach for which they hold themselves mutually accountable.

"Down with bosses! Up with teams! is the new battle cry of the world's leading organizations."—Charles C. Manz and Henry P. Sims Jr., leading authorities on the emergence of teams in organizations[4]

Teams include people with a mix of skills appropriate to the tasks to be done. Three types of skills are usually required in a team. First, the team needs to have members with the technical or functional skills to do the jobs. Some types of engineering, scientific, technological, legal, or business skills may be necessary. Second, some team members need to have problem-solving and decision-making skills to help the team identify problems, determine priorities, evaluate alternatives, analyze tradeoffs, and make decisions about the direction of the team. Third, members need interpersonal skills to manage communication flow, resolve conflict, direct questions and discussion, provide support, and recognize the interests of all members of the team. Not all members will have all of the required skills, especially when the team first convenes; different members will have different skills. However, as the team grows, develops, and matures, team members will come to have more of the necessary skills.[5] The "Working with Diversity" box illustrates how the diverse talents of team members at a Florida medical center led to its better performance.

Having a common purpose and common performance goals sets the tone and direction of the team. A team comes together to take action to pursue a goal, un-

WORKING WITH DIVERSITY

Diversity of Talents = High-Performing Teams

What's the first thing that you think of when someone mentions "diversity"? Perhaps race, gender, or age. With more thought, additional characteristics such as marital status or education may come to mind. However, if the goal is to assemble a group that will be creative, another important element would be employee talents, which have a profound impact on the way people think and work in groups.

"[A great] team should be made up of people who think differently," claims Mike Maerz, CEO of etrieve, Inc. This idea has recently been adopted by a Florida hospital, the St. Lucie Medical Center. The hospital was expanding due to an aging local population, but patient, staff, and doctor dissatisfaction was growing, too, giving the company a 35 percent annual turnover rate. To engineer a turnaround, St. Lucie first identified high-performing employees. "We realized that better understanding our own individual talents as well as the talents of our peers would be one of the keys to our success," says Nancy Hilton, St. Lucie's Chief Nursing Officer. Then the hospital conducted a companywide survey of employee traits and opinions. The results showed that the best employees had talents that were not being fully used. In addition, although the worst employees also had some talents, those talents were unrelated to their jobs.

Based on survey results, personnel were reassigned, and workflow was redesigned. Team members were se-

"We realized that better understanding our own individual talents as well as the talents of our peers would be one of the keys to our success."—Nancy Hilton, Chief Nursing Officer, St. Lucie Medical Center

lected to maximize the synergy of diverse talents. For example, nurses with better time-management skills were given the scheduling tasks for their teams whereas nurses with more empathy spent more time in patient interaction. Kelley Charles, director of laboratory services, explains, "If I know this person is, by nature, extremely positive, always looking for the silver lining, and [another] person is instinctively drawn to identifying problems that need to be fixed, then the complementarity of their talents will make it easier for them to have a valuable impact on the performance of the group."

Marcus Buckingham and Curt Coffman, authors of the bestseller *First, Break All the Rules*, assert that employees must feel that they "have the opportunity to do what they do best every day." St. Lucie is following that precept, and the results thus far are quite good.

References: "First, Break All the Rules," *Gallup Management Journal* web site. www.gallupjournal.com on May 11, 2002; Regina Fazio Maruca, "What Makes Teams Work?" *Fast Company*, November 2000 www.fastcompany.com on May 11, 2002; Brad Black, "The Road to Recovery," *Gallup Management Journal*, Winter 2001, pp. 10–12 (quotation p. 11). See www.gallupjournal.com; Marcus Buckingham and Curt Coffman, *First, Break All the Rules: What the World's Greatest Managers Do Differently* (New York: Simon and Schuster, May 1999).

like a work group, in which members merely report to the same supervisor or work in the same department. The purpose becomes the focus of the team, which makes all decisions and takes all actions in pursuit of the goal. Teams often spend days or weeks establishing the reason for their existence, an activity which builds strong identification and fosters commitment to the team. This process also helps team members develop trust in one another.[6] Usually, the defining purpose comes first, followed by development of specific performance goals.

For example, a team of local citizens, teachers, and parents may come together for the purpose of making the local schools the best in the state. Then the team establishes specific performance goals to serve as guides for decision making, to maintain the focus on action, to differentiate this team from other groups who may want to improve schools, and to challenge people to commit themselves to the team. One further note on the importance of purpose and performance goals for teams: Katzenbach and Smith studied more than thirty teams and found that demanding, high-performance goals often challenge members to create a real team—

Teams have become an increasingly important mechanism for organizations to use in getting things done. For example, some large companies are beginning to suggest that small suppliers work together as partners to win major contracts. In order to facilitate such partnerships each supplier generally provides one or more team members who work together to coordinate their effort. Woodrow Hall, owner of a plastic packaging business called Film Fabricators Inc., and Robert Johnson, owner of Johnson-Bryce Corp., a plastic bag manufacturer and printer, are working together as a team in pursuit of a major contract from Procter & Gamble.

as opposed to being merely a group— because when goals are truly demanding, members must pull together, find resources within themselves, develop and use the appropriate skills, and take a common approach to reach the goals.[7]

Agreeing on a common approach is especially important for teams because it is often the approach that differentiates one team from others. The team's approach usually covers how work will be done, social norms regarding dress, attendance at meetings, tardiness, norms of fairness and ethical behavior, and what will and will not be included in the team activities.

Finally, the definition states that teams hold themselves mutually accountable for results rather than merely meeting a manager's demands for results, as in the traditional approach. If the members translate accountability to an external manager into internal, or mutual, accountability, the group moves toward acting like a team. Mutual accountability is essentially a promise that members make to each other to do everything possible to achieve their goals, and it requires the commitment and trust of all members. It is the promise of each member to hold herself or himself accountable for the team's goals that earns each individual the right to express her or his views and expect them to get a fair and constructive hearing. With this promise, members maintain and strengthen the trust necessary for the team to succeed. The clearly stated high-performance goals and the common approach serve as the standards to which the team holds itself. Because teams are mutually accountable for meeting performance goals, three other differences between groups and teams become important: job categories, authority, and reward systems. The differences for traditional work groups and work teams are shown in Table 12.1.

Job Categories

The work of conventional groups is usually described in terms of highly specialized jobs that require minimal training and moderate effort. Tens or even hundreds of people may have similar job descriptions and see little relationship between their

table 12.1

Differences Between
Teams and Traditional
Work Groups

Issue	Conventional Work Groups	Teams
Job Categories	Many narrow categories	One or two broad categories
Authority	Supervisor directly controls daily activities	Team controls daily activities
Reward System	Depends on the type of job, individual performance, and seniority	Based on team performance and individual breadth of skills

Reference: Adapted from Jack D. Osburn, Linda Moran, and Ed Musselwhite, with Craig Perrin, *Self-Directed Work Teams: The New American Challenge* (Homewood, Ill.: Business One Irwin, 1990), p. 11.

effort and the end result or finished product. In teams, on the other hand, members have many different skills that fit into one or two broad job categories. Neither workers nor management worries about who does what job as long as the team puts out the finished product or service and meets its performance goals.[8]

Authority

As shown in Table 12.1, in conventional work groups, the supervisor directly controls the daily activities of workers. In teams, the team discusses what activities need to be done and determines for itself who has the necessary skills and will do each task. The team, rather than the supervisor, makes the decisions. If a "supervisor" remains on the team, the person's role usually changes to that of coach, facilitator, or one who helps the team make decisions rather than remain the traditional role of decision maker and controller.

Reward Systems

How employees are rewarded is vital to the long-term success of an organization. The traditional reward and compensation systems suitable for individual motivation (discussed in Chapter 8) are simply not appropriate in a team-based organization. In conventional settings, employees are usually rewarded on the basis of their individual performance, their seniority, or their job classification. In a team-based situation, team members are rewarded for mastering a range of skills needed to meet team performance goals, and rewards are sometimes based on team performance. Such a pay system tends to promote the flexibility that teams need to be responsive to changing environmental factors. Three types of reward systems are common in a team environment: skill-based pay, gain-sharing systems, and team bonus plans.

Skill-Based Pay   Skill-based pay systems require team members to acquire a set of the core skills needed for their particular team plus additional special skills, depending on career tracks or team needs. Some programs require all members to acquire the core skills before any member receives additional pay. Usually employees can increase their base compensation by some fixed amount, say $0.30 per hour for each additional skill acquired, up to some fixed maximum. Companies using skill-based pay systems include Eastman Chemical Company, Colgate-Palmolive Company, and Pfizer.

Gain-Sharing Systems   Gain-sharing systems usually reward all team members from all teams based on the performance of the organization, division, or plant. Such a system requires a baseline performance that must be exceeded for team members to receive some share of the gain over the baseline measure. Westinghouse gives equal one-time, lump-sum bonuses to everyone in the plant based on improvements in productivity, cost, and quality. Employee reaction is usually positive because when employees work harder to help the company, they share in the profits they helped generate. On the other hand, when business conditions or other factors beyond their control make it impossible to generate improvements over the preset baseline, employees may feel disappointed and even disillusioned with the process.

Team Bonus Plans   Team bonus plans are similar to gain-sharing plans except that the unit of performance and pay is the team rather than a plant, a division, or the entire organization. Each team must have specific performance targets or baseline measures that the team considers realistic for the plan to be effective. Companies using team bonus plans include Milwaukee Insurance Company, Colgate-Palmolive, and Harris Corporation.

Changes in an organizational compensation system can be traumatic and threatening to most employees. However, matching the reward system to the way that work is organized and accomplished can have very positive benefits. The three types of team-based reward systems presented can be used in isolation for simplicity or in some combination to address different types of issues for each organization.

Benefits and Costs of Teams in Organizations

With the popularity of teams increasing so rapidly around the world, it is possible that some organizations are starting to use teams simply because everyone else is doing it, which is obviously the wrong reason. The reason for a company to create teams should be that teams make sense for that particular organization. The best reason to start teams in any organization is to recap the positive benefits that can result from a team-based environment: enhanced performance, employee benefits, reduced costs, and organizational enhancements. Four categories of benefits and some examples are shown in Table 12.2.

Enhanced Performance

Enhanced performance can come in many forms, including improved productivity, quality, and customer service. Working in teams enables workers to avoid wasted effort, reduce errors, and react better to customers, resulting in more output for each unit of employee imput.

"I learned a long time ago that a team will always defeat an individual."
—John Chambers, CEO of Cisco Systems, Inc.[9]

Such enhancements result from pooling of individual efforts in new ways and from continuously striving to improve for the benefit of the team. For example, a General Electric plant in North Carolina experienced a 20 percent increase in productivity after team implementation.[10] K Shoes reported a 19 percent increase in productivity and significant reductions in rejects in the manufacturing process. The "Talking Technology" box discusses how technological advances mandated

table 12.2

Benefits of Teams in Organizations

Type of Benefit	Specific Benefit	Organizational Examples
Enhanced Performance	• Increased productivity • Improved quality • Improved customer service	Ampex: On-time customer delivery rose 98%. K Shoes: Rejects per million dropped from 5,000 to 250. Eastman: Productivity rose 70%.
Employee Benefits	• Quality of work life • Lower stress	Milwaukee Mutual: Employee assistance program usage dropped to 40% below industry average.
Reduced Costs	• Lower turnover, absenteeism • Fewer injuries	Kodak: Reduced turnover to one-half the industry average. Texas Instruments: Reduced costs more than 50%. Westinghouse: Costs down 60%.
Organizational Enhancements	• Increased innovation, flexibility	IDS Mutual Fund Operations: Improved flexibility to handle fluctuations in market activity. Hewlett-Packard: Innovative order-processing system.

References: Adapted from Richard S. Wellins, William C. Byham, and George R. Dixon, *Inside Teams* (San Francisco: Jossey-Bass, 1994); Charles C. Manz and Henry P. Sims Jr., *Business Without Bosses* (New York: Wiley, 1993).

that scientists at Roche Group begin working in collaborative groups to best utilize their new knowledge.

Employee Benefits

Employees tend to benefit as much as organizations in a team environment. Much attention has been focused on the differences between the baby-boom generation and the "postboomers" in their attitudes toward work, its importance to their lives, and what they want from it. In general, younger workers tend to be less satisfied with their work and the organization, to have lower respect for authority and supervision, and to want more than a paycheck every week. Teams can provide the sense of self-control, human dignity, identification with work, and sense of self-worth and self-fulfillment for which current workers seem to strive. Rather than relying on the traditional, hierarchical, manager-based system, teams give employees the freedom to grow and to gain respect and dignity by managing themselves, making decisions about their work, and really making a difference in the world around them.[11] As a result, employees have a better work life, face less stress at work, and make less use of employee assistance programs.

Reduced Costs

As empowered teams reduce scrap, make fewer errors, file fewer worker compensation claims, and reduce absenteeism and turnover, organizations based on teams are

Technology Changes the Culture at Roche

Conducting one million genomics* experiments a day? Testing over 3 million new compounds annually? It sounds impossible, but it's not—it's the new reality for pharmaceutical firms. Of the myriad technological developments and applications of the 1990s, perhaps none are so rapid in their evolution or so startling in their outcomes as the recent advances in bioengineering. Industries as diverse as agriculture and petrochemicals are impacted as the pharmaceutical industry is experiencing an unprecedented upheaval.

The technological revolution began with the decoding of human DNA. Innovative equipment now uses that knowledge to match compounds with their affected genes. Promising compounds are then tested to ensure their effectiveness against cancer-causing genes and to determine whether they have adverse effects on other body organs.

Before these advances, Swiss drug manufacurer Roche Group had a competitive culture that pitted development teams against each other. The system worked when the firm was occupied with finding ideas for new blockbuster drugs. However, breakthroughs in technology made that culture obsolete, pushing the firm to adopt a more collaborative team approach. One incentive for more teamwork is to reduce the number of experiments, given their cost in computer capacity and researcher time. One Roche scientist explains, "Back when we were working on one gene, we could do fishing experiments. [How-

ever, W]hen you get [information] from 12,000 genes, you need to be careful. . . . If it isn't useful, you can waste a lot of time looking at it." Teams found that they needed members from all parts of the organization in order to access specialized knowledge. Roche researcher Barry Goggin re-

> *"We'd just get together in the corridors and design all sorts of small projects."—Barry Goggin, Roche research scientist*

calls, "We'd just get together in the corridors and design all sorts of small projects." At first, team members had trouble communicating, but they learned how to share information effectively. "It was almost as if two different languages were being spoken by the geneticists and the oncologists," Goggin says. "We had to bridge the gap."

Although the increase in collaboration and cross-specialty communication is good for the firm, some workers are suffering. The changing technology and the increased capacity of robotic equipment have caused Roche to lay off some R & D staff. Although this move will reduce costs, Roche must proceed cautiously to avoid upsetting its new and effective collaborative organization culture.

*Genomics is the study of DNA nucleotide sequences.

References: "Roche in the Sciences and Medicine," "Innovative R & D," Roche web site. www.roche.com on May 11, 2002; Jesse Eisinger, "Roche's Planned Job Cuts Look Desperate, Not Smart," *Wall Street Journal*, June 1, 2001. See interactive.wsj.com/archive on May 11, 2002; George Anders, "Roche's New Scientific Method," *Fast Company*, January 2002, pp. 60–67 (quotation p. 64). See www.fastcompany.com.

showing significant cost reductions. Team members feel that they have a stake in the outcomes, want to make contributions because they are valued, and are committed to their team and do not want to let it down. Wilson Sporting Goods reported saving $10 million per year for five years thanks to its teams. Colgate-Palmolive reported that technician turnover was extremely low—more than 90 percent of technicians were retained after five years—once it changed to a team-based approach.

Organizational Enhancements

Other improvements in organizations that result from moving from a hierarchically based, directive culture to a team-based culture include increased innovation, creativity, and flexibility.[12] Use of teams can eliminate redundant layers of bureaucracy

Moving to a team-based approach to work often results in numerous unexpected organizational enhancements. For example, the New York Police Department Bomb Squad, a world-renowned team, has helped develop several innovations that help not only its own team members but many others as well. Two of the more effective innovations that the team has helped create are multi-layered Kevlar suits and robot assistants.

and flatten the hierarchy in large organizations. Employees feel closer and more in touch with top management. Employees who think their efforts are important are more likely to make significant contributions. In addition, the team environment constantly challenges teams to innovate and solve problems creatively. If the "same old way" does not work, empowered teams are free to throw it out and develop a new way. With increasing global competition, organizations must constantly adapt to keep abreast of changes. Teams provide the flexibility to react quickly. One of Motorola's earliest teams challenged a long-standing top-management policy regarding supplier inspections in order to reduce the cycle times and improve delivery of crucial parts.[13] After several attempts, management finally allowed the team to change the system and consequently reaped the expected benefits.

Costs of Teams

The costs of teams are usually expressed in terms of the difficulty of changing to a team-based organization. Managers have expressed frustration and confusion about their new roles as coaches and facilitators, especially if they developed their managerial skills under the old traditional hierarchical management philosophy. Some managers have felt as if they were working themselves out of a job as they turned over more and more of their old directing duties to a team.[14]

Employees may also feel like losers during the change to a team culture. Some traditional staff groups, such as technical advisory staffs, may feel that their jobs are in jeopardy as teams do more and more of the technical work formerly done by technicians. New roles and pay scales may need to be developed for the technical staff in these situations. Often, technical people have been assigned to a team or a small group of teams and become members who fully participate in team activities.

Unfortunately, this person probably isn't going to be a very effective team member. That's too bad, because working in teams can result in enhanced performance, a reduction in errors, and an overall enhancement in performance. An organization that promotes a team environment can see positive results in terms of worker creativity, productivity, and job satisfaction.

Reference: ©Randy Glasbergen

"Before I begin, I'd just like to make it known that I didn't volunteer to do this presentation."

Another cost associated with teams is the slowness of the process of full team development. As discussed elsewhere in this chapter, it takes a long time for teams to go through the full development cycle and become mature, efficient, and effective. If top management is impatient with the slow progress, teams may be disbanded, returning the organization to its original hierarchical form with significant losses for employees, managers, and the organization.

Probably the most dangerous cost is premature abandonment of the change to a team-based organization. If top management gets impatient with the team change process and cuts it short, never allowing teams to develop fully and realize benefits, all the hard work of employees, middle managers, and supervisors is lost. As a result, employee confidence in management in general and in the decision makers in particular may suffer for a long time.[15] The losses in productivity and efficiency will be very difficult to recoup. Management must therefore be fully committed before initiating a change to a team-based organization.

Types of Teams

M any different types of teams exist in organizations today. Some evolved naturally in organizations that permit various types of participative and empowering management programs. Others have been formally created at the suggestion of enlightened management. One easy way to classify teams is by what they do; for example, some teams make or do things, some teams recommend things, and some teams run things. The most common types of teams are quality circles, work teams, and problem-solving teams; management teams are also quite common.

Quality circles are small groups of employees from the same work area who regularly meet to discuss and recommend solutions to workplace problems.

Quality Circles

Quality circles (QCs) are small groups of employees from the same work area who meet regularly (usually weekly or monthly) to discuss and recommend solutions to workplace problems.[16] QCs were the first type of team created in U.S. organizations, becoming most popular during the 1980s in response to growing Japanese competition. QCs had some success in reducing rework and cutting defects on the shop floors of many manufacturing plants. Some attempts have been made to use QCs in offices and service operations, too. They exist alongside the traditional management structure and are relatively permanent. The role of QCs is to investigate a variety of quality problems that might come up in the workplace. They do not replace the work group or make decisions about how the work is done. Interest in QCs has dropped somewhat, although many companies still have them.[17] QCs are teams that make recommendations.

Work Teams

Work teams include all the people working in an area, are relatively permanent, and do the daily work, making decisions regarding how the work of the team is done.

Work teams tend to be permanent, like QCs, but they, rather than auxiliary committees, are the teams that do the daily work.[18] A team of nurses, orderlies, and various technicians responsible for all patients on a floor or wing in a hospital is a work team. Rather than investigate a specific problem, evaluate alternatives, and recommend a solution or change, a work team does the actual daily work of the unit. The difference between a traditional work group of nurses and the patient care team is that the latter has the authority to decide how the work is done, in what order, and by whom; the entire team is responsible for all patient care. When the team decides how the work is to be organized or done, it becomes a self-managing team, to which accrue all of the benefits described in this chapter. Work teams are teams that make or do things.

Problem-Solving Teams

Problem-solving teams are temporary teams established to attack specific problems in the workplace.

Problem-solving teams are temporary teams established to attack specific problems in the workplace. Teams can use any number of methods to solve the problem, as discussed in Chapter 15. After solving the problem, the team is usually disbanded, allowing members to return to their normal work. One survey found that 91 percent of U.S. companies utilize problem-solving teams regularly.[19] High-performing problem-solving teams are often cross-functional, meaning that team members come from many different functional areas. Crisis teams are problem-solving teams created only for the duration of an organizational crisis and are usually composed of people from many different areas. Problem-solving teams are teams that make recommendations for others to implement.

Management Teams

Management teams consist of managers from various areas; they coordinate work teams.

Management teams consist of managers from various areas and coordinate work teams. They are relatively permanent because their work does not end with the completion of a particular project or the resolution of a problem. Management teams must concentrate on the teams that have the most impact on overall corporate performance. The primary job of management teams is to coach and counsel other teams to be self-managing by making decisions within the team. The second most important task of management teams is to coordinate work between work teams that are interdependent in some manner. Digital Equipment Corporation recently announced it was abandoning its team matrix structure because the matrix of teams was not well organized and coordinated. Team members at all levels reported spending hours and hours in meetings trying to coordinate among teams, leaving too little time to get the real work done.[20]

"I couldn't do this job if I didn't have them."—Jack Welch, former CEO of General Electric, on the importance of his top-management team[21]

Product development teams are combinations of work teams and problem-solving teams that create new designs for products or services that will satisfy customer needs.

Product development teams are very commonly used in organizations today. For example, Apple hardware chief Jon Rubinstein and industrial designer Jonathan Ive worked with a group of other specialists to help create the new Apple iPod. The team managed to design the product and get it into production in just eight months.

Top-management teams may have special types of problems. First, the work of the top-management team may not be conducive to teamwork. Vice presidents or heads of divisions may be in charge of different sets of operations that are not related and do not need to be coordinated. Forcing that type of top-management group to be a team may be inappropriate. Second, top managers often have reached high levels in the organization because they have certain characteristics or abilities to get things done. For successful managers to alter their style, to pool resources, and to sacrifice their independence and individuality can be very difficult.[22]

Product Development Teams

Product development teams are combinations of work teams and problem-solving teams that create new designs for products or services that will satisfy customer needs. They are similar to problem-solving teams because when the product is fully developed and in production, the team may be disbanded. As global competition and electronic information storage, processing, and retrieving capabilities increase, companies in almost every industry are struggling to cut product development times. The primary organizational means of accomplishing this important task is the "blue-ribbon" cross-functional team. Boeing's team that developed the 777 commercial airplane and the platform teams of Chrysler are typical examples.

The rush to market with new designs can lead to numerous problems for product development teams. The primary problems of poor communication and coordination of typical product development processes in organizations can be rectified by creating self-managing cross-functional product development teams.[23]

Virtual Teams

Virtual teams work together by computer and other electronic communication utilities; members move in and out of meetings and the team itself as the situation dictates.

Virtual teams are teams that may never actually meet together in the same room—their activities take place on the computer via teleconferencing and other electronic information systems. Engineers in the United States can directly connect audibly and visually with counterparts all around the globe, sharing files via Internet, electronic mail, and other communication utilities. All participants can look at the same drawing, print, or specification, so decisions are made much faster. With electronic communication systems, team members can move in or out of a team or a team discussion as the issues warrant.

Implementing Teams in Organizations

Implementing teams in organizations is not easy; it takes a lot of hard work, time, training, and patience. Changing from a traditional organizational structure to a team-based structure is much like other organizational changes (which we discuss in Chapter 19). It is really a complete cultural change for the organization. Typically, the organization is hierarchically designed in order to provide clear direction and control. However, many organizations need to be able to react quickly to a dynamic environment. Team procedures artificially imposed on existing processes are a recipe for disaster. In this section we present several essential elements peculiar to an organizational change to a team-based situation.

Planning the Change

The change to a team-based organization requires a lot of analysis and planning before it is implemented; the decision cannot be made overnight and quickly implemented. It is such a drastic departure from the traditional hierarchy and authority-and-control orientation that significant planning, preparation, and training are prerequisites. The planning actually takes place in two phases, the first leading to the decision about whether to move to a team-based approach and the second while preparing for implementation.

Making the Decision   Prior to making the decision, top management needs to establish the leadership for the change, develop a steering committee, conduct a feasibility study, and then make the go/no-go decision, as shown in Table 12.3. Top management must be sure that the team culture is consistent with its strategy, as we discuss in Chapter 18. Quite often the leadership for the change is the chief executive officer, the chief operating officer, or another prominent person in top management. Regardless of the position, the person leading the change needs to (1) have a strong belief that employees want to be responsible for their own work, (2) be able to demonstrate the team philosophy, (3) articulate a coherent vision of the team environment, and (4) have the creativity and authority to overcome obstacles as they surface.

The leader of the change needs to put together a steering committee to help explore the organization's readiness for the team environment and lead it through the planning and preparation for the change. The steering committee can be of any workable size, from two to ten people who are influential and know the work and the organization. Members may include plant or division managers, union representatives, human resource department representatives, and operational-level

Implementing teams in organizations is a complex and multi-step process. But if done well the payoffs can be dramatic. For instance, India's Wipro Technologies moved to a team organization as a way of competing more effectively with other international software solutions firms such as EDS and IBM Global Solutions. This team helped the firm win a major contract from Home Depot. Other teams have worked effectively with clients such as General Electric and Nokia as Wipro's annual revenues approach $400 million.

employees. The work of the steering committee includes visits to sites that might be candidates for utilizing work teams, visits to currently successful work teams, data gathering and analysis, low-key discussions, and deliberating and deciding whether to use a consultant during the change process.

A feasibility study is a necessity before making the decision to use teams. The steering committee needs to know if the work processes are conducive to team use, if the employees are willing and able to work in a team environment, if the managers in the unit to be converted are willing to learn and apply the hands-off managerial style necessary to make teams work, if the organization's structure and culture are ready to accommodate a team-based organization, if the market for the unit's products or services is growing or at least stable enough to absorb the increased productive capacity that teams will be putting out, and if the community will support the transition teams. Without answers to these questions, management is merely guessing and hoping that teams will work and may be destined for many surprises that could doom the effort.

After the leadership has been established, the steering committee has been set up, and a feasibility study has been conducted, the go/no-go decision can be made. The committee and top management will need to decide jointly to go ahead if conditions are right. On the other hand, if the feasibility study indicates that questions exist as to whether the organizational unit is ready, the committee can decide to postpone implementation while changes are made in personnel, organizational structure, organizational policies, or market condi-

table 12.3

The First Four Steps of Planning to Change to Teams

Step 1: Establish leadership

Step 2: Develop a steering committee

Step 3: Conduct a feasibility study

Step 4: Make the go/no-go decision

Reference: Jack D. Orsburn, Linda Moran, and Ed Musselwhite, with Craig Perrin, *Self-Directed Work Teams: The New American Challenge* (Homewood, Ill.: Business One Irwin, 1990), pp. 35–49.

tions. The committee could also decide to implement training and acculturation for employees and managers in the unit in preparation for later implementation.

Preparing for Implementation   Once the decision is made to change to a team-based organization, much needs to be done before implementation can begin. Preparation consists of the following five steps: clarifying the mission, selecting the site for the first work teams, preparing the design team, planning the transfer of authority, and drafting the preliminary plan.

The mission statement is simply an expression of purpose that summarizes the long-range benefits the company hopes to gain by moving to a team environment. It must be consistent with the organization's strategy as it establishes a common set of assumptions for executives, middle managers, support staff, and the teams. In addition, it sets the parameters or boundaries within which the change will take place. It may identify which divisions or plants will be involved or what levels will be converted to teams. The mission statement attempts to stimulate and focus the energy of those people who need to be involved in the change. The mission can focus on continuous improvement, employee involvement, increasing performance, competition, customer satisfaction, and contributions to society. The steering committee should involve many people from many different areas to foster fuller involvement in the change.

Once the mission is established, the steering committee needs to decide where teams will be implemented first. Selection of the first site is crucial because it sets the tone for the success of the total program. The best initial site would be one that includes workers from multiple job categories, one where improving performance or reaching the targets set in the mission is feasible, and one where workers accept the idea of using teams. Also valuable are a tradition or history of success and a staff that is receptive to training, especially training in interpersonal skills. One manufacturing company based its choice of sites for initial teams not on criteria such as these but on the desire to reward the managers of successful divisions or to "fix" areas performing poorly. Team implementation in that company consequently was very slow and not very successful.[24] Initial sites must also have a local "champion" of the team concept.

Once the initial sites have been identified, the steering committee needs to set up the team that will design the other teams. The design team is a select group of employees, supervisors, and managers who will work out the staffing and operational details to make the teams perform well. The design team selects the initial team members, prepares members and managers for teams, changes work processes for use with the team design, and plans the transition from the current state to the new self-managed teams. The design team usually spends the first three months learning from the steering committee, visiting sites where teams are being used successfully, and spending a significant amount of time in classroom training. Considering the composition of the teams is one of the most important decisions the design team has to make.

Planning the transfer of authority from management to teams is the most important phase of planning the implementation. It is also the most distinctive and difficult part of moving to a team-based organization. It is difficult because it is so different from the traditional, hierarchical organization management system. It is a gradual process, one that takes from two to five years in most situations. Teams must learn new skills and make new decisions related to their work, all of which take time. It is, essentially, a cultural change for the organization.

The last stage of planning the implementation is to write the tentative plan for the initial work teams. The draft plan combines the work of the steering and design committees and becomes the primary working document that guides the continuing work of the design teams and the first work teams. The draft plan (1) recommends a process for selecting the people who will be on the first teams; (2) describes roles and responsibilities for all the people who will be affected (team members, team leaders, facilitators, support teams, managers, and top management); (3) explains what training the several groups will need; (4) identifies specifically which work processes will be involved; (5) describes what other organizational systems will be affected; and (6) lays out a preliminary master schedule for the next two to three years. Once the steering committee and top management approve the preliminary plan, the organization is ready to start the implementation.

Phases of Implementation

Implementation of self-managing work teams is a long and difficult process, often taking two to five years. During this period, the teams go through a number of phases (Figure 12.1); these phases are not, however, readily apparent at the times the team is going through them.

Phase 1: Start-Up   In phase 1, team members are selected and prepared to work in teams so that the teams have the best possible chance of success. Much of the initial training is informational or "awareness" training that sends the message that top management is firmly committed to teams and that teams are not experimental. The steering committee usually starts the training at the top, and the training and information are passed down the chain to the team members. Training covers the rationale for moving to a team-based organization, how teams were selected, how they work, the roles and responsibilities of teams, compensation, and job security. In general, training covers the technical skills necessary to do the work of the team, the administrative skills necessary for the team to function within the organization, and the interpersonal skills necessary to work with people in the team and throughout the organization. Sometimes the interpersonal skills are important. Perhaps most important is establishing the idea that teams are not "unmanaged" but are "differently managed." The difference is that the new teams manage themselves. Team boundaries are also identified, and the preliminary plan is adjusted to fit the particular team situations. Employees typically feel that much is changing during the first few months, enthusiasm runs high, and the anticipation of employees is quite positive. Performance by teams increases at start-up because of this initial enthusiasm for the change.

Phase 2: Reality and Unrest   After perhaps six to nine months, team members and managers report frustration and confusion about the ambiguities of the new situation. For employees, unfamiliar tasks, more responsibility, and worry about job security replace hope for the opportunities presented by the new approach. All of the training and preparation, as important as it is, is never enough to prepare for the storm and backlash. Cummins Engine Company held numerous "prediction workshops" in an effort to prepare employees and managers for the difficulties that lay ahead, all to no avail. Its employees reported the same problems that employees of other companies did. The best advice is to perform phase 1 very well and then make managers very visible, continue to work to clarify the roles and responsibilities of everyone involved, and reinforce the positive behaviors that do occur.

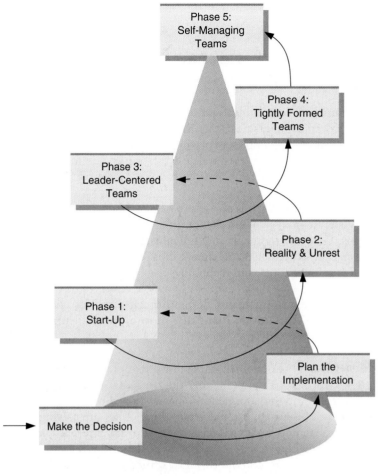

figure 12.1

Phases of Team Implementation

Implementation of teams in organizations is a long and arduous process. After the decision is made to initiate teams, the steering committee develops the plans for the design team, which plans the entire process. The goal is for teams to become self-managing. The time it takes for each stage varies with the organization.

Some managers make the mistake of staying completely away from the newly formed teams, thinking that the whole idea is to let teams manage themselves. In reality, managers need to be very visible to provide encouragement, to monitor team performance, to act as intermediaries between teams, to help teams acquire needed resources, to foster the right type of communication, and sometimes to protect teams from those who want to see them fail. Managers, too, feel the unrest and confusion. The change they supported results in more work for them. In addition, there is the real threat, at least initially, that work will not get done, projects may not get finished, or orders will not get shipped on time and that they will be blamed for the problems.[25] Managers also report that they still have to intervene and solve problems for the teams because the teams do not know what they are doing.

Phase 3: Leader-Centered Teams   As the discomfort and frustrations of the previous phase peak, teams usually long for a system that resembles the old manager-centered organizational structure (see Figure 12.1). However, members are learning about self-direction and leadership from within the team and usually start to focus on a single leader in the team. In addition, the team begins to think of itself as a unit as members learn to manage themselves. Managers begin to get a sense of the positive possibilities of organizing in teams and begin to withdraw slowly from the daily operation of the unit to begin focusing on standards, regulations, systems, and resources for the team.[26] This phase is not a setback to team development, although it may seem like one, because development of and reliance on one internal leader is a move away from focusing on the old hierarchy and traditional lines of authority.

The design and steering committees need to be sure that two things happen during this phase. First, they need to encourage the rise of strong internal team leaders. The new leaders can either be company appointed or team appointed. Top management sometimes prefers the additional control they get from appointing the team leaders, assuming that production will continue through the team transition. On the other hand, if the company-appointed leaders are the former managers, team members have trouble believing that anything has really changed.

Team-appointed leaders can be a problem if the leaders are not trained properly and oriented toward team goals.

"The most important thing that a captain can do is to see the ship from the eyes of the crew."—D. Michael Abrashoff, U.S. Navy[27]

If the team-appointed leader is ineffective, the team usually recognizes the problem and makes the adjustments necessary to get the team back on track. Another possibility for team leadership is a rotating system in which the position changes every quarter, month, week, or even day. A rotating system fosters professional growth of all members of the team and reinforces the strength of the team's self-management.

The second important issue for this phase is to help each team develop its own sense of identity. Visits to observe mature teams in action can be a good step for newly formed teams. Recognizing teams and individuals for good performance is always powerful, especially when the teams choose the recipients. Continued training in problem-solving steps, tools, and techniques is imperative. Managers need to push as many problem-solving opportunities as possible down to the team level. Finally, as team identity develops, teams develop social activities and display T-shirts, team names, logos, and other items that show off their identity. All of these are a sure sign that the team is moving into phase 4.

Phase 4: Tightly Formed Teams   The fourth phase of team implementation is when teams become tightly formed to the point that their internal focus can become detrimental to other teams and to the organization as a whole. Such teams are usually extremely confident of their ability to do everything. They are solving problems, managing their schedule and resources, and resolving internal conflicts. However, communication with external teams begins to diminish, the team covers up for underperforming members, and interteam rivalries can turn sour, leading to unhealthy competition.

To avoid the dangers of the intense team loyalty and isolation inherent in phase 4, managers need to make sure that teams continue to do the things that have enabled them to prosper thus far. First, teams need to keep the communication channels with other teams open through councils of rotating team representatives who meet regularly to discuss what works and what does not; teams who communicate and cooperate with other teams should be rewarded. At the Digital Equipment plant in Connecticut, team representatives meet weekly to share successes and failures so that all can avoid problems and improve the ways their teams operate.[28] Second, management needs to provide performance feedback through computer terminals in the work area that give up-to-date information on performance, or via regular feedback meetings. At TRW plants, management introduced peer performance appraisal at this stage of the team implementation process. It found that in phase 4, teams were ready to take on this administrative task but needed significant training in how to perform and communicate appraisals. Third, teams need to follow the previously developed plan to transfer authority and responsibility to the teams and to be sure that all team members have followed the plan to get training in all of the skills necessary to do the work of the team. By the end of phase 4, the team should be ready to take responsibility for managing itself.

Phase 5: Self-Managing Teams   Phase 5 is the end result of the months or years of planning and implementation. Mature teams are meeting or exceeding their performance goals. Team members are taking responsibility for team-related leadership functions. Managers and supervisors have withdrawn from the daily operations and are planning and providing counseling for teams. Probably most important, mature teams are flexible—taking on new ideas for improvement; making changes as needed to membership, roles, and tasks; and doing whatever it takes to meet the strategic objectives of the organization. Although the teams are mature and functioning quite well, several things need to be done to keep them on track. First and foremost, individuals and teams need to continue their training in job skills and team and interpersonal skills. Second, support systems need to be constantly improved to facilitate team development and productivity. Third, teams always need to improve their internal customer and supplier relationships within the organization. Partnerships among teams throughout the organization can help the internal teams continue to meet the needs of external customers.

Essential Team Issues

T his chapter has described the many benefits of teams and the process of changing to a team-based organization. Teams can be utilized in small and large organizations, on the shop floor and in offices, and in countries around the world. Teams must be initiated for performance-based business reasons, and proper planning and implementation strategies must be used. In this section we discuss two essential issues that cannot be overlooked as organizations move to a team-based setup: team performance and starting at the top. Another interesting team issue, norm conformity, which is relevant in professional sports, is discussed in the "Business of Ethics" box.

Team Performance

Organizations typically expect too much too soon when they implement teams. In fact, things often get worse before they get better.[29] Figure 12.2 shows how, shortly after implementation, team performance often declines and then rebounds to rise to the original levels and above. Management at Investors Diversified Services, the financial services giant in Minneapolis, Minnesota, expected planning for team start-up to take three or four months.

"Every project we take on starts with a question: How can we do what's never been done before?"—Stuart Hornery, chairman, Lend Lease Corp.[30]

The actual planning took eight and a half months.[31] It often takes a year or more before performance levels return to at least their before-team levels. If teams are implemented without proper planning, their performance may never return to prior levels. The long lead time for improving performance can be discouraging to managers who reacted to the fad for teams and expected immediate returns.

The phases of implementation discussed in the previous sections correspond to key points on the team performance curve. At the start-up, performance is at its normal levels, although sometimes the anticipation of, and enthusiasm for, teams cause a slight increase in performance. In phase 2, reality and unrest, teams are often confused and frustrated with the training and lack of direction from top

▶ BUSINESS OF ETHICS

▶ *The Morality of Injury*

It could be a tabloid headline: "National heroes, top athletes are liars!!!" Sports figures are heroes for many Americans, but the players and their teams stand accused of lying about injuries in order to gain an advantage over their rivals. This situation highlights one of the darker aspects of teams: They are wonderful when they motivate workers, set high performance norms, and foster creativity. However, a potential downside is norm conformity, and that is problematic when the norms reward low performance or are unethical.

Most players and team managers are honest, but it can be tempting for them to stretch the truth a little. Under NBA rules, each team can carry just twelve players. When a player is injured, a substitute is named. Then, when the injured player recovers, teams will move somebody onto the injured list to keep the player available for future games, if needed. Rod Thorn, former NBA official and president of the New Jersey Nets, claims that as many as 40 percent of players on the injured list are in fact healthy. Some claim that the system isn't unethical. "It's just something that you do as part of the business," according to Joe Dumars of the Detroit Pistons. General Manager of the Atlanta Hawks Pete Babcock strongly disagrees, maintaining, "It just isn't ethical. It's a lie perpetuated. It kind of makes a mockery of the whole system."

Jerry Sloan, coach of the Utah Jazz, holds a mixed opinion, saying, "I've never liked [the practice]. I think it's a phony thing. But if you're going to compete, you have to go along with whatever is acceptable." Herein lies the

> *"[I]f you're going to compete, you have to go along with whatever is acceptable."* — Jerry Sloan, head coach, Utah Jazz basketball team

problem. Working together in a league, each team feels the pressure to adopt group norms. And the group norms in this case, although disputed by a few, seem to permit such behavior. One solution is to institute more rules and more policing, but they may not help. As long as the incentive is there, some teams will find a way to bend the rules. As with most ethical dilemmas, finding an effective long-term solution will not depend on changing the laws but rather on changing the attitudes of those involved.

References: D.J. Glombowski, "How the NBA Proposes Sacrifice," Sports Ethics Institute web site. www.sports-ethics.com on May 23, 2002; "NSD and NBA Make Great Partners, "Institute for International Sport web site. www.internationalsport.com on May 23, 2002; Cam Crews, "Fake NBA Injuries Tarnish Fair Play," The Tartan (student newspaper of Carnegie Mellon University, Pittsburgh, Pennsylvania), March 25, 2002. www.thetartan.org on May 23, 2002; Rick Wartzman, "Practice of Faking One for the Team Has Become Regular Drill in the NBA," Wall Street Journal, March 20, 2002, p. A1. See www.wsj.com. "Spurs' Robinson Honored for Sportsmanship," press release on the NBA web site. www.nba.com on May 23, 2002.

management to the point that actual performance may decline. In phase 3, leader-centered teams become more comfortable with the team idea and refocus on the work of the team. They once again have established leadership, although it is with an internal leader rather than an external manager or supervisor. Thus, their performance usually returns to at least their former levels. In phase 4, teams are beginning to experience the real potential of teamwork and are producing above their prior levels. Finally, in phase 5, self-managing teams are mature, flexible, and usually setting new records for performance.

Organizations changing to a team-based arrangement need to recognize the time and effort involved in making such a change. Hopes for immediate, positive results can lead to disappointment. The most rapid increases in performance occur between the leader-centered phase and the team-centered phase because teams have managed to get past the difficult, low-performance stages, have had a lot of training, and are ready to utilize their independence and freedom to make decisions about their own work. Team members are deeply committed to each other and to the success of the team. In phase 5, management needs to make sure that

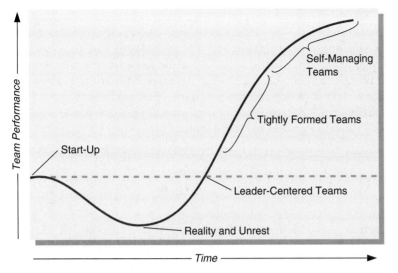

figure 12.2

Performance and Implementation of Teams

The team performance curve shows that performance initially drops as reality sets in, and team members experience frustration and unrest. However, performance soon increases and rises to record levels as the teams mature and become self-managing.

Reference: Reprinted by permission of Harvard Business School Press. From *The Wisdom of Teams: Creating the High Performance Organization* by Jon R. Katzenbach and Douglas K. Smith Boston, MA. 1993, p. 84. Copyright © 1993 by McKinley & Company, Inc., all rights reserved.

teams are focused on the strategic goals of the organization.

Start at the Top

The question of where to start in team implementation is really no issue at all. Change starts at the top in every successful team implementation. Top management has three important roles to play. First, top management must decide to go to a team-based organization for sound business performance–related reasons. A major cultural change cannot be made because it is the fad, because the boss went to a seminar on teams, or because a quick fix is needed. Second, top management is instrumental in communicating the reasons for the change to the rest of the organization. Third, top management has to support the change effort during the difficult periods. As discussed previously, performance usually goes down in the early phases of team implementation. Top-management support may involve verbal encouragement of team members, but organizational support systems for the teams are also needed. Examples of support systems for teams include more efficient inventory and scheduling systems, better hiring and selection systems, improved information systems, and appropriate compensation systems.

Synopsis

Groups and teams are not the same. A team is a small number of people with complementary skills who are committed to a common purpose, common performance goals, and a common approach for which they hold themselves mutually accountable. Teams differ from traditional work groups in their job categories, authority, and reward systems.

Teams are used because they make sense for a specific organization. Organizational benefits include enhanced performance, employee benefits, and reduced costs, among others.

Many different types of teams exist in organizations. Quality circles are small groups of employees from the same work area who meet regularly to discuss and recommend solutions to workplace problems. Work teams perform the daily operations of the

organization and make decisions about how to do the work. Problem-solving teams are temporarily established to solve a particular problem. Management teams consist of managers from various areas; these teams are relatively permanent and coach and counsel the new teams. Product development teams are teams assigned the task of developing a new product or service for the organization. Members of virtual teams usually meet via teleconferencing, may never actually sit in the same room together, and often have a fluid membership.

Planning the change entails all the activities leading to the decision to utilize teams and then preparing the organization for the initiation of teams. Essential steps include establishing leadership for the change, creating a steering committee, conducting a feasibility study, and making the go/no-go decision. After the decision to utilize teams has been made, preparations include clarifying the mission of the change, selecting the site for the first teams, preparing the design team, planning the transfer of authority, and drafting the preliminary plan.

Implementation includes five phases: start-up, reality and unrest, leader-centered teams, tightly formed teams, and self-managing teams. Implementation of teams is really a cultural change for the organization.

For teams to succeed, the change must start with top management, who must decide why the change is needed, communicate the need for the change, and support the change. Management must not expect too much too soon because team performance tends to decrease before it returns to prior levels and then increases to record levels.

Discussion Questions

1. Why is it important to make a distinction between "group" and "team"? What kinds of behaviors might be different in these assemblages?

2. How are other organizational characteristics different for a team-based organization?

3. Some say that changing to a team-based arrangement "just makes sense" for organizations. What are the four primary reasons why this might be so?

4. If employees are happy working in the traditional boss-hierarchical organization, why should a manager even consider changing to a team-based organization?

5. How are the six types of teams related to each other?

6. Explain the circumstances under which a cross-functional team is useful in organizations.

7. Which type of team is the most common in organizations? Why?

8. Why is planning the change important in the implementation process?

9. What can happen if your organization prematurely starts building a team-based organization by clarifying the mission and then selecting the site for the first work teams?

10. What are two of the most important issues facing team-based organizations?

Organizational Behavior Case for Discussion

None of Us Is as Smart as All of Us

Are you unhappy about your recent encounters with the medical profession? Do you think that doctors are too rushed and impersonal, insurance companies have too much control, fees are too high, and procedures and tests are not thoroughly explained? You're not alone. National consumer surveys show a low level of satisfaction with health care, but at the Mayo Clinic in Rochester, Minnesota, patient satisfaction soars above the average. At the same time, costs are lower and the staff is happier than those at most other hospitals. Teamwork is the key to the clinic's remarkable success.

The Mayo Clinic was founded by Dr. William W. Mayo, a Minnesota physician, and his two sons, William J. and Charles, also physicians. After a catastrophic tornado in 1883, the doctors joined forces with nurses from the Sisters of St. Francis, and the arrangement was made permanent with the opening of St. Mary's Hospital in 1889. The Mayo brothers recruited more physicians, hiring technicians and business managers and creating one of the first group medical practices. The closeness of the two siblings, as well as advances in medicine, helped guide the development of Mayo's team-based culture. Harry Harwick, their first business manager, claims, "The first and perhaps greatest lesson I learned from the Mayos was that of teamwork. For 'my brother and I' was no mere convenient term of reference, but rather the expression of a basic, indivisible philosophy of life." Dr. William J. Mayo said, "It has become necessary to develop medicine as a cooperative science; the clinician, the specialist, and the laboratory workers uniting for the good of the patient. Individualism in medicine can no longer exist."

The team approach permeates the culture of the entire organization. It begins with staff and physician recruiting. Mayo runs its own medical school and residency programs and hires many of its own graduates. The clinic selects only those with the "right" attitude, the ones who are willing to put patients' needs first. All clinic medical staff, including doctors, nurses, and technicians, call each other "consultants," a term which emphasizes collaboration and also reduces status barriers, enabling all workers to participate as equals in patient-care decisions. The CEO is a physician; every committee is headed by medical personnel, with business staffers working as advisors only. The Mayo brothers turned their life savings into the Mayo Foundation, which funds the clinic's operation as well as medical education and research. Doctors at Mayo are employees, not owners, so they receive a salary, ensuring that they will make decisions in the best interests of their patients, not for personal gain. Without worries about turf battles, collaboration is the norm. Oncologist Lynn Hartman explains, "I take great comfort in the proximity of expertise. I feel much more confident in the accuracy of my diagnosis because I've got some very, very smart people next to me who have expertise that I don't have."

A typical patient's experience at Mayo is something like this: A cancer patient would have multiple professionals involved in his or her care, from oncologists to nurses to radiologists to surgeons to social workers, and the group would meet as a team with the patient to work out a joint strategy for treatment. Cancer patients typically feel that they have little control, but Mayo doctors know that getting patients actively involved in their own care dramatically increases the odds of successful treatment. Hartman claims, "Most patients today want a more interactive style . . . so [that] they can be part of the decision. They're on the Internet; they're doing their own research. What they're looking for is someone who can help them sort through that information." With help from the professionals, patients can work out a treatment that makes sense for their particular circumstances. When a patient's needs or questions change, the team adapts. "We work in teams, and each team is driven by the medical problems involved in a case and by the patient's preferences. Sometimes that means that a team must be expanded—or taken apart and reassembled," says Hartman.

Part of Mayo's success comes because of past successes—for example, when its medical school graduates refer patients to the clinic. The foresight of Will and Charlie Mayo in providing financially for the clinic is another factor. Mayo's reputation also creates opportunities, such as Mayo physician Donald D. Hensrud's recurring column for *Fortune* readers and the award-winning web site mayoclinic.com. But most of it is due to the passion for teamwork expressed in the founders' philosophy: "No one is big enough to be independent of others. None of us is as smart as all of us."

"It has become necessary to develop medicine as a cooperative science . . . Individualism in medicine can no longer exist."—William J. Mayo, M.D., cofounder of the Mayo Clinic

References: 2000 Mayo Foundation Annual Report. www.mayoclinic.org on May 23, 2002; "History," "Mayo's Mission," "The Tradition," Mayo clinic web site (quotation from "History"). www.mayoclinic.org on May 23, 2002; Paul Roberts, "The Agenda—Total Teamwork," *Fast Company*, April 1999. www.fastcompany.com on May 23, 2002.

Case Questions

1. Would you consider the patient-care groups at the Mayo Clinic to be teams? Explain your answer in terms of job categories, authority, and reward system. (Hint: See Table 12.1 for guidance.)

2. What team-related benefits can you find described in this case? What are the possible team-related costs?

3. What type of team are the patient-care teams? What factors led you to arrive at your answer?

Experiencing Organizational Behavior

Using Teams

Introduction: The use of groups and teams is becoming more common in organizations throughout the world. The following assessment surveys your beliefs about the effective use of teams in work organizations.

Instructions: You will agree with some of the statements and disagree with others. In some cases, you may find making a decision difficult, but you should force a choice. Record your answers next to each statement according to the following scale:

4 =   Agree Strongly
3 =   Agree Somewhat
2 =   Disagree Somewhat
1 =   Disagree Strongly

_____ 1. Each individual in a work team should have a clear assignment so that individual accountability can be maintained.

_____ 2. For a team to function effectively, the team must be given complete authority over all aspects of the task.

_____ 3. One way to get teams to work is to simply assemble a group of people, tell them in general what needs to be done, and let them work out the details.

_____ 4. Once a team "gets going," management can turn its attention to other matters.

_____ 5. To ensure that a team develops into a cohesive working unit, managers should be especially careful not to intervene in any way during the initial start-up period.

_____ 6. Training is not critical to a team because the team will develop any needed skills on its own.

_____ 7. It's easy to provide teams with the support they need because they are basically self-motivating.

_____ 8. Teams need little or no structure to function effectively.

_____ 9. Teams should set their own direction, with managers determining the means to the selected end.

_____ 10. Teams can be used in any organization.

For interpretation, see the Interpretation Guide in the *Instructor's Resource Manual.*

Reference: Adapted from J. Richard Hackman (ed.), *Groups That Work (and Those That Don't)*, pp. 493–504. Copyright © 1990. This material is used by permission of Jossey-Bass, Inc., a subsidiary of John Wiley & Sons, Inc.

Self-Assessment Exercise

Understanding the Benefits of Teams

Purpose: This exercise will help you understand some of the benefits of teamwork.

Format: Your instructor will divide the group into teams of four to six people. (These could be previously formed teams or new teams.) Teams should arrange their desks or chairs so that they can interact and communicate well with each other.

Procedure: Consider that your team is an engineering design team assigned to work out this difficult problem whose solution would be the key to getting a major purchase contract from a large influential buyer. The task seems simple, but working out such tasks (at different levels of complexity) can be very important to organizations.

1. It is important for your team to work together to develop your solution.

2. Look at the following figure. Your task is to create a single square by making only **two** straight-line cuts and then reassembling the pieces so that all material is used in the final product.

The Figure:

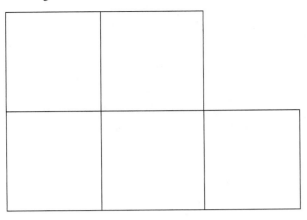

3. It might be easier to trace the design onto stiff paper or cardboard to facilitate working with the pieces.

4. Your instructor has access to the correct answer key from the *Instructor's Resource Manual*.

Follow-up Questions

1. How did the other members of your team help or hinder your ability to solve the problem?

2. Did your team have a leader throughout the exercise? If so, can you identify why that person emerged as the leader?

3. What type of training would have helped your team solve the problem better or faster?

Reference: From John W. Newstrom and Edward E. Scannell, *Games Trainers Play: Experiential Learning Exercises*, p. 259. Copyright © 1980 by McGraw-Hill Companies. Used with permission.

OB Online

1. Identify an example of a team in which you are interested and find out as much as you can about it on the Internet. An example might be your favorite sports team or performing arts company.

2. In what ways might the Internet reshape organizational thinking about teams?

3. Which do you think would result in a more effective team, one that is first formed electronically and then begins to work together face to face, or vice versa? Why?

4. Use the Internet to find one example of each of the types of teams identified in the chapter.

Building Managerial Skills

Exercise Overview: Groups and teams are becoming ever more important in organizations. This exercise will allow you to practice your conceptual skills as they apply to work teams in organizations.

Exercise Background: A variety of highly effective groups exists outside the boundaries of typical business organizations. For example, each of the following represents a team:

1. A basketball team

2. An elite military squadron

3. A government policy group such as the presidential cabinet

4. A student planning committee

Exercise Task

1. Identify an example of a real team, such as one just listed. Choose one (1) that is not part of a normal business and (2) that you can argue is highly effective.

2. Determine the reasons for the team's effectiveness.

3. Determine how a manager could learn from this particular team and use its success determinants in a business setting.

13 Leadership Models and Concepts

Management Preview

▶ The mystique of leadership makes it one of the most widely debated, studied, and sought-after commodities of organizational life. Managers talk about the characteristics that make an effective leader, and organizational scientists have extensively studied leadership and myriad related phenomena. We begin this chapter, the first of two devoted to leadership, with a discussion of the meaning of leadership, including its definition and the distinctions between leadership and management. Then we turn to historical views of leadership, focusing on the trait and behavioral approaches. Next, we examine three contemporary leadership theories that have formed the basis for most leadership research: the LPC theory developed by Fiedler, the path-goal theory, and Vroom's decision tree approach to leadership. We conclude by describing two other popular models of leadership. In our next chapter we explore other elements of leadership, focusing more specifically on influence processes in organizations. First, though, we examine the odyssey of one leader and his amazing transformation.

▼ ▼ ▼

This is a story about a man, a man who ruled his businesses through fear and punishment and then learned to govern with respect—and even love—for his workers. The man in question is Andrall (Andy) Pearson, Chairman of Tricon Global Restaurants, a Pepsi spinoff that owns Pizza Hut, Taco Bell, and KFC (Kentucky Fried Chicken). His evolution from feared dictator to beloved guru is quite a journey.

A snapshot of the old Andy: A graduate of USC, armed with a Harvard M.B.A., Pearson sums up the first fifty years of his career by saying, "I proved that I was smart by finding fault with other people's ideas." He began at the strategic consulting firm McKinsey & Co., rising to the position of senior director in charge of the firm's marketing practice. During his fourteen-year stint as president and COO of PepsiCo, he was known for being abrasive, numbers oriented, and hard to please. His favorite phrase was "So what?" *Fortune* named him one of the top ten toughest bosses in 1980, in part because he often drove employees to tears or to quitting if they failed to meet his expectations. In fact, he helped people out the door—his policy was to fire the lowest performing 10 to 20 percent of all his employees each year.

As a tenured professor at the Harvard Business School, he contributed articles to the prestigious *Harvard Business Review* with titles such as "Tough-Minded Ways to Get Innovative." He was invited to join Tricon by CEO David Novak, who saw that Pearson's no-nonsense style would complement his own people-oriented approach. When Pearson first came to Tricon, "he was brutal," according to Aylwin Lewis, Tricon's COO. "One time he told us, 'A room full of monkeys could do better than this!'"

"Great leaders find a balance between getting results and how they get them."
—Andy Pearson, Chairman of Tricon Global Restaurants

Now, a picture of the new Andy: Employees still weep, but this time it's with gratitude for praise from Pearson. Managers who are mentored by Pearson tell him that the experience is life changing, and Pearson says, "I get letters that would just bring tears to your eyes." Pearson is greeted with loud cheers when he tells a crowd, "My experience at Tricon represents the capstone of my career." At the beginning, Novak told Pearson, "We can learn from each other," and when Pearson arrived at headquarters, hundreds of employees were cheering and a band was playing. "All the time I was at Pepsi, nothing remotely like this had ever happened. It was overwhelming," says Pearson. "I knew something was going on that was fundamentally very powerful. If we could learn how to harness that spirit with something systematic, then we would have something unique."

Pearson has softened, been transformed. When he says, "If I could only unleash the power of everybody in the organization, instead of just a few people, . . . we'd be a much better company," he seems to truly care about employees. And his thinking about leadership has matured. Now he says, "Great leaders find a balance between getting results and how they get them. A lot of people make the mistake of thinking that getting results is all there is to a job. . . . Your real job is to get results and to do it in a way that makes your organization a great place to work."

References: "Our Vision," Tricon web site. www.triconglobal.com on May 15, 2002; "America's Most Admired Companies: 2002 All-Stars: Food Service," *Fortune*, March 4, 2002. www.fortune.com on May 15, 2002; Gerry Khermouch, "Tricon's Fast-Food Smorgasbord," *Business Week*, February 11, 2002. www.businessweek.com on May 15, 2002; Brian O'Keefe, "The New Future: Global Brands," *Fortune*, November 26, 2001. www.fortune.com on May 15, 2002; Aixa Pascual, "Taco Bell Hopes It Has a Menu to Go," *Business Week*, October 16, 2001. www.businessweek.com on May 15, 2002; David Dorsey, "Andy Pearson Finds Love," *Fast Company*, August 2001, pp. 78–86 (quotation p. 84). See www.fastcompany.com; Joseph Weber, "The Best Performers," *Business Week*, March 23, 2001. www.businessweek.com on May 15, 2002.

Andy Pearson represents two extremes of leadership—the harsh and brutal autocrat and the caring and considerate supportive leader. As we will see in this chapter, there may be times and places when each approach is necessary. There also appear to be some leaders capable of using either approach while other leaders are unable to change their behavior. As we will also see, in some organizational settings leaders make the difference between enormous success and overwhelming failure. However, in others, leaders may appear to have no significant effect on the organization whatsoever. And although some leaders are effective in one organization but not in others, some succeed no matter where they are. Yet despite hundreds of studies on leadership, researchers have found no simple way to account for these inconsistencies. Why, then, should we study leadership? First, leadership is of great practical importance to organizations. Second, researchers have isolated and verified some key variables that influence leadership effectiveness.[1]

The Nature of Leadership

Leadership is both a process and a property. As a *process*, leadership involves the use of noncoercive influence. As a *property*, leadership is the set of characteristics attributed to someone who is perceived to use influence successfully.

Because "leadership" is a term that is often used in everyday conversation, you might assume that it has a common and accepted meaning. In fact, just the opposite is true—like several other key organizational behavior terms such as "personality" and "motivation," "leadership" is used in a variety of ways. Thus, we first clarify its meaning as it is used in this book.

Leadership is both a complex and a compelling phenomenon. Whether the setting is a business, a government, an educational, or an athletic setting, most people would agree that having a good leader is desirable. Take the recent World Cup soccer tournament for example. Led by captain Claudio Reyna, the U.S. soccer team advanced to the quarterfinals and went on to lose a close final game to the powerhouse German team. While the team was comprised of many talented athletes, the leadership of Reyna played a critical role in the team's success.

The Meaning of Leadership

We will define **leadership** in terms of both process and property.[2] As a process, leadership is the use of noncoercive influence to direct and coordinate the activities of group members to meet a goal. As a property, leadership is the set of characteristics attributed to those who are perceived to use such influence successfully.[3] From an organizational viewpoint, leadership is vital because it has such a powerful influence on individual and group behavior.[4] Moreover, because the goal toward which the group directs its efforts is often the desired goal of the leader, it may or may not mesh with organizational goals.

Leadership involves neither force nor coercion. A manager who relies solely on force and formal authority to direct the behavior of subordinates is not exercising leadership. Thus, as discussed more fully in the next section, a manager or supervisor may or may not also be a leader. It is also important to note that a leader may possess the characteristics attributed to him or her; on the other hand, the leader may merely be perceived as possessing them.

Leadership Versus Management

From these definitions, it should be clear that leadership and management are related, but they are not the same. A person can be a manager, a leader, both, or neither.[5] Some of the basic distinctions between the two are summarized in Table 13.1. On the left side of the table are four elements that differentiate leadership from management. The two columns show how each element differs when considered from a management and a leadership point of view. For example, when executing plans, managers focus on monitoring results, comparing them with goals, and correcting deviations. In contrast, the leader focuses on energizing people to overcome bureaucratic hurdles to help reach goals. Thus, when Andy Pearson monitors the performance of his Tricon employees, he is playing the role of manager. But when he inspires them to work harder at achieving their goals, he is playing the role of leader.

To further underscore the differences, consider the various roles that might typify managers and leaders in a hospital setting. The chief of staff of a large hospital is clearly a manager by virtue of the position itself. At the same time, this individual may not be respected or trusted by others and may have to rely solely on the authority vested in the position to get people to do things. But an emergency-room nurse with no formal authority may be quite effective at taking charge of a chaotic situation and directing others in how to deal with specific patient problems. Others in the emergency room may respond because they trust the nurse's judgment and have confidence in the nurse's decision-making skills.

And the head of pediatrics, supervising a staff of twenty other doctors, nurses, and attendants, may also enjoy the staff's complete respect, confidence, and trust.

table 13.1
Distinctions Between Management and Leadership

Activity	Management	Leadership
Creating an Agenda	**Planning and budgeting.** Establishing detailed steps and timetables for achieving needed results; allocating the resources necessary to make those needed results happen	**Establishing direction.** Developing a vision of the future, often the distant future, and strategies for producing the changes needed to achieve that vision
Developing a Human Network for Achieving the Agenda	**Organizing and staffing.** Establishing some structure for accomplishing plan requirements, staffing that structure with individuals, delegating responsibility and authority for carrying out the plan, providing policies and procedures to help guide people, and creating methods or systems to monitor implementation	**Aligning people.** Communicating the direction by words and deeds to all those whose cooperation may be needed to influence the creation of teams and coalitions that understand the vision and strategies and accept their validity
Executing Plans	**Controlling and problem solving.** Monitoring results vs. plan in some detail, identifying deviations, and then planning and organizing to solve these problems	**Motivating and inspiring.** Energizing people to overcome major political, bureaucratic, and resource barriers to change by satisfying very basic, but often unfulfilled, human needs
Outcomes	Produces a degree of predictability and order and has the potential to consistently produce major results expected by various stakeholders (e.g., for customers, always being on time; for stockholders, being on budget)	Produces change, often to a dramatic degree, and has the potential to produce extremely useful change (e.g., new products that customers want, new approaches to labor relations that help make a firm more competitive)

Reference: Reprinted with the permission of The Free Press, an imprint of Simon & Schuster Adult Publishing Group, from *A Force for Change: How Leadership Differs from Management*, by John P. Kotter, 1990. Copyright © 1990 by John P. Kotter, Inc.

They readily take her advice and follow directives without question, and often go far beyond what is necessary to help carry out the unit's mission. Thus, being a manager does not ensure that a person is also a leader—any given manager may or may not also be a leader. Similarly, a leadership position can also be formal, as when someone appointed to head a group has leadership qualities, or informal, as when a leader emerges from the ranks of the group according to a consensus of the members. The chief of staff described earlier is a manager but not a leader. The emergency-room nurse is a leader but not a manager. And the head of pediatrics is both.

Managers "know how to write business plans, while leaders get companies—and people—to change."—Carol Bartz, CEO of Autodesk, Inc.[6]

Organizations need both management and leadership if they are to be effective. For example, leadership is necessary to create and direct change and to help the organization get through tough times.[7] And management is necessary to achieve coordination and systematic results and to handle administrative activities during times of stability and predictability. Management in conjunction with leadership can help achieve planned orderly change, and leadership in conjunction with management can keep the organization properly aligned with its environment. In addition, managers and leaders also play a major role in establishing the moral climate of the organization and in determining the role of ethics in its culture.[8] The "Mastering Change" box illustrates how both leadership and management have helped Johnson & Johnson.

Early Approaches to Leadership

Although leaders and leadership have profoundly influenced the course of human events, careful scientific study of them began only about a century ago. Early study focused on the traits, or personal characteristics, of leaders.[9] Later research shifted to examine actual leader behaviors.

Trait Approaches to Leadership

The trait approach to leadership attempted to identify stable and enduring character traits that differentiated effective leaders from nonleaders.

Lincoln, Napoleon, Joan of Arc, Hitler, and Gandhi are names that most of us know quite well. Early researchers believed that notable leaders such as these had some unique set of qualities or traits that distinguished them from their peers. Moreover, these traits were presumed to be relatively stable and enduring. Following this **trait approach,** these researchers focused on identifying leadership traits, developing methods for measuring them, and using the methods to select leaders.

Hundreds of studies guided by this research agenda were conducted during the first several decades of the twentieth century. The earliest writers believed that important leadership traits included intelligence, dominance, self-confidence, energy, activity, and task-relevant knowledge. The results of subsequent studies gave rise to a long list of additional traits. Unfortunately, the list quickly became so long that it lost any semblance of practical value. In addition, the results of many studies were inconsistent.

For example, one early argument was that effective leaders such as Lincoln tended to be taller than ineffective leaders. But critics were quick to point out that Hitler and Napoleon, both effective leaders in their own way, were not tall. Some

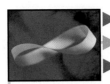

MASTERING CHANGE

▶ *Leading Change at Johnson & Johnson*

Pharmaceutical giant Johnson & Johnson is known for the eloquent expression of its corporate values. In part, its "Credo" says, "We must be mindful of ways to help our employees fulfill their family responsibilities," and "We must be good citizens—support good works and charities and bear our fair share of taxes." But J & J is no wimpy, "touchy-feely" organization. In fact, Jim Collins, author of *Built to Last*, maintains, "J & J is a team of nice guys until you get on the football field with them, and then they hit really hard." CEO Bill Weldon, appointed in 2002, agrees, explaining, "Our values are the ante you need to play in the game, but to stay in the game, you need results."

Alex Taylor, writing for *Fortune*, claims, "The company [has a] Jekyll-and-Hyde culture—smile, and squeeze very hard." J & J's hard-hitting approach has helped its stock price rise 19 percent in the last year while the industry average fell 14 percent, a sign of investor confidence in the firm. In a break with industry tradition, J & J diversified beyond prescription drugs into consumer products and medical devices. The drug manufacturer thinks of itself as a retail competitor rather than a scientific pioneer dedicated to the selfless task of curing disease.

J & J is more willing than its rivals to acquire drug ideas from outsiders—four of its six top sellers spring from acquisitions or collaborations. To avoid diluting that famous corporate culture, the firm investigates every potential acquisition carefully. "We've looked at organizations that weren't the right fit with our culture," Weldon

> *"The company [has a] Jekyll-and-Hyde culture—smile, and squeeze very hard."—Alex Taylor III,* Fortune *magazine writer*

says. "It is one of those walk-away points." When the firm acquired a maker of artificial joints, J & J managers spent a year coaching the company's staff in order to minimize corporate culture clash.

With Weldon at the helm, Johnson & Johnson is likely to become an even stronger competitor. The new CEO claims he isn't heavy-handed, adding, "God forbid that I should dictate to somebody who knows the business better than I do." However, Weldon's tough-guy attitude may be just what J & J needs to maintain its leadership in a risky and volatile industry.

References: Alex Taylor III, "Can J & J Keep the Magic Going?" *Fortune*, May 27, 2002, pp. 117–122 (quotation p. 118). See www.fortune.com; "Fast Facts," "Our Credo," Johnson & Johnson web site. www.jnj.com on May 25, 2002; Patricia O'Connell, "At J & J, New Boss, Same Strategy," *Business Week*, May 14, 2002. www.businessweek.com on May 25, 2002.

writers have even tried to relate leadership to such traits as body shape, astrological sign, or handwriting patterns. The trait approach also had a significant theoretical problem in that it could neither specify nor prove how presumed leadership traits are connected to leadership per se. For these and other reasons, the trait approach was all but abandoned several decades ago.

In recent years, however, the trait approach has received renewed interest. For example, some researchers have sought to reintroduce a limited set of traits into the leadership literature. These traits include drive, motivation, honesty and integrity, self-confidence, cognitive ability, knowledge of the business, and charisma (which is discussed in Chapter 14).[10] Some people even believe that biological factors may play a role in leadership. Although it is too early to know whether these traits have validity from a leadership perspective, it does appear that a serious and scientific assessment of appropriate traits may further our understanding of the leadership phenomenon.

Similarly, other work has also started examining the role of gender and other diversity factors in leadership. For example, do women and men tend to lead differently? Some early research suggests that there are indeed fundamental differences in leadership as practiced by women and men.[11] Given that most leadership theories and research studies have focused on male leaders, developing a better understanding of how females lead is clearly an important next step. Similarly, are there differences in the leadership styles exhibited by individuals of different ethnicity? Or between younger and older leaders? Again, few answers exist for these questions, but researchers are beginning to address them.

The role of national culture may also be important. For instance, there may be important leadership differences in different cultures.[12] U.S. business leaders often talk about growth, profits, strategy, and competition. But Japanese leaders are more prone to stress group cohesiveness and identity. And Kim Sang Phi, chair of South Korea's Samsung group, is fond of talking about management morality and etiquette.[13] The "World View" box explores how leadership at Samsung has emulated both Japanese and American styles to bring the company to the forefront of the electronics industry. Thus, as they have with gender, ethnicity, and age, researchers need to focus attention on cultural differences in terms of leadership traits, roles, and behaviors.

Behavioral Approaches to Leadership

The behavioral approach to leadership tried to identify behaviors that differentiated effective leaders from non-leaders.

In the late 1940s, most researchers began to shift away from the trait approach and to look at leadership as an observable process or activity. The goal of the so-called **behavioral approach** was to determine what behaviors are associated with effective leadership.[14] The researchers assumed that the behaviors of effective leaders differed somehow from the behaviors of less effective leaders and that the behaviors of effective leaders would be the same across all situations. The behavioral approach to the study of leadership included the Michigan studies, the Ohio State studies, and the leadership grid.

"Well, it wasn't too many years ago that the dictatorial approach, the command-and-control management style, was accepted. Today, it's more about working through people, being more of a leader and empowering other executives on the team to carry out the mission."—Thomas Neff, leadership expert[15]

The Michigan leadership studies defined job-centered and employee-centered leadership as opposite ends of a single leadership dimension.

The Michigan Studies   The **Michigan leadership studies** were a program of research conducted at the University of Michigan.[16] The goal of this work was to determine the pattern of leadership behaviors that results in effective group performance. From interviews with supervisors and subordinates of high- and low-productivity groups in several organizations, the researchers collected and analyzed descriptions of supervisory behavior to determine how effective supervisors differed from ineffective ones. Two basic forms of leader behavior were identified—job-centered and employee-centered—as shown in the top portion of Figure 13.1.

Job-centered leader behavior involves paying close attention to the work of subordinates, explaining work procedures, and demonstrating a strong interest in performance.

The leader who exhibits **job-centered leader behavior** pays close attention to the work of subordinates, explains work procedures, and is mainly interested in performance. The leader's primary concern is efficient completion of the task. The leader who engages in **employee-centered leader behavior** attempts to build effective work groups with high performance goals. The leader's main concern is with high performance, but that is to be achieved by paying attention to the human aspects of the group. These two styles of leader behavior were presumed to be at opposite ends of a single dimension. Thus, the Michigan researchers suggested that any given leader could exhibit either job-centered or employee-centered

Employee-centered leader behavior involves attempting to build effective work groups with high performance goals.

WORLD VIEW

New Leadership Styles Propel Samsung Ahead

For decades the Japanese firms Fujitsu, Hitachi, Matsushita, NEC, Sony, and Toshiba have dominated the international electronics industry, but recently they have been suffering from slower sales and lower profits at home. A former "copycat" of the Japanese firms, Korean-based Samsung Electronics, is taking over their position, rapidly becoming Korea's first multinational powerhouse. "Five years ago, we had to buy chips from Sony or Matsushita, so we were always behind," says Chin Dae Je, head of Samsung's digital media division. "Now, we can be number one. There's no doubt in my mind."

Samsung is following the same path to success that the Japanese employed after World War II—imitating market leaders and perfecting their processes. The Japanese adopted practices from American manufacturing; now they find themselves emulated, and bettered, by companies from Pacific Rim rival nations Taiwan, Malaysia, Singapore, and Korea. Samsung's products already are the leaders in Russia and China, and the firm is now turning its attention to the largest market in the world: the United States. It is significant that Samsung CEO Yun John Yong speaks Japanese, having spent part of his career in Japan, and two of his three top executives were educated in the United States and are fluent in English.

How have Samsung managers led their company to the vanguard of the electronics industry? Heavy investments in R & D led to innovations, so Samsung now ranks fifth in the world in the number of patents it holds. The firm has adopted a Western-style corporate governance, with open books and non-Koreans on its board of directors. The most radical change, however, has occurred

"We used to benchmark [foreign firms] for the phone business. Now, we have nobody to benchmark against."
—*Lee Sang Chul, CEO of KT*

within the firm's culture, which has changed from a top-down, bureaucratic style to one that is aggressive, flexible, and results oriented. Yun believes in pay for performance and has even fired low-performing managers, both of which are highly unusual practices in Korea.

Samsung is not the only Korean firm following this strategy. Lee Sang Chul, CEO of KT, formerly Korea Telecom, says, "We used to benchmark BT (which is English), NTT (Japanese), and AT & T for the phone business. Now, we have nobody to benchmark against." As success follows success for Korean companies, will we soon see American companies "copycatting" them?

References: Brian Bremner, "Watch Out Japan, Korea Is Gaining," *Business Week*, May 9, 2002. www.businessweek.com on May 16, 2002; William J. Holstein, "Samsung's Golden Touch," *Fortune*, April 1, 2002, pp. 89–94. See www.fortune.com; Moon Ihlwan, "South Korea: High-Speed Profits Ahead," *Business Week*, March 18, 2002 (quotation). www.businessweek.com on May 16, 2002; Anthony Paul, "The Pyongyang Paradox," *Fortune*, May 28, 2001. www.fortune.com on May 16, 2002.

leader behavior, but not both at the same time. Moreover, they suggested that employee-centered leader behavior was more likely to result in effective group performance than was job-centered leader behavior.

The Ohio State leadership studies defined leader consideration and initiating-structure behaviors as independent dimensions of leadership.

Consideration behavior involves being concerned with subordinates' feelings and respecting subordinates' ideas.

The Ohio State Studies   The **Ohio State leadership studies** were conducted about the same time as the Michigan studies (in the late 1940s and early 1950s).[17] During this program of research, behavioral scientists at Ohio State University developed a questionnaire, which they administered in both military and industrial settings, to assess subordinates' perceptions of their leaders' behavior. The Ohio State studies identified several forms of leader behavior but tended to focus on the two most significant ones: consideration and initiating-structure.

When engaging in **consideration behavior,** the leader is concerned with the subordinates' feelings and respects subordinates' ideas. The leader-subordinate relationship is characterized by mutual trust, respect, and two-way communication. The

Leader behaviors have long played a fundamental role in various leadership models and theories. Moreover, certain behaviors are especially common in different approaches to leadership. One such behavior, variously termed employee-centered behavior, consideration behavior, or concern for people, obviously relates to how leaders treat their subordinates. But as Charlie Brown will no doubt learn from Lucy, the effectiveness of consideration behavior by the leader may be substantially diminished when others have to ask for it!

Reference: PEANUTS Reprinted by permission of United Feature Syndicate, Inc.

Initiating-structure behavior involves clearly defining the leader-subordinate roles so that subordinates know what is expected of them.

cartoon illustrates this form of behavior. When using **initiating-structure behavior,** on the other hand, the leader clearly defines the leader-subordinate roles so that subordinates know what is expected of them. The leader also establishes channels of communication and determines the methods for accomplishing the group's task.

Unlike the employee-centered and job-centered leader behaviors, consideration and initiating structure were not thought to be on the same continuum. Instead, as shown in the bottom portion of Figure 13.1, they were seen as independent dimensions of the leader's behavioral repertoire. As a result, a leader could exhibit high initiating-structure behavior and low consideration or low initiating-structure behavior and high consideration. A leader could also exhibit high or low levels of each behavior simultaneously. For example, a leader may clearly define subordinates' roles and expectations but exhibit little concern for their feelings. Alternatively, she or he may be concerned about subordinates' feelings but fail to define roles and expectations clearly. But the leader might also demonstrate concern for performance expectations and employee welfare simultaneously.

The Ohio State researchers also investigated the stability of leader behaviors over time. They found that a given individual's leadership pattern appeared to change little as long as the situation remained fairly constant.[18] Another topic they looked at was the combinations of leader behaviors that were related to effectiveness. At first, they believed that leaders who exhibit high levels of both behaviors would be most effective. An early study at International Harvester (now Navistar Corporation), however, found that employees of supervisors who ranked high on initiating-structure behavior were higher performers but also expressed lower levels of satisfaction. Conversely, employees of supervisors who ranked high on consideration had lower performance ratings but also had fewer absences from work.[19] Later research showed that these conclusions were misleading because the studies did not consider all the important variables. In other words, the situational context limits the extent to which consistent and uniform relationships exist between leader behaviors and subordinate responses. As a result, there are no simple explanations of what constitutes effective leader behavior because leader effectiveness varies from one situation to another.

The **Leadership Grid** evaluates leader behavior along two dimensions, concern for production and concern for people, and suggests that effective leadership styles include high levels of both behaviors.

The Leadership Grid   The **Leadership Grid** was developed as a framework for portraying types of leadership behavior and their various potential combinations.[20] Created

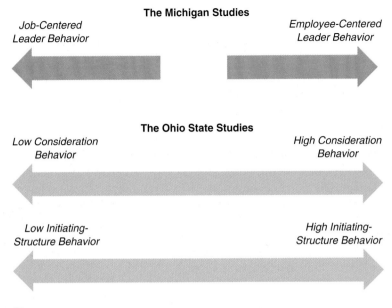

figure 13.1

Early Behavioral Approaches to Leadership

Two of the first behavioral approaches to leadership were the Michigan and Ohio State studies. The results of the Michigan studies suggested that there are two fundamental types of leader behavior, job-centered and employee-centered, which were presumed to be at opposite ends of a single continuum. The Ohio State studies also found two similar kinds of leadership behavior, "consideration" and "initiating-structure," but this research suggested that these two types of behavior were actually independent dimensions.

primarily as a consulting tool to apply the Ohio State findings, the grid consists of two dimensions. The first dimension is concern for production. A manager's concern for production is rated on a nine-point scale, on which 9 represents high concern and 1 indicates low concern. A manager who has high concern for production is task-oriented and focuses on getting results or accomplishing the mission. The second dimension is concern for people, also rated on a nine-point scale, with 9 for high and 1 for low. As might be expected, a manager who has a high concern for people avoids conflict and strives for friendly relations with subordinates.

These two dimensions are combined and integrated to form a nine-by-nine grid. The grid thus identifies an array of possible leader behavior combinations. The developers of the grid suggest that the 9, 9 combination of leadership behaviors is the most effective leadership style; that is, a manager who has a high concern for people and production simultaneously will be the most effective leader. This recommendation, although based on the grid developers' experiences as consultants to

firms like Gulf Oil (now a part of Chevron) and Exxon and on anecdotal evidence from managers who have used the grid, has been shown to be less than optimal in many situations.[21]

The Michigan, Ohio State, and grid behavioral models attracted considerable attention from managers and behavioral scientists. Unfortunately, later research on each model revealed significant weaknesses. For example, the models were not always supported by research and were even found to be ineffective in some settings.[22] The behavioral approaches were valuable in that they identified several fundamental leader behaviors that are still used in most leadership theories today. Moreover, they moved leadership research away from the narrow trait theory. The Michigan and Ohio State studies were exploratory in nature, and they have given researchers several fundamental insights into basic leadership processes. However, in trying to precisely specify a set of leader behaviors effective in all situations, as attempted by the Leadership Grid, the studies overlooked the enormous complexities of individual behavior in organizational settings.

In the end, their most basic shortcoming was that they failed to meet their primary goal—to identify universal leader-behavior and follower-response patterns and relationships. Managers and behavioral scientists thus realized that still different approaches were needed to accommodate the complexities of leadership. Consequently, they began to focus on contingency theories to better explain leadership and its consequences. These theories assume that appropriate leader behavior will vary across settings. Their focus is on better understanding how different situations call for different forms of leadership. As related at the beginning of this chapter, Andy Pearson at Tricon has clearly changed his behavior as a leader. The three major contingency theories are discussed next, beginning with the LPC theory.

The LPC Theory of Leadership

The LPC theory of leadership suggests that a leader's effectiveness depends on the situation.

F red Fiedler developed the **LPC theory of leadership.** The LPC theory attempts to explain and reconcile both the leader's personality and the complexities of the situation.[23] (This theory was originally called the "contingency theory of leadership." However, because this label has come to have generic connotations, new labels are being used to avoid confusion. "LPC" stands for "least-preferred coworker," a concept we explain later in this section.) The LPC theory contends that a leader's effectiveness depends on the situation and, as a result, some leaders may be effective in one situation or organization but not in another. The theory also explains why this discrepancy may occur and identifies leader-situation matches that should result in effective performance.

Task Versus Relationship Motivation

Fiedler and his associates maintain that leadership effectiveness depends on the match between the leader's personality and the situation. Fiedler devised special terms to describe a leader's basic personality traits in relation to leadership: "task motivation" versus "relationship motivation." He also conceptualized the situational context in terms of its favorableness for the leader, ranging from highly favorable to highly unfavorable.

The LPC theory suggests that what constitutes effective leadership is determined by the situation. These Native American elders, for example, have helped gain formal recognition for the Cowlitz tribe and have recruited over 2,000 members. The leadership style they used to accomplish this task was partially dictated by what they wanted to accomplish. Now, the leadership style needed to lead the tribe in its formative stages may be different. And finally, when the tribe becomes a mature and fully functional entity yet another style may be needed.

In some respects, the ideas of task and relationship motivation resemble the basic concepts identified in the behavioral approaches. Task motivation closely parallels job-centered and initiating-structure leader behavior, and relationship motivation is similar to employee-centered and consideration leader behavior. A major difference, however, is that Fiedler viewed task versus relationship motivation as being grounded in personality in a way that is basically constant for any given leader.

The least-preferred coworker (LPC) scale presumes to measure a leader's motivation.

The degree of task or relationship motivation in a given leader is measured by the **least-preferred coworker (LPC) scale**. The LPC instructions ask respondents (i.e., leaders) to think of all the persons with whom they have worked and to then select their least-preferred coworker. Respondents then describe this coworker by marking a series of sixteen scales anchored at each end by a positive or negative quality or attribute.[24] For example, three of the items Fiedler uses in the LPC are

Pleasant	8 7 6 5 4 3 2 1	Unpleasant
Inefficient	1 2 3 4 5 6 7 8	Efficient
Unfriendly	1 2 3 4 5 6 7 8	Friendly

The higher numbers on the scales are associated with a positive evaluation of the least-preferred coworker. (Note that the higher scale numbers are associated with the more favorable term and that some items reverse both the terms and the scale values. The latter feature forces the respondent to read the scales more carefully and to provide more valid answers.) Respondents who describe their least-preferred coworker in relatively positive terms receive a high LPC score whereas those who use relatively negative terms receive a low LPC score.

Fiedler assumed that these descriptions actually say more about the leader than about the least-preferred coworker. He believed, for example, that everyone's least preferred coworker is likely to be equally "unpleasant" and that differences in descriptions actually reflect differences in personality traits among the leaders responding to the LPC scale. Fiedler contended that high-LPC leaders are basically more concerned with interpersonal relations whereas low-LPC leaders are more concerned with task-relevant problems. Not surprisingly, controversy has always surrounded the LPC scale. Researchers have offered several interpretations of the LPC score, arguing that it may be an index of behavior, personality, or some other unknown factor. Indeed, the LPC measure—and its interpretation—have long been among the most debated aspects of this theory.

Situational Favorableness

Fiedler also identified three factors that determine the favorableness of the situation. In order of importance (from most to least important), these factors are leader-member relations, task structure, and leader position power.

Leader-member relations refers to the personal relationship that exists between subordinates and their leader. It is based on the extent to which subordinates trust, respect, and have confidence in their leader, and vice versa. A high degree of mutual trust, respect, and confidence obviously indicates good leader-member relations, and a low degree indicates poor leader-member relations.

Task structure is the second most important determinant of situational favorableness. A structured task is routine, simple, easily understood, and unambiguous. The LPC theory presumes that structured tasks are more favorable because the leader need not be closely involved in defining activities and can devote time to other matters. On the other hand, an unstructured task is one that is nonroutine, ambiguous, and complex. Fiedler argues that this task is more unfavorable because the leader must play a major role in guiding and directing the activities of subordinates.

Finally, *leader position power* is the power inherent in the leader's role itself. If the leader has considerable power to assign work, reward and punish employees, and recommend them for promotion, position power is high and favorable. If, however, the leader must have job assignments approved by someone else, does not control rewards and punishment, and has no voice in promotions, position power is low and unfavorable; that is, many decisions are beyond the leader's control.

Leader Motivation and Situational Favorableness   Fiedler and his associates conducted numerous studies examining the relationships among leader motivation, situational favorableness, and group performance. Table 13.2 summarizes the results of these studies.

To begin interpreting the results, let's first examine the situational favorableness dimensions shown in the table. The various combinations of these three dimensions result in eight different situations, as arrayed across the first three lines of the table. These situations in turn define a continuum ranging from very favorable to very unfavorable situations from the leader's perspective. Favorableness is noted in the fourth line of the table. For example, good relations, a structured task, and either high or low position power result in a very favorable situation for the leader. But poor relations, an unstructured task, and either high or low position power create very unfavorable conditions for the leader.

The table also identifies the leadership approach that is supposed to achieve high group performance in each of the eight situations. These linkages are shown in the bottom line of the table. A task-oriented leader is appropriate for very favorable as well as very unfavorable situations. For example, the LPC theory predicts that if leader-member relations are poor, the task is unstructured, and leader position power is low, a task-oriented leader will be effective. It also predicts that a task-oriented leader will be effective if leader-member relations are good, the task is structured, and leader position power is high. Finally, for situations of intermediate favorableness, the theory suggests that a person-oriented leader will be most likely to achieve high group performance.

Leader-Situation Match   What happens if a person-oriented leader faces a very favorable or very unfavorable situation, or a task-oriented leader faces a situation of intermediate favorableness? Fiedler considers these leader-situation combinations

table 13.2

The LPC Theory of Leadership

Leader-Member Relations	Good				Poor			
Task Structure	Structured		Unstructured		Structured		Unstructured	
Position Power	High	Low	High	Low	High	Low	High	Low
Situational Favorableness	Very favorable		Moderately favorable				Very unfavorable	
Recommended Leader Behavior	↓ Task-oriented behavior		↓ Person-oriented behavior				↓ Task-oriented behavior	

to be "mismatches." Recall that a basic premise of his theory is that leadership behavior is a personality trait. Thus, the mismatched leader cannot readily adapt to the situation and achieve effectiveness. Fiedler contends that when a leader's style and the situation do not match, the only available course of action is to change the situation through "job engineering."[25]

For example, Fiedler suggests that if a person-oriented leader ends up in a situation that is very unfavorable, the manager should attempt to improve matters by spending more time with subordinates to improve leader-member relations and by laying down rules and procedures to provide more task structure. Fiedler and his associates have also developed a widely used training program for supervisors on how to assess situational favorableness and to change the situation, if necessary, to achieve a better match.[26] Weyerhauser and Boeing are among the firms that have experimented with Fiedler's training program. Although not directly tied to the LPC theory, the "Working with Diversity" box provides an excellent example of a leader and situation at Kraft Foods that are very well matched.

Evaluation and Implications

The validity of Fiedler's LPC theory has been heatedly debated because of the inconsistency of the research results. Apparent shortcomings of the theory are that the LPC measure lacks validity, the theory is not always supported by research, and Fiedler's assumptions about the inflexibility of leader behavior are unrealistic.[27] The theory itself, however, does represent an important contribution because it returned the field to a study of the situation and explicitly considered the organizational context and its role in effective leadership.

The Path-Goal Theory of Leadership

Another important contingency approach to leadership is the path-goal theory. Developed jointly by Martin Evans and Robert House, the path-goal theory focuses on the situation and leader behaviors rather than on fixed traits of the leader.[28] In contrast to the LPC theory, the path-goal theory suggests that leaders can readily adapt to different situations.

Basic Premises

The path-goal theory has its roots in the expectancy theory of motivation discussed in Chapter 6. Recall that expectancy theory says that a person's attitudes and behaviors can be predicted from the degree to which the person believes job performance will lead to various outcomes (expectancy) and the value of those outcomes (valences) to the individual. The **path-goal theory of leadership** argues that subordinates are motivated by their leader to the extent that the behaviors of that leader influence their expectancies. In other words, the leader affects subordinates' performance by clarifying the behaviors (paths) that will lead to desired rewards (goals). Ideally, of course, getting a reward in an organization depends on effective performance. Path-goal theory also suggests that a leader may behave in different ways in different situations.

The path-goal theory of leadership suggests that effective leaders clarify the paths (behaviors) that will lead to desired rewards (goals).

Leader Behaviors   As Figure 13.2 shows, path-goal theory identifies four kinds of leader behavior: directive, supportive, participative, and achievement-oriented. With *directive leadership*, the leader lets subordinates know what is expected of them, gives specific guidance as to how to accomplish tasks, schedules work to be done, and

WORKING WITH DIVERSITY

▶ *It Takes One to Know One*

No one sells more groceries or markets as many "category killers" as Kraft Foods. The company's brands include Miracle Whip, Oreos, Kool-Aid, Oscar Mayer, Velveeta, Ritz, Jell-O, Maxwell House, Lunchables, Life Savers, Planter's, Nabisco, Post, and more. In an industry in which 80 percent of the products are purchased by married women with children, firms must understand the needs of the target customers—mothers. So it's no surprise that Kraft's newly appointed co-chief executive is Betsy Holden, a former fourth-grade teacher and suburban mom of two.

Holden taught elementary school while moonlighting as a toy developer for PlaySkool. She then became fascinated with marketing and left teaching to earn her M.B.A. at Northwestern University, graduating first in her class. Holden began working for General Foods (which merged with Kraft in 1989) as an assistant brand manager, working her way up the corporate ladder. In 2001, Holden assumed the co-CEO job with responsibility for North America while her co-CEO, Roger Deromedi, ran the international division.

Holden makes communication with customers a top priority. She meets face to face two days each month with managers of grocery chains, and her staff spends about one-half of their time with customers. One of Holden's competitors explains her success by saying, "Betsy understood that cooperation builds categories. And she was wildly cooperative." Regarding meetings with customers, Holden says, "We're there to listen. If we're not the best

vendor, we want to know who is." Kraft understands the changing needs of customers, as its range of new products demonstrates: Boca meat alternatives, convenient microwavable macaroni and cheese, prepackaged puddings and Jell-O, and trendy Altoids mints.

Kraft's commitment to women is reflected in its philan-

"Betsy understood that cooperation builds categories."
—A competitor of Kraft Foods, commenting on Kraft Co-CEO Betsy Holden

thropies—domestic abuse causes—and a top corporate team in which three of seven executives are female. However, the company's North American top executives include fifteen men and ten women whereas its international executives include just one female in a group of fourteen. Recent reports indicate that Kraft is having difficulties overseas, with only 27 percent of its revenues being generated abroad (compared with 50 percent for McDonald's or 80 percent for Coca-Cola). Perhaps the international division should take a lesson from Holden's operations book: If you want to market successfully, you'd better get close to your customers.

References: "About Kraft Foods," "History," "Kraft Cares," "Management Bios," Kraft Foods web site. www.kraft.com on May 25, 2002; "Key Facts," "Supermarket Facts," Food Marketing Institute web site. www.fmi.org on May 25, 2002; Brandon Copple, "Shelf Determination," *Forbes*, April 15, 2002, pp. 131-142 (quotation p. 140). See www.forbes.com; Julie Foster, "Can Kraft Be a Big Cheese Abroad?" *Business Week*, June 4, 2001. www.businessweek.com on May 25, 2002; "What's Cooking at Kraft," *Business Week*, June 4, 2001. www.businessweek.com on May 25, 2002.

maintains definitive standards of performance for subordinates. A leader exhibiting *supportive leadership* is friendly and shows concern for subordinates' status, well-being, and needs. With *participative leadership*, the leader consults with subordinates about issues and takes their suggestions into account before making a decision. Finally, *achievement-oriented leadership* involves setting challenging goals, expecting subordinates to perform at their highest level, and showing strong confidence that subordinates will put forth effort and accomplish the goals. Unlike the LPC theory, path-goal theory assumes that leaders can change their behavior and exhibit any or all of these leadership styles. The theory also predicts that the appropriate combination of leadership styles depends on situational factors.

Situational Factors   The path-goal theory proposes two types of situational factors that influence how leader behavior relates to subordinate satisfaction: the personal characteristics of the subordinates and the characteristics of the environment (see Figure 13.2).

The path-goal theory of leadership encompasses four kinds of leader behavior. Andrea Jung, Chair and CEO of Avon, uses each of these behaviors on a regular basis. For example, she occasionally uses directive behavior to set performance expectations and provide guidance. Jung also demonstrates supportive behavior through her care and interest in those she works with. She frequently uses participative leadership as well by soliciting input from other executives in the firm. Finally, she also uses achievement-oriented leadership in that she sets challenging goals and provides constant encouragement for everyone to work toward those goals.

Two important personal characteristics of subordinates are locus of control and perceived ability. Locus of control, discussed in Chapter 4, refers to the extent to which individuals believe that what happens to them results from their own behavior or from external causes. Research indicates that individuals who attribute outcomes to their own behavior may be more satisfied with a participative leader (since they feel their own efforts can make a difference) whereas individuals who attribute outcomes to external causes may respond more favorably to a directive leader (since they think their own actions are of little consequence). Perceived ability pertains to how people view their own ability with respect to the task. Employees who rate their own ability relatively high are less likely to feel a need for directive leadership (since they think they know how to do the job) whereas those who perceive their own ability to be relatively low may prefer directive leadership (since they think they need someone to show them how to do the job).

Important environmental characteristics are task structure, the formal authority system, and the primary work group. The path-goal theory proposes that leader behavior will motivate subordinates if it helps them cope with environmental uncertainty created by those characteristics. In some cases, however, certain forms of leadership will be redundant, decreasing subordinate satisfaction. For example, when task structure is high, directive leadership is less necessary and therefore less effective; similarly, if the work group gives the individual plenty of social support, a supportive leader will not be especially attractive. Thus, the extent to which leader behavior matches the people and environment in the situation is presumed to influence subordinates' motivation to perform.

For another example, consider the success of Barbara Samson, founder of Intermedia, a Florida telephone company. To get her idea from the drawing board into the business world, Samson had to use directive leadership to organize her employees. But she also had to use supportive leadership to help them get through the tough times during the early days of start-up. When she met with investors, she had to demonstrate achievement-oriented leadership to convey her goals and strategies. And as her business has grown, she has increasingly used participative leadership to spread decision-making authority throughout the firm.[29]

figure 13.2

The Path-Goal Theory of Leadership

The path-goal theory of leadership specifies four kinds of leader behavior: directive, supportive, participative, and achievement-oriented. Leaders are advised to vary their behaviors in response to such situational factors as personal characteristics of subordinates and environmental characteristics.

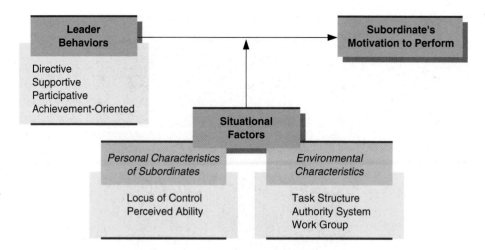

Evaluation and Implications

The path-goal theory was designed to provide a general framework for understanding how leader behavior and situational factors influence subordinate attitudes and behaviors. But the intention of the path-goal theorists was to stimulate research on the theory's major propositions, not to offer definitive answers. Researchers hoped that a more fully developed, formal theory of leadership would emerge from continued study. Further work actually has supported the theory's major predictions, but it has not validated the entire model. Moreover, many of the theory's predictions remain overly general and have not been fully refined and tested.

Vroom's Decision Tree Approach to Leadership

Vroom's decision tree approach to leadership attempts to prescribe how much participation subordinates should be allowed in making decisions.

The third major contemporary approach to leadership is **Vroom's decision tree approach.** The earliest version of this model was proposed by Victor Vroom and Philip Yetton and later revised and expanded by Vroom and Arthur Jago.[30] Most recently, Vroom has developed yet another refinement of the original model.[31] Like the path-goal theory, this approach attempts to prescribe a leadership style appropriate to a given situation. It also assumes that the same leader may display different leadership styles. But Vroom's approach concerns itself with only a single aspect of leader behavior: subordinate participation in decision making.

Basic Premises

Vroom's decision tree approach assumes that the degree to which subordinates should be encouraged to participate in decision making depends on the characteristics of the situation. In other words, no one decision-making process is best for all situations. After evaluating a variety of problem attributes (characteristics of the problem or decision), the leader determines an appropriate decision style that specifies the amount of subordinate participation.

"Wellington would spend hours every day meeting with his officers on strategy. He pulled the strings, but he didn't even carry a weapon."—Ralph Hayles, expert in military leadership[32]

Vroom's current formulation suggests that managers should use one of two different decision trees.[33] To do so, the manager first assesses the situation in terms of several factors. This assessment involves determining whether the given factor is "high" or "low" for the decision that is to be made. For instance, the first factor is decision significance. If the decision is extremely important and may have a major impact on the organization (i.e., choosing a location for a new plant), its significance is high. But if the decision is routine, and its consequences not terribly important (i.e., selecting a logo for the firm's softball team uniforms), its significance is low. This assessment guides the manager through the paths of the decision tree to a recommended course of action. One decision tree is to be used when the manager is primarily interested in making the decision on the most timely basis possible; the other is to be used when time is less critical, and the manager is interested in helping subordinates to improve and develop their own decision-making skills.

The two decision trees are shown in Figures 13.3 and 13.4. The problem attributes (situational factors) are arranged along the top of the decision tree. To use the model, the decision-maker starts at the left side of the diagram and assesses the first problem attribute (decision significance). The answer determines the path to the second node on the decision tree, where the next attribute (importance of commitment) is assessed. This process continues until a terminal node is reached. In this way, the manager identifies an effective decision-making style for the situation.

The various decision styles reflected at the ends of the tree branches represent different levels of subordinate participation that the manager should attempt to adopt in a given situation. The five styles are defined as follows:

Decide: The manager makes the decision alone and then announces or "sells" it to the group.

Vroom's Decision Tree approach to leadership suggests that leaders should vary the degree of participation they provide to subordinates in making decisions. In the wake of financial scandal after financial scandal, some top managers have begun to systematically increase communication and participation throughout the ranks of their organization. For instance, Steve Odland (standing) is the CEO of AutoZone. He now insists that all top managers fully participate in discussions and decisions regarding the firm's finances. Indeed, he requires that each top manager certify the accuracy of his or her unit's financial performance before the results are submitted to him.

Decision Significance	Importance of Commitment	Leader Expertise	Likelihood of Commitment	Group Support	Group Expertise	Team Competence	
H	H	H	H	-	-	-	Decide
			L	H	H	H	Delegate
						L	Consult (Group)
					L	-	Consult (Group)
				L	-	-	Consult (Group)
		L	H	H	H	H	Facilitate
						L	Consult (Individually)
					L	-	Consult (Individually)
				L	-	-	Consult (Individually)
			L	H	H	H	Facilitate
						L	Consult (Group)
					L	-	Consult (Group)
				L	-	-	Consult (Group)
	L	H	-	-	-	-	Decide
		L	-	H	H	H	Facilitate
						L	Consult (Individually)
					L	-	Consult (Individually)
				L	-	-	Consult (Individually)
L	H	-	H	-	-	-	Decide
			L	-	-	H	Delegate
						L	Facilitate
	L	-	-	-	-	-	Decide

(Left column spanning all rows: PROBLEM STATEMENT)

figure 13.3

Vroom's Time-Driven Decision Tree

This matrix is recommended for situations in which time is of the highest importance in making a decision. The matrix operates like a funnel. You start at the left with a specific decision problem in mind. The column headings denote situational factors that may or may not be present in that problem. You progress by selecting High or Low (H or L) for each relevant situational factor. Proceed down from the funnel, judging only those situational factors for which a judgment is called for, until you reach the recommended process.

Reference: Victor H. Vroom's Time-Driven Model from *A Model of Leadership Style,* copyright 1998.

	Decision Significance	Importance of Commitment	Leader Expertise	Likelihood of Commitment	Group Support	Group Expertise	Team Competence	
P R O B L E M S T A T E M E N T	H	H	-	H	H	H	H	Decide
							L	Facilitate
						L	-	Consult (Group)
					L	-	-	Consult (Group)
				L	H	H	H	Delegate
							L	Facilitate
						L	-	Facilitate
					L	-	-	Consult (Group)
		L	-	-	H	H	H	Delegate
							L	Facilitate
						L	-	Consult (Group)
					L	-	-	Consult (Group)
	L	H	-	H	-	-	-	Decide
				L	-	-	-	Delegate
		L	-	-	-	-	-	Decide

figure 13.4

Vroom's Development-Driven Decision Tree

This matrix is to be used when the leader is more interested in developing employees than in making the decision as quickly as possible. Just as with the time-driven tree shown in Figure 13.3, the leader assesses up to seven situational factors. These factors, in turn, funnel the leader to a recommended process for making the decision.

Reference: Victor H. Vroom's Development-Driven Model from *A Model of Leadership Style,* copyright 1998.

Delegate: The manager allows the group to define for itself the exact nature and parameters of the problem and to then develop a solution.

Consult (Individually): The manager presents the program to group members individually, obtains their suggestions, and then makes the decision.

Consult (Group): The manager presents the problem to group members at a meeting, gets their suggestions, and then makes the decision.

Facilitate: The manager presents the problem to the group at a meeting, defines the problem and its boundaries, and then facilitates group member discussion as members make the decision.

Vroom's decision tree approach represents a very focused but quite complex perspective on leadership. To compensate for this difficulty, Vroom has developed elaborate expert system software to help managers assess a situation accurately and quickly and then make an appropriate decision regarding employee participation. Many firms, including Halliburton Company, Litton Industries, and Borland International, have provided their managers with training in how to use the various versions of this model.

Evaluation and Implications

Because Vroom's current approach is relatively new, it has not been fully scientifically tested. The original model and its subsequent refinement, however, attracted a great deal of attention and were generally supported by research.[34] For example, there is some support for the idea that individuals who make decisions consistent with the predictions of the model are more effective than those who make decisions inconsistent with it. The model therefore appears to be a tool that managers can apply with some confidence in deciding how much subordinates should participate in the decision-making process.

Other Contemporary Approaches to Leadership

Because leadership is such an important area, managers and researchers continue to study it. As a result, new ideas, theories, and perspectives are continuously being developed. Two of the better known are the LMX model and the Hersey and Blanchard theory.

The Leader-Member Exchange Model

The leader-member exchange (LMX) model of leadership stresses the fact that leaders develop unique working relationships with each of their subordinates.

The **leader-member exchange model (LMX)** of leadership, conceived by George Graen and Fred Dansereau, stresses the importance of variable relationships between supervisors and each of their subordinates.[35] Each superior-subordinate pair is referred to as a "vertical dyad." The model differs from earlier approaches in that it focuses on the differential relationship leaders often establish with different subordinates. Figure 13.5 shows the basic concepts of the leader-member exchange theory.

figure 13.5

The Leader-Member Exchange (LMX) Model

The LMX model suggests that leaders form unique independent relationships with each of their subordinates. As illustrated here, a key factor in the nature of this relationship is whether the individual subordinate is in the leader's out-group or in-group.

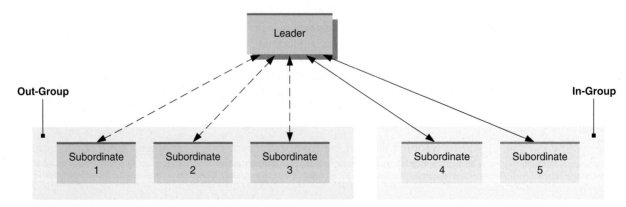

The model suggests that supervisors establish a special relationship with a small number of trusted subordinates referred to as the in-group. The in-group usually receives special duties requiring responsibility and autonomy; they may also receive special privileges. Subordinates who are not a part of this group are called the out-group, and they receive less of the supervisor's time and attention. Note in the figure that the leader has a dyadic, or one-to-one, relationship with each of the five subordinates.

Early in his or her interaction with a given subordinate, the supervisor initiates either an in-group or out-group relationship. It is not clear how a leader selects members of the in-group, but the decision may be based on personal compatibility and subordinates' competence. Research has confirmed the existence of in-groups and out-groups. In addition, studies generally have found that in-group members have a higher level of performance and satisfaction than out-group members.[36]

The Hersey and Blanchard Model

The Hersey and Blanchard model of leadership identifies different combinations of leadership presumed to work best with different levels of readiness on the part of followers.

Another popular perspective among practicing managers is the **Hersey and Blanchard model.** Like the grid discussed earlier, this model was developed as a consulting tool. The Hersey and Blanchard model is based on the notion that appropriate leader behavior depends on the readiness of the leader's followers.[37] In this instance, readiness refers to the subordinate's degree of motivation, competence, experience, and interest in accepting responsibility. Figure 13.6 shows the basic model.

The figure suggests that as the readiness of followers improves, the leader's basic style should also change. When subordinate readiness is low, for example, the leader should rely on a "telling" style by providing direction and defining roles. When low to moderate readiness exists, the leader should use a "selling" style by offering direction and role definition accompanied by explanation and information. In a case of moderate-to-high follower readiness, the leader should use a "participating" style, allowing followers to share in decision making. Finally, when follower readiness is high, the leader is advised to use a "delegating" style by allowing followers to work independently with little or no overseeing.

figure 13.6

The Hersey and Blanchard Theory of Leadership

The Hersey and Blanchard theory suggests that leader behaviors should vary in response to the readiness of followers. This figure shows the nature of this variation. The curved line suggests that relationship leader behavior should start low, gradually increase, but then decrease again as follower readiness increases. But task behavior, shown by the straight line, should start high when followers lack readiness and then continuously diminish as they gain readiness.

Reference: The Situational Leadership Model is the registered trademark of the Center for Leadership Studies, Escondido, CA. Excerpt from P. Hersey, *Management Organizational Behavior Utilizing Human Resources,* 3rd ed., 1977, p. 165.

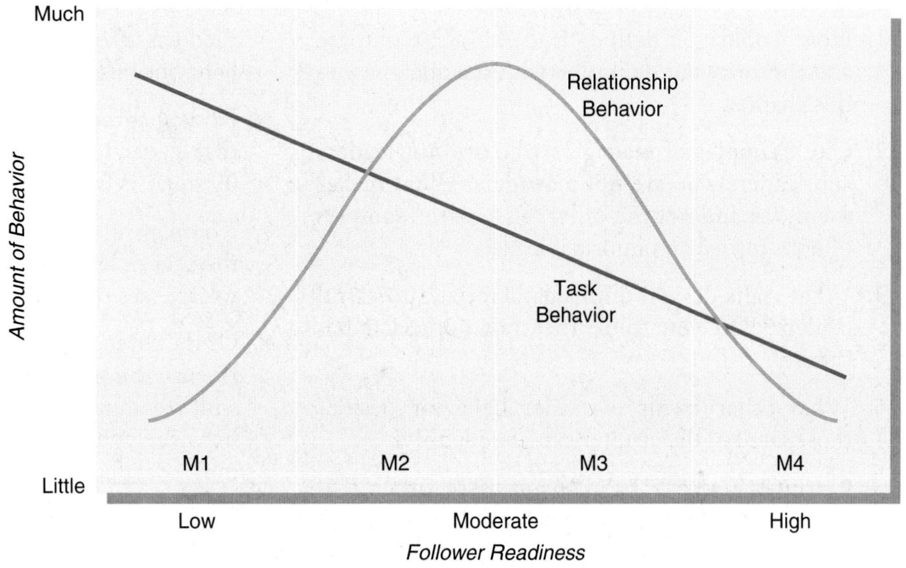

Synopsis

Leadership is both a process and a property. Leadership as a process is the use of noncoercive influence to direct and coordinate the activities of group members to meet goals. As a property, leadership is the set of characteristics attributed to those who are perceived to use such influence successfully. Leadership and management are related but distinct phenomena.

Early leadership research primarily attempted to identify important traits and behaviors of leaders. The Michigan and Ohio State studies each identified two kinds of leader behavior, one focusing on job factors, the other on people factors. The Michigan studies viewed these behaviors as points on a single continuum whereas the Ohio State studies suggested that they were separate dimensions. The Leadership Grid suggests that the most effective leaders are those who have a high concern for both people and production.

Newer contingency theories of leadership attempt to identify appropriate leadership styles on the basis of the situation. Fiedler's LPC theory states that leadership effectiveness depends on a match between the leader's style (viewed as a trait of the leader) and the favorableness of the situation. Situation favorableness, in turn, is determined by task structure, leader-member relations, and leader position power. Leader behavior is presumed to reflect a constant personality trait and therefore cannot easily be changed.

The path-goal theory focuses on appropriate leader behavior for various situations. The path-goal theory suggests that directive, supportive, participative, or achievement-oriented leader behavior may be appropriate, depending on the personal characteristics of subordinates and the characteristics of the environment. Unlike the LPC theory, this view presumes that leaders can alter their behavior to best fit the situation.

Vroom's decision tree approach suggests appropriate decision-making styles based on situation characteristics. This approach focuses on deciding how much subordinates should participate in the decision-making process. Managers assess situational attributes and follow a series of paths through a decision tree that subsequently prescribes for them how they should make a particular decision.

Two recent perspectives that are not rooted in traditional leadership theories are the leader-member exchange theory and the Hersey and Blanchard model. The leader-member exchange model focuses on specific relationships between a leader and individual subordinates. The Hersey and Blanchard model acknowledges that leader behavior toward a particular group needs to change as a function of the readiness of the followers.

Discussion Questions

1. How would you define "leadership"? Compare and contrast your definition with the one given in this chapter.

2. Cite examples of managers who are not leaders and leaders who are not managers. What makes them one and not the other? Also, cite examples of both formal and informal leaders.

3. What traits do you think characterize successful leaders? Do you think the trait approach has validity?

4. What other forms of leader behavior besides those cited in the chapter can you identify?

5. Critique Fiedler's LPC theory. Are other elements of the situation important? Do you think

Fiedler's assertion about the inflexibility of leader behavior makes sense? Why or why not?

6. Do you agree or disagree with Fiedler's assertion that leadership motivation is basically a personality trait? Why?

7. Compare and contrast the LPC and path-goal theories of leadership. What are the strengths and weaknesses of each?

8. Of the three major leadership theories—the LPC theory, the path-goal theory, and Vroom's decision tree approach—which is the most comprehensive? Which is the narrowest? Which has the most practical value?

9. How realistic do you think it is for managers to attempt to use Vroom's decision tree approach as prescribed? Explain.

10. Which of the two contemporary theories of leadership do you believe holds the most promise? Why?

11. Could either of the two contemporary perspectives be integrated with any of the three major theories of leadership? If so, how?

Organizational Behavior Case for Discussion

How Do You Manage Magic?

According to science fiction writer Arthur C. Clarke, "Any significantly advanced technology is indistinguishable from magic." This statement aptly describes much of biotechnology. Manufacturing biotech pharmaceuticals is a complex, technical, and expensive process, with millions of pages of data, daily costs of $1 million, and an 80 percent failure rate. The entire process of getting a new product to market takes ten to twelve years, and there are numerous hurdles that must be cleared along the way. The challenge for biotech managers, then, is how to manage complex processes as well as how to lead workers who are more knowledgeable and highly educated than their bosses.

The process begins with a test tube of cells being injected with a human gene. The gene creates a naturally occurring compound in the human body (interferon is one), but these cells have now been altered to make only that compound. The cells then reproduce and are moved into increasingly larger containers until the volume of the fluid is about 2,000 liters. The fluid is purified, yielding two liters of concentrated drug. All told, the procedure takes about five weeks, and if the batch has problems, they won't be discovered until the end. In spite of facilities so clean that they are more sterile than hospital operating rooms, bad batches can occur. The compounds are hundreds of times more complex than traditional drugs. For example, aspirin has a molecular weight (a crude measure of a compound's complexity) of about 180; biotech's average is 25,000.

The scientists who develop and manipulate this complicated process have M.D.s or Ph.D.s in subjects such as analytical chemistry, microbiology, or pharmacology. Biogen CEO James C. Mullen has a B.S. in chemical engineering and an M.B.A., has held engineering positions at pharmaceutical firms since 1980, and is no intellectual lightweight, yet it's impossible for anyone to fully understand the firm's variety of specialized disciplines. Michael Gilman, Biogen's senior vice president of research, himself a research scientist, says, "I am completely ignorant about three-quarters of the stuff that goes on. And my colleagues on the senior management team? They are 98 percent ignorant."

Mullen is the right kind of person for the top job—open to debate, eager for input, yet decisive and tough-minded. He relies on objective data, asking, "Is this a fact, an opinion, or a guess?" "We're often making decisions in uncertainty," Mullen asserts. "If the organization is running correctly, the only decisions that get to my desk are the ones with high uncertainty." One development team couldn't answer Mullen's questions. Mullen says, "I was asking questions more from a commercial or a customer's point of view. I kept meeting resistance. Really, it was an attitude problem." Finally, in exasperation, Mullen demanded to see the raw data and analyzed it himself, finding trends the experts hadn't spotted. Mullen uses that experience as a lesson in how *not* to lead. He explains, "That group had the wrong values for this company. They no longer work at Biogen."

Another challenge is to focus on the end result while not losing track of the details. One team proposed a 180-day timetable for completing their FDA application; Mullen insisted it could be done in ninety. According to Mullen, "Sometimes, you get more creativity when you're in a box than when you can do anything. In really difficult situations, sometimes you get the most interesting thinking." After Mullen pointed out to the scientists that an extra ninety days of drug sales might be worth $125 million, they completed the application in ninety-eight days. The ten-year development process is also a target. Mullen says, "People don't relate to ten-year product cycles. Half the people here haven't even worked for ten years. You have to break the time frames down so [that] a person can have an impact and see the impact."

Mullen wants more emphasis on the bottom line without sacrificing innovation. The CEO focuses intently on one thing at a time; he doesn't believe in multitasking. When teams are undisciplined, he ends the meeting by stating, "You aren't prepared. Call me when you're ready." Mullen reduced the number of people reporting to him from fifteen to nine to increase accountability. "The campfire culture doesn't work here anymore, with people sitting around telling each other what's going on," maintains Mullen, who is changing Biogen's culture. "We need to demand results."

Biogen's web site's statement of corporate values claims, "Biogen's success is based on its people. Everyone here is a leader. The core of leadership is integrity and courage. . . . These shared values describe how we aspire to lead and work together." Mullen's leadership at Biogen is moving the firm toward the accomplishment of that vision.

"If the organization is running correctly, the only decisions that get to my desk are the ones with high uncertainty." — James C. Mullen, CEO of Biogen

References: "Career Opportunities," "Our History," "Vision, Mission, Values," Biogen web site. www.biogen.com on May 17, 2002; David Shook, "Biogen Could Use This Shot in the Arm," *Business Week*, May 16, 2002. www.businessweek.com on May 17, 2002; Catherine Arnst, "The Tech Outlook: Biotech," *Business Week*, March 25, 2002. www.businessweek.com on May 17, 2002; Charles Fishman, "Isolating the Leadership Gene," *Fast Company*, March 2002, pp. 83–90 (quotation pp. 86–87). See www.fastcompany.com; Julie Creswell, "Investor's Guide 2000: The Next Big Things," *Fortune*, December 20, 1999. www.fortune.com on May 17, 2002.

Case Questions

1. In what ways is Mullen acting as a manager? In what ways is he acting as a leader? (Hint: For a good summary of the differences, see Table 13.1, "Distinctions Between Management and Leadership.")

2. Answer these questions based on Fielder's LPC theory. Does Mullen seem to be motivated more by tasks or relationships? Is the situation at Biogen more favorable or unfavorable? Considering the match or mismatch between leader motivation and situation favorableness, what outcomes would Fiedler predict?

3. Using the path-goal theory of leadership, tell whether you think Mullen is using the appropriate kind of leader behavior. Explain why or why not.

Experiencing Organizational Behavior

Understanding Successful and Unsuccessful Leadership

Purpose: This exercise will help you better understand the behaviors of successful and unsuccessful leaders.

Format: You will be asked to identify contemporary examples of successful and unsuccessful leaders and then to describe how these leaders differ.

Procedure:
1. Working alone, each student should list the names of ten people he or she thinks of as leaders in public life. Note that the names should not necessarily be confined to "good" leaders but instead should also identify "strong" leaders.

2. Next, students should form small groups and compare their lists. This comparison should focus on common and unique names as well as on the kinds of individuals listed (i.e., male or female, contemporary or historical, business or nonbusiness, and so on).

3. From all the lists, choose two leaders whom most people would consider very successful and two who would be deemed unsuccessful.

4. Identify similarities and differences between the two successful leaders and between the two unsuccessful leaders.

5. Relate the successes and failures to at least one theory or perspective discussed in the chapter.

6. Select one group member to report your findings to the rest of the class.

Follow-up Questions

1. What role does luck play in leadership?

2. Are there factors about the leaders you researched that might have predicted their success or failure before they achieved leadership roles?

3. What are some criteria of successful leadership?

Self-Assessment Exercise

Applying Vroom's Decision Tree Approach

This skillbuilder will help you better understand your own leadership style regarding employee participation in decision making. Mentally play the role described in the following scenario, then make the comparisons suggested at the end of the exercise.

You are the southwestern United States branch manager of an international manufacturing and sales organization. The firm's management team is looking for ways to increase efficiency. As one part of this effort, the company recently installed an integrated computer network linking sales representatives, customer service employees, and other sales support staff. Sales were supposed to increase and sales expenses to drop as a result.

However, exactly the opposite has occurred: Sales have dropped a bit, and expenses are up. You have personally inspected the new system and believe the hardware is fine. However, you believe the software linking the various computers is less than ideal.

The subordinates you have quizzed about the system, on the other hand, think the entire system is fine. They attribute the problems to a number of factors, including inadequate training in how to use the system, a lack of incentive for using it, and generally poor morale. Whatever the reasons given, each worker queried had strong feelings about the issue.

Your boss has just called you and expressed concern about the problems. He has indicated that he has confidence in your ability to solve the problem and will leave it in your hands. However, he wants a report on how you plan to proceed within one week.

First, think of how much participation you would normally be inclined to allow your subordinates in making this decision. Next, apply Vroom's decision tree approach to the problem and see what it suggests regarding the optimal level of participation. Compare your normal approach with the recommended solution.

OB Online

1. Using your favorite search engine, do an Internet search using simply the word "leadership." How many sites were identified? What conclusions can you draw based on this result?
2. Identify a historical figure whom you consider a highly effective leader. Use the Internet to find two or three sites that specifically address this individual as a leader.
3. Repeat the previous exercise for a contemporary figure.
4. Describe how a web site might be created that would allow managers to input their situation and, using Vroom's tree diagram model, get advice on how much participation to allow their subordinates in making a decision. How popular do you think such a site would be? How much do you think managers might be willing to pay to use it?

Building Managerial Skills

Exercise Overview: Conceptual skills refer to the manager's ability to think in the abstract. This exercise will enable you to apply your conceptual skills to better understanding the distinction between leadership and management.

Exercise Task: First, identify someone who currently occupies a management and/or leadership position. This individual can be a manager in a large business, the owner of a small business, the president of a campus organization, or any other similar kind of position. Next, interview this individual and ask them the following questions:

1. Name three recent tasks or activities that were primarily management in nature, requiring little or no leadership.

2. Name three recent tasks or activities that were primarily leadership in nature, requiring little or no management.

3. Do you spend most of the time working as a manager or a leader?

4. How easy or difficult is it to differentiate activities on the basis of them being management versus leadership?

Finally, after you have completed the interview break up into small groups with your classmates and discuss your results. What have you learned about leadership from this activity?

14 Leadership and Influence Processes

Management Preview

▶ As we learned in Chapter 13, leadership is a powerful, complex, and amorphous concept. This chapter explores many of the skills and personal resources that affect leaders and leadership. We first revisit the role of influence in leadership. We then introduce and discuss two contemporary influence-based perspectives on leadership, transformational leadership and charismatic leadership. Next, we discuss various substitutes for leadership that may exist in organizations. We then describe power and political behavior in organizations, influence-based phenomena that often involve leadership. Finally, we introduce and explore impression management, a related but distinct concept. First, though, we discuss the challenges facing some of today's newest business leaders.

▼ ▼ ▼

The twenty-first century has thus far been quite challenging for corporate leaders, especially so for new leaders, who must learn to lead while facing a very tough business environment. ABC Entertainment; Kinko's, Inc.; and Southwest Airlines are among the major businesses whose new CEOs have had to weather the current business climate.

Susan Lyne, president of ABC Entertainment, assumes responsibility for the network's television programming. She first worked in print publishing—the *Village Voice*, *Premiere*—and later managed ABC's TV miniseries division. Her top priority is "getting the younger creative people at the network to feel comfortable speaking up." Lyne wants to change the television giant, which she says is "quick to blame and slow to celebrate." Also on her agenda are increasing managers' entrepreneurial spirit and focusing on unfilled market niches when choosing new shows.

When entrepreneur-turned-CEO Gary Kusin became leader of Kinko's, he knew that the store employees had the best information about the state of the firm. He visited with 2,500 associates, finding that business customers were demanding more services, more technology, and closer working partnerships. He spent time listening and learning about his new firm, but he also brought renewed attention to efficiency and costs. He says, "As far as running a tight operation is concerned, it's always good to play very defensively. When things are good, people become lax. We've taken this opportunity to get buttoned down. Then, even if the economy lifts[,] . . . we will not lose that focus."

"Cutting jobs should be the last thing a company does rather than the first thing."
—James Parker, CEO, Southwest Airlines

Southwest's James Parker has been with the airline since 1986, assuming the top position when Herb Kelleher stepped down. Three months after he became chief executive, the events of September 11 devastated airlines. Unlike most of his competitors, Parker decided not to lay off any workers. He explains, "We have a lot of people who worked hard for more than thirty years so that they can have job security in hard times. . . . Cutting jobs should be the last thing a company does rather than the first thing." Parker cut costs elsewhere, such as by delaying aircraft purchases, and spent time reassuring employees.

The job of CEO is ever varied, requiring leaders to utilize their skills with both people and processes. Leaders need to build on their own strengths, but they also need to be adaptable in order to face the challenges in a variety of situations.

References: Alison Overholt, "New Leaders, New Agendas," *Fast Company*, May 2002, pp. 52–62 (quotation p. 62). See www.fastcompany.com; Geoffrey Colvin, "Who's Smiling Through This Recession?" *Business Week*, October 26, 2001. www.businessweek.com on May 16, 2002; Ron Grover, "ABC's Next Hit Could Co-Star the Internet," *Business Week*, March 26, 2001. www.businessweek.com on May 16, 2002.

The leaders just described are dealing with one of the most significant challenges any leader can face—the need to transform an organization from one thing into something different. In order to have any chance for success, they have to rely on power and political processes to facilitate key changes. In her or his own way, each is also attempting to influence the organization in new and profound ways. And influence, as we will see, is the foundation of effective leadership.

Leadership as Influence

Recall that in Chapter 13 we defined leadership (from a process perspective) as the use of noncoercive influence to direct and coordinate the activities of group members to meet goals. We then described a number of leadership models and theories based variously on leadership traits, behaviors, and contingencies. Unfortunately, most of these models and theories essentially ignore the influence component of leadership. That is, they tend to focus on the characteristics of the leader (traits, behaviors, or both) and the responses from followers (satisfaction, performance, or both, for instance) with little regard for how the leader actually exercises influence in an effort to bring about the desired responses from followers.

But influence should actually be seen as the cornerstone of the process. Regardless of the leader's traits or behaviors, leadership only matters if influence actually occurs. That is, a person's effectiveness in affecting the behavior of others

Influence, the ability to influence the perceptions, attitudes, or behaviors of others, is a fundamental cornerstone of leadership. Childhood friends Rameck Hunt, Sampson Davis, and George Jenkins vowed to defy the limitations of their inner city upbringings and become doctors together. Throughout the rigors of college and medical school the friends pushed each other to do their best. And there is little doubt in any of their minds that their mutual influence was the catalyst for each of them to succeed. Now they do their best to exert that same positive influence on others who face similar challenges.

through influence is the ultimate determinant of whether she or he is really a leader. No one can truly be a leader without the ability to influence others. And if someone does have the ability to influence others, he or she clearly has the potential to become a leader.

Influence can be defined as the ability to affect the perceptions, attitudes, or behaviors of others.[1] If a person can make another person recognize that her working conditions are more hazardous than she currently believes them to be (change in perceptions), influence has occurred. Likewise, if an individual can convince someone else that the organization is a much better place to work than he currently believes it to be (change in attitude), influence has occurred. And if someone can get others to work harder or to file a grievance against their boss (change in behavior), influence has occurred.[2] Note, too, that influence can be used in ways that are beneficial or harmful. Someone can be influenced to help clean up a city park on the weekend as part of a community service program, for example, or be influenced to use or sell drugs.

"In a network, all you have is influence. That's all you've got. . . . In a hierarchy the CEO is always CEO, but in networks leadership is always shifting."—Jessica Lipnack, communications consultant[3]

Influence-Based Approaches to Leadership

Influence is the ability to affect the perceptions, attitudes, or behaviors of others.

Influence has become a more significant component of some leadership models and concepts in recent years.[4] The two contemporary approaches to leadership discussed in this section, for example, are each tied directly or indirectly to influence. These approaches are transformational leadership and charismatic leadership.

Transformational Leadership

Transformational leadership, a relative newcomer to the leadership literature, focuses on the basic distinction between leading for change and leading for stability.[5] According to this viewpoint, much of what a leader does occurs in the course of normal, routine work related transactions—assigning work, evaluating performance, making decisions, and so forth. Occasionally, however, the leader has to initiate and manage major change, such as managing a merger, creating a work group, or defining the organization's culture. The first set of issues involves transactional leadership whereas the second entails transformational leadership.[6]

Recall from Chapter 13 the distinction between management and leadership. *Transactional leadership* is essentially the same as management in that it involves routine, regimented activities. Closer to the general notion of leadership, however, is **transformational leadership,** the set of abilities that allows the leader to recognize the need for change, to create a vision to guide that change, and to execute the change effectively. Only a leader with tremendous influence can hope to perform these functions successfully. Some experts believe that change is such a vital organizational function that even successful firms need to change regularly to avoid complacency and stagnation; accordingly, leadership for change is also important.[7]

Moreover, some leaders can adopt either transformational or transactional perspectives, depending on their circumstances. Others are able to do one or the other, but not both. The first CEO of Compaq Computer, Ron Canion, was clearly an excellent transactional leader. He built the firm from a single new idea and managed it efficiently and profitably for several years. But the environment changed to the point that Compaq needed to change as well, and Canion was apparently unable to recognize the need for change, to lead the firm through those changes, or both. His replacement, Eckhard Pfeiffer, apparently excelled at transformational leadership as he led the firm through several very successful new initiatives and transformations. But when this work was done and Compaq needed to refocus on efficient and effective operations best directed by a transactional leader, Pfeiffer faltered, and he too was replaced. The new CEO, Michael Capellas, then successfully negotiated a merger for Compaq with Hewlett-Packard.

Charismatic Leadership

Perspective based on charismatic leadership, like the trait theories discussed in Chapter 13, assume that charisma is an individual characteristic of the leader. **Charisma** is a form of interpersonal attraction that inspires support and acceptance. **Charismatic leadership** is accordingly a type of influence based on the leader's personal charisma. All else being equal, then, someone with charisma is more likely to be able to influence others than someone without charisma. For example, a highly charismatic supervisor will be more successful in influencing subordinate behavior than a supervisor who lacks charisma. Thus, influence is again a fundamental element of this perspective.[8]

"What I learned as a leader is that you don't [mess with] people under hostile circumstances. You tell them the truth."—Robert Swan, explorer and acknowledged charismatic leader[9]

Robert House first proposed a theory of charismatic leadership based on research findings from a variety of social science disciplines.[10] His theory suggests that charismatic leaders are likely to have a lot of self-confidence, firm confidence in their beliefs and ideals, and a strong need to influence people. They also tend to communicate high expectations about follower performance and to express confidence in their followers. Gordon Bethune, CEO of Continental Airlines, is an excellent example of a charismatic leader. Bethune possesses a unique combina-

Transformational leadership is the set of abilities that allows the leader to recognize the need for change, to create a vision to guide that change, and to execute that change effectively.

Charisma is a form of interpersonal attraction that inspires support and acceptance from others.

Charismatic leadership is a type of influence based on the leader's personal charisma.

Charismatic leadership is a type of influence based on an individual's personal charisma. Evangelist Franklin Graham, son of famed Reverend Billy Graham, is clearly a charismatic leader. His crusades and revival meetings attract standing room crowds, and people leave them feeling that they have heard a master orator. Graham has the ability to inspire support and win acceptance of his ideas and energizes those who hear him.

tion of executive skill, honesty, and playfulness. These qualities have attracted a group of followers at Continental who are willing to follow his lead without question and to dedicate themselves to carrying out his decisions and policies with unceasing passion.[11]

Figure 14.1 portrays the three elements of charismatic leadership in organizations that most experts acknowledge today.[12] First, the leader needs to be able to envision the future, to set high expectations, and to model behaviors consistent with meeting those expectations. Next, the charismatic leader must be able to energize others by demonstrating personal excitement, personal confidence, and patterns of success. Finally, the charismatic leader enables others by supporting them, empathizing with them, and expressing confidence in them.[13]

Charismatic leadership ideas are quite popular among managers today and are the subject of numerous books and articles. Unfortunately, few studies have specifically attempted to test the meaning and impact of charismatic leadership. Lingering ethical concerns about charismatic leadership also trouble some people. They stem from the fact that some charismatic leaders inspire such blind faith in their followers that they may engage in inappropriate, unethical, or even illegal behaviors just because the leader instructed them to do so. Taking over a leadership role

figure 14.1

The Charismatic Leader

The charismatic leader is characterized by three fundamental attributes. As illustrated here, these are behaviors resulting in envisioning, energizing, and enabling. Charismatic leaders can be a powerful force in any organizational setting.

Reference: David A. Nadler and Michael L. Tushman, "Beyond the Charismatic Leader: Leadership and Organizational Change," *California Management Review*, Winter 1990, pp. 70–97.

The Charismatic Leader		
Envisioning	*Energizing*	*Enabling*
Articulating a compelling vision Setting high expectations Modeling consistent behaviors	Demonstrating personal excitement Expressing personal confidence Seeking, finding, and using success	Expressing personal support Empathizing Expressing confidence in people

MASTERING CHANGE

▶ Inheriting the Family Business at Tyson

When John Tyson, nearly fifty years old, was named CEO of family-owned Tyson Foods, he faced a demanding transition. "I don't think many people have a whole lot of confidence in John," a former senior manager says. "He's always just been daddy's kid." "Daddy" is Don Tyson, whose astute decisions, such as the development of prepackaged convenience products, took the company from being a regional firm to being the largest poultry supplier in the world. Under Don's leadership, the chicken industry grew explosively, with individual consumption growing from 9 pounds per person in 1952 to 78 pounds in 2000.

While living up to his father's legacy, John Tyson also faces two additional challenges. The first is reversing the company's declining profitability brought on by the expensive acquisition of IBP, the red meat supplier. John hopes to gain synergies and size advantages, such as increased sales to Wal-Mart. The discounter has announced that it will sell only prepackaged meats, the kind that Tyson supplies, in order to cut costs. Convincing smaller retailers to abandon their traditional methods may be tougher.

The second challenge is hiring enough labor for Tyson's processing plants. The job is unappealing, dirty, and dangerous, with high turnover—between 40 and 100 per-

cent annually. So Tyson and other firms recruit immigrants, who may have relatively few employment options. But the firm is quick to point out that the company's workers are well treated: paid $9 per hour, given health benefits, and

"My responsibility is to be the head cheerleader for the organization and its new culture."—John Tyson, CEO, Tyson Foods

protected by a labor union. "Labor is such an important part of our business. [Workers are] just too valuable for us to . . . [be] abusers of labor" says co-COO Greg Lee.

Even a seasoned, well-respected leader might struggle in this situation; however, it's unclear whether John possesses his father's business savvy. Although he talks to Don every day, John is more willing to delegate than his dad was. "I've got some philosophical things I believe in, and one of them is for people to make their own decisions," he says. "My responsibility is to be the head cheerleader for the organization and its new culture."

References: "About Tyson Foods," "News Releases," Tyson Foods web site. www.tyson.com on May 28, 2002; Nicholas Stein, "Son of a Chicken Man," *Fortune*, May 13, 2002, pp. 137–145 (quotation p. 145). See www.fortune.com; Wendy Zellner, "Hiring Illegals: The Risk Grows," *Business Week*, May 13, 2002. www. businessweek.com on May 28, 2002; Julie Foster, "Hungry for Convenience," *Business Week*, January 14, 2002. www.businessweek.com on May 28, 2002.

from someone with substantial personal charisma is also a challenge, as illustrated in the "Mastering Change" box's description of new CEO John Tyson's situation at Tyson Foods.

Leadership Substitutes: Can Leadership Be Irrelevant?

Another interesting twist on leadership is the premise that it may sometimes be unnecessary or irrelevant. An implicit assumption made by each leadership and influence perspective described thus far is that the leader and the follower can be differentiated. That is, one person, the leader, is trying to influence or control another, the follower. But the concept of leadership substitutes points out that in some situations leadership may not be necessary.

The Nature of Leadership Substitutes

Leadership substitutes are individual, task, and organizational characteristics that tend to outweigh the leader's ability to affect subordinates' satisfaction and performance.[14] In other words, if certain factors are present, the employee will perform his or

Leadership substitutes are individual, task, and organizational characteristics that tend to outweigh the leader's ability to affect subordinates' satisfaction and performance.

Leadership substitutes allow people to perform effectively without the direction or supervision of a leader. The Dragon Slayers, shown here, are a volunteer group of high school girls who provide the only round-the-clock emergency care available for 3,000 people in a region of Alaska that is the size of Maryland. The girls voluntarily undergo 200 hours of medical training and respond to about 450 calls a year. And they function without supervision and without a formal leader—they simply know what to do, and then get it done in order to save lives and help people.

her job capably without the direction of a leader. Unlike traditional theories, which assume that hierarchical leadership is always important, the premise of the leadership substitutes perspective is that leader behaviors are irrelevant in many situations.

Workplace Substitutes

Ability, experience, training, knowledge, need for independence, professional orientation, and indifference to organizational rewards are individual characteristics that may neutralize leader behaviors. For example, an employee who has the skills and abilities to perform her job and a high need for independence may not need—and may even resent—a leader who tries to provide direction and structure.

A task characterized by routine, a high degree of structure, frequent feedback, and intrinsic satisfaction may also render leader behavior irrelevant. Thus, if the task gives the subordinate enough intrinsic satisfaction, she or he may not need support from a leader.

Explicit plans and goals, rules and procedures, cohesive work groups, a rigid reward structure, and physical distance between supervisor and subordinate are organizational characteristics that may substitute for leadership. For example, if job goals are explicit, and there are many rules and procedures for task performance, a leader providing directions may not be necessary. Preliminary research has provided support for the concept of leadership substitutes, but additional research is needed to identify other potential substitutes and their impact on leadership effectiveness.[15]

Superleadership

Superleadership occurs when a leader gradually and purposefully turns over power, responsibility, and control to a self-managing work group.

A relatively new addition to the literature on leadership substitutes is the notion of superleadership. **Superleadership** occurs when a leader gradually turns over power, responsibility, and control to a self-managing work group. As we discussed more fully in Chapter 12, many firms today are making widespread use of work teams that function without a formal manager. A big challenge faced by these firms is what to do with the existing group leader. Although some managers cannot handle this change and leave, a superleader can alter his or her own personal style and become more of a coach or facilitator than a supervisor.

"Leaders are lonely, because they must think and dream about their work—all day, every day, day after day."—Lorraine Monroe, principal of Harlem's Frederick Douglass School, considered one of New York's greatest educational success stories[16]

Power in Organizations

Influence is also closely related to the concept of power. Power is one of the most significant forces that exists in organizations. Moreover, it can be an extremely important ingredient in organizational success—or organizational failure. In this section we first describe the nature of power. Then we examine the types and uses of power.

The Nature of Power

Power is the potential ability of a person or group to exercise control over another person or group.

Power has been defined in dozens of different ways; no one definition is generally accepted. Drawing from the more common meanings of the term, we define **power** as the potential ability of a person or group to exercise control over another person or group.[17] Power is distinguished from influence due to the element of control; the more powerful control the less powerful. Thus, power might be thought of as an extreme form of influence.

One obvious aspect of our definition is that it expresses power in terms of potential; that is, we may be able to control others but may choose not to exercise that control. Nevertheless, simply having the potential may be enough to influence others in some settings. We should also note that power may reside in individuals (such as managers and informal leaders), in formal groups (such as departments and committees), and in informal groups (such as a clique of influential people). Finally, we should note the direct link between power and influence. If a person can convince another person to change his or her opinion on some issue, to engage in or refrain from some behavior, or to view circumstances in a certain way, that person has exercised influence—and used power.

Considerable differences of opinion exist about how thoroughly power pervades organizations. Some people argue that virtually all interpersonal relations are influenced by power whereas others believe that exercise of power is confined to only certain situations. Whatever the case, power is undoubtedly a pervasive part of organizational life. It affects decisions ranging from the choice of strategies to the color of the new office carpeting. It makes or breaks careers. And it enhances or limits organizational effectiveness.

Types of Power

Within the broad framework of our definition, there obviously are many types of power. These types usually are described in terms of bases of power and position power versus personal power.

Bases of Power   The most widely used and recognized analysis of the bases of power is the classic framework developed by John R. P. French and Bertram Raven.[18] French and Raven identified five general bases of power in organizational settings: legitimate, reward, coercive, expert, and referent power.

Legitimate power is power that is granted by virtue of one's position in the organization.

Legitimate power, essentially the same thing as authority, is granted by virtue of one's position in an organization. Managers have legitimate power over their subordinates. The organization specifies that it is legitimate for the designated individual to direct the activities of others. The bounds of this legitimacy are defined partly by the formal nature of the position involved and partly by informal norms and traditions. For example, it was once commonplace for managers to expect their secretaries not only to perform work-related activities such as typing and filing but also to run personal errands such as picking up laundry and buying gifts. In highly centralized, mechanistic, and bureaucratic organizations such as the military, the legitimate power inherent in each position is closely specified, widely known, and strictly followed. In more organic organizations such as research and development labs and software firms, the lines of legitimate power often are blurry. Employees may work for more than one boss at the same time, and leaders and followers may be on a nearly equal footing.

Reward power is the extent to which a person controls rewards that another person values.

Reward power is the extent to which a person controls rewards that are valued by another. The most obvious examples of organizational rewards are pay, promotions, and work assignments. If a manager has almost total control over the pay his subordinates receive, can make recommendations about promotions, and has considerable discretion to make job assignments, he or she has a high level of reward power. Reward power can extend beyond material rewards. As we noted in our discussions of motivation theory in Chapters 5 and 6, people work for a variety of reasons in addition to pay. For instance, some people may be motivated primarily by a desire for recognition and acceptance. To the extent that a manager's praise and acknowledgment satisfy those needs, that manager has even more reward power.

Coercive power is the extent to which a person has the ability to punish or physically or psychologically harm someone else.

Coercive power exists when someone has the ability to punish or physically or psychologically harm another person. For example, some managers berate subordinates in front of everyone, belittling their efforts and generally making their lives miserable. Certain forms of coercion may be subtle. In some organizations, a particular division may be notorious as a resting place for people who have no future with the company. Threatening to transfer someone to a dead-end branch or some other undesirable location is thus a form of coercion. Clearly, the more negative the sanctions a person can bring to bear on others, the stronger is her or his coercive power. At the same time, the use of coercive power carries a considerable cost in employee resentment and hostility.

"Colleagues know immediately when the boss is upset. His blue eyes flash with anger, and he intimidates subordinates with long silences. Indeed, in an era when team-building and employee empowerment are in vogue, Piëch prefers fear as a motivator."—David Woodruff and Keith Naughton, business writers, referring to Volkswagen CEO Ferdinand Piëch[19]

Control over expertise or, more precisely, over information is another source of power. For example, to the extent that an inventory manager has information that a sales representative needs, the inventory manager has **expert power** over the sales representative. The more important the information, and the fewer the alternative sources for getting it, the greater the power. Expert power can reside in many niches in an organization; it transcends positions and jobs. Although legitimate, reward, and coercive power may not always correspond exactly to formal authority, they often do. Expert power, on the other hand, may be associated much less with formal authority. Upper-level managers usually decide on the organization's strategic agenda, but individuals at lower levels in the organization may have the expertise those managers need to do the tasks. A research scientist may have crucial information about a technical breakthrough of great importance to the organization and its strategic decisions. Or an assistant may take on so many of the boss's routine and mundane activities that the manager loses track of such details and comes to depend on the assistant to keep things running smoothly. In other situations, lower-level participants are given power as a way to take advantage of their expertise.

Referent power is power through identification. If José is highly respected by Adam, José has referent power over Adam. Like expert power, referent power does not always correlate with formal organizational authority. In some ways, referent power is similar to the concept of charisma in that it often involves trust, similarity, acceptance, affection, willingness to follow, and emotional involvement. Referent power usually surfaces as imitation. For example, suppose a new department manager is the youngest person in the organization to have reached that rank. Further, it is widely believed that she is being groomed for the highest levels of the company. Other people in the department may begin to imitate her, thinking that they too may be able to advance. They may begin dressing like her, working the same hours, and trying to pick up as many work-related pointers from her as possible.

Position Versus Personal Power   The French and Raven framework is only one approach to examining the origins of organizational power. Another approach categorizes power in organizations in terms of position or personal power.

Position power is power that resides in the position, regardless of who holds it. Thus, legitimate, reward, and some aspects of coercive and expert power can all contribute to position power. Position power is thus similar to authority. In creating a position, the organization simultaneously establishes a sphere of power for the person filling that position. He or she will generally have the power to direct the activities of subordinates in performing their jobs, to control some of their potential rewards, and to have a say in their punishment and discipline. There are, however, limits to a manager's position power. A manager cannot order or control activities that fall outside his or her sphere of power—for instance, directing a subordinate to commit crimes, to perform personal services, or to take on tasks that clearly are not part of the subordinate's job.

Personal power is power that resides with an individual, regardless of his or her position in the organization. Thus, the primary bases of personal power are referent and some traces of expert, coercive, and reward power. Charisma may also contribute to personal power. Someone usually exercises personal power through rational persuasion or by playing on followers' identification with him or her. An individual with personal power often can inspire greater loyalty and dedication in followers than someone who has only position power. The stronger influence stems from the fact that the followers are acting more from choice than from ne-

Expert power is the extent to which a person controls information that is valuable to someone else.

Referent power exists when one person wants to be like or imitates someone else.

Position power resides in the position, regardless of who is filling that position.

Personal power resides in the person, regardless of the position he or she is filling.

cessity (as dictated, for example, by their organizational responsibilities) and thus will respond more readily to requests and appeals. Of course, the influence of a leader who relies only on personal power is limited because followers may freely decide not to accept his or her directives or orders.

The distinctions between formal and informal leaders are also related to position and personal power. A formal leader will have, at minimum, position power. And an informal leader will similarly have some degree of personal power. Just as a person may be both a formal and an informal leader, he or she can have both position and personal power simultaneously. Indeed, such a combination usually has the greatest potential influence on the actions of others. Figure 14.2 illustrates how personal and position power may interact to determine how much overall power a person has in a particular situation. An individual with both personal and position power will have the strongest overall power. Likewise, an individual with neither personal nor position power will have the weakest overall power. Finally, when either personal or position power is high, but the other is low, the individual will have a moderate level of overall power.

The Uses of Power in Organizations

Power can be used in many ways in an organization. But because of the potential for its misuse and the concerns that it may engender, it is important that managers fully understand the dynamics of using power. Gary Yukl has presented a useful perspective for understanding how power may be wielded.[20] His perspective includes two closely related components. The first relates power bases, requests from individuals possessing power, and probable outcomes in the form of prescriptions for the manager. Table 14.1 indicates the three outcomes that may result when a leader tries to exert power. These outcomes depend on the leader's base of power, how that base is operationalized, and the subordinate's individual characteristics (for example, personality traits or past interactions with the leader).

Commitment will probably result from an attempt to exercise power if the subordinate accepts and identifies with the leader. Such an employee will be highly motivated by requests that seem important to the leader. For example, a leader might explain that a new piece of software will greatly benefit the organization if it is developed soon. A committed subordinate will work just as hard as the leader to complete the project, even if that means working overtime. Sam Walton once asked all Wal-Mart employees to start greeting customers with a smile and an offer to help. Because Wal-Mart employees generally were motivated by and loyal to Walton, most of them accepted his request.

figure 14.2

Position Power and Personal Power

Position power resides in a job whereas personal power resides in an individual. When these two types of power are broken down into high and low levels and related to one another, the two-by-two matrix shown here is the result. For example, the upper-right cell suggests that a leader with high levels of both position and personal power will have the highest overall level of power. Other combinations result in differing levels of overall power.

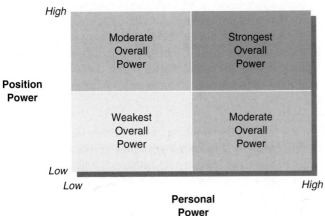

table 14.1

Uses and Outcomes of Power

Source of Leader Influence	Type of Outcome		
	Commitment	Compliance	Resistance
Referent Power	Likely	Possible	Possible
	If request is believed to be important to leader	If request is perceived to be unimportant to leader	If request is for something that will bring harm to leader
Expert Power	Likely	Possible	Possible
	If request is persuasive and subordinates share leader's task goals	If request is persuasive but subordinates are apathetic about leader's task goals	If leader is arrogant and insulting, or subordinates oppose task goals
Legitimate Power	Possible	Likely	Possible
	If request is polite and very appropriate	If request or order is seen as legitimate	If arrogant demands are made or request does not appear proper
Reward Power	Possible	Likely	Possible
	If used in a subtle, very personal way	If used in a mechanical, impersonal way	If used in a manipulative, arrogant way
Coercive Power	Very Unlikely	Possible	Likely
		If used in a helpful, nonpunitive way	If used in a hostile or manipulative way

Reference: From Dorwin P. Cartwright (ed.). Studies in Social Power, 1959. Reprinted with permission from the Institute for Social Research, University of Michigan, Ann Arbor, Michigan.

Compliance means the subordinate is willing to carry out the leader's wishes as long as doing so will not require extra effort. That is, the person will respond to normal, reasonable requests that are perceived to be clearly within the normal boundaries of the job. But the person will not be inclined to do anything extra or to go beyond the normal expectations for the job. Thus, the subordinate may work at a reasonable pace but refuse to work overtime, insisting that the job will still be there tomorrow. Many ordinary requests from a boss meet with compliant responses from subordinates.

Resistance occurs when the subordinate rejects or fights the leader's wishes. For example, suppose an unpopular leader asks employees to volunteer for a company-sponsored community activity project. The employees may reject this request, largely because of their feelings about the leader. A resistant subordinate may even deliberately neglect the project to ensure that it is not done as the leader wants. When Frank Lorenzo ran Continental Airlines, some employees occasionally disobeyed his mandates as a form of protest against his leadership of the firm.

table 14.2

Guidelines for Using Power

Basis of Power	Guidelines for Use
Referent Power	Treat subordinates fairly Defend subordinates' interests Be sensitive to subordinates' needs, feelings Select subordinates similar to oneself Engage in role modeling
Expert Power	Promote image of expertise Maintain credibility Act confident and decisive Keep informed Recognize employee concerns Avoid threatening subordinates' self-esteem
Legitimate Power	Be cordial and polite Be confident Be clear and follow up to verify understanding Make sure request is appropriate Explain reasons for request Follow proper channels Exercise power regularly Enforce compliance Be sensitive to subordinates' concerns
Reward Power	Verify compliance Make feasible, reasonable requests Make only ethical, proper requests Offer rewards desired by subordinates Offer only credible rewards
Coercive Power	Inform subordinates of rules and penalties Warn before punishing Administer punishment consistently and uniformly Understand the situation before acting Maintain credibility Fit punishment to the infraction Punish in private

Reference: Reprinted from Gary A. Yukl, *Leadership in Organization*, 2nd ed., © 1989, pp. 44–49, Prentice Hall, Inc., Englewood Cliffs, N.J.

Table 14.2 suggests ways for leaders to use various kinds of power most effectively. By effective use of power we mean using power in the way that is most likely to engender commitment, or at the very least, compliance, and that is least likely to engender resistance. For example, to suggest a somewhat mechanistic approach, managers may enhance their referent power by choosing subordinates with backgrounds similar to their own. They might, for instance, build a referent power base by hiring several subordinates who went to the same college they did. A more subtle way to exercise referent power is through role modeling: The leader behaves as she or he wants subordinates to behave. As noted earlier, since subordinates relate to and identify with the leader with referent power, they may subsequently attempt to emulate that person's behavior.

In using expert power, managers can subtly make others aware of their education, experience, and accomplishments. To maintain credibility, a leader should not

Leaders are expected to use their expert power to inform, guide, and direct the actions of others. When their expertise is relevant and important, and when it is provided in a supportive fashion with employee development in mind, others value and appreciate both the leader and the information. But when the information is actually trivial or is presented in a condescending or demeaning manner, people may be offended and resist what the leader is trying to accomplish. In this illustration, the boss's clumsy attempt to provide information results in Dilbert expressing sarcasm and disrespect.

Reference: DILBERT reprinted by permission of United Feature Syndicate, Inc.

pretend to know things that he or she really does not know. A leader whose pretensions are exposed will rapidly lose expert power. A confident and decisive leader demonstrates a firm grasp of situations and takes charge when circumstances dictate. Managers should also keep themselves informed about developments related to tasks that are valuable to the organization and relevant to their expertise.

A leader who recognizes employee concerns works to understand the underlying nature of these issues and takes appropriate steps to reassure subordinates. For example, if employees feel threatened by rumors that they will lose office space after an impending move, the leader might ask them about this concern and then find out just how much office space there will be and tell the subordinates. Finally, to avoid threatening the self-esteem of subordinates, a leader should be careful not to flaunt expertise or behave like a "know-it-all." The cartoon illustrates the consequences of doing so.

In general, a leader exercises legitimate power by formally requesting that subordinates do something. The leader should be especially careful to make requests diplomatically if the subordinate is sensitive about his or her relationship with the leader. This might be the case, for example, if the subordinate is older or more experienced than the leader. But although the request should be polite, it should be made confidently. The leader is in charge and needs to convey his or her command of the situation. The request should also be clear. Thus, the leader may need to follow up to ascertain that the subordinate has understood it properly. To ensure that a request is seen as appropriate and legitimate to the situation, the leader may need to explain the reasons for it. Often subordinates do not understand the rationale behind a request and consequently are unenthusiastic about it. It is important, too, to follow proper channels when dealing with subordinates.

Suppose a manager has asked a subordinate to spend his day finishing an important report. Later, while the manager is out of the office, her boss comes by and asks the subordinate to drop that project and work on something else. The subordinate will then be in the awkward position of having to decide which of two higher-ranking individuals to obey. Exercising authority regularly will reinforce its presence and legitimacy in the eyes of subordinates. Compliance with legitimate power should be the norm because if employees resist a request, the leader's power base may diminish. Finally, the leader exerting legitimate power should attempt to be responsive to subordinates' problems and concerns in the same ways that we outlined for using expert power.

Reward power is, in some respects, the easiest base of power to use. Verifying compliance simply means that leaders should find out whether subordinates have carried out their requests before giving rewards; otherwise, subordinates may not recognize a performance-reward linkage. The request that is to be rewarded must be both reasonable and feasible because even the promise of a reward will not motivate a subordinate who thinks a request should not or cannot be carried out.

The same can be said for a request that seems improper or unethical. Among other things, the follower may see a reward linked to an improper or unethical request as a bribe or other shady offering. Finally, if the leader promises a reward that subordinates know she or he cannot actually deliver, or if they have little use for a reward the manager can deliver, they will not be motivated to carry out the request. Further, they may grow skeptical of the leader's ability to deliver rewards that are worth something to them.

Coercion is certainly the most difficult form of power to exercise. Because coercive power is likely to cause resentment and to erode referent power, it should be used infrequently, if at all. Compliance is about all one can expect from using coercive power, and that only if the power is used in a helpful, nonpunitive way—that is, if the sanction is mild and fits the situation and if the subordinate learns from it. In most cases, resistance is the most likely outcome, especially if coercive power is used in a hostile or manipulative way.

The first guideline for using coercive power—that subordinates should be fully informed about rules and the penalties for violating them—will prevent accidental violations of a rule, which pose an unpalatable dilemma for a leader. Overlooking an infraction on the grounds that the perpetrator was ignorant may undermine the rule or the leader's legitimate power, but carrying out the punishment probably will create resentment. One approach is to provide reasonable warning before inflicting punishment, responding to the first violation of a rule with a warning about the consequences of another violation. Of course, a serious infraction such as a theft or violence warrants immediate and severe punishment.

The disciplinary action needs to be administered consistently and uniformly because doing so shows that punishment is both impartial and clearly linked to the infraction. Leaders should obtain complete information about what has happened before they punish because punishing the wrong person or administering uncalled-for punishment can stir great resentment among subordinates. Credibility must be maintained because a leader who continually makes threats but fails to carry them out loses both respect and power. Similarly, if the leader uses threats that subordinates know are beyond his or her ability to impose, the attempted use of power will be fruitless. Obviously, too, the severity of the punishment generally should match the seriousness of the infraction. Finally, punishing someone in front of others adds humiliation to the penalty, which reflects poorly on the leader and makes those who must watch and listen uncomfortable as well.

Politics and Political Behavior

Organizational politics are activities carried out by people to acquire, enhance, and use power and other resources to obtain their desired outcomes.

A concept closely related to power in organizational settings is politics, or political behavior. We can define **organizational politics** as activities people perform to acquire, enhance, and use power and other resources to obtain their preferred outcomes in a situation in which there is uncertainty or disagreement. Thus, political behavior is the general means by which people attempt to obtain and use power. Put simply, the goal of such behavior is to get one's own way about things. A recent example of how political behavior can translate into business practice is discussed in the examination of Boeing's questionable accounting practices in the "Business of Ethics" box.

The Pervasiveness of Political Behavior

One classic survey provides some interesting insights into how managers perceive political behavior in their organizations.[21] Roughly one-third of the 428 managers who responded to this survey believed political behavior influenced salary decisions in their organizations whereas 28 percent felt it affected hiring decisions. Moreover, three-quarters of them also believed that political behavior is more prevalent at higher levels of the organization than at lower levels. More than half believed that politics is unfair, unhealthy, and irrational but also acknowledged that successful executives must be good politicians and that it is necessary to behave politically to get ahead. The survey results suggest that managers see political behavior as an undesirable but unavoidable facet of organizational life.

Politics often is viewed as being synonymous with dirty tricks or backstabbing and therefore as something distasteful and best left to others. But the results of the survey just described demonstrate that political behavior in organizations, like power, is pervasive. Thus, rather than ignoring or trying to eliminate political behavior, managers might more fruitfully consider when and how organizational politics can be used constructively.

Figure 14.3 presents an interesting model of the ethics of organizational politics.[22] In the model, a political behavior alternative (PBA) is a given course of action, largely political in character, in a particular situation. The model considers political behavior ethical and appropriate under two conditions: (1) if it respects the rights of all affected parties, and (2) if it adheres to the canons of justice (that is, to a commonsense judgment of what is fair and equitable). Even if the political behavior does not meet these tests, it may be ethical and appropriate under certain circumstances. For example, politics may provide the only possible basis for deciding which employees to let go during a recessionary period of cutbacks. In all cases where nonpolitical alternatives exist, however, the model recommends rejecting political behavior that abrogates rights or justice.

To illustrate how the model works, consider Susan Jackson and Bill Thompson, both assistant professors of English. University regulations stipulate that only one of the assistant professors may be tenured; the other must be let go. (Some universities actually follow this practice.) Both Susan and Bill submit their credentials for review. By most objective criteria, such as number of publications and teaching evaluations, the two faculty members' qualifications are roughly the same. Because he fears termination, Bill begins an active political campaign to support a tenure decision favoring him. He continually reminds the tenured faculty of his intangible contributions, such as his friendship with influential campus administra-

BUSINESS OF ETHICS

Five Years' of Accounting Secrets at Boeing

The legality of an action is determined by interpretation of the language of a legal code. Whether that same action is socially responsible is determined by a different standard: The action should protect and contribute to the social environment. Thus, it is quite possible that an action can be socially responsible but not legal—or legal but not socially responsible.

The latter is the case with the actions of Boeing executives, which were publicly disclosed in May 2002. The firm began to experience cost overruns in 1996, as noted by auditors Deloitte Touche, because of faulty inventory scheduling, a high defect rate, and increased overtime pay. According to generally accepted accounting principles (GAAP), reporting of expenses may be spread over the life of a project under normal conditions whereas expenses must be reported at occurrence if the conditions are considered abnormal. Deloitte called the expenses abnormal; Boeing officials insisted that these were normal costs and that normal costs fluctuate. Boeing's view prevailed, and the increased expenses were not made public until October 1997. This action was found to be legal, but many considered it unethical and socially irresponsible. The motive seems clear: Boeing was merging with rival McDonnell-Douglas and feared that disclosure would nix the deal. Debra Smith, a former auditor, says, "Boeing basically decided in the short run that [underreporting expenses] was a lesser evil than losing the merger." Boeing managers "were hoping against hope that none of the problems would bubble up before they got the deal done," says a Boeing ex-official.

Investors were hard hit by the announcement when it finally came, dropping Boeing's stock price 20 percent in

> *"[Boeing managers] were hoping against hope that none of the problems would bubble up before they got the deal done."— former Boeing official commenting on the company's proposed merger with rival McDonnell-Douglas*

one week and wiping out $10.7 billion dollars in value. Also hurt were employees and suppliers due to the resulting layoffs and reduced spending. Customers suffered, too, when new planes were delivered late. Ultimately, some customers defected to rivals, and several Boeing managers lost their jobs, but CEO Phil Condit retained his. The firm paid $92 million to settle a lawsuit without admitting guilt. The use of accounting technicalities to mask production inefficiencies is continuing at the firm, and an accurate picture of its financial state is as remote as ever. Fallout from the incident continues. When *Business Week* published its investigative report in May 2002, the company's stock had declined yet again.

References: "Dow Jones Industrial Average," Dow Jones Index web site. www.djindexes.com on May 27, 2002; Stanley Holmes and Mike France, "Boeing's Secret, *Business Week*, May 20, 2002, pp. 110–120 (quotation p. 110). See www.businessweek.com; Stanley Holmes and David Henry, "And Where Were the Auditors?" *Business Week*, May 20, 2002, p. 120. See www.businessweek.com; Bethany McLean, "Markets Suffer Indigestion," *Fortune*, May 10, 2002. www.fortune.com on May 27, 2002.

tors. Susan, on the other hand, decides to say nothing and let her qualifications speak for themselves. The department ultimately votes to give Bill tenure and let Susan go.

Was Bill's behavior ethical? Assuming that his comments about himself were accurate and that he said nothing to disparage Susan, his behavior did not affect her rights; that is, she had an equal opportunity to advance her own cause but chose not to do so. Bill's efforts did not directly hurt Susan but only helped himself. On the other hand, it might be argued that Bill's actions violated the canons of justice because clearly defined data on which to base the decision were available. Thus, one could argue that Bill's calculated introduction of additional information into the decision was unjust.

This model has not been tested empirically. Indeed, its very nature may make it impossible to test. Further, as the preceding example demonstrates, it often is difficult to give an unequivocal yes or no answer to the question, even under the

figure 14.3

A Model of Ethical Political Behavior

Political behavior can serve both ethical and unethical purposes. This model helps illustrate circumstances in which political behavior is most and least likely to have ethical consequences. By following the paths through the model, a leader concerned about the ethics of an impending behavior can gain insights into whether ethical considerations are really a central part of the behavior.

Reference: Gerald F. Cavanaugh, Dennis J. Moberg, and Manuel Velasques, "The Ethics of Organizational Politics." *Academy of Management Review*, July 1981, p. 368. Used with permission.

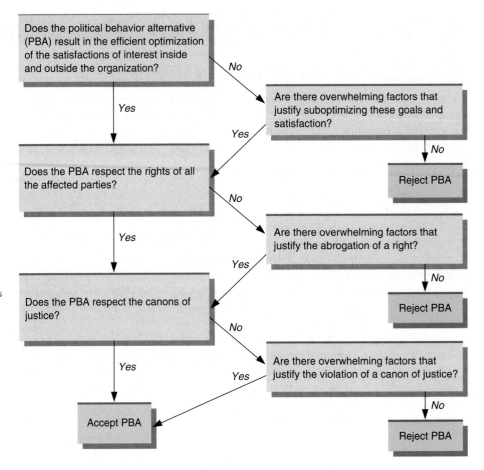

simplest circumstances. Thus, the model serves as a general framework for understanding the ethical implications of various courses of action managers might take.

How, then, should managers approach the phenomenon of political behavior? Trying to eliminate political behavior will seldom, if ever, work. In fact, such action may well increase political behavior because of the uncertainty and ambiguity it creates. At the other extreme, universal and freewheeling use of political behavior probably will lead to conflict, feuds, and turmoil. In most cases, a position someplace in between is best: The manager does not attempt to eliminate political activity, recognizing its inevitability, and may try to use it effectively, perhaps following the ethical model just described. At the same time, the manager can take certain steps to minimize the potential dysfunctional consequences of abusive political behavior.

Managing Political Behavior

Managing organizational politics is not easy. The very nature of political behavior makes it tricky to approach in a rational and systematic way. Success will require a basic understanding of three factors: the reasons for political behavior, common techniques for using political behavior, and strategies for limiting the effects of political behavior.

Political behavior, of course, is an integral part of most government functions. For example, John Ashcroft, Robert Mueller, Tom Ridge, and George Tenet have been key figures in the U.S. war on terrorism. In order to work effectively together, these individuals and their colleagues have had to learn new methods for sharing intelligence information to avoid another terrorist attack. But at the same time, turf issues among such operations as the FBI, the CIA, and the newly created Department of Homeland Security also make it politically difficult to be totally open.

Reasons for Political Behavior   Political behavior occurs in organizations for five basic reasons: ambiguous goals, scarce resources, technology and environment, nonprogrammed decisions, and organizational change (see Figure 14.4).

Most organizational goals are inherently ambiguous. Organizations frequently espouse goals such as "increasing our presence in certain new markets" or "increasing our market share." The ambiguity of such goals provides an opportunity for political behavior because people can view a wide range of behaviors as helping to meet the goal. In reality, of course, many of these behaviors may actually be designed for the personal gain of the individuals involved. For example, a top manager might argue that the corporation should pursue its goal of entry into a new market by buying out another firm instead of forming a new division. The manager may appear to have the good of the corporation in mind—but what if he owns some of the target firm's stock and stands to make money on a merger or acquisition?

Whenever resources are scarce, some people will not get everything they think they deserve or need. Thus, they are likely to engage in political behavior as a means of inflating their share of the resources. In this way, a manager seeking a larger budget might present accurate but misleading or incomplete statistics to inflate the perceived importance of her department. Because no organization has unlimited resources, incentives for this kind of political behavior are always present.

Technology and environment may influence the overall design of the organization and its activities. The influence stems from the uncertainties associated with nonroutine technologies and dynamic, complex environments. These uncertainties favor the use of political behavior because in a dynamic and complex environment, it is imperative that an organization respond to change. An organization's response generally involves a wide range of activities, from purposeful activities to uncertainty to a purely political response. In the last case, a manager might use an environmental shift as an argument for restructuring his or her department to increase his or her own power base.

Political behavior is also likely to arise whenever many nonprogrammed decisions need to be made. Nonprogrammed-decision situations involve ambiguous circumstances that allow ample opportunity for political maneuvering. The two faculty members competing for one tenured position is an example. The nature of the decision allowed political behavior, and in fact, from Bill's point of view, the nonprogrammed decision demanded political action.

As we discuss in Chapter 19, changes in organizations occur regularly and can take many forms. Each such change introduces some uncertainty and ambiguity into the organizational system, at least until it has been completely institutionalized. The period during which this is occurring usually affords much opportunity for political activity. For instance, a manager worried about the consequences of a reorganization may resort to politics to protect the scope of his or her authority.

The Techniques of Political Behavior   Several techniques are used in practicing political behavior. Unfortunately, because these techniques have not been systematically studied, our understanding of them is based primarily on informal observation and inference.[23] To further complicate this problem, the participants themselves may not even be aware that they are using particular techniques. Figure 14.4 also summarizes the most frequently used techniques.[24]

One technique of political behavior is to control as much information as possible. The more critical the information and the fewer people who have access to it, the larger the power base and influence of those who do. For example, suppose a top manager has a report compiled as a basis for future strategic plans. Rather than distributing the complete report to peers and subordinates, he shares only parts of it with the few managers who must have the information. Because no one but the manager has the complete picture, he has power and is engaging in politics to control decisions and activities according to his own ends.

Similarly, some people create or exploit situations to control lines of communication, particularly access to others in the organization. Secretaries frequently control access to their bosses. A secretary may put visitors in contact with the boss, send them away, delay the contact by ensuring that phone calls are not returned promptly, and so forth. People in these positions often find that they can use this type of political behavior quite effectively.

Using outside experts, such as consultants or advisers, can be an effective political technique. The manager who hires a consultant may select one whose views match her own. Because the consultant realizes that the manager was responsible for selecting him, he feels a certain obligation to her. Although the consultant truly attempts to be objective and unbiased, he may unconsciously recommend courses of

figure 14.4

Use of Political Behavior: Reasons, Techniques, and Possible Consequences

People choose to engage in political behavior for many reasons. Depending on the reasons and circumstances, a person interested in using political behavior can employ a variety of techniques, which will produce a number of intended—and possibly unintended—consequences.

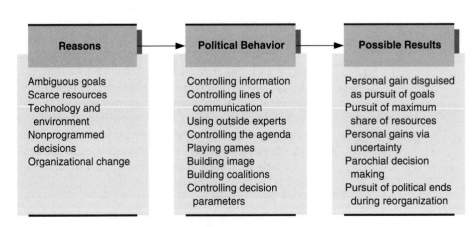

Reasons	Political Behavior	Possible Results
Ambiguous goals	Controlling information	Personal gain disguised as pursuit of goals
Scarce resources	Controlling lines of communication	Pursuit of maximum share of resources
Technology and environment	Using outside experts	Personal gains via uncertainty
Nonprogrammed decisions	Controlling the agenda	Parochial decision making
Organizational change	Playing games	Pursuit of political ends during reorganization
	Building image	
	Building coalitions	
	Controlling decision parameters	

action favored by the manager. Given the consultant's presumed expertise and neutrality, others in the organization accept his recommendations without challenge. By using an outside expert, the manager has ultimately gotten what she wants.

Controlling the agenda is another common political technique. Suppose a manager wants to prevent a committee from approving a certain proposal. The manager first tries to keep the decision off the agenda entirely, claiming that it is not yet ready for consideration, or attempts to have it placed last on the agenda. As other issues are decided, he sides with the same set of managers on each decision, building up a certain assumption that they are a team. When the controversial item comes up, he can defeat it through a combination of collective fatigue, the desire to get the meeting over with, and the support of his carefully cultivated allies. This technique, then, involves group polarization. A less sophisticated tactic is to prolong discussion of prior agenda items so that the group never reaches the controversial one. Or the manager may raise so many technical issues and new questions about the proposal that the committee decides to table it. In any of these cases, the manager will have used political behavior for his or her own ends.

Game playing is a complex technique that may take many forms. When playing games, managers simply work within the rules of the organization to increase the probability that their preferred outcomes will come about. Suppose a manager is in a position to cast the deciding vote on an upcoming issue. She does not want to alienate either side by voting on it. One game she might play is to arrange to be called out of town on a crucial business trip when the vote is to take place. Assuming that no one questions the need for the trip, she will successfully maintain her position of neutrality and avoid angering either opposing camp.

Another game would involve using any of the techniques of political behavior in a purely manipulative or deceitful way. For example, a manager who will soon be making recommendations about promotions tells each subordinate, in "strictest confidence," that he or she is a leading candidate and needs only to increase his or her performance to have the inside track. Here the manager is using his control over information to play games with his subordinates. A power struggle at W. R. Grace a few years ago further illustrates manipulative practices. One senior executive fired the CEO's son and then allegedly attempted to convince the board of directors to oust the CEO and to give the executive his job. The CEO, in response, fired his rival and then publicly announced that the individual had been forced out because he had sexually harassed Grace employees.[25]

The technique of building coalitions has as its general goal convincing others that everyone should work together to accomplish certain things. A manager who believes she does not control enough votes to pass an upcoming agenda item may visit with other managers before the meeting to urge them to side with her. If her preferences are in the best interests of the organization, this may be a laudable strategy for her to follow. But if she herself is the principal beneficiary, the technique is not desirable from the organization's perspective.

At its extreme, coalition building, which is frequently used in political bodies, may take the form of blatant reciprocity. In return for Roberta Kline's vote on an issue that concerns him, José Montemayor agrees to vote for a measure that does not affect his group at all but is crucial to Kline's group. Depending on the circumstances, this practice may benefit or hurt the organization as a whole.

The technique of controlling decision parameters can be used only in certain situations and requires much subtlety. Instead of trying to control the actual decision, the manager backs up one step and tries to control the criteria and tests on which the decision is based. This allows the manager to take a less active role in the actual decision but still achieve his or her preferred outcome. For example, suppose a district manager wants a proposed new factory to be constructed on a site in his region. If he tries to influence the decision directly, his arguments will be seen as biased and self-serving. Instead, he may take a very active role in defining the criteria on which the decision will be based, such as target population, access to rail transportation, tax rates, distance from other facilities, and the like. If he is a skillful negotiator, he may be able to influence the decision parameters such that his desired location subsequently appears to be the ideal site as determined by the criteria he has helped shape. Hence, he gets just what he wants without playing a prominent role in the actual decision.

Limiting the Effects of Political Behavior   Although it is virtually impossible to eliminate political activity in organizations, managers can limit its dysfunctional consequences. The techniques for checking political activity target both the reasons that it occurs in the first place and the specific techniques that people use for political gain.

Opening communication is one very effective technique for restraining the impact of political behavior. For instance, with open communication the basis for allocating scarce resources will be known to everyone. This knowledge, in turn, will tend to reduce the propensity to engage in political behavior to acquire those resources because people will already know how decisions will be made. Open communication also limits the ability of any single person to control information or lines of communication.

A related technique is to reduce uncertainty. Several of the reasons that political behavior occurs—ambiguous goals, nonroutine technology, an unstable environment, and organizational change—and most of the political techniques themselves are associated with high levels of uncertainty. Political behavior can be limited if the manager can reduce uncertainty. Consider an organization about to transfer a major division from Florida to Michigan. Many people will resist the idea of moving north and may resort to political behavior to forestall their own transfer. However, the manager in charge of the move could announce who will stay and who will go at the same time that news of the change spreads throughout the company, thereby curtailing political behavior related to the move.

The adage "forewarned is forearmed" sums up the final technique for controlling political activity. Simply being aware of the causes and techniques of political behavior can help a manager check their effects. Suppose a manager anticipates that several impending organizational changes will increase the level of political activity. As a result of this awareness, the manager quickly infers that a particular subordinate is lobbying for the use of a certain consultant only because the subordinate thinks the consultant's recommendations will be in line with his own. Attempts to control the agenda, engage in game playing, build a certain image, and control decision parameters often are transparently obvious to the knowledgeable observer. Recognizing such behaviors for what they are, an astute manager may be able to take appropriate steps to limit their impact.

Impression Management in Organizations

Impression management   A direct and intentional effort by someone to enhance his or her own image in the eyes of others.

Impression management is a subtle form of political behavior that deserves special mention. **Impression management** is a direct, intentional effort by someone to enhance his or her image in the eyes of others. People engage in impression management for a variety of reasons. For one thing, they may do so to further their own careers. By making themselves look good, they think that they are more likely to receive rewards, attractive job assignments, and promotions. They may also engage in impression management to boost their own self-esteem. When people have a solid image in an organization, others make them aware of it through their compliments, respect, and so forth. Another reason people use impression management is to acquire more power and hence more control.

People attempt to manage how others perceive them through a variety of mechanisms. Appearance is one of the first things people think of. Hence, a person motivated by impression management will pay close attention to choice of attire, selection of language, and the use of manners and body posture. People interested in impression management are also likely to jockey to be associated only with successful projects. By being assigned to high-profile projects led by highly successful managers, a person can begin to link his or her own name with such projects in the minds of others.

Sometimes people too strongly motivated by impression management become obsessed by it and resort to dishonest or unethical means. For example, some people have been known to take credit for others' work in an effort to make themselves look better. People have also been known to exaggerate or even falsify their personal accomplishments in an effort to enhance their image.

Synopsis

Influence can be defined as the ability to affect the perceptions, attitudes, or behaviors of others. Influence is a cornerstone of leadership. Whereas the basic leadership models discussed in Chapter 13 acknowledge influence, they do not directly include it as part of the leadership process.

In recent years, new leadership approaches have attempted to consider the use of influence more directly. Transformational leadership, one such approach, is the set of abilities that allow a leader to recognize the need for change, to create a vision to guide that change, and to execute the change effectively. Another influence-based approach to leadership considers charismatic leadership. Charisma, the basis of this approach, is a form of interpersonal attraction that inspires support and acceptance.

Leadership substitutes are individual, task, and organizational characteristics that tend to outweigh a leader's ability to affect subordinates' satisfaction and performance. Superleadership, a special type of leadership substitute, occurs when a leader gradually and purposefully turns over power, responsibility, and control to a self-managing work group.

Power is the potential ability of a person or group to exercise control over another person or group. The five bases of power are legitimate power (granted by virtue of one's position in the organization), reward power (control of rewards valued by others), coercive power (the ability to punish or harm), expert power (control over information that is valuable to the organization), and referent power (power through personal identification). Position power is tied to a position regardless of the individual who holds it. Personal power is power that resides in a person regardless of position. Attempts to use power can result in commitment, compliance, or resistance.

Organizational politics is activities people perform to acquire, enhance, and use power and other resources to obtain their preferred outcomes in a situation in which uncertainty or disagreement exists. Research indicates that most managers do not advocate use of political behavior but acknowledge that it is a necessity of organizational life. Because managers cannot eliminate political activity in the organization, they must learn to cope with it. Understanding how to manage political behavior requires understanding why it occurs, what techniques it employs, and the strategies for limiting its effects.

Impression management is a direct, intentional effort by someone to enhance his or her image in the eyes of others. People engage in impression management for a variety of reasons and use a variety of methods to influence how others see them.

Discussion Questions

1. Can a person without influence be a leader? Does having influence automatically make someone a leader?

2. Do all organizations need transformational leaders? Do all organizations need transactional leaders? Why are some leaders able to play both roles whereas others can perform only one?

3. Who are some of the more charismatic leaders today?

4. What might happen if two people, each with significant, equal power, attempt to influence each other?

5. Cite examples based on a professor-student relationship to illustrate each of the five bases of organizational power.

6. Is there a logical sequence in the use of power bases that a manager might follow? For instance, should the use of legitimate power usually precede the use of reward power, or vice versa?

7. Cite examples in which you have been committed, compliant, or resistant as a result of efforts to influence you. Think of times when your attempts to influence others led to commitment, compliance, or resistance.

8. Do you agree or disagree with the assertion that political behavior is inevitable in organizational settings?

9. The term "politics" is generally associated with governmental bodies. Why do you think it has also come to be associated with the behavior in organizations described in the chapter?

10. Recall examples of how you have either used or observed others using the techniques of political behavior identified in the chapter. What other techniques can you suggest?

11. Have you ever engaged in impression management? Some people might think that as long as it doesn't get out of hand, impression management is fine; others may think that it is misleading and always inappropriate. What do you think?

Organizational Behavior Case for Discussion

A Corporate Marriage Made in Heaven (Not!)

Enron was 2002's biggest business scandal, but the Hewlett-Packard/Compaq merger was a close runner-up. The story, which has been compared to both a soap opera and a prizefight, began with the appointment in 1999 of Carly Fiorina to the chief executive spot at HP. Fiorina took charge of a company that had degenerated from the once-great computer giant envisioned by founders William Hewlett and David Packard into an unfocused, tradition-bound, and ailing jumble of unrelated business segments. A slowing economy had stalled profits in 2000, and in July 2001, Fiorina announced that she and Compaq CEO Michael Capellas wanted a merger in order to give the combined firm a strong position in both PCs and PC peripherals. Howard Schultz, an HP customer and chairman of Starbucks, believed the merger would be beneficial. At the time, he said, "It's clear to me the best model in an industry that is rapidly consolidating is for this to happen."

The board agreed, but David W. Packard and Walter Hewlett, sons of the HP founders and individuals held in high regard by HP employees and investors, publicly opposed it; together they controlled 18 percent of the company's voting shares. Refuting their position, HP board member Tom Perkins said, "If Walter Hewlett wins this battle, HP will be another Polaroid or Xerox: conservative, risk averse, too reliant on its technology. This is really a proxy battle for the heart and soul of Hewlett-Packard."

The fight quickly became personal and emotional. Hewlett, who serves on HP's board, initially voted in favor of the merger, along with the rest of the board. However, on November 6, 2001, Hewlett told reporters that he would vote against the merger, giving Fiorina thirty minutes' notice of his decision. In January 2002, HP ran print ads claiming that "Bill and Dave" would have approved the merger and sent a letter to stockholders calling Hewlett "an academic and a musician," implying that he doesn't understand business. In response, Packard printed a retort in the *Wall Street Journal* that concludes, "There is now a real danger that HP will die of a broken heart." Hewlett threatened to resign from the board if the merger was completed; Fiorina threatened to resign as CEO if it was blocked.

Perceptions and prejudices were highlighted during the conflict. Walter Hewlett is soft-spoken, but he also earned three graduate degrees from Stanford, competes in marathons and long-distance bicycle races, and plays ten instruments. While appearing in court, Hewlett was described as "rumpled," "off-guard," and "uncomfortable." In contrast, the words "cool," "assertive," and "professional" were used to describe Fiorina. She has excellent business skills and experience, but because she is female, she might be perceived as ineffectual in a tough battle. "I think she's judged by a much harsher and colder metric than a male CEO would be," says Donna Hoffman, a Vanderbilt University management professor. However, according to Jeffrey Christian, Fiorina's executive recruiter, "She has proven [that] a woman can take the heat, stand up to major conflict, and not give up[,] no matter what the odds." Nancy Rothbard, a management professor at the University of Pennsylvania, agrees, noting, "[Fiorina] demonstrates that there are a lot of styles out there. That's great for women. It makes a nice contrast to some of our stereotypical notions of women in leadership roles."

The fighting was followed by a too-close-to-call proxy vote, so even small investors got personalized attention through numerous mailings, emails, and phone calls. "Enough is enough already," protested an owner with less than two-tenths of 1 percent share of HP. In a scene reminiscent of the Bush-Gore presidential race, it took six weeks for all of the mailed-in votes to be counted; in the meantime, each side claimed victory. In the end, the merger was approved by a 51.4 percent majority. Many of those opposing the deal were HP employees—75 percent of shares in employee retirement accounts voted "No."

The legacy of the fighting is a divided firm as Fiorina and Capellas work to merge two giants with very different cultures and history. HP employees fear the inevitable layoffs in which 15,000 to 24,000 employees are likely to lose their jobs. At the April 2002 annual stockholders' meeting, Fiorina said, "I hope we can put the rancor of this campaign behind us and find common ground," but Hewlett later received standing ovations whereas Fiorina was booed. Hewlett lost his position on the board, and he sued the company, claiming that managers "coerced and enticed" Deutsche Bank, a major stockholder, to cast its votes in favor of the merger because Deutsche is providing a $4 billion loan to HP to help pay for the merger. According to *Business Week* writer Peter Burrows, "If [HP] can't get the details right, the honeymoon could be painfully short." It's not yet clear if the divided firm can heal itself. After the eight-month battle, HP survives but remains in danger of dying of a broken heart.

"There is now a real danger that HP will die of a broken heart." —David W. Packard, son of Hewlett-Packard founder David Packard, commenting on the HP-Compaq merger.

References: "Biography: Carleton S. (Carly) Fiorina," Hewlett-Packard Company web site. thenew.hp.com on May 28, 2002; Peter Burrows, "What's In Store for This Happy Couple?" *Business Week*, May 20, 2002. www.businessweek.com on May 28, 2002; Adam Lashinsky, "Hanging Chads: Take 2," *Fortune*, May 13, 2002. www.fortune.com on May 28, 2002; Peter Burrows, "Walter Hewlett's Last Stand?" *Business Week*, April 25, 2002. www.businessweek.com on May 28, 2002; David Kirkpatrick, "After the Accolades, Now What?" *Fortune*, April 15, 2002. www.fortune.com on May 28, 2002; David Rocks, "Hewlett's Challenge: Proving It," *Business Week*, April 9, 2002. www.businessweek.com on May 28, 2002; Peter Burrows and Andrew Park, "How Investors Could Win the HP Battle," *Business Week*, April 4, 2002. www.businessweek.com on May 28, 2002; Amy Tsao, "Fiorina's Stereotype-Smashing Performance," *Business Week*, April 3, 2002. www.businessweek.com on May 28, 2002; Peter Burrows and Andrew Park, "What Price Victory at Hewlett-Packard?" *Business Week*, April 1, 2002. www.businessweek.com on May 28, 2002; Andrew Park and Peter Burrows, "The HP Fight Is Still Too Close to Call," *Business Week*, March 25, 2002. www.businessweek.com on May 28, 2002; David Kirkpatrick, "Carly's New Way," *Fortune*, March 20, 2002. www.fortune.com on May 28, 2002; Peter Burrows, "What's the Truth about Walter Hewlett?" *Business Week*, February 11, 2002. www.businessweek.com on May 19, 2002; "Table: A Corporate Soap Opera," *Business Week*, February 11, 2002 (quotation). www.businessweek.com on May 19, 2002; Adam Lashinsky, "The Defiant Ones," *Fortune*, January 7, 2002. www.fortune.com on May 28, 2002.

Case Questions

1. Based on information from the case, what types of power are demonstrated by Ms. Fiorina? By Mr. Hewlett?

2. Based on information from the case, describe as many instances of the use of political techniques as you can. Consider the actions of all of the involved parties in your answer.

3. In your opinion, what are the likely consequences of the political behavior demonstrated during the HP-Compaq merger?

Experiencing Organizational Behavior

Learning About Ethics and Power

Purpose: This exercise will help you appreciate some of the ambiguities involved in assessing the ethics of power and political behavior in organizations.

Format: First, you will identify examples of more and less ethical uses of power and political behavior. Then you will discuss, compare, and contrast your examples with those generated by some of your classmates.

Procedure:

1. Identify and write down three examples of situations in which you think it would be ethical to use power and political behavior. For example, you might think it is ethical to use them to save the job of a coworker whom you think is a very good—but misunderstood—employee.

2. Identify and write down three examples of situations in which you think it would be unethical to use power and political behavior. For instance, you might think it is unethical to use power and political behavior to gain a job for which you are really not qualified.

3. Form small groups of three or four members each. Each member of the group should read his or her examples of ethical and unethical uses of power and political behavior.

4. Discuss the extent to which the group members agree on the ethics for each situation.

5. See if your group members can think of different situations in which the ethical context changes. For example, if everyone agrees that a given situation is ethical, see if the group can think of slightly different circumstances in which, in essentially the same situation, using power and political behavior would become more unethical.

Follow-up Questions

1. How realistic was this exercise? What did you learn from it?

2. Could you assess real-life situations relating to the ethics of political activity using this same process?

Self-Assessment Exercise

Are You a Charismatic Leader?

Introduction: Charismatic leaders articulate a vision, show concern for group members, communicate high expectations, and create high-performing organizations. This assessment exercise measures your charismatic potential.

Instructions: The following statements refer to the possible ways in which you might behave toward others when you are in a leadership role. Please read each statement carefully and decide to what extent it applies to you. Then put a check on the appropriate number.

To a very great extent   = 5
To a considerable extent = 4
To a moderate extent   = 3
To a slight extent   = 2
To little or no extent   = 1

1. I pay close attention to what others say when they are talking.   1 2 3 4 5

2. I communicate clearly.   1 2 3 4 5

3. I am trustworthy.   1 2 3 4 5

4. I care about other people.   1 2 3 4 5

5. I do not put excessive energy into avoiding failure.   1 2 3 4 5

6. I make the work of others more meaningful.   1 2 3 4 5

7. I seem to focus on the key issues in a situation.   1 2 3 4 5

8. I get across my meaning effectively, often in unusual ways.   1 2 3 4 5

9. I can be relied on to follow
through on commitments.   1 2 3 4 5

10. I have a great deal of self-respect.   1 2 3 4 5

11. I enjoy taking carefully
calculated risks.   1 2 3 4 5

12. I help others feel more competent
in what they do.   1 2 3 4 5

13. I have a clear set of priorities.   1 2 3 4 5

14. I am in touch with how others
feel.   1 2 3 4 5

15. I rarely change once I have
taken a clear position.   1 2 3 4 5

16. I focus on strengths, of myself
and of others.   1 2 3 4 5

17. I seem most alive when deeply
involved in some project.   1 2 3 4 5

18. I show others that they are all
part of the same group.   1 2 3 4 5

19. I get others to focus on the issues
I see as important.   1 2 3 4 5

20. I communicate feelings as well as
ideas.   1 2 3 4 5

21. I let others know where I stand.   1 2 3 4 5

22. I seem to know just how I "fit"
into a group.   1 2 3 4 5

23. I learn from mistakes and do not
treat errors as disasters but rather
as learning experiences.   1 2 3 4 5

24. I am fun to be around.   1 2 3 4 5

For interpretation, see the Interpretation Guide in the *Instructor's Resource Manual.*

The questionnaire measures six facets of charismatic leadership. Your score can range from 4 to 20 for each section. Each question is stated as a measure of the extent to which you engage in the behavior—or elicit the feelings. The higher your score, the more you demonstrate charismatic leader behaviors.

Index 1: Management of Attention (1, 7, 13, 19).
Your score: ____. You pay especially close attention to people with whom you are communicating. You are also "focused in" on the key issues under discussion and help others to see clearly these key points. You have clear ideas about the relative importance or priorities of different issues under discussion.

Index 2: Management of Meaning (2, 8, 14, 20).
Your score: ____. This set of items centers on your communication skills, specifically your ability to get the meaning of a message across, even if this means devising some quite innovative approach.

Index 3: Management of Trust (3, 9, 15, 21).
Your score: ____. The key factor is your perceived trustworthiness as shown by your willingness to follow through on promises, to avoid "flip-flop" shifts in position, and to take clear positions.

Index 4: Management of Self (4, 10, 16, 22).
Your score: ____. This index concerns your general attitudes toward yourself and others—that is, your overall concern for others and their feelings as well as for "taking care of" feelings about yourself in a positive sense (e.g., self-regard).

Index 5: Management of Risk (5, 11, 17, 23).
Your score: ——. Effective charismatic leaders are deeply involved in what they do and do not spend excessive amounts of time or energy on plans to "protect" themselves against failure. These leaders are willing to take risks, not on a hit-or-miss basis, but after careful estimation of the odds of success or failure.

Index 6: Management of Feelings (6, 12, 18, 24).
Your score: ____. Charismatic leaders seem to consistently generate a set of positive feelings in others. Others feel that their work becomes more meaningful and that they are the "masters" of their own behavior—that is, they feel competent. They feel a sense of community, a "we-ness" with their colleagues and coworkers.

Reference: Marshall Sashkin and William C. Morris, *Experiential Exercises in Management Book*, p. 132. Copyright © 1987, Addison-Wesley Publishing Company, Inc. Reprinted by permission of Addison-Wesley Longman, Inc.

OB Online

1. Use a search engine to identify web sites that deal with power and politics. What conclusions can you draw from your findings?

2. Identify a leader whose behavior you would consider transformational. Then use the Internet to find articles and/or other material that either supports or refutes your belief.

3. Think of three individuals who are both leaders and who have their own personal web sites. Review the sites to see what role, if any, impression management plays in how others perceive these individuals.

4. Describe how the Internet and related forms of information technology might serve as substitutes for leadership.

Building Managerial Skills

Exercise Overview: Diagnostic skills help a manager visualize appropriate responses to a situation. One situation managers often face is whether to use power to solve a problem. This exercise will help you develop your diagnostic skills as they relate to using different types of power in different situations.

Exercise Background: Several methods have been identified for using power. These include the following:

1. *Legitimate request*—The manager requests that the subordinate comply because the subordinate recognizes that the organization has given the manager the right to make the request. Most day-to-day interactions between manager and subordinate are of this type.

2. *Instrumental compliance*—In this form of exchange, a subordinate complies to get the reward the manager controls. Suppose that a manager asks a subordinate to do something outside the range of the subordinate's normal duties, such as working extra hours on the weekend, terminating a relationship with a long-standing buyer, or delivering bad news. The subordinate complies and, as a direct result, reaps praise and a bonus from the manager. The next time the subordinate is asked to perform a similar activity, that subordinate will recognize that compliance could be instrumental in her getting more rewards. Hence the basis of instrumental compliance is clarifying important performance-reward contingencies.

3. *Coercion*—This is used when the manager suggests or implies that the subordinate will be punished, fired, or reprimanded if he or she does not do something.

4. *Rational persuasion*—This is when the manager can convince the subordinate that compliance is in the subordinate's best interest. For example, a manager might argue that the subordinate should accept a transfer because it would be good for the subordinate's career. In some ways, rational persuasion is like reward power except that the manager does not really control the reward.

5. *Personal identification*—This is when a manager who recognizes that she has referent power over a subordinate can shape the behavior of that subordinate by engaging in desired behaviors. The manager consciously becomes a model for the subordinate and exploits personal identification.

6. *Inspirational appeal*—This is when a manager can induce a subordinate to do something consistent with a set of higher ideals or values through inspirational appeal. For example, a plea for loyalty represents an inspirational appeal.

Exercise Task: With these ideas in mind, do the following:

1. Relate each of the uses of power just listed to the five types of power identified in the chapter. That is, indicate which type or types of power are most closely associated with each use of power, which type or types may be related to each use of power, and which type or types are unrelated to each use of power.

2. Is a manager more likely to be using multiple forms of power at the same time or to be using a single type of power?

3. Identify other methods and approaches to using power.

4. What are some of the dangers and pitfalls associated with using power?

15 Decision Making and Negotiation

Management Preview

▶ Making decisions is the most basic of all management activities. Some decisions involve major events, such as buying another company or launching an expensive new product line, and will have a dramatic impact on a firm's future growth, profits, and even survival. Others, such as choosing the colors of the office's new carpet or deciding when to reorder office supplies, are much less significant. But all decisions are important on some level, so managers need to understand how decisions are made.

This chapter explores decision making in detail. We start by examining the nature of decision making. Next, we describe several different approaches to understanding the decision-making process. We then identify and discuss two related behavioral aspects of decision making. Next, we discuss several important issues in group decision making. We conclude with a discussion of negotiation, a common management activity closely related to decision making. But first we describe how effective decision making has been a boon to both MTV and its parent company, Viacom.

▼ ▼ ▼

When Bill Roedy became president of MTV's Networks International division, he probably didn't count on singing *Madame Butterfly* arias alone and unaccompanied in front of dozens of Chinese executives and his boss. But Roedy, a fifty-three-year-old West Point graduate, was willing to do it, so intent is he on doing whatever it takes to cultivate long-term relationships with potential partners. Listeners took Roedy's opera performance as a sign of his understanding of Chinese customs, which can include impromptu classical singing at business dinners. Roedy was persuading Chinese cable TV operators to carry MTV—and the performance must have been effective because MTV today is seen in 60 million Chinese homes on over forty cable systems.

In addition to his vocal talents, Roedy's decision-making skills are also paying off for MTV. Early on, it was decided that programming in other countries should consist primarily of local performers (70 percent local, 30 percent American, currently). This move was part marketing genius—allowing MTV to attract both conservative and adventurous listeners—and part brilliant negotiation strategy. "We've had very little resistance once we explain that we're not in the business of exporting American culture," says Roedy. The mix allows MTV's parent company, Viacom, to obtain the rights to the best international performers for introduction to the American market. To overcome regulatory opposition, Roedy has dined with former Israeli Prime Minister Shimon Peres, Chinese president Jiang Zemin, and even Fidel Castro, the Cuban leader.

"We've had very little resistance once we explain that we're not in the business of exporting American culture."—Bill Roedy, MTV Networks International president

A key decision was to focus on regions with high numbers of teens and in high growth television ownership, such as India, Brazil, and China. Currently, MTV is viewed by 84.6 million households in North America, 124.1 million in Europe, 28.1 million in Latin America, and 137.9 million in Asia. "Everyone who has a TV knows there's something called MTV," claims Chantara Kapahi, a student at Jai Hind College of Bombay, India. The decision to focus on countries with an increased standard of living pays a double bonus: As consumer buying power increases, local businesses are more willing and able to pay for MTV advertisements. In countries where public sentiment or government policy makes it difficult for American companies to compete, such as Italy and Brazil, MTV partners with a local cable provider.

Viacom cleverly decided to move into many aspects of the media and the entertainment industry, leading to name recognition and other synergies. Among other holdings, Viacom owns CBS, UPN, Paramount, MTV, Nickelodeon, BET, VH1, CNN, CMT, Comedy Central, Showtime, Blockbuster movie rentals, and the Simon and Schuster publishing house. Viacom plans to use MTV to break ground in new regional markets and then follow up with its other cable offerings. "Let's face it, the way people know Viacom is through MTV," says Viacom Chief Operating Officer and President Mel Karmazin. Sound choices have put the firm on the path to success—its latest achievement is a broadcast of the May 2002 China Central TV-MTV Mandarin Music awards. The show will reach 300 million households in China and another 300 million around the world, making it one of the most-watched broadcasts ever.

References: "Businesses," "Viacom Chairman Sumner Redstone Meets with China's President Jiang Zemin in Beijing, to Reaffirm Viacom's Commitment to China," Viacom web site. www.viacom.com on May 13, 2002; John Simmons, "Come Se Dice Must-See TV?" *Fortune*, April 15, 2002. www.fortune.com on May 13, 2002; Tom Lowry, "Viacom: A Survivor—and Much More," *Business Week*, April 3, 2002. www.businessweek.com on May 13, 2002; Kerry Capell, "How MTV Conquered Italy," *Business Week*, February 18, 2002, p. 84. See www.businessweek.com; Kerry Capell, "MTV's World," *Business Week*, February 18, 2002, pp. 81–84 (quotation p. 82). See www.businessweek.com.

The man or woman at the top of an organization, such as Bill Roedy at MTV, is paid to make both tough and easy decisions. Regardless of which decisions are made, though, it is almost certain that some observers will criticize and others will applaud. Indeed, in the rough-and-tumble world of business, there are few simple or easy decisions to make. Some managers claim to be focused on the goal of what is good for the company in the long term and make decisions accordingly. Others clearly focus on the here-and-now. Some decisions deal with employees, some with investors, and others with dollars and cents. But all require careful thought and consideration. This chapter describes many different perspectives of decision making.

The Nature of Decision Making

Decision making is the process of choosing from among several alternatives.

Decision making is choosing one alternative from among several. Consider football, for example. The quarterback can run any of perhaps a hundred plays. With the goal of scoring a touchdown always in mind, he chooses the play that seems to promise the best outcome. His choice is based on his understanding of the game situation, the likelihood of various outcomes, and his preference for each outcome.

Figure 15.1 shows the basic elements of decision making. A decision maker's actions are guided by a goal. Each of several alternative courses of action is linked with various outcomes. Information is available on the alternatives, on the likelihood that each outcome will occur, and on the value of each outcome relative to the goal. The decision maker chooses one alternative on the basis of his or her evaluation of the information.

Decisions made in organizations can be classified according to frequency and to information conditions. In a decision-making context, frequency is how often a particular decision situation recurs, and information conditions describe how much information is available about the likelihood of various outcomes.

A programmed decision is a decision that recurs often enough for a decision rule to be developed.

A decision rule is a statement that tells a decision maker which alternative to choose based on the characteristics of the decision situation.

Types of Decisions

The frequency of recurrence determines whether a decision is programmed or nonprogrammed. A **programmed decision** recurs often enough for decision rules to be developed. A **decision rule** tells decision makers which alternative to choose once they have predetermined information about the decision situation. The appropriate decision rule is used whenever the same situation is encountered. Programmed decisions usually are highly structured; that is, the goals are clear

figure 15.1

Elements of Decision Making

A decision maker has a goal, evaluates the outcomes of alternative courses of action in terms of the goal, and selects one alternative to be implemented.

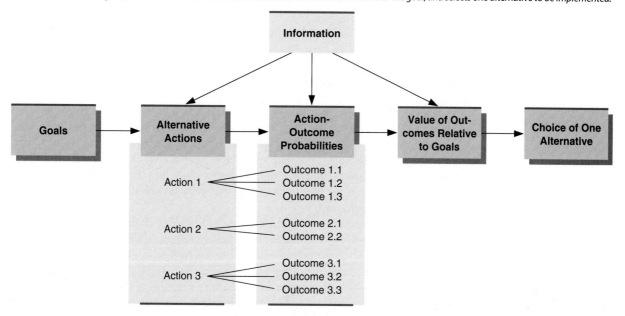

and well known, the decision-making procedure is already established, and the sources and channels of information are clearly defined.[1]

Airlines use established procedures when an airplane breaks down and cannot be used on a particular flight. Passengers may not view the issue as a programmed decision because they experience this situation relatively infrequently. But the airlines know that equipment problems that render a plane unfit for service arise regularly. Each airline has its own set of clear procedures to use in the event of equipment problems. A given flight may be delayed, canceled, or continued on a different plane, depending on the nature of the problem and other circumstances (such as the number of passengers booked, the next scheduled flight for the same destination, and so forth).

When a problem or decision situation has not been encountered before, however, a decision maker cannot rely on previously established decision rules. Such a decision is called a **nonprogrammed decision,** and it requires problem solving. **Problem solving** is a special form of decision making in which the issue is unique—it requires developing and evaluating alternatives without the aid of a decision rule. Nonprogrammed decisions are poorly structured because information is ambiguous, there is no clear procedure for making the decision, and the goals are often vague. Many of the decisions that had to be made by government, military, and business leaders in the wake of the events of September 11, 2001, were clearly this type.

A nonprogrammed decision is a decision that recurs infrequently and for which there is no previously established decision rule.

Problem solving is a form of decision making in which the issue is unique and alternatives must be developed and evaluated without the aid of a programmed decision rule.

"Solve it, solve it quickly, solve it right or wrong. If you solved it wrong, it would come back and slap you in the face, and then you could solve it right."—Thomas J. Watson Jr., CEO and son of the founder of IBM[2]

Table 15.1 summarizes the characteristics of programmed and nonprogrammed decisions. Note that programmed decisions are more common at the lower levels of the organization whereas a primary responsibility of top management is to make the difficult, nonprogrammed decisions that determine the organization's long-term effectiveness. By definition, the strategic decisions for which top management is responsible are poorly structured and nonroutine and have far-reaching consequences.[3] Programmed decisions, then, can be made according to previously tested rules and procedures. Nonprogrammed decisions generally require that the decision maker exercise judgment and creativity. In other words, all problems require a decision, but not all decisions require problem solving.

Information Required for Decision Making

Decisions are made to bring about desired outcomes, but the information available about those outcomes varies. The range of available information can be considered as a continuum whose endpoints represent complete certainty when all alternative outcomes are known and complete uncertainty when alternative outcomes are unknown. Points between the two extremes create risk—the decision maker has some information about the possible outcomes and may be able to estimate the probability of their occurrence.

Different information conditions present different challenges to the decision maker.[4] For example, suppose the marketing manager of PlayStation is trying to determine whether to launch an expensive promotional effort for a new video game (see Figure 15.2). For simplicity, assume there are only two alternatives: to promote the game or not to promote it. Under a **condition of certainty,** the manager knows the outcomes of each alternative. If the new game is promoted heavily,

Under the condition of certainty, the manager knows the outcomes of each alternative.

table 15.1

Characteristics of Programmed and Nonprogrammed Decisions

Characteristics	Programmed Decisions	Nonprogrammed Decisions
Type of Decision	Well structured	Poorly structured
Frequency	Repetitive and routine	New and unusual
Goals	Clear, specific	Vague
Information	Readily available	Not available, unclear channels
Consequences	Minor	Major
Organizational Level	Lower levels	Upper levels
Time for Solution	Short	Relatively long
Basis for Solution	Decision rules, set procedures	Judgment and creativity

the company will realize a $10 million profit. Without promotion, the company will realize only a $2 million profit. Here the decision is simple: Promote the game. (Note: These figures are created for the purposes of this example and are not actual profit figures for any company.)

Under the condition of risk, the decision maker cannot know with certainty what the outcome of a given action will be but has enough information to estimate the probabilities of various outcomes.

Under a **condition of risk,** the decision maker cannot know with certainty what the outcome of a given action will be but has enough information to estimate the probabilities of various outcomes. Thus, working from information gathered by the market research department, the marketing manager in our example can estimate the likelihood of each outcome in a risk situation. In this case, the alternatives are defined by the size of the market. The probability for a large video game market is 0.6, and the probability for a small market is 0.4. The manager can calculate the expected value of the promotional effort based on these probabilities and the expected profits associated with each. To find the expected value of an alternative, the manager multiplies each outcome's value by the probability of its occurrence. The sum of these calculations for all possible outcomes represents that alternative's expected value. In this case, the expected value of alternative 1—to promote the new game—is as follows:

$$0.6 \times \$10,000,000 = \$6,000,000$$

$$+ \ 0.4 \times \$2,000,000 = \quad \$800,000$$

Expected value of alternatives 1 = $6,800,000

The expected value of alternative 2—not to promote the new game—is $1,400,000 (see Figure 15.2). The marketing manager should choose the first alternative, because its expected value is higher. The manager should recognize, however, that although the numbers look convincing, they are based on incomplete information and are only estimates of probability.

Under the condition of uncertainty, the decision maker lacks enough information to estimate the probability of possible outcomes.

The decision maker who lacks enough information to estimate the probability of outcomes (or perhaps even to identify the outcomes at all) faces a **condition of uncertainty.** In the PlayStation example, this might be the case if sales of video games had recently collapsed, and it was not clear whether the precipitous drop was temporary or permanent or when information to clarify the situation would be available. Under such circumstances, the decision maker may wait for more information to reduce uncertainty or rely on judgment, experience, and intuition to make the decision.

figure 15.2

Alternative Outcomes Under Different Information Conditions

The three decision-making conditions of certainty, risk, and uncertainty for the decision about whether to promote a new video game to the market.

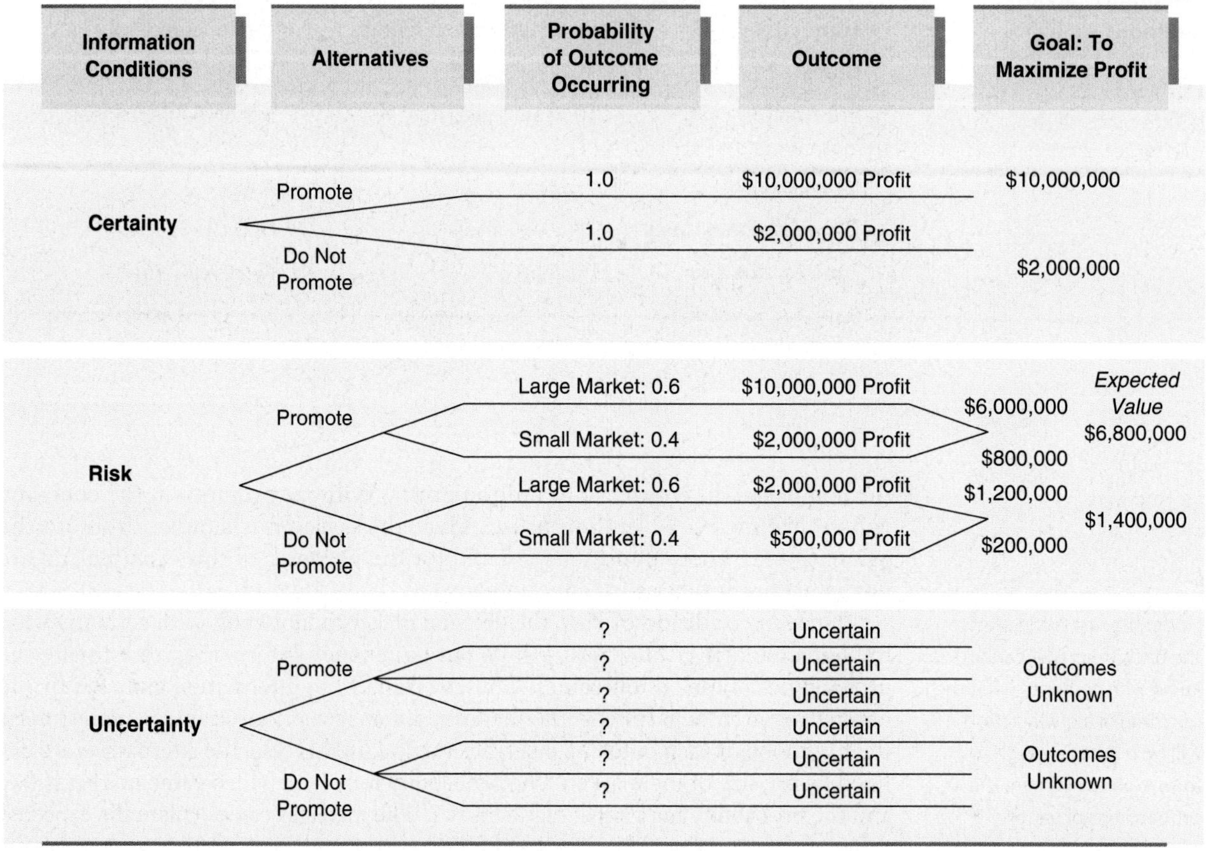

Information Conditions	Alternatives	Probability of Outcome Occurring	Outcome	Goal: To Maximize Profit
Certainty	Promote	1.0	$10,000,000 Profit	$10,000,000
	Do Not Promote	1.0	$2,000,000 Profit	$2,000,000
Risk	Promote	Large Market: 0.6	$10,000,000 Profit	$6,000,000 — *Expected Value* $6,800,000
		Small Market: 0.4	$2,000,000 Profit	$800,000
	Do Not Promote	Large Market: 0.6	$2,000,000 Profit	$1,200,000 — $1,400,000
		Small Market: 0.4	$500,000 Profit	$200,000
Uncertainty	Promote	?	Uncertain	Outcomes Unknown
		?	Uncertain	
		?	Uncertain	
	Do Not Promote	?	Uncertain	Outcomes Unknown
		?	Uncertain	
		?	Uncertain	

Decision making, however, is not always so easy to classify in terms of certainty, uncertainty, and risk. Some individuals are more likely to take risks than others are, as was discussed in Chapter 4. In addition, in some parts of the world it may be more common to take risks than in others, as was discussed in Chapter 3.

"When you look at companies that get themselves into trouble, they're often taking steps of great, lurching bravado rather than quiet, deliberate understanding."
—*Jim Collins, decision-making writer and expert*[5]

The Decision-Making Process

Several approaches to decision making offer insights into the process by which managers arrive at their decisions. The rational approach is appealing because of its logic and economy. Yet these very qualities raise questions about this approach because actual decision making often is not a wholly rational process. The behavioral approach, meanwhile, attempts to account for the limits on rationality in decision making. The practical approach combines features of the rational and behavioral approaches. Finally, the personal approach focuses on the decision-making processes individuals use in difficult situations.

The Rational Approach

The rational decision-making approach is a systematic, step-by-step process for making decisions.

The **rational decision-making approach** assumes that managers follow a systematic, step-by-step process. It further assumes the organization is economically based and managed by decision makers who are entirely objective and have complete information.[6] Figure 15.3 identifies the steps of the process, starting with

figure 15.3

The Rational Decision-Making Process

The rational model follows a systematic, step-by-step approach from goals to implementation, measurement, and control.

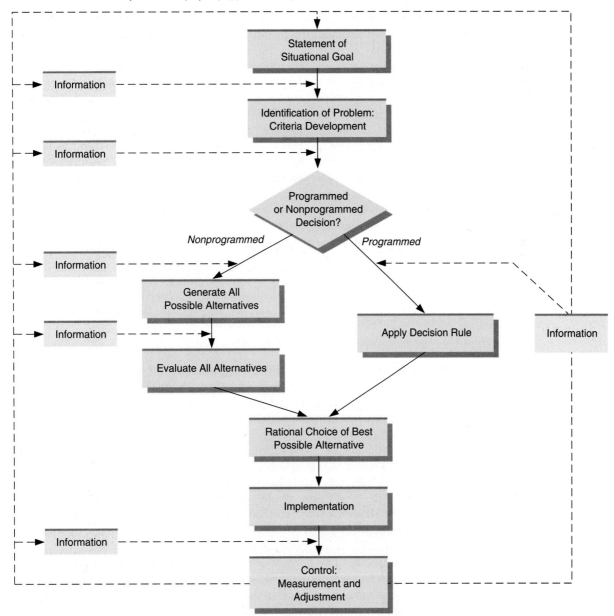

MASTERING CHANGE

▶ Technical Developments Drive "People" Changes

Faced with stagnant U.S. sales and consumer caution, manufacturers are turning to a quality initiative called Six Sigma for help. The process limits the number of defective products to just 3.4 per 1 million items produced. Businesses are required to identify customer requirements, measure performance, analyze performance gaps, make improvements, and ensure ongoing compliance. Thus, Six Sigma is a structured, systematic, quantitative process for making decisions. Many different types of companies, from automakers to insurers to hospitals, have benefited from using the program. The following are some Six Sigma success stories.

Shea Homes, a Phoenix homebuilder, used Six Sigma to reduce its defects from 80 percent to just 20 percent one year later. The company worked closely with its numerous subcontractors, a group whose opinions are not usually valued by homebuilders. After one meeting with a framing subcontractor, Buddy Satterfield of Shea Homes said, "Six Sigma . . . brings home our goal for a zero-defect delivery."

GE's former CEO Jack Welch claims Six Sigma saved the firm over $1 billion annually. For example, GE made a plastic that was used in car mirrors, and United Technologies Automotive molded and painted the mirrors. GE engineers worked with United to change the plastic's composition for better paint adherence, resulting in less waste, lower expenses, and increased customer satisfaction.

> "[Six Sigma is] not about fixing things. It's about reinventing them."—Max Allway, vice president of consulting for Six Sigma Academy of Scottsdale, Arizona

Dow Chemical sends its employees to four week-long Six Sigma training sessions. "People come from around the world and [from] every part of Dow, so you have a manufacturing engineer sitting next to a seller, sitting next to an IT person. It's very diverse," according to Tom Gurd, Dow's vice president for quality.

One benefit of using Six Sigma is participants' willingness to scrap previous processes and begin anew. Gurd says, "We realized that this was not something we wanted to do as an evolution. It was going to be a transformation." Max Allway of the Six Sigma Academy claims, "Six Sigma has been called a new corporate DNA because it's not about fixing things. It's about reinventing them." Six Sigma provides the perfect example of how developments in technical fields such as engineering can have a profound impact on an organization's "people" processes—communicating, organizing, and decision making.

References: "Six Sigma—What is Six Sigma?" iSixSigma web site. www.isixsigma.com on May 14, 2002; Catherine Reagor, "Simplify and Save," *Arizona Republic* (Phoenix), January 27, 2002, p. D1 (quotation. See www.azcentral.com; Kristine Ellis, "Mastering Six Sigma," *Training,* December 2001. See www.trainingmag.com.

stating a goal and running logically through the process until the best decision is made, implemented, and controlled. The "Mastering Change" box discusses how some firms are applying a rational, structured decision-making process called Six Sigma to their quality improvement initiatives.

State the Situational Goal   The rational decision-making process begins with the statement of a situational goal—that is, a goal for a particular situation. The goal of a marketing department, for example, may be to obtain a certain market share by the end of the year. (Some models of decision making do not start with a goal. We include it because it is the standard used to determine whether there is a decision to be made.)

Identify the Problem   The purpose of problem identification is to gather information that bears on the goal. If there is a discrepancy between the goal and the actual state, action may be needed. In the marketing example, the group may gather information about the company's actual market share and compare it with the desired market share. A difference between the two represents a problem that necessitates a decision. Reliable information is very important in this step. Inaccurate information can lead to an unnecessary decision or no decision when one is required.

"The formulation of a problem is often more essential than its solution."—Rolf Smith, president of Virtual Thinking Expedition Company, quoting Albert Einstein[7]

Determining Decision Type   Next, the decision makers must determine if the problem represents a programmed or a nonprogrammed decision. If a programmed decision is needed, the appropriate decision rule is invoked, and the process moves on to the choice among alternatives. A programmed marketing decision may be called for if analysis reveals that competitors are outspending the company on print advertising. Because creating print advertising and buying space for it are well-established functions of the marketing group, the problem requires only a programmed decision.

Although it may seem simple to diagnose a situation as programmed, apply a decision rule, and arrive at a solution, mistakes can still occur. Choosing the wrong decision rule or assuming the problem calls for a programmed decision when a nonprogrammed decision actually is required can result in poor decisions. The same caution applies to the determination that a nonprogrammed decision is called for. If the situation is wrongly diagnosed, the decision maker wastes time and resources seeking a new solution to an old problem, or "reinventing the wheel."

Generate Alternatives   The next step in making a nonprogrammed decision is to generate alternatives. The rational process assumes that decision makers will generate all the possible alternative solutions to the problem. However, this assumption is unrealistic because even simple business problems can have scores of possible solutions. Decision makers may rely on education and experience as well as knowledge of the situation to generate alternatives. In addition, they may seek information from other people such as peers, subordinates, and supervisors. Decision makers may analyze the symptoms of the problem for clues or fall back on intuition or judgment to develop alternative solutions.[8] If the marketing department in our example determines that a nonprogrammed decision is required, it will need to generate alternatives for increasing market share.

Evaluate Alternatives   Evaluation involves assessing all possible alternatives in terms of predetermined decision criteria. The ultimate decision criterion is "Will this alternative bring us nearer to the goal?" In each case, the decision maker must examine each alternative for evidence that it will reduce the discrepancy between the desired state and the actual state. The evaluation process usually includes (1) describing the anticipated outcomes (benefits) of each alternative, (2) evaluating the anticipated costs of each alternative, and (3) estimating the uncertainties and risks associated with each alternative.[9] In most decision situations, the decision maker does not have perfect information regarding the outcomes of all alternatives. At one extreme, as shown earlier in Figure 15.2, outcomes may be known with certainty; at the other, the decision maker has no information whatsoever, so the outcomes are entirely uncertain. But risk is the most common situation.

Choose an Alternative   Choosing an alternative is usually the most crucial step in the decision-making process. Choosing consists of selecting the alternative with the highest possible payoff, based on the benefits, costs, risks, and uncertainties of all alternatives. In the PlayStation promotion example, the decision maker evaluated the two alternatives by calculating their expected values. Following the rational approach, the manager would choose the alternative with the largest expected value.

Even with the rational approach, however, difficulties can arise in choosing an alternative. First, when two or more alternatives have equal payoffs, the decision maker must obtain more information or use some other criterion to make the choice. Second, when no single alternative will accomplish the objective, some combination of two or three alternatives may have to be implemented. Finally, if no alternative or combination of alternatives will solve the problem, the decision maker must obtain more information, generate more alternatives, or change the goals.[10]

An important part of the choice phase is the consideration of **contingency plans**—alternative actions that can be taken if the primary course of action is unexpectedly disrupted or rendered inappropriate.[11] Planning for contingencies is part of the transition between choosing the preferred alternative and implementing it. In developing contingency plans, the decision maker usually asks such questions as "What if something unexpected happens during the implementation of this alternative?" or "If the economy goes into a recession, will the choice of this alternative ruin the company?" or "How can we alter this plan if the economy suddenly rebounds and begins to grow?"

Implement the Plan   Implementation puts the decision into action. It builds on the commitment and motivation of those who participated in the decision-making process (and may actually bolster individual commitment and motivation). To succeed, implementation requires the proper use of resources and good management skills. Following the decision to promote the new PlayStation game heavily, for example, the marketing manager must implement the decision by assigning the project to a work group or task force. The success of this team depends on the leadership, the reward structure, the communications system, and group dynamics. Sometimes the decision maker begins to doubt a choice already made. This doubt is called *post-decision dissonance*, or more generally, **cognitive dissonance**.[12] To reduce the tension created by the dissonance, the decision maker may seek to rationalize the decision further with new information.

Control: Measure and Adjust   In the final stage of the rational decision-making process, the outcomes of the decision are measured and compared with the desired goal. If a discrepancy remains, the decision maker may restart the decision-making process by setting a new goal (or reiterating the existing one). The decision maker, unsatisfied with the previous decision, may modify the subsequent decision-making process to avoid another mistake. Changes can be made in any part of the process, as Figure 15.3 illustrates by the arrows leading from the control step to each of the other steps. Decision making therefore is a dynamic, self-correcting, and ongoing process in organizations.

Suppose a marketing department implements a new print advertising campaign. After implementation, it constantly monitors market research data and compares its new market share with the desired market share. If the advertising has the desired effect, no changes will be made in the promotion campaign. If, however, the data indicate no change in the market share, additional decisions and implementation of a contingency plan may be necessary. For example, when Nissan introduced its luxury car line Infiniti, it relied on a Zen-like series of ads that featured images of rocks, plants, and water—but no images of the car. At the same time, Toyota was featuring pictures of its new luxury car line, Lexus, which quickly

Contingency plans are alternative actions to take if the primary course of action is unexpectedly disrupted or rendered inappropriate.

Cognitive dissonance is doubt about a choice that has already been made.

established itself as a market leader. When Infiniti managers realized their mistake, they quickly pulled the old ads and started running new ones centered around images of their car.[13]

Strengths and Weaknesses of the Rational Approach   The rational approach has several strengths. It forces the decision maker to consider a decision in a logical, sequential manner, and the in-depth analysis of alternatives enables the decision maker to choose on the basis of information rather than emotion or social pressure. But the rigid assumptions of this approach often are unrealistic.[14] The amount of information available to managers usually is limited by either time or cost constraints, and most decision makers have limited ability to process information about the alternatives. In addition, not all alternatives lend themselves to quantification in terms that will allow for easy comparison. Finally, because they cannot predict the future, it is unlikely that decision makers will know all possible outcomes of each alternative.

The decision-making process is supposed to be logical and rational but is instead often affected by behavioral, practical, and personal considerations. Consider, for example, Gabrielle Melchionda. Ms. Melchionda is a Maine entrepreneur whose skin-care product business is booming. She was recently offered a lucrative contract to begin exporting her products to Turkey. But she turned it down when she learned that the exporter also sold weapons. Had rational decision-making prevailed she would have jumped on the idea. But her own personal values kept her focused on what was important to her as a person—and it wasn't just the money!

The Behavioral Approach

Whereas the rational approach assumes that managers operate logically and rationally, the behavioral approach acknowledges the role and importance of human behavior in the decision-making process. In particular, a crucial assumption of the behavioral approach is that decision makers operate with bounded rationality rather than with the perfect rationality assumed by the rational approach. **Bounded rationality** is the idea that although individuals seek the best solution to a problem, the demands of processing all the information bearing on the problem, generating all possible solutions, and choosing the single best solution are beyond the capabilities of most decision makers. Thus, they accept less-than-ideal solutions based on a process that is neither exhaustive nor entirely rational. For example, one recent study found that under time pressure, groups usually eliminate all but the two most favorable alternatives and then process the remaining two in great detail.[15] Thus, decision makers operating with bounded rationality limit the inputs to the decision-making process and base decisions on judgment and personal biases as well as on logic.[16]

Bounded rationality is the idea that decision makers cannot deal with information about all the aspects and alternatives pertaining to a problem and therefore choose to tackle some meaningful subset of it.

The behavioral approach uses rules of thumb, suboptimizing, and satisficing in making decisions.

The **behavioral approach** is characterized by (1) the use of procedures and rules of thumb, (2) suboptimizing, and (3) satisficing. Uncertainty in decision making can initially be reduced by relying on procedures and rules of thumb. If, for example, increasing print advertising has increased a company's market share in the past, that linkage may be used by company employees as a rule of thumb in decision making. When the previous month's market share drops below a certain level, the company might increase its print advertising expenditures by 25 percent during the following month.

Suboptimizing is knowingly accepting less than the best possible outcome. Frequently it is not feasible to make the ideal decision in a real-world situation given organizational constraints. The decision maker often must suboptimize to avoid unintended negative effects on other departments, product lines, or decisions.[17] An automobile manufacturer, for example, can cut costs dramatically and increase efficiency if it schedules the production of one model at a time. Thus, the production group's optimal decision is single-model scheduling. But the marketing group, seeking to optimize its sales goals by offering a wide variety of models, may demand the opposite production schedule: short runs of entirely different models. The groups in the middle, design and scheduling, may suboptimize the benefits the production and marketing groups seek by planning long runs of slightly different models. This is the practice of the large auto manufacturers such as General Motors and Ford, which make several body styles in numerous models on the same production line.

The final feature of the behavioral approach is **satisficing**: examining alternatives only until a solution that meets minimal requirements is found and then ceasing to look for a better one.[18] The search for alternatives usually is a sequential process guided by procedures and rules of thumb based on previous experiences with similar problems. The search often ends when the first minimally acceptable choice is encountered. The resulting choice may narrow the discrepancy between the desired and the actual states, but it is not likely to be the optimal solution. As the process is repeated, incremental improvements slowly reduce the discrepancy between the actual and desired states.

> Suboptimizing is knowingly accepting less than the best possible outcome to avoid unintended negative effects on other aspects of the organization.

> Satisficing is examining alternatives only until a solution that meets minimal requirements is found.

The Practical Approach

Because of the unrealistic demands of the rational approach and the limited, short-run orientation of the behavioral approach, neither is entirely satisfactory. However, the worthwhile features of each can be combined into a practical approach to decision making, shown in Figure 15.4. The steps in this process are the same as in the rational approach; however, the conditions recognized by the behavioral approach are added to provide a more realistic process. For example, the **practical approach** suggests that rather than generating all alternatives, the decision maker should try to go beyond rules of thumb and satisficing limitations and generate as many alternatives as time, money, and other practicalities of the situation allow. In this synthesis of the two other approaches, the rational approach provides an analytical framework for making decisions whereas the behavioral approach provides a moderating influence.

> The practical approach to decision making combines the steps of the rational approach with the conditions in the behavioral approach to create a more realistic approach for making decisions in organizations.

In practice, decision makers use some hybrid of the rational, behavioral, and practical approaches to make the tough day-to-day decisions in running organizations. Some decision makers use a methodical process of gathering as much information as possible, developing and evaluating alternatives, and seeking advice from knowledgeable people before making a decision. Others fly from one decision to another, making seemingly hasty decisions and barking out orders to subordinates. The second group would seem not to use much information or a rational approach to making decisions. Recent research, however, has shown that managers who make decisions very quickly probably are using just as much, or more, information and generating and evaluating as many alternatives as slower, more methodical decision makers.[19]

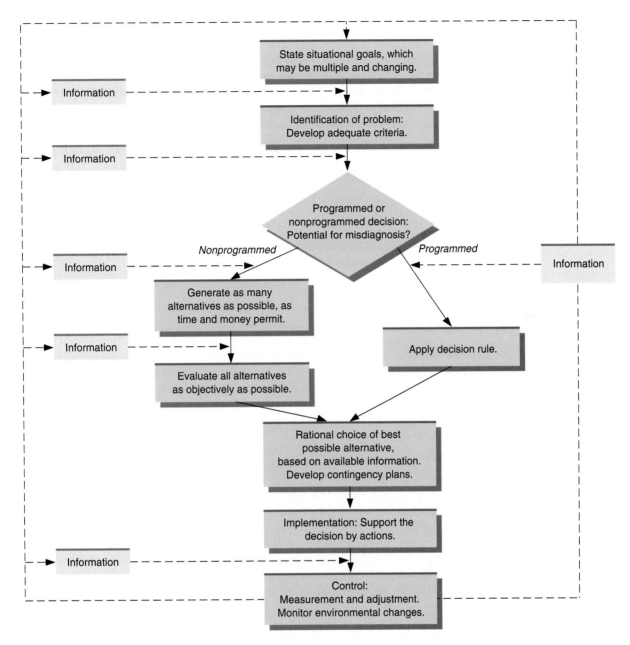

figure 15.4

Practical Approach to Decision Making with Behavioral Guidelines

The practical model applies some of the conditions recognized by the behavioral approach to the rational approach to decision making. Although similar to the rational model, the practical approach recognizes personal limitations at each point (or step) in the process.

The Personal Approach

Although the models just described have provided significant insight into decision making, they do not fully explain the processes people engage in when they are nervous, worried, and agitated over making a decision that has major implications for them, their organization, or their families. In short, they still do not reflect the conditions under which many decisions are made. One attempt to provide a more realistic view of individual decision making is the model presented by Irving Janis and Leon Mann.[20] The Janis-Mann concept, called the **conflict model,** is based on research in social psychology and individual decision processes and is a very personal approach to decision making. Although the model may appear complex, if you examine it one step at a time and follow the example in this section, you should easily understand how it works. The model has five basic characteristics:

> The conflict model is a very personal approach to decision making because it deals with the personal conflicts that people experience in particularly difficult decision situations.

1. It deals only with important life decisions—marriage, schooling, career, and major organizational decisions—that commit the individual or the organization to a certain course of action following the decision.
2. It recognizes that procrastination and rationalization are mechanisms by which people avoid making difficult decisions and coping with the associated stress.
3. It explicitly acknowledges that some decisions probably will be wrong and that the fear of making an unsound decision can be a deterrent to making any decision at all.
4. It provides for **self-reactions**—comparisons of alternatives with internalized moral standards. Internalized moral standards guide decision making as much as economic and social outcomes do. A proposed course of action may offer many economic and social rewards, but if it violates the decision maker's moral convictions, it is unlikely to be chosen.
5. It recognizes that at times the decision maker is ambivalent about alternative courses of action; in such circumstances, it is very difficult to make a wholehearted commitment to a single choice. Major life decisions seldom allow compromise, however; usually they are either-or decisions that require commitment to one course of action.

> Self-reactions are comparisons of alternatives with internalized moral standards.

The Janis-Mann conflict model of decision making is shown in Figure 15.5. A concrete example will help explain each step. Our hypothetical individual is Richard, a thirty-year-old engineer with a working wife and two young children. Richard has been employed at a large manufacturing company for eight years. He keeps abreast of his career situation through visits with peers at work and in other companies, through feedback from his manager and others regarding his work and future with the firm, through the alumni magazine from his university, and through other sources.

At work one morning, Richard learns that he has been passed over for a promotion for the second time in a year. He investigates the information, which can be considered negative feedback, and confirms it. As a result, he seeks out other information regarding his career at the company, the prospect of changing employers, and the possibility of going back to graduate school to get an M.B.A. At the same time, he asks himself, "Are the risks serious if I do not make a change?" If the answer is "no," Richard will continue his present activities. In the model's terms, this option is called **unconflicted adherence.** If instead the answer is "yes" or "maybe," Richard will move to the next question in the model.

> Unconflicted adherence entails continuing with current activities if doing so does not entail serious risks.

The second step asks, "Are the risks serious if I do make a change?" If Richard goes on to this step, he will gather information about potential losses from making a change. He may, for example, find out whether he would lose health insurance and pension benefits if he changed jobs or went back to graduate school. If he believes that changing presents no serious risks, Richard will make the change, called an **unconflicted change.** Otherwise, Richard will move on to the next step.

> Unconflicted change involves making decisions in present activities if doing so presents no serious risks.

But suppose Richard has determined that the risks are serious whether or not he makes a change. He believes he must make a change because he will not be pro-

Antecedent Conditions   **Mediating Processes**   **Consequences**

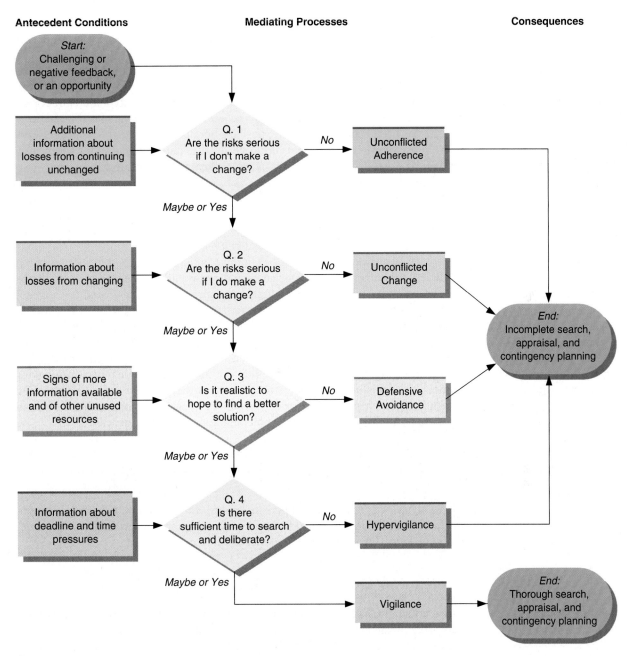

figure 15.5

Janis-Mann Conflict Model of Decision Making

A decision maker answering "yes" to all four questions will engage in vigilant information processing.

Reference: Adapted with the permission of The Free Press, an imprint of Simon & Schuster Adult Publishing Group from *Decision Making: A Psychological Analysis of Conflict, Choice, and Commitment,* by Irving L. Janis and Leon Mann. Copyright ©1977 by The Free Press.

moted further in his present company, yet serious risks are also associated with making a change—perhaps loss of benefits, uncertain promotion opportunities in another company, or lost income from going to graduate school for two years. In the third step, Richard wonders, "Is it realistic to hope to find a better solution?" He continues to look for information that can help him make the decision. If the

Defensive avoidance entails making no changes in present activities and avoiding further contact with associated issues because there appears to be no hope of finding a better solution.

Hypervigilance is frantic, superficial pursuit of some satisfising strategy.

Vigilant information processing involves thoroughly investigating all possible alternatives, weighing their costs and benefits before making a decision, and developing contingency plans.

answer to this third question is "no," Richard may give up hope of finding anything better and opt for what Janis and Mann call **defensive avoidance;** that is, he will make no change and avoid any further contact with the issue. A positive response, however, will move Richard onward to the next step.

Here the decision maker, who now recognizes the serious risks involved yet expects to find a solution, asks, "Is there sufficient time to search and deliberate?" Richard now asks himself how quickly he needs to make a change. If he believes that he has little time to deliberate, perhaps because of his age, he will experience what Janis and Mann call **hypervigilance.** In this state, he may suffer severe psychological stress and engage in frantic, superficial pursuit of some satisfising strategy. (This might also be called "panic"!) If, on the other hand, Richard believes that he has two or three years to consider various alternatives, he will undertake vigilant information processing, in which he will thoroughly investigate all possible alternatives, weigh their costs and benefits before making a choice, and develop contingency plans.

Negative answers to the questions in the conflict model lead to responses of unconflicted adherence, unconflicted change, defensive avoidance, and hypervigilance. All are coping strategies that result in incomplete search, appraisal, and contingency planning. A decision maker who gives the same answer to all the questions will always engage in the same coping strategy. However, if the answers change as the situation changes, the individual's coping strategies may change as well. The decision maker who answers "yes" to each of the four questions is led to **vigilant information processing,** a process similar to that outlined in the rational decision-making model. The decision maker objectively analyzes the problem and all alternatives, thoroughly searches for information, carefully evaluates the consequences of all alternatives, and diligently plans for implementation and contingencies.

Related Behavioral Aspects of Decision Making

The behavioral, practical, and personal approaches each have behavioral components, but the manager must consider two additional behavioral aspects of decision making. These are ethics and escalation of commitment.

Ethics and Decision Making

Ethics are an individual's personal beliefs about what is right and wrong or good and bad.

As we noted in Chapter 2, **ethics** are a person's beliefs about what constitutes right and wrong behavior. Ethical behavior is that which conforms to generally accepted social norms; unethical behavior does not conform to generally accepted social norms. Some decisions made by managers may have little or nothing to do with their own personal ethics, but many other decisions are influenced by the manager's ethics. For example, decisions involving such disparate issues as hiring and firing employees, dealing with customers and suppliers, setting wages and assigning tasks, and maintaining one's expense account are all subject to ethical influences.

In general, ethical dilemmas for managers may center on direct personal gain, indirect personal gain, or simple personal preferences. Consider, for example, a top executive contemplating a decision about a potential takeover. His or her stock option package may result in enormous personal gain if the decision goes one way, even though stockholders may benefit more if the decision goes the other way. An indirect personal gain may result when a decision does not directly add value to a

Ethics and decision-making have become very visibly linked in recent times. And indeed, so critical are ethics today that some MBA programs have started screening potential students on the basis of their integrity. In the words of Rose-marie Martinelli, director of MBA admissions for the Wharton School, "Everybody has ethics on the mind right now."

manager's personal worth but does enhance her or his career. Or the manager may face a choice about relocating a company facility in which one of the options is closest to his or her residence.

"Every day everybody in the company has to make decisions about what they're going to put first and what they're going to put second."—Clayton Christensen, Harvard Business School[21]

Managers should carefully and deliberately consider the ethical context of every one of their decisions. The goal, of course, is for the manager to make the decision that is in the best interest of the firm, as opposed to the best interest of the manager. Doing this requires personal honesty and integrity. Managers also find it helpful to discuss potential ethical dilemmas with colleagues. Others can often provide an objective view of a situation that may help a manager avoid unintentionally making an unethical decision. One recent situation that revolved around ethical decision making, Imclone's decision to present a cancer-fighting drug, Erbitux, for FDA approval, is discussed in the "Business of Ethics" feature.

Escalation of Commitment

Escalation of commitment is the tendency to persist in an ineffective course of action when evidence reveals that the project cannot succeed.

Sometimes people continue to try to implement a decision despite clear and convincing evidence that substantial problems exist. **Escalation of commitment** is the tendency to persist in an ineffective course of action when evidence indicates that the project is doomed to failure. A good example is the decision by the government of British Columbia to hold EXPO '86 in Vancouver. Originally, the organizers expected the project to break even financially so that the province would not have to increase taxes to pay for it. However, as work progressed, it became clear that expenses were far greater than had been projected. But organizers considered it too late to call off the event, despite the huge losses that obviously would occur. Eventually, the province conducted a $300 million lottery to try to cover the

BUSINESS OF ETHICS

► *How Fast Is Too Fast?*

On one side are ill patients desperate for a wonder drug. On the other side are pharmaceutical companies, from tiny biotechnology start-ups to giant multinational corporations, eager to find blockbuster drugs. In the middle is the Food and Drug Administration (FDA), charged with ensuring drug safety but also aware of the terrible need for quick action. In this mix there is plenty of potential for trouble.

Consider the case of Erbitux, a cancer-fighting drug under development by small Imclone, Inc., working in partnership with giant Bristol-Myers Squibb. The drug showed promise in clinical trials, so much promise that the FDA gave it fast-track status to hasten its final approval. Dr. Robert J. Mayer, an oncologist, says, "There is no doubt that the compound works. We have had people who benefited quite dramatically."

In December, 2001, however, the FDA rejected the Erbitux application, and then the blaming started. Imclone and Bristol managers claim the rejection was unexpected. Industry observers note that sometimes the federal agency has abruptly changed the rules for approval, causing expensive delays. The approval process itself is cumbersome and complex, and requires input from many different constituencies. Drug approval decisions are poorly structured and nonprogrammed, with both sides facing significant uncertainties.

On their side, FDA officials claim that Imclone managers received warnings but did not heed them. Imclone managers seemed to be in a hurry, not sending complete data to the FDA. Imclone is not profitable, and financial pressure might have caused management to push too hard for quick approval of the drug. FDA officials emphasize that

"A lot of biotech companies get into survival mode instead of success mode."—Richard B. Brewer, CEO, Scios, Inc.

the decision stakes in such a situation are high, with many lives at risk, and that an incorrect decision can be lethal.

Richard B. Brewer, CEO of small drug manufacturer Scios, Inc., understands the ethical issues all too well—his company had a heart medication rejected by the FDA last year—but he believes that it's up to Imclone executives to ensure that the process stays on track. "A lot of biotech companies get into survival mode instead of success mode. They forget that the FDA is not here to get your drug approved. It's here to protect patients." Hopefully, the two sides can come to an agreement soon because those cancer patients are waiting for a resolution.

References: Andrew Serwer, "Bristol's Bad Medicine," *Fortune*, April 29, 2002. www.fortune.com on May 13, 2002; Andrew Serwer, "The Socialite Scientist," *Fortune*, April 15, 2002. www.fortune.com on May 13, 2002; "The Trials of Erbitux," *Fortune*, April 15, 2002. www.fortune.com on May 13, 2002; Catherine Arnst, "Where Imclone Went Wrong," *Business Week*, February 18, 2002, pp. 68–71 (quotation p. 68). See www.businessweek.com.

costs.[22] Similar examples abound in stock market investments, in political and military situations, and in organizations developing any type of new project.

There are several possible reasons for escalation of commitment.[23] Some projects require much front-end investment and offer little return until the end, so the investor must stay in all the way to get any payoff. These "all or nothing" projects require unflagging commitment. Furthermore, investors' or project leaders' egos often become so involved with the project that their identities are totally wrapped up in it. Failure or cancellation seems to threaten their reason for existence. They therefore continue to push the project as potentially successful despite strong evidence to the contrary. At other times, the social structure, group norms, and group cohesiveness support a project so strongly that cancellation is impossible. Organizational inertia also may force an organization to maintain a failing project. Thus, escalation of commitment is a phenomenon that has a strong foundation.

How can an individual or organization recognize that a project needs to be stopped before it results in throwing good money after bad? Several suggestions have been made; some are easy to put to use, and others are more difficult. Having good information about a project is always a first step in preventing the escalation problem. Usually it is possible to schedule regular sessions to discuss the project, its progress, the assumptions on which it originally was based, the current validity of these assumptions, and any problems with the project. An objective review is necessary to maintain control.

Some organizations have begun to make separate teams responsible for the development and implementation of a project to reduce ego involvement. Often the people who initiate a project are those who know the most about it, however, and their expertise can be valuable in the implementation process. Experts suggest that a general strategy for avoiding the escalation problem is to try to create an "experimenting organization" in which every program and project is reviewed regularly, and managers are evaluated on their contribution to the total organization rather than to specific projects.[24]

Group Decision Making

People in organizations work in a variety of groups—formal and informal, permanent and temporary. Most of these groups make decisions that affect the welfare of the organization and the people in it. The cartoon shows one example of how these processes can occur. Here we discuss several issues surrounding how groups make decisions: group polarization, groupthink, and group problem solving.

Group Polarization

Members' attitudes and opinions with respect to an issue or a solution may change during group discussion. Some studies of this tendency have showed the change to be a fairly consistent movement toward a more risky solution, called "risky shift."[25] Other studies and analyses have revealed that the group-induced shift is not always toward more risk; the group is just as likely to move toward a more conservative view.[26] Generally, **group polarization** occurs when the average of the group members' postdiscussion attitudes tends to be more extreme than average prediscussion attitudes.[27]

Group polarization is the tendency for a group's average postdiscussion attitudes to be more extreme than its average prediscussion attitudes.

Group decision making can occur in many different ways. As we discuss in this chapter, managers can control group decision-making processes in a variety of ways so as to increase the chances for making a high-quality decision. But managers can also foul things up by making any number of mistakes in group decision-making settings. This manager, for instance, is clearly letting everyone know that he expects them to agree with him and that those who care to disagree may pay a big price! As a result, the next time that he wants a decision made by a group, there will be even less disagreement and debate, perhaps resulting in a poorer quality decision.

Several features of group discussion contribute to polarization. When individuals discover during group discussion that others share their opinions, they may become more confident about their opinions, resulting in a more extreme view. Persuasive arguments also can encourage polarization. If members who strongly support a particular position are able to express themselves cogently in the discussion, less avid supporters of the position may become convinced that it is correct. In addition, members may believe that because the group is deciding, they are not individually responsible for the decision or its outcomes. This diffusion of responsibility may enable them to accept and support a decision more radical than those they would make as individuals.

Polarization can profoundly affect group decision making. If group members are known to lean toward a particular decision before a discussion, it may be expected that their postdecision position will be even more extreme. Understanding this phenomenon may be useful for one who seeks to affect their decision.

Groupthink

As discussed in Chapters 11 and 12, highly cohesive groups and teams often are very successful at meeting their goals, although they sometimes have serious difficulties as well. One problem that can occur is groupthink. According to Irving L. Janis, **groupthink** is "a mode of thinking that people engage in when they are deeply involved in a cohesive in-group, when the members' strivings for unanimity override their motivation to realistically appraise alternative courses of action."[28] When groupthink occurs, then, the group unknowingly makes unanimity rather than the best decision its goal. Individual members may perceive that raising objections is not appropriate. Groupthink can occur in many decision-making situations in organizations. The current trend toward increasing use of teams in organizations may increase instances of groupthink because of the susceptibility of self-managing teams to this type of thought.[29]

Groupthink is a mode of thinking that occurs when members of a group are deeply involved in a cohesive in-group, and the desire for unanimity offsets their motivation to appraise alternative courses of action.

Symptoms of Groupthink   The three primary conditions that foster the development of groupthink are cohesiveness, the leader's promotion of his or her preferred solution, and insulation of the group from experts' opinions. Based on analysis of the disaster associated with the explosion of the space shuttle *Challenger* in 1986, the original idea of groupthink symptoms was enhanced to include the effects of increased time pressure and the role of the leader in not stimulating critical thinking in developing the symptoms of groupthink.[30] Figure 15.6 outlines the revised groupthink process.

A group in which groupthink has taken hold exhibits eight well-defined symptoms:

1. An *illusion of invulnerability*, shared by most or all members, that creates excessive optimism and encourages extreme risk taking
2. *Collective efforts to rationalize or discount warnings* that might lead members to reconsider assumptions before recommitting themselves to past policy decisions
3. An *unquestioned belief in the group's inherent morality*, inclining members to ignore the ethical and moral consequences of their decisions
4. *Stereotyped views of "enemy" leaders* as too evil to warrant genuine attempts to negotiate or as too weak or stupid to counter whatever risky attempts are made to defeat their purposes

figure 15.6

The Groupthink Process

Groupthink can occur when a highly cohesive group with a directive leader is under time pressure; it can result in a defective decision process and low probability of successful outcomes.

Reference: Gregory Moorhead, Richard Ference, and Chris P. Neck, "Group Decision Fiascoes Continue: Space Shuttle *Challenger* and a Revised Groupthink Framework," *Human Relations*, 1991, vol. 44, pp. 539–550.

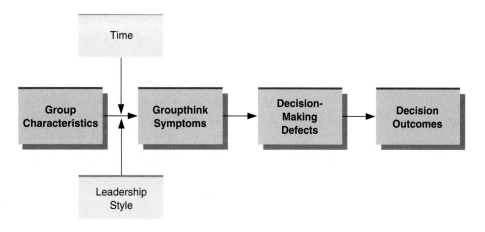

5. *Direct pressure on a member* who expresses strong arguments against any of the group's stereotypes, illusions, or commitments, making clear that such dissent is contrary to what is expected of loyal members

6. *Self-censorship of deviations* from the apparent group consensus, reflecting each member's inclination to minimize the importance of his or her doubts and counterarguments

7. A *shared illusion of unanimity*, resulting partly from self-censorship of deviations, augmented by the false assumption that silence means consent[31]

8. *The emergence of self-appointed "mindguards,"* members who protect the group from adverse information that might shatter their shared complacency about the effectiveness and morality of their decisions[32]

Janis contends that the members of the group involved in the Watergate cover-up—Richard Nixon, H. R. Haldeman, John Ehrlichman, and John Dean—may have been victims of groupthink. Evidence of most of the groupthink symptoms can be found in the unedited transcripts of the group's deliberations.[33]

Decision-Making Defects and Decision Quality   When groupthink dominates group deliberations, the likelihood that decision-making defects will occur increases. The group is less likely to survey a full range of alternatives and may focus on only a few (often one or two). In discussing a preferred alternative, the group may fail to examine it for nonobvious risks and drawbacks. The group may not reexamine previously rejected alternatives for nonobvious gains or some means of reducing apparent costs, even when they receive new information. The group may reject expert opinions that run counter to its own views and may choose to consider only information that supports its preferred solution. The decision to launch the space shuttle *Challenger* in January 1986 may have been a product of groupthink because due to the increased time pressure to make a decision and the leaders' style, negative information was ignored by the group that made the decision. Finally, the group may not consider any potential setbacks or countermoves by competing groups and therefore may fail to develop contingency plans. It should be noted that Janis contends that these six defects may arise from other common problems as well: fatigue, prejudice, inaccurate information, information overload, and ignorance.[34]

Defects in decision making do not always lead to bad outcomes or defeats. Even if its own decision-making processes are flawed, one side can win a battle because of the poor decisions made by the other side's leaders. Nevertheless, decisions produced by defective processes are less likely to succeed.

Although the arguments for the existence of groupthink are convincing, the hypothesis has not been subjected to rigorous empirical examination. Research supports parts of the model but leaves some questions unanswered.[35]

Prevention of Groupthink   Several suggestions have been offered to help managers reduce the probability of groupthink in group decision making. Summarized in Table 15.2, these prescriptions fall into four categories, depending on whether they apply to the leader, the organization, the individual, or the process. All are designed to facilitate the critical evaluation of alternatives and discourage the single-minded pursuit of unanimity.

Participation

A major issue in group decision making is the degree to which employees should participate in the process. Early management theories, such as those of the scientific management school, advocated a clear separation between the duties of managers and workers: Management was to make the decisions, and employees were to implement them.[36] Other approaches have urged that employees be allowed to participate in decisions to increase their ego involvement, motivation, and satisfaction.[37] Numerous research studies have shown that whereas employees who seek responsibility and challenge on the job may find participation in the decision-making process both motivating and enriching, other employees may regard such participation as a waste of time and a management imposition.[38]

Whether employee participation in decision making is appropriate depends on the situation. In tasks that require an estimation, a prediction, or a judgment of accuracy—usually referred to as judgmental tasks—groups typically are superior to individuals simply because more people contribute to the decision-making process. However, one especially capable individual may make a better judgment than a group.

In problem-solving tasks, groups generally produce more and better solutions than do individuals. But groups take far longer than individuals to develop solutions

table 15.2

Prescriptions for Preventing Groupthink

A. Leader prescriptions
  1. Assign everyone the role of critical evaluator.
  2. Be impartial; do not state preferences.
  3. Assign the devil's advocate role to at least one group member.
  4. Use outside experts to challenge the group.
  5. Be open to dissenting points of view.

B. Organizational prescriptions
  1. Set up several independent groups to study the same issue.
  2. Train managers and group leaders in groupthink prevention techniques.

C. Individual prescriptions
  1. Be a critical thinker.
  2. Discuss group deliberations with a trusted outsider; report back to the group.

D. Process prescriptions
  1. Periodically break the group into subgroups to discuss the issues.
  2. Take time to study external factors.
  3. Hold second-chance meetings to rethink issues before making a commitment.

and make decisions. An individual or very small group may be able to accomplish some things much faster than a large, unwieldy group or organization. In addition, individual decision making avoids the special problems of group decision making such as groupthink or group polarization. If the problem to be solved is fairly straightforward, it may be more appropriate to have a single capable individual concentrate on solving it. On the other hand, complex problems are more appropriate for groups. Such problems can often be divided into parts and the parts assigned to individuals or small groups who bring their results back to the group for discussion and decision making.

"When good people are given good information, they typically make good decisions."—Jim Lyons, general manager, Consolidated Diesel Co.[39]

An additional advantage of group decision making is that it often creates greater interest in the task. Heightened interest may increase the time and effort given to the task, resulting in more ideas, a more thorough search for solutions, better evaluation of alternatives, and improved decision quality.

The Vroom decision tree approach to leadership (discussed in Chapter 13) is one popular way of determining the appropriate degree of subordinate participation.[40] The model includes decision styles that vary from "decide" (the leader alone makes the decision) to "delegate" (the group makes the decision, with each member having an equal say). The choice of style rests on seven considerations that concern the characteristics of the situation and the subordinates.

Participation in decision making is also related to organizational structure. For example, decentralization involves delegating some decision-making authority throughout the organizational hierarchy. The more decentralized the organization, the more its employees tend to participate in decision making. Whether one views participation in decision making as pertaining to leadership, organization structure, or motivation, it remains an important aspect of organizations that continues to occupy managers and organizational scholars.[41]

Group Problem Solving

A typical interacting group may have difficulty with any of several steps in the decision-making process. One common problem arises in the generation-of-alternatives phase: the search may be arbitrarily ended before all plausible alternatives have been identified. Several types of group interactions can have this effect. If members immediately express their reactions to the alternatives as they are first proposed, potential contributors may begin to censor their ideas to avoid embarrassing criticism from the group. Less confident group members, intimidated by members who have more experience, higher status, or more power, also may censor their ideas for fear of embarrassment or punishment. In addition, the group leader may limit idea generation by enforcing requirements concerning time, appropriateness, cost, feasibility, and the like.

To improve the generation of alternatives, managers may employ any of three techniques to stimulate the group's problem-solving capabilities: brainstorming, the nominal group technique, or the Delphi technique.

Brainstorming   **Brainstorming,** a technique made popular in the 1950s, is most often used in the idea-generation phase of decision making and is intended to solve problems that are new to the organization and have major consequences. In brain-

Brainstorming is a technique used in the idea-generation phase of decision making that assists in development of numerous alternative courses of action.

storming, the group convenes specifically to generate alternatives. The members present ideas and clarify them with brief explanations. Each idea is recorded in full view of all members, usually on a flip chart. To avoid self-censoring, no attempts to evaluate the ideas are allowed. Group members are encouraged to offer any ideas that occur to them, even those that seem too risky or impossible to implement. (The absence of such ideas, in fact, is evidence that group members are engaging in self-censorship.) In a subsequent session, after the ideas have been recorded and distributed to members for review, the alternatives are evaluated.

The intent of brainstorming is to produce totally new ideas and solutions by stimulating the creativity of group members and encouraging them to build on the contributions of others. Brainstorming does not provide the resolution to the problem, an evaluation scheme, or the decision itself. Instead, it should produce a list of alternatives that is more innovative and comprehensive than one developed by the typical interacting group.

The Nominal Group Technique   The **nominal group technique** is another means of improving group decision making. Whereas brainstorming is used primarily to generate alternatives, this technique may be used in other phases of decision making, such as identification of the problem and of appropriate criteria for evaluating alternatives. To use this technique, a group of individuals convenes to address an issue. The issue is described to the group, and each individual writes a list of ideas; no discussion among the members is permitted. Following the five-to-ten-minute idea-generation period, individual members take turns reporting their ideas, one at a time, to the group. The ideas are recorded on a flip chart, and members are encouraged to add to the list by building on the ideas of others. After all ideas have been presented, the members may discuss them and continue to build on them or proceed to the next phase. This part of the process can also be carried out without a face-to-face meeting or by mail, telephone, or computer. A meeting, however, helps members develop a group feeling and puts interpersonal pressure on the members to do their best in developing their lists.

After the discussion, members privately vote on or rank the ideas or report their preferences in some other agreed-upon way. Reporting is private to reduce any feelings of intimidation. After voting, the group may discuss the results and continue to generate and discuss ideas. The generation-discussion-vote cycle can continue until an appropriate decision is reached.

The nominal group technique has two principal advantages. It helps overcome the negative effects of power and status differences among group members, and it can be used to explore problems to generate alternatives, or to evaluate them. Its primary disadvantage lies in its structured nature, which may limit creativity.

The Delphi Technique   The **Delphi technique** was originally developed by Rand Corporation as a method to systematically gather the judgments of experts for use in developing forecasts. It is designed for groups that do not meet face to face. For instance, the product development manager of a major toy manufacturer might use the Delphi technique to probe the views of industry experts to forecast developments in the dynamic toy market.

The manager who wants the input of a group is the central figure in the process. After recruiting participants, the manager develops a questionnaire for them to complete. The questionnaire is relatively simple in that it contains straightforward questions that deal with the issue, trends in the area, new technological developments, and other factors the manager is interested in. The manager

With the nominal group technique, group members follow a generate-discussion-vote cycle until they reach an appropriate decision.

The Delphi technique is a method of systematically gathering judgments of experts for use in developing forecasts.

summarizes the responses and reports back to the experts with another question-naire. This cycle may be repeated as many times as necessary to generate the information the manager needs.

The Delphi technique is useful when experts are physically dispersed, anonymity is desired, or the participants are known to have trouble communicating with one another because of extreme differences of opinion. This method also avoids the intimidation problems that may exist in decision-making groups. On the other hand, the technique eliminates the often fruitful results of direct interaction among group members.

Negotiation

Negotiation is the process in which two or more parties (people or groups) reach agreement even though they have different preferences.

O ne special way that decisions are made in organizations is through negotiation. **Negotiation** is the process in which two or more parties (people or groups) reach agreement even though they have different preferences. In its simplest form the parties involved may be two individuals who are trying to decide who will pay for lunch. A little more complexity is involved when two people, such as an employee and manager, sit down to decide on personal performance goals for the next year against which the employee's performance will be measured. Even more complex are the negotiations that take place between labor unions and the management of a company or between two companies as they negotiate the terms of a joint venture. The "World View" box illustrates the problems inherent in an international acquisition. The key issues in such negotiations are that at least two parties are involved, their preferences are different, and they need to reach agreement.

Approaches to Negotiation

Interest in negotiation has grown steadily in recent years.[42] Four primary approaches to negotiation have dominated this study: individual differences, situational characteristics, game theory, and cognitive approaches. Each of these is briefly described in the following sections.

Individual Differences   Early psychological approaches concentrated on the personality traits of the negotiators.[43] Traits investigated have included demographic characteristics and personality variables. Demographic characteristics have included age, gender, and race, among others. Personality variables have included risk taking, locus of control, tolerance for ambiguity, self-esteem, authoritarianism, and Machiavellianism. The assumption of this type of research was that the key to successful negotiation was selecting the right person to do the negotiating, one who had the appropriate demographic characteristics or personality. This assumption seemed to make sense because negotiation is such a personal and interactive process. However, the research rarely showed the positive results expected because situational variables negated the effects of the individual differences.[44]

Situational Characteristics   Situational characteristics are the context within which negotiation takes place. They include such things as the types of communication between negotiators, the potential outcomes of the negotiation, the relative power of the parties (both positional and personal), the time frame available for negotiation, the number of people representing each side, and the presence of other

WORLD VIEW

Wanted: Skilled Negotiator for GM, Daewoo Acquisition

It's a negotiator's nightmare: In September 2001, General Motors agreed to buy a controlling interest in Korea's Daewoo Motor Co., and the transaction was scheduled for December. GM wanted access to the Korean market in which Daewoo is the number two brand as well as to the rest of Asia, and Daewoo needed a cash infusion to remain profitable, so both parties agreed upon the $400 million price tag. But in May 2002, the deal still remained undone, and it's not clear when, or even if, it can be finalized.

"It's not desirable to delay. . . . But, you can't neglect important negotiations."—Jim Nyum, Korea's Finance and Economy Minister

Imagine the problems of completing any acquisition when the two parties are located in different regions, with different cultures and languages. Add to that the unique features of this situation—GM wants ownership in only some, not all, of Daewoo assets, and Daewoo is huge and diversified, with exports to 180 countries and annual sales of $6 billion.

Another significant difficulty is that the Korean autoworkers union is passionately opposed to the sale because it fears that manufacturing workers will be laid off. Radical workers recently staged a year-long sit-in near Daewoo's plant at Bupyeong, which is the least efficient and most likely to be closed. Suppliers, too are suffering. Joe Hang Kyun, whose company sells components to Daewoo, says, "Many of us could go belly-up unless cash flow improves soon."

The Korean government's usual policy is to prop up ailing businesses with cash, but reforms are moving Korea toward a more market-driven economy in which compa-

nies are allowed to succeed or fail on their own. Jim Nyum, Korea's Finance and Economy Minister, says, "It's not desirable to delay. . . . But, you can't neglect important negotiations." Korean officials could serve as mediators; however, since 2002 is an election year, "nobody in the government is willing to stick out his neck," according to Korea Labor Institute researcher Bae Kiu Sik.

In the meantime, Daewoo is getting weaker, losing market share, operating at only one-third of its usual capacity, and cutting back on new-car development investments. GM and Daewoo knew about the risks when they undertook this purchase. Now it remains to be seen if the two firms can bring together those involved—including workers, suppliers, and regulators—to hammer out a solution that will be acceptable to all.

References: "Global Net: Daewoo Makes Its Cars Around the World—For the World," Daewoo web site. www.daewoous.com on May 14, 2002; Joe Miller, "GM Near Pact to Take Over Daewoo," *Detroit News*, April 11, 2002. detnews.com on May 14, 2002; Samuel Len, "GM Says Major Issues Resolved in Daewoo Motor Talks," *Reuters Business*, April 9, 2002. biz.yahoo.com on May 14, 2002; "GM, Daewoo Sale Talks in Final Stage," *Financial Express*, March 21, 2002. www.financialexpress.com on May 14, 2002; Moon Ihlwan, "Daewoo: Stuck in Neutral," *Business Week*, February 18, 2002, p. 54 (quotation p. 54). See www.businessweek.com.

parties. Some of this research has contributed to our understanding of the negotiation process. However, the shortcomings of the situational approach are similar to those of the individual characteristics approach. Many situational characteristics are external to the negotiators and beyond their control. Often the negotiators cannot change their relative power positions or the setting within which the negotiation occurs. So, although we have learned a lot from research on the situational issues, we still need to learn much more about the process.

Game Theory   Game theory was developed by economists using mathematical models to predict the outcome of negotiation situations. It requires that every alternative and outcome be analyzed with probabilities and numerical outcomes reflecting the preferences for each outcome. In addition, the order in which different parties can make choices and every possible move are predicted, along with associated preferences for outcomes. The outcomes of this approach are exactly what negotiators

Win-win negotiations strategies involve trying to reach agreements that benefit all parties. Jimmy de Castro provides a good example. Mr. de Castro, a former athlete and disc jockey, is shown here leading an aerobics class—something he does for fun. But the rest of his day will be spent leading AOL Interactive Services. In that role he works tirelessly with company executives and media partners to identify new opportunities that will benefit AOL, its subscribers, its advertisers, and its investors. In short, de Castro wants them to all win together, rather than some parties winning at the expense of others.

want: a predictive model of how negotiation should be conducted. One major drawback is that it requires the ability to describe all possible options and outcomes for every possible move in every situation before the negotiation starts. This is often very tedious, if possible at all. Another problem is that this theory assumes that negotiators are rational at all times. Other research in negotiation has shown that negotiators often do not act rationally. Therefore, this approach, although elegant in its prescriptions, is usually unworkable in a real negotiation situation.

Cognitive Approaches   The fourth approach is the cognitive approach, which recognizes that negotiators often depart from perfect rationality during negotiation; it tries to predict how and when negotiators will make these departures. Howard Raiffa's decision analytic approach focuses on providing advice to negotiators actively involved in negotiation.[45] Bazerman and Neale have added to Raiffa's work by specifying eight ways in which negotiators systematically deviate from rationality.[46] The types of deviations they describe include escalation of commitment to a previously selected course of action, overreliance on readily available information, assuming that the negotiations can produce fixed-sum outcomes, and anchoring negotiation in irrelevant information. These cognitive approaches have advanced the study of negotiation a long way beyond the early individual and situational approaches. Negotiators can use them to attempt to predict in advance how the negotiation might take place.

Win-Win Negotiation

In addition to the approaches to negotiation previously described, a group of approaches proposed by consultants and advisors is meant to give negotiators a specific model to use in carrying out difficult negotiations. One of the best of these is the "Win-Win Negotiator" developed by Ross Reck and his associates.[47] The Win-Win approach (see Figure 15.7) does not treat negotiation as a game in which there are winners and losers. Instead, it approaches negotiation as an opportunity for both sides to be winners, to get what they want out of the agreement. The focus is on both parties reaching agreement such that both are committed to fulfilling their own end of the agreement and to returning for more agreements in the

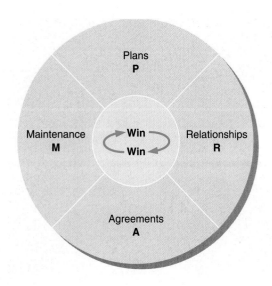

figure 15.7

The PRAM Model of Negotiation

The PRAM model shows the four steps in setting up negotiation so that both parties win.

Reference: Reprinted with the permission of Pocket Books, a division of Simon & Schuster Adult Publishing Group, from *The Win-Win Negotiator: How to Negotiate Favorable Agreements That Last,* by Ross R. Reck, Ph.D., and Brian Q. Long, Ph.D. Copyright © 1985, 1987 by Brian G. Long and Ross R. Reck.

The PRAM model guides the negotiator through the four steps of planning for agreement, building relationships, reaching agreements, and maintaining relationships.

future. In other words, both parties want to have their needs satisfied. In addition, this approach does not advocate either a "tough guy" or a "nice guy" approach to negotiation, both of which are popular in the literature. It assumes that both parties work together to find ways to satisfy both parties at the same time.

The Win-Win approach is a four-step approach illustrated in the **PRAM model** shown in Figure 15.7. The PRAM four-step approach proposes that proper planning, building relationships, getting agreements, and maintaining the relationships are the key steps to successful negotiation.

Planning requires that each negotiator set his or her own goals, anticipate the goals of the other, determine areas of probable agreement, and develop strategies for reconciling areas of probable disagreement.

Developing Win-Win *relationships* requires that negotiators plan activities that enable positive personal relationships to develop, cultivate a sense of mutual trust, and allow relationships to develop fully before discussing business in earnest. The development of trust between the parties is probably the single most important key to success in negotiation.

Forming Win-Win *agreements* requires that each party confirm the other party's goals, verify areas of agreement, propose and consider positive solutions to reconcile areas of disagreement, and jointly resolve any remaining differences. The key in reaching agreement is to realize that both parties share many of the goals. The number of areas of disagreement is usually small.

Finally, Win-Win *maintenance* entails providing meaningful feedback based on performance, each of the parties holding up an end of the agreement, keeping in contact, and reaffirming trust between the parties. The assumption is that both parties want to keep the relationship going so that future mutually beneficial transactions can occur. Both parties must uphold their ends of the agreement and do what they said they would do. Finally, keeping in touch is as easy as making a telephone call or meeting for lunch.

In summary, the PRAM model provides simple advice for conducting negotiations. The four steps are easy to remember and carry out as long as games played by other parties do not distract the negotiator. The focus is on planning, agreeing on goals, trust, and keeping commitments.

Synopsis

Decision making is the process of choosing one alternative from among several. The basic elements of decision making include choosing a goal; considering alternative courses of action; assessing potential outcomes of the alternatives, each with its own value relative to the goal; and choosing one alternative based on an evaluation of the outcomes. Information is available regarding the alternatives, outcomes, and values.

Programmed decisions are well-structured, recurring decisions made according to set decision rules. Nonprogrammed decisions involve nonroutine, poorly structured situations with unclear sources of information; these decisions cannot be made according to existing decision rules. Decision making may also be classified according to the information available. The classifications—certainty, risk, and uncertainty—reflect the amount of information available regarding the outcomes of alternatives.

The rational approach views decision making as a completely rational process in which goals are established, a problem is identified, alternatives are generated and evaluated, a choice is made and implemented, and control is exercised. The use of procedures and rules of thumb, suboptimizing, and satisficing characterize the behavioral model. The rational and behavioral views can be combined into a practical model. The Janis-Mann conflict model recognizes the personal anxiety individuals face when they must make important decisions.

Two related behavioral aspects of decision making are escalation of commitment and ethics. Escalation of commitment to an ineffective course of action occurs in many decision situations. Psychological, social, ego, and organizational factors may cause it. Ethics also play an important role in many managerial decisions.

Group decision making involves problems as well as benefits. One possible problem is group polarization, the shift of members' attitudes and opinions to a more extreme position following group discussion. Another difficulty is groupthink, a mode of thinking in which the urge toward unanimity overrides the critical appraisal of alternatives. Yet another concern involves employee participation in decision making. The appropriate degree of participation depends on the characteristics of the situation.

Negotiation is the process through which two or more parties (people or groups) reach agreement even though they have different preferences. Research on negotiation has examined individual differences, situational characteristics, game theory, and cognitive approaches. The Win-Win approach provides a simple four-step model to successful negotiation: planning, relationships, agreement, and maintenance.

Discussion Questions

1. Some have argued that people, not organizations, make decisions and that the study of "organizational" decision making is therefore pointless. Do you agree with this argument? Why or why not?

2. What information did you use in deciding to enter the school you now attend?

3. When your alarm goes off each morning, you have a decision to make: whether to get up and go to school or work, or to stay in bed and sleep longer. Is this a programmed or nonprogrammed decision? Why?

4. Describe at least three points in the decision-making process at which information plays an important role.

5. How does the role of information in the rational model of decision making differ from the role of information in the behavioral model?

6. Why does it make sense to discuss several different models of decision making?

7. Can you think of a time when you satisficed when making a decision? Have you ever suboptimized?

8. Describe a situation in which you experienced escalation of commitment to an ineffective course of action. What did you do about it? Do you wish you had handled it differently? Why or why not?

9. How are group polarization and groupthink similar? How do they differ?

10. Describe a situation in which you negotiated an agreement, perhaps when buying a car or a house. How did the negotiation process compare with the PRAM approach? How did it differ? Were you satisfied with the result of the negotiation?

Organizational Behavior Case for Discussion

The Most Stressful Conditions

How can effective choices be made when there is no time, when your employees, your company, and your community are in imminent danger? Decision making under these conditions takes on a different character, as shown in the response of Sidley Austin Brown & Wood to the tragic events of September 11, 2001.

The giant law firm was formed in May 2001 when Brown & Wood merged its Wall Street financial law offices with those of Chicago-based Sidley & Austin, corporate law specialists, creating the nation's fourth-largest practice, with 1,400 lawyers worldwide. Many of the firm's lawyers are headquartered in New York City, with 600 formerly housed at 1 World Trade Center on floors 52 to 57 and another 100 seven miles away in midtown Manhattan. On September 11, the first plane struck overhead. Workers noticed the explosion's tremors and the smell of jet fuel. Director of Administration John Connelly asked workers to evacuate, helping the frightened and confused employees to the stairs. Being unaware of the extent of the danger, Connelly and others went from floor to floor to ensure that everyone was safely out, then left the building just as it collapsed. Only one company employee perished in the attack.

In the aftermath, with damaged facilities and workers in shock, Sidley Austin employees faced the most trying circumstances of their careers. When their attempts to contact the midtown building failed because cell phone towers had been destroyed, many employees walked to the site. At the midtown location, partner Alan S. Weil anticipated the need for additional office space and called his landlord, who granted immediate leases on two floors and also got another law firm to give up two newly leased floors. By the end of the day, hundreds of desks, computers, and cell phones were arriving, and contractors were installing computer cables. "It's just amazing what you can get in New York overnight," says partner Thomas R. Smith Jr. According to *New York Times* writer John Schwartz, "The normal rules of business engagement—deliberate negotiation, adversarial wrangling and jockeying for advantage—were swept away. The infamously in-your-face New York attitude was nowhere to be found."

The partnership's directors were supposed to meet in Los Angeles on September 12 but were stranded elsewhere as airlines ceased operations. The executives used conference calls to begin "issue-spotting," according to Thomas Cole, partner. He explained, "The lawyers who assembled that day and in the days thereafter were people who had spent their entire working lives engaged in solving complex problems for clients. . . . But that was under normal conditions. Would we succeed under the most stressful conditions . . . ?" Issues involving people, insurance, and communications were complex; for example, the people issue covered such items as payroll continuity, trauma counseling, and safety and security. The organization pulled together—staffers from the Chicago headquarters drove all night to assist. When the firm's backup data tapes needed transport from a New Jersey warehouse to Chicago, the storage companies offered to have their employees drive overnight because no planes were flying. Dennis J. O'Donovan, head of the firm's technology section, says, "[Disaster recovery seminars] always prepare you for the worst—people not being available, people not being cooperative; the opposite has happened."

On September 17, firm employees met, and partner Charles W. Douglas told the crowd, "The assets of the law firm are not the desks in the offices, the woodwork that's on the walls or the paintings that are hung in the corridors. The assets of the law firm are its people." Smith agreed, saying, "Being able to keep the business going is great, but it's the people that count." Employees and partners at Sidley Austin have taken on the added work with few complaints; many say that work is therapeutic. The lawyers have completed many financial deals on time, believing that it's their patriotic duty to continue working as before. Employees claim that the tragedy drew them closer together, creating intimate friendships. Others are still suffering from stress, and some may choose paid disability leave. Nancy L. Karen, chief information officer, says the firm has learned a lot about crisis conditions. "We ought to be able to recover in less than a day next time," she says, adding with a nervous laugh, "God forbid!" Perhaps Thomas Cole best sums up the firm's response, saying, "I have been asked . . . if the disaster has been a setback to the full realization of the anticipated benefits of our merger. I answer that "[b]ecause of the way we have risen to this challenge together, the most important yet most elusive goal in any merger integration, namely the creation of a true partnership, occurred overnight."

> ## "The normal rules of business engagement—deliberate negotiation, adversarial wrangling and jockeying for advantage—were swept away."—John Schwartz, *New York Times* reporter

References: "About Sidley," "Our Offices," "Our Practices," Sidley Austin Brown & Wood web site. www.sidley.com on May 25, 2002; "Sidley Austin Brown & Wood Top Issuer Counsel in 1Q02," Thomson Financial web site. www.tfibcm.com on May 25, 2002; Thomas Cole, "Our Test," *American Lawyer*, November 2001. www.american.lawyer on May 25, 2002; John Schwartz, "Rebuilding a Day at a Time: Law Firm Pushes 2 Steps Forward for Every Step Back, Rebuilds a Day at a Time," *New York Times*, December 14, 2001. www.nytimes.com on May 25, 2002; John Schwartz, "Up from the Ashes: *N.Y. Times* Profile of Sidley Austin Brown & Wood's Response to the World Trade Center Tragedy," *New York Times*, September 16, 2001 (quotation). www.nytimes.com on May 25, 2002.

Case Questions

1. Using the rational approach to decision making, describe the ways in which these crisis conditions affected each step of the decision-making process.

2. Based on your answer to question 1, what are some potential problems that firms should be aware of when they must make decisions during a crisis? What are some steps that firms can take to avoid those problems or to minimize their negative impact?

3. Due to the extraordinary circumstances in New York City during and just after September 11, many individuals and firms changed their behavior, acting more altruistically and ethically. In your opinion, why did this occur? Do you think the change is likely to endure for a long time, or is it only temporary?

 # Experiencing Organizational Behavior

Programmed and Nonprogrammed Decisions

Purpose: This exercise will allow you to take part in making a hypothetical decision and help you understand the difference between programmed and nonprogrammed decisions.

Format: You will be asked to perform a task both individually and as a member of a group.

Procedure: The following is a list of typical organizational decisions. Your task is to determine whether they are programmed or nonprogrammed. Number your paper, and write *P* for programmed or *N* for nonprogrammed next to each number.

Your instructor will divide the class into groups of four to seven. All groups should have approximately the same number of members. Your task as a group is to make the determinations just outlined. In arriving at your decisions, do not use techniques such as voting or negotiating ("Okay, I'll give in on this one if you'll give in on that one.") The group should discuss the difference between programmed and nonprogrammed decisions and each decision situation until all members at least partly agree with the decision.

Decision List

1. Hiring a specialist for the research staff in a highly technical field

2. Assigning workers to daily tasks

3. Determining the size of dividend to be paid to shareholders in the ninth consecutive year of strong earnings growth

4. Deciding whether to officially excuse an employee's absence for medical reasons

5. Selecting the location for another branch of a 150-branch bank in a large city

6. Approving the appointment of a new law school graduate to the corporate legal staff

7. Making annual assignments of graduate assistants to faculty

8. Approving an employee's request to attend a local seminar in his or her special area of expertise

9. Selecting the appropriate outlets for print advertisements for a new college textbook

10. Determining the location for a new fast-food restaurant in a small but growing town on the major interstate highway between two very large metropolitan areas

Follow-up Questions

1. To what extent did group members disagree about which decisions were programmed and which were nonprogrammed?

2. What primary factors did the group discuss in making each decision?

3. Were there any differences between the members' individual lists and the group lists? If so, discuss the reasons for the differences.

Self-Assessment Exercise

Rational Versus Practical Approaches to Decision Making

Managers need to recognize and understand the different models that they use to make decisions. They also need to understand the extent to which they are predisposed to be relatively autocratic or relatively participative in making decisions. To develop your skills in these areas, perform the following activity.

First, assume you are the manager of a firm that is rapidly growing. Recent sales figures strongly suggest the need for a new plant to produce more of your firm's products. Key issues include where the plant might be built and how large it might be (for example, a small, less expensive plant to meet current needs that could be expanded in the future versus a large and more expensive plant that might have excess capacity today but could better meet long-term needs).

Using the rational approach diagrammed in Figure 15.3, trace the process the manager might use to make the decision. Note the kinds of information that might be required and the extent to which other people might need to be involved in making a decision at each point.

Next, go back and look at various steps in the process where behavioral processes might intervene and affect the overall process. Will bounded rationality come into play? How about satisficing?

Finally, use the practical approach shown in Figure 15.4 and trace through the process again. Again note where other input may be needed. Try to identify places in the process where the rational and practical approaches are likely to result in the same outcome and places where differences are most likely to occur.

OB Online

1. Assume you need to make decisions about where to locate a new plant. The options have been narrowed down to Madison, Wisconsin; Columbia, Missouri; and Bryan, Texas. You now need to find information about tax rates, unemployment statistics, and airport access for each community. Use the Internet to search for this information.

2. In what ways do you think the emergence of the Internet has affected how managers make decisions? Give concrete examples to support your ideas.

3. Describe ways in which information technology might be used to manage brainstorming, the nominal group technique, and the Delphi technique more efficiently than using these techniques in more traditional ways.

4. Pair up with one of your classmates and conduct a hypothetical negotiation via email. Then discuss the pros and cons of electronic negotiation versus face-to-face negotiation based on your experience.

Building Managerial Skills

Exercise Overview: Interpersonal skills refer to the manager's ability to understand and motivate individuals and groups. This exercise will allow you to practice your interpersonal skills in a role-playing exercise.

Exercise Background: You supervise a group of six employees who work in an indoor facility in a relatively isolated location. The company you work for has recently adopted an ambiguous policy regarding smoking. Essentially, the policy states that all company work sites are to be smoke free unless the employees at a specific site choose differently and at the discretion of the site supervisor.

Four members of the work group you supervise are smokers. They have come to you with the argument that since they constitute the majority, they should be allowed to smoke at work. The other two members of the group, both nonsmokers, have heard about this request and have also discussed the situation with you. They argue that the health-related consequences of secondary smoke should outweigh the preferences of the majority.

To compound the problem further, your boss wrote the new policy and is quite defensive about it—numerous individuals have already criticized the policy. You know that your boss will get very angry with you if you also raise concerns about the policy. Finally, you are personally indifferent to the issue. You do not smoke yourself, but your spouse does smoke. Secondary smoke does not bother you, and you do not have strong opinions about it. Still, you have to make a decision about what to do. You see that your choices are to (1) mandate a smoke-free environment, (2) allow smoking in the facility, or (3) ask your boss to clarify the policy.

Exercise Task: Based on the background previously presented, assume that you are the supervisor and do the following:

1. Assume that you have chosen option 1. Write down an outline that you will use to announce your decision to the four smokers.

2. Assume that you have chosen option 2. Write down an outline that you will use to announce your decision to the two nonsmokers.

3. Assume that you have chosen option 3. Write down an outline that you will use when you meet with your boss.

4. Are there other alternatives?

5. What would you do if you were actually the group supervisor?

The Downfall of Enron—The Leadership

Part II ended with a description of the anger and betrayal felt by Enron employees. Their justifiable anger at losing their jobs and their retirement funds is sharpened by a perception that those who should have been looking out for their interests, Enron's top managers and board of directors, were either too incompetent or too disinterested to exercise effective oversight. Some unhappy former employees go further, alleging that the managers and directors must have been involved in a deliberate swindle. The courts will be the judge of criminal intent, but the evidence seems to support the claim that those at the highest levels of Enron were aware of, and chose to ignore, signs of serious problems at the firm.

Enron has had two CEOs: Kenneth Lay, who served from the company's founding in 1985 until February 2001, and Jeffrey Skilling, who served for just six months, resigning in August 2001, after which Lay resumed the chief executive role. The two men had worked closely together, and their combined impact on the firm they helped to shape has been considerable. Lay holds a bachelor's degree, master's degree, and Ph.D. in economics, having graduated Phi Beta Kappa. He worked on energy policy issues for the federal government and then held increasingly responsible positions at several energy firms before being named the CEO of Houston Natural Gas in 1984. When that company merged with InterNorth, Inc., in 1985 to form Enron, Lay became CEO and chairman of the board for the combined firm. Skilling earned a Harvard M.B.A. prior to his employment at McKinsey & Co., a consulting firm, which put him in charge of the Enron account. Lay hired Skilling in 1990, when gas prices were dragging Enron's profitability down. Lay saw the hiring of Skilling as an opportunity to move the firm into a trading role in which it could profitably serve as an intermediary without the expense of owning expensive physical assets such as gas pipelines. Although Lay was the visionary, Skilling was the master implementer who carried the plans into action. Insiders called Lay the "good cop" to Skilling's "bad cop." Skilling's boldness led to some outrageous behavior. When it was rumored that Royal Dutch/Shell, the sixth-largest company in the world, might acquire Enron, Skilling was asked what he would do in that case. He answered, "I'd run Shell."

Lay's management style, described as "smooth" and "charming," contrasts with that of the "brash" or "abrasive" Skilling. Lay was perpetually optimistic about Enron's future and fierce in his defense of the company he had built. When a long-time critic of the firm, financial analyst John Olson, publicly questioned Enron's accounting practices, Lay sent him a note saying, "John Olson has been wrong about Enron for over 10 years[,] and he is still wrong. But he is consistent." (Olson framed the letter.) However, in spite of evidence suggesting that he knew about the unethical dealings, Lay was treated as a mentor and father figure by customers, investors, and employees because of his obvious devotion to the firm, his generous charitable giving, and his personal interest in his employees. After the firm's demise, there was a backlash of anger directed at Lay and his "Mr. Do-Good" image. One energy consultant said, "Maybe he's a bumbling figurehead. Or maybe he just played the good old boy and he's the shrewdest guy on the planet."

One former employee describes his reaction to a post-bankruptcy encounter with the CEO in the office: "[Lay] stepped into the elevator and pressed the button for floor 50[,] a floor that once inspired awe and now provokes disgust and anger. . . . [H]ow tense it was on that tiny elevator. . . . [We] didn't know whether to hate or admire him." Another writes about his first suspicion of Lay's culpability, which came at an address to an all-employee meeting on November 20, 2001: "Now Dr. Lay was a legend at Enron and in the Houston community[,] something of a kindly patriarch who would always look after his Enron family. But as he danced around explanations[,] . . . one of the questions written on a 3x5 card came forward. 'Dear Ken: Are you on crack?' There was a bit of a gasp among the employees present, followed by laughter, including Ken's. But somehow that marked the tide change. The aura of invincibility had been pierced. From then on he was just another suit who had sold us out for his own gain. For the damage done to his reputation now, it probably would have been better had he been on drugs."

Whereas Lay is now criticized by most and hated by some, Skilling had long been vilified by virtually everyone for his crudeness and insensitivity. In an April 2001 conference call, Skilling was pressed by stock analysts to explain why the company did not release all of its financial statements at the same time since simultaneous release is the norm. After a heated discussion, analyst Richard Grubman stated in frustration, "You're the only financial institution that can't produce a balance sheet or a cash flow statement with their earnings." Skilling's nonresponsive reply was "Well, thank you very much. We appreciate it." Skilling then muttered an obscenity, causing his Houston colleagues to laugh, but the listening analysts were stunned. In another incident, Skilling was introduced to an audience as the "Number one CEO in the entire country." He then thoughtlessly offered an insensitive joke, outraging California state officials. After speaking about that state's energy crisis, he asked the audience, "Do you know what the difference is between the state of California and the Titanic?" He followed with the punch line: "At least when the Titanic went down, the lights were on."

Skilling also seems to have had a continual problem with honesty. While testifying before Congress on February 7, 2002, he was confronted with the testimonies of other Enron employees. He responded, "On the date I left the company, on August 14, 2001, I had every reason to believe the company was financially stable. And you can say today that everybody agrees there was a problem. I challenge that. I challenge that." For this and other testimony that was perceived as absurdly dishonest, Skilling found himself contradicted and mocked, first by politicians and then by the media. After hearing Skilling assert his ignorance, Senator Barbara Boxer replied, "You're very smart. That's why I don't believe you." Representative Edward J. Markey also questioned Skilling's truthfulness. Frustrated with Skilling's claim that he had forgotten most of the important events leading up to the bankruptcy, Markey said, "What you have done today is invoked the 'Hogan's Heroes' Sergeant Schultz defense of 'I see nothing, I hear nothing, I know nothing.'" The quotation from the 1960s sitcom was used to convey a willful ignorance. The show's creator, Albert S. Ruddy, explains, "Shultz always knew what was going on. He would turn a blind eye. He just didn't want to get involved."

One puzzling aspect of the Enron debacle is the issue of executive compensation because the two CEOs missed or avoided opportunities to maximize their gains. On the one hand, they both earned about $200 million annually in salary, stocks, and other compensation. In addition, Lay had a $7.5 million line of credit from Enron and used the funds to purchase real estate, repaying with company stock. On the other hand, Enron investors claim in their lawsuit that twenty-nine managers sold $1.1 billion dollars of Enron stock in the three years preceding the bankruptcy, but Lay and Skilling sold only trivial amounts. And Lay could have received a $25 million "golden parachute" by resigning, but he stayed until January 2002 and ultimately received no severance package.

Although Lay, Skilling, and other managers received the majority of the blame for Enron's misdeeds, many astute observers also asked about the board of directors' failure to provide oversight. The board's auditing committee, for example, should have noticed when top Enron executives sold more than $1 billion of stock, but three of the board's six members were located in London, Hong Kong, and Rio de Janeiro, too far away to provide close supervision. In the aftermath of the scandal, most board members have quit, some under pressure from other boards on which they serve.

Today, the former Enron CEOs are living a life of quiet luxury punctuated by court appearances. After Lay avoided testifying before Congress by invoking the Fifth Amendment, avoiding self-incrimination, he began focusing on rebuilding his status within the Houston social and business community. The task will be formidable. After news of Enron's scandal broke, Lay and his wife Linda were greeted with shocked gasps from other diners upon entering a restaurant in their upscale neighborhood. Since then, the couple has eased back into fashionable Houston society, attending charity fundraisers along with local figures such as former First Lady Barbara Bush. Skilling and Fastow have also been keeping a low profile and spending time with family.

It's clear, however, that Enron's top executives are not lacking in funds. Mrs. Lay appeared on the *Today* show on January 28, 2002, to defend her husband. She maintained, "Never, never, not for one second would he have allowed anything to go on that was illegal. There are some things he wasn't told." (In an ironic twist, when Mrs. Lay opened up to a national audience about her husband's work, she could have waived her "marital privilege," the right of spouses not to testify about private conversations with their mates. Prosecutors will now be able to use her admission to show that Lay never intended his conversations to be private, so Mrs. Lay may be called as a witness against her husband.) Through tears, she told rapt viewers,

"We've lost everything." However, the Lays have sold $40 million worth of real estate, including a house in Aspen, so the claim of poverty seems rather exaggerated. Fastow, too, seems to be flush with cash and is building a 12,000-square-foot home in the posh River Oaks neighborhood of Houston, where Lay and Skilling, who owns a $4 million home, will be his neighbors. Mrs. Lay is opening a furnishings and antiques boutique that will offer decorative items from the homes the Lays have sold. As one can imagine, all of this apparent wealth is disturbing to former Enron employees and investors, many of whom are in ruinous financial conditions.

"What you have done today is invoked the 'Hogan's Heroes' Sergeant Schultz defense of 'I see nothing, I hear nothing, I know nothing.'"—Representative Edward J. Markey, responding to Jeffrey Skilling's testimony before Congress

References: "Enron Vice Chairman Cliff Baxter Resigns," Enron press release. www.enron.com on June 28, 2002; David Barboza, "From Enron's Rubble, Life on a Luxury Tightrope," *New York Times*, May 19, 2002, BUI. See www.nytimes.com; Lorraine Woellert, "Skilling's Sequel: Clueless," *Business Week*, February 27, 2002. www.businessweek.com on June 27, 2002; Warren Bennis, "A Corporate Fear of Too Much Truth," *New York Times*, February 17, 2002, p. WK11; Mike France, "Up Front," *Business Week*, February 11, 2002. www.businessweek.com on June 28, 2002; Kurt Eichenwald, "Enron Buffed Image to a Shine Even as It Rotted from Within," *New York Times*, February 10, 2002, pp. 1, 28, 29. See www.nytimes.com; Reed Abelson, "Endgame? Some Enron Board Members Quit or Face Ouster at Other Companies," *New York Times*, February 9, 2002, p. C5. See www.nytimes. com; "Excerpts from the House Subcommittee Hearings on the Enron Collapse," testimony of Jeffrey K. Skilling, recorded in a February 7, 2002, hearing before the House Energy and Commerce Subcommittee, published in the *New York Times*, February 9, 2002, p. C4 (quotation). See www.nytimes.com; Richard A. Oppel Jr., "Enron's Lay Is to Appear Before Panel," *New York Times*, February 9, 2002, pp. C1, C4. See www.nytimes.com; "Enron Letters," *Houston Chronicle*, February 7–8, 2002. www.chron.com on June 26, 2002; Nancy Rivera Brooks, "Powerful Figures Behind Firm's Rise—And Crash," *Los Angeles Times*, January 26, 2002. www.latimes.com on June 27, 2002; Sherri Day, "Police Say Former Enron Executive Committed Suicide," *Truthout* online magazine, January 25, 2002. wwwtruthout.org on June 28, 2002; "Kenneth L. Lay, Chairman and Chief Executive Officer, Enron," Strategos Revolutionaries Conference 2000, October 2000. www. crashingbull.com on June 27, 2002.

Integrative Case Questions

1. What impact did the backgrounds, experience, and personalities of Kenneth Lay and Jeffrey Skilling have on Enron?

2. Describe the leadership capabilities of Lay and Skilling. In what ways were they effective leaders? In what ways were they ineffective leaders?

3. What types of power did Lay and Skilling display? Give examples of the various types.

16 Dimensions of Organization Structure

Management Preview

It seems as if organizations are always "restructuring." They rearrange the organization chart and make people report to different managers. What they are really doing is trying to find the best way to set up the structure of the organization. This is the first in a two-chapter sequence in which we explore how the structure of an organization can be a major factor in how successfully the organization achieves its goals. In this chapter, we present the basics of organization structure, its building blocks, and the classical ways of designing organization structures. Chapter 17 integrates the basic elements of structure, taking into consideration other factors such as the environment and technology, and presents several perspectives on organization design.

In this chapter, we begin with an overview of organizations and organization structure, defining both terms and placing organization structure in the context of organizational goals and strategy. Second, we discuss the two major perspectives of organizing, the structural configuration view and the operational view. We then discuss the often confusing concepts of responsibility and authority and present an alternative view of authority. Finally, we explain several of the classic views of how organizations should be structured. But first we describe some of the organizational challenges faced by AOL Time Warner.

Whether you call it integration, synergy, or "convergence," AOL chairman Steve Case's favorite word, it is the driving force behind the organization structures of so-called "New Economy" firms, based on the hypothetical benefits of owning a variety of related business units. Since the future of technology remains uncertain it makes sense for firms to hedge their bets by owning many different technologies. Case, a visionary leader, says, "We are moving into an era of convergence where the lines between industries will blur." However, it is clear that owning widely diversified businesses does not yet contribute to profitability, perhaps because an overly diversified corporate structure is difficult to manage.

AOL Time Warner is struggling with this issue today. The huge firm, with $38 billion in revenue, today comprises dozens of major brands. An exhaustive, and exhausting, list of brands includes Internet businesses such as AOL, Compu-Serve, Road Runner, icq, Instant Messenger, Netscape, and Mapquest; cable networks HBO, Cinemax, CNN, the Cartoon Network, TNT, TBS Superstation, Turner Classic Movies, the WB; movie studios Warner Brothers, Castle Rock Entertainment, and New Line Cinema; magazines such as *Time, People, Sports Illustrated, Fortune, InStyle, Money, Entertainment Weekly, marie claire, MAD* comics, and over one hundred other specialty titles; the Time Warner cable provider and four local TV stations; the Atlanta Braves baseball team, the Atlanta Hawks basketball team, and the Atlanta Thrashers hockey team; book publishers; the Looney Tunes animation studio; and Atlantic, Elektra, Rhino, and other recording companies.

Thus far, the much-hyped benefits have failed to materialize. According to Case, the slow start was to be expected. He says, "I've always said this is a marathon, not a sprint." The firm is effectively cross-selling products, for example, by advertising its other products on its web portals and cable stations. But it could do more. Case maintains, "The merger was never about cross-divisional promotion. It was about cross-divisional innovation." The firm has taken the first step, adding divisions with responsibility for achieving synergies, but some obvious moves, such as offering movie sneak previews exclusively to AOL subscribers, have been widely discussed but never implemented.

"I've always said this is a marathon, not a sprint."—Steve Case, chairman of the board of AOL Time Warner

The challenge for CEO Richard Parsons is to create an organization structure that will harness the power of these combined businesses, realizing synergies and sparking innovation, while also maintaining control. Parsons, who assumed the top spot in May 2002, began with a reorganization, asking some top executives who had previously reported to Case to report directly to him and changing other reporting relationships at the firm's top level. The change will give more formal authority and public visibility to several top executives, mainly those in strategic planning, external communications, and technology development. Parsons also plans to concentrate on making each business unit successful on its own, downplaying the importance of convergence. According to a senior AOL executive, Parsons feels that "if we set convergence as a dramatic target, we set ourselves up for a fall because it's clearly going to take longer than we thought." The new CEO is also attempting to respond to investors, who are clamoring for a simplified, more easily understood structure.

The firm's missteps, along with the slump in the technology sector, have caused the company's stock price to fall, erasing more than $100 billion of shareholder value since the 2001 merger of AOL and Time Warner. Still, Case believes that a convergence strategy will ultimately yield the best results. He points out, "The Internet phenomenon, the trend toward more of a connected society, is unabated." Now it is up to Parsons to find a way to organize the entity so as to capture Case's vision and then to make that organization profitable.

References: "AOL Time Warner 2002 Factbook," "Corporate Information: Timeline," "Overview," AOL Time Warner web site. www.aoltimewarner.com on June 5, 2002; Martin Peers, "AOL CEO Parsons Reorganizes Reporting Lines for Senior Aides," *Wall Street Journal*, May 24, 2002. online.wsj.com on June 5, 2002; Marc Gunther and Stephanie N. Mehta, "Can Steve Case Make Sense of This Beast?" *Fortune*, May 13, 2002 (quotation). www.fortune.com on April 30, 2002; Martin Peers, "In New Turn, AOL Time Warner Will De-Emphasize 'Convergence,'" *Wall Street Journal*, May 13, 2002. online.wsj.com on June 5, 2002.

▼ ▼ ▼

AOL Time Warner is faced with developing an organization structure that allows the synergies it expected when the two companies merged yet still enables management to have some control over operations. This is not unusual in business and industry these days as companies struggle to remain competitive in a rapidly changing world. This chapter introduces many of the key concepts of organization structure and sets the stage for understanding the many aspects of developing the appropriate organization design, which is discussed in Chapter 17.

The Nature of Organization Structure

In other chapters we discuss key elements of the individual and the factors that tie the individual and the organization together. In a given organization, these factors must fit together within a common framework: the organization's structure.

Organization Defined

An organization is a group of people working together to attain common goals.

An **organization** is a group of people working together to achieve common goals.[1] Top management determines the direction of the organization by defining its purpose, establishing goals to meet that purpose, and formulating strategies to achieve the goals.[2] The definition of its purpose gives the organization reason to exist; in effect, it answers the question "What business are we in?"

Organizational goals are objectives that management seeks to achieve in pursuing the firm's purpose.

Establishing goals converts the defined purpose into specific, measurable performance targets. **Organizational goals** are objectives that management seeks to achieve in pursuing the purpose of the firm. Goals motivate people to work together. Although each individual's goals are important to the organization, it is the organization's overall goals that are most important. Goals keep the organization on track by focusing the attention and actions of the members. They also give the organization a forward-looking orientation. They do not address past success or failure; rather, they force members to think about and plan for the future.

"We needed to give people a beacon that they could follow when they were having a tough time with prioritization, leadership, where to go, what hills to take."—Steven A. Ballmer, the new CEO of Microsoft, describing why the software giant was reorganizing[3]

Finally, strategies are specific action plans that enable the organization to achieve its goals and thus its purpose. Pursuing a strategy involves developing an organization structure and the processes to do the organization's work.

Organization Structure

Organization structure is the system of task, reporting, and authority relationships within which the organization does its work.

Organization structure is the system of task, reporting, and authority relationships within which the work of the organization is done. Thus, structure defines the form and function of the organization's activities. Structure also defines how the parts of an organization fit together, as is evident from an organization chart.

The purpose of an organization's structure is to order and coordinate the actions of employees to achieve organizational goals. The premise of organized effort is that people can accomplish more by working together than they can separately. The work must be coordinated properly, however, if the potential gains of collective effort are to be realized. Consider what might happen if the thousands of employees at Dell Computers worked without any kind of structure. Each person might try to build a computer that he or she thought would sell. No two computers would be alike, and each would take months or years to build. The costs of making the computers would be so high that no one would be able to afford them. To produce computers that are both competitive in the marketplace and profitable for the company, Dell must have a structure in which its employees and managers work together in a coordinated manner. DaimlerChrysler was faced with similar coordination problems following its merger, due to duplication of capabilities, facilities, and product lines, as discussed in the "Mastering Change" box.

The task of coordinating the activities of thousands of workers to produce cars or computers that do the work expected of them and that are guaranteed and easy to maintain may seem monumental. Yet whether the goal is to mass produce computers or to make soap, the requirements of organization structure are similar. First, the structure must identify the various tasks or processes necessary for the organization to reach its goals. This dividing of tasks into smaller parts is often called "division of labor." Even small organizations (those with fewer than one hundred employees) use division of labor.[4] Second, the structure must combine and coordinate the divided tasks to achieve a desired level of output. The more interdependent the divided tasks, the more coordination is required.[5] Every organization structure addresses these two fundamental requirements.[6] The various ways of approaching these requirements are what make one organization structure different from another.

Organization structure can be analyzed in three ways. First, we can examine its configuration—that is, its size and shape—as depicted on an organization chart. Second, we can analyze its operational aspects or characteristics, such as separation

Africa native Florence Wambugu has developed genetically modified foods, such as bananas and sweet potatoes, to help the starving people of her homeland. However, some governments in Africa object to genetically altered food, and people are starving despite the availability of the controversial crops. Wambugu has created a new organization, A Harvest Biotech Foundation International, to serve as a pan-African voice on the issue. With the organizational goal of increasing the availability of genetically modified crops in Africa, the organization will be better able to stay on track and continue its forward momentum.

MASTERING CHANGE

DaimlerChrysler Revs Up

In 1999, German automaker Daimler, which manufactures Mercedes cars, merged with Chrysler, one of America's Big Three, and DaimlerChrysler, as the new firm is called, then purchased a 34 percent stake in Japan-based Mitsubishi Motors. Although the merger seemed like a brilliant move, combining powerhouses from three continents, the results have been weak thus far.

The German-born CEO Jurgen Schrempp is trying to combine the firm's disparate units into an integrated whole. "The chief executive should not be the one who just sort of guides the board on vision and strategy. You also have to know what you are talking about," Schrempp says. To advise him, Schrempp created a chairman's council of eleven outsiders, including IBM's Lou Gerstner. He also established an executive automotive committee whose members are the heads of Mercedes, Chrysler, and Mitsubishi; he hopes the group can improve coordination.

One problematic area is cost control. The merger resulted in duplication of capabilities, facilities, and product lines, consequently increasing expenses. Combined with the effect of slower sales and increased competition, the cost increase caused the firm to lose $589 million in 2001, compared with a 2000 gain of $7 billion. Three years after the merger, the firm is still seeking closer integration in some functions. Schrempp asks, "Why not combine parts departments, workshops and things like that?" Sharing components across the three major divisions could bring significant savings; for example, using the Mercedes

gearbox in Chrysler sedans could save as much as $100 million.

Another problem is the potential dilution of Daimler-Chrysler's brands. For example, Schrempp wants to avoid the perception that a Mercedes is just an expensive

> *"The chief executive should not be the one who just sort of guides the board on vision and strategy."—Jurgen Schrempp, DaimlerChrysler CEO*

Chrysler. Garel Rhys, professor at Cardiff Business School, warns, "[Mercedes] is not doing as well as it was. It is widening its share with cars that have lower margins."

A third problem is the need to jump-start synergy and creativity across the divisions. The new Crossfire roadster is a Chrysler brand engineered by Mercedes, that shares components with both Mitsubishi and Mercedes. The innovative Pacifica station wagon/minivan hybrid is due in 2003, and Schrempp promises a pipeline of new designs through 2005. He recently announced the formulation of a ten-year plan for closer integration, but investors and customers are hoping that the merger benefits become evident long before then.

References: Alex Taylor III, "Schrempp Shifts Gears," *Fortune*, March 18, 2002 (quotation). www.fortune.com on June 6, 2002; Christine Tierney and Joann Muller, "DaimlerChrysler's Foggy Forecast," *Business Week*, February 14, 2002. www.businessweek.com on June 6, 2002; "DaimlerChrysler Chief Seeks Greater Brand Integration," as reported in the *Financial Times*, reprinted in *Wall Street Journal Online*, May 21, 2002. online.wsj.com on June 6, 2002. Joann Muller, "Daimler and Chrysler Have a Baby," *Business Week*, January 14, 2002. www.businessweek.com on June 6, 2002.

of specialized tasks, rules and procedures, and decision making. Finally, we can examine responsibility and authority within the organization. In this chapter, we describe organization structure from all three points of view.

Structural Configuration

An organization chart is a diagram showing all people, positions, reporting relationships, and lines of formal communication in the organization.

The structure of an organization is most often described in terms of its organization chart. See Figure 16.1 for an example. A complete **organization chart** shows all people, positions, reporting relationships, and lines of formal communication in the organization. (However, as we discussed in Chapter 10, communication is not limited to these formal channels.) For large organizations, several charts may be necessary to show all positions. For example, one chart may show top management, including the board of directors, the chief executive officer, the president, all vice presidents, and important headquarters staff units. Subsequent charts may show the structure of each department and staff unit. Figure 16.1 depicts two organization charts for a large firm; top management is shown in the upper portion of the figure and the manufacturing department in the lower portion. Notice that the structures of the different manufacturing groups are given in separate charts.

An organization chart depicts reporting relationships and work group memberships and shows how positions and small work groups are combined into departments, which together make up the **configuration,** or shape, of the organization. The configuration of organizations can be analyzed in terms of how the two basic requirements of structure—division of labor and coordination of the divided tasks—are fulfilled.

The configuration of an organization is its shape, which reflects the division of labor and the means of coordinating the divided tasks.

Division of Labor

Division of labor is the extent to which the organization's work is separated into different jobs to be done by different people. Division of labor is one of the seven primary characteristics of structuring described by Max Weber,[7] but the concept

The division of labor is the way the organization's work is divided into different jobs to be done by different people.

figure 16.1

Examples of Organization Charts

These two charts show the similarities between a top-management chart and a department chart. In each, managers have four other managers or work groups reporting to them.

Top Management Chart

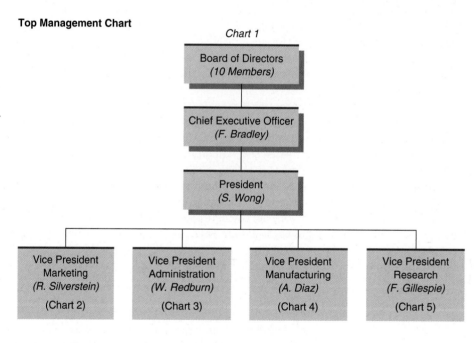

Department Chart

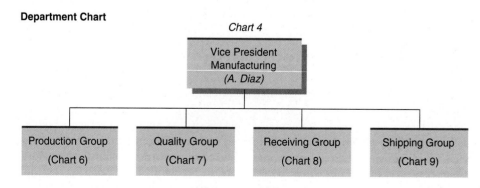

Larger and fancier hotels have many employees providing service to the guests, including bellhops, reception desk personnel, concierge, floor attendants, room service providers, and many more. These tasks are separated and usually assigned to different functional departments. This separation means that these employees usually work pretty independently from those in other departments. However, some hotels are finding that the work of these employees often needs to be better coordinated in order to provide better guest service. One way they are doing this is equipping all of them with tiny two-way radios with which they can better coordinate. One added feature is the ability to tell each other the names of guests as they enter the facility. In this case, this bellhop is able to tell the reception desk the names of the arriving guests so the guests can be greeted by name as they approach the reception desk. Hotels are finding that high-end guests love it.

can be traced back to the eighteenth-century economist Adam Smith. As we noted in Chapter 7, Smith used a study of pin making to promote the idea of dividing production work to increase productivity.[8] Division of labor grew more popular as large organizations became more prevalent in a manufacturing society. This trend has continued, and most research indicates that large organizations usually have more division of labor than smaller ones.[9]

Division of labor has been found to have both advantages and disadvantages (see Table 16.1). Modern managers and organization theorists are still struggling with the primary disadvantage: Division of labor often results in repetitive, boring jobs that undercut worker satisfaction, involvement, and commitment.[10] In addition, extreme division of labor may be incompatible with new, integrated computerized manufacturing technologies that require teams of highly skilled workers.[11]

However, division of labor need not result in boredom. Visualized in terms of a small organization such as a basketball team, it can be quite dynamic. A basketball team consists of five players, each of whom plays a different role on the team. In professional basketball the five positions typically are center, power forward, small forward, shooting guard, and point guard. The tasks of the players in each position are quite different, so players of different sizes and skills are on the floor at any one time. The teams that win championships, such as the Los Angeles Lakers and the Chicago Bulls, use division of labor by having players specialize in doing specified tasks, and doing them impeccably. Similarly, organizations must have specialists who are highly trained and know their specific jobs very well.

table 16.1
Advantages and Disadvantages of Division of Labor

Advantages	Disadvantages
Efficient use of labor	Routine, repetitive jobs
Reduced training costs	Reduced job satisfaction
Increased standardization and uniformity of output	Decreased worker involvement and commitment
Increased expertise from repetition of tasks	Increased worker alienation
	Possible incompatibility with computerized manufacturing technologies

Coordinating the Divided Tasks

Three basic mechanisms are used to help coordinate the divided tasks: departmentalization, span of control, and administrative hierarchy. These mechanisms focus on grouping tasks in some meaningful manner, creating work groups of manageable size and establishing a system of reporting relationships among supervisors and managers. When companies reorganize, they are usually changing the ways in which the division of labor is coordinated. To some people affected by a reorganization, it may seem that things are still just as disorganized as they were before, as the cartoon illustrates. But there really is a purpose for such reorganization efforts. Top management expects that the work will be better coordinated under the new system.

Departmentalization   **Departmentalization** is the manner in which divided tasks are combined and allocated to work groups. It is a consequence of the division of labor. Because employees engaged in specialized activities can lose sight of overall organizational goals, their work must be coordinated to ensure that it contributes to the welfare of the organization.

There are many possible ways to group, or departmentalize, tasks. The five groupings most often used are business function, process, product or service, customer, and geography. The first two, function and process, derive from the internal operations of the organization; the others are based on external factors. Most organizations tend to use a combination of methods, and departmentalization often changes as organizations evolve.[12]

Departmentalization by business function is based on traditional business functions such as marketing, manufacturing, and human resource administration (see Figure 16.2). In this configuration employees most frequently associate with those engaged in the same function, a situation which helps in communication and cooperation. In a functional group, employees who do similar work can learn from one

Departmentalization is the manner in which divided tasks are combined and allocated to work groups.

It seems that organizations are always reorganizing from one type of disorganization to another. Reorganizing too often may leave employees confused about whom they report to and who reports to them. Usually, however, companies reorganize so that the activities of the people who really do the work will be better coordinated.

Reference: © Randy Glasbergen

© 1999 Randy Glasbergen.
www.glasbergen.com

**"Our reorganization is finally completed.
Our old disorganized system has been
replaced by our new disorganized system."**

figure 16.2

Departmentalization by Business Function and by Process

These two charts compare departmentalization by business function and by process. "Functions" are the basic business function whereas "processes" are the specific categories of jobs that people do.

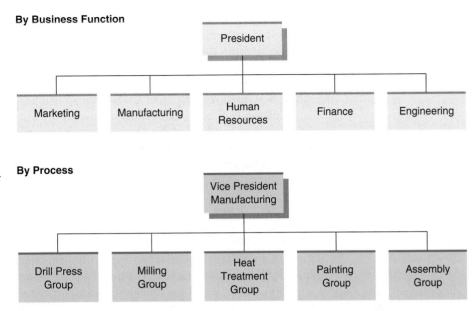

another by sharing ideas about opportunities and problems they encounter on the job. Unfortunately, functional groups lack an automatic mechanism for coordinating the flow of work through the organization.[13] In other words, employees in a functional structure tend to associate little with those in other parts of the organization. The result can be a narrow focus that limits the coordination of work among functional groups, as when the engineering department fails to provide marketing with product information because it is too busy testing materials to think about sales.

Departmentalization by process is similar to functional departmentalization except that the focus is much more on specific jobs grouped according to activity. Thus, as Figure 16.2 illustrates, the firm's manufacturing jobs are divided into certain well-defined manufacturing processes: drilling, milling, heat treatment, painting, and assembly. Hospitals often use process departmentalization, grouping the professional employees such as therapists according to the types of treatment they provide.

Process groupings encourage specialization and expertise among employees, who tend to concentrate on a single operation and share information with departmental colleagues. A process orientation may develop into an internal career path and managerial hierarchy within the department. For example, a specialist might become the "lead" person for that specialty—that is, the lead welder or lead press operator. As in functional grouping, however, narrowness of focus can be a problem. Employees in a process group may become so absorbed in the requirements and execution of their operations that they disregard broader considerations such as overall product flow.[14]

Departmentalization by product or service occurs when employees who work on a particular product or service are members of the same department regardless of their business function or the process in which they are engaged. In the late 1980s, IBM reorganized its operations into five autonomous business units: personal computers, medium-size office systems, mainframes, communications equipment, and components.[15] Although the reorganization worked for a while, the company took quite a downturn in the early 1990s.

Facing the Internet age at the beginning of the new century, IBM added several new divisions: a global computer services group to provide computing services; an Internet division to develop, manufacture, and distribute products for the new Internet age; and the Pervasive Computing Division to develop strategies centered on devices, software, and services that make the Internet accessible anywhere, anytime. These new divisions continued IBM's departmentalization by product or service.

Colgate-Palmolive changed its organization structure by eliminating the typical functional divisions such as basic research, processing, and packaging. Instead, employees were organized into teams based on products such as pet food, household products, and oral hygiene products. This configuration is shown in Figure 16.3. Since the reorganization, new-product development has increased significantly, and cost savings are estimated to be about $40 million.[16]

Departmentalization according to product or service obviously enhances interaction and communication among employees who produce the same product or service and may reduce coordination problems. In this type of configuration, there may be less process specialization but more specialization in the peculiarities of the specific product or service. IBM expected that the new alignment would allow all employees, from designers to manufacturing workers to marketing experts, to become specialists in a particular product line. The disadvantage is that employees may become so interested in their particular product or service that they miss technological improvements or innovations developed in other departments.

Departmentalization by customer is often called "departmentalization by market." Many lending institutions in Texas, for example, have separate departments for retail, commercial, agriculture, and petroleum loans similar to those shown in Figure 16.4. When significant groups of customers differ substantially from one another, organizing along customer lines may be the most effective way to provide the best product or service possible. This is why hospital nurses often are grouped by the type of illness they handle; the various maladies demand different treatment and specialized knowledge.[17] Deutsche Bank has recently changed its organization structure from a regional structure to one based on client groups, as discussed in the "World View" box.

With customer departmentalization there is usually less process specialization because employees must remain flexible to do whatever is necessary to enhance the relationship with customers. This configuration offers the best coordination of the

figure 16.3

Departmentalization by Product or Service
a) Colgate-Palmolive's Old Functional Departmentalization
b) Colgate-Palmolive's New Product Departmentalization

Colgate-Palmolive changed its departmentalization scheme and increased its new-product development with cost savings estimated at $40 million.

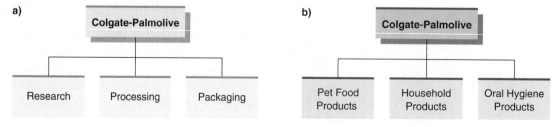

WORLD VIEW

Corporate Structure Moves Deutsche Bank into the Twenty-first Century

As firms become increasingly more global, many find that their traditional, local ways of doing business no longer serve them well. This realization is apparent at German-based Deutsche Bank, which is changing its structure and management to expand its international presence and to appeal to more international investors.

German tax law and business culture favor practices that are different from those of American-style firms. Most German firms have a large management board that makes decisions based on group consensus and gets involved in a variety of issues, including some midlevel, operational ones. It is common for German corporations to have cross-shareholdings, in which firms hold each other's shares. Deutsche Bank, for example, owns a significant share of DaimlerChrysler, insurer Allianz, and other German firms. These practices can lead to problems such as inflexibility and a tendency to downplay internationalization. Some German firms also risk losing their global competitiveness.

In response, Deutsche Bank is divesting some of its nonbank holdings while restoring its focus on banking. CEO Rolf Breuer says, "The logic behind business enterprise must today be found in corporate strategy. . . . The focus is on value creation." The bank has a new organization structure built around client groups rather than regions. Incoming CEO Josef Ackerman reduced the management board from eight to five members and increased diversity while removing the board's authority over day-to-day operations. He has created a new executive committee and given it responsibility for strategy and oversight, thus increasing the CEO's power. The appointment of Ackerman, a Swiss investment banker, signals the firm's international intentions as well as a shift toward more lucrative investment markets.

"The logic behind business enterprise must today be found in corporate strategy."—Rolf Breuer, CEO of Deutsche Bank

Breuer explains the impact of the changes by saying, "[They] made more of a mental difference than a change to daily operations [would have]. We [now] have another culture in the bank[,] . . . not just in the U.S., but also in Europe, even in Germany." Although some of the bank's older workers are concerned that the firm will change its headquarters location or lose its German heritage, many of the younger staff and many outsiders think that this new strategy and structure will help the firm shed its "dinosaur" image and move into the top ranks of the world banking industry.

References: "Speech by Rolf E. Breuer at the General Meeting of Deutschen Bank AG, May 22, 2002, (quotation)" "Fact Sheets," "Organizational Structure," Deutsche Bank web site. group.deutsche-bank.de on June 7, 2002; Marcus Walker, "Lean New Guard at Deutsche Bank Sets Global Agenda—But Cultural Rifts Prevent More-Aggressive Cost Cuts—The Traditionalists Haven't Gone Quietly," *Wall Street Journal*, February 14, 2002. www.wsj.com on April 4, 2002; Stephen Graham, "Deutsche Bank Says 2001 Profit Plummeted, Proceeds with Management Shake-Up," *National Business Stream*, January 31, 2002; "Deutsche Bank Names Next CEO, Continuity Seen," *National Business Stream*, September 21, 2000.

work flow to the customer; however, it may isolate employees from others in their special areas of expertise. For example, if each of a company's three metallurgical specialists is assigned to a different market-based group, these individuals are unlikely to have many opportunities to discuss the latest technological advances in metallurgy.

Departmentalization by geography means that groups are organized according to a region of the country or world. Sales or marketing groups often are arranged by geographic region. As Figure 16.4 illustrates, the marketing effort of a large multinational corporation can be divided according to major geographical divisions. Using a geographically based configuration may result in significant cost savings and better market coverage. On the other hand, it may isolate work groups from activities in the organization's home office or in the technological community because

figure 16.4

Departmentalization by Customer and by Geographic Region

Departmentalization by customer or by geographic region is often used in marketing or sales departments in order to focus on specific needs or locations of customers.

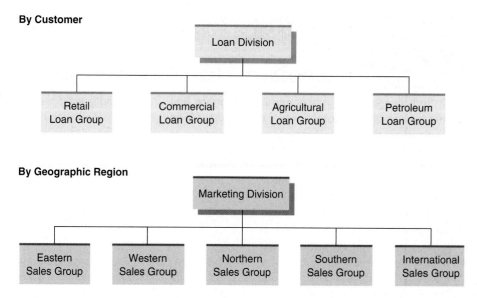

the focus of the work group is solely on affairs within the region. Such a regional focus may foster loyalty to the work group that exceeds commitment to the larger organization. In addition, work-related communication and coordination among groups may be somewhat inefficient.

Many large organizations use a mixed departmentalization scheme. Such organizations may have separate operating divisions based on products, but within each division, departments may be based on business function, process, customers, or geographic region (see Figure 16.5). Which methods work best depends on the organization's activities, communication needs, and coordination requirements. Another type of mixed structure often occurs in joint ventures, which are becoming increasingly popular.

The span of control is the number of people who report to a manager.

Span of Control   The second dimension of organizational configuration, **span of control,** is the number of people reporting to a manager; thus, it defines the size of the organization's work groups. Span of control is also called "span of management." A manager who has a small span of control can maintain close control over workers and stay in contact with daily operations. If the span of control is large, close control is not possible. Figure 16.6 shows examples of small and large spans of control. Supervisors in the upper portion of the figure have a span of control of sixteen whereas in the lower portion, supervisors have a span of control of eight.

A number of formulas and rules have been offered for determining the optimal span of control in an organization,[18] but research on the topic has not conclusively identified a foolproof method.[19] Henry Mintzberg concluded that the optimal unit size, or span of control, depends on five conditions:

1. The coordination requirements within the unit, including factors such as the degree of job specialization
2. The similarity of the tasks in the unit
3. The type of information available or needed by unit members
4. Differences in the members' need for autonomy
5. The extent to which members need direct access to the supervisor[20]

figure 16.5

Mixed Departmentalization

A mixed departmentalization scheme is often used in very large organizations with more complex structures. Headquarters is organized based on products. Industrial products and consumer products are departmentalized on the basis of function. The manufacturing department is based on process. Sales is based on customer. Marketing is based on geographical regions.

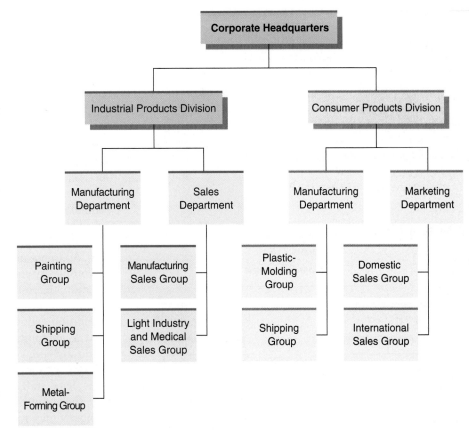

For example, a span of control of sixteen (as shown in Figure 16.6) might be appropriate for a supervisor in a typical manufacturing plant in which experienced workers do repetitive production tasks. On the other hand, a span of control of eight or fewer (as shown in Figure 16.6) might be appropriate in a job shop or custom-manufacturing facility in which workers do many different things and the tasks and problems that arise are new and unusual.[21]

The administrative hierarchy is the system of reporting relationships in the organization, from the lowest to the highest managerial levels.

Administrative Hierarchy   The **administrative hierarchy** is the system of reporting relationships in the organization, from the first level up through the president or CEO. It results from the need for supervisors and managers to coordinate the activities of employees. The size of the administrative hierarchy is inversely related to the span of control: Organizations with a small span of control have many managers in the hierarchy; those with a large span of control have a smaller administrative hierarchy. Companies often rearrange their administrative hierarchies to achieve more efficient operations. Gateway 2005 rearranged its management and moved the company's headquarters from South Dakota to San Diego, California, in order to develop an organization that will enable it to provide many different computer-related products and services.[22]

Using Figure 16.6 again, we can examine the effects of small and large spans of control on the number of hierarchical levels. The smaller span of control for the supervisors in the lower portion of the figure requires that there be four supervisors rather than two. Correspondingly, another management layer is needed to keep the

Large Span of Control

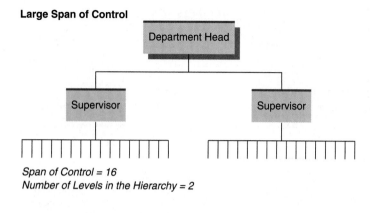

Span of Control = 16
Number of Levels in the Hierarchy = 2

Small Span of Control

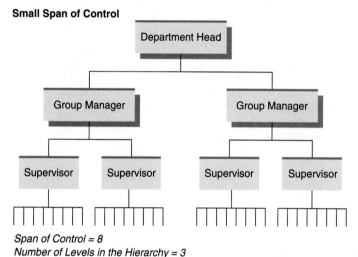

Span of Control = 8
Number of Levels in the Hierarchy = 3

figure 16.6

Span of Control and Levels in the Administrative Hierarchy

These charts show how span of control and the number of levels in the administrative hierarchy are inversely related. The thirty-two first-level employees are in two groups of sixteen in the top chart and in four groups of eight in the bottom chart. Either may be appropriate, depending on the work situation.

department head's span of control at two. Thus, when the span of control is small, the workers are under tighter supervision, and there are more administrative levels. When the span of control is large, as in the upper portion of the figure, production workers are not closely supervised, and there are fewer administrative levels. Because it measures the number of management personnel, or administrators, in the organization, the administrative hierarchy is sometimes called the "administrative component," "administrative intensity," or "administrative ratio."

The size of the administrative hierarchy also relates to the overall size of the organization. As an organization's size increases, so do its complexity and the requirements for coordination, necessitating proportionately more people to manage the business. However, this conclusion defines the administrative component as including the entire administrative hierarchy—that is, all of the support staff groups, such as personnel and financial services, legal staff, and others. Defined in this way, the administrative component in a large company may seem huge compared with the number of production workers. On the other hand, research that separates the support staff and clerical functions from the management hierarchy has found that the ratio of managers to total employees actually decreases with increases in the organization's size. Other, more recent research has shown that the size of the administrative hierarchy and the overall size of the organization are not related in a straightforward manner, especially during periods of growth and decline.[23]

"There used to be eleven layers between me and the lowest-level employees; now there are five."—William Stavropoulos, CEO of Dow Chemical, describing Dow's new organization structure[24]

The popular movement of downsizing has been partially a reaction to the complexity that comes with increasing organization size. Much of the literature on organizational downsizing has proposed that it results in lower overhead costs, less bureaucracy, faster decision making, smoother communications, and increases in productivity.[25]

These expectations are due to the effort to reduce the administrative hierarchy by cutting out layers of middle managers. Unfortunately, many downsizing efforts have resulted in poorer communication, reduced productivity, and lower employee morale because the downsizing is done indiscriminately, without regard for the jobs that people actually do, the coordination needs of the organization, and the additional training that may be necessary for the survivors.[26]

Structure and Operations

Some important aspects of organization structure do not appear on the organization chart and thus are quite different from the configurational aspects discussed in the previous section. In this section, we examine the structural policies that affect operations and prescribe or restrict how employees behave in their organizational activities.[27] The two primary aspects of these policies are centralization of decision making and formalization of rules and procedures.

Centralization

Centralization is a structural policy in which decision-making authority is concentrated at the top of the organizational hierarchy.

The first structural policy that affects operations is **centralization,** wherein decision-making authority is concentrated at the top of the organizational hierarchy. At the opposite end of the continuum is decentralization, in which decisions are made throughout the hierarchy.[28] Increasingly, centralization is being discussed in terms of participation in decision making.[29] In decentralized organizations, lower-level employees participate in making decisions. The changes that Jack Smith made in 1993 and 1996 at General Motors were intended to decentralize decision making throughout the company. Smith dismantled the old divisional structure, created a single unit called North American Operations, and abolished a tangle of management committees that slowed down decision making. Managers are now encouraged to make decisions on new designs and pricing that used to take weeks to circulate through the committee structure on their way to the top.[30]

"Decisions weren't getting made because of structural impediments."—Ben Rosen, chairman of the board of Compaq, describing the reasons for Compaq's 1999 change in management[31]

Decision making in organizations is more complex than the simple centralized-decentralized classification indicates. In Chapter 15, we discussed organizational decision making in more depth. One of the major distinctions we made there was that some decisions are relatively routine and require only the application of a decision rule. These decisions are programmed decisions whereas those that are not routine are nonprogrammed. The decision rules for programmed decisions are formalized for the organization. This difference between programmed and nonprogrammed decisions tends to cloud the distinction between centralization and decentralization. For even if decision making is decentralized, the decisions themselves may be programmed and tightly circumscribed.

If there is little employee participation in decision making, then decision making is centralized, regardless of the nature of the decisions being made. At the other extreme, if individuals or groups participate extensively in making nonprogrammed decisions, the structure can be described as truly decentralized. If individuals or groups participate extensively in decision making but mainly in programmed decisions, the structure is called "formalized decentralization." Formalized decentralization is a common way to provide decision-making involvement for employees at many different levels in the organization while maintaining control and predictability.

Participative management has been described as a total management system in which people are involved in the daily decision making and management of the organization. As part of an organization's culture, participative management can contribute significantly to the long-term success of an organization.[32] It has been described as effective and, in fact, morally necessary in organizations. Thus, for many people, participation in decision making has become more than a simple aspect of organization structure. Caution is required, however, because if middle managers are to make effective decisions, as participative management requires, they must have sufficient information.[33] Honda Motor Co. originally chose a product departmentalization strategy when it introduced the Acura.[34] Honda of America, however, later changed its structure by decentralizing and using more participation with great success.[35] One of the highly touted benefits of the "Information Age" was that all employees throughout the organization would have more information and would therefore be able to participate more in decisions affecting their work, thus creating more decentralized organizations. However, some have suggested that all of this new information in organizations has had the opposite effect by enabling top managers to have more information about the organization's operations and to keep the decisions to themselves, thus creating more centralized organizations.[36]

Formalization

Formalization is the degree to which rules and procedures shape the jobs and activities of employees.

Formalization is the degree to which rules and procedures shape employees' jobs and activities. The purpose of formalization is to predict and control how employees behave on the job.[37] Rules and procedures can be both explicit and implicit. Explicit rules are set down in job descriptions, policy and procedures manuals, or office memos. (In one large company that continually issues directives attempting to limit employee activities, workers refer to them as "Gestapo" memos because they require employees to follow harsh rules.) Implicit rules may develop as employees become accustomed to doing things in a certain way over a period of time.[38] Though unwritten, these established ways of getting things done become standard operating procedures and have the same effect on employee behavior as written rules.

We can assess formalization in organizations by looking at the proportion of jobs that are governed by rules and procedures and the extent to which those rules permit variation. More formalized organizations have a higher proportion of rule-bound jobs and less tolerance for rule violations.[39] Increasing formalization may affect the design of jobs throughout the organization[40] as well as employee motivation[41] and work group interactions.[42] The specific effects of formalization on employees are still unclear, however.[43]

Organizations tend to add more rules and procedures as the need for control of operations increases. Some organizations have become so formalized that they have rules for how to make new rules! One large state university created such rules in the form of a three-page document entitled "Procedures for Rule Adoption" that was added to the four-inch-thick Policy and Procedures Manual. The new policy first defines terms such as "university," "board," and "rule" and lists ten exceptions that describe when this policy on rule adoptions does not apply. It then presents a nine-step process for adopting a new rule within the university.

Other organizations are trying to become less formalized by reducing the number of rules and procedures employees must follow. In this effort, Chevron cut the number of its rules and procedures from over four hundred to eighteen. Highly detailed procedures for hiring were eliminated in favor of letting managers make hiring decisions based on common sense.[44]

Another approach to organizational formalization attempts to describe how, when, and why good managers should bend or break a rule.[45] Although rules exist in some form in almost every organization, how strictly they are enforced varies significantly from one organization to another and even within a single organization. Some managers argue that "a rule is a rule" and that all rules must be enforced to control employee behaviors and prevent chaos in the organization. Other managers act as if "all rules are made to be broken" and see rules as stumbling blocks on the way to effective action. Neither point of view is better for the organization; rather, a more balanced approach is recommended.

The test of a good manager in a formalized organization may be how well he or she uses appropriate judgment in making exceptions to rules. A balanced approach to making exceptions to rules should do two things. First, it should recognize that individuals are unique and that the organization can benefit from making exceptions that capitalize on exceptional capabilities. For example, suppose an engineering design department with a rule mandating equal access to tools and equipment acquires a limited amount of specialized equipment such as personal computers. The department manager decides to make an exception to the equal-access rule by assigning the computers to the designers the manager believes will use them the most and with the best results instead of making them available for use by all. Second, a balanced approach should recognize the commonalities among employees. Managers should make exceptions to rules only when there is a true and meaningful difference between individuals rather than base exceptions on features such as race, sex, appearance, or social factors.

Responsibility and Authority

R esponsibility and authority are related to both configurational and operational aspects of organization structure. For example, the organization chart shows who reports to whom at all levels in the organization. From the operational perspective, the degree of centralization defines the locus of decision-making authority in the organization. However, often there is some confusion about what responsibility and authority really mean for managers and how the two terms relate to each other.

Responsibility

Responsibility is an obligation to do something with the expectation of achieving some act or output.

Responsibility is an obligation to do something with the expectation that some act or output will result. For example, a manager may expect an employee to write and present a proposal for a new program by a certain date; thus, the employee is responsible for preparing the proposal.

Responsibility ultimately derives from the ownership of the organization. The owners hire or appoint a group, often a board of directors, to be responsible for managing the organization, making the decisions, and reaching the goals set by the owners. A downward chain of responsibility is then established. The board hires a Chief Executive Officer (CEO) or president to be responsible for running the organization. The CEO or president hires more people and holds them responsible for accomplishing designated tasks that enable her or him to produce the results expected by the board and the owners. Jack Welch became famous for the way he ran GE for twenty years. Over the years he hired many managers and delegated responsibility for running various parts of the business. However, in the end, Jack Welch was responsible for all of the activities of the organization, including the degree to which business was conducted ethically. The "Business of Ethics" box discusses how some of GE's actions have recently come under closer scrutiny.

"I think it's a mistake to designate a No. 2 to run the business. I like a CEO who does that job himself."—Warren Buffett, commenting on the lack of a No. 2 person at Coca-Cola[46]

The chain extends throughout the organization because each manager has an obligation to fulfill: to appropriately employ organizational resources (people, money, and equipment) to meet the owners' expectations. Although managers seemingly pass responsibility on to others to achieve results, each manager is still held responsible for the outputs of those to whom he or she delegates tasks.

A manager responsible for a work group assigns tasks to members of the group. Each group member is then responsible for doing his or her task, yet the manager still remains responsible for each task and for the work of the group as a whole. This means that managers can take on the responsibility of others but cannot shed their own responsibility onto those below them in the hierarchy.

Authority is power that has been legitimized within a particular social context.

Authority

Authority is power that has been legitimized within a specific social context.[47] (Power is discussed in Chapter 14.) Only when power is part of an official organizational role does it become authority. Authority includes the legitimate right to use resources to accomplish expected outcomes. As we discussed in the previous section, the authority to make decisions may be restricted to the top levels of the organization or dispersed throughout the organization.

Like responsibility, authority originates in the ownership of the organization. The owners establish a group of directors who are responsible for managing the organization's affairs. The directors, in turn, authorize people in the organization to make decisions and to use organizational resources. Thus, they delegate authority, or power in a social context, to others.

Authority is linked to responsibility because a manager responsible for accomplishing certain results must have the authority to use resources to achieve those results.[48] The relationship be-

Heidi Barrett is a wine consultant, one of approximately 100 in the wine industry. Consultants such as Barrett are hired by small to medium sized wineries to advise on creating top-quality wines. A job usually handled within the winery by internal wine makers, the work of these specialists means they are paid (often a lot of money) to provide advice on planting and picking methods for the grapes, barreling, blending, and tasting. In effect, these wineries have contracted to outsiders the authority and the responsibility to make good wine. Last year, a bottle of wine, crafted by Barrett, was sold at auction for $500,000. Now that's a lot of responsibility!

BUSINESS OF ETHICS

Should GE Be a Corporate Role Model?

Few American CEOs have earned the widespread approval, even adulation, that has been garnered by General Electric's former chief executive Jack Welch, who retired in 2001. "I think history is just going to remember [that] Jack Welch was one of the greatest industrial managers of our time," says John Inch, a Bear Stearns analyst. "Every conglomerate in America wants to grow up to be GE." Under Welch's twenty-year reign, GE grew to become the sixth-largest U.S. company. However, as Welch was stepping down, several ethical issues were emerging.

First, a GE acquisition of Honeywell, which manufactures products similar to GE's, was approved by the U.S. Federal Trade Commission (the FTC), which ruled that the deal did not violate antitrust regulations. However, the acquisition was not approved by the European Competition Commission, the FTC's European equivalent. Many international firms protested to the European Commission although few firms did so in the United States, probably because the European commission's hearings are private whereas the FTC's are public. Companies were unwilling to criticize GE publicly, fearing a backlash of higher prices for their purchases.

Second, GE is involved in an ugly battle over PCB chemicals that it dumped into the Hudson River for thirty years, beginning in the 1940s. The Environmental Protection Agency (EPA) ordered the firm to pay the $460 million cleanup cost; GE responded with an aggressive public relations campaign that spread misinformation. The EPA then directed the firm to pay an additional $37 million to cover the government's cost of conducting additional studies and publicizing their results. "This [action] is a direct message to GE that the EPA means business," claims

> *"Every conglomerate in America wants to grow up to be GE."*
> — *John Inch, Bear Stearns analyst*

Janet MacGillivray, senior attorney with the environmental group Riverkeeper.

Third, GE may be the victim of its own success. The firm's ability to maintain a steady 10 percent increase in earnings and always meet quarterly earnings targets is legendary—Welch missed the target only once in twenty years. But given the climate of investor distrust in the post-Enron era, GE's earnings have suddenly become questionable. Although no one suspects the firm of Enron-style fraud, Jeff Immelt, Welch's successor at GE, must now defend the company's earnings policy. He asks, "Would a miss be more honest? . . . I think that's terrible. [Should I say,] 'I missed my numbers—aren't you proud of me?'" How Immelt chooses to handle these issues will reveal a lot about him, and about GE.

References: Justin Fox, "What's So Great About GE?" *Fortune*, March 4, 2002. www.fortune.com on June 6, 2002; Dina Cappiello, "GE Ordered to Pick Up $37M Dredging-Plan Tab," *Times Union* (Albany, N.Y.), February 13, 2002. www.timesunion.com on June 7, 2002; "Despite Failed Merger, GE's Image Still Strong," *Arizona Republic*, July 9, 2001, pp. D1, D4 (quotation p. D4). See www.azcentral.com; Philip Shishkin, "EU Makes It Official: No Honeywell for GE—Regulatory Policy Hits a Continental Divide," *Wall Street Journal*, July 4, 2001. See www.wsj.com.

tween responsibility and authority must be one of parity; that is, the authority over resources must be sufficient to enable the manager to meet the output expectations of others.

But authority and responsibility differ in significant ways. Responsibility cannot be delegated down to others (as discussed in the previous section), but authority can. One complaint often heard from employees is that they have too much responsibility but not enough authority to get the job done. This indicates a lack of parity between responsibility and authority. Managers usually are quite willing to hold individuals responsible for specific tasks but are reluctant to delegate enough authority to do the job. In effect, managers try to rid themselves of responsibility for results (which they cannot do), yet they rarely like to give away their cherished authority over resources.

Delegation is the transfer of authority to make decisions and use organizational resources to others. Delegation of authority to make decisions to lower-level

Delegation is the transfer to others of authority to make decisions and use organizational resources.

managers is common in organizations today. The important thing is to give lower-level managers authority to carry out the decisions they make. Managers typically have difficulty in delegating successfully. In the Self-Assessment Exercise at the end of this chapter, you will have a chance to practice delegation.

The Iran-Contra affair of 1987–1988 is a good example of the difference between authority and responsibility. Some believe the Reagan administration confused delegation of authority with abdication of responsibility.[49] President Reagan delegated a great deal of authority to subordinates but did not require that they keep him informed, and they made no effort to do so. Hence, delegation of authority by the administration was appropriate and necessary, but its failure to require progress reports to keep informed and in control of operations resulted in the administration's trying to avoid responsibility. Although the president did hold his subordinates responsible for their actions, he ultimately—and rightfully—retained full responsibility.

An Alternative View of Authority

So far we have described authority as a "top-down" function in organizations; that is, authority originates at the top and is delegated downward as the managers at the top consider appropriate. In author Chester Barnard's alternative perspective, authority is seen as originating in the individual, who can choose whether or not to follow a directive from above. The choice of whether to comply with a directive is based on the degree to which the individual understands it, feels able to carry it out, and believes it to be in the best interests of the organization and consistent with personal values.[50] This perspective has been called the **acceptance theory of authority** because it means that the manager's authority depends on the subordinate's acceptance of the manager's right to give the directive and to expect compliance.

For example, assume that you are a marketing analyst, and your company has a painting crew in the maintenance department. For some reason, your manager has told you to repaint your own office over the weekend. You probably would question your manager's authority to make you do this work. In fact, you would probably refuse to do it. If you received a similar request to work over the weekend to finish a report, you would be more likely to accept it and carry it out. Thus, by either accepting or rejecting the directives of a supervisor, workers can limit supervisory authority.[51] In most organizational situations, employees accept a manager's right to expect compliance on normal, reasonable directives because of the manager's legitimate position in the organizational hierarchy or in the social context of the organization. They may choose to disobey a directive and must accept the consequences if they do not accept the manager's right.

> The acceptance theory of authority says that the authority of a manager depends on the subordinate's acceptance of the manager's right to give directives and to expect compliance with them.

Classic Views of Structure

The earliest views of organization structure combined the elements of organization configuration and operation into recommendations on how organizations should be structured. These views have often been called "classical organization theory" and include Max Weber's concept of the ideal bureaucracy, the classic organizing principles of Henri Fayol, and the human organization view of Rensis

Likert. Although all three are universal approaches, their concerns and structural prescriptions differ significantly.

Ideal Bureaucracy

Weber's ideal bureaucracy is characterized by a hierarchy of authority and a system of rules and procedures designed to create an optimally effective system for large organizations.

Weber's **ideal bureaucracy,** presented in Chapter 1, was an organizational system characterized by a hierarchy of authority and a system of rules and procedures that, if followed, would create a maximally effective system for large organizations. Weber, writing at a time when organizations were inherently inefficient, claimed that the bureaucratic form of administration is superior to other forms of management with respect to stability, control, and predictability of outcomes.[52]

Weber's ideal bureaucracy had seven essential characteristics and utilized several of the building blocks discussed in this chapter, including the division of labor, hierarchy of authority, and rules and procedures. Weber intended these characteristics to ensure order and predictability in relationships among people and jobs in the bureaucracy. But it is easy to see how the same features can lead to sluggishness, inefficiency, and red tape. The administrative system can easily break down if any of the characteristics are carried to an extreme or are violated. For example, if endless arrays of rules and procedures bog down employees who must find the precise rule to follow every time they do something, responses to routine client or customer requests may slow to a crawl. Moreover, subsequent writers have said that Weber's view of authority is too rigid and have suggested that the bureaucratic organization may impede creativity and innovation and result in a lack of compassion for the individual in the organization.[53] In other words, the impersonality that is supposed to foster objectivity in a bureaucracy may result in serious difficulties for both employees and the organization. However, some organizations retain some characteristics of a bureaucratic structure while remaining innovative and productive.

"The challenge is to find ways to constantly refresh the components of bureaucracy so that it remains the healthy kind rather than the destructive kind."—Roger R. Klene, president and COO of Mott Corporation[54]

Paul Adler has recently countered the currently popular movements of "bureaucracy busting" by noting that large-scale, complex organizations still need some of the basic characteristics that Weber described—hierarchical structure, formalized procedures, and staff expertise—in order to avoid chaos and ensure efficiency, conformance quality, and timeliness. Adler further proposes a second type of bureaucracy that essentially serves an enabling function in organizations.[55] The need for bureaucracy is not past. Bureaucracy, or at least some of its elements, is still critical for designing effective organizations.

The Classic Principles of Organizing

The management functions set forth by Henri Fayol include planning, organizing, command, coordination, and control.

Henri Fayol, a French engineer and chief executive officer of a mining company, presented a second classic view of the organization structure at the beginning of the twentieth century. Drawing on his experience as a manager, Fayol was the first to classify the essential elements of management—now usually called **management functions**—as planning, organizing, command, coordination, and control.[56]

table 16.2

**Fayol's Classic Principles
of Organizing**

Principle	Fayol's Comments
1. Division of work	Individuals and managers work on the same part or task.
2. Authority and responsibility	Authority—right to give orders; power to exact obedience; goes with responsibility for reward and punishment.
3. Discipline	Obedience, application, energy, behavior. Agreement between firm and individual.
4. Unity of command	Employee receives orders from one superior.
5. Unity of direction	One head and one plan for activities with the same objective.
6. Subordination of individual interest to general interest	Objectives of the organization come before objectives of the individual.
7. Remuneration of personnel	Pay should be fair to the organization and the individual; discussed various forms.
8. Centralization	Proportion of discretion held by the manager compared to that allowed to subordinates.
9. Scalar chain	Line of authority from lowest to top.
10. Order	A place for everyone and everyone in his or her place.
11. Equity	Combination of kindness and justice; equality of treatment.
12. Stability of tenure of personnel	Stability of managerial personnel; time to get used to work.
13. Initiative	Power of thinking out and executing a plan.
14. Esprit de corps	Harmony and union among personnel is strength.

Reference: From *General and Industrial Management*, by Henri Fayol. Copyright © Lake Publishing 1984, Belmont, CA 94002. Used with permission.

In addition, he presented fourteen principles of organizing that he considered an indispensable code for managers (see Table 16.2).

Fayol's principles have proved extraordinarily influential; they have served as the basis for the development of generally accepted means of organizing. For example, Fayol's "unity of command" principle means that employees should receive directions from only one person, and "unity of direction" means that tasks with the same objective should have a common supervisor. Combining these two principles with division of labor, authority, and responsibility results in a system of tasks and reporting and authority relationships that is the very essence of organizing. Fayol's principles thus provide the framework for the organization chart and the coordination of work.

The classic principles have been criticized on several counts. First, they ignore factors such as individual motivation, leadership, and informal groups—the human element in organizations. This line of criticism asserts that the classic principles result in a mechanical organization into which people must fit, regardless of their interests, abilities, or motivations. The principles have also been criticized for their lack of operational specificity in that Fayol described the principles as universal truths but did not specify the means of applying many of them. Finally, Fayol's principles have been discounted because they were not supported by scientific evidence; Fayol presented them as universal principles, backed by no evidence other than his own experience.[57]

Human Organization

Rensis Likert's human organization approach is based on supportive relationships, participation, and overlapping work groups.

Rensis Likert called his approach to organization structure the **human organization**.[58] Because Likert, like others, had criticized Fayol's classic principles for overlooking human factors, it is not surprising that his approach centered on the principles of supportive relationships, employee participation, and overlapping work groups.

The term "supportive relationships" suggests that in all organizational activities, individuals should be treated in such a way that they experience feelings of support, self-worth, and importance. By "employee participation," Likert meant that the work group needs to be involved in decisions that affect it, thereby enhancing the employee's sense of supportiveness and self-worth. The principle of "overlapping work groups" means that work groups are linked, with managers serving as the "linking pins." Each manager (except the highest ranking) is a member of two groups: a work group that he or she supervises and a management group composed of the manager's peers and their supervisor. Coordination and communication grow stronger when the managers perform the linking function by sharing problems, decisions, and information both upward and downward in the groups to which they belong. The human organization concept rests on the assumption that people work best in highly cohesive groups oriented toward organizational goals. Management's function is to make sure the work groups are linked for effective coordination and communication.

Likert described four systems of organizing, which he called management systems, whose characteristics are summarized in Table 16.3. System 1, the exploitive authoritative system, can be characterized as the classic bureaucracy. System 4, the participative group, is the organization design Likert favored. System 2, the benevolent authoritative system, and system 3, the consultative system, are less extreme than either system 1 or system 4.

Likert described all four systems in terms of eight organizational variables: leadership processes, motivational forces, communication processes, interaction-influence processes, decision-making processes, goal-setting processes, control processes, and performance goals and training. Likert believed that work groups should be able to overlap horizontally as well as vertically where necessary to accomplish tasks. This feature is directly contrary to the classic principle that advocates unity of command. In addition, rather than the hierarchical chain of command, Likert favored the linking-pin concept of overlapping work groups for making decisions and resolving conflicts.

Research support for Likert's human organization emanates primarily from Likert and his associates' work at the Institute for Social Research at the University of Michigan. Although their research has upheld the basic propositions of the approach, it is not entirely convincing. One review of the evidence suggested that although research has shown characteristics of system 4 to be associated with positive worker attitudes and, in some cases, increased productivity, it is not clear that the characteristics of the human organization "caused" the positive results.[59] It may have been that positive attitudes and high productivity allowed the organization structure to be participative and provided the atmosphere for the development of supportive relationships. Likert's design has also been criticized for focusing almost exclusively on individuals and groups and not dealing extensively with structural issues. Overall, the most compelling support for this approach is at the individual and work-group levels. In some ways, Likert's system 4 is much like the team-based organization popular today.

table 16.3   Characteristics of Likert's Four Management Systems

Characteristic	System 1: Exploitive Authoritative	System 2: Benevolent Authoritative	System 3: Consultative	System 4: Participative Group
Leadership				
• Trust in subordinates	None	None	Substantial	Complete
• Subordinates' ideas	Seldom used	Sometimes used	Usually used	Always used
Motivational Forces				
• Motives tapped	Security, status	Economic, ego	Substantial	Complete
• Level of satisfaction	Overall dissatisfaction	Some moderate satisfaction	Moderate satisfaction	High satisfaction
Communication				
• Amount	Very little	Little	Moderate	Much
• Direction	Downward	Mostly downward	Down, up	Down, up, lateral
Interaction-Influence				
• Amount	None	None	Substantial	Complete
• Cooperative teamwork	None	Virtually none	Moderate	Substantial
Decision Making				
• Locus	Top	Policy decided at top	Broad policy decided at top	All levels
• Subordinates involved	Not at all	Sometimes consulted	Usually consulted	Fully involved
Goal Setting				
• Manner	Orders	Orders with comments	Set after discussion	Group participation
• Acceptance	Covertly resisted	Frequently resisted	Sometimes resisted	Fully accepted
Control Processes				
• Level	Top	None	Some below top	All levels
• Information	Incomplete, inaccurate	Often incomplete, inaccurate	Moderately complete, accurate	Complete, accurate
Performance				
• Goals and Training	Mediocre	Fair to good	Good	Excellent

Reference: Adapted from Rensis Likert, *New Patterns of Management* (New York: McGraw-Hill, 1961), pp. 223–233; and Rensis Likert, *The Human Organization* (New York: McGraw-Hill, 1967), pp. 197, 198, 201, 203, 210, and 211.

Thus, the classic views of organization embody the key elements of organization structure. Each view, however, combined these key elements in different ways and with other management elements. These three classic views are typical of how the early writers attempted to prescribe a universal approach to organization structure that would be best in all situations. In the next chapter we describe other views of organization structure that may be effective, depending on the organizational situation.

Synopsis

The structure of an organization is the system of task, reporting, and authority relationships within which the organization does its work. The purpose of organization structure is to order and coordinate the actions of employees to achieve organizational goals. Every organization structure addresses two fundamental issues: dividing available labor according to the tasks to be performed and combining and coordinating divided tasks to ensure that tasks are accomplished.

An organization chart shows reporting relationships, work group memberships, departments, and formal lines of communication. In a broader sense, an organization chart shows the configuration, or shape, of the organization. Configuration has four dimensions: division of labor, departmentalization, span of control, and administrative hierarchy. Division of labor is the separation of work into different jobs to be done by different people. Departmentalization is the manner in which the divided tasks are combined and allocated to work groups for coordination. Tasks can be combined into departments on the basis of business function, process, product, customer, and geographic region. Span of control is the number of people reporting to a manager; it also defines the size of work groups and is inversely related to the number of hierarchical levels in the organization. The administrative hierarchy is the system of reporting relationships in the organization.

Structural policies prescribe how employees should behave in their organizational activities. Such policies include formalization of rules and procedures and centralization of decision making. Formalization is the degree to which rules and procedures shape employees' jobs and activities. The purpose of formalization is to predict and control how employees behave on the job. Explicit rules are set down in job descriptions, policy and procedures manuals, and office memos. Implicit rules develop over time as employees become accustomed to doing things in certain ways.

Centralization concentrates decision-making authority at the top of the organizational hierarchy; under decentralization, decisions are made throughout the hierarchy.

Responsibility is an obligation to do something with the expectation of achieving some output. Authority is power that has been legitimized within a specific social context. Authority includes the legitimate right to use resources to accomplish expected outcomes. The relationship between responsibility and authority needs to be one of parity; that is, employees must have enough authority over resources to meet the expectations of others.

Weber's ideal bureaucracy, Fayol's classic principles of organizing, and Likert's human organization cover many of the key features of organization structure. Weber's bureaucratic form of administration was intended to ensure stability, control, and predictable outcomes. Rules and procedures, division of labor, a hierarchy of authority, technical competence, separation of ownership, rights and property differentiation, and documentation characterize the ideal bureaucracy.

Fayol's classic principles included departmentalization, unity of command, and unity of direction; they came to be generally accepted as means of organizing. Taken together, the fourteen principles provided the basis for the modern organization chart and for coordinating work.

Likert's human organization was based on the principles of supportive relationships, employee participation, and overlapping work groups. Likert described the human organization in terms of eight variables based on the assumption that people work best in highly supportive and cohesive work groups oriented toward organization goals.

Discussion Questions

1. Define "organization structure" and explain its role in the process of managing the organization.

2. What is the purpose of organization structure? What would an organization be like without a structure?

3. In what ways are aspects of the organization structure analogous to the structural parts of the human body?

4. How is labor divided in your college or university? In what other ways could your college or university be departmentalized?

5. What types of organizations could benefit from a small span of control? What types might benefit from a large span of control?

6. Discuss how increasing formalization might affect the role conflict and role ambiguity of employees.

7. How might the impact of formalization differ for research scientists, machine operators, and bank tellers?

8. How might centralization or decentralization affect the job characteristics specified in job design?

9. When a group makes a decision, how is responsibility for the decision apportioned among the members?

10. Why do employees typically want more authority and less responsibility?

11. Consider the job you now hold or one that you held in the past. Did your boss have the authority to direct your work? Why did he or she have this authority?

12. Describe at least four features of organization structure that were important parts of the classic view of organizing.

Organizational Behavior Case for Discussion

A Company Divided Against Itself Cannot Stand

Would you feel respect and loyalty for U.S. President George W. Bush if he held the title of co-president? Bush enjoys a high approval rating, but what if he shared power with another person? (Given Bush's perceived strengths and weaknesses, perhaps an ideal co-president would be an elderly Ph.D. holder from a northern state.) At least for Americans, a single leader is almost universally preferred. Yet several large U.S. corporations, including Southwest Airlines and SAP, are using a co-CEO structure, in which the chief executive position is jointly held by two persons.

Stuart Moore and Jerry Greenberg together founded Sapient, an Internet consultancy firm, in 1991. They come from very different backgrounds, educations, and lifestyles but function well together. In addition to having complementary skills, Moore and Greenberg possess the other two requisite qualities for sharing the CEO role—they have a long-established history of trust in each other as well as "power motivation." ("Power motivation refers not to dictatorial behavior but to a desire to have impact, to be strong and influential," say professors David McClelland and David Burnham, who coined the term. A person who has high power motivation wants to lead in order to build a great institution, not merely to exercise personal power.) Moore and Greenberg make all decisions jointly; a tie-breaking mechanism was developed, but has never been used. The two travel together, work at desks just two inches apart, and split everything 50/50, including profits, ownership, and responsibility.

One important reason to split the CEO role is to increase the skills and experiences available to the leaders. "I don't think power sharing is natural. I think

it's very, very difficult," says professor Warren Bennis of the University of Southern California. "But [with] the warp speed companies are traveling at, the amazing number of alliances that are springing up, [and] everyone's fear of being taken over by some disruptive technology—right now you need a lot of eyes. I don't think anyone can do it all."

Another valid reason is to utilize executives' complementary styles. Dave Pottruck, the co-CEO of Schwab, claims he was "too competitive; too driven, making everybody around [him] uncomfortable." Sharing the CEO position with founder Charles Schwab allowed Pottruck to develop company-specific expertise and prepare for someday handling the job alone while also honing his people skills.

At Golden West Financial, founders and spouses Marion and Herbert Sandler ensure that a man's and a woman's point of view are equally represented. *Working Woman* ranked the company third in the United States for supporting women, and Marion maintains that she is making the best hires. Elaborating on her hiring practices, she confidently asserts, "You're not looking for figureheads. You don't want to make any compromises."

Yet another common reason for the use of co-CEOs is to facilitate the transition after a merger, especially one of two equally powerful firms. Verizon, created by the merger of GTE and Bell Atlantic, was for a time headed by Ivan Seidenberg, co-CEO and former CEO of Bell Atlantic, and Charles R. Lee, co-CEO and former head of GTE. However, after sharing the top spot for just twenty-one months, Lee became the chairman of the board, leaving the CEO position completely to Seidenberg. Mark L. Sirower, an advisor with Boston Consulting Group, notes,

"The inherent instability of the co-CEO relationship makes the structure particularly problematic in mergers and acquisitions—transitory at best and downright destructive at worst."

The co-CEO relationship also went awry at Citigroup. Sanford Weill, former head of Travelers Insurance, and John Reed, former CEO of Citibank, agreed to share the top position when the two firms merged in 1998, but the structure endured less than two years. The original motivation for the arrangement was to ease the post-merger transition, but it clearly did not work out that way. Instead, as *Fortune* writer Patricia Sellers describes, "John Reed lost. Sandy Weill won." As Reed fell from power, many of his protégés left Citigroup. Although the combined firm is performing well financially, many insiders admit that the two cultures never really coalesced and that the talent drain continues today.

Although co-CEO arrangements have the potential to work in some limited circumstances—for example, in situations in which there is considerable shared history and trust—they appear risky in a merger. Sirower worries about the lack of a unified corporate culture and is quite negative about the arrangement, claiming, "If there is ever a time when a company needs clear direction, leadership and rapid decision making, it is in the postmerger integration phase, when managers must . . . bring together two distinct organizations while protecting the day-to-day business. . . . It seems likely that the organizational disruption caused by the co-CEO model generally is not worth the perceived benefits, especially since most companies will eventually revert [back] to the single-CEO model."

"[T]he co-CEO relationship [is] transitory at best and downright destructive at worst."—Mark L. Sirower, corporate development advisor, Boston Consulting Group

References: "Corporate Information," "Following the Leader," "Golden West Financial Corporation Board of Directors," Golden West Financial web site. www.worldsavings.com on June 10, 2002; "Profile: Charles Schwab Corp." Yahoo! Finance web site. biz.yahoo.com on June 10, 2002; "Senior Leadership Profiles," Verizon web site. investor.verizon.com on June 10, 2002; "Who's Who," Schwab web site. www.aboutschwab.com on June 10, 2002; Patricia Sellers, "Hubby, Wife Are Golden Duo," *Fortune*, March 4, 2002. www.fortune.com on June 10, 2002; Kathleen Melymuka, "Taking Stock," *Computerworld*, June 26, 2000. www.computerworld.com on June 10, 2002; Patricia Sellers, "CEO Deathmatch!" *Fortune*, March 20, 2000. www.fortune.com on June 10, 2002; David Whitford, "The Two-Headed Manager," *Fortune*, January 24, 2000. www.fortune.com on June 10, 2002; Mark L. Sirower, "One Head Is Better Than Two," *Wall Street Journal*, October 18, 1999 (quotation). interactive.wsj.com on October 26, 1999.

Case Questions

1. Describe ways in which a firm could use the three forms of coordination (departmentalization, span of control, and administrative hierarchy) to help manage the CEO's job when that position is being filled by two co-CEOs.

2. Would an organization that utilizes co-CEOs be more likely to be centralized or decentralized than one with a single CEO? Would it be more likely to be formal or informal? Explain your answers.

3. In your opinion, is the use of co-CEOs more likely to be successful in the long term when the two individuals have complementary skills and viewpoints, or when there is substantial similarity and agreement between them? Why?

 # Experiencing Organizational Behavior

Understanding Organization Structure

Purpose: This exercise will help you understand the configurational and operational aspects of organization structure.

Format: You will interview at least five employees in different parts of either the college or university you attend or a small- to medium-sized organization and analyze its structure. (You may want to coordinate this exercise with the exercise in Chapter 17.)

Procedure: If you use a local organization, your first task is to find one with fifty to five hundred employ-

ees. The organization should have more than two hierarchical levels, but it should not be too complex to understand in a short period of study. You may want to check with your professor before contacting the company. Your initial contact should be with the highest-ranking manager, if possible. Be sure that top management is aware of your project and gives its approval.

If you use your local college or university, you could talk to professors, secretaries, and other administrative staff in the admissions office, student services department, athletic department, library, or many other areas. Be sure to represent a variety of jobs and levels in your interviews.

Using the material in this chapter, interview employees to obtain the following information on the structure of the organization.

1. The type of departmentalization (business function, process, product, customer, geographic region)
2. The typical span of control at each level of the organization
3. The number of levels in the hierarchy
4. The administrative ratio (ratio of managers to total employees and ratio of managers to production employees)
5. The degree of formalization (to what extent are rules and procedures written down in job descriptions, policy and procedures manuals, and memos?)
6. The degree of decentralization (to what extent are employees at all levels involved in making decisions?)

Interview three to five employees of the organization at different levels and in different departments. One should hold a top-level position. Be sure to ask the questions in a way that is clear to the respondents; they may not be familiar with the terminology used in this chapter.

Students should produce a report with a paragraph on each configurational and operational aspect of structure listed in this exercise as well as an organization chart of the company, a discussion of differences in responses from the employees interviewed, and any unusual structural features (for example, a situation in which employees report to more than one person or to no one). You may want to send a copy of your report to the company's top management.

Follow-up Questions

1. Which aspects of structure were the hardest to obtain information about? Why?
2. If there were differences in the responses of the employees you interviewed, how do you account for them?

 # Self-Assessment Exercise

Making Delegation Work

Tasks and decisions must be delegated to others if what remains of middle management is to survive. With all of the recent downsizing, those who are left must do more with less time and fewer resources. In addition, the essence of total quality management is allowing others—teams and individuals—to make decisions about their work. On the other hand, many managers and supervisors complain that they do not know how to delegate effectively. The following twelve points should improve your delegation.

If you hold any type of managerial assignment or job at work or in a student club or association, you could delegate some job or task to another person. Try the following simple steps.

1. Choose a specific task and time frame. Know exactly what task is to be delegated and by when.
2. Specify in writing exactly why you are delegating this task.

3. Put down in writing exactly what you expect to be done and how it will be measured.
4. Be sure that the person or team is competent to do the task, or at least knows how to acquire the competence if they do not have it initially.
5. Be certain that those who must do the tasks really want to take on more responsibility.
6. Measure or oversee the work without being conspicuous and bothersome to those doing the task.
7. Predict how much it will cost to correct mistakes that might be made.
8. Make sure that YOUR boss knows that you are delegating this task and approves.
9. Be sure that you will be able to provide the appropriate rewards to the person or team who takes on this additional responsibility if they succeed.

10. Be ready with another task to delegate when the person or team succeeds with this one.

11. Be sure to delegate both responsibility for the task and the authority to utilize the appropriate resources to get the job done.

References: Selwyn W. Becker, "TQM Does Work: Ten Reasons Why Misguided Attempts Fail," *Management Review*, May 1993, pp. 30–33; Janet Houser Carter, "Minimizing the Risks from Delegation," *Supervisory Management*, February 1993, pp. 1–2; John Lawrie, "Turning Around Attitudes About Delegation," *Supervisory Management*, December 1990, pp. 1–2.

OB Online

1. Some large, publicly traded organizations have a type of organization chart that at least shows the way that their top level is structured. Using the Internet, look up the organization charts of several organizations. You may have to go to documents that are reported to the Securities and Exchange Commission in order to find them. Pick four companies in different industries for which you can find good and recent organization charts.

2. Describe the configurational aspects of the structure of each organization.

3. By reviewing the charts and reading the annual report for each company, see if you can describe any of the operational aspects of the structure as delineated in this chapter.

Building Managerial Skills

Exercise Overview: Managers typically inherit an existing organization structure when they are promoted or hired into a position as manager. Often, however, after working with the existing structure for a while, they feel the need to rearrange the structure to increase the productivity or performance of the organization. This exercise provides you with the opportunity to restructure an existing organization.

Exercise Background: Recall the analysis you did in the "Experiencing Organizational Behavior" exercise on page 453 in which you analyzed the structure of an existing organization. In that exercise you described the configurational and operational aspects of the structure of a local organization or department at your college or university.

Exercise Task: Develop a different organization structure for that organization. You may utilize any or all of the factors described in this chapter. For example, you could alter the span of control, the administrative hierarchy, and the method of departmentalization as well as the formalization and centralization of the organization. Remember, the key to structure is to develop a way to coordinate the divided tasks. You should draw a new organization chart and develop a rationale for your new design.

Conclude by addressing the following questions:

1. How difficult was it to come up with a different way of structuring the organization?

2. What would it take to convince the current head of that organization to go along with your suggested changes?

17 Organization Design

Management Preview

▶ Why is it that when some companies' products mature, the economy changes, or low-cost foreign competition enters the market, some companies die, but others adjust and become stronger than ever? One key reason is organization design. Within the organization, design coordinates the efforts of the people, work groups, and departments. Designing a system of task, reporting, and authority relationships that leads to the efficient accomplishment of organizational goals is a challenge managers must be prepared to face. In Chapter 16, we discussed the tools with which managers design a system that enables the organization to be effective. In this chapter, we integrate these basic elements of structure; take into consideration other factors such as the environment, technology, and strategy; and present several perspectives on organization design. We begin this chapter by discussing organization designs based on the contingency approach. In this discussion we describe how an organization's size, technology, and environment combine with its strategy to determine various aspects of organization design. Next, we examine several organization designs: mechanistic and organic designs, the sociotechnical systems perspective, the Mintzberg framework for classifying organization structures, matrix designs, and virtual organizations. We conclude with an examination of contemporary organization design issues. But first, we describe the many factors that may have caused the death of "Ma Bell."

▽ ▼ ▽

In 1876, Alexander Graham Bell uttered the first words ever heard over a telephone: "Mr. Watson, come here, I want you," and forever changed the history of communications. American Telephone and Telegraph Company, AT&T, was created as a Bell subsidiary in 1885 to provide national long-distance communications. In a landmark case in 1913, AT&T settled a federal antitrust lawsuit by agreeing to divest its telegraph holdings, thereby creating Western Union, in exchange for a government-sanctioned monopoly if the firm guaranteed universal access. Over the decades, AT&T has had many "firsts," including the first transatlantic telephone cable, the first communications satellite, and the first commercial-use fiber-optic cable. Consumers who have no choice in selecting local or long-distance providers refer either affectionately or sarcastically to the giant firm as "Ma Bell." After dominating the industry for more than a century, AT&T today is a firm in decline. Analyst Ken McGee says, "We really are witnessing the death of an American icon."

The first blow to the seemingly invincible firm was also the most dramatic. Between 1982 and 1984, AT&T negotiated an antitrust settlement requiring the divestiture of its local telephone operations that created seven regional companies called the "Baby Bells." The parent company retained long-distance and R&D services. Throughout the 1990s, AT&T, looking to the future, made strategic acquisitions in computers and wireless technology. But in 1995, AT&T sold its computer holdings to NCR and spun off its product businesses into Lucent Technologies. In 2001, the company split into four separate firms—wireless, broadband (including cable and Internet), business customers, and consumer businesses.

"We really are witnessing the death of an American icon."—Ken McGee, analyst, the Gartner Group

One cause of AT&T's court-ordered breakup and its abrupt changes in strategy was the firm's monopoly status, which had led to the creation of a bureaucratic and tradition-bound culture. For example, monopoly pricing caused the company to overcharge for some services while providing others virtually free, thus losing sight of its own cost structure. Bad decisions played a part, too—when the telephone market was saturated, AT&T managers felt they had to move into new industries in order to grow. With its innovation stifled, the firm became vulnerable to outsiders like MCI. One former executive claims, "People who took risks and failed . . . got killed." Under the threat of competition in the 1970s, the firm wasted valuable years fighting in court rather than becoming more competitive in the marketplace. In the 1980s, regulation shifted to allow the Baby Bells to offer long-distance service, so AT&T faced strong competition for the first time with no legal protection. "AT&T thrived in eras when it crafted the rules," says analyst Brian Adamik. "Then the Telecom Act came along, and now they're in a struggle for survival."

All of these changes—restructurings, acquisitions, mergers, spinoffs, and divestitures—are likely to result in the firm's demise once it has sold off every one of its businesses. At best, AT&T will be a much smaller firm, serving the least profitable industry segments such as consumer long-distance. AT&T CEO Mike Armstrong says that even if the firm's name is gone, its legacy will endure: "Whether we end up standing alone, merging, or [becoming] part of an industry consolidation, if what we have become is an attractive company, that's good for shareholder value."[1]

References: "About AT&T," "AT&T History," "AT&T To Create Family of Four New Companies," AT&T web site. www.att.com on June 11, 2002; Martha McKay, "AT&T To Cut Another 5,000 Jobs This Year—Layoffs Spur Speculation About Possible Merger," *The Record* (Hackensack, N.J.), January 5, 2002. See www.bergen.com; Stephanie N. Mehta, "Say Goodbye to AT&T," *Fortune*, October 1, 2001, pp. 135–146 (quotation p. 136). www.fortune.com on June 11, 2002.

AT&T is not alone in trying to change itself in order to survive in an ever-changing environment. Many companies are constantly reorganizing to try to increase their performance, productivity, and response times—or just to survive. The primary issue is how to determine which organizational form is right for a given organization. In this chapter we describe several approaches to organization design.

Contingency Approaches to Organization Design

In the universal approach to organization design, prescriptions or propositions are designed to work in any circumstances.

Under the contingency approach to organization design, the desired outcomes for the organization can be achieved in several ways.

Organization designs vary from rigid bureaucracies to flexible matrix systems. Most theories of organization design take either a universal or a contingency approach. A **universal approach** is one whose prescriptions or propositions are designed to work in any situation. Thus, a universal design prescribes the "one best way" to structure the jobs, authority, and reporting relationships of the organization, regardless of factors such as the organization's external environment, the industry, and the type of work to be done. The classical approaches discussed in Chapter 16 are all universal approaches. A **contingency approach,** on the other hand, suggests that organizational efficiency and effectiveness can be achieved in several ways. In a contingency design, specific conditions such as the environment, technology, and the organization's workforce determine the structure. Figure 17.1 shows the distinction between the universal and contingency approaches. This distinction is similar to the one between universal and contingency approaches to motivation (Chapters 5 and 6), job design (Chapter 7), and leadership (Chapters 13 and 14). Although no one particular form of organization is generally accepted, the contingency approach most closely represents current thinking.

Weber, Fayol, and Likert (see Chapter 16) each proposed an organization design that is independent of the nature of the organization and its environment. Although each of their approaches contributed to our understanding of the organizing process and the practice of management, none has proved to be universally applicable. In this chapter we turn to several contingency designs, which attempt to specify the conditions, or contingency factors, under which they are likely to be most effective. The contingency factors include such things as the strategy of the

figure 17.1

Universal and Contingency Approaches to Organization Design

The universal approach looks for the single best way to design an organization regardless of situational issues. The contingency approach designs the organization to fit the situation.

The Universal Design Approach (Ideal Bureaucracy, Classic Principles of Organizing, Human Organization)

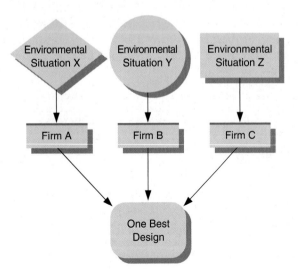

The Contingency Design Approach (Sociotechnical Systems, Structural Imperatives, Strategy and Strategic Choice)

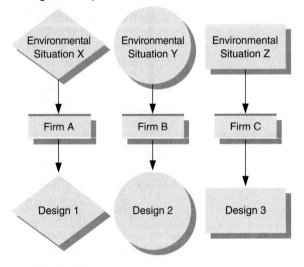

organization, its technology, the environment, the organization's size, and the social system within which the organization operates.

"Sony started as a small venture company with a strong orientation towards international markets in the early postwar years. Over the past decades, Sony has turned into a huge multinational enterprise. A reorganization has become inevitable."—Mario Tokoro, president, Sony Computer Science Laboratories; corporate executive vice president and director, Information & Network Technologies Laboratory, Sony Corporation[2]

The contingency approach has been criticized as being unrealistic because managers are expected to observe a change in one of the contingency factors and to make a rational structural alteration. On the other hand, Donaldson has argued that it is reasonable to expect organizations to respond to lower organizational performance, which may result from a lack of response to some significant change in one or several contingency factors.[3]

Strategy, Structural Imperatives, and Strategic Choice

The decision about how to design the organization structure is based on numerous factors. In this section, we present several views of the determinants of organization structure and integrate them into a single approach. We begin with the strategic view.

Strategy

Strategy is the plans and actions necessary to achieve organizational goals.

A **strategy** is the plans and actions necessary to achieve organizational goals.[4] Kellogg, for example, has attempted to be the leader in the ready-to-eat cereal industry by pursuing a strategy that combines product differentiation and market segmentation. Over the years, Kellogg has successfully introduced new cereals made from different grains in different shapes, sizes, colors, and flavors in its effort to provide any type of cereal the consumer might want.[5]

After studying the history of seventy companies, Alfred Chandler drew certain conclusions about the relationship between an organization's structure and its business strategy.[6] Chandler observed that a growth strategy to expand into a new product line is usually matched with some type of decentralization, a decentralized structure being necessary to deal with the problems of the new product line.

Chandler's "structure follows strategy" concept seems to appeal to common sense. Management must decide what the organization is to do and what its goals are before deciding how to design the organization structure, which is how the organization will meet those goals. This perspective assumes a purposeful approach to designing the structure of the organization.

Structural Imperatives

The structural-imperatives approach to organization design probably has been the most discussed and researched contingency perspective of the last thirty years. This perspective was not formulated by a single theorist or researcher, and it has

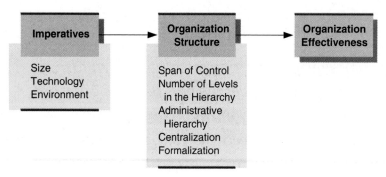

figure 17.2

The Structural Imperatives Approach

Organizational size, environment, and technology determine how an organization should be structured to be effective.

Structural imperatives—size, technology, and environment—are the three primary determinants of organization structure.

not evolved from a systematic and cohesive research effort. Rather, it gradually emerged from a vast number of studies that sought to address the question "What are the compelling factors that determine how the organization must be structured to be effective?" As Figure 17.2 shows, the three factors that have been identified as **structural imperatives** are size, technology, and environment.

Size   The size of an organization can be gauged in many ways. Usually it is measured in terms of total number of employees, value of the organization's assets, total sales in the previous year (or number of clients served), or physical capacity. The method of measurement is very important, although the different measures usually are correlated.[7]

Generally, larger organizations have a more complex structure than smaller ones. Peter Blau and his associates concluded that large size is associated with greater specialization of labor, a larger span of control, more hierarchical levels, and greater formalization.[8] These multiple effects are shown in Figure 17.3. Increasing size leads to more specialization of labor within a work unit, which increases the amount of differentiation among work units and the number of levels in the hierarchy, resulting in a need for more intergroup formalization. With greater specialization within the unit, there is less need for coordination within groups; thus, the span of control can be larger. Larger spans of control mean fewer first-line managers, but the need for more intergroup coordination may require more second- and third-line managers and staff personnel to coordinate them. Large organizations may therefore be more efficient because of their large spans

figure 17.3

Impact of Large Size on Organization Structure

As organizations grow larger, their structures usually change in predictable ways. Larger organizations tend to have more complex structures, larger spans of control, and more rules and procedures.

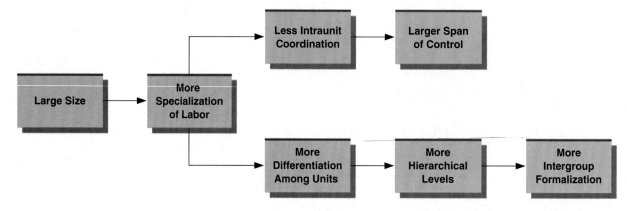

Real estate companies are making a concerted effort to reach out to a multicultural society. Minority homeownership is increasing at a rapid pace, leading the real estate industry to search for ways to better serve the minority and immigrant groups within the area. Based on their assessment of changes in the real estate environment, companies are developing new business strategies, resulting in new hiring practices, training programs, and revised marketing efforts.

of control and reduced administrative overhead; however, the greater differentiation among units makes the system more complex. Studies by researchers associated with the University of Aston in Birmingham, England, and others have shown similar results.[9]

Economies of scale are another advantage of large organizations. In a large operation, fixed costs—for example, plant and equipment—can be spread over more units of output, thereby reducing the cost per unit. In addition, some administrative activities such as purchasing, clerical work, and marketing can be accomplished for a large number of units at the same cost as for a small number. Their cost can then be spread over the larger number of units, again reducing unit cost.

Companies such as AT&T Technologies, General Electric's Aircraft Engines products group, and S. C. Johnson & Son have gone against the conventional wisdom that larger is always better in manufacturing plants. They cite as their main reasons the smaller investment required for smaller plants, the reduced need to produce a variety of products, and the desire to decrease organizational complexity (that is, reduce the number of hierarchical levels and shorten lines of communication). In a number of instances, smaller plants have resulted in increased team spirit, improved productivity, and higher profits.[10] Other studies have found that the relationship between size and structural complexity is less clear than the Blau results indicate. These studies suggest that size must be examined in relation to the technology of the organization.[11]

Traditionally, as organizations have grown, several layers of advisory staff have been added to help coordinate the complexities inherent in any large organization. In contrast, a current trend is to cut staff throughout the organization. Known as **organizational downsizing,** this popular trend is aimed primarily at reducing the size of corporate staff and middle management to reduce costs. The results of downsizing have been mixed, with some observers noting that indiscriminate across-the-board cuts may leave the organization weak in certain key areas. Companies such as NYNEX, Eastman Kodak, Digital Equipment Corporation, and RJR Nabisco have made cutbacks with disastrous results. NYNEX Corporation, the telephone company, had to hire back hundreds of employees who had taken an early retirement program to try to build back its reputation for customer service. In addition, the New York Public Service Commission ordered NYNEX to rebate $50 million to 5 million customers because it had fallen behind in responding to problems due to its staff reductions. Eastman Kodak is paying more for contract workers who are doing the work that laid-off workers used to do. In addition, Kodak is rehiring some of those laid off at increased salaries and incurring the costs of

Organizational downsizing is a popular trend aimed at reducing the size of corporate staff and middle management to reduce costs.

There are often unintended consequences of downsizing. Often those employees who survive the downsizing usually are required to pick up the work of those who have left. This poor guy got a promotion and a new title, but he now has more jobs to do.

Reference: © Randy Glasbergen

"I downsized our staff so effectively, they promoted me to Executive Vice President. They also made me custodian, receptionist and parking garage attendant."

recruiting and rehiring. And Digital Equipment Corporation does not even exist anymore. There are always some unintended consequences of downsizing, as shown in the cartoon.

In sales, cutting costs can be disastrous. Digital Equipment Company eliminated hundreds of sales and marketing staff members because it reported losing $3 million per day! Customers then reported never seeing a DEC representative for months and subsequently began to use other computer equipment suppliers such as IBM and Hewlett-Packard. In fact, some of the laid-off salespeople were hired by the competitors and immediately pulled former DEC customers with them. Following a merger, RJR Nabisco decided to merge sales forces for its foods group, which handles Grey Poupon Mustard and Milkbone dog biscuits, with the Planters Life Savers Company, which makes gums, candies, and nuts. Problems arose when the lack of compatibility in product types and in outlets began to surface. Sales representatives had trouble covering the much broader array of products and selling to twice as many outlets. As a result, customers were not called on promptly, and sales suffered significantly. Initially, profit margins did improve, but the next year operating earnings fell to 25 percent of their former levels.[12]

However, positive results often include quicker decision making because fewer layers of management must approve every decision. One review of research on organizational downsizing found that it had both psychological and sociological impacts. This study suggested that in a downsizing environment, size affects organization design in very complex ways.[13]

Organizational technology refers to the mechanical and intellectual processes that transform inputs into outputs.

Technology   **Organizational technology** consists of the mechanical and intellectual processes that transform raw materials into products and services for customers. For example, the primary technology employed by major oil companies transforms crude oil (input) into gasoline, motor oil, heating oil, and other petroleum-based products (outputs). Prudential Insurance uses actuarial tables and information-processing technologies to produce its insurance services. Of course, most organizations use multiple technologies. Oil companies use research and information-processing technologies in their laboratories, where new petroleum products and processes are generated.

table 17.1

Summary of Approaches to Technology

Approach	Classification of Technology	Example
Woodward (1958 and 1965) (cit. no. 14)	Unit or small-batch	Customized parts made one at a time
	Large-batch or mass production	Automobile assembly line
	Continuous process	Chemical plant, petroleum refinery
Burns and Stalker (1961) (cit. no. 15)	Rate of technological change	Slow: large manufacturing; rapid: computer industry
Perrow (1967) (cit. no. 16)	Routine	Standardized products (Procter & Gamble, General Foods)
	Nonroutine	New technology products or processes (computers, telecommunications)
Thompson (1967) (cit. no. 17)	Long-linked	Assembly line
	Mediating	Bank
	Intensive	General hospital
Aston studies: Hickson, Pugh, and Pheysey (1969) (cit. no. 18)	Workflow integration; operations, materials, and knowledge technologies	Technology differs in various parts of the organization

Although there is general agreement that technology is important, the means by which this technology has been evaluated and measured have varied widely. Five approaches to examining the technology of the organization are shown in Table 17.1. For convenience, we have classified these approaches according to the names of their proponents.

In an early study of the relationship between technology and organization structure, Joan Woodward categorized manufacturing technologies by their complexity: unit or small-batch, large-batch or mass production, and continuous process.[14] Tom Burns and George Stalker proposed that the rate of change in technology determines the best method of structuring the organization.[15] Charles Perrow developed a technological continuum, with routine technologies at one end and nonroutine technologies at the other, and claimed that all organizations could be classified on his routine-to-nonroutine continuum.[16] Thompson claimed that all organizations could be classified into one of three technological categories: long-linked, mediating, and intensive.[17] Finally, a group of English researchers at the University of Aston developed three categories of technology based on the type of workflow involved: operations, material, and knowledge.[18] These perspectives on technology are somewhat similar in that all (except the Aston typology) address the adaptability of the technological system to change. Large-batch or mass production, routine, and long-linked technologies are not very adaptable to change. At the opposite end of the continuum, continuous-process, nonroutine, and intensive technologies are readily adaptable to change.

One major contribution of the study of organizational technology is the recognition that organizations have more than one important "technology" that enables them to accomplish their tasks. Instead of examining technology in isolation, the

Aston group recognized that size and technology are related in determining organization structure.[19] They found that in smaller organizations, technology had more direct effects on the structure. In large organizations, however, they, like Blau, found that structure depended less on the operations technology and more on size considerations such as the number of employees. In large organizations, each department or division may have a different technology that determines how that department or division should be structured. In short, in small organizations the structure depended primarily on the technology whereas in large organizations the need to coordinate complicated activities was the most important factor. Thus, both organizational size and technology are important considerations in organization design.

Global technology variations come in two forms: variations in available technology and variations in attitudes toward technology. The technology available affects how organizations can do business. Many underdeveloped countries, for example, lack electric power sources, telephones, and trucking equipment, not to mention computers and robots. A manager working in such a country must be prepared to deal with many frustrations. Some Brazilian officials convinced a U.S. company to build a high-tech plant in their country. Midway through construction, however, the government of Brazil decided it would not allow the company to import some accurate measuring instruments that it needed to produce its products. The new plant was abandoned before it opened.[20]

Attitudes toward technology also vary across cultures. Surprisingly, Japan only began to support basic research in the 1980s. For many years, the Japanese government encouraged its companies to take basic research findings discovered elsewhere (often in the United States) and figure out how to apply them to consumer products (applied research). In the mid-1980s, however, the government changed its stance and started to encourage basic research as well.[21] Most Western nations have a generally favorable attitude toward technology whereas until the 1990s, China and other Asian countries (with the exception of Japan) did not.

Despite all of the emphasis on technology's role as a primary determinant of structure, there is some support for viewing it from the perspective that the strategy and structure of the organization determine what types of technology are appropriate. For example, Wal-Mart and Dell Computers are careful to only use new information technology in ways that support their strategy and structure, as described in the "Talking Technology" box.

Environment   The **organizational environment** includes all of the elements—people, other organizations, economic factors, objects, and events—that lie outside the boundaries of the organization. The environment is composed of two layers: the general environment and the task environment. The **general environment** includes all of a broad set of dimensions and factors within which the organization operates, including political-legal, social, cultural, technological, economic, and international factors. The **task environment** includes specific organizations, groups, and individuals who influence the organization. People in the task environment include customers, donors, regulators, inspectors, and shareholders. Among the organizations in the task environment are competitors, legislatures, and regulatory agencies. Economic factors in the task environment might include interest rates, international trade factors, and the unemployment rate in a particular area. Objects in the task environment include such things as buildings, vehicles, and trees. Events that may affect organizations include weather, elections, or war.

It is necessary to determine the boundaries of the organization to understand where the environment begins. These boundaries may be somewhat elusive, or at

The organizational environment is everything outside an organization and includes all elements—people, other organizations, economic factors, objects, and events—that lie outside the boundaries of the organization.

The general environment includes the broad set of dimensions and factors within which the organization operates, including political-legal, sociocultural, technological, economic, and international factors.

The task environment includes specific organizations, groups, and individuals who influence the organization.

TALKING TECHNOLOGY

▶ *Two Technology Titans*

Contemplate two companies that, at least superficially, appear to be vastly different: Wal-Mart and Dell Computers. Wal-Mart has 1.3 million employees in 4,300 stores worldwide, which sell thousands of items to over 100 million customers weekly. At heart it is a traditional firm—a folksy, bricks-and-mortar company. On the other hand, Dell makes a limited product line at just six locations, then sells the products online and by phone. It is one of the exemplar firms of the New Economy—a cool, "clicks-and-mortar" company.

Wal-Mart, founded in 1962 by Sam Walton with a single store in Rogers, Arkansas, and Dell Computers, established when Michael Dell started selling PCs from his University of Texas dorm in 1984, began as low-tech enterprises. Nevertheless, today these two seemingly different firms are savvy users of technology in their quest to achieve low costs and market dominance.

Wal-Mart's information systems keep track of its inventory from receipt to shelf placement to purchase. The firm uses checkout information to develop purchasing profiles, employs satellites to unite its many facilities, and requires employees to analyze sales printouts. Wal-Mart creates more than 90 percent of the software that it uses in order to focus on its particular needs. "What we've built here doesn't exist anywhere else," says Chief Information Officer Randy Mott.

Dell uses technology to optimize its manufacturing processes; the firm's engineers hold two hundred process-related patents. Like Wal-Mart, Michael Dell also requires immediate sales information. He says, "I know that yesterday we sold 77, 850 computers. I know it by customer types, by product type, by geography, and what the mix was." The firm also pioneered a way to link with suppliers

> *"All those fancy systems are just tools . . . the means to an end."*—Eryn Brown, magazine writer, Fortune

for just-in-time parts deliveries. Suppliers are able to re-supply Dell every two hours by basing their orders on real-time parts data they receive from the production floor.

Because the companies started with low-tech processes and then adopted new technologies over time, the technology clearly was a result of each firm's structure and strategy, and not the other way around. *Fortune* writer Eryn Brown says, "All those fancy systems are just tools[,] . . . the means to an end. It's that attitude—the unwillingness to get mired in technology for technology's sake—that keeps both companies ahead of the pack."

References: "About Wal-Mart," "Wal-Mart Stores, Inc., at a Glance," Wal-Mart web site. www.walmartstores.com on June 12, 2002; "Dell at a Glance." "Dell Worldwide." Dell web site. www.dell.com on June 12, 2002; Brian Dumaine, "What Michael Dell Knows That You Don't," *Fortune*, June 3, 2002. www.fortune.com on June 12, 2002; Andy Serwer, "Dell Does Domination," *Fortune*, January 21, 2002, pp. 71–75. See www.fortune.com; Eryn Brown, "America's Most Admired Companies," *Fortune*, March 1, 1999, pp. 68–73 (quotation p. 70). See www.fortune.com.

least changeable, and thus difficult to define. Many companies are spinning off some business units but then continuing to do business with them as suppliers. Therefore, one day a manager may be a member of an organization and the next day be a part of the environment of that organization. But for the most part, we can say that certain people, groups, or buildings are either in the organization or in the environment. For example, a college student shopping for a personal computer is part of the environment of Apple, Dell, IBM, and other computer manufacturers. However, if the student works for one of these computer manufacturers, he or she is not part of that company's environment but is within the boundaries of the organization.

This definition of organizational environment emphasizes the expanse of the environment within which the organization operates. It may give managers the false impression that the environment is outside their control and interest. But because the environment completely encloses the organization, managers must be constantly concerned about it. Most managers these days are aware that the environment is changing rapidly. The difficulty for most is to determine how those changes affect the company.

"The company has changed and the world has changed, but Michael hasn't changed. Now he's got to change."—former Disney executive speaking about Michael Eisner, chairman of Walt Disney [22]

The manager, then, faces an enormous, only vaguely specified environment that somehow affects the organization. Managing the organization within such an environment may seem like an overwhelming task. The alternatives for the manager are to (1) ignore the environment because of its complexity and focus on managing the internal operations of the company, (2) exert maximum energy in gathering information on every part of the environment and in trying to react to every environmental factor, and (3) pay attention to specific aspects of the task environment, responding only to those that most clearly affect the organization.

To ignore environmental factors entirely and focus on internal operations leaves the company in danger of missing major environmental shifts such as changes in customer preferences, technological breakthroughs, and new regulations. To expend large amounts of energy, time, and money exploring every facet of the environment may take more out of the organization than the effort may return.

The third alternative—to analyze carefully segments of the environment that most affect the organization and to respond accordingly—is the most prudent course. The issue, then, is to determine which parts of the environment should receive the manager's attention. In the remainder of this section, we examine two perspectives on the organizational environment: the analysis of environmental components and environmental uncertainty.

Forces in the environment have different effects on different companies. Hospital Corporation of America, for example, is very much influenced by government regulations and medical and scientific developments. Quite different environmental forces, on the other hand, affect McDonald's—consumer demand, disposable income, the cost of meat and bread, and gasoline prices. Thus, the task environment, the specific set of environmental forces that influence the operations of an organization, varies among organizations.

Environmental uncertainty exists when managers have little information about environmental events and their impact on the organization.

Environmental complexity is the number of environmental components that impinge on organizational decision making.

Environmental dynamism is the degree to which environmental components that impinge on organizational decision making change.

The environmental characteristic that brings together all of these different environmental influences and appears to have the most effect on the structure of the organization is uncertainty. **Environmental uncertainty** exists when managers have little information about environmental events and their impact on the organization. [23] Uncertainty has been described as resulting from complexity and dynamism in the environment. **Environmental complexity** is the number of environmental components that impinge on organizational decision making. **Environmental dynamism** is the degree to which these components change. [24] With these two dimensions, we can determine the degree of environmental uncertainty, as illustrated in Figure 17.4.

In cell 1, a low-uncertainty environment, there are few important components, and they change infrequently. A company in the cardboard container industry might have a highly certain environment when demand is steady, manufacturing processes are stable, and government regulations have remained largely unchanged.

In contrast, in cell 4, many important components are involved in decision making, and they change often. Thus, cell 4 represents a high-uncertainty envi-

	Simple →	**Complex**

Cell 1:
Low Perceived Uncertainty

1. Small number of factors and components in the environment.
2. Factors and components are somewhat similar to one another.
3. Factors and components remain basically the same.

Example: cardboard container industry

Cell 2:
Moderately Low Perceived Uncertainty

1. Large number of factors and components in the environment.
2. Factors and components are not similar to one another.
3. Factors and components remain basically the same.

Example: state universities

Cell 3:
Moderately High Perceived Uncertainty

1. Small number of factors and components in the environment.
2. Factors and components are somewhat similar to one another.
3. Factors and components of the environment continually change.

Example: fashion industry

Cell 4:
High Perceived Uncertainty

1. Large number of factors and components in the environment.
2. Factors and components are not similar to one another.
3. Factors and components of environment continually change.

Example: banking industry

Static / *Dynamic* — **Rate of Environmental Change**

Environmental Complexity — *Simple* / *Complex*

figure 17.4

Classification of Environmental Uncertainty

This four-cell matrix describes all four levels of environmental dynamism and complexity and shows how they combine to create low or high environmental uncertainty.

Reference: Reprinted from "Characteristics of Organizational Environments and Perceived Uncertainty," by Robert B. Duncan, published in *Administrative Science Quarterly*, vol. 17, no. 3 (Sept. 1972), p. 320, by permission of *Administrative Science Quarterly*. © Johnson Graduate School of Management, Cornell University.

ronment. The banking environment is now highly uncertain. With deregulation and the advent of interstate operations, banks today must compete with insurance companies, brokerage firms, real estate firms, and even department stores. The toy industry also is in a highly uncertain environment. As they develop new toys, toy companies must stay in tune with movies, television shows, and cartoons, as well as with public sentiment. Between 1983 and 1988, Saturday morning cartoons were little more than animated stories about children's toys. Recently, however, due to the disappointing sales of many toys presented in cartoons designed to promote them, most toy companies have left the toy-based cartoon business. Many toys that are now sold are based on movies.[25]

Environmental characteristics and uncertainty have been important factors in explaining organization structure, strategy, and performance. For example, the characteristics of the environment affect how managers perceive the environment, which in turn affects how they adapt the structure of the organization to meet environmental demands.[26] The environment has also been shown to affect the degree to which a firm's strategy enhances its performance.[27] That is, a certain strategy will enhance organizational performance to the extent that it is appropriate for the environment in which the organization operates. Finally, the environment is directly related to organizational performance.[28] The environment and the organization's response to it are crucial to success.

An organization attempts to continue as a viable entity in a dynamic environment. The environment completely encloses the organization, and managers must be constantly concerned about it. The organization as a whole, as well as departments and divisions within it, is created to deal with different challenges, problems, and uncertainties. James Thompson suggested that organizations design a structure to protect the dominant technology of the organization, smooth out any problems, and keep down coordination costs.[29] Thus, organization structures are designed to coordinate relevant technologies and protect them from outside disturbances. Structural components such as inventory, warehousing, and shipping help buffer the technology used to transform inputs into outputs. For instance, demand for products usually is cyclical or seasonal and is subject to many disturbances, but the warehouse inventory helps the manufacturing system function as if the environment accepted output at a steady rate, maximizing technological efficiency and helping the organization respond to fluctuating demands of the market.

Organizations with international operations must contend with additional levels of complexity and dynamism, both within and across cultures. Many cultures have relatively stable environments. For example, the economies of Sweden and the United States are fairly stable. Although competitive forces within each country's economic system vary, each economy remains strong. In contrast, the environments of other countries are much more dynamic. For example, France's policies on socialism versus private enterprise tend to change dramatically with each election. At present, far-reaching changes in the economic and management philosophies of most Western European countries make their environments far more dynamic than that of the United States.

Environments also vary widely in terms of their complexity. The Japanese culture, which is fairly stable, is also quite complex. Japanese managers are subject to an array of cultural norms and values that are far more encompassing and resistant to change than those U.S. managers face. India too has an extremely complex environment, which continues to be influenced by its old caste system. The "World View" box describes the environmental uncertainties faced by foreign firms doing business in China.

Strategic Choice

The previous two sections described how structure is affected by the strategy of the organization and by the structural imperatives of size, technology, and environment. These approaches may seem to contradict each other since both approaches attempt to specify the determinants of structure. This apparent clash has been resolved by refining the strategy concept to include the role of the top management decision maker in determining the organization's structure.[30] In effect, this view inserts the manager as the decision maker who evaluates the imperatives and the organization strategy and then designs the organization structure. The role of top management in determining the structure of the organization is significant. The "Business of Ethics" box describes how the values and choices of the CEO can have a dramatic impact on the way an organization does business by examining the devastating effect Sam Waksal's lifestyle had on his company, ImClone.

The importance of the role of top management can be understood by comparing Figure 17.5 with Figure 17.2. Figure 17.5 shows structural imperatives as contextual factors within which the organization must operate and that affect the purposes and goals of the organization. The manager's choices for organization structure are affected by the organization's strategy (purposes and goals), the imperatives (contextual

WORLD VIEW

How Do You Say "M&A" In Chinese?

Mergers and acquisitions (M&A) comprise one of the most difficult and complex business arenas in the United States today, requiring an understanding of legal requirements, intricate financial transactions, organization culture, and much more. That complexity increases when the M&A activity occurs between firms from two different countries with vastly different business practices and national cultures. When one of the firms is from a country with a tradition of state-owned enterprise, the situation is further complicated. This challenging environment is faced by international companies that want to enter China, where foreign firms must partner with a local business in order to win government approval.

China presents a tempting target—it offers a market that is ten times the size of America's. Charles Tharp, president of Environmental Dynamics, says, "Who could snub such an opportunity, no matter how great the challenge?" And the nation is trying to reduce its investment in state-owned businesses, by seeking a cash infusion. During the period from 2001 to 2005, China needs foreign investments of at least $250 billion to maintain its economic growth. However, the maze of legal restrictions and cultural barriers that foreign firms must face can be daunting.

For example, the government charges foreign firms high fees to process their labor and payroll paperwork. Private firms can do the work more cheaply, but few foreign-

"Who could snub such an opportunity, no matter how great the challenge?"—Charles Tharp, president of Environmental Dynamics, maker of water treatment systems, commenting on doing business in China

ers know about them. One businessman says that when dealing with Chinese officials, "Everyone tells you a different story. All you can hope for is a degree of certainty." Even infrastructure and suppliers can be a problem. Some areas lack warehouses or adequate roads. Computer software is often difficult to obtain because China's weak copyright protection causes many suppliers to refuse sales from the region. Language and customs also present barriers. For example, in China, high performance is valued so greatly that when one employee botched a task, he ran for the exit and was never seen again.

In spite of threats of terrorism and an economic downturn, American-Chinese alliances continue to increase. "The economic downturn at home has made doing business abroad more of a priority," according to Tharp. "It's a way to grow your customer base and develop new revenue streams when domestic business dries up."

References: Lori Ioannou, "American Invasion," *Fortune*, May 13, 2002 (quotation). www.fortune.com on June 12, 2002; Jesse Wong, "How to Start a Business Without a Road Map," *Fortune*, April 1, 2002. www.fortune.com on June 12, 2002; Camilla Ojansivu, "Strategy for a Stronger Market Economy: Corporate Restructuring the PRC," *Business Beijing*, November, 2001, pp. 38–39.

figure 17.5

The Strategic Choice Approach to Organization Design

The integration of the structural imperative approach to organization design with the strategic choice approach takes into account the role of the manager, whose perspective on contextual factors and the organization, along with personal preferences, values, and experience, help determine the structure of the organization.

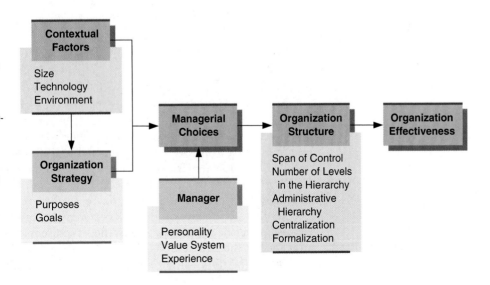

BUSINESS OF ETHICS

▶ Socialite CEO's Legacy at ImClone

Wouldn't it be a terrific achievement to invent a cancer-fighting drug? And wouldn't it be fun to pal around with Mick Jagger and Martha Stewart? What if you could do both? If you could, you would be living the unique and complex life of Sam Waksal, cofounder (with brother Harlan, a physician) and former CEO of biotech firm ImClone Systems. However, Sam's sometimes outrageous lifestyle caused problems for his firm, leading to delays in getting medication to market and depriving patients of needed treatment.

> *"The greatest frustration . . . is that there is a highly useful drug gathering dust in a back room due to a regulatory morass."—Robert J. Mayer, M.D., director of gastrointestinal oncology at Dana-Farber Cancer Institute in Boston*

Waksal, a doctor of immunology, is a good scientist, claims Richard Mulligan, a Harvard Medical School professor. Mulligan feels Waksal "has far more scientific knowledge and depth of understanding than the majority of CEOs in biotech." However, he also invests in celebrity restaurants and is a social climber—an image at odds with his technical background. According to a private investigator, Waksal has a long history of broken business dealings, questionable associates, and missed debt payments.

Sam Waksal's history is important because it affects his firm. ImClone has been developing Erbitux, a cancer treatment that showed early promise, gaining FDA fast-track status. But questions have since arisen: How can Waksal afford a $20 million private art collection? Is it a coincidence that he and his family members repeatedly sold stock the day before an adverse announcement about the drug's FDA status lowered stock prices? Did Sam misrepresent Erbitux's results to investors at Bristol-Myers Squibb, who invested $2 billion in ImClone in the biggest single-product pharmaceutical deal ever?

After the FDA refused to accept ImClone's application and new test results disappointed, the biotech's price fell from $84 in March 2000 to just $7.45 in June 2002. Shareholders are suing, and Bristol is renegotiating a lower-priced deal. Sam Waksal was forced to resign as CEO but was succeeded by his brother Harlan, raising doubts about any meaningful change.

Wall Street's impatience is partly to blame—investors expect to see quick and decisive results, which are rare for biotech products. The FDA is also under fire as it continues to make inconsistent and unclear decisions. Physician Robert J. Mayer, who is investigating cancer treatments, says, "The greatest frustration . . . is that there is a highly useful drug gathering dust in a back room due to a regulatory morass." But the overriding issue is whether ImClone can overcome the Waksals' reputations and forge an ethical organization. In the meantime, cancer patients still await better medication.

References: Catherine Arnst, "Commentary: Patience, Biotech Investors, Patience," *Business Week*, June 10, 2002. www.businessweek.com on June 11, 2002; Andrew Serwer, "The Socialite Scientist," *Fortune*, April 15, 2002. www.fortune.com on June 11, 2002; Catherine Arnst, "Where ImClone Went Wrong," *Business Week*, February 18, 2002 (quotation). www.businessweek.com on June 11, 2002.

factors), and the manager's personal value system and experience.[31] Organizational effectiveness depends on the fit among the size, the technology, the environment, the strategies, and the structure. The Thermos Company noted new environmental conditions, reinvented its approach, and came up with an innovative new product, an electric cooking grill.[32] When Citicorp and Travelers Group merged in 1998, they installed both former CEOs as co-CEOs to run the merged company. This dual CEO arrangement dramatically affected the ways in which the new company was structured and run for several years.[33]

Another perspective on the link between strategy and structure is that the relationship may be reciprocal; that is, the structure may be set up to implement the strategy, but the structure may then affect the process of decision making, influencing such matters as the centralization or decentralization of decision making and the formalization of rules and procedures.[34] Thus, strategy determines structure, which in turn affects strategic decision making. A more complex view, suggested by Herman Boschken, is that strategy is a determinant of structure and long-term performance, but only when the subunits doing the planning have the ability to do the planning well.[35]

The relationship between strategic choice and structure is actually more complicated than the concept that "structure follows strategy" conveys. However, this relationship has received less research attention than the idea of structural imperatives. And, of course, some might view strategy simply as another imperative, along with size, technology, and environment. But the strategic-choice view goes beyond the imperative perspective because it is a product of both the analyses of the imperatives and the organization's strategy.

Organizational Designs

The previous section described several factors that determine how organizations are structured. In this section we present several different organizational designs that have been created to adapt organizations to the many contingency factors they face. We discuss mechanistic and organic structures, the sociotechnical system perspective, Mintzberg's designs, matrix designs, and virtual organizations.

Mechanistic and Organic Designs

A mechanistic structure is primarily hierarchical; interactions and communications typically are vertical, instructions come from the boss, knowledge is concentrated at the top, and loyalty and obedience are required to sustain membership.

As we discussed in the previous section, most theorists believe that organizations need to be able to adapt to changes in the technology. For example, if the rate of change in technology is slow, the most effective design is bureaucratic or, to use Burns and Stalker's term, "mechanistic." As summarized in Table 17.2, a **mechanistic structure** is primarily hierarchical in nature, interactions and communications are mostly vertical, instructions come from the boss, knowledge is concentrated at the top, and continued membership requires loyalty and obedience.

"Informality gives you speed."—Jack Welch, former CEO of GE[36]

An organic structure is set up like a network; interactions and communications are horizontal, knowledge resides wherever it is most useful to the organization, and membership requires a commitment to the organization's tasks.

But if the technology is changing rapidly, the organization needs a structure that allows more flexibility and faster decision making so that it can react quickly to change. This design is called "organic." An **organic structure** resembles a network—interactions and communications are more lateral, knowledge resides wherever it is most useful to the organization, and membership requires a commitment to the tasks of the organization. An organic organization is generally expected to be faster at reacting to changes in the environment.

Sociotechnical Systems Designs

A system is an interrelated set of elements that function as a whole.

The foundation of the sociotechnical systems approach to organizing is systems theory, discussed in Chapter 1. There we defined a **system** as an interrelated set of elements that function as a whole. A system may have numerous subsystems, each of which, like the overall system, includes inputs, transformation processes, outputs, and feedback. We also defined an **open system** as one that interacts with its environment. A complex system is made up of numerous subsystems in which the

An open system is a system that interacts with its environment.

table 17.2

Mechanistic and Organic Organization Designs

Characteristic	Mechanistic	Organic
Structure	Hierarchical	Network based on interests
Interactions, Communication	Primarily vertical	Lateral throughout
Work Directions, Instructions	From supervisor	Through advice, information
Knowledge, Information	Concentrated at top	Throughout
Membership, Relationship with Organization	Requires loyalty, obedience	Commitment to task, progress, expansion

The sociotechnical systems approach to organization design views the organization as an open system structured to integrate the technical and social subsystems into a single management system.

A technical (task) subsystem is the means by which inputs are transformed into outputs.

A social subsystem includes the interpersonal relationships that develop among people in organizations.

outputs of some are the inputs to others. The **sociotechnical systems approach** views the organization as an open system structured to integrate the two important subsystems: the technical (task) subsystem and the social subsystem.

The **technical (task) subsystem** is the means by which inputs are transformed into outputs. The transformation process may take many forms. In a steel foundry, it would entail the way steel is formed, cut, drilled, chemically treated, and painted. In an insurance company or financial institution, it would be the way information is processed. Often, significant scientific and engineering expertise is applied to these transformation processes to get the highest productivity at the lowest cost. For example, Fireplace Manufacturers of Santa Ana, California, a manufacturer of prefabricated metal fireplaces, implemented "just in time" (JIT) manufacturing and inventory systems to improve the productivity of its plant.[37] Under this system, component parts arrive "just in time" to be used in the manufacturing process, reducing the costs of storing them in a warehouse until they are needed. In effect, JIT redesigns the transformation process, from the introduction of raw materials to the shipping of the finished product. In three years, Fireplace Manufacturers' inventory costs dropped from $1.1 million to $750,000 while sales doubled during the same period. The transformation process usually is regarded as technologically and economically driven; that is, whatever process is most productive and costs the least is generally the most desirable.

The **social subsystem** includes the interpersonal relationships that develop among people in organizations. Employees learn one another's work habits, strengths, weaknesses, and preferences while developing a sense of mutual trust. The social relationships may be manifested in personal friendships and interest groups. Communication, about both work and employees' common interests, may be enhanced by friendship or hampered by antagonistic relationships. The Hawthorne studies (discussed in Chapter 1) were the first serious studies of the social subsystems in organizations.[38]

The sociotechnical systems approach was developed by members of the Tavistock Institute of England as an outgrowth of a study of coal mining. The study concerned new mining techniques that were introduced to increase productivity but failed because they entailed splitting up well-established work groups.[39] The Tavistock researchers concluded that the social subsystem had been sacrificed to the technical subsystem. Thus, improvements in the technical subsystem were not realized because of problems in the social subsystem. More recently, Lifeline Systems, a manufacturer of electronic medical equipment that implemented just-in-time systems, recognized the potential problems of employee acceptance and emphasized the role of management in getting employees to go along with the changes.[40]

The Tavistock group proposed that an organization's technical and social subsystems could be integrated through autonomous work groups. The aim of **autonomous work groups** is to make technical and social subsystems work together for the benefit of the larger system. These groups are developed using concepts of task design, particularly job enrichment, and ideas about group interaction, supervision, and other characteristics of organization design. To structure the task, authority, and reporting relationships around work groups, organizations should delegate to the groups themselves decisions regarding job assignments, training, inspection, rewards, and punishments. Management is responsible for coordinating the groups according to the demands of the work and task environment. Autonomous work groups often evolve into self-managing teams, as was discussed in Chapter 12.

Organizations in turbulent environments tend to rely less on hierarchy and more on the coordination of work among autonomous work groups. Sociotechnical systems theory asserts that the role of management is twofold: to monitor the environmental factors that impinge on the internal operations of the organization and to coordinate the social and technical subsystems. Although the sociotechnical systems approach has not been thoroughly tested, it has been tried with some success in the General Foods plant in Topeka, Kansas; the Saab-Scania project in Sweden; and the Volvo plant in Kalmar, Sweden.[41] The development of the sociotechnical systems approach is significant in its departure from the universal approaches to organization design and in its emphasis on jointly harnessing the technical and human subsystems. The popular movements in management today include many of the principles of the sociotechnical systems design approach. The development of cross-functional teams to generate and design new products and services is a good example (see Chapter 12).

Mintzberg's Designs

In this section we describe the concrete organization designs proposed by Henry Mintzberg. The universe of possible designs is large, but fortunately we can divide designs into a few basic forms. Mintzberg proposed that the purpose of organizational design was to coordinate activities, and he suggested a range of coordinating mechanisms that are found in operating organizations.[42] In Mintzberg's view, organization structure reflects how tasks are divided and then coordinated. He described five major ways in which tasks are coordinated: by mutual adjustment, by direct supervision, and by standardization of worker (or input) skills, work processes, or outputs (see Figure 17.6). These five methods can exist side by side within an organization.

Coordination by mutual adjustment (1 in Figure 17.6) simply means that workers use informal communication to coordinate with one another whereas coordination by direct supervision (2 in Figure 17.6) means that a manager or supervisor coordinates the actions of workers. As noted, *standardization* may be used as a coordination mechanism in three different ways: (1) We can standardize the *input skills* (3 in Figure 17.6)—that is, the worker skills that are inputs to the work process; (2) we can standardize the *work processes* themselves (4 in Figure 17.6)—that is, the methods workers use to transform inputs into outputs; and (3) we can standardize the *outputs* (5 in Figure 17.6)—that is, the products or services or the performance levels expected of workers. Standardization usually is developed by staff analysts and

Autonomous work groups are used to integrate an organization's technical and social subsystems for the benefit of the larger system.

figure 17.6

Mintzberg's Five Coordinating Mechanisms

Mintzberg described five methods of coordinating the actions of organizational participants. The dashed lines in each diagram show the five different means of coordination: (1) mutual adjustment, (2) direct supervision, and standardization of (3) input skills, (4) work processes, and (5) outputs.

Reference: Henry Mintzberg, *The Structuring of Organizations: A Synthesis of the Research.* © 1979, p. 4. Reprinted by permission of Prentice Hall, Inc., Englewood Cliffs, N.J.

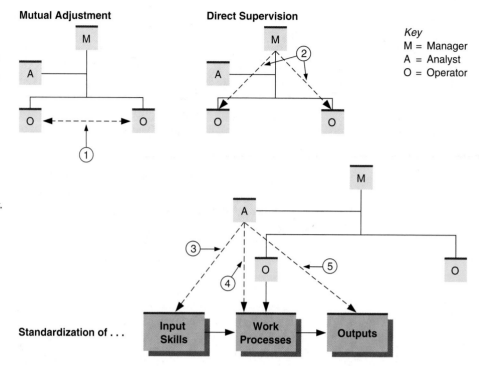

enforced by management such that skills, processes, and output meet predetermined standards.

Mintzberg further suggested that the five coordinating mechanisms roughly correspond to stages of organizational development and complexity. In the very small organization, individuals working together communicate informally, achieving coordination by mutual adjustment. As more people join the organization, coordination needs become more complex, and direct supervision is added. For example, two or three people working in a small fast-food business can coordinate the work simply by talking to each other about the incoming orders for hamburgers, fries, and drinks. However, direct supervision becomes necessary in a larger restaurant with more complex cooking and warming equipment and several shifts of workers.

In large organizations, standardization is added to mutual adjustment and direct supervision to coordinate the work. The type of standardization depends on the nature of the work situation—that is, the organization's technology and environment. Standardization of work processes may achieve the necessary coordination when the organization's tasks are fairly routine. Thus, the larger fast-food outlet may standardize the making of hamburger patties: The meat is weighed, put into a hamburger press, and compressed into a patty. McDonald's is well known for this type of standardized process.

In other complex situations, standardization of the output may allow employees to do the work in any appropriate manner as long as the output meets specifications. Thus, the cook may not care how the hamburger is pressed, only being concerned that the right amount of meat is used and that the patty is the correct diameter and thickness. In other words, the worker may use any process as long as the output is a standard burger.

A third possibility is to coordinate work by standardizing worker skills. This approach is most often adopted in situations in which processes and outputs are difficult to standardize. In a hospital, for example, each patient must be treated as a special situation; the hospital process and output therefore cannot be standardized. Similar diagnostic and treatment procedures may be used with more than one patient, but the hospital relies on the skills of the physicians and nurses, which are standardized through their professional training, to coordinate the work. Organizations may have to depend on workers' mutual adjustment to coordinate their own actions in the most complex work situations or when the most important elements of coordination are the workers' professional training and communication skills. In effect, mutual adjustment can be an appropriate coordinating mechanism in both the simplest and the most complex situations. Analysis of the success of McDonald's shows that some part of its success is due to the degree of standardization.

Mintzberg pointed out that the five methods of coordination can be combined with the basic components of structure to develop five structural forms: the simple structure, the machine bureaucracy, the professional bureaucracy, the divisionalized form, and the adhocracy. Mintzberg called these structures pure or ideal types of designs.

Simple Structure   The **simple structure** characterizes relatively small, usually young organizations in a simple, dynamic environment. The organization has little specialization and formalization, and its overall structure is organic. Power and decision making are concentrated in the chief executive, often also the owner-manager, and the flow of authority is from the top down. The primary coordinating mechanism is direct supervision. The organization must adapt quickly to survive because of its dynamic and often hostile environment. Most small businesses—a car dealership, a locally owned retail clothing store, or a candy manufacturer with only regional distribution—have a simple structure.

> The simple structure, typical of relatively small or new organizations, has little specialization or formalization; power and decision making are concentrated in the chief executive.

Machine Bureaucracy   The **machine bureaucracy** is typical of large, well-established companies in simple, stable environments. Work is highly specialized and formalized, and decision making is usually concentrated at the top. Standardization of work processes is the primary coordinating mechanism. This highly bureaucratic structure does not have to adapt quickly to changes because the environment is both simple and stable. Examples include large mass-production firms such as Container Corporation of America, some automobile companies, and providers of services to mass markets, such as insurance companies.

> In machine bureaucracy, which typifies large, well-established organizations, work is highly specialized and formalized, and decision making is usually concentrated at the top.

Professional Bureaucracy   Usually found in a complex and stable environment, the **professional bureaucracy** relies on standardization of skills as the primary means of coordination. There is much horizontal specialization by professional areas of expertise but little formalization. Decision making is decentralized and takes place where the expertise is. The only means of coordination available to the organization is standardization of skills—those of the professionally trained employees.

Although it lacks centralization, the professional bureaucracy stabilizes and controls its tasks with rules and procedures developed in the relevant profession. Hospitals, universities, and consulting firms are examples.

> A professional bureaucracy is characterized by horizontal specialization by professional areas of expertise, little formalization, and decentralized decision making.

Divisionalized Form   The **divisionalized form** is characteristic of old, very large firms operating in a relatively simple, stable environment with several diverse markets. It resembles the machine bureaucracy except that it is divided according to the various markets it serves. There is some horizontal and vertical specialization between the divisions (each defined by a market) and headquarters. Decision making

> The divisionalized form, typical of old, very large organizations, is divided according to the different markets served; horizontal and vertical specialization exists between divisions and headquarters, decision making is divided between headquarters and divisions, and outputs are standardized.

This dog is wearing the latest in specialty doggy wear, Doggles, created by Roni and Ken DiLullo for their pet, MidKnight. Not just providing protection from the sun, these anti-UVA doggie goggles can protect dogs' eyes from external materials following surgery or from harmful debris when searching building explosions or natural disasters. This small million-dollar company has a very simple structure composed of the DiLullos, who primarily do marketing and distribution of the Doggles while the product is manufactured in Asia.

is clearly split between headquarters and the divisions, and the primary means of coordination is standardization of outputs. The mechanism of control required by headquarters encourages the development of machine bureaucracies in the divisions.

The classic example of the divisionalized form is General Motors, which, in a reorganization in the 1920s, adopted a design that created divisions for each major car model.[43] Although the divisions have been reorganized and the cars changed several times, the concept of the divisionalized organization is still very evident at GM.[44] General Electric uses a two-tiered divisionalized structure, dividing its numerous businesses into strategic business units, which are then further divided into sectors.[45]

In an adhocracy, typically found in young organizations in highly technical fields, decision making is spread throughout the organization, power resides with the experts, horizontal and vertical specialization exists, and there is little formalization.

Adhocracy　The **adhocracy** is typically found in young organizations engaged in highly technical fields in which the environment is complex and dynamic. Decision making is spread throughout the organization, and power is in the hands of experts. There is horizontal and vertical specialization but little formalization, resulting in a very organic structure. Coordination is by mutual adjustment through frequent personal communication and liaison. Specialists are not grouped together in functional units but are instead deployed into specialized market-oriented project teams.

The typical adhocracy is usually established to foster innovation, something to which the other four types of structures are not particularly well suited. Numerous U.S. organizations—Johnson & Johnson, Procter & Gamble, Monsanto, and 3M, for example—are known for their innovation and constant stream of new products.[46] These organizations are either structured totally as adhocracies or have large divisions set up as adhocracies. Johnson & Johnson established a new-products division over thirty years ago to encourage continued innovation, creativity, and risk taking. The division continues to succeed; Johnson & Johnson in the United States has introduced more than two hundred new products in the past several years. Most of the new start-up 'dot-com' companies were most likely structured as adhocracies.

Mintzberg believed that fit among parts is the most important consideration in designing an organization. Not only must there be a fit among the structure, the structural imperatives (technology, size, and environment), and organizational strategy, but the components of structure (rules and procedures, decision making, specialization) must also fit together and be appropriate for the situation. Mintzberg suggested that an organization cannot function effectively when these characteristics are not put together properly.[47]

Matrix Organization Design

One other organizational form deserves attention here: the matrix organization design. Matrix design is consistent with the contingency approach because it is useful only in certain situations. One of the earliest implementations of the matrix design was at TRW Systems Group in 1959.[48] Following TRW's lead, other firms in aerospace and high technology fields created similar matrix structures.

The matrix design combines two different designs to gain the benefits of each; typically combined are a product or project departmentalization scheme and a functional structure.

The **matrix design** attempts to combine two different designs to gain the benefits of each. The most common matrix form superimposes product or project departmentalization on a functional structure (see Figure 17.7). Each department and project has a manager; each employee, however, is a member of both a functional department and a project team. The dual role means that the employee has two supervisors, the department manager and the project leader.

A matrix structure is appropriate when three conditions exist:

1. There is external pressure for a dual focus, meaning that factors in the environment require the organization to focus its efforts equally on responding to multiple external factors and on internal operations.
2. There is pressure for a high information-processing capacity.
3. There is pressure for shared resources.[49]

In the aerospace industry in the early 1960s, all these conditions were present. Private companies had a dual focus: their customers, primarily the federal government, and the complex engineering and technical fields in which they were engaged. Moreover, the environments of these companies were changing very rapidly. Technological sophistication and competition were increasing, resulting in growing environmental uncertainty and an added need for information processing. The final condition stemmed from the pressure on the companies to excel in a very competitive environment despite limited resources. The companies concluded that it was inefficient to assign their highly professional—and highly compensated—scientific and engineering personnel to just one project at a time.

Built into the matrix structure is the capacity for flexible and coordinated responses to internal and external pressures. Members can be reassigned from one project to another as demands for their skills change. They may work for a month on one project, be assigned to the functional home department for two weeks, and then be reassigned to another project for the next six months. The matrix form improves project coordination by assigning project responsibility to a single leader

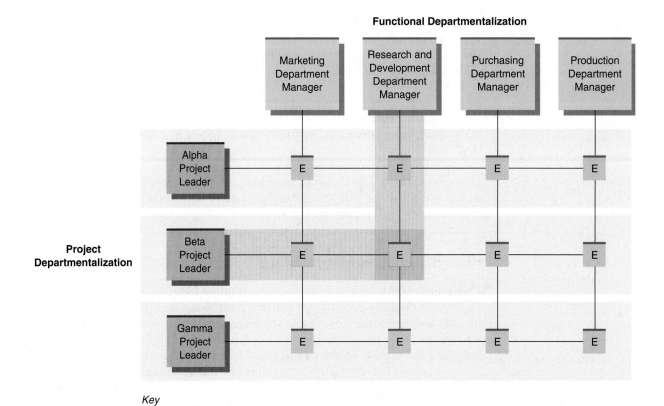

Functional Departmentalization

Key
E = Employee

figure 17.7

A Matrix Organization Design

A matrix organization design superimposes two different types of departmentalization onto each other—for example, a functional structure and a project structure.

rather than dividing it among several functional department heads. Furthermore, it improves communication because employees can talk about the project with members of both the project team and the functional unit to which they belong. In this way, solutions to project problems may emerge from either group. Many different types of organizations have used the matrix form of organization, notably large-project manufacturing firms, banks, and hospitals.[50]

The matrix organizational form thus provides several benefits for the organization. It is not, however, trouble-free. Typical problems include the following:

1. The dual reporting system may cause role conflict among employees.
2. Power struggles may occur over who has authority on which issues.
3. Matrix organization often is misinterpreted to mean that a group must make all decisions; as a result, group decision-making techniques may be used when they are not appropriate.
4. If the design involves several matrices, each laid on top of another, there may be no way to trace accountability and authority.[51]

Only under the three conditions listed earlier is the matrix design likely to work. In any case, it is a complex organizational system that must be carefully coordinated and managed to be effective.

Virtual Organizations

Some companies do one or two things very well, such as sell to government clients, but struggle with most others, such as manufacturing products with very tight precision. Other companies might be great at close-tolerance manufacturing but lousy at reaching out to certain types of clients. Wouldn't it be nice if those two organizations could get together to utilize each other's strengths but still retain their independence? They can, and many are doing so in what are called "virtual organizations."

A **virtual organization** is a temporary alliance between two or more organizations that band together to accomplish a specific venture. Each partner contributes to the partnership what it does best. The opportunity is usually something that needs a quick response to maximize the market opportunity. A slow response will probably result in losses. Therefore, a virtual organization allows different organizations to bring their best capabilities together without worrying about learning how to do something that they have never done before. Thus, the reaction time is faster, mistakes are fewer, and profits are quicker. Sharing of information among partners is usually facilitated by electronic technology such as computers, faxes, and electronic mail systems, thereby avoiding the expenses of renting new office space for the venture or costly travel time between companies.

There are no restrictions on how large or small organizations or projects need to be to take advantage of this type of alliance. In fact, some very small organizations are working together quite well. In Phoenix, Arizona, a public relations firm, a graphic design firm, and an advertising firm are working together on projects that have multiple requirements beyond those offered by any single firm. Rather than turn down the business or try to hire additional staff to do the extra work, the three firms work together to better serve client needs. The clients like the arrangement because they get high-quality work and do not have to shop around for someone to do little pieces of work. The networking companies feel that the result is better creativity, more teamwork, more efficient use of resources, and better service for their clients.

More typically, however, large companies create virtual organizations. Corning is involved in nineteen partnerships on many different types of projects, and it is pleased with most of its ventures and plans to do more. Intel worked with two Japanese organizations to manufacture flash memory chips for computers. One of the Japanese companies was not able to complete its part of the project, leaving Intel with a major product-delivery problem. Intel's chairman at the time, Andrew Grove, was not too happy about that venture and may not participate in others.[52]

The virtual organization is not just another management fad. It has become one way to deal with the rapid changes brought about by evolving technology and global competition. Management scholars have mixed opinions on the effectiveness of such arrangements. Although it may seem odd, this approach can produce substantial benefits in some situations.

A virtual organization is a temporary alliance between two or more organizations that band together to undertake a specific venture.

Contemporary Organization Design

The current proliferation of design theories and alternative forms of organization gives practicing managers a dizzying array of choices. The task of the manager or organization designer is to examine the firm and its situation and to design a form of organization that meets its needs. A partial list of contemporary alternatives includes such approaches as downsizing, rightsizing, reengineering the organization, team-based organizations, and the virtual organization. These approaches often make use of total quality management, employee empowerment, employee involvement and participation, reduction in force, process innovation, and networks of alliances. Practicing managers must deal with the new terminology, the temptation to treat such new approaches as fads, and their own organizational situation before making major organization design shifts. In this section we describe two currently popular approaches—reengineering and rethinking the organization—as well as global organization structure and design issues. We conclude with a summary of the dominant themes in contemporary organization design.

Reengineering the Organization

Reengineering is the radical redesign of organizational processes to achieve major gains in cost, time, and provision of services.

Reengineering is the radical redesign of organizational processes to achieve major gains in cost, time, and provision of services. It forces the organization to start from scratch to redesign itself around its most important processes rather than beginning with its current form and making incremental changes. It assumes that if a company had no existing structure, departments, jobs, rules, or established ways of doing things, reengineering would design the organization as it should be for future success. The process starts with determining what the customers actually want from the organization and then developing a strategy to provide it. Once the strategy is in place, strong leadership from top management can create a core team of people to design an organizational system to achieve the strategy.[53] Reengineering is a process of redesigning the organization that does not necessarily result in any particular organizational form.

Rethinking the Organization

Rethinking the organization means looking at organization design in totally different ways, perhaps even abandoning the classic view of organization as a pyramid.

Also currently popular is the concept of rethinking the organization. **Rethinking** the organization is also a process for restructuring that throws out traditional assumptions that organizations should be structured with boxes and horizontal and vertical lines. Robert Tomasko makes some suggestions for new organizational forms for the future.[54] He suggests that the traditional pyramid shape of organizations may be inappropriate for current business practices. Traditional structures, he contends, may have too many levels of management arranged in a hierarchy to be efficient and to respond to dynamic changes in the environment.

"Every year for the past 14 years, we've been a new company."—Ted Waitt, founder and chairman of the board, Gateway 2005[55]

Rethinking organizations might entail thinking of the organization structure as a dome rather than a pyramid, the dome being top management, which acts as an umbrella, covering and protecting those underneath but also leaving them alone to do their work. Internal units underneath the dome would have the flexibility to interact with each other and with environmental forces. Companies such as Microsoft Corporation and Royal Dutch Petroleum have some of the characteristics of this dome approach to organization design. American Express Financial Advisors restructured from a vertical organization into a horizontal organization as a result of its rethinking everything about the ways it needed to meet customers' needs.[56]

The Americanization of Toyota is well underway. Facing a shrinking car market at home, Toyota is increasingly looking like a well-run American company. They sold more cars and trucks in the U.S. than in Japan in 2001. They employ 123,000 Americans in their factories and dealerships, more than Coca-Cola, Microsoft, and Oracle combined. Most of their top executives in the U.S. are locals rather than expatriate Japanese. And their biggest selling products in the U.S. were designed mostly for the U.S. market. It is close to becoming number three in the U.S. big three automakers, displacing DaimlerChrysler. They have publicly acknowledged that the U.S. market is their number one priority. But despite this, between-culture issues arise, such as color schemes for interiors and overall vehicle size and roominess.

Global Organization Structure and Design Issues

Managers working in an international environment must consider not only similarities and differences among firms in different cultures but also the structural features of multinational organizations.

Between-Culture Issues   "Between-culture issues" are variations in the structure and design of companies operating in different cultures. As might be expected, such companies have both differences and similarities. For example, one study compared the structures of fifty-five U.S. and fifty-one Japanese manufacturing plants. Results suggested that the Japanese plants had less specialization, more "formal" centralization (but less "real" centralization), and taller hierarchies than their U.S. counterparts. The Japanese structures were also less affected by their technology than the U.S. plants.[57]

Many cultures still take a traditional view of organization structure not unlike the approaches used in this country during the days of classical organization theory. For example, Tom Peters, a leading U.S. management consultant and co-author of *In Search of Excellence*, spent some time lecturing to managers in China. They were not interested in his ideas about decentralization and worker participation, however. Instead, the most frequently asked question concerned how a manager determined the optimal span of control.[58]

In contrast, many European companies are increasingly patterning themselves after successful U.S. firms, a move stemming in part from corporate raiders in Europe emulating their U.S. counterparts and partly from the managerial workforce becoming better educated. Together, these two factors have caused many European firms to become less centralized and to adopt divisional structures by moving from functional to product departmentalization.[59]

Multinational Organization   More and more firms have entered the international arena and have found it necessary to adapt their designs to better cope with different cultures.[60] For example, after a company has achieved a moderate level of international activity, it often establishes an international division, usually at the same organizational level as other major functional divisions. Levi-Strauss uses this organization design. One division, Levi-Strauss International, is responsible for the company's business activities in Europe, Canada, Latin America, and Asia.

For an organization that has become more deeply involved in international activities, a logical form of organization design is the international matrix. This type of matrix arrays product managers across the top. Project teams headed by foreign market managers cut across the product departments. A company with three basic product lines, for example, might establish three product departments (of course, it would include domestic advertising, finance, and operations departments as well). Foreign market managers can be designated for, say, Canada, Japan, Europe, Latin America, and Australia. Each foreign market manager is then responsible for all three of the company's products in his or her market.[61]

Finally, at the most advanced level of multinational activity, a firm might become an international conglomerate. Nestlé and Unilever N.V. fit this type. Each has an international headquarters (Nestlé in Vevey, Switzerland, and Unilever in Rotterdam, the Netherlands) that coordinates the activities of businesses scattered around the globe. Nestlé has factories in fifty countries and markets its products in virtually every country in the world. Over 96 percent of its business is done outside of Switzerland, and only about 7,000 of its 160,000 employees reside in its home country.

Dominant Themes of Contemporary Designs

The four dominant themes of current design strategies are (1) the effects of technological and environmental change, (2) the importance of people, (3) the necessity of staying in touch with the customer, and (4) the global organization. Technology and the environment are changing so fast and in so many unpredictable ways that no organization structure will be appropriate for long. The changes in electronic information processing, transmission, and retrieval alone are so vast that employee relationships, information distribution, and task coordination need to be reviewed almost daily.[62] The emphasis on productivity through people that was energized by Thomas Peters and Robert Waterman Jr. in the 1980s continues in almost every aspect of contemporary organization design.[63] In addition, Peters and Austin further emphasized the importance of staying in touch with customers at the initial stage in organization design.[64]

These popular contemporary approaches and the four dominant factors argue for a contingency design perspective. Unfortunately, there is no "one best way." Managers must consider the impact of multiple factors—sociotechnical systems, strategy, the structural imperatives, changing information technology, people, global considerations, and a concern for end users—on their particular organization and design the organization structure accordingly.

Synopsis

Universal approaches to organization design attempt to specify the one best way to structure organizations for effectiveness. Contingency approaches, on the other hand, propose that the best way to design organization structure depends on a variety of factors.

Important contingency approaches to organization design center on the organizational strategy, the determinants of structure, and strategic choice.

Initially, strategy was seen as the determinant of structure: the structure of the organization was designed to implement its purpose, goals, and strategies. Taking managerial choice into account in determining organization structure is a modification of this view. The manager designs the structure to accomplish organizational goals, guided by an analysis of the contextual factors, the strategies of the organization, and personal preferences.

The structural imperatives are size, technology, and environment. In general, large organizations have more complex structures and usually more than one technology. The structures of small organizations, on the other hand, may be dominated by one core operations technology. The structure of the organization is also established to fit with the environmental demands and buffer the core operating technology from environmental changes and uncertainties.

Organization designs can take many forms. A mechanistic structure relies on the administrative hierarchy for communication and directing activities. An organic design is structured like a network; communications and interactions are horizontal and diagonal across groups and teams throughout the organization.

In the sociotechnical systems view, the organization is an open system structured to integrate two important subsystems: the technical (task) subsystem and the social subsystem. According to this approach, organizations should structure the task, authority, and reporting relationships around the work group, delegating to the group decisions on job assignments, training, inspection, rewards, and punishments. The task of management is to monitor the environment and coordinate the structures, rules, and procedures.

Mintzberg's ideal types of organization design were derived from a framework of coordinating mechanisms. The five types are simple structure, machine bureaucracy, professional bureaucracy, divisionalized form, and adhocracy. Most organizations have some characteristics of each type, but one is likely to predominate. Mintzberg believed that the most important consideration in designing an organization is the fit among parts of the organization.

The matrix design combines two types of structure (usually functional and project departmentalization) to gain the benefits of each. It usually results in a multiple command and authority system. Benefits of the matrix form include increased flexibility, cooperation, and communication and better use of skilled personnel. Typical problems are associated with the dual reporting system and the complex management system needed to coordinate work.

Virtual organizations are temporary alliances between several organizations that agree to work together on a specific venture. Reaction time to business opportunities can be very fast with these types of alliances. In effect, organizations create a network of other organizations to enable them to respond to changes in the environment.

Contemporary organization design is contingency oriented. Currently popular design strategies are reengineering the organization and rethinking the organization. Four factors influencing design decisions are the changing technological environment, concern for people as valued resources, the need to keep in touch with customers, and global impacts on organizations.

Discussion Questions

1. What are the differences between universal approaches and contingency approaches to organization design?

2. Define "organizational environment" and "organizational technology." In what ways do these concepts overlap?

3. Identify and describe some of the environmental and technological factors that affect your college or university. Give specific examples of how they affect you as a student.

4. How does organization design usually differ for large and small organizations?

5. What might be the advantages and disadvantages of structuring the faculty members at your college or university as an autonomous work group?

6. What do you think are the purposes, goals, and strategies of your college or university? How are they reflected in its structure?

7. Which of Mintzberg's pure forms is best illustrated by a major national political party (Democratic or Republican)? A religious organization? A football team? The U.S. Olympic Committee?

8. In a matrix organization, would you rather be a project leader, a functional department head, or a highly trained technical specialist? Why?

9. Discuss what you think the important design considerations will be for organization designers in the year 2020.

10. How would your college or university be different if you rethought or reengineered the way in which it is designed?

Organizational Behavior Case for Discussion

Restructuring at Cisco

Changing an organization's structure is a difficult, time-consuming, and expensive task. Therefore, organizations tend to maintain a structure for a considerable period of time, often for decades. Nevertheless, it is clear that organization structure must also be somewhat flexible in order to adapt to internal and external changes. In addition, some organizations, notably high-tech firms, compete in rapidly and radically changing industries. How, then, can a high-tech company structure itself in order to prepare for an uncertain future? Networking firm Cisco is one high-tech company that recently restructured its divisions. "We're building a base for the future," says Cisco CEO and President John Chambers. "If we do this right, it will position us to break away even faster [when the economy improves]."

Cisco is a provider of networking hardware, software, services, and support. It makes the big routers and servers that carry most of the Internet traffic, smaller routers and servers for local area networks, and components such as hubs, fiber optics, switches, and security software. The reorganization shifted the company from a customer orientation to a product orientation. It used to have three divisions: small businesses, large businesses, and service providers. That structure facilitated good relations with each customer segment. However, a product developed for one customer group might not have been shared with the other groups, causing duplication of effort—at times, Cisco had as many as eight teams working to develop similar technology. The former structure also separated marketing from engineering. "What our [former] organizational structure had done is create a lot of overlap in technology developments," says Chief Marketing Officer James Richardson.

Cisco's new organization structure has eleven divisions, each one concentrating on a specific set of related technologies such as access, core routing, storage, and wireless. Thus, duplication of effort is eliminated while engineering and marketing join more closely to work together to develop and sell a particular technology set. The reorganization was accomplished by reassigning personnel and promoting six managers to the senior vice president level. The restructuring followed layoffs that have reduced the firm's workforce by about 17 percent, or 8,500 jobs, and have resulted in fewer managers—twelve instead of fifteen—reporting directly to Chambers.

The publicly stated reasons for the shake-up were to provide better customer service, eliminate duplication, highlight the central role of technology, and strengthen the relationship between engineering and marketing. However, other explanations also exist, including the slowdown in high-tech industries. After years of strong growth, Cisco's sales dropped rapidly in 2001—for example, falling 25 percent in just one quarter. Chambers claims this "may be the fastest any industry our size has ever decelerated." U.S. markets for networking equipment are saturated, and customers are waiting for the next major breakthrough before making more purchases, asking, "How many times do I need another router?" Chambers claims that the recent leveling-off of high-tech sales aids the reorganization effort. "You make these transitions at times when you're stable," he says.

Another motivation for the changes was suggested by the departure of Kevin Kennedy, the former head of the service provider division. This group contributed half of Cisco's revenues, but sales were slowing and technology stagnating. The official explanation is that Kennedy, in spite of efforts to keep him with the firm, left Cisco to "pursue other opportunities." But it is not clear whether Kennedy left for better career options, had a disagreement with Cisco leadership, or left involuntarily, an action which could be a signal that Cisco is losing interest in the service provider segment.

Richardson denies the loss of interest; saying, "There's nothing to be read into that. The catalyst of all this is [Kennedy's] deciding to leave the company. As a result, [Chambers] said, 'If I'm going to change to a functional organization, I might as well do it now.'" Whatever Kennedy's motivation for quitting, Frank Dzubeck, industry observer, says, "Kevin [Kennedy] lost the fire in the belly and he literally wanted out. He's not the only one [who's] going to be going[,] either."

It is not yet certain whether the reorganization will be beneficial for Cisco. Tam Dell'Oro, a consultant, says it will. "When a company has tighter control [of its divisions], it knows more about what's happening in the business, and it may be able to move faster," she asserts. Others disagree. Technology researcher Bill Lesieur says the shake-up "creates the perception that Cisco is not fully committed to [becoming] a top-three player" in the service-provider segment. The CEO, however, denies that Cisco is giving up on any customers. "This should not be viewed as a shift in strategy," Chambers says.

> **"If we do this right, it will position us to break away even faster [when the economy improves]."**
> **—John Chambers, CEO and President, Cisco**

References: "Chief Development Officer—Technology Groups," "Company Overview," "Mario Mazzola Gives Update on Cisco's Technology Organization," Cisco web site. newsroom.cisco.com on June 13, 2002; Jim Duffy, "Shakeup at Cisco—Service Provider Business Lost in the Sauce in Enterprise-Heavy Reorganization," *Network World*, August 31, 2001. Republished at www.tbri.com on June 13, 2002; Jim Duffy, "Cisco Restructures Around 11 Core Technologies," *Network World*, August 27, 2001, pp. 8–10. See www.networkworld.com; David R. Baker, "Networking Company Streamlines, Consolidates in Major Restructuring," *San Francisco Chronicle*, August 24, 2001, p. B1 (quotation). See www.sfchron.com; Scott Thurm, "Cisco Shake-Up Streamlines Operations—Three Units Are Eliminated in Effort to Centralize Engineering, Marketing," *Wall Street Journal*, August 24, 2001, p. A3. See www.wsj.com; Stephen Lee, "Slumping Cisco Restructures," *InfoWorld*, April 23, 2001, p. 10. See www.infoworld.com.

Case Questions

1. How did Cisco's strategy affect decisions about its new organization structure?

2. How did Cisco's structural imperatives—size, technology, and environment—affect decisions about its new organization structure?

3. How would you resolve the "strategy versus structure" debate in Cisco's case? In other words, which came first, its strategy or its structure? Provide specific details to support your answer.

 # Experiencing Organizational Behavior

Studying a Real Organization

Purpose: This exercise will help you understand the factors that determine the design of organizations.

Format: You will interview at least five employees in different parts of the college or university that you attend or employees of a small- to medium-sized organization and analyze the reasons for its design. (You may want to coordinate this exercise with the "Experiencing Organizational Behavior" exercise in Chapter 16.)

Procedure: If you use a local organization, your first task is to find one with between fifty and five hundred employees. (It should not be part of your college or university.) If you did the exercise for Chapter 16, you can use the same company for this exercise. The organization should have more than two hierarchical levels, but it should not be too complex to understand with a short period of study. You may want to check with your professor before contacting the company. Your initial contact should be with the highest-ranking manager you can reach. Make sure that top management is aware of your project and gives its approval.

If you use your local college or university, you could talk to professors, secretaries, and other administrative staff in the admissions office, student services department, athletic department, library, and many others. Be sure to include employees from a variety of jobs and levels in your interviews.

Using the material in this chapter, you will interview employees to obtain the following information on the structure of the organization:

1. What is the organization in business to do? What are its goals and its strategies for achieving them?

2. How large is the company? What is the total number of employees? How many work full-time? How many work part-time?

3. What are the most important components of the organization's environment?

4. Is the number of important environmental components large or small?

5. How quickly or slowly do these components change?

6. Would you characterize the organization's environment as certain, uncertain, or somewhere in between? If in between, describe approximately how certain or uncertain.

7. What is the organization's dominant technology; that is, how does it transform inputs into outputs?

8. How rigid is the company in its application of rules and procedures? Is it flexible enough to respond to environmental changes?

9. How involved are employees in the daily decision making related to their jobs?

10. What methods are used to ensure control over the actions of employees?

Interview at least five employees of the college or company at different levels and in different departments. One should hold a top-level position. Be sure to ask the questions in a way the employees will understand; they may not be familiar with some of the terminology used in this chapter.

The result of the exercise should be a report describing the technology, environment, and structure of the company. You should discuss the extent to which the structure is appropriate for the organization's strategy, size, technology, and environment. If it does not seem appropriate, you should explain the reasons. If you also used this company for the exercise in Chapter 16, you can comment further on the organization chart and its appropriateness for the company. You may want to send a copy of your report to the cooperating company.

Follow-up Questions

1. Which aspects of strategy, size, environment, and technology were the most difficult to obtain information about? Why?

2. If there were differences in the responses of the employees you interviewed, how do you account for them?

3. If you were the president of the organization you analyzed, would you structure it in the same way? Why or why not? If not, how would you structure it differently?

4. How did your answers to questions 2 and 3 differ from those in the exercise in Chapter 16?

 # Self-Assessment Exercise

Diagnosing Organization Structure

Introduction: You are probably involved with many different organizations—the place you work, a social or service club, a church, the college or university you attend. This assessment will help you diagnose the structure of one of those organizations. You could use this assessment on the organization that you analyzed in the preceding "Experiencing Organizational Behavior" exercise.

Instructions: First, pick one of the organizations you belong to or know a lot about. Then read each of the following statements and determine the degree to which you agree or disagree with that statement about your organization by using the following scale.

5	4	3	2	1
Strongly Agree	Agree	Don't Know	Disagree	Strongly Disagree

Then place the number of the response that best represents your organization in the space before each statement.

_____ 1. If people believe that they have the right approach to carrying out their job, they can usually go ahead without checking with their superior.

_____ 2. People in this organization don't always have to wait for orders from their superiors on important matters.

_____ 3. People in this organization share ideas with their superior.

_____ 4. Different individuals play important roles in making decisions.

_____ 5. People in this organization are likely to express their feelings openly on important matters.

_____ 6. People in this organization are encouraged to speak their minds on important matters, even if it means disagreeing with their superior.

_____ 7. Talking to other people about the problems someone might have in making decisions is an important part of the decision-making process.

_____ 8. Developing employees' talents and abilities is a major concern of this organization.

_____ 9. People are encouraged to make suggestions before decisions are made.

_____10. In this organization, most people can have their point of view heard.

_____11. Superiors often seek advice from subordinates before making decisions.

_____12. Subordinates play an active role in running this organization.

_____13. For many decisions, the rules and regulations are developed as we go along.

_____14. It is not always necessary to go through channels in dealing with important matters.

_____15. Employees do not consistently follow the same rules and regulations.

_____16. There are few rules and regulations for handling any kind of problem that may arise in making most decisions.

_____17. People from different departments are often put together in task forces to solve important problems.

_____18. For special problems, we usually set up a temporary task force until we meet our objectives.

_____19. Jobs in this organization are not clearly defined.

_____20. In this organization, adapting to changes in the environment is important.

_____ = Total Score

When you have finished, add up the numbers to get a total score. Your instructor can help you interpret your scores by referring to the *Instructor's Resource Manual*.

Reference: From Ricky W. Griffin, *Management*, 5/e, which is adapted from Robert T. Keller, *Type of Management System*. Griffin copyright © 1996 by Houghton Mifflin Company. Keller copyright © 1988. Used by permission of Houghton Mifflin Company and Robert T. Keller.

 # OB Online

1. Pick one organization that you think would have a "Low Perceived Uncertainty" type of environment (Cell 1 in Figure 17.4) and one organization that you think would have a "High Perceived Uncertainty" type of environment (Cell 4 in Figure 17.4) and look them up on the Internet. Most companies have references and/or links to media articles about their company and their annual report. Read as much as you can about these two companies and the environments in which they operate.

2. Given the information you found about the two companies, do you think your original classifications of them were accurate? What information either changed your mind or supported your original thoughts?

3. What impact do you think the type of environment had on the way that each firm structured the company?

Building Managerial Skills

Exercise Overview: When organizations utilize a matrix organizational structure (see Figure 17.7), every employee and manager in the system has dual reporting relationships, a situation which puts additional pressure on the managerial skills of everybody in the system. This exercise provides you with opportunity to analyze some of the managerial requirements for success in a matrix organizational structure.

Exercise Background: The matrix organizational structure was initially established to overcome the inadequacies of traditional structures when the environment and technology of certain organizations required additional information-processing capabilities. It has been hailed as a great innovation in certain situations, but it has also caused some problems when utilized in other organizations.

Exercise Task: Working alone, look again at the managerial roles and critical managerial skills described in Chapter 2. See if you can describe how each of these managerial roles and skills is affected when an

organization uses a matrix structure. Go through each role and each skill, first listing each one along with a simple one-sentence description. Then, reread the section on matrix organizations in this chapter and write a description of the roles and skills required of managers in a matrix structure.

Exchange papers with a classmate or share papers in a small group. Make notes about how others saw the roles and skills differently than you did. Discuss the differences and similarities that you find.

Conclude by addressing the following questions:

1. To what extent does the matrix organization structure put additional pressure on managers?

2. What should organizations using a matrix structure do to help their managers be prepared for those additional pressures?

3. Would you like to work in a matrix organizational structure? Why or why not?

18 Organization Culture

Management Preview

▶ Many organizations attribute their success to a strong and entrenched culture. Companies such as Sony, Boeing, Nike, Hewlett-Packard, and many others are successful because they each have a culture that is unique and appropriate just for them. But culture is an often elusive concept that can be easily misunderstood. In this chapter we describe the organization cultures of several different organizations and show how organizations can develop their own. We begin this chapter by exploring the nature and historical foundations of organization culture. Next, we describe the process of creating the culture. We then examine two basic approaches to describing the characteristics of organization culture and discuss three important issues in organization culture. Finally, we show how organization culture can be managed to enhance the organization's effectiveness. But first, we describe an unusual corporate culture at Southwest Airlines.

▼ ▼ ▼

It was a move that had been widely anticipated but dreaded—the resignation of a popular leader who had propelled his company to the forefront of its highly competitive industry. In June 2001, Southwest Airlines' founder, CEO, president, and chairman, seventy-year-old Herb Kelleher, stepped down, keeping only his chairman position. (Kelleher also maintains an active involvement in the firm by serving as a sort of "community ambassador.") In his place, Colleen Barrett assumed the roles of president and chief operating officer while James A. Parker tackled the CEO job. Although observers had confidence in the abilities of both Parker and Barrett—they have almost sixty years of combined experience at Southwest and were handpicked by Kelleher—there was concern that Southwest might lose its culture along with its flamboyant founder.

But such fears proved to be unfounded. Kelleher says, "We wanted to be sure that the culture of Southwest Airlines would continue." Southwest has a strong culture that produces loyal and motivated employees, leading to high organization performance. The airline has acted to nurture its culture since Kelleher's resignation, starting with the appointment of the two insiders to the top positions. After the September 11, 2001, terrorist attacks, many airlines laid off workers, but Southwest chose not to do so. However, workers insisted on helping the company maintain profitability—some volunteered to mow lawns; others worked "off the clock." When asked how the firm achieves such unity, Barrett answers, "It's a matter of getting buy-in from each new hire; making [ours] a culture they want to be part of. . . . We want [employees] to start thinking in terms of 'we' immediately. . . . You have a lot of mentoring going on, a lot of coaching, and a lot of storytelling."

"[Y]ou have to hold people accountable to whatever you want your core values to be."—Colleen Barrett, Southwest Airlines chief operating officer and president

Another Southwest value is "doing your own thing," even if that means overturning conventional wisdom. Kelleher's vision for the firm was a no-frills operation, with repetitive, short-haul flights and no seat assignments or food service. Unlike other airlines, Southwest only sells tickets on its own web site. Parker claims, "Independence is the way we do things. Customers are not surprised when we do something different. They expect that." He adds that other airlines have tried to mimic Southwest's culture and practices but have failed. He explains, "They want to be Southwest, but they also want to assign seats, or offer a first class or serve hot meals. We've been very disciplined about what we are, and we stick to it, evolving with our vision." Barrett advises cultural copycats, "[Don't] mimic anybody. If you want a culture that's similar [to ours,] . . . you have to hold people accountable to whatever you want your core values to be."

Parker and Barrett will work together to help maintain the company, and the culture, that Herb built. When asked if filling Kelleher's shoes will be difficult, Barrett replies, "Herb is who Herb is. Anyone who would even think they were going to emulate that would be crazy." Parker also acknowledges his indebtedness to Kelleher, saying, "One thing I'll always think about is 'What would Herb do?' . . . This is a superb company that has been successful. My challenge is just [not to] screw it up."[1]

References: Erika Rasmusson, "Flying High," *Sales and Marketing Management*, December 2001, p. 55 (quotation); Shaun McKinnon, "New Faces, Old Methods," *Arizona Republic* (Phoenix), July 29, 2001, pp. D1, D11. See www.azcentral.com; Wendy Zellner, "Southwest: After Kelleher, More Blue Skies," *Business Week*, April 2, 2001, p. 45. See www.businessweek.com.

Southwest Airlines has developed a culture that reflects its founder's philosophy and is just right for the company. Herb Kelleher had the vision and set the expectations for Southwest from the very start. But what about other companies? All companies have some sort of culture, but it is not easy to create this kind of successful culture for every organization.

The Nature of Organization Culture

In the early 1980s, organization culture became a central concern in the study of organizational behavior. Hundreds of researchers began to work in this area. Numerous books were published, important academic journals dedicated entire issues to the discussion of culture, and almost overnight, organizational behavior textbooks that omitted culture as a topic of study became obsolete.

Interest in organization culture was not limited to academic researchers. Businesses expressed a far more intense interest in culture than in other aspects of organizational behavior. *Business Week, Fortune,* and other business periodicals published articles that touted culture as the key to an organization's success and suggested that managers who could manage through their organization's culture almost certainly would rise to the top.[2]

Although the enthusiasm of the early 1980s has waned somewhat, the study of organization culture remains important. The assumption is that organizations with a strong culture perform at higher levels than those without a strong culture.[3] For example, studies have shown that organizations with strong cultures that are strategically appropriate and that have norms that permit the organization to change actually do perform well.[4] Other studies have shown that different functional units may require different types of cultures.[5] The research on the impact of culture on organizational performance is mixed, however, depending on how the research is done and what variables are measured.

Many researchers have begun to weave the important aspects of organization culture into their research on more traditional topics. Now there are fewer headline stories in the popular business press about culture and culture management, but organization culture has become a common topic for managers interested in improving organizational performance, as the opening case about Southwest Airlines illustrates. The enormous amount of research on culture completed in the last twenty years has fundamentally altered the way both academics and managers look at organizations. Some of the concepts developed in the analysis of organization culture have become basic parts of the business vocabulary, and the analysis of organization culture is one of the most important specialties in the field of organizational behavior.

What Is Organization Culture?

A surprising aspect of the recent rise in interest in organization culture is that the concept, unlike virtually every other concept in the field, has no single widely accepted definition. Indeed, it often appears that authors feel compelled to develop their own definitions, which range from very broad to highly specific. For example, Deal and Kennedy define a firm's culture as "the way we do things around here."[6] This very broad definition presumably could include the way a firm manufactures its products, pays its bills, treats its employees, and performs any other organizational operation. More specific definitions include those of Schein ("the pattern of basic assumptions that a given group has invented, discovered, or developed in learning to cope with its problems of external adaptation and internal integration"[7]) and Peters and Waterman ("a dominant and coherent set of shared values conveyed by such symbolic means as stories, myths, legends, slogans, anecdotes, and fairy tales"[8]). Table 18.1 lists these and other important definitions of organization culture. In the "World View" box, we describe the values that ING Group is trying to develop with all of its many different companies that it has acquired. Notice the repeated references to family, children, being friendly, and having a human face.

Despite the apparent diversity of these definitions, a few common attributes emerge. First, all the definitions refer to some set of values held by individuals in a firm. These values define what is good or acceptable behavior and what is bad or unacceptable behavior. In some organizations, for example, it is unacceptable to blame customers when problems arise. Here the value "the customer is always

table 18.1

**Definitions of
Organization Culture**

Definition	Source
"A belief system shared by an organization's members"	J. C. Spender, "Myths, Recipes and Knowledge-Bases in Organizational Analysis" (Unpublished manuscript, Graduate School of Management, University of California at Los Angeles, 1983), p. 2.
"Strong, widely shared core values"	C. O'Reilly, "Corporations, Cults, and Organizational Culture: Lessons from Silicon Valley Firms" (Paper presented at the Annual Meeting of the Academy of Management, Dallas, Texas, 1983), p. 1.
"The way we do things around here"	T. E. Deal and A. A. Kennedy, *Corporate Cultures: The Rites and Rituals of Corporate Life* (Reading, Mass.: Addison-Wesley, 1982), p. 4.
"The collective programming of the mind"	G. Hofstede, *Culture's Consequences: International Differences in Work-Related Values* (Beverly Hills, Calif.: Sage, 1980), p. 25.
"Collective understandings"	J. Van Maanen and S. R. Barley, "Cultural Organization: Fragments of a Theory" (Paper presented at the Annual Meeting of the Academy of Management, Dallas, Texas, 1983), p. 7.
"A set of shared, enduring beliefs communicated through a variety of symbolic media, creating meaning in people's work lives"	J. M. Kouzes, D. F. Caldwell, and B. Z. Posner, "Organizational Culture: How It Is Created, Maintained, and Changed" (Presentation at OD Network National Conference, Los Angeles, October 9, 1983).
"A set of symbols, ceremonies, and myths that communicates the underlying values and beliefs of that organization to its employees"	W. G. Ouchi, *Theory Z: How American Business Can Meet the Japanese Challenge* (Reading, Mass.: Addison-Wesley, 1981), p. 41.
"A dominant and coherent set of shared values conveyed by such symbolic means as stories, myths, legends, slogans, anecdotes, and fairy tales"	T. J. Peters and R. H. Waterman Jr., *In Search of Excellence: Lessons from America's Best-Run Companies* (New York: Harper & Row, 1982), p. 103.
"The pattern of basic assumptions that a given group has invented, discovered, or developed in learning to cope with its problems of external adaptation and internal integration"	E. H. Schein, "The Role of the Founder in Creating Organizational Culture," *Organizational Dynamics,* Summer 1985, p. 14.

right" tells managers what actions are acceptable (not blaming the customer) and what actions are not acceptable (blaming the customer). In other organizations, the dominant values might support blaming customers for problems, penalizing employees who make mistakes, or treating employees as the firm's most valuable assets. In each case, values help members of an organization understand how they should act.

WORLD VIEW

A Big Family with a Lot of Children

The worldwide banking deregulation of the 1990s created new opportunities for financial institutions. For the first time, banks were allowed to sell a wide range of products, including consumer and commercial banking, investments, and insurance. In 1991, a Dutch insurer and a Dutch bank joined forces to create ING Group. Since its founding, the company has acquired over fifty financial institutions, ranging from United Kingdom-based Baring's to American insurer Aetna, and today serves 50 million clients in 65 countries.

So how does ING manage this diverse stable of businesses? ING supervisory board member Godfried van der Lugt says, "In Europe, you have to be mindful of cultural differences and local identities. Therefore, we allow our companies to keep their names, their identities and[,] to a certain extent[,] their independence. . . . [T]he trick is to find the right balance between local affinity and global reach." He claims that the disparate units are able to coordinate and work for shared goals, explaining, "The way I see it, we are a big family with a lot of children who have different first names and a common last name."

Although it is huge, with 110,000 employees worldwide, the company is "not combative or internally competitive," according to ING manager Valerie Brown. The bank emphasizes relationship and consensus, and she attributes this focus to the firm's "Dutch roots, where people

don't believe in sticking your head above the dike." In a physical display of its eclectic culture, the company is building a strikingly avant-garde headquarters in Amsterdam. Chairman Ewald Kist says that because the firm produces only paperwork, "We need to show our employees

> *"[W]e are a big family with a lot of children who have different first names and a common last name."—Godfried van der Lugt, member of the supervisory board, ING*

and our clients that we have a human face. We have to show the outside world that we're not dull."

van der Lugt believes that the firm's success has been driven largely by its culture of autonomy for each unit. He says, "I would never have gotten the support of the various managements of the companies we bought if I had tried to impose the ING name on them. . . . It's very important not to be seen as unfriendly. I can't afford to have the image of the whole group damaged by one ugly squabble. We only do friendly takeovers."

References: "History of ING," "Mission and Strategy," "Products and Services," "Profile," ING web site. www.ing.com on June 14, 2002; Milton Moskowitz and Robert Levering, "10 Great Companies to Work for: Combining Style and Substance, These European Companies Stand Out," *Fortune Europe*, February 4, 2002. See www.fortune.com; John Carreyrou, "Managers & Managing: ING Thrives with Hands-Off Takeover Style—Firms It Absorbs Retain Their Names, Some Autonomy," *Wall Street Journal*, September 28, 1999, p. 4 (quotation). See www.wsj.com.

A second attribute common to many of the definitions in Table 18.1 is that the values that make up an organization's culture are often taken for granted; that is, they are basic assumptions made by the firm's employees rather than prescriptions written in a book or made explicit in a training program. It may be as difficult for an organization to articulate these basic assumptions as it is for people to express their personal beliefs and values. Several authors have argued that organization culture is a powerful influence on individuals in firms precisely because it is not explicit but instead becomes an implicit part of employees' values and beliefs.[9]

Some organizations have been able to articulate the key values in their cultures. Some have even written down these values and made them part of formal training procedures. E*Trade Group, Inc., the online stock and mutual fund trading company, uses unique ways of creating the company culture. Chief Executive Officer Christos M. Cotsakos is building a culture that is edgy, a bit bizarre, and sometimes brilliant that he sums up in five words, "a lust for being different." He tells new recruits that the company has to be on the offensive and predatory, like infantrymen in a war. He once asked his newly hired vice president of international business development to stand on a chair and reveal something about himself to forty strangers in the company.[10]

Even when firms can articulate and describe the basic values that make up their cultures, however, the values most strongly affect actions when people in the organization take them for granted. An organization's culture is not likely to influence behavior powerfully when employees must constantly refer to a handbook to remember what the culture is. When the culture becomes part of them—when they can ignore what is written in the book because they already have embraced the values it describes—the culture can have an important impact on their actions.

"I began to realize that my own values were no longer in alignment with those of the organization."—Richard Barrett, partner in Barrett and Associates[11]

The final attribute shared by many of the definitions in Table 18.1 is an emphasis on the symbolic means through which the values in an organization's culture are communicated. Although, as we noted, companies sometimes could directly describe these values, their meaning is perhaps best communicated to employees through the use of stories, examples, and even what some authors call "myths" or "fairy tales." Stories typically reflect the important implications of values in a firm's culture. Often they develop a life of their own. As they are told and retold, shaped and reshaped, their relationship to what actually occurred becomes less important than the powerful impact the stories have on the way that people behave every day. Nike uses a group of technical representatives called "Ekins" ("Nike" spelled backwards) who run a nine-day training session for large retailers, telling them stories about Nike's history and traditions, such as the stories about CEO Phil Knight selling shoes from the trunk of his car and cofounder Bill Bowerman using the family's waffle iron to create the first waffle-soled running shoe.[12]

Some organization stories have become famous. At E*Trade, CEO Cotsakos has done many things that have become famous around the company because he does not follow the rules for the typical investment company. To make people move faster, he organized a day of racing in Formula One cars at speeds of around 150 miles per hour. To create a looser atmosphere around the office, he has employees carry around rubber chickens or wear propeller beanies. To bond the employees together, he organized gourmet-cooking classes.[13] The stories of these incidents and others are told to new employees and are spread throughout the company, thus affecting the behavior of many more people than those who actually took part in each event.

We can use the three common attributes of definitions of culture just discussed to develop a definition with which most authors probably could agree: **Organization culture** is the set of shared values, often taken for granted, that help people in an organization understand which actions are considered acceptable and which are considered unacceptable. Often these values are communicated through stories and other symbolic means.

Organization culture is the set of values that helps the organization's employees understand which actions are considered acceptable and which are unacceptable.

Historical Foundations

Although research on organization culture exploded onto the scene in the early 1980s, the antecedents of this research can be traced to the origins of social science. Understanding the contributions of other social science disciplines is partic-

Students and the Dean of Northwestern University's Kellogg School of Management are celebrating the school being ranked number one in the Business Week rankings of MBA programs. Kellogg attributes its lofty ranking to its "go-to-any-lengths" culture. Because new graduates are facing the most difficult job market in recent memory, deans work individually with students and use their personal contacts to help them find jobs. Students feel that they are the deans' and the schools top priority.

ularly important in the case of organization culture because many of the dilemmas and debates that continue in this area reflect differences in historical research traditions.

Anthropological Contributions   Anthropology is the study of human cultures.[14] Of all the social science disciplines, anthropology is most closely related to the study of culture and cultural phenomena. Anthropologists seek to understand how the values and beliefs that make up a society's culture affect the structure and functioning of that society. Many anthropologists believe that to understand the relationship between culture and society, it is necessary to look at a culture from the viewpoint of the people who practice it—from the "native's point of view."[15] To reach this level of understanding, anthropologists immerse themselves in the values, symbols, and stories that people in a society use to bring order and meaning to their lives. Anthropologists usually produce book-length descriptions of the values, attitudes, and beliefs that underlie the behaviors of people in one or two cultures.[16]

Whether the culture is that of a large, modern corporation or a primitive tribe in New Guinea or the Philippines, the questions asked are the same: How do people in this culture know what kinds of behavior are acceptable and what kinds are unacceptable? How is this knowledge understood? How is this knowledge communicated to new members? Through intense efforts to produce accurate descriptions, the values and beliefs that underlie actions in an organization become clear. However, these values can be fully understood only in the context of the organization in which they developed. In other words, a description of the values and beliefs of one organization is not transferable to those of other organizations; each culture is unique.

Sociological Contributions   Sociology is the study of people in social systems such as organizations and societies. Sociologists have long been interested in the causes and consequences of culture. In studying culture, sociologists have most often focused on informal social structure. Émile Durkheim, an important early sociologist, argued that the study of myth and ritual is an essential complement to the study of structure and rational behavior in societies.[17] By studying rituals, Durkheim argued, we can understand the most basic values and beliefs of a group of people.

Many sociological methods and theories have been used in the analysis of organization cultures. Sociologists use systematic interviews, questionnaires, and other quantitative research methods rather than the intensive study and analysis of anthropologists. Practitioners using the sociological approach generally produce a fairly simple typology of cultural attributes and then show how the cultures of a relatively large number of firms can be analyzed with this typology.[18] The major pieces of research on organization culture that later spawned widespread business interest—including Ouchi's *Theory Z*, Deal and Kennedy's *Corporate Cultures*, and Peters and Waterman's *In Search of Excellence*[19]—used sociological methods. Later in this chapter, we review some of this work in more detail.

Social Psychology Contributions   Social psychology is a branch of psychology that includes the study of groups and the influence of social factors on individuals. Although most research on organization culture has used anthropological or sociological methods and approaches, some has borrowed heavily from social psychology. Social psychological theory, with its emphasis on the creation and manipulation of symbols, lends itself naturally to the analysis of organization culture.

For example, research in social psychology suggests that people tend to use stories or information about a single event more than they use multiple observations to make judgments.[20] Thus, if your neighbor had trouble with a certain brand of automobile, you will probably conclude that the brand is bad even though the car company can generate reams of statistical data to prove that the situation with your neighbor's car was a rarity.

The impact of stories on decision making suggests an important reason that organization culture has such a powerful influence on the people in an organization. Unlike other organizational phenomena, culture is best communicated through stories and examples, and these become the basis that individuals in the organization use to make judgments. If a story says that blaming customers is a bad thing to do, then blaming customers is a bad thing to do. This value is communicated much more effectively through the cultural story than through some statistical analysis of customer satisfaction.[21]

Economics Contributions   The influence of economics on the study of organization culture is substantial enough to warrant attention, although it has been less significant than the influence of anthropology and sociology. Economic analysis treats organization culture as one of a variety of tools that managers can use to create some economic advantage to the organization.

The economics approach attempts to link the cultural attributes of firms with their performance rather than simply describing the cultures of companies as the sociological and anthropological perspectives do. In *Theory Z*, for example, Ouchi does not just say that Type Z companies differ from other kinds of companies—he asserts that Type Z firms outperform other firms.[22] When Peters and Waterman say they are in search of excellence, they define "excellence," in part, as consistently high financial performance.[23] These authors are using cultural explanations of financial success.

Researchers disagree about the extent to which culture affects organization performance. Several authors have investigated the conditions under which organization culture is linked with superior financial performance.[24] This research sug-

WORKING WITH DIVERSITY

▶ *Where Are Wal-Mart's Women Executives?*

In 2002, mega-retailer Wal-Mart rose to the top slot of the Fortune 500, the first service company ever to occupy that position. The company is flying high, but one potentially disastrous cloud is looming on the horizon—accusations about a lack of diversity, and even deliberate discrimination, particularly against women.

Wal-Mart publicly and proudly claims a commitment to diversity. Its web site mentions "respect the individual" as one of the firm's basic beliefs and then expands further: "We have very different backgrounds, different colors and different beliefs, but we do believe that every individual deserves to be treated with respect and dignity." Wal-Mart's founder, Sam Walton, described how to build a successful business in his 1992 book, *Made in America*. Of Walton's ten rules, six directly relate to the importance of employees and include advice such as "celebrate success," "listen to everyone," "appreciate," and "treat employees as partners."

Nevertheless, despite Wal-Mart's hiring a staff that is 59 percent women, some female workers describe a hostile culture that includes sexual talk, unwanted sexual advances, and even the showing of pornographic videos in the employee lounge. These women also note that 72 percent of the sales staff is female, but only one-third of managers are, despite the company's promote-from-within policy.

Wal-Mart's proportion of female managers is below that of other retailers—who average 56 percent—and even worse, is below the other retailers' levels of 25 years ago. As a result, Wal-Mart has been the subject of a number of discrimination lawsuits, and it has a history of aggressively fighting such suits by stonewalling or even violating court orders. Equal Employment Opportunity Commission lawyer Mary Jo O'Neill says, "I have never seen this kind of blatant disregard for the law. . . . Wal-Mart[,] . . . at

> *"I have never seen this kind of blatant disregard for the law."*
> —Mary Jo O'Neill, lawyer, Equal Employment Opportunity Commission

the top, isn't committed to taking . . . federal employment laws seriously."

In its defense, Wal-Mart maintains that its size and geographic spread make it hard to closely supervise every one of its worldwide locations. Spokesman Jay Allen says, "When you have a million people, you're going to have a few people out there who don't do things right." Still, it is difficult for a company that purports to be "so centralized that it can keep tabs on every last light bulb in its more than 3,100 stores" to claim ignorance about its employment discrimination.

References: "3 Basic Beliefs," "Sam's Rules for Building a Business," Wal-Mart web site. www.walmartstores.com on June 21, 2002; Cait Murphy, "Wal-Mart Rules: Now That Wal-Mart Is America's Largest Corporation, the Service Economy Wears the Crown," *Fortune*, April 15, 2002. www.fortune.com on June 21, 2002; "More Jobs for Women," *Fortune*, February 4, 2002. www.fortune.com on June 21, 2002; "The 100 Best Companies to Work for in America," *Fortune*, February 4, 2002. www.fortune.com on June 21, 2002; Wendy Zellner, "How Well Does Wal-Mart Travel?" *Business Week*, September 3, 2001. www.businessweek.com on June 21, 2002; Michelle Conlin, "Is Wal-Mart Hostile to Women?" *Business Week*, July 16, 2001. www.businessweek.com on June 21, 2002.

gests that under some relatively narrow conditions, a link between culture and performance may exist. However, the fact that a firm has a culture does not mean it will perform well; indeed, a variety of cultural traits can actually hurt performance. For example, a firm could have a culture that includes values like "customers are too ignorant to be of much help," "employees cannot be trusted," "innovation is not important," and "quality is too expensive." The firm would have a strong culture, but the culture might impair its performance. Wal-Mart, known for its retailing expertise and its culture of respect for individuals, is also becoming known as a company whose culture does not lead to success for women, as the "Working with Diversity" box discusses. The relationship between culture and performance depends, to some extent at least, on the values expressed in the organization's culture.

Culture Versus Climate

During the past twenty years, since the concept of organization culture has become popular, managers have often asked about the similarities and differences between organization culture and organization climate. Some people, managers and researchers alike, have argued that they are really the same thing, although their research bases are different, as we explain next.

The two concepts are similar in that both are concerned with the overall work atmosphere of an organization. In addition, they both deal with the social context in organizations, and both are assumed to affect the behaviors of people who work in organizations.[25]

The two concepts differ in several significant ways, however. Much of the study of climate was based in psychology whereas the study of organization culture was based in anthropology and sociology. **Organization climate** usually refers to current situations in an organization and the linkages among work groups, employees, and work performance. Climate, therefore, is usually more easily manipulated by management to directly affect the behavior of employees. Organization culture, on the other hand, usually refers to the historical context within which a situation occurs and the impact of this context on the behaviors of employees. Organization culture is generally considered much more difficult to alter in short-run situations because it has been defined over the course of years of history and tradition.

The two concepts also differ in their emphases. Organization culture is often described as the means through which people in the organization learn and communicate what is acceptable and unacceptable in an organization—its values and norms.[26] Most descriptions of organization climate do not deal with values and norms. Therefore, descriptions of organization climate are concerned with the current atmosphere in an organization whereas organization culture is based on the history and traditions of the organization and emphasizes values and norms about employee behavior.

> Organization climate usually refers to current situations in an organization and the linkages among work groups, employees, and work performance.

Creating the Organization Culture

To the entrepreneur who starts a business, creating the culture of the company may seem secondary to the basic processes of creating a product or service and selling it to customers or clients. However, as the company grows and becomes successful, it usually develops a culture that distinguishes it from other companies and that is one of the reasons for its success. In other words, a company succeeds as a result of what the company does, its strategy, and how it does it, its culture. The culture is linked to the strategic values, whether one is starting up a new company or trying to change the culture of an existing company.[27] The process of creating an organization culture is really a process of linking its strategic values with its cultural values, much as the structure of the organization is linked to its strategy, as we described in Chapter 17. The process is shown in Table 18.2.

Establish Values

> Strategic values are the basic beliefs about an organization's environment that shape its strategy.

The first two steps in the process involve establishing values. First, management must determine the strategic values of the organization. **Strategic values** are the basic beliefs about an organization's environment that shape its strategy. They are

Step1—Formulate Strategic Values

Step 2—Develop Cultural Values

Step 3—Create Vision

Step 4—Initiate Implementation Strategies

Step 5—Reinforce Cultural Behaviors

table 18.2

Creating Organization Culture

Cultural values are the values
that employees need to have
and act on for the organization to act on the strategic
values.

developed following an environmental scanning process and strategic analysis that evaluate economic, demographic, public policy, technological, and social trends to identify needs in the market-place that the organization can meet. Strategic values, in effect, link the organization with its environment. Dell Computer believed that customers would buy computers from a catalogue if the price were right, rather than go to computer stores as the conventional wisdom dictated they would. The $6.8 billion business resulted.[28] The second set of required values is the cultural values of the organization. **Cultural values** are the values employees need to have and to act on for the organization to carry out its strategic values. They should be grounded in the organization's beliefs about how and why the organization can succeed. Organizations that attempt to develop cultural values that are not linked to their strategic values may end up with an empty set of values that have little relationship to their business. In other words, employees need to value work behaviors that are consistent with and support the organization's strategic values: low-cost production, customer service, or technological innovation.

"So my biggest concern is that somehow, through maladroitness, through inattention, through misunderstanding, we lose the esprit de corps, the culture, the spirit. If we ever do lose that, we will have lost our most valuable competitive asset."—Herb Kelleher, former CEO of Southwest Airlines[29]

Create Vision

After developing its strategic and cultural values, the organization must establish a vision of its direction. This "vision" is a picture of what the organization will be like at some point in the future. It portrays how the strategic and cultural values will combine to create the future. For example, an insurance company might establish a vision of "protecting the lifestyles of 2 million families by the year 2005." In effect, it synthesizes both the strategic and cultural values as it communicates a performance target to employees. The conventional wisdom has been that the vision statement is written first, but experience suggests that the strategic and cultural values must be established first for the vision to be meaningful.

Initiate Implementation Strategies

The next step, initiating implementation strategies, builds on the values and initiates the action to accomplish the vision. The strategies cover many factors, from developing the organization design to recruiting and training employees who share the values and will carry them out. Consider a bank that has the traditional orientation of handling customer loans, deposits, and savings. If the bank changes, placing more emphasis on customer service, it may have to recruit a different type of employee, one who is capable of building relationships. The bank will also have to

Students and faculty at Alverno College are jointly involved in creating a new kind of learning environment. Alverno, a small liberal arts college for women in Milwaukee, Wisconsin, is recognized internationally for its educational innovations. There are no grades and students take an ability-based curriculum. They created this new culture by intense internal analysis of their core values and then by building a new system based on those values. Faculty, students, and administration believe that education must be related to life and students should demonstrate competence in eight categories, from communication to effective citizenship. From that they developed new curricula, teaching methodologies, and assessment techniques.

commit to serious, long-term training of its current employees to teach them the new service-oriented culture. The strategic and cultural values are the stimuli for the implementation practices.

Reinforce Cultural Behaviors

The final step is to reinforce the behaviors of employees as they act out the cultural values and implement the organization's strategies. Reinforcement can take many forms. First, the formal reward system in the organization must reward desired behaviors in ways that employees value. Second, stories must be told throughout the organization about employees who engaged in behaviors that epitomize the cultural values. Third, the organization must engage in ceremonies and rituals that emphasize employees doing the things that are critical to carrying out the organization's vision. In effect, the organization must "make a big deal out of employees doing the right things." For example, if parties are held only for retirement or to give out longevity and service pins, the employees get the message that retirement and length of service are the only things that matter. On the other hand, holding a ceremony for a group of employees who provided exceptional customer service reinforces desirable employee behaviors. Reinforcement practices are the final link between the strategic and cultural values and the creation of the organization culture.

Approaches to Describing Organization Culture

The models discussed in this section provide valuable insights into the dimensions along which organization cultures vary. No single framework for describing the values in organization cultures has emerged; however, several frameworks have been suggested. Although these frameworks were developed in the 1980s, their ideas about organization culture are still influential today. Some of the "excellent" companies that they described are not as highly lauded now, but the concepts are still in use in companies all over the world. Managers should evaluate the various parts of the frameworks described and use the parts that fit the strategic and cultural values of their own organizations.

The Ouchi Framework

One of the first researchers to focus explicitly on analyzing the cultures of a limited group of firms was William G. Ouchi. Ouchi analyzed the organization cultures of three groups of firms, which he characterized as (1) typical U.S. firms, (2) typical Japanese firms, and (3) **Type Z** U.S. firms.[30]

The Type Z firm is committed to retaining employees; evaluates workers' performance based on both qualitative and quantitative information; emphasizes broad career paths; exercises control through informal, implicit mechanisms; requires that decision making occur in groups and be based on full information-sharing and consensus; expects individuals to take responsibility for decisions; and emphasizes concern for people.

Through his analysis, Ouchi developed a list of seven points on which these three types of firms can be compared. He argued that the cultures of typical Japanese firms and U.S. Type Z firms are very different from those of typical U.S. firms, and that these differences explain the success of many Japanese firms and U.S. Type Z firms and the difficulties faced by typical U.S. firms. The seven points of comparison developed by Ouchi are presented in Table 18.3.

Commitment to Employees   According to Ouchi, typical Japanese and Type Z U.S. firms share the cultural value of trying to keep employees. Thus, both types of firms lay off employees only as a last resort. In Japan, the value of "keeping employees on" often takes the form of lifetime employment, although some Japanese companies, reacting to the economic troubles of the past few years, are challenging this value. A person who begins working at some Japanese firms usually has a virtual guarantee that he or she will never be fired. In U.S. Type Z companies, this cultural value is manifested in a commitment to what Ouchi called "long-term employment." Under the Japanese system of lifetime employment, employees usually cannot be fired. Under the U.S. system, workers and managers can be fired, but only if they are not performing acceptably.

Ouchi suggested that typical U.S. firms do not have the same cultural commitment to employees that Japanese firms and U.S. Type Z firms do. In reality, U.S. workers and managers often spend their entire careers in a relatively small number

table 18.3

The Ouchi Framework

Cultural Value	Expression in Japanese Companies	Expression in Type Z U.S. Companies	Expression in Typical U.S. Companies
Commitment to Employees	Lifetime employment	Long-term employment	Short-term employment
Evaluation	Slow and qualitative	Slow and qualitative	Fast and quantitative
Careers	Very broad	Moderately broad	Narrow
Control	Implicit and informal	Implicit and informal	Explicit and formal
Decision Making	Group and consensus	Group and consensus	Individual
Responsibility	Group	Individual	Individual
Concern for People	Holistic	Holistic	Narrow

of companies. Still, there is a cultural expectation that if there is a serious down-turn in a firm's fortunes, change of ownership, or a merger, workers and managers will be let go. For example, when Wells Fargo Bank bought First Interstate Bank in Arizona, it expected to lay off about 400 employees in Arizona and 5,000 in the corporation as a whole. However, eight months after the purchase, Wells Fargo had eliminated over 1,000 employees in Arizona alone and laid off a total of 10,800 workers. Wells Fargo has a reputation as a vicious cutter following a takeover and seems to be living up to it.[31]

Evaluation   Ouchi observed that in Japanese and Type Z U.S. companies, appropriate evaluation of workers and managers is thought to take a very long time—up to ten years—and requires the use of qualitative as well as quantitative information about performance. For this reason, promotion in these firms is relatively slow, and promotion decisions are made only after interviews with many people who have had contact with the person being evaluated. In typical U.S. firms, on the other hand, the cultural value suggests that evaluation can and should be done rapidly and should emphasize quantitative measures of performance. This value tends to encourage short-term thinking among workers and managers.

Careers   Ouchi next observed that the careers most valued in Japanese and Type Z U.S. firms span multiple functions. In Japan, this value has led to very broad career paths, which may lead to employees' gaining experience in six or seven distinct business functions. The career paths in Type Z U.S. firms are somewhat narrower.

However, the career path valued in typical U.S. firms is considerably narrower. Ouchi's research indicated that most U.S. managers perform only one or two different business functions in their careers. This narrow career path reflects, according to Ouchi, the value of specialization that is part of so many U.S. firms.

Control   All organizations must exert some level of control to achieve coordinated action. Thus, it is not surprising that firms in the United States and Japan have developed cultural values related to organizational control and how to manage it. Most Japanese and Type Z U.S. firms assume that control is exercised through informal, implicit mechanisms. One of the most powerful of these mechanisms is the organization's culture. In contrast, typical U.S. firms expect guidance to come through explicit directions in the form of job descriptions, delineation of authority, and various rules and procedures, rather than from informal and implicit cultural values.

From a functional perspective, organization culture could be viewed as primarily a means of social control based on shared norms and values.[32] Control comes from knowing that someone who matters is paying close attention to what we do and will tell us if our actions are appropriate or not. In organizations, control can come from formal sources, such as the organization structure or your supervisor, or from social sources, such as the organization's culture. In Ouchi's view, control is based in formal organizational mechanisms in typical U.S. firms whereas control is more social in nature and derived from the organization culture's shared norms and values in Japanese and Type Z U.S. firms.

Decision Making   Japanese and Type Z U.S. firms have a strong cultural expectation that decision making occurs in groups and is based on principles of full information sharing and consensus. In most typical U.S. firms, individual decision making is considered appropriate.

Responsibility   Closely linked to the issue of group versus individual decision making are ideas about responsibility. Here, however, the parallels between Japanese firms and Type Z U.S. firms break down. Ouchi showed that in Japan, strong cultural norms support collective responsibility; that is, the group as a whole, rather than a single person, is held responsible for decisions made by the group. In both Type Z U.S. firms and typical U.S. firms, individuals expect to take responsibility for decisions.

Linking individual responsibility with individual decision making, as typical U.S. firms do, is logically consistent. Similarly, group decision making and group responsibility, the situation in Japanese firms, seem to go together. But how do Type Z U.S. firms combine the cultural values of group decision making and individual responsibility?

Ouchi suggested that the answer to this question depends on a cultural view we have already discussed: slow, qualitative evaluation. The first time a manager uses a group to make a decision, it is not possible to tell whether the outcomes associated with that decision resulted from the manager's influence or from the quality of the group. However, if a manager works with many groups over time, and if these groups consistently do well for the organization, it is likely that the manager is skilled at getting the most out of the groups. This manager can be held responsible for the outcomes of group decision-making processes. Similarly, managers who consistently fail to work effectively with the groups assigned to them can be held responsible for the lack of results from the group decision-making process.

Concern for People   The last cultural value examined by Ouchi deals with a concern for people. Not surprisingly, in Japanese firms and Type Z firms, the cultural value that dominates is a holistic concern for workers and managers. Holistic concern extends beyond concern for a person simply as a worker or manager to concern about that person's home life, hobbies, personal beliefs, hopes, fears, and aspirations. In typical U.S. firms, the concern for people is a narrow one that focuses on the workplace. A culture that emphasizes a strong concern for people, rather than one that emphasizes a work or task orientation, can decrease worker turnover.[33]

Theory Z and Performance   Ouchi argued that the cultures of Japanese and Type Z firms help them outperform typical U.S. firms. Toyota imported the management style and culture that succeeded in Japan into its manufacturing facilities in North America. Toyota's success has often been attributed to the ability of Japanese and Type Z firms to systematically invest in their employees and operations over long periods, resulting in steady and significant improvements in long-term performance.

The Peters and Waterman Approach

Tom Peters and Robert Waterman, in their bestseller *In Search of Excellence*, focused even more explicitly than Ouchi on the relationship between organization culture and performance. Peters and Waterman chose a sample of highly successful U.S. firms and sought to describe the management practices that led to their success.[34] Their analysis rapidly turned to the cultural values that led to successful management practices. These "excellent" values are listed in Table 18.4.

Bias for Action   According to Peters and Waterman, successful firms have a bias for action. Managers in these firms are expected to make decisions even if all the facts are not in. Peters and Waterman argued that for many important decisions, all the

table 18.4

The Peters and Waterman Framework

Attributes of an Excellent Firm	
1. Bias for action	5. Hands-on management
2. Stay close to the customer	6. Stick to the knitting
3. Autonomy and entrepreneurship	7. Simple form, lean staff
4. Productivity through people	8. Simultaneously loose and tight organization

facts will never be in. Delaying decision making in these situations is the same as never making a decision. Meanwhile, other firms probably will have captured whatever business initiative existed. On average, according to these authors, organizations with cultural values that include a bias for action outperform firms without such values.

Stay Close to the Customer   Peters and Waterman believe that firms whose organization cultures value customers over everything else outperform firms without this value. The customer is a source of information about current products, a source of ideas about future products, and the ultimate source of a firm's current and future financial performance. Focusing on the customer, meeting the customer's needs, and pampering the customer when necessary all lead to superior performance. After losing money for years, Scandinavian Airlines focused its culture on customer service and finally started making money in 1989, when many other airlines were experiencing financial difficulties.[35]

"The only thing that matters to me is that we are using information technology to make our customers happy."—Tom Siebel, chairman and CEO of Siebel Systems[36]

Autonomy and Entrepreneurship   Peters and Waterman maintained that successful firms fight the lack of innovation and the bureaucracy usually associated with large size. They do this by breaking the company into smaller, more manageable pieces and then encouraging independent, innovative activities within smaller business segments. Stories often exist in these organizations about the junior engineer who takes a risk and influences major product decisions, or of the junior manager, dissatisfied with the slow pace of a product's development, who implements a new and highly successful marketing plan.

Productivity Through People   Like Ouchi, Peters and Waterman believe successful firms recognize that their most important assets are their people—both workers and managers—and that the organization's purpose is to let its people flourish. It is a basic value of the organization culture—a belief that treating people with respect and dignity is not only appropriate but essential to success.

Hands-on Management   Peters and Waterman noted that the firms they studied insisted that senior managers stay in touch with the firms' essential business. It is an expectation, reflecting a deeply embedded cultural norm, that managers should manage not from behind the closed doors of their offices but by "wandering around" the plant, the design facility, the research and development department, and so on.

Stick to the Knitting   Another cultural value characteristic of excellent firms is their reluctance to engage in business outside their areas of expertise. These firms reject the concept of diversification, the practice of buying and operating businesses in unrelated industries. This notion is currently referred to as relying on the company's "core competencies," or what the company does best.

Simple Form, Lean Staff   According to Peters and Waterman, successful firms tend to have few administrative layers and relatively small corporate staff groups. In excellently managed companies, importance is measured not only by the number of people who report to a manager but also by the manager's impact on the organization's performance. The cultural values in these firms tell managers that their staffs' performance rather than their size is important.

Simultaneously Loose and Tight Organization   The final attribute of organization culture identified by Peters and Waterman appears contradictory. How can a firm be simultaneously loosely and tightly organized? The resolution of this apparent paradox is found in the firms' values. The firms are tightly organized because all their members understand and believe in the firms' values. This common cultural bond is a strong glue that holds the firms together. At the same time, however, the firms are loosely organized because they tend to have less administrative overhead, fewer staff members, and fewer rules and regulations. The result is increased innovation and risk taking and faster response times.

The loose structure is possible only because of the common values held by people in the firm. When employees must make decisions, they can evaluate their options in terms of the organization's underlying values—whether the options are consistent with a bias for action, service to the customer, and so on. By referring to commonly held values, employees can make their own decisions about what actions to take. In this sense, the tight structure of common cultural values makes possible the loose structure of fewer administrative controls.

Emerging Issues in Organization Culture

As the implementation of organization culture continues, it inevitably changes and develops new perspectives. Many new ideas about productive environments build on earlier views such as those of Ouchi, Peters and Waterman, and others. Typical of these approaches are the total quality management movement, worker participation, and team-based management, which were discussed in earlier chapters. Three other movements are briefly discussed in this section: innovation, empowerment, and procedural justice.

Innovation

Innovation is the process of creating and doing new things that are introduced into the marketplace as products, processes, or services.

Innovation is the process of creating and doing new things that are introduced into the marketplace as products, processes, or services. Innovation involves every aspect of the organization, from research through development, manufacturing, and marketing. One of the organization's biggest challenges is to bring innovative technology to the needs of the marketplace in the most cost-effective manner possible.[37] Note that innovation does not only involve the technology to create new products. True organizational innovation is pervasive throughout the organization. According to *Fortune* magazine, the most admired organizations are those that are the most innovative.[38] Those companies are innovative in every way—staffing, strategy, research, and business processes.

Many risks are associated with being an innovative company. The most basic is the risk that decisions about new technology or innovation will backfire. As research proceeds, and engineers and scientists continue to develop new ideas or solutions to problems, there is always the possibility that the innovation will fail to perform as expected. For this reason, organizations commit considerable resources to testing innovations.[39] A second risk is the possibility that a competitor will make decisions enabling it to get an innovation to the market first. The marketplace has become a breeding ground for continuous innovation. Motorola, for example, is striving to build a company in which customer needs shape new-product development without crippling the firm's technological leadership in its basic products.

"I could sit here and beat estimates by a penny a share the rest of my life, and two years from now be annihilated by the freight train that's the Internet. . . . Or I can step up to the gallows today to be hanged, but do so proactively."—David Dunkel, CEO of Romac International [40]

Types of Innovation   Innovation can be either radical, systems, or incremental. A **radical innovation** is a major breakthrough that changes or creates whole industries. Examples include xerography (which was invented by Chester Carlson in 1935 and became the hallmark of Xerox Corporation), steam engines, and the internal combustion engine (which paved the way for today's automobile industry). **Systems innovation** creates a new functionality by assembling parts in new ways. For example, the gasoline engine began as a radical innovation and became a systems innovation when it was combined with bicycle and carriage technology to create automobiles. **Incremental innovation** continues the technical improvement and extends the applications of radical and systems innovations. There are many more incremental innovations than there are radical and systems innovations. In fact, several incremental innovations are often necessary to make radical and systems innovations work properly. Incremental innovations force organizations to continuously improve their products and keep abreast or ahead of the competition.

Radical innovation is a major breakthrough that changes or creates whole industries.

Systems innovation creates a new functionality by assembling parts in new ways.

Incremental innovation continues the technical improvement and extends the applications of radical and systems innovations.

New Ventures   New ventures based on innovations require entrepreneurship and good management to work. The profile of the entrepreneur typically includes a need for achievement, a desire to assume responsibility, a willingness to take risks, and a focus on concrete results. Entrepreneurship can occur inside or outside large organizations. Outside entrepreneurship requires all of the complex aspects of the innovation process. Inside entrepreneurship occurs within a system that usually discourages chaotic activity.

Large organizations typically do not accept entrepreneurial types of activities. Thus, for a large organization to be innovative and develop new ventures, it must actively encourage entrepreneurial activity within the organization. This form of activity, often called **intrapreneurship,** usually is most effective when it is a part of everyday life in the organization and occurs throughout the organization rather than in the research and development department alone.

Intrapreneurship is entrepreneurial activity that takes place within the context of a large corporation.

Corporate Research   The most common means of developing innovation in the traditional organization is through corporate research, or research and development. Corporate research is usually set up to support existing businesses, provide incremental innovations in the organization's businesses, and explore potential new

Ed Sabol and his son, Steve, developed NFL Films into a $50 million business by doing what they love: watching and filming professional football. Based on Ed's passions for football and videotaping his son's football games, the company has become an innovator in the industry. Its first foray into filming the professional game focused on showing the beauty and passion of the game. Since then, in the face of mountains of competition, it still innovates in the use of color, camera positioning, the use of music, and narration. As a result the company has 89 Emmy awards. Always the creative one, Steve has been president since 1987. They used to give a $1,000 award to the most spectacular failure in order to stimulate ingenuity, innovation, and risk taking. Each cameraperson is his or her own director by selecting location and shots, all of which encourages creativity.

technology bases. It often takes place in a laboratory, either on the site of the main corporate facility or some distance away from normal operations.

Corporate researchers are responsible for keeping the company's products and processes technologically advanced. Product life cycles vary a great deal, depending on how fast products become obsolete and whether substitutes for the product are developed. Obviously, if a product becomes obsolete or some other product can be substituted for it, the profits from its sales will decrease. The job of corporate research is to prevent this from happening by keeping the company's products current.

The corporate culture can be instrumental in fostering an environment in which creativity and innovation occur. Sony and Hewlett-Packard are examples of two companies that are trying to change their organization cultures to be more innovative. The "Mastering Change" box describes how Hewlett-Packard, now merging with Compaq Computers to become HP-Compaq, is now struggling with combining its culture with Compaq's to create a new, innovative culture.

Empowerment

One of the most popular buzzwords in management today is "empowerment." Almost every new approach to quality, meeting the competition, getting more out of employees, productivity enhancement, and corporate turnarounds deals with employee empowerment. As

Empowerment is the process of enabling workers to set their own work goals, make decisions, and solve problems within their sphere of responsibility and authority.

we discussed in Chapter 7, **empowerment** is the process of enabling workers to set their own goals, make decisions, and solve problems within their spheres of responsibility and authority. Fads are often dismissed as meaningless and without substance because they are misused and overused, and the concept of empowerment, too, can be taken too lightly.

Empowerment is simple and complex at the same time. It is simple in that it tells managers to quit bossing people around so much and to let them do their jobs. It is complex in that managers and employees typically are not trained to do that. A significant amount of time, training, and practice may be needed to truly empower employees. In Chapter 7, we discussed some techniques for utilizing empowerment and conditions in which empowerment can be effective in organizations.

MASTERING CHANGE

▶ Will the HP Way Become the HP-Compaq Way?

Hewlett-Packard was founded in 1939 by Stanford University electrical engineering graduates Bill Hewlett and Dave Packard. Their first product, a sound equipment tester, was a smashing success—Disney ordered eight for its new movie, *Fantasia*. The two men worked together closely, using management practices considered radical at the time. They compiled the company's first written set of corporate objectives, an unusual practice for the period, in 1957; today these are known as the "HP Way." The seven objectives include the needs to make a sufficient but fair profit; to manufacture high-quality products; to explore new, related technologies; to seek corporate growth; to provide safety, job security, participation, and recognition for employees; to foster creativity; and to be socially responsible. As the company prospered, HP employees continued to be guided by the HP Way; in fact, employees still make decisions by asking, "What would Bill (or Dave) do?"

Today, however, the company with the strongly ingrained culture is merging with PC-manufacturer Compaq, and observers fear a culture clash. The merger makes strategic sense because the firms are moving toward a common goal. But does it make cultural sense? HP values tradition and history, moves slowly when making major changes, provides a high level of job security and benefits to employees, and tends to be bureaucratic and conservative. On the other hand, Compaq reinvents itself every few years, with radical shifts in strategy. HP CEO Carly Fiorina is a driving force behind the merger. She claims that the HP Way does not preclude changes. "This company has never been about looking in the rear-view mirror," says Fiorina, "though some people are more comfortable doing [that]."

> *"This company has never been about looking in the rear-view mirror."—Carly Fiorina, CEO of Hewlett-Packard*

A team of six hundred employees from both companies are developing an integrated culture during the transition, calling themselves "cultural astronauts." The team will not issue culture "directives" but instead will look for problems and deal with them one at a time. It is interesting that the merged firm is recognizing the need to focus on this often-overlooked area. Given that worker surveys at both Hewlett-Packard and Compaq show a high level of dissatisfaction with the merger, the combined firm is going to need all the help it can get.

References: "About HP: History and Facts—1950s," Hewlett-Packard web site. www.hp.com on June 21, 2002; Michael Davis, "Melding Cultures High on To-Do List: Compaq, HP Forge a Common Ground," *Houston Chronicle*, March 10, 2002, p. 1. See www.chron.com; Steve Lohr, "Hewlett Chief Battles for Her Deal and Her Career," *New York Times*, December 10, 2001 (quotation). www.nytimes.com on January 2, 2002; Mark Larson, "HP's Employee-Friendly Culture in Flux," *Sacramento Business Journal*, August 3, 2001. See www.bizjournals.com/sacramento; Eric Nee, "The Hard Truth Behind a Shotgun Wedding," *Fortune*, October 1, 2001. pp. 109–114. See www.fortune.com.

Empowerment can be much more than a motivational technique, however. In some organizations it is the cornerstone of organizational culture. At E*Trade, CEO Cotsakos believes that people should be empowered and then encouraged to take responsibility and solve their own problems. When the chief information officer and the chief financial officer got into what seemed to be an irresolvable spat, they turned to Cotsakos for resolution. He insisted that they work it out between them for the good of the company. He sent them each a bouquet of roses bearing the message "We're a team. Let's work it out." and made each think that the other had sent the flowers. The two executives resolved their problems and developed a better understanding of each other's role in the company.[41]

Empowerment can be viewed as liberating employees, but sometimes "empowerment" entails little more than delegating a task to an employee and then watching over the employee too closely. Employees may feel that this type of participation is superficial and that they are not really making meaningful decisions. The concept of liberating employees suggests that they should be free to do what they think is best without fear that the boss is standing by to veto or change the work they do.[42]

Procedural Justice

Procedural justice is the extent to which the dynamics of an organization's decision-making processes are judged to be fair by those most affected by them.

Another movement in management that may be viewed as a cultural issue is procedural justice. **Procedural justice** is the extent to which the dynamics of an organization's decision-making processes are judged to be fair by those most affected by them. Especially in the United States, employees are demanding more say in determining work rules and in matters pertaining to health and safety on the job and the provision of certain benefits for all employees. Furthermore, each generation of new employees may feel more entitled to having certain kinds of influence in the organization, especially on matters pertaining to their work. Employees who expect to have more input into decision making may or may not comply with decisions or directives from top management in which they have had little or no part.

The lack of procedural justice may lead to less compliant attitudes on the part of lower-level managers. This has been shown to come into play in strategic decision making in multinational organizations. The exercise of procedural justice can be an effective way to engender compliance from subsidiary managers in large multinationals.[43] The extent to which this movement continues may depend on the overall cultural shifts in society and the extent to which the employee empowerment becomes entrenched in organizations and in management practice.

Managing Organization Culture

The work of Ouchi, Peters and Waterman, and many others demonstrates two important facts. First, organization cultures differ among firms; second, these different organization cultures can affect a firm's performance. Based on these observations, managers have become more concerned about how to best manage the cultures of their organizations. The three elements of managing organization culture are (1) taking advantage of the existing culture, (2) teaching organization culture, and (3) changing the organization culture.

Taking Advantage of the Existing Culture

Most managers are not in a position to create an organization culture; rather, they work in organizations that already have cultural values. For these managers, the central issue in managing culture is how best to use the cultural system that already exists. It may be easier and faster to alter employee behaviors within the existing culture than it is to change the history, traditions, and values that already exist.[44]

"The benefit of having a strong culture is [that] it's binding."—John S. Reed, co-CEO of Citigroup[45]

To take advantage of an existing cultural system, managers must first be fully aware of the culture's values and what behaviors or actions those values support. Becoming fully aware of an organization's values usually is not easy, however; it involves more than reading a pamphlet about what the company believes in. Managers must

Procter & Gamble Co. is selling the nation's best-selling toothbrush, the $5 SpinBrush: a product they did not invent or develop, or even market initially. Its four developers did all that for them. P&G simply bought it from its developers for $475 million. In the highly competitive world of toothpaste and toothbrushes, a $5 spinning toothbrush was competing and winning lots of market share. They utilized the expertise and entrepreneurial spirit of its original developers by hiring them to work for P&G for a year and a half to make sure the well-entrenched culture of the 165-year-old company did not kill the new product. It worked, although it faced the old culture every step of the way, in terms of manufacturing, packaging, shipping, and advertising. The old company recognized that its culture, one that had worked so well for myriads of products over the years, would not work for this new one.

Socialization is the process through which individuals become social beings.

Organizational socialization is the process through which employees learn about the firm's culture and pass their knowledge and understanding on to others.

develop a deep understanding of how organizational values operate in the firm—an understanding that usually comes only through experience.

This understanding, once achieved, can be used to evaluate the performances of others in the firm. Articulating organizational values can be useful in managing others' behaviors. For example, suppose a subordinate in a firm with a strong cultural value of "sticking to its knitting" develops a business strategy that involves moving into a new industry. Rather than attempting to argue that this business strategy is economically flawed or conceptually weak, the manager who understands the corporate culture can point to the company's organizational value: "In this firm, we believe in sticking to our knitting."

Senior managers who understand their organization's culture can communicate that understanding to lower-level individuals. Over time, as these lower-level managers begin to understand and accept the firm's culture, they will require less direct supervision. Their understanding of corporate values will guide their decision making.

Teaching the Organization Culture: Socialization

Socialization is the process through which individuals become social beings.[46] As studied by psychologists, it is the process through which children learn to become adults in a society—how they learn what is acceptable and polite behavior and what is not, how they learn to communicate, how they learn to interact with others, and so on. In complex societies, the socialization process takes many years.

Organizational socialization is the process through which employees learn about their firm's culture and pass their knowledge and understanding on to others. Employees are socialized into organizations, just as people are socialized into societies; that is, they come to know over time what is acceptable in the organization and what is not, how to communicate their feelings, and how to interact with others. They learn both through observation and through efforts by managers to communicate this information to them. Research into the process of socialization indicates that for many employees, socialization programs do not necessarily

Fortunately, while most organizations have a distinct corporate culture with specific organizational values, not all employees would classify their office "families" as "dysfunctional." A strong organizational culture can enhance performance and create loyal employees. However, not all organizations have cultures that value and promote high performance, and in these cases attempting to change the organization's culture, while often difficult, can be rewarding in terms of productivity and performance.

Reference: © Randy Glasbergen

**"At my office we're not just coworkers,
we're like a family. A very dysfunctional family."**

change their values, but instead they make employees more aware of the differences between personal and organization values and help them develop ways to cope with the differences.[47]

A variety of organizational mechanisms can affect the socialization of workers in organizations. Probably the most important are the examples that new employees see in the behavior of experienced people. Through observing examples, new employees develop a repertoire of stories they can use to guide their actions. When a decision needs to be made, new employees can ask, "What would my boss do in this situation?" This is not to suggest that formal training, corporate pamphlets, and corporate statements about organization culture are unimportant in the socialization process. However, these factors tend to support the socialization process based on people's close observations of the actions of others.

In some organizations, the culture described in pamphlets and presented in formal training sessions conflicts with the values of the organization as they are expressed in the actions of its people. For example, a firm may say that employees are its most important asset but treat employees badly. In this setting, new employees quickly learn that the rhetoric of the pamphlets and formal training sessions has little to do with the real organization culture. Employees who are socialized into this system usually come to accept the actual cultural values rather than those formally espoused.

Changing the Organization Culture

Much of our discussion to this point has assumed that an organization's culture enhances its performance. When this is the case, learning what an organization's cultural values are and using those values to help socialize new workers and managers is very important, for such actions help the organization succeed. However, as Ouchi's and Peters and Waterman's research indicates, not all firms have cultural values that are consistent with high performance. Ouchi found that Japanese firms and U.S. Type Z firms have performance-enhancing values. Peters and Waterman identified performance-enhancing values associated with successful companies. By implication, some firms not included in Peters and Waterman's study must have had performance-reducing values. What should a manager who works in a company with performance-reducing values do?

The answer to this question is, of course, that top managers in such firms should try to change their organization's culture. However, this is a difficult thing to do.[48] Organization culture resists change for all the reasons that it is a powerful influence on behavior—it embodies the firm's basic values, it is often taken for granted, and it is typically communicated most effectively through stories or other symbols. When managers attempt to change organization culture, they are attempting to change people's basic assumptions about what is and is not appropriate behavior in the organization. Changing from a traditional organization to a team-based organization (discussed in Chapter 12) is one example of an organization culture change. Another is Boeing's decision in 1999 to change from a family culture to a performance culture.[49]

Despite these difficulties, some organizations have changed their cultures from performance-reducing to performance-enhancing.[50] This change process is described in more detail in Chapter 19. The earlier section on creating organization culture describes the importance of linking the strategic values and the cultural values in creating a new organization culture. We briefly discuss other important elements of the cultural change process in the following sections.

Managing Symbols   Research suggests that organization culture is understood and communicated through the use of stories and other symbolic media. If this is correct, managers interested in changing cultures should attempt to substitute stories and myths that support new cultural values for those that support old ones. They can do so by creating situations that give rise to new stories.

Suppose an organization traditionally has held the value "employee opinions are not important." When management meets in this company, the ideas and opinions of lower-level people—when discussed at all—are normally rejected as foolish and irrelevant. The stories that support this cultural value tell about managers who tried to make a constructive point only to have that point lost in personal attacks from superiors.

An upper-level manager interested in creating a new story, one that shows lower-level managers that their ideas are valuable, might ask a subordinate to prepare to lead a discussion in a meeting and follow through by asking the subordinate to take the lead when the topic arises. The subordinate's success in the meeting will become a new story, one that may displace some of the many stories suggesting that the opinions of lower-level managers do not matter.

The Difficulty of Change   Changing a firm's culture is a long and difficult process. A primary problem is that upper-level managers, no matter how dedicated they are to implementing some new cultural value, may sometimes inadvertently revert to old patterns of behavior. This happens, for example, when a manager dedicated to implementing the value that lower-level employees' ideas are important vehemently attacks a subordinate's ideas.

This mistake generates a story that supports old values and beliefs. After such an incident, lower-level managers may believe that the boss seems to want employee input and ideas, but nothing could be further from the truth. No matter what the boss says or how consistent his/her behavior is, some credibility has been lost, and cultural change has been made more difficult.

The Stability of Change   The process of changing a firm's culture starts with a need for change and moves through a transition period in which efforts are made to adopt new values and beliefs. In the long run, a firm that successfully changes its culture will find that the new values and beliefs are just as stable and influential as the old ones. Value systems tend to be self-reinforcing. Once they are in place, changing them requires an enormous effort. Thus, if a firm can change its culture from performance-reducing to performance-enhancing, the new values are likely to remain in place for a long time.

Synopsis

Organization culture has become one of the most discussed subjects in the field of organization behavior. It burst on the scene in the 1980s with books by Ouchi, Peters and Waterman, and others. Interest has not been restricted to academics, however. Practicing managers are also interested in organization culture, especially as it relates to performance.

There is little agreement about how to define organization culture. A comparison of several important definitions suggests that most have three things in common: They define culture in terms of the values that individuals in organizations use to prescribe appropriate behavior, they assume that these values are usually taken for granted, and they emphasize the stories and other symbolic means through which the values are typically communicated.

Current research on organization culture reflects various research traditions. The most important contributions have come from anthropology and sociology. Anthropologists have tended to focus on the organization cultures of one or two firms and have used detailed descriptions to help outsiders understand organization culture from the "natives' point of view." Sociologists typically have used survey methods to study the organization cultures of larger numbers of firms. Two other influences on current work in organization culture are social psychology, which emphasizes the manipulation of symbols in organizations, and economics. The economics approach sees culture both as a tool used to manage and as a determinant of performance.

Creating organization culture is a five-step process. It starts with formulating strategic and cultural values for the organization. Next, a vision for the organization is created, followed by the institution of implementation strategies. The final step is reinforcing the cultural behaviors of employees.

Although no single framework for describing organization culture has emerged, several have been suggested. The most popular efforts in this area have been Ouchi's comparison of U.S. and Japanese firms and Peters and Waterman's description of successful firms in the United States. Ouchi and Peters and Waterman suggested several important dimensions along which organization values vary, including treatment of employees, definitions of appropriate means for decision making, and assignment of responsibility for the results of decision making.

Emerging issues in the area of organization culture include innovation, employee empowerment, and procedural justice. Innovation is the process of creating and doing new things that are introduced into the marketplace as products, processes, or services. The organization culture can either help or hinder innovation. Employee empowerment, in addition to being similar to employee participation as a motivation technique, is now viewed by some as a type of organization culture. Empowerment occurs when employees make decisions, set their own work goals, and solve problems in their own area of responsibility. Procedural justice is the extent to which the dynamics of an organization's decision-making processes are judged to be fair by those most affected by them.

Managing the organization culture requires attention to three factors. First, managers can take advantage of cultural values that already exist and use their knowledge to help subordinates understand them. Second, employees need to be properly socialized, or trained, in the cultural values of the organization, either through formal training or by experiencing and observing the actions of higher-level managers. Third, managers can change the culture of the organization through managing the symbols, addressing the extreme difficulties of such a change, and relying on the durability of the new organization culture once the change has been implemented.

Discussion Questions

1. A sociologist or anthropologist might suggest that the culture in U.S. firms simply reflects the dominant culture of the society as a whole. Therefore, to change the organization culture of a company, one must first deal with the inherent values and beliefs of the society. How would you respond to this claim?

2. Psychology has been defined as the study of individual behavior. Organizational psychology is the study of individual behavior in organizations. Many of the theories described in the early chapters of this book are based in organizational psychology. Why was this field not identified as a contributor to the study of organization culture along with anthropology, sociology, social psychology, and economics?

3. Describe the culture of an organization with which you are familiar. It might be one in which you currently work, one in which you have worked, or one in which a friend or family member works. What values, beliefs, stories, and symbols are significant to employees of the organization?

4. Discuss the similarities and differences between the organization culture approaches of Ouchi and Peters and Waterman.

5. Describe how organizations use symbols and stories to communicate values and beliefs. Give some examples of how symbols and stories have been used in organizations with which you are familiar.

6. What is the role of leadership (discussed in Chapters 13 and 14) in developing, maintaining, and changing organization culture?

7. Review the characteristics of organization structure described in earlier chapters and compare them with the elements of culture described by Ouchi and Peters and Waterman. Describe the similarities and differences, and explain how some characteristics of one may be related to characteristics of the other.

8. Discuss the role of organization rewards in developing, maintaining, and changing the organization culture.

9. How are empowerment and procedural justice similar? How do they differ?

10. Describe how the culture of an organization can affect innovation.

Organizational Behavior Case for Discussion

Microsoft: Cult or Culture?

The words "culture" and "cult" sprang from a common source, the Latin word "colere," which means "to cultivate." From that origin, two distinct meanings emerged—"culture" became defined as "socially transmitted behavior patterns, arts, beliefs, and other products of human work and thought" while "cult" took on a somewhat different connotation as "a system or community of religious worship and ritual." The words have separate meanings, but both have been significant in describing Microsoft Corporation under the direction of founder Bill Gates and CEO Steve Ballmer.

Gates began Microsoft in 1976 with Paul Allen. Their first blockbuster product, MS-DOS, was released in 1981. Windows was introduced to the public in 1985, and since then the company has saturated the PC software market with products covering the entire range of applications, from word processing to video editing to web surfing. The software giant has continued to grow internally and through acquisitions until today it employs almost 50,000 people worldwide.

Throughout the expansion, Microsoft's culture has remained recognizable and extremely effective. Its core values include an us-versus-them mentality, a fierce competitiveness, an ethic of hard work, and a strong bonding of coworkers. One former employee says, "By the time I was in my 20s, Microsoft was my whole identity." Another ex-employee, Scott Sandell, states, "Microsoft has a cult-like culture. It [either] assimilates you or spits you out." Microsoft has been humorously compared to the science-fictional "Borg" race of the *Star Trek: The Next Generation* television series, whose motto is "You will be assimilated. Resistance is futile." The analogy works both for Microsoft's attitudes toward competitors—they are either acquired or imitated—as well as toward its employees.

Marc Andreessen, formerly CEO of Netscape and cofounder of Loudcloud, believes that a start-up's founder has a strong influence on the development of the organization's culture and the employees' behavior. "These companies are like organisms. It's as if you took a DNA sample from the chief executive and blew it up to monstrous size. The founder and the company share all the same strengths and weaknesses," he explains. That certainly seems to be the case with Microsoft since employees have copied every detail of Gates's behavior, including his dress and speaking style. And the phenomenon extends beyond Microsoft. Other founders who have shaped their enterprises include Sam Walton, whose plain spoken, down-home style is still evident at Wal-Mart; and Arthur Andersen, whose military-style discipline shaped the accounting partnership's reporting structure and career paths.

In January of 2000, Gates resigned as CEO, and Steve Ballmer, who had been president, assumed the top role. At the time there was speculation that Microsoft might soften its competitive stance, lose its sharp focus on innovation, or even agree to split the firm in order to settle the Department of Justice's antitrust suit. None of those things happened, and, in fact, the company structure has remained very much the same, and business is being conducted as usual. If anything, Microsoft today is regarded as an even more unrepentant monopolist. This is not surprising, given that Ballmer has worked at Microsoft since 1980 and is often described as Gates's "best friend."

Is this conformity to a strong organization culture an asset or a liability? Some believe that the question is beside the point because they feel that a "personality cult" around the company founder is inevitable in high-tech startups. "Other industries hire people for jobs. The assets are in real estate or a factory. But in high tech, the people are the assets. So you need a charismatic leader to attract the people," former Microsoft executive Naveen Jain says. Although some individuals have become disenchanted, many more remain in awe of Gates's accomplishments in creating a cohesive and high-performance culture that has endured even his resignation as CEO.

In Microsoft's latest configuration, CEO Ballmer is in charge of strategy, marketing, and public relations while president Richard Belluzzo takes over finance, logistics, and other operations, leaving Gates

the task of creating software architecture. Together the three decided that the firm's old vision—a computer on every desk and in every home—had essentially been realized and that a new vision was needed. The firm's new vision is to "empower people through great software—any time, any place, and on any device," and it seems to be working. *Fortune* writer Brent Schlender says, "A new cohesion of purpose and sense of inventiveness pervade the company." As the company's culture continues to grow stronger, its challengers are disappearing or retreating. And it seems destined to continue its domination of the high-tech industry. Mark Eppley, CEO of specialty software maker Laplink, describes Microsoft's position as the ultimate in "assimilation," saying, "Microsoft is the ocean. The rest of us are fish swimming in it."

"Microsoft is the ocean. The rest of us are fish swimming in it."—Mark Eppley, CEO, Laplink, provider of Internet remote access technology

References: Jay Greene, "Ballmer's Microsoft," *Business Week*, June 17, 2002. www.businessweek.com on June 18, 2002; Eryn Brown, "Just Another Product Launch," *Fortune*, November 12, 2001. www.fortune.com on June 18, 2002; Fred Vogelstein, "The Long Shadow of XP," *Fortune*, November 12, 2001 (quotation). www.fortune.com on June 18, 2002; Brent Schlender, "The Beast Is Back," *Fortune*, June 11, 2001. www.fortune.com on June 18, 2002; David Streitfeld, "Gates Leads Company Cult of Personality," *Arizona Republic* (Phoenix), May 8, 2000, pp. D1, D4. See www.azcentral.com; *Webster's Revised Unabridged Dictionary*, Random House, 1998. www.dictionary.com on June 18, 2002.

Case Questions

1. Using the Ouchi framework, describe Microsoft's organization culture. (Hint: Use Table 18.3 of your text.) Address each of the seven cultural values. Is Microsoft more like a Type Z firm or like a typical U.S. firm. Why?

2. What are the advantages of Microsoft's culture for the firm? What are the disadvantages? In your opinion, is there anything that Microsoft managers can do to lessen or eliminate the disadvantages?

3. Can you give examples of the effects of a founder or other influential leader on an organization's culture other than those mentioned in the case? Consider, for example, a religious institution, a sports team, a classroom, or a company at which you have worked. Was the influence direct, such as an order or a policy, or was it indirect?

Experiencing Organizational Behavior

Culture of the Classroom

Purpose: This exercise will help you appreciate the fascination as well as the difficulty of examining culture in organizations.

Format: The class will divide into groups of four to six. Each group will analyze the organization culture of a college class. Students in most classes that use this book will have taken many courses at the college they attend and therefore should have several classes in common.

Procedure: The class is divided into groups of four to six on the basis of classes the students have had in common.

1. Each group should first decide which class it will analyze. Each person in the group must have attended the class.

2. Each group should list the cultural factors to be discussed. Items to be covered should include

   a. Stories about the professor
   b. Stories about the exams
   c. Stories about the grading
   d. Stories about other students
   e. The use of symbols that indicate the students' values
   f. The use of symbols that indicate the instructor's values
   g. Other characteristics of the class as suggested by the frameworks of Ouchi and Peters and Waterman.

3. Students should carefully analyze the stories and symbols to discover their underlying meanings. They should seek stories from other members of the group to ensure that all aspects of the class culture are covered. Students should take notes as these items are discussed.

4. After twenty to thirty minutes of work in groups, the instructor will reconvene the entire class and ask each group to share its analysis with the rest of the class.

Follow-up Questions

1. What was the most difficult part of this exercise? Did other groups experience the same difficulty?

2. How did your group overcome this difficulty? How did other groups overcome it?

3. Do you believe your group's analysis accurately describes the culture of the class you selected? Could other students who analyzed the culture of the same class come up with a very different result? How could that happen?

4. If the instructor wanted to try to change the culture in the class you analyzed, what steps would you recommend that he or she take?

Self-Assessment Exercise

An Empowering Culture: What It Is and What It Is Not

What does it mean to empower people? Below is a brief definition, along with three behaviors that masquerade as empowerment, often with devastating results. See how well you can distinguish among them by choosing the one that best describes the supervisory behavior. Answers appear in *the Instructor's Resource Manual*. The quiz and answers were prepared by Donna Deeprose of Deeprose Consulting in New York.

Empower: To enable an employee to set work goals, make decisions, and solve problems

Exploit: To take advantage of an employee to meet an unspoken goal of one's own

Abandon: To delegate but provide no support

Delude: To give the appearance of empowering but to withhold the freedom the employee needs to be successful

1. A supervisor gives an employee authority to handle a project. When the employee complains about difficulties, the supervisor responds, "Don't worry, I'll handle it from now on."

   Behavior: _____

2. Same situation as (1), except that when the employee comes to the supervisor for help, the supervisor's response is "This is your project. You take care of it."

   Behavior: _____

3. Same as (1) and (2), except that the supervisor discusses the problem with the employee and guides the employee into determining an appropriate next move.

   Behavior: _____

4. An employee has asked for additional responsibilities. The supervisor delegates to the employee total responsibility for a time-consuming report. The supervisor leaves at 5 P.M. each day while the employee works late to complete the report.

   Behavior: _____

5. A supervisor keeps up with the company's changing mission, objectives, and plans, and keeps employees informed of how well all these changes influence the work unit.

   Behavior: _____

Reference: Reprinted from "Understanding the E-Word," *Supervisory Management*, November 1993, pp. 7–8. American Management Association International. Reprinted by permission of American Management Association International, New York, NY. All rights reserved.

 # OB Online

1. As you near graduation, you may become interested in interviewing for a job you can take after graduation. Pick several companies that you think you might want to work for. Rank-order the companies in the order in which you would choose to work for them (at least at this point). Then, starting from the top, look up articles on the management of each company, searching specifically for articles that describe something about the culture of the company. Not all companies have articles written about them that describe their culture, so it may take several tries to find articles that do. Remember, an article that has a description of an organization's culture may not always use the word "culture," so read carefully.

2. Describe the kinds of information you were able to locate. How much valuable information on culture did the articles provide?

3. What other information do you need to better understand the culture of these companies?

4. Would you change your initial preference ranking based on the information that you found?

 # Building Managerial Skills

Exercise Overview: Typically, managers are promoted or selected to fill jobs in an organization with a given organization culture. As they begin to work, they must recognize the culture and either learn how to work within it or figure out how to change it. If the culture is a performance-reducing one, managers must figure out how to change the culture to a performance-enhancing one. This exercise will give you a chance to develop your own ideas about changing organization culture.

Exercise Background: Assume that you have just been appointed to head the legislative affairs committee of your local student government. As someone with a double major in business management and government, you are eager to take on this assignment and really make a difference. This committee has existed at your university for several years, but it has done little because the members use the committee as a social group and regularly throw great parties. In all the years of its existence, the commitee has done nothing to impact the local state legislature in relation to the issues important to university students, such as tuition. Since you know that the issue of university tuition will come before the state legislature during the current legislative session, and you know that many students could not afford a substantial raise in tuition, you are determined to use this committee to ensure that any tuition increase is as small as possible. However, you are worried that the party culture of the existing committee may make it difficult for you to use it to work for your issues. You also know that you cannot "fire" any of the volunteers on the committee and can only add two people to the committee.

Exercise Task: Using this information as context, do the following:

1. Design a strategy for utilizing the existing culture of the committee to help you impact the legislature regarding tuition.

2. Assuming that the existing culture is a performance-reducing culture, design a strategy for changing it to a performance-enhancing culture.

19 Organization Change and Development

Management Preview

▶ Companies constantly face pressures to change. Significant decreases in revenues and profits, forecasts of changing economic conditions, consumer purchasing patterns, technological and scientific factors, and competition, both foreign and domestic, can force top management to evaluate their organization and consider significant changes.

This chapter presents several perspectives on change in organizations. First, we examine the forces for change and discuss several approaches to planned organization change. Then, we consider organization development processes and the resistance to change that usually occurs. The chapter briefly covers several international and cross-cultural factors that affect organization change processes. Finally, we disuss how to manage organization change and development efforts in organizations. First, however, we describe how Jean-Marie Messier has changed a small water company in France into a media and entertainment giant.

▼ ▼ ▼

In 1996, when Jean-Marie Messier was name chairman of the French conglomerate Compagnie Générale des Eaux, the appointing board did not anticipate the wild ride of changes that were in store for the tradition-bound firm. CGE, which roughly translates as the "General Water Company," has a proud history; it was founded in 1853 by decree of Emperor Napoleon III, nephew of Napoleon I, to sell municipal water to Lyons. For more than one hundred years, the firm expanded slowly into other utilities, such as waste management and energy. It began to move into cable and other media ventures, and in 1988 changed its name to Vivendi to reflect its growing diversification.

Messier began with a reorganization, creating two divisions—environment and communications—and selling all other assets. The CEO then made an aggressive series of acquisitions to move the company into the entertainment and consumer-products industries, forming four divisions: music, publishing, TV and film, and Internet. The conglomerate now has acquired more than three hundred companies and brands, artistic management and production enterprises, and entertainment products. Among the recognizable names on its roster are *American Pie*, *A Beautiful Mind*, Blink 182, Crash Bandicoot video games, Curious George children's books, *E. T.*, Elton John, Enrique Iglesias, George Strait, Houghton Mifflin Company (which publishes this textbook), the *Jerry Springer Show*, Jump Start educational software, *Jurassic Park*, *Law and Order*, Limp Bizkit, Mary J. Blige, MCA Records, Motown Records, mp3.com, tenor Placido Domingo, *Rolling Stone* magazine, the Sci-Fi Channel, Spencer Gifts, *The Mummy*, U2, Universal Studios and Theme Parks, the USA Network, and European web portal Vivazzi. Messier says, "For the first time in five years, we can now say that there are no parts missing in the strategy."

Some remain skeptical of Vivendi's phenomenal growth during Messier's tenure as CEO. In spite of a $30.8 billion acquisition-related debt, synergies among units have been slow to develop. European companies have a poor track record in American media. And the company's hands-off management style, promised as part of many of its acquisition deals, could lead to a problematic lack of corporate control. Messier has tangled with the French government— he refused to pay particularly high telecom licensing fees. When Messier fired several low-performing but top-level managers, he was accused of ruining a French "national treasure" (Canal+, a French cable system). Messier is also battling government labor regulations, including a mandatory 35-hour workweek.

> *"It's rare to have a CEO who succeeds in expressing his personal emotions. That's the way I am, and it's too late to change myself."—Jean-Marie Messier, CEO of Vivendi*

Europeans resent what some regard as the "Americanization" of Messier and Vivendi. Ever since his public-service days, when he championed privatization of French industries, Messier has been accused of promoting "Anglo-Saxon capitalism." The contention is well founded. Vivendi shifted to American accounting principles to make the company more transparent and acceptable to American investors. Messier, who speaks perfect English, calls himself "the most un-French Frenchman you'll ever meet." When he received the French Legion of Honor, the typically elegant and dull event was transformed into a gaudy multimedia show. French society reacted with shock and outrage, exactly what Messier intended, his supporters say. Expressing a sentiment more American than French, Messier claims, "It's rare to have a CEO who succeeds in expressing his personal emotions. That's the way I am, and it's too late to change myself." It is unclear how, or if, Messier will overcome his problems, which, according to *Business Week* writer Ron Grover, include the fact that "he isn't American enough to satisfy U.S. investors[,] . . . and he isn't French enough to satisfy the hometown crew, who worry that he has gone Hollywood."[1]

References: "2001—The Year in Brief," "Company Profile," "Executive Bio," "Our Leaders," "The Group History," "What We Do," Vivendi web site. www.vivendiuniversal.com on June 22, 2002; Janet Guyon, "Getting Messier by the Minute," *Fortune*, June 10, 2002. www.fortune.com on June 22, 2002; Ron Glover, "A Loser's Race for Media Moguls," *Business Week*, June 6, 2002. www.businessweek.com on June 22, 2002; Geoffrey Colvin, "Culture in Peril? Mais Oui!" *Fortune*, May 13, 2002. www.fortune.com on June 22, 2002; Richard Tomlinson, "The Nouveau CEO," *Fortune*, December 10, 2001. www.fortune.com on June 22, 2002; Devin Leonard, "Mr. Messier Is Ready For His Close-Up," *Fortune*, September 3, 2001 (quotation). www.fortune.com on June 22, 2002.

Jean-Marie Messier made many changes at Vivendi that he thought were necessary given his vision of what the strategy for the company should be. This was not a turn-around situation for a company in trouble. In this case, his view of what the company should be in order to maximize shareholder wealth was the trigger for the changes that he made. Undoubtedly, Messier (who resigned his position in July of 2002) saw opportunities in the environment that matched the capabilities of the organization, so he sought to exploit them. In this case, there was great resistance to the changes he made, both to the actual changes as well as to the ways in which he made them. The changes at Vivendi illustrate many key issues regarding change in organizations.

Forces for Change

An organization is subject to pressures for change from far too many sources that can be discussed here. Moreover, it is difficult to predict what types of pressures for change will be most significant in the next decade because the complexity of events and the rapidity of change are increasing. However, it is possible—and important—to discuss the broad categories of pressures that probably will have major effects on organizations. The four areas in which the pressures for change appear most powerful involve people, technology, information processing and communication, and competition. Table 19.1 gives examples of each of these categories.

People

Approximately 56 million people were born between 1945 and 1960. These baby boomers differ significantly from previous generations with respect to education, expectations, and value systems.[2] As this group has aged, the median age of the U.S. population has gradually increased, passing 32 for the first time in 1988[3] and further increasing to 35.6 in 1999.[4] The special characteristics of baby boomers show up in distinct purchasing patterns that affect product and service innovation, technological change, and marketing and promotional activities.[5] Employment practices, compensation systems, promotion and managerial succession systems, and the entire concept of human resource management are also affected.

table 19.1

Pressures for Organization Change

Category	Examples	Type of Pressure for Change
People	Generation X Baby boomers Senior citizens Workforce diversity	Demands for different training, benefits, workplace arrangements, and compensation systems
Technology	Manufacturing in space Internet Artificial Intelligence	More education and training for workers at all levels, more new products, products move faster to market
Information Processing and Communication	Computer, satellite communications Videoconferencing	Faster reaction times, immediate responses to questions, new products, different office arrangements, telecommuting
Competition	Worldwide markets International trade agreements Emerging nations	Global competition, more competing products with more features and options, lower costs, higher quality

Other population-related pressures for change involve the generations that sandwich the baby boomers: the increasing numbers of senior citizens and those born after 1960. The parents of the baby boomers are living longer, healthier lives than previous generations, and today they expect to live the "good life" that they missed when they were raising their children. The impact of the large number of senior citizens is already evident in part-time employment practices, in the marketing of everything from hamburgers to packaged tours of Asia, and in service areas such as health care, recreation, and financial services. The post-1960 generation of workers who are entering the job market also differ from the baby boomers. These changes in demographics extend to the composition of the workforce, family lifestyles, and purchasing patterns worldwide. The makeover of Avon in response to changes in the population and workforce is described in the "Working with Diversity" box.

The increasing diversity of the workforce in coming years will mean significant changes for organizations. This increasing diversity was discussed in some detail in Chapter 3. In addition, employees are facing a different work environment in the twenty-first century. The most descriptive word for this new work environment is "change." Employees must be prepared for constant change. Change is occurring in organizations' cultures, structures, work relationships, and customer relationships, as well as in the actual jobs that people do. People will have to be completely adaptable to new situations while maintaining productivity under the existing system.[6]

Technology

Not only is technology changing, but the rate of technological change is also increasing. In 1970, for example, all engineering students owned slide rules and used them in almost every class. By 1976, slide rules had given way to portable electronic calculators. In the mid-1980s, some universities began issuing microcomputers to entering students or assumed that those students already owned them. In 1993, the Scholastic Aptitude Test (SAT), which many college-bound students take to get into college, allowed calculators to be used during the test! Today students cannot make it through the university without owning or at least having ready access to a personal computer. The dormitory rooms at many universities are wired for direct computer access for email and class assignments and for connection to the Internet. Technological development is increasing so rapidly in almost every field that it is quite difficult to predict which products will dominate ten years from now. DuPont is an example of a company that is making major changes due to new technological developments. Although its business had been based on petrochemicals since the end of the nineteenth century, as new technology has developed in the life sciences, DuPont has changed its basic business strategy, reorganized its eighty-one business units into three, and invested heavily in agrichemicals and the life sciences. Realizing that a biotechnology-based business changes much more rapidly than a petrochemical-based business, Chairman Chad Holliday has had to make cultural changes as well as structural ones in order to make the strategy work.[7]

Interestingly, organization change is self-perpetuating. With the advances in information technology, organizations generate more information, and it circulates more quickly. Consequently, employees can respond more quickly to problems, so the organization can respond more quickly to demands from other organizations, customers, and competitors.[8]

WORKING WITH DIVERSITY

A Makeover at Avon

What could possibly be more dated than the 1950s version of the Avon Lady, perfectly dressed down to her white gloves, ringing doorbells on weekday mornings to sell lipstick and perfume to stay-at-home moms? "Ding-dong. Avon calling." Yet today, thanks to savvy business moves by CEO Andrea Jung, the retailer is thriving, and so is the Avon Lady.

Today's Avon Lady is likely to be a young professional woman who supplements her income by selling products ranging from perfume and cosmetics to exercise equipment and vitamins to both men and women. She profits not only from sales but also from recruitment bonuses she earns for attracting new representatives, and she uses the Internet to find customers, place orders, and advertise. All of these changes were either introduced or advanced by Jung, who took the CEO role in 2000. Her other strategies for change include selling a new line of cosmetics in mall kiosks and at J. C. Penney's under the brand name "Becoming" and focusing more on the international market, where 62 percent of the firm's sales occur.

Jung, the first woman to head Avon, has teamed with President Susan Kropf to improve back-office operations, reducing costs in R&D, purchasing, and logistics while also getting innovative products to market faster. Jung and Kropf agree that a female executive has only a minor advantage in the glamour industry. "You go home and try on a new mascara, and I guess a male CEO can't do that," Jung wryly notes. Kropf points out, "Maybe, on the periphery, there is a greater personal affinity for the products we sell.

"You go home and try on a new mascara. . . . I guess a male CEO can't do that."—Andrea Jung, CEO, Avon Products

[But] in terms of leadership, the strategy, the disciplines, [and] the analytical rigor, it doesn't matter if you're a man, woman, dog, or cat. There is no gender consideration."

The two leaders do believe, however, that their gender allows them to relate well to the company's 500,000 representatives, the majority of whom are female. Jung asserts, "[Women] see that the glass ceiling has been broken at Avon."

References: "Let's Talk About Avon," Avon web site. www.avoncompany.com on June 18, 2002; Diane Brady, "A Makeover Has Avon Looking Good," *Business Week*, January 22, 2002. www.businessweek.com on June 18, 2002; Patricia O'Connell, "Meet the Avon Ladies-In-Chief," *Business Week*, January 22, 2002. www.businessweek.com on June 18, 2002; Katrina Booker, "It Took a Lady To Save Avon," *Fortune*, October 15, 2001. pp. 202–208. See www.fortune.com; Jennifer Pellet, "Ding-dong Avon Stalling?" *Chief Executive*, June 2000, pp. 26–31 (quote). See www.chiefexecutive.net.

New technology will affect organizations in ways we cannot yet predict. Artificial intelligence—computers and software programs that think and learn in much the same way as humans do—is already assisting in geological exploration.[9] Several companies are developing systems to manufacture chemicals and exotic electronic components in space. The Internet and the World Wide Web are changing the way companies and individuals communicate, market, buy, and distribute faster than organizations can respond. Thus, as organizations react more quickly to changes, change occurs more rapidly, which in turn necessitates more rapid responses.

Information Processing and Communication

Advances in information processing and communication have paralleled each other. A new generation of computers, which will mark another major increase in processing power, is being designed. Satellite systems for data transmission are already in use. Today people carry telephones in their briefcases along with their portable computers, pocket-size televisions, music players, and pagers.

Cell phone giants such as Nokia, Motorola, and Erikson have had a stranglehold on the worldwide cellular phone market. All three have major operations in China, manufacturing and selling in Asia as well as the rest of the world. That world is changing fast, however. The new competition may soon be from Chinese companies. More than 30 Chinese companies are now manufacturing cellular phones and working with software providers Microsoft and Qualcomm Inc. to develop much lower priced handsets. Nokia and the others had better watch out!

In the future, people may not need offices as they work with computers and communicate through new data transmission devices. Work stations, both in and outside of offices, will be more electronic than paper and pencil. For years, the capability has existed to generate, manipulate, store, and transmit more data than managers could use, but the benefits were not fully realized. Now the time has come to utilize all of that information-processing potential, and companies are making the most of it. Typically, companies received orders by mail in the 1970s, by toll-free telephone numbers in the 1980s, by fax machine in the late 1980s and early 1990s, and by electronic data exchange in the mid-1990s. Orders used to take a week; now they are placed instantaneously, and companies must be able to respond immediately, all because of changes in information processing and communication.[10] As described in the "Talking Technology" box, systems integrators such as Context Integration are providing new knowledge management systems to help companies outthink their competition.

Competition

Although competition is not a new force for change, competition today has some significant new twists. First, most markets are international because of decreasing transportation and communication costs and the increasing export orientation of business. The adoption of trade agreements such as the North American Free Trade Agreement (NAFTA) and the presence of the World Trade Organization (WTO) have changed the way business operates. In the future, competition from industrialized countries such as Japan and Germany will take a back seat to competition from the booming industries of developing nations. The Internet is creating new competitors overnight and in ways that could not have been imagined five years ago.

"There are always challengers. We've seen them before. They are good for us. They make us work harder."—John Chambers, Cisco CEO[11]

Companies in developing nations may soon offer different, newer, cheaper, or higher-quality products while enjoying the benefits of low labor costs, abundant supplies of raw materials, expertise in certain areas of production, and financial protec-

TALKING TECHNOLOGY

▶ *Outthinking the Competition at Context Integration*

It was Sunday morning, and technology consultant Ken Sheldon was in trouble. An e-commerce project with a Monday deadline had run into a snag, and Sheldon could not find the fix. It sounds like a recipe for disaster—missed deadline, unhappy client, lost credibility. But Sheldon got some expert advice, fixed the problem, and met the deadline, all thanks to the knowledge management system in place at his employer, Houston-based Context Integration.

Context Integration is an e-commerce systems integrator whose power derives from its ability to solve clients' problems with technical expertise. *Fast Company* writer Chuck Salter describes the situation at Context Integration and other knowledge-based firms by saying, "Winning companies don't just outhustle or outmuscle the competition. They out-think the competition. Business today is about brains, not brawn. It's about how many ideas you generate, not how many factories you own." Context Integration also must quickly and efficiently share the group's collective knowledge with employees scattered around the country.

Context Integration programmers developed a knowledge-management system called IAN (Intellectual Assets Network). IAN combines a database of project summaries, skills inventories, employee résumés, client information, and other relevant information with a web-based interface for ease of data entry and retrieval. Employees can also access IAN via cell phone or pager. A full-time knowledge manager who monitors usage, enforces organization, and purges outdated information oversees IAN.

Some users were initially reluctant. Bruce Strong, an IAN developer, says, "Coming out of the gate, we had a ton of good will. Then the challenge of real-world pressures

> *"Winning companies don't just outhustle or outmuscle the competition. They out-think the competition."—Chuck Salter, Fast Company, writer*

start beating down on [our] head[s]." An easy-to-use design helped; so did the experience of the knowledge manager, but more was still needed. Some felt that using IAN was too much trouble. Others did not like publicly admitting that they needed help. Some managers opposed the rigid structure required by IAN's database.

Context Integration CEO Stephen Sharp made using IAN a part of everyone's job description, recognized strong contributors, and even based 10 percent of each employee's quarterly bonus on IAN contributions and usage. As a result, IAN participation doubled. Today, the tool has become a valuable part of the company. "You don't want to be the person [who] doesn't use IAN at all," says Sharp. "It's your performance—it's how we view you."

References: "Intellectual Assets Network (IAN)," "Our Approach," Context Integration web site. www.context.com on June 19, 2002; Suzanne Koudsi, "Actually, It Is Like Brain Surgery," *Fortune*, March 20, 2000, pp. 233–234. See www.fortune.com; Chuck Salter, "Ideas.com," *Fast Company*, September 1999, p. 292 (quotation). See www.fastcompany.com.

tion from their governments that may not be available to firms in older industrialized states. Nokia, a Finnish company, is locked in a battle with Motorola and Ericcson for the worldwide cellular phone market. In order to meet the global competitive challenges, Nokia changed its approach to marketing by holding global strategy sessions and training managers to think globally yet act locally by developing a good understanding of local cultures. The firm had to adjust to the fact that mass marketing differs widely among the United States, Europe, and Asia.[12] Organizations that are not ready for these new sources of competition may not last long in the new century.

Processes for Planned Organization Change

External forces may impose change on an organization. Ideally, however, the organization will not only respond to change but will also anticipate it, prepare for it through planning, and incorporate it in the organization strategy. Organization change can be viewed from a static point of view, such as that of Lewin (see next section), or from a dynamic perspective.

Lewin's Process Model

Planned organization change requires a systematic process of movement from one condition to another. Kurt Lewin suggested that efforts to bring about planned change in organizations should approach change as a multistage process.[13] His model of planned change is made up of three steps—unfreezing, change, and refreezing—as shown in Figure 19.1.

Unfreezing is the process by which people become aware of the need for change.

Unfreezing is the process by which people become aware of the need for change. If people are satisfied with current practices and procedures, they may have little or no interest in making changes. The key factor in unfreezing is making employees understand the importance of a change and how their jobs will be affected by it. The employees who will be most affected by the change must be made aware of why it is needed, which in effect makes them dissatisfied enough with current operations to be motivated to change.

Change itself is the movement from the old way of doing things to a new way. Change may entail installing new equipment, restructuring the organization, implementing a new performance appraisal system—anything that alters existing relationships or activities.

Refreezing is the process of making new behaviors relatively permanent and resistant to further change.

Refreezing makes new behaviors relatively permanent and resistant to further change. Examples of refreezing techniques include repeating newly learned skills in a training session and role playing to teach how the new skill can be used in a real-life work situation. Refreezing is necessary because without it, the old ways of doing things might soon reassert themselves while the new ways are forgotten. For example, many employees who attend special training sessions apply themselves diligently and resolve to change things in their organizations. But when they return to the workplace, they find it easier to conform to the old ways than to make waves. There usually are few, if any, rewards for trying to change the organizational status quo. In fact, the personal sanctions against doing so may be difficult to tolerate. Learning theory and reinforcement theory (see Chapter 6) can play important roles in the refreezing phase.

The Continuous Change Process Model

Perhaps because Lewin's model is very simple and straightforward, virtually all models of organization change use his approach. However, it does not deal with several important issues. A more complex, and more helpful, approach is illustrated

figure 19.1

Lewin's Process of Organization Change

In Lewin's three-step model, change is a systematic process of transition from an old way of doing things to a new way. Inclusion of an "unfreezing" stage indicates the importance of preparing for the change. The refreezing stage reflects the importance of following up on the change to make it permanent.

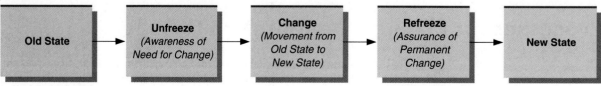

in Figure 19.2. This approach treats planned change from the perspective of top management and indicates that change is continuous. Although we discuss each step as if it were separate and distinct from the others, it is important to note that as change becomes continuous in organizations, different steps are probably occurring simultaneously throughout the organization. The model incorporates Lewin's concept into the implementation phase.

In this approach, top management perceives that certain forces or trends call for change, and the issue is subjected to the organization's usual problem-solving and decision-making processes (see Chapter 15). Usually, top management defines its goals in terms of what the organization or certain processes or outputs will be like after the change. Alternatives for change are generated and evaluated, and an acceptable one is selected.

Early in the process, the organization may seek the assistance of a **change agent**—a person who will be responsible for managing the change effort. The change agent may also help management recognize and define the problem or the need for the change and may be involved in generating and evaluating potential plans of action. The change agent may be a member of the organization, an outsider such as a consultant, or even someone from headquarters whom employees view as an outsider. An internal change agent is likely to know the organization's people, tasks, and political situations, which may be helpful in interpreting data and understanding the system; but an insider may also be too close to the situation to view it objectively. (In addition, a regular employee would have to be removed from his or her regular duties to concentrate on the transition.) An outsider, then, is often received better by all parties because of his or her assumed impartiality. Under the direction and management of the change agent, the organization implements the change through Lewin's unfreeze, change, and refreeze process.

A change agent is a person responsible for managing a change effort.

figure 19.2

Continuous Change Process Model of Organization Change

The continuous change process model incorporates the forces for change, a problem-solving process, a change agent, and transition management. It takes a top-management perspective and highlights the fact that in organizations today, change is a continuous process.

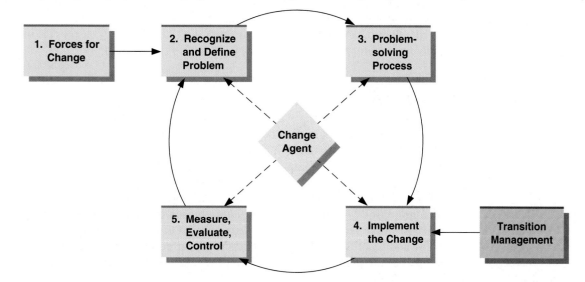

The final step is measurement, evaluation, and control. The change agent and the top management group assess the degree to which the change is having the desired effect; that is, they measure progress toward the goals of the change and make appropriate changes if necessary. The more closely the change agent is involved in the change process, the less distinct the steps become. The change agent becomes a "collaborator" or "helper" to the organization as she or he is immersed in defining and solving the problem with members of the organization. When this happens, the change agent may be working with many individuals, groups, and departments within the organization on different phases of the change process. When the change process is moving along from one stage to another, it may not be readily observable because of the total involvement of the change agent in every phase of the project. Throughout the process, however, the change agent brings in new ideas and viewpoints that help members look at old problems in new ways. Change often arises from the conflict that results when the change agent challenges the organization's assumptions and generally accepted patterns of operation.

"One of the foremost things we need is a change agent—and Dick Brown fits the bill."—James Baker III, former U.S. secretary of state and EDS board member[14]

Through the measurement, evaluation, and control phase, top management determines the effectiveness of the change process by evaluating various indicators of organizational productivity and effectiveness or employee morale. It is hoped that the organization will be better after the change than before. However, the uncertainties and rapid change in all sectors of the environment make constant organization change a certainty for most organizations.

Transition management is
the process of systematically
planning, organizing, and implementing change.

Transition management is the process of systematically planning, organizing, and implementing change, from the disassembly of the current state to the realization of a fully functional future state within an organization.[15] Once change begins, the organization is in neither the old state nor the new state, yet business must go on. Transition management ensures that business continues while the change is occurring; therefore, it must begin before the change occurs. The members of the regular management team must take on the role of transition managers and coordinate organizational activities with the change agent. An interim management structure or interim positions may be created to ensure continuity and control of the business during the transition. Communication about the changes to all involved, from employees to customers and suppliers, plays a key role in transition management.[16]

Organization Development

On one level, organization development is simply the way organizations change and evolve. Organization change can involve personnel, technology, competition, and other areas. Employee learning and formal training, transfers, promotions, terminations, and retirements are all examples of personnel-related changes. Thus, in the broadest sense, organization development means organization change.[17] However, the term as used here means something more specific. Over the past thirty years, organization development has emerged as a distinct field of study and practice. Experts now substantially agree as to what constitutes organization development in general, although arguments about details continue.[18] Our definition of organization development is an attempt to describe a very complex process in a simple manner. It is also an attempt to capture the best points of several definitions offered by writers in the field.

Organization Development Defined

Organization development is the process of planned change and improvement of organizations through the application of knowledge of the behavioral sciences. Three points in this definition make it simple to remember and use. First, organization development involves attempts to plan organization changes, which excludes spontaneous, haphazard initiatives. Second, the specific intention of organization development is to improve organizations. This point excludes changes that merely imitate those of another organization, are forced on the organization by external pressures, or are undertaken merely for the sake of changing. Third, the planned improvement must be based on knowledge of the behavioral sciences such as organizational behavior, psychology, sociology, cultural anthropology, and related fields of study rather than on financial or technological considerations. Under our definition, the replacement of manual personnel records with a computerized system would not be considered an instance of organization development. Although such a change has behavioral effects, it is a technology-driven reform rather than a behavioral one. Likewise, alterations in record keeping necessary to support new government mandated reporting requirements are not a part of organization development because the change is obligatory and the result of an external force. The three most basic types of techniques are systemwide, task and technological, and group and individual.

Organization development is the process of planned change and improvement of the organization through application of knowledge of the behavioral sciences.

Systemwide Organization Development

The most comprehensive type of organization change involves a major reorientation or reorganization—usually referred to as a **structural change** or a systemwide rearrangement of task division and authority and reporting relationships. A structural change affects performance appraisal and rewards, decision making, and communication and information-processing systems. As we discussed in Chapter 17, reengineering and rethinking the organizations are two contemporary approaches to systemwide structural change. Reengineering can be a difficult process, but it has great potential for organizational improvement. It requires that managers challenge long-held assumptions about everything they do and set outrageous goals and expect that they will be met.

Structural change is a systemwide organization development involving a major restructuring of the organization or instituting programs such as quality of work life.

"One of the wonderful things about business: You have to work hard to forget what you know. If I like the business model I have now, I am not going to like it in five years."—Larry Bossidy, former CEO of AlliedSignal (before its merger with Honeywell)[19]

An organization may change the way it divides tasks into jobs, combines jobs into departments and divisions, and arranges authority and reporting relationships among positions. It may move from functional departmentalization to a system based on products or geography, for example, or from a conventional linear design to a matrix or a team-based design. Other changes may include dividing large groups into smaller ones or merging small groups into larger ones. In addition, the degree to which rules and procedures are written down and enforced, as well as the locus of decision-making authority, may be altered. Supervisors may become "coaches" or "facilitators" in a team-based organization. The organization will have transformed both the configurational and the operational aspects of its structure if all of these changes are made.

No systemwide structural change is simple.[20] A company president cannot just issue a memo notifying company personnel that on a certain date they will report to a different supervisor and be responsible for new tasks and expect everything to change overnight. Employees have months, years, and sometimes decades of experience in dealing with people and tasks in certain ways. When these patterns are disrupted, employees need time to learn the new tasks and to settle into the new relationships. Moreover, they may resist the change for a number of reasons; we discuss resistance to change later in this chapter. Therefore, organizations must manage the change process.

Ford Motor Company is pretty typical of organizations that have had to make major organization-wide and worldwide changes. Over the years, Ford had developed several regional fiefdoms, such as Ford of Europe, Ford United States, and Ford Australia, which all operated relatively independently. When Jacques Nasser was named CEO, he set out to tear down those regionally based organizations and to create a truly globally integrated car manufacturer. As his plan was unfolding, however, Ford continued to lose market share, so on October 30, 2001, Nasser was replaced as CEO by Ford family member William Clay Ford Jr., who is continuing to develop the global car idea.[21] Only time will tell if the new plan will work.

Another systemwide change is the introduction of quality-of-work-life programs. J. Lloyd Suttle defined **quality of work life** as the "degree to which members of a work organization are able to satisfy important personal needs through their experiences in the organization."[22] Quality-of-work-life programs focus strongly on providing a work environment conducive to satisfying individual needs. The emphasis on improving life at work developed during the 1970s, a period of increasing inflation and deepening recession. The development was rather surprising because an expanding economy and substantially increased resources are the conditions that usually induce top management to begin people-oriented programs. However, top management viewed improving life at work as a means of improving productivity.

> Quality of work life is the extent to which workers can satisfy important personal needs through their experiences in the organization.

Any movement with broad and ambiguous goals tends to spawn diverse programs, each claiming to be based on the movement's goals, and the quality-of-work-life movement is no exception. These programs vary substantially, although most espouse a goal of "humanizing the workplace." Richard Walton divided them into the eight categories shown in Figure 19.3.[23] Obviously, many types of programs can be accommodated by the categories, from changing the pay system to establishing an employee bill of rights that guarantees workers the rights to privacy, free speech, due process, and fair and equitable treatment.

Total quality management, which was discussed in several earlier chapters, can also be viewed as a systemwide organization development program. In fact, some might consider total quality management as a broad program that includes structural change as well as quality of work life. It differs from quality of work life in that it emphasizes satisfying customer needs by making quality-oriented changes rather than focusing on satisfying employee needs at work. Often, however, the employee programs are very similar to it.

The benefits gained from quality-of-work-life programs differ substantially, but generally they are of three types. A more positive attitude toward the work and

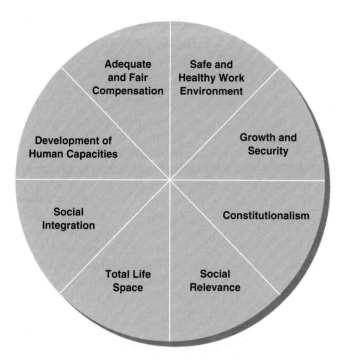

figure 19.3

Walton's Categorization of Quality-of-Work-Life Programs

Quality-of-work-life programs can be categorized into eight types. The expected benefits of these programs are increased employee morale, productivity, and organizational effectiveness.

Reference: Adapted from Richard E. Walton, "Quality of Work Life: What Is It?" *Sloan Management Review*, Fall 1973, pp. 11–21, by permission of the publisher. Copyright © 1973 by the Sloan Management Review Association. All rights reserved.

the organization, or increased job satisfaction, is perhaps the most direct benefit.[24] Another is increased productivity, although it is often difficult to measure and separate the effects of the quality-of-work-life program from the effects of other organizational factors. A third benefit is increased effectiveness of the organization as measured by its profitability, goal accomplishment, shareholder wealth, or resource exchange. The third gain follows directly from the first two: If employees have more positive attitudes about the organization and their productivity increases, everything else being equal, the organization should be more effective.

Task and Technological Change

Another way to bring about systemwide organization development is through changes in the tasks involved in doing the work, the technology, or both. The direct alteration of jobs usually is called "task redesign." Changing how inputs are transformed into outputs is called "technological change" and also usually results in task changes. Strictly speaking, changing the technology is typically not part of organization development whereas task redesign usually is.

The structural changes discussed in the preceding section are explicitly systemwide in scope. Those we examine in this section are more narrowly focused and may not seem to have the same far-reaching consequences. It is important to remember, however, that their impact is felt throughout the organization. The discussion of task design in Chapter 7 focused on job definition and motivation and gave little attention to implementing changes in jobs. Here we discuss task redesign as a mode of organization change.

Several approaches to introducing job changes in organizations have been proposed. One is by a coauthor of this book, Ricky W. Griffin. Griffin's approach is an integrative framework of nine steps that reflect the complexities of the interfaces between individual jobs and the total organization.[25] The process, shown in Table 19.2, includes the steps usually associated with change such as recognizing the need for a change, selecting the appropriate intervention, and evaluating the change. But Griffin's approach inserts four additional steps into the standard sequence: diagnosis of the overall work system and context, including examination of the jobs, workforce, technology, organization design, leadership, and group dynamics; evaluating the costs and benefits of the change; formulating a redesign strategy; and implementing supplemental changes.

Diagnosis includes analysis of the total work environment within which the jobs exist. It is important to evaluate the organization structure, especially the work

Step 1: Recognition of a need for a change
Step 2: Selection of task redesign as a potential intervention
Step 3: Diagnosis of the work system and context
    a. Diagnosis of existing jobs
    b. Diagnosis of existing workforce
    c. Diagnosis of technology
    d. Diagnosis of organization design
    e. Diagnosis of leader behavior
    f. Diagnosis of group and social processes
Step 4: Cost-benefit analysis of proposed changes
Step 5: Go/no-go decision
Step 6: Formulation of the strategy for redesign
Step 7: Implementation of the task changes
Step 8: Implementation of any supplemental changes
Step 9: Evaluation of the task redesign effort

Reference: Ricky W. Griffin, *Task Design: An Integrative Framework* (Glenview, Ill.: Scott, Foresman, 1982), p. 208. Used by permission.

table 19.2

Integrated Framework for Implementation of Task Redesign in Organizations

rules and decision-making authority within a department, when job changes are being considered.[26] For example, if jobs are to be redesigned to give employees more freedom in choosing work methods or scheduling work activities, diagnosis of the present system must determine whether the rules will allow that to happen. Diagnosis must also include evaluation of the work group and teams and intragroup dynamics (discussed in Chapters 11 and 12). Furthermore, it must determine whether workers have or can easily obtain the new skills to perform the redesigned task.

It is extremely important to recognize the full range of potential costs and benefits associated with a job redesign effort. Some are direct and quantifiable; others are indirect and not quantifiable. Redesign may involve unexpected costs or benefits; although these cannot be predicted with certainty, they can be weighed as possibilities. Factors such as short-term role ambiguity, role conflict, and role overload can be major stumbling blocks to a job redesign effort.

Implementing a redesign scheme takes careful planning, and developing a strategy for the intervention is the final planning step. Strategy formulation is a four-part process. First, the organization must decide who will design the changes. Depending on the circumstances, the planning team may consist of only upper-level management or may include line workers and supervisors. Next, the team undertakes the actual design of the changes based on job design theory and the needs, goals, and circumstances of the organization. Third, the team decides the timing of the implementation, which may require a formal transition period during which equipment is purchased and installed, job training takes place, new physical layouts are arranged, and the bugs in the new system are worked out. Fourth, strategy planners must consider whether the job changes require adjustments and supplemental changes in other organizational components such as reporting relationships and the compensation system.

Group and Individual Change

Groups and individuals can be involved in organization change in a vast number of ways. Retraining a single employee can be considered an organization change if the training affects the way the employee does his or her job. Familiarizing managers with the Leadership grid or the Vroom decision tree (Chapter 13) is an attempt at change. In the first case, the goal is to balance management concerns for production and people; in the second, the goal is to increase the participation of rank-and-file employees in the organization's decision making. In this section, we present an overview of four popular types of people-oriented change techniques: training, management development programs, team building, and survey feedback.

Top Gun training for corporate execs? What can military pilots possibly have that highly paid corporate executives would pay for? Combat planning, preparedness, reaction to unforeseen emergencies, contingency planning, discipline, and knowing your competitors are among the lessons that Afterburner Seminars is selling and delivering to top management of companies, including, Dell, Charles Schwab, Ford Motor, IBM, Pfizer, and Sun Microsystems. Former and reservist pilots utilize a mock military squadron bunker to plan air strikes on enemy targets to teach managers that business is like combat where you can win and survive, or lose and not come home.

Training   Training generally is designed to improve employees' job skills. Employees may be trained to run certain machines, taught new mathematical skills, or acquainted with personal growth and development methods. Stress management programs are becoming popular for helping employees, particularly executives, understand organizational stress and develop ways to cope with it.[27] Training may also be used in conjunction with other, more comprehensive organization changes. For instance, if an organization is implementing a management-by-objectives program, training in establishing goals and reviewing goal-oriented performance is probably needed. One important type of training that is becoming increasingly more common is training people to work in other countries. Companies such as Motorola give extensive training programs to employees at all levels before they start an international assignment. Training includes intensive language courses, cultural courses, and courses for the family.

Among the many training methods, the most common are lecture, discussion, a lecture-discussion combination, experiential methods, case studies, and films or videotapes. Training can take place in a standard classroom, either on company property or in a hotel, at a resort, or at a conference center. On-the-job training provides a different type of experience in which the trainee learns from an experienced worker. Most training programs use a combination of methods determined by the topic, the trainees, the trainer, and the organization.

A major problem of training programs is transferring employee learning to the workplace. Often an employee learns a new skill or a manager learns a new management technique, but upon returning to the normal work situation, he or she finds it easier to go back to the old way of doing things. As we discussed earlier, the process of refreezing is a vital part of the change process, and some way must be found to make the accomplishments of the training program permanent.

Management Development Programs   Management development programs, like employee training programs, attempt to foster certain skills, abilities, and perspectives. Often, when a highly qualified technical person is promoted to manager of a work group, he or she lacks training in how to manage or deal with people. In such cases, management development programs can be important to organizations, both for the new manager and for his or her subordinates.

Typically, management development programs use the lecture-discussion method to some extent but rely most heavily on participative methods such as case studies and role playing. Participative and experiential methods allow the manager to experience the problems of being a manager as well as the feelings of frustration, doubt, and success that are part of the job. The subject matter of this type of training program is problematic, however, in that management skills, including communication, problem diagnosis, problem solving, and performance appraisal, are not as easy to identify or to transfer from a classroom to the workplace as the skills required to run a machine. In addition, rapid changes in the external environment can make certain managerial skills obsolete in a very short time. As a result, some companies are approaching the development of their management team as an ongoing, career-long process and require their managers to attend refresher courses periodically.

One training approach involves managers in an intense exercise that simulates the daily operation of a real company. Such simulations emphasize problem-solving behavior rather than competitive tactics and usually involve extensive debriefing during which a manager's style is openly discussed and criticized by trained observers as the first step to improvement. IBM and AT&T have commissioned experts to create a simulation specifically for their managers. Although the cost of custom simulations is high, it is reportedly repaid in benefits from individual development.[28]

As corporate America invests hundreds of millions of dollars in management development, certain guiding principles are evolving: (1) Management development is a multifaceted, complex, and long-term process to which there is no quick or simple approach; (2) organizations should carefully and systematically identify their unique developmental needs and evaluate their programs accordingly; (3) management development objectives must be compatible with organizational objectives;(4) the utility and value of management development remain more an article of faith than a proven fact.[29]

Team Building   When interaction among group members is critical to group success and effectiveness, team development, or team building, may be useful. Team building emphasizes members' working together in a spirit of cooperation and generally has one or more of the following goals:

1. To set team goals and priorities
2. To analyze or allocate the way work is performed
3. To examine how a group is working—that is, to examine processes such as norms, decision making, and communications
4. To examine relationships among the people doing the work[30]

Total quality management efforts usually focus on teams, and the principles of team building must be applied to make them work. Team participation is especially important in the data-gathering and evaluation phases of team development. In data gathering, the members share information on the functioning of the group. The opinions of the group thus form the foundation of the development process. In the evaluation phase, members are the source of information about the effectiveness of the development effort.[31]

Like total quality management and many other management techniques, team building should not be thought of as a one-time experience, perhaps something undertaken on a retreat from the workplace; rather, it is a continuing process. It may take weeks, months, or years for a group to learn to pull together and function as a team. Team development can be a way to train the group to solve its own problems in the future. Research on the effectiveness of team building as an organization development tool so far is mixed and inconclusive. For more details on developing teams in organizations, please refer to Chapter 12.

Survey Feedback   Survey feedback techniques can form the basis for a change process. In this process, data are gathered, analyzed, summarized, and returned to those who generated them to identify, discuss, and solve problems. A survey feedback process is often set in motion either by the organization's top management or by a consultant to management. By providing information about employees' beliefs and attitudes, a survey can help management diagnose and solve an organization's problems. A consultant or change agent usually coordinates the process and is responsible for data gathering, analysis, and summary. The three-stage process is shown in Figure 19.4.[32]

The use of survey feedback techniques in an organization development process differs from their use in traditional attitude surveys. In an organization development process, data are (1) returned to employee groups at all levels in the organization and (2) used by all employees working together in their normal work groups to identify and solve problems. In traditional attitude surveys, top management reviews the data and may or may not initiate a new program to solve problems the survey has identified.

In the data-gathering stage, the change agent interviews selected personnel from appropriate levels to determine the key issues to be examined. Information from these interviews is used to develop a survey questionnaire, which will be distributed to a large sample of employees. The questionnaire may be a standardized instrument, an instrument developed specifically for the organization, or a combination of the two. The questionnaire data are analyzed and aggregated by group or department to ensure that respondents remain anonymous.[33] Then the change agent prepares a summary of the results for the group feedback sessions. From this point on, the consultant is involved in the process as a resource person and expert.

The feedback meetings generally involve only two or three levels of management. Meetings are usually held serially, first with a meeting of the top management group, which is then followed by meetings of employees throughout the organization. The group manager rather than the change agent typically leads sessions to transfer "ownership" of the data from the change agent to the work group. The feedback consists primarily of profiles of the group's attitudes toward the organization, the work, the leadership, and other topics on the questionnaire. During the feedback sessions, participants discuss reasons for the scores and the problems that the data reveal.

In the process analysis stage, the group examines the process of making decisions, communicating, and accomplishing work, usually with the help of the consultant. Unfortunately, groups often overlook this stage as they become absorbed in the survey data and the problems revealed during the feedback sessions. Occasionally, group managers simply fail to hold feedback and process analysis sessions. Change agents should ensure that managers hold these sessions and that they are rewarded for doing so. The process analysis stage is important because its purpose is to develop action plans to make improvements. Several sessions may be

figure 19.4

The Survey Feedback Process

The survey feedback process has three distinct stages, which must be fully completed for the process to be most effective. As an organization development process, its purpose is to fully involve all employees in data analysis, problem identification, and development of solutions.

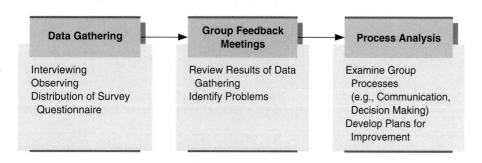

United Way of America is the corporate parent of many local United Way organizations across the United States. Typically, the United Way serves as a unified means of raising money for community charities. Basically, they raise the money and give it away to community charitable organizations. New CEO Brian Gallagher is changing that model and facing stiff opposition. Back in his home state of Ohio, rather than just raise the money and give it away, he worked with locals to find the root cause of the homeless problem and developed ways to help homeless families get low cost housing, day jobs, and child care. Funding went to support this new effort instead of to the existing homeless shelters. Taking that model to the national level is creating quite a stir among many existing local agencies that fear their source of funding will dry up or at least that they may have to follow directives from the national organization. Efforts to change have cost the previous two CEOs their jobs. Only time will tell if Gallagher can survive his own efforts to change the United Way.

required to discuss the process issues fully and to settle on a strategy for improvements. Groups often find it useful to document the plans as they are discussed and to appoint a member to follow up on implementation. Generally, the follow-up assesses whether communication and communication processes have actually been improved. A follow-up survey can be administered several months to a year later to assess how much these processes have changed since they were first reported.

The survey feedback method is probably one of the most widely used organization change and development interventions. If any of its stages are compromised or omitted, however, the technique becomes less useful. A primary responsibility of the consultant or change agent, then, is to ensure that the method is fully and faithfully carried through.

Resistance to Change

Change is inevitable; so is resistance to change. Paradoxically, organizations both promote and resist change. As an agent for change, the organization asks prospective customers or clients to change their current purchasing habits by switching to the company's product or service, asks current customers to change by increasing their purchases, and asks suppliers to reduce the costs of raw materials. The organization resists change in that its structure and control systems protect the daily tasks of producing a product or service from uncertainties in the environment. The organization must have some elements of permanence to avoid mirroring the instability of the environment, yet it must also react to external shifts with internal change to maintain currency and relevance in the marketplace.

"There has to be a crisis to push us to take a risk. But often we lack a sense of urgency. And in a company as big as ours, urgency can be a difficult thing to feel."—Jeff Leppla, Procter & Gamble employee[34]

A commonly held view is that all resistance to change needs to be overcome, but that is not always the case. Resistance to change can be used for the benefit of the organization and need not be eliminated entirely. By revealing a legitimate concern that a proposed change may harm the organization or that other alternatives might be better, resistance may alert the organization to reexamine the change.[35] For example, an organization may be considering acquiring a company in a completely different industry. Resistance to such a proposal may cause the organization to examine the advantages and disadvantages of the move more carefully. Without resistance, the decision might be made before the pros and cons have been sufficiently explored.

Resistance may come from the organization, the individual, or both. Determining the ultimate source is often difficult, however, because organizations are composed of individuals. Table 19.3 summarizes various types of organizational and individual sources of resistance.

Organizational Sources of Resistance

Daniel Katz and Robert Kahn have identified six major organizational sources of resistance: overdetermination, narrow focus of change, group inertia, threatened expertise, threatened power, and changes in resource allocation.[36] Of course, not every organization or every change situation displays all six sources.

Overdetermination   Organizations have several systems designed to maintain stability. For example, consider how organizations control employees' performance. Job candidates must have certain specific skills so that they can do the job the

table 19.3

Organizational and Individual Sources of Resistance

Organizational Sources	Examples
Overdetermination	Employment system, job descriptions, evaluation, and reward system, organization culture
Narrow Focus of Change	Structure changed with no concern given to other issues, e.g., jobs, people
Group Inertia	Group norms
Threatened Expertise	People move out of area of expertise
Threatened Power	Decentralized decision making
Resource Allocation	Increased use of part-time help

Individual Sources	Examples
Habit	Altered tasks
Security	Altered tasks or reporting relationships
Economic Factors	Changed pay and benefits
Fear of the Unknown	New job, new boss
Lack of Awareness	Isolated groups not heeding notices
Social Factors	Group norms

MASTERING CHANGE

▶ EDS Is "Cool" Again

What happens when the immovable object (an Old Economy firm) meets the irresistible force (the New Economy)? Electronic Data Systems Corporation (EDS), founded in 1962 by Ross Perot, invented the computer services business. Acquired by General Motors in 1984, EDS prospered, but as profits stagnated, GM spun off EDS in 1996. Revenue per employee was 55 percent below that of rival IBM, probably because one-third of the sales force had not made a sale in two years. Even worse, EDS had a stodgy reputation after missing important industry changes, notably the increasing use of the Internet. John Wilkerson, an EDS executive, recalls, "When [CEO] Scott McNealy of Sun Microsystems first had us do a piece of a contract for him, he wouldn't let us publicize the deal, because he thought we were too Old Economy. Sun was cool. We were the knuckle draggers." Seeing the need for radical change, the board searched for an outsider to shake the place up, ultimately hiring experienced CEO Dick Brown.

Brown found that EDS had no clear direction from the top, lacked a performance culture, and was bloated with employees. He cut 5,000 jobs in a move that employees call "Brown-sizing." He introduced a forced-ranking employee evaluation system and tied pay to the rankings. When Brown wanted to answer his own telephone calls and send regular emails to every employee, he was unable to do so because the previous CEO had had the phone wires cut, and the high-tech firm had no companywide messaging system! After addressing these problems, Brown reorganized around four global customer-focused lines of business and also developed six industry-specific teams. He then changed the corporate logo from a square

> *"Sun [Microsystems] was cool. We were the knuckle draggers."*
> —*John Wilkerson, president of the EDS Global Indirect Markets unit*

to a circle, possibly as a symbolic representation of the e-business dot that is driving the company's future.

Brown's biggest challenge was changing the complacent corporate culture. "Most business leaders are afraid to talk about culture. They're far more comfortable with numbers," the CEO says. "While I am very numbers focused, you can't change a business with numbers. Numbers are the end result. You change a business by changing the behavior of its people." When managers began insisting on frank customer evaluations and sharing their financial results with the entire organization, Brown knew that his changes had worked. Today, EDS is no longer the square company it was, thanks to Dick Brown.

References: Bill Breen, "How EDS Got Its Groove Back," *Fast Company*, October 2001, pp. 105–117 (quotation p. 108). See www.fastcompany.com; Leah Beth Ward, "Electronic Data Systems Rounds Off Logo," *Knight-Ridder/Tribune Business News*, January 20, 2000, p. ITEM 00021038; "Fast and Unafraid," *Economist*, January 8, 2000, p. 68. See www.economist.com; Nancy Williams, "EDS Unveils Leadership Teams as Company Completes New Business Approach," *PR Newswire*, November 30, 1999, p. 1488. See www.prnewswire.com; Neil Weinberg, "A Shock to the System," *Forbes*, May 31, 1999, pp. 178–182. See www.forbes.com.

Overdetermination, or structural inertia, occurs because numerous organizational systems are in place to ensure that employees and systems behave as expected to maintain stability.

organization needs them to do. New employees are given a job description, and the supervisor trains, coaches, and counsels the employee in job tasks. The new employee usually serves some type of probationary period that culminates in a performance review; thereafter, the employee's performance is regularly evaluated. Finally, rewards, punishment, and discipline are administered, depending on the level of performance. Such a system is said to be characterized by **overdetermination,** or **structural inertia,**[37] in that one could probably have the same effect on employee performance with fewer procedures and safeguards. In other words, the structure of the organization produces resistance to change because it was designed to maintain stability. Another important source of overdetermination is the culture of the organization. As discussed in Chapter 18, the culture of an organization can have powerful and long-lasting effects on the behavior of its employees. New CEO Dick Brown faced resistance in his efforts to radically change the culture at EDS, as the "Mastering Change" box discusses.

Narrow Focus of Change   Many efforts to create change in organizations adopt too narrow a focus. Any effort to force change in the tasks of individuals or groups must take into account the interdependencies among organizational elements such as people, structure, tasks, and the information system. For example, some attempts at redesigning jobs fail because the organization structure within which the jobs must function is inappropriate for the redesigned jobs.[38]

Group Inertia   When an employee attempts to change his or her work behavior, the group may resist by refusing to change other behaviors that are necessary complements to the individual's changed behavior. In other words, group norms may act as a brake on individual attempts at behavior change.

Threatened Expertise   A change in the organization may threaten the specialized expertise that individuals and groups have developed over the years. A job redesign or a structural change may transfer responsibility for a specialized task from the current expert to someone else, threatening the specialist's expertise and building his or her resistance to the change.

Threatened Power   Any redistribution of decision-making authority, such as with reengineering or team-based management, may threaten an individual's power relationships with others. If an organization is decentralizing its decision making, managers who wielded their decision-making powers in return for special favors from others may resist the change because they do not want to lose their power base.

Resource Allocation   Groups that are satisfied with current resource allocation methods may resist any change they believe will threaten future allocations. Resources in this context can mean anything from monetary rewards and equipment to additional seasonal help to more computer time.

These six sources explain most types of organization-based resistance to change. All are based on people and social relationships. Many of these sources of resistance can be traced to groups or individuals who are afraid of losing something—resources, power, or comfort in a routine.

Individual Sources of Resistance

Individual sources of resistance to change are rooted in basic human characteristics such as needs and perceptions. Researchers have identified six reasons for individual resistance to change: habit, security, economic factors, fear of the unknown, lack of awareness, and social factors (see Table 19.3).[39]

Habit   It is easier to do a job the same way every day if the steps in the job are repeated over and over. Learning an entirely new set of steps makes the job more difficult. For the same amount of return (pay), most people prefer to do easier rather than harder work.

Security   Some employees like the comfort and security of doing things the same old way. They gain a feeling of constancy and safety from knowing that some things stay the same despite all the change going on around them. People who believe their security is threatened by a change are likely to resist the change.

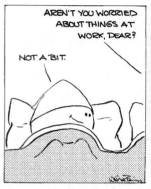

This little guy brags to his coworkers that he is not worried about the reorganization when he really *is* worried about it. In any organization change, most people worry about how the changes will affect their job and their future. Most people learn how to survive in the job and the work environment and fear the unknowns that changes might bring.

Reference: © 2003 Grantland Enterprises, Inc. All Rights Reserved.

Economic Factors   Change may threaten employees' steady paychecks. Workers may fear that change will make their jobs obsolete or reduce their opportunities for future pay increases.

Fear of the Unknown   Some people fear anything unfamiliar. Changes in reporting relationships and job duties create anxiety for such employees. Employees become familiar with their bosses and their jobs and develop relationships with others within the organization, such as contact people for various situations. These relationships and contacts help facilitate their work. Any disruption of familiar patterns may create fear because it can cause delays and foster the belief that nothing is getting accomplished. The cartoon shows how people sometimes appear brave, but when alone, they worry about what the changes might bring.

Lack of Awareness   Because of perceptual limitations such as lack of attention or selective attention, a person may not recognize a change in a rule or procedure and thus may not alter his or her behavior. People may pay attention only to things that support their point of view. As an example, employees in an isolated regional sales office may not notice—or may ignore—directives from headquarters regarding a change in reporting procedures for expense accounts. They may therefore continue the current practice as long as possible.

Social Factors   People may resist change for fear of what others will think. As we mentioned before, the group can be a powerful motivator of behavior. Employees may believe change will hurt their image, result in ostracism from the group, or simply make them "different." For example, an employee who agrees to conform to work rules established by management may be ridiculed by others who openly disobey the rules.

Managing Successful Organization Change and Development

In conclusion, we offer seven keys to managing change in organizations. They relate directly to the problems identified earlier and to our view of the organization as a comprehensive social system. Each can influence the elements of the so-

table 19.4

Keys to Managing Successful Organization Change and Development

Key	Impact
Consider international issues.	Keeps in touch with the latest global developments and how change is handled in different cultures
Take a holistic view of the organization.	Helps anticipate the effects of change on the social system and culture
Start small.	Works out details and shows the benefits of the change to those who might resist
Secure top management support.	Gets dominant coalition on the side of change: safeguards structural change, heads off problems of power and control
Encourage participation by those affected by the change.	Minimizes transition problems of control, resistance, and task redefinition
Foster open communication.	Minimizes transition problems of resistance and information and control systems
Reward those who contribute to change.	Minimizes transition problems of resistance and control systems

cial system and may help the organization avoid some of the major problems in managing the change. Table 19.4 lists the points and their potential impacts.

Consider International Issues

One factor to consider is how international environments dictate organization change. As we have already noted, the environment is a significant factor in bringing about organization change. Given the additional environmental complexities multinational organizations face, it follows that organization change may be even more critical to them than it is to purely domestic organizations.

A second point to remember is that acceptance of change varies widely around the globe. Change is a normal and accepted part of organization life in some cultures. In other cultures, change causes many more problems. Managers should remember that techniques for managing change that have worked routinely back home may not work at all and may even trigger negative responses if used indiscriminately in other cultures.[40]

Take a Holistic View

Managers must take a holistic view of the organization and the change project. A limited view can endanger the change effort because the subsystems of the organization are interdependent. A holistic view encompasses the culture and dominant coalition as well as the people, tasks, structure, and information subsystems.

Start Small

Peter Senge claims that every truly successful, systemwide change in large organizations starts small.[41] He recommends that change start with one team, usually an executive team. One team can evaluate the change, make appropriate adjustments along the way, and most importantly, show that the new system works and gets desired results. If the change makes sense, it begins to spread to other teams, groups, and divisions throughout the system. Senge described how at Shell and Ford, significant changes started small, with one or two parallel teams, and then spread as others reconized the benefits of the change. When others see the benefits, they automatically drop their inherent resistance and join in. They can voluntarily join and be committed to the success of the change effort.

"Just as nothing in nature starts big, so the way to start creating a change is with a pilot group—a growth seed."—*Peter Senge, author and expert on organization change*[42]

Secure Top Management Support

The support of top management is essential to the success of any change effort. As the organization's probable dominant coalition, it is a powerful element of the social system, and its support is necessary to deal with control and power problems. For example, a manager who plans a change in the ways in which tasks are assigned and responsibility is delegated in his or her department must notify top management and gain its support. Complications may arise if disgruntled employees complain to high-level managers who have not been notified of the change or do not support it. The employees' complaints may jeopardize the manager's plan—and perhaps her or his job.

Encourage Participation

Problems related to resistance, control, and power can be overcome by broad participation in planning the change. Allowing people a voice in designing the change may give them a sense of power and control over their own destinies, which may help to win their support during implementation.

Foster Open Communication

Open communication is an important factor in managing resistance to change and overcoming information and control problems during transitions. Employees typically recognize the uncertainties and ambiguities that arise during a transition and seek information on the change and their place in the new system. In the absence of information, the gap may be filled with inappropriate or false information, which may endanger the change process. Rumors tend to spread through the grapevine faster than accurate information can be disseminated through official channels. A manager should always be sensitive to the effects of uncertainty on employees, especially during a period of change; any news, even bad news, seems better than no news.

Reward Contributors

Although this last point is simple, it can easily be neglected. Employees who contribute to the change in any way need to be rewarded. Too often, the only people acknowledged after a change effort are those who tried to stop it. Those who quickly grasp new work assignments, work harder to cover what otherwise might not get done during the transition, or help others adjust to changes deserve special credit—perhaps a mention in a news release or the internal company newspaper, special consideration in a performance appraisal, a merit raise, or a promotion. From a behavioral perspective, individuals need to benefit in some way if they are to willingly help change something that eliminates the old, comfortable way of doing the job.

In the current dynamic environment, managers must anticipate the need for change and satisfy it with more responsive and competitive organization systems. These seven keys to managing organization change may also serve as general guidelines for managing organizational behavior because organizations must change or face elimination.

Synopsis

Change may be forced on an organization, or an organization may change in response to the environment or an internal need. Forces for change are interdependent and influence organizations in many ways. Currently, the areas in which the pressures for change seem most powerful involve people, technology, information and communication, competition, and social trends.

Planned organization change involves anticipating change and preparing for it. Lewin described organization change in terms of unfreezing, the change itself, and refreezing. In the continuous change process model, top management recognizes forces encouraging change, engages in a problem-solving process to design the change, and implements and evaluates the change.

Organization development is the process of planned change and improvement of organizations through the application of knowledge of the behavioral sciences. It is based on a systematic change process and focuses on managing the culture of the organization. The most comprehensive change involves altering the structure of the organization through reorganization of departments, reporting relationships, or authority systems.

Quality-of-work-life programs focus on providing a work environment in which employees can satisfy individual needs. Task and technological changes alter the way the organization accomplishes its primary tasks. Along with the steps usually associated with change, task redesign entails diagnosis, cost-benefit analysis, formulation of a redesign strategy, and implementation of supplemental changes.

Frequently used group and individual approaches to organization change are training and management development programs, team building, and survey feedback techniques. Training programs are usually designed to improve employees' job skills, to help employees adapt to other organization changes (such as a management-by-objectives program), or to develop employees' awareness and understanding of problems such as workplace safety or stress. Management development programs attempt to foster in current or future managers the skills, abilities, and perspectives important to good management. Team-building programs are designed to help a work team or group develop into a mature, functioning team by helping it define its goals or priorities, analyze its tasks and the way they are performed, and examine relationships among the people doing the work. As used in the organization development process, survey feedback techniques involve gathering data, analyzing and summarizing them, and returning them to employees and groups for discussion and to identify and solve problems.

Resistance to change may arise from several individual and organizational sources. Resistance may indicate a legitimate concern that the change is not good for the organization and may warrant a reexamination of plans.

To manage change in organizations, international issues must be considered, and managers should take a holistic view of the organization and start small. Top management support is needed, and those most affected by the change must participate. Open communication is important, and those who contribute to the change effort should be rewarded.

Discussion Questions

1. Is most organization change forced on the organization by external factors or fostered from within? Explain.

2. What broad category of pressures for organization change other than the four discussed in the chapter can you think of? Briefly describe it.

3. Which sources of resistance to change present the most problems for an internal change agent? For an external change agent?

4. Which stage of the Lewin model of change do you think is most often overlooked? Why?

5. What are the advantages and disadvantages of having an internal change agent rather than an external change agent?

6. How does organization development differ from organization change?

7. How and why would organization development differ if the elements of the social system were not interdependent?

8. Do quality-of-work-life programs rely more on individual or organizational aspects of organizational behavior? Why?

9. Describe how the job of your professor could be redesigned. Include a discussion of other subsystems that would need to be changed as a result.

10. Which of the seven keys for successfully managing an organizational change effort seem to be the most difficult to manage? Why?

Organizational Behavior Case for Discussion

Change of Direction at Schwab

The Charles Schwab Company has long provided individual investors with an alternative to traditional investment firms. Unlike its Wall Street competitors, Schwab does not give investment advice; it merely facilitates trades that are chosen by the investors themselves. Schwab also has no investments of its own and does not employ any commissioned brokers, so there is no conflict of interest—the company is free to concentrate on each investor's needs. This unique philosophy has made Schwab a leader in its industry—that is, until now. Due to the bear market and a post-Enron loss of investor confidence, the number of daily trades executed by the firm was down 18 percent from the previous year, causing Schwab to lay off 6,000 workers in 2001. In the face of these challenges, Schwab, known as a company that thrives on change, is making an abrupt departure from business as usual.

Although every investments firm has suffered in this age of lowered expectations and distrust, Schwab has been hit especially hard. Other investment banks have institutional trades, merger and acquisition involvement, and other types of financial transactions to provide ongoing funds when one area dries up, but stock trades are Schwab's only business. Schwab's past success has led to another problem. As the company grew during the boom years, it added workers, bought servers, and opened more facilities, all of which lead to higher costs. Unfortunately, the firm's greatest spending spree occurred just before the stock market bubble burst, leaving an unfavorable cost structure.

After having relinquished more and more leadership to co-CEO David Pottruck in the previous months, the crisis brought founder and co-CEO Charles Schwab back. One of his first moves was to return the company to making money the old-fashioned way—by raising prices and lowering costs. The firm is introducing higher fees for customers who do not trade very often so that high-volume customers will no longer have to subsidize them. "We feel very strongly about our heritage of helping people become investors and teaching people how to invest," Pottruck says, "but there is a tension in that, because it's also very expensive." The firm is also making its web site more easily accessible, which should encourage customers to make more trades online rather than through a costly phone system.

Offering advice is perhaps the biggest change yet because it comes close to changing Charles Schwab's vision of an investments firm focused on the needs of clients, with no conflicts of interest. The company has developed a computerized stock analysis program that will compare each investor's risk profile and current holdings against a list of recommended stocks and then notify the customer of any suggested changes. Charles Schwab insists that the firm will still be differentiated from competitors because the advice will be free of bias. The program builds upon the expertise of Schwab's financial advisors, so it will be a low-cost way to increase customer service. And that customer service is sorely needed at discounter Schwab. One perplexing problem has been finding a way to keep customers who, although they started small with Schwab's discount trading system, have increased their wealth significantly. When they can pay for more sophisticated support, they often abandon Schwab and move up to a full-service investment firm.

Moreover, as Schwab shifts closer to the full-service sector of the industry, it will begin competing against heavyweights such as Merrill Lynch and Fidelity for a shrinking number of investors. As *Fortune* writer Fred Vogelstein explains, "It is true that Schwab's advantage is that it is building a new business rather than trying to dismantle an old one. That's the problem facing the full-service brokerages, which understand full well that their commission-based pay structure is ultimately untenable. Pottruck likens it to the choice between adding ten stories to a building or taking ten stories away. He believes adding is less risky to the underlying structure than taking away."

The change presents a new set of challenges for Schwab employees as well as for Charles Schwab and Pottruck. Maintaining a harmonious relationship has been problematic for the two CEOs in the past, with Pottruck threatening to quit if Shwab did not share more of the decision-making power. Pottruck changed his management style, too, losing his aggressive, edgy, "East Coast" approach in order to appeal to Schwab's more laid-back West Coast workers. Still ahead for the firm is the task of inspiring workers to adapt to the changes while not losing Schwab's unique culture. Schwab Chief Information Officer Dawn Lepore believes that the company's vision of "no conflicts of interest" remains intact and inspiring to employees. "People will work for money, but they'll give a piece of their lives for meaning," she maintains.

> ## "[It's] the choice between adding ten stories to a building or taking ten stories away. . . . [A]dding is less risky to the underlying structure than taking away." —Fred Vogelstein, Fortune writer, quoting Schwab Co-CEO David Pottruck.

References:" "June 2002 Monthly Report," Charles Schwab Company web site. aboutschwab.com on June 20, 2002; Fred Vogelstein, "Can Schwab Get Its Mojo Back?" *Fortune*, September 17, 2001, pp. 93–98. See www.fortune.com; Clinton Wilder, "Leaders of the Net Era," *InformationWeek*, November 27, 2000. pp. 44–56 (quotation). See www.informationweek.com; Kathleen Melymuka, "Taking Stock," *Computerworld*, June 26, 2000, pp. 66-69. See www.computerworld.com; Jerry Useem, "Internet Defense Strategy: Cannibalize Yourself," *Fortune*, September 6, 1999. pp. 121–134. See www.fortune.com.

Case Questions

1. What are the forces for change at Charles Schwab? (Hint: Use Table 19.1 of your textbook for ideas.) Be specific in naming examples from the case that fit within each category.

2. What types of resistance to change is Schwab experiencing? (Hint: Use Table 19.3 of your textbook.) Give specific examples. Consider the behavior of both Schwab employees and Schwab customers.

3. In your opinion, what are some actions that Schwab leaders could undertake to attempt either to support the forces for change or to overcome the resistance to change, as mentioned in your answers to questions 1 and 2? In your opinion, are the actions likely to be successful? Why or why not?

Experiencing Organizational Behavior

Planning a Change at the University

Purpose: This exercise will help you understand the complexities of change in organizations.

Format: Your task is to plan the implementation of a major change in an organization.

Procedure:

Part 1

The class will divide into five groups of approximately equal size. Your instructor will assign each group one of the following changes:

1. A change from the semester system to the quarter system (or the opposite, depending on the school's current system).

2. A requirement that all work—homework, examinations, term papers, problem sets—be done on computer and submitted via computers.

3. A requirement that all students live on campus.

4. A requirement that all students have reading, writing, and speaking fluency in at least three languages, including English and Japanese, to graduate.

5. A requirement that all students room with someone in the same major

First, decide what individuals and groups must be involved in the change process. Then decide how the change will be implemented using Lewin's process of organization change (Figure 19.1) as a framework. Consider how to deal with resistance to change, using Tables 19.3 and 19.4 as guides. Decide whether a change agent (internal or external) should be used. Develop a realistic timetable for full implementation of the change. Is transition management appropriate?

Part 2

Using the same groups as in Part 1, your next task is to describe the techniques you would use to imple-

ment the change described in Part 1. You may use structural changes, task and technology methods, group and individual programs, or any combination of these. You may need to go to the library to gather more information on some techniques.

You should also discuss how you will utilize the seven keys to successful change management discussed at the end of the chapter.

Your instructor may make this exercise an in-class project, but it is also a good semester-ending project for groups to work on outside class. Either way, the exercise is most beneficial when the groups report their implementation programs to the entire class. Each group should report on which change techniques are to be used, why they were selected, how they will be implemented, and how problems will be avoided.

Follow-up Questions

Part 1

1. How similar were the implementation steps for each change?

2. Were the plans for managing resistance to change realistic?

3. Do you think any of the changes could be successfully implemented at your school? Why or why not?

Part 2

1. Did various groups use the same technique in different ways or to accomplish different goals?

2. If you did outside research on organization development techniques for your project, did you find any techniques that seemed more applicable than those in this chapter? If so, describe one of them.

Self-Assessment Exercise

Support for Change

Introduction: The following questions are designed to help people understand the level of support or opposition to change within an organization. Scores on this scale should be used for classroom discussion only.

Instructions: Think of an organization for which you have worked in the past or an organization to which you currently belong and consider the situation when a change was imposed at some point in the recent past. Then circle the number that best represents your feeling about each statement or question.

1. **Values and Vision**

   (Do people throughout the organization share values or vision?)

1	2	3	4	5	6	7
Low						High

2. **History of Change**

   (Does the organization have a good track record in handling change?)

1	2	3	4	5	6	7
Low						High

3. **Cooperation and Trust**

   (Do they seem high throughout the organization?)

1	2	3	4	5	6	7
Low						High

4. **Culture**

   (Is it one that supports risk taking and change?)

1	2	3	4	5	6	7
Low						High

5. **Resilience**

   (Can people handle more?)

1	2	3	4	5	6	7
Low						High

6. **Rewards**

   (Will this change be seen as beneficial?)

1	2	3	4	5	6	7
Low						High

7. **Respect and Face**

   (Will people be able to maintain dignity and self-respect?)

1	2	3	4	5	6	7
Low						High

8. **Status Quo**

   (Will this change be seen as mild?)

1	2	3	4	5	6	7
Low						High

A Guide to Scoring and explanation is available in the *Instructor's Resource Manual.*

Reference: From Rick Maurer, *Beyond the Wall of Resistance*, 1996 (Austin: Bard Press), pp. 104–105. Used by permission of Bard Press.

OB Online

1. Use any available search engine to look up two of the companies that are discussed in this chapter as being involved in making organizational changes (Vivendi, Ford, DuPont, EDS, Context Integration, Avon, Schwab, Nokia, Honeywell/Allied Signal). You should look up the companies' web sites and utilize any of several databases that have magazine, newspaper, and journal articles.

2. Create an update report about these companies by describing how well the changes have worked, whether the companies have continued the changes, and whether they have made even more changes.

Building Managerial Skills

Exercise Overview: Many organizations utilize surveys to assess the needs and concerns of their employees. On the basis of the results of such surveys, many organizations make significant organizational changes. This exercise will help you understand more about organizational surveys.

Exercise Background: Your organization has a new CEO who has been brought in to make changes. Her first priority is to survey all employees to find out what employees think about the company, what they want from the company, and what their needs and concerns are.

Exercise Task: You have been assigned to find several organizational surveys that could be used by your company. Search the Internet for resources that might assist you in finding several different surveys and other related resources. Describe the kinds of information you were able to locate and explain its likely value to you.

Finally, respond to the following questions:

1. What additional information would you need, besides what was available on the Internet, to actually use one of the surveys that you found?

2. How would the type of survey you use be different if you were a large multinational company as opposed to a small manufacturing company with employees at only one location?

The Downfall of Enron—The Organization

Parts I, II, and III outline several contributing factors in the downfall of Enron. But there is yet another culprit—the flawed design of the organization itself. The failures at Enron were caused not only by accounting irregularities or allegedly corrupt leadership but also by the company's organization structure and culture. Specifically, critics of Enron assert that the company's emphasis on flexibility, "loose-tight" design, "creative destruction," decentralization, lack of reporting and control, and competitive culture were also factors in one of the biggest and most rapidly developing corporate calamities. Enron's decentralized organization structure made control difficult because managers in different businesses could act without the knowledge or permission of others. Many of the key players in the scandal reported directly to Skilling, an example of "letting the fox guard the henhouse"—giving oversight responsibility to the very person who was encouraging the risk taking.

Additionally, Skilling used a set of principles developed at McKinsey & Co., his previous employer. The "loose-tight" principle allowed workers freedom to innovate but also maintained some central control. Risk taking increased, as did innovation. Skilling believed in the necessity of taking big risks, saying, "No shots, no ducks." Another McKinsey principle, "creative destruction," based on the work of economist Joseph Schumpeter, required that a firm constantly reinvent itself. Under Skilling, Enron employees utilized this principle by continuously reconfiguring the organization, thus creating a moving target that was hard to understand and even harder to manage and control.

Enron's design was weak in external reporting and control requirements. The board of directors, expert stock analysts, management scholars, and even Enron's own CEOs all maintained that they had been unaware of key events at the firm. On the day Enron declared bankruptcy, it claimed to have $3 billion in the bank, but only $1 billion was found. Could a company really lose $2 billion and not notice? If that was truly an error and not a scam, then the firm's reporting and authority structures must have been grossly ineffectual. A former Enron manager declares, "The environment was ripe for abuse. Nobody at corporate was asking the right questions. It was completely hands-off management. A situation like that requires tight controls. Instead, it was a runaway train."

Enron's corporate culture rewarded employees for innovation regardless of the outcomes. According to the firm's 1999 Annual Report, Enron valued creativity highly. It states: "Our culture of innovation is difficult to duplicate. Individuals are empowered to do what they think is best, and most of our outstanding initiatives in 1999 came directly from our own ranks. Our philosophy is to not stand in the way of our employees, so we don't insist on hierarchical approval." In the hindsight, the company did just that—and risk taking mushroomed. The Annual Report continues by noting, "We insist on results, and the results have been quite good." However, the results the firm was measuring were revenues, not earnings. And the risks and expenses of obtaining those sales revenues were not accurately reported or successfully controlled.

The firm also failed to communicate accurately with those inside and outside the corporation. Warren Bennis, a professor at the University of Southern California, relates the story of Samuel Goldwyn discussing recent failures and stating jokingly, "I want you to tell me exactly what's wrong with me and M.G.M.—even if it means losing your job." That willingness to examine one's own weaknesses was lacking at Enron, Bennis asserts. In his *New York Times* article entitled "A Corporate Fear of Too Much Truth," Bennis writes, "Mr. Lay's failing is . . . his inability to create a company culture open to reality, one that does not discourage management from delivering bad news. No organization can be honest with the public if it is not honest with itself."

How did things go so wrong so quickly? The reasons are many. In spite of the checks and balances in our economic system, catastrophic failures of seemingly sound firms can happen. Ambiguous and vague regulations provide one reason for the failures. Most of what Enron did, although unethical, nevertheless complies with accounting standards and is legal. Another reason is the low priority of investigating white-collar crime for most law enforcement agencies. In addition, the complexity of the company's deals made it difficult for authorities to establish the facts. Representative John Dingell says, "What we're looking at here is an example of superbly complex financial results. They didn't have to lie. All they had to do was to obfuscate it with sheer complexity—although they probably lied too." Prosecutors must prove intent to defraud, which can be impossible to do. And wealthy executives are rarely sentenced to prison even if they are found guilty.

As for the long-term effects, there will be consequences for many individuals and entities, including former employees, investors and the analysts who advise them, corporations, the accounting profession, the energy industry, government regulators, and the U.S. economy.

Some employees are making light of their situation—you can buy a coffee cup emblazoned with "Enron Retirement Planning" for $300 on eBay; an "Enron Code of Ethics" manual costs $175. Former Enron employee Meredith M. Stewart explains, "There's only so much sadness you can take till you just need a break." She has recorded a sardonic rap-style composition: "We danced at parties and drank the booze[.] Stock was up[,] no way to lose. Now less than zero and falling fast[.] Got no severance and my savings are trashed." Another song, sung to the tune of "Da Do Run Run," includes these lyrics: "The accountants said that everything was A-O.K., At Enron Ron, At Enron Ron. Now the moving vans are taking all the desks away, From Enron Ron, From Enron Ron."

Other former employees are not coping as well, as evidenced by a surge in individual bankruptcies and home foreclosures. In the most tragic case, the scandal cost a life. Enron Vice Chairman J. Clifford Baxter, who sold shares valued at $12 million, resigned in May 2001. Sherron Watkins claims, "Cliff Baxter complained mightily to Skilling and all who would listen about the inappropriateness of our transactions." Baxter shot and killed himself on January 25, 2002, apparently believing that his reputation had been ruined.

Investors named Enron and Andersen as defendants in several fraud cases. Investors are also battling with the surviving partnerships for their non-Enron assets. The U.S. District Court in Houston will try the cases, and the potential for conflicts of interest is high, given Enron's generous contributions to local judges. Some financial firms are also defendants because they had advised clients to purchase stock, which benefited their companies' brokerage units but hurt most investors.

Corporations such as Credit Suisse and Citicorp that invested in partnerships with Enron are scrambling to salvage their assets and reputations. The association also taints companies with close relationships to Enron, such as Andersen, McKinsey & Co., and Merrill Lynch; observers wonder why they didn't

see the impending crisis. Meanwhile, all corporations will be held to higher accounting standards. Already, Tyco International and Xerox have restated their earnings, adjusting past profits by billions of dollars. Corporations want to avoid being accused of "Enronitis," an overemphasis on earnings. For example, General Electric CEO Jeff Immelt says, "I'm not worried about being like [Enron]. But any of us could see it would have a fairly big impact on . . . the way companies are run."

Andersen stands accused of obstruction of justice for untimely shredding of audit documents. Andersen was driven out of business, but skeptics note that the partners who established its dysfunctional culture have accepted other high-paying jobs. And the accounting profession as a whole is being criticized. Accounting principles are regarded as too flexible; for example, they allow companies to recognize estimated future profits—but the estimates are often inaccurate. Paul A. Volcker Jr., the former chairman of the Federal Reserve has declared, "Accounting and auditing in this country are in a state of crisis."

The energy industry is also coming under higher scrutiny. Before Enron's collapse, in just four years, twenty-four states, including California and Texas, passed deregulation statutes, primarily as a result of lobbying efforts by Enron. So is it a coincidence that California governor Gray Davis received $97,500 in campaign contributions from Enron, and Texas governor Rick Perry received $212,000? California officials complain that in 2001 they overpaid by millions of dollars and received too little energy, a situation that resulted in brownouts, thanks to Enron's manipulation of the industry's energy supply and pricing. States are now insisting on more industry oversight.

A record thirteen subcommittees of Congress are investigating the scandal. This interest is fueled, in part, by the desire of Democratic politicians to connect members of the Bush administration with Enron managers. (Vice President Dick Cheney refused to release notes of his meetings with Enron leaders, and President Bush refused to order Cheney to relinquish the information.) Congress is also considering many related issues, including increased regulation of accounting standards, auditors, the makeup of retirement accounts, executive stock options, and energy trading practices, as well as beefing up the budget of the SEC. The legislature has already restricted the connections between a firm's analysts, who claim to be independent, and its brokers, who represent clients, to minimize conflicts of interest. Some object to the proposed regulations. Labor Secretary Elaine L. Chao claims, "Washington shouldn't be allowed to dictate to workers how much company stock they can own." However, despite some opposition, regulation is likely in every one of these areas.

Long-term fallout from the Enron debacle might even include disastrous effects on the U.S. economy. Pointing to historical examples of scandals that had a similarly large scope, such as the Teapot Dome scandal of the 1920s, experts predict a lower level of participation in the stock market. Investors have lost confidence. Alex Berenson, writing for the *New York Times*, says, "The fact that a company as large and well-known as Enron could essentially be vaporized in a matter of months has shaken even the most cynical investors on Wall Street." Investors' skepticism is well founded. Two-thirds of chief financial officers are asked to misrepresent earnings; 12 percent admit doing so. Stock prices have fallen—the S&P index dropped 4 percent. Earnings restatements will further lower profitability, driving stock prices down. Ultimately, companies will pay more for funds, and the increased costs will be passed along to consumers.

As the Enron saga continues to unwind, and as more is learned about what happened and why, the tendency to point fingers becomes stronger. "Blame is a natural, self-protecting tendency," claims Laura P. Hartman, a professor at DePaul University. "Given ourselves or someone else, we are far more likely to blame other people." Daryl Koehn, a professor at the University of St. Thomas, agrees: "All of us were happy to see our stock portfolios soar in value and did not want to look closely at the practices that were generating our capital gains. When the market went south, we all looked for someone to scapegoat." Of course, anyone who engaged in fraudulent activity should be held accountable. But investors and employees who turned a blind eye to wrongdoing also must take some responsibility. The scandal has become a mirror, showing us both the good and the bad inherent in our economic system and ourselves. After the facts are known and the blame apportioned, it will be time for reform. *New York Times* writer Jeffrey L. Seglin has the right idea when he says, "Then we should figure out ways to ensure that these fine messes don't happen again."

"The environment was ripe for abuse. . . . [Enron] was a runaway train."—a former Enron manager in Enron's energy services unit

References: "A Hollow Victory Against Andersen," *Business Week*, July 1, 2002. www.businessweek.com on June 25, 2002; Mike France and Dan Carney, "Why Corporate Crooks Are Tough to Nail," *Business Week*, July 1, 2002. www.businessweek.com on June 25, 2002; Joseph Kahn, "Will It Be California Redux?" *New York Times*, May 12, 2002, p. BU1, 10. See www.nytimes.com; Steve Shepard, "Online Extra: Q&A with GE's Jeff Immelt," *Business Week*, April 29, 2002. www.businessweek.com on April 29, 2002; Gretchen Morgenson, "Time for Accountability at the Corporate Candy Store," *New York Times*, March 31, 2002, p. BU1. See www.nytimes.com; Leslie Wayne, "Chagrined Enron Partners Try to Stave Off Both Losses and Scandal's Taint," *New York Times*, March 31, 2002, p. 20. See www.nytimes.com; John Schwartz, "An Enron Auditor and an Elephant Walk Into a Bar . . ." *New York Times*, March 3, 2002, p. BU9. See www.nytimes.com; John A. Byrne, "At Enron, 'The Environment Was Ripe for Abuse,'" *Business Week*, February 25, 2002 (quotation). www.businessweek. com on June 25, 2002; Alex Berenson, "Three-Decade-Old Echoes, Awakened by Enron," *New York Times*, February 24, 2002, p. BU1. See www.nytimes.com; Tom Zeller, "Taking Enron Scraps to Auction," *New York Times*, February 17, 2002, p. WK4. See www.nytimes.com; Alex Berenson, "The Biggest Casualty of Enron's Collapse: Confidence," *New York Times*, February 10, 2002, p. WK1, 6. See www.nytimes.com; Adam Clymer, "Never Have So Many Missed the Forest," *New York Times*, February 10, 2002, p. WK6. See www.nytimes.com; David Leonhardt, "How Will Washington Read the Signs?" *New York Times*, February 10, 2002, p. BU1, 13. See www.nytimes. com; Gretchen Morgenson, "Scandal's Ripple Effect: Earnings Under Threat," *New York Times*, February 10, 2002, pp. BU1, 12. See www.nytimes.com; Stuart Elliott, "TV Catch Phrase from the 1960's Is Evoked in a Hearing over Enron," *New York Times*, February 9, 2002, p. C4. See www.nytimes.com; Steven Greenhouse, "Plan to Put Limits on 401(k) Holdings Draws Fire," *New York Times*, February 9, 2002, pp. C1, 5. See www.nytimes.com; Leslie Wayne, "Enron, Preaching Deregulation, Worked the Statehouse Circuit," *New York Times*, February 9, 2002, pp. C1, 5. See www.nytimes.com; Bethany McLean, "Why Enron Went Bust," *Fortune*, December 24, 2001. www.fortune.com on June 27, 2002; "To Our Shareholders," Enron 1999 Annual Report. www.enron.com on June 28, 2002.

Integrative Case Questions

1. Describe Enron's organization structure, including its division of labor, coordination, and responsibility. What could Enron managers have done differently in designing the company's structure to make the problems it experienced less likely to occur?

2. List as many of Enron's cultural values and norms as possible. Then, looking at your list, tell how the values and norms helped Enron to be effective. Looking at the list again, describe how those same values and norms also contributed to Enron's downfall.

3. Enron's policy of creative destruction emphasizes the firm's commitment to continual change. In what ways does continual change provide benefits for firms? In what ways does it increase risks?

Appendix A
Research Methods in Organizational Behavior

We have referred to theories and research findings as a basis for our discussion throughout this book. In this appendix, we further examine how theories and research findings about organizational behavior are developed. First, we highlight the role of theory and research. We then identify the purposes of research and describe the steps in the research process, types of research designs, and methods of gathering data. We conclude with a brief discussion of some related issues.

The Role of Theory and Research

Some managers—and many students—fail to see the need for research. They seem confused by what appears to be an endless litany of theories and by sets of contradictory research findings. They often ask, "Why bother?"

Indeed, few absolute truths have emerged from studies of organizational behavior. Management in general and organizational behavior in particular, however, are in many ways fields of study still in their infancy. Thus, it stands to reason that researchers in these fields have few theories that always work. In addition, their research cannot always be generalized to settings other than those in which the research was originally conducted.

Still, theory and research play valuable roles.[1] Theories help investigators organize what they do know. They provide a framework that managers can use to diagnose problems and implement changes. They also serve as road signs that help managers solve many problems involving people. Research also plays an important role. Each study conducted and published adds a little more to the storehouse of knowledge available to practicing managers. Questions are posed and answers developed. Over time, researchers can become increasingly more confident of findings as they are applied across different settings.[2]

Purposes of Research

Scientific research is the systematic investigation of hypothesized propositions about the relationships among natural phenomena.

Basic research is concerned with discovering new knowledge rather than solving specific problems.

Applied research is conducted to solve particular problems or answer specific questions.

As much as possible, researchers try to approach problems and questions of organizational behavior scientifically. **Scientific research** is the systematic investigation of hypothesized propositions about the relationships among natural phenomena. The aims of science are to describe, explain, and predict phenomena.[3] Research can be classified as basic or applied. **Basic research** is concerned with discovering new knowledge rather than solving particular problems. The knowledge made available through basic research may not have much direct application to organizations, at least when it is first discovered.[4] Research scientists and university professors are the people who most often conduct basic research in organizational behavior.

Applied research, on the other hand, is conducted to solve particular problems or answer specific questions. The findings of applied research are, by definition, immediately applicable to managers. Consultants, university professors, and managers themselves conduct much of the applied research performed in organizations.

The Scientific Research Process

To result in valid findings, research should be conducted according to the scientific process shown in Figure AA.1. The starting point is a question or problem.[5] For example, a manager wants to design a new reward system to enhance employee motivation but is unsure about what types of rewards to offer or how to tie them to performance. Therefore, this manager's questions are "What kinds of rewards will motivate my employees?" and "How should those rewards be tied to performance?"

The next step is to review existing literature to determine what is already known about the phenomenon. Something has probably been written about most problems or questions today's managers face. Thus, the goal of the literature review is to avoid "reinventing the wheel" by finding out what others have already learned. Basic research generally is available in journals such as the *Academy of Management Journal, Academy of Management Review, Administrative Science Quarterly, Journal of Applied Psychology, Organizational Behavior and Human Decision Processes, Journal of*

figure AA.1

The Research Process

The scientific research process follows a logical and rational sequence of activities. Using this process enables researchers to place greater confidence in their findings. Of course, in some instances compromises may be necessary in order to study some phenomena in certain settings. For example, studying potentially controversial subjects like power, politics, or ethics may be difficult if the process is followed rigidly.

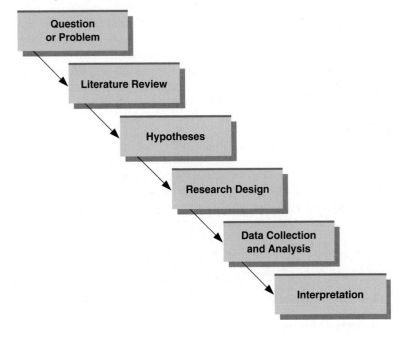

Management, and *Organization Science*. Applied research findings are more likely to be found in such sources as the *Harvard Business Review, Academy of Management Executive, Organizational Dynamics, HRMagazine*, and *Personnel Psychology*.

Based on the original question and the review of the literature, researchers formulate hypotheses—predictions of what they expect to find. The hypothesis is an important guide for the researcher's design of the study because it provides a very clear and precise statement of what the researcher wants to test. That means that study can be specifically designed to test the hypothesis.

The research design is the plan for doing the research. (We discuss the more common research designs later.) As part of the research design, the researcher must determine how variables will be measured. Thus, if satisfaction is one factor being considered, the researcher must decide how to measure it.

After data have been collected, they must be analyzed. (We also discuss common methods for gathering data later.) Depending on the study design and hypotheses, data analysis may be relatively simple and straightforward or may require elaborate statistical procedures. Methods for analyzing data are beyond the scope of this discussion.

Finally, the results of the study are interpreted; that is, the researcher figures out what they mean. They may provide support for the hypothesis, fail to support the hypothesis, or suggest a relationship other than that proposed in the hypothesis. An important part of the interpretation process is recognizing the limitations imposed on the findings by weaknesses in the research design.

Many researchers go a step further and try to publish their findings. Several potential sources for publication are the journals mentioned in the discussion of literature review. Publication is important because it helps educate other researchers and managers and also provides additional information for future literature reviews.[6]

Types of Research Designs

A research design is the set of procedures used to test the predicted relationships among natural phenomena.

A **research design** is the set of procedures used to test the predicted relationships among natural phenomena. The design addresses such issues as how the relevant variables are to be defined, measured, and related to one another. Managers and researchers can draw on a variety of research designs, each with its own strengths and weaknesses. Four general types of research designs often are used in the study of organizational behavior (see Table AA.1); each type has several variations.[7]

Case Study

A case study is an in-depth analysis of one setting.

A **case study** is an in-depth analysis of a single setting. This design frequently is used when little is known about the phenomena being studied and the researcher wants to look at relevant concepts intensively and thoroughly. A variety of methods are used to gather information, including interviews, questionnaires, and personal observation.[8]

The case study research design offers several advantages. First, it allows the researcher to probe one situation in detail, yielding a wealth of descriptive and explanatory information. The case study also facilitates the discovery of unexpected relationships. Because the researcher observes virtually everything that happens in a given situation, she or he may learn about issues beyond those originally chosen for study.

table AA.1

Types of Research Designs

Type	Dominant Characteristic
Case Study	Useful for thorough exploration of unknown phenomena
Field Survey	Provides easily quantifiable data
Laboratory Experiment	Allows researcher high control of variables
Field Experiment	Takes place in realistic setting

The case study design also has several disadvantages. The data it provides cannot be readily generalized to other situations because the information is so closely tied to the situation being studied. In addition, case study information may be biased by the researcher's closeness to the situation. Case study research also tends to be very time-consuming.

Nevertheless, the case study can be an effective and useful research design as long as the researcher understands its limitations and takes them into account when formulating conclusions.

Field Survey

A field survey typically relies on a questionnaire distributed to a sample of people selected from a larger population.

A **field survey** usually relies on a questionnaire distributed to a sample of people chosen from a larger population.

If a manager is conducting the study, the sample often is drawn from a group or department within her or his organization. If a researcher is conducting the study, the sample typically is negotiated with a host organization interested in the questions being addressed. The questionnaire generally is mailed or delivered by hand to participants at home or at work and may be returned by mail or picked up by the researcher. The respondents answer the questions and return the questionnaire as directed. The researcher analyzes the responses and tries to make inferences about the larger population from the representative sample.[9] Field surveys can focus on a variety of topics relevant to organizational behavior, including employees' attitudes toward other people (such as leaders and coworkers), attitudes toward their jobs (such as satisfaction with the job and commitment to the organization), and perceptions of organizational characteristics (such as the challenge inherent in the job and the degree of decentralization in the organization).[10]

Field surveys provide information about a much larger segment of the population than do case studies. They also provide an abundance of data in easily quantifiable form, which facilitates statistical analysis and the compilation of normative data for comparative purposes.

Field surveys also have several disadvantages. First, survey information may reveal only superficial feelings and reactions to situations rather than deeply held feelings, attitudes, or emotions. Second, the design and development of field surveys require a great deal of expertise and can be very time-consuming. Furthermore, relationships among variables tend to be accentuated in responses to questionnaires because of what is called "common method variance." This means that people may tend to answer all the questions in the same way, creating a misleading impression. A final, very important point is that field surveys give the researcher little or no control. The researcher may lack control over who completes the questionnaire, when it is filled out, the mental or physical state of the respondent, and many other important conditions. Thus, the typical field survey has many inherent sources of potential error.[11]

Nonetheless, surveys can be a very useful means of gathering large quantities of data and assessing general patterns of relationships among variables.

Laboratory Experiment

A laboratory experiment involves creating an artificial setting similar to a real work situation to allow control over almost every possible factor in that setting.

The **laboratory experiment** gives the researcher the most control. By creating an artificial setting similar to a real work situation, the researcher can control almost every possible factor in that setting. He or she can then manipulate the variables in the study and examine their effects on other variables.[12]

As an example of how laboratory experiments work, consider the relationship between how goals are developed for subordinates and the subordinates' subsequent level of satisfaction. To explore this relationship, the researcher structures a situation in which some subjects (usually students but occasionally people hired or recruited from the community) are assigned goals while others determine their own goals. Both groups then work on a hypothetical task relevant to the goals, and afterward all subjects fill out a questionnaire designed to measure satisfaction. Differences in satisfaction between the two groups could be attributed to the method used for goal setting.

Laboratory experiments prevent some of the problems of other types of research. Advantages include a high degree of control over variables and precise measurement of variables. A major disadvantage is the lack of realism; rarely does the laboratory setting exactly duplicate the real-life situation. A related problem is the difficulty in generalizing the findings to organizational settings. Finally, some organizational situations, such as plant closings or employee firings, cannot be realistically simulated in a laboratory.

Field Experiment

A field experiment is similar to a laboratory experiment but is conducted in a real organization.

A **field experiment** is similar to a laboratory experiment except that it is conducted in a real organization. In a field experiment, the researcher attempts to control certain variables and to manipulate others to assess the effects of the manipulated variables on outcome variables. For example, a manager interested in the effects of flexible working hours on absenteeism and turnover might design a field experiment in which one plant adopts a flexible work schedule program and another plant, one as similar as possible to the first, serves as a control site. Attendance and turnover are monitored at both plants. If attendance increases and turnover decreases in the experimental plant and there are no changes at the control site, the manager probably will conclude that the flexible work schedule program was successful.

The field experiment has certain advantages over the laboratory experiment. The organizational setting provides greater realism, making generalization to other organizational situations more valid. Disadvantages include the lack of control over other events that might occur in the organizational setting (such as additional changes the firm could introduce); contamination of the results if the various groups discover their respective roles in the experiment and behave differently because of that knowledge, greater expense, and the risk that the experimental manipulations will contribute to problems within the company.

Methods of Gathering Data

T he method of gathering data is a critical concern of the research design. Data-gathering methods may be grouped into four categories: questionnaires, interviews, observation, and nonreactive measures.[13]

Questionnaires

A *questionnaire* is a collection of written questions about the respondents' attitudes, opinions, perceptions, demographic characteristics, or some combination of these factors. Usually the respondent fills out the questionnaire and returns it to the researcher. To facilitate scoring, the researcher typically uses questions with a variety of answers, each of which has an associated score. Some questionnaires have a few open-ended questions that allow respondents to elaborate on their answers. Designing a questionnaire that will provide the information the researcher desires is a very complex task and one that has received considerable attention. Some researchers have recently begun using computer networks to distribute questionnaires and collect responses.

Interviews

An *interview* resembles a questionnaire, but the questions are presented to the respondent orally by an interviewer. The respondent usually is allowed to answer questions spontaneously rather than being asked to choose among alternatives defined by the researcher. Interviews generally take much more time to administer than questionnaires, and they are more difficult to score. The benefit of interviews is the opportunity for the respondent to speak at length on a topic, thereby providing a richness and depth of information not normally yielded by questionnaires.

Observation

Observation, in its simplest form, is watching events and recording what is observed. Researchers use several types of observation. In structured observation, the observer is trained to look for and record certain activities or types of events. In participant observation, the trained observer actually participates in the organizational events as a member of the work team and records impressions and observations in a diary or daily log. In hidden observation, the trained observer is not visible to the subjects. A hidden camera or a specially designed observation room may be used.

Nonreactive Measures

When a situation is changed because of data gathering, we say the activity has caused a reaction in the situation. *Nonreactive measures*, also called "unobtrusive measures," have been developed for gathering data without disturbing the situation being studied. When questionnaires, interviews, and obtrusive observations may cause problems in the research situation, the use of nonreactive measures may be an appropriate substitute. Nonreactive measures include examination of physical traces, use of archives, and simple observation. At some universities, for example, sidewalks are not laid down around a new building until it has been in use for some time. Rather than ask students and faculty about their traffic patterns or try to anticipate them, the designers observe the building in use, see where the grass is most heavily worn, and put sidewalks there.

Related Issues in Research

Three other issues are of particular interest to researchers: causality, reliability and validity, and ethical concerns.[14]

Causality

Scientific research attempts to describe, explain, and predict phenomena. In many cases, the purpose of the research is to reveal causality; that is, researchers attempt to describe, explain, and predict the cause of a certain event. In everyday life, people commonly observe a series of events and infer causality about the relationship among them. For example, you might observe that a good friend is skipping one of her classes regularly. You also know that she is failing that class. You might infer that she is failing the class because of her poor attendance. But the causal relationship may be just the reverse: Your friend may have had a good attendance record until her poor performance on the first test destroyed her motivation and led her to stop attending class. Given the complexities associated with human behavior in organizational settings, the issues of causality, causal inference, and causal relations are of considerable interest to managers and researchers alike.

In the behavioral sciences, causality is difficult to determine because of the interrelationships among variables in a social system. Causality cannot always be empirically proven, but it may be possible to infer causality in certain circumstances. In general, two conditions must be met for causality to be attributed to an observed relationship among variables. The first is temporal order: If x causes y, then x must occur before y. Many studies, especially field surveys, describe the degree of association among variables with highly sophisticated mathematical techniques, but inferring a causal relationship is difficult because the variables are measured at the same point in time. On the basis of such evidence, we cannot say whether one variable or event caused the other, whether they were both caused by another variable, or whether they are totally independent of each other.

The second condition is the elimination of spuriousness. If we want to infer that x caused y, we must eliminate all other possible causes of y. Often a seemingly causal relationship between two variables is due to their joint association with a third variable, z. To be able to say the relationship between x and y is causal, we must rule out z as a possible cause of y. In the behavioral sciences, so many variables may influence one another that tracing causal relationships is like walking in an endless maze. Yet despite the difficulties of the task, we must continue trying to describe, explain, and predict social phenomena in organizational settings if we are to advance our understanding of organizational behavior.[15]

Reliability and Validity

The margin: *The reliability of a measure is the extent to which it is consistent over time.*

The **reliability** of a measure is the extent to which it is consistent over time. Suppose that a researcher measures a group's job satisfaction today with a questionnaire and then measures the same thing again in two months. Assuming that nothing has changed, individual responses should be very similar. If they are, the measure can be assessed as having a high level of reliability. Likewise, if question 2 and question 10 ask about the same thing, responses to these questions should be consistent. If measures lack reliability, little confidence can be placed in the results they provide.

Validity is the extent to which a measure actually reflects what it was intended to measure.

Validity describes the extent to which research measures what it was intended to measure. Suppose that a researcher is interested in employees' satisfaction with their jobs. To determine this, he asks them a series of questions about their pay, supervisors, and working conditions. He then averages their answers and uses the average to represent job satisfaction. We might argue that this is not a valid measure. Pay, supervision, and working conditions, for example, may be unrelated to the job itself. Thus, the researcher has obtained data that do not mean what he thinks they mean—they are not valid. The researcher, then, must use measures that are valid as well as reliable.[16]

Ethical Concerns

Last, but certainly not least, the researcher must contend with ethical concerns. Two concerns are particularly important.[17] First, the researcher must provide adequate protection for participants in the study and not violate their privacy without their permission. For example, suppose that a researcher is studying the behavior of a group of operating employees. A good way to increase people's willingness to participate is to promise that their identities will not be revealed. Having made such a guarantee, the researcher is obligated to keep it.

Likewise, participation should be voluntary. All prospective subjects should have the right to not participate or to withdraw their participation after the study has begun. The researchers should explain all procedures in advance to participants and should not subject them to any experimental conditions that could harm them either physically or psychologically. Many government agencies, universities, and professional associations have developed guidelines for researchers to use to guarantee protection of human subjects.

The other issue involves how the researcher reports the results. In particular, it is important that research procedures and methods be reported faithfully and candidly. This enables readers to assess for themselves the validity of the results reported. It also allows others to do a better job of replicating (repeating) the study, perhaps with a different sample, to learn more about how its findings generalize.

Appendix B
Career Dynamics

Now that baby boomers are moving up the corporate ladder into middle management, a problem has become apparent: Some people of the following generation, often called the "busters," do not like working for some of the boomers. This group of workers born after 1965 has also been called "Generation X." In fact some members of Generation X are leaving the corporate world for small businesses, often starting their own.[1] Career paths are not what they used to be.

As companies downsize, reengineer, and rethink the corporation, there are fewer jobs in the middle and at the top, and thus fewer opportunities to climb the ladder. Many of the boomers have either been downsized into redeployment groups and eventually laid off, or they have become disillusioned with their middle-level management positions. Some finally discover that they are in the wrong occupation. Many have quit for a variety of personal and professional reasons. For example, many parents are reducing their hours on the job and taking pay cuts to spend more time with their families. Mark Jefferson, an architect in Phoenix, reduced his hours to coach his seven-year-old son's baseball team. In a recent survey by Robert Half International, 76 percent of those surveyed would give up rapid career advancement for more family or personal time.[2] Many members of Generation X are unhappy, unsuccessful, or both because they are in the wrong occupation or profession. This means that nearly 30 million people are unhappy in their jobs. The impact on organizational productivity is immense.

A new type of worker is becoming common in many companies: the high-tech nomad. These are people who do freelance work as consultants or contract workers on a project-by-project basis for companies around the world. A job may last a week or six months. The hourly rate is high, but the worker gives up the job security and benefits that typically come from a permanent position with an established company. These types of jobs are on the increase because of the massive downsizing by many companies.[3] Globally, the situation is different. Joblessness is increasing worldwide. Almost one-third of the Earth's 2.8 billion workers are unemployed or underemployed.[4]

An underemployed worker is one who is doing a job for which she or he is overqualified. A combination of factors is causing this global jobs problem. In industrialized countries, most companies are struggling to become more efficient to remain competitive globally. In the developing and transitional-economy countries, the struggle is to modernize the means of production and train workers to do the jobs.

Clearly, on a global basis, people may just be happy to have a job. But even those who have jobs seem to be dissatisfied with them and looking for something more. If these problems are to be solved, both individuals and organizations need to know more about jobs, careers, career choices, and career management.

Why are so many people dissatisfied with their jobs and careers? How can organizations help employees pursue the careers that offer the greatest benefit to both employees and the organization? Why do so many people change not only their jobs but also the type of work they do several times during their work lives? How can organizations ensure that when employees leave the company, either by quitting or by retiring, highly qualified people will quickly and efficiently replace them? The issues reflected in these questions have led organizations to invest large amounts of money, time, and effort in developing career management programs. In addition, researchers have begun to study careers systematically.

In this appendix, we examine individual and organizational perspectives on careers. We describe several aspects of career choices. Then we explore the career stages and conclude by discussing organizational career planning.

Individual and Organizational Perspectives on Careers

A career is a perceived sequence of attitudes and behaviors associated with work-related experiences and activities over the person's life span.

People often use the word "career" to refer to the professional occupations of others and not to their own work or job. Indeed, many people do not even expect to have careers—they expect to have jobs.[5] A **career** is a "perceived sequence of attitudes and behaviors associated with work-related experiences and activities over the span of the person's life."[6] Whereas a job is what a person does to bring home a paycheck, a career is a more satisfying and productive activity.[7] Thus, a career involves a long-term series of jobs and work experiences.

People's careers may reflect their personal interests. As people evaluate job opportunities, those with a career perspective usually are concerned with factors such as those listed in Table AB.1. Note how these matters reflect a long-term perspective: People are concerned about the future of technological change, economic conditions, and personal advancement. Many see opportunities for advancement slowing as more people enter popular career fields. They see the rate of technical obsolescence accelerating with the advent of new and better computers and automated manufacturing processes. People trying to establish their careers may worry when the rate of economic growth is declining. They also see that new entrants are treated better than people already in the labor market—getting higher starting salaries, better opportunities, and the like. Furthermore, companies are reorganizing and downsizing, which is increasing uncertainty and decreasing opportunities for advancement. Finally, aging is a concern; as people get older, their career options frequently narrow and their opportunities shrink.[8]

table AB.1

Individual Career Issues

Career Issues	Examples
Opportunity for Advancement Slowing	More people entering popular careers
Technical Obsolescence Accelerating	Rapidly changing automation, computerization
Rate of Economic Growth Declining	Economy not expanding, fewer jobs created
New Entrants into the Labor Market Receiving More Favorable Treatment	Higher starting salaries and prerequisites for new hires
Companies Reorganizing	Downsizing, reducing layers of middle management
Aging	Career options narrow, fewer opportunities

Reference: Adapted from C. Hymowitz, "Stable Cycles of Executive Careers Shattered by Upheaval in Business," *Wall Street Journal,* May 26, 1987, p. 31. Republished with permission of Dow Jones, from the *Wall Street Journal*, May 26, 1987; permission conveyed through Copyright Clearance Center, Inc.

Organizations have a different perspective on careers.[9] They want to ensure that managerial succession is orderly and efficient so that when managers need to be replaced because of promotion, retirement, accident or illness, termination, or resignation, highly qualified people can replace them quickly and easily. Organizations also want their employees to pursue careers in which they are interested and for which they have been properly trained. If employees are unhappy with their career choices and opportunities, they may not perform well or choose to leave the organization. Thus, to achieve high levels of performance and lower levels of turnover, organizations have an investment in ensuring that people and careers match.

Clearly, although their perspectives are not identical, employees and organizations can both benefit from working together to improve career management. Career choices, however, remain in the hands of individuals.

Career Choices

Career choices arise more than once during a lifetime because both people and career opportunities change. People need not be "locked in" to a particular career choice. Knowing that they can change careers can help individuals avoid becoming poor performers in their jobs as a result of career frustration.

Career choices are not something to take lightly, however; they are important in their own right, and they form the basis for future career decisions. As Figure AB.1 indicates, making a career choice involves six steps. First, the person must become aware that a career choice is needed. This awareness may arise in a variety of ways. A recent high school graduate may recognize the need to make a choice after being urged to find a job or declare a college major. A person already pursuing a career may consider choosing a new one after receiving a negative performance evaluation, being turned down for a big promotion, or being fired or laid off.

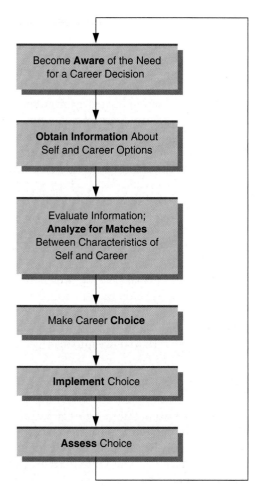

figure AB.1

A Simplified Model of Individual Career Choice

People are never "locked in" to a particular job, occupation, or organization. Periodically, they make career choices just as they make other decisions. Good information is the key to making important life and work career decisions.

Second, the worker must obtain information about himself or herself and about available career options. Personal interests, skills, abilities, and desires can be identified by self-reflection as well as by formal and informal consultations with others. In addition, information about the demands and rewards of various careers is available from numerous sources, including career counselors, placement officers, friends, and family.

The third step in the career choice process involves evaluating the information and looking for matches between the person's wants and needs and the characteristics of potential careers. This can be frustrating and confusing as the person finds that every job has advantages as well as disadvantages. Although the help of a competent advisor or counselor is valuable, the next step—the career decision—rests with the individual. In the fourth step, the individual must make a commitment to a career or a set of highly similar careers. Commitment means making the decision and initiating the next step, implementation.

Implementing the decision involves actively pursuing the career; preparing through training, education, or internships; obtaining a position; and finally, working. After a time, the individual must assess the choice. As long as the result of the assessment is satisfactory, the individual continues to pursue the career. If the conclusion is unsatisfactory, the individual becomes aware of the need for another career choice and the process begins again.

In making career decisions, people are subjected to a number of pressures. As indicated in Figure AB.2, these pressures may be personal, social, or work related. An individual's personality and goals may be better suited to some careers than to others, and lack of agreement between the types of careers that suit the person's personality and those appropriate to his or her personal goals can create internal conflicts. Social factors that create career pressure include urging from family or friends to quit a job or to take one job rather than another. Some people are now evaluating the balance between certain life and social issues and the time devoted to work. In a recent survey, two-thirds of Americans indicated they would accept lower pay to obtain more personal and leisure time. Many of the respondents said they were not willing to give up their personal lives for the benefit of a company that

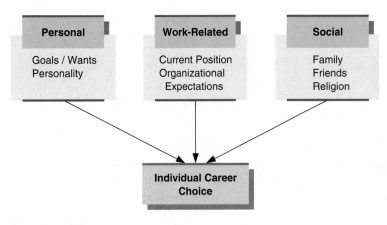

figure AB.2

Pressures on Individual Career Choice

Many different pressures force people to make choices regarding their careers. These pressures may have conflicting influences on career decisions.

could lay them off at any time.[10] Religious dictates also impose powerful career-related pressures on some people.

Work factors can also create career-related pressures. A person's current position in an organization may open certain career options, but other options may simply be unavailable to one in that position. This is true of some state government jobs; if one wants to run for political office, one must resign from any other government job first. In addition to formal requirements, informal expectations are associated with most jobs. Certain job and career-related behaviors may be expected from a person in a particular position, which usually puts pressure on the job holder to do the things expected. For example, coworkers may expect a colleague to seek managerial jobs to advance in the organization whereas the person may enjoy the current job and not wish to move into management.

Choice of Occupation

An occupation or occupational field is a group of jobs that are similar in terms of the types of tasks and training involved.

One major career decision is choice of occupation. An **occupation,** or **occupational field,** is a group of jobs that are similar in terms of the type of tasks and training involved. Occupations can usually be pursued in many different organizations whereas jobs are organization-specific. The United States Census Bureau identifies hundreds of occupations, including accountant, auctioneer, baker, carpenter, cashier, dancer, embalmer, farmer, furrier, huckster, loom fixer, railroad conductor, receptionist, stock handler, waiter, weaver, and weigher.[11] Of course, these occupations are not equally appealing to people. Rankings of the desirability of occupations have been generally stable. For instance, professions dominate the upper end of such evaluations. The occupation of physician is nearly always among those ranked as having the highest prestige, as are college and university professor, judge, and lawyer. The lowest-prestige occupations are more mixed. Bellhops, bootblacks, cleaners and janitorial workers, teamsters, and ushers are among those consistently rated low in prestige.

Theories that explain how people choose among the many occupations available to them emphasize either content or process.[12] Content theories deal with factors that influence career decisions, such as prestige, pay, and working conditions. Process theories, on the other hand, deal with how people make these decisions.

Content theories focus on six major factors that influence the occupations people choose:

1. The values and attitudes of the individual's family, especially parents[13]
2. Interests and needs[14]
3. Skills and abilities[15]
4. Education
5. General economic conditions
6. Political and social conditions

table AB.2

Holland Typology of Personality and Sample Occupations

Realistic	
Personal characteristics	Shy, genuine, materialistic, persistent, stable
Sample occupations	Mechanical engineer, drill press operator, aircraft mechanic, dry cleaner, waitress
Investigative	
Personal characteristics	Analytical, cautious, curious, independent, introverted
Sample occupations	Economist, physicist, actuary, surgeon, electrical engineer
Artistic	
Personal characteristics	Disorderly, emotional, idealistic, imaginative, impulsive
Sample occupations	Journalist, drama teacher, advertising manager, interior decorator, architect
Social	
Personal characteristics	Cooperative, generous, helpful, sociable, understanding
Sample occupations	Interviewer, history teacher, counselor, social worker, clergy
Enterprising	
Personal characteristics	Adventurous, ambitious, energetic, domineering, self-confident
Sample occupations	Purchasing agent, real estate salesperson, market analyst, attorney, personnel manager
Conventional	
Personal characteristics	Efficient, obedient, practical, calm, conscientious
Sample occupations	File clerk, CPA, typist, keypunch operator, teller

Reference: Table from *Career Management,* by Jeffrey H. Greenhaus, copyright © 1987 by The Dryden Press. Adapted from J. L. Holland, *Making Vocational Choices: A Theory of Careers.* Prentice Hall, Englewood Cliffs, N.J.: 1973.

Process theories suggest that people make occupational choices in stages over time, seeking to match their needs and occupational demands. According to this approach, although people begin considering occupations when they are very young, their thinking evolves and becomes more specific over time.[16]

One process model of occupational choice has been proposed by J. L. Holland. According to Holland, there are six basic personality types—realistic, investigative, artistic, social, enterprising, and conventional—each of which is characterized by a set of preferences, interests, and values. Occupations can also be grouped: working with things, working with observations and data, working with people, working in very ordered ways, exercising power, and using self-expression.[17] As people evaluate occupations over time, they attempt to match their occupational activities to their personality types. Table AB.2 shows Holland's proposed match between personality types and various occupational activities.

Another process model is similar to the expectancy model of motivation introduced in Chapter 6. This framework assumes that people base their occupational choices on their probability of success.[18] Thus, in an expectancy approach, a person uses information on the anticipated outcomes of being employed in a given occupation and the probability of obtaining those outcomes to assess the attractiveness of the occupation.

This process may be used in comparing two occupations. For example, some people face a new occupational choice after several years in their chosen field. From an expectation point of view, the person may attempt to compare the costs and benefits of remaining in his or her current field against the advantages and disadvantages of a new occupation. The costs may include loss of such benefits as seniority, pension, and earning power if extensive retraining is involved. But the employee may gain benefits such as higher long-term earnings, a different lifestyle, and daily activities that seem inherently more enjoyable.

The choice of occupation is more difficult now than it has ever been. Rather than being based in organizations and positions, new careers will be a series of tasks accomplished, skills mastered, and projects completed.[19] Managerial careers will also be vastly different in the twenty-first century. A group of human resource managers and executive recruiters agreed that managerial careers of this century will be based on a knowledge-based technical specialty, cross-functional and international experience, competence in collaborative leadership, self-management skills, and personal traits such as flexibility, integrity, and trustworthiness.[20]

Choice of Organization

People must choose not only an occupation but also an organization in which to pursue that occupation. This is an important choice—being an engineer for a municipal government, for instance, may be far different from being an engineer for a private aerospace corporation. Indeed, some organizational differences—such as profit or not for profit, large or small, private or governmental, and military or nonmilitary—may greatly influence the individual's ability to reach his or her goals and have a satisfying career.

Research suggests that in choosing an organization, individuals generally seek companies that can provide some minimally acceptable level of economic return—a sort of "base pay." Beyond that, the most frequently desired features of the organization involve the chance it gives employees to engage in interesting, challenging, or novel activities.[21] The type and size of the organization, its reputation, and its geographic location do not seem as important to people making career choices as the level of economic return and the nature of the activities they will be doing.[22]

Changes in Midcareer

As people change, grow older, and mature, they may need to reevaluate their careers and make new choices. Someone who dropped out of school early in life, for example, may decide that that choice restricted career options too much and may return to school to open up new career opportunities. Life experiences may broaden a person's skills so that new career options become available. One increasingly popular career change option is to take one or more part-time jobs. Some research suggests that the part-time option may benefit the employee as well as the organization.[23] Another increasingly popular choice is to become a "permanent" temporary, or contract, worker. Companies are finding that this option can benefit both the organization and the temporary worker.[24]

Sometimes people find that as they have changed, their definition of career success has also changed. Although these people may not need to move from one occupation to another, some adaptation may be in order. Career adaptation may involve retraining to perform better on the job or to move to another job within the same career field. Adaptation may also mean changing organizations while pursuing the same general occupation. Adaptation may be caused by organizational changes such as mergers, acquisition, downsizing, and layoffs. Often, employees choose to make major changes during periods of organizational change because of perceived shifts in the work environment, the economy, or technology. Andy Grove, former chairman and CEO of Intel Corporation, pointed out that the Internet and the hundreds of mergers and acquisitions are causing virtually all workers to reevaluate their career options and become more adaptable in their perspectives of their career.[25]

Career Stages

Career stages are the periods in which the person's work life is characterized by specific needs, concerns, tasks, and activities.

The gradual changes that occur over time in careers are called **career stages**, which are periods in which the individual's work life is characterized by distinctive needs, concerns, tasks, and activities. Career stages are changing as the organizational, technological, and economic environments change. Even the definition of career success is changing. Whereas once career success was measured by how high a level in the organization a person reached or how much money he or she earned, in the future career success will be measured in psychological terms. Psychological success is "the feeling of pride and personal accomplishment that comes from achieving one's most important goals in life, be they achievement, family happiness, inner peace, or something else."[26]

And although it was once the norm for people to stay with one organization for their entire careers, that no longer is the case. In fact, in the future, people are likely to change occupations as well as organizations several times during their lives. Figure AB.3 shows how career stages may progress as people move from one occupation and organization to another over their entire careers. Within each major stage are five substages: entry (exploration), trial (socialization), establishment, mastery, and exit (withdrawal).

Entry

The entry stage (exploration stage) is characterized by self-examination, role tryouts, and occupational exploration.

The **entry stage** is also known as the **exploration stage.** Exploration may be the more accurate label for the early part of the stage, in which self-examination, role tryouts, and occupational exploration occur. This is the stage during which education and training are most commonly pursued. During the latter part of the stage, the person begins work by trying out jobs associated with the career. This trial period may involve many different jobs as the individual explores a variety of organizations, occupations, and careers. Performance during this stage is represented in Figure AB.3 as a dashed line to indicate unpredictability.[27]

Trial

During the trial stage (socialization stage), individuals more specifically explore jobs, and performance begins to improve.

The **trial,** or **socialization,** stage usually begins with a period (shown in the figure by a dashed line) during which the individual continues to explore jobs, but much more narrowly than before. Then, as he or she focuses on a specific job,

figure AB.3

A Model of Career Stages

Career stages differ for different people. Some people have few major career changes; some people have many. At each major career change, however, a person may go through a five-step progression: entry, trial, establishment, mastery, and exit. This figure indicates there may be several segments in a person's career, each one going through the five stages. The dashed lines and question marks indicate/signify the uncertainties people face.

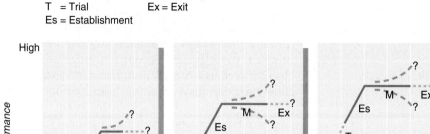

Key
En = Entry   M = Mastery
T = Trial   Ex = Exit
Es = Establishment

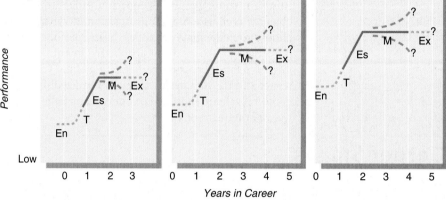

Reference: Adapted from Douglas T. Hall, "Protean Careers of the 21st Century," *Academy of Management Executive,* November 1996, p. 9. Used with permission of the author.

performance begins to improve. The person is in the early phases of becoming established in the career. The sequence of getting established has been found to consist of three phases: "getting in" (entry), "breaking in" (trial period), and "settling in" (establishment).[28]

During the socialization stage, people begin to form attachments and make commitments, both to others (new friends and coworkers) and to the organizations for which they work. Employees begin to learn the organization's goals, norms, values, and preferred ways of doing things; in other words, they learn the culture of the organization (see Chapter 18). In particular, they learn an appropriate set of role behaviors and develop work skills and abilities particular to their jobs and organizations. They begin to demonstrate that, at least to some degree, they are learning to accept the values and norms of the organization.[29]

During the socialization period, people must make many adjustments. They must learn to accept the fact that the organization and its people may be quite different from what they had anticipated. When they discover, for example, that other people do not appreciate their ideas, they must learn to deal with resistance to change. Employees must also be prepared to face dilemmas that involve making on-the-job decisions. Dilemmas may pit loyalties to the job, to good performance, to the boss, and to the organization against one another. Career dilemmas may also involve ethical considerations.[30]

An organization can take action to ensure that this stage is successful.[31] It can provide a relaxed orientation program for new personnel. It can see to it that the first job is challenging and that relevant training is provided. It can ensure that timely and reliable feedback is provided to people in this early stage of their careers. Finally, it can place new personnel in groups with high standards to encourage modeling of acceptable norms.

Establishment

The **establishment stage,** also known as the **settling-down stage,** evolves as the person is recognized for the improved performance that comes with development and growth. The individual is learning his or her career and performing well in it. Soon he or she becomes less dependent on others.

As in the other stages, adjustments are often necessary. Some individuals, of course, are less likely than others to make adjustments and learn. Those who are unsuccessful may change careers or adapt in another way—by job hopping. **Job hopping** occurs when people make fewer adjustments within organizations and instead move to different organizations to advance their careers. This practice has gained acceptance and has increased in recent years as more organizations have used outsiders to replace key managers to improve organization performance.[32] Workers are cautioned not to "job-hop" too fast but instead to make sure the new job fits their skills and goal aspirations.[33]

Vertical and horizontal, or lateral, movement also occurs frequently in this stage. Vertical movement involves promotions whereas lateral movement involves transfers. These kinds of movements teach people about various jobs in the organization, a broadening experience that can benefit both the individuals and the organization. Organizations meet their staffing needs through such movement, and individuals satisfy their needs for achievement and recognition.

Job moves, whether to a new organization or within the same organization, can cause problems, however. Invariably, higher-level jobs bring increased demands for performance, and frequently managers moving into these jobs receive little preparation. They usually are expected to step right into top executive positions and perform well, with little time for socialization into a new system. Furthermore, moves often necessitate relocation to other parts of the country, placing stress not only on the jobholder but also on his or her family.

Organizations can take steps to manage promotions and transfers to reduce problems. Longer-term, careful career planning may reduce the need to relocate since much of the broadening may be accomplished at one location. The timing and spacing of moves can be coordinated with, or at least adjusted to, the individual's family situation. More important, better training can be provided to enable the individual to make the move more readily and with substantially less stress.

Mastery

In the **mastery stage,** individuals develop a stronger attachment to their organizations and, hence, lose some career flexibility. Performance varies considerably in this stage. It may continue to grow, level off, or decline. If performance continues to grow, this stage progresses as a direct extension of the establishment stage. If performance levels or drops, career changes may result.

If leveling off occurs, the individual is said to have reached a "plateau" in her or his career. Responses to plateauing can be effective or ineffective for the individual and the organization. Those who respond effectively to plateaus have been termed "solid citizens"; they have little chance for further advancement but continue to make valuable contributions to the organization. Those whose responses are ineffective are referred to as "deadwood"; they too have little chance for promotion, but they also contribute little to the organization.[34]

Solid citizens become interested in establishing and guiding the next generation of organization members. As a result, they frequently begin to act as mentors for younger people in the organization (we discuss mentoring later). As mentors, they show younger members the ins and outs of organization politics and help them learn the values and norms of the organization. These individuals also begin to reexamine their own goals in life and rethink their long-term career plans. In some cases, this reflection leads to new values (or the reemergence of older ones) that cause the individuals to quit their jobs or pass up chances for promotions.[35] In other cases, individuals achieve new insights and begin to move upward again; such individuals are known as "late bloomers."[36]

Individuals who have become deadwood are more difficult to deal with. Their knowledge, loyalty, and understanding of plateauing, however, represent value to the organization and could make them salvageable. Perhaps rewards other than advancement can keep these persons productive. Their jobs may be redesigned (see Chapters 7 and 17) to facilitate performance, or they may be reassigned within the organization. And, of course, career counseling programs (discussed later in this appendix) could help them reach a better understanding of their situations and opportunities.[37]

If performance declines, the individual may be experiencing some type of midlife crisis, which is associated with such matters as awareness of physical aging and the nearness of death, reduced career performance, the recognition that life goals may not be met, and changes in family and work relationships. Individuals handle midlife crises differently. Some develop new patterns for coping with the pressures of careers. They may change careers or modify the way they are handling their current careers. Others have a more difficult time and may need professional assistance.

Changing jobs during the mastery stage has become fairly common. Many such moves prove highly beneficial to the person. Several "executive dropouts," for example, have become successful entrepreneurs, such as James L. Patterson, who left IBM to cofound Quantum Corporation.[38] Of course, not all job changes at this stage lead to success. Some job changers find, much to their dismay, that the grass is not greener in the new job, and they experience just as much frustration and disappointment as they did in the old job.[39]

Exit

In the exit (withdrawal) stage, the general pattern is one of decreasing performance as individuals prepare to move on or retire.

The final stage—**exit,** or **withdrawal**—frequently involves the end of this major career stage as individuals move to another occupation, organization, or both. For older workers, it may be the end of full-time employment as they face retirement and other options. The general pattern is one of decreasing performance as people recognize their loss of interest or productivity and begin to search for alternatives. Again, individual adaptation may be positive—beginning a new career, helping others, or learning to accept retirement—or it may be negative—becoming indifferent, giving up, or developing abnormally strong dependence on family and friends. As shown in Figure AB.3, a new and different career stage may begin with new exploration and training and a new period of performance and growth. People may go through two, three, or more of these major career stages during their working lives.

Although legislation may restrict an organization's power to force retirement at age sixty-five, many individuals nevertheless quit full-time employment at about that age, and many organizations encourage even earlier retirement for many of their members. Problems may arise for people who are not prepared for the changes retirement brings. A person who is not ready to retire or feels forced to do so may have an especially difficult time adapting to those changes. To help employees adjust, many organizations are initiating preretirement programs that include information on health, housing, financial planning, legal issues, time management, and social programs for maintaining involvement in the community.

Hall and Hall have argued that the use of the career growth cycle can help organizations manage careers, especially at this crucial stage.[40] The career growth cycle suggests that the organization should provide employees with challenging job goals, support, feedback, and proper counseling to foster career growth for employees. Initially, the organization ensures that jobs offer challenging goals and supports employees' efforts to achieve those goals. If feedback is positive, the employees experience psychological success, which enhances their self-esteem and leads to greater involvement. Less positive feedback, however, which people often receive in the withdrawal stage, has the opposite effect. In this instance, the organization provides counseling to help the individual adapt to the changing circumstances.

Mentoring

Mentoring occurs when an older, more experienced person helps a younger employee grow and advance by providing advice, support, and encouragement.

Mentoring programs can be an excellent way for an organization to help manage the career stages of its employees. **Mentoring** is an arrangement in which more experienced workers help less experienced workers grow and advance by providing advice, support, and encouragement. Despite some criticisms of formal mentoring programs, many organizations have implemented them, and many others rely on more traditional informal networks. These companies believe that creating a bond between a senior and a junior employee helps both and benefits the company as well. From the protégé, the mentor often learns about the feelings and attitudes of a younger generation, and he or she may learn about new research and techniques as well. The mentoring process can breathe new life into the career of a person who may be nearing the withdrawal stage.[41] The younger colleague can pick up practical skills from the mentor and gain insights into the organization culture and philosophy that otherwise might take years to discover. A strong, secure bond between the two can lead one or both to do more innovative, important work than they might do on their own.[42]

For the company, this kind of bond can pay off in a number of ways. As the baby boom generation ages and the Generation X workers burst onto the scene, businesses have to try harder to find and keep good employees. An employee who feels secure in the company because of a good mentoring relationship is less likely to think about looking for another job. Mentors can be especially important for employees who might have trouble fitting into the organization. To move up in a company dominated by an "old-boy" network, for instance, women and minority employees often need contacts of their own in the company's higher ranks. Similarly, multinational corporations may find mentors useful in helping managers from other countries fit into the culture of the corporation. Mentors can also help executives of merged companies adjust to the philosophies and expectations of their new employees.[43]

To get the most out of mentoring programs, experts say, companies must do more than just put two people together and hope for the best.[44] They need to determine what the goals of the program are: to teach specific skills, help new people get along with other employees, or introduce employees to corporate philosophies. Clarifying these goals should help the organization decide who will make the best mentors. Middle managers may be best at helping new people develop specific skills whereas senior managers may be more effective at passing on the company's vision. In any case, a key element in any mentoring program is matching the two individuals, for the protégé needs to believe that he or she is gaining a friend rather than another boss.

Research into the career stages of people in organizations continues. A recent phenomenon among managers is the occurrence of gaps in career development. These may occur because of changing lifestyles, taking time off for childbearing and child rearing, or for a variety of other reasons. A recent study, however, showed that such career gaps seem to have more negative effects on the careers of men than on those of women.[45]

Organizational Career Planning

In career planning, individuals evaluate their abilities and interests, consider alternative career opportunities, establish career goals, and plan practical development activities.

Career planning, the process of planning one's life work, involves evaluating abilities and interests, considering alternative career opportunities, establishing career goals, and planning practical development activities.[46] Organizations have a vested interest in the careers of their members, and career planning and development programs help them enhance employees' job performance and thus the overall effectiveness of the organization.

Purposes of Career Planning

Organizational career planning programs can help companies identify qualified personnel and future managers, improve job satisfaction and other attitudes, increase the involvement of key employees, and improve the vital match between individual and organizational wants and needs.[47] The purpose of career planning, then, is to ensure that such enhanced individual and organizational performance occurs.

Organizational career planning is a complex process involving many conflicting concerns, some of which are listed in Figure AB.4. Reliable and valid personnel decision techniques must be used to ensure that career planning achieves its purposes. Careers should offer employees broad enough experience to develop their skills. The organization must ensure that women and minorities are hired, especially in managerial positions, and that they are compensated fairly. These concerns also involve issues such as nepotism, dual careers, and age discrimination. Career planning may also involve establishing a functional stress management program (see Chapter 9).

figure AB.4

Organizational Career-Planning Concerns

Organizations, like individuals, must address many different issues in their career-planning efforts, which makes career planning a difficult and complex process.

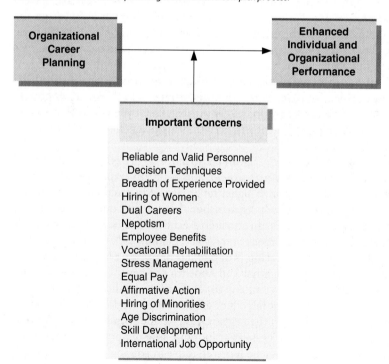

Types of Career Programs

Research suggests that organizational career planning programs fit into seven general categories: career pathing, career counseling, human resource planning, career information systems, management development, training, and special programs.[48]

Career pathing is the identification of a certain sequence of jobs in a career that represents a progression through the organization.

Career Pathing   **Career pathing** is identifying career tracks, or sequences of jobs, that represent a coherent progression vertically and laterally through the organization. Figure AB.5 illustrates two such paths for college graduates, one for an engineering or technical career and one for a sales or marketing career. Some organizations clearly specify paths such as these whereas others allow far more flexibility. Most organizations do not adhere too strictly to specific career paths because doing so might limit the full utilization of individual potential, and there are always many exceptions to particular specified paths.[49] Such organizations give employees opportunities for both horizontal and vertical movement to develop their skills and breadth of experience. Some career paths include assignments overseas to help prospective top managers understand the organization's international operations. Career paths usually have a time frame (frequently five to ten years), may be updated periodically, and may be developed to ensure that the work experiences are relevant to a particular target (that is, higher-level) position in the organization.

Career Counseling   Organizations use both informal and formal approaches to career counseling.[50] Counseling occurs informally as part of the day-to-day supervisor-subordinate relationship and often during employment interviews and performance evaluations as well. More formally, the human resources department often offers career counseling to all personnel, especially those who are being moved up, down, or out of the organization.[51]

Human resource planning involves forecasting the organization's human resource needs, developing replacement charts (charts showing a planned succession of personnel) for all levels of the organization, and preparing inventories of the skills and abilities individuals need to move within the organization.

Human Resource Planning   **Human resource planning** involves forecasting the organization's human resource needs, developing replacement charts (charts showing a planned succession of personnel) for all levels of the organization, and preparing inventories of the skills and abilities individuals need to move within the organization. Human resource planning and development systems can be quite complex and involve both individual and organizational activities. Basically, however, such systems involve developing plans, matching organizations and individuals, assessing needs, and implementing the plans. It is the specific applications that lead to the complexity of the system.

Career Information Systems   When internal job markets are combined with formal career counseling, the result is a career information system. Internal job markets exist when the organization first announces job openings to organization members. News about openings may appear on bulletin boards, in newsletters, and in memoranda. A career information center keeps up-to-date information about such openings as well as information about employees who are seeking other jobs or careers within the organization. Career information systems, then, can serve not only to develop the organization's resources but also to provide information that may increase employees' motivation to perform.

Management Development   Management development programs vary considerably. They may consist simply of policies that hold managers directly responsible for the development of their successors, or they may outline elaborate formal educational

figure AB.5

Two Examples of Possible Career Paths

These two career paths are for illustration only and do not necessarily map out a specific career for any one individual. In the future, either of these paths could represent just one major career stage, leading into another, totally different stage in a few years.

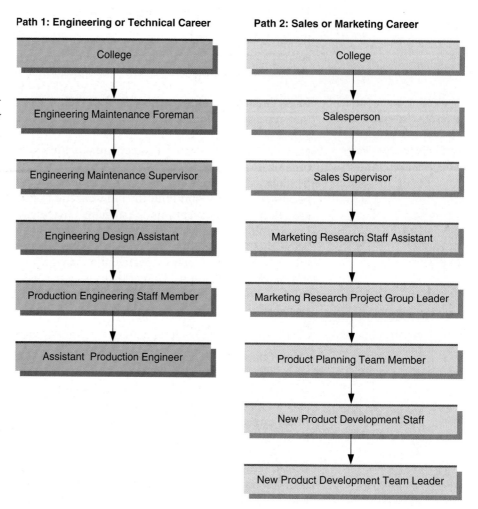

Path 1: Engineering or Technical Career

- College
- Engineering Maintenance Foreman
- Engineering Maintenance Supervisor
- Engineering Design Assistant
- Production Engineering Staff Member
- Assistant Production Engineer

Path 2: Sales or Marketing Career

- College
- Salesperson
- Sales Supervisor
- Marketing Research Staff Assistant
- Marketing Research Project Group Leader
- Product Planning Team Member
- New Product Development Staff
- New Product Development Team Leader

programs. Management development is receiving increasing attention in all types of organizations. On average, managers are participating in from twenty to forty hours per year of education and development activities dealing with topics such as time management, problem solving and decision making, strategic planning, and leadership.[52] Developmental programs in smaller organizations (those with fewer than one thousand employees) tend to focus on management and supervisory skills, communication, and behavioral skills. In larger organizations, development activities typically concentrate on executive development, new management techniques, and computer literacy.[53] Management development is discussed in more detail in Chapter 19.

Training   More specialized efforts to improve skills usually are termed "training." These activities include on-the-job training, formalized job rotation programs, in-house training sessions to develop specific technical job skills, programs on legal and political changes that affect specific jobs, tuition reimbursement programs, and student intern programs. The emphasis is usually on specific job skills, immediate performance being of greater concern than long-term career development. Of course, continued improvement in job performance carries implications of evolving career opportunities.

Special Programs   Training and development programs may be designed for and offered to special groups within the organization. Examples include preretirement programs and programs designed to help organization members cope with midlife career crises. Many organizations now offer outplacement counseling—programs designed to help employees who are leaving the organization, either voluntarily or involuntarily.[54] Outplacement programs help people preserve their dignity and sense of self-worth when they are fired, and they can reduce negative feelings toward the organization. Other special programs have been developed for women, minorities, and differently abled personnel to help them solve their special career problems.[55] Some organizations also have special programs to help personnel move from technical to managerial positions. Still other organizations have begun programs to deal with smokers because it has become clear that they pose health risks not only to themselves but also to others.[56]

Career Management

Career management is the process of implementing organizational career planning.

Career management is the implementation of organizational career planning. As Table AB.3 shows, top management support is needed to establish a climate that fosters career development. All human resource activities within the organization must be coordinated, and human resource managers from various areas should be involved at least as consultants. The career-planning programs must be open to all members of the organization, so they must be flexible to accommodate individual differences. Realistic feedback should be provided to participants, with the focus on psychological success rather than simply on advancement. Implementation of new programs should begin with small pilot programs that emphasize periodic assessment of both employee skills and the program itself.[57]

It is extremely important that supervisors be involved and that they be trained carefully lest they neglect or mishandle their roles and negate the positive effects of career-planning programs. The roles of supervisors include communicating information about careers; counseling to help subordinates identify their skills and understand their options; evaluating subordinates' performance, strengths, and

table AB.3

Key Ingredients for Career Management

- Top management support
- Coordination with other human resource activities
- Involvement of supervisors
- Use of human resource managers as consultants
- Periodic skill assessment
- Realistic feedback about career progress

- Equal access and open enrollment
- Focus on psychological success rather than on advancement
- Flexibility for individual needs
- Climate setting for career development
- Small pilot programs
- Periodic program assessment

Reference: From *Managing Careers in Organizations,* by Daniel C. Feldman. Copyright © 1988 by Scott, Foresman and Company.

weaknesses; coaching or teaching skills and behaviors to those who need support; advising about the realities of the organization; serving as mentors or role models for subordinates; brokering, or bringing together subordinates and those who might have positions better suited to them; and informing subordinates about opportunities.[58]

Results of Career Planning

Organizational career planning has many important results.[59] Employees develop a more realistic sense of what is expected of them on the job and what their future with the organization will entail. Planning clarifies supervisory roles in career counseling, increases personal career-planning ability through knowledge and education, and uses human resource systems more effectively. All of these effects strengthen career commitment as individuals develop plans to take charge of their careers. Ultimately, then, the organization can better use the talent of its members, reduce turnover, and improve individual and corporate performance.

These benefits are not, however, guaranteed. If the existence of an organizational career-planning program raises individuals' expectations unrealistically, dysfunctional consequences may result. Anxiety may increase, supervisors may spend too much time counseling their subordinates, and human resource systems may become overloaded. These effects lead to frustration, disappointment, and reduced commitment. In the end, talent is inadequately used, turnover increases, and individual and organizational performance suffers. The key to keeping employee expectations realistic is for all supervisors and managers to be trained to provide only factual information about jobs and employees' true prospects. Clearly, organizations must use career-planning programs carefully to ensure positive results.

Endnotes

Chapter 1

1. For a classic discussion of the meaning of "organizational behavior," see Larry Cummings, "Toward Organizational Behavior," *Academy of Management Review*, January 1978, pp. 90–98. For recent updates, see the annual series *Research in Organizational Behavior* (Greenwich, Conn.: JAI Press) and *Trends in Organizational Behavior* (New York: John Wiley and Sons).

2. Daniel A. Wren, *The Evolution of Management Thought*, 4th ed. (New York: John Wiley and Sons, 1994), Chapters 1 and 2. See also Stephen J. Carroll and Dennis A. Gillen, "Are the Classical Management Functions Useful in Describing Managerial Work?" *Academy of Management Review*, January 1987, pp. 38–51; and Daniel A. Wren, "Management History: Issues and Ideas for Teaching and Research," *Journal of Management*, Summer 1987, pp. 339–350.

3. Quoted in "Why Business History?" *Audacity*, Fall 1992, p. 15.

4. Alfred Kieser, "Why Organization Theory Needs Historical Analyses—And How This Should Be Performed," *Organization Science*, November 1994, pp. 608–617.

5. Frederick W. Taylor, *Principles of Scientific Management* (New York: Harper, 1911).

6. Quoted in Alan Farnham, "The Man Who Changed Work Forever," *Forbes*, July 21, 1997, p. 114.

7. See "The Line Starts Here," *Wall Street Journal*, January 11, 1999, pp. R25–R28.

8. For critical analyses, see Charles D. Wrege and Amedeo G. Perroni, "Taylor's Pig-Tale: A Historical Analysis of Frederick W. Taylor's Pig-Iron Experiment," *Academy of Management Journal*, March 1974, pp. 6–27; and Charles D. Wrege and Ann Marie Stoka, "Cooke Creates a Classic: The Story Behind Taylor's Principles of Scientific Management," *Academy of Management Review*, October 1978, pp. 736–749. For a more favorable review, see Edwin A. Locke, "The Ideas of Frederick W. Taylor: An Evaluation," *Academy of Management Review*, January 1982, pp. 14–24. See Oliver E. Allen, "'This Great Mental Revolution,'" *Audacity*, Summer 1996, pp. 52–61, for a discussion of the practical value of Taylor's work.

9. Max Weber, *Theory of Social and Economic Organization*, trans. A. M. Henderson and T. Parsons (London: Oxford University Press, 1921).

10. Hugo Münsterberg, *Psychology and Industrial Efficiency* (Boston: Houghton Mifflin, 1913); and Wren, *Evolution of Management Thought*. See also Frank J. Landy, "Hugo Münsterberg: Victim or Visionary?" *Journal of Applied Psychology*, 1992, vol. 77, no. 6, pp. 787–802; and Frank J. Landy, "Early Influences on the Development of Industrial and Organizational Psychology," *Journal of Applied Psychology*, 1997, vol. 82, no. 4, pp. 467–477.

11. Elton Mayo, *The Human Problems of Industrial Civilization* (New York: Macmillan, 1933); Fritz J. Roethlisberger and William J. Dickson, *Management and the Worker* (Cambridge, Mass.: Harvard University Press, 1939).

12. Alex Carey, "The Hawthorne Studies: A Radical Criticism," *American Sociological Review*, June 1967, pp. 403–416; Lyle Yorks and David A. Whitsett, "Hawthorne, Topeka, and the Issue of Science Versus Advocacy in Organizational Behavior," *Academy of Management Review*, January 1985, pp. 21–30.

13. Douglas McGregor, *The Human Side of Enterprise* (New York: McGraw-Hill, 1960); Abraham Maslow, "A Theory of Human Motivation," *Psychological Review*, July 1943, pp. 370–396. See also Paul R. Lawrence, "Historical Development of Organizational Behavior," in Jay W. Lorsch (ed.), *Handbook of Organizational Behavior* (Engle-wood Cliffs, N.J.: Prentice Hall, 1987), pp. 1–9.

14. See "Conversation with Lyman W. Porter," *Organizational Dynamics*, Winter 1990, pp. 69–79.

15. Jeffrey Pfeiffer and John F. Veiga, "Putting People First for Organizational Success," *Academy of Management Executive*, 1999, vol. 13, no. 2, pp. 37–48. See also Richard Chase and Sriram Dasu, "Want to Perfect Your Company's Service? Use Behavioral Science," *Harvard Business Review*, June 2001, pp. 79–89.

16. Joseph W. McGuire, "Retreat to the Academy," *Business Horizons*, July–August 1982, pp. 31–37; Kenneth Thomas and Walter G. Tymon, "Necessary Properties of Relevant Research: Lessons from Recent Criticisms of the Organizational Sciences," *Academy of Management Review*, July 1982, pp. 345–353. See also Jeffrey Pfeiffer, "The Theory-Practice Gap: Myth or Reality?" *Academy of Management Executive*, February 1987, pp. 31–32.

17. Fremont Kast and James Rosenzweig, "General Systems Theory: Applications for Organization and Management," *Academy of Management Journal*, December 1972, pp. 447–465.

18. See Fremont Kast and James Rosenzweig (eds.), *Contingency Views of Organization and Management* (Chicago: SRA, 1973), for a classic overview and introduction.

19. James Terborg, "Interactional Psychology and Research on Human Behavior in Organizations," *Academy of Management Review*, October 1981, pp. 569–576; Benjamin Schneider, "Interactional Psychology and Organizational Behavior," in Larry Cummings and Barry Staw (eds.), *Research in Organizational Behavior* (Greenwich, Conn.: JAI Press, 1983), vol. 5, pp. 1–32; Daniel B. Turban and Thomas L. Keon, "Organizational Attractiveness: An Interactionist Perspective," *Journal*

of Applied Psychology, 1993, vol. 78, no. 2, pp. 184–193.

20. See Milton Hakel, "The Past, Present, and Future of OB Applications by Consulting Academicians," in Jerald Greenberg (ed.), *Organizational Behavior–The State of the Science* (Hillsdale, N.J.: Lawrence Erlbaum Associates, 1994), pp. 275–288.

21. Martha Finney, "Books That Changed Careers," *HRMagazine*, June 1997, p. 141.

22. Nanette Fondas, "Feminization Unveiled: Management Qualities in Contemporary Writings," *Academy of Management Review*, 1997, vol. 22, no. 1, pp. 257–282; see also Anne Fisher, "What Women Can Learn from Machiavelli," *Fortune*, April 14, 1997, p. 162.

Chapter 2

1. Henry Mintzberg, "Rounding Out the Manager's Job," *Sloan Management Review*, Fall 1994, pp. 11–26; see also "All in a Day's Work," *Harvard Business Review*, December 2001, pp. 55–60.

2. Brian Dumaine, "The New Non-Manager Managers," *Fortune*, February 22, 1993, pp. 80–84. See also "In Praise of Middle Managers," *Harvard Business Review*, September 2001, pp. 72–81.

3. Mauro F. Guillen, "The Age of Eclecticism: Current Organizational Trends and the Evolution of Managerial Models," *Sloan Management Review*, Fall 1994, pp. 75–86.

4. Quoted in Ram Charan and Geoffrey Colvin, "Why CEOs Fail," *Fortune*, June 21, 1999, pp. 68–78 (quotation on p. 74).

5. John P. Kotter, "What Effective General Managers Really Do," *Harvard Business Review*, March–April 1999, pp. 145–159; see also David H. Freedman, "Is Management Still a Science?" *Harvard Business Review*, November– December 1992, pp. 26–38.

6. For an overview of the management process, see Ricky W. Griffin, *Fundamentals of Management*, 3rd ed. (Boston: Houghton Mifflin, 2003).

7. Henry Mintzberg, "The Manager's Job: Folklore and Fact," *Harvard Business Review*, July–August 1975, pp. 49–61.

8. Robert L. Katz, "The Skills of an Effective Administrator," *Harvard Business Review*, September–October 1987, pp. 90–102.

9. "Most Important Qualities for a CEO," *USA Today*, March 11, 2002, p. A1.

10. Quoted in Associated Press news report published as "Kellogg Workers to Lose Jobs," *Bryan-College Station Eagle*, August 15, 1999, p. C4.

11. Patricia L. Nemetz and Sandra L. Christensen, "The Challenge of Cultural Diversity: Harnessing a Diversity of Views to Understand Multiculturalism," *Academy of Management Review*, 1996, vol. 21, no. 2, pp. 434–462; Frances J. Milliken and Luis L. Martins, "Searching for Common Threads: Understanding the Multiple Effects of Diversity in Organizational Groups," *Academy of Management Review*, 1996, vol. 21, no. 2, pp. 402–433.

12. Geoffrey Colvin, "The 50 Best Companies for Asians, Blacks, and Hispanics," *Fortune*, July 19, 1999, pp. 52–57.

13. Craig L. Pearce and Charles P. Osmond, "Metaphors for Change: The ALPS Model of Change Management," *Organizational Dynamics*, Winter 1996, pp. 23–35.

14. Quoted in "Virtually There?" *Fast Company*, March 2002, p. 110.

15. Rick Tetzeli and Mary Cronin, "Getting Your Company's Internet Strategy Right," *Fortune*, March 18, 1996, pp. 72–78.

16. "The E-Gang," *Forbes*, July 26, 1999, pp. 145–157.

17. Rahul Jacob, "The Struggle to Create an Organization for the 21st Century," *Fortune*, April 3, 1995, pp. 90–99; Susan Sonnesyn Brooks, "Managing a Horizontal Revolution," *HRMagazine*, June 1995, pp. 52–57.

18. Michael Porter, *Competitive Strategy* (New York: Free Press, 1980).

19. Jeffrey Pfeiffer, "Producing Sustainable Competitive Advantage Through the Effective Management of People," *The Academy of Management Executive*, 1995, vol. 9, no. 1, pp. 55–69; Carl Long and Mary Vickers-Koch, "Using Core Capabilities to Create Competitive Advantage," *Organiza-*

tional Dynamics, Summer 1995, pp. 39–55.

20. For an overview, see Ricky W. Griffin and Michael W. Pustay, *International Business—A Managerial Perspective*, 3rd ed. (Upper Saddle River, N.J.: 2002).

21. David M. Messick and Max H. Bazerman, "Ethical Leadership and the Psychology of Decision Making," *Sloan Management Review*, Winter 1996, pp. 9–22.

22. Ross Johnson and William O. Winchell, *Management and Quality* (Milwaukee: American Society for Quality Control, 1989).

Chapter 3

1. R. Roosevelt Thomas Jr., "Redefining Diversity," *HRFOCUS*, April 1996, pp. 6–7.

2. Ibid.

3. Jeremy Kahn, "Diversity Trumps the Downturn," *Fortune*, July 9, 2001, pp. 114–116.

4. "America's 50 Best Companies for Minorities," *Fortune*, July 9, 2001, pp. 122–128.

5. "Diversity Today: Developing and Retaining the Best Corporate Talent," *Fortune*, June 21, 1999, pp. S2–S4.

6. Michael L. Wheeler, "Diversity: Making the Business Case," *Business Week*, December 9, 1996; special advertising section.

7. Elaine Carter, Elaine Kepner, Malcolm Shaw, and William Brooks Woodson, "The Effective Management of Diversity," *S. A. M. Advanced Management Journal*, Autumn 1982, pp. 49–53.

8. Marilyn Loden and Judy B. Rosener, *Workforce America! Managing Employee Diversity as a Vital Resource* (Homewood, Ill.: Business One Irwin, 1991), pp. 58–62.

9. Ibid., p. 60.

10. Ibid., pp. 68–70.

11. Howard N. Fullerton Jr. and Mitra Toossi, "Labor Force Projections to 2010: Steady Growth and Changing Composition," *Monthly Labor Review*, November 2001, pp. 21–38.

12. Ibid, p. 37.

13. Ibid, p. 22.

14. Michael Crawford, "The New Office Etiquette," *Canadian Business*, May 1993, pp. 22–31.

15. Harish C. Jain and Anil Verma, "Managing Workforce Diversity for Competitiveness: The Canadian Experience" *International Journal of Manpower*, April–May 1996, pp. 14–30.

16. "Plenty of Muck, Not Much Money," *Economist*, May 8, 1999, p. 52.

17. Barry Louis Rubin, "Europeans Value Diversity," *HRMagazine*, January 1991, pp. 38–41, 78.

18. Ron Corben, "Thailand Faces a Shrinking Work Force," *Journal of Commerce and Commercial*, December 26, 1996, p. 5a.

19. "Lone Knights: Knight Ridder Is a Rare Beacon Among Newspapers," *Fortune*, July 19, 1999, p. 68.

20. Martha Irvine, "EEOC Sues Illinois Company Over 'English-Only' Policy." *Legal Intelligence*, September 2, 1999, p. 4.

21. Wheeler, "Diversity: Making the Business Case."

22. Lennie Copeland, "Making the Most of Cultural Differences at the Workplace," *Personnel*, June 1988, pp. 52–60.

23. M. J. Gent, "Theory X in Antiquity, or the Bureaucratization of the Roman Army," *Business Horizons*, January–February 1984, pp. 53–54.

24. "Saybolt Inc. Pleads Guilty and Is Fined $1.5 Million for Bribery of Panamanian Officials, Reports U.S Attorney," *PR Newswire*, January 21, 1999.

25. Henry W. Lane and Joseph J. DiStefano, *International Management Behavior* (Ontario: Nelson, 1988).

26. Brian O'Reilly, "Your New Global Workforce," *Fortune*, December 14, 1992, pp. 58–66.

27. Christopher Knowlton, "What America Makes Best," *Fortune*, March 28, 1988, pp. 40–54.

28. Alex Taylor III, "Why GM Leads the Pack in Europe," *Fortune*, May 17, 1993, pp. 83–86.

29. Richard M. Steers and Edwin L. Miller, "Management in the 1990s: The International Challenge," *Academy of Management Executive*, February 1988, pp. 21–22.

30. Simcha Ronen and Oded Shenkar, "Clustering Countries on Attitudinal Dimension: A Review and Synthesis," *Academy of Management Review*, July 1985, pp. 435–454.

31. Nancy J. Adler, Robert Doktor, and Gordon Redding, "From the Atlantic to the Pacific Century," *Journal of Management*, Summer 1986, pp. 295–318.

32. Brian O'Reilly, "Japan's Uneasy U.S. Managers," *Fortune*, April 25, 1988, pp. 245–264.

33. "Learning to Accept Cultural Diversity," *Wall Street Journal*, September 12, 1990, pp. B1, B9.

34. Tamotsu Yamaguchi, "The Challenge of Internationalization," *Academy of Management Executive*, February 1988, pp. 33–36.

35. Geert Hofstede, *Culture's Consequences: International Differences in Work-Related Values* (Beverly Hills: Sage Publications, 1980).

36. Loden and Rosener, *Workforce America!* p. 19.

37. Fullerton, "Labor Force 2006," p. 36.

38. Sar A. Levitan, "Older Workers in Today's Economy," presentation at the Textbook Author's Conference, Washington, D.C., October 21, 1992.

39. Fullerton and Toossi, "Labor Force 2006," p. 21.

40. Beverly Hynes-Grace, "To Thrive, Not Merely Survive," presentation at the Textbook Author's Conference, Washington, D.C., October 21, 1992.

41. Ibid.

42. Wheeler, "Diversity: Making the Business Case."

43. Copeland, "Making the Most of Cultural Differences at the Workplace," pp. 52–60.

44. Charlene Marmer Soloman, "The Corporate Response to Workforce Diversity," *Personnel Journal*, August 1989, pp. 42–54.

45. Susan Faludi, *Backlash: The Undeclared War Against American Women* (New York: Doubleday, 1991).

46. Loden and Rosener, *Workforce America!* pp. 85–86.

47. Richard L. Drach, "Making Reasonable Accommodations Under the ADA," *Employment Relations Today*, Summer 1992, pp. 167–175.

48. Toby B. Gooley, "Ready, Willing and Able!" *Traffic Management*, October 1993, pp. 63–67.

49. Thomas A. Stewart, "Gay in Corporate America," *Fortune*, December 16, 1991, pp. 42–56.

50. Ibid., p. 45.

51. Wheeler, "Diversity: Making the Business Case."

52. André Laurent, "The Cultural diversity of Western Conceptions of Management," *International Studies of Management and Organization*, Spring–Summer 1983, pp. 75–96.

53. See Brian O'Reilly, "Your New Global Workforce," *Fortune*, December 14, 1992, pp. 58–66; Richard I. Kirkland Jr., "Europe's New Managers," *Fortune*, September 29, 1986, pp. 56–60.

54. Bill Leonard, "Ways to Make Diversity Programs Work," *HRMagazine*, April 1991, pp. 37–39, 98.

55. Taylor H. Cox and Stacy Blake, "Managing Cultural Diversity: Implications for Organizational Competitiveness," *Academy of Management Executive*, August 1991, pp. 45–56.

56. Taylor H. Cox, "The Multicultural Organizational," *Academy of Management Executive*, May 1991, pp. 34–47.

57. Ibid., p. 42.

Chapter 4

1. Denise M. Rousseau and Judi McLean Parks, "The Contracts of Individuals and Organizations," in Larry L. Cummings and Barry M. Staw (eds.), *Research in Organizational Behavior*, vol. 15 (Greenwich, Conn.: JAI Press, 1993), pp. 1–43.

2. Denise M. Rousseau, "Changing the Deal While Keeping the People," *Academy of Management Executive*, February 1996, pp. 50–58.

3. Quoted in Nina Munk, "The New Organization Man," *Fortune*, March 16, 1998, p. 68.

4. Richard A. Guzzo, Katherine A. Noonan, and Efrat Elron, "Expatriate Managers and the Psychological Contract," *Journal of Applied Psychology*, vol. 79, no. 4, pp. 617–626.

5. Amy L. Kristof, "Person-Organization Fit: An Integrative Review of Its Conceptualizations, Measurement, and Implications," *Personnel Psychology*, Spring 1996, pp. 1–49.

6. J. B. Rotter, "Generalized Expectancies for Internal vs. External Control of Reinforcement," *Psychological Monographs*, 1966, vol. 80, pp. 1–28; Bert De Brabander and Christopher Boone, "Sex Differences in Perceived Locus of Control," *Journal of Social Psychology*, 1990, vol. 130, pp. 271–276.

7. T. W. Adorno, E. Frenkel-Brunswick, D. J. Levinson, and R. N. Sanford, *The Authoritarian Personality* (New York: Harper & Row, 1950).

8. Leon Festinger, *A Theory of Cognitive Dissonance* (Palo Alto: Stanford University Press, 1957).

9. Patricia C. Smith, L. M. Kendall, and Charles Hulin, *The Measurement of Satisfaction in Work and Behavior* (Chicago: Rand-McNally, 1969).

10. Linda Grant, "Happy Workers, High Returns," *Fortune*, January 12, 1998, p. 81.

11. See Timothy Judge, Carl Thoresen, Joyce Bono, and Gregory Patton, "The Job Satisfaction–Job Performance Relationship: A Qualitative and Quantitative Review," *Psychological Bulletin*, 2001, vol. 127, no. 3, pp. 376–407.

12. James R. Lincoln, "Employee Work Attitudes and Management Practice in the U.S. and Japan: Evidence from a Large Comparative Study," *California Management Review*, Fall 1989, pp. 89–106.

13. See Michael Riketta, "Attitudinal Organizational Commitment and Job Performance: A Meta-Analysis," *Journal of Organizational Behavior*, 2002, vol. 23, no. 3, pp. 257–266.

14. Lincoln, "Employee Work Attitudes and Management Practice."

15. Leslie E. Palich, Peter W. Hom, and Roger W. Griffeth, "Managing in the International Context: Testing Cultural Generality of Sources of Commitment to Multinational Enterprises," *Journal of Management*, 1995, vol. 21, no. 4, pp. 671–690.

16. For an example of research in this area, see Jennifer M. George and Gareth R. Jones, "The Experience of Mood and Turnover Intentions: Interactive Effects of Value Attainment, Job Satisfaction, and Positive Mood," *Journal of Applied Psychology*, 1996, vol. 81, no. 3, pp. 318–325; for a recent review, see Arthur P. Brief and Howard M. Weiss, "Organizational Behavior: Affect in the Workplace," in *Annual Review of Psychology*, vol. 53 (Palo Alto: Annual Reviews, 2002), pp. 279–307.

17. Quoted in Ronald B. Lieber, "Why Employees Love These Companies," *Fortune*, January 12, 1998, p. 73.

18. "One Man's Accident Is Shedding New Light on Human Perception," *Wall Street Journal*, September 30, 1993, pp. A1, A13.

19. William H. Starbuck and John M. Mezias, "Opening Pandora's Box: Studying the Accuracy of Managers' Perceptions," *Journal of Organizational Behavior*, 1996, vol. 17, pp. 99–117.

20. Quoted in Dan Seligman, "In Defense of Stereotypes," *Forbes*, December 1, 1997, p. 114.

21. Mark J. Martinko and William L. Gardner, "The Leader/Member Attribution Process," *Academy of Management Review*, April 1987, pp. 235–249; Jeffrey D. Ford, "The Effects of Causal Attributions on Decision Makers' Responses to Performance Downturns," *Academy of Management Review*, October 1985, pp. 770–786.

22. See Richard W. Woodman, John E. Sawyer, and Ricky W. Griffin, "Toward a Theory of Organizational Creativity," *Academy of Management Review*, April 1993, pp. 293–321.

23. Emily Thornton, "Japan's Struggle to Be Creative," *Fortune*, April 19, 1993, pp. 129–134.

24. Quoted in Ed Brown, "A Day at Innovation U.," *Fortune*, April 12, 1999, p. 164.

25. "Chick-fil-A Cuts Job Turnover Rates," *Houston Chronicle*, January 9, 2002, p. B3.

26. See Anne O'Leary-Kelly, Ricky W. Griffin, and David J. Glew, "Organization-Motivated Aggression: A Research Framework," *Academy of Management Review*, January 1996, pp. 225–253.

27. See Dennis W. Organ, "Personality and Organizational Citizenship Behavior," *Journal of Management*, 1994, vol. 20, no. 2, pp. 465–478. For more recent information, see Jeffrey LePine, Amir Erez, and Diane Johnson, "The Nature and Dimensionality of Organizational Citizenship Behavior: A Critical Review and Meta-Analysis," *Journal of Applied Psychology*, 2002, vol. 87, no. 1, pp. 52–65.

Chapter 5

1. Richard M. Steers, Gregory A. Bigley, and Lyman W. Porter, *Motivation and Leadership at Work*, 6th ed. (New York: McGraw-Hill, 1996). See also Ruth Kanfer, "Motivational Theory and Industrial and Organizational Psychology," in M. D. Dunnette and L. M. Hough (eds.), *Handbook of Industrial and Organizational Psychology*, 2nd ed. (Palo Alto: Consulting Psychologists Press), vol. 1, pp. 75–170; and M. L. Ambrose, "Old Friends, New Faces: Motivation Research in the 1990s," *Journal of Management*, 1999, vol. 25, no. 2, pp. 110–131.

2. Roland E. Kidwell Jr. and Nathan Bennett, "Employee Propensity to Withhold Effort: A Conceptual Model to Intersect Three Avenues of Research," *Academy of Management Review*, July 1993, pp. 429–456.

3. Jeffrey Pfeiffer, *The Human Equation* (Boston: Harvard Business School Press, 1998).

4. E. L. Deci and R. M. Ryan, "The 'What' and 'Why' of Goal Pursuits: Human Needs and the Self-Determination of Behavior," *Psychological Inquiry*, 2000, vol. 11, no. 4, pp. 227–269.

5. Craig Pinder, *Work Motivation in Organizational Behavior* (Upper Saddle River, N. J.: Prentice Hall, 1998).

6. Frederick W. Taylor, *Principles of Scientific Management* (New York: Harper, 1911).

7. Ibid., pp. 46–47.

8. See Charles D. Wrege and Amedeo G. Perroni, "Taylor's Pig-Tale: A Historical Analysis of Frederick W. Taylor's Pig-Iron Experiment," *Academy of Management Journal*, March 1974, pp. 6–27.

9. Pinder, *Work Motivation in Organizational Behavior*. See also Daniel Wren, *The Evolution of Management Thought*, 4th ed. (New York: John Wiley and Sons, 1994).

10. Gerald R. Salancik and Jeffrey Pfeiffer, "An Examination of Need-Satisfaction Models of Job Attitudes,"

Administrative Science Quarterly, September 1977, pp. 427–456.

11. Abraham H. Maslow, "A Theory of Human Motivation," *Psychological Review,* 1943, vol. 50, pp. 370–396; Abraham H. Maslow, *Motivation and Personality* (New York: Harper & Row, 1954). Maslow's most famous work includes Abraham Maslow, Deborah C. Stephens, and Gary Heil, *Maslow on Management* (New York: John Wiley and Sons, 1998); and Abraham Maslow and Richard Lowry, *Toward a Psychology of Being* (New York: John Wiley and Sons, 1999).

12. Quoted in "Living Overtime: A Factory Workaholic," *Wall Street Journal,* October 13, 1998, p. B1.

13. See Nancy Adler, *International Dimensions of Organizational Behavior,* 3rd ed. (Boston: PWS-Kent), 1997.

14. Mahmond A. Wahba and Lawrence G. Bridwell, "Maslow Reconsidered: A Review of Research on the Need Hierarchy Theory," *Organizational Behavior and Human Performance,* April 1976, pp. 212–240.

15. Clayton P. Alderfer, *Existence, Relatedness, and Growth* (New York: Free Press, 1972).

16. Ibid.

17. Frederick Herzberg, Bernard Mausner, and Barbara Synderman, *The Motivation to Work* (New York: John Wiley and Sons, 1959); Frederick Herzberg, "One More Time: How Do You Motivate Employees?" *Harvard Business Review,* January–February 1968, pp. 53–62.

18. Herzberg, Mausner, and Synderman, *The Motivation to Work.*

19. Ibid.

20. Quoted in "Can Trees and Jogging Trails Lure Techies to Kansas?" *Wall Street Journal,* October 21, 1998, p. B1.

21. Herzberg, "One More Time"; Ricky W. Griffin, *Task Design: An Integrative Approach* (Glenview, Ill.: Scott, Foresman, 1982).

22. Pinder, *Work Motivation in Organizational Behavior.*

23. Frederick Herzberg, *Work and the Nature of Man* (Cleveland: World, 1966); Valerie M. Bookman, "The Herzberg Controversy," *Personnel Psychology,* Summer 1971, pp. 155–189; Benedict Grigaliunas and Frederick Herzberg, "Relevance in the Test of Motivation-Hygiene Theory," *Journal of Applied Psychology,* February 1971, pp. 73–79.

24. Marvin Dunnette, John Campbell, and Milton Hakel, "Factors Contributing to Job Satisfaction and Job Dissatisfaction in Six Occupational Groups," *Organizational Behavior and Human Performance,* May 1967, pp. 143–174; Charles L. Hulin and Patricia Smith, "An Empirical Investigation of Two Implications of the Two-Factor Theory of Job Satisfaction," *Journal of Applied Psychology,* October 1967, pp. 396–402.

25. Adler, *International Dimensions of Organizational Behavior.*

26. David McClelland, *The Achieving Society* (Princeton, N.J.: Nostrand, 1961). See also David C. McClelland, *Human Motivation* (Cambridge, UK: Cambridge University Press, 1988).

27. Quoted in "The Daddy Trap," *Business Week,* September 21, 1998, p. 62.

28. Michael J. Stahl, "Achievement, Power, and Managerial Motivation: Selecting Managerial Talent with the Job Choice Exercise," *Personnel Psychology,* Winter 1983, pp. 775–790.

29. McClelland, *The Achieving Society.*

30. Stanley Schachter, *The Psychology of Affiliation* (Palo Alto: Stanford University Press, 1959).

31. David McClelland and David H. Burnham, "Power Is the Great Motivator," *Harvard Business Review,* March–April 1976, pp. 100–110.

32. Pinder, *Work Motivation in Organizational Behavior;* McClelland and Burnham, "Power Is the Great Motivator."

33. Pinder, *Work Motivation in Organizational Behavior.*

Chapter 6

1. See Craig Pinder, *Work Motivation in Organizational Behavior* (Upper Saddle River, N.J.: Prentice Hall, 1998).

2. J. Stacy Adams, "Toward an Understanding of Inequity," *Journal of Abnormal and Social Psychology,* November 1963, pp. 422–436. See also Richard T. Mowday, "Equity Theory Predictions of Behavior in Organizations," in Richard M. Steers and Lyman W. Porter (eds.), *Motivation and Work Behavior,* 4th ed. (New York: McGraw-Hill, 1987), pp. 89–110.

3. Priti Pradham Shah, "Who Are Employees' Social Referents? Using a Network Perspective to Determine Referent Others," *Academy of Management Journal,* 1998, vol. 41, no. 3, pp. 249–268.

4. J. Stacy Adams, "Inequity in Social Exchange," in L. Berkowitz (ed.), *Advances in Experimental Social Psychology,* vol. 2 (New York: Academic Press, 1965), pp. 267–299.

5. Craig Pinder, *Work Motivation in Organizational Behavior* (Upper Saddle River, N.J.: Prentice Hall, 1998).

6. See Kerry Sauler and Arthur Bedeian, "Equity Sensitivity: Construction of a Measure and Examination of Its Psychometric Properties," *Journal of Management,* 2000, vol. 26, no. 5, pp. 885–910; Mark Bing and Susan Burroughs, "The Predictive and Interactive Effects of Equity Sensitivity in Teamwork-Oriented Organizations," *Journal of Organizational Behavior,* 2001, vol. 22, pp. 271–290.

7. Quoted in "Holiday on Ice: Stuck at the Office," *USA Today,* November 18, 1998, p. B5.

8. Edward C. Tolman, *Purposive Behavior in Animals* (New York: Appleton-Century-Crofts, 1932); Kurt Lewin, *The Conceptual Representation and the Measurement of Psychological Forces* (Durham, N.C.: Duke University Press, 1938).

9. Victor Vroom, *Work and Motivation* (New York: John Wiley and Sons, 1964).

10. Quoted in "Perks That Work," *Time,* November 9, 1998, p. 86.

11. Lyman W. Porter and Edward E. Lawler, *Managerial Attitudes and Performance* (Homewood, Ill.: Dorsey Press, 1968).

12. See Terence R. Mitchell, "Expectancy Models of Job Satisfaction, Occupational Preference, and Effort: A Theoretical, Methodological, and Empirical Appraisal," *Psychological Bulletin,* 1974, vol. 81, pp. 1096–1112; and John P. Campbell and Robert D. Pritchard, "Motivation Theory in Industrial and Organizational Psychology," in Marvin D. Dunnette (ed.), *Handbook of Industrial and Organizational Psychology* (Chicago: Rand McNally, 1976), pp. 63–130, for reviews.

13. Pinder, *Work Motivation and Organizational Behavior.*

14. Ibid.

15. Campbell and Pritchard, "Motivation Theory in Industrial and Organizational Psychology."

16. Nancy Adler, *International Dimensions of Organizational Behavior,* 3rd ed. (Boston: PWS-Kent, 1997).

17. David A. Nadler and Edward E. Lawler, "Motivation: A Diagnostic Approach," in J. Richard Hackman, Edward E. Lawler, and Lyman W. Porter (eds.), *Perspectives on Behavior in Organizations,* 2nd ed. (New York: McGraw-Hill, 1983), pp. 67–78.

18. Ivan P. Pavlov, *Conditional Reflexes* (New York: Oxford University Press, 1927).

19. Albert Bandura, "Social Cognitive Theory: An Agentic Perspective," *Annual Review of Psychology,* 2001, vol. 52, pp. 1–26.

20. B. F. Skinner, *Science and Human Behavior* (New York: Macmillian, 1953), and *Beyond Freedom and Dignity* (New York: Knopf, 1972).

21. Fred Luthans and Robert Kreitner, *Organizational Behavior Modification and Beyond* (Glenview, Ill.: Scott, Foresman, 1985).

22. "Workers: Risks and Rewards," *Time,* April 15, 1991, pp. 42–43.

23. See Richard Arvey and John M. Ivancevich, "Punishment in Organizations: A Review, Propositions, and Research Suggestions," *Academy of Management Review,* April 1980, pp. 123–132 for a review of the literature on punishment.

24. Quoted in "Net Pro," *Profiles,* November 1996, p. 42.

25. Fred Luthans and Robert Kreitner, *Organizational Behavior Modification* (Glenview, Ill.: Scott, Foresman, 1975); Luthans and Kreitner, *Organizational Behavior Modification and Beyond.*

26. Alexander D. Stajkovic, "A Meta-Analysis of the Effects of Organizational Behavior Modification on Task Performance, 1975–95," *Academy of Management Journal,* 1997, vol. 40, no. 5, pp. 1122–1149.

27. "At Emery Air Freight: Positive Reinforcement Boosts Performance,"
Organizational Dynamics, Winter 1973, pp. 41–50; W. Clay Hamner and Ellen P. Hamner, "Organizational Behavior Modification on the Bottom Line," *Organizational Dynamics,* Spring 1976, pp. 3–21.

28. Hamner and Hamner, "Organizational Behavior Modification on the Bottom Line."

29. Quoted in Garry M. Ritzky, "Turner Bros. Wins Safety Game with Behavioral Incentives," *HRMagazine,* June 1998, p. 80.

30. Edwin Locke, "The Myths of Behavior Mod in Organizations," *Academy of Management Review,* 1977, vol. 2, pp. 543–553.

Chapter 7

1. Ricky W. Griffin and Gary C. McMahan, "Motivation Through Job Design," in Jerald Greenberg (ed.), *Organizational Behavior: State of the Science* (New York: Lawrence Erlbaum and Associates, 1994), pp. 23–44.

2. For a recent example, see Bart Victor, Andrew Boynton, and Theresa Stephens-Jahng, "The Effective Design of Work Under Total Quality Management," *Organization Science,* 2000, vol. 11, no. 1, pp. 102–117.

3. Adam Smith, *An Inquiry into the Nature and Causes of the Wealth of Nations* (New York: Modern Library, 1937). Originally published in 1776.

4. Charles Babbage, *On the Economy of Machinery and Manufactures* (London: Charles Knight, 1832).

5. Frederick W. Taylor, *The Principles of Scientific Management* (New York: Harper & Row, 1911).

6. Quoted in "These Six Growth Jobs Are Dull, Dead-End, Sometimes Dangerous," *Wall Street Journal,* December 1, 1994, pp. A1.

7. C. R. Walker and R. Guest, *The Man on the Assembly Line* (Cambridge, Mass.: Harvard University Press, 1952).

8. Jia Lin Xie and Gary Johns, "Job Scope and Stress: Can Job Scope Be Too High?" *Academy of Management Journal,* 1995, vol. 38, no. 5, pp. 1288–1309.

9. Ricky W. Griffin, *Task Design: An Integrative Approach* (Glenview, Ill.: Scott, Foresman, 1982).
10. "These Six Growth Jobs Are Dull, Dead-End, Sometimes Dangerous," *Wall Street Journal,* December 1, 1994, pp. A1, A8, A9.

11. H. Conant and M. Kilbridge, "An Interdisciplinary Analysis of Job Enlargement: Technology, Cost, Behavioral Implications," *Industrial and Labor Relations Review,* 1965, vol. 18, no. 7, pp. 377–395.

12. Frederick Herzberg, "One More Time: How Do You Motivate Employees?" *Harvard Business Review,* January–February 1968, pp. 53–62; Frederick Herzberg, "The Wise Old Turk," *Harvard Business Review,* September–October 1974, pp. 70–80.

13. R. N. Ford, "Job Enrichment Lessons from AT & T," *Harvard Business Review,* January–February 1973, pp. 96–106.

14. E. D. Weed, "Job Enrichment 'Cleans Up' at Texas Instruments," in J. R. Maher (ed.), *New Perspectives in Job Enrichment* (New York: Van Nostrand, 1971).

15. Griffin, *Task Design;* Griffin and McMahan, "Motivation Through Job Design."

16. J. Richard Hackman and Greg Oldham, "Motivation Through the Design of Work: Test of a Theory," *Organizational Behavior and Human Performance,* 1976, vol. 16, pp. 250–279. See also Michael A. Campion and Paul W. Thayer, "Job Design: Approaches, Outcomes, and Trade-Offs," *Organizational Dynamics,* Winter 1987, pp. 66–78.

17. J. Richard Hackman, "Work Design," in J. Richard Hackman and J. L. Suttle (eds.), *Improving Life at Work: Behavioral Science Approaches to Organizational Change* (Santa Monica, Calif.: Goodyear, 1977).

18. Griffin, *Task Design.*

19. Griffin, *Task Design.* See also Karlene H. Roberts and William Glick, "The Job Characteristics Approach to Task Design: A Critical Review," *Journal of Applied Psychology,* 1981, vol. 66, pp. 193–217; and Ricky W. Griffin, "Toward an Integrated Theory of Task Design," in Larry L. Cummings and Barry M. Staw (eds.), *Research in Organizational Behavior*

(Greenwich, Conn.: JAI Press, 1987), vol. 9, pp. 79–120.

20. Ricky W. Griffin, M. Ann Welsh, and Gregory Moorhead, "Perceived Task Characteristics and Employee Performance: A Literature Review," *Academy of Management Review*, October 1981, pp. 655–664.

21. For a recent discussion of these issues, see Timothy Butler and James Waldroop, "Job Sculpting," *Harvard Business Review*, September–October 1999, pp. 144–152.

22. Gerald Salancik and Jeffrey Pfeiffer, "An Examination of Need-Satisfaction Models of Job Attitudes," *Administrative Science Quarterly*, 1977, vol. 22, pp. 427–456; Gerald Salancik and Jeffrey Pfeiffer, "A Social Information Processing Approach to Job Attitudes and Task Design," *Administrative Science Quarterly*, 1978, vol. 23, pp. 224–253.

23. Joe Thomas and Ricky W. Griffin, "The Social Information Processing Model of Task Design: A Review of the Literature," *Academy of Management Review*, October 1983, pp. 672–682. See also Griffin, "Toward an Integrated Theory of Task Design."

24. Charles A. O'Reilly and D. F. Caldwell, "Informational Influence as a Determinant of Perceived Task Characteristics and Job Satisfaction," *Journal of Applied Psychology*, 1979, vol. 64, pp. 157–165; Ricky W. Griffin, "Objective and Social Sources of Information in Task Redesign: A Field Experiment," *Administrative Science Quarterly*, June 1983, pp. 184–200. See also Griffin, "Toward an Integrated Theory of Task Design," and Donald J. Campbell, "Task Complexity: A Review and Analysis," *Academy of Management Review*, January 1988, pp. 40–52.

25. "Offenders Can Spread Ill Will from the Top Down," *USA Today*, September 9, 1998, pp. B1, B2.

26. David J. Glew, Anne M. O'Leary-Kelly, Ricky W. Griffin, and David D. Van Fleet, "Participation in Organizations: A Preview of the Issues and Proposed Framework for Future Analysis," *Journal of Management*, 1995, vol. 21, no. 3, pp. 395–421;

for a recent update, see Russ Forrester, "Empowerment: Rejuvenating a Potent Idea," *Academy of Management Executive*, 2002, vol. 14, no. 1, pp. 67–78.

27. John A. Wagner III, "Participation's Effects of Performance and Satisfaction: A Reconsideration of Research Evidence," *Academy of Management Review*, 1994, vol. 19, no. 2, pp. 312–330.

28. See Putai Jin, "Work Motivation and Productivity in Voluntarily Formed Work Teams: A Field Study in China," *Organizational Behavior and Human Decision Processes*, 1993, vol. 54, pp. 133–155, for an interesting example.

29. Quoted in "Herb Kelleher Has One Main Strategy: Treat Employees Well," *Wall Street Journal*, August 31, 1999, p. B1.

30. "9 to 5 Isn't Working Anymore," *Business Week*, September 20, 1999, pp. 94–98.

31. A. R. Cohen and H. Gadon, *Alternative Work Schedules: Integrating Individual and Organizational Needs* (Reading, Mass.: Addison-Wesley, 1978).

32. See Barbara Rau and MaryAnne Hyland, "Role Conflict and Flexible Work Arrangements: The Effects on Applicant Attraction," *Personnel Psychology*, 2002, vol. 55, no. 1, pp. 111–136.

33. Quoted in "Perks That Work," *Time*, November 9, 1998, p. 55.

34. For a recent analysis, see Sumita Raghuram, Raghu Garud, Batia Wiesenfeld, and Vipin Gupta, "Factors Contributing to Virtual Work Adjustment," *Journal of Management*, 2001, vol. 27, pp. 383–405.

Chapter 8

1. Jon R. Katzenbach and Jason A. Santamaria, "Firing Up the Front Line," *Harvard Business Review*, May–June 1999, pp. 107–117.

2. A. Bandura, *Social Learning Theory* (Englewood Cliffs, N.J.: Prentice-Hall, 1977).

3. See Edwin A. Locke, "Toward a Theory of Task Performance and Incentives," *Organizational Behavior*

and Human Performance, 1968, vol. 3, pp. 157–189.

4. Gary P. Latham and Gary Yukl, "A Review of Research on the Application of Goal Setting in Organizations," *Academy of Management Journal*, 1975, vol. 18, pp. 824–845.

5. Gary P. Latham and J. J. Baldes, "The Practical Significance of Locke's Theory of Goal Setting," *Journal of Applied Psychology*, 1975, vol. 60, pp. 187–191.

6. Gary P. Latham, "The Importance of Understanding and Changing Employee Outcome Expectancies for Gaining Commitment to an Organizational Goal," *Personnel Psychology*, 2001, vol. 54, pp. 707–720.

7. Quoted in Jim Collins, "Turning Goals Into Results: The Power of Catalytic Mechanisms," *Harvard Business Review*, July–August 1999, p. 72.

8. H. John Bernardin and Richard W. Beatty, *Performance Appraisal: Assessing Human Behavior at Work* (Boston: Kent, 1984).

9. Quoted in "Performance Reviews: Some Bosses Try a Fresh Approach," *Wall Street Journal*, December 1, 1998, p. B1.

10. See Bruce Pfau and Ira Kay, "Does 360-Degree Feedback Negatively Affect Company Performance?" *HRMagazine*, June 2002, pp. 54–59.

11. Joan Brett and Leanne Atwater, "360° Feedback: Accuracy, Reactions, and Perceptions of Usefulness," *Journal of Applied Psychology*, 2001, vol. 86, no. 5, pp. 930–942; Terry Beehr, Lana Ivanitskaya, Curtiss Hansen, Dmitry, and David Gudanowski, "Evaluation of 360-Degree Feedback Ratings: Relationships with Each Other and with Performance and Selection Predictors," *Journal of Organizational Behavior*, 2001, vol. 22, pp. 775–788.

12. Vanessa Urch Druskat and Steven B. Wolff, "Effects and Timing of Developmental Peer Appraisals in Self-Managing Work Groups," *Journal of Applied Psychology*, 1999, vol. 84, no. 1, pp. 58–74.

13. Peter Senge, *The Fifth Discipline* (New York: The Free Press, 1993).

14. See Edward E. Lawler, *Pay and Organization Development* (Reading, Mass.: Addison-Wesley, 1981).

15. Brian Boyd and Alain Salamin, "Strategic Reward Systems: A Contingency Model of Pay System Design," *Strategic Management Journal*, 2001, vol. 22, pp. 777–792.

16. Quoted in "Tight Labor Market Squeezes Pay Raises," *USA Today*, November 23, 1998, p. B1.

17. Alfred Rappaport, "New Thinking on How to Link Executive Pay with Performance," *Harvard Business Review*, March–April 1999, pp. 91–99.

18. Steve Bates, "Piecing Together Executive Compensation," *HRMagazine*, May 2002, pp. 60–69.

19. "Rich Benefit Plan Gives GM Competitors Cost Edge," *Wall Street Journal*, March 21, 1996, pp. B1, B4.

20. "Painless Perks," *Forbes*, September 6, 1999, p. 138. See also "Does Rank Have Too Much Privilege?" *The Wall Street Journal*, February 26, 2002, pp. B1, B4.

21. John R. Deckop, Robert Mangel, and Carol C. Cirka, "Getting More Than You Pay For: Organizational Citizenship Behavior and Pay-for-Performance Plans," *Academy of Management Journal*, 1999, vol. 42, no. 4, pp. 420–428.

22. Charlotte Garvey, "Steering Teams with the Right Pay," *HRMagazine*, May 2002, pp. 70–80.

23. Andrea Poe, "Selection Savvy," *HRMagazine*, April 2002, pp. 77–80.

24. Ricky W. Griffin and Michael W. Pustay, *International Business— A Managerial Perspective*, 3rd ed. (Upper Saddle River, N.J.: Prentice Hall, 2002).

Chapter 9

1. For a recent review, see Richard S. DeFrank and John M. Ivancevich, "Stress on the Job: An Executive Update," *Academy of Management Executive*, 1998, vol. 12, no. 3, pp. 55–65.

2. See James C. Quick and Jonathan D. Quick, *Organizational Stress and Preventive Management* (New York: McGraw-Hill, 1984), for a review.

3. Hans Selye, *The Stress of Life* (New York: McGraw-Hill, 1976).

4. For example, see Steve M. Jex and Paul D. Bliese, "Efficacy Beliefs as a Moderator of the Impact of Work-Related Stressors: A Multilevel Study," *Journal of Applied Psychology*, 1999, vol. 84, no. 3, pp. 349–361.

5. Meyer Friedman and Ray H. Rosenman, *Type A Behavior and Your Heart* (New York: Knopf, 1974).

6. Quoted in "Stress in the Valley," *Forbes*, September 6, 1999, p. 208.

7. "Prognosis for the 'Type A' Personality Improves in a New Heart Disease Study," *Wall Street Journal*, January 14, 1988, p. 27.

8. Susan C. Kobasa, "Stressful Life Events, Personality, and Health: An Inquiry Into Hardiness," *Journal of Personality and Social Psychology*, January 1979, pp. 1–11; Susan C. Kobasa, S. R. Maddi, and S. Kahn, "Hardiness and Health: A Prospective Study," *Journal of Personality and Social Psychology*, January 1982, pp. 168–177.

9. Professor Cooper's findings were reported by Carol Kleiman, *Chicago Times*, March 31, 1988, p. B1.

10. Todd D. Jick and Linda F. Mitz, "Sex Differences in Work Stress," *Academy of Management Review*, October 1985, pp. 408–420; Debra L. Nelson and James C. Quick, "Professional Women: Are Distress and Disease Inevitable?" *Academy of Management Review*, April 1985, pp. 206–218.

11. "Complex Characters Handle Stress Better," *Psychology Today*, October 1987, p. 26.

12. Quoted in "Some Employers Find Way to Ease Burden of Changing Shifts," *Wall Street Journal*, March 25, 1998, p. B1.

13. Robert L. Kahn, D. M. Wolfe, R. P. Quinn, J. D. Snoek, and R. A. Rosenthal, *Organizational Stress: Studies in Role Conflict and Role Ambiguity* (New York: John Wiley and Sons, 1964).

14. David R. Frew and Nealia S. Bruning, "Perceived Organizational Characteristics and Personality Measures as Predictors of Stress/Strain in the Work Place," *Academy of Management Journal*, December 1987, pp. 633–646.

15. Thomas H. Holmes and Richard H. Rahe, "The Social Readjustment Rating Scale," *Journal of Psychosomatic Research*, 1967, vol. 11, pp. 213–218.

16. Evelyn J. Bromet, Mary A. Dew, David K. Parkinson, and Herbert C. Schulberg, "Predictive Effects of Occupational and Marital Stress on the Mental Health of a Male Workforce," *Journal of Organizational Behavior*, 1988, vol. 9, pp. 1–13.

17. Quoted in "The New Paternalism," *Forbes*, November 2, 1998, p. 70.

18. "Employers on Guard for Violence," *Wall Street Journal*, April 5, 1995, pp. 3A; Joel H. Neuman and Robert A. Baron, "Workplace Violence and Workplace Aggression: Evidence Concerning Specific Forms, Potential Causes, and Preferred Targets," *Journal of Management*, 1998, vol. 24, no. 3, pp. 391–419.

19. Raymond T. Lee and Blake E. Ashforth, "A Meta-Analytic Examination of the Correlates of the Three Dimensions of Job Burnout," *Journal of Applied Psychology*, 1996, vol. 81, no. 2, pp. 123–133.

20. For a recent update, see Iain Densten, "Re-thinking Burnout," *Journal of Organizational Behavior*, 2001, vol. 22, pp. 833–847.

21. John M. Kelly, "Get a Grip on Stress," *HRMagazine*, February 1997, pp. 51–57.

22. John W. Lounsbury and Linda L. Hoopes, "A Vacation from Work: Changes in Work and Nonwork Outcomes," *Journal of Applied Psychology*, 1986, vol. 71, pp. 392–401.

23. "Overloaded Staffers Are Starting to Take More Time Off Work," *Wall Street Journal*, September 23, 1998, p. B1.

24. "Eight Ways to Help You Reduce the Stress in Your Life," *Business Week Careers*, November 1986, p. 78. See also Holly Weeks, "Taking the Stress out of Stressful Conversations," *Harvard Business Review*, July–August 2001, pp. 112–116.

25. Quoted in "Workplace Hazard Gets Attention," *USA Today*, May 5, 1998, p. 1B.

26. Richard A. Wolfe, David O. Ulrich, and Donald F. Parker, "Employee Health Management Programs: Review, Critique, and Research Agenda,"

Journal of Management, Winter 1987, pp. 603–615.

27. "Workplace Hazard Gets Attention," *USA Today*, May 5, 1998, pp. 1B, 2B.

28. Quoted in "The Daddy Trap," *Business Week*, September 21, 1998, p. 56.

29. "Work and Family," *Business Week*, September 15, 1997, pp. 96–99.

Chapter 10

1. Otis W. Baskin and Craig E. Aronoff, *Interpersonal Communication in Organizations* (Santa Monica, Calif.: Goodyear, 1980), p. 2.

2. "How Merrill Lynch Moves Its Stock Deals All Around the World," *Wall Street Journal*, November 9, 1987, pp. 1, 8.

3. Quoted in "Email's Limits Create Confusion, Hurt Feelings," *USA Today*, February 5, 2002, p. 1B.

4. Jeanne D. Maes, Teresa G. Weldy, and Marjorie L. Icenogle, "A Managerial Perspective: Oral Communication Competency Is Most Important for Business Students in the Workplace," *Journal of Business Communication*, January 1997, pp. 67–80.

5. Melinda Knight, "Writing and Other Communication Standards in Undergraduate Business Education: A Study of Current Program Requirements, Practices, and Trends," *Business Communication Quarterly*, March 1999, p. 10.

6. Robert Nurden, "Graduates Must Master the Lost Art of Communication," *The European*, March 20, 1997, p. 24.

7. Silvan S. Tompkins and Robert McCarter, "What and Where Are the Primary Affects? Some Evidence for a Theory," *Perceptual and Motor Skills*, February 1964, pp. 119–158.

8. See Everett M. Rogers and Rekha Agarwala-Rogers, *Communication in Organizations* (New York: Free Press, 1976), for a brief review of the background and development of the source-message-channel-receiver model of communication.

9. Charles A. O'Reilly III, "Variations in Decision Makers' Use of Information Sources: The Impact of Quality and Accessibility of Information," *Academy of Management Journal*, December 1982, pp. 756–771.

10. Quoted in Cynthia L. Kemper, "Sacre Bleu! English as a Global Lingua Franca? Why English Is Rapidly Achieving Worldwide Status," *Communication World*, June–July 1999, p. 41.

11. See Jerry C. Wofford, Edwin A. Gerloff, and Robert C. Cummins, *Organizational Communication* (New York: McGraw-Hill, 1977), for a discussion of channel noise.

12. Donald R. Hollis, "The Shape of Things to Come: The Role of IT," *Management Review*, June 1996, p. 62.

13. Quoted in "Like It or Not, You've Got Mail," *Business Week*, October 4, 1999, p. 184.

14. Kym France, "Computer Commuting Benefits Companies," *Arizona Republic*, August 16, 1993, pp. E1, E4.

15. Paul S. Goodman and Eric D. Darr, "Exchanging Best Practices Through Computer-Aided Systems," *Academy of Management Executive*, May 1996, pp. 7–18.

16. Jenny C. McCune, "The Intranet: Beyond E-Mail," *Management Review*, November 1996, pp. 23–27.

17. See Daniel Katz and Robert L. Kahn, *The Social Psychology of Organizations*, 2nd ed. (New York: John Wiley and Sons, 1978), for more about the role of organizational communication networks.

18. For good discussions of small-group communication networks and research on this subject, see Wofford, Gerloff, and Cummins, *Organizational Communication*; and Marvin E. Shaw, *Group Dynamics: The Psychology of Small Group Behavior*, 3rd ed. (New York: McGraw-Hill, 1981), pp. 150–161.

19. See R. Wayne Pace, *Organizational Communication: Foundations for Human Resource Development* (Englewood Cliffs, N.J.: Prentice Hall, 1983), for further discussion of the development of communication networks.

20. David Krackhardt and Lyman W. Porter, "The Snowball Effect: Turnover Embedded in Communication Networks," *Journal of Applied Psychology*, February 1986, pp. 50–55.

21. "Has Coke Been Playing Accounting Games?" *Business Week*, May 13, 2002, pp. 98–99.

22. See "E-mail's Limits Create Confusion, Hurt Feelings," *USA Today*, February 5, 2002, pp. 1B, 2B.

23. "Talk of Chapter 11 Bruises Kmart Stock," *USA Today*, January 3, 2002, p. 1B.

24. Thomas J. Peters and Robert H. Waterman Jr., *In Search of Excellence: Lessons from America's Best-Run Companies* (New York: Harper & Row, 1982), p. 121.

25. Shari Caudron, "Monsanto Responds to Diversity," *Personnel Journal*, November 1990, pp. 72–78; "Trading Places at Monsanto," *Training and Development Journal*, April 1993, pp. 45–49.

Chapter 11

1. Blake E. Ashforth and Fred Mael, "Social Identity Theory and the Organization," *Academy of Management Review*, January 1989, pp. 20–39.

2. Marvin E. Shaw, *Group Dynamics: The Psychology of Small Group Behavior*, 3rd ed. (New York: McGraw-Hill, 1981), p. 11.

3. Joseph P. Shapiro, "You Guys Are Outta Here!" *U.S. News & World Report*, September 13, 1999, p. 55.

4. Francis J. Yammarino and Alan J. Dubinsky, "Salesperson Performance and Managerially Controllable Factors: An Investigation of Individual and Work Group Effects," *Journal of Management*, 1990, vol. 16, pp. 87–106.

5. Rob Cross and Laurence Prusak, "The People Who Make Organizations Go—Or Stop," *Harvard Business Review*, June 2002, pp. 104–114.

6. William L. Sparks, Dominic J. Monetta, and L. M. Simmons Jr., "Affinity Groups: Developing Complex Adaptive Organizations," working paper, The PAM Institute, Washington, D.C., 1999.

7. Shawn Tully, "The Vatican's Finances," *Fortune*, December 21, 1987, pp. 28–40.

8. Dominic J. Monetta, "The POWER of Affinity Groups," *Management Review*, November 1998, p. 70.

9. Bernard M. Bass and Edward C. Ryterband, *Organizational Psychology*, 2nd ed. (Boston: Allyn & Bacon, 1979), pp. 252–254. See also Scott Lester, Bruce

Meglino, and M. Audrey Korsgaard, "The Antecedents and Consequences of Group Potency: A Longitudinal Investigation of Newly Formed Work Groups," *Academy of Management Journal*, 2002, vol. 45, no. 2, pp. 352–368.

10. Quoted in Charles Fishman, "Whole Foods Is All Teams," *Fast Company*, September 1998, p. 105.

11. Susan Long, "Early Integration in Groups: A Group to Join and a Group to Create," *Human Relations*, April 1984, pp. 311–332.

12. For example, see Mary Waller, Jeffrey Conte, Cristina Gibson, and Mason Carpenter, "The Effect of Individual Perceptions of Deadlines on Team Performance," *Academy of Management Review*, 2001, vol. 26, no. 4, pp. 586–600.

13. Steven L. Obert, "Developmental Patterns of Organizational Task Groups: A Preliminary Study," *Human Relations*, January 1983, pp. 37–52.

14. Bass and Ryterband, *Organizational Psychology*, pp. 252–254.

15. Bernard M. Bass, "The Leaderless Group Discussion," *Psychological Bulletin*, September 1954, pp. 465–492.

16. Jill Lieber, "Time to Heal the Wounds," *Sports Illustrated*, November 2, 1987, pp. 86–91.

17. Connie J. G. Gersick, "Marking Time: Predictable Transitions in Task Groups," *Academy of Management Journal*, 1989, vol. 32, pp. 274–309.

18. James H. Davis, *Group Performance* (Reading, Mass.: Addison-Wesley, 1964), pp. 82–86.

19. Shaw, *Group Dynamics*.

20. Charles A. O'Reilly III, David F. Caldwell, and William P. Barnett, "Work Group Demography, Social Integration, and Turnover," *Administrative Science Quarterly*, March 1989, vol. 34, pp. 21–37.

21. See Sheila Simsarian Webber and Lisa Donahue, "Impact of Highly and Less Job-Related Diversity on Work Group Cohesion and Performance: A Meta-Analysis," *Journal of Management*, 2001, vol. 27, pp. 141–162.

22. Nancy Adler, *International Dimensions of Organizational Behavior*, 3rd ed. (Boston: PWS-Kent, 1997), pp. 132–133.

23. Shaw, *Group Dynamics*, pp. 173–177.

24. Quoted in Todd Balf, "Wanna Score?" *Fast Company*, January 1999, p. 164.

25. See Jennifer Chatman and Francis Flynn, "The Influence of Demographic Heterogeneity on the Emergence and Consequences of Cooperative Norms in Work Teams," *Academy of Management Journal*, 2001, vol. 44, no. 5, pp. 956–974.

26. Daniel C. Feldman, "The Development and Enforcement of Group Norms," *Academy of Management Review*, January 1984, pp. 47–53.

27. John Tower, Edmund Muskie, and Brent Skowcroft, *The Tower Commission Report* (New York: joint publication of Bantam Books and Times Books, 1987); *Taking the Stand: The Testimony of Lieutenant Colonel Oliver L. North* (New York: Pocket Books, 1987).

28. Tower, Muskie, and Skowcroft, *The Tower Commission Report*, pp. 37–38.

29. William E. Piper, Myriam Marrache, Renee Lacroix, Astrid M. Richardson, and Barry D. Jones, "Cohesion as a Basic Bond in Groups," *Human Relations*, February 1983, pp. 93–108.

30. Robert T. Keller, "Predictors of the Performance of Project Groups in R & D Organizations," *Academy of Management Journal*, December 1986, pp. 715–726.

31. Irving L. Janis, *Groupthink*, 2nd ed. (Boston: Houghton Mifflin, 1982), p. 9.

32. Blake E. Ashforth and Fred Mael, "Social Identity Theory and the Organization," *Academy of Management Review*, January 1989, pp. 20–39.

33. "Now That It's Cruising, Can Ford Keep Its Foot to the Gas?" *Business Week*, February 11, 1985, pp. 48–52; Reed E. Nelson, "The Strength of Strong Ties: Social Networks and Intergroup Conflict in Organizations," *Academy of Management Journal*, June 1989, pp. 377–401, reprinted by permission.

34. See Stephen P. Robbins, *Managing Organizational Conflict* (Englewood Cliffs, N.J.: Prentice Hall, 1974), for a classic review.

35. Charles R. Schwenk, "Conflict in Organizational Decision Making: An Exploratory Study of Its Effects in For-Profit and Not-for-Profit Organizations," *Management Science*, April 1990, pp. 436–448.

36. Robbins, *Managing Organizational Conflict*, 1974.

37. Kenneth Thomas, "Conflict and Conflict Management," in Marvin Dunnette (ed.), *Handbook of Industrial and Organizational Psychology* (Chicago: Rand McNally, 1976), pp. 889–935.

38. Alfie Kohn, "How to Succeed Without Even Vying," *Psychology Today*, September 1986, pp. 22–28.

39. See Carsten K.W. De Dreu and Annelies E. M. Van Vianen, "Managing Relationship Conflict and the Effectiveness of Organizational Teams," *Journal of Organizational Behavior*, 2001, vol. 22, pp. 309–328.

40. Quoted in Joe Torre with Henry Dreher, *Joe Torre's Ground Rules for Winners* (New York: Hyperion Press, 1999), p. 89.

41. Patrick Nugent, "Managing Conflict: Third-Party Interventions for Managers," *Academy of Management Executive*, 2002, vol. 16, no. 1, pp. 139–148.

Chapter 12

1. Eric L. Trist and K. W. Bamforth, "Some Social and Psychological Consequences of the Longwall Method of Goal-Getting," *Human Relations*, February 1951, pp. 3–38; Jack D. Orsburn, Linda Moran, and Ed Musselwhite, with John Zenger, *Self-Directed Work Teams: The New American Challenge* (Homewood, Ill.: Business One Irwin, 1990).

2. See Jon R. Katzenbach and Douglas K. Smith, *The Wisdom of Teams: Creating the High-Performance Organization* (Boston: Harvard Business School Press, 1993), p. 45.

3. See Ruth Wageman, "How Leaders Foster Self-Managing Team Effectiveness: Design Choices Versus Hands-on Coaching," *Organization Science*, 2001, vol. 12, no. 5, pp. 559–577.

4. Charles C. Manz and Henry P. Sims, *Business Without Bosses: How Self-Managing Teams Are Building High-Performance Companies* (New York: John Wiley and Sons, 1993) p. 1.

5. See Michelle Marks, John Mathieu, and Stephen Zaccaro, "A Temporally Based Framework and Taxonomy of Team Processes," *Academy of Management Review*, 2001, vol. 26, no. 3, pp. 356–376.

6. Michele Williams, "In Whom We Trust: Group Membership as an Affective Context for Trust Development," *Academy of Management Review*, 2001, vol. 26, no. 3, pp. 377–396.

7. Katzenbach and Smith, *The Wisdom of Teams*, p. 3.

8. See Michelle Marks, Mark Sabella, C. Shawn Burke, and Stephen Zaccaro, "The Impact of Cross-Training on Team Effectiveness," *Journal of Applied Psychology*, 2002, vol. 87, no. 1, pp. 3–13.

9. Quoted in John A. Byrne, "The Global Corporation Becomes the Leaderless Corporation," *Business Week*, August 30, 1999, p. 90.

10. Orsburn, Moran, Musselwhite, and Zenger, *Self-Directed Work Teams*, p. 15.

11. Manz and Sims, *Business Without Bosses*, pp. 10–11.

12. See Deborah Ancona, Henrik Bresman, and Katrin Kaeufer, "The Competitive Advantage of X-Teams," *Sloan Management Review*, Spring 2002, pp. 33–42.

13. Katzenbach and Smith, *The Wisdom of Teams*, pp. 184–189.

14. Manz and Sims, *Business Without Bosses*, pp. 74–76.

15. Jason Colquitt, Raymond Noe, and Christine Jackson, "Justice in Teams: Antecedents and Consequences of Procedural Justice Climate," *Personnel Psychology*, 2002, vol. 55, pp. 83–95.

16. Nigel Nicholson (ed.), *Encyclopedic Dictionary of Organizational Behavior* (Cambridge, Mass.: Blackwell, 1995), p. 463.

17. Brian Dumaine, "The Trouble with Teams," *Fortune*, September 5, 1994.

18. Ibid.

19. Ibid.

20. Ibid.

21. Quoted in John A. Byrne, "The Global Corporation Becomes the Leaderless Corporation," *Business Week*, August 30, 1999, p. 90.

22. Ellen Hart, "Top Teams," *Management Review*, February 1996, pp. 43–47.

23. Dan Dimancescu and Kemp Dwenger, "Smoothing the Product Development Path," *Management Review*, January 1996, pp. 36–41.

24. Ibid.

25. Manz and Sims, *Business Without Bosses*, pp. 27–28.

26. Ibid., pp. 29–31.

27. Quoted in "Make Yourself a Leader," *Fast Company*, June 1999 (insert following p. 128).

28. Ibid., p. 130.

29. Manz and Sims, *Business Without Bosses*, p. 200.

30. Quoted in Polly Labarre, "The Company Without Limits," *Fast Company*, September 1999, p. 165.

31. Manz and Sims, *Business Without Bosses*, p. 200

Chapter 13

1. Ralph M. Stogdill, *Handbook of Leadership* (New York: Free Press, 1974). See also Bernard Bass, *Bass and Stogdill's Handbook of Leadership*, 3rd ed. (Riverside, N.J.: Free Press, 1990) and "In Search of Leadership," *Business Week*, November 15, 1999, pp. 172–176.

2. See Gary Yukl and David D. Van Fleet, "Theory and Research on Leadership in Organizations," in M. D. Dunnette and L. M. Hough (eds.), *Handbook of Industrial and Organizational Psychology*, vol. 3 (Palo Alto, Calif.: Consulting Psychologists Press, 1992), pp. 148–197.

3. Arthur G. Jago, "Leadership: Perspectives in Theory and Research," *Management Science*, March 1982, pp. 315–336.

4. Melvin Sorcher and James Brant, "Are You Picking the Right Leaders?" *Harvard Business Review*, February 2002, pp. 78–85.

5. See John P. Kotter, "What Leaders Really Do," *Harvard Business Review*, May–June 1990, pp. 103–111. See also Abraham Zaleznik, "Managers and Leaders: Are They Different?" *Harvard Business Review*, March–April 1992, pp.126–135; and John Kotter, "What Leaders Really Do," *Harvard Business Review*, December 2001, pp. 85–94.

6. Quoted in "Some Managers Are More Than Bosses—They're Leaders, Too," *Wall Street Journal*, November 16, 1999, p. B1.

7. Ronald Heifetz and Marty Linsky, "A Survival Guide for Leaders," *Harvard Business Review*, June 2002, pp. 65–74.

8. Frederick Reichheld, "Lead for Loyalty," *Harvard Business Review*, July–August 2001, pp. 76–83.

9. David D. Van Fleet and Gary A. Yukl, "A Century of Leadership Research," in D. A. Wren and J. A. Pearce II (eds.), *Papers Dedicated to the Development of Modern Management* (Chicago: The Academy of Management, 1986), pp. 12–23.

10. Shelly A. Kirkpatrick and Edwin A. Locke, "Leadership: Do Traits Matter?" *Academy of Management Executive*, May 1991, pp. 48–60; see also Robert J. Sternberg, "Managerial Intelligence: Why IQ Isn't Enough," *Journal of Management*, 1997, vol. 23, no. 3, pp. 475–493.

11. Russell L. Kent and Sherry E. Moss, "Effects of Sex and Gender Role on Leader Emergence," *Academy of Management Journal*, 1994, vol. 37, no. 5, pp. 1335–1346.

12. For example, see Sheila Puffer, "Understanding the Bear: A Portrait of Russian Business Leaders," *Academy of Management Executive*, 1994, vol. 8, no. 1, pp. 41–49.

13. "Korea's Samsung Plans Very Rapid Expansion into Autos, Other Lines," *Wall Street Journal*, March 2, 1995, pp. A1, A14.

14. Philip M. Podsakoff, Scott B. MacKenzie, Mike Ahearne, and William H. Bommer, "Searching for a Needle in a Haystack: Trying to Identify the Illusive Moderators of Leadership Behaviors," *Journal of Management*, 1995, vol. 21, no. 3, pp. 422–470.

15. Quoted in "In Search of Leadership," *Business Week*, November 15, 1999, p. 172.

16. Rensis Likert, *New Patterns of Management* (New York: McGraw-Hill, 1961).

17. Edwin Fleishman, E. F. Harris, and H. E. Burtt, *Leadership and Supervision in Industry* (Columbus, Ohio: Bureau of Educational Research, Ohio State University, 1955).

18. See Edwin A. Fleishman, "Twenty Years of Consideration and Structure," in Edward A. Fleishman and James G. Hunt (eds.), *Current Developments in the Study of Leadership* (Carbondale, Ill.: Southern Illinois University Press, 1973), pp. 1–40.

19. Fleishman, Harris, and Burtt, *Leadership and Supervision in Industry.*

20. See Robert R. Blake and Anne Adams McCanse, *Leadership Dilemmas—Grid Solutions* (Houston: Gulf, 1991); Robert R. Blake and Jane S. Mouton, *The Managerial Grid* (Houston: Gulf, 1964).

21. See P. C. Nystrom, "Managers and the Hi-Hi Leader Myth," *Academy of Management Journal*, 1978, vol. 21, pp. 325–331; L. L. Larson, J. G. Hunt, and R. N. Osborn, "The Great Hi-Hi Leader Behavior Myth: A Lesson from Occam's Razor," *Academy of Management Journal*, 1976, vol. 19, pp. 628–641.

22. See Gary A. Yukl, *Leadership in Organizations*, 3rd ed. (Englewood Cliffs, N.J.: Prentice-Hall, 1994).

23. See Fred E. Fiedler, *A Theory of Leadership Effectiveness* (New York: McGraw-Hill, 1967).

24. From Fred E. Fiedler, *A Theory of Leadership Effectiveness* (New York: McGraw-Hill, 1967). Reprinted by permission of the author.

25. See Fred E. Fiedler, "Engineering the Job to Fit the Manager," *Harvard Business Review*, September–October 1965, pp. 115–122.

26. See Fred E. Fiedler, Martin M. Chemers, and Linda Mahar, *Improving Leadership Effectiveness: The Leader Match Concept* (New York: John Wiley and Sons, 1976).

27. Chester A. Schriesheim, Bennett J. Tepper, and Linda A. Tetrault, "Least Preferred Co-Worker Score, Situational Control, and Leadership Effectiveness: A Meta-Analysis of Contingency Model Performance Predictions," *Journal of Applied Psychology*, 1994, vol. 79, no. 4, pp. 561–573.

28. See Martin G. Evans, "The Effects of Supervisory Behavior on the Path-Goal Relationship," *Organizational Behavior and Human Performance*, May 1970, pp. 277–298; Robert J. House, "A Path-Goal Theory of Leadership Effectiveness," *Administrative Science Quarterly*, September 1971, pp. 321–339; Robert J. House and Terence R. Mitchell, "Path-Goal Theory of Leadership," *Journal of Contemporary Business*, Autumn 1974, pp. 81–98.

29. "Woman with a Mission," *Forbes*, September 25, 1995, pp. 172–173.

30. See Victor H. Vroom and Philip H. Yetton, *Leadership and Decision Making* (Pittsburgh: University of Pittsburgh Press, 1973); Victor H. Vroom and Arthur G. Jago, *The New Leadership* (Englewood Cliffs, N.J.: Prentice-Hall, 1988).

31. Victor Vroom, "Leadership and the Decision-Making Process," *Organizational Dynamics*, Spring 2000.

32. Quoted in "Out of Tragedy at War, Lessons for Leaders on the Job," *Wall Street Journal*, August 15, 1999, p. B12.

33. Vroom and Jago, *The New Leadership.*

34. See Madeline E. Heilman, Harvey A. Hornstein, Jack H. Cage, and Judith K. Herschlag, "Reaction to Prescribed Leader Behavior as a Function of Role Perspective: The Case of the Vroom-Yetton Model," *Journal of Applied Psychology*, February 1984, pp. 50–60; R. H. George Field, "A Test of the Vroom-Yetton Normative Model of Leadership," *Journal of Applied Psychology*, February 1982, pp. 523–532.

35. George Graen and J. F. Cashman, "A Role-Making Model of Leadership in Formal Organizations: A Developmental Approach," in J. G. Hunt and L. L. Larson (eds.), *Leadership Frontiers* (Kent, Ohio: Kent State University Press, 1975), pp. 143–165; Fred Dansereau, George Graen, and W. J. Haga, "A Vertical Dyad Linkage Approach to Leadership Within Formal Organizations: A Longitudinal Investigation of the Role-Making Process," *Organizational Behavior and Human Performance*, 1975, vol. 15, pp. 46–78.

36. See Charlotte R. Gerstner and David V. Day, "Meta-Analytic Review of Leader-Member Exchange Theory: Correlates and Construct Issues," *Journal of Applied Psychology*, 1997, vol. 82, no. 6, pp. 827–844; John Maslyn and Mary Uhl-Bien, "Leader-Member Exchange and Its Dimensions: Effects of Self-Effort and Others' Effort on Relationship Quality," *Journal of Applied Psychology*, 2001, vol. 86, no. 4, pp. 697–708.

37. Paul Hersey and Kenneth H. Blanchard, *Management of Organizational Behavior: Utilizing Human Resources*, 3rd ed. (Englewood Cliffs, N.J.: Prentice Hall, 1977).

Chapter 14

1. Robert W. Allen and Lyman W. Porter (eds.), *Organizational Influence Processes* (Glenview, Ill.: Scott, Foresman, 1983).

2. Alan L. Frohman, "The Power of Personal Initiative," *Organizational Dynamics*, Winter 1997, pp. 39–48; see also James H. Dulebohn and Gerald R. Ferris, "The Role of Influence Tactics in Perceptions of Performance Evaluations' Fairness," *Academy of Management Journal*, 1999, vol. 42, no. 3, pp. 288–303.

3. Quoted in Thomas A. Stewart, "Get with the New Power Game," *Fortune*, January 13, 1997, p. 61.

4. Gary Williams and Robert Miller, "Change the Way You Persuade," *Harvard Business Review*, May 2002, pp. 65–75.

5. See James MacGregor Burns, *Leadership* (New York: Harper & Row, 1978), and Karl W. Kuhnert and Philip Lewis, "Transactional and Transformational Leadership: A Constructive/Developmental Analysis," *Academy of Management Review*, October 1987, pp. 648–657. See also Nick Turner, Julian Barling, Olga Epitropaki, Vicky Butcher, and Caroline Milner, "Transformational Leadership and Moral Reasoning," *Journal of Applied Psychology*, vol. 87, no. 3, pp. 304–311.

6. Francis J. Yammarino and Alan J. Dubinsky, "Transformational Leadership Theory: Using Levels of Analysis to Determine Boundary Conditions," *Personnel Psychology*, 1994, vol. 47, pp. 787–800.

7. Vicki Goodwin, J. C. Wofford, and J. Lee Whittington, "A Theoretical and Empirical Extension to the Transformational Leadership Construct,"

Journal of Organizational Behavior, 2001, vol. 22, pp. 759–774.

8. Juan-Carlos Pastor, James Meindl, and Margarita Mayo, "A Network Effects Model of Charisma Attributions," *Academy of Management Journal,* 2002, vol. 45, no. 2, pp. 410–420.

9. Quoted in Curtis Sittenfeld, "Leader on the Edge," *Fast Company,* October 1999, p. 220.

10. See Robert J. House, "A 1976 Theory of Charismatic Leadership," in J. G. Hunt and L. L. Larson (eds.), *Leadership: The Cutting Edge* (Carbondale, Ill.: Southern Illinois University Press, 1977), pp. 189–207. See also Jay A. Conger and Rabindra N. Kanungo, "Toward a Behavioral Theory of Charismatic Leadership in Organizational Settings," *Academy of Management Review,* October 1987, pp. 637–647.

11. "Play Hard, Fly Right," *Time, Bonus Section: Inside Business,* June 2002, pp. Y15–Y22.

12. David A. Nadler and Michael L. Tushman, "Beyond the Charismatic Leader: Leadership and Organizational Change," *California Management Review,* Winter 1990, pp. 77–97.

13. David A. Waldman and Francis J. Yammarino, "CEO Charismatic Leadership: Levels-of-Management and Levels-of-Analysis Effects," *Academy of Management Review,* 1999, vol. 24, no. 2, pp. 266–285.

14. See Steven Kerr and John M. Jermier, "Substitutes for Leadership: Their Meaning and Measurement," *Organizational Behavior and Human Performance,* 1978, vol. 22, pp. 375–403. See also Charles C. Manz and Henry P. Sims Jr., "Leading Workers to Lead Themselves: The External Leadership of Self-Managing Work Teams," *Administrative Science Quarterly,* March 1987, pp. 106–129.

15. Jon P. Howell, David E. Bowen, Peter W. Dorfman, Steven Kerr, and Philip Podsakoff, "Substitutes for Leadership: Effective Alternatives to Ineffective Leadership," *Organizational Dynamics,* Summer 1990, pp. 20–38. See also Philip M. Podsakoff, Scott B. Mackenzie, and William H. Bommer, "Transformational Leader Behaviors

and Substitutes for Leadership as Determinants of Employee Satisfaction, Commitment, Trust, and Organizational Citizenship Behaviors," *Journal of Management,* 1996, vol. 22, no. 2, pp. 259–298.

16. Quoted in Keith H. Hammonds, "The Monroe Doctrine," *Fast Company,* October 1999, p. 232.

17. For reviews of the meaning of power, see Henry Mintzberg, *Power in and Around Organizations* (Englewood Cliffs, N.J.: Prentice Hall, 1983); Jeffrey Pfeiffer, *Power in Organizations* (Marshfield, Mass.: Pitman Publishing, 1981); John Kenneth Galbraith, *The Anatomy of Power* (Boston: Houghton Mifflin, 1983); Gary A. Yukl, *Leadership in Organizations,* 3rd ed. (Englewood Cliffs, N.J.: Prentice Hall, 1994).

18. John R. P. French and Bertram Raven, "The Bases of Social Power," in Darwin Cartwright (ed.), *Studies in Social Power* (Ann Arbor, Mich.: University of Michigan Press, 1959), pp. 150–167. See also Philip M. Podsakoff and Chester A. Schriesheim, "Field Studies of French and Raven's Bases of Power: Critique, Reanalysis, and Suggestions for Future Research," *Psychological Bulletin,* 1985, vol. 97, pp. 387–411.

19. Quoted in "Hard-Driving Boss," *Business Week,* October 5, 1998, p. 84.

20. Yukl, *Leadership in Organizations,* Chapter X.

21. Victor Murray and Jeffrey Gandz, "Games Executives Play: Politics at Work," *Business Horizons,* December 1980, pp. 11–23. See also Jeffrey Gandz and Victor Murray, "The Experience of Workplace Politics," *Academy of Management Journal,* June 1980, pp. 237–251.

22. Gerald F. Cavanaugh, Dennis J. Moberg, and Manuel Valasquez, "The Ethics of Organizational Politics," *Academy of Management Review,* July 1981, pp. 363–374.

23. Pfeiffer, *Power in Organizations;* Mintzberg, *Power in and Around Organizations.*

24. The techniques in Figure 13.5 are based on Pfeiffer, *Power in Organizations;* Mintzberg, *Power in and Around*

Organizations; and Galbraith, *Anatomy of Power.*

25. "How the 2 Top Officials of Grace Wound Up in a Very Dirty War," *Wall Street Journal,* May 18, 1995, pp. Al, A8.

Chapter 15

1. Herbert Simon, *The New Science of Management Decision* (New York: Harper & Row, 1960), p. 1.

2. Quoted in Thomas A. Stewart, Alex Taylor III, Peter Petre, and Brent Schlender, "Henry Ford, Alfred P. Sloan, Tom Watson Jr., "Bill Gates: The Businessman of the Century," *Fortune,* November 22, 1999, p. 118.

3. Nandini Rajagopalan, Abdul M. A. Rasheed, and Deepak K. Datta, "Strategic Decision Processes: Critical Review and Future Directions," *Journal of Management,* Summer 1993, vol. 19, no. 2, pp. 349–384.

4. See George P. Huber, *Managerial Decision Making* (Glenview, Ill.: Scott, Foresman, 1980), pp. 90–115, for a discussion of decision making under conditions of certainty, risk, and uncertainty.

5. Quoted in "Why Companies Fail," *Fortune,* May 27, 2002, p. 62.

6. See David Garvin and Michael Roberto, "What You Don't Know About Making Decisions," *Harvard Business Review,* September 2001, pp. 108–115.

7. Quoted in Anna Muoio, "Idea Summit," *Fast Company,* January–February 2000, p. 156.

8. "'90s Style Brainstorming," *Forbes ASAP,* October 25, 1993, pp. 44–61.

9. Henry Mintzberg, Duru Raisinghani, and Andre Thoret, "The Structure of 'Unstructured' Decision Processes," *Administrative Science Quarterly,* June 1976, pp. 246–275; Milan Zeleny, "Descriptive Decision Making and Its Application," *Applications of Management Science,* 1981, vol. 1, pp. 327–388.

10. See E. Frank Harrison, *The Managerial Decision-Making Process,* 5th ed. (Boston: Houghton Mifflin, 1999), pp. 55–60, for more on choice processes.

11. Ari Ginsberg and N. Ventraka-man, "Contingency Perspectives of Organizational Strategy: A Critical Review of the Empirical Research," *Academy of Management Review*, July 1985, pp. 412–434; Donald C. Ham-brick and David Lei, "Toward an Empirical Prioritization of Contin-gency Variables for Business Strategy," *Academy of Management Journal*, December 1985, pp. 763–788.

12. Leon Festinger, *A Theory of Cognitive Dissonance* (Palo Alto, Calif.: Stanford University Press, 1957).

13. Patricia Sellers, "The Dumbest Marketing Ploys," *Fortune*, October 5, 1992, pp. 88–94.

14. See Harrison, *The Managerial Decision-Making Process*, pp. 74–100, for more on the rational approach to decision making.

15. Craig D. Parks and Rebecca Cowlin, "Group Discussion as Affected by Number of Alternatives and by a Time Limit," *Organizational Behavior and Human Decision Processes*, 1995, vol. 62, no. 3, pp. 267–275.

16. See James G. March and Herbert A. Simon, *Organizations* (New York: Wiley, 1958), for more on the concept of bounded rationality.

17. Herbert A. Simon, *Administrative Behavior: A Study of Decision Making Processes in Administrative Organiza-tions*, 3rd ed. (New York: Free Press, 1976).

18. Richard M. Cyert and James G. March, *A Behavioral Theory of the Firm* (Englewood Cliffs, N.J.: Prentice Hall, 1963), p. 113; Simon, *Administrative Behavior*.

19. Kathleen M. Eisenhardt, "Making Fast Strategic Decisions in High-Velocity Environments," *Academy of Management Journal*, September 1989, pp. 543–576.

20. Irving L. Janis and Leon Mann, *Decision Making: A Psychological Analy-sis of Conflict, Choice, and Commitment* (New York: Free Press, 1977).

21. Quoted in "Internet Defense Strategy: Cannibalize Yourself," *Fortune*, September 6, 1999, p. 128.

22. Jerry Ross and Barry M. Staw, "Expo 86: An Escalation Prototype," *Administrative Science Quarterly*, June 1986, pp. 274–297.

23. Barry M. Staw, "Escalation of Commitment to a Course of Action," *Academy of Management Review*, October 1981, pp. 577–587.

24. Barry M. Staw and Jerry Ross, "Good Money After Bad," *Psychology Today*, February 1988, pp. 30–33.

25. M. A. Wallach, N. Kogan, and D. J. Bem, "Group Influence on Indi-vidual Risk Taking," *Journal of Abnor-mal and Social Psychology*, August 1962, pp. 75–86; James A. F. Stoner, "Risky and Cautious Shifts in Group Deci-sions: The Influence of Widely Held Values," *Journal of Experimental Social Psychology*, October 1968, pp. 442–459.

26. Dorwin Cartwright, "Risk Taking by Individuals and Groups: An Assess-ment of Research Employing Choice Dilemmas," *Journal of Personality and Social Psychology*, December 1971, pp. 361–378.

27. S. Moscovici and M. Zavalloni, "The Group as a Polarizer of Atti-tudes," *Journal of Personality and Social Psychology*, June 1969, pp. 125–135.

28. Irving L. Janis, *Groupthink*, 2nd ed. (Boston: Houghton Mifflin, 1982), p. 9.

29. Gregory Moorhead, Christopher P. Neck, and Mindy West, "The Tendency Toward Defective Decision Making Within Self-Managing Teams: Relevance of Groupthink for the 21st Century," *Organizational Behavior and Human Decision Processes*, February–March 1998, pp. 327–351.

30. Gregory Moorhead, Richard Ference, and Chris P. Neck, "Group Decision Fiascoes Continue: Space Shuttle *Challenger* and a Revised Groupthink Framework," *Human Relations*, 1991, vol. 44, pp. 539–550.

31. See Robert Cross and Susan Brodt, "How Assumptions of Consen-sus Undermine Decision Making," *Sloan Management Review*, Winter 2001, pp. 86–95.

32. Irving L. Janis, *Victims of Group-think* (Boston: Houghton Mifflin, 1972), pp. 197–198.

33. Janis, *Groupthink*.

34. Janis, *Groupthink*, pp. 193–197; Gregory Moorhead, "Groupthink: Hypothesis in Need of Testing," *Group & Organization Studies*, December 1982, pp. 429–444.

35. Gregory Moorhead and John R. Montanari, "Empirical Analysis of the Groupthink Phenomenon," *Human Relations*, May 1986, pp. 399–410; John R. Montanari and Gregory Moorhead, "Development of the Groupthink Assessment Inventory," *Educational and Psychological Measure-ment*, Spring 1989, pp. 209–219.

36. Frederick W. Taylor, *The Princi-ples of Scientific Management* (New York: Harper & Row, 1911).

37. Chris Argyris, *Personality and Organization* (New York: Harper & Row, 1957); Rensis Likert, *New Patterns of Management* (New York: McGraw-Hill, 1961).

38. Lester Coch and John R. P. French, "Overcoming Resistance to Change," *Human Relations*, 1948, vol. 1, pp. 512–532; N. C. Morse and E. Reimer, "The Experimental Change of a Major Organizational Variable," *Journal of Abnormal and Social Psychol-ogy*, January 1956, pp. 120–129.

39. Quoted in Curtis Sittenfeld, "Powered by the People," *Fast Com-pany*, July–August 1999, p. 189.

40. Victor Vroom, "Leadership and the Decision-Making Process," *Or-ganizational Dynamics* (Spring 2000).

41. For a recent example, see Carsten K. W. De Dreu and Michael West, "Minority Dissent and Team Innova-tion: The Importance of Participation in Decision Making," *Journal of Ap-plied Psychology*, 2001, vol. 86, no. 6, pp. 1191–1201.

42. See Kimberly Wade-Benzoni, Andrew Hoffman, Leigh Thompson, Don Moore, James Gillespie, and Max Bazerman, "Barriers to Resolution in Ideologically Based Negotiations: The Role of Values and Institutions," *Academy of Management Review*, 2002, vol. 27, no. 1, pp. 41–57.

43. J. Z. Rubin and B. R. Brown, *The Social Psychology of Bargaining and Negotiation* (New York: Academic Press, 1975).

44. R. J. Lewicki and J. A. Litterer, *Ne-gotiation* (Homewood, Ill.: Irwin, 1985).

45. Howard Raiffa, *The Art and Science of Negotiation* (Cambridge, Mass.: Belknap, 1982).

46. K. H. Bazerman and M. A. Neale, *Negotiating Rationally* (New York: Free Press, 1992).

47. Ross R. Reck and Brian G. Long, *The Win-Win Negotiator* (Escondido, Calif.: Blanchard Training and Development, 1985).

Chapter 16

1. See Richard Daft, *Organization Theory and Design*, 2nd ed. (St. Paul, Minn.: West, 1986), p. 9, for further discussion of the definition of *organization*.

2. John R. Montanari, Cyril P. Morgan, and Jeffrey S. Bracker, *Strategic Management* (Hinsdale, Ill.: Dryden Press, 1990), pp. 1–2.

3. Quoted in Michael Moeller, Steve Hamm, and Timothy J. Mullaney, "Remaking Microsoft," *Business Week*, May 17, 1999, p. 106.

4. A. Bryman, A. D. Beardworth, E. T. Keil, and J. Ford, "Organizational Size and Specialization," *Organization Studies*, September 1983, pp. 271–278.

5. Joseph L. C. Cheng, "Interdependence and Coordination in Organizations: A Role System Analysis," *Academy of Management Journal*, March 1983, pp. 156–162.

6. Henry Mintzberg, *The Structuring of Organizations* (Englewood Cliffs, N.J.: Prentice Hall, 1979), for further discussion of the basic elements of structure.

7. Max Weber, *The Theory of Social and Economic Organization*, trans. A. M. Henderson and Talcott Parsons (New York: Free Press, 1947).

8. Adam Smith, *An Inquiry into the Nature and Causes of the Wealth of Nations* (London: Dent, 1910).

9. Nancy M. Carter and Thomas L. Keon, "The Rise and Fall of the Division of Labour, the Past 25 Years," *Organization Studies*, 1986, pp. 54–57.

10. Glenn R. Carroll, "The Specialist Strategy," *California Management Review*, Spring 1984, pp. 126–137.

11. "Management Discovers the Human Side of Automation," *Business Week*, September 29, 1986, pp. 70–75.

12. See Robert H. Miles, *Macro Organizational Behavior* (Santa Monica, Calif.: Goodyear, 1980), pp. 28–34, for a discussion of departmentalization schemes.

13. Mintzberg, *The Structuring of Organizations*, p. 125.

14. Miles, *Macro Organizational Behavior*, pp. 122–133.

15. "Big Blue Wants to Loosen Its Collar," *Fortune*, February 29, 1988, p. 8; "Inside IBM: Internet Business Machines," *Business Week*, December 13, 1999, pp. EB20–28.

16. Ronald Henkoff, "Cost Cutting: How to Do It Right," *Fortune*, April 9, 1990, pp. 40–50.

17. Peggy Leatt and Rodney Schneck, "Criteria for Grouping Nursing Subunits in Hospitals," *Academy of Management Review*, March 1984, pp. 150–165.

18. Lyndall F. Urwick, "The Manager's Span of Control," *Harvard Business Review*, May–June 1956, pp. 39–47.

19. Dan R. Dalton, William D. Tudor, Michael J. Spendolini, Gordon J. Fielding, and Lyman W. Porter, "Organization Structure and Performance: A Critical Review," *Academy of Management Review*, January 1980, pp. 49–64.

20. Mintzberg, *The Structuring of Organizations*, pp. 133–147.

21. See David Van Fleet, "Span of Management Research and Issues," *Academy of Management Journal*, September 1983, pp. 546–552, for an example of research on span of control.

22. "New Home. New CEO. Gateway Is Moo and Improved," *Fortune*, December 20, 1999, pp. 44–46; "Weitzen to Become Gateway's New CEO; Waitt Still Chairman," *Wall Street Journal*, December 9, 1999, p. B16; William J. Holstein and Susan Gregory Thomas, "Gateway Gets Citified," *U.S. News & World Report*, May 3, 1999, p. 42; Elizabeth Corcoran, "Gateway 2005," *Forbes*, March 8, 1999, p. 52.

23. John R. Montanari and Philip J. Adelman, "The Administrative Component of Organizations and the Rachet Effect: A Critique of Cross-Sectional Studies," *Journal of Management Studies*, March 1987, pp. 113–123.

24. Quoted in Richard M. Hodgetts, "Dow Chemical's CEO William Stavropoulos on Structure and Decision Making," *Academy of Management Executive*, November 1999, p. 30.

25. D. A. Heenan, "The Downside of Downsizing," *Journal of Business Strategy*, November–December 1989, pp. 18–23.

26. Wayne F. Cascio, "Downsizing: What Do We Know? What Have We Learned?" *Academy of Management Executive*, February 1993, pp. 95–104.

27. Dalton et al., "Organization Structure and Performance."

28. See John Child, *Organization: A Guide to Problems and Practice*, 2nd ed. (New York: Harper & Row, 1984), pp. 145–153, for a detailed discussion of centralization.

29. Richard H. Hall, *Organization: Structure and Process*, 3rd ed. (Englewood Cliffs, N.J.: Prentice Hall, 1982), pp. 87–96.

30. "Can Jack Smith Fix GM?" *Business Week*, November 1, 1993, pp. 126–131; John McElroy, "GM's Brand Management Might Work," *Automotive Industries*, September 1996, p. 132.

31. Quoted in Alex Taylor III, "Compaq Looks Inside for Salvation," *Fortune*, August 16, 1999, p. 126.

32. Daniel R. Denison, "Bringing Corporate Culture to the Bottom Line," *Organizational Dynamics*, Autumn 1984, pp. 4–22.

33. Leonard W. Johnson and Alan L. Frohman, "Identifying and Closing the Gap in the Middle of Organizations," *Academy of Management Executive*, May 1989, pp. 107–114.

34. "The Selling of Acura—A Honda That's Not a Honda," *Business Week*, March 17, 1986, p. 93.

35. Brian S. Moskal, "Supervision (or Lack of It)," *Industry Week*, December 3, 1990, pp. 54–57; Roger Schreffler, "A Decade of Progress," *Automotive Industries*, November 1992, pp. 46–48; Alison Rogers, "GM vs. Honda: A Morality Tale," *Fortune*, February 8, 1993, pp. 11–12; "The Dangers of Running Too Lean," *Fortune*, June 14, 1993, pp. 114–116; Keith Naughton, "America's No. 1 Car Exporter Is Japan?" *Business Week*, February 26, 1996, p. 113.

36. Michael Schrage, "I Know What You Mean, and I Can't Do Anything About It," *Fortune*, April 2, 2001, p. 186.

37. Mintzberg, *The Structuring of Organizations*, pp. 83–84.

38. Arthur P. Brief and H. Kirk Downey, "Cognitive and Organizational Structures: A Conceptual Analysis of Implicit Organizing Theories," *Human Relations*, December 1983, pp. 1065–1090.

39. Jerald Hage, "An Axiomatic Theory of Organizations," *Administrative Science Quarterly*, December 1965, pp. 289–320.

40. Gregory Moorhead, "Organizational Analysis: An Integration of the Macro and Micro Approaches," *Journal of Management Studies*, April 1981, pp. 191–218.

41. J. Daniel Sherman and Howard L. Smith, "The Influence of Organizational Structure on Intrinsic Versus Extrinsic Motivation," *Academy of Management Journal*, December 1984, pp. 877–885.

42. John A. Pearce II and Fred R. David, "A Social Network Approach to Organizational Design-Performance," *Academy of Management Review*, July 1983, pp. 436–444.

43. Eileen Farihurst, "Organizational Rules and the Accomplishment of Nursing Work on Geriatric Wards," *Journal of Management Studies*, July 1983, pp. 315–332.

44. "Chevron Corp. Has Big Challenge Coping with Worker Cutbacks," *Wall Street Journal*, November 4, 1986, pp. 1, 25.

45. Neil F. Brady, "Rules for Making Exceptions to Rules," *Academy of Management Review*, July 1987, pp. 436–444.

46. Quoted in Patricia Sellers, "Crunch Time for Coke," *Fortune*, July 19, 1999, p. 78.

47. See Jeffrey Pfeiffer, *Power in Organizations* (Boston: Pittman, 1981), pp. 4–6, for a discussion of the relationship between power and authority.

48. John B. Miner, *Theories of Organizational Structure and Process* (Hinsdale, Ill.: Dryden Press, 1982), p. 360.

49. "Management Lesson of Irangate," *Wall Street Journal*, March 24, 1987, p. 36.

50. Chester Barnard, *The Functions of the Executive* (Cambridge, Mass.: Harvard University Press, 1938), pp. 161–184.

51. Pfeiffer, *Power in Organizations*, pp. 366–367.

52. Weber, *The Theory of Social and Economic Organization*.

53. For more discussion of these alternative views, see John B. Miner, *Theories of Organizational Structure and Process*, p. 386.

54. Quoted in Roger R. Klene, commentary on Paul S. Adler, "Building Better Bureaucracies," *Academy of Management Executive*, November 1999, pp. 36–47, 47–48.

55. Paul S. Adler, "Building Better Bureaucracies," *Academy of Management Executive*, November 1999, pp. 36–46.

56. This summary of the classic principles of organizing is based on Henri Fayol, *General and Industrial Management*, trans. Constance Storrs (London: Pittman, 1949); Miner, *Theories of Organizational Structure and Process*, pp. 358–381; and the discussions in Bedeian, *Organizations: Theory and Analysis*, 2nd ed. (Chicago: Dryden, 1984), pp. 58–59.

57. Miner, *Theories of Organizational Structure and Process*, pp. 358–381.

58. See Rensis Likert, *New Patterns of Management* (New York: McGraw-Hill, 1961); and Rensis Likert, *The Human Organization: Its Management and Value* (New York: McGraw-Hill, 1967), for a complete discussion of the human organization.

59. Miner, *Theories of Organizational Structure and Process*, pp. 17–53.

Chapter 17

1. "About AT&T," "AT&T History," "AT&T to Create Family of Four New Companies," AT&T web site. www.att.com on June 11, 2002. Martha McKay, "AT&T to Cut Another 5,000 Jobs This Year—Layoffs Spur Speculation About Possible Merger," *The Record* (Hackensack, N.J.), January 5, 2002. See www. bergen.com. Stephanie N. Mehta, "Say Goodbye to AT&T," *Fortune*, October 1, 2001, pp. 135–146 (quotation p. 136). www.fortune.com on June 11, 2002.

2. Quoted in "Sony Restructures to Embrace Digital Economy," *Research Technology Management*, September 1999, p. 4.

3. Lex Donaldson, "Strategy and Structural Adjustment to Regain Fit and Performance: In Defense of Contingency Theory," *Journal of Management Studies*, January 1987, pp. 1–24.

4. John R. Montanari, Cyril P. Morgan, and Jeffrey Bracker, *Strategic Management* (Hinsdale, Ill.: Dryden Press, 1990), p. 114.

5. See Arthur A. Thompson Jr. and A. J. Strickland III, *Strategic Management*, 3rd ed. (Plano, Tex.: Business Publications, 1984), pp. 19–27.

6. Alfred D. Chandler, *Strategy and Structure: Chapters in the History of the American Industrial Enterprise* (Cambridge, Mass.: MIT Press, 1962).

7. John R. Kimberly, "Organizational Size and the Structuralist Perspective: A Review, Critique, and Proposal," *Administrative Science Quarterly*, December 1976, pp. 571–597.

8. Peter M. Blau and Richard A. Schoenherr, *The Structure of Organizations* (New York: Basic Books, 1971).

9. The results of these studies are thoroughly summarized in Richard H. Hall, *Organizations: Structure and Process*, 3rd ed. (Englewood Cliffs, N.J.: Prentice Hall, 1982), pp. 89–94. For a recent study in this area, see John H. Cullen and Kenneth S. Anderson, "Blau's Theory of Structural Differentiation Revisited: A Theory of Structural Change or Scale?" *Academy of Management Journal*, June 1986, pp. 203–229.

10. "Small Is Beautiful Now in Manufacturing," *Business Week*, October 22, 1984, pp. 152–156.

11. Richard H. Hall, J. Eugene Haas, and Norman Johnson, "Organizational Size, Complexity, and Formalization," *American Sociological Review*, December 1967, pp. 903–912.

12. Catherine Arnst, "Downsizing out One Door and in Another," *Business Week*, January 22, 1996, p. 41; Peter Elstrom, "Dial A for Aggravation," *Business Week*, March 11, 1996, p. 34; Alex Markels and Matt Murray, "Call It Dumbsizing: Why Some Companies Regret Cost-Cutting," *Wall Street Journal*, May 14, 1996, pp. A1, A5.

13. Robert I. Sutton and Thomas D'Anno, "Decreasing Organizational

Size: Untangling the Effects of Money and People," *Academy of Management Review*, May 1989, pp. 194–212.

14. Joan Woodward, *Management and Technology: Problems of Progress in Industry*, no. 3 (London: Her Majesty's Stationery Office, 1958); Joan Woodward, *Industrial Organizations: Theory and Practice* (London: Oxford University Press, 1965).

15. Tom Burns and George M. Stalker, *The Management of Innovation* (London: Tavistock, 1961).

16. Charles B. Perrow, "A Framework for the Comparative Analysis of Organizations," *American Sociological Review*, April 1967, pp. 194–208.

17. James D. Thompson, *Organizations in Action* (New York: McGraw-Hill, 1967).

18. David J. Hickson, Derek S. Pugh, and Diana C. Pheysey, "Operations Technology and Organization Structure: An Empirical Reappraisal," *Administrative Science Quarterly*, September 1969, pp. 378–397.

19. Hickson, Pugh, and Pheysey, "Operations Technology and Organization Structure."

20. Andrew Kupfer, "How to Be a Global Manager," *Fortune*, March 14, 1988, pp. 52–58.

21. "Going Crazy in Japan—In a Break from Tradition, Tokyo Begins Funding a Program for Basic Research," *Wall Street Journal*, November 10, 1986, p. D20.

22. Quoted in Marc Gunther, "Eisner's Mouse Trap," *Fortune*, September 6, 1999, p. 114.

23. Richard L. Daft, *Organization Theory and Design*, 2nd ed. (St. Paul, Minn.: West, 1986), p. 55.

24. Robert B. Duncan, "Characteristics of Organizational Environments and Perceived Uncertainty," *Administrative Science Quarterly*, September 1972, pp. 313–327.

25. "Toy Makers Lose Interest in Tie-Ins with Cartoons," *Wall Street Journal*, April 28, 1988, p. 29.

26. Masoud Yasai-Ardekani, "Structural Adaptations to Environments," *Academy of Management Review*, January 1986, pp. 9–21.

27. John E. Prescott, "Environments as Moderators of the Relationship Between Strategy and Performance," *Academy of Management Journal*, June 1986, pp. 329–346.

28. Timothy M. Stearns, Alan N. Hoffman, and Jan B. Heide, "Performance of Commercial Television Stations as an Outcome of Interorganizational Linkages and Environmental Conditions," *Academy of Management Journal*, March 1987, pp. 71–90.

29. Thompson, *Organizations in Action*, pp. 51–82.

30. For more information on managerial choice, see John Child, "Organizational Structure, Environment, and Performance: The Role of Strategic Choice," *Sociology*, January 1972, pp. 1–22; John R. Montanari, "Managerial Discretion: An Expanded Model of Organizational Choice," *Academy of Management Review*, April 1978, pp. 231–241.

31. H. Randolph Bobbitt and Jeffrey D. Ford, "Decision Maker Choice as a Determinant of Organizational Structure," *Academy of Management Review*, January 1980, pp. 13–23.

32. "Thermos Fires Up Grill Lines," *Weekly Home Furnishings Newspaper*, August 24, 1992, p. 54; Brian Dumaine, "Payoff from the New Management," *Fortune*, December 13, 1993, pp. 102–110.

33. "Three's Company," *Economist*, October 30, 1999, p. 80; "Citigroup: So Much for 50–50," *Business Week*, August 16, 1999, p. 80; Carol J. Loomis, "Citigroup: Scenes from a Merger," *Fortune*, January 11, 1999, pp. 76–88.

34. James W. Frederickson, "The Strategic Decision Process and Organization Structure," *Academy of Management Review*, April 1986, pp. 280–297.

35. Herman L. Boschken, "Strategy and Structure: Reconceiving the Relationship," *Journal of Management*, March 1990, pp. 135–150.

36. Quoted in John Huey and Geoffrey Colvin, "The Jack and Herb Show," *Fortune*, January 11, 1999, p. 164.

37. "Small Manufacturers Shifting to 'Just-In-Time' Techniques," *Wall Street Journal*, December 21, 1987, p. 25.

38. Elton Mayo, *The Human Problems of an Industrial Civilization* (New York: Macmillan, 1933); F. J. Roethlisberger and W. J. Dickson, *Management and the Worker* (Cambridge, Mass.: Harvard University Press, 1939).

39. Eric L. Trist and K. W. Bamforth, "Some Social and Psychological Consequences of the Longwall Method of Coal-Getting," *Human Relations*, February 1951, pp. 3–38.

40. "Small Manufacturers Shifting to 'Just-In-Time' Techniques."

41. Richard E. Walton, "How to Counter Alienation in the Plant," *Harvard Business Review*, November–December 1972, pp. 70–81; Pehr G. Gyllenhammar, "How Volvo Adapts Work to People," *Harvard Business Review*, July–August 1977, pp. 102–113; Richard E. Walton, "Work Innovations at Topeka: After Six Years," *Journal of Applied Behavioral Science*, July–August–September 1977, pp. 422–433.

42. Henry Mintzberg, *The Structuring of Organizations: A Synthesis of the Research* (Englewood Cliffs, N.J.: Prentice Hall, 1979).

43. See Harold C. Livesay, *American Made: Men Who Shaped the American Economy* (Boston: Little, Brown, 1979), pp. 215–239, for a discussion of Alfred Sloan and the development of the divisionalized structure at General Motors.

44. Anne B. Fisher, "GM Is Tougher Than You Think," *Fortune*, November 10, 1986, pp. 56–64.

45. Thompson and Strickland, *Strategic Management*, p. 212.

46. Kenneth Labich, "The Innovators," *Fortune*, June 6, 1988, pp. 51–64.

47. Henry Mintzberg, "Organization Design: Fashion or Fit," *Harvard Business Review*, January–February 1981, pp. 103–116.

48. Harvey F. Kolodny, "Managing in a Matrix," *Business Horizons*, March–April 1981, pp. 17–24.

49. Stanley M. Davis and Paul R. Lawrence, *Matrix* (Reading, Mass.: Addison-Wesley, 1977), pp. 11–36.

50. Lawton R. Burns, "Matrix Management in Hospitals: Testing Theories of Matrix Structure and Development,"

Administrative Science Quarterly, September 1989, pp. 355–358.

51. Ibid., pp. 129–154.

52. "The Virtual Corporation," *Business Week*, February 8, 1993, pp. 98–102; William H. Carlile, "Virtual Corporation a Real Deal," *Arizona Republic*, August 2, 1993, pp. E1, E4.

53. Thomas A. Stewart, "Reengineering: The Hot New Managing Tool," *Fortune*, August 23, 1993, pp. 41–48.

54. Robert Tomasko, *Rethinking the Corporation* (New York: AMA-COM, 1993).

55. Quoted in William J. Holstein and Susan Gregory Thomas, "Gateway Gets Citified," *U.S. News & World Report*, May 3, 1999, p. 42.

56. Rahul Jacob, "The Struggle to Create an Organization for the 21st Century," *Fortune*, April 3, 1995, pp. 90–99; Gene G. Marcial, "Don't Leave Your Broker Without It?" *Business Week*, February 5, 1996, p. 138; Jeffrey M. Laderman, "Loading Up on No-Loads," *Business Week*, May 27, 1996, p. 138.

57. James R. Lincoln, Mitsuyo Hanada, and Kerry McBride, "Organizational Structures in Japanese and U.S. Manufacturing," *Administrative Science Quarterly*, September 1986, pp. 338–364.

58. "The Inscrutable West," *Newsweek*, April 18, 1988, p. 52.

59. Richard I. Kirkland Jr., "Europe's New Managers," *Fortune*, September 29, 1980, pp. 56–60; Shawn Tully, "Europe's Takeover Kings," *Fortune*, July 20, 1987, pp. 95–98.

60. Henry W. Lane and Joseph J. DiStefano, *International Management Behavior* (Ontario: Nelson, 1988).

61. William H. Davison and Philippe Haspeslagh, "Shaping a Global Product Organization," *Harvard Business Review*, July–August 1982, pp. 125–132.

62. John Child, *Organizations: A Guide to Problems and Practice* (New York: Harper & Row, 1984), p. 246.

63. Thomas J. Peters and Robert H. Waterman Jr., *In Search of Excellence: Lessons from America's Best-Run Companies* (New York: Harper & Row, 1982), pp. 235–278.

64. Thomas J. Peters and Nancy K. Austin, "A Passion for Excellence," *Fortune*, May 13, 1985, pp. 20–32.

Chapter 18

1. Erika Rasmusson, "Flying High," *Sales and Marketing Management*, December 2001, p. 55 (quotation), Shaun McKinnon, "New Faces, Old Methods," *Arizona Republic* (Phoenix), July 29, 2001, pp. D1, D11; Wendy Zellner, "Southwest: After Kelleher, More Blue Skies," *Business Week*, April 2, 2001, p. 45.

2. See "Corporate Culture: The Hard-to-Change Values That Spell Success or Failure," *Business Week*, October 27, 1980, pp. 148–160; Charles G. Burck, "Working Smarter," *Fortune*, June 15, 1981, pp. 68–73.

3. Charles A. O'Reilly and Jennifer A. Chatman, "Culture as Social Control: Corporations, Cults, and Commitment," in Barry M. Staw and L. L. Cummings (eds.), *Research in Organizational Behavior* (Stamford, Conn.: JAI Press, 1996), vol. 18, pp. 157–200.

4. J. P. Kotter and J. L. Heskett, *Corporate Culture and Performance* (New York: Free Press, 1992).

5. Michael Tushman and Charles A. O'Reilly, *Staying on Top: Managing Strategic Innovation and Change for Long-Term Success* (Boston: Harvard Business School Press, 1996).

6. T. E. Deal and A. A. Kennedy, *Corporate Cultures: The Rites and Rituals of Corporate Life* (Reading, Mass.: Addison-Wesley, 1982), p. 4.

7. E. H. Schein, "The Role of the Founder in Creating Organizational Culture," *Organizational Dynamics*, Summer 1983, p. 14.

8. Thomas J. Peters and Robert H. Waterman Jr., *In Search of Excellence: Lessons from America's Best-Run Companies* (New York: Harper & Row, 1982), p. 103.

9. See M. Polanyi, *Personal Knowledge* (Chicago: University of Chicago Press, 1958); E. Goffman, *The Presentation of Self in Everyday Life* (New York: Doubleday, 1959); and P. L. Berger and T. Luckman, *The Social Construction of Reality* (Garden City, N.Y.: Anchor Books, 1967).

10. Louise Lee, "Tricks of E*Trade," *Business Week E.Biz*, February 7, 2000, pp. EB18–EB31.

11. Quoted in David Dorsey, "The New Spirit of Work," *Fast Company*, 1998, vol. 16, pp. 125–128.

12. Eric Ransdell, "The Nike Story? Just Tell It!" *Fast Company*, January–February 2000, pp. 44–46 (quotation on p. 46); Claude Solnik, "Co-Founder of Nike Dies Christmas Eve," *Footwear News*, January 3, 2000, p. 2; Rosemary Feitelberg, "Bowerman's Legacy Runs On," *WWD*, December 30, 1999, p. 8.

13. Louise Lee, "Tricks of E*Trade," pp. EB18–EB31.

14. A. L. Kroeber and C. Kluckhohn, "Culture: A Critical Review of Concepts and Definitions," in *Papers of the Peabody Museum of American Archaeology and Ethnology*, vol. 47, no. 1 (Cambridge, Mass.: Harvard University Press, 1952).

15. C. Geertz, *The Interpretation of Cultures* (New York: Basic Books, 1973).

16. See, for example, B. Clark, *The Distinctive College* (Chicago: Adline, 1970).

17. E. Durkheim, *The Elementary Forms of Religious Life*, trans. J. Swain (New York: Collier, 1961), p. 220.

18. See Ouchi, *Theory Z*; and Peters and Waterman, *In Search of Excellence*.

19. See Ouchi, *Theory Z*; Deal and Kennedy, *Corporate Cultures*; and Peters and Waterman, *In Search of Excellence*.

20. E. Borgida and R. E. Nisbett, "The Differential Impact of Abstract vs. Concrete Information on Decisions," *Journal of Applied Social Psychology*, July–September 1977, pp. 258–271.

21. J. Martin and M. Power, "Truth or Corporate Propaganda: The Value of a Good War Story," in Pondy et al., pp. 93–108.

22. W. G. Ouchi, "Markets, Bureaucracies, and Clans," *Administrative Science Quarterly*, March 1980, pp. 129–141; A. Wilkins and W. G. Ouchi, "Efficient Cultures: Exploring the Relationship Between Culture and Organizational Performance," *Administrative Science Quarterly*, September 1983, pp. 468–481.

23. Peters and Waterman, *In Search of Excellence*.

24. J. B. Barney, "Organizational Culture: Can It Be a Source of Sustained Competitive Advantage?" *Academy* *of Management Review*, July 1986, pp. 656–665.

25. Daniel R. Denison, "What Is the Difference Between Organizational Culture and Organizational Climate? A Native's Point of View on a Decade of Paradigm Wars," *Academy of Management Review*, July 1996, pp. 619–654.

26. O'Reilly and Chatman, "Culture as Social Control."

27. Richard L. Osborne, "Strategic Values: The Corporate Performance Engine," *Business Horizons*, September–October 1996, pp. 41–47.

28. See Osborne, "Strategic Values: The Corporate Performance Engine"; and Gary McWilliams, "Dell's Profit Rises Slightly, As Expected," *Wall Street Journal*, February 11, 2000, p. A3.

29. Quoted in "The Jack and Herb Show," *Fortune*, January 11, 1999, p. 166.

30. Ouchi, *Theory Z*.

31. Catherine Reagor, "Wells Fargo Riding Roughshod in State, Some Say," *Arizona Republic*, September 8, 1996, pp. D1, D4; Catherine Reagor, "Wells Fargo to Cut 3,000 Additional Jobs," *Arizona Republic*, December 20, 1996, pp. E1, E2.

32. O'Reilly and Chatman, "Culture as Social Control."

33. John E. Sheridan, "Organizational Culture and Employee Retention," *Academy of Management Journal*, December 1992, pp. 1036–1056; Lisa A. Mainiero, "Is Your Corporate Culture Costing You?" *Academy of Management Executive*, November 1993, pp. 84–85.

34. Peters and Waterman, *In Search of Excellence*.

35. Kenneth Labich, "An Airline That Soars on Service," *Fortune*, December 31, 1990, pp. 94–96.

36. Quoted in Geoffrey Brewer, "Tom Siebel Is Bulking Up," *Sales & Marketing Management*, September 1998, p. 59.

37. Watts S. Humphrey, *Managing for Innovation: Leading Technical People* (Englewood Cliffs, N.J.: Prentice Hall, 1987).

38. Brian O'Reilly, "Secrets of the Most Admired Corporations: New Ideas and New Products," *Fortune*, March 3, 1997, pp. 60–64.

39. Laurie K. Lewis and David R. Seibold, "Innovation Modification During Intraorganizational Adoption," *Academy of Management Review*, April 1993, vol. 10, no. 2, pp. 322–354.

40. Quoted in Jerry Useem, "Internet Defense Strategy: Cannibalize Yourself," *Fortune*, September 6, 1999, p. 128.

41. Louise Lee, "Tricks of E*Trade."

42. Oren Harari, "Stop Empowering Your People," *Management Review*, November 1993, pp. 26–29.

43. W. Chan Kim and Renee A. Mauborgne, "Procedural Justice, Attitudes, and Subsidiary Top Management Compliance with Multinationals' Corporate Strategic Decisions," *Academy of Management Journal*, June 1993, pp. 502–526.

44. See Warren Wilhelm, "Changing Corporate Culture—Or Corporate Behavior? How to Change Your Company," *Academy of Management Executive*, November 1992, pp. 72–77.

45. Quoted in Gary Silverman, Leah Nathans Spiro, John Rossant, and Owen Ullmann, "Is This Marriage Working?" *Business Week*, June 7, 1999, p. 134.

46. "Socialization" has also been defined as "the process by which culture is transmitted from one generation to the next." See J. W. M. Whiting, "Socialization: Anthropological Aspects," in D. Sils (ed.), *International Encyclopedia of the Social Sciences*, vol. 14 (New York: Free Press, 1968), p. 545.

47. J. E. Hebden, "Adopting an Organization's Culture: The Socialization of Graduate Trainees," *Organizational Dynamics*, Summer 1986, pp. 54–72.

48. J. B. Barney, "Organizational Culture: Can It Be a Source of Sustained Competitive Advantage?" *Academy of Management Review*, July 1986, pp. 656–665.

49. Bellamy Pailthorp, "Safe Landing for Boeing," *U.S. News & World Report*, September 13, 1999, p. 43; Janet Rae-Dupree, "Can Boeing Get Lean Enough?" *Business Week*, August 30, 1999, p. 182; Aaron Bernstein, "Boeing's Unions Are Worried About Job Security—The CEO's," *Business Week*, July 5, 1999, p. 30; Kenneth Labich, "Boeing Finally Hatches a Plan," *Fortune*, March 1, 1999, pp. 101–106 (quotation on p. 102).

50. James R. Norman, "A New Teledyne," *Forbes*, September 27, 1993, pp. 44–45.

Chapter 19

1. "2001—The Year in Brief," "Company Profile," "Executive Bio," "Our Leaders," "The Group History," "What We Do," Vivendi web site. www.vivendiuniversal.com on June 22, 2002; Devin Leonard, "Mr. Messier is Ready For His Close-Up," *Fortune*, September 3, 2001 (quotation); Geoffrey Colvin, "Culture in Peril? Mais Oui!" *Fortune*, May 13, 2002; Janet Guyon, "Getting Messier by the Minute," *Fortune*, June 10, 2002; Richard Tomlinson, "The Nouveau CEO," *Fortune*, December 10, 2001; Ron Glover, "A Loser's Race for Media Moguls," *Business Week*, June 6, 2002.

2. "Baby Boomers Push for Power," *Business Week*, July 2, 1984, pp. 52–56.

3. "Americans' Median Age Passes 32," *Arizona Republic*, April 6, 1988, pp. A1, A5.

4. "Population Estimates Program," Population Division, U.S. Census Bureau, Washington, D.C.

5. Geoffrey Colvin, "What the Baby Boomers Will Buy Next," *Fortune*, October 15, 1984, pp. 28–34.

6. John Huey, "Managing in the Midst of Chaos," *Fortune*, April 5, 1993, pp. 38–48.

7. "DuPont Adopts New Direction in China," Xinhua News Agency, September 7, 1999, p. 1008250h0104; Alex Taylor III, "Why DuPont Is Trading Oil for Corn," *Fortune*, April 26, 1999, pp. 154n–160; Jay Palmer, "New DuPont: For Rapid Growth, an Old-Line Company Looks to Drugs, Biotechnology," *Barron's*, May 11, 1998, p. 31.

8. Peter Nulty, "How Personal Computers Change Managers' Lives," *Fortune*, September 3, 1984, pp. 38–48.

9. "Artificial Language Is Here," *Business Week*, July 9, 1984, pp. 54–62.

10. Thomas A. Stewart, "Welcome to the Revolution," *Fortune*, December 13, 1993, pp. 66–80.

11. Quoted in Andy Serwer, "There's Something About Cisco," *Fortune*, May 15, 2000, p. 116.

12. "Nokia's Restructured," *Television Digest*, September 4, 1995, p. 15; Rahul Jacob, "Nokia Fumbles, but Don't Count It Out," *Fortune*, February 19, 1996, pp. 86–88; Gail Edmondson, "At Nokia, A Comeback—and Then Some," *Business Week*, December 2, 1996, p. 106.

13. Kurt Lewin, *Field Theory in Social Science* (New York: Harper & Row, 1951).

14. Quoted in Neil Weinberg, "A Shock to the System," *Forbes*, May 31, 1999, p. 179.

15. Linda S. Ackerman, "Transition Management: An In-Depth Look at Managing Complex Change," *Organizational Dynamics*, Summer 1982, pp. 46–66; David A. Nadler, "Managing Transitions to Uncertain Future States," *Organizational Dynamics*, Summer 1982, pp. 37–45.

16. Noel M. Tichy and David O. Ulrich, "The Leadership Challenge—A Call for the Transformational Leader," *Sloan Management Review*, Fall 1984, pp. 59–68.

17. W. Warner Burke, *Organization Development: Principles and Practices* (Boston: Little, Brown, 1982).

18. Michael Beer, *Organization Change and Development* (Santa Monica, Calif.: Goodyear, 1980); Burke, *Organization Development*.

19. Quoted in Thomas A. Stewart, "How to Leave It All Behind," *Fortune*, December 6, 1999, p. 348.

20. Danny Miller and Peter H. Friesen, "Structural Change and Performance: Quantum Versus Piecemeal-Incremental Approaches," *Academy of Management Journal*, December 1982, pp. 867–892.

21. "Ford Enters New Era of E-Communication: New Web Sites Connect Dealers, Consumer, Suppliers," *PR Newswire*, January 24, 2000, p. 7433; Suzy Wetlaufer, "Driving Change," *Harvard Business Review*, March–April 1999, pp. 77–85; "Ford's Passing Fancy," *Business Week*, March 15, 1999, p. 42.

22. J. Lloyd Suttle, "Improving Life at Work—Problems and Prospects," in J. Richard Hackman and J. Lloyd Suttle (eds.), *Improving Life at Work: Behavioral Science Approaches to Organizational Change* (Santa Monica, Calif.: Goodyear, 1977), p. 4.

23. Richard E. Walton, "Quality of Work Life: What Is It?" *Sloan Management Review*, Fall 1983, pp. 11–21.

24. Daniel A. Ondrack and Martin G. Evans, "Job Enrichment and Job Satisfaction in Greenfield and Redesign QWL Sites," *Group & Organization Studies*, March 1987, pp. 5–22.

25. Ricky W. Griffin, *Task Design: An Integrative Framework* (Glenview, Ill.: Scott, Foresman, 1982).

26. Gregory Moorhead, "Organizational Analysis: An Integration of the Macro and Micro Approaches," *Journal of Management Studies*, April 1981, pp. 191–218.

27. James C. Quick and Jonathan D. Quick, *Organizational Stress and Preventive Management* (New York: McGraw-Hill, 1984).

28. Peter Petre, "Games That Teach You to Manage," *Fortune*, October 29, 1984, pp. 65–72.

29. Kenneth N. Wexley and Timothy T. Baldwin, "Management Development," *1986 Yearly Review of Management of the Journal of Management*, in the *Journal of Management*, Summer 1986, pp. 277–294.

30. Richard Beckhard, "Optimizing Team-Building Efforts," *Journal of Contemporary Business*, Summer 1972, pp. 23–27, 30–32.

31. Bernard M. Bass, "Issues Involved in Relations Between Methodological Rigor and Reported Outcomes in Evaluations of Organizational Development," *Journal of Applied Psychology*, February 1983, pp. 197–201; William M. Vicars and Darrel D. Hartke, "Evaluating OD Evaluations: A Status Report," *Group & Organization Studies*, June 1984, pp. 177–188.

32. Beer, *Organization Change and Development*.

33. Jerome L. Franklin, "Improving the Effectiveness of Survey Feedback," *Personnel*, May–June 1978, pp. 11–17.

34. Quoted in Anna Muoio, "Idea Summit," *Fast Company*, January–February 2000, p. 156.

35. Paul R. Lawrence, "How to Deal with Resistance to Change," *Harvard Business Review*, May–June 1954, reprinted in Gene W. Dalton, Paul R. Lawrence, and Larry E. Greiner (eds.), *Organizational Change and Development* (Homewood, Ill.: Irwin, 1970), pp. 181–197.

36. Daniel Katz and Robert L. Kahn, *The Social Psychology of Organizations*, 2nd ed. (New York: John Wiley and Sons, 1978), pp. 36–68.

37. See Michael T. Hannah and John Freeman, "Structural Inertia and Organizational Change," *American Sociological Review*, April 1984, pp. 149–164, for an in-depth discussion of structural inertia.

38. Moorhead, "Organizational Analysis: An Integration of the Macro and Micro Approaches."

39. G. Zaltman and R. Duncan, *Strategies for Planned Change* (New York: John Wiley and Sons, 1977); David A. Nadler, "Concepts for the Management of Organizational Change," in J. Richard Hackman, Edward E. Lawler III, and Lyman W. Porter (eds.), *Perspectives on Behavior in Organizations*, 2nd ed. (New York: McGraw-Hill, 1983), pp. 551–561.

40. Alfred M. Jaeger, "Organization Development and National Culture: Where's the Fit?" *Academy of Management Review*, January 1986, pp. 178–190.

41. Alan M. Webber, "Learning for a Change," *Fast Company*, May 1999, pp. 178–188.

42. Quoted in Alan M. Webber, "Learning for a Change," *Fast Company*, May 1999, p. 186.

Appendix A

1. Jeffrey Pfeiffer, "The Theory-Practice Gap: Myth or Reality?" *Academy of Management Executive*, February 1987, pp. 31–33.

2. Eugene Stone, *Research Methods in Organizational Behavior* (Santa Monica, Calif.: Goodyear, 1978).

3. Fred N. Kerlinger and Howard B. Lee, *Foundations of Behavioral Research*, 4th ed. (New York: Harcourt College Publishers, 1999).

4. Richard L. Daft, Ricky W. Griffin, and Valerie Yates, "Retrospective Accounts of Research Factors Associated with Significant and Not-So-Significant Research Outcomes," *Academy of Management Journal*, December 1987, pp. 763–785.

5. Richard L. Daft, "Learning the Craft of Organizational Research," *Academy of Management Review*, October 1983, pp. 539–546.

6. Larry L. Cummings and Peter Frost, *Publishing in Organizational Sciences* (Homewood, Ill.: Irwin, 1985). See also Ellen R. Girden, *Evaluating Research Articles from Start to Finish* (Beverly Hills, Calif.: Sage, 1996).

7. D. T. Campbell and J. C. Stanley, *Experimental and Quasi-Experimental Designs for Research* (Boston: Houghton Mifflin, 1966).

8. R. Yin and K. Heald, "Using the Case Study Method to Analyze Policy Studies," *Administrative Science Quarterly*, June 1975, pp. 371–381.

9. Kerlinger and Lee, *Foundations of Behavioral Research*.

10. Ramon J. Aldag and Timothy M. Stearns, "Issues in Research Methodology," *Journal of Management*, June 1988, pp. 253–276.

11. See C. A. Schriesheim et al., "Improving Construct Measurement in Management," *Journal of Management*, Summer 1993, pp. 385–418.

12. Cynthia D. Fisher, "Laboratory Experiments," in Thomas S. Bateman and Gerald R. Ferris (eds.), *Method and Analysis in Organizational Research* (Reston, Va.: Reston, 1984); Edwin Locke (ed.), *Generalizing from Laboratory to Field Settings* (Lexington, Mass.: Lexington Books, 1986).

13. Stone, *Research Methods in Organizational Behavior*.

14. Phillip M. Podsakoff and Dan R. Dalton, "Research Methodology in Organizational Studies," *Journal of Management*, Summer 1987, pp. 419–441.

15. Stone, *Research Methods in Organizational Behavior*.

16. Kerlinger and Lee, *Foundations of Behavioral Research*.

17. Mary Ann Von Glinow, "Ethical Issues in Organizational Behavior,"
Academy of Management Newsletter, March 1985, pp. 1–3.

Appendix B

1. Suneel Ratan, "Generational Tension in the Office: Why Busters Hate the Boomers," *Fortune*, October 4, 1993, pp. 56–70.

2. Julie Amparano, "Parents Cut Pay, Hours to Rear Kids," *Arizona Republic*, June 22, 1996, pp. A1, A19.

3. Bernard Wysocki Jr., "High-Tech Nomads Write New Program for Future Work," *Wall Street Journal*, August 19, 1996, pp. A1, A6.

4. Ray Marshall, "The Global Jobs Crisis," *Foreign Policy*, Fall 1995, pp. 50–68.

5. M. W. McCall and E. E. Lawler III, "High School Students' Perceptions of Work," *Academy of Management Journal*, March 1976, pp. 17–24.

6. D. T. Hall, *Careers in Organizations* (Santa Monica, Calif.: Goodyear, 1976), p. 4.

7. M. Breidenbach, *Career Development: Taking Charge of Your Career* (Englewood Cliffs, N.J.: Prentice Hall, 1988).

8. "Stable Cycles of Executive Careers Shattered by Upheaval in Business," *Wall Street Journal*, May 26, 1987, p. 31.

9. D. B. Miller, *Careers '79* (Saratoga, Calif.: Vitality Associates, 1979).

10. Amparano, "Parents Cut Pay, Hours to Rear Kids," pp. A1, A19.

11. U.S. Census Bureau, Housing and Household Economic Statistics Division, *Census 2000: Alphabetical Index of Industries and Occupations*, Washington, D.C., created February 27, 2001.

12. D. C. Feldman, *Managing Careers in Organizations* (Glenview, Ill.: Scott, Foresman, 1988), pp. 189–192.

13. P. M. Blau, J. W. Gustad, R. Jesson, H. S. Parnes, and R. C. Wilcox, "Occupational Choices: A Conceptual Hall, Careers in Organizations Framework," *Industrial and Labor Relations Review*, July 1956, pp. 531–543.

14. J. L. Holland, *Making Vocational Choices* (Englewood Cliffs, N.J.: Prentice Hall, 1973).

15. D. C. Feldman and H. J. Arnold, "Personality Types and Career Patterns: Some Empirical Evidence on Holland's
Model," *Canadian Journal of Administrative Science*, June 1985, pp. 192–210.

16. E. Ginzberg, S. W. Ginzberg, W. Axelrod, and J. L. Herna, *Occupational Choice: An Approach to a General Theory* (New York: Columbia University Press, 1951); Hall, *Careers in Organizations*.

17. Holland, *Making Vocational Choices*.

18. T. R. Mitchell and B. W. Knudsen, "Instrumentality Theory Predictions of Students' Attitudes Toward Business and Their Choice of Business as an Occupation," *Academy of Management Journal*, March 1973, pp. 41–52; S. L. Rynes and J. Lawler, "A Policy-Capturing Investigation of the Role of Expectancies in Decisions to Pursue Job Alternatives," *Journal of Applied Psychology*, November 1983, pp. 620–631.

19. Michael B. Arthur and Denise M. Rousseau, "A Career Lexicon for the 21st Century," *Academy of Management Executive*, November 1996, pp. 28–39.

20. Brent B. Allred, Charles C. Snow, and Raymond E. Miles, "Characteristics of Managerial Careers in the 21st Century," *Academy of Management Executive*, November 1996, pp. 17–27.

21. P. A. Renwick, E. E. Lawler III, and staff, "What You Really Want from Your Job," *Psychology Today*, May 1978, pp. 53–65.

22. D. C. Feldman and H. J. Arnold, "Position Choice: Comparing the Importance of Job and Organizational Factors," *Journal of Applied Psychology*, December 1978, pp. 706–710.

23. Ellen F. Jackofsky and Lawrence H. Peters, "Part-Time Versus Full-Time Employment Status Differences: A Replication and Extension," *Journal of Occupational Behavior*, January 1987, pp. 1–9.

24. Courtney von Hippel, Stephen L. Mangum, David B. Greenberger, Robert L. Heneman, and Jeffrey D. Skoglind, "Temporary Employment: Can Organizations and Employees Both Win?" *Academy of Management Executive*, February 1997, pp. 93–104.

25. Andrew S. Grove, *Only the Paranoid Survive* (New York: Doubleday, 1999).

26. Douglas T. Hall, "Protean Careers of the 21st Century," *Academy of Management Executive*, November 1996, p. 8.

27. Hall, *Careers in Organizations*.

28. D. C. Feldman, "A Socialization Process That Helps New Recruits Succeed," *Personnel*, March–April 1980, pp. 11–23.

29. D. C. Feldman, "The Multiple Socialization of Organization Members," *Academy of Management Review*, April 1981, pp. 309–318.

30. R. A. Webber, "Career Problems of Young Managers," *California Management Review*, Summer 1976, pp. 19–33; E. Schein, *Career Dynamics: Matching Individual and Organizational Needs* (Reading, Mass.: Addison-Wesley, 1978).

31. D. C. Feldman, "A Practical Program for Employee Socialization," *Organizational Dynamics*, Autumn 1976, pp. 64–80.

32. "Should Companies Groom New Leaders or Buy Them?" *Business Week*, September 22, 1986, pp. 94–96.

33. Harvey Mackay, "Use Your Head in Leaving Job You Hate," *Arizona Republic*, January 5, 1997, p. D3.

34. T. P. Ference, J. A. F. Stoner, and E. K. Warren, "Managing the Career Plateau," *Academy of Management Review*, October 1977, pp. 602–612.

35. D. LaBier, "Madness Stalks the Ladder Climbers," *Fortune*, September 1, 1986, pp. 79–84.

36. F. Rice, "Lessons from Late Bloomers," *Fortune*, August 31, 1987, pp. 87–91.

37. R. C. Payne, "Mid-Career Block," *Personnel Journal*, April 1984, pp. 38–48.

38. J. Main, "Breaking Out of the Company," *Fortune*, May 25, 1987, pp. 81–88.

39. "Crushed Hopes: When a New Job Proves to Be Something Different," *Wall Street Journal*, June 10, 1987, p. 27.

40. D. T. Hall and F. S. Hall, "What's New in Career Management," *Organizational Dynamics*, Summer 1976, pp. 17–33.

41. Kerry D. Carson and Paula Phillips Carson, "Career Entrenchment: A Quiet March Toward Occupational Death?" *Academy of Management Executive*, February 1997, pp. 62–75.

42. Dan Hurley, "The Mentor Mystique," *Psychology Today*, May 1988, pp. 39–43.

43. Michael G. Zey, "A Mentor for All Reasons," *Personnel Journal*, January 1988, pp. 47–51.

44. "Guidelines for Successful Mentoring," *Training*, December 1984, p. 125.

45. Joy A. Schneer and Frieda Reitman, "Effects of Employment Gaps on the Careers of MBAs More Damaging for Men Than for Women," *Academy of Management Journal*, June 1990, pp. 391–406.

46. J. Walker, "Does Career Planning Rock the Boat?" *Human Resource Management*, Spring 1978, pp. 2–7.

47. C. S. Granrose and J. D. Portwood, "Matching Individual Career Plans and Organizational Career Management," *Academy of Management Journal*, December 1987, pp. 699–720.

48. M. A. Morgan, D. T. Hall, and A. Martier, "Career Development Strategies in Industry—Where Are We and Where Should We Be?" *Personnel*, March–April 1979, pp. 13–30.

49. T. A. DiPrete, "Horizontal and Vertical Mobility in Organizations," *Administrative Science Quarterly*, December 1987, pp. 422–444.

50. N. C. Hill, "Career Counseling: What Employees Should Do—and Expect," *Personnel*, August 1985, pp. 41–46.

51. J. C. Latack and J. B. Dozier, "After the Ax Falls: Job Loss as a Career Transition," *Academy of Management Review*, April 1986,

pp. 375–392; W. Kiechel III, "Passed Over," *Fortune*, October 13, 1986, pp. 189–191.

52. E. H. Burack, *Creative Human Resource Planning and Applications: A Strategic Approach* (Englewood Cliffs, N.J.: Prentice Hall, 1988).

53. Ibid.

54. T. M. Camden, "Using Outplacement as a Career Development Tool," *Personnel Administrator*, January 1982, pp. 35–44.

55. See, for example, D. D. Van Fleet and J. Saurage, "Recent Research on Women in Leadership and Management," *Akron Business and Economic Review*, Summer 1984, pp. 15–24; E. M. Van Fleet and D. D. Van Fleet, "Entrepreneurship and Black Capitalism," *American Journal of Small Business*, Fall 1985, pp. 31–40; D. D. Bowen and R. D. Hisrich, "The Female Entrepreneur: A Career Development Perspective," *Academy of Management Review*, April 1986, pp. 393–407; "Male vs. Female: What a Difference It Makes in Business Careers," *Wall Street Journal*, December 9, 1986, p. 1; "In Dad's Footsteps: More Women Find a Niche in the Family Business," *Wall Street Journal*, May 28, 1987, p. 29.

56. "Cigarette Smoking Is Growing Hazardous to Careers in Business," *Wall Street Journal*, April 23, 1987, pp. 1, 19.

57. Adapted from Feldman, *Managing Careers in Organizations*, pp. 189–192. See also K. B. McRae, "Career-Management Planning: A Boon to Managers and Employees," *Personnel*, May 1985, pp. 56–61.

58. Z. B. Leibowitz and N. K. Schlossberg, "Training Managers for Their Role in a Career Development System," *Training and Development Journal*, July 1981, pp. 72–79.

59. Walker, "Does Career Planning Rock the Boat?"

Glossary

absenteeism Failure to show up for work. (4)

acceptance theory of authority The theory that the manager's authority depends on the subordinate's acceptance of the manager's right to give directives and to expect compliance with them. (16)

accommodation Occurs when the parties' goals are compatible and the interaction between groups is relatively unimportant to the goals' attainment. (11)

adhocracy This structure is typically found in young organizations in highly technical fields. Within it, decision making is spread throughout the organization, power resides with the experts, horizontal and vertical specialization exists, and there is little formalization. (17)

administrative hierarchy The system of reporting relationships in the organization, from the lowest to the highest managerial levels. (16)

affect A person's feelings toward something. (4)

affinity group Collections of employees from the same level in the organization who meet on a regular basis to share information, capture emerging opportunities, and solve problems. (11)

agreeableness A person's ability to get along with others. (4)

all-channel network In this type of network, all members communicate with all other members. (10)

applied research Conducted to solve particular problems or answer specific questions. (Appendix A)

assimilation The process through which a minority group learns the ways of the dominant group. In organizations, this means that when people of different types and backgrounds are hired, the organization attempts to mold them to fit the existing organizational culture. (3)

attitudes A person's complexes of beliefs and feelings about specific ideas, situations, or other people. (4)

attribution theory Suggests that we attribute causes to behavior based on observations of certain characteristics of that behavior. Employees observe their own behavior, determine whether it is a response to external or internal factors, and shape their future motivated behavior accordingly. (4, 6)

authoritarianism The belief that power and status differences are appropriate within hierarchical social systems such as organizations. (4)

authority Power that has been legitimized within a particular social context. (16)

autonomous work groups Groups used to integrate an organization's technical and social systems for the benefit of large systems. (17)

avoidance (negative reinforcement) The opportunity to avoid or escape from an unpleasant circumstance after exhibiting behavior. Avoidance occurs when the interacting parties' goals are incompatible and the interaction between groups is relatively unimportant to the attainment of the goals. (6, 11)

basic research Involves discovering new knowledge rather than solving specific problems. (Appendix A)

behavioral approach Approach to leadership that tries to identify behaviors that differentiate effective leaders from nonleaders. It uses rules of thumb, suboptimizing, and satisficing in making decisions. (13, 15)

benefits An important form of indirect compensation. (8)

"big five" personality traits A set of fundamental traits that are especially relevant to organizations. (4)

bounded rationality The idea that decision makers cannot deal with information about all the aspects and alternatives pertaining to a problem and therefore choose to tackle some meaningful subset of it. (15)

brainstorming A technique used in the idea-generation phase of decision making that assists in the development of numerous alternative courses of action. (15)

burnout A general feeling of exhaustion that develops when an individual simultaneously experiences too much pressure and has too few sources of satisfaction. (9)

career A perceived sequence of attitudes and behaviors associated with work-related experiences and activities over a person's life span. (Appendix B)

career management   The process of implementing organizational career planning. (Appendix B)

career pathing   The identification of a certain sequence of jobs in a career that represents a progression through the organization. (Appendix B)

career planning   Process in which individuals evaluate their abilities and interests, consider alternative career opportunities, establish career goals, and plan practical development activities. (Appendix B)

career stages   The periods in which an individual's work life is characterized by specific needs, concerns, tasks, and activities. (Appendix B)

case study   An in-depth analysis of one setting. (Appendix A)

centralization   A structural policy in which decision-making authority is concentrated at the top of the organizational hierarchy. (16)

certainty   Condition under which the manager knows the outcomes of each alternative. (15)

chain network   In this type of network, each member communicates with the person above and below, except for the individuals on each end, who each communicate with only one person. (10)

change agent   A person responsible for managing a change effort. (19)

channel noise   A disturbance in communication that is primarily a function of the medium. (10)

charisma   A form of interpersonal attraction that inspires support and acceptance from others. (14)

charismatic leadership   A type of influence based on the leader's personal charisma. (14)

circle network   In this type of network, each member communicates with the people on both sides but with no one else. (10)

classical conditioning   A simple form of learning that links a conditioned response with an unconditioned stimulus. (6)

classical organization theory   An early approach to management that focused on how organizations can be structured most effectively to meet their goals. (1)

coercive power   The extent to which a person has the ability to punish or physically or psychologically harm someone else. (14)

cognition   The knowledge a person presumes to have about something. (4)

cognitive dissonance   The anxiety a person experiences when he or she simultaneously possesses two sets of knowledge or perceptions that are contradictory or incongruent. (4, 15)

collaboration   Occurs when the interaction between groups is very important to goal attainment and the goals are compatible. (11)

collectivism   The extent to which people emphasize the good of the group or society. (3)

command group   A relatively permanent, formal group with functional reporting relationships; usually included in the organization chart. (11)

communication   The social process in which two or more parties exchange information and share meaning. (10)

communication and decision making   The stage of group development where members discuss their feelings more openly and agree on group goals and individual roles in the group. (11)

communication networks   Networks that form spontaneously and naturally as the interactions among workers continue over time. (10)

compensation package   The total array of money (wages, salary, commission), incentives, benefits, perquisites, and awards provided by the organization to an employee. (8)

competition   Occurs when the goals are incompatible and the interactions between groups are important to meeting goals. (11)

competitive strategy   An outline of how a business intends to compete with other firms in the same industry. (2)

compressed workweek   A situation in which employees work a full forty-hour week in fewer than the traditional five days. (7)

compromise   Occurs when the interaction is moderately important to meeting goals and the goals are neither completely compatible nor completely incompatible. (11)

conceptual skills   Used to think in the abstract. (2)

configuration   An organization's shape, which reflects the division of labor and the means of coordinating the divided tasks. (16)

conflict   A disagreement among parties. It has both positive and negative characteristics. (11)

conflict model   A very personal approach to decision making because it deals with the personal conflicts that people experience in particularly difficult decision situations. (15)

conflict resolution Occurs when a manager resolves a conflict that has become harmful or serious. (11)

conflict stimulation The creation and constructive use of conflict by a manager. (11)

conscientiousness The number of goals on which a person focuses. (4)

consideration behavior Involves being concerned with subordinates' feelings and respecting subordinates' ideas. (13)

contingency approach An approach to organization design in which the desired outcomes for the organization can be achieved in several ways. (17)

contingency perspective Suggests that in most organizations, situations and outcomes are contingent on, or influenced by, other variables. (1)

contingency plans Alternative actions to take if the primary course of action is unexpectedly disrupted or rendered inappropriate. (15)

continuous improvement Perspective suggesting that performance should constantly be enhanced. (8)

continuous reinforcement With this type of reinforcement, behavior is rewarded every time it occurs. (6)

contributions An individual's contributions to an organization include such things as effort, skills, ability, time, and loyalty. (4)

control and organization The stage of group development when the group is mature; members work together and are flexible, adaptive, and self-correcting. (11)

controlling The process of monitoring and correcting the actions of the organization and its members to keep them directed toward their goals. (2)

cosmopolite Links the organization to the external environment and may also be an opinion leader in the group. (10)

creativity A person's ability to generate new ideas or to conceive of new perspectives on existing ideas. (4)

cultural values The values that employees need to have and act on for the organization to act on the strategic values. (18)

decision making The process of choosing from among several alternatives. (15)

decision-making roles There are four basic decision-making roles: the entrepreneur, the disturbance handler, the resource allocator, and the negotiator. (2)

decision rule A statement that tells a decision maker which alternative to choose based on the characteristics of the decision situation. (15)

decoding The process by which the receiver of the message interprets its meaning. (10)

defensive avoidance Entails making no changes in present activities and avoiding any further contact with associated issues because there appears to be no hope of finding a better solution. (15)

delegation The transfer to others of the authority to make decisions and use organizational resources. (16)

Delphi technique A method of systematically gathering judgments of experts for use in developing forecasts. (15)

departmentalization The manner in which divided tasks are combined and allocated to work groups. (16)

diagnostic skills Used to understand cause-and-effect relationships and to recognize the optimal solutions to problems. (2)

distress The unpleasant stress that accompanies negative events. (9)

division of labor The way the organization's work is divided into different jobs to be done by different people. (16)

divisionalized form This structure is typical of old, very large organizations. Within it, the organization is divided according to the different markets served. Horizontal and vertical specialization exists between divisions and headquarters, decision making is divided between headquarters and divisions, and outputs are standardized. (17)

downsizing The process of purposely becoming smaller by reducing the size of the workforce or shedding divisions or businesses. (2)

dual-structure theory Identifies motivation factors, which affect satisfaction, and hygiene factors, which affect dissatisfaction. (5)

dysfunctional behaviors Those that detract from organizational performance. (4)

effort-to-performance expectancy A person's perception of the probability that effort will lead to performance. (6)

employee-centered leader behavior Involves attempting to build effective work groups with high performance goals. (13)

empowerment The process of enabling workers to set their own work goals, make decisions, and solve problems within their sphere of responsibility and authority. (7, 18)

encoding The process by which the message is translated from an idea or thought into transmittable symbols. (10)

entry stage (exploration stage) Characterized by self-examination, role tryouts, and occupational exploration. (Appendix B)

environmental complexity The number of environmental components that impinge on organizational decision making. (17)

environmental dynamism The degree to which environmental components that impinge on organizational decision making change. (17)

environmental uncertainty Exists when managers have little information about environmental events and their impact on the organization. (17)

equity The belief that we are being treated fairly in relation to others. (6)

equity theory Focuses on people's desire to be treated with what they perceive as equity and to avoid perceived inequity. (6)

ERG theory Describes existence, relatedness, and growth needs. (5)

escalation of commitment The tendency to persist in an ineffective course of action when evidence reveals that the project cannot succeed. (15)

establishment stage (settling-down stage) Stage at which the individual gets more recognition for improvement. (Appendix B)

ethics An individual's personal beliefs about what is right and wrong or good and bad. (2, 15)

eustress The pleasurable stress that accompanies positive events. (9)

exit (withdrawal) stage Characterized by a pattern of decreasing performance as individuals prepare to move on or retire. (Appendix B)

expectancy theory Suggests that people are motivated by how much they want something and the likelihood they perceive of getting it. (6)

expert power The extent to which a person controls information that is valuable to someone else. (14)

extinction Decreases the frequency of behavior by eliminating a reward or desirable consequence that follows that behavior. (6)

extraversion The quality of being comfortable with relationships; the opposite extreme, introversion, is characterized by more social discomfort. (4)

feedback The process in which the receiver returns a message to the sender that indicates receipt of the message. (10)

fidelity The degree of correspondence between the message intended by the source and the message understood by the receiver. (10)

field experiment Similar to a laboratory experiment but is conducted in a real organization. (Appendix A)

field survey Typically relies on a questionnaire distributed to a sample of people selected from a larger population. (Appendix A)

fixed-interval reinforcement Provides reinforcement on a fixed time schedule. (6)

fixed-ratio reinforcement Provides reinforcement after a fixed number of behaviors. (6)

flexible reward system Allows employees to choose the combination of benefits that best suits their needs. (8)

flexible work schedules (flextime) These schedules give employees more personal control over the hours they work each day. (7)

formal group Formed by an organization to do its work. (11)

formalization The degree to which rules and procedures shape the jobs and activities of employees. (16)

friendship group A group that is relatively permanent and informal and draws its benefits from the social relationships among its members. (11)

gatekeeper An individual who has a strategic position in the network that allows him or her to control information moving in either direction through a channel. (10)

general adaptation syndrome (GAS) Identifies three stages of response to a stressor: alarm, resistance, and exhaustion. (9)

general environment The broad set of dimensions and factors within which the organization operates, including political-legal, sociocultural, technological, economic, and international factors. (17)

goal A desirable objective. (8)

goal acceptance The extent to which a person accepts a goal as his or her own. (8)

goal commitment The extent to which a person is personally interested in reaching a goal. (8)

goal compatibility The extent to which the goals of more than one person or group can be achieved at the same time. (11)

goal difficulty The extent to which a goal is challenging and requires effort. (8)

goal specificity The clarity and precision of a goal. (8)

grapevine An informal system of communication that coexists with the formal system. (10)

group Two or more people who interact with one another such that each person influences and is influenced by each other person. (11)

group cohesiveness The extent to which a group is committed to staying together. (11)

group composition The degree of similarity or difference among group members on factors important to the group's work. (11)

group performance factors Composition, size, norms, and cohesiveness. They affect the success of the group in fulfilling its goals. (11)

group polarization The tendency for a group's average postdiscussion attitudes to be more extreme than its average prediscussion attitudes. (15)

group size The number of members of the group; it affects the number of resources available to perform the task. (11)

groupthink Occurs when a group's overriding concern is a unanimous decision rather than critical analysis of alternatives. (11, 15)

hardiness A person's ability to cope with stress. (9)

Hawthorne studies Conducted between 1927 and 1932, these studies led to some of the first discoveries of the importance of human behavior in organizations. (1)

Hersey and Blanchard model Identifies different combinations of leadership presumed to work best with different levels of organizational maturity on the part of followers. (13)

hierarchy of needs theory Abraham Maslow's hierarchy that assumes human needs are arranged in a hierarchy of importance. (5)

human organization Rensis Likert's approach that is based on supportive relationships, participation, and overlapping work groups. (16)

human relations approach Suggested that favorable employee attitudes result in motivation to work hard. (5)

human relations movement An approach to management based on the assumption that employee satisfaction is a key determinant of performance. It marked the beginning of organizational behavior. (1)

human resource planning Forecasting the organization's human resource needs, developing replacement charts (charts showing planned succession of personnel) for all levels of the organization, and preparing inventories of the skills and abilities individuals need to move within the organization. (Appendix B)

hygiene factors These factors are extrinsic to the work itself. They include factors such as pay and job security. (5)

hypervigilance A frantic, superficial pursuit of some satisficing strategy. (15)

ideal bureaucracy Weber's model that is characterized by a hierarchy of authority and a system of rules and procedures designed to create an optimally effective system for large organizations. (16)

impression management A direct and intentional effort by someone to enhance his or her own image in the eyes of others. (14)

incentive systems Plans in which employees can earn additional compensation in return for certain types of performance. (8)

incremental innovation Continues the technical improvement and extends the applications of radical and systems innovations. (18)

incubation A period of less intense conscious concentration during which a creative person lets the knowledge and ideas acquired during preparation mature and develop. (4)

individual differences Personal attributes that vary from one person to another. (4)

individualism The extent to which people place primary value on themselves. (3)

inducements The tangible and intangible rewards provided by organizations to individuals. (4)

inequity The belief that we are being treated unfairly in relation to others. (6)

influence The ability to affect the perceptions, attitudes, or behaviors of others. (14)

informal group A group that is established by its members. (11)

informational roles The monitor, the disseminator, and the spokesperson. (2)

initiating-structure behavior Involves clearly defining the leader-subordinate roles so that subordinates know what is expected of them. (13)

innovation The process of creating and doing new things that are introduced into the marketplace as products, processes, or services. (18)

insight The stage in the creative process when all the scattered thoughts and ideas that were maturing during incubation come together to produce a breakthrough. (4)

intention A component of an attitude that guides a person's behavior. (4)

interactionalism Suggests that individuals and situations interact continuously to determine individuals' behavior. (1)

interest group A group that is relatively temporary and informal and is organized around a common activity or interest of its members. (11)

interpersonal demands Stressors associated with group pressures, leadership, and personality conflicts. (9)

interpersonal roles There are three important interpersonal roles: the figurehead, the leader, and the liaison. (2)

interpersonal skills Used to communicate with, understand, and motivate individuals and groups. (2)

intrapreneurship Entrepreneurial activity that takes place within the context of a large corporation. (18)

isolate Individual who tends to work alone and to interact and communicate little with others. (10)

isolated dyad Two people who tend to work alone and to interact and communicate little with others. (10)

jargon The specialized or technical language of a trade, profession, or social group. (10)

job analysis The process of systematically gathering information about specific jobs to use in developing a performance measurement system, to write job or position descriptions, and to develop equitable pay systems. (8)

job-centered leader behavior Involves paying close attention to the work of subordinates, explaining work procedures, and demonstrating a strong interest in performance. (13)

job characteristics approach Focuses on the motivational attributes of jobs. (7)

job characteristics theory Identifies three critical psychological states: experienced meaningfulness of the work, experienced responsibility for work outcomes, and knowledge of results. (7)

job design How organizations define and structure jobs. (7)

job enlargement Involves giving workers more tasks to perform. (7)

job enrichment Entails giving workers more tasks to perform and more control over how to perform them. (7)

job hopping Occurs when an individual makes fewer adjustments within the organization and moves to different organizations to advance his or her career. (Appendix B)

job rotation Systematically moving workers from one job to another in an attempt to minimize monotony and boredom. (7)

job satisfaction The extent to which a person is gratified or fulfilled by his or her work. (4)

job sharing A situation in which two or more part-time employees share one full-time job. (7)

job specialization Advocated by scientific management. It can help improve efficiency, but it can also promote monotony and boredom. (7)

laboratory experiment Involves creating an artificial setting similar to a real work situation to allow control over almost every possible factor in that setting. (Appendix A)

leader-member exchange (LMX) model This model of leadership stresses the fact that leaders develop unique working relationships with each of their subordinates. (13)

leadership Both a process and a property. As a process, leadership involves the use of noncoercive influence. As a property, leadership is the set of characteristics attributed to someone who is perceived to use influence successfully. (13)

Leadership Grid Evaluates leadership behavior along two dimensions, concern for production and concern for people, and suggests that effective leadership styles include high levels of both behaviors. (13)

leadership substitutes Individual, task, and organizational characteristics that tend to outweigh the leader's ability to affect subordinates' satisfaction and performance. (14)

leading The process of getting the organization's members to work together toward the organization's goals. (2)

learning A relatively permanent change in behavior or behavioral potential resulting from direct or indirect experience. (6)

learning organization An organization that works to facilitate the lifelong learning and personal development of all of its employees while continually transforming itself to respond to changing demands and needs. (8)

least-preferred coworker (LPC) scale Presumes to measure a leader's motivation. (13)

legitimate power Power that is granted by virtue of one's position in the organization. (14)

liaison An individual who serves as a bridge between groups, tying groups together and facilitating the communication flow needed to integrate group activities. (10)

life change Any meaningful change in a person's personal or work situation; too many life changes can lead to health problems. (9)

life trauma Any upheaval in an individual's life that alters his or her attitudes, emotions, or behaviors. (9)

linking role A position for a person or group that serves to coordinate the activities of two or more organizational groups. (11)

locus of control The extent to which people believe their circumstances are a function of their own actions versus external factors beyond their control. (4)

long-term orientation Focused on the future. (3)

LPC theory of leadership Suggests that a leader's effectiveness depends on the situation. (13)

Machiavellianism A personality trait. People who possess this trait behave to gain power and to control the behavior of others. (4)

machine bureaucracy This structure is typical of large, well-established organizations. Work is highly specialized and formalized, and decision making is usually concentrated at the top. (17)

management by objectives (MBO) A collaborative goal-setting process through which organizational goals cascade down throughout the organization. (8)

management functions Set forth by Henri Fayol; they include planning, organizing, command, coordination, and control. (16)

management teams Consist of managers from various areas; they coordinate work teams. (12)

masculinity The extent to which the dominant values in a society emphasize aggressiveness and the acquisition of money and material goods, rather than concern for people, relationships among people, and the overall quality of life. (3)

mastery stage The stage at which individuals develop a stronger attachment to their organizations and lose some career flexibility; performance may vary. (Appendix B)

matrix design Combines two different designs to gain the benefits of each; typically combined are a product or project departmentalization scheme and a functional structure. (17)

mechanistic structure This structure is primarily hierarchical. Within it, interactions and communications are typically vertical, instructions come from the boss, knowledge is concentrated at the top, and loyalty and obedience are required to sustain membership. (17)

medium The channel or path through which the message is transmitted. (10)

mentoring Occurs when an older, more experienced person helps a younger employee grow and advance by providing advice, support, and encouragement. (Appendix B)

Michigan leadership studies These studies defined job-centered and employee-centered leadership as opposite ends of a single leadership continuum. (13)

motivation The set of forces that lead people to behave in particular ways. (5)

motivation and productivity The stage of group development in which members cooperate, help each other, and work toward accomplishing tasks. (11)

motivation factors These factors are intrinsic to the work itself. They include factors such as achievement and recognition. (5)

motive A factor that determines a person's choice of one course of behavior from among several possibilities. (5)

multicultural organization　The multicultural organization has six characteristics: pluralism, full structural integration, full integration of informal networks, an absence of prejudice and discrimination, equal identification among employees with organizational goals for majority and minority groups, and low levels of intergroup conflict. (3)

mutual acceptance　The stage of group development that is characterized by members sharing information about themselves and getting to know each other. (11)

need　Anything an individual requires or wants. (5)

need for achievement　The desire to accomplish a task or goal more effectively than in the past. (5)

need for affiliation　The need for human companionship. (5)

need for power　The desire to control the resources in one's environment. (5)

need theories of motivation　These theories assume that need deficiencies cause behavior. (5)

negative affectivity　People who possess this trait are generally downbeat and pessimistic, see things in a negative way, and seem to be in a bad mood. (4)

negative emotionality　Characterized by moodiness and insecurity; those who have little negative emotionality are better able to withstand stress. (4)

negative reinforcement (avoidance)　The opportunity to avoid or escape from an unpleasant circumstance after exhibiting behavior. (6)

negotiation　The process in which two or more parties (people or groups) reach agreement even though they have different preferences. (15)

noise　Any disturbance in the communication process that interferes with or distorts communication. (10)

nominal group technique　Technique in which group members follow a generate-discussion-vote cycle until they reach an appropriate decision. (15)

nonprogrammed decision　A decision that recurs infrequently and for which there is no previously established decision rule. (15)

norm　A standard against which the appropriateness of a behavior is judged. (11)

occupation or **occupational field**　A group of jobs that are similar with respect to the type of tasks and training involved. (Appendix B)

Ohio State leadership studies　These studies defined leader consideration and initiating-structure behaviors as independent dimensions of leadership. (13)

open system　A system that interacts with its environment. (17)

openness　The capacity to entertain new ideas and to change as a result of new information. (4)

optimism　The extent to which a person sees life in relatively positive or negative terms. (9)

organic structure　This structure is set up like a network. Within it, interactions and communications are horizontal, knowledge resides wherever it is most useful to the organization, and membership requires a commitment to the organization's tasks. (17)

organization　A group of people working together to attain common goals. (16)

organization chart　A diagram showing all people, positions, reporting relationships, and lines of formal communication in the organization. (16)

organization climate　Current situations in an organization and the linkages among work groups, employees, and work performance. (18)

organization culture　The set of values that helps the organization's employees understand which actions are considered acceptable and which unacceptable. (18)

organization development　The process of planned change and improvement of the organization through application of knowledge of the behavioral sciences. (19)

organization structure　The system of task, reporting, and authority relationships within which the organization does its work. (16)

organizational behavior　The study of human behavior in organizational settings, the interface between human behavior and the organization, and the organization itself. (1)

organizational behavior modification (OB mod)　The application of reinforcement theory to people in organizational settings. (6)

organizational citizenship　The extent to which a person's behavior makes a positive overall contribution to the organization. (4)

organizational commitment　A person's identification with and attachment to an organization. (4)

organizational downsizing　A popular trend aimed at reducing the size of corporate staff and middle management to reduce costs. (17)

organizational environment Everything outside an organization. It includes all elements, people, other organizations, economic factors, objects, and events that lie outside the boundaries of the organization. (17)

organizational goals Objectives that management seeks to achieve in pursuing the firm's purpose. (16)

organizational politics Activities carried out by people to acquire, enhance, and use power and other resources to obtain their desired outcomes. (14)

organizational socialization The process through which employees learn about the firm's culture and pass their knowledge and understanding on to others. (18)

organizational stressors Factors in the workplace that can cause stress. (9)

organizational technology The mechanical and intellectual processes that transform inputs into outputs. (17)

organizing The process of designing jobs, grouping jobs into units, and establishing patterns of authority between jobs and units. (2)

outcome Anything that results from performing a particular behavior. (6)

overdetermination Occurs because numerous organizational systems are in place to ensure that employees and systems behave as expected to maintain stability. (19)

participation The process of giving employees a voice in making decisions about their own work. (7)

path-goal theory of leadership Suggests that effective leaders clarify the paths (behaviors) that will lead to desired rewards (goals). (13)

perception The set of processes by which an individual becomes aware of and interprets information about the environment. (4)

performance behaviors The total set of work-related behaviors that the organization expects the individual to display. (4)

performance measurement (performance appraisal) The process by which someone (1) evaluates an employee's work behaviors by measurement and comparison with previously established standards, (2) documents the results, and (3) communicates the results to the employee. (8)

performance plan An understanding between an employee and a manager concerning what and how a job is to be done such that both parties know what is expected and how success is defined and measured. (8)

performance-to-outcome expectancy An individual's perception of the probability that performance will lead to certain outcomes. (6)

perquisites Special privileges awarded to selected members of an organization, usually top managers. (8)

personal power Resides in the person, regardless of the position he or she fills. (14)

personality The relatively stable set of psychological attributes that distinguish one person from another. (4)

person-job fit The extent to which the contributions made by the individual match the inducements offered by the organization. (4)

physical demands Stressors associated with the job's physical setting, such as the adequacy of temperature and lighting and the physical requirements the job makes on the employee. (9)

planning The process of determining an organization's desired future position and the best means of getting there. (2)

pluralistic organization An organization that has diverse membership and takes steps to fully involve all people who differ from the dominant group. (3)

position power Resides in the position, regardless of who is filling that position. (14)

positive affectivity People who possess this trait are upbeat and optimistic, have an overall sense of well-being, and see things in a positive light. (4)

positive reinforcement A reward or other desirable consequence that a person receives after exhibiting behavior. (6)

power The potential ability of a person or group to exercise control over another person or group. (14)

power distance The extent to which less powerful persons accept the unequal distribution of power. (3)

practical approach The approach to decision making that combines the steps of the rational approach with the conditions in the behavioral approach to create a more realistic process for making decisions in organizations. (15)

PRAM model This model guides the negotiator through the four steps of planning for agreement, building relationships, reaching agreements, and maintaining relationships. (15)

prejudices   Judgments about others that reinforce beliefs about superiority and inferiority. (3)

preparation   Usually the first stage in the creative process. It includes education and formal training. (4)

primary dimensions of diversity   Factors that are either inborn or exert extraordinary influence on early socialization: age, ethnicity, gender, physical abilities, race, and sexual orientation. (3)

primary needs   The basic physical requirements necessary to sustain life. (5)

problem solving   A form of decision making in which the issue is unique and alternatives must be developed and evaluated without the aid of a programmed decision rule. (15)

problem-solving teams   Temporary teams established to attack specific problems in the workplace. (12)

procedural justice   The extent to which the dynamics of an organization's decision-making processes are judged to be fair by those most affected by them. (18)

process-based perspectives   These perspectives focus on how people behave in their efforts to satisfy their needs. (6)

product development teams   Combinations of work teams and problem-solving teams that create new designs for products or services that will satisfy customer needs. (12)

productivity   An indicator of how much an organization is creating relative to its inputs. (2)

professional bureaucracy   This structure is characterized by horizontal specialization by professional area of expertise, little formalization, and decentralized decision making. (17)

programmed decision   A decision that recurs often enough for a decision rule to be developed. (15)

psychological contract   A person's set of expectations regarding what he or she will contribute to the organization and what the organization, in return, will provide to the individual. (4)

punishment   An unpleasant, or aversive, consequence that results from behavior. (6)

quality   The total set of features and characteristics of a product or service that determine its ability to satisfy stated or implied needs. (2)

quality circles   Small groups of employees from the same work area who regularly meet to discuss and recommend solutions to workplace problems. (12)

quality of work life   The extent to which workers can satisfy important personal needs through their experiences in the organization. (19)

radical innovation   A major breakthrough that changes or creates whole industries. (18)

rational decision-making approach   A systematic, step-by-step process for making decisions. (15)

receiver   The individual, group, or organization that perceives the encoded symbols; the receiver may or may not decode them and try to understand the intended message. (10)

reengineering   The radical redesign of organizational processes to achieve major gains in cost, time, and provision of services. (17)

referent power   Exists when one person wants to be like or imitates someone else. (14)

refreezing   The process of making new behaviors relatively permanent and resistant to further change. (19)

reinforcement   The consequences of behavior. (6)

reinforcement discrimination   The process of recognizing differences between behavior and reinforcement in different settings. (6)

reinforcement generalization   The process through which a person extends recognition of similar or identical behavior-reinforcement relationships to different settings. (6)

reinforcement theory   This theory is based on the idea that behavior is a function of its consequences. (6)

reliability   The extent to which a measure is consistent over time. (Appendix A)

research design   The set of procedures used to test the predicted relationships among natural phenomena. (Appendix A)

responsibility   An obligation to do something with the expectation of achieving some act or output. (16)

rethinking   Looking at organization design in totally different ways, perhaps even abandoning the classic view of the organization as a pyramid. (17)

reward power   The extent to which a person controls rewards that another person values. (14)

reward system The system that consists of all organizational components, including people, processes, rules and procedures, and decision-making activities, involved in allocating compensation and benefits to employees in exchange for their contributions to the organization. (8)

risk Condition under which the decision maker cannot know with certainty what the outcome of a given action will be but has enough information to estimate the probabilities of various outcomes. (15)

risk propensity The degree to which a person is willing to take chances and make risky decisions. (4)

role A set of expected behaviors associated with a particular position in a group or organization. (9)

role ambiguity Arises when a role is unclear. (9)

role conflict Occurs when the messages and cues constituting a role are clear but contradictory or mutually exclusive. (9)

role demands Stressors associated with the role a person is expected to play. (9)

role overload Occurs when expectations for the role exceed the individual's capabilities. (9)

satisficing Examining alternatives only until a solution that meets minimal requirements is found. (15)

schedules of reinforcement Indicate when or how often managers should reinforce certain behaviors. (6)

scientific management One of the first approaches to management. It focused on the efficiency of individual workers and assumed that employees are motivated by money. (1, 5)

scientific research The systematic investigation of hypothesized propositions about the relationships among natural phenomena. (Appendix A)

secondary dimensions of diversity Factors that are important to us as individuals and that to some extent define us to others but are less permanent and can be adapted or changed: educational background, geographic location, income, marital status, military experience, parental status, religious beliefs, and work experience. (3)

secondary needs The requirements learned from the environment and culture in which the person lives. (5)

selective perception The process of screening out information that we are uncomfortable with or that contradicts our beliefs. (4)

self-efficacy The extent to which we believe we can accomplish our goals even if we failed to do so in the past. (4, 8)

self-esteem The extent to which a person believes he or she is a worthwhile and deserving individual. (4)

self-reactions Comparisons of alternatives with internalized moral standards. (15)

semantics The study of language forms. (10)

short-term orientation Focused on the past or present. (3)

simple structure This structure is typical of relatively small or new organizations and has little specialization or formalization. Within this structure, power and decision making are concentrated in the chief executive. (17)

social learning Occurs when people observe the behaviors of others, recognize their consequences, and alter their own behavior as a result. (6)

social loafing The tendency of some members of groups to put forth less effort in a group than they would when working alone. (11)

social responsibility An organization's social responsibility is its obligation to protect and contribute to the social environment in which it functions. (2)

social subsystem Includes the interpersonal relationships that develop among people in organizations. (17)

socialization The process through which individuals become social beings. (18)

sociotechnical systems approach An approach to organization design that views the organization as an open system structured to integrate the technical and social subsystems into a single management system. (17)

source The individual, group, or organization interested in communicating something to another party. (10)

span of control The number of people who report to a manager. (16)

stereotypes Rigid judgments about others that ignore the specific person and the current situation. Acceptance of stereotypes can lead to the dangerous process of prejudice toward others. (3)

stereotyping The process of categorizing or labeling people on the basis of a single attribute. (4)

strategic values The basic beliefs about an organization's environment that shape its strategy. (18)

strategy The plans and actions necessary to achieve organizational goals. (17)

stress A person's adaptive response to a stimulus that places excessive psychological or physical demands on that person. (9)

structural change A systemwide organization development involving a major restructuring of the organization or instituting programs such as quality of work life. (19)

structural imperatives The three structural imperatives, environment, technology, and size, are the three primary determinants of organization structure. (17)

suboptimizing Knowingly accepting less than the best possible outcome to avoid unintended negative effects on other aspects of the organization. (15)

superleadership Occurs when a leader gradually and purposefully turns over power, responsibility, and control to a self-managing work group. (14)

superordinate goal An organizational goal that is more important to the well-being of the organization and its members than the more specific goals of interacting parties. (11)

surface value The objective meaning or worth a reward has to an employee. (8)

symbolic value The subjective and personal meaning or worth a reward has to an employee. (8)

system A set of interrelated elements functioning as a whole. (1, 17)

systems innovation Creates a new functionality by assembling parts in new ways. (18)

task demands Stressors associated with the specific job a person performs. (9)

task environment This environment includes specific organizations, groups, and individuals that influence the organization. (17)

task group A relatively temporary, formal group established to do a specific task. (11)

team A small number of people with complementary skills who are committed to a common purpose, common performance goals, and approach for which they hold themselves mutually accountable. (12)

technical (task) subsystem The means by which inputs are transformed into outputs. (17)

technical skills The skills necessary to accomplish specific tasks within the organization. (2)

technology The mechanical and intellectual processes used to transform inputs into products and services. (2)

telecommuting A work arrangement in which employees spend part of their time working off-site. (7)

Theory X Concept described by Douglas McGregor indicating an approach to management that takes a negative and pessimistic view of workers. (1)

Theory Y Concept described by Douglas McGregor reflecting an approach to management that takes a positive and optimistic perspective on workers. (1)

360-degree feedback Performance management system in which people receive performance feedback from those on all sides of them in the organization: their boss, their colleagues and peers, and their own subordinates. (8)

total quality management (TQM) A form of management that focuses on the customer, an environment of trust and openness, working in teams, breaking down internal organizational barriers, team leadership and coaching, shared power, and continuous improvement. Use of this approach often involves fundamental changes in the organization's culture. (8)

trait approach This approach attempted to identify stable and enduring character traits that differentiated effective leaders from nonleaders. (13)

transformational leadership The set of abilities that allows the leader to recognize the need for change, to create a vision to guide that change, and to execute that change effectively. (14)

transition management The process of systematically planning, organizing, and implementing change. (19)

transmission The process through which the symbols that represent a message are sent to the receiver. (10)

trial stage (socialization stage) Stage in which individuals more specifically explore jobs and performance begins to improve. (Appendix B)

turnover When people quit their jobs. (4)

Type A People who are extremely competitive, highly committed to work, and have a strong sense of time urgency. (9)

Type B People who are less competitive, less committed to work, and have a weaker sense of time urgency. (9)

Type Z firm This type of firm is committed to retaining employees; evaluates workers' performance based on both qualitative and quantitative information; emphasizes broad career paths; exercises control through informal, implicit mechanisms; requires that decision making occur in groups and be based on full information sharing and consensus; expects individuals to take responsibility for decisions; and emphasizes concern for people. (18)

uncertainty Condition under which the decision maker lacks enough information to estimate the probability of possible outcomes. (15)

uncertainty avoidance The extent to which people prefer to be in clear and unambiguous situations. (3)

unconflicted adherence Continuing with current activities if doing so does not entail serious risks. (15)

unconflicted change Involves making changes in present activities if doing so presents no serious risks. (15)

unfreezing The process by which people become aware of the need for change. (19)

universal approach An approach to organization design in which prescriptions or propositions are designed to work in any circumstance. (17)

valence The degree of attractiveness or unattractiveness a particular outcome has for a person. (6)

validity The extent to which a measure actually reflects what it was intended to measure. (Appendix A)

valuing diversity Means putting an end to the assumption that everyone who is not a member of the dominant group must assimilate. The first step is to recognize that diversity exists in organizations so that we can begin to manage it. (3)

variable-interval reinforcement Varies the amount of time between reinforcements. (6)

variable-ratio reinforcement Varies the number of behaviors between reinforcements. (6)

verification The final stage of the creative process in which the validity or truthfulness of the insight is determined. (4) The feedback portion of communication in which the receiver sends a message to the source indicating receipt of the message and the degree to which he or she understood the message. (10)

vigilant information processing Involves thoroughly investigating all possible alternatives, weighing their costs and benefits before making a decision, and developing contingency plans. (15)

virtual organization A temporary alliance between two or more organizations that band together to undertake a specific venture. (17)

virtual teams Teams that work together by computer and other electronic communication utilities; members move in and out of meetings and the team itself as the situation dictates. (12)

Vroom's decision tree approach to leadership This model attempts to prescribe how much participation subordinates should be allowed in making decisions. (13)

wheel network In this type of network, information flows between the person at the end of each spoke and the person in the middle. (10)

work teams Include all the people working in an area, are relatively permanent, and do the daily work, making decisions regarding how the work of the team is done. (12)

workforce diversity The similarities and differences in such characteristics as age, gender, ethnic heritage, physical abilities and disabilities, race, and sexual orientation among the employees of organizations. (3)

work-life relationships The interrelationships between a person's work life and personal life. (9)

workplace behavior The pattern of action by the members of an organization that directly or indirectly influences organizational effectiveness. (4)

Name Index

Abrashoff, D. Michael, 330
Ackerman, Josef, 439
Ackerman, Linda S., 598
Adamik, Brian, 459
Adams, J. Stacy, 583
Adelman, Philip J., 593
Adler, Nancy, 581, 583, 584, 588
Adler, Paul, 449, 594
Adorno, T. W., 582
Aeppel, Timothy, 147n, 220n
Agar, Michael, 257
Agarwala-Rogers, Rekha, 587
Ahearne, Mike, 589
Aldag, Ramon J., 599
Alderfer, Clayton, 125, 131, 583
Alexander, Karen, 239n
Alford, C. Fred, 96
Allday, Erin, 276n
Allen, Jay, 499
Allen, Oliver E., 579
Allen, Paul, 516
Allen, Robert W., 590
Allred, Brent B.
Allway, Max, 400
Ambrose, M. L., 582
Amparano, Julie, 599
Ancona, Deborah, 589
Anderson, Kenneth S., 594
Andreessen, Marc, 517
Andrews, Robert, 39n
Ansberry, Clare, 164
Ante, Spencer E., 169n, 282n
Arent, Lindsey, 53n
Argyris, Chris, 592
Aristotle, 5
Armour, Stephanie, 13n
Armstrong, Mike, 459
Arnold, H. J., 599
Arnst, Catherine, 239n, 362n, 410n, 472n, 594
Aronoff, Craig E., 587
Arvey, Richard, 584
Ashcroft, John, 383
Ashforth, Blake E., 586, 587, 588
Atwater, Leanne, 585
Austin, Nancy K., 116n, 596
Axelrod, Beth, 147n
Axelrod, W., 599

Babbage, Charles, 166, 167, 584
Babcock, Pete, 332
Bailey, Darren, 169
Bailey, Kent, 114
Baker, David R., 487n
Baker, James, III, 530
Baker, Wayne E., 72n
Baldes, J. J., 585
Baldwin, Timothy T., 598
Balf, Todd, 588
Ballmer, Steven A., 431, 516, 517
Bamforth, K. W., 588, 595
Bandura, Albert, 584, 585
Banks, Gloria Mayfield, 100
Banks, Walter, 160n
Barboza, David, 84n, 428n
Barley, S. R., 494
Barling, Julian, 590

Barnard, Chester, 448, 594
Barnett, William P., 588
Barney, J. B., 596, 597
Barnholt, Ned, 275, 276
Baron, Robert A., 242n, 586
Barrett, Colleen, 491
Barrett, Heidi, 446
Barrett, Richard, 496
Bartz, Carol, 342
Baskin, Otis W., 587
Bass, Bernard, 587, 589, 598
Bates, Steve, 90n, 586
Baxter, J. Clifford, 552
Bazerman, K. H., 593
Bazerman, Max, 419, 580, 592
Beardworth, A. D., 593
Beatty, Richard W., 585
Beazley, Hamilton, 72
Beck, Juelene, 53
Beckhard, Richard, 598
Bedeian, Arthur, 583
Beehr, Terry, 585
Beer, Michael, 598
Beitia, Angelina, 159
Belkin, Lisa, 119n, 223n, 239n
Bell, Alexander Graham, 458
Bell, George, 224
Belluzzo, Richard, 517
Belson, Ken, 206n
Bem, D. J., 592
Benavidez, Brian, 232
Bennett, Nathan, 582
Bennis, Warren, 428n, 454, 551
Benson, Alex, 553, 553n
Berger, P. L., 596
Bernardin, H. John, 585
Bernstein, Aaron, 147n, 597
Bethune, Gordon, 27-28, 34, 35, 368-369
Biggs, Mary, 39n
Bigley, Gregory A., 582
Bing, Mark, 583
Birnbaum, Jeffrey H., 43n
Black, Brad, 315n
Blake, Robert R., 590
Blake, Stacy, 74n, 581
Blanchard, Kenneth H., 590
Blau, Peter, 462, 466, 594, 599
Bliese, Paul D., 586
Blot, Harry, 48
Bobbitt, H. Randolph, 595
Bobo, Stephen, 13
Bollenbach, Stephen, 39
Bommer, William H., 589, 591
Bono, Joyce, 585
Booker, Katrina, 525n
Bookman, Valerie M., 583
Boone, Christopher, 582
Borgida, E., 596
Boschken, Herman, 473, 595
Boswell, Wendy, 223
Boudreau, John, 223
Bowen, D. D., 600
Bowen, David E., 591
Bowerman, Bill, 496
Boyd, Brian, 586
Boyle, Dennis, 106

Boynton, Andrew, 584
Bracker, Jeffrey, 593, 594
Brady, Diane, 525n
Brady, Neil F., 594
Bragganti, Nancy, 251n
Brant, James, 589
Breen, Bill, 49n, 540n
Breienbach, M., 599
Bremner, Brian, 345n
Bresman, Henrik, 589
Brett, Joan, 585
Breuer, Rolf, 439
Brewer, Geoffrey, 597
Brewer, Richard B., 410
Bridwell, Lawrence G., 583
Brief, Arthur P., 582, 594
Brodt, Susan, 592
Bromet, Evelyn J., 586
Brooker, Katrina, 249n
Brooks, Nancy Rivera, 428n
Brooks, Susan Sonnesyn, 580
Brown, Denise, 181
Brown, Derek, 249
Brown, Dick, 540
Brown, Ed, 582
Brown, Eryn, 467, 517n
Brown, Louise, 134
Brown, R. R., 592
Brown, Valerie, 495
Bruning, Nealia S., 586
Brunson, Lee, 134
Bryman, A., 593
Buckingham, Marcus, 315n
Buffett, Warren, 446
Burack, E. H., 600
Burck, Charles G., 596
Burgage, Tom, 48, 49
Burke, C. Shawn, 589
Burke, W. Warner, 598
Burnham, David H., 454, 583
Burns, James MacGregor, 590
Burns, Lawton R., 595
Burns, Tom, 465, 595
Burroughs, Susan, 583
Burrows, Peter, 389
Burtt, H. E., 589
Bush, Barbara, 427
Bush, George W., 63, 454, 552
Butcher, Vicky, 590
Butler, Timothy, 585
Byrne, John A., 247n, 553n, 589
Bzomowski, Steve, 294

Cage, Jack H., 590
Caldwell, David F., 494, 585, 588
Calipari, John, 153-154
Camden, T. M., 600
Campbell, D. T., 599
Campbell, Donald J., 585
Campbell, John, 583
Campbell, Laurel, 72n
Campion, Michael A., 584
Canabou, Christine, 167n
Canion, Rod, 19, 20, 368
Cantu, Carlos, 277
Capell, Kerry, 308n, 394n
Capellas, Michael, 20, 368, 388, 389

Caple, William, 262
Cappelli, Peter, 164
Cappiello, Dina, 447n
Carey, Alex, 579
Carlile, William H., 596
Carlson, Chester, 508
Carmichael, Pat, 203
Carnegie, Dale, 114
Carney, Dan, 553n
Carpenter, Mason, 588
Carreyrou, John, 495n
Carroll, Glenn R., 593
Carroll, Stephen J., 579
Carson, Kerry D., 600
Carson, Paula Phillips, 600
Carter, Elaine, 580
Carter, Nancy M., 593
Cartwright, Dorwin, 376n, 592
Cascio, Wayne F., 593
Case, John, 185n
Case, Steve, 429, 430
Casey, William, 295
Cashman, J. F., 590
Castro, Fidel, 394
Caudron, Shari, 587
Causey, Richard A., 83, 84
Cavanaugh, Gerald F., 382n, 591
Chambers, John, 318, 486, 487, 526
Chambers, Karen, 313n
Champy, James A., 281
Chandler, Alfred, 5, 461, 594
Chao, Elaine L., 553
Charan, Ram, 580
Chase, Richard, 579
Chatman, Jennifer, 588, 596, 597
Chemers, Martin M., 590
Cheney, Dick, 552
Cheng, Joseph L. C., 593
Chihuly, Dale, 313
Child, John, 593, 595, 596
Christensen, Clayton, 409
Christensen, Sandra L., 580
Christian, Jeffrey, 389
Chul, Lee Sang, 345
Cirka, Carol C., 586
Clark, B., 596
Clarke, Arthur C., 361
Clarke, Virginia, 78, 203
Clemmons, Lynda, 245
Clymer, Adam, 553n
Coch, Lester, 592
Coffman, Curt, 315n
Cohen, A. R., 585
Cole, Thomas, 422
Collins, Jim, 343, 398, 585
Colquitt, Jason, 589
Colvin, Geoffrey, 366n, 522n, 580, 595, 597
Comes, Shelley, 181
Conant, H., 584
Condit, Phil, 381
Conger, Jay, 245, 591
Conlin, Michelle, 86n, 116n, 198, 499n
Connelly, John, 422
Conte, Jeffrey, 588

614

Cooper, Gary, 225-226
Cooper, James, 198n, 586
Copeland, Lennie, 581
Copple, Brandon, 352n
Corben, Ron, 581
Corcoran, Elizabeth, 593
Covey, Stephen, 21
Cowlin, Rebecca, 592
Cox, Taylor H., 74n, 581
Crawford, Michael, 580
Creswell, Julie, 362n
Crews, Cam, 332n
Crisman, Thomas, 72
Cronin, Mary, 580
Cross, Robert, 587, 592
Crowley, Clifford, 164
Cullen, John H., 594
Culloton, Dan, 72n
Cummings, Larry, 579, 581, 584-585, 596, 599
Cummins, Robert C., 587
Curvin, Wendy, 190
Cyert, Richard M., 592

Daft, Douglas, 55, 206
Daft, Richard, 593, 595, 599
Dalton, Dan R., 593, 599
Dalton, Gene W., 598
Danchisko, John, 307, 308
D'Anno, Thomas, 594
Dansereau, Fred, 358, 590
Darr, Eric D., 587
Dasu, Sriram, 579
Datta, Deepak K., 591
David, Fred R., 594
Davis, Gray, 552
Davis, James H., 588
Davis, Michael, 510n
Davis, Sampson, 367
Davis, Stanley M., 595
Davison, William H., 596
Day, David V., 590
Day, Sherri, 428n
Deal, T. E., 21, 494, 498, 596
Dean, John, 413
De Brabander, Bert, 582
de Castro, Jimmy, 419
Deci, E. L., 582
Deckop, John R., 586
De Dreu, Carsten K. W., 588, 592
DeFrank, Richard S., 586
Delebohn, James H., 590
Dell, Michael, 467
Dell'Oro, Tam, 487
Deming, W. Edwards, 199
Denison, Daniel R., 593, 597
Densten, Iain, 586
Deromedi, Roger, 352
Deutsch, Claudia H., 206n
Devine, Elizabeth, 251n
Dew, Mary A., 586
Dickens, Charles, 275
Dickson, W. J., 595
Dickson, William, 8, 579
DiFlorio, Dennis, 137-138
Dillard, Richard, 163, 164
DiLullo, Ken, 478
DiLullo, Roni, 478
Dimancescu, Dan, 589
Dingell, John, 551-552
DiPrete, T. A., 600
DiStefano, Joseph J., 581, 596
Doktor, Robert, 581
Donahue, Lisa, 588
Donaldson, Lex, 594
Dorfman, Peter W., 591

Dornheim, Michael A., 49n
Dorsey, David, 339n, 596
Douglas, Charles W., 422
Downey, H. Kirk, 594
Doyle, Rodger, 90n
Dozier, J. B., 600
Drach, Richard L., 581
Dreher, Henry, 588
Druskat, Vanessa Urch, 585
Druyun, Darleen, 48
Dubinsky, Alan J., 587, 590
Duffy, Jim, 487n
Dumaine, Brian, 185n, 467n, 580, 589
Dumars, Joe, 332
Duncan, David B., 246
Duncan, R., 598
Duncan, Robert B., 469n, 595
Dunnette, Marvin D., 301n, 582, 583, 589
Durkheim, Émile, 497-498, 596
Dusek, Dorothy E., 244n
Dutta, Ronojoy, 31
Dwenger, Kemp, 589
Dzubeck, Frank, 487

Eaton, Leslie, 220n
Ebert, Ronald J., 185n
Edmondson, Gail, 598
Ehrenreich, Barbara, 215
Ehrlichman, John, 413
Eichenwald, Kurt, 84n, 247n, 428n
Einhart, Nancy, 167n
Eisenhardy, Kathleen M., 592
Eisner, Michael, 468
Elkind, Peter, 84n
Elliott, Stuart, 553n
Ellis, Kristine, 400n
Ellison, Jill Darby, 167
Ellison, Larry, 299
Elron, Efrat, 581
Emerson, Harrington, 6
Enbar, Nadav, 282n
Epitropaki, Olga, 590
Eppley, Mark, 517
Erb, David, 147
Erez, Amir, 582
Evans, Donald L., 84
Evans, Martin, 351, 590, 598
Everly, George S., Jr., 244n

Faludi, Susan, 581
Farhnam, Alan, 579
Farihurst, Eileen, 594
Fastow, Andrew S., 83, 245, 427
Favre, Brett, 144
Fayol, Henri, 7, 448-450, 460
Feitelberg, Rosemary, 596
Feldman, Daniel C., 557n, 588, 599, 600, 601
Ference, Richard, 413n, 592
Ference, T. P., 600
Ferris, Gerald R., 590, 599
Festinger, Leon, 582, 592
Fiedler, Fred, 348-351, 590
Fielding, Gordon J., 593
Finley, Michael, 299n
Finney, Darrell, 220
Finney, Martha, 21, 580
Fiorina, Carly, 140, 388, 389, 510
Fisher, Anne, 114n, 140n, 282n, 580, 595
Fisher, Cynthia D., 599
Fishman, Charles, 362n, 588
Fleishman, Edwin, 589
Flood, Frances, 159-160

Flynn, Francis, 588
Follett, Mary Parker, 8, 10
Fondas, Nanette, 580
Fooley, Toby B., 581
Ford, J., 593
Ford, Jeffrey D., 582, 595
Ford, R. N., 584
Ford, William Clay, Jr., 532
Fortune, Stan, 109, 110
Forward, Gordon, 184
Foster, Julie, 352n, 370n
Foust, Dean, 86n
Fox, Justin, 447n
France, Kym, 587
France, Mike, 381n, 428n, 553n
Frank, Amy, 181
Franklin, Jerome L., 598
Fraser, Claire, 34
Frederickson, James W., 595
Freedman, David H., 580
Freeman, John, 598
French, John R. P., 373, 591, 592
Frenkel-Brunswick, E., 582
Frew, David R., 586
Friedman, Meyer, 222-224, 586
Friesen, Peter H., 598
Frohman, Alan L., 590, 593
Frost, Peter, 599
Fuld, Richard S., Jr., 39
Fullerton, Howard, Jr., 57, 580, 581
Furst, Bonnie, 69
Fustad, J. W., 599

Gadbow, Daryl, 313n
Gadon, H., 585
Galbraith, John Kenneth, 591
Gallagher, Brian, 538
Galvin, Christopher, 39
Gandz, Jeffrey, 591
Ganwal, Rakesh, 31
Gardner, William L., 582
Garman, Sarah, 203n
Garud, Raghu, 585
Garvey, Charlotte, 586
Garvin, David, 591
Gates, Bill, 21, 130, 516, 517
Geertz, C., 596
Gent, M. J., 581
Gentner, Russell, 159
George, Jennifer M., 582
George, Tischelle, 86n
Gerloff, Edwin A., 587
Germer, Erika, 167n
Gersick, Connie J. G., 588
Gerstner, Charlotte R., 590
Gerstner, Louis V., Jr., 39, 433
Gibara, Samir, 31
Gibson, Cristina, 588
Gilbreth, Frank, 6
Gilbreth, Lillian, 6
Gillen, Dennis A., 579
Gillespie, James, 592
Gilman, Michael, 361
Gilmore, Patty, 241
Gimein, Mark, 110, 215n
Ginsberg, Ari, 592
Ginzberg, E., 599
Ginzberg, S. W., 592
Girdano, Daniel A., 244n
Girden, Ellen R., 599
Glenn, Ethel C., 278n
Glew, David J., 582, 585
Glick, William, 584
Glocer, Tom, 248-249
Glombowski, D. J., 332n

Glover, Ron, 522n, 597
Goffman, E., 596
Goggin, Barry, 320
Gogoi, Pallavi, 249n
Goldman, Lea, 160n
Goldwyn, Samuel, 551
Goluboff, Nicole, 182
Goodman, Paul S., 587
Goodwin, Vicki, 590
Googins, Bradley, 233
Graen, George, 358, 590
Graham, Franklin, 369
Graham, Nicholas, 167
Graham, Stephen, 439n
Granrose, C. S., 600
Grant, Linda, 582
Grasso, Jen, 167n
Grazier, Peter, 113, 114
Green, Dick, 72
Greenberg, Jerald, 580, 584
Greenberg, Jerry, 454
Greenberger, David B., 599
Greene, Jay, 517n
Greenhaus, Jeffrey H., 567n
Greenhouse, Steven, 553n
Greenspan, Alan, 84
Greiner, Larry E., 598
Griffeth, Roger W., 582
Griffin, Ricky W., 124n, 184n-185n, 489n, 533, 580, 582, 583, 584, 586, 598, 599
Grigaliunas, Benedict, 583
Grossman, Robert J., 190n
Grove, Andrew, 569, 600
Grover, Ron, 366n
Grubman, Richard, 427
Gudanowski, David, 585
Gudonis, Paul R., 281, 282n
Guest, R., 584
Guillen, Mauro F., 580
Gunther, Marc, 72n, 430n, 595
Gupta, Vipin, 585
Gurd, Tom, 400
Guyon, Janet, 522n, 597
Guzzo, Richard A., 581
Gyllenhammar, Pehr G., 595

Haas, J. Eugene, 594
Hackman, J. Richard, 173, 174n, 584, 598
Haga, W. J., 590
Hage, Jerald, 594
Hakel, Milton, 580, 583
Haldeman, H. R., 413
Hall, Douglas T., 570n, 599, 600
Hall, F. S., 600
Hall, Richard H., 593, 594
Hall, Woodrow, 316
Hambly, Drew, 206
Hambrick, Donald C., 592
Hamel, Gary, 21
Hamm, Mia, 143
Hamm, Steve, 593
Hammett, Lee, 190
Hammonds, Keith H., 28n, 591
Hamner, Ellen P., 584
Hamner, W. Clay, 584
Hanada, Mitsuyo, 596
Handfield-Jones, Helen, 147n
Handley, Nancy, 214-215
Hannah, Michael T., 598
Hansen, Curtiss, 585
Harris, E. F., 589
Harris, Jay, 59
Harrison, Derek, 241
Harrison, E. Frank, 591

Harrison, Laird, 134n
Hart, Ellen, 589
Hartke, Darrel D., 598
Hartman, Laura P., 553
Hartman, Lynn, 335
Harwick, Harry, 334-335
Haspeslagh, Philippe, 596
Hassan, Fred, 31
Hayles, Ralph, 354
Haynes, Stephanie, 109
Heald, K., 599
Hebden, J. E., 597
Heenan, D. A., 593
Heide, Jan B., 595
Heifetz, Ronald, 589
Heil, Gary, 583
Heilman, Madeline E., 590
Heim, Axel, 86
Helliker, Kevin, 127
Henderson, A. M., 579
Henderson, Jill, 87-88
Heneman, Robert L., 599
Henkoff, Ronald, 593
Henry, David, 381n
Hensrud, Donald D., 335
Heraclitus, 39
Herna, J. L., 599
Herschlag, Judith K., 590
Hersey, P., 359n
Hersey, Paul, 590
Herzberg, Frederick, 126-128, 131, 583, 584
Heskett, J. L., 596
Hewlett, Sylvia Ann, 239
Hewlett, Walter, 388, 389
Hewlett, William, 34, 275, 388, 510
Hickman, Jonathon, 203n
Hickson, David J., 595
Higley, Rick, 307
Hill, E. Jeffrey, 164
Hill, N. C., 600
Hill, Vernon, 137
Hilton, Nancy, 315
Hisrich, R. D., 600
Hodgetts, Richard M., 593
Hoffman, Alan N., 595
Hoffman, Andrew, 592
Hoffman, Donna, 389
Hofstede, G., 494
Hofstede, Geert, 64-66, 581
Holden, Betsy, 352
Holland, J. L., 567, 599
Holliday, Chad, 524
Hollis, Donald R., 587
Holmes, Stanley, 381n
Holmes, Thomas, 230, 232, 586
Holstein, William J., 345n, 593, 596
Hom, Peter W., 582
Hoopes, Linda L., 586
Hoover, J. Edgar, 269
Hornery, Stuart, 331
Hornstein, Harvey A., 590
Horwitz, Tony, 168
Hough, L. M., 582, 589
House, Robert, 351, 368, 590, 591
Howell, Jon P., 591
Hrabowski, Freeman, 200
Huber, George P., 591
Huey, John, 595, 597
Hulin, Charles, 582, 583
Humphrey, Watts S., 597
Hunt, James G., 590, 591
Hunt, Rameck, 367
Hurley, Dan, 600
Hyland, MaryAnne, 585
Hymowitz, Carol, 43n, 69n, 564n
Hynes-Grace, Beverly, 581

Icenogle, Marjorie L., 587
Ihlwan, Moon, 345n, 418n
Immelt, Jeff, 447
Inch, John, 447
Ioannou, Lori, 471n
Irvine, Martha, 581
Iso, Ariko, 67
Ivancevich, John M., 584, 586
Ivanitskaya, Lana, 585
Ive, Jonathan, 324

Jackofsky, Ellen F., 599
Jackson, Christine, 589
Jacob, Rahul, 580, 596
Jaeger, Alfred M., 598
Jago, Arthur, 354, 589, 590
Jain, Harish C., 581
Jain, Naveen, 517
James, Edgerrin, 207
Janis, Irving L., 406-408, 412, 413, 588, 592
Janson, R., 174n
Je, Chin Dae, 345
Jefferson, Mark, 562
Jenkins, George, 367
Jermier, John M., 591
Jesson, R., 599
Jex, Steve M., 586
Jick, Todd D., 586
Jin, Putai, 585
Jobs, Steve, 34, 130
Johns, Gary, 584
Johnson, Diane, 582
Johnson, Leonard W., 593
Johnson, Norman, 594
Johnson, Robert, 316
Johnson, Roberta Ann, 96
Johnson, Ross, 580
Jones, Barry D., 588
Jones, Del, 31n, 116n
Jones, Gareth R., 582
Judge, Timothy, 582
Jung, Andrea, 31, 140, 353, 525

Kaeufer, Katrin, 589
Kahn, Jeremy, 78n, 84n, 203n, 580
Kahn, Joseph, 553n
Kahn, Robert, 539, 586, 587, 598
Kahn, S., 586
Kanfer, Ruth, 582
Kanigel, Robert, 6
Kanungo, Rabindra N., 591
Kapahi, Chantara, 394
Karen, Nancy L., 422
Karmazin, Mel, 394
Kast, Fremont, 579
Katz, Daniel, 539, 587, 598
Katz, Robert, 580
Katzenbach, Jon, 245, 258, 281-282, 315, 333n, 585, 588
Kay, Ira, 585
Keenan, Faith, 282n
Keil, E. T., 593
Kelleher, Herb, 177, 366, 491, 501
Keller, Robert T., 489n, 588
Kelly, Jim, 169
Kelly, John M., 586
Kelly, Marilyn, 134
Kemper, Cynthia L., 587
Kendall, L. M., 582
Kennan, Faith, 169n
Kennedy, A. A., 21, 494, 498, 596
Kennedy, Kevin, 486, 487
Kent, Russell L., 589
Keon, Thomas L., 579, 593
Kepner, Elaine, 580
Kerlinger, Fred N., 598
Kerr, Steven, 591

Khermouch, Gerry, 339n
Kidwell, Roland E., Jr., 582
Kiechel, W., III, 600
Kieser, Alfred, 579
Kilbridge, M., 584
Killen, Heather, 140
Kim, W. Chan, 597
Kimberly, John R., 594
Kinsman, Michael, 220n, 223n
Kirkland, Richard I., Jr., 581, 596
Kirkpatrick, David, 389n
Kirkpatrick, Shelly A., 589
Kist, Ewald, 495
Klein, Karen E., 198n
Kleinman, Carol, 586
Klene, Roger R., 449, 594
Klinefelter, Jeff, 109
Kluckhohn, C., 596
Knight, Melinda, 587
Knight, Phil, 496
Knowlton, Christopher, 581
Knudsen, B. W., 599
Kobasa, Susan C., 586
Koehn, Daryl, 553
Kogan, N., 592
Kohn, Alfie, 588
Kolodny, Harvey F., 595
Konrad, Rachel, 72n
Korsgaard, M. Audrey, 588
Kosiyanon, Rochana, 69
Kosnett, Jeffery R., 138
Kotter, John P., 21, 341, 580, 589, 596
Koudsi, Suzanne, 527n
Kouzes, J. M., 494
Krackhardt, David, 587
Kraemer, Harry, 236
Kreitner, Robert, 584
Kristof, Amy L., 581
Kroeber, A. L., 596
Kropf, Susan, 525
Kuhnert, Karl W., 590
Kumar, Sanjay, 31
Kupfer, Andrew, 595
Kusin, Gary, 365-366
Kyun, Joe Hang, 418

Laabs, Jennifer Koch, 308n
Labarre, Polly, 589
Labich, Kenneth, 595, 597
LaBier, D., 600
Lacroix, Renee, 588
Laderman, Jeffrey M., 596
Landy, Frank J., 579
Lane, Henry W., 581, 596
Langley, Rich, 313
Lapore, Dawn, 547
Larson, L. L., 590, 591
Larson, Mark, 510n
Lashinsky, Adam, 389n
Latack, J. C., 600
Latham, Gary, 192, 193n, 585
Lau, Doris, 69
Lauren, Dylan, 300
Laurent, André, 581
Lawler, Edward E., 145, 146n, 583, 584, 586, 598, 599
Lawler, J., 599
Lawrence, Paul R., 579, 595, 598
Lay, Kenneth, 82-84, 96, 245, 246, 426-428, 551
Lay, Linda, 427-428
Leatt, Peggy, 593
Lechler, Katherine, 145
Lee, Charles, 39, 454
Lee, Howard B., 598
Lee, Louise, 596, 597

Lee, Raymond T., 586
Lee, Stephen, 487n
Lei, David, 592
Leibowitz, Z. B., 601
Len, Samuel, 418n
Leonard, Bill, 581
Leonard, Devin, 522n, 597
Leonhard, David, 86n, 553n
LePine, Jeffrey, 582
Lepore, Dawn G., 140
Leppla, Jeff, 538
Lesieur, Bill, 487
Lester, Scott, 587
Levering, Robert, 495n
Levitan, Sar A., 581
Lewicki, R. J., 592
Lewin, Kurt, 143, 528, 529, 583, 598
Lewis, Aylwin, 339
Lewis, Bill, 78
Lewis, Laurie K., 597
Lewis, Philip, 590
Lieber, Jill, 588
Lieber, Ronald B., 582
Likert, Rensis, 448-449, 451, 452, 460, 589, 592, 594
Lincoln, James R., 582, 596
Linden, Dana Wechsler, 10n
Linsky, Marty, 589
Lipnack, Jessica, 367
Litterer, J. A., 592
Livesay, Harold C., 595
Locke, Edwin, 191, 192, 579, 584, 585, 589, 599
Loden, Marilyn, 61n, 580, 581
Lohr, Steve, 510n
Long, Brian G., 420, 593
Long, Carl, 580
Long, Susan, 588
Loomis, Carol J., 595
LoRash-Neuenschwander, Heidi, 147
Lorenzo, Frank, 98-99, 376
Lounsbury, John W., 586
Lowry, Richard, 583
Lowry, Tom, 249n, 394n
Lublin, Joann S., 96n
Luckman, T., 596
Luthans, Fred, 584
Lyne, Susan, 365
Lyons, Jim, 415

Mace, Flora, 313
MacGillivray, Janet, 447
Machiavelli, Niccolo, 94
Mackay, Harvey, 600
MacKenzie, Scott B., 589, 591
Mackey, John, 288
Maddi, S. R., 586
Madigan, Kathleen, 198n
Mael, Fred, 587, 588
Maerz, Mike, 315
Maes, Jeanne D., 587
Magliochetti, Joe, 116
Mahar, Linda, 590
Maher, J. R., 584
Main, J., 600
Mainiero, Lisa A., 597
Mangel, Robert, 586
Mangum, Stephen L., 599
Mann, Leon, 406-408, 592
Manning, John, 138
Manz, Charles C., 314, 588, 591
Mao Zedong, 69
March, James G., 592
Marcial, Gene G., 596
Markels, Alex, 594
Markey, Edward J., 428
Marks, Michelle, 589

Marrache, Myriam, 588
Marris, Mary C., 140
Marshall, Ray, 599
Marshall, Samantha, 69n
Martier, A., 600
Martin, J., 596
Martinko, Mark J., 582
Martins, Luis L., 580
Maruca, Regina Fazio, 315n
Maslow, Abraham, 11, 121-125, 131, 583
Maslyn, John, 590
Mathieu, John, 589
Mauborgne, Renee A., 597
Mausner, Bernard, 583
Maxeiner, James R., 239
Mayer, Robert J., 410, 472
Mayo, Charles, 334, 335
Mayo, Elton, 8, 579, 595
Mayo, Margarita, 591
Mayo, William, 334, 335
McBride, Kerry, 596
McCall, M. W., 599
McCanse, Anne Adams, 590
McCarter, Robert, 587
McClelland, David, 128, 130, 454, 583
McCune, Jenny C., 588
McElroy, John, 593
McFarlane, Robert, 295
McGee, Ken, 459
McGeehan, Patrick, 96n
McGregor, Douglas, 11, 12n, 121, 579
McGuire, Joseph W., 579
McKay, Martha, 459n
McKinnon, Shaun, 492n, 596
McLaughlin, Martin, 48
McLean, Bethany, 83, 84, 247n, 381n
McMahan, Gary C., 584
McNealy, Scott, 540
McRae, K. B., 601
McWilliams, Gary, 597
Mean, David H., 62
Meglino, Bruce, 587-588
Mehta, Stephanie N., 78n, 203n, 430n, 459n, 594
Meindl, James, 591
Melchionda, Gabrielle, 403
Melymuka, Kathleen, 547n
Mendels, Pamela, 90n
Merritt, Jennifer, 78n
Messick, David M., 580
Messier, Jean-Marie, 521-523
Meyerson, Debra, 140
Mezias, John M., 582
Miles, Raymond E., 599
Miles, Robert H., 593
Miller, D. B., 599
Miller, Danny, 598
Miller, David, 72
Miller, Edwin L., 581
Miller, Joe, 418n
Miller, Mary, 53n
Miller, Robert, 590
Milligan, Jack, 138
Milliken, Frances J., 580
Milner, Caroline, 590
Miner, John B., 594
Mintz, Jordan, 83, 84
Mintzberg, Henry, 32, 440, 475-479, 580, 591, 593, 595
Mitchell, Cynthia, 78n
Mitchell, Terence R., 583, 590, 599
Mitz, Linda F., 586
Moberg, Dennis J., 382n, 591
Moeller, Michael, 593

Monaghan. Tom, 72
Monetta, Dominic J., 287, 587
Monroe, Lorraine, 372
Montanari, John R., 592, 593, 594, 595
Moore, Dinah, 203
Moore, Don, 592
Moore, Stuart, 454
Moorhead, Gregory, 413n, 585, 592, 594, 598
Moran, Linda, 588
Morgan, Cyril P., 593, 594
Morgan, M. A., 600
Morgenson, Gretchen, 553n
Morse, David, 105
Morse, N. C., 592
Moscovici, S., 592
Moskal, Brian S., 593
Moskowitz, Milton, 495n
Moss, Sherry E., 589
Mott, Randy, 467
Mounton, Jane S., 590
Mowday, Richard T., 583
Moy-Bruno, Donna, 463
Mueller, Robert, 383
Mullaney, Timothy J., 593
Mullen, James C., 361, 362
Muller, Joann, 215n, 433n
Munk, Nina, 88, 581
Münsterberg, Hugo, 8, 579
Muoio, Anna, 591, 598
Murphy, Cait, 499n
Murray, Matt, 594
Murray, Victor, 591
Muskie, Edmund, 588
Musselwhite, Ed, 326n, 588

Nadler, David A., 369n, 584, 591, 598
Nasser, Jacques, 31, 532
Naughton, Keith, 373, 593
Neale, M. A., 593
Neck, Christopher P., 413n, 592
Nelson, Debra L., 586
Nelson, Reed E., 588
Nemetz, Patricia L., 580
Neubauer, Joseph, 31
Neuman, Joel H., 242n, 586
Newman, Tom, 85
Nicholson, Nigel, 589
Nisbett, R. E., 596
Nixon, Richard, 413
Noe, Raymon d, 589
Noonan, Katherine A., 581
Norman, James R., 597
North, Oliver, 295
Novak, David, 339
Nugent, Patrick, 588
Nulty, Peter, 597
Nurden, Robert, 587
Nusbaum, Marci Alboher, 96n
Nyberg, Lars, 31
Nystrom, P. C., 590
Nyum, Jim, 418

Obert, Steven L., 588
O'Connell, Patricia, 343, 525n
Odland, Steve, 355
O'Donovan, Dennis J., 422
Ojansivu, Camilla, 471n
O'Keefe, Brian, 110, 339n
Oldham, G. R., 173, 174n
Oldham, Greg, 584
O'Leary-Kelly, Anne, 582, 585
Olson, John, 426
Ondrack, Daniel A., 598
O'Neill, Mary Jo, 499
O'Neill, Paul H., 84

Oppel, Richard A., Jr., 428n
O'Reilly, Brian, 581, 597
O'Reilly, C., 494
O'Reilly, Charles A., 585, 587, 596, 597
Organ, Dennis W., 582
Orsburn, Jack D., 326n, 588
Osborn, R. N., 590
Osbourne, Richard L., 597
Osmond, Charles P., 580
O'Toole, James, 245
Ouchi, William G., 21, 494, 498, 503-505, 511, 513, 596, 597
Overholt, Alison, 167n, 366n
Owen, Robert, 8

Pace, R. Wayne, 587
Packard, David, 34, 275, 388-389, 510
Pailthorp, Bellamy, 597
Palich, Leslie E., 582
Parades, Hugo, 77
Park, Andrew, 389n
Parker, Donald F., 586
Parker, James, 366, 491
Parker, Sir Peter, 10
Parker-Pope, Tara, 53n
Parkinson, David K., 586
Parks, Craig D., 592
Parks, Judi McLean, 581
Parnes, H. S., 599
Parsons, Richard, 430
Parsons, T., 579
Pascaul, Aixa, 339n
Pastor, Juan-Carlos, 591
Patterson, James L., 572
Patton, Gregory, 582
Paul, Anthony, 345n
Pavlov, Ivan P., 584
Pawley, Dennis, 98
Payne, Melanie, 119n
Payne, R. C., 600
Pearce, Craig, 580
Pearce, John A., II, 589, 594
Pearson, Andrall (Andy), 338-339, 341, 348
Peck, Ross, 419, 420n
Peden, Mark, 281
Peers, Martin, 430n
Pellet, Jennifer, 525n
Pepper, John E., 53
Perera, Rick, 86n
Peres, Shimon, 394
Perot, Ross, 540
Perrin, Craig, 326n
Perrone, Jennifer, 138
Perroni, Amedeo G., 579, 582
Perrow, Charles, 465, 595
Perry, Rick, 552
Peters, Lawrence H., 599
Peters, Thomas, 21, 272, 273, 483, 484, 493, 494, 498, 505-507, 511, 513-514, 587, 596
Petre, Peter, 591, 598
Pfau, Bruce, 585
Pfeiffer, Eckhard, 20, 368, 591
Pfeiffer, Jeffrey, 579, 580, 582, 585, 594, 598
Pheysey, Diana C., 595
Phi, Kim Sang, 344
Philbrick, Tim, 214
Piëch, Ferdinand, 373
Pinder, Craig, 582, 584
Pink, Daniel H., 262n
Piper, William E., 588
Plato, 5
Podsakoff, Philip, 589, 591, 599

Poe, Andrea, 586
Polanyi, M., 596
Pond, Elliott A., 278n
Porter, Lyman W., 145, 146n, 579, 582, 583, 584, 587, 590, 593, 598
Porter, Michael, 21, 580
Portwood, J. D., 600
Posner, B. Z., 494
Pottruck, David, 454, 546, 547
Power, M., 596
Preiffer, Jeffrey, 582
Prescott, John E., 595
Pritchard, Robert D., 583
Pruneau, Steve, 198
Prusak, Laurence, 587
Puffer, Sheila, 589
Pugh, Derek S., 595
Purdy, K., 174n
Pustay, Michael W., 124n, 580, 586
Pyo, Ken, 190

Quick, James C., 226n, 586, 598
Quick, Jonathan D., 226n, 586, 598
Quinn, R. P., 586
Quittner, Jeremy, 182n

Rae-Dupree, Janet, 597
Raghuram, Sumita, 585
Rahe, Richard, 230, 232, 586
Raiffa, Howard, 419, 592
Raisinghani, Duru, 591
Rajagopalan, Nandini, 591
Ransdell, Eric, 596
Rappaport, Alfred, 586
Rasheed, Abdul M. A., 591
Rasmusson, Erika, 492n, 596
Ratan, Suneel, 599
Rau, Barbara, 585
Raven, Bertram, 373, 591
Reagan, Ronald, 295, 448
Reagor, Catherine, 400n, 597
Reck, Ross R., 593
Redding, Gordon, 581
Reed, John, 105, 455, 511
Reichheld, Frederick, 589
Reimer, E., 592
Reitman, Frieda, 600
Reitz, Bonnie, 27, 28
Renwick, P. A., 599
Rhys, Garel, 433
Rice, F., 600
Richardson, Astrid M., 588
Richardson, James, 486, 487
Ricks, David A., 251n
Ridge, Tom, 38, 383
Riketta, Michael, 582
Ritter, Andy, 189
Ritzky, Garry M., 157, 584
Robbins, Stephen P., 588
Roberto, Michael, 591
Roberts, Karlene H., 584
Roberts, Paul, 335n
Robertson, Tim, 219
Robinson, Debra, 36
Rocks, David, 389n
Rockwell, David, 281
Roedy, Bill, 393-394
Roethlisberger, Fritz, 8, 579, 595
Rogers, Alison, 593
Rogers, Everett M., 587
Ronen, Simcha, 581
Rosch, Paul, 237
Rose, Taryn, 192
Rosekind, Mark, 220
Rosen, Ben, 443
Rosen, Corey, 134

Rosener, Judy B., 61n, 580, 581
Rosenman, Ray, 222–224, 586
Rosenthal, R. A., 586
Rosenzweig, James, 579
Ross, Jerry, 592
Rossant, John, 597
Rossler, Joann, 241
Rossler, Lisa, 242
Rossler, Walter Charles, 241
Roth, Daniel, 276n
Rothbard, Nancy, 389
Rotter, J. B., 582
Rousseau, Denise M., 581, 599
Rubin, Barry Louis, 581
Rubin, J. Z., 592
Rubin, Jeff, 300
Rubinstein, Jon, 324
Ruhm, Christopher J., 220
Ryan, R. M., 582
Rynes, S. L., 599
Ryterband Edward C., 587

Sabella, Mark, 589
Sabol, Ed, 509
Sabol, Steve, 509
Salamin, Alain, 586
Salancik, Gerald, 582, 585
Salter, Chuck, 527
Samson, Barbara, 353
Sandell, Scott, 516
Sanders, Tim, 114
Sandler, Herbert, 454
Sandler, Marion, 140, 454
Sandlund, Chris, 182n, 229n
Sanford, R. N., 582
Santamaria, Jason A., 585
Sauler, Kerry, 583
Saurage, J., 600
Sauter, James, 197
Sawatzki, Susan, 160n
Sawyer, John E., 582
Schachter, Stanley, 583
Scharf, Charlie, 266
Schein, E., 494, 596, 600
Schempp, Jurgen, 433
Schiefflin, Allison K., 96
Schlender, Brent, 517, 591
Schlossberg, N. K., 601
Schneck, Rodney, 593
Schneer, Joy A., 600
Schoenherr, Richard A., 594
Schrage, Michael, 593
Schriesheim, Chester A., 590, 591, 599
Schulberg, Herbert C., 586
Schultz, George P., 295
Schultz, Howard, 388
Schultz, Quentin, 253
Schumacher, Thomas, 86
Schumpeter, Joseph, 551
Schwab, Charles, 546, 547
Schwartz, John, 422, 553n
Schwenk, Charles R., 588
Scott, Lee, 34, 109
Screffler, Roger, 593
Seglin, Jeffrey L., 43n, 553
Seibold, David R., 597
Seidel, Michael, 39n
Seidenberg, Ivan, 39, 454
Seligman, Dan, 101, 582
Sellers, Patricia, 23n, 455, 592, 594
Selye, Hans, 221, 222, 586
Senge, Peter, 21, 98, 543–544, 585
Serwer, Andrew, 410n, 472n, 597
Shah, Priti Pradham, 583
Shannon, Kyle, 262
Shapiro, Joseph P., 587

Shapley, Deborah, 276n
Al Sharif, Khalid, 124
Sharp, Stephen, 527
Shaw, George Bernard, 116
Shaw, Malcolm, 580
Shaw, Marvin E., 587, 588
Sheldon, Ken, 527
Shellenbarger, Sue, 114n, 223n
Shenkar, Oded, 581
Shepard, Steve, 553n
Sheridan, John E., 597
Sherman, J. Daniel, 594
Sherwood, Kaitlin Duck, 252
Shishkin, Philip, 447n
Shook, David, 362n
Sidhu, Jay, 31
Siebel, Tom, 506
Sils, D., 597
Silverman, Gary, 597
Simmons, John, 262n, 394n
Simmons, L. M., Jr., 587
Simon, Herbert, 591, 592
Simpson, Eric, 299
Simpson, James Daniel, 241–242
Sims, Henry P., 314, 588, 591
Sirois, Bill, 219
Sirower, Mark L., 454–455
Sittenfeld, Curtis, 167n, 591, 592
Skilling, Jeffrey, 82–84, 245, 246, 426–428, 551
Skinner, B. F., 149, 584
Skoglind, Jeffrey D., 599
Skowcroft, Brent, 588
Sloan, Alfred, 595
Sloan, Jerry, 332
Smith, Adam, 166–167, 435, 584, 593
Smith, Douglas K., 333n, 588
Smith, Howard L., 594
Smith, Jack, 443
Smith, Patricia, 582, 583
Smith, Rolf, 401
Smith, Thomas R., Jr., 422
Snoek, J. D., 586
Snow, Charles C., 599
Snyder, Nancy, 285
Solero, Carlos, 59
Solnik, Claude, 596
Soloman, Charlene Marmer, 581
Sorcher, Melvin, 589
Soupata, Lea, 78
Sparks, William L., 587
Spender, J. C., 494
Spendolini, Michael J., 593
Spiro, Leah Nathans, 597
Stack, Jack, 134
Stahl, Michael J., 583
Stajkovic, Alexander D., 584
Stalker, George, 465, 595
Stanley, J. C., 599
Starbuck, William H., 582
Staw, Barry, 579, 581, 584, 592, 596
Stearns, Timothy M., 595, 599
Steers, Richard M., 581, 582
Stein, Nicholas, 370n
Stephens, Deborah C., 583
Stephens-Jahng, Theresa, 584
Stern, Carolyn, 175
Sternberg, Robert J., 589
Stewart, Martha, 23, 299
Stewart, Meredith M., 552
Stewart, Thomas A., 581, 590, 591, 596, 597
Stoddard, Sherri, 142
Stogdill, Ralph M., 589
Stoka, Ann Marie, 579
Stone, Amey, 249n

Stone, Eugene, 598
Stoner, James A. F., 592, 600
Strauss, Gary, 206n
Strauss, John, 86n
Streitfeld, David, 517n
Strickland, A. J., III, 594, 595
Strong, Bruce, 527
Stropki, John, 164
Suttle, J. Lloyd, 532, 584, 598
Sutton, Robert I., 594
Swan, Robert, 368
Synderman, Barbara, 583

Taylor, Alex, III, 343, 433n, 581, 591, 593, 597
Taylor, Frederick W., 6–7, 120, 121, 168, 579, 582, 584, 592
Taylor, Martin, 48
Tenet, George, 383
Tepper, Bennett J., 590
Terborg, James, 579
Teslick, Sarah, 206
Tetlow, Richard, 43
Tetrault, Linda A., 590
Tetzeli, Rick, 580
Tharahirunchote, Wiwam, 69
Tharp, Charles, 471
Thayer, Paul W., 584
Thomas, Arthur A., Jr., 594
Thomas, Joe, 585
Thomas, Kenneth, 301n, 579, 588
Thomas, R. Roosevelt, Jr., 580
Thomas, Susan Gregory, 593, 596
Thompson, James, 470, 595
Thompson, Leigh, 592
Thompson, Loren, 49
Thomson, Arthur A., Jr., 595
Thoresen, Carl, 582
Thoret, Andre, 591
Thorn, Rod, 332
Thornton, Emily, 582
Thurm, Scott, 487n
Tichy, Noel M., 598
Tierney, Christine, 433n
Tokoro, Mario, 461
Tolman, Edward, 143, 583
Tomasko, Robert, 596
Tomlinson, Richard, 241, 522n, 597
Tompkins, Silvan S., 587
Toner, Robin, 239n
Toosi, Mitra, 57, 580, 581
Torre, Joe, 588
Tower, John, 588
Trist, Eric L., 588, 595
Trump, Donald, 299
Tucker, Michael, 220
Tudor, William D., 593
Tulgan, Bruce, 142
Tully, Shawn, 587
Turban, Daniel B., 579
Turner, Nick, 590
Tushman, Michael, 369n, 591, 596
Tuson, John, 370
Tymon, Walter G., 579
Tyson, Don, 370

Uhl-Bien, Mary, 590
Ullmann, Owen, 597
Ulrich, David O., 586, 598
Urwick, Lyndall, 7, 593
Useem, Jerry, 547n, 597

Valasquez, Manuel, 591
van der Lugt, Godfried, 495
Vanderslice, Virginia, 134
Van Fleet, David D., 585, 589, 593, 600

Van Maanen, J., 494
Van Vianen, Annelies E. M., 588
Veiga, John F., 579
Velasques, Manuel, 382n
Ventrakaman, N., 592
Verma, Anil, 581
Vernon, Lillian, 140
Vicars, William M., 598
Vicker-Koch, Mary, 580
Victor, Bart, 584
Vogelstein, Fred, 517n, 547
Volcker, Paul A., Jr., 552
Von Glinow, Mary Ann, 599
von Hippel, Courtney, 599
Vroom, Victor, 143, 354–358, 583, 590, 592

Wade-Benzoni, Kimberly, 592
Wageman, Ruth, 588
Wagner, John A. III, 585
Wahba, Mahmond A., 583
Wahlgren, Eric, 198n
Waitt, Ted, 482
Waksal, Harlan, 472
Waksal, Sam, 470, 472
Walch, Jeffrey, 238
Waldman, David A., 591
Waldroop, James, 585
Walker, C. R., 584
Walker, J., 600, 601
Walker, Marcus, 439n
Wallace, Marc, 205
Wallach, M. A., 592
Waller, Mary, 588
Walls, Julius, Jr., 72
Walton, Richard E., 532, 533, 595, 598
Walton, Sam, 109, 110, 375, 467, 499, 517
Ward, Leah Beth, 540n
Warner, Fara, 98n, 285n
Warren, E. K., 600
Wartzman, Rick, 332n
Waterman, Robert, 21, 272, 273, 484, 493, 494, 498, 505–507, 511, 513–514, 587, 596
Watkins, Sherron S., 83, 96, 246, 552
Watson, Noshua, 203n
Watson, Thomas J., Jr., 396
Wayne, Leslie, 553n
Webber, Alan M., 98n, 598
Webber, R. A., 600
Webber, Sheila Simsarian, 588
Weber, Joseph, 339n
Weber, Max, 7, 8, 40, 434, 448, 449, 460, 579, 593
Weed, E. D., 584
Weeks, Holly, 587
Weil, Alan W., 422
Weill, Sanford, 455
Weinberg, Neil, 540n, 598
Weinberger, Caspar W., 295
Weisman, Jeb, 281
Weiss, Howard M., 582
Welch, Jack, 21, 30, 116, 281, 324, 400, 446, 447, 473
Welch, James, 1–2
Weldon, Bill, 343
Weldy, Teresa G., 587
Welsh, M. Ann, 585
Wenning, Werner, 308
West, Michael, 592
West, Mindy, 592
Wetlaufer, Suzy, 598
Wexley, Kenneth N., 598
Wheat, Alynda, 203n
Wheeler, Michael L., 580, 581

Whitford, David, 455n
Whiting, J. W. M., 597
Whitsett, David A., 579
Whittington, J. Lee, 590
Wiesenfeld, Batia, 585
Wilcox, R. C., 599
Wilder, Clinton, 547n
Wilhelm, Warren, 597
Wilkerson, John, 540
Wilkins, A., 596
Willard, Rick, 164
Williams, Gary, 590
Williams, Michele, 589
Williams, Nancy, 540n
Williams, Serena, 115
Williams, Venus, 115
Willman, Jim, 189-190

Wilson, Patti, 86
Winchell, William O., 580
Winfrey, Oprah, 22-23
Woellert, Lorraine, 428n
Wofford, Jerry C., 587, 590
Wolfe, D. M., 586
Wolfe, Richard A., 586
Wolff, Steven B., 585
Wonderlic, Charles, 90
Wong, Anny, 253
Wong, Jesse, 471n
Woodman, Richard W., 582
Woodruff, David, 373
Woodson, William Brooks, 580
Woodward, Joan, 465, 595
Wozniak, Steve, 34
Wrege, Charles D., 579, 582

Wren, D. A., 589
Wren, Daniel, 10n, 579, 582
Wysocki, Bernard, Jr., 599

Xie, Jia Lin, 584

Yamaguchi, Tamotsu, 581
Yammarino, Francis J., 587, 590, 591
Yasai-Ardekani, Masoud, 595
Yates, Jacquelyn, 134
Yates, Valerie, 599
Yetton, Philip H., 590
Yin, R., 599
Yong, Yun John, 345
Yorks, Lyle, 579
Yoshino, Hiroyuki, 190n

Yukl, Gary, 375, 377n, 585, 589, 590, 591
Yunus, Mohammed, 229

Zaccaro, Stephen, 589
Zaleznik, Abraham, 589
Zaltman, G., 598
Zavalloni, M., 592
Zeleny, Milan, 591
Zeller, Tom, 247n
Zellner, Wendy, 96n, 370n, 492n, 499n, 596
Zemin, Jiang, 394
Zenger, John, 588
Zey, Michael G., 600
Zollars, Bill, 1-3
Zuckerman, Seth, 167

Organization Index

ABC Entertainment, 365
ActivityOne.com, 167
Advantica, 203
Afterburn Seminars, 535
Agency.com, 262
Agilent Technology, 86, 275–276
Alabama Industrial Development Training, 190
Alcatel, 63
Alcoa, 194
Alertness Solutions, 220
Allianz, 439
Alverno College, 502
Amadeus Global Travel Distribution, 58
American Cyanamid, 171
American Express, 482
America Online (AOL), 419, 429–430
Amoco Chemicals, 179
Arthur Andersen, 84, 96, 517, 552
Anderson School (UCLA), 53
Anheuser-Busch, 273
AOL Time Warner, 429–431
Apple Computer, 34, 37, 68, 70, 130, 324, 467
Applied Materials, 203
Aramark, 31
A & R Welding, 164
Atlantic Richfield, 179
AT&T, 36, 53, 171, 172, 174, 197, 227, 261, 275, 458–459, 463, 536
AutoZone, 355
Avon Products, 31, 73, 140, 353, 525

BAE, 48
Baker International, 171
Banc One, 266
Bank of Montreal, 180
Baxter International, 236
Bayer Corporation, 307–308
L. L. Bean, 238
Beck Group, 202
BEEJ, Business Leaders for Excellence, Ethics, and Justice, 72
Bell Atlantic, 39, 454
BellSouth, 203
Bethlehem Steel, 6, 120, 121
Bic, 41
Biogen, 361–362
Black & Decker, 194
Blackhawk Automotive Plastics, 164
Blistex, 72
BMW, 41, 62, 63
Boeing, 48, 70, 324, 381, 491, 514
Borland International, 358
Robert Bosch GmbH, 208
BP Amoco, 62
Bristol-Myers Squibb, 410, 472
British Airways, 198
British Petroleum, 58
British Sterling, 62
Brown & Wood, 421
Burlington Industries, 13
Burrows, Peter, 389

Calvin Klein, 41
Caterpillar, 253
Chaparral Steel, 183–184
Charles Schwab Company, 140, 454, 535, 546–547
Chase Manhattan Bank, 197

Chevron, 347, 444–445
Chick-fil-A, 107
Children's Hospital (Montefiore), 281
Chrysler, 63, 324
Cisco Systems, Inc., 318, 486–487
Citibank, 105, 455
Citicorp, 472, 552
ClearOne Communications, 160
Cloud Cap Glass, 313
Coca-Cola, 42, 55, 206, 270, 483
Colgate-Palmolive Company, 317, 318, 438
Colonial Life Insurance Company, 171
Commerce Bancorp, 137–139
Compagnie Générale des Eaux, 521–522
Compaq Computer Corporation, 19–20, 275, 368, 388, 509, 510
Computer Associates, 31
Container Corporation, 477
Continental Airlines, 27–28, 34, 35, 44, 368–369, 376
Corning, 105, 220, 481
Credit Suisse, 552
Crown Mold and Machine, 164
Cummins Engine Company, 328

Daewoo Motor Co., 418
Daimler-Benz, 63
DaimlerChrysler, 433, 439, 483
D'Ancono and Pflaum, 13
Deci, 158
Dell Computers, 432, 466, 467, 501, 535
Deloitte Touche, 381
Denny's, 53
Deutsch Bank, 438, 439, dai389
Digital Equipment Corporation, 58, 70, 73, 226, 323–324, 330, 463, 464
Domino's Pizza, 72
Dow Chemical, 400
DuPont, 70, 194, 524
Dynergy, 84

Eastman Chemical Company, 317
Eastman Kodak, 21, 70, 203, 463–464
EchoMail, 275
Ecotrust, 167
Electronic Data Systems Corporation (EDS), 326, 540
Eli Lilly, 262
Emery Air Freight, 157
Enron Corporation, 13, 43, 82–84, 96, 245–247, 270, 388, 426–428, 551–553
Environmental Protection Agency (EPA), 447
Erikson, 526, 527
Ernst and Young, 53
E*Trade, 496, 510
Exide Technologies, 219
Exxon Mobil Corporation, 62, 109, 347

Federal Express, 286
Federal Trade Commission (FTC), 447
Fidelity, 547
Fiesta Mart, 41
Film Fabricators, Inc., 316
Fireplace Manufacturers, 474
First Interstate Bank, 504
Fleet-Boston, 181
Food and Drug Administration (FDA), 472

Ford Motor Company, 31, 62, 63, 86, 171, 404, 532, 535
Friedman-Jacobs Company, 211
Fujitsu, 58, 345

Gateway 2005, 441
General Electric, 8, 9, 32, 116, 211, 238, 273, 281, 285, 318, 326, 400, 447, 463, 478, 552
General Foods, 172, 194, 475
General Mills, 312
General Motors, 36, 44, 109, 162, 207–208, 214, 215, 265–266, 281, 286, 312, 404, 418, 443, 478, 540
Gentner Communications, 159–160
Georgia-Pacific Corporation, 169
Global Crossing, 43
Golden West Financial, 140, 454
Goldman Sachs, 140
B. F. Goodrich, 157
Goodyear, 31
W. L. Gore, 133–134
W. R. Grace, 385
Graphic Controls, 211
Greater Boston Rehabilitation Services, 70
Greyston Bakery, 72
GTE, 39, 454
Gulf Oil, 347

Halliburton Company, 358
John Hancock, 179
Harley-Davidson, 41
Harpo, Inc., 22
Harris Corporation, 318
Hewlett-Packard, 20, 34, 58, 73, 140, 275, 312, 368, 388–389, 464, 491, 509, 510
Hilton hotels, 39
Hitachi, 345
Home Depot, 4, 326
Homeland Security Department, 38
Honda Motor Co., 41, 44, 189–190, 208, 444
Honeywell, 447
Hospital Corporation of America, 468
Houston Natural Gas Production Company, 82

IBM, 21, 32, 36, 39, 172, 261, 326, 437–438, 464, 467, 535, 536, 540, 572
ImClone Systems, 470, 472
Ingersol Milling Machine, 261
ING Group, 493, 495
Institute for Genomic Research, 34
Institute for Social Research (University of Michigan), 451
Intel Corporation, 481, 569
Intermedia, 353
Internal Revenue Service, 208
International Harvester, 133, 346
InterNorth, Inc., 82
Investors Diversified Services, 331
Ivron Systems, 160

Jaguar, 63
Joe Boxer, 167
Johnson-Bryce Corp., 316
Johnson & Johnson, 342, 343, 478, 479
S. C. Johnson & Son, 463
Justin Industries, 36

Kawasaki, 41
Kellogg Company, 36, 461
Kellogg School of Management (Northwestern University), 497
Kinko's, Inc., 365
Kmart, 109, 271
Kraft Foods, 352
K Shoes, 318
KT, 345

Lean Learning, 98
Legatus, 72
Lehman Brothers, 39
Levi Strauss, 70, 484
Lifeline systems, 474–475
Lincoln Electric, 163–164
Lionel Train Company, 89
Litton Industries, 358
Lockheed Martin, 48–49, 94, 238, 281
Lotus Development, 70
LTV, 13
Lucent Technologies, 86, 140, 459

Mars, 58
Mary Kay, Inc., 100
Matsushita, 345
Mayo Clinic, 334–335
Maytag, 171, 285
Mazda, 62
McDonald's, 6, 7, 37, 42, 54, 124, 273, 468, 476, 477
McDonnell-Douglas, 48, 273, 381
MCI, 459
McKinsey & Co., 338, 551, 552
Mercedes, 62
Merck, 106
Merrill Lynch, 87–88, 252–253, 547, 552
Michigan Bell, 157
Microsoft Corporation, 116, 130, 482, 483, 516–517, 526
Midvale Steel Company, 6
Milliken & Company, 163
Milwaukee Insurance Company, 318
Monsanto Company, 272, 478
Motorola, 74, 261, 321, 508, 526, 527
MTV, 393–394

RJR Nabisco, 463, 464
National Athletic Trainers' Association, 67
National Black MBA Association, 284
National Bureau of Economic Research, 164
National Football League, 67
National Institute of Occupational Safety and Health (NIOSH), 223
National Labor Relations Board, 211
National School Board Association, 180
Navistar Corporation, 346
NCR Corporation, 31, 459
NEC, 345
Nestlé, 42, 62, 163, 197, 484
New York Police Department, 321
New York Public Service Commission, 463
NeXT Computer, 130
NFL Films, 509
Nike, 14, 275, 491, 496
Nikon, 41
Nissan, 62, 208, 402–403

Nokia, 63, 326, 526, 527
Northrup Grumman, 48
Northwestern University, 497
NYNEX Corporation, 463

Occupational Safety and Health Administration (OSHA), 169, 182
OMRON, 63
Oracle, 483
OTG Software, 36, 53, 171, 172, 174, 197, 227, 261
Oxygen Media, 22

Pace Foods, 74
Pavlov, Ivan, 148
PepsiCo., 338
Pfizer, 53, 317, 535
Pharmacia, 31
Pier 1 Imports, 198
Pilgrim's Pride, 171
Pitney Bowes, 53, 197
Pittsburgh Steelers, 67
Planters Life Savers Company, 464
Polaroid, 13
J. D. Powers, 44
Praxis Consulting, 134
Pret A Manger, 4
Procter & Gamble, 52–53, 312, 316, 478, 512
Prudential Insurance, 171, 172
Publix Super Markets, 133, 134

Qualcomm Inc., 526
Quantum Corporation, 572

Rand Corporation, 416
Rent-A-Center, 90
Reuters Group, 248, 249
R. J. Reynolds, 179
Roche Group, 319, 320
Rolex, 40–41
Romac Industries, 211
Royal Caribbean Cruise Lines, 42
Royal Dutch/Shell, 62, 482
Rubbermaid, 105–106

Saab-Scania, 475
Safeway, 140, 227
SAIC, 133
Samsung Electronics, 344, 345
San Francisco Forty-Niners, 291
SAP, 454
Sapient, 454
Saybolt, Inc., 62
Scandinavian Airlines, 506
Scios, Inc., 410
Sears, 32
Securities and Exchange Commission (SEC), 84
ServiceMaster, 72
Shea Homes, 400
Shell Oil Company, 18, 21, 42, 70, 179, 202
Sidley Austin Brown & Wood, 421–422
Siemens, 86
Silicon Graphics, 54
Simonds Rolling Machine Company, 6
Six Sigma Academy, 400
Sony Corporation, 345, 461, 491, 509

Southwest Airlines, 134, 365, 454, 491–492, 501
Sovereign Bank, 31
Spencer Stuart, 78, 203
Springfield Remanufacturing, 133, 134
St. Lucie Medical Center, 315
Standard Oil of Ohio, 157
Sun Microsystems, 116, 535, 540

Target, 90
Tavistock Institute, 312, 474, 475
Team Building, Inc., 113
Techneglas, Inc., 147
Tenneco, 194
Teradyne, Inc., 85
Texaco, 62
Texas Instruments, 41, 172, 174
Thermos Company, 472
3Com, 140
3M, 54, 105–106, 174, 478
Timex, 41
Toshiba, 345
Toyota, 62, 208, 402–403, 483
Travelers Group, 472
Tricon Global Restaurants, 338, 339, 341, 348
TRW, 330, 479
Tyco International, 42, 552
Tyson Foods, 370

Unilever N.V., 484
United Airlines, 31, 134, 180
United Auto Workers (UAW), 214
United Food and Commercial Workers Union (UFCW), 133
United Parcel Service (UPS), 7, 77–78
United Way of America, 538
University of Maryland Baltimore County, 200
University of Michigan, 451
UNUM Corporation, 211
U.S. Civil Service, 171
U.S. Senate, 275
US Airways, 31

Vault.com, 262
Verizon, 39, 454
Viacom, 22, 394
Vivendi, 521–522
Volkswagen, 62
Volvo, 174, 475

Wal-Mart, 34, 109–110, 204, 214, 215, 375, 466, 467, 499, 517
Walt Disney, 86
Walter Rossler Company, 241
Wells Fargo Bank, 140, 504
Westinghouse, 318
Weyerhaeuser, 157, 191
Whirlpool, 285
Whistler Corporation, 44
Wipro Technologies, 326
Wonderlic Testing, 89

Xerox Corporation, 68, 70, 73, 86, 174, 312, 508, 552

Yale University, 281
Yellow Freight, 1–3

Subject Index

Absenteeism, 46, 107
Acceptance theory of authority, 448
Accommodation, 301–302
Achievement, 128–130
Achievement-oriented leadership, 352
Acquisitions, 471
Adhocracy, 478–479
Administrative hierarchy, 441–443
Affect, 96, 100
Affiliation, 130
Affinity groups, 286, 287
Affirmative action, 68
Afghanistan, 71
African Americans, 38, 203. *See also* Culture;
    Diversity; Ethnic groups; Minority groups
Age, 66–67
Agreeableness, 92
All-channel network, 263
Americans with Disabilities Act, 38, 70
Anthropology, 14, 497
Applied research, 555
Appraisal. *See* Performance measurement
Asian Americans, 38
Asian countries, 69
Assertiveness, 65
Assimilation, 59–60
Attitudes
    affective component of, 100
    change in, 97–99
    explanation of, 95
    formation of, 95–97
    individual, 46
    stress and, 234
    work-related, 99
Attribution theory, 102, 158
Authoritarianism, 94
Authority
    acceptance theory of, 448
    delegation of, 447–448
    explanation of, 446–447
    of teams and groups, 317
Autonomous work groups, 475
Avoidance
    explanation of, 150–151
    as reaction to conflict, 301
Awards, 208–209

Bankruptcy, 13
Basic research, 555
Behavior. *See* Individual behavior
Behavioral approach to decision making, 403–404
Behavioral approach to leadership
    explanation of, 344, 347–348
    Leadership Grid and, 346–347
    Michigan studies and, 344–345, 347
    Ohio State studies and, 345–347
Behavior modification. *See* Organizational
    behavior modification (OB mod)
Belongingness needs, 122, 123
Benefits
    cost of providing, 207–208
    types of, 206–207
The "Bodacious" Success of Oprah (Case Study),
    22–23
Body language, 255
Bonus plans, 13, 318
Bonus systems, 205
Bounded rationality, 403
Brainstorming, 415–416
Burnout, 234

Canada
    cultural attitudes and behaviors in, 65
    workforce diversity in, 57–58
Career counseling, 575
Career information systems, 575
Career management, 577–578
Career pathing, 575
Career planning
    explanation of, 574
    implementation of, 577–578
    programs for, 575–577
    purposes of, 574
    results of, 578
Careers
    changes in, 568–569
    choices regarding, 564–566
    explanation of, 563
    individual and organizational perspectives on,
        563–564
    occupation choices and, 566–568
    organization choices and, 568
    overview of, 562–563
Career stages
    entry, 569
    establishment, 571
    exit, 572–573
    mastery, 571–572
    mentoring, 573–574
    trial, 569–570
Case studies
    The "Bodacious" Success of Oprah, 22–23
    Change of Direction at Schwab, 546–547
    A Company Divided Against Itself
        Cannot Stand, 454–455
    A Corporate Marriage Made in Heaven (Not!),
        388–389
    The Downfall of Enron, 82–84, 245–247,
        426–428, 551–553
    Employee Participation at Chaparral Steel,
        183–185
        explanation of, 556–557
    Gentner Communications, 159–160
    How Do You Manage Magic?, 361–362
    Microsoft: Cult or Culture?, 516–517
    The Most Stress Conditions, 421–422
    None of Us Is as Smart as All of Us, 334–335
    Over the Edge, 241–242
    Restructuring at Cisco, 486–487
    Rewarding the Hourly Worker, 214–215
    The Sky's the Limit at Lockheed Martin,
        48–49
    A Tale of Two Companies, 275–276
    UPS Delivers Diversity to Diverse World,
        77–78
    Using Groups to Get Things Done, 307–308
    Valuing Employees at the World's Largest
        Firm, 109–110
    When Employees Are Owners, 133–134
Causality, 560
Cell phones, 229
Central Europe, 58, 63
Centralization, 443–444
Chain network, 263
Challenger space shuttle, 412, 413
Challenge stress, 223
Change. *See* Organization change
Change agent, 529
Change of Direction at Schwab (Case Study),
    546–547
Channel noise, 259–260

Charisma, 368, 374
Charismatic leadership, 368–370
Cheaper by the Dozen, 6
Chief executive officers (CEOs)
    compensation for, 140, 205–206
    corporate hierarchy and, 30
    foreign-born, 31
China
    cultural attitudes and behaviors in, 65
    economic development in, 42
    employment opportunities for women in, 69
    international business alliances with, 471
    manufacturing in, 63, 526
Circle network, 263
Classical conditioning, 148–149
Classical organization theory, 7
Coalition building, 385
Coercive power, 373, 376, 379
Cognition, 97, 149
Cognitive approach, 419
Cognitive dissonance, 97, 402
Cognitive process, 149
Cohesiveness, 295–296
Collaboration, 302
Collateral programs, 237–238
Collectivism, 64
Command groups, 286, 287
Commitment
    escalation of, 409–411
    power and, 375, 377
Communication
    across cultures, 250–253
    explanation of, 250
    informal, 272–273
    nonverbal, 251, 255–256
    oral, 254–255
    organization change and, 525–526, 544
    purposes of, 253
    written, 253–254
Communication and decision-making stage, 289
Communication fidelity, 268
Communication networks
    negative impacts of, 267
    organizational, 265–268
    small-group, 263–265
Communication process
    decoding and, 257–258, 269–270
    encoding and, 257, 269–270
    feedback and, 259, 271
    improving organizational factors in,
        271–273
    methods to improve, 268–271
    noise and, 259–260
    receiver and, 259, 270–271
    source and, 256–257, 268–269
    transmission and, 257
Communication technologies
    advances in, 248–249
    electronic information processing and
        telecommunications and, 260–262
    language use and, 252
    stress and, 229
A Company Divided Against Itself Cannot Stand
    (Case Study), 454–455
Compensation
    for CEOs, 140, 205–206
    executive, 13, 30, 31, 140, 205–206
    expatriate, 211–213
    for minorities, 203
    as reward, 204

Compensation package
  awards and, 208–209
  base pay and, 204–205
  benefits and, 206–208
  incentive systems and, 205–206
  perquisites and, 208
Competition
  explanation of, 300, 302
  organization change and, 526–527
Competitive advantage, 73, 74
Competitive strategy, 40–41
Compliance, 376, 377, 379
Compressed work week, 179
Compromise, 302–303
Conceptual skills, 34
Condition of certainty, 396–398
Condition of risk, 397, 398
Condition of uncertainty, 397–398
Configuration, 434
Conflict
  explanation of, 298
  in groups and organizations, 298–300
  management of, 303–304
  nature of, 300
  reactions to, 301–303
  role, 229–230
Conflict model, 406–408
Conflict resolution, 303
Conflict stimulation, 304
Conscientiousness, 92
Consideration behavior, 345–346
Context integration, 527
Contingency approach
  explanation of, 19–20
  to organization design, 460–461
Contingency plans, 402
Continuous change process model, 528–530
Continuous operations, 219–220
Continuous reinforcement, 152
Contributions, 87
Control and organization stage, 290–291
Controlling, 32
A Corporate Marriage Made in Heaven (Not!)
  (Case Study), 388–389
Corporate Cultures (Kennedy), 21
Corporate research, 508–509
Cosmopolite, 267
Cost leadership strategy, 41
Creativity
  background experiences and, 103
  cognitive abilities and, 103–104
  explanation of, 102–103
  personal traits and, 103
  promotion of, 105–106
  stages in, 104–105
Cross-training, 164
Culture. *See also* Diversity; Minority groups;
    Organization culture; Workforce diversity
  attitudes and behaviors and, 64–66, 128
  communication across, 250–253
  differences and similarities in, 63–64
  explanation of, 4, 14
  international business alliances and, 471
  managerial behavior across, 71–73
  organization structure and design and, 483
  stress and, 225–226
  view of technology and, 466
Cybercrime, 182

Decision making
  behavioral approach to, 403–404
  centralization of, 443–444
  escalation of commitment and, 409–411
  ethics and, 408–410
  explanation of, 395
  group, 411–417, 504
  information required for, 396–398
  personal approach to, 405–408
  practical approach to, 404, 405
  rational approach to, 399–403

Decision rule, 395
Decisions
  nonprogrammed, 396
  programmed, 396, 397
  types of, 395–396
Decoding
  explanation of, 257–258
  problems with, 269–270
Defensive avoidance, 408
Delegation, 447–448
Delphi technique, 416–417
Denmark, 65
Departmentalization
  by business function, 436–437
  by customer, 438–439
  explanation of, 436
  by geography, 439–440
  by process, 437
  by product or service, 437–438
Diagnostic skills, 35–36
Differentiation strategy, 40–41
Directive leadership, 351–352
Disability benefits, 207
Discrimination, 69
Disseminators, 33
Distress, 222
Disturbance handlers, 33
Diversification, 507
Diversity. *See also* Culture; Ethnic groups; Minor-
    ity groups; Workforce diversity
  age and, 66–67
  different abilities and, 70
  explanation of, 37, 69
  gender and, 68–70, 140
  needs and, 123, 124
  primary dimensions of, 66–71
  race and ethnicity and, 67–68
  secondary dimensions of, 71
  sexual orientation and, 70–71
  on teams, 315
  value of, 58–61
  workforce, 37–38, 54–61
Divisionalized form, 477–478
Division of labor, 434–435
The Downfall of Enron (Case Study), 82–84,
    245–247, 426–428, 551–553
Downsizing
  effects of, 442–443
  explanation of, 36, 463
Dual-structure theory of motivation
  development of, 126–127
  evaluation of, 127–128, 131, 132
  job enrichment and, 172
  role of, 126
Dysfunctional behaviors, 106–107

Economics
  achievement and, 130
  explanation of, 14
  organization culture and, 498–499
Effectiveness
  managing for, 45–47
  organizational fit and, 472
Effort-to-performance expectancy, 143, 145
Email
  ethical problems related to, 262
  language use and, 252
  monitoring of, 262
  use of, 260, 261
Email management systems, 262
Email response software, 275
Employee appraisal. *See* Performance
  measurement
Employee-centered leader behavior,
    344–345
Employee Participation at Chaparral Steel (Case
  Study), 183–185
Employee perquisites, 86
Employee stock option plans, 205
Employee turnover, 46, 107

Empowerment
  early perspectives on, 176
  explanation of, 176, 509
  organization culture and, 510–511
  techniques and issues in, 177–178
Encoding
  explanation of, 257
  problems with, 269–270
Engineering, 14
Entrepreneurs, 33, 506
Entry stage, 569
Environment
  communication and, 264
  complexity of, 468, 470
  dynamic, 468, 469
  general, 466
  organizational, 466–467
  organization design and, 466–470
  task, 466
Environmental uncertainty, 468, 469
Equal employment opportunities
  for individuals with disabilities, 38
  performance measurement and, 201
  for women, 68–70
Equity
  explanation of, 139
  perceptions of, 139–140
  responses to, 140–141
Equity theory
  evaluation of, 141–142
  explanation of, 139–141
ERG theory, 125, 131, 132
Escalation of commitment, 409–411
Establishment stage, 571
Esteem needs, 122, 123
Ethical issues
  accounting techniques and, 381
  decision making and, 408–410
  email and, 262
  employee stock ownership and, 43
  explanation of, 42–43
  General Electric and, 447
  leadership and, 369
  medication availability and, 472
  organizational behavior modification and,
    157–158
  political behavior and, 381, 382
  psychological testing and, 90
  related to research, 561
  rewards and, 116
  safety issues for telecommuting employees and,
    182
Ethnic groups. *See also* Culture; Diversity;
    Minority groups
  cultural differences between, 67–68
  in workplace, 38
Europe, 58, 206
European Union, 42, 58
Eustress, 222
Executives
  compensation for, 13, 30, 31, 140, 205–206
  work-life issues and, 239
Exercise, 235
Existence needs, 125
Exit stage, 572–573
Expansion, 37
Expatriates
  compensation for, 211–213
  management of psychological contracts
    for, 89
Expectancy
  effort-to-performance, 143, 145
  performance-to-outcome, 144, 145
Expectancy theory of motivation
  evaluation and implications of, 146–148
  explanation of, 143–145
  occupational choice and, 567–568
  Porter-Lawler of, 145–146
Expert power, 374, 376
Exploratory stage, 569

Extinction, 151
Extraversion, 92

Facial expressions, 255
Fatigue, 220, 223
Federal Insurance Contributions Act
    (FICA), 206
Feedback, 259, 271
Fidelity, communication, 268
Field experiments, 558
Field surveys, 557–558
Figureheads, 33
Filtering, 268–269
Fitness programs, 238
Fixed-interval reinforcement, 152
Fixed-ratio reinforcement, 152–153
Flexible reward systems, 210–211
Flexible work schedules, 179–180
Focus strategy, 41
Foreign Corrupt Practices Act, 62
Formal groups, 286–287
Formalization, 444–445
Formalized decentralization, 443–444
401(k) plans, 43
Friendship groups, 287, 288
Friendships, 114–115
Full structural integration, 75

Gain-sharing programs, 205, 318
Game playing, 385
Game theory, 418–419
Gatekeepers, 267
Gender. *See also* Men; Women
    CEO compensation and, 140
    employment opportunities and, 68–70
    leadership and, 343–344
    stress and, 226
General adaptation syndrome (GAS), 221–222
General environment, 466
Generation X, 38, 562
Germany
    CEO compensation in, 206
    cultural attitudes and behaviors in, 65, 71–72
    tax law and business culture in, 439
    unification of, 42, 63
    workforce diversity in, 58
Glass ceiling, 68, 71
Globalization. *See also* International
    business; Multinational organizations
    explanation of, 41–42
    workforce diversity and, 61
Goals
    acceptance of, 192
    commitment to, 192–193
    compatibility of, 301
    difficulty of, 191
    explanation of, 191
    specificity of, 192
Goal-setting theory
    evaluation and implications of, 194–195
    explanation of, 191–193
    perspectives on, 193–194
Grapevine, 272
Great Britain, 71–72
Group decision making. *See also* Decision making
    groupthink and, 412–414
    organization culture and, 504
    participation and, 414–415
    polarization and, 411–412
Group development stages
    communication and decision-making, 289
    control and organization, 290–291
    motivation and productivity, 289
    mutual acceptance, 288
Group performance factors
    cohesiveness as, 295–296
    composition as, 292–293
    explanation of, 291–292
    norms as, 294–295

size and, 293–294
Groups
    authority in, 317
    explanation of, 282–283
    formal, 286–287
    formation of, 284–286
    heterogeneous, 292
    homogeneous, 292
    importance of studying, 283–284
    inertia in, 541
    informal, 287–288
    interactions within, 297–298
    job categories and, 316–317
    management of, 304–305
    organization change and, 534–538
    outcomes of, 46
    polarization in, 411–412
    problem solving in, 415–417
    teams vs., 313–318
    work, 314
Groupthink
    decision-making defects and quality and,
        413–414
    explanation of, 296, 412
    prevention of, 414
    symptoms of, 412–413
Growth needs, 125

Hardiness, 225
Hawthorne studies, 8–10
Health, 223, 233
Health insurance programs, 207
Hedonism, 120
Hersey and Blanchard model, 359
Hierarchy of needs
    explanation of, 121–125, 131, 132
    tradeoffs in, 119
Hispanics, 38, 203. *See also* Culture; Diversity;
    Ethnic groups; Minority groups
Homosexuals, 70–71
Hong Kong, 42, 65, 69
How Do You Manage Magic? (Case Study),
    361–362
Human organization, 451–452
Human relations movement, 10–12, 121
Human resource planning, 575
The Human Side of Enterprise (McGregor), 11
Hygiene factors, 127
Hypervigilance, 408

IAN (Intellectual Assets Network), 527
Ideal bureaucracy, 449
Illness. *See* Health
Immigrants, 38
Impression management, 386–387
Incentive systems, 205
Incremental innovation, 508
Incubation, 104–105
India, 42
Individual behavior
    absenteeism and, 46
    affect and mood and, 100
    attitude formation and, 95–99
    creativity and, 102–106
    dysfunctional behaviors and, 106–107
    individual differences and, 91
    organizational citizenship and, 107–108
    perception and, 100–102
    performance and, 45–46, 106
    personality traits and, 91–95
    person-job fit and, 89–91
    productivity and, 45
    psychological contracts and, 87–89
    work-related attitudes and, 99
Individual differences, 90, 417
Individualism, 64
Individuals with disabilities, 38, 70
Indonesia, 65
Inducements, 87

Industrial Revolution, 166, 167
Inequity
    explanation of, 139
    responses to, 140–141
Influence
    charismatic leadership and, 368–370
    explanation of, 367
    leadership as, 366–368
    transformational leadership and, 368
Informal groups, 287–288
Information technology. *See also* Technology
    impact of, 40
    for performance measurement, 198
    use of, 260, 261, 466273
Initiating-structure behavior, 346
Innovation
    corporate research to develop, 508–509
    explanation of, 507–508
    new ventures based on, 508
    types of, 508
Inputs, 139, 140
*An Inquiry into the Nature and Causes of the Wealth
    of Nations* (Smith), 166–167
In Search of Excellence (Waterman), 21
Insight, 105
Institutional programs, 237
Intention, 97
Interactionalism, 20
Interest groups, 287, 288
Intergroup conflict, 76
Intergroup dynamics
    explanation of, 297–298
    management of, 304–305
International business. *See also* Globalization;
    Multicultural organizations
    cross-cultural similarities and differences and,
        63–66
    growth of, 61–62
    mergers and acquisitions and, 471
    organization structure and design and, 483–484
    psychological contracts and, 88–89
    trends in, 62–63
Internet
    competition and, 526
    ethical issues related to, 262
    use of, 260
Interpersonal demands, 230
Interpersonal roles, 32–33
Interpersonal skills, 34
Interrole conflict, 229
Interviews, 559
Intranet, 262
Intrapreneurship, 508
Intrarole conflict, 229
Intrasender conflict, 229
Iran-Contra Affair, 295, 448
Isolate, 267
Isolated dyad, 267
Israel, 65
Italy, 65, 71, 72

Janis-Mann conflict model, 406–408
Japan
    CEO compensation in, 206
    cultural attitudes and behaviors in, 64, 65, 71
    economy in, 42
    employee participation in, 177
    employment opportunities for women in, 69,
        239
    organization culture in, 503–505
    performance measurement in, 198
Jargon, 269–270
Job categories, 316–317
Job-centered leader behavior, 344–345
Job characteristics approach, 172
Job characteristics theory
    explanation of, 173–174
    implementation of, 174
    research on, 175

Job design
    enlargement and, 171
    enrichment and, 171–172
    evolution of, 166–167
    explanation of, 166
    rotation and, 170–171
    social information and, 175–176
    specialization and, 168–170
Job enlargement, 171
Job enrichment, 171–172
Job hopping, 571
Job rotation
    examples of, 163–164
    explanation of, 170–171
Jobs, 227
Job satisfaction, 99, 119
Job security, 227
Job sharing, 180, 181
Job specialization
    early alternatives to, 170–171
    explanation of, 168–170
Job titles, 167
Just in time (JIT) manufacturing, 474

Laboratory experiments, 558
Language, 251–252
Leader-member exchange model (LMX), 358–359
Leaders
    managers as, 33
    power exerted by, 378–379
Leadership
    achievement-oriented, 352
    behavioral approaches to, 344–348
    charismatic, 368–370
    directive, 351–352
    explanation of, 32, 340
    Hersey and Blanchard model of, 359
    as influence, 366–367
    leader-member exchange model of, 358–359
    LPC theory of, 348–351
    management vs., 340–342
    participative, 352, 353
    path-goal theory of, 351–354
    stress and styles of, 230
    supportive, 352
    on teams, 332
    trait approaches to, 342–344
    transformational, 367–368
    Vroom's decision tree approach to, 354–358, 415
Leadership Grid, 346–347, 534
Leadership substitutes
    nature of, 370–371
    superleadership and, 372
    workplace substitutes and, 371
Learning
    classical conditioning and, 148–149
    reinforcement discrimination and, 153–154
    reinforcement generalization and, 153
    reinforcement theory and, 149–153
    social, 154
Learning organizations, 201–202
Least-preferred coworker (LPC) scale, 349. See also LPC theory of leadership
Legitimate power, 373, 376
Lesbians, 70–71
Liaison, 267
Liaisons, 33
Life change, 230–232
Life insurance programs, 207
Life stressors, 230–232
Life trauma, 232
Linking roles, 305
Locus of control, 93–94, 353
Long-term compensation, 205
Long-term orientation, 65
LPC theory of leadership
    evaluation and implications of, 351
    explanation of, 348

situational favorableness and, 349–351
task vs. relationship motivation and, 348–349

Machiavellianism, 94–95, 120
Machine bureaucracy, 477
Management
    for group- and team-level outcomes, 46
    impression, 386–387
    for individual-level outcomes, 45–46
    leadership vs., 340–342
    for organization-level outcomes, 46–47
    participative, 176, 444
Management by objectives (MBO), 193, 194
Management development programs, 535–536, 575–576
Management functions, 449–450
Management teams, 323–324. See also Teams
Managers
    expatriate, 89
    functions of, 30–32
    roles of, 32–34
    skills of, 34–36
Manufacturing industry
    changes in, 163
    continuous operations in, 219–220
    technology use in, 44
Masculinity, 65
Mastery stage, 571–572
Materialism, 65
Matrix design, 479–480
Mechanistic structure, 473, 474
Medium, 257
Men. See also Gender
    leadership and, 343–344
    stress and, 226
    work-life issues and, 239
Mentoring, 573–574
Mergers, 471
Merit pay plans, 205
Mexico, 65
Michigan leadership studies, 344–345, 347
Microsoft: Cult or Culture? (Case Study), 516–517
Minority groups. See also Culture; Diversity; specific groups, Ethnic groups
    cultural differences between, 67–68
    full structural integration of, 75
    gaining input from, 74
    home ownership and, 463
    rewards for, 203
    support networks for, 75
Mission statement, 327
Mommy track, 239
Monitors, 33
The Most Stress Conditions (Case Study), 421–422
Motivation. See also Needs
    achievement needs and, 128–130
    affiliation needs and, 130
    dual-structure theory of, 126–128, 172
    employee performance and, 165–166
    enhancing employee, 114–115
    equity theory of, 139–142
    ERG theory of, 125
    ethics and, 116
    expectancy theory of, 143–148
    explanation of, 115
    framework for, 117
    goal setting and, 191–195
    historical perspective on, 120–121
    importance of, 115–117
    learning and, 148–154
    needs theories of, 113–114, 121–125, 131–132
    in organizations, 118–119
    personal relationships and, 114–115
    power needs and, 130–131
    process-based perspectives on, 137–139 (See also Process-based perspective)
    technology and, 147

Motivation and productivity stage, 289
Motives, 118–119
Multicultural organizations. See also Organizations
    characteristics of, 74–76
    as competitive advantage, 73, 74
    explanation of, 71
    managerial behaviors in, 71–73
Multinational organizations. See also Globalization; International business
    organization change in, 543
    organization structure and design and, 483–484
Mutual acceptance stage, 288
Myer-Briggs Type Indicator (MBTI), 93
National Labor Relations Act, 211
Needs
    achievement, 128–130
    affiliation, 130
    cultural diversity and, 123, 124
    dual-structure theory of, 126–128, 131, 132
    ERG theory of, 125, 131, 132
    explanation of, 117
    hierarchy of, 119, 121–125, 131, 132
    motives, behavior and, 118
    power, 130–131
    primary, 118
    secondary, 118
    theories of, 121
Negative affectivity, 100
Negative emotionality, 92
Negative reinforcement, 150–151
Negotiation
    approaches to, 417–419
    explanation of, 417
    Win-Win, 419–420
Negotiators, 33–34
Netherlands, 65
Nine-eighty schedule, 179
Noise, 259–260, 272
Nominal group technique, 416
None of Us Is as Smart as All of Us (Case Study), 334–335
Nonprogrammed decisions, 396
Nonreactive measures, 559–560
Nonverbal communication
    cultural differences in, 251–252
    explanation of, 255–256
Norms, 294–295
North American Free Trade Agreement (NAFTA), 42, 526

Observation, 559
Occupational field, 566
Occupations, 566
Ohio State leadership studies, 345–347
On the Economy of Machinery and Manufacturers (Babbage), 167
Openness, 93
Open systems, 473–474
Optimism, 225
Oral communication, 254–255
Organic structure, 473, 474
Organizational behavior
    basic concepts of, 15–17
    classical organizational theory and, 7
    contemporary applied perspectives on, 21
    contingency perspective on, 19–20
    descriptive nature of, 15
    emergence of, 12
    explanation of, 3–4
    Hawthorne studies and, 8–10
    historical background of, 5–7
    human relations movement and, 10–12
    interactionalism perspective on, 20
    interdisciplinary focus of, 13–15
    managerial perspectives on, 29–30
    precursors of, 8

research methods in, 552–561 (*See also* Research; Research designs)
scientific management and, 6–7
systems perspective on, 17–19
Organizational behavior modification (OB mod)
effectiveness of, 157
ethics of, 157–158
explanation of, 155–157
Organizational citizenship, 107–108
Organizational goals, 431
Organizational politics, 380
Organizational psychology, 13–14
Organizational socialization, 512–513
Organizational stressors
explanation of, 226
interpersonal demands as, 230
physical demands as, 228
role demands as, 228–230
task demands as, 226–228
Organizational technology. *See* Technology
Organization change
attitudes and, 17, 97–99
competition and, 526–527
coping with, 39
cultivation of, 98
information processing and communication and, 525–526, 544
management of, 542–545
organization culture and, 514–515
people and, 523–524
processes for planned, 527–530
resistance to, 538–542
technology and, 524–525
Organization charts
communication channels in, 265, 267
explanation of, 433–434
Organization climate, 500
Organization culture. *See also* Culture
approaches to, 502–507
creation of, 500–502
definitions of, 494
empowerment and, 509–511
explanation of, 493–496
historical foundations of, 496–499
innovation and, 507–509
interest in, 492–493
making use of, 511–512
methods for changing, 513–515
organization climate vs., 500
Ouchi framework and, 503–505
Peters and Waterman approach to, 505–507
socialization and, 512–513
Organization design
contemporary, 481–484
contingency approaches to, 460–461
environment and, 466–470
global organization structure and, 483–484
matrix, 479–480
mechanistic and organic, 473
Mintzberg's, 475–479
organization size and, 462–464
reengineering and, 482
rethinking the organization and, 482
sociotechnical systems, 473–475
strategic choice and, 471–473
strategy for, 461
structural imperatives for, 461–470
technology and, 464–466
virtual organizations and, 481
Organization development
explanation of, 530–531
management of, 542–545
systemwide, 531–533
through group and individual change, 534–538
through task and technological change, 533–534
Organizations
affect and mood in, 100
attitudes in, 95–100

attributes reinforced by culture in, 61
authority in, 446–448
changing diversity in, 37–38
characteristics of new workforce in, 38–39
commitment to, 99
competitive strategy in, 40–41
creativity in, 102–106
employee-owned, 133–134
environmental change in, 39–40
ethics and social responsibility and, 42–43
expansion and reduction of, 36–37
explanation of, 431
globalization and, 41–42
holistic view of, 543
individual rewards in, 202–209 (*See also* Rewards)
learning, 201–202
managing technology in, 44
multicultural, 71–76 (*See also* Multicultural organizations)
outcomes of, 46–47
perception in, 100–102
pluralistic, 74
quality and productivity in, 44
responsibility in, 445–446
virtual, 481
Organization size, 462–464
Organization structure
administrative hierarchy in, 441–443
analysis of, 432–433
centralization in, 443–444
classic principles of organizing and, 450
departmentalization in, 436–440
division of labor in, 434–435
explanation of, 431–433
formalization in, 444–445
human organization and, 451–452
ideal bureaucracy and, 449
span of control in, 440–441
Organizing
classic principles of, 449–450
explanation of, 32
Orientation to authority, 64–65
Ouchi framework, 503–505
Outcomes
explanation of, 139, 144
group- and team-level, 46
individual-level, 45–46
organization-level, 46–47
valences of, 144–145
Overdetermination, 540
Overload, 227–228
Over the Edge (Case Study), 241–242

Pakistan, 65
Participation
areas of, 177
early perspectives on, 176
explanation of, 176
in group decision making, 414–415
Participative leadership, 352, 353
Participative management, 176, 444
Participative pay systems, 211
Path-goal theory of leadership
explanation of, 350–351
situational factors and, 352–353
Pay, base, 204–205
Pay systems
gain-sharing, 318
participative, 211
secret, 211
skill-based, 317
for teams, 317–318
Pension plans, 207
Perception
attribution and, 102
explanation of, 100
selective, 101
stereotyping and, 101

Performance
of individuals, 45
management by objectives and, 194
motivation and, 115–117, 165–166
rewards for, 116, 210
stress and, 234
of teams, 318–319, 331–333
Type Z firms and, 505
Performance behaviors, 106
Performance management, 195
Performance management system (PMS)
elements of successful, 200–201
explanation of, 195–196
total quality management and, 200
Performance measurement
elements of, 196–197
explanation of, 195–196
frequency of, 197–198
high-tech, 198
purposes of, 196
total quality management and, 199–202
Performance plans, 201
Performance-to-outcome expectancy, 144, 145
Perquisites, 208
Persian Gulf War, 71
Personal approach to decision making, 405–408
Personal digital assistants (PDAs), 229
Personality, 91, 93
Personality profiles
stress and, 222–224
test for, 243–244
Personality traits
authoritarianism as, 94
big five, 91–93
locus of control as, 93–94
Machiavellianism as, 94–95
risk propensity as, 95
self-efficacy as, 94
self-esteem as, 95
Personal power, 374–375
Person-job fit
explanation of, 89–91
importance of, 119
Person-role conflict, 229–230
Physical demands, 228
Physiological needs, 122, 123
Piecework programs, 205
Planning, 31–32
Pluralistic organizations, 74–76
Polarization, 411–412
Political behavior
management of, 382
pervasiveness of, 380–382
reasons for, 383–384
reducing effects of, 386
techniques of, 384–386
Political science, 14
Politics, 380
Porter-Lawler expectancy model, 145–147
Position power, 374
Positive affectivity, 100
Positive reinforcement, 150, 151
Post-decision dissonance, 402
Power
bases of, 373–374
nature of, 372
need for, 94–95, 120, 130–131
position vs. personal, 374–375
reward, 379
threatened, 541
uses of, 375–379
Power distance, 64–65
Practical approach to decision making, 404, 405
PRAM model, 420
Prejudices, 55–56
Preparation, 104
Primary needs, 118
Principles of Scientific Management (Taylor), 6
Privacy issues, 262

Problem solving. *See also* Decision making
  explanation of, 396
  group, 415–417
Problem-solving teams, 323. *See also* Teams
Procedural justice, 511
Process-based perspective. *See also* Motivation
  attribution and motivation and, 158
  behavior modification and, 155–158
  equity theory of motivation and, 139–142
  expectancy theory of motivation and, 143–148
  explanation of, 137–139
  learning and motivation and, 148–154
  performance and, 165
Process models, 528–530
Product development teams, 324. *See also* Teams
Productivity
  explanation of, 44
  of individuals, 45
  stress and, 234
Professional bureaucracy, 477
Profit-sharing plans, 205
Programmed decisions, 395–396
Psychological contracts, 87–89
Psychological testing, 90
Psychology, 13–14
Punishment, 151

Quality, 44
Quality circles (QCs), 322–323
Quality-of-work-life programs, 532–533
Questionnaires, 559

Racial harassment, 107
Radical innovation, 508
Rational decision-making approach
  explanation of, 399–400
  steps in, 400–403
  strengths and weaknesses of, 403
Receiver, communication, 259, 270–271
Reengineering, 482
Referent power, 374, 376
Refreezing, 528
Rehabilitation Act, 70
Reinforcement
  motivation and, 191
  negative, 150–151
  in organizations, 150–151
  positive, 150, 151
  schedules of, 151–153
Reinforcement discrimination, 153–154
Reinforcement generalization, 153
Reinforcement theory, 149–153
Relatedness needs, 125
Relaxation, 235
Reliability, 560–561
Religion, 71, 72
Research
  applied, 555
  basic, 555
  causality and, 560
  data gathering for, 559–560
  ethical issues related to, 561
  innovation and, 508–509
  purposes of, 555–556
  reliability and validity of, 560–551
  role of theory and, 552
  scientific, 555
Research designs
  case study, 556–557
  field experiment, 558
  field survey, 557–558
  laboratory experiment, 558
Resistance
  to change, 538–542
  individual sources of, 541–542
  organizational sources of, 539–541
  power and, 376, 377
Resource allocation, 33, 541

Responsibility
  authority vs., 448
  collective, 505
  explanation of, 445–446
Restructuring at Cisco (Case Study), 486–487
Rethinking organizations, 482–484
Retirement plans, 207
Rewarding the Hourly Worker (Case Study), 214–215
Reward power, 373, 376, 379
Rewards
  explanation of, 203
  flexible, 210–211
  linking performance and, 210
  management by objectives and, 194
  management of, 209–213
  for minority employees, 203
  for organization change contributions, 544–545
  overview of, 190
  for performance, 116
Reward systems
  roles, purposes, and meanings of, 203–204
  for teams, 317–318
  types of, 204–209
Risk propensity, 94, 95
Role demands, 228–230
Role management, 236–237
Roles
  ambiguity of, 228
  conflict between, 229–230
  explanation of, 228
  overload in, 230
Russia, 65

Safety, 169, 182
Satisficing, 404
Saudi Arabia, 124
Scientific management
  background of, 167, 168
  explanation of, 6–7, 120–121
Scientific research, 555
Scientific research process, 555–556
Secondary needs, 118
Security needs, 122, 123
Selective perception, 101
Self-actualization, 122, 123
Self-efficacy, 94, 191
Self-esteem, 95
Semantics, 269
Settling-down stage, 571
Sexual harassment, 107
Sexual orientation, 70–71
Short-term orientation, 65
Simple structure, 477
Simulations, 536
Situational favorableness, 349–351
Six Sigma, 400
Size. *See* Organization size
Skill-based pay, 317
The Sky's the Limit at Lockheed Martin (Case Study), 48–49
Small-group networks, 263–265
Social information, 175–176
Socialization , 512–513
Socialization stage, 569–570
Social learning, 154
Social loafing, 294
Social psychology, 498
Social responsibility, 42–43
Social Security, 206, 207
Social subsystems, 474–475
Sociology, 14, 497–498
Sociotechnical systems designs, 473–475
Soldiering, 6
Source, communication, 256–257, 268–269, 271
South Korea, 42
Span of control, 440–442
Spirituality, 71, 72

Spokespersons, 33
Stereotypes, 55–56, 101
Stock ownership, 43
Strategic choice, 470–473
Strategic values, 500–501
Strategy, 461
Stress
  benefits and drawbacks of, 223
  burnout as consequences of, 234
  causes of, 226–232
  distress and eustress and, 222
  employment status and, 220
  explanation of, 221
  function of, 46
  general adaptation syndrome and, 221–222
  hardiness and optimism and, 225–226
  individual consequences of, 233
  organizational consequences of, 233–234
  personality profiles and, 222–224
  work-life issues and, 239
Stress management
  individual coping strategies for, 235–237
  methods for, 234–235
  organizational coping strategies for, 237–238
Stressors
  life, 230–232
  organizational, 226–230
Structural change, 531–533
Structural-imperatives approach
  environment and, 466–470
  explanation of, 461–462
  size and, 462–464
  technology and, 464–466
Structural inertia, 540
Suboptimizing, 404
Superleadership, 372
Superordinate goals, 304
Support groups, 237
Supportive leadership, 352
Surface value, of rewards, 204
Survey feedback techniques, 536–538
Sweden, 65, 73
Symbolic value, of rewards, 204
Systems
  explanation of, 17–18, 473
  open, 473–474
Systems innovation, 508
Systems perspective, 17–19

Taiwan, 42
Task demands, 226–228
Task environment, 466
Task groups, 286, 287
Task redesign, 533–534
Taxes, 213
Team building, 536
Teams
  authority in, 317
  benefits of being on, 319
  bonus plans for, 318
  costs reductions and, 319–320
  drawbacks of, 321–322, 332
  ethical issues related to, 332
  explanation of, 314
  groups vs., 313–318
  implementation phases for, 328–331
  job categories and, 316–317
  management, 323–324
  organizational enhancements of, 320–321
  outcomes of, 46
  performance of, 318–319, 331–333
  planning for, 325–328, 333
  problem-solving, 323
  product development, 324
  reward systems for, 317–318
  types of, 322–325
  use of, 312–313
  value of, 299

virtual, 325
work, 323
Teapot Dome scandal, 553
Technical skills, 34
Technical subsystems, 474
Technological change, 533–534
Technology. *See also* Communication technologies; Information technology
culture and views of, 466
electronic information processing and telecommunications, 260–262
explanation of, 44
growth in international business and, 61
impact of, 40
as motivator, 147
organization change and, 524–525
organization design and, 464–470
performance measurement and, 198
service, 44
stress and, 229
teamwork and, 320
worker safety and, 169
Telecommuting
advances in, 260, 261
explanation of, 181
legal aspects of, 182
Terrorist attacks of September 11, 2001
decision making and, 421–422
effects of, 27, 114, 491–492
rescue activities following, 290
spirituality and, 72
stress following, 225, 232
Testing, psychological, 90
Thailand, 69
Theories, 552
Theory X, 11, 12, 121
Theory Y, 11, 12, 121
360-degree feedback, 197
Time management, 235–236
Total quality management (TQM)
explanation of, 199
performance measurement and, 200
performance plans and, 201
as systemwide organization development, 532
team building and, 536

Training
benefits of, 189, 535
methods used for, 535, 576–577
prehire, 189–190
worker safety, 169
Trait approach, 342–344
Transformational leadership, 368
Transition management, 530
Transmission, 257
Trial stage, 569–570
Type A personality, 223–224
Type B personality, 223–224
Type Z companies, 498, 503–505

Uncertainty avoidance, 65
Uncertainty reduction, 386
Unconflicted adherence, 406
Unconflicted change, 406
Unemployment, 220
Unemployment compensation, 207
Unfreezing, 528
United States, 65, 71–72
Universal approach, 19, 460
UPS Delivers Diversity to Diverse World (Case Study), 77–78
Using Groups to Get Things Done (Case Study), 307–308

Valences, 144–145
Validity, 561
Valuing Employees at the World's Largest Firm (Case Study), 109–110
Variable-interval reinforcement, 152
Variable-ratio reinforcement, 153
Variable work schedules, 178–179
Venezuela, 65
Verification, 105, 271
Videoconferencing, 258
Vietnam, 42
Vigilant information processing, 408
Virtual organizations, 481
Virtual teams, 325. *See also* Teams
Voicemail, 254–255
Vroom's decision tree approach to leadership, 354–358, 415, 534

Watergate Affair, 413
West Africa, 65
Wheel network, 263
Whistleblowers, 96
Win-Win negotiation, 419–420
Withdrawal, 234
Withdrawal stage, 572–573
Women. *See also* Gender
employment opportunities for, 68–70
leadership and, 343–344
stress and, 226
in top management positions, 53, 499, 525
in workforce, 37, 239
work-life issues and, 239
Work, preoccupation with, 129–130
Workers' compensation benefits, 207
Workforce
median age of, 66
women in, 37, 239
Workforce diversity. *See also* Diversity
assimilation and, 59–60
explanation of, 54–56
global, 57–58
outlook for, 56–57
trends in, 37–38
value of, 58–59
Work groups, 314, 475. *See also* Groups
Work-life relationships
creating balance in, 239–240
explanation of, 238–239
Workplace, 38–39
Workplace behavior
dysfunctional behavior as, 106–107
explanation of, 106
organizational citizenship as, 107–108
performance behavior as, 106
Work schedules
flexible, 179–180
variable, 178–179
Work teams, 323. *See also* Teams
World Trade Organization (WTO), 526
Written communication
effective, 269
explanation of, 253–254

Supplements Designed to Aid Instructors and Students

For Students:

Student Web Site. This site provides additional information, study aids, activities, and resources that help reinforce the concepts presented in the text.

- **Learning Objectives** for each chapter help guide students in their reading and studying.

- A brief **Chapter Outline** provides a quick framework for each chapter.

- The **Chapter Summary** helps students review key points.

- The **OB Online** exercises from the text are repeated with relevant links and any necessary updates.

- **ACE Self-Tests** give students an opportunity to assess their knowledge.

- The **Glossary** from the main text is provided for easy reference.

- **Flash Cards** help students review the key terms that are boldfaced in the text.

- **Additional Cases** are provided in case instructors and students want extra opportunity to apply the concepts.

- Convenient **Chapter Links** to the organizations highlighted in the chapter-opening vignettes, boxes, and cases allow students to gain further insight into the practices of these businesses.

- A **Resource Center** provides links to various sites of general organizational behavior interest.

OB in Action. This book of exercises and cases provides hands-on experiential activities to help students bridge the gap between theory and practice. Working individually or in teams, students explore issues, tackle problems, and find solutions, using organizational behavior theories as their foundation.